CASES AND MATERIALS

# CORPORATIONS AND OTHER BUSINESS ORGANIZATIONS

CONCISE EIGHTH EDITION

*by*

MELVIN ARON EISENBERG
Koret Professor of Law
University of California at Berkeley

NEW YORK, NEW YORK
FOUNDATION PRESS
2000

                    395 Hudson Street
                    New York, NY 10014
                    Phone Toll Free 1–877–888–1330
                    Fax (212) 367–6799
                    fdpress.com

**ISBN** 1–56662–906–3

∞

1st Reprint — 2001

# PREFACE

In many areas of corporate law, it is difficult to fully understand the issues and the legal rules without some background knowledge of basic accounting and financial concepts. Accordingly, this casebook includes introductory materials on such topics as financial statements, the present-value rule, diversification, valuation, the efficient capital market hypothesis, and dividend policy. These materials have been chosen and edited with an eye to ensuring that they are accessible to students who don't have an accounting and financial background. The materials are introduced gradually, at relevant points throughout the book, so that students are not faced with an onslaught of unfamiliar concepts.

Because of the importance of statutes in corporation law, students should refer to the Statutory Supplement whenever a cross-reference to that Supplement appears. When a cross-referenced statutory provision includes an Official Comment, the Comment should be read as well. Other cross-references to the Statutory Supplement (for example, references to excerpts from the Restatement (Second) of Agency) should be treated the same way.

In the preparation of this casebook, the following conventions have been used: Where a portion of the text of an original source (such as a case) has been omitted, the omission is indicated by ellipses The omission of footnotes from original sources is not indicated, but the original footnote numbers are used for those footnotes that are retained.

The American Law Institute's Principles of Corporate Governance: Analysis and Recommendations (1994) is cited simply as ALI, Principles of Corporate Governance.

I thank Uriel Procaccia for wonderful suggestions concerning the organization of the chapter on distributions to shareholders; David Ruder for valuable help on the Williams Act; Pilar Sansone for excellent work as a research assistant; Sue Smith for exceeding skill and diligence in preparing the manuscript for publication; and Elizabeth Erdinger, Marlene Harmon, Ginny Irving, Debby Kearney, Janice Kelly, Michael Levy, and Alice Youmans, Reference Librarians at the Law School at the University of California at Berkeley, and Kathleen Vanden Heuvel, the Library's Associate Director, for their thorough, accurate, fast, unflagging, and marvelous responses to the innumerable problems I sent them.

*

# SUMMARY OF CONTENTS

**CHAPTER XIV  The Public Distribution of Securities** ............ 901

*

# ANALYTICAL TABLE OF CONTENTS

# TABLE OF CASES

Principal cases are in bold type. Non-principal cases are in roman type. References are to Pages.

\*

CASES AND MATERIALS

# CORPORATIONS AND OTHER BUSINESS ORGANIZATIONS

*

# CHAPTER I

# AGENCY

## SECTION 1.  INTRODUCTION

Courses in corporations or business associations are, in large part, courses in organizational law. The most common forms of business organization in this country are sole proprietorships, corporations, general and limited partnerships, and limited liability companies. Based on tax filings, as of 1995 there were 16,424,000 sole proprietorships in the United States (exclusive of farms), 4,474,000 corporations, and 1,581,000 partnerships. U.S. Bureau of the Census, Statistical Abstract of the United States 541 (1998).

A *sole proprietorship* is a business organization that is owned by a single individual, and is not cast in a special legal form of organization, such as a corporation, that can be utilized only by filing an organic document with the state pursuant to an authorizing statute.

The term *business organization* may seem to be an inappropriate characterization of a form that involves only a single owner. That terminology can, however, be justified on at least two grounds.

First, a business enterprise that is owned by an individual is likely to have a degree of psychological and sociological identity separate from that of the individual. This separateness of a sole proprietor's enterprise is often expressed by giving the enterprise its own name, like "Acme Shoe Company." Furthermore, a sole proprietor usually will consider only a certain portion of his property and cash as invested in the business, and will keep a separate set of financial records for the enterprise, as if the enterprise's finances were separate from her own.

Thus, if Alice Adams begins a new business in 2000—say, Acme Shoe Company—she is likely to issue a balance sheet for the business that does not show all of her assets and liabilities, but only those assets dedicated to, and those liabilities arising out of, the enterprise's operations. (See Section 4, An Introduction to Financial Statements, infra.) In short, as a psychological matter Adams, and to a certain extent those who deal with her, are likely to regard Acme Shoe Company as an enterprise or firm that has a certain degree of separateness from Adams herself, and a certain amount of capital. As a matter of law, however, a sole proprietorship has no separate identity from its owner. If Adams takes no special legal step, like incorporating the enterprise, all of her wealth will be effectively committed to the enterprise, because an individual who owns a sole proprietorship has unlimited personal liability for obligations incurred in the conduct of the business.

1

The second reason for calling a sole proprietorship an organization is that a sole proprietor typically will not conduct the business by herself, but will engage various people—salespersons, mechanics, managers—to act on her behalf, and subject to her control, in conducting the business. The employment by one person, *P*, of another, *A,* to act on *P*'s behalf, and subject to her control, brings us to the most elementary form of organizational law, known as the law of agency. An *agent* is a person who by mutual assent acts on behalf of another and subject to the other's control. Restatement, Second, Agency § 1. The person for whom the agent acts is a *principal.* Id. Agency law governs: (1) The relationship between agents and principals. (2) The relationship between agents and third persons with whom an agent deals, or purports to deal, on a principal's behalf. (3) The relationship between principals and third persons when an agent deals, or purports to deal, with a third person on the principal's behalf.

Although agency is a consensual relationship, whether an agency relationship has been created does not turn on whether the parties *think of themselves* as or *intend* to be agent and principal. "Agency is a legal concept which depends upon the existence of required factual elements: the manifestation by the principal that the agent shall act for him, the agent's acceptance of the undertaking and the understanding of the parties that the principal is to be in control of the undertaking. The relation which the law calls agency does not depend upon the intent of the parties to create it, nor their belief that they have done so. To constitute the relation, there must be an agreement, but not necessarily a contract, between the parties; if the agreement results in the factual relation between them to which are attached the legal consequences of agency, an agency exists although the parties did not call it agency and did not intend the legal consequences of the relation to follow. Thus, when one . . . asks a friend to do a slight service for him, such as to return for credit goods recently purchased from a store, [an agency relationship may be created although] neither one may have any realization that they are creating an agency relation or be aware of the legal obligations which would result from performance of the service." Restatement (Second) of Agency § 1, Comment b.

## SECTION 2.   AUTHORITY

## Morris Oil Co. v. Rainbow Oilfield Trucking, Inc.

New Mexico Court of Appeals, 1987.
106 N.M. 237, 741 P.2d 840.

■ GARCIA, JUDGE. . . .

Defendant Dawn appeals from the judgment rendered against it in favor of Morris Oil Company, Inc. (Morris), based upon a determination that Rainbow Oilfield Trucking, Inc. (Rainbow) was Dawn's agent when it incurred indebtedness with Morris. We affirm the trial court.

### FACTS

Appellant Dawn, the holder of a certificate of public convenience and necessity, is engaged in the oilfield trucking business in the Farmington area. Rainbow was a New Mexico corporation established for the purpose of operating an oilfield trucking business in the Hobbs area. Defendant corporations entered into several contracts whereby Rainbow would be permitted to use Dawn's certificate of public convenience and necessity in operating a trucking enterprise in Hobbs. Dawn reserved the right to full and complete control over the operations of Rainbow in New Mexico. Dawn was to collect all charges due and owing for transportation conducted by Rainbow and, after deducting a $1,000 per month "clerical fee" and a percentage of the gross receipts, was to remit the balance to Rainbow. Under a subcontract entered into by defendants, Rainbow was to be responsible for payment of operating expenses, including fuel; further, the subcontract provides that all operations utilizing fuel were to be under the direct control and supervision of Dawn. All billing for services rendered by Rainbow would be made under Dawn's name, with all monies to be collected by Dawn.

Defendants also entered into a terminal management agreement which provided that Dawn was to have complete control over Rainbow's Hobbs operation. The agreement further recited that Rainbow was not to become the agent of Dawn and was not empowered to incur or create any debt or liability of Dawn "other than in the ordinary course of business relative to terminal management." The agreement recited that Rainbow was to be an independent contractor and not an employee, and that liability on the part of Rainbow for creating charges in violation of the agreement would survive the termination of the agreement. Dawn was to notify Rainbow of any claim of such charges whereby Rainbow would assume the defense, compromise or payment of such claims.

Rainbow operated the oilfield trucking enterprise under these contractual documents, during which time Rainbow established a relationship with plaintiff Morris, whereby Morris installed a bulk dispenser at the Rainbow terminal and periodically delivered diesel fuel for use in the trucking operation. The enterprise proved unprofitable, however, and Rainbow ceased its operations and ultimately declared bankruptcy, owing Morris approximately $25,000 on an open account.

When Morris began its collection efforts against Rainbow, it determined that Rainbow had ceased its operations, everyone associated with Rainbow had moved back to Texas and it did not appear likely that the account would be paid. Morris was directed by Rainbow's representative in Texas to Dawn for payment of the account.

When Rainbow ceased its operations, Dawn was holding some $73,000 in receipts from the Hobbs operation. Dawn established an escrow account through its Roswell attorneys to settle claims arising from Rainbow's Hobbs operation. When Morris contacted Dawn with regard to the outstanding account, it was notified of the existence of the escrow account and was asked to forbear upon collection efforts, indicting that payment would be forthcoming from the escrow account. Dawn's representatives indicated that it was necessary to wait for authorization from Rainbow's parent Texas corporation before paying the account. At no time did Rainbow or Dawn question the amount or legitimacy of Morris' open account balance.

Dawn's principal [owner] further testified that the subcontract and terminal management agreement were cancelled by Dawn when he learned that Rainbow was incurring debts in Dawn's name. The charges owing to Morris, however, were incurred in the name of Rainbow and not Dawn.

Although some claims were paid from the attorneys' escrow account established by Dawn, there was no explanation at trial why the Morris claim was not paid. When Morris learned that the escrow funds had been disbursed without payment of its charges, it instituted this action and also sought to garnish the remaining $13,000 held by Dawn from the impounded funds. Rainbow did not defend, and the trial court entered a default judgment against Rainbow, from which it does not appeal.

### DISCUSSION

The trial court found that Dawn retained the right to direct control and supervision of Rainbow's New Mexico operations, and that in the course of those operations, Rainbow incurred a balance of almost $25,000 on an open account with Morris for fuel used in the New Mexico operations. The trial court further found that when Rainbow defaulted on payments on Morris' account, Dawn made representations over a period of time concerning the existence of a fund held by Dawn to settle indebtedness created by Rainbow operating under the subcontract. The court determined that Morris delayed its collection efforts pending disbursement of the funds, and that Dawn was aware that Morris was relying upon Dawn's representations that payment would be made from the impounded fund. The trial court concluded that Rainbow was at all times in its dealings with Morris the agent of Dawn and, therefore, Dawn was responsible for the account balance.

Dawn urges one point of error on appeal; that the trial court erred in finding liability based on a principal-agent relationship between the defendants. Dawn relies upon the language in the terminal management agreement which states:

4.   Rainbow is not appointed and shall not become the agent of Dawn and is not empowered to incur or create any debt or liability of Dawn other than in the ordinary course of business relative to terminal management. Rainbow shall not enter into or cause Dawn to become a party to any agreement without the express written consent of Dawn.

5.   Rainbow shall be considered an independent contractor and not an employee of Dawn.

Dawn's reliance upon these paragraphs of the agreement is unpersuasive for two reasons. First, the agreement specifically states that Rainbow may create liabilities of Dawn in the ordinary course of business of operating the terminal. There is no question that the liability to Morris was incurred in the ordinary course of operating the trucking business. Second, the recitation of the parties in their contractual documents need not bind third parties who deal with one of them in ignorance of those instructions. See South Second Livestock Auction, Inc. v. Roberts, 69 N.M. 155, 364 P.2d 859 (1961); see also Great Northern R.R. Co. v. O'Connor, 232 U.S. 508, 34 S.Ct. 380, 58 L.Ed. 703 (1914).

While Dawn argues from cases discussing apparent authority, we view this as a case of undisclosed agency. Rainbow contracted in its own name and not in the name of Dawn Enterprises, Inc. Thus, this case involves concepts relating to undisclosed agency rather than to apparent authority, and is governed by principles of undisclosed principal-agent contracts. See, e.g., 3 Am.Jur.2d Agency § 316 (1986).

It is well established that an agent for an undisclosed principal subjects the principal to liability for acts done on his account if they are usual or necessary in such transactions. Restatement (Second) of Agency § 194 (1958). This is true even if the principal has previously forbidden the agent to incur such debts so long as the transaction is in the usual course of business engaged in by the agent. Id.

The indebtedness in the instant case is squarely governed by well-established principles of agency where an undisclosed principal entrusts the agent with the management of his business. The undisclosed principal is subject to liability to third parties with whom the agent contracts where such transactions are usual in the business conducted by the agent, even if the contract is contrary to the express directions of the principal. Restatement (Second) of Agency § 195 (1958).

Dawn's reliance upon Bloodgood v. Woman's Ben. Ass'n, 36 N.M. 228, 13 P.2d 412 (1932) is misplaced. Indeed, the case stands for the proposition that a principal may limit an agent's authority, and further, that the limitation will be binding upon a third party dealing with the agent if the third party has knowledge of the limitation of authority. Here there is no evidence that Morris had any actual knowledge of the existence of the Rainbow-Dawn agency, let alone any claimed limitations by Dawn on Rainbow's authority. It is undisputed that Morris thought it was dealing solely with Rainbow when it sold fuel.

Morris correctly observes that secret instructions or limitations placed upon the authority of an agent must be known to the party dealing with the agent, or the principal is bound as if the limitations had not been made. Chevron Oil Co. v. Sutton, 85 N.M. 679, 515 P.2d 1283 (1973) . . . .

Moreover, assuming arguendo that Dawn was not responsible for the indebtedness to Morris for the reasons urged on appeal, it is clear that Dawn ratified the open account after learning of its existence when Morris contacted Dawn regarding payment. A principal may be held liable for the unauthorized acts of his agent if the principal ratifies the transaction after acquiring knowledge of the material facts concerning the transaction. Ulibarri Landscaping Material, Inc. v. Colony Materials, Inc., 97 N.M. 266, 639 P.2d 75 (Ct.App.1981).

It was undisputed that in several telephone conversations between the principals of Dawn and Morris, the material facts of the Morris open account were disclosed to Dawn. At no time did Dawn dispute the legitimacy or amount of the open account, and indeed assured Morris that payment would be forthcoming from the funds retained from Rainbow's revenues. Despite this, Dawn used the fund to pay itself a $1,000 per month clerical fee, to pay legal fees incurred as a result of its agency with Rainbow and to settle other claims arising from the Rainbow operations. Where the principal retains the benefits or proceeds of its business relations with an agent with knowledge of the material facts, the principal is deemed to have ratified the methods employed by the agent in generating the proceeds. See id. See also 3 Am.Jur.2d Agency § 194 (1986). The diesel fuel provided by Morris was used in Rainbow's trucking operation. Dawn collected the receipts due to Rainbow. Dawn seeks to retain the benefits of the agency with Rainbow, and yet at the same time disclaims responsibility for the business of the agent by which the benefits were generated. This it cannot do. Ulibarri Landscaping Material, Inc. v. Colony Materials, Inc.

In sum, for the foregoing reasons, we affirm.

IT IS SO ORDERED . . . .

■ BIVINS and MINZNER, JJ., concur.

----

## NOTE ON AUTHORITY

1. *Terminology.* An *agent* is a person who acts on behalf and subject to the control of another. For some purposes, agents are classified as general or special. A *general agent* is an agent who is authorized to conduct a series of transactions involving continuity of service. A *special agent* is an agent who is authorized to conduct only a single transaction, or only a series of transactions not involving continuity of service.

A *principal* is a person on whose behalf and subject to whose control an agent acts. Principals are conventionally divided into three classes: disclosed, partially disclosed, and undisclosed.

A principal is *disclosed* if at the time of a transaction between the agent and a third person, the third person knows that the agent is acting on behalf of a principal and knows the principal's identity.

A principal is *partially disclosed* if at the time of the transaction the third person knows that the agent is acting on behalf of a principal, but does not know the principal's identity.

A principal is *undisclosed* if the agent, in dealing with the third person, purports to be acting on his own behalf. An undisclosed principal is liable for her agent's authorized activities, even though, because the agent does not disclose his agency, the third person believes the agent is acting strictly on his own behalf. One reason the undisclosed principal is liable is that she set the transaction in motion and stood to gain from it. A second reason is this: Even if the undisclosed principal was not directly liable to the third person, the agent would be. Therefore, the third person could sue the agent. If he did so, the agent could then sue the principal for indemnification of the damages he had to pay the third person. See Section 6 of this Note, infra. Accordingly, allowing the third person to sue the undisclosed principal does not materially enlarge the principal's liability, and collapses two lawsuits into one.

In the area of torts, a principal is usually referred to as a master and an agent is usually referred to as a servant. A *master* is a principal who controls or has the right to control the *physical conduct* of an agent in the performance of the agent's services. A *servant* is an agent whose physical conduct in the performance of services for the principal is subject to the control of the principal. Restatement (Second) Agency § 2. Both terms are purely technical, and "do not denote menial or manual service. Many servants perform exacting work requiring intelligence rather than muscle. Thus the officers of a corporation or a ship, [and the intern] in a hospital . . . are servants. . . ." Id., Comment c.

The liability of a master for the tort of a servant is referred to as liability in *respondeat superior.* Under the doctrine of respondeat superior, a master is liable for torts of servant if the servant's physical conduct in the performance of services for the master is subject to the master's control, and the tort is committed while the servant is acting within the scope of her employment.

A variety of problems can arise out of an actual or alleged principal-agency relationship. Perhaps the most common problem is what liabilities arise out of a certain transaction between the agent and a third person? Most of the issues implicated by that question are addressed by the legal rules governing *authority.* This Note will emphasize the liability of the principal to the third person (Section 2), but will also consider the liability of the third person to the principal (Section 3); the liability of the agent to the third person (Section 4); and the duties and liabilities of the agent and the principal to each other (Sections 5 and 6). Although the law of agency encompasses liabilities in tort as well as in contract, for the most part this Note will address only issues that relate to contractual transactions.

2. *Liability of Principal to Third Person.* Under the law of agency, a principal becomes liable to a third person as a result of an act or transaction by another, A, on the principal's behalf, if A had actual, apparent, or inherent authority, or was an agent by estoppel, or if the principal ratified the act or transaction.

a. *Actual authority.* An agent has *actual authority* to act in a given way on a principal's behalf if the principal's words or conduct would lead a reasonable person in the agent's position to believe that the principal had authorized him to so act.

Actual authority may be either *express* or *implied:* "It is possible for a principal to specify minutely what the agent is to do. To the extent that he does this, the agent may be said to have express authority. But most authority is created by implication. Thus, in the authorization to 'sell my automobile', the only fully expressed power is to transfer title in exchange for money or a promise to give money. In fact, under some circumstances ... there may ... be power to take or give possession of the automobile or to extend credit or to accept something in partial exchange. These powers are all implied or inferred from the words used, from customs and from the relations of the parties. They are described as 'implied authority.' " Restatement (Second) of Agency § 7, Comment c.

A common type of implied actual authority is *incidental authority,* which is the authority to do incidental acts that are reasonably necessary to accomplish an actually authorized transaction, or that usually accompany it. If the principal has authorized the agent to engage in a given transaction, and certain acts are reasonably necessary to accomplish the transaction, or usually accompany it, a reasonable person in the agent's position would believe that the authority to engage in the transaction also conferred authority to engage in those acts.

Note that if an agent has actual authority, the principal is bound even if the third person did not know that the agent had actual authority, and indeed even if the third person thought the agent was herself the principal, not merely an agent. These issues will be discussed below.

On the issues discussed in this section, see Restatement (Second) of Agency §§ 26, 32, 33, 35, 39, 43, 144, 186 in the Statutory Supplement.*

b. *Apparent authority.* An agent has *apparent authority* to act in a given way on a principal's behalf in relation to a third person, T, if the words or conduct of the principal would lead a reasonable person in T's position to believe that the principal had authorized the agent to so act.

In most cases, actual and apparent authority go hand in hand, as Restatement (Second) of Agency § 8, Illustration 1, supra, suggests.

---

* Corporations and Other Business Organizations—Statutes, Rules, Materials, and Forms (Foundation Press; M. Eisenberg ed.).

For example, if P Bank appoints A as cashier, and nothing more is said, A will reasonably believe she has the authority that cashiers normally have, and third persons who deal with A will reasonably believe the same thing. Apparent authority becomes salient in such a case if P Bank does not actually give A all the authority that cashiers usually have, and a customer deals with A knowing that A is a cashier, but not knowing that P Bank has placed special limits on A's authority.

The apparent authority of A in the cashier hypothetical is a special type of apparent authority known as *power of position*. "... [A]pparent authority can be created by appointing a person to a position, such as that of manager or treasurer, which carries with it generally recognized duties; to those who know of the appointment there is apparent authority to do the things ordinarily entrusted to one occupying such a position, regardless of unknown limitations which are imposed upon the particular agent. . . . If a principal puts an agent into, or knowingly permits him to occupy, a position in which according to the ordinary habits of persons in the locality, trade or profession, it is usual for such an agent to have a particular kind of authority, anyone dealing with him is justified in inferring that he has such authority, in the absence of reason to know otherwise." Restatement (Second) of Agency § 27, Comment a, § 49, Comment c.

On apparent authority, see Restatement (Second) of Agency §§ 27, 49, 159 in the Statutory Supplement.

c. *Agency by estoppel.* Still another type of authority is known as "agency by estoppel." The core of agency by estoppel is described as follows in Restatement (Second) of Agency § 8B:

(1) A person who is not otherwise liable as a party to a transaction purported to be done on his account, is nevertheless subject to liability to persons who have changed their positions because of their belief that the transaction was entered into by or for him, if

(a) he intentionally or carelessly caused such belief, or

(b) knowing of such belief and that others might change their positions because of it, he did not take reasonable steps to notify them of the facts.

The concept of agency by estoppel is so close to the concept of apparent authority that for most practical purposes the former concept can be subsumed in the latter.

d. *Inherent authority.* Under the doctrine of *inherent authority*, an agent may bind a principal in certain cases even when the agent had neither actual nor apparent authority. Although the doctrine of inherent authority is relatively well established, its exact contours are not always clear. Restatement (Second) of Agency § 8A provides that "Inherent agency power is a term used ... to indicate the power of an agent which is derived not from actual authority, apparent authority or estoppel, but solely from the agency relation and exists for the protection of persons harmed by or dealing with a servant or other agent."

Section 161 of the Restatement concerns the inherent authority of general agents of disclosed or partially disclosed principals. Under Section 161, a disclosed or partially disclosed principal is liable for an act done on his behalf by a general agent, even if the principal had forbidden the agent to do the act, if (i) the act usually accompanies or is incidental to transactions that the agent is authorized to conduct, and (ii) the third person reasonably believes the agent is authorized to do the act. But this leaves open the issue, under what circumstances is a third person reasonable in believing that an agent has authority that, by hypothesis, is beyond the agent's apparent authority?

Section 194 of the Restatement concerns the inherent authority of agents for undisclosed principals. It provides that "A general agent for an undisclosed principal authorized to conduct transactions subjects his principal to liability for acts done on his account, if usual or necessary in such transactions, although forbidden by the principal to do them." Unlike Section 161, Section 194 does not require that the third person reasonably believes the agent is authorized to act. Indeed, such a requirement could not be imposed, because in the case of an undisclosed principal the third person will not know that he is dealing with an agent.

On the issues discussed in this section, see Restatement (Second) of Agency §§ 8A, 159–161A, 194, 195A, 219, 220, 228–231 in the Statutory Supplement.

e. *Ratification.* Even if an agent has neither actual, apparent, nor inherent authority, the principal will be bound to the third person if the agent purported to act on the principal's behalf, and the principal, with knowledge of the material facts, either (1) affirms the agent's conduct by manifesting an intention to treat the agent's conduct as authorized, or (2) engages in conduct that is justifiable only if he has such an intention.

*Manifesting an intention* to treat the agent's conduct as authorized is sometimes known as *express ratification.*

*Engaging in conduct* that is justifiable only if the principal intends to treat the agent's conduct as authorized is sometimes known as *implied ratification.* The most common example is the case where, as a result of the purported agent's transaction, the principal, with knowledge of the facts, receives or retains something to which he would otherwise not be entitled.

Ratification need not be communicated to the third person to be effective, although it must be objectively manifested. Restatement (Second) of Agency § 95. However, to be effective a ratification must occur before either (1) the third person has withdrawn, (2) the agreement has otherwise terminated, or (3) the situation has so materially changed that it would be inequitable to bind the third person, and the third person elects not to be bound. See Restatement (Second) of Agency §§ 88, 89.

f. *Acquiescence.* A concept that is comparable to, but different from, ratification is authority by *acquiescence.* "[I]f the agent performs a series of acts of a similar nature, the failure of the principal to object to them is an indication that he consents to the performance of similar acts in the future under similar conditions." Restatement (Second) of Agency § 43, Comment b. Suppose, for example, an agent engages in a series of comparable purchases on the principal's behalf. Prior to the first purchase, a reasonable person in the agent's position would not have thought she had authority to enter into such a transaction. Nevertheless, the principal did not object either to that purchase or to a later such purchase when he learned of them. At that point, a reasonable person in the agent's position would assume that the principal approved the agent's engaging in such purchases. Accordingly, the principal's acquiescence gives rise to actual authority. As to third persons who know of the acquiescence, the acquiescence also gives rise to apparent authority.

On the concepts of ratification and acquiescence, see Restatement (Second) of Agency §§ 43, 82–85, 87–90, 93, 94, 97–100A, 143 in the Statutory Supplement.

g. *Termination of agent's authority.* As a general rule, a principal has the *power* to terminate an agent's authority at any time, even if doing so violates a contract between the principal and the agent, and even if it had been agreed that the agent's authority was irrevocable. This rule rests largely on the ground that contracts relating to personal services will not be specifically enforced. (There is an important but limited exception to this rule, which applies to a type of relationship known as an *agency coupled with an interest.* This exception will be discussed in Chapter 6, infra.) Accordingly, a contractual provision under which an agent's authority cannot be terminated by either party normally cannot be specifically enforced. However, such a provision is effective to create *liability* (damages) for wrongful termination.

On the revocability of agency powers, see Restatement (Second) of Agency § 118 in the Statutory Supplement.

3. *Liability of Third Person to Principal.* Section 2 considered the liability of a principal to a third person. What is the liability of the third person to the principal? The general rule is that if an agent and a third person enter into a contract under which the agent's principal is liable to the third person, then the third person is liable to the principal. Restatement (Second) of Agency § 292. The major exception is that the third person is not liable to an undisclosed principal if the agent or the principal knew that the third person would not have dealt with the principal if she had known the principal's identity. Id., Comment c.

4. *Liability of Agent to Third Person.*

a. *Where the principal is bound.* Where the agent has actual, apparent, or inherent authority, so that the principal is bound to the third person, the agent's liability to the third person depends in part on whether the principal was disclosed, partially disclosed, or undisclosed.

(i) *Undisclosed principal.* If the principal was undisclosed (that is, if at the time of the transaction the agent purported to act on her own behalf), the general rule is that the agent is bound, even though the principal is bound too. Restatement (Second) of Agency § 322. The theory is that the third person must have expected the agent to be a party to the contract, because that is how the agent presented the transaction. However, there is a quirk in the law here. Under the majority rule, if the third person, after learning of an undisclosed principal's identity, obtains a judgment against the principal, the agent is discharged from liability even if the judgment is not satisfied. Similarly, the undisclosed principal is discharged if the third person obtains a judgment against the agent. Under the minority rule, which is sounder, neither the agent nor the principal is discharged by a judgment against the other, but only by satisfaction of the judgment.

(ii) *Partially disclosed principal.* If the principal was partially disclosed (that is, if at the time of the transaction the third person knew that the agent was acting on behalf of a principal, but did not know the principal's identity), the general rule is that the agent as well as the principal is bound to the third person. Restatement (Second) of Agency § 321. The theory is that if the third person did not know the identity of the principal, and therefore could not investigate the principal's credit or reliability, he probably expected that the agent would be liable, either solely or as a co-promisor or surety. Id., Comment a.

(iii) *Disclosed principal.* Assume now that the principal was disclosed (that is, at the time of the transaction the third person knew that the agent was acting on behalf of a principal and knew the principal's identity). If the principal is bound by the agent's act because the agent had actual, apparent, or inherent authority, or because the principal ratified the act, the general rule is that the agent is not bound to the third person. Restatement (Second) of Agency § 320. The theory is that in such a case the third person did not expect the agent to be bound; he did expect the principal to be bound; and he gets just what he expects.

b. *Where the principal is not bound.* If the principal is *not* bound by the agent's act, because the agent did not have actual, apparent, or inherent authority, the general rule is that the agent is liable to the third person. The agent's liability is usually based on the theory that an agent makes an implied warranty of authority to the third person, although a few authorities have adopted a theory that the agent can be held liable on the contract itself. In principle, the difference between the two theories might lead to a difference in the measure of damages. Under the liability-on-the-contract theory, the third person will recover the gains that he would have derived under the contract—essentially, expectation damages. In contrast, under the implied-warranty theory it might seem that the third person would recover only the losses he suffered by having entered into the transaction—essentially, reliance damages. However, Restatement (Second) of Agency § 329, while adopting the implied-warranty theory, provides for an expectation measure of damages, just as if it had adopted the contract theory: "The third person can recover in damages not only for the harm caused to him by the fact that the agent was unauthorized, but also for the amount by which he would have benefitted had the authority existed." Id., Comment j.

On the agent's liability to the third person, see Restatement (Second) of Agency §§ 320–322, 328–330 in the Statutory Supplement.

5. *Liability of Agent to Principal.* If an agent takes an action that she has no actual authority to perform, but the principal is nevertheless bound because the agent had apparent authority, the agent is liable to the principal for any resulting damages. Restatement (Second) of Agency § 383, Comment e. Whether an agent is liable to the principal for an act that binds the principal by virtue of the agent's inherent but not actual authority is an unsettled point.

6. *Liability of Principal to Agent.* If an agent has acted within her actual authority, the principal is under a duty to indemnify the agent for payments authorized or made necessary in executing the principal's affairs. This includes authorized payments made by the agent on the principal's behalf; payments made by the agent to a third person on contracts upon which the agent was authorized to make herself liable (as where the agent acted on behalf of a partially disclosed or undisclosed principal); payments of damages to third parties that the agent incurs because of an authorized act that constituted a breach of contract; and expenses in defending actions brought against the agent by third parties because of the agent's authorized conduct.

On the agent's right to indemnification, see Restatement (Second) of Agency §§ 438–440 in the Statutory Supplement.

---

## SECTION 3.   THE AGENT'S DUTY OF LOYALTY

---

## Tarnowski v. Resop

Supreme Court of Minnesota, 1952.
236 Minn. 33, 51 N.W.2d 801.

■ KNUTSON, JUSTICE.

Plaintiff desired to make a business investment. He engaged defendant as his agent to investigate and negotiate for the purchase of a route of coin-operated music machines. On June 2, 1947, relying upon the advice of defendant and the investigation he had made, plaintiff purchased such a business from Phillip Loechler and Lyle Mayer of Rochester, Minnesota, who will be referred to hereinafter as the sellers. The business was located at LaCrosse, Wisconsin, and throughout the surrounding territory. Plaintiff alleges that defendant represented to him that he had made a thorough investigation of the route; that it had 75 locations in operation; that one or more machines were at each location; that the equipment at each location was not more than six months old; and that the gross income from all locations amounted to more than $3,000 per month. As a matter of fact, defendant had made only a superficial investigation and had investigated only five of the locations. Other than that, he had adopted false representations of the sellers as to the other locations and had passed them on to plaintiff as his own. Plaintiff was to pay $30,620 for the business. He paid $11,000 down. About six weeks after the purchase, plaintiff discovered that the representations made to him by defendant were false, in that there were not more than 47 locations; that at some of the locations there were no machines and at others there were machines more than six months old, some of them being seven years old; and that the gross income was far less than $3,000 per month. Upon discovering the falsity of defendant's representations and those of the sellers, plaintiff rescinded the sale. He offered to return what he had received, and he demanded the return of his money. The sellers refused to comply, and he brought suit against them in the district court of Olmsted county. The action was tried, resulting in a verdict of $10,000 for plaintiff. Thereafter, the sellers paid plaintiff $9,500, after which the action was dismissed with prejudice pursuant to a stipulation of the parties.

In this action, brought in Hennepin county, plaintiff alleges that defendant, while acting as agent for him, collected a secret commission from the sellers for consummating the sale, which plaintiff seeks to recover under his first cause of action. In his second cause of action, he seeks to recover damages for [losses caused by defendant's wrong].

1.   With respect to plaintiff's first cause of action, the principle that all profits made by an agent in the course of an agency belonging to the principal, whether they are the fruits of performance or the violation of an agent's duty, is firmly established and universally recognized. Smitz v. Leopold, 51 Minn. 455, 53 N.W. 719. . . .

It matters not that the principal has suffered no damage or even that the transaction has been profitable to him. Raymond Farmers Elevator Co. v. American Surety Co., 207 Minn. 117, 290 N.W. 231, 126 A.L.R. 1351.

The rule and the basis therefor are well stated in Lum v. Clark, 56 Minn. 278, 282, 57 N.W. 662, where, speaking through Mr. Justice Mitchell, we said: "Actual injury is not the principle the law proceeds on, in holding such transactions void. Fidelity in the agent is what is aimed at, and, as a means of securing it, the law will not permit him to place himself in a position in which he may be tempted by his own private interests to disregard those of his principal. . . . It is not material that no actual injury to the company [principal] resulted, or that the policy recommended may have been for its best interest. Courts will not inquire into these matters. It is enough to know that the agent in fact placed himself in such relations that he might be tempted by his own interests to disregard those of his principal. The transaction was nothing more or less than the acceptance by the agent of a bribe to perform his duties in the manner desired by the person who gave the bribe. Such a contract is void. This doctrine rests on such plain principles of law, as well as common business honesty, that the citation of authorities is unnecessary."

The right to recover profits made by the agent in the course of the agency is not affected by the fact that the principal, upon discovering a fraud, has rescinded the contract and recovered that with which he parted. Restatement, Agency, § 407(2). Comment e on Subsection (2) reads: "If an agent has violated a duty of loyalty to the principal so that the principal is entitled to profits which the agent has thereby made, the fact that the principal has brought an action against a third person and has been made whole by such action does not prevent the principal from recovering from the agent the profits which the agent has made. Thus, if the other contracting party has given a bribe to the agent to make a contract with him on behalf of the principal, the principal can rescind the transaction, recovering from the other party anything received by him, or he can maintain an action for damages against him; in either event the principal may recover from the agent the amount of the bribe."

It follows that, insofar as the secret commission of $2,000 received by the agent is concerned, plaintiff had an absolute right thereto, irrespective of any recovery resulting from the action against the sellers for rescission.

2.   Plaintiff's second cause of action is brought to recover damages for (1) losses suffered in the operation of the business prior to rescission; (2) loss of time devoted to operation; (3) expenses in connection with rescission of the sale and investigation therewith; (4) nontaxable expenses in connection with the prosecution of the suit against the sellers; and (5) attorneys' fees in connection with the suit.

The case comes to us on a bill of exceptions. No part of the testimony of the witnesses is included, so we must assume that the evidence establishes the items of damage claimed by plaintiff. Our inquiry is limited to a consideration of the question whether a principal may recover of an agent who has breached his trust the items of damage mentioned after a successful prosecution of an action for rescission against the third parties with whom the agent dealt for his principal.

The general rule is stated in Restatement, Agency, § 407(1), as follows: "If an agent has received a benefit as a result of violating his duty of loyalty, the principal is entitled to recover from him what he has so received, its value, or its proceeds, and also the amount of damage thereby caused, except that if the violation consists of the wrongful disposal of the principal's property, the principal cannot recover its value and also what the agent received in exchange therefor."

In Comment a on Subsection (1) we find the following: "... In either event, whether or not the principal elects to get back the thing improperly dealt with or to recover from the agent its value or the amount of benefit which the agent has improperly received, he is, in addition, entitled to be indemnified by the agent for any loss which has been caused to his interest by the improper transaction. Thus, if the purchasing agent for a restaurant purchases with the principal's money defective food, receiving a bonus therefor, and the use of the food in the restaurant damages the business, the principal can recover from the agent the amount of money improperly expended by him, the bonus which the agent received, and the amount which will compensate for the injury to the business."

The general rule with respect to damages for a tortious act is that "The wrong-doer is answerable for all the injurious consequences of his tortious act, which according to the usual course of events and the general experience were likely to ensue, and which, therefore, when the act was committed, he may reasonably be supposed to have foreseen and anticipated." 1 Sutherland, Damages (4 ed.) § 45, quoted with approval in Sargent v. Mason, 101 Minn. 319, 323, 112 N.W. 255, 257. . . .

Bergquist v. Kreidler, 158 Minn. 127, 196 N.W. 964, involved an action to recover attorneys' fees expended by plaintiffs in an action seeking to enforce and protect their right to the possession of real estate. Defendant, acting as the owner's agent, had falsely represented to plaintiffs that they could have possession on August 1, 1920. It developed after plaintiffs had purchased the premises that a tenant had a lease running to August 1, 1922, on a rental much lower than the actual value of the premises. Defendant (the agent) conceded that plaintiffs were entitled to recover the loss in rent, but contended that attorneys' fees and disbursements expended by plaintiffs in testing the validity of the tenant's lease were not recoverable. In affirming plaintiffs' right to recover we said, 158 Minn. 132, 196 N.W. 966: "... the litigation in which plaintiffs became involved was the direct, legitimate, and a to be expected result of appellant's misrepresentation. The loss sustained by plaintiffs in conducting that litigation 'is plainly traceable' to appellant's wrong and he should make compensation accordingly."

So far as the right to recover attorneys' fees is concerned, the same may be said in this case. Plaintiff sought to return what had been received and demanded a return of his down payment. The sellers refused. He thereupon sued to accomplish this purpose, as he had a right to do, and was successful. His attorneys' fees and expenses of suit were directly traceable to the harm caused by defendant's wrongful act. As such, they are recoverable.

... The general rule applicable here is stated in 15 Am.Jur., Damages, § 144, as follows: "It is generally held that where the wrongful act of the defendant has involved the plaintiff in litigation with others or placed him in such relation with others as makes it necessary to incur expense to protect his interest, such costs and expenses, including attorneys' fees, should be treated as the legal consequences of the original wrongful act and may be recovered as damages.''

The same is true of the other elements of damage involved. . . .

Affirmed.

———

## RESTATEMENT (SECOND) OF AGENCY
### §§ 13, 387–396, 401, 403, 404, 407

[See Statutory Supplement]

———

## Jensen & Meckling, Theory of the Firm: Managerial Behavior, Agency Costs and Ownership Structure

3 J. Financial Economics 305, 308 (1976).

We define an agency relationship as a contract under which one or more persons (the principal(s)) engage another person (the agent) to perform some service on their behalf which involves delegating some decision making authority to the agent. If both parties to the relationship are utility maximizers there is good reason to believe that the agent will not always act in the best interests of the principal. The *principal* can limit divergences from his interest by establishing appropriate incentives for the agent and by incurring monitoring costs designed to limit the aberrant activities of the agent. In addition in some situations it will pay the *agent* to expend resources (bonding costs) to guarantee that he will not take certain actions which would harm the principal or to ensure that the principal will be compensated if he does take such actions. However, it is generally impossible for the principal or the agent at zero cost to ensure that the agent will make optimal decisions from the principal's viewpoint. In most agency relationships the principal and the agent will incur positive monitoring and bonding costs (non-pecuniary as well as pecuniary), and in addition there will be some divergence between the agent's decisions and those decisions which would maximize the welfare of the principal. The dollar equivalent of the reduction in welfare experienced by the principal due to this divergence is also a cost of the agency relationship, and we refer to this latter cost as the "residual loss". We define *agency costs* as the sum of:

(1) the monitoring expenditures by the principal,

(2) the bonding expenditures by the agent,

(3) the residual loss.

## SECTION 4.   AN INTRODUCTION TO FINANCIAL STATEMENTS

The law of business associations is about enterprises that are organized for profit. Accordingly, issues concerning such matters as accounting, valuation, and portfolio theory often lurk behind the legal rules and the cases in this area, and sometimes take center stage. It would be impossible to develop these issues in a really meaningful way in a book like this, which is devoted to explicitly legal materials. However, from time to time in this book, beginning here, materials will be set out that at least provide a vocabulary concerning these issues.

---

## D. Herwitz, Materials on Accounting for Lawyers 1–3, 11–12

1980.

### . . . THE BALANCE SHEET

The object of bookkeeping is to make it as easy as possible for anyone who understands the language to get a clear and accurate summary of how well a business is doing. Suppose we want a financial picture of E. Tutt, who recently graduated from law school. Certainly one important facet is how much he owns. Since we really are concerned with his business and not his personal affairs, we forget his car, his clothes, and other personal property, and we look to see what he has in his office:

(a) Office furniture

(b) Office equipment

(c) Stationery and supplies

(d) Library

(e) Cash in the bank [of $1,000]

All of these would be understood by laymen to be what the accountant calls them: *assets.*

We would also want some measurement of these assets; i.e., we would want to put a dollar figure on them. And since the price at which the property was bought is ordinarily much easier to ascertain and less subjective than the "present value" of the property, it would make sense to record E. Tutt's assets at *cost.*

If E. Tutt bought all his property out of his own funds and has not yet earned anything, we could simply add up the assets to find out how E. Tutt stands in his business. But if he has borrowed money from a bank to buy some of his assets or, perhaps more likely, has bought some on credit, E. Tutt's personal "stake" in the business would not be as large as if he had bought everything from his own funds. In order to give a true picture of his financial position, we would want to know where the money came from to buy the assets. Suppose we find that he acquired the assets as follows:

(a) Office furniture: bought on credit from Frank Co. for $400;

(b) Office equipment: bought on credit from Elmer Co. for $300;

(c) Stationery and supplies: bought from Stanley for $100 on a promissory note;

(d) Library: purchased for $200 cash, out of Tutt's original "stake" of $1,000;

(e) $800 cash: balance of Tutt's original "stake" remaining.

We could then list, in parallel columns, the assets and their sources:

| Assets | | Sources | |
|---|---|---|---|
| (a) Office furniture | $ 400 | Frank Co. | $ 400 (a) |
| (b) Office equipment | 300 | Elmer Co. | 300 (b) |
| (c) Stationery and supplies | 100 | Stanley | 100 (c) |
| (d) Library | 200 | | |
| (e) Cash (balance remaining) | 800 | E. Tutt | 1,000 (d, e) |
| | $1,800 | | $1,800 |

This parallel listing of assets and their sources is what the accountant calls a *balance sheet*. It shows, at any point in time, what assets the business now has and where the money came from to acquire them. Since that is all it is, no matter how complicated the business or how long its history the totals of the two columns are always equal.

To give a somewhat clearer picture of how well off E. Tutt himself is, we can separate the sources of assets into two groups: "outside" sources, or here, money owed by the business to outsiders; and "inside" sources, here, what Tutt himself has put into the business. The outside sources, which are usually called *"Liabilities"*, may be money owed on open account, usually called an "account payable;" another "outside" source is money advanced on a note, a "note payable". The "inside" source here is E. Tutt's contribution (his "stake" or equity in the business) which is often called *"Proprietorship"*. We might also rearrange the assets, listing them in the order in which they are likely to be used up. The result would be a somewhat more refined balance sheet that might look like this:

| Assets | | Liabilities & Proprietorship | |
|---|---|---|---|
| | | Liabilities: | |
| (e) Cash | $ 800 | Accounts Payable | |
| (c) Supplies | 100 | Frank Co. | $ 400 (a) |
| (a) Furniture | 400 | Elmer Co. | 300 (b) |
| (b) Equipment | 300 | Notes Payable | |
| | | Stanley | 100 (c) |
| (d) Library | 200 | Proprietorship | 1,000 (d, e) |
| | $1,800 | | $1,800 |

Note that no change has been made except a change in presentation. The essential meaning is the same. But because clear disclosure is one of the accountant's main concerns, matters of presentation are important. . . .

## . . . THE INCOME STATEMENT

The balance sheet shows the present status of the assets and the "sources of assets" resulting from all transactions since the business was formed. It is drawn up at regular intervals which will vary with the needs of the business. There is another, and increasingly more important, basic financial statement: the *income statement.* The income statement is a statement for a period of time, giving a summary of earnings between balance sheet dates. A fundamental distinction between the two is that the balance sheet speaks as of a particular date, while the income statement covers a period of time between successive balance sheet dates....

It may be easiest to start by drawing up an income statement for E. Tutt, say for the month of June. Suppose that during the month he receives legal fees of $600 and $400.

|     |                     |       |
|-----|---------------------|-------|
| (1) | Professional Income | $600  |
| (2) | Professional Income | $400  |

To find his net income, we have to subtract his expenses for the month. Suppose that the operating expenses were as follows:

|     |              |       |
|-----|--------------|-------|
| (3) | Rent         | $200  |
| (4) | Secretary    | $230  |
| (5) | Telephone    | $ 15  |
| (6) | Heat & Light | $  5  |
| (7) | Miscellaneous| $  5  |

In addition, during the month Tutt suffered a loss when a thief broke into his office and stole $20 cash. This loss is treated as just another expense:

|     |            |       |
|-----|------------|-------|
| (8) | Theft loss | $ 20  |

There is no particular form required for an income statement, so long as it is a clear and fair statement of the information. An acceptable one might look like this:

### INCOME STATEMENT—E. TUTT, JUNE

| (1 & 2) Professional Income | | | ...$1,000 |
|---------|--------------|------|--------|
| | Less: Expenses | | |
| (3) | Rent | $200 | |
| (4) | Secretary | 230 | |
| (5) | Telephone | 15 | |
| (6) | Heat & Light | 5 | |
| (7) | Miscellaneous | 5 | |
| (8) | Theft Loss | 20 | |
| | Total Expenses | | 475 |
| | NET INCOME | | $525 |

To get started on seeing how the income statement fits into the balance sheet we might ask where "net income" shows up on a balance sheet. In lay terms, it is an increase in the owner's stake in the business, which we call "Proprietorship". Hence, if no other change in Proprietorship occurs, the balance sheet figure for Proprietorship on June 30 should be $525 larger than on June 1.

# R. Hamilton, Fundamentals of Modern Business 154–55

1989.

    ... *[E]very transaction entered into by a business must be recorded in at least two ways if the balance sheet is to continue to balance.* This last point underlies the concept of that mysterious subject, *double entry bookkeeping*, and is the cornerstone on which modern accounting is built.

    Assume that we have a new business, just starting out, in which the owner has invested $10,000 in cash.... The opening balance sheet will look like this:

| Assets: | | Liabilities | –0– |
|---|---|---|---|
| Cash | 10,000 | Owner's Equity | 10,000 |

Now let us assume that the owner buys a used truck for $3,000 cash. The effect of this transaction is to reduce cash by $3,000 and create a new asset on the balance sheet:

| Assets: | | Liabilities | –0– |
|---|---|---|---|
| Cash | 7,000 | Owner's Equity | 10,000 |
| Used Truck | 3,000 | | |
| | 10,000 | | 10,000 |

Voila! The balance sheet still balances. Let us assume next that the owner goes down to the bank and borrows an additional $1,000. This also has a dual effect: it increases cash by $1,000 (since the business is receiving the proceeds of the loan) and increases liabilities by $1,000 (since the business thereafter has to repay the loan). Yet another balance sheet can be created showing the additional effect of this second transaction:

| Assets: | | Liabilities | |
|---|---|---|---|
| Cash | 8,000 | Debt to Bank | 1,000 |
| Used Truck | 3,000 | Owner's Equity | 10,000 |
| | 11,000 | | 11,000 |

---

## NOTE ON BALANCE SHEETS

    The fundamental accounting equation is Assets − Liabilities = Owner's Equity (or "Proprietorship" or "Net Worth"). Rearranging the terms of this equation, Assets = Liabilities + Owner's Equity. The latter form of the equation parallels the form of a balance sheet, which represents the equation in the form of a chart, with Assets on the left of the chart and Liabilities and Owner's Equity on the right. However, in evaluating a balance sheet it must be borne in mind that the entries do not necessarily reflect real or market values. Instead, the entries are (or should be) constructed according to generally accepted accounting principles ("GAAP"), and typically reflect only "book value," that is, the value (more precisely, the amount) at which various assets and liabilities are recorded or "booked" on the financial statements. Thus, under generally accepted accounting principles a building is normally shown on the balance sheet at the original cost of the asset, minus depreciation (that is, the assumed loss of value of the asset over its useful life). Depreciation, in turn, is determined by a formula, rather than by actual loss in value. For example, under "straight-line" depreciation, a plant built at a cost of $1 million might be depreciated by deducting 5% of that cost every year during a projected twenty-year life. After four years, therefore, the value of the plant shown on the books (the "book value") would be $800,000 ($1 million cost minus $50,000 annual depreciation for each of four years), even though the fair market value of the plant—the price the owner could get for the plant if he sold it—was, say, $1.4 million. Because balance-sheet net worth is simply balance-sheet assets minus balance-sheet liabilities, actual net worth may be much higher or much lower than the figure for owner's equity recorded on the balance sheet.

# CHAPTER II

# PARTNERSHIP

---

## INTRODUCTORY NOTE

Although partnership had a rich history under the common law, it has long been governed by statute. Until recently, the relevant statute was the Uniform Partnership Act ("the UPA"), which was promulgated by the National Conference of Commissioners on Uniform State Laws (NCCUSL) in 1914 and was adopted in every state except Louisiana.

In 1994, NCCUSL adopted the Revised Uniform Partnership Act (RUPA), which is intended to supersede the UPA. As of early 2000, RUPA had been enacted in a number of states, but by no means all states. Accordingly, the UPA continues to be important.

Under RUPA § 1006, RUPA normally applies not only to all partnerships formed after RUPA is adopted in any given state but, after a transition period, to all partnerships, even those formed before RUPA was adopted.

The cases and materials in this Section will largely concern the UPA, partly because as of this writing (2000) the UPA is still in effect in many states, partly because RUPA is so new that it has not yet spawned much case law, and partly because RUPA continues many of the rules of the UPA. In general, however, where RUPA makes a material change in a relevant UPA rule the changes will be discussed in a Text Note.

---

As of 1996, there were 1,116,054 general partnerships in the United States, with an average of 4 partners in each partnership. Alan Zempel, Partnership Returns, 1996, 18 Statistics of Income Bulletin No. 2, at 49–50 (1998).

This chapter will consider the basic partnership form, general partnerships. Two special partnership forms, limited partnerships and limited liability partnerships, will be considered in Chapter 7, infra.

---

## SECTION 1.   PARTNERSHIP FORMATION

---

### UNIFORM PARTNERSHIP ACT §§ 6, 7

---

**REVISED UNIFORM PARTNERSHIP ACT §§ 101(6), 202**

[See Statutory Supplement]

———

## Martin v. Peyton

New York Court of Appeals, 1927.
246 N.Y. 213, 158 N.E. 77.

Appeal from Supreme Court, Appellate Division, First Department.

Action by Charles S. Martin against William C. Peyton and others. A judgment of the Special Term, entered on the report of a referee in favor of the defendants was affirmed by the Appellate Division (219 App.Div. 297, 220 N.Y.S. 29), and plaintiff appeals. Affirmed.

ANDREWS, J. Much ancient learning as to partnership is obsolete. Today only those who are partners between themselves may be charged for partnership debts by others. (Partnership Law [Cons. Laws, ch. 39], sec. 11.) There is one exception. Now and then a recovery is allowed where in truth such relationship is absent. This is because the debtor may not deny the claim. (Sec. 27.)

Partnership results from contract, express or implied. If denied it may be proved by the production of some written instrument; by testimony as to some conversation; by circumstantial evidence. If nothing else appears the receipt by the defendant of a share of the profits of the business is enough. (Sec. 11.)

Assuming some written contract between the parties the question may arise whether it creates a partnership. If it be complete; if it expresses in good faith the full understanding and obligation of the parties, then it is for the court to say whether a partnership exists. It may, however, be a mere sham intended to hide the real relationship. Then other results follow. In passing upon it effect is to be given to each provision. Mere words will not blind us to realities. Statements that no partnership is intended are not conclusive. If as a whole a contract contemplates an association of two or more persons to carry on as co-owners a business for profit a partnership there is. (Sec. 10.) On the other hand, if it be less than this no partnership exists. Passing on the contract as a whole, an arrangement for sharing profits is to be considered. It is to be given its due weight. But it is to be weighed in connection with all the rest. It is not decisive. It may be merely the method adopted to pay a debt or wages,as interest on a loan or for other reasons.

An existing contract may be modified later by subsequent agreement, oral or written. A partnership may be so created where there was none before. And again, that the original agreement has been so modified may be proved by circumstantial evidence—by showing the conduct of the parties.

In the case before us the claim that the defendants became partners in the firm of Knauth, Nachod & Kuhne, doing business as bankers and brokers, depends upon the interpretation of certain instruments. There is nothing in their subsequent acts determinative of or indeed material upon this question. And we are relieved of questions that sometimes arise. "The plaintiff's position is not," we are told, "that the agreements of June 4, 1921, were a false expression or incomplete expression of the intention of the parties. We say that they express defendants' intention and that that intention was to create a relationship which as a matter of law constitutes a partnership." Nor may the claim of the plaintiff be rested on any question of estoppel. "The plaintiff's claim," he stipulates, "is a claim of actual partnership, not of partnership by estoppel...."

Remitted then, as we are, to the documents themselves, we refer to circumstances surrounding their execution only so far as is necessary to make them intelligible. And we are to remember that although the intention of the parties to avoid liability as partners is clear, although in language precise and definite they deny any design to then join the firm of K.N. & K.; although they say their interests in profits should be construed merely as a measure of compensation for loans, not an interest in profits as such; although they provide that they shall not be liable for any losses or treated as partners, the question still remains whether in fact they agree to so associate themselves with the firm as to "carry on as co-owners a business for profit."

In the spring of 1921 the firm of K.N. & K. found itself in financial difficulties. John R. Hall was one of the partners. He was a friend of Mr. Peyton. From him he obtained the loan of almost $500,000 of Liberty bonds, which K.N. & K. might use as collateral to secure bank advances. This, however, was not sufficient. The firm and its members had engaged in unwise speculations, and it was deeply involved. Mr. Hall was also intimately acquainted with George W. Perkins, Jr., and with Edward W. Freeman. He also knew Mrs. Peyton and Mrs. Perkins and Mrs. Freeman. All were anxious to help him. He, therefore, representing K.N. & K., entered into negotiations with them. While they were pending a proposition was made that Mr. Peyton, Mr. Perkins and Mr. Freeman or some of them should become partners. It met a decided refusal. Finally an agreement was reached. It is expressed in three documents, executed on the same day, all a part of the one transaction. They were drawn with care and are unambiguous. We shall refer to them as "the agreement," "the indenture" and "the option."

We have no doubt as to their general purpose. The respondents were to loan K.N. & K. $2,500,000 worth of liquid securities, which were to be returned to them on or before April 15, 1923. The firm might hypothecate them to secure loans totaling $2,000,000, using the proceeds as its business necessities required. To insure respondents against loss K.N. & K. were to turn over to them a large number of their own securities which may have been valuable, but which were of so speculative a nature that they could not be used as collateral for bank loans. In compensation for the loan the respondents were to receive 40 per cent of the profits of the firm until the return was made, not exceeding, however, $500,000 and not less than $100,000. Merely because the transaction involved the transfer of securities and not of cash does not prevent its being a loan within the meaning of section 11. The respondents also were given an option to join the firm if they or any of them expressed a desire to do so before June 4, 1923.

Many other detailed agreements are contained in the papers. Are they such as may be properly inserted to protect the lenders? Or do they go further? Whatever their purpose, did they in truth associate the respondents with the firm so that they and it together thereafter carried on as co-owners a business for profit? The answer depends upon an analysis of these various provisions.

As representing the lenders, Mr. Peyton and Mr. Freeman are called "trustees." The loaned securities when used as collateral are not to be mingled with other securities of K.N. & K., and the trustees at all times are to be kept informed of all transactions affecting them. To them shall be paid all dividends and income accruing therefrom. They may also substitute for any of the securities loaned securities of equal value. With their consent the firm may sell any of its securities held by the respondents, the proceeds to go, however, to the trustees. In other similar ways the trustees may deal with these same securities, but the securities loaned shall always be sufficient in value to permit of their hypothecation for $2,000,000. If they rise in price the excess may be withdrawn by the defendants. If they fall they shall make good the deficiency.

So far there is no hint that the transaction is not a loan of securities with a provision for compensation. Later a somewhat closer connection with the firm appears. Until the securities are returned the directing management of the firm is to be in the hands of John R. Hall, and his life is to be insured for $1,000,000, and the policies are to be assigned as further collateral security to the trustees. These requirements are not unnatural. Hall was the one known and trusted by the defendants. Their acquaintance with the other members of the firm was of the slightest. These others had brought an old and established business to the verge of bankruptcy. As the respondents knew, they also had engaged in unsafe speculation. The respondents were about to loan $2,500,000 of good securities. As collateral they were to receive others of problematical value. What they required seems but ordinary caution. Nor does it imply an association in the business.

The trustees are to be kept advised as to the conduct of the business and consulted as to important matters. They may inspect the firm books and are entitled to any information they think important. Finally they may veto any business they think highly speculative or injurious. Again we hold this but a proper precaution to safeguard the loan. The trustees may not initiate any transaction as a partner may do. They may not bind the firm by any action of their own. Under the circumstances the safety of the loan depended upon the business success of K.N. & K. This success was likely to be compromised by the inclination of its members to engage in speculation. No longer, if the respondents were to be protected, should it be allowed. The trustees, therefore, might prohibit it, and that their prohibition might be effective, information was to be furnished them. Not dissimilar agreements have been held proper to guard the interests of the lender.

As further security each member of K.N. & K. is to assign to the trustees their interest in the firm. No loan by the firm to any member is permitted and the amount each may draw is fixed. No other distribution of profits is to be made. So that realized profits may be calculated the existing capital is stated to be $700,000, and profits are to be realized as promptly as good business practice will permit. In case the trustees think this is not done, the question is left to them and to Mr. Hall, and if they differ then to an arbitrator. There is no obligation that the firm shall continue the business. It may dissolve at any time. Again we conclude there is nothing here not properly adapted to secure the interest of the respondents as lenders. If their compensation is dependent on a percentage of the profits still provision must be made to define what these profits shall be.

The "indenture" is substantially a mortgage of the collateral delivered by K.N. & K. to the trustees to secure the performance of the "agreement." It certainly does not strengthen the claim that the respondents were partners.

Finally we have the "option." It permits the respondents or any of them or their assignees or nominees to enter the firm at a later date if they desire to do so by buying 50 per cent or less of the interests therein of all or any of the members at a stated price. Or a corporation may, if the respondents and the members agree, be formed in place of the firm. Meanwhile, apparently with the design of protecting the firm business against improper or ill-judged action which might render the option valueless, each member of the firm is to place his resignation in the hands of Mr. Hall. If at any time he and the trustees agree that such resignation should be accepted, that member shall then retire, receiving the value of his interest calculated as of the date of such retirement.

This last provision is somewhat unusual, yet it is not enough in itself to show that on June 4, 1921, a present partnership was created nor taking these various papers as a whole do we reach such a result. It is quite true that even if one or two or three like provisions contained in such a contract do not require this conclusion, yet it is also true that when taken together a point may come where stipulations immaterial separately cover so wide a field that we should hold a partnership exists. As in other branches of the law a question of degree is often the determining factor. Here that point has not been reached. . . .

The judgment appealed from should be affirmed, with costs.

■ CARDOZO, CH. J., POUND, CRANE, LEHMAN, KELLOGG and O'BRIEN, JJ., concur.

Judgment affirmed, etc.

———

# Lupien v. Malsbenden

Supreme Judicial Court of Maine, 1984.
477 A.2d 746.

■ Before McKusick, C.J., and Nichols, Roberts, Wathen, Glassman and Scholnik, JJ.

■ McKusick, Chief Justice.

Defendant Frederick Malsbenden appeals a judgment of the Superior Court (York County) holding him to partnership liability on a written contract entered into between plaintiff Robert Lupien and one Stephen Cragin doing business as York Motor Mart.[1] The sole issue asserted on appeal is whether the Superior Court erred in its finding that Malsbenden and Cragin were partners in the pertinent part of York Motor Mart's business. We affirm.

On March 5, 1980, plaintiff entered into a written agreement with Stephen Cragin, doing business in the town of York as York Motor Mart, for the construction of a Bradley automobile.[2] Plaintiff made a deposit of $500 towards the purchase price of $8,020 upon signing the contract, and made a further payment of $3,950 one week later on March 12. Both the purchase order of March 5, 1980, and a later bill of sale, though signed by Cragin, identified the seller as York Motor Mart. At the jury-waived trial, plaintiff testified that after he signed the contract he made visits to York Motor Mart on an average of once or twice a week to check on the progress being made on his car. During those visits plaintiff generally dealt with Malsbenden because Cragin was seldom present. On one such visit in April, Malsbenden told plaintiff that it was necessary for the latter to sign over ownership of his pickup truck, which would constitute the balance of the consideration under the contract, so that the proceeds from the sale of the truck could be used to complete construction of the Bradley. When plaintiff complied, Malsbenden provided plaintiff with a rental car, and later with a "demo" model of the Bradley, for his use pending the completion of the vehicle he had ordered. When it was discovered that the "demo" actually belonged to a third person who had entrusted it to York Motor Mart for resale, Malsbenden purchased the vehicle for plaintiff's use. Plaintiff never received the Bradley he had contracted to purchase.

In his trial testimony, defendant Malsbenden asserted that his interest in the Bradley operation of York Motor Mart was only that of a banker. He stated that he had loaned $85,000 to Cragin, without interest, to finance the Bradley portion of York Motor Mart's business.[3] The loan was to be repaid from the proceeds of each car sold.

---

**1.** Cragin "disappeared" several months before this action was commenced. Plaintiff Lupien originally named Cragin as a co-defendant. However, since Cragin was never served with process, the Superior Court at the behest of both Lupien and defendant Malsbenden dismissed the claim against Cragin.

**2.** A Bradley automobile is a "kit car" constructed on a Volkswagen chassis.

**3.** Malsbenden's testimony indicated that Cragin carried on an automotive repair business at the York Motor Mart that was unrelated to the Bradley operation. Malsbenden testified, without contradiction, that he had no involvement with that other business.

Malsbenden acknowledged that Bradley kits were purchased with his personal checks and that he had also purchased equipment for York Motor Mart. He also stated that after Cragin disappeared sometime late in May 1980, he had physical control of the premises of York Motor Mart and that he continued to dispose of assets there even to the time of trial in 1983.

The Uniform Partnership Act, adopted in Maine at 31 M.R.S.A. §§ 281–323 (1978 & Supp.1983–1984), defines a partnership as "an association of 2 or more persons ... to carry on as co-owners[4] a business for profit." 31 M.R.S.A. § 286 (1978). Whether a partnership exists is an inference of law based on established facts. *See Dalton v. Austin,* 432 A.2d 774, 777 (Me.1981); *Roux v. Lawand,* 131 Me. 215, 219, 160 A. 756, 757 (1932); *James Bailey Co. v. Darling,* 119 Me. 326, 328, 111 A. 410, 411 (1920). A finding that the relationship between two persons constitutes a partnership may be based upon evidence of an agreement, either express or implied,

> to place their money, effects, labor, and skill, or some or all of them, in lawful commerce or business with the understanding that a community of profits will be shared.... No one factor is alone determinative of the existence of a partnership....

*Dalton v. Austin,* 432 A.2d at 777; *Cumberland County Power & Light Co. v. Gordon,* 136 Me. 213, 218, 7 A.2d 619, 622 (1939). *See James Bailey Co. v. Darling,* 119 Me. at 328, 111 A. at 411. If the arrangement between the parties otherwise qualifies as a partnership, it is of no matter that the parties did not expressly agree to form a partnership or did not even intend to form one:

> It is possible for parties to intend no partnership and yet to form one. If they agree upon an arrangement which is a partnership in fact, it is of no importance that they call it something else, or that they even expressly declare that they are not to be partners. The law must declare what is the legal import of their agreements, and names go for nothing when the substance of the arrangement shows them to be inapplicable.

*James Bailey Co. v. Darling,* 119 Me. at 328, 111 A. at 411 (quoting *Beecher v. Bush,* 45 Mich. 188, 193–94, 7 N.W. 785, 785–86 (1881)).

Here the trial justice concluded that, notwithstanding Malsbenden's assertion that he was only a "banker," his "total involvement" in the Bradley operation was that of a partner. The testimony at trial, both respecting Malsbenden's financial interest in the enterprise and his involvement in day-to-day business operations, amply supported the Superior Court's conclusion. Malsbenden had a financial interest of $85,000 in the Bradley portion of York Motor Mart's operations. Although Malsbenden termed the investment a loan, significantly he conceded that the "loan" carried no interest. His "loan" was not

---

**4.** As we made clear in *Dalton v. Austin,* 432 A.2d 774, 777 (Me.1981), the term "co-owners" as used in the statute does not necessarily mean joint title to all assets. On the contrary, "the right to participate in control of the business is the essence of co-ownership." *Id.*

made in the form of a fixed payment or payments, but was made to the business, at least in substantial part, in the form of day-to-day purchases of Bradley kits, other parts and equipment, and in the payment of wages. Furthermore, the "loan" was not to be repaid in fixed amounts or at fixed times, but rather only upon the sale of Bradley automobiles.

The evidence also showed that, unlike a banker, Malsbenden had the right to participate in control of the business and in fact did so on a day-to-day basis.[5] According to Urbin Savaria, who worked at York Motor Mart from late April through June 1980, Malsbenden during that time opened the business establishment each morning, remained present through part of every day, had final say on the ordering of parts, paid for parts and equipment, and paid Savaria's salary. On plaintiff's frequent visits to York Motor Mart, he generally dealt with Malsbenden because Cragin was not present. It was Malsbenden who insisted that plaintiff trade in his truck prior to the completion of the Bradley because the proceeds from the sale of the truck were needed to complete the Bradley. When it was discovered that the "demo" Bradley given to plaintiff while he awaited completion of his car actually belonged to a third party, it was Malsbenden who bought the car for plaintiff's use. As of three years after the making of the contract now in litigation, Malsbenden was still doing business at York Motor Mart, "just disposing of property."

Malsbenden and Cragin may well have viewed their relationship to be that of creditor-borrower, rather than a partnership. At trial Malsbenden so asserts, and Cragin's departure from the scene in the spring of 1980 deprives us of the benefit of his view of his business arrangement with Malsbenden. In any event, whatever the intent of these two men as to their respective involvements in the business of making and selling Bradley cars, there is no clear error in the Superior Court's finding that the Bradley car operation represented a pooling of Malsbenden's capital and Cragin's automotive skills, with joint control over the business and intent to share the fruits of the enterprise. As a matter of law, that arrangement amounted to a partnership under 31 M.R.S.A. § 286.

The entry is:

Judgment affirmed.

All concurring.

------

## NOTE ON THE FORMATION OF PARTNERSHIPS

1. *Formalities.* Corporations, limited partnerships, and limited liability companies can be organized (formed) only if certain formalities are complied with and a filing is made with the state. In contrast,

**5.** Thus its facts clearly distinguish the case at bar from *James Bailey Co. v. Darling,* 119 Me. 326, 332, 111 A. 410, 413 (1920), where although the defendant advanced money for the purchase of automobiles that was to be repaid upon the sale of individual automobiles, the defendant had no control over the business.

general partnerships can be organized with no formalities and no filing. The absence of a filing requirement reflects in part a conception that partnership status depends on the factual characteristics of a relationship between two or more persons, not on whether the persons think of themselves as having entered into a partnership.

Although no filings are *required* under either the UPA or RUPA, RUPA *permits* certain filings. See, e.g., Note on the Authority of Partners Under RUPA, infra.

2. *The Four-Element Test, Mutual Right of Control, and Loss-Sharing*. It is sometimes said that where there is no express partnership agreement, a relationship will be considered a partnership only if four elements are present—an agreement to share profits, an agreement to share losses, a mutual right of control or management of the business, and a community of interest in the venture. See, e.g., Weingart v. C & W Taylor Partnership, 248 Mont. 76, 809 P.2d 576 (1991); Corpus Christi v. Bayfront Associates, Ltd., 814 S.W.2d 98 (Tex.App.1991). This four-element test departs from the statutory test of both UPA § 6(a) and RUPA § 202, which provide simply that with certain exceptions a partnership is "an association of two or more persons to carry on as co-owners a business for profit," and say nothing about control or loss-sharing.

Although the Comments to both UPA § 6(a) and RUPA § 202 say that "to state that partners are co-owners of a business is to state that they each have the power of ultimate control," in fact even explicit partnership agreements frequently do not involve either ultimate control or loss-sharing for every partner. For example, many partnership agreements vest control in only one or more managing partners, or create elaborate allocations of voting power in which some partners do not share. Similarly, not every partnership agreement provides for loss sharing by every partner. If *explicit* partnership agreements do not always include control and loss-sharing as elements of the partnership relation, why should courts require those elements as a condition to finding an *implicit* partnership?

A better approach is that the presence or absence of the four specified elements, including mutual control and loss-sharing, is evidence, but not a requirement, of a partnership relation. This approach was taken, for example, in Beckman v. Farmer, 579 A.2d 618, 627 (D.C.App.1990), where the court said that "[t]he customary attributes of partnership, such as loss sharing and joint control of decisionmaking are necessary guideposts of inquiry, but none is conclusive." Other cases have held that once profit-sharing has been shown, it is not essential to show that there was an agreement to share in the losses. See Hansford v. Maplewood Station Business Park, 621 N.E.2d 347 (Ind.App.1993); Endsley v. Game–Show Placements, Ltd., 401 N.E.2d 768 (Ind.App.1980).

# SECTION 2.    THE LEGAL NATURE OF A PARTNERSHIP

## UNIFORM PARTNERSHIP ACT § 6

---

## REVISED UNIFORM PARTNERSHIP ACT §§ 101(6), 201

[See Statutory Supplement]

---

## NOTE ON THE LEGAL NATURE OF A PARTNERSHIP: ENTITY OR AGGREGATE STATUS

1.  *Entity v. Aggregate.* Individuals may associate in a wide variety of forms, and the issue often arises whether a given form of association has a legal status separate from that of its members. Frequently, this issue is stated in terms of whether a particular form of association is—or is not—a "separate legal entity" or a "legal person" (as opposed to a natural person, that is, an individual). A variety of issues may turn on the answer to this question—for example, whether the association can sue and be sued in its own name, and whether it can hold property in its own right.

In the history of English and American law this issue arose in the context of many different kinds of associations, such as universities, charitable institutions, and even municipalities. In most cases the issue was eventually resolved in a straightforward way, but in the case of partnerships it continued to be vexing. The predominant although not exclusive view under the common law was that a partnership was not an entity, but merely an aggregate of its members, so that a partnership was no more a legal person than was a friendship.

2.  *The UPA.* In 1902, when the Conference of Commissioners on Uniform State Laws determined to promulgate a Uniform Partnership Act, Dean James Barr Ames of Harvard Law School was appointed to draft the Act. Subsequently, the Commissioners instructed Dean Ames, at his own urging, to draft the Act on the theory that a partnership is a legal entity. Accordingly, in the drafts submitted by Dean Ames a partnership was defined as "*a legal person* formed by the association of two or more individuals for the purpose of carrying on business with a view to profit," and various provisions of the drafts reflected the entity theory. Dean Ames died before the work was completed, however, and his successor, Dean William Draper Lewis of the University of Pennsylvania Law School, was distinctly unfriendly to the entity view. Ultimately, Dean Lewis convinced the Commissioners to instruct him to draft the Act on the aggregate theory. UPA Section 6 therefore provides simply that "A partnership is an association of two or more persons to carry on as co-owners a business for profit." Although the language of this provision does not in itself render the issue free from doubt, it is pretty clear that the Act was intended to adopt the aggregate rather than the entity theory of partnership.

However, that is not the end of the story. Having adopted the aggregate theory in principle, in practice the UPA deals with a number of specific issues (such as the ownership of partnership property) *as if* a partnership is an entity. For many purposes, this approach works pretty well. Generally speaking, however, the entity theory of partnership works much better than the aggregate theory. In cases where the UPA treats the partnership as if it is an entity despite the aggregate theory, the results are good but the manner in which the statute reaches those results involves needlessly complex mechanics. In cases where the UPA does not treat the partnership as if it is an entity, the results tend to be bad and in need of legislative revision.

3.   *Other Statutes.* The question often arises whether a partnership that operates in a UPA jurisdiction is to be treated as an aggregate or an entity for the purpose of statutes *other* than the UPA. See, e.g., United States v. A & P Trucking Co., 358 U.S. 121, 79 S.Ct. 203, 3 L.Ed.2d 165 (1958). This question is a matter of legislative intent under the relevant statute. As in all such matters, the answer will depend on the language employed and the purposes manifested in the statute. The fact that the UPA adopts the aggregate theory will be relevant, but not dispositive, in answering that question. A legislature may choose to treat a partnership as an entity for purposes of another statute, even though a partnership is defined as an association under the U.P.A. See,e.g., United States v. A & P Trucking Co., 358 U.S. 121, 79 S.Ct. 203, 3 L.Ed.2d 165 (1958).

4.   *RUPA.* In contrast to the UPA, RUPA confers entity status on partnerships. RUPA § 101, like UPA § 6, defines a partnership as "an association of two or more persons to carry on as co-owners a business for profit." However, RUPA § 201 then squarely provides that "A partnership is an entity."

# SECTION 3.   THE ONGOING OPERATION OF PARTNERSHIPS

———

## (a) MANAGEMENT

———

### UNIFORM PARTNERSHIP ACT §§ 18(e), (g), (h), 19, 20

———

### REVISED UNIFORM PARTNERSHIP
### ACT §§ 103, 401(f), (i), (j), 403

[See Statutory Supplement]

———

## Summers v. Dooley

Supreme Court of Idaho, 1971.
94 Idaho 87, 481 P.2d 318.

■ DONALDSON, JUSTICE.

This lawsuit, tried in the district court, involves a claim by one partner against the other for $6,000. The complaining partner asserts that he has been required to pay out more than $11,000 in expenses without any reimbursement from either the partnership funds or his partner. The expenditure in question was incurred by the complaining partner (John Summers, plaintiff-appellant) for the purpose of hiring an additional employee. The trial court denied him any relief except for ordering that he be entitled to one half $966.72 which it found to be a legitimate partnership expense.

The pertinent facts leading to this lawsuit are as follows. Summers entered a partnership agreement with Dooley (defendant-respondent) in 1958 for the purpose of operating a trash collection business. The business was operated by the two men and when either was unable to work, the non-working partner provided a replacement at his own expense. In 1962, Dooley became unable to work and, at his own expense, hired an employee to take his place. In July, 1966, Summers approached his partner Dooley regarding the hiring of an additional employee but Dooley refused. Nevertheless, on his own initiative, Summers hired the man and paid him out of his own pocket. Dooley, upon discovering that Summers had hired an additional man, object-ed, stating that he did not feel additional labor was necessary and refused to pay for the new employee out of the partnership funds. Summers continued to operate the business using the third man and in October of 1967 instituted suit in the district court for $6,000 against his partner, the gravamen of the complaint being that Summers has been required to pay out more than $11,000 in expenses, incurred in the hiring of the additional man, without any reimbursement from either the partnership funds or his partner. After trial before the court, sitting without a jury, Summers was granted only partial relief[1] and he has appealed. He urges in essence that the trial court erred by failing to conclude that he should be reimbursed for expenses and costs connected in the employment of extra help in the partnership business.

The principal thrust of appellant's contention is that in spite of the fact that one of the two partners refused to consent to the hiring of additional help, nonetheless, the non-consenting partner retained profits earned by the labors of the third man and therefore the non-consenting partner should be estopped from denying the need and value of the employee, and has by his behavior ratified the act of the other partner who hired the additional man.

---

1. The trial court did award Summers one half of $966.72 which it found to be a legitimate partnership expense.

The issue presented for decision by this appeal is whether an equal partner in a two man partnership has the authority to hire a new employee in disregard of the objection of the other partner and then attempt to charge the dissenting partner with the costs incurred as a result of his unilateral decision.

The State of Idaho has enacted specific statutes with respect to the legal concept known as "partnership." Therefore any solution of partnership problems should logically begin with an application of the relevant code provision.

In the instant case the record indicates that although Summers requested his partner Dooley to agree to the hiring of a third man, such requests were not honored. In fact Dooley made it clear that he was "voting no" with regard to the hiring of an additional employee.

An application of the relevant statutory provisions and pertinent case law to the factual situation presented by the instant case indicates that the trial court was correct in its disposal of the issue since a majority of the partners did not consent to the hiring of the third man. I.C. § 53–318(8) provides:

> "Any difference arising as to ordinary matters connected with the partnership business may be decided by a *majority of the partners*...." (emphasis supplied) ...

The intent of the legislature may be implied from the language used, or inferred on grounds of policy or reasonableness.... A careful reading of the statutory provision indicates that subsection 5 bestows *equal rights in the management and conduct of the partnership business* upon all of the partners. The concept of equality between partners with respect to management of business affairs is a central theme and recurs throughout the Uniform Partnership law, I.C. § 53–301 et seq., which has been enacted in this jurisdiction. Thus the only reasonable interpretation of I.C. § 53–318(8) is that business differences must be decided by a majority of the partners provided no other agreement between the partners speaks to the issues....

In the case at bar one of the partners continually voiced objection to the hiring of the third man. He did not sit idly by and acquiesce in the actions of his partner. Under these circumstances it is manifestly unjust to permit recovery of an expense which was incurred individually and not for the benefit of the partnership but rather for the benefit of one partner.

Judgment affirmed. Costs to respondent.

■ McQUADE, C.J., and McFADDEN, SHEPARD and SPEAR, JJ., concur.

---

## QUESTION

Suppose that A, B, and C form a partnership. A contributes 90% of the capital, and by agreement is entitled to 90% of any profits and is responsible for 90% of any losses. B and C each contribute 5% of the capital and by agreement each is entitled to 5% of any profits, and responsible for 5% of any losses. Nothing is said in the agreement concerning how decisions will be made. If A votes one way on an ordinary matter connected with the partnership, and B and C vote another way, who prevails?

---

### NOTE ON THE MANAGEMENT OF PARTNERSHIPS

1.  *Voting.* The cases and authorities are divided on the issue raised in Summers v. Dooley. In accord with *Summers* is Covalt v. High, 100 N.M. 700, 675 P.2d 999 (App.1983). But see National Biscuit Co. v. Stroud, 249 N.C. 467, 106 S.E.2d 692 (1959).

2.  *Participation.* Because UPA Section 18(h) provides that partnership action requires a majority vote, what is added by UPA Section 18(e), which provides that all partners have equal rights in the management and conduct of the partnership business? Presumably, the effect of this Section is that absent contrary agreement, every partner must be *consulted* in partnership decisions.

> For a majority of partners to say; We do not care what one partner may say, we, being the majority, will do what we please, is, I apprehend, what this Court will not allow. So, again, with respect to making Mr. *Robertson* the treasurer, Mr. *Const* had a right to be consulted; his opinion might be overruled, and honestly over-ruled, but he ought to have had the question put to him and discussed: In all partnerships ... the partners are bound to be true and faithful to each other: They are to act upon the joint opinion of all, and the discretion and judgment of anyone cannot be excluded: What weight is to be given to it is another question. ...

Const v. Harris, 37 Eng.Rep. 1191, 1202 (Ch.1824) (Lord Chancellor Eldon). Thus absent contrary agreement, a majority of partners who made decisions without consulting a minority partner would violate § 18(e), even though the majority could have overridden the minority partner after he had been consulted.

RUPA § 401(f) continues the rule of UPA § 18(e), by conferring on each partner the right to participate in management. The Comment to § 401(f) notes that UPA § 18(e) "has been interpreted broadly to mean that, absent contrary agreement, each partner has a continuing right to participate in the management of the partnership and to be informed about the partnership business, even if his assent ... is not required."

---

## (b) INDEMNIFICATION AND CONTRIBUTION

---

**UNIFORM PARTNERSHIP ACT §§ 18(a), (b), (c), (d), (f)**

———

**REVISED UNIFORM PARTNERSHIP ACT §§ 401(a)–(e), (h)**

[See Statutory Supplement]

———

## NOTE ON INDEMNIFICATION AND CONTRIBUTION

As discussed in Section 5, infra, partners are individually liable to partnership creditors for partnership obligations. As between the partners, however, each partner is liable only for his share of partnership obligations. Thus if one partner pays off a partnership obligation in full (or, for that matter, if he simply pays more than his share), he is entitled to *indemnification* from the *partnership* for the difference between what he paid and his share of the liability.

Indemnification should be distinguished from *contribution*. In a proper case, a partner has a right to be indemnified by the partnership. In contrast, in a proper case the partnership has a right to require *contribution* from one or more *partners*. Thus the obligation to indemnify a partner is a partnership liability, and the obligation to make contribution is a liability of a partner. Partners may, for example, be required to make contribution to fund a partnership obligation to indemnify another partner, so that all partners share a burden that was initially placed on only one. Contribution may also be required for other purposes—in particular, paying off partnership creditors and equalizing capital losses.

"Indemnification resolves the apparent conflict between a partner's joint or joint and several liability, whereby a partner may be called upon to pay the entire amount of partnership debt to third parties under UPA § 15 and RUPA § 306 and the proportionate sharing of profits and losses among the partners under UPA § 18(a) and RUPA § 401(b). A partner who pays or incurs a personal liability to a third party on behalf of the partnership becomes a creditor of the partnership in the amount of the payment or liability, in effect subrogated to the rights of the creditor.... If a going partnership indemnifies the partner, all partners incur a detriment in proportion to their profit shares if the business is profitable, or otherwise according to their loss shares. If the partnership is unable to pay, all partners must contribute to make up the resulting deficit under UPA §§ 18(a) and 40(b)(11) and (d) and RUPA §§ 401(b) and 807(b) according to their loss shares. If the partners are unable to contribute or cannot be sued, the paying partner, rather than the third party, bears the loss." Bromberg & Ribstein on Partnership § 6.02(f).

———

## (c) DISTRIBUTIONS, REMUNERATION, AND CAPITAL CONTRIBUTIONS

---

### UNIFORM PARTNERSHIP ACT §§ 18(a), (b), (c), (d), (f)

---

### REVISED UNIFORM PARTNERSHIP ACT § 401(a)–(e), (h)

[See Statutory Supplement]

---

### QUESTION

Suppose A, B, and C form a partnership. A contributes 90% of the capital, and B and C each contribute 5%. All work full-time in the partnership business, with roughly equal responsibilities. Nothing is said in the partnership agreement concerning how partnership profits will be divided. If the partnership makes a profit in a given year, how is it to be divided?

---

## SECTION 4.   THE AUTHORITY OF A PARTNER

---

### UNIFORM PARTNERSHIP ACT §§ 3, 4(3), 9, 10, 11, 12, 13, 14

---

### REVISED UNIFORM PARTNERSHIP ACT
### §§ 301, 302, 303, 304, 305, 306, 308

[See Statutory Supplement]

---

**BURNS v. GONZALEZ**, 439 S.W.2d 128 (Tex.Civ.App.1969). Bosquez and Gonzalez were partners in a business that sold broadcast time on a radio station located in Mexico. The station was owned and operated by a Mexican corporation, Radiodifusora. Bosquez and Gonzalez each owned 50% of Radiodifusora's stock, and Bosquez was its president. In 1957, Radiodifusora made a contract with Burns, which it failed to perform. Subsequently, Bosquez, purporting to act on his own behalf and on behalf of the partnership, executed a $40,000 promissory note payable to Burns, partly in exchange for Burns's promise not to sue Radiodifusora. Burns sued Bosquez and Gonzalez on the note, as partners. Gonzalez argued that Bosquez had no authority to execute the note on the partnership's behalf. In reviewing a jury verdict in favor of defendants, the court stated:

> [Because the] express limitation on the authority of Bosquez was unknown to Burns, then, under the language of [UPA] Sec. 9(1), his act in executing the note would bind the partnership if such act can be classified as an act "for apparently carrying on in the usual way the business of the partnership."
>
> As we interpret Sec. 9(1), the act of a partner binds the firm, absent an express limitation of authority known to the party dealing with such partner, if such act is for the purpose of "apparently carrying on" the business of the partnership in the way in which other firms engaged in the same business in the locality usually transact business, or in the way in which the particular partnership usually transacts its business. In this case, [however,] there is no evidence relating to the manner in which firms engaged in the sale of advertising time on radio stations usually transact business.

---

## NOTE ON THE AUTHORITY OF PARTNERS

The basic rule governing a partner's actual authority under the UPA is that each partner is an agent of the partnership for the purpose of its business. This rule interacts with the UPA's rule on a partner's apparent authority. For most practical purposes, the major difference between the UPA and RUPA concerning a partner's authority is that RUPA § 301(1) makes clear, as the UPA did not, that a partnership is bound by an act of the partner for apparently carrying on in the usual way (i) the partnership business or (ii) business *of the kind* carried on by the partnership. The Comment to § 301(1) states:

> Section 301(1).... clarifies that a partner's apparent authority includes acts for carrying on in the ordinary course "business of the kind carried on by the partnership," not just the business of the particular partnership in question. The UPA is ambiguous on this point, but there is some authority for an expanded construction.... See, e.g., Burns v. Gonzalez, 439 S.W.2d 128, 131 (Tex.Civ.App.1969) (dictum)....

The treatment of authority under RUPA also differs from the UPA in certain other respects. For example, RUPA § 302 provides elaborate rules concerning when a transfer of partnership property is binding. In addition:

1. RUPA § 301 makes subtle shifts in determining when a third person's knowledge or notice of a restriction on a partner's authority will be effective to prevent partnership liability from arising. "Under UPA section 9(1), the partnership was not bound by the unauthorized actions of a partner if the third party had 'knowledge' of the partner's lack of authority. Under UPA section 9(1), a third party had knowledge

when he or she had actual knowledge or 'when he [or she] has knowledge of such other facts as in the circumstances shows bad faith.' This latter language creates an implied or inquiry notice, the exact parameters of which are ill-defined. Under RUPA, the third party will not be placed under a duty of inquiry or be deemed to have notice from the facts and circumstances. Only actual knowledge or receipt of a notification of a partner's lack of authority will meet the standard." Merrill, Partnership Property and Partnership Authority Under the Revised Uniform Partnership Act, 49 Bus.Law. 83, 88–89 (1993).

2. RUPA § 303 enables a partnership to file a "Statement of Partnership Authority." Under § 303, a *grant* of authority set forth in such a Statement is normally conclusive in favor of third persons, even if they have no actual knowledge of the Statement, unless they have actual knowledge that the partner has no such authority. However, a *limitation* on a partner's authority that is contained in such a Statement, other than a limitation on the partner's authority to transfer real property, will not be effective unless the third party knows of the limitation or the Statement has been delivered to him. A limitation, in a Statement of Partnership Authority, of a partner's authority to transfer partnership real property is effective against all third persons if a certified copy of the Statement is filed in the real-property recording office.

Why would a partnership want to file a Statement that may expand a partner's authority, but will not limit a partner's authority unless it is not only filed but also delivered? One answer is that persons who deal with a partnership may require such a Statement to ensure themselves that the partnership will be bound. Furthermore, "[in] the process of searching for the grant of authority, the third party will acquire actual knowledge of any restriction on authority in a filed statement. [And] the ... partners may protect themselves by delivering the statement to all known creditors, actual or potential." Merrill, supra, at 89.

## SECTION 5. LIABILITY FOR PARTNERSHIP OBLIGATIONS

———

### UNIFORM PARTNERSHIP ACT §§ 9, 13, 14, 15, 16, 17, 36

———

### REVISED UNIFORM PARTNERSHIP ACT §§ 305, 306, 307, 308

[See Statutory Supplement]

———

**NOTE ON LIABILITY FOR PARTNERSHIP OBLIGATIONS**

1.   *UPA.* The provisions of the Uniform Partnership Act governing liability for partnership obligations reflect an amalgam of the entity and aggregate theories. On the one hand, UPA §§ 9, 13, and 14 make "the partnership" liable for defined acts of the partners. It might seem to follow that this liability could be enforced by a suit against the partnership. However, the UPA does not authorize such a suit, because it does not recognize a partnership as an entity, and unless authorized by statute, suit normally cannot be brought against an association that is not an entity. Indeed, the UPA goes to the opposite extreme. Under UPA § 15(a), partners are *jointly and severally* liable for wrongful acts and omissions of the partnership (such as torts)and breaches of trust. Under UPA § 15(b), however, partners are only *jointly* liable "for all other debts and obligations of the partnership." At common law, if an obligation is "joint and several" the obligors can be sued either jointly or separately. If, however, an obligation is only "joint" the obligee must join all the obligors in the same suit (subject to a few exceptions where jurisdiction over all the obligors cannot be obtained). See C. Clark, Handbook of the Law of Code Pleading 373–74 (2d ed. 1947). Thus under the UPA, an action on a partnership's contractual obligation must be brought against all the partners, and if even one partner is not joined, the action can be dismissed on motion by the partners who were joined.

The inability of a partnership creditor to sue a partnership in its own name, under the UPA, is obviously undesirable, and many states have statutorily patched up the UPA rule by adopting Common Name Statutes, which explicitly allow a partnership to be sued in its own name. An example is N.Y.Civ.Prac.L. & R. § 1025: "Two or more persons conducting a business as a partnership may sue or be sued in the partnership name . . . ." Under such statutes, a judgment is binding on the partnership property and on the individual property of all partners who are served.

The need to join all the partners in a suit to establish liability on a contract claim is also undesirable. Some states address this issue by making all partnership liabilities joint and several, rather than joint. Other states have adopted Joint Debtor Statutes, which provide that a suit against joint obligors can proceed even if some of the obligors are not joined. See, e.g., Cal.Civ.Proc.Code § 410.70. Under such statutes, a judgment is binding on both the joint (partnership) property and on the property of those partners who are served.

2.   *RUPA.* Unlike the UPA, RUPA § 307(a) specifically provides that a partnership may both *sue* and *be sued* in its own name. Furthermore, RUPA § 306 provides that partners are jointly and severally liable for *all* obligations of the partnership. However, RUPA adds a new barrier to *collecting* against an individual partner. Under RUPA § 307, a judgment against a partner based on a claim against the partnership normally cannot be satisfied against the partner's individual assets, unless and until a judgment on the same claim has been rendered against the partnership and a writ of execution on the

judgment has been returned unsatisfied. To put this differently, RUPA § 307 adopts an exhaustion rule, under which partnership assets must be exhausted before a partner's individual assets can be reached. (The exhaustion rule is made subject to certain exceptions, one of which is that the rule does not apply if the partnership is in bankruptcy.) Thus as the Comment to RUPA § 306 points out, "Joint and several liability under RUPA differs ... from the classic model [of joint and several liability outside RUPA], which permits a judgment creditor to proceed immediately against any of the joint and several judgment debtors."

In effect, RUPA takes an aggregate-like approach to a partner's *liability*, but an entity-like approach to *collecting judgments* based on that liability. (RUPA § 307 also provides that, subject to certain exceptions, a judgment against a partnership is not by itself a judgment against a partner, and cannot be satisfied from a partner's assets unless there is also a judgment against the partner.)

## SECTION 6.   PARTNERSHIP INTERESTS AND PARTNERSHIP PROPERTY

———

**UNIFORM PARTNERSHIP ACT §§ 8, 18(g), 24, 25, 26, 27, 28**

———

**REVISED UNIFORM PARTNERSHIP ACT §§ 203, 204, 501, 502, 503, 504**

[See Statutory Supplement]

———

### NOTE ON PARTNERSHIP PROPERTY

1.   *The UPA.* Property that is used by a partnership may be either partnership property or the property of individual partners that is in effect loaned to the partnership. The issue whether property used by the partnership is partnership property or the property of individual partners may be important for several different reasons. First, the issue may be important for purposes of determining who has the power to transfer the property. Property owned by the partnership can be transferred by the partnership. Property loaned to the partnership cannot be. Second, the issue may be important if creditors of the partnership are competing with creditors of an individual partner, and the question arises whether any given property is owned by the partnership or owned by the partner and loaned to the partnership. Third, the issue may be important if the partnership is dissolved: If property used by the partnership is partnership property, on dissolution the property must be sold along with other partnership assets,

and the proceeds of the sale must be distributed among the partners. In contrast, if property used by the partnership is the individual property of a partner, on dissolution the property must normally be returned directly to that partner, rather than sold for the account of all the partners.[1] This third issue may be especially important if the property is crucial to the partnership's business, so that as a practical matter whoever owns the property has the ability to continue the business.

If the aggregate theory of the UPA was strictly applied, a partnership could not own property. Rather, the property that the partners think of as partnership property would as a matter of law be held by the individual partners as joint tenants or tenants in common. For a variety of reasons, such a regime would be wholly impracticable. Accordingly, in the matter of partnership property, as in several other matters, the UPA lays down rules that effectively treat the partnership *as if* it were an entity.

This objective is accomplished largely with smoke and mirrors. UPA § 8 recognizes the concept of "partnership property," and explicitly permits real property to be held in the partnership's name. (Even before the UPA, it was well settled that personal property could be so held.) However, UPA § 25(1) provides that "partnership property" is owned by the *partners,* under the ingenuous nomenclature, *tenancy in partnership.* UPA § 25(2) then systematically strips from the individual partners every incident normally associated with ownership. Under § 25(2)(a), a partner has no right to possess partnership property as an individual. Under § 25(2)(b), a partner cannot individually assign his rights in specific partnership property. Under § 25(2)(c), a partner's rights in specific partnership property cannot be subject to attachment or execution by a creditor of the partner in the latter's individual capacity. Under § 25(2)(d), when the partner dies his right in specific partnership property does not devolve on his heirs or legatees. Under Section 25(2)(e), widows, heirs, and next of kin cannot claim dower, curtesy,or allowances in the partner's right to specific partnership property. In short, under the UPA in theory individual partners own the partnership property, but in practice all the incidents of ownership are vested in the partnership, so that the "tenan[cy] in partnership" rule of the UPA has no real-world significance.

2. *RUPA*, which confers entity status on partnerships, drops the elaborate tenancy-in-partnership apparatus of the UPA. RUPA § 203 provides that "Property acquired by a partnership is property of the partnership and not the partners individually." RUPA § 204 then sets out a series of rules and presumptions concerning whether any given property is partnership property or the separate property of a partner. These provisions are supplemented by § 501, which provides that "A partner is not a co-owner of partnership property and has no interest

---

1. But see Pav–Saver Corp. v. Vasso Corp., 143 Ill.App.3d 1013, 97 Ill.Dec. 760, 493 N.E.2d 423 (1986) (wrongfully dissolving partner held not entitled to return of property).

in partnership property which can be transferred, either voluntarily or involuntarily." The purpose of § 501 is to explicitly abolish the UPA concept of tenancy in partnership.

_____

### NOTE ON PARTNERSHIP INTERESTS

1. *The Partner's Interest in the Partnership*. Although a partner does not own partnership property under the UPA except in some metaphysical sense, he does own his *interest* in the partnership, that is, his share of the partnership. The net result is a functional two-level ownership structure that is somewhat comparable to the two-level ownership structure in a corporation. In the case of a corporation, the corporation owns the corporate property, and the shareholder owns her shares in the corporation. In the case of a UPA partnership, in practice (although not in theory) the partnership owns the partnership property, and the partner owns her interest in the partnership.

2. *Assignment*. As compared to ordinary property interests, a partnership interest is conditioned in one very important respect. Normally, the owner of a property interest can freely sell it, and a creditor can freely levy on it. In contrast, although a partnership interest is assignable, a partner cannot make an assignment of his partnership interest that would substitute the transferee as a partner in the transferor's place, because no person can become a partner without the consent of all the partners. Correspondingly, a creditor cannot levy on a partnership interest in such a way as to be substituted as a partner; nor can a creditor recover her debt by selling the partnership interest to a third party who will be substituted as a partner. Accordingly, the assignee of a partnership interest does not become a partner (unless all the other partners consent), and has no right to information about the partnership and no right to inspect the partnership books. However, as long as the partnership continues in existence, the assignee of a partnership interest does have a right to receive the distributions to which the assigning partner would other-wise be entitled; and on dissolution the assignee has a right to receive the assigning partner's interest. In practice, despite the limitations on the assignor's rights partnership interests have a fairly high degree of assignability. See A. Bromberg, Enforcement of Partnership Obligations—Who is Sued for The Partnership?, 71 Neb. L. Rev. 143, 240 (1992).

A partner who has assigned her partnership interest remains a partner. However, RUPA § 601(4)(ii) explicitly permits the nonassigning partners to expel the assignor from the partnership, and UPA § 31(c) permits the nonassigning partners to dissolve the partnership as of right even if the partnership is not at will.

3. *Partnership Creditors*.

a. *UPA*. A partner's *separate creditor* (that is a creditor who has extended credit to a partner as an individual, rather than extending credit to a partnership) is in a position somewhat comparable to the assignee of a partnership interest. Under UPA § 28, if such a creditor obtains a judgment, he can get a *charging order* on the partner's partnership interest. Such an order will effectively give the creditor the right to be paid the partnership distributions to which the debtor-partner would be otherwise entitled. The creditor can foreclose on the partnership interest under UPA § 28, and thereby cause its sale. In that case, the buyer of the interest has the right to compel dissolution if (i) the term of the partnership has expired, or (ii) the partnership is at will. Alternatively, the creditor may put the individual partner into bankruptcy, which will result in dissolution of the partnership under UPA § 31(5).

b. *RUPA*. RUPA § 504 continues UPA § 28 largely unchanged in substance. RUPA § 504 does add some details that are not found in UPA § 28, but for the most part these details are consistent with the case law under § 28. Like the UPA, RUPA § 801(a) provides that a transferee of a partner's transferable interest is entitled to judicial dissolution on the partnership (i) at any time in a partnership at will, and (ii) after the expiration of the partnership's term or the completion of the undertaking in a partnership for a particular undertaking.

## SECTION 7.   THE PARTNER'S DUTY OF LOYALTY

---

### UNIFORM PARTNERSHIP ACT § 21

---

### REVISED UNIFORM PARTNERSHIP ACT
### §§ 103(a),(b) (3), (5), 104, 403, 404, 405

[See Statutory Supplement]

---

## Meinhard v. Salmon

New York Court of Appeals, 1928.
249 N.Y. 458, 164 N.E. 545.

Appeal from a judgment of the Appellate Division of the Supreme Court in the first judicial department, entered June 28, 1928, modifying and affirming as modified a judgment in favor of plaintiff entered upon the report of a referee.

■ CARDOZO, CH. J. On April 10, 1902, Louisa M. Gerry leased to the defendant Walter J. Salmon the premises known as the Hotel Bristol at the northwest corner of Forty-second street and Fifth avenue in the city of New York. The lease was for a term of twenty years, commencing May 1, 1902, and ending April 30, 1922. The lessee undertook to change the hotel building for use as shops and offices at a cost of $200,000. Alterations and additions were to be accretions to the land.

Salmon, while in course of treaty with the lessor as to the execution of the lease, was in course of treaty with Meinhard, the plaintiff, for the necessary funds. The result was a joint venture with terms embodied in a writing. Meinhard was to pay to Salmon half of the moneys requisite to reconstruct, alter, manage and operate the property. Salmon was to pay to Meinhard 40 per cent of the net profits for the first five years of the lease and 50 per cent for the years thereafter. If there were losses, each party was to bear them equally. Salmon, however, was to have sole power to "manage, lease, underlet and operate" the building. There were to be certain pre-emptive rights for each in the contingency of death.

The two were coadventurers, subject to fiduciary duties akin to those of partners (King v. Barnes, 109 N.Y. 267). As to this we are all agreed. The heavier weight of duty rested, however, upon Salmon. He was a coadventurer with Meinhard, but he was manager as well. During the early years of the enterprise, the building, reconstructed, was operated at a loss. If the relation had then ended, Meinhard as well as Salmon would have carried a heavy burden. Later the profits became large with the result that for each of the investors there came a rich return. For each, the venture had its phases of fair weather and of foul. The two were in it jointly, for better or for worse.

When the lease was near its end, Elbridge T. Gerry had become the owner of the reversion. He owned much other property in the neighborhood, one lot adjoining the Bristol Building on Fifth avenue and four lots on Forty-second street. He had a plan to lease the entire tract for a long term to some one who would destroy the buildings then existing, and put up another in their place. In the latter part of 1921, he submitted such a project to several capitalists and dealers. He was unable to carry it through with any of them. Then, in January, 1922, with less than four months of the lease to run, he approached the defendant Salmon. The result was a new lease to the Midpoint Realty Company, which is owned and controlled by Salmon, a lease covering the whole tract, and involving a huge outlay. The term is to be twenty years, but successive covenants for renewal will extend it to a maximum of eighty years at the will of either party. The existing buildings may remain unchanged for seven years. They are then to be torn down, and a new building to cost $3,000,000 is to be placed upon the site. The rental, which under the Bristol lease was only $55,000, is to be from $350,000 to $475,000 for the properties so combined. Salmon personally guaranteed the performance by the lessee of the covenants of the new lease until such time as the new building had been completed and fully paid for.

The lease between Gerry and the Midpoint Realty Company was signed and delivered on January 25, 1922. Salmon had not told Meinhard anything about it. Whatever his motive may have been, he had kept the negotiations to himself. Meinhard was not informed even of the bare existence of a project. The first that he knew of it was in February when the lease was an accomplished fact. He then made demand on the defendants that the lease be held in trust as an asset of the venture, making offer upon the trial to share the personal obligations incidental to the guaranty. The demand was followed by refusal, and later by this suit. A referee gave judgment for the plaintiff, limiting the plaintiff's interest in the lease, however, to 25 per cent. The limitation was on the theory that the plaintiff's equity was to be restricted to one-half of so much of the value of the lease as was contributed or represented by the occupation of the Bristol site. Upon cross-appeals to the Appellate Division, the judgment was modified so as to enlarge the equitable interest to one-half of the whole lease. With this enlargement of plaintiff's interest, there went, of course, a corresponding enlargement of his attendant obligations. The case is now here on an appeal by the defendants.

Joint adventurers, like copartners, owe to one another, while the enterprise continues, the duty of the finest loyalty. Many forms of conduct permissible in a workaday world for those acting at arm's length, are forbidden to those bound by fiduciary ties. A trustee is held to something stricter than the morals of the market place. Not honesty alone, but the punctilio of an honor the most sensitive, is then the standard of behavior. As to this there has developed a tradition that is unbending and inveterate. Uncompromising rigidity has been the attitude of courts of equity when petitioned to undermine the rule of undivided loyalty by the "disintegrating erosion" of particular exceptions (Wendt v. Fischer, 243 N.Y. 439, 444). Only thus has the level of conduct for fiduciaries been kept at a level higher than that trodden by the crowd. It will not consciously be lowered by any judgment of this court.

The owner of the reversion, Mr. Gerry, had vainly striven to find a tenant who would favor his ambitious scheme of demolition and construction. Baffled in the search, he turned to the defendant Salmon in possession of the Bristol, the keystone of the project. He figured to himself beyond a doubt that the man in possession would prove a likely customer. To the eye of an observer, Salmon held the lease as owner in his own right, for himself and no one else. In fact he held it as a fiduciary, for himself and another, sharers in a common venture. If this fact had been proclaimed, if the lease by its terms had run in favor of a partnership, Mr. Gerry, we may fairly assume, would have laid before the partners, and not merely before one of them, his plan of reconstruction. The pre-emptive privilege, or, better, the pre-emptive opportunity, that was thus an incident of the enterprise, Salmon appropriated to himself in secrecy and silence. He might have warned Meinhard that the plan had been submitted, and that either would be free to compete for the award. If he had done this, we do not need to say whether he would have been under a duty, if successful in the competition, to hold the lease so acquired for the benefit of a venture then about to end, and thus prolong by indirection its responsibilities and duties. The trouble about his conduct is that he excluded his coadventurer from any chance to compete, from any chance to enjoy the opportunity for benefit that had come to him alone by virtue of his agency. This chance, if nothing more, he was under a duty to concede. The price of its denial is an extension of the trust at the option and for the benefit of the one whom he excluded.

No answer is it to say that the chance would have been of little value even if seasonably offered. Such a calculus of probabilities is beyond the science of the chancery. Salmon, the real estate operator, might have been preferred to Meinhard, the woolen merchant. On the other hand, Meinhard might have offered better terms, or reinforced his offer by alliance with the wealth of others. Perhaps he might even have persuaded the lessor to renew the Bristol lease alone, postponing for a time, in return for higher rentals, the improvement of adjoining lots. We know that even under the lease as made the time for the enlargement of the building was delayed for seven years. All these opportunities were cut away from him through another's intervention. He knew that Salmon was the manager. As the time drew near for the expiration of the lease, he would naturally assume from silence, if from nothing else, that the lessor was willing to extend it for a term of years, or at least to let it stand as a lease from year to year. Not impossibly the lessor would have done so, whatever his protestations of unwillingness, if Salmon had not given assent to a project more attractive. At all events, notice of termination, even if not necessary, might seem, not unreasonably, to be something to be looked for, if the business was over and another tenant was to enter. In the absence of such notice, the matter of an extension was one that would naturally be attended to by the manager of the enterprise, and not neglected altogether. At least, there was nothing in the situation to give warning to any one that while the lease was still in being, there had come to the manager an offer of extension which he had locked within his breast to be utilized by himself alone. The very fact that Salmon was in control with exclusive powers of direction charged him the more obviously with the duty of disclosure, since only through disclosure could opportunity be equalized. If he might cut off renewal by a purchase for his own benefit when four months were to pass before the lease would have an end, he might do so with equal right while there remained as many years (cf. Mitchell v. Reed, 61 N.Y. 123, 127). He might steal a march on his comrade under cover of the darkness, and then hold the captured ground. Loyalty and comradeship are not so easily abjured....

We have no thought to hold that Salmon was guilty of a conscious purpose to defraud. Very likely he assumed in all good faith that with the approaching end of the venture he might ignore his coadventurer and take the extension for himself. He had given to the enterprise time and labor as well as money. He had made it a success. Meinhard, who had given money, but neither time nor labor, had already been richly paid. There might seem to be something grasping in his insistence upon more. Such recriminations are not unusual when coadventurers fall out. They are not without their force if conduct is to be judged by the common standards of competitors. That is not to say that they have pertinency here. Salmon had put himself in a position in which thought of self was to be renounced, however hard the abnegation. He was much more than a coadventurer. He was a managing coadventurer (Clegg v. Edmondson, 8 D.M. & G. 787, 807). For him and for those like him, the rule of undivided loyalty is relentless and supreme (Wendt v. Fischer, supra; Munson v. Syracuse, etc., R.R. Co., 103 N.Y. 58, 74). A different question would be here if there were lacking any nexus of relation between the business conducted by the manager and the opportunity brought to him as an incident of management (Dean v. MacDowell, 8 Ch.D. 345, 354; Aas v. Benham, 1891, 2 Ch. 244, 258; Latta v. Kilbourn, 150 U.S. 524). For this problem, as for most, there are distinctions of degree. If Salmon had received from Gerry a proposition to lease a building at a location far removed, he might have held for himself the privilege thus acquired, or so we shall assume. Here the subject-matter of the new lease was an extension and enlargement of the subject-matter of the old one. A managing coadventurer appropriating the benefit of such a lease without warning to his partner might fairly expect to be reproached with conduct that was underhand, or lacking, to say the least, in reasonable candor, if the partner were to surprise him in the act of signing the new instrument. Conduct subject to that reproach does not receive from equity a healing benediction.

A question remains as to the form and extent of the equitable interest to be allotted to the plaintiff. The trust as declared has been held to attach to the lease which was in the name of the defendant corporation. We think it ought to attach at the option of the defendant Salmon to the shares of stock which were owned by him or were under his control. The difference may be important if the lessee shall wish to execute an assignment of the lease, as it ought to be free to do with the consent of the lessor. On the other hand, an equal division of the shares might lead to other hardships. It might take away from Salmon the power of control and management which under the plan of the joint venture he was to have from first to last. The number of shares to be allotted to the plaintiff should, therefore, be reduced to such an extent as may be necessary to preserve to the defendant Salmon the expected measure of dominion. To that end an extra share should be added to his half.

Subject to this adjustment, we agree with the Appellate Division that the plaintiff's equitable interest is to be measured by the value of half of the entire lease, and not merely by half of some undivided part. A single building covers the whole area. Physical division is impracticable along the lines of the Bristol site, the keystone of the whole. Division of interests and burdens is equally impracticable. Salmon, as tenant under the new lease, or as guarantor of the performance of the tenant's obligations, might well protest if Meinhard, claiming an equitable interest, had offered to assume a liability not equal to Salmon's, but only half as great. He might justly insist that the lease must be accepted by his coadventurer in such form as it had been given, and not constructively divided into imaginary fragments. What must be yielded to the one may be demanded by the other. The lease as it has been executed is single and entire. If confusion has resulted from the union of adjoining parcels, the trustee who consented to the union must bear the inconvenience (Hart v. Ten Eyck, 2 Johns. Ch. 62). . . .

[Three judges dissented. Andrews, J., who wrote the dissenting opinion, agreed that "(w)ere this a general partnership I should have little doubt as to the correctness of this result assuming the new lease to be an offshoot of the old," but concluded that the parties' joint venture "had in view a very limited object and was to end at a limited time."]

_____

## NOTE ON JOINT VENTURES

The line between a joint venture and a partnership is exceedingly thin. "[M]ost courts have [distinguished] between isolated transactions and continuing enterprises by classifying the former as joint ventures." 1 A. Bromberg & L. Ribstein, Partnership 2:42–2:43 (1994).

Some authorities take the position that joint ventures are generally governed by partnership law. See, e.g., id. at 192 ("Whether a [joint venture] is considered a partnership or merely analogized to one, the venturers are governed by the rules applicable to partners"); Comment, The Joint Venture: Problem Child of Partnership, 38 Calif.L.Rev. 860 (1950). In contrast, other commentators argue that joint ventures are not merely a form of partnership, and not entirely subject to partnership rules. See, e.g., Jaeger, Partnership or Joint Venture?, 37 Notre Dame Law. 138 (1961). The same split is found in the cases. Some cases suggest that it makes no legal difference whether an enterprise is characterized as a partnership or a joint venture, while others suggest that special rules apply to joint ventures.

_____

**LATTA v. KILBOURN**, 150 U.S. 524, 541, 14 S.Ct. 201, 37 L.Ed. 1169 (1893). It is "well settled that one partner cannot, directly or indirectly use partnership assets for his own benefit; that he cannot in conducting the business of a partnership, take any profit clandestinely for himself; that he cannot carry on the business of the partnership for his private advantage; that he cannot carry on another business in competition or rivalry with that of the firm, thereby depriving it of the benefit of his time, skill, and fidelity, without being accountable to his copartners for any profit that may accrue to him therefrom; that he cannot be permitted to secure for himself that which it is his duty to obtain, if at all, for the firm of which he is a member; nor can he avail himself of knowledge or information which may be properly regarded as the property of the partnership, in the sense that it is available or useful to the firm for any purpose within the scope of the partnership business."

_____

## SECTION 8.   DISSOLUTION (I): DISSOLUTION BY RIGHTFUL ELECTION

———

**UNIFORM PARTNERSHIP ACT §§ 29, 30, 31(1), 38(1), 40**

———

**REVISED UNIFORM PARTNERSHIP ACT §§ 601, 602, 603, 701, 801, 802, 803, 804, 807**

[See Statutory Supplement]

———

**GIRARD BANK v. HALEY,** 460 Pa. 237, 332 A.2d 443 (1975). Mrs. Reid, a partner in an at-will UPA partnership, had sent the following letter to the other three partners: "I am terminating the partnership which the four of us entered into on the 28th day of September, 1958." The issue was whether this letter caused a dissolution of the partnership. The chancellor, at trial, held that it did not, because neither in the letter nor at trial did Mrs. Reid offer evidence to justify a termination of the partnership. Reversed.

In supposing that justification was necessary the learned court below fell into error. Dissolution of a partnership is caused, under § 31 of the [UPA], "by the express will of any partner." The expression of that will need not be supported by any justification. If no "definite term or particular undertaking [is] specified in the partnership agreement," such an at-will dissolution does not violate the agreement between the partners; indeed, an expression of a will to dissolve is effective as a dissolution even if in contravention of the agreement. Ibid. We have recognized the generality of a dissolution at will. If the dissolution results in breach of contract, the aggrieved partners may recover damages for the breach and, if they meet certain conditions, may continue the firm business for the duration of the agreed term or until the particular undertaking is completed. See § 38 of the Act....

The remaining question is whether or not the unilateral dissolution made by Mrs. Reid violated the partnership agreement. The agreement contains no provision fixing a definite term, and the sole "undertaking" to which it refers is that of maintaining and leasing real property. This statement is merely one of general purpose, however, and cannot be said to set forth a "particular undertaking" within the meaning of that phrase as it is used in the Act. A "particular undertaking" under the statute must be capable of accomplishment at some time, although the exact time may be unknown and unascertainable at the date of the agreement. Leasing property, like many other trades or businesses, involves entering into a business relationship which may continue indefinitely; there is nothing "particular" about it. We thus conclude, on the record before us, that the dissolution of the partnership was not in contravention of the agreement.

---

## Dreifuerst v. Dreifuerst

Wisconsin Court of Appeals, 1979.
90 Wis.2d 566, 280 N.W.2d 335.

■ Before Brown, P.J., Bode, J., and Robert W. Hansen, Reserve Judge.

■ Brown, P.J. The plaintiffs and the defendant, all brothers, formed a partnership. The partnership operated two feed mills, one located at St. Cloud, Wisconsin and one located at Elkhart Lake, Wisconsin. There were no written Articles of Partnership governing this partnership.

On October 4, 1975, the plaintiffs served the defendant with a notice of dissolution and wind-up of the partnership. The action for dissolution and wind-up was commenced on January 27, 1976. The dissolution complaint alleged that the plaintiffs elected to dissolve the partnership. There was no allegation of fault, expulsion or contravention of an alleged agreement as grounds for dissolution. The parties were unable, however, to agree to a winding-up of the partnership.

Hearings on the dissolution were held on October 18, 1976 and March 4, 1977. Testimony was presented regarding the value of the partnership assets and each partner's equity. At the March 4, 1977 hearing, the defendant requested that the partnership be sold pursuant to sec. 178.33(1), Stats., and that the court allow a sale, at which time the partners would bid on the entire property. By such sale, the plaintiffs could continue to run the business under a new partnership, and the defendant's partnership equity could be satisfied in cash.

On February 20, 1978, the trial court, by written decision, denied the defendant's request for a sale and instead divided the partnership assets in-kind according to the valuation presented by the plaintiffs. The plaintiffs were given the physical assets from the Elkhart Lake mill, and the defendant was given the physical assets from the St. Cloud mill. The defendant appeals this order and judgment dividing the assets in-kind.

Under sec. 178.25(1), Stats., a partnership is dissolved when any partner ceases to be associated in the carrying on of the business. The partnership is not terminated, but continues, until the winding-up of the partnership is complete. Sec. 178.25(2), Stats. The action started by the plaintiffs, in this case, was an action for dissolution and wind-up. The plaintiffs were not continuing the partnership and, therefore, secs. 178.36 and 178.37, Stats.,[3] do not apply. The sole question in this case is whether, in the absence of a written agreement to the contrary, a partner, upon dissolution and wind-up of the partnership, can force a sale of the partnership assets.

At the outset, we note, and the parties agree, that the appellant was not in contravention of the partnership agreement since there was no partnership agreement. The partnership was a partnership at will. They also agree there was no written agreement governing distribution of partnership assets upon dissolution and wind-up. The dispute, in this case, is over the authority of the trial court to order in-kind distribution in the absence of any agreement of the partners.

Section 178.33(1), Stats., provides:

> When dissolution is caused in any way, except in contravention of the partnership agreement, each partner, as against his copartners and all persons claiming through them in respect to their interests in the partnership, *unless otherwise agreed*, may have the partnership property applied to discharge its liabilities, and the surplus applied to pay *in cash* the net amount owing to the respective partners. [Emphasis supplied.]

The appellant contends this statute grants him the right to force a sale of the partnership assets in order to obtain his fair share of the partnership assets in cash upon dissolution. He claims that in the absence of an agreement of the partners to in-kind distribution, the trial court had no authority to distribute the assets in-kind. He is entitled to an in-cash settlement after judicial sale.

The respondents contend the statute does not entitle the appellant to force a sale and grants the trial court the power to distribute the assets in-kind if in-kind distribution is equitably possible and doesn't jeopardize the rights of creditors.

We do not believe that the statute can be read in any way to permit in-kind distribution unless the partners agree to in-kind distribution or unless there is a partnership agreement calling for in-kind distribution at the time of dissolution and wind-up.

A partnership at will is a partnership which has no definite term or particular undertaking and can rightfully be dissolved by the express will of any partner. Sec. 178.26(1)(b), Stats.; J. Crane and A. Bromberg, Law of Partnership § 74(b) (1968) [hereinafter cited as Crane and Bromberg]. In the present case, the respondents wanted to dissolve the partnership. This being a partnership at will, they could rightfully dissolve this partnership with or without the consent of the appellant. In addition, the respondents have never claimed the appellant was in violation of any partnership agreement. Therefore, neither the appellant nor the respondents have wrongfully dissolved the partnership.

---

**3.** Sections 178.36 and 178.37 deal with cases where the partnership is not wound up, but continues after one partner leaves.

Unless otherwise agreed, partners who have not wrongfully dissolved a partnership have a right to wind up the partnership. Sec. 178.32, Stats. Winding-up is the process of settling partnership affairs after dissolution. Winding-up is often called liquidation and involves reducing the assets to cash to pay creditors and distribute to partners the value of their respective interests. Crane and Bromberg, supra, §§ 73 and 80(c). Thus, lawful dissolution (or dissolution which is caused in any way except in contravention of the partnership agreement) gives each partner the right to have the business liquidated and his share of the surplus paid *in cash*. Young v. Cooper, 30 Tenn.App. 55, 203 S.W.2d 376 (1947); sec. 178.33(1), Stats.; Crane and Bromberg, supra, § 83A. In-kind distribution is permissible only in very limited circumstances. If the partnership agreement permits in-kind distribution upon dissolution or wind-up or if, at any time prior to wind-up, all partners agree to in-kind distribution, the court may order in-kind distribution. Logoluso v. Logoluso, 43 Cal.Rptr. 678 (1965); Gathright v. Fulton, 122 Va. 17, 94 S.E. 191, 194 (1917). . . .

. . . There was no showing that there were no creditors who would be paid from the proceeds, nor was there a showing that no one other than the partners would be interested in the assets. These factors are important if an in-kind distribution is to be allowed. Section 178.33(1) and § 38 of the Uniform Partnership Act are intended to protect creditors as well as partners. In-kind distributions may affect a creditor's right to collect the debt owed since the assets of the partnership, as a whole, may be worth more than the assets once divided up. Thus, the creditor's ability to collect from the individual partners may be jeopardized. Secondly, if others are interested in the assets, a sale provides a more accurate means of establishing the market value of the assets and, thus, better assuring each partner his share in the value of the assets. Where only the partners are interested in the assets, a fair value can be determined without the necessity of a sale. The sale would be merely the partners bidding with each other without any competition. This process could be accomplished through negotiations or at trial with the court as a final arbitrator of the value of the assets. . . .

However, even assuming the respondents in this case can show that there are no creditors to be paid, no one other than the partners are interested in the assets, and in-kind distribution would be fair to all partners, we cannot read § 38 of the Uniform Partnership Act or sec. 178.33(1), Stats. (the Wisconsin equivalent), as permitting an in-kind distribution under any circumstances, unless all partners agree. The statute and § 38 of the Uniform Partnership Act are quite clear that if a partner may force liquidation, he is entitled to his share of the partnership assets, after creditors are paid *in cash*. . . . We, therefore, must hold the trial court erred in ordering an in-kind distribution of the assets of the partnership.

The last question that arises is whether the appellant can force an actual sale of the assets or whether the trial court can determine the fair market value of the assets and order the respondents to pay the appellant in cash an amount equal to his share in the assets.

As discussed above, a sale is the best means of determining the true fair market value of the assets. Generally, liquidation envisions some form of sale. Since the statutes provide that, unless otherwise agreed, any partner who has not wrongfully dissolved the partnership has the right to wind up the partnership and force liquidation, he likewise has a right to force a sale, unless otherwise agreed. Fortugno v. Hudson Manure Co., 51 N.J.Super. 482, 144 A.2d 207, 218–19 (1958); Young v. Cooper, 30 Tenn.App. 55, 203 S.W.2d 376 (1947). See also Crane and Bromberg, supra, § 83A; 4 Vill.L.Rev. 457 (1959). While judicial sales in some instances may cause economic hardships, these hardships can be avoided by the use of partnership agreements.

*By the Court.*—Judgment reversed and cause remanded for further proceedings not inconsistent with this opinion.

-------

### NOTE ON NICHOLES v. HUNT

Nicholes v. Hunt, 273 Or. 255, 541 P.2d 820 (1975), was a case of rightful dissolution of a partnership between Nicholes and Hunt. Hunt had contributed an operating business to the partnership and Nicholes had contributed cash and services. The trial court refused to order a sale of the partnership's assets. Instead, it awarded the operating assets to Hunt, and ordered that Nicholes be paid the value of his partnership interest in cash. Affirmed. "We conclude, as defendant contends and as the trial court found, that the equities lie with the defendant in this case. . . . The defendant conceived and designed the machinery and the method of operation, which was successfully operated for a number of years before formation of the partnership at will." See also Swann v. Mitchell, 435 So.2d 797 (Fla.1983); Wiese v. Wiese, 107 So.2d 208 (Fla.App.1958); Schaefer v. Bork, 413 N.W.2d 873 (Minn.App.1987).

-------

**PAGE v. PAGE**, 55 Cal.2d 192, 10 Cal.Rptr. 643, 359 P.2d 41 (1961). Plaintiff and defendant entered into an oral partnership agreement in 1949. Within the first two years, each partner contributed approximately $43,000 for the purchase of land, machinery, and linen needed to begin the business. From 1949 to 1957 the enterprise was unprofitable, losing approximately $62,000. The partnership's major creditor was a corporation, wholly owned by plaintiff, that supplied the linen and machinery necessary for the day-to-day operation of the business. This corporation held a $47,000 demand note of the partnership. The partnership operations began to improve in 1958. Despite this improvement, plaintiff wished to dissolve the partnership.

Defendant contended that plaintiff was acting in bad faith by attempting to use his superior financial position to appropriate the now profitable business of the partnership. The fact that plaintiff's wholly owned corporation held a $47,000 demand note of the partnership might make it difficult to sell the business as a going concern. Defendant therefore feared that upon dissolution he would receive very little and that plaintiff, who was the managing partner and knew how to conduct the operations of the partnership, would receive a business that had become very profitable because of the establishment of Vandenberg Air Force Base in its vicinity. Defendant charged that plaintiff had been content to share the losses, but now that the business had become profitable, he wished to keep all the gains.

The trial court ruled that the plaintiff could not rightfully terminate the partnership, because the partnership was impliedly for a term. The California Supreme Court reversed that ruling, but held that even though the partnership was at will, the power to dissolve could only be exercised in good faith.

"Even though the Uniform Partnership Act provides that a partnership at will may be dissolved by the express will of any partner [under UPA § 31(1)(b)], this power like any other power held by a fiduciary, must be exercised in good faith. . . .

"A partner at will is not bound to remain in a partnership, regardless of whether the business is profitable or unprofitable. A partner may not, however, by use of adverse pressure 'freeze out' a copartner and appropriate the business to his own use. A partner may not dissolve a partnership to gain the benefits of the business for himself, unless he fully compensates his copartner for his share of the prospective business opportunity. In this regard his fiduciary duties are at least as great as those of a shareholder of a corporation.

" . . . If . . . it is proved that plaintiff acted in bad faith and violated his fiduciary duties by attempting to appropriate to his own use the new prosperity of the partnership without adequate compensation to his copartner, the dissolution would be wrongful and the plaintiff would be liable [under UPA § 38(2)(a)] (rights of partners upon wrongful dissolution) for violation of the implied agreement not to exclude defendant wrongfully from the partnership business opportunity."

---

## NOTE ON PARTNERSHIP BREAKUP UNDER THE UPA

One of the most difficult issues in partnership law is how to treat cases in which either a person's status as a partner is terminated, the partnership is to be terminated as a going concern, or both. (The complexity of these issues is illustrated by the fact that they occupy about a third of the text and comment of RUPA.) The difficult substantive issues raised by these issues have been made even more complex by the nomenclature that partnership law has employed. The UPA and RUPA take different strategies toward both the nomenclature and the underlying substantive issues. This Note will focus on dissolution under the UPA. A Note in Section 9, infra, will concern partnership breakup under RUPA.

Before getting directly into the legal issues, it is useful to outline the business economics involved.

Assume that a partnership is to be terminated as a going concern. Typically, the termination process will fall into three phases.

(i) The first phase consists of an event—which may be a decision of a partner or a court—that sets the termination in motion.

(ii) The second phase consists of the process of actually terminating the partnership's business. Inevitably, some period of time must elapse between the moment at which the event that sets termination in motion occurs and the time at which termination of the partnership's business is completed. For example, if the partnership is in the manufacturing business, to terminate the business the partnership will need to pay off its debts, settle its contracts with employees and suppliers, find a purchaser for the factory, and so forth.

(iii) The final phase consists of the completion of the second phase and an end to the partnership as a going concern.

Under the UPA, the first phase is referred to as "dissolution," the second phase is referred to as "winding up," and the third phase is referred to as "termination." The principal draftsman of the UPA explained as follows the manner in which that statute uses the term "dissolution":

> [The term "dissolution" is used in the UPA to designate] a change in the relation of the partners caused by any partner ceasing to be associated in the carrying on of the business. As thus used "dissolution" does not terminate the partnership, it merely ends the carrying on of the business in that partnership. The partnership continues until the winding up of partnership affairs is completed.

Lewis, The Uniform Partnership Act, 24 Yale L.J. 617, 626–27 (1915).

To put all of this somewhat differently, "dissolution" is used in the UPA to describe a change in the *legal status* of the partners and the partnership. "Winding-up" is used to describe the *economic* event of liquidation that follows dissolution.

Under the UPA, any termination of a person's status as a partner effects a dissolution of the partnership. It's not easy to see why this should be so when, as often happens, the remaining partners rightfully carry on the partnership's business after one partner has departed. Basically, the UPA's treatment of this issue seems to have been driven by a form of conceptualism. The UPA treats a partnership as an aggregation of persons to carry on business for profit as co-owners, rather than as an entity. Because the UPA treats a partnership as an aggregation, the drafters seemed to have believed that it followed "logically" that any change in the identity of the partners "necessarily" worked a dissolution of the partnership. If a partnership is conceptualized as an aggregation of the partners, and if the partners in Partnership P are A, B, C, and D, then it may have seemed to the drafters of the UPA that if D ceases to be a partner, Partnership P "must be" dissolved, because there is no longer an aggregation of A, B, C, and D. Following this line, UPA § 29 defines dissolution as "the change in the relation of partners caused by any partner ceasing to be associated in the carrying on" of the partnership's business.

The law, however, should not be built on deductive logic, but on policy, morality, and experience. We make rules because they are desirable, not because they are deducible. If a person ceases to be a partner, the law can treat the partnership as either dissolved or not dissolved. Which course the law takes should depend on which treatment better protects expectations and best reflects social policy. This, in turn, depends on what consequences the law should and does attach to dissolution.

Broadly speaking, the law may attach consequences to dissolution (1) among the partners themselves, (2) between the partners as a group and third persons, such as individuals or firms with whom the partnership has contracted, and (3) for tax purposes. The remainder of this Note will consider each of these areas.

1. *Consequences Among the Partners.* Under the UPA, upon the occurrence of dissolution—which, remember, under the UPA means simply that any partner ceases to be a partner—then unless otherwise agreed the partnership normally must sell its assets for cash and distribute the proceeds of the sale among all the partners. See Dreifuerst v. Dreifuerst, supra. (If, however, a partner, *W, wrongfully* causes dissolution, UPA § 38(2)(b) provides that although the *partnership* is dissolved, the remaining partners can continue the partnership's *business*. To do so, the remaining partners must either: (i) Pay *W* the value of her partnership interest (but without counting the value of the partnership's good will), minus any damages caused by the dissolution; or (ii) Put up a bond to secure such a payment, and indemnify *W* against present and future partnership liabilities. See Section 9, infra.)

UPA § 38(1) provides that "[w]hen dissolution is [rightfully] caused ... each partner ... *unless otherwise agreed*, may have the partnership property applied to discharge its liabilities, and the surplus applied to pay in cash the net amount owing to the respective partners." (Emphasis added.) It is well accepted that under the "unless" clause, the partnership agreement can provide that after the termination of a person's status as a partner (and, therefore, after the dissolution of the partnership under the UPA) the remaining partners can continue the partnership *business*, even if the partnership has been dissolved and the dissolution is rightfully caused. See, e.g., Meehan v. Shaughnessy, 404 Mass. 419, 535 N.E.2d 1255 (1989); Adams v. Jarvis, 23 Wis.2d 453, 127 N.W.2d 400 (1964).

Agreements that enable remaining partners to continue the business after dissolution are common, especially in large partnerships, such as law partnerships. Such agreements are usually known as business-continuation agreements or, more simply, continuation agreements. Typically, continuation agreements include not only the right of the remaining partners to continue the partnership's business, but also the terms on which the partner who causes dissolution (or his estate) will be compensated for his partnership interest.

2. *Effect of Dissolution on the Relationship Between the Partnership and Third Parties.* As among the partners, it often won't matter very much whether the withdrawal of a partner does or does not cause dissolution, because as among the partners a continuation agreement can override the substantive effects that dissolution would otherwise have. However, dissolution may also affect the relationship of the partnership to third persons.

For example, suppose that Partnership P, consisting of partners A, B, C, and D, is dissolved by the withdrawal of D, but the business of the partnership is continued by A, B, and C under a continuation agreement. Because P has been dissolved, the partnership of A, B, and C may be deemed a "new" partnership for legal purposes, so that P's assets and agreements, such as leases, licenses, or franchises, must be "transferred" to the new partnership. See Report of the ABA Subcommittee on the Revision of the U.P.A., 43 Bus.Law. 121, 160–62 (1987). In a much remarked-on case, Fairway Development Co. v. Title Insurance Co., 621 F.Supp. 120 (N.D.Ohio 1985), Fairway, a partnership, sued Title Insurance Co. under a title guarantee policy. The policy had been issued at a time when the partners in Fairway were B, S, and W. Subsequently, B and S transferred their partnership interests to W and a third party, V. W and V apparently continued Fairway's business under the Fairway name. The court nevertheless held that Title Insurance was not bound under its policy because the partnership to which it had issued the policy had been legally dissolved.

A debated point under the UPA is whether a partnership agreement can provide not only that the partnership business may be continued after dissolution, but also that the withdrawal of a partner will not cause dissolution, so that the partnership's relation with third parties will not be affected by a partner's withdrawal, as happened in the *Fairway* case. The prevailing (but not unanimous) answer is no, on the ground that UPA § 31 expressly states that "[d]issolution is caused" by the withdrawal of a partner.

3. *Tax Consequences.* The tax-law treatment of dissolution is relatively straightforward, and largely unimpeded by conceptualism. Internal Revenue Code § 708 provides that a partnership's existence does not terminate for tax purposes until either "(A) no part of any business, financial operation, or venture of the partnership continues to be carried on by any of [the] partners in a partnership, or (B) within a twelve-month period there is a sale or exchange of fifty percent or more of the total interest in partnership capital and profits." Accordingly, dissolution under partnership law is normally a

non-event for federal income tax purposes. (Warning: Despite IRC § 708, dissolution may have tax effects on a partner who does not continue, or on his estate. Even these effects, however, can normally be avoided by a continuation agreement.)

---

## SECTION 9.   DISSOLUTION (II): DISSOLUTION BY JUDICIAL DECREE AND WRONGFUL DISSOLUTION

---

### UNIFORM PARTNERSHIP ACT §§ 31(2), 32, 38(2)

### REVISED UNIFORM PARTNERSHIP ACT §§ 601, 602, 603, 701, 801, 802, 803, 804, 807

[See Statutory Supplement]

---

### Drashner v. Sorenson

Supreme Court of South Dakota, 1954.
75 S.D. 247, 63 N.W.2d 255.

■ SMITH, P.J. In January 1951 the plaintiff, C.H. Drashner, and defendants, A.D. Sorenson and Jacob P. Deis, associated themselves as co-owners in the real estate, loan and insurance business at Rapid City. For a consideration of $7500 they purchased the real estate and insurance agency known as J. Schumacher Co. located in an office room on the ground floor of the Alex Johnson Hotel building. The entire purchase price was advanced for the partnership by the defendants, but at the time of trial $3,000 of that sum had been repaid to them by the partnership. Although, as will appear from facts presently to be outlined, their operations were not unsuccessful, differences arose and on June 15, 1951 plaintiff commenced this action in which he sought an accounting, dissolution and winding up of the partnership. The answer and counterclaim of defendants prayed for like relief.

The cause came on for trial September 4, 1951. The court among others made the following findings. VII. "That thereafter the plaintiff violated the terms of said partnership agreement, in that he demanded a larger share of the income of the said partnership than he was entitled to receive under the terms of said partnership agreement; that the plaintiff was arrested for reckless driving and served a term in jail for said offense; that the plaintiff demanded that the defendants permit him to draw money for his own personal use out of the moneys held in escrow by the partnership; that the plaintiff spent a large amount of time during business hours in the Brass Rail Bar in Rapid City, South Dakota, and other bars, and neglected his duties in connection with the business of the said partnership. ... That the plaintiff, by his actions hereinbefore set forth, has made it impossible to carry on the partnership." The conclusions adopted read as follows: I "That the defendants are entitled to continue the partnership and have the value of the plaintiff's interest in the partnership business determined, upon the filing and approval of a good and sufficient bond, conditioned upon the release of the plaintiff from any liability arising out of the said partnership, and further conditioned upon the payment by the defendants to the plaintiff of the value of plaintiffs' interest in the partnership as determined by the Court." II "That in computing the value of the plaintiff's interest in the said partnership, the value of the good will of the business shall not be considered." III "That the value of the partnership shall be finally determined upon a hearing before this Court, . . ." and IV "That the plaintiff shall be entitled to receive one-third of the value of the partnership property owned by the partnership on the 12th day of September, 1951, not including the good will of the business, after the payment of the liabilities of the partnership and the payment to the defendants of the invested capital in the sum of $4,500.00." Judgment was accordingly entered dissolving the partnership as of September 12, 1951.

After hearing at a later date the court found: I "That the value of the said partnership property on the 12th day of September, 1951, was the sum of Four Thousand Four Hundred Ninety-eight and 90/100 Dollars ($4498.90), and on said date there was due and owing by the partnership for accountant's services the sum of Four Hundred Eighty Dollars ($480.00), and that on said date the sum of Four Thousand Five Hundred Dollars ($4500.00) of the capital invested by the defendants had not been returned to the defendants." and II "That there is not sufficient partnership property to reimburse the defendants for their invested capital." Thereupon the court decreed "that the plaintiff had no interest in the property of the said partnership", and that the defendants were the sole owners thereof.

The assignments of error are predicated upon insufficiency of the evidence to support the findings and conclusions. Of these assignments, only those which question whether the court was warranted in finding that (a) the plaintiff caused the dissolution wrongfully, and (b) the value of the partnership property, exclusive of good will, was $4498.90 on the 12th day of September, 1951, merit discussion. A preliminary statement is necessary to place these issues in their framework.

The agreement of the parties contemplated an association which would continue at least until the $7500 advance of defendants had been repaid from the gross earnings of the business. Hence, it was not a partnership at will. Vangel v. Vangel, 116 Cal.App.2d 615, 254 P.2d 919; Zeibak v. Nasser, 12 Cal.2d 1, 82 P.2d 375. In apparent recognition of that fact, both plaintiff and defendants sought dissolution in contravention of the partnership agreement, see SDC 49.0603(2) under SDC 49.0604(1)(d) on the ground that the adverse party had caused the dissolution wrongfully by willfully and persistently committing a breach of the partnership agreement, and by so conducting himself in matters relating to the partnership business as to render impracticable the carrying on of the business in partnership with him.

[The court here quoted U.P.A. Section 38(2)].

From this background we turn to a consideration of the evidence from which the trial court inferred that plaintiff caused the dissolution wrongfully.

The breach between the parties resulted from a continuing controversy over the right of plaintiff to withdraw sufficient money from the partnership to defray his living expenses. Plaintiff was dependent upon his earnings for the support of his family. The defendants had other resources. Plaintiff claimed that he was to be permitted to draw from the earnings of the partnership a sufficient amount to support himself and family. The defendants asserted that there was a definite arrangement for the allocation of the income of the partnership and there was no agreement for withdrawal by plaintiff of more than his allotment under that plan. Defendants' version of the facts was corroborated by a written admission of plaintiff offered in evidence. From evidence thus sharply in conflict, the trial court made a finding, reading as follows: "That the oral partnership agreement between the parties provided that each of the three partners were to draw as compensation one-third of one-half of the commissions earned upon sales made by the partners; that the other one-half of the commissions earned on sales made by the partners and one-half of the commissions earned upon sales made by salesmen employed by the partnership, together with the earnings from the insurance business carried on by the partnership, was to be placed in a fund to be used for the payment of the operating expenses of the partnership, and after the payment of such operating expenses to be used to reimburse the defendants for the capital advanced in the purchase of the Julius Schumacher business and the capital advanced in the sum of Eight Hundred Dollars ($800.00) for the operating expenses of the business."

As an outgrowth of this crucial difference, there was evidence from which a court could reasonably believe that plaintiff neglected the business and spent too much time in a nearby bar during business hours. At a time when plaintiff had overdrawn his partners and was also indebted to one of defendants for personal advances, he requested $100 and his request was refused. In substance he then said, according to the testimony of the defendant Deis, that he would see that he "gets some money to run on", if they "didn't give it to him he was going to dissolve the partnership and see that he got it." Thereafter plaintiff pressed his claims through counsel, and eventually brought this action to dissolve the partnership. The claim so persistently asserted was contrary to the partnership agreement found by the court.

The foregoing picture of the widening breach between the parties is drawn almost entirely from the evidence of defendants. Of course, plaintiff's version of the agreement of the parties, and of the ensuing differences, if believed, would have supported findings of a different order by the trier of the fact. It cannot be said, we think, that the trial court acted unreasonably in believing defendants, and we think it equally clear the court could reasonably conclude that the insistent and continuing demands of the plaintiff and his attendant conduct rendered it reasonably impracticable to carry on the business in partnership with him. It follows, we are of the opinion, the evidence supports the finding that plaintiff caused the dissolution wrongfully. Zeibak v. Nasser, 12 Cal.2d 1, 82 P.2d 375; Owen v. Cohen, 19 Cal.2d 147, 119 P.2d 713; Meherin v. Meherin, 93 Cal.App.2d 459, 209 P.2d 36; and Vangel v. Vangel, 116 Cal.App.2d 615, 254 P.2d 919.

This brings us to a consideration of the sufficiency of the evidence to support the finding of the court that the property of the partnership was of the value of $4498.90 as of the date of dissolution.

Bitter complaint is made because the trial court refused to consider the good will of this business in arriving at its conclusion. The feeling of plaintiff is understandable. These partners must have placed a very high estimate upon the value of the good will of this agency because they paid Mr. Schumacher $7500 to turn over that office with its very moderate fixtures and its listing of property, together with an agreement that he would not engage in the business in Rapid City for at least two years. No doubt they attached some of this good will value to the location of the business which was under only a month to month letting. Cf. 38 C.J.S., Good Will, § 3, page 951; In re Brown's Will, 242 N.Y. 1, 150 N.E. 581, 44 A.L.R. 510, at page 513. Their estimate of value was borne out by the subsequent history of the business. Its real estate commissions, earned but only partly received, grossed $21,528.25 and its insurance commissions grossed $661.21 in the period January 15 to August 31, 1951. In that period the received commissions paid all expenses, including the commissions of salesmen, retired $3,000 of the $7500 purchase price advanced by defendants, and all of $800 of working capital so advanced, allowed the parties to withdraw $1453.02 each, and accumulated a cash balance of $2221.43. In addition the partnership has commissions due. ... Notwithstanding this indication of the great value of the good will of this business, the statute does not require the court to take it into consideration in valuing the property of the business in these circumstances. The statute provides such a sanction for causing the dissolution of a partnership wrongfully. SDC 49.0610(2)(c)(2) quoted supra. The court applied the statute....

That the $1500 value placed on [the assets other than good will] was conservative we do not question. However, after mature study and reflection we have concluded that the court's finding is not against the clear weight of the evidence appearing in this record. Hence we are not at liberty to disturb it.

The brief of plaintiff includes some discussion of his right to a share in the profits from the date of the dissolution until the final judgment. It does not appear from the record that this claim was presented to the trial court, or that the net profit of the business during that period was evidenced. Because that issue was not presented below, it is not before us.

The judgment of the trial court is affirmed.

All the Judges concur.

------

### NOTE ON WRONGFUL DISSOLUTION

Drashner v. Sorenson illustrates that drastic consequences can befall a wrongfully dissolving partner under the UPA, in the form of (i) damages; (ii) a valuation of his interest that does not reflect the real value of the interest because goodwill is not taken into account; and (iii) a continuation of the business without him. These consequences may have a special impact in a partnership without an expressly specified term. Suppose one of the partners, A, elects to dissolve such a partnership on the theory that the partnership is at will. If the court finds that the partnership is for a term as a matter of implication, A will have dissolved the partnership in contravention of the partnership agreement. The penalties for guessing wrong on whether the court will make such a finding "may act as significant disincentives to dissolution [and may therefore] tend to stabilize the partnership." Hillman, The Dissatisfied Participant in the Solvent Business Venture: A Consideration of the Relative Permanence of Partnerships and Close Corporations, 67 Minn.L.Rev. 1, 34 (1982). For comparable reasons, a partner who believes that other partners have engaged in wrongful conduct is taking a risk if she tries to dissolve a partnership through a self-help election, as opposed to going to court for a decree under UPA Section 32. The other side of the coin, of course, is that judicial proceedings entail delay.

------

### NOTE ON PARTNERSHIP BREAKUP UNDER RUPA

RUPA's provisions on partnership breakup are even more complex than those of the UPA. To begin with nomenclature, RUPA continues to use the terms "dissolution," "winding up," and "termination." However, RUPA adds a new term, "dissociation," to describe the termination of a person's status as a partner.

1. *Events of Dissociation.* Although the term "dissociation" is new, the concept is not. Even under the UPA, a variety of events result in the termination of a person's status as a partner, and there is a very substantial overlap between the UPA and RUPA concerning the description of those events. For example, RUPA § 602(a) continues the rule of the UPA that every partner has the right to withdraw (dissociate) from the partnership at any time, rightfully or wrongfully, by express will. RUPA § 602(c) provides that a partner who wrongfully dissociates is liable to the partnership and to the other partners for damages caused by the dissociation. Furthermore, if a partner wrongfully dissociates, the partnership can continue without him.

2. *Rightful and Wrongful Dissociation.* RUPA § 602 distinguishes between events of dissociation that involve rightful conduct by the dissociated partner and events of dissociation that involve wrongful conduct. An event of dissociation is rightful unless it is specified as wrongful in § 602(b). The major types of wrongful dissociation are: (i) A dissociation that is in breach of an express provision of the partnership agreement. (ii) A withdrawal of a partner by the partner's express will before the expiration of the partnership term or the completion of an undertaking for which the partnership was formed. (iii) A partner engaged in wrongful conduct that adversely and materially affected the partnership business. (iv) A partner willfully or persistently committed a material breach of the partnership agreement or of a duty of care, loyalty, good faith, and fair dealing owed to the partnership or the other partners under § 404.

The Comment to RUPA § 602 states:

> [Under 602(a)] . . . a partner has the power to dissociate at any time by expressing a will to withdraw, even in contravention of the partnership agreement. The phrase "rightfully or wrongfully" reflects the distinction between a partner's *power* to withdraw in contravention of the partnership agreement and a partner's *right* to do so. In this context, although a partner can not be enjoined from exercising the power to dissociate, the dissociation may be wrongful under subsection (b). . . .
>
> . . . The significance of a wrongful dissociation is that it may give rise to damages under subsection (c) and, if it results in the dissolution of the partnership, the wrongfully dissociating partner is not entitled to participate in winding up the business. . . .

3. *Consequences of Dissociation.* The partnership-breakup provisions of RUPA are driven by functional considerations rather than by the "nature" of a partnership (although the Comments occasionally lapse into conceptual justifications based on the entity theory). Along these lines, RUPA, unlike the UPA, does not provide that every termination of a person's status as a partner—every dissociation—causes dissolution. Instead, the key issue is whether *dissociation* has occurred, and what are the consequences of the kind of dissociation that occurred.

There is an important distinction here between the partnership and the partnership's business. Under the UPA, if the partnership is dissolved because the partnership status of one or more partners is terminated, the remaining partners might continue the business, albeit as a new partnership. For example, the remaining partners might agree on a buyout price with the departing partners, or might buy the partnership business at an auction pursuant to winding up, or might continue the business under a continuation agreement. Under RUPA, the partnership agreement can provide that the departure of a partner does not cause dissolution at all. In fact, under RUPA the dissociation of a partner does not necessarily cause dissolution. For example, upon a wrongful dissociation, or a dissociation by death, the partnership is not dissolved—and therefore the partnership's business continues—

unless within ninety days a majority of the remaining partners dissociate or agree to wind up.

Under RUPA, dissociation leads to two forks in the statutory road: winding up under Article 8, or mandatory buyout under Article 7. Which fork must be taken depends on the nature of the event of dissociation.

*First Fork: Winding Up.* The events of dissociation that require the partnership to be wound up under RUPA are described in § 801. The Official Comment adds:

> . . . Under RUPA, not every partner dissociation causes a dissolution of the partnership. Only certain departures trigger a dissolution. The basic rule is that a partnership is dissolved, and its business must be wound up, only upon the occurrence of one of the events listed in Section 801. All other dissociations result in a buyout of the partner's interest under Article 7 and a continuation of the partnership entity and business by the remaining partners.

> Section 801 continues two basic rules from the UPA. First, it continues the rule that any member of an *at-will* partnership has the right to force a liquidation. Second, by negative implication, it continues the rule that the partners who wish to continue the business of a *term* partnership can not be forced to liquidate the business by a partner who withdraws prematurely in violation of the partnership agreement.

*Second Fork: Buyout.* If, upon the dissociation of a partner, winding up is not required under § 801, then RUPA § 701 requires a mandatory buyout of the dissociated partner's interest by the partnership. However, if the dissociation was wrongfully caused by the dissociated partner, § 701(c) provides that the buyout price under § 701(b) is to be reduced by damages for the wrongful dissociation. Furthermore, under § 701(h) a partner who wrongfully dissociates before the expiration of a definite term, or the completion of a particular undertaking, is not entitled to payment of any portion of the buyout price until the expiration of the term or completion of the undertaking, unless the partner establishes to the satisfaction of the court that earlier payment will not cause undue hardship to the business of the partnership. A deferred payment must be adequately secured and bear interest. Under § 701(b), the buyout price of a dissociated partner's interest is the amount that would have been distributable to the dissociating partner if, on the date of dissociation, the assets of the partnership were sold at a price equal to the greater of the liquidation value or the value based on a sale of the entire business as a going concern, without the dissociated partner, and the partnership was wound up as of that date.

# CHAPTER III

# THE CORPORATE FORM

## SECTION 1. THE CHARACTERISTICS OF THE CORPORATION

1. *Publicly Held Enterprises.* The corporation has traditionally been the preferred choice of form for business enterprises that are to be publicly held (that is, whose ownership interests are to be held by members of the public, as opposed to owner-managers). This preference results from five central attributes of the corporate form.

   *a. Limited liability.* Shareholders are not personally liable for corporate obligations. This legal rule is conventionally expressed by the statement that shareholders have *limited liability*. The *managers* of a corporation are also normally not personally liable for corporate obligations: As long as corporate managers act on the corporation's behalf and within their authority, they are treated like agents, not principals, for liability purposes.

   *b. Free Transferability of Ownership Interests.* Ownership (or "equity") interests in corporations—represented by shares of stock—are freely transferable.

   *c. Continuity of existence.* The legal existence of a corporation is perpetual, unless a shorter term is stated in the certificate of incorporation. As a result, a corporation is relatively secure against early termination. This may have a beneficial impact on long-term planning. See Rock & Wachter, *Waiting for the Omelet to Set*, 24 J. Corp. L. 913 (1999).

   *d. Centralized management.* Under the corporate statutes, a corporation is normally managed by or under the direction of a board of directors, and a shareholder as such has no right to participate in management.

   *e. Entity status.* A corporation is a "legal person" or "legal entity." As a result, a corporation can exercise power and have rights in its own name. For example, a corporation can sue or be sued, and can hold property.

2. *Privately Held Enterprises.* If an enterprise is not to be publicly held, the choice of form is much more complex. Today, such a firm might be either a close corporation, a general partnership, a limited liability partnership, a limited partnership, or a limited liability company. The general-partnership form has been considered in Chapter 2. Close corporations will be considered in Chapter 6. The remaining forms will be considered in Chapter 7.

## SECTION 2.   SELECTING A STATE OF INCORPORATION

### NOTE ON COMPETITION AMONG THE STATES FOR INCORPORATIONS

Under traditional choice-of-law rules, a firm can incorporate wherever it chooses, and a corporation's internal affairs are governed by the law of its state of incorporation—even if the corporation has no business contacts with that state.

A corporation with only a few owners—a "close corporation"—will almost invariably incorporate locally, that is, in the state where it has its principal place of business. Partly this is for tax reasons. If a corporation *does business* in a state, the state will impose a doing-business tax on the corporation on a basis that reflects the amount of that business. If a corporation is *incorporated* in a state, the state will impose a franchise tax for the privilege of incorporation, even if the corporation does not do business in that state. Elements of the doing-business and franchise taxes may overlap, so that if a corporation is doing business mainly in one state, its total tax bill usually will be less if it is also incorporated in that state. Furthermore, local attorneys, familiar with local corporate law, may be hesitant about rendering formal opinions on the laws of other states, and are likely to recommend local incorporation.

In the case of a publicly held corporation, a different calculus prevails. Publicly held corporations usually do business in a great number of states. The costs attendant on incorporation in any given state are likely to be inconsequential in comparison with the corporation's total revenues. On the state's side of the equation, franchise-tax revenues may represent a potentially enormous source of revenue to a state with a small fiscal base. A small state therefore has a great economic incentive to design a corporation law that will attract incorporation (or reincorporation from another state), particularly by large publicly held corporations. If the state is successful in attracting incorporation, the resulting franchise-tax revenues can subsidize a large portion of its budget, because the out-of-pocket cost of maintaining such a regime will be negligible, while the social and economic costs of any defects in the regime will be borne largely by the citizens of other states. Delaware is by far the most successful state in attracting publicly held corporations. As of 1996, Delaware accounted for 56% of all corporations listed on major stock exchanges (up from 50% in 1981), and 62% of New York Stock Exchange corporations (up from 54% in 1981). See Daines, Does Delaware Law Improve Firm Value? (1999).

Because the law of the state of incorporation normally governs internal corporate affairs, and because Delaware is preeminent for publicly held corporations, the Delaware statute provides a major axis of this book. A second major axis is provided by the Revised Model Business Corporation Act, promulgated by the Committee on Corporate Laws of the ABA's Section of Business Law. Although the Model Act itself has no official status, it has served as a template for the statutes of many states. Recurring reference will also be made to the California and New York statutes, because these states account for a significant portion of total corporations, as a result of the size of their populations and their commercial significance.

---

## SECTION 3. ORGANIZING A CORPORATION

Once a decision has been made to incorporate, and the state of incorporation has been selected, the next step is to create or *organize* the corporation. To begin this process, an *incorporator* files a *certificate of incorporation, articles of incorporation, or charter* (the nomenclature varies from state to state) with a designated state office—usually the office of the Secretary of State.

---

### DEL. GEN. CORP. LAW §§ 101, 102, 103, 106, 107, 108, 109

[See Statutory Supplement]*

---

### REV. MODEL BUS. CORP. ACT §§ 2.01, 2.02, 2.03, 2.05, 2.06

[See Statutory Supplement]

---

### FORM OF CERTIFICATE OF INCORPORATION

[See Statutory Supplement]

---

### NOTE ON AUTHORIZED AND ISSUED STOCK AND ON PREEMPTIVE RIGHTS

An important function of a certificate of incorporation is to designate the classes of stock, and the number of shares of each class, that the corporation is *authorized* to issue. If the corporation's authorized stock consists of one class of common stock, the certificate need only designate the number of authorized shares. If there is to be more than one class of stock, and particularly if there is to be one or

---

* References in this book to the "Statutory Supplement" are to Corporations and Other Business Organizations; Statutes, Rules, Materials, and Forms (M. Eisenberg ed.).

more classes of preferred stock (that is, stock that carries a preference as to dividends, on liquidation, or both, over common stock), the certificate of incorporation must either (i) designate the terms of each class or (ii) authorize the board to issue portions of the authorized class in series from time to time and to designate the terms of each series as it is issued. A sale of stock by the corporation is known as an *issuance of stock*. Only stock that has been authorized in the certificate of incorporation can be issued. Authorized stock that has not yet been issued is known as *unauthorized but unissued* stock. Authorized stock that has been issued is known as *authorized and issued stock*, or *authorized and outstanding stock*. Sometimes a corporation repurchases stock that it has previously issued. Such stock may sometimes be referred to as *treasury stock* or *unauthorized and issued but not outstanding stock*.

The power to issue authorized but unissued stock, and the price at which the stock will be issued, is in the hands of the board, subject only to certain very limited constraints. At common law, one of these constraints was that each existing shareholder had the right to subscribe to her proportionate part of a new issue of stock of the class she held. This is known as the *preemptive right*. The right was riddled with exceptions—for example, it did not apply to stock that was issued for property rather than cash. Modern statutes provide that shareholders have no preemptive rights unless the certificate of incorporation provides such a right. Few do.

Even where shareholders have no preemptive rights, the board may not issue stock for the purpose of reallocating or perpetuating control. See, e.g., Schwartz v. Marien, 37 N.Y.2d 487, 373 N.Y.S.2d 122, 335 N.E.2d 334 (1975). And under basic fiduciary principles, the board cannot issue stock to individual directors at an unfairly low price. The right to prohibit a non-pro-rata stock issuance for an improper purpose is sometimes referred to as the "quasi-preemptive right."

-------

### NOTE ON THE BASIC MODES OF CORPORATE FINANCE

An initial question for a corporation is how to finance its business. The three major modes of corporate finance are common stock, debt, and preferred stock.

1. *Common Stock.* Traditionally, shares of common stock are conceived as ownership or *equity* interests in the corporation, so that the body of common shareholders are the corporation's owners. Normally, but not invariably, common stock carries the right to vote in the election of directors and certain other matters. Typically, or at least often, dividends are paid on common stock, but many corporations do not pay dividends, and in any event whether dividends are paid, and if so in what amount, is generally in the discretion of the board. As a result, common stock has no fixed claim on the corporation. Partly for this reason, modern financial theory often conceives of common stock

in terms other than ownership. Under one such conception, common stock is regarded as ultimate or *residual* ownership. "Common shareholders are often thought of as the owners of the firm or as the holders of the *equity* interest in the firm.... The equity interest is sometimes usefully thought of as the *residual* interest—the claim to what is left after all senior claimants have been satisfied." W. Klein & J. Coffee, Business Organization and Finance 271 (7th ed. 2000) (emphasis added). The "senior claimants" to which Coffee & Klein refer are debt and preferred stock.

2. *Debt. Debt* is a fixed claim against the corporation for principal and interest. The major types of corporate debt are *trade debt, bank debt, bonds, debentures*, and *notes.*

(a) *Trade debt.* When a business purchases goods or services, payment is typically not due for thirty, sixty, or ninety days. Trade debt consists principally of amounts that a corporation owes for such goods and services at any point in time. Trade debt appears on a corporation's balance sheet as Accounts Payable.

(b) *Bank debt.* A business will often be financed in significant part by commercial-bank loans. Bank loans appear on a corporation's balance sheet under captions such as Loans Payable.

(c) *Bonds and debentures.* Another method of financing a corporation is to issue bonds or debentures. Essentially, bonds and debentures are promises, embodied in an instrument, to repay amounts that the firm has borrowed on a long-term basis, typically, on the general market or on some special market. Bonds appear on a corporation's balance sheet under captions such as Bonds Payable, or under a caption that describes specific bond issues, such as 7.5% Senior Debentures. Unlike bank loans, bonds and debentures normally represent money borrowed from the public, or at least from a significant group of lenders or investors. "As a matter of historical practice, bonds and debentures are long term obligations issued under indentures, bonds generally being *secured* obligations and debentures being *unsecured* obligations." V. Brudney & W. Bratton, Corporate Finance— Cases and Materials 150–52 (4th ed. 1993) (emphasis added).

> A bond [or] debenture ... is simply a promise by the borrower to pay a specified amount on a specified date, together with interest at specified times, on the terms and subject to the conditions spelled out in a governing indenture ... Bonds [and] debentures ... are, then ... issued pursuant to and governed by [a contract known as an *indenture*]. Some of the governing terms and conditions will be set out on the face of the [bond or debenture]. Most terms, however, will be in the [indenture] that governs the instrument and will be merely referred to on its face. The note incorporates the [indenture] by reference.
>
> It is the practice in both financial and legal writing to use "bond" as a generic term for all long term debt securities....

Id.

Brudney & Bratton describe an *indenture* as follows:

An indenture is a contract entered into between the borrowing corporation and a trustee. The trustee administers the payments of interest and principal, and monitors and enforces compliance with other obligations on behalf of the bondholders as a group. The indenture defines the assorted obligations of the borrower, the rights and remedies of the holders of the bonds, and the role of the trustee.

The borrower contracts with a trustee rather than directly with the holders of the bonds so as to permit the bonds to be sold in small denominations to large numbers of scattered investors. Given widespread ownership in small amounts, unilateral monitoring and enforcement by each holder is not cost effective. The device of the trust solves this problem....

The student should keep in mind a distinction between the "bonds" and the "indenture." The bonds set out a promise to pay that runs to the holders of the bonds. The indenture is a bundle of additional promises (including a backup promise to pay) that run to the trustee. The holders of the bonds are third party beneficiaries of the promises in the indenture. Even though the promises in the bonds run directly to the holders, the bonds are subject to the indenture, and therefore may be enforced directly by the holders only to the extent that the indenture allows. Indentures generally constrain the unilateral enforcement rights of small holders, channelling enforcement through the central agency of the trustee. The device of the trust indenture, then, not only facilitates enforcement by the widely scattered holders, but also restrains such enforcement. It facilitates borrowing in small amounts from large numbers of widely scattered lenders not only by constraining the issuer as against the holders, but by protecting the issuer from the holders.

(d) *Notes.* There is no legally recognized distinction between bonds and debentures, on the one hand, and notes, on the other. However,

Under the historical practice, notes may be long term or short term obligations, but in either case are not issued pursuant to an indenture. Recent practice has changed this. Today, "notes" often are issued pursuant to indentures as unsecured long term obligations. But they tend to be intermediate term securities, coming due in ten years or less, where "debentures" tend to mature in ten years or more.

V. Brudney & W. Bratton, supra.

3. *Preferred Stock.* Preferred stock is a hybrid that combines the ownership element of common stock and the senior nature of debt. The basic elements of preferred stock are described as follows in Hunt, Williams & Donaldson, Basic Business Finance 358–61 (5th ed. 1974):

From the purely legal point of view ... preferred stock is a type of ownership and thus takes a classification similar to that of the common stock.... Unlike [a] bond, ... preferred stock does not contain any promise of repayment of the original investment; and as far as the shareholders are concerned, this must be considered as a permanent investment for the life of the company. Further, there is no legal obligation to pay a fixed rate of return on the investment.

The special character of the preferred stock lies in its relationship to the common stock. When a preferred stock is used as a part of the corporate capital structure, the rights and responsibilities of the owners as the residual claimants to the asset values and earning power of the business no longer apply equally to all shareholders. Two types of owners emerge, representing a voluntary subdivision of the overall ownership privileges. Specifically, the common shareholders agree that the preferred shareholder shall have "preference" or first claim in the event that the directors are able and willing to pay a dividend. In the case of what is termed a nonparticipating or *straight preferred stock*, which is the most frequent type, the extent of this priority is a fixed percentage of the par value of the stock or a fixed number of dollars per share in the case of stock without a nominal or par value....

In most cases the prior position of preferred stock also extends to the disposition of assets in the event of liquidation of the business. Again, the priority is only with reference to the common stock and does not affect the senior position of creditors in any way....*

Typically, preferred stock carries a dividend that is payable periodically—often, quarterly—in the board's discretion. Thus the most obvious difference between debt and preferred stock is that debtholders have a fixed claim on the corporation for interest and principal, while preferred shareholders normally have no fixed claims for distributions. Instead, the claims of preferred stock for distributions are only contingent: *If* the corporation proposes to pay a dividend on common, *then* it must first pay a designated dividend to the preferred. *If* the corporation liquidates, *then* before it distributes anything to the common it must satisfy the preferred's liquidation preference.

Often, the preferred's dividend preference is "cumulative"—that is, no dividend can be paid on common unless all prior dividends on the preferred have been paid. (If a preferred is noncumulative, a dividend can be paid on common as long as the current dividend on the preferred is paid.) Often too, preferred is given the right to vote on the election of directors if, but only if, preferred dividends are in default for a designated number of periods.

4. *Convertibles, Classified Stock, and Derivatives.* In the modern world, the basic elements of common stock, preferred stock, and

* As quoted in V. Brudney & W. Bratton,    36 (4th ed. 1993). Corporate Finance—Cases and Material 335–

debt are often disaggregated, and their fragments are combined to design more exotic corporate securities. For example, preferred stock is often issued in several classes, and common stock may be issued in several classes as well (*classified common*). In such cases, each class enjoys somewhat different rights than the others in respect of voting, dividend, or liquidation rights, or all three. Many preferred stocks, and some bonds, are made convertible into common stock at the option of the holder, on specified terms. Furthermore, new types of securities may be"derived" from common stock, in the sense that although the securities are not themselves common stock, their value largely depends on the value of a corporation's common stock and on the terms of their relationship to the common stock. The simplest example is a "right" or "warrant," which is a security issued by the corporation that gives the holder a right or option to purchase common stock on specified terms.

---

## NOTE ON INITIAL DIRECTORS

Once a corporation is under way, its board of directors is elected by the shareholders. However, a corporation has no shareholders until stock is issued, and the function of issuing stock is normally vested in the board. Accordingly, there must be a mechanism either for naming initial directors before stock is issued, or for issuing stock before directors are elected by the shareholders. There are two basic mechanisms to solve this problem. Under the law of some states, like New York, the corporation's incorporators have the powers of shareholders until stock is issued, and the powers of directors until directors are elected. N.Y.Bus.Corp.Law §§ 404(a), 615(c). Under such a statute, the incorporators will typically adopt by-laws, fix the number of directors, and elect initial directors to serve until the first annual meeting of shareholders. See N.Y.Bus.Corp.Law § 404(a). Under the law of other states, the initial directors can be named in the corporation's certificate of incorporation. Del.Gen.Corp.Law §§ 107, 108. If the initial directors are named in the certificate of incorporation, the functions of the incorporators pass to the directors when the certificate is filed and recorded. Del.Gen.Corp.Law §§ 107, 108(a).

Once the initial directors are named, either by the incorporators or by the certificate of incorporation, they will hold an organization meeting. A typical agenda for such a meeting is reflected in the Form of Minutes of Organization Meeting that follows.

---

## FORM OF MINUTES OF ORGANIZATION MEETING

[See Statutory Supplement]

---

## NOTE ON SUBSCRIPTIONS FOR SHARES

Normally, stock is issued by a corporation in a simultaneous exchange for cash or property. In some cases, however, a would-be shareholder enters into a "subscription agreement," under which he agrees to purchase a corporation's stock when it is issued to him at some future date. Typically, in such cases, the corporation has not yet been formed. (The agreement is then made on the would-be corporation's behalf by incorporators, agents, or trustees.) Agreements of this type are called pre-incorporation subscription agreements.

There is a good deal of old law on various aspects of such agreements. The general rule was that a pre-incorporation subscription was only a continuing offer by the subscriber, and that a subscriber therefore was not bound if he made a timely revocation. Under this rule, a subscriber could revoke his agreement until the moment of incorporation or, in the alternative, until the corporation, once formed, issued stock to the subscriber. There was an exception where the mutual promises of subscribers were expressed as consideration for each other. In that case, a contract was deemed to be formed immediately. In addition, subscription agreements entered into *after* the corporation was formed were treated as ordinary contracts, and raised no special problems of enforceability.

This treatment of pre-incorporation subscription agreements has been changed by the modern corporate statutes. Most statutes now provide that pre-incorporation subscriptions are irrevocable for a specified period of time unless all the subscribers consent to a revocation or the agreement otherwise provides. See, e.g., Del.Gen. Corp.Law § 165 (preincorporation subscription agreements irrevocable for six months except with the consent of all other subscribers); RMBCA § 6.20(a) (same). Because of these statutory changes, the law relating to subscriptions is of greatly diminished importance, and current cases on the subject are rare.

––––––

## FORM OF BY–LAWS

[See Statutory Supplement]

––––––

## FORM OF STOCK CERTIFICATE

[See Statutory Supplement]

––––––

## DEL. GEN. CORP. LAW § 109

[See Statutory Supplement]

––––––

**REV. MODEL BUS. CORP. ACT §§ 2.06, 10.20–10.21**

[See Statutory Supplement]

---

## SECTION 4. PREINCORPORATION TRANSACTIONS BY PROMOTERS

A *promoter* is a person who transforms an idea into a business by bringing together the needed persons and assets, and superintending the various steps required to bring the new business into existence. Often, a promoter of a corporation makes contracts for the benefit of the corporation even before the corporation has been formed. If, as is usually the case, the corporation is later formed, and benefits from such a contract, issues may arise regarding who is liable under the contract.

(a) *Liability of the promoter.* The general rule is that when a promoter makes a contract for the benefit of a contemplated corporation, the promoter is personally liable on the contract and remains liable even after the corporation is formed.

An exception to the general rule is that if the party who contracted with the promoter knew that the corporation was not in existence at the time of contracting, and nevertheless agreed to look solely to the corporation for performance, the promoter is not deemed a party to the contract. Such an agreement may be express or implied. As a practical matter, it is often difficult to predict whether a court will or will not find an implied contract of this sort.

For example, in Goodman v. Darden, Doman & Stafford Associates, 100 Wash.2d 476, 670 P.2d 648 (1983), Goodman had proposed to renovate an apartment building owned by Darden, Doman & Stafford Associates (DDS). During the course of negotiations, Goodman informed DDS that he would be forming a corporation to limit his personal liability. In August 1979, a contract was made between DDS and "BUILDING DESIGN AND DEVELOPMENT INC. (In Formation) John A. Goodman, President." DDS knew that the corporation was not yet in existence.

On November 1, Goodman filed articles of incorporation. Between August and December 1979 DDS made five progress payments on the contract. The first check was made out to "Building Design and Development Inc.—John Goodman." Goodman struck out his name and endorsed the check "Bldg. Design & Dev. Inc., John A. Goodman, Pres." He instructed DDS to make further payments to the corporation only, and DDS did so. The court held that Goodman was liable on the contract:

> . . . The fact that a contracting party knows that the corporation is nonexistent does not indicate any agreement to release the promoter. To the contrary, such knowledge alone would seem to

indicate that the members of DDS intended to make Goodman a party to the contract. They could not hold the corporation, a nonexistent entity, responsible and of course they would expect to have recourse against someone (Goodman) if default occurred....

The only other evidence of the parties' intent to make the corporation the sole party to the contract is that the progress payments were made payable to the corporation. However, they were so written only at the instruction of Goodman and in fact the first check written by DDS after the signing of the contract was written to the corporation *and* Goodman as an individual. This evidence does not show by reasonable certainty that DDS intended to contract only with the corporation....

In contrast, in Company Stores Development Corp. v. Pottery Warehouse, Inc., 733 S.W.2d 886 (Tenn.App.1987), Company Stores leased a store to Pottery Warehouse, Inc., for five years. Pottery Warehouse was not incorporated at the time of the lease. The lease recited that the corporation was to be organized, and was signed as follows:

THE POTTERY WAREHOUSE, INC.

a corporation to be formed under the laws of the State of Tennessee

BY *Jane M. Vosseller*

   *Its President....*

The court held that the promoter was not liable:

In the instant case, the stipulations of fact establish the plaintiff intended to look solely to Pottery Warehouse, Inc., for satisfaction of the obligation arising under the lease at the time of execution. At the time the lease was signed, plaintiff was aware of the nonexistence of the corporate entity and did not require Vosseller to sign the agreement in an individual capacity but as a president of a future corporate entity. The lease imputes no intention on the part of Vosseller to be bound personally.

(b) *Liability of the corporation.* A corporation that is formed after a promoter has entered into a contract on its behalf is not bound by the contract, without more. The reason is that the corporation was not in existence when the contract was made, and therefore did not authorize—and indeed could not have authorized—the promoter to enter into the contract on its behalf. However, after the corporation has been formed it may become bound in one of several ways. "The usual grounds that have been suggested are ratification, adoption, novation, and that the proposition made to the promoters is a continuing offer to be accepted or rejected by the corporation when it comes into being, and upon acceptance becomes an original contract on its part; and the liability has also been sustained on the ground that the corporation, by accepting the benefits of a contract, takes it cum onere, and is estopped to deny its liability on the contract." Clifton v.

Tomb, 21 F.2d 893 (4th Cir.1927). In Illinois Controls, Inc. v. Langham, 70 Ohio St.3d 512, 639 N.E.2d 771 (1994), the court held that if a promoter is liable under a contract under the law of promoter's liability, the fact that the corporation also becomes liable on the contract, by adopting it, does not relieve the promoter of liability. Instead, in such a case the promoter and the corporation are jointly and severally liable.

---

## RESTATEMENT (SECOND) OF AGENCY § 326

### [See Statutory Supplement]

---

## SECTION 5.    CONSEQUENCES OF DEFECTIVE INCORPORATION

---

## Cantor v. Sunshine Greenery, Inc.

Superior Court of New Jersey, Appellate Division, 1979.
165 N.J.Super. 411, 398 A.2d 571.

■ Larner, J.

This appeal involves the propriety of a personal judgment against defendant William J. Brunetti for the breach of a lease between plaintiffs and a corporate entity known as Sunshine Greenery, Inc., and more particularly whether there was a *de facto* corporation in existence at the time of the execution of the lease.

Plaintiffs brought suit for damages for the breach of the lease against Sunshine Greenery, Inc. and Brunetti. Default judgment was entered against the corporation and a nonjury trial was held as to the liability of the individual. The trial judge in a letter opinion determined that plaintiffs were entitled to judgment against Brunetti individually on the theory that as of the time of the creation of the contract he was acting as a promoter and that his corporation, Sunshine Greenery, Inc., was not a legal or *de facto* corporation.

The undisputed facts reveal the following: Plaintiffs prepared the lease naming Sunshine Greenery, Inc. as the tenant, and it was signed by Brunetti as president of that named entity. Mr. Cantor, acting for plaintiffs, knew that Brunetti was starting a new venture as a newly formed corporation known as Sunshine Greenery, Inc. Although Cantor had considerable experience in ownership and leasing of commercial property to individuals and corporations, he did not request a personal guarantee from Brunetti, nor did he make inquiry as to his financial status or background. Without question, he knew and expected that thelease agreement was undertaken by the corporation and not by Brunetti individually, and that the corporation would be responsible thereunder.

At the time of the signing of the lease on December 16, 1974 in Cantor's office, Brunetti was requested by Cantor to give him a check covering the first month's rent and the security deposit. When Brunetti stated that he was not prepared to do so because he had no checks with him, Cantor furnished a blank check which was filled out for $1,200, with the name of Brunetti's bank and signed by him as president of Sunshine Greenery, Inc. The lease was repudiated by a letter from counsel for Sunshine Greenery, Inc. dated December 17, 1974, which in turn was followed by a response from Cantor to the effect that he would hold the "client" responsible for all losses. The check was not honored because Brunetti stopped payment, and in any event because Sunshine Greenery, Inc. did not have an account in the bank.

The evidence is clear that on November 21, 1974 the corporate name of Sunshine Greenery, Inc. had been reserved for Brunetti by the Secretary of State, and that on December 3, 1974 a certificate of incorporation for that company was signed by Brunetti and Sharyn N. Sansoni as incorporators. The certificate was forwarded by mail to the Secretary of State on that same date with a check for the filing fee, but for some unexplained reason it was not officially filed until December 18, 1974, two days after the execution of the lease.*

In view of the late filing, Sunshine Greenery, Inc. was not a *de jure* corporation on December 16, 1974 when the lease was signed. See N.J.S.A. 14A:2–7(2). Nevertheless, there is ample evidence of the fact that it was a *de facto* corporation in that there was a *bona fide* attempt to organize the corporation some time before the consummation of the contract and there was an actual exercise of the corporate powers by the negotiations with plaintiffs and the execution of the contract involved in this litigation. When this is considered in the light of the concession that plaintiffs knew that they were dealing with that corporate entity and not with Brunetti individually, it becomes evident that the *de facto* status of the corporation suffices to absolve Brunetti from individual liability. Plaintiffs in effect are estopped from attacking the legal existence of the corporation collaterally because of the nonfiling in order to impose liability on the individual when they have admittedly contracted with a corporate entity which had *de facto* status. . . . In fact, their prosecution of the claim against the corporation to default judgment is indicative of their recognition of the corporation as the true obligor and theoretically inconsistent with the assertion of the claim against the individual.

The trial judge's finding that Sunshine Greenery, Inc. was not a *de facto* corporation is unwarranted under the record facts herein. The mere fact that there were no formal meetings or resolutions or

---

\* We note that the letter enclosing the certificate of incorporation is addressed to "Mortimer G. Newman, Jr., Secretary of State, State House Annex, Trenton, New Jersey." Whether this misidentification of the person holding the office of Secretary of State accounts for the filing delay we are unable to say from the record.

issuance of stock is not determinative of the legal or *de facto* existence of the corporate entity, particularly under the simplified New Jersey Business Corporation Act of 1969, which eliminates the necessity of a meeting of incorporators. See N.J.S.A. 14A:2–6 and Commissioners' Comment thereunder. The act of executing the certificate of incorporation, the *bona fide* effort to file it and the dealings with plaintiffs in the name of that corporation fully satisfy the requisite proof of the existence of a *de facto* corporation. To deny such existence because of a mere technicality caused by administrative delay in filing runs counter to the purpose of the *de facto* concept, and would accomplish an unjust and inequitable result in favor of plaintiffs contrary to their own contractual expectations. . . .

In view of the foregoing, the judgment entered against defendant William J. Brunetti is reversed and set aside, and the matter is remanded to the Law Division to enter judgment on the complaint in favor of William J. Brunetti.

---

**McLEAN BANK v. NELSON,** 232 Va. 420, 350 S.E.2d 651 (1986). "It is the corporate form that provides limited liability. Without the corporation . . . personal liability exists. The limited liability provided by a de jure corporation is the exception, not the rule. . . . [I]f a group of individuals have not done the things necessary to secure or retain de jure corporate status, then they will not have corporate protection. They will be exposed to personal liability. . . ."

---

**McCHESNEY, DOCTRINAL ANALYSIS AND STATISTICAL MODELING IN LAW: THE CASE OF DEFECTIVE INCORPORATION,** 71 Wash. U. L.Q. 493, 498–99 (1993). "Three requirements are typically cited for application of the de facto corporation doctrine. There must have been: (1) a statute in existence by which incorporation was legally possible; (2) a 'colorable' attempt to comply with the statute; and (3) some actual use or exercise of corporate privileges. Because every state has a corporation statute and defendants ordinarily have been acting under the aegis of a supposed corporation, the three factors typically dissolve into one: whether defendants' attempts to incorporate had gone far enough to be deemed 'colorable compliance.' For example, an attempt to file the articles of incorporation, albeit unsuccessful, has frequently sufficed as the necessary attempt at statutory compliance. 'In addition, some cases and commentators have added good faith of corporation or associates as a fourth element. [The good faith requirement] is often omitted, however, because a colorable compliance with the incorporation statute usually encompasses a good faith attempt to incorporate.' "

---

**HARRIS v. LOONEY**, 43 Ark.App. 127, 862 S.W.2d 282 (1993).
"On February 1, 1988, appellant, Robert L. Harris, sold his business
and its assets to J & R Construction. The articles of incorporation for J
& R Construction were signed by the incorporators on February 1,
1988, but were not filed with the Secretary of State's office until
February 3, 1988. In 1991, J & R Construction defaulted on its contract
and promissory note, and appellant sued the incorporators of J & R
Construction, Joe Alexander and appellees, Avanell Looney and Rita
Alexander, for judgment jointly and severally on the corporation's debt
of $49,696.21. In his amended complaint, appellant alleged that the
incorporators were jointly and severally liable for the debt of J & R
Construction because its articles of incorporation had not been filed
with the Secretary of State's Office at the time Joe Alexander, on behalf
of the corporation, entered into the contract with appellant. After a
bench trial, the circuit court held that Joe Alexander was personally
liable for the debts of J & R Construction because he was the
contracting party who dealt on behalf of the corporation. The court
refused, however, to hold appellees, Avanell Looney and Rita Alexander, liable, because neither of them had acted for or on behalf of the
corporation pursuant to Ark.Code Ann. § 4–27–204 (Repl.1991)....

"In 1987, the Arkansas General Assembly ... adopted the Arkansas Business Corporation Act. Section 204 of this Act, Ark.Code Ann.
§ 4–27–204, concerns liability for pre-incorporation transactions and
is identical to Section 2.04 of the Revised Model Business Corporation
Act. It states: 'All persons purporting to act as or on behalf of a
corporation, knowing there was no incorporation under this Act, are
jointly and severally liable for all liabilities created while so acting.'
. . .

"In passing this Act, the Arkansas General Assembly adopted a
heightened standard for imposing personal liability for transactions
entered into before incorporation. The Act requires that, in order to
find liability under § 4–27–204, there must be a finding that the
persons sought to be charged acted as or on behalf of the corporation
and knew there was no incorporation under the Act.

"The evidence showed that the contract to purchase appellant's
business and the promissory note were signed only by Joe Alexander
on behalf of the corporation. The only evidence introduced to support
appellant's allegation that appellees were acting on behalf of the
corporation was Joe Alexander's and Avanell Looney's statements that
they were present when the contract with appellant was signed;
however, these statements were disputed by appellant and his wife.
Appellant testified that he, his wife, Kathryn Harris, and Joe Alexander
were present when the documents were signed to purchase his
business and he did not remember appellee Avanell Looney being
present. Kathryn Harris testified that appellees were not present when
the contract was signed.

"The trial court denied appellant judgment against appellees
because he found that appellees had not acted for or on behalf of J &
R Construction as required by § 4–27–204. The findings of fact of a
trial judge sitting as the factfinder will not be disturbed on appeal

unless the findings are clearly erroneous or clearly against the prepon-derance of the evidence, giving due regard to the opportunity of the trial court to assess the credibility of the witnesses. Arkansas Poultry Fed'n Ins. Trust v. Lawrence, 34 Ark.App. 45, 805 S.W.2d 653 (1991). From our review of the record, we cannot say that the trial court's finding in this case is clearly against the preponderance of the evi-dence, and we find no error in the court's refusal to award appellant judgment against appellees.''

---

**WEIR v. KIRBY CONSTRUCTION COMPANY**, 213 Ga.App. 832, 446 S.E.2d 186 (1994). "[Under the former version of the Model Act,] liability was imposed without regard to . . . lack of knowledge that the certificate of incorporation had not issued. . . .

"[In contrast, Revised Model Act § 2.04] . . . applies to 'all persons purporting to act as or on behalf of a corporation, knowing there was no incorporation.'

"To the extent that common law [liability] was based on what a person 'should have known,' it is inconsistent with [Model Act § 2.04,] which imposes liability only on persons 'purporting to act as . . . a corporation, knowing there was no incorporation.' . . . To 'purport' one thing while 'knowing' another requires culpable knowl-edge. This language replaced a statute which had made liable persons who merely 'assumed' to act for a corporation without knowing the charter of incorporation had not been issued. Under [the prior version of the Model Act], innocent mistake, lack of actual knowledge, or even equitable estoppel would not help such persons. . . . The inequity of such a statute is obvious. . . . . [Revised Model Act § 2.04] requires actual knowledge that there was no incorporation.

---

## REV. MODEL BUS. CORP. ACT §§ 2.03, 2.04

[See Statutory Supplement]

---

## DEL. GEN. CORP. LAW §§ 106, 329

[See Statutory Supplement]

---

## NOTE ON ESTOPPEL

1. *Estoppel Theory Compared With De Facto Theory*. In many cases in which neither a de jure nor a de facto corporation has been formed, the courts have held that a party who has dealt with an

enterprise on the basis that it is corporation is estopped from denying the enterprise's corporate status. Neither the precise contours of the estoppel theory nor its relationship to the de facto theory has ever been entirely clear. It is sometimes said that the estoppel theory differs from the de facto theory in that estoppel is effective for only a specific transaction. However, the de facto theory also may be effective only for a specific transaction: A decision in one suit that a corporation has de facto status will normally not be res judicata in a suit brought by an unrelated plaintiff on an unrelated transaction.

As a practical matter, however, there is likely to be a difference between the *precedential* effect of decisions based on estoppel theory and decisions based on de facto theory. Because a decision based on estoppel theory will normally turn heavily on the plaintiff's conduct, it may have only a limited precedential effect on future cases involving other plaintiffs and other transactions. In contrast, a decision based on de facto theory will normally turn on the defendant's conduct in attempting to organize a corporation. Because that conduct will be the focus of any future de facto case involving those defendants, a decision that a de facto corporation was formed by the conduct will have a precedential effect.

2.  *Disaggregating Estoppel.* A problem with the estoppel theory is that in fact it is not a single theory, but a cluster of very different rules covering cases that fall into very different categories, only one of which involves a true estoppel, that is, reliance by one party on the other's representation.

a.  *Denial of corporate status by the would-be shareholders.* In one kind of estoppel case, an enterprise and its owners, who have claimed corporate status in an earlier transaction with a third party, T, later deny that status in a suit brought by T against the would-be corporation. This is a true estoppel case, at least if T relied on the initial claim of corporate status.

b.  *Technical contexts.* In another kind of estoppel case, the question of corporate status is raised in a technical, procedural context. For example, in a suit brought by a would-be corporation, the defendant may seek to raise the defense that the plaintiff is not really a corporation and therefore cannot sue in a corporate name. The courts tend to regard such defenses as nonmeritorious and to brush them off, using "estoppel" as a handy tool to do so.

c.  *Liability of would-be shareholders.* In the most important category of estoppel cases, a third party who has dealt with an enterprise on the basis that it is a corporation seeks to impose personal liability on the would-be shareholders, who in turn raise estoppel as a defense. Here the issue is whether, as a matter of equity, the claimant, having dealt with the enterprise as if it were a corporation, should be prevented—"estopped"—from treating it as anything else. A leading case in this category is Cranson v. International Business Mach. Corp., 234 Md. 477, 200 A.2d 33 (1964). I.B.M. had sold typewriters to Real Estate Service Bureau on credit. I.B.M. dealt with Bureau as if Bureau were a corporation. In fact, it wasn't, because, without the knowledge of the would-be shareholders, their attorney had negligently failed to file the certificate of incorporation before the transaction with the third party. The court held that the estoppel doctrine could be applied even when a corporation did not have de facto existence, and that although the organizational defects in the case might have prevented the Bureau from being a de facto corporation, "we think that I.B.M. having dealt with the Bureau as if it were a corporation and relied on its credit rather than that of [the would-be shareholders], is estopped to assert that the Bureau was not incorporated at the time the typewriters were purchased."

In this third category of cases, estoppel theory is comparable in its function to de facto theory. However, the two theories differ in two important ways in their application:

*First,* the nub of estoppel theory in such cases is that the third party has dealt with the business as if it were a corporation. Presumably, therefore, the theory would not apply to a tort claimant or other involuntary creditor who was a stranger to the business before his claim arose. In contrast, the de facto theory can be applied to such claimants.

*Second,* the would-be shareholders would not need to resort to the estoppel theory if they could establish that their business had de facto corporate status. Presumably, therefore, less in the way of corporateness must be shown to establish a corporation by estoppel than to establish a de facto corporation. (Thus in Cranson v. International Business Mach., supra, the court applied the estoppel theory only after observing that because the certificate of incorporation had not been filed at the time of the transaction, the de facto theory might not be applicable.)

There is an obvious relationship between the first and second points. A tort claimant or other involuntary creditor has a stronger claim against would-be shareholders than a contract creditor, because a contract creditor who transacts with a would-be corporation expects only limited liability, while the expectation of a typical tort or other involuntary creditor is usually not so limited. Accordingly, the assertion of limited liability against a contact creditor should be easier than the assertion of limited liability against a tort creditor. This result is accomplished by estoppel theory, which allows easier assertion of limited liability than does de facto theory, but is effectively limited to contract creditors.

----

### NOTE ON QUO WARRANTO

A traditional although rarely used method for testing the validity of a would-be corporation's status is through a quo warranto proceeding brought by the state. This form of proceeding derives from an ancient prerogative writ issued on behalf of the King against one who falsely claimed an office or franchise. Most states provide by statute for proceedings in the nature of quo warranto, often without using that name. See, e.g., N.Y. Bus. Corp. Law § 109; California Corp. Code § 1801(a). Such a proceeding can be maintained even against a de facto corporation, because de facto theory is a defense only against a "collateral attack" on corporate status—in effect, only against a challenge raised by private actors—not against a challenge by the state itself.

Even a quo warranto proceeding, however, will not always succeed against a would-be corporation that has failed to satisfy all of the statutory requirements for incorporation. An enterprise that fails to meet all the requirements for incorporation may be deemed a corporation *de jure* if the noncompliance is extremely insubstantial. De jure status, unlike de facto status, is a good defense even against a quo warranto proceeding. For example, in People v. Ford, 294 Ill. 319, 128 N.E. 479 (1920), the Attorney General filed an action in the nature of quo warranto against three would-be incorporators who had failed to comply with a statute that provided that the statement of incorporation was to be sealed. The incorporators had used the Secretary of State's incorporation forms, which neither contained nor mentioned a seal. The court concluded that de jure status had been attained. The provision for a seal, the court said, was only "directory," not "mandatory," because the purpose of the statute was to make a public record, and a seal did not further that purpose.

## SECTION 6.   THE CLASSICAL ULTRA VIRES DOCTRINE

---

### INTRODUCTORY NOTE

1. *The Classical Ultra Vires Doctrine.* Under the classical theory of corporate existence, the corporation is regarded as a fictitious person, endowed with life and capacity only insofar as provided in its charter. Early corporate charters tended to narrowly circumscribe the activities in which a corporation could permissibly engage. Transactions outside that sphere were characterized by the courts as *ultra vires* (beyond the corporation's power) and unenforceable—unenforceable *against* the corporation because beyond the corporation's powers, and unenforceable *by* the corporation on the ground of lack of mutuality. A leading example is Ashbury Railway Carriage & Iron Co. v. Riche, 7 L.R.–Eng. & Ir.App. 653, 33 L.T.R. 450 (1875). Ashbury was authorized by its charter "to make and sell, or lend on hire, railway-carriages and wagons, and all kinds of railway plant, fittings, machinery, and rolling-stock; to carry on the business of mechanical engineers and general contractors; to purchase and sell, as merchants, timber, coal, metals, or other materials; and to buy and sell any such materials on commission, or as agents." 7 L.R.–Eng. & Ir.App. at 654. Ashbury purchased a concession to construct with authority and operate a railway line in Belgium, and Riche contracted to do the

construction. After Riche had done some of the work, Ashbury repudiated the contract. Riche brought suit. The House of Lords held for Ashbury, on the ground that it lacked the power under its charter to build a railroad, and therefore lacked the power to contract for that purpose.

The original purpose of the ultra vires doctrine seems to have been to protect the public or the state from unsanctioned corporate activity. Accordingly, under classical English law even unanimous shareholder ratification would not be a bar to an ultra vires defense ifthe transaction was outside the objects of the corporation. See *Ashbury,* supra; Frommel, Reform of the Ultra Vires Rule: A Personal View, 8 The Company Lawyer 11 (1987).

2. *Powers and Purposes.* In theory, the classical ultra vires doctrine was applicable to two somewhat different kinds of questions. The first question was whether a corporation had acted beyond its *purposes,* that is, had engaged in a type of business activity not permitted under its certificate. The second question was whether the corporation had exercised a *power* not specified in its certificate. In practice, the two questions tended to merge. For example, certificates of incorporation commonly contained clauses that described the corporation's various purposes and powers as both purposes and powers.

3. *Recurring Problems.* A number of problems concerning specific types of corporate transactions tended to recur under the classical vires doctrine. One of these recurring problems concerned the power of a corporation to guarantee a third party's debts. Early cases often held that such guarantees were ultra vires, in the absence of a provision in the certificate of incorporation that explicitly conferred the power to guarantee. See, e.g., Brinson v. Mill Supply Co., 219 N.C. 498, 14 S.E.2d 505 (1941). Present-day statutes make this problem moot by explicitly empowering corporations to make guarantees. See, e.g., Del. Gen. Corp. Law § 123.

Another recurring problem concerned the power of a corporation to be a general partner. Early cases often held that a corporation had no power to enter into a partnership unless that power was explicitly granted by a statute or by the certificate of incorporation. See, e.g., Whittenton Mills v. Upton, 76 Mass. (10 Gray) 582 (1858); Central R.R. Co. v. Collins, 40 Ga. 582 (1869). The concern was that a corporate partner would be bound by the acts and decisions of copartners who were not its duly appointed officers, thereby improperly impinging on the board's power and duty to manage the corporation. (The cases did permit corporations to enter into joint ventures, which are usually temporary in nature and created for a limited purpose.) Present-day statutes make this problem moot by explicitly empowering corporations to become partners. See, e.g., Del. Gen. Corp. Law § 122(11); N.Y.Bus.Corp.Law § 202(15); Rev. Model Bus. Corp. Act § 3.02(9).

4. *Limitations on the Ultra Vires Doctrine.* Ultra vires was always regarded by the commentators as an unsound doctrine. For example, Ballantine, writing in 1927, argued that "in general the objects and purposes clause of the articles should operate simply like by-laws or

articles of partnership, as limitations on the actual authority of the directors and officers to bind the corporation, but not upon their ostensible or apparent authority, unless reasonably to be inferred or actually known." Ballantine, Proposed Revision of the Ultra Vires Doctrine, 12 Cornell L.Q. 453, 455 (1927). Neither the courts nor, for the most part, the legislatures, ever went quite that far, but the history of the doctrine is one of steady erosion by the courts and the bar, resulting in large part from the widespread view that the doctrine was unsound. This erosion proceeded along a variety of fronts:

(i) It was established even in early cases that corporate powers could be implied as well as explicit. See Sutton's Hospital Case, 10 Coke 23a (1613). The courts eventually became very liberal in finding implied powers, including implied powers to enter into business activities not specified in the certificate. Thus in Jacksonville, Mayport, Pablo Ry. & Navigation Co. v. Hooper, 160 U.S. 514, 526, 16 S.Ct. 379, 40 L.Ed. 515 (1896), the Supreme Court held that a Florida company whose purpose, under its charter, was to run a railroad, could also engage in leasing and running a resort hotel. "Undoubtedly the main business of a corporation is to be confined to that class of operations which properly appertain to the general purposes for which its charter was granted. But it may also enter into and engage in transactions which are auxiliary or incidental to its main business." Similarly, in John B. Waldbillig, Inc. v. Gottfried, 22 A.D.2d 997, 254 N.Y.S.2d 924 (1964), aff'd 16 N.Y.2d 773, 209 N.E.2d 818, 262 N.Y.S.2d 498 (1965), the court held that a corporation organized to "engage in the business of building, construction, and contracting" could have incidental or implied power to practice engineering.

(ii) Generally speaking, ultra vires was not a defense to corporate tort or criminal liability. Furthermore, even in areas where ultra vires was a defense it could not be used to reverse completed transactions. Accordingly, the major impact of the doctrine was confined to executory contracts.

(iii) Even as applied to executory contracts, the ambit of the doctrine was limited. The difficult case occurred where only one party had performed under the contract, and the nonperforming party then sought to assert ultra vires as a defense for its nonperformance. Under the majority view, the nonperforming party, having received a benefit under the contract, was "estopped" from asserting the ultra vires defense. See, e.g., Joseph Schlitz Brewing Co. v. Missouri Poultry & Game Co., 287 Mo. 400, 229 S.W. 813 (1921). Under the minority view—known as the "federal rule"—part performance did not have an estoppel effect, on the theory that an ultra vires contract was prohibited by law and therefore void. Even the cases taking this view, however, usually permitted the performing party to recover in restitution for the value of any benefit conferred. See Central Transportation Co. v. Pullman's Palace Car Co., 139 U.S. 24, 11 S.Ct. 478, 35 L.Ed. 55 (1891).

(iv) Under American law, unanimous shareholder approval barred the ultra vires defense unless creditors would be injured. See Note, 83 U.Pa.L.Rev. 479, 488–92 (1935).

(v) The final source of erosion of the ultra vires doctrine was the decreasing significance of the certificate of incorporation as a limit on the corporation's purposes and powers. Draftsmen began writing endless and crushingly boring certificate-of-incorporation provisions that enumerated every possible business purpose and power imaginable. Eventually, most statutes made this kind of draftsmanship unnecessary, by stating that the certificate of incorporation could provide simply that the corporation could engage in any lawful business, and by setting out a laundry list of powers that are conferred on every corporation even without enumeration in the certificate.

(vi) The final step was the adoption, in modern statutes, of provisions that almost (but not quite) abolish the doctrine. The Delaware and Model Act provisions in the following cross-references are examples. Similar statutes have been adopted in all but a few states. See Schaeftler, Ultra Vires—Ultra Useless: The Myth of State Interest in Ultra Vires Acts of Business Corporations, 9 J.Corp.Law 81, 81–83 & n. 6 (1983).

———

### DEL. GEN. CORP. LAW §§ 101(b), 102(a)(3), 121, 122, 124

[See Statutory Supplement]

———

### REV. MODEL BUS. CORP. ACT §§ 3.01(a), 3.02, 3.04

[See Statutory Supplement]

———

## Goodman v. Ladd Estate Co.

Supreme Court of Oregon, 1967.
246 Or. 621, 427 P.2d 102.

■ Before McALLISTER, C.J., and SLOAN, GOOMWIN, HOLMAN[2] and LUSK, JJ.

■ LUSK, JUSTICE.

Plaintiffs brought this suit to enjoin the defendant Ladd Estate Company, a Washington corporation, from enforcing a guaranty agreement executed by Westover Tower, Inc., a corporation, in favor of Ladd Estate. From a decree dismissing the suit plaintiffs appeal.

In 1961 the defendant Walter T. Liles[1] held all the common shares of Westover and he, Dr. Edmond F. Wheatley and Samuel H. Martin were its directors.

---

**2.** Did not participate in this decision. (Footnote by the court.)

**1.** Pursuant to stipulation, the suit was dismissed as to Liles and Westover. The stip-

On September 8, 1961, Dr. Wheatley borrowed $10,000 from Citizens Bank of Oregon and gave his promissory note therefor, which was endorsed by Ladd Estate. Contemporaneously with this transaction Liles, individually, and Westover, by Liles as president, and Martin, as secretary, executed an agreement in writing by which they unconditionally guaranteed Ladd Estate against loss arising out of the latter's endorsement of the Wheatley note to Citizens Bank. The agreement was also signed by Ladd Estate. It recited that it was made at the request of Liles and Westover and that Ladd Estate would not have guaranteed payment of the Wheatley note without the guarantee of Liles and Westover to Ladd Estate.

Wheatley defaulted on his note, Ladd Estate paid to Citizens Bank the amount owing thereon, $9,583.61, and demanded reimbursement from Westover. Upon the latter's rejection of the demand Ladd filed an action at law upon the guaranty agreement against Liles and Westover.

The plaintiffs Morton J. Goodman and Edith Goodman, husband and wife, came into the case in this manner: On September 27, 1963, plaintiffs purchased all the common shares of Westover from a receiver appointed by the Circuit Court for Multnomah County who was duly authorized to make such sale. At the time of such purchase, plaintiffs were fully aware of the guaranty agreement given by Westover and Liles to Ladd Estate. It is conceded that the guaranty agreement was ultra vires the corporation. Plaintiffs, as stockholders, brought this suit pursuant to the provisions of ORS 57.040. [ORS 57.040 is comparable to Del.G.C.L. § 124, supra] . . . .

It will be noticed that the court may set aside and enjoin the performance of the ultra vires contract if it deems such a course equitable. Plaintiffs argue that to deny them the relief they seek would be "shocking," because Westover executed the guaranty agreement in order to enable one of its directors, Wheatley, to obtain a loan of money to be used for purposes entirely foreign to any corporate purpose. We see nothing shocking or even inequitable about it. The corporation was organized for the purposes, among others, to engage in the business of providing housing for rent or sale and to obtain contracts of mortgage insurance from the Federal Housing Commissioner, pursuant to the provisions of the National Housing Act, 12 U.S.C.A. § 1701 et seq. Authorized capital stock comprised 30,100 shares of which 100 shares, having a par value of $1 per share and designated preferred stock, were issued to the Commissioner, pursuant to § 1743(b)(1), U.S.C.A. and 30,000 shares, having a par value of $1 per share and designated common stock, were issued to Liles. Voting rights of the shareholders were vested exclusively in the holders of the common stock. The guaranty agreement recites that, at the request of Liles and Westover, Ladd Estate guaranteed payment of the Wheatley note. Ladd Estate made good on its endorsement when Wheatley defaulted and now calls upon Westover to honor its obligation. The agent of the plaintiffs, who purchased the shares for them,

---

ulation provided that "this suit may proceed in the same manner as if the said Walter T. Liles and Westover Tower, Inc. were parties hereto."

testified that he considered the question whether the guaranty was a valid obligation of the corporation before making the purchase and concluded that it was not. The fact that he guessed wrong does not in any way enhance plaintiffs' claim to equitable consideration.

Neither would it be inequitable to enforce the agreement because of the purpose which the guaranty was intended to serve. Even before the enactment of ORS 57.040 a corporation might properly enter into a guaranty agreement in the legitimate furtherance of its business or purposes: Depot R. Syndicate v. Enterprise B. Co., 87 Or. 560, 562, 170 P. 294, 171 P. 223, L.R.A. 1918C, 1001; 19 Am.Jur.2d 493, Corporations § 1030; that the agreement does not further such purposes is what makes it ultra vires. But the statute says the agreement is enforceable even though ultra vires, and to accept the plaintiffs' argument would be to say that because it is ultra vires the agreement is inequitable and, therefore, unenforceable. This would effectually emasculate the statute.

Moreover, plaintiffs are in no position to invoke the aid of a court of equity. Liles, the former holder of their shares—all the voting shares of Westover—induced Ladd Estate to endorse Wheatley's note by procuring Westover to execute the guaranty agreement. If a shareholder himself has participated in the ultra vires act he cannot thereafter attack it as ultra vires: 7 Fletcher, Cyc. of Corporations (perm. ed., 1964 rev.) 613, § 3453. This would seem to be emphatically so of a shareholder who exercises the entire voting power of the corporation. Plaintiffs, as purchasers of Liles' shares, are in no better position than he would have been to raise the question: McCampbell v. Fountain Head R. Co., 111 Tenn. 55, 75, 77 S.W. 1070, 102 Am.St.Rep. 731; 7 Fletcher, op. cit. 614, § 3456.

It should be added that no rights of creditors of Westover are involved and there is nothing to indicate that the security of any mortgage guaranteed by the Federal Housing Commissioner would be impaired by enforcement of the agreement here in question....

We are of the opinion that plaintiffs are not entitled to equitable relief. The decree is affirmed.

---

**INTER–CONTINENTAL CORP. v. MOODY**, 411 S.W.2d 578 (Tex. Civ.App.1966). Inter–Continental Corp., a Texas corporation, guaranteed a note given by Shively, its president, to Moody. Moody knew or should have known that the guarantee was given for Shively's personal benefit. Shively lost control of Inter–Continental and Moody brought suit on the guarantee. Texas had a statute comparable to Del.Gen. Corp.Law § 124. Inter–Continental defended on the ground of ultra vires, and also arranged for a minority shareholder to intervene for the purpose of enjoining payment of the note on the same ground. (Inter–

Continental's attorney drafted the shareholder's petition, promised to pay his legal expenses, and contacted his lawyer, who testified that he had never talked to the shareholder.) The court held that a defense of ultra vires by the corporation is barred under the statute even if the third party actually knew that the corporation lacked authority to enter into the transaction. However, the court continued, a shareholder can intervene to enjoin an ultra vires act even if he has been solicited to do so by the corporation, provided the shareholder is not the corporation's agent.

———

**711 KINGS HIGHWAY CORP. v. F.I.M.'S MARINE REPAIR SERV., INC.,** 51 Misc.2d 373, 273 N.Y.S.2d 299 (Spec.Term 1966). Kings Highway leased a motion-picture theater to Mariner Repair for fifteen years, beginning July 1, 1966. Before July 1, Kings Highway brought an action for a declaratory judgment to invalidate the lease, on the ground that it was void because it would be ultra vires for Mariner Repair to conduct a motion-picture theater business. The New York statute, Bus.Corp.Law § 203, was comparable to Del.Gen.Corp. Law § 124. Held, for Mariner Repair. "It is undisputed that the present case does not fall within the stated exceptions contained in Section 203. . . . Neither is there merit to the plaintiff's contention that Section 203 applies only where ultra vires is raised as a defense. Notwithstanding the fact that this section is entitled 'Defense of ultra vires' it seems that except in the three stated situations set forth in the section, which are not applicable to the instant case, ultra vires may not be invoked as a sword in support of a cause of action any more than it can be utilized as a defense. . . ."

———

## SECTION 7. THE OBJECTIVE AND CONDUCT OF THE CORPORATION

The question considered in this Section is, to what extent may a corporation act in a manner that is not intended to maximize corporate profits. This question is often put in terms of whether a given act would be "ultra vires," but it penetrates much more deeply into the nature of the corporate institution, and its place in society, than does the classical ultra vires issue.

———

## (a) THE SHAREHOLDERS' INTERESTS, THE PRESENT-VALUE RULE, AND DIVERSIFICATION

———

## Richard A. Brealey & Steward C. Myers Principles of Corporate Finance

Sixth ed., 2000.*

### INTRODUCTION TO PRESENT VALUE ...

Your apartment house has burned down, leaving you with a vacant lot worth $50,000 and a check for $200,000 from the fire insurance company. You consider rebuilding, but your real estate adviser suggests putting up an office building instead. The construction cost would be $300,000, and there would also be the cost of the land, which might otherwise be sold for $50,000. On the other hand, your adviser foresees a shortage of office space and predicts that a year from now the new building would fetch $400,000 if you sold it. Thus you would be investing $350,000 now in the expectation of realizing $400,000 a year hence. You should go ahead if the **present value (PV)** of the expected $400,000 payoff is greater than the investment of $350,000. Therefore, you need to ask yourself, "What is the value today of $400,000 to be received one year from now, and is that present value greater than $350,000?"

### *Calculating Present Value*

The present value of $400,000 one year from now must be less than $400,00. After all, *a dollar today is worth more than a dollar tomorrow,* because the dollar today can be invested to start earning interest immediately. This is the first basic principle of finance. Thus, the present value of a delayed payoff may be found by multiplying the payoff by a discount factor which is less than 1. (If the discount factor were more than 1, a dollar today would be worth *less* than a dollar tomorrow.) If $C_1$ denotes the expected payoff at time period 1 (1 year hence), then

$$\text{Present value (PV)} = \text{discount factor} \times C_1$$

This discount factor is expressed as the reciprocal of 1 plus a *rate of return:*

$$\text{Discount factor} = \frac{1}{1 + r}$$

The rate of return $r$ is the reward that investors demand for accepting delayed payment.

Now we can value the real estate investment, assuming for the moment that the $400,000 payoff is a sure thing. The office building is not the only way to obtain $400,000 a year from now. You could invest in United States government securities maturing in a year. Suppose these securities yield 7 percent interest. How much would you have to invest in them in order to receive $400,000 at the end of the year? That's easy: you would have to invest $400,000/1.07, which is $373,832. Therefore, at an interest rate of 7 percent, the present value of $400,000 1 year from now is $373,832.

Let's assume that, as soon as you've committed the land and begun construction on the building, you decide to sell your project. How much could you sell it for? That's another easy question. Since the property produces $400,000, investors would be willing to pay $373,832 for it today. That's what it would cost them to get a $400,000 payoff from investing in government securities. Of course you could always sell your property for less, but why sell for less than the market will bear? The $373,832 present value is the only feasible price that satisfies both buyer and seller. Therefore, the present value of the property is also its market price.

To calculate present value, we discount expected future payoffs by the rate of return offered by comparable investment alternatives in the capital markets. This rate of return is often referred to as the **discount rate, hurdle rate,** or **opportunity cost of capital.** It is called the *opportunity cost* because it is the return forgone by investing in the project rather than investing in securities. In our example the opportunity cost was 7 percent. Present value was obtained by dividing $400,000 by 1.07:

$$PV = \text{discount factor} \times C_1 = \frac{1}{1 + r} \times C_1 = \frac{400,000}{1.07} = \$373,832$$

### Net Present Value

The building is worth $373,832, but this does not mean that you are $373,832 better off. You committed $350,000, and therefore your **net present value (NPV)** is $23,832. Net present value (**NPV**) is found by subtracting the required investment:

NPV = PV − required investment = 373,832 − 350,000 = $23,832

In other words, your office development is worth more than it costs— it makes a *net* contribution to value. The formula for calculating NPV can be written as

$$NPV = C_0 + \frac{C_1}{1 + r}$$

remembering that $C_0$, the cash flow at time period 0 (that is, today) will usually be a negative number. In other words, $C_0$ is an investment and therefore a cash *outflow*. In our example, $C_0 = -\$350,000$.

### A Comment on Present Value

We made one unrealistic assumption in our discussion of the office development: Your real estate adviser cannot be *certain* about future values of office buildings. The $400,000 figure represents the best *forecast,* but it is not a sure thing.

If the future value of the building is risky, our calculation of NPV is wrong. Investors could achieve $400,000 with certainty by buying $373,832 worth of United States government securities, so they would not buy your building for that amount. You would have to cut your asking price to attract investors' interest.

Here we can invoke a second basic financial principle: *A safe dollar is worth more than a risky one.* Most investors avoid risk when they can do so without sacrificing return. However, the concepts of present value and the opportunity cost of capital still make sense for risky investments. It is still proper to discount the payoff by the rate of return offered by a comparable investment. But we have to think of *expected* payoffs and the *expected* rates of return on other investments.

Not all investments are equally risky. The office development is riskier than a government security but is probably less risky than a start-up biotech venture. Suppose you believe the project is as risky as investment in the stock market and that stock market investments are forecasted to return 12 percent. Then 12 percent becomes the appropriate opportunity cost of capital. That is what you are giving up by not investing in comparable securities. You can now recompute NPV:

$$PV = \frac{400,000}{1.12} = \$357,143$$

$$NPV = PV - 350,000 = \$7143$$

If other investors agree with your forecast of a \$400,000 payoff and your assessment of a its risk, then your property ought to be worth \$357,143 once construction is under way. If you tried to sell it for more than that, there would be no takers, because the property would then offer an expected rate of return lower than the 12 percent available in the stock market. The office building still makes a net contribution to value, but it is much smaller than our earlier calculations indicated.

The value of the office building depends on the timing of the cash flows and their uncertainty. The \$400,000 payoff would be worth exactly that if it could be realized instantaneously. If the office building is as risk-free as government securities, the one–year delay reduces value to \$373,382. If the office building is as risky as investment in the stock market, then uncertainty reduces value by a further \$16,689 to \$357,143. . . .

*Present Values*

We have decided that construction of the office building is a smart thing to do, since it is worth more than it costs—it has a positive net present value. To calculate how much it is worth, we worked out how much one would have to pay to achieve the same income by investing directly in securities. The project's present value is equal to its future income discounted at the rate of return offered by these securities.

We can say this in another way: Our property venture is worth undertaking because its rate of return exceeds the cost of capital. The return on the capital invested is simply the profit as a proportion of the initial outlay:

$$\text{Return} = \frac{\text{profit}}{\text{investment}} = \frac{400{,}000 - 350{,}000}{350{,}000} = .14 \text{ or } 14\%$$

The cost of capital is once again the return forgone by *not* investing in securities. In our present case, if the office building is as risky as investing in the stock market, the return forgone is 12 percent. Since the 14 percent return on the office building exceeds the 12 percent cost, you should go ahead with the project.

Here then we have two equivalent decision rules for capital investment.

1. *Net present value rule.* Accept investments that have positive net present values.

2. *Rate-of-return rule.* Accept investments that offer rates of return in excess of their opportunity costs of capital. . . .

### A FUNDAMENTAL RESULT

Our justification of the present value rule was restricted to two periods and to a certain cash flow. However, the rule also makes sense for uncertain cash flows that extend far into the future. The argument goes like this:

1. A financial manager should act in the interest of the firm's owners, its stockholders. Each stockholder wants three things:

   (*a*) To be as rich as possible, that is, to maximize current wealth.

   (*b*) To transform that wealth into whatever time pattern of consumption he or she desires.

   (*c*) To choose the risk characteristics of that consumption plan.

2. But stockholders do not need the financial manager's help to reach the best time pattern of consumption. They can do that on their own, providing they have free access to competitive capital markets. They can also choose the risk characteristics of their consumption plan by investing in more or less risky securities.

3. How then can the financial manager help the firm's stockholders? There is only one way: increasing the market value of each stockholder's stake in the firm. The way to do that is to seize all investment opportunities that have a positive net present value.

Despite the fact that shareholders have different preferences, they are unanimous in the amount that they want to invest in real assets. This means that they can cooperate in the same enterprise and can safely delegate operation of that enterprise to professional managers. These managers do not need to know anything about the tastes of their shareholders and should not consult their own tastes. Their task is to maximize net present value. If they succeed, they can rest assured that they have acted in the best interest of their shareholders.

This gives us the fundamental condition for successful operation of a modern capitalist economy. Separation of ownership and control is essential for most corporations, so authority to manage has to be delegated. It is good to know that managers can all be given one simple instruction: Maximize net present value.

---

## Hu, New Financial Products, The Modern Process of Financial Innovation, and the Puzzle of Shareholder Welfare

69 Tex.L.Rev. 1273, 1278–1283 (1991).

The most basic principle of corporate law is that a corporation is to be primarily run for the pecuniary benefit of its shareholders. Apart from the impact of nonstockholder constituency statutes and notions of social responsibility generally, few would disagree with this principle as a general matter.

But what does this principle mean in the usual day-to-day operation of publicly held corporations? . . .

The traditional conception of the basic pecuniary goals of a corporation is based on the simple premise that what is good for the corporation is good for the shareholder. If corporate welfare is furthered, as through the maximization of earnings or earnings per share, shareholder welfare is presumed to be furthered as well. . . .

The traditional conception is based on two related assumptions. First, accounting-based measures such as earnings or earnings per share are appropriate indicators of corporate performance. Second, the welfare of a shareholder is largely coincident with the welfare of the corporation.

Unfortunately, both of these classic assumptions are of limited validity. Financial theorists have long argued—and corporate managers are starting to realize—that maximization of total corporate earnings or even earnings per share does not necessarily maximize shareholder wealth. Earnings growth as a sole measure of corporate performance fails to measure the risk characteristics of corporate investments, the extent of investments in working and fixed capital needed to sustain the firm, dividend policy, and the time value of money. . . .

The second assumption underlying the traditional conception, that the welfare of the corporation is coincident with the welfare of its shareholder, is also fundamentally flawed. For example, there may be a conflict of interest concerning risk between the corporation and its shareholders. . . . [M]odern financial theory suggests that corporations concerned about the well-being of shareholders will generally take more risks than corporations concerned about the entity's own well-being; shareholders can, by holding a portfolio of stocks, diversify away much of the risk that a corporation might itself find daunting. Similarly, there may be a conflict of interest as to time. For example, from the point of view of shareholders, the best thing to do with the typical company in a dying industry may be to liquidate the company immediately, pay the net proceeds to shareholders, and allow shareholders to put the money to better use. From the point of view of the company itself—and its managers and employees—long-term decline may be preferable.

[A second, competing] conception of the pecuniary goals of a corporation is directly focused on the welfare of the shareholder. Under this view, shareholder wealth maximization is sought directly, rather than as a by-product of corporate welfare. Managers should seek to take those actions that maximize the wealth of shareholders through a combination of maximizing the actual short-or long-term trading price of each share of common stock and the dividends they actually receive. There is no focus on measures of corporate perfor-mance like accounting earnings and no concern for the corporation independent of the welfare of its shareholders.

The shift to this second conception has been gradual but discerni-ble. Most academics now believe that shareholder wealth maximization is the basic pecuniary objective of the modern publicly held corpora-tion. Judges have typically subscribed to this standard only in the most limited of circumstances, typically in the context of a sale of the entire company.

---

## Hu, Risk, Time, and Fiduciary Principles in Corporate Investment

38 U.C.L.A. L.Rev. 277, 291–94, 299–300 (1990).

### ... *The Paramount Importance of Nondiversifiable Risk*

Assume that ... a corporation is trying to decide between Project B and Project C. [Project B has a projected return of 10%. Project C has a projected return of 15%.] The variability of returns on the two projects suggests that Project C is riskier than Project B. Thus, it follows that management should choose Project C only if it believes that the additional return [on Project C] is somehow worth the additional risk.

This view ignores diversification effects. If a shareholder invests exclusively in one corporation and that corporation invests in Project C, the shareholder would be intensely interested in what happens in a year; the one "flip of the coin" would determine whether the share-holder makes money or loses it. In a close corporation setting, the shareholder may well have all or a substantial part of his wealth in shares of one corporation. That corporation's financial welfare can be equated to the shareholder's; if the corporation does badly, the shareholder does badly.

In the typical publicly held corporation setting, however, a share-holder is usually able to avoid keeping all his eggs in one basket. Assume that the publicly held corporation ("Corporation I") invests in Project C and the economy has other publicly held corporations (Corporations II, III, IV, and so forth), each of which also invests in projects with risks and returns similar to Project C. If the shareholder can invest half his funds in Corporation I and half his funds in Corporation II, and if the economic forces affecting Corporation I and those affecting Corporation II are completely unrelated, then the chances of both such companies ending up with a loss is only 25%, not 50%; there are two flips of the coin, and there is only a 25% chance both coins would end up tails. By the simple act of investing in two companies, the investor will cut in half the possibility of disaster.

The investor could extend this diversification further. Intuition and statistics suggest that the investor who invests in 100 such corporations that in turn invest in projects with characteristics like Project C (all with flips of the coin which are completely independent of each other) is virtually certain to receive a return very close to 15%. Under these circumstances, because of diversification, Project C is really no riskier than Project B. Thus, if all of the risk associated with Projects B and C can be diversified away—if both have zero "systematic" or "nondiversifiable" risk—a corporation should invest in Project C because it provides a higher expected return than Project B.

What does this first type of diversification effect suggest to managers dedicated to maximizing shareholder wealth? If shareholders are diversified and the risk associated with a project can be diversified away, managers can concentrate on expected returns and pay relatively little attention to such "diversifiable," "unique," or "unsystematic" risk. Stated more generally, if shareholders hold diversified portfolios (as is usually presumed for publicly held corporations), corporate managers dedicated to acting consistently with shareholder optimality should pay relatively little attention to unsystematic risk in judging among investment alternatives. . . .

---

## (b) INTERESTS OTHER THAN MAXIMIZATION OF THE SHAREHOLDERS' ECONOMIC WEALTH

### NOTE ON DODGE v. FORD MOTOR CO.

One of the most famous of all corporation-law cases is Dodge v. Ford Motor Co., 204 Mich. 459, 170 N.W. 668 (1919). The case is unusual in its early consideration of the issue (or at least one aspect of the issue) that is now known as corporate social responsibility.

Ford Motor had been incorporated in 1903. Henry Ford owned 58% of Ford Motor's stock and controlled the board. Two Dodge brothers owned 10%, and five other shareholders owned the balance. From 1908 on, Ford Motor had paid a regular annual dividend of $1.2 million, and between December 1911 and October 1915 it paid special dividends totaling $41 million. At the close of its July 31, 1916, fiscal year, Henry Ford, who controlled the board, declared it to be the settled policy of the company not to pay in the future any special dividends, but to put back into the business for the future all of the earnings of the company, other than the regular dividend of $1.2 million. "My ambition," declared Mr. Ford, "is to employ still more men; to spread the benefits of this industrial system to the greatest possible number, to help them build up their lives and their homes. To do this, we are putting the greatest share of our profits back into the business." At the time of the announcement, Ford Motor had a surplus of $112 million, including $52.5 million in cash and $1.3 million in municipal bonds.

The Dodge brothers then brought a suit whose objects included compelling a dividend equal to 75% of the accumulated cash surplus. The trial court ordered Ford Motor to declare a dividend of $19.3 million—equal to half of its cash surplus as of July 31, 1916, minus special dividends paid between the time the complaint was filed and July 31, 1917. The Michigan Supreme Court affirmed this portion of the trial court's decree:

> When plaintiffs made their complaint and demand for further dividends the Ford Motor Company had concluded its most prosperous year of business. The demand for its cars at the price of the preceding year continued.... [I]t reasonably might have expected a profit for the year [beginning August 1, 1916], of upwards of $60,000,000.... Considering [the facts of this case] a refusal to declare and pay further dividends appears to be not an exercise of discretion on the part of the directors, but an arbitrary refusal to do what the circumstances required to be done. These facts and others call upon the directors to justify their action, or failure or refusal to act. In justification, the defendants have offered testimony [proving that: Ford Motor had a general policy to reduce the price of its cars every year while maintaining or improving quality. It could have produced 600,000 cars in the year beginning August 1, 1916, and sold them for $440 each. However, the policy of reducing prices called for the cars to be sold at $360 each, a difference of $48 million.]
>
> The plan, as affecting the profits of the business for the year beginning August 1, 1916, and thereafter, calls for a reduction in the selling price of the cars.... In short, the plan does not call for and is not intended to produce immediately a more profitable business but a less profitable one; not only less profitable than formerly but less profitable than it is admitted it might be made. The apparent immediate effect will be to diminish the value of shares and the returns to shareholders.
>
> It is the contention of plaintiffs that the apparent effect of the plan is intended ... to continue the corporation henceforth as a semieleemosynary institution and not as a business institution. In support of this contention they point to the attitude and to the expressions of Mr. Henry Ford....
>
> ... [Mr. Ford's] testimony creates the impression, also, that he thinks the Ford Motor Company has made too much money, has had too large profits, and that although large profits might be

still earned, a sharing of them with the public, by reducing the price of the output of the company, ought to be undertaken. We have no doubt that certain sentiments, philanthropic and altruistic, creditable to Mr. Ford, had large influence in determining the policy to be pursued by the Ford Motor Company—the policy which has been herein referred to.

It is said by his counsel that—

> "Although a manufacturing corporation cannot engage in humanitarian works as its principal business, the fact that it is organized for profit does not prevent the existence of implied powers to carry on with humanitarian motives such charitable works as are incidental to the main business of the corporation."
> . . .

The difference between an incidental humanitarian expenditure of corporate funds for the benefit of the employees, like the building of a hospital for their use and the employment of agencies for the betterment of their condition, and a general purpose and plan to benefit mankind at the expense of others, is obvious. There should be no confusion (of which there is evidence) of the duties which Mr. Ford conceives that he and the stockholders owe to the general public and the duties which in law he and his codirectors owe to protesting, minority stockholders. A business corporation is organized and carried on primarily for the profit of the stockholders. The powers of the directors are to be employed for that end. The discretion of directors is to be exercised in the choice of means to attain that end and does not extend to a change in the end itself, to the reduction of profits or to the nondistribution of profits among stockholders in order to devote them to other purposes.

. . . As we have pointed out, and the proposition does not require argument to sustain it, it is not within the lawful powers of a board of directors to shape and conduct the affairs of a corporation for the merely incidental benefit of shareholders and for the primary purpose of benefitting others, and no one will contend that if the avowed purpose of the defendant directors was to sacrifice the interests of shareholders it would not be the duty of the courts to interfere.

---

## A.P. Smith Mfg. Co. v. Barlow

Supreme Court of New Jersey, 1953.
13 N.J. 145, 98 A.2d 581, appeal dismissed, 346 U.S. 861, 74 S.Ct. 107, 98 L.Ed. 373 (1953).

■ JACOBS, J. The Chancery Division, in a well-reasoned opinion by Judge Stein, determined that a donation by the plaintiff The A.P. Smith Manufacturing Company to Princeton University was *intra vires.* Because of the public importance of the issues presented, the appeal duly taken to the Appellate Division has been certified directly to this court under Rule 1:5–1(*a*).

The company was incorporated in 1896 and is engaged in the manufacture and sale of valves, fire hydrants and special equipment, mainly for water and gas industries. Its plant is located in East Orange and Bloomfield and it has approximately 300 employees. Over the years the company has contributed regularly to the local community chest and on occasions to Upsala College in East Orange and Newark University, now part of Rutgers, the State University. On July 24, 1951 the board of directors adopted a resolution which set forth that it was in the corporation's best interests to join with others in the 1951 Annual Giving to Princeton University, and appropriated the sum of $1,500 to be transferred by the corporation's treasurer to the university as a contribution towards its maintenance. When this action was questioned by stockholders the corporation instituted a declaratory judgment action in the Chancery Division and trial was had in due course.

Mr. Hubert F. O'Brien, the president of the company, testified that he considered the contribution to be a sound investment, that the public expects corporations to aid philanthropic and benevolent institutions, that they obtain good will in the community by so doing, and that their charitable donations create favorable environment for their business operations. In addition, he expressed the thought that in contributing to liberal arts institutions, corporations were furthering their self-interest in assuring the free flow of properly trained personnel for administrative and other corporate employment. Mr. Frank W. Abrams, chairman of the board of the Standard Oil Company of New Jersey, testified that corporations are expected to acknowledge their public responsibilities in support of the essential elements of our free enterprise system. He indicated that it was not "good business" to disappoint "this reasonable and justified public expectation," nor was it good business for corporations "to take substantial benefits from their membership in the economic community while avoiding the normally accepted obligations of citizenship in the social community." Mr. Irving S. Olds, former chairman of the board of the United States Steel Corporation, pointed out that corporations have a self-interest in the maintenance of liberal education as the bulwark of good government. He stated that "Capitalism and free enterprise owe their survival in no small degree to the existence of our private, independent universities" and that if American business does not aid in their maintenance it is not "properly protecting the long-range interest of its stockholders, its employees and its customers." Similarly, Dr. Harold W. Dodds, President of Princeton University, suggested that if private institutions of higher learning were replaced by governmental institutions our society would be vastly different and private enterprise in other fields would fade out rather promptly. Further on he stated that "democratic society will not long endure if it does not nourish within itself strong centers of non-governmental fountains of knowledge, opinions of all sorts not governmentally or politically originated. If the time comes when all these centers are absorbed into government, then freedom as we know it, I submit, is at an end."

The objecting stockholders have not disputed any of the foregoing testimony nor the showing of great need by Princeton and other private institutions of higher learning and the important public service being rendered by them for democratic government and industry alike. Similarly, they have acknowledged that for over two decades there has been state legislation on our books which expresses a strong public policy in favor of corporate contributions such as that being questioned by them. Nevertheless, they have taken the position that (1) the plaintiff's certificate of incorporation does not expressly authorize the contribution and under common-law principles the company does not possess any implied or incidental power to make it, and (2) the New Jersey statutes which expressly authorize the contribution may not constitutionally be applied to the plaintiff, a corporation created long before their enactment. See *R.S.* 14:3–13; *R.S.* 14:3–13.1 *et seq.*

In his discussion of the early history of business corporations Professor Williston refers to a 1702 publication where the author stated flatly that "The general intent and end of all civil incorporations is for better government." And he points out that the early corporate charters, particularly their recitals, furnish additional support for the notion that the corporate object was the public one of managing and ordering the trade as well as the private one of profit for the members. See 3 *Select Essays on Anglo–American Legal History* 201 (1909); 1 *Fletcher, Corporations* (*rev. ed.* 1931), 6.... However, with later economic and social developments and the free availability of the corporate device for all trades, the end of private profit became generally accepted as the controlling one in all businesses other than those classed broadly as public utilities. *Cf. Dodd, For Whom Are Corporate Managers Trustees?*, 45 *Harv.L.Rev.* 1145, 1148 (1932). As a concomitant the common-law rule developed that those who managed the corporation could not disburse any corporate funds for philanthropic or other worthy public cause unless the expenditure would benefit the corporation. *Hutton v. West Cork Railway Company*, 23 Ch.D. 654 (1883); *Dodge v. Ford Motor Co.*, 204 Mich. 459, 170 N.W. 668, 3 A.L.R. 413 (Sup.Ct.1919).... During the 19th Century when corporations were relatively few and small and did not dominate the country's wealth, the common-law rule did not significantly interfere with the public interest. But the 20th Century has presented a different climate. *Berle and Means, The Modern Corporation and Private Property* (1948). Control of economic wealth has passed largely from individual entrepreneurs to dominating corporations, and calls upon the corporations for reasonable philanthropic donations have come to be made with increased public support. In many instances such contributions have been sustained by the courts within the common-law doctrine upon liberal findings that the donations tended reasonably to promote the corporate objectives....

... [C]ourts, while adhering to the terms of the common-law rule, have applied it very broadly to enable worthy corporate donations with indirect benefits to the corporations. In *State ex rel. Sorensen v. Chicago B. & Q.R. Co.*, 112 *Neb.* 248, 199 *N.W.* 534, 537

(1924), the Supreme Court of Nebraska, through Justice Letton, went even further and without referring to any limitation based on economic benefits to the corporation said that it saw ... "no reason why a railroad corporation may not, to a reasonable extent, donate funds or services to aid in good works." ...

When the wealth of the nation was primarily in the hands of individuals they discharged their responsibilities as citizens by donating freely for charitable purposes. With the transfer of most of the wealth to corporate hands and the imposition of heavy burdens of individual taxation, they have been unable to keep pace with increased philanthropic needs. They have therefore, with justification, turned to corporations to assume the modern obligations of good citizenship in the same manner as humans do. Congress and state legislatures have enacted laws which encourage corporate contributions, and much has recently been written to indicate the crying need and adequate legal basis therefor.... In actual practice corporate giving has correspondingly increased. Thus, it is estimated that annual corporate contributions throughout the nation aggregate over 300 million dollars with over 60 million dollars thereof going to universities and other educational institutions. Similarly, it is estimated that local community chests receive well over 40% of their contributions from corporations; these contributions and those made by corporations to the American Red Cross, to Boy Scouts and Girl Scouts, to 4–H Clubs and similar organizations have almost invariably been unquestioned.

During the first world war corporations loaned their personnel and contributed substantial corporate funds in order to insure survival; during the depression of the '30s they made contributions to alleviate the desperate hardships of the millions of unemployed; and during the second world war they again contributed to insure survival. They now recognize that we are faced with other, though nonetheless vicious, threats from abroad which must be withstood without impairing the vigor of our democratic institutions at home and that otherwise victory will be pyrrhic indeed. More and more they have come to recognize that their salvation rests upon sound economic and social environment which in turn rests in no insignificant part upon free and vigorous nongovernmental institutions of learning. It seems to us that just as the conditions prevailing when corporations were originally created required that they serve public as well as private interests, modern conditions require that corporations acknowledge and discharge social as well as private responsibilities as members of the communities within which they operate. Within this broad concept there is no difficulty in sustaining, as incidental to their proper objects and in aid of the public welfare, the power of corporations to contribute corporate funds within reasonable limits in support of academic institutions. But even if we confine ourselves to the terms of the common-law-rule in its application to current conditions, such expenditures may likewise readily be justified as being for the benefit of the corporation; indeed, if need be the matter may be viewed strictly in terms of actual survival of the corporation in a free enterprise system....

In 1930 a statute was enacted in our State which expressly provided that any corporation could cooperate with other corporations and natural persons in the creation and maintenance of community funds and charitable, philanthropic or benevolent instrumentalities conducive to public welfare, and could for such purposes expend such corporate sums as the directors "deem expedient and as in their judgment will contribute to the protection of the corporate interests." ... In 1950 a more comprehensive statute was enacted. *L.* 1950, *c.* 220; *N.J.S.A.* 14:3–13.1 *et seq.* In this enactment the Legislature declared that it shall be the public policy of our State and in furtherance of the public interest and welfare that encouragement be given to the creation and maintenance of institutions engaged in community fund, hospital, charitable, philanthropic, educational, scientific or benevolent activities or patriotic or civic activities conducive to the betterment of social and economic conditions; and it expressly empowered corporations acting singly or with others to contribute reasonable sums to such institutions, provided, however, that the contribution shall not be permissible if the donee institution owns more than 10% of the voting stock of the donor and provided, further, that the contribution shall not exceed 1% of capital and surplus unless the excess is authorized by the stockholders at a regular or special meeting. To insure that the grant of express power in the 1950 statute would not displace preexisting power at common law or otherwise, the Legislature provided that the "act shall not be construed as directly or indirectly minimizing or interpreting the rights and powers of corporations, as heretofore existing, with reference to appropriations, expenditures or contributions of the nature above specified." *N.J.S.A.* 14:3–13.3. It may be noted that statutes relating to charitable contributions by corporations have now been passed in 29 states. See *Andrews, supra,* 235.

The appellants contend that the foregoing New Jersey statutes may not be applied to corporations created before their passage. Fifty years before the incorporation of The A.P. Smith Manufacturing Company our Legislature provided that every corporate charter thereafter granted "shall be subject to alteration, suspension and repeal, in the discretion of the legislature." L.1846, p. 16; *R.S.* 14:2–9. A similar reserved power was placed into our State Constitution in 1875 (Art. IV, Sec. VII, par. 11), and is found in our present Constitution....

... We are entirely satisfied that within the orbit of above authorities the legislative enactments found in *R.S.* 14:3–13 and *N.J.S.A.* 14:3–13.1 *et seq.* and applied to pre-existing corporations do not violate any constitutional guarantees afforded to their stockholders.

... And since in our view the corporate power to make reasonable charitable contributions exists under modern conditions, even apart from express statutory provision, its enactments simply constitute helpful and confirmatory declarations of such power, accompanied by limiting safeguards.

In the light of all of the foregoing we have no hesitancy in sustaining the validity of the donation by the plaintiff. There is no suggestion that it was made indiscriminately or to a pet charity of the corporate directors in furtherance of personal rather than corporate ends. On the contrary, it was made to a preeminent institution of higher learning, was modest in amount and well within the limitations imposed by the statutory enactments, and was voluntarily made in the reasonable belief that it would aid the public welfare and advance the interests of the plaintiff as a private corporation and as part of the community in which it operates. We find that it was a lawful exercise of the corporation's implied and incidental powers under common-law principles and that it came within the express authority of the pertinent state legislation. As has been indicated, there is now wide-spread belief throughout the nation that free and vigorous non-governmental institutions of learning are vital to our democracy and the system of free enterprise and that withdrawal of corporate authority to make such contributions within reasonable limits would seriously threaten their continuance. Corporations have come to recognize this and with their enlightenment have sought in varying measures, as has the plaintiff by its contribution, to insure and strengthen the society which gives them existence and the means of aiding themselves and their fellow citizens. Clearly then, the appellants, as individual stock-holders whose private interests rest entirely upon the well-being of the plaintiff corporation, ought not be permitted to close their eyes to present-day realities and thwart the long-visioned corporate action in recognizing and voluntarily discharging its high obligations as a con-stituent of our modern social structure.

The judgment entered in the Chancery Division is in all respects Affirmed.

■ *For affirmance*—CHIEF JUSTICE VANDERBILT, and JUSTICES HEHER, OLIPHANT, WACHENFELD, BURLING and JACOBS—6.

*For reversal*—None.

———

## DEL. GEN. CORP. LAW § 122(9), (12)

[See Statutory Supplement]

———

## REV. MODEL BUS. CORP. ACT § 3.02(12)–(14)

[See Statutory Supplement]

## NOTE ON THE CONDUCT OF THE CORPORATION

1. Virtually all states have now adopted statutory provisions relating to corporate contributions that are comparable to Del.Gen. Corp.Law § 122(9) and Rev.Model Bus.Corp.Act § 3.02(13). Although typically these provisions do not explicitly incorporate a limit of

reasonableness, the commentators generally agree that such a limit is to be implied. Of particular significance is the commentary of Ray Garrett, a principal figure in the drafting history of the Model Act:

> Donations should be reasonable in amount in the light of the corporation's financial condition, bear some reasonable relation to the corporation's interest, and not be so "remote and fanciful" as to excite the opposition of shareholders whose property is being used. Direct corporate benefit is no longer necessary, but corporate interest remains as a motive.

Garrett, Corporate Donations, 22 Bus.Law. 297, 301 (1967).

2.  There is very little direct authority on the permissibility of taking ethical considerations into account in framing corporate action where doing so might not enhance profits. However, statutory provisions like Rev.Model Bus.Corp.Act § 3.02(13) provide indirect support for doing so, since it would be anomalous to permit the corporation to donate money it has already earned for public welfare or charitable purposes, while prohibiting the corporation from forgoing a limited amount of profits in the service of generally recognized ethical principles.

3.  The median level of corporate contributions has normally been around 1% of pretax income. See The Conference Board, Corporate Contributions in 1997 (1999).

---

**MILTON FRIEDMAN, THE SOCIAL RESPONSIBILITY OF BUSINESS IS TO INCREASE ITS PROFITS,** N.Y. Times, Sept. 13, 1970, § 6 (magazine) at 32. "In a free-enterprise, private-property system, a corporate executive is an employee of the owners of the business. He has direct responsibility to his employers. That responsibility is to conduct the business in accordance with their desires, which generally will be to make as much money as possible while conforming to the basic rules of the society, both those embodied in law and those embodied in ethical custom."

---

### AMERICAN LAW INSTITUTE, PRINCIPLES OF CORPORATE GOVERNANCE §§ 2.01, 6.02

[See Statutory Supplement]

---

### CONN. GEN. STATS. ANN. §§ 33–756

[See Statutory Supplement]

---

**INDIANA CODE ANN. § 23–1–35–1**

[See Statutory Supplement]

———

**N.Y. BUS. CORP. LAW § 717**

[See Statutory Supplement]

———

**PENNSYLVANIA CONSOL. STATS. ANN. TITLE
15, §§ 1711, 1715, 1716, 1717, 2502**

[See Statutory Supplement]

---

## SECTION 8.  THE NATURE OF CORPORATE LAW

———

**M. EISENBERG, THE STRUCTURE OF THE CORPORATION 1**
(1976). "corporate law is constitutional law; that is, its dominant
function is to regulate the manner in which the corporate institution is
constituted, to define the relative rights and duties of those participating in the institution, and to delimit the powers of the institution vis-à-
vis the external world."

———

## Melvin A. Eisenberg, The Conception that the Corporation is a Nexus of Contracts, and the Dual Nature of the Firm

24 J. Corp. Law 819 (1998).

### I.  INTRODUCTION

In 1976 by Michael Jensen and William Meckling formulated the
conception that the corporation is a nexus of contracts in their famous
article *The Theory of the Firm: Managerial Behavior, Agency Costs,
and Ownership Structure.*[1] Since that time, the conception has dominated the law-and-economics literature in corporate law. The validity
of this conception, however, cannot be established by economic
analysis. That does not make the conception invalid, but it does mean
that its validity must be examined along other dimensions. . . .

---

**1.** Michael C. Jensen & William H.
Meckling, *The Theory of the Firm: Manageri-*
*al Behavior, Agency Costs, and Ownership*
*Structure,* 3 J. Fin. Econ. 305 (1976).

## II.  A BRIEF INTELLECTUAL HISTORY

It is useful to begin by developing the intellectual history of the Jensen and Meckling article. That history begins with Ronald Coase's landmark paper, *The Nature of the Firm.*[3] In that paper, Coase characterized the boundaries of the firm as the range of exchanges over which the market system was superseded and resource allocation was accomplished instead by authority and direction:

> [I]n economic theory we find that the allocation of factors of production between different uses is determined by the price mechanism. The price of factor *A* becomes higher in *X* than in *Y*. As a result, *A* moves from *Y* to *X* until the difference between the prices in *X* and *Y*, except insofar as it compensates for other differential advantages, disappears. Yet in the real world, we find that there are many areas where this does not apply. If a workman moves from department *Y* to department *X*, he does not go because of a change in relative prices, but because he is ordered to do so.
>
> .... Outside the firm, price movements direct production, which is co-ordinated through a series of exchange transactions on the market. Within a firm, these market transactions are eliminated and in place of the complicated market structure with exchange transactions is substituted the entrepreneur-coordinator, who directs production.

Coase argued that activities will be included within a firm when the costs of using markets—that is, contracts—are greater than the costs of direction by authority. The essential issue in the theory of the firm, therefore, was why some economic activity takes place within firms, so that the activity is directed by authority, while other economic activity takes place across markets, so that the activity is determined by contract.

Coase did not explicitly define the firm in this paper. Implicitly, however, he defined the firm to consist of the activities under the direction of the entrepreneur, who in turn was defined as the person or persons who take the place of the price mechanism in the direction of resources. Coase stated that the question what constitutes a firm can be approached in practice by considering the relationship of employer and employee. One of the essentials of this relationship, he said, is that the employer must have the right to control the work of the employee.[4] "We thus see," he concluded, "that it is the fact of direction which is the essence of the legal concept of employer and employee"—and, by extension, of the firm.

In their paper *Production, Information Costs, and Economic Organization,*[10] Alchian and Harold Demsetz objected to the Coasian conception of the firm, and emphasized instead the role of team

---

**3.** Ronald H. Coase, *The Nature of the Firm,* 4 Economica 386 (1937).

**4.** *Id.* at 404–05.

**10.** Armen A. Alchian and Harold Demsetz, Production, Information Costs, and Economic Organization, 62 AM. ECON. REV. 777 (1972).

production within the firm and the role of agreement and monitoring in team production. It is a "delusion," they said, "to see the firm characterized by the power to settle issues by fiat, by authority, or by disciplinary action superior to that available in the conventional market."[11] Rather,

> [The firm] has no power of fiat, no authority, no disciplinary action any different in the slightest degree from ordinary market contracting between any two people. [In the case of a contract between me and you,] I can "punish" you only by withholding future business or by seeking redress in the courts for any failure to honor our exchange agreement. That is exactly all that any employer can do. He can fire or sue, just as I can fire my grocer by stopping purchases from him or sue him for delivering faulty products. What then is the content of the presumed power to manage and assign workers to various tasks? Exactly the same as one little consumer's power to manage and assign his grocer to various tasks. The single consumer can assign his grocer to the task of obtaining whatever the customer can induce the grocer to provide at a price acceptable to both parties. That is precisely all that an employer can do to an employee. To speak of managing, directing, or assigning workers to various tasks is a deceptive way of noting that the employer continually is involved in renegotiation of contracts on terms that must be acceptable to both parties. Telling an employee to type this letter rather than to file that document is like my telling a grocer to sell me this brand of tuna rather than that brand of bread.... Wherein then is the relationship between a grocer and his employee different from that between a grocer and his customers? It is in a *team* use of inputs and a centralized position of some party in the contractual arrangements of *all* other inputs. It is the *centralized contractual agent in a team productive process*—not some superior authoritarian directive or disciplinary power.[12]

Jensen and Meckling applauded Alchian and Demsetz's objection to Coase's theory of the firm, but concluded that Alchian and Demsetz had not gone far enough in rejecting Coase:

> Alchian and Demsetz ... object to the notion that activities within the firm are governed by authority, and correctly emphasize the role of contracts as a vehicle for voluntary exchange. They emphasize the role of monitoring in situations in which there is joint input or team production. We sympathize with the importance they attach to monitoring, but we believe the emphasis which Alchian–Demsetz place on joint input production is too narrow and therefore misleading. Contractual relations are the essence of the firm, not only with employees but with suppliers, customers, creditors, etc.

11. Id. at 777.  

12. *Id.* at 777–78 (emphasis in original).

Jensen and Meckling therefore substituted, for Coase's conception of the firm, the competing conception that the firm was a nexus of contracts—and, more particularly, "that most organizations are simply *legal fictions which serve as a nexus for a set of contracting relationships among individuals....*"[14]

Before proceeding further, it is necessary to clarify the meaning of the nexus-of-contracts conception. The conception neither can nor does mean what it literally says. In ordinary language, the term *contract* means an agreement. In law, the term means a legally enforceable promise. Pretty clearly, however, the nexus-of-contracts conception does not mean either that the corporation is a nexus of agreements or that it is a nexus of legally enforceable promises. Instead, the conception means that the corporation is a nexus of reciprocal arrangements. But then why is the term *contracts*, rather than the term *reciprocal arrangements*, used in the nexus-of-contracts conception?

One possible explanation is that the term *nexus of contracts* was coined by economists, and "[e]conomists tend to view contracts as relationships characterized by reciprocal relations and behavior."[15] . . . Whatever the explanation, . . . I will use the term *nexus of contracts* in the way it is meant, that is, a nexus of reciprocal arrangements. . . .

### IV. THE PROBLEM OF MANDATORY LEGAL RULES

A central issue raised by the nexus-of-contracts conception is how to deal with the rules of corporate law. Clearly, these rules are basic to the constitution of the corporation. Equally clearly, they are not reciprocal arrangements; in particular, some important rules of corporation law, such as the federal laws that govern insider trading and tender offers, are mandatory.

Some commentators deal with this issue by taking the position that none of the rules of corporation law are really mandatory. . . .

The strategy of denying that there are mandatory rules of corporate law is not only untenable; it is unnecessary. Nothing in the nexus-of-contracts conception requires a denial that there are mandatory corporate rules. After all, even real contracts are governed by a number of mandatory rules, such as the rules that concern consideration, unconscionability, and good faith. Accordingly, the nexus-of-contracts conception could easily be interpreted to mean that the corporation is a nexus of reciprocal arrangements made within a framework of mandatory legal rules, just as many other reciprocal arrangements, like contracts, trusts, and marriages, are made within a framework of mandatory legal rules.

Unfortunately, it has proved tempting to confuse the positive proposition the corporation is a nexus of reciprocal arrangements with

---

**14.** [Jensen and Meckling, *supra* note 1] at 310–11 (emphasis in original).

**15.** Oliver Hart, An Economist's Perspective on The Theory of the Firm, 89 Co-lum.L.Rev. 1757, 1764 n.30. Hart builds here on Jeffrey N. Grodon, The Mandatory Structure of Corporate Law, 89 Colum.L.Rev. 1549 (1989).

the normative proposition that the persons who constitute a corporation should be free to make whatever reciprocal arrangements they choose, without the constraints of any mandatory legal rules. For example, Stephen Bainbridge states that "The nexus of contracts model has important implications for a range of corporate law topics, the most obvious of which is the debate over the proper role of mandatory legal rules."[20] However, insofar as the nexus of contracts is a positive conception, it has no implications for the proper role of mandatory legal rules. To reason from the nexus-of-contracts conception to a rejection of mandatory legal rules is to mistakenly reason from is to *ought*.

Whether any rules of corporation law should be mandatory, and if so, what those rules should be, are important and difficult questions. Contracts—real contracts—should normally be respected and legally enforced. Under appropriate conditions, so should certain other forms of private ordering. In the corporate context, however, contracts and other forms of private ordering are subject to special problems. For example, there are a number of potential limits on the force of shareholder consent to corporate actions. The consent may be fictitious—as where the approval is given in part by nonshareholders with power to vote, like brokers who hold stock in street name. The consent may be tainted by a conflict of interest—as where a majority of the approving shareholders benefit from the approval in a way that other shareholders do not. The consent may be coerced—as where the shareholders are threatened that unless they approve a proposal, management will refuse to take some action that is in the shareholders' interests, like the payment of dividends. The consent may be impoverished—as where shareholders approve an action they deem second best because management's control of the agenda prevents them from voting on an action they deem first best, or where the shareholders have only a weak, incomplete, or nonexistent idea of a proposal for which they vote.

Furthermore, the respect that is normally due to contracts and other forms of private ordering is significantly diminished when the contract or private ordering creates adverse third-party effects—negative externalities. The possibility of such effects is especially salient in the corporate context, because of the interdependence of individuals and groups who are interested in the corporation but may not be parties to a given arrangement. For example, a shareholders' agreement between two of three shareholders in a close corporation may have a significant negative effect on the third shareholder. A contract between the board and the chief executive officer may have a significant negative effects on the shareholders as a group. A restructuring of the corporation initiated by the board and approved by the shareholders may have a significant negative effect on bondholders.

**20.** Stephen M. Bainbridge, Community and Statism: A Conservative Contractarian Critique of Progressive Corporate Law Scholarship, 82 Cornell L.Rev. 856, 860 (1997)....

Given the special problems of contract and private ordering in the corporate context, whether any particular rule of corporate law should be mandatory must be examined on a rule-by-rule basis in light of the extent, if any, to which the power to contract around the given rule may implicate these problems. One of the defects of the nexus-of-contracts conception is that it too easily leads to a substitution of conclusory thinking for careful rule-by-rule analysis of these issues.

## VI.   THE DUAL NATURE OF THE FIRM

Recall that Coase's conception of the firm turned on the entrepreneur's *authority* (that is, his power) to direct his subordinates through rules and orders. Recall too that in contrast, Alchian and Demsetz argued that the concept of authority in the firm was a delusion. "The firm," they said, "has no power of fiat, no authority, no disciplinary action any different in the slightest degree from ordinary market contracting between any two people." Accordingly, they said, there is no difference between the employer-employee relationship and the grocer-customer relationship:

> To speak of managing, directing, or assigning workers to various tasks is a deceptive way of noting that the employer continually is involved in renegotiation of contracts on terms that must be acceptable to both parties. Telling an employee to type this letter rather than to file that document is like my telling a grocer to sell me this brand of tuna rather than that brand of bread.[32]

This analysis, in turn, is a lynchpin of Jensen and Meckling's nexus-of-contracts conception.

This analysis is not exactly wrong. But neither is it exactly right. It catches half the truth, but only half. To begin with, many or most of the contracts in a corporation are sticky. It is usually easy to switch grocers, but it is usually not easy to quit jobs. Consider, for example, an employee with firm-specific skills, or with great seniority, unvested stock options, or other benefits that will be lost if he resigns.

Much more important, the position that there is no difference between contracting to do an act and being ordered or directed to do an act lacks all correspondence with reality. Corporations are hierarchical organizations. Anyone who has worked in a hierarchical organization knows that the way in which directions are experienced by supervisors and subordinates is entirely different from the way in which contracts are experienced by contracting parties. To use Alchian and Demsetz's example, both employer and employee experience employer's direction to type a letter in a very different way than customer and grocer experience grocer's trying to sell tuna rather than bread.

This difference is qualitative, not merely quantitative. When a consumer needs to decide whether to buy bread or tuna, his decision will be based on whether bread or tuna is the best choice (by whatever metric of best he employs), all things considered—that is, considering,

---

**32.** Alchian and Demsetz, supra note 10, at 777.

on the merits, all the reasons for and against each alternative. In contrast, when a subordinate is given a direction by a superior, the fact of the direction normally excludes the subordinate from considering any reason for action except the direction. Thus a subordinate normally follows a direction more or less reflexively, whether he likes the direction or not, and whether or not he considers the direction best, all things considered. As Bainbridge has observed, "there is a sharp disconnect between Alchian and Demsetz's argument and the real world of work. Command-and-control is the norm in most workplaces. Workers generally accept hierarchical authority and perceive obedience to authority as an integral part of their job: 'for the majority, disobedience is unthinkable.' "[35] . . .

All this is of great psychological and sociological importance, because most people work in hierarchical organizations. But it is of economic importance as well, just because it is of psychological and sociological importance. Just as a subordinate experiences getting a direction differently than making a real contract, so too does a superior experience giving a direction differently than making a real contract. There are costs to inducing action by making real contracts, and there are costs to inducing action by giving directions. Firms exist in part when the cost of inducing action through giving directions is less than the cost of inducing action through making real contracts.

Furthermore, a corporation—or more generally, a firm—is not only a hierarchical organization; it is a *bureaucratic* hierarchical organization. That means, among other things, that much of the activity in a corporation is organized by established bureaucratic rules that are not open to continued re-examination, let alone negotiation. To paraphrase a remark of Benjamin Klein, an organization is embedded in its human capital, but is greater than the sum of its parts. Employees come and go, but the organization maintains the memory of how things are done.[38]

More generally, an organization consists not only of assets, persons, and relationships among persons, but of the rules that organize those assets, persons, and relationships. Some of those rules are contractual, but most are bureaucratic in the sense that they are hierarchically adopted and persist over time as persons, assets, and relationships come and go.

To put this differently, the corporation has a dual nature. In the first quarter of the twentieth century, it was discovered that light, theretofore described and understood as a wave (a portion of the electromagnetic spectrum), can alternatively be described and understood as a particle (a photon) and that, correspondingly, the building-blocks of atoms, such as electrons, theretofore described and under-

---

**35.** Bainbridge, Participatory Management Within a Theory of the Firm, 21 J. Corp. L. 657, 663–64 (1996) (quoting John F. Witte, Democracy, Authority, and Alienation in Work: Workers' Participation in an American Corporation 38 (1980). . . .

**38.** See Klein, Vertical Integration as Organizational Ownership: The Fisher Body–General Motors Relationship Revisited, 4 J.L. ECON. & ORGANIZATION 199; 208 (1988).

stood as particles, can alternatively be described and understood as waves. So too the firm can be described and understood either as a set of reciprocal arrangements or as a bureaucratic hierarchical organization. To describe and understand firms purely as bureaucratic hierarchical organizations misses the voluntary element of many of the arrangements that constitute a firm. To describe firms purely as a set of reciprocal arrangements misses the extent to which firms are organized by bureaucratic rules and operate by hierarchical directions issued by superiors to subordinates. . . .

# CHAPTER IV

# CORPORATE STRUCTURE

## SECTION 1. SHAREHOLDERSHIP IN PUBLICLY HELD CORPORATIONS

### NOTE ON SHAREHOLDERSHIP IN PUBLICLY HELD CORPORATIONS

Until recently, corporation law reflected what might be called the traditional model of formal corporate decisionmaking. Under this model, the board of directors manages the corporation's business and makes business policy; the officers act as agents of the board and execute its decisions; and the shareholders elect the board and decide on "major corporate actions" or "fundamental" changes. The model is an inverted pyramid in form. At the top of the inverted pyramid are the shareholders, who own the corporation, who elect the board of directors, and whose approval is required for fundamental corporate actions. At the next level down is the board, which constitutes the policymaking body of the corporation and selects the officers. At the bottom of the inverted pyramid are the officers, who have some discretion but are limited to execution of policies formulated by the board.

This model was first called into drastic question in 1932, with the publication of Berle & Means's classic work, *The Modern Corporation and Private Property*. One of this book's principal conclusions, almost revolutionary at the time, was that in publicly held corporations, *control* had come to be divorced from *ownership*. The modern publicly held corporation has thousands or even hundreds of thousands of shareholders. However, the separation of ownership from control documented by Berle & Means did not result only from large *numbers* of *shareholders*, but from the *dispersal of shareholdings*, that is, from patterns of shareholdings in which no single individual, firm, or compact group owns more than a tiny fraction of a corporation's stock. Where shareholdership is highly dispersed, the corporation will be controlled not by the shareholders, but by management— that is what Berle & Means meant by the separation of *ownership*, which still lay with the shareholders, and *control*, which had shifted to management.

As a result of this separation of ownership and control, the inherent conflict between principal and agent (the agency-cost problem) is compounded, because when the principal consists of a highly dispersed group, it faces not only an agency-cost problem but coordination costs (the collective-action problem). There are two basic reasons why dispersion of shareholdings presents a severe collective-action problem.

First, if a shareholder owns only a tiny amount of a corporation's stock, it is not cost-effective for her to spend a significant amount of time on the corporation's affairs. Such a shareholder, therefore, will be "rationally apathetic." If all shareholders in a corporation own only tiny percentages of the corporation's stock, then all the corporation's shareholders will be rationally apathetic.

Second, when a corporation's stock is held by thousands of shareholders living across the country, voting must be done by proxy rather than in person. Typically, in such a corporation, management controls the corporate proxy machinery and has cost-free access to that machinery. In contrast, shareholders who want to oppose a management action must find a way to coordinate, which will be difficult enough, and then must pay the expense of a proxy contest out of their own pockets. If a proxy contest does occur, management has in its favor not only its cost-free access to the corporate proxy machinery, but the legitimacy that goes with being management. Moreover, a shareholder who is extremely dissatisfied with management will often prefer "exit" to "voice" that is, will often prefer to sell, rather than to vote against management—so that the market siphons off many potential anti-management shareholders. Thus in a corporation with a great number of shareholders and highly dispersed shareholdings, incumbent management, rather than shareholders, will normally have control.

Since Berle & Means wrote, however, there has been a major shift in the pattern of shareholdings, from highly dispersed to relatively concentrated, because a very large and increasing proportion of equities (shares) in American corporations have come to be held by institutional investors.

In the U.S., almost all institutional shareholders fall into six basic categories:

1. *Private Pension Funds*. Private pension funds are normally established by private employers, to assure income for the sponsor's employees after they have retired. The most important provisions of these plans, for present purposes, concern decisionmaking power on (i) the acquisition and disposition of the plan's portfolio assets ("portfolio decisions") and (ii) how to vote portfolio stocks ("voting decisions"). Portfolio and voting decisions are often delegated by the employer to fiduciaries, such as banks, who are hired to administer the plan. Particularly among larger corporations, however, part or all of the decisionmaking power may be retained by the employer's management. In such cases, the employer usually exercises its portfolio and voting decisionmaking powers through portfolio managers on its own payroll.

2. *Public Pension Funds*. Public pension funds are established by governmental employers, such as states and cities, to assure retirement income for public employees. As in the case of private pension funds, decisionmaking powers may be either retained or delegated to fiduciaries. Often, portfolio decisions are delegated while voting decisions are retained.

3. *Banks*. Bank trust departments often manage the funds of pension plans, and commonly serve as trustees for individuals and estates.

4. *Investment Companies*. Investment companies manage money on behalf of individuals or, less commonly, other entities. The most common type of investment company is the mutual fund, which is an open-end company, in the sense that investors can withdraw their investment at any time, based on the value of the fund's assets at the time of demand. The other major type of investment company is a closed-end company. A closed-end company is a corporation that raises funds for investment by selling its shares. The owners of shares in a closed-end company have no right to withdraw their investments, but they can sell their shares in the company on the open market.

5. *Insurance Companies*. Insurance companies accumulate huge liquid funds based on the premiums paid by their insureds. These funds are invested by the insurance companies in portfolios that include equities.

6. *Foundations*. Foundations (including universities and religious institutions) typically have endowments, which they invest either through outside professional managers or on their own behalf.

Table 1 shows the percentage of total institutional-investor assets held by the leading types of institutional investors as of 1994:

**TABLE 1**

| TYPE OF INSTITUTION | ASSETS HELD |
|---|---|
| Private Pension Funds | 35% |
| Public Pension Funds | 13% |
| Investment Advisors | 0% |
| Investment Companies | 19% |
| Insurance Companies | 20% |
| Banks | 12% |
| Foundations | 2% |

Source: *The Brancato Report on Institutional Investment* (January 1996). (figures are rounded, and therefore add up to more than 100%).

Institutional-investor holdings now account for about 50% of all equities. Most important for present purposes, institutional-investor holdings account for about 57% of equities in the 1,000 largest U.S. corporations. Brancato, *supra*, at 19–20. As Table 1 shows, pension funds account for almost half of institutional-investor assets. Pension funds also accounted for the largest dollar increase of assets held by any type of institutional investors between 1980 and 1995. Public pension funds have been growing even faster than private pension funds.

The growth of equity holdings by institutional investors has fundamental implications for American corporate governance. Unlike individual shareholdings, institutional shareholdings tend to be very large in absolute terms, so that an investment in governance can be cost-justified. Moreover, institutional shareholdings tend to be *concentrated* rather than dispersed. As a result, coordination becomes substantially easier.

The increased concentration of shareholdings in publicly held corporations, due to the dramatic increase of shareholdings by institutional investors, has set the stage for a dramatic increase in the shareholder role in the modern publicly held corporation. As shareholders get more sophisticated, the costs of playing an active shareholder role decreases. As shareholdings get larger, the cost-benefit ratio for investing time playing that role improves. As shareholdings become more *concentrated*, coordination between shareholders becomes easier.

However, setting the stage is one thing; putting on the play is another.

A number of social and legal forces affect the role of institutional investors in corporate governance in the United States. Some of these forces point in very different directions.

Paramount among the *social* forces is the problem of conflicts of interest. Many institutional investors have ties to management that inhibit voting against management's wishes. For example, if the trust department of Bank *B* holds the stock of Corporation C in a pension portfolio, and C is also a client of Bank B's commercial department, a trust officer of Bank B will think long and hard before voting against a proposal made by C's management, or in favor of a proposal that C's management opposes. Insurance companies, like banks, often have extensive commercial contacts with corporations whose stock they hold in their investment portfolios. Mutual funds may want to stay on management's good side to keep open their lines of access for getting information about a corporation's business. Corporate managers of corporate pension funds will be uncomfortable voting against other corporate managers. External managers of private pension funds may fear that if they vote against management positions, the sponsors will switch to other external managers.

In addition, at least until about 15 years ago there was a cultural norm, shared by many institutional investors, under which voting against management "wasn't done." A governing rule was the so-called Wall Street Rule—If you don't like management, sell. The corollary of that Rule was, if you don't sell, support management. In addition, prior to 1992 the SEC's Proxy Rules made it very expensive for institutional shareholders to communicate with each other to determine whether it was in their mutual interests to combine forces in connection with voting on a management proposal or initiating a proposal of their own.

The SEC's 1992 revision of its Proxy Rules removed a constraint on institutional investors. Another federal agency, the U.S. Department of Labor ("DOL"), has been a major agent of change. One of the DOL's responsibilities is the administration of the Employee Retirement Income Security Act ("ERISA"). Pension plans are the dominant kinds of institutional investors, and among other things ERISA imposes certain fiduciary obligations of the managers of pension plans. Under ERISA, whoever exercises discretion over plan assets must manage those assets "solely in the interest of the participants and beneficiaries and for the exclusive purpose of providing benefits to participants and their beneficiaries." This is known as the "exclusive benefit rule." In 1988, the DOL issued a well-publicized letter, which stated that the fiduciary duties of managing pension-plan assets included not only portfolio decisions but voting decisions.

Under ERISA, therefore, a private pension-fund trustee must take voting decisions seriously, and cannot simply follow the Wall Street Rule. Well-informed observers believe that, partly as result of the DOL's activities and partly for other reasons, the institutional-investor community has come to accept and practice the idea that voting is important. The result has been a significant shift from a passivity norm to an activity norm.

Much of the current institutional-shareholder activism in the United States has been led by public-pension funds. In part this is because public-pension funds have fewer ties to management than other types of institutional investors, and are therefore not as subject to conflict-of-interest problems. In part too, this activism is related to the fact that public-pension funds often follow indexation strategies. An investment fund that uses indexation essentially mimics the market, in the sense that the fund contains the same proportion of each equity on a given market as does the market itself. There are two ideas behind indexation: (1) Under the efficient-capital-markets hypothesis, it is difficult and perhaps not possible to outguess the market, or at least to outguess the market by a margin sufficient to cover the costs of analysis and trading. (2) Under the theory of diversification, a diversified portfolio eliminates important risks. Institutional investors such as pension funds pursue indexation because they believe they cannot beat the market averages by a margin sufficient to cover the higher transaction costs of trading in a more active portfolio. Under such a strategy, a shareholder who disapproves of the management of a corporation cannot simply sell its stock (because that would defeat the concept of indexation), and therefore has a greater incentive to become active in voting and monitoring.

Although public-pension funds and, to a lesser extent, unions have taken the lead in institutional investor activity, other institutional investors seem to be stepping up their activities as well. Partly this is because there has been an increased perception that some level of activism can increase the value of a portfolio; partly it is because there has been a shift in the culture of institutional investors; and partly it is because once public-pension funds take a position that is clearly proper, it is not easy for other institutional investors to hide.

Despite these legal and cultural shifts, there remain important constraints on the extent to which institutional investors can be expected to be active monitors of the corporations in which they hold stock. One of these constraints consists of limits on holdings. Under modern portfolio theory, an institutional investor should diversify its portfolio. That objective will normally prevent any given institutional investor from putting too many eggs in any single corporate basket, particularly in light of the huge capitalization of many large American publicly held corporations. In addition, certain kinds of institutional investors are statutorily forbidden to hold more than a fixed percentage of the stock of any given corporation. As a result of these economic and legal constraints, typically any one institutional investor will have limited holdings in any one corporation.

The significance of limited holdings by an given institutional investor in any given portfolio corporation is that it reduces the investor's cost-benefit ratio for active involvement, and leads to a free-rider problem. Any expenses the institutional investor incurs for beyond-the-ordinary-course shareholder activities will benefit the other shareholders more than itself. Suppose, for example, Institution S holds 1% of Corporation C's stock. Corporation C has a governance rule that diminishes C's value. A proxy contest to repeal the rule, and thereby increase the value of C stock, would cost $500,000. Assume that if S runs the contest by itself, it will derive no economic benefit except the increased value of its C stock. In that case, if S does run the contest in effect it will spend $5,000 on itself and $495,000 on behalf of the other shareholders, who will free ride at S's expense.

The free-rider problem shows that institutional investors are not likely to engage in monitoring or voting activity that (i) goes beyond the monitoring and voting activity in which the investor can be expected to engage in the normal course of its shareholding capacity, (ii) would require significant expenditures, (iii) would increase the value of the institution's holding in its portfolio companies by less than the costs of the activity, and (iv) would result in no private economic benefit to the investor beyond the increased value of that holding. However, monitoring and voting activity may be engaged in if all of these conditions are *not* satisfied. In fact, all of these conditions frequently aren't satisfied, for a variety of reasons.

*First*. Much voting activity requires very little effort. Furthermore, in many cases the same issue recurs in a number of corporations for example, how to deal with anti-takeover provisions of various kinds so that the investor need only make a one-time expenditure of effort to determine its general position, and can then amortize the expenditure over a number of votes.

*Second*. A vote on a recurring issue, like a certain type of corporate-governance rule, may send a message to all portfolio corporations, and may therefore have an economic benefit to the investor beyond its impact on the immediate portfolio corporation.

*Third.* Unless an investor has adopted an indexing strategy, it must monitor its portfolio corporations in any event, to determine whether to hold or sell.

*Fourth.* The costs of playing a shareholder role have been dramatically reduced by the development of firms like Institutional Shareholders Services and Investors Responsibility Research Center. These firms analyze a huge number of proxy materials, and report those analyses in bulletins that are distributed regularly to institutional-investor clients. In effect, the clients of these services form a sort of *research coalition,* by pooling their funds through the subscription prices they pay for the costs of the services' analyses.

*Fifth.* In many cases, a voting decision has a very obvious and dramatic effect on the value of a portfolio stock, as where the vote concerns a merger or a value-decreasing anti-takeover provision. In such cases, beyond-ordinary-course voting activity will often be cost-justified.

*Sixth.* Even in less dramatic cases, there has been an increasing acceptance of the idea that changes in a corporation's governance rules, and often in its management, can increase the value of the corporation's stock, so that it may be more cost-effective to hold and vote than to sell.

*Seventh.* Under ERISA, as interpreted by the DOL, many institutional investors are legally obliged to vote in a way that maximizes the value of their shares. Institutional investors that don't fall within the coverage of ERISA may be under a comparable fiduciary obligation.

The bottom line is that institutional investors have grown increasingly activist. The question then arises, what is the competence of institutional shareholders as shareholders? Certainly, institutional shareholders are not equipped to make, or even meaningfully assesses, individual business decisions in the ordinary course. There are, however, several areas in which institutional shareholders can play a meaningful role.

● Institutional shareholders can meaningfully assess the corporation's governance structure—for example, its rules concerning take-over defenses, or the conduct of elections. Managers are usually self-interested as to governance rules, because such rules typically bear on the preservation and enhancement of managerial positions. Even apart from the problem of managerial self-interest, institutional shareholders may have special competence in this area because they can review such rules across corporations as a class.

● Institutional shareholders can meaningfully assess proposed structural changes, like mergers. Again, managers will often be self-interested in such proposals, if only because structural changes will normally threaten to reduce or promise to enhance managerial positions. Even apart from the problem of managerial self-interest, institutional shareholders may have special competence to assess such proposals, because managers are typically trained in making operational business decisions, while institutional shareholders specialize in making financial decisions. Moreover, often the market will react to such proposals, and institutional shareholders can use the market's reaction as strong evidence of the proposal's merit.

● Institutional shareholders can meaningfully assess overall management performance, both by comparing the financial results of management's performance with the performance of managers in like corporations, and by taking into account the evaluation of a particular management by the business community as a whole.

● Finally, institutional investors may play a role in corporate business and policy and in the dismissal of chief executive officers. For example, in the past ten years institutional investors have induced various corporations to restructure their operations by spinning off some businesses to focus on core businesses. In other cases, pressures from institutional investors have helped lead boards to dismiss chief executive officers who were viewed as ineffective.

The next issue is the *forms* that institutional involvement in corporate governance may take.

1. The simplest form of institutional involvement is taking an active posture in voting on management or shareholder proposals.

2. A more aggressive form of involvement is not only to *vote* on shareholder proposals, but to *make* shareholder proposals. The most common types of proposals made by institutional investors concern the *structure* or *rules* of corporate governance—for example, a requirement of a majority of independent directors, or the deletion of an anti-takeover rule.

3. Another possible form of institutional activity is the election of individuals as directors to represent institutional investors. In general, institutional investors in the United States have not followed this path, perhaps partly because of concerns that trading in a corporation's stock by an investor with a representative on the corporation's board might be deemed insider trading. However, institutions sometimes have joined movements begun by others to oust directors and replace them with new directors. In such cases, the new directors would not be representatives of, or even selected by, the institutional investors, so that the insider-trading problem is not salient.

4. An extremely important process through which the concerns of institutional investors are expressed is that of consultation. Many large institutional investors get their points across, without voting, by consultation with management. Consultation can concern either specific issues, such as a proposed merger, or general corporate policies. As a practical matter, institutional investors probably get more done through consultation than through voting on management or shareholder proposals. However, there is an important interrelation between the consultation process and the voting process, because the implied or actual threat that an institutional investor will bring an issue to a vote (either on a shareholder proposal or in the election of

directors) is an important incentive for managers to take seriously the concerns expressed by institutional investors in the consultation process.

## SECTION 2.  THE ALLOCATION OF LEGAL POWER BETWEEN MANAGEMENT AND SHAREHOLDERS

### DEL. GEN. CORP. LAW § 141(a)

[See Statutory Supplement]

### REV. MODEL BUS. CORP. ACT § 8.01(b)

[See Statutory Supplement]

## Charlestown Boot & Shoe Co. v. Dunsmore

New Hampshire Supreme Court, 1880.
60 N.H. 85.

CASE. Demurrer to the declaration in which the following facts were alleged:—The plaintiffs are a manufacturing corporation having for its object a dividend of profits, and commenced business in 1871. Dunsmore was elected director in 1871 and Willard in 1873, and entered upon the discharge of their duties, and have continued so to act by virtue of successive elections until the present time. December 10, 1874, the corporation[1] voted to choose a committee to act with the directors to close up its affairs, and chose one Osgood for such committee. Osgood tendered his services, but the defendants refused to act with him, and contracted new debts to a larger extent than allowed by law. By their negligence, debts due to the corporation to the amount of $2,161.23 have been wholly lost. By their negligence in disposing of the goods of the corporation, a loss has accrued of $3,300.40. By their neglect to sell the buildings and machinery of the corporation when they might and ought, and were urged by Osgood to sell, the same depreciated in value to the extent of $20,000.

Also for that the plaintiffs owned and possessed a certain shop of the value of $10,000, and a large amount of machinery and fixtures of the value of $10,000; "and whereas it was the duty of said defendants, directors as aforesaid, to procure sufficient and proper insurance against fire to be made on said property, and keep the same so

---

1. By "the corporation," in this phrase and some others, the court seems to mean the body of shareholders. (Footnote by ed.)

sufficiently insured, of all which the said defendants had notice, yet they did not and would not keep the said property so insured, and afterwards, to wit, on the 28th day of April, 1878, while the said property was so remaining without insurance, the same was wholly consumed by fire and wholly lost to the plaintiff, whereby the plaintiff suffered great loss and damage, to wit, $20,000.''

■ SMITH, J. The provision of the statute is, that the business of a dividend paying corporation shall be managed by the directors. The statute reads, "The business of every such corporation shall be managed by the directors thereof, subject to the by-laws and votes of the corporation, and under their direction by such officers and agents as shall be duly appointed by the directors or by the corporation." G.L., *c. 148, s. 3*; Gen.Stats., *c. 134, s. 3*. The only limitation upon the judgment or discretion of the directors is such as the corporation by its by-laws and votes shall impose. It may define its business, its nature and extent, prescribe rules and regulations for the government of its officers and members, and determine whether its business shall be wound up or continued; but when it has thus acted, the business as thus defined and limited is to be managed by its directors, and by such officers and agents under their direction as the directors or the corporation shall appoint. The statute does not authorize a corporation to join another officer with the directors, nor compel the directors to act with one who is not a director. They are bound to use ordinary care and diligence in the care and management of the business of the corporation, and are answerable for ordinary negligence. *March v. Railroad,* 43 N.H. 516, 529; *Scott v. Depeyster,* 1 Edw. Ch. 513, 543; Ang. & Ames Corp., *s. 314*. There is no difference in this respect between the agents of corporations and those of natural persons, unless expressly made by the charter or by-laws. *Id., s. 315*. It would be unreasonable to hold them responsible for the management of the affairs of the corporation if compelled to act with one who to a greater or less extent could control their acts. The statute not only entrusts the management of the business of the corporation to the directors, but places its other officers and agents under their direction. When a statute provides that powers granted to a corporation shall be exercised by any set of officers or any particular agents, such powers can be exercised only by such officers or agents, although they are required to be chosen by the whole corporation; and if the whole corporation attempts to exercise powers which by the charter are lodged elsewhere, its action upon the subject is void. *Insurance Co. v. Keyser,* 32 N.H. 313, 315. The vote choosing Osgood a committee to act with the directors in closing up the affairs of the plaintiff corporation was inoperative and void.

The declaration also alleges that it was the duty of the defendants, as directors, to keep the property of the corporation insured. There is no statute that makes it the duty of the directors of a corporation to keep its property insured, and there are no facts alleged from which we can say, as matter of law, that it was the duty of the defendants to insure the property of the corporation.

*Demurrer sustained.*

■ STANLEY, J., did not sit: the others concurred.

---

**PEOPLE EX REL. MANICE v. POWELL,** 201 N.Y. 194, 200–01, 94 N.E. 634, 637 (1911). " 'The board of directors of a corporation do not stand in the same relation to the corporate body which a private agent holds towards his principal. . . . In corporate bodies the powers of the board of directors are, in a very important sense, original and undelegated.' (*Hoyt v. Thompson's Executors,* 19 N.Y. 207, 216; *Beveridge v. N.Y.E.R.R. Co.,* 112 N.Y. 1, 22, 23.)

"While the ordinary rules of law relating to an agent are applicable in considering the acts of a board of directors in behalf of a corporation when dealing with third persons, the individual directors making up the board are not mere employees, but a part of an elected body of officers constituting the executive agents of the corporation. They hold such office charged with the duty to act for the corporation according to their best judgment, and in so doing they cannot be controlled in the reasonable exercise and performance of such duty. As a general rule the stockholders cannot act in relation to the ordinary business of the corporation, nor can they control the directors in the exercise of the judgment vested in them by virtue of their office.

"The relation of the directors to the stockholders is essentially that of trustee and *cestui que trust.* The peculiar relation that they bear to the corporation and the owners of its stock grows out of the inability of the corporation to act except through such managing officers and agents. The corporation is the owner of the property, but the directors in the performance of their duty possess it, and act in every way as if they owned it."

---

**DEL. GEN. CORP. LAW § 141(k)**

[See Statutory Supplement]

---

**CAL. CORP. CODE §§ 303, 304**

[See Statutory Supplement]

---

**N.Y. BUS. CORP. LAW § 706**

[See Statutory Supplement]

---

## NOTE ON REMOVAL OF DIRECTORS

1.  *Removed by the Shareholders*. The shareholders can remove a director for cause, even in the absence of a statute that so provides. See, e.g., Auer v. Dressel, 306 N.Y. 427, 118 N.E.2d 590 (1954); Campbell v. Loew's, Inc., 36 Del.Ch. 563, 134 A.2d 852 (1957). Shareholders cannot remove a director without cause in the absence of specific authority to do so under the statute, the certificate of incorporation, or the by-laws. See, e.g., Frank v. Anthony, 107 So.2d 136 (Fla.App.1958). Some statutes permit the shareholders to remove a director without cause. See, e.g., Cal.Corp.Code § 303(a); Rev.Model Bus.Corp.Act § 8.08. A few statutes permit the shareholders to remove a director without cause if the certificate or by-laws so provide. See, e.g., N.Y.Bus.Corp.Law § 706(b). A certificate or by-law provision can permit the removal without cause only of directors elected after the provision has been adopted. See, e.g., Everett v. Transnation Development Corp., 267 A.2d 627 (Del.Ch.1970).

2.  *Removal by the Board*. In the absence of statute, the board cannot remove a director, with or without cause. See, e.g., Bruch v. National Guarantee Credit Corp., 13 Del.Ch. 180, 116 A. 738 (1922). Whether the certificate of incorporation can change this rule is uncertain. See Dillon v. Berg, 326 F.Supp. 1214 (D.Del.1971), aff'd 453 F.2d 876 (3d Cir.); Bruch v. National Guarantee Credit Corp., supra. However, some statutes permit the board to remove a director for cause, see, e.g., Mass.Gen.Laws ch. 156B, § 51(c), or for specified reasons, such as conviction of a felony, see, e.g., Calif.Corp.Code § 302. A few statutes permit the board to remove a director for cause or for specified reasons if the certificate of incorporation so provides. See, e.g., N.J.Stat.Ann. § 14A:6–6.

3.  *Removal by the Court*. The cases are split on whether a court can remove directors for cause. Compare Webber v. Webber Oil Co., 495 A.2d 1215 (Me.1985) (courts do not have power to remove directors) with Ross v. 311 North Central Avenue Building Corp., 130 Ill.App.2d 336, 264 N.E.2d 406 (1970) (courts have power to remove directors, at least for fraud or the like). However, some statutes permit the courts to remove a director for specified reasons, such as fraudulent or dishonest acts. These statutes usually provide that a petition for such removal can be brought only by a designated percentage of the shareholders (most commonly 10%), by the attorney general, or in some cases, by either. See, e.g., Calif.Corp.Code § 304; N.Y.Bus.Corp. Law § 706(d).

---

## Schnell v. Chris–Craft Industries, Inc.

Supreme Court of Delaware, 1971.
285 A.2d 437.

■ HERRMANN, JUSTICE (for the majority of the court):

This is an appeal from the denial by the Court of Chancery of the petition of dissident stockholders for injunctive relief to prevent management[1] from advancing the date of the annual stockholders' meeting from January 11, 1972, as previously set by the by-laws, to December 8, 1971.

The opinion below is reported at 285 A.2d 430. This opinion is confined to the frame of reference of the opinion below for the sake of brevity and because of the strictures of time imposed by the circumstances of the case.

It will be seen that the Chancery Court considered all of the reasons stated by management as business reasons for changing the date of the meeting; but that those reasons were rejected by the Court below in making the following findings:

> "I am satisfied, however, in a situation in which present management has disingenuously resisted the production of a list of its stockholders to plaintiffs or their confederates and has otherwise turned a deaf ear to plaintiffs' demands about a change in management designed to lift defendant from its present business doldrums, management has seized on a relatively new section of the Delaware Corporation Law for the purpose of cutting down on the amount of time which would otherwise have been available to plaintiffs and others for the waging of a proxy battle. Management thus enlarged the scope of its scheduled October 18 directors' meeting to include the by-law amendment in controversy after the stockholders committee had filed with the S.E.C. its intention to wage a proxy fight on October 16.

> "Thus plaintiffs reasonably contend that because of the tactics employed by management (which involve the hiring of two established proxy solicitors as well as a refusal to produce a list of its stockholders, coupled with its use of an amendment to the Delaware Corporation Law to limit the time for contest), they are given little chance, because of the exigencies of time, including that required to clear material at the S.E.C., to wage a successful proxy fight between now and December 8 . . . . "

In our view, those conclusions amount to a finding that management has attempted to utilize the corporate machinery and the Delaware Law for the purpose of perpetuating itself in office; and, to that end, for the purpose of obstructing the legitimate efforts of dissident stockholders in the exercise of their rights to undertake a proxy contest against management. These are inequitable purposes, contrary to established principles of corporate democracy. The advancement by directors of the by-law date of a stockholders' meeting, for such purposes, may not be permitted to stand. Compare Condec Corporation v. Lunkenheimer Company, Del.Ch., 230 A.2d 769 (1967).

When the by-laws of a corporation designate the date of the annual meeting of stockholders, it is to be expected that those who intend to contest the reelection of incumbent management will gear

---

1. We use this word as meaning "managing directors".

their campaign to the by-law date. It is not to be expected that management will attempt to advance that date in order to obtain an inequitable advantage in the contest.

Management contends that it has complied strictly with the provisions of the new Delaware Corporation Law in changing the by-law date. The answer to that contention, of course, is that inequitable action does not become permissible simply because it is legally possible. . . .

We are unable to agree with the conclusion of the Chancery Court that the stockholders' application for injunctive relief here was tardy and came too late. . . .

Accordingly, the judgment below must be reversed and the cause remanded, with instructions to nullify the December 8 date as a meeting date for stockholders; to reinstate January 11, 1972 as the sole date of the next annual meeting of the stockholders of the corporation; and to take such other proceedings and action as may be consistent herewith regarding the stock record closing date and any other related matters.

[The dissenting opinion of Chief Justice Wolcott is omitted.]

———

**A.A. BERLE & G. MEANS, THE MODERN CORPORATION AND PRIVATE PROPERTY** 220 (rev. ed. 1967). "[A]n underlying thesis in corporation law . . . could be applied to each and every power in the whole corporate galaxy. Succinctly stated, the thesis [is] that all powers granted to a corporation or to the management of a corporation, or to any group within the corporation, whether derived from statute or charter or both, are necessarily and at all times exercisable only for the ratable benefit of all the shareholders as their interest appears. That, in consequence, the *use* of the power is subject to equitable limitation when the power has been exercised to the detriment of their interest, however absolute the grant of power may be in terms, and however correct the technical exercise of it may have been."

———

# Blasius Industries, Inc. v. Atlas Corp.

Court of Chancery of Delaware, 1988.
564 A.2d 651.

## OPINION

■ ALLEN, CHANCELLOR.

Two cases pitting the directors of Atlas Corporation against that company's largest (9.1%) shareholder, Blasius Industries, have been consolidated and tried together. Together, these cases ultimately require the court to determine who is entitled to sit on Atlas' board of directors. . . .

The first of the cases was filed on December 30, 1987. As amended, it challenges the validity of board action taken at a telephone meeting of December 31, 1987 that added two new members to Atlas' seven member board. That action was taken as an immediate response to the delivery to Atlas by Blasius the previous day of a form of stockholder consent that, if joined in by holders of a majority of Atlas' stock, would have increased the board of Atlas from seven to fifteen members and would have elected eight new members nominated by Blasius.

As I find the facts of this first case, they present the question whether a board acts consistently with its fiduciary duty when it acts, in good faith and with appropriate care, for the primary purpose of preventing or impeding an unaffiliated majority of shareholders from expanding the board and electing a new majority. For the reasons that follow, I conclude that, even though defendants here acted on their view of the corporation's interest and not selfishly, their December 31 action constituted an offense to the relationship between corporate directors and shareholders that has traditionally been protected in courts of equity. As a consequence, I conclude that the board action taken on December 31 was invalid and must be voided. . . .

The facts set forth below represent findings based upon a preponderance of the admissible evidence, as I evaluate it.

I.

*Blasius Acquires a 9% Stake in Atlas.*

Blasius is a new stockholder of Atlas. It began to accumulate Atlas shares for the first time in July, 1987. On October 29, it filed a Schedule 13D with the Securities Exchange Commission disclosing that, with affiliates, it then [owned] 9.1% of Atlas' common stock. It stated in that filing that it intended to encourage management of Atlas to consider a restructuring of the Company or other transaction to enhance shareholder values. It also disclosed that Blasius was exploring the feasibility of obtaining control of Atlas, including instituting a tender offer or seeking "appropriate" representation on the Atlas board of directors.

Blasius has recently come under the control of two individuals, Michael Lubin and Warren Delano, who after experience in the commercial banking industry, had, for a short time, run a venture capital operation for a small investment banking firm. Now on their own, they apparently came to control Blasius with the assistance of Drexel Burnham's well noted junk bond mechanism. Since then, they have made several attempts to effect leveraged buyouts, but without success. . . .

The prospect of Messrs. Lubin and Delano involving themselves in Atlas' affairs, was not a development welcomed by Atlas' management. Atlas had a new CEO, defendant Weaver, who had, over the course of the past year or so, overseen a business restructuring of a sort. Atlas had sold three of its five divisions. It had just announced (September 1, 1987) that it would close its once important domestic uranium operation. The goal was to focus the Company on its gold mining business. By October, 1987, the structural changes to do this had been largely accomplished. Mr. Weaver was perhaps thinking that the restructuring that had occurred should be given a chance to produce benefit before another restructuring (such as Blasius had alluded to in its Schedule 13D filing) was attempted, when he wrote in his diary on October 30, 1987:

> 13D by Delano & Lubin came in today. Had long conversation w/MAH & Mark Golden [of Goldman Sachs] on issue. All agree we must dilute these people down by the acquisition of another Co. w/stock, or merger or something else.

### The Blasius Proposal of A Leverage Recapitalization Or Sale.

Immediately after filing its 13D on October 29, Blasius' representatives sought a meeting with the Atlas management. Atlas dragged its feet. A meeting was arranged for December 2, 1987 following the regular meeting of the Atlas board. Attending that meeting were Messrs. Lubin and Delano for Blasius, and, for Atlas, Messrs. Weaver, Devaney (Atlas' CFO), Masinter (legal counsel and director) and Czajkowski (a representative of Atlas' investment banker, Goldman Sachs).

At that meeting, Messrs. Lubin and Delano suggested that Atlas engage in a leveraged restructuring and distribute cash to shareholders. In such a transaction, which is by this date a commonplace form of transaction, a corporation typically raises cash by sale of assets and significant borrowings and makes a large one time cash distribution to shareholders. The shareholders are typically left with cash and an equity interest in a smaller, more highly leveraged enterprise. Lubin and Delano gave the outline of a leveraged recapitalization for Atlas as they saw it.

Immediately following the meeting, the Atlas representatives expressed among themselves an initial reaction that the proposal was infeasible. On December 7, Mr. Lubin sent a letter detailing the proposal. In general, it proposed the following: (1) an initial special cash dividend to Atlas' stockholders in an aggregate amount equal to (a) $35 million, (b) the aggregate proceeds to Atlas from the exercise of option warrants and stock options, and (c) the proceeds from the sale or disposal of all of Atlas' operations that are not related to its continuing minerals operations; and (2) a special non-cash dividend to Atlas' stockholders of an aggregate $125 million principal amount of 7% Secured Subordinated Gold–Indexed Debentures. The funds necessary to pay the initial cash dividend were to principally come from (i) a "gold loan" in the amount of $35,625,000, repayable over a three to five year period and secured by 75,000 ounces of gold at a price of $475 per ounce, (ii) the proceeds from the sale of the discontinued Brockton Sole and Plastics and Ready–Mix Concrete businesses, and

(iii) a then expected January, 1988 sale of uranium to the Public Service Electric & Gas Company. . . .

The proposal met with a cool reception from management. . . .

On December 30, 1987, Blasius caused Cede & Co. (the registered owner of its Atlas stock) to deliver to Atlas a signed written consent (1) adopting a precatory resolution recommending that the board develop and implement a restructuring proposal, (2) amending the Atlas bylaws to, among other things, expand the size of the board from seven to fifteen members—the maximum number under Atlas' charter, and (3) electing eight named persons to fill the new directorships. . . .

The reaction was immediate. Mr. Weaver conferred with Mr. Masinter, the Company's outside counsel and a director, who viewed the consent as an attempt to take control of the Company. They decided to call an emergency meeting of the board, even though a regularly scheduled meeting was to occur only one week hence, on January 6, 1988. The point of the emergency meeting was to act on their conclusion (or to seek to have the board act on their conclusion) "that we should add at least one and probably two directors to the board . . ." (Tr. 85, Vol. II). A quorum of directors, however, could not be arranged for a telephone meeting that day. A telephone meeting was held the next day. At that meeting, the board voted to amend the bylaws to increase the size of the board from seven to nine and appointed John M. Devaney and Harry J. Winters, Jr. to fill those newly created positions. Atlas' Certificate of Incorporation creates staggered terms for directors; the terms to which Messrs. Devaney and Winters were appointed would expire in 1988 and 1990, respectively.

### The Motivation of the Incumbent Board In Expanding the Board and Appointing New Members.

In increasing the size of Atlas' board by two and filling the newly created positions, the members of the board realized that they were thereby precluding the holders of a majority of the Company's shares from placing a majority of new directors on the board through Blasius' consent solicitation, should they want to do so. Indeed the evidence establishes that that was the principal motivation in so acting.

The conclusion that, in creating two new board positions on December 31 and electing Messrs. Devaney and Winters to fill those positions the board was principally motivated to prevent or delay the shareholders from possibly placing a majority of new members on the board, is critical to my analysis of the central issue posed by the first filed of the two pending cases. If the board in fact was not so motivated, but rather had taken action completely independently of the consent solicitation, which merely had an incidental impact upon the possible effectuation of any action authorized by the shareholders, it is very unlikely that such action would be subject to judicial nullification. See, e.g., Frantz Manufacturing Company v. Eac Industries, Del.Supr., 501 A.2d 401, 407 (1985); Moran v. Household International, Inc., Del.Ch., 490 A.2d 1059, 1080, aff'd, Del.Supr., 500 A.2d 1346 (1985). The board, as a general matter, is under no fiduciary obligation to suspend its active management of the firm while the consent solicitation process goes forward. . . .

. . . I conclude that, while the addition of these qualified men would, under other circumstances, be clearly appropriate as an independent step, such a step was in fact taken in order to impede or preclude a majority of the shareholders from effectively adopting the course proposed by Blasius. . . .

## II.

Plaintiff attacks the December 31 board action as a selfishly motivated effort to protect the incumbent board from a perceived threat to its control of Atlas. Their conduct is said to constitute a violation of the principle, applied in such cases as Schnell v. Chris–Craft Industries, Del.Supr., 285 A.2d 437 (1971), that directors hold legal powers [subject] to a supervening duty to exercise such powers in good faith pursuit of what they reasonably believe to be in the corporation's interest. The December 31 action is also said to have been taken in a grossly negligent manner, since it was designed to preclude the recapitalization from being pursued, and the board had no basis at that time to make a prudent determination about the wisdom of that proposal, nor was there any emergency that required it to act in any respect regarding that proposal before putting itself in a position to do so advisedly.

Defendants, of course, contest every aspect of plaintiffs' claims. They claim the formidable protections of the business judgment rule. See, e.g., Aronson v. Lewis, Del.Supr., 473 A.2d 805 (1984); Grobow v. Perot, Del.Supr., 539 A.2d 180 (1988); In re J.P. Stevens & Co., Inc. Shareholders Litigation, Del.Ch., 542 A.2d 770 (1988).

They say that, in creating two new board positions and filling them on December 31, they acted without a conflicting interest (since the Blasius proposal did not, in any event, challenge *their* places on the board), they acted with due care (since they well knew the persons they put on the board and did not thereby preclude later consideration of the recapitalization), and they acted in good faith (since they were motivated, they say, to protect the shareholders from the threat of having an impractical, indeed a dangerous, recapitalization program foisted upon them). Accordingly, defendants assert there is no basis to conclude that their December 31 action constituted any violation of the duty of the fidelity that a director owes by reason of his office to the corporation and its shareholders.

Moreover, defendants say that their action was fair, measured and appropriate, in light of the circumstances. Therefore, even should the court conclude that some level of substantive review of it is appropriate under a legal test of fairness, or under the intermediate level of review authorized by *Unocal Corp. v. Mesa Petroleum Co.*, Del.Supr., 493 A.2d 946 (1985), defendants assert that the board's decision must be sustained as valid in both law and equity.

III. . . .

On balance, I cannot conclude that the board was acting out of a self-interested motive in any important respect on December 31. I conclude rather that the board saw the "threat" of the Blasius recapitalization proposal as posing vital policy differences between itself and Blasius. It acted, I conclude, in a good faith effort to protect its incumbency, not selfishly, but in order to thwart implementation of the recapitalization that it feared, reasonably, would cause great injury to the Company.

The real question the case presents, to my mind, is whether, in these circumstances, the board, even if it *is* acting with subjective good faith (which will typically, if not always, be a contestable or debatable judicial conclusion), may validly act for the principal purpose of preventing the shareholders from electing a majority of new directors. The question thus posed is not one of intentional wrong (or even negligence), but one of authority *as between the fiduciary and the beneficiary* (not simply legal authority, *i.e.*, as between the fiduciary and the world at large).

## IV.

It is established in our law that a board may take certain steps— such as the purchase by the corporation of its own stock—that have the effect of defeating a threatened change in corporate control, when those steps are taken advisedly, in good faith pursuit of a corporate interest, and are reasonable in relation to a threat to legitimate corporate interests posed by the proposed change in control. See Unocal Corp. v. Mesa Petroleum Co., Del.Supr., 493 A.2d 946 (1985); Kors v. Carey, Del.Ch., 158 A.2d 136 (1960); Cheff v. Mathes, Del. Supr., 199 A.2d 548 (1964); Kaplan v. Goldsamt, Del.Ch., 380 A.2d 556 (1977). Does this rule—that the reasonable exercise of good faith and due care generally validates, in equity, the exercise of legal authority even if the act has an entrenchment effect—apply to action designed for the primary purpose of interfering with the effectiveness of a stockholder vote? Our authorities, as well as sound principles, suggest that the central importance of the franchise to the scheme of corporate governance, requires that, in this setting, that rule not be applied and that closer scrutiny be accorded to such transaction.

1. *Why the deferential business judgment rule does not apply to board acts taken for the primary purpose of interfering with a stockholder's vote, even if taken advisedly and in good faith.*

A. *The question of legitimacy.*

The shareholder franchise is the ideological underpinning upon which the legitimacy of directorial power rests. Generally, shareholders have only two protections against perceived inadequate business performance. They may sell their stock (which, if done in sufficient numbers, may so affect security prices as to create an incentive for altered managerial performance), or they may vote to replace incumbent board members.

It has, for a long time, been conventional to dismiss the stockholder vote as a vestige or ritual of little practical importance. It may be that we are now witnessing the emergence of new institutional voices and arrangements that will make the stockholder vote a less predictable affair than it has been. Be that as it may, however, whether the vote is seen functionally as an unimportant formalism, or as an important tool of discipline, it is clear that it is critical to the theory that legitimates the exercise of power by some (directors and officers) over vast aggregations of property that they do not own. Thus, when viewed from a broad, institutional perspective, it can be seen that matters involving the integrity of the shareholder voting process involve [considerations] not present in any other context in which directors exercise delegated power.

B. *Questions of this type raise issues of the allocation of authority as between the board and the shareholders.*

The distinctive nature of the shareholder franchise context also appears when the matter is viewed from a less generalized, doctrinal point of view. From this point of view, as well, it appears that the ordinary considerations to which the business judgment rule originally responded are simply not present in the shareholder voting context. That is, a decision by the board to act for the primary purpose of preventing the effectiveness of a shareholder vote inevitably involves the question who, as between the principal and the agent, has authority with respect to a matter of internal corporate governance. That, of course, is true in a very specific way in this case which deals with the question who should constitute the board of directors of the corporation, but it will be true in every instance in which an incumbent board seeks to thwart a shareholder majority. A board's decision to act to prevent the shareholders from creating a majority of new board positions and filling them does not involve the exercise of *the corporation's power* over its property, or with respect to *its* rights or obligations; rather, it involves allocation, between shareholders as a class and the board, of effective power with respect to governance of the corporation. This need not be the case with respect to other forms of corporate action that may have an entrenchment effect—such as the stock buybacks present in *Unocal, Cheff* or *Kors v. Carey*. Action designed principally to interfere with the effectiveness of a vote inevitably involves a conflict between the board and a shareholder majority. Judicial review of such action involves a determination of the legal and equitable obligations of an agent towards his principal. This is not, in my opinion, a question that a court may leave to the agent finally to decide so long as he does so honestly and competently; that is, it may not be left to the agent's business judgment.

2. *What rule does apply: per se invalidity of corporate acts intended primarily to thwart effective exercise of the franchise or is there an intermediate standard?*

Plaintiff argues for a rule of *per se* invalidity once a plaintiff has established that a board has acted for the primary purpose of thwarting the exercise of a shareholder vote. Our opinions in Canada

Southern Oils, Ltd. v. Manabi Exploration Co., Del.Ch., 96 A.2d 810
(1953) and Condec Corporation v. Lunkenheimer Company, Del.Ch.,
230 A.2d 769 (1967) could be read as support for such a rule of *per se*
invalidity....

... A *per se* rule that would strike down, in equity, any board
action taken for the primary purpose of interfering with the effectiveness of a corporate vote would have the advantage of relative clarity
and predictability.[4] It also has the advantage of most vigorously
enforcing the concept of corporate democracy. The disadvantage it
brings along is, of course, the disadvantage a *per se* rule always has: it
may sweep too broadly. In two recent cases dealing with shareholder
votes, this court struck down board acts done for the primary purpose
of impeding the exercise of stockholder voting power. In doing so, a
per se rule was not applied. Rather, it was said that, in such a case, the
board bears the heavy burden of demonstrating a compelling justification for such action. [Aprahamian v. HBO & Co., 531 A.2d 1204 (1987)
(Del.Ch.1987); Phillips v. Insituform, C.A.No. 9173, Del.Ch. 1987).]

In my view, our inability to foresee now all of the future settings
in which a board might, in good faith, paternalistically seek to thwart a
shareholder vote, counsels against the adoption of a *per se* rule
invalidating, in equity, every board action taken for the sole or primary
purpose of thwarting a shareholder vote, even though I recognize the
transcending significance of the franchise to the claims to legitimacy of
our scheme of corporate governance. It may be that some set of facts
would justify such extreme action. This, however, is not such a case.

3.  *Defendants have demonstrated no sufficient justification for
the action of December 31 which was intended to prevent an unaffiliated majority of shareholders from effectively exercising their right to
elect eight new directors.*

The board was not faced with a coercive action taken by a
powerful shareholder against the interests of a distinct shareholder
constituency (such as a public minority). It was presented with a
consent solicitation by a 9% shareholder. Moreover, here it had time
(and understood that it had time) to inform the shareholders of its
views on the merits of the proposal subject to stockholder vote. The
only justification that can, in such a situation, be offered for the action
taken is that the board knows better than do the shareholders what is
in the corporation's best interest. While that premise is no doubt true
for any number of matters, it is irrelevant (except insofar as the
shareholders wish to be guided by the board's recommendation) when
the question is who should comprise the board of directors. The
theory of our corporation law confers power upon directors as the
agents of the shareholders; it does not create Platonic masters. It may
be that the Blasius restructuring proposal was or is unrealistic and
would lead to injury to the corporation and its shareholders if

---

**4.** While it must be admitted that any
rule that requires for its invocation the finding of a subjective mental state (*i.e.*, a primary purpose) necessarily will lead to controversy concerning whether it applies or not,
nevertheless, once it is determined to apply,
this *per se* rule would be clearer than the
alternative discussed below.

pursued. Having heard the evidence, I am inclined to think it was not a sound proposal. The board certainly viewed it that way, and that view, held in good faith, entitled the board to take certain steps to evade the risk it perceived. It could, for example, expend corporate funds to inform shareholders and seek to bring them to a similar point of view. See, e.g. Hall v. Trans–Lux Daylight Picture Screen Corporation, Del.Ch., 171 A. 226, 227 (1934); Hibbert v. Hollywood Park, Inc., Del.Supr., 457 A.2d 339 (1983). But there is a vast difference between expending corporate funds to inform the electorate and exercising power for the primary purpose of foreclosing effective shareholder action. A majority of the shareholders, who were not dominated in any respect, could view the matter differently than did the board. If they do, or did, they are entitled to employ the mechanisms provided by the corporation law and the Atlas certificate of incorporation to advance that view. They are also entitled, in my opinion, to restrain their agents, the board, from acting for the principal purpose of thwarting that action.

I therefore conclude that, even finding the action was taken in good faith, it constituted an unintended violation of the duty of loyalty that the board owed to the shareholders. I note parenthetically that the concept of an unintended breach of the duty of loyalty is unusual but not novel. . . . That action will, therefore, be set aside by order of this court. . . .

[During the pendency of the case involving Blasius's attack on the action of the directors in adding two members to the board, Blasius presented Atlas with shareholder consents purporting to show that a majority of Atlas's shareholders had adopted Blasius's proposals to enlarge the board from seven to fifteen, elect eight new directors nominated by Blasius, and take certain other actions. Atlas appointed Manufacturers Hanover Trust Company to act as judge of the shareholders' "vote." Manufacturers reported that the vote had been extremely close, but that none of Blasius's proposals had succeeded. Blasius then brought a second case, in which it challenged certain of Manufacturers' determinations. That case was consolidated with Blasius's attack on the action of the directors in adding two members to the board. The court upheld most of Manufacturers' determinations and Manufacturers' conclusion that Blasius had lost the vote, and rendered judgment in the second case for the defendants.]

---

## NOTE ON THE BUSINESS JUDGMENT RULE

Corporate law employs a number of different standards of judicial review of the conduct of directors and officers, depending on the type of conduct involved. The most lenient standard—the standard that is easiest for officers and directors to satisfy—is the business judgment rule, referred to in *Blasius*. The meaning and application of this rule will be considered in depth in Chapter VIII, The Duty of Care. At this point, suffice to say that under the business judgment rule, if certain conditions are satisfied a director or officer will not be liable for the consequences of a decision unless the decision was irrational. In *Blasius*, Chancellor Allen in effect concluded that conduct that interferes with shareholder voting is not reviewed the business judgment rule. Instead, a much more stringent standard of review—the standard of compelling justification—should be applied.

----

## NOTE ON TAKEOVERS

Until around the mid–1960s, it was very difficult to oust an incumbent management. In principle, ouster could be achieved through a proxy fight, in which insurgents mobilized support among other shareholders to vote the incumbents out of office. However, for a variety of reasons proxy fights were not often launched and were only intermittently successful. Correspondingly, it was difficult to acquire a corporation against the objections of its managers, because the principal forms of acquisitions, such as mergers or the purchase of all or substantially all of an acquired corporation's assets, require approval by the board of the corporation proposed to be acquired.

In the mid–1960s, however, hostile takeovers came to be an important way to both oust incumbent managements and effect acquisitions. In a hostile takeover, Corporation A makes a public offer—called a *bid* or *tender offer*—to purchase stock in Corporation B, up to a stated amount and subject to certain conditions. The tender offer is made to B's shareholders, not to B. The tender-offer price is invariably well above the prevailing market price for B's stock.

Because a tender offer is made to B's shareholders, rather than to B, the approval of B's board is not required. Nevertheless, despite the fact that a tender offer is made to shareholders rather than to the corporation, incumbent managers tend to resist takeovers by causing the corporation to take defensive actions to stymie a bid. Takeover bids, and defensive actions in response to such bids, will be considered at length in Chapter XII. For now, what is important is that much of present corporate law and practice is motivated, directly or indirectly, by the takeover phenomenon. For example, the potential ability of management to block takeover bids has led to renewed emphasis on proxy fights or—as in *Blasius*—consent solicitations. This, in turn, has led to attempts by incumbent managers to take various kinds of actions—again as in *Blasius*—to prevent their removal by shareholder vote or shareholder consent.

----

## NOTE ON STROUD v. GRACE

In Stroud v. Grace, 606 A.2d 75 (Del.1992), the Delaware Supreme Court approved both Schnell and Blasius, although holding that the principles established in those cases were not applicable on the facts of the case before the Court:

> [W]e accept the basic legal tenets of ... *Blasius* ... [As *Blasius* recognized,] where boards of directors deliberately employed various legal strategies either to frustrate or completely disenfranchise a shareholder vote ... [t]here can be no dispute that such conduct violates Delaware law....

> ... [In this case, however,] a fully-informed majority of Milliken's shareholders ratified the Amendments. Therefore, the factual predicate of unilateral board action intended to inequitably manipulate the corporate machinery is compely absent here.... The result of the vote, ceding greater authority to the board, does not under the circumstances implicate ... *Blasius*.

## NOTE ON WEIGHTED VOTING IN PUBLICLY HELD CORPORATIONS

In the majority of publicly held corporations, only common shareholders have voting rights, and each share of common stock carries one vote. However, voting rights can be conferred on preferred stock, or even on bonds. Furthermore, a corporation may have two or more classes of common stock, each with different voting rights. When there are two or more classes of common stock, often one class has voting power all out of proportion to its equity interests. Such structures are sometimes referred to as dual-class common, super-voting stock, or weighted voting. Although not new, the incidence of such structures increased during the takeover movement in the 1980s, when they were often installed as an anti-takeover defense.

In theory, the creation of such a structure affects only the relative rights of different shareholders, not the allocation of power between managers and shareholders. As the use of such structures to defend against takeovers suggests, however, in practice these structures usually involve the issuance of super-voting stock to members of a control group with the objective of allowing control to be maintained with a minimum investment.

In Stroh v. Blackhawk Holding Corp., 48 Ill.2d 471, 272 N.E.2d 1 (1971), noted, 85 Harv.L.Rev. 1676 (1972), 26 Sw.L.J. 618 (1972), Blackhawk's certificate authorized a Class A and a Class B stock. Class B voted share for share with Class A, but was entitled neither to dividends nor to participate in the proceeds of liquidation. After Blackhawk's formation, its promoters purchased 500,000 shares of Class B at a quarter of a cent per share, and 87,868 shares of Class A at $3.40 per share, and thereafter sold Class A stock to the public at $4 per share. As of June 1968, Blackhawk had outstanding 1,237,681 Class A shares and 500,000 Class B shares, the latter representing an investment of $1250 but carrying 28.78% of the total vote. The court upheld the validity of the B stock.

... Section 14 of the Business Corporation Act ... provides that shares of stock in an Illinois corporation may be divided into classes,

"with such designations, preferences, qualifications, limitations, restrictions and such special or relative rights as shall be stated in the articles of incorporation. The articles of incorporation shall not limit or deny the voting power of the shares of any class.... "

Section 14 ... clearly expresses the intent of the legislature to be that parties to a corporate entity may create whatever restrictions and limitations they may want with regard to their corporate stock by expressing such restrictions and limitations in the articles of incorporation....

... It has long been the common practice in Illinois to classify shares of stock such that one may invest less than another in a corporation, and yet have control. One of two shareholders may purchase ten shares of a class of stock issued at its par value of $1,000 per share, and his business partner may purchase 100 shares of another class of the corporate stock issued at its par value of $10 per share. The parties, for varying reasons, may be very willing that the party investing the $1,000 have control of the management of the corporation, as opposed to the party having the investment of $10,000....

In this case the parties went one step further than is customary. The stock which could be bought cheaper, and yet carry the same voting power per share, was not permitted to share at all in the dividends or assets of the corporation. This additional step did not invalidate the stock.

In Providence & Worcester Co. v. Baker, 378 A.2d 121 (Del.1977), a form of weighted voting was achieved by limiting the number of votes that could be cast by any one shareholder. P & W's certificate provided that each holder of common stock had one vote per share for his first 50 shares, but only one vote per 20 shares for all shares over 50. The validity of these limitations was challenged by the trustees in bankruptcy of Penn Central, who held 28% of P & W's stock, but were effectively restricted to 3% of the total voting power. The court upheld the restrictions under Del. § 212(a), which states that "[u]nless otherwise provided in the certificate of incorporation ... each stockholder shall be entitled to 1 vote for each share of capital stock held by such stockholder." The court concluded that "if the General Assembly intended to bar the type of restriction on stockholders' voting rights here under review, such prohibition would appear in § 212.... Under § 212(a), voting rights of stockholders may be varied from the 'one share-one vote' standard by the certificate of incorporation...." See also Lacos Land Co. v. Arden Group Inc., 517 A.2d 271 (Del.Ch.1986); 1 F.H. O'Neal & R. Thompson, O'Neal's Close Corporations § 3.16 (3d ed. 1992).

In a few states, weighted voting in publicly held corporations is controlled to varying extents by the Blue Sky administrator, and in several situations Congress has acted to prevent abuses in this area.

For example, § 18 of the Investment Company Act of 1940, 15 U.S.C.A. § 80a–18, forbids the issuance of nonvoting stock by companies subject to that Act, except in a few special cases.

The rules of the New York Stock Exchange, the American Stock Exchange and NASDAQ, set certain limits on weighted voting in listed corporations.

See generally Gordon, Ties that Bond: Dual Class Common Stock and the Problem of Shareholder Choice, 76 Calif.L.Rev. 1 (1988); Gilson, Evaluating Dual Class Common Stock: The Relevance of Substitutes, 73 Va.L.Rev. 807 (1987).

---

## NEW YORK STOCK EXCHANGE, LISTED COMPANY MANUAL § 313.00

[See Statutory Supplement]

---

### NOTE ON WILLIAMS v. GEIER

In Williams v. Geier, 671 A.2d 1368 (Del.1996), Cincinnati Milacron adopted a recapitalization plan by an amendment to Milacron's certificate of incorporation. The recapitalization provided for a form of "tenure voting." Holders of common stock on the record date for voting on the Amendment would have ten votes per share. Upon sale or other transfer, however, each share would revert to one-vote-per-share status until that share was held by its owner for three years. Williams argued that (1) the recapitalization disproportionately and invalidly favored stockholders who were part of a majority bloc in Milacron and disfavored the minority stockholders, and (2) the sole purpose of the recapitalization was to entrench Milacron management in office and allow the majority block to sell a portion of its holdings while retaining control of the corporation. The Delaware Supreme Court upheld the recapitalization:

> We hold that [the *Blasius* standard is not] implicated here because there was no unilateral board action. Here, there was stockholder approval of the Amendment. Accordingly, the Board action was not unilateral. The Board recommended that stockholders vote in favor of the Amendment. We must examine, therefore, both the Board action and the validity of the stockholder approval. . . .
>
> *Blasius*' burden of demonstrating a "compelling justification" is quite onerous, and is therefore applied rarely. As this Court noted in Stroud v. Grace, Del.Supr., 606 A.2d 75, 92 (1992) ("*Stroud II*"), the application of the "compelling justification" standard set forth in *Blasius* is appropriate only where the "'primary purpose' of the board's action [is] to interfere with or

impede exercise of the shareholder franchise," and the stockholders are not given a "full and fair opportunity to vote."

We can find no evidence to support Williams' claim that the Defendants' primary purpose in adopting the Recapitalization was a desire to impede the Milacron stockholders' vote. The record does not rebut the business judgment rule presumption that the Board acted independently, with due care, in good faith and in the honest belief that its actions were in the stockholders' best interests.... According to the Proxy, the directors were motivated by a desire to:

> promote long-term planning and values by enhancement of voting rights of long-term shareholders ...[;] permit the issuance of additional shares of common stock for financing or other purposes with minimal dilution of voting rights of long-term shareholders ... [; and] discourage hostile takeovers and put the Board of Directors in the best position to represent the interests of all shareholders.

Proxy at 14. Plaintiff has submitted no evidence to the contrary....

Williams contends that the action of the Board in recommending the Amendment and Recapitalization to the stockholders constituted either a breach of fiduciary duty or an impermissible effort at entrenchment, both of which are claimed to rebut the business judgment presumption and implicate entire fairness review. We disagree. These contentions are conclusory and have no factual support in this record.

There was on this record: (1) no non-pro rata or disproportionate benefit which accrued to the Family Group on the face of the Recapitalization, although the dynamics of how the Plan would work in practice had the effect of strengthening the Family Group's control; (2) no evidence adduced to show that a majority of the Board was interested or acted for purposes of entrenching themselves in office; (3) no evidence offered to show that the Board was dominated or controlled by the Family Group; and (4) no violation of fiduciary duty by the Board.

Only by demonstrating that the Board breached its fiduciary duties may the presumption of the business judgment rule be rebutted, thereby shifting the burden to the Board to demonstrate that the transaction complained of was entirely fair to the stockholders....

Based on the undisputed evidence in this record, we conclude that the Board's action in recommending the Amendment and Recapitalization to the stockholders for approval, pursuant to 8 Del.C. § 242(b)(1), is protected by the business judgment rule. We now turn to the issue of the validity of the stockholder vote....

We put to one side those cases, not relevant here, where stockholders are called upon to ratify action which may involve a transaction with an interested director or where the transaction approved by the board may otherwise be voidable. . . .

Our analysis here involves an entirely different application of the Delaware General Corporation Law—namely, the effect of corporate action which, in order to become operative, requires and receives both approval by the board of directors and the stockholders. Three examples are common: amendments to the certificate of incorporation (8 Del.C. § 242); mergers or consolidations of domestic corporations (8 Del.C. § 251); and sales of all or substantially all of a corporation's assets (8 Del.C. § 271, which permits a sequence that may vary from the sequences applicable to amendments or mergers). There are, of course, other examples. . . .

We find that *Stroud II* is applicable here. In *Stroud II*, this Court held that the stockholder vote, being both fully informed and devoid of any fraud, waste, manipulative or other inequitable conduct, effectively implemented the board recommendations adopting amendments to the certificate of incorporation and approving a bylaw change, both of which allegedly benefited the incumbent controlling majority. *Stroud II*, 606 A.2d at 83. The presence of a controlling majority stockholder did not undermine the validity of the stockholder vote.

In the instant case, like *Stroud II*, the Board recommended the advisability of the Amendment to the stockholders who voted in favor of the Amendment. On its face, therefore, the corporate action was authorized and regular. Stockholders (even a controlling stockholder bloc) may properly vote in their own economic interest, and majority stockholders are not to be disenfranchised because they may reap a benefit from corporate action which is regular on its face. . . .

------

## General Datacomm Industries, Inc. v. Wisconsin Investment Board

Delaware Chancery Court, 1999.
1999 WL 66533.

### I.

In this matter, the plaintiff, General DataComm Industries, Inc., ("GDC"), a Delaware corporation, seeks declaratory and injunctive relief regarding the validity of a bylaw proposed for consideration at GDC's upcoming annual meeting by the defendant, State of Wisconsin Investment Board ("SWIB"). The proposed "Repricing Bylaw" provides as follows:

> Option Repricing. [GDC] shall not reprice any stock options already issued and outstanding to a lower strike price at any time during the term of such option, without the prior approval of the shareholders.

Compl. P 8.

GDC contends that this proposed Repricing Bylaw "restricts unlawfully and in a material way the directors' statutory power and authority, as well as the directors' fiduciary duty, to make decisions on matters of management policy. Because no provision limiting the board's managerial authority is contained in the GDC certificate of incorporation, SWIB's proposed Repricing Bylaw is invalid." Compl. P 15.

Before me now is GDC's motion to expedite proceedings, which was filed on January 28, 1999. GDC's annual meeting is scheduled for February 4, 1999.

According to GDC, "this matter needs prompt resolution so that GDC is not required to suffer a facially invalid bylaw and its directors are not impaired in the management of [GDC's] incentive compensation program for recruitment and retention of key employees due to uncertainty, as long as this dispute remains unresolved, over their authority to act without stockholder approval." P1.'s Mot. P 9.

After a consideration of GDC's motion, I believe that the issues raised in its complaint are not yet ripe for judicial resolution and therefore deny its motion for expedited proceedings. However, in the event that the Repricing Bylaw is adopted by the GDC stockholders, I will promptly, upon renewed application by GDC, consider whether a schedule for expedited proceedings to address the issues raised by its complaint should be put in place.

## II.

SWIB first submitted the Repricing Bylaw to GDC for consideration on September 2, 1998. According to GDC, Securities and Exchange Commission ("SEC") rules require GDC to include the Repricing Bylaw proposal in GDC's proxy materials unless an applicable SEC exclusion applies.

Throughout the fall, GDC attempted to obtain SEC approval to exclude the Repricing Bylaw proposal from its proxy materials. In particular, GDC argued that exclusion was proper under SEC Rule 14a–8(i)(1), which enables exclusion if the "proposal is not a proper subject for action by shareholders under the laws of the jurisdiction of the company's organization." Compl. P 11, Ex. B.

SWIB, through the Delaware law firm of Grant & Eisenhofer, disputed this contention. On December 9, 1998, the SEC advised GDC that it could not exclude the Repricing Bylaw from its proxy materials on the basis of Rule 14a–8(i)(1), stating: "Neither counsel for you nor for the proponent has opined as to any compelling state law precedent. In view of the lack of any decided legal authority the Division has determined not to express any view with respect to the application of rule 14a–8(i)(1) to the proposal." Compl. PP 12–13, Ex. D.

On December 14, 1998, GDC sent its stockholders proxy materials setting forth SWIB's proposed Repricing Bylaw, SWIB's supporting statement, and the management response of GDC. Compl. P 14, Ex. E. A particularly pertinent part of the management response provides:

> Requiring the Corporation to submit option repricing to stockholders at the next annual meeting or at a special meeting is both cumbersome and untimely and would effectively eliminate the ability to reprice options for employees who are otherwise leaving their employment. The Corporation has also been advised by its Delaware counsel that in their opinion, the proposal if implemented would violate Delaware law since such restrictions are only permitted in the Certificate of Incorporation. Should the stockholders approve the proposal, the Corporation reserves the right to challenge its validity in appropriate Delaware court proceedings.
>
> ACCORDINGLY, THE BOARD OF DIRECTORS UNANIMOUSLY RECOMMENDS THAT THE STOCKHOLDERS VOTE AGAINST THE PROPOSED BY–LAW ADDITION RESTRICTING OPTION REPRICING.

Compl. P 14, Ex. E at 14.

On January 22, 1999, some three weeks after the Delaware Supreme Court issued its decision in *Quickturn Design Sys., Inc. v. Shapiro, Del. Supr., Nos. 511, 512, 721 A.2d 1281, 1998 WL 954752 (1998)*, GDC wrote SWIB asking it to withdraw the Repricing Bylaw on the ground that Quickturn made it clear that the Repricing Bylaw was invalid, or in the alternative, to advise the GDC stockholders that the proposed Repricing Bylaw was invalid. Three days later, GDC wrote to the SEC to advise it of the Quickturn decision and to urge it to reconsider GDC's request to exclude the Repricing Bylaw from its proxy materials. GDC has heard back from neither SWIB nor the SEC.

On January 28, 1999, GDC brought this action seeking declaratory and injunctive relief, to wit: a declaratory judgment that the Repricing Bylaw is invalid; a declaratory judgment that the SWIB proxy discussion of the Repricing Bylaw is false and misleading; an order enjoining SWIB from soliciting votes for the Repricing Bylaw or otherwise seeking adoption of that Bylaw; an order directing that supplemental proxy materials be sent to GDC stockholders advising them of the removal of the Repricing Bylaw from consideration at the annual meeting; and an order permitting GDC to adjourn or postpone the meeting or any vote on the Repricing Bylaw pending the adjudication of its claims in this case. Compl. pp. 8–9, PP A–F.

Earlier today, an office conference was held to consider GDC's motion for expedited proceedings.

### III.

GDC seeks to have this court determine the validity of a yet to be adopted bylaw. Therefore, I must weigh the reasons "for not rendering a hypothetical opinion. . . . against the benefits to be derived from the rendering of a declaratory judgment." *Stroud v. Milliken Enter., Inc., Del. Supr., 552 A.2d 476, 480 (1989)*. Even in a situation where more substantial corporate interests were at stake, I would be reluctant to grant an advisory opinion in a situation like this. In this matter, where no irreparable harm is threatened, prudence dictates that judicial action regarding whether the Repricing Bylaw is valid should await an affirmative stockholder vote....

... [T]he stockholders can cast an informed vote if the proxy materials disclose that there are differing views regarding the validity of the Repricing Bylaw. In fact, the GDC materials already state GDC's view that the Repricing Bylaw is invalid. Compl. P 14, Ex. E at 14.

... [A] post-meeting adjudication would not unduly disrupt the corporation's affairs. At most, the Repricing Bylaw will inhibit the GDC board's ability to reprice options in the event that in the board's business judgment such repricing becomes necessary in the period between the Repricing Bylaw's adoption at the annual meeting (if that occurs) and a post-adoption adjudication of its validity by this court. The speculative nature of these eventualities, the availability of prompt injunctive relief, and the fact that this court has committed to consider promptly a request to expedite a post-adoption adjudication eliminates any necessity for a pre-adoption adjudication of the Repricing Bylaw's validity....

This lack of urgency cuts against the need to determine a potentially important issue of Delaware law in haste. It may be that GDC is correct in stating that the Repricing Bylaw is obviously invalid under the teaching of *Quickturn*. But the question of whether a stockholder-approved bylaw that can potentially be repealed at any time by the GDC board of directors exercising its business judgment, see 8 Del. C. § 109(a)[1], is clearly invalid under the teaching of a case involving a board-approved contractual rights plan precluding, by contract, a new board majority from redeeming the rights under the plan until six months after election seems to me to be a question worthy of careful consideration.[2]

---

1. Under § 109(a) of the Delaware General Corporation Law, the GDC certificate may permissibly vest authority to amend the corporation's bylaws in its board of directors and at oral argument GDC's counsel indicated that the GDC certificate so empowers its board. The question of whether a stockholder-approved bylaw may be repealed by a board of directors with such authority has not clearly been answered by a Delaware Court. However, the Supreme Court's decision in *Centaur Partners, IV v. Nat'l Intergroup, Inc.,* Del. Supr., 582 A.2d 923, 929 (1990) and the views of a learned commentator suggests that the affirmative answer may be the correct one. Lawrence Hamermesh, Corporate Democracy and Stockholder-Adopted By-Laws: Taking Back the Street?, 73 Tul. L. Rev. 409, 467–479 (1998). But see 1 R. Franklin Balotti & Jesse A. Finkelstein, The Delaware Law of Corporations & Business Organizations, § 1.11 at 1–16 (1998) (suggesting that the negative answer is correct).

2. At minimum, the question would seem to require consideration of several provisions of the Delaware General Corporation Law, including § 102, § 109, § 141, § 153, and § 157, as well as relevant case law, including *Quickturn*. A recently published article which addresses the subject of stockholder-adopted bylaws in a sophisticated and comprehensive manner, states well the difficulties this subject generally raises:

Just as this nascent effort to shift the balance of corporate power from directors to stockholders through the use of stockholder-adopted by-law provisions is gaining momentum, however, it has exposed a critical dearth of precedent. For while stockholders have unquestioned power to adopt by-laws covering a broad range of subjects, it is also well established in corporate law that stockholders may not directly manage the business and affairs of the corporation, at least without specific authorization either by statute or in the certificate or articles of incorporation.

As a result, I believe that GDC has not shown a compelling justification sufficient to persuade me to rule on its claims at this time. My reticence to issue a ruling at this time is, I must admit, also influenced by my reluctance to encourage corporations to seek advisory opinions about important issues of Delaware corporation law as a method of shaping their annual meeting proxy materials. *Stroud*, 552 A.2d at 479 (Declaratory Judgment Act not to be used as a means of obtaining advisory rulings from Delaware courts). If this option were routinely available, this court could find itself playing a parallel role to the SEC, which is regularly involved, pursuant to its statutory and regulatory authority, in the proxy preparation process. This court's traditional commitment to prompt justice should ordinarily be sufficient to address any legitimate corporate interests threatened by the adoption by stockholders of an invalid bylaw. Absent an imminent threat of irreparable injury, there seems to be no need and much risk for this court to step into the void when the SEC concludes that state law is not clear enough for its Rule 14a–8(i)(1) to exclude a proposal. The SEC's judgment in such a situation would suggest that the issue involved is of a difficult nature and that it deserves careful scrutiny: that is, that the issue is of precisely the sort about which this court should be reluctant to opine until the issue is ripe for judicial resolution. Cf *Stroud*, 552 A.2d at 481 (finding that unripe claim raising issues "novel and important . . . to Delaware corporate law" should be dismissed).

## IV.

For the foregoing reasons, GDC's motion to expedite proceedings is hereby DENIED. IT IS SO ORDERED.

## SECTION 3.   THE LEGAL STRUCTURE OF MANAGEMENT

There is an obvious zone of conflict between these precepts: in at least some respects, attempts by stockholders to adopt by-laws limiting or influencing director authority inevitably offend the notion of management by the board of directors. However, neither the courts, the legislators, the SEC, nor legal scholars have clearly articulated the means of resolving this conflict and determining whether a stockholder-adopted by-law provision that constrains director managerial authority is legally effective.

Related to this gap in legal authority is a less substantive but nearly as important area of legal uncertainty. Even if the stockholders could validly initiate and adopt a by-law limiting the authority of the directors, such a by-law amendment would accomplish little or nothing if the board of directors could simply repeal it after the stockholders adopted it. In some jurisdictions, of course, there is no question that such repeal can be prevented. Under many statutory schemes, the board of directors may not repeal a stockholder-adopted by-law if that by-law expressly prohibits such repeal. In other jurisdictions, however, notably Delaware and New York, the corporation statutes allow the board of directors to amend the by-laws if the certificate or articles of incorporation so provide and place no express limits on the application of such director amendment authority to stockholder-adopted by-laws. The second significant legal uncertainty, therefore is whether, in the absence of an explicitly controlling statute, a stockholder-adopted by-law can be made immune from repeal or modification by the board of directors.

Hamermesh, 73 Tul. L. Rev, at 415–417. Cf. *Int'l Brotherhood of Teamsters Gen. Fund v. Fleming Cos., Inc.*, 975 P.2d 907, 1999 OK 3, 1999 WL 35227, at *1 (Okla.1999). . . .

## NOTE ON THE STRUCTURE OF THE CORPORATION

1. *The Traditional Legal Model.* The most striking aspect of the traditional legal model of the corporation is the distinctive position of the board. Simple business organizations are managed either by the owners or by persons who are legally agents of the owners. Under the traditional legal model of the corporation, however, the board of directors manages the corporation's business, and the board is conceived as an independent institution, not as an agent of the shareholders. For example, although an agent must normally follow his principal's instructions, shareholders have no legal power to give binding instructions to the board on matters within the board's exclusive power. Similarly, although the authority of an agent can normally be terminated by his principal at any time, directors are normally removable by shareholders only for good cause.

2. *Modern Corporate Practice.* Despite the central *legal* role of the board, under modern corporate practice in publicly held corporations, the management function is ordinarily located not in the board, but in the executives, and the central figure in the corporation is not the board, but the chief executive officer (CEO). The limited role of the board in managing the corporation is the result of several critical constraints imposed by modern board practice.

a. *Constraints of time.* Boards of publicly held corporations meet an average of 8 times a year, and outside directors spend an average of 157 hours a year on board matters, including preparation time and travel time. Korn/Ferry International, 25th Annual Board of Directors Study 20 (1999). If it is assumed, pretty conservatively, that travel time averages 4 hours a meeting, that means that directors average about 125 hours a year on board matters, that is, the equivalent of fifteen working days. It is obvious that by reason of time constraints alone the typical board could not possibly "manage" the business of a large publicly held corporation in the normal sense of that term: Such businesses are far too complex to be managed by persons who put in the equivalent of fifteen working days a year.

b. *Constraints of information.* The distribution of information in the corporation is highly asymmetrical: the officers typically not only have much more information than the board, but control much of the flow of information to the board. By controlling the information that the board receives, the officers heavily shape the decisions that the board makes.

c. *Constraints of composition.* The typical board includes a number of directors who are economically or psychologically tied to the corporation's executives, particularly to the CEO. Indeed, a number of seats on a board are usually held by inside directors, that is, by the corporation's own executives. The inside director, dependent on the CEO for both retention and promotion, and on other executives for day-to-day support, is highly unlikely to dissent at a board meeting from the inside line determined by the CEO prior to the meeting.

Outside directors may have economic ties to the corporation, and ties of friendship, colleagueship, or both, to the CEO.

3. *The Monitoring Board.* Because of the unrealistic nature of the monitoring model, in the last twenty years there has been a relatively sudden shift from a managing model to a monitoring model.

The monitoring model of the board recognizes that in a publicly held corporation the management function is exercised not by the board, but by the senior executives. Under the monitoring model, therefore, the primary although not exclusive function of the board of a publicly held corporation is, not to manage the business of the corporation, but to select, regularly evaluate, fix the compensation of, and, where appropriate, replace the senior executives, and to monitor the conduct of the corporation's business to evaluate whether the business is being properly managed.

This functional component of the monitoring model is complemented by a structural component. If the board has the function of monitoring the senior executives, it must be structured to effectuate that function. Effectuating that function requires that the board consist of at least a majority of directors who are independent of the senior executives, and that the board have audit, nominating, and compensation committees, composed exclusively of such independent directors, to aid in implementing that function.

Today, the monitoring model of the board has been almost universally accepted and adopted in large publicly held corporations. Ultimately, the acceptance and adoption of the monitoring model of the board rests on its perceived economic advantage in providing an additional system to monitor the efficiency of management—in particular, of the CEO. The monitoring board, taken alone, is an imperfect mechanism to achieve that end, but because all systems to monitor the efficiency of the management of publicly held corporations are imperfect, it is important to construct a web of overlapping and even redundant monitoring systems. The monitoring board is one important part of that web.

---

## AMERICAN LAW INSTITUTE, PRINCIPLES OF CORPORATE GOVERNANCE §§ 3.01, 3.02, 3.05, 3A.01–3A.05

[See Statutory Supplement]

---

## AMERICAN LAW INSTITUTE, PRINCIPLES OF CORPORATE GOVERNANCE § 3.03

[See Statutory Supplement]

## SECTION 4.  FORMALITIES REQUIRED FOR ACTION BY THE BOARD

### DEL. GEN. CORP. LAW §§ 141(b), (f), (i), 229

[See Statutory Supplement]

### REV. MODEL BUS. CORP. ACT §§ 8.20, 8.21, 8.22, 8.23, 8.24

[See Statutory Supplement]

### NOTE ON FORMALITIES REQUIRED FOR ACTION BY THE BOARD

The validity of an action by the board of directors is governed by rules concerning the formalities required for meeting, notice, quorum, and voting. These rules can be considered at two levels. At the first level are rules that govern the formalities for board action. At the second level are rules concerning the consequence of noncompliance with the first-level rules.

*Level 1: The Governing Rules.* Unless otherwise indicated, the following account is based on predominant statutory patterns.

(i) *Meetings.* A single director, as such, has no power. Instead, directors can act only as a body. Normally, directors must act at a duly convened meeting at which a quorum is present. Most statutes provide that a meeting of the board can be conducted by conference telephone, or by any other means of communication through which all participating directors can simultaneously hear each other. In addition, most statutes also permit the board to act by unanimous written consent without a meeting of any kind.

(ii) *Notice.* Formal notice is not required for a regular board meeting: If the meeting is a regular one, the directors are already on notice of its date, time, and place. In the case of a special meeting, notice of date, time, and place must be given to every director. The notice need not state the purpose of a meeting unless the certificate of incorporation or the bylaws otherwise provide. The statutes usually provide that notice must be given a stated number of days in advance of the meeting, but then add that the stated period may be made shorter or longer by the certificate of incorporation or by-laws. Most statutes provide that notice can be waived in writing before or after a meeting, and that attendance at a meeting constitutes a waiver unless the director attends merely to protest against holding the meeting.

(iii) *Quorum.* A quorum of a board consists of a majority of the *full board,* that is, a majority of the authorized number of directors (not simply a majority of the directors then in office, which may be less than the authorized number because of board vacancies). A majority of statutes permit the certificate of incorporation or bylaws to require a greater number for a quorum than a majority of the full board. A substantial minority of the statutes, including the Delaware statute and the Model Act, permit the certificate or bylaws to set a lower number, but usually no less than one-third of the full board.

(iv) *Voting.* Assuming that a quorum is present when a vote is taken, the affirmative vote of a majority of those present (not simply a majority of those voting) is required for action. Most statutes provide that the articles or bylaws can require a greater-than-majority vote for board action.

*Level 2: Consequences of Noncompliance.* The consequences of noncompliance with the rules that govern the formalities required for board action are not always clear. In publicly held corporations, where bureaucratic order usually prevails, lack of a quorum, lack of the requisite affirmative vote, or an uncured defect of notice, will usually render board action ineffective. However, in closely held corporations, where formalities are seldom followed and the shareholders tend to make their own rules, the results of a failure to observe proper formalities are much less clear-cut. Unless otherwise indicated, the balance of this Note concerns cases involving closely held corporations.

(i) *Unanimous explicit, but informal, approval.* Some cases, most of which are quite old, have held that informal approval by directors—that is, approval without following the requisite formalities—is ineffective, even if the approval is explicit and unanimous. A leading case was Baldwin v. Canfield, 26 Minn. 43, 54, 1 N.W. 261, 270 (1879). Cases like *Baldwin* are of doubtful validity today. More characteristic of modern authority is Gerard v. Empire Square Realty Co., 195 App.Div. 244, 187 N.Y.S. 306 (1921). Plaintiff brought an action against several related corporations to recover damages for breach of an employment contract. The corporations' shares were owned by five persons, all of whom were directors. Owing to dissension, no shareholders' or directors' meetings were held, but there was evidence that each director had separately agreed to the hiring of the plaintiff. The court held that on these facts the corporations would be bound:

> I think that under the circumstances of the case we are considering, where the directors own all the capital stock of the corporations, where they are members of the same family but so at variance that directors' and stockholders' meetings are not held, their action, concurred in by all, although separately and not as a body, binds the corporation. We must recognize the fact that [corporations] are, in perhaps the majority of instances, conducted by officers and directors little informed in the law of corporations, who often act informally, sometimes without meetings or

even by-laws. To hold that in all instances technical conformity to the requirements of the law of corporations is a condition to a valid action by the directors, would be to lay down a rule of law which could be used as a trap for the unwary who deal with corporations, and to permit corporations sometimes to escape liability to which an individual in the same circumstances would be subjected.

The results in this area are too disparate to be captured by a single clear rule. In general, however, it is fair to say that most modern courts would hold that at least in the context of a closely held corporation, explicit but informal approval by all the directors is effective where a person who has contracted with a corporate officer has been led to regard his transaction with the corporation as valid, and all the shareholders either are directors or have acquiesced in the transaction or in a past practice of informal board action. See Anderson v. K.G. Moore, Inc., 6 Mass.App.Ct. 386, 376 N.E.2d 1238 (1978), cert. denied 439 U.S. 1116, 99 S.Ct. 1020, 59 L.Ed.2d 74 (1979).

Indeed, today many cases involving unanimous explicit but informal approval probably are governed by the modern statutory rule that the board can act without a meeting, by written consent. It might be argued that the negative implication of these statutes is that no effect should be given to informal unanimous approval unless it is in writing. Thus, in Village of Brown Deer v. City of Milwaukee, 16 Wis.2d 206, 114 N.W.2d 493 (1962), cert. denied 371 U.S. 902, 83 S.Ct. 205, 9 L.Ed.2d 164, the court stated that, "The legislature has said that the corporation could act informally, without a meeting, by obtaining the consent in writing of all of the directors. In our opinion, this pronouncement has preempted the field and prohibits corporations from acting informally without complying with the statute." In *Brown Deer*, however, apparently only a majority of the directors knew of the transaction in question, so there was no unanimous approval, formal or informal. Other cases decided in jurisdictions that have unanimous-written-consent statutes have held that the corporation was bound by unanimous oral consent. See Note, Corporations: When Informal Action by Corporate Directors Will Be Permitted to Bind the Corporation, 53 B.U.L.Rev. 101, 120 (1973).

(ii) *Explicit majority approval coupled with acquiescence by remaining directors.* In the type of case just considered, all the directors informally but explicitly approve a transaction. Suppose that a majority of the directors explicitly approve a transaction, while the remaining directors knew of the transaction and took no action to disavow it, so that they may be said to have acquiesced in the transaction. The difference between this case and the case in which all the directors explicitly but informally approve is not very significant. Accordingly, the courts will normally treat cases alike. See, e.g., Winchell v. Plywood Corp., 324 Mass. 171, 85 N.E.2d 313 (1949). The same result will normally follow even if there is no explicit approval by a majority of the directors, but all the directors acquiesce. See e.g.,

Juergens v. Venture Capital Corp., 1 Mass.App.Ct. 274, 295 N.E.2d 398 (1973); Pierce v. Astoria Fish Factors, Inc., 31 Wash.App. 214, 640 P.2d 40 (1982).

(iii) *Majority approval or acquiescence.* Suppose, finally, that a majority of the directors of a closely held corporation approve a transaction, explicitly or by acquiescence, but the remaining directors lack knowledge of the transaction. Some courts have refused to hold the corporation liable under these circumstances. See, e.g., Hurley v. Ornsteen, 311 Mass. 477, 42 N.E.2d 273 (1942). Other courts have held the corporation liable, at least if the *shareholders* acquiesced in the transaction or the shareholders or the remaining directors acquiesced in a practice of informal action by the directors. One theory is that the remaining directors would have known of the transaction if they had been properly active. Another is that the shareholders, if they have tolerated informal action by the directors over a period of time, have by that acquiescence authorized the directors to act in that manner. See, e.g., Holy Cross Gold Mining & Milling Co. v. Goodwin, 74 Colo. 532, 223 P. 58 (1924).

---

**NOTE ON COMMITTEES**

The boards of publicly held corporations almost invariably accomplish much of their work through committees. Committees can be advisory to the board, but alternatively the board may delegate to a committee the power to make decisions about specific matters or a range of matters. Most statutes contain a list of matters that cannot be delegated, but generally speaking there is very little that cannot be delegated. In general, the rules governing board procedures—such as the rules concerning notice and quorum—are applicable to committees as well.

---

**DEL. GEN. CORP. LAW § 141(c)**

[See Statutory Supplement]

---

**REV. MODEL BUS. CORP. ACT § 8.25**

[See Statutory Supplement]

---

**SECTION 5. AUTHORITY OF CORPORATE OFFICERS**

---

### DEL. GEN. CORP. LAW § 142

[See Statutory Supplement]

———

### REV. MODEL BUS. CORP. ACT §§ 8.40, 8.41

[See Statutory Supplement]

———

### NOTE ON AUTHORITY

[See Chapter 1, supra]

———

## NOTE ON THE AUTHORITY OF CORPORATE OFFICERS

Legal questions concerning the authority of a corporate officer typically arise in the context of a transaction between a third person and the corporation in which an officer, rather than the board, acted on the corporation's behalf. The application of the principle of apparent authority in such cases may rest on the officer's position, that is, his title.

1. *President.* There are a great number of cases concerning the apparent authority of a president by virtue of his title. Some cases hold that a president does not have any apparent authority by virtue of his position—that instead, he has only the actual authority that the board has conferred upon him. For example, in Federal Services Finance Corp. v. Bishop Nat. Bank of Hawaii at Honolulu, 190 F.2d 442 (9th Cir.1951), supplemented 205 F.2d 11 (9th Cir.1953), the court held that the president had no presumed power by virtue of his office to cash checks payable to the company's order.

However, the prevalent modern rule is that the president has apparent authority to bind his company to contracts in the usual and regular course of business, but not to contracts of an "extraordinary" nature. See, e.g., in Lee v. Jenkins Bros., 268 F.2d 357 (2d Cir.1959), cert. denied 361 U.S. 913, 80 S.Ct. 257, 4 L.Ed.2d 183. The difficulty lies in drawing a line between what is "ordinary" and what is "extraordinary." Some cases have been restrictive in determining the apparent authority of a president, perhaps influenced by statutory language that the business of the corporation shall be managed by the board. See, e.g., Liebermann v. Princeway Realty Corp., 17 A.D.2d 258, 233 N.Y.S.2d 1001 (1962), aff'd 13 N.Y.2d 999, 245 N.Y.S.2d 390, 195 N.E.2d 57 (1963). Other cases, like Lee v. Jenkins Brothers, supra, determine the president's apparent authority in a more expansive manner. An expansive interpretation reflects both the reality that the management of the business of the corporation is normally conducted by or under the supervision of its executives, rather than its board, and a sound understanding of the normal expectations of third persons in such cases.

Any attempt at precision in determining the apparent authority of a president would almost certainly be futile, because the issue is highly dependent on the context in which it arises, and the types of business transactions that may arise are endlessly variable. Nevertheless, certain boundaries can be identified. To begin with, some matters, such as the declaration of dividends, are required by statute to be decided by the board. Typically, the statutes also enumerate certain matters that the board cannot delegate to a committee, such as approval of an action that requires approval by both the board and the shareholders pursuant to statute. By analogy, it would normally not be within the apparent authority of the president to take binding action on these matters.

Beyond these boundaries, among the elements to be taken into account for purposes of determining what constitutes an "extraordinary" action, that would normally be outside the apparent authority of the president, are the economic magnitude of the action in relation to corporate assets and earnings, the extent of risk involved, the time-span of the action's effect, and the cost of reversing the action. Examples of extraordinary acts for these purposes include the creation of long-term or other significant debt, the reacquisition of equity or debt securities, significant capital investments, significant business combinations, the disposition of significant businesses, entry into important new lines of business, significant acquisitions of stock in other corporations, and actions that would foreseeably expose the corporation to significant litigation or significant new regulatory problems. A useful generalization is that decisions that would make a significant change in the structure of the business enterprise, or in the structure of control over the enterprise, are extraordinary corporate actions and therefore normally outside the president's apparent authority.

Of course, the president, or any other officer, may have actual authority that is greater than his apparent authority. The president's actual authority may be found in the certificate of incorporation, the by-laws, or board resolutions, or may derive from a pattern of past acquiescence by the board, or from the board's ratification of a specific transaction.

2. *Chairman of the Board.* There is little case-law on the apparent authority of a chairman of the board by virtue of his position, in part because the actual authority of the chairman varies significantly. Often, but not always, the chairmanship title is simply piled on to the CEO title. However, "In some [corporations, the chairman's office] is held by a chief executive officer who has relinquished day-by-day operations to a younger man while still holding the reins of power; in others it is held by a retired chief executive officer whose counsel and advice are still valued; in still others it provides a formula for dividing up between two relatively equal principals the control of the corpora-

tion." American Express Co. v. Lopez, 72 Misc.2d 648, 340 N.Y.S.2d 82 (Civ.Ct.1973).

3. *Vice-Presidents.* The case-law on the apparent authority of vice-presidents is also sparse. Under the relatively strict outlook of the earlier cases, a vice-president, as such, had little or no apparent authority. See James F. Monaghan, Inc. v. M. Lowenstein & Sons, 290 Mass. 331, 195 N.E. 101 (1935). There is some indication that courts today may follow a more expansive approach to the authority of a vice-president, at least if the vice-president has the appearance of standing close to the top of the corporate hierarchy. See Kanavos v. Hancock Bank & Trust Co., 14 Mass.App.Ct. 326, 439 N.E.2d 311 (1982).

4. *Secretary.* The secretary of a corporation has apparent authority to certify the records of the corporation, including resolutions of the board. A secretary's certificate that a given resolution was duly adopted by the board is conclusive in favor of third party relying on the certificate. See, e.g., Diamond Paint Co. of Houston v. Embry, 525 S.W.2d 529 (Tex.Civ.App.1975). The significance of the secretary's power of certification is demonstrated in In re Drive–In Development Corp., 371 F.2d 215, 219–20 (7th Cir.1966), cert. denied Creditors' Committee of Drive–In Development Corp. v. National Boulevard Bank of Chicago, 387 U.S. 909, 87 S.Ct. 1691, 18 L.Ed.2d 626 (1967), which involved the question whether a corporation was bound by a guaranty:

> . . . [T]he referee found that Drive In's minute book did not show that a resolution authorizing Maranz to sign the guaranty was adopted by the directors and that Dick [the corporate secretary] could not recall a specific directors' meeting at which such a resolution was approved. From these findings, the referee concluded that Maranz, who signed the guaranty on behalf of Drive In, had no authority, "either actual or implied or apparent," to bind Drive In. This conclusion was erroneous. Drive In was estopped to deny Maranz' express authority to sign the guaranty because of the certified copy of a resolution of Drive In's board of directors purporting to grant such authority furnished to the bank by Dick, whether or not such a resolution was in fact formally adopted.

Other than the very important power of certification, a secretary's apparent authority by virtue of his position, is close to nil. See, e.g., Ideal Foods, Inc. v. Action Leasing Corp., 413 So.2d 416, 417 (Fla.App. 1982) ("The secretary of a corporation, merely as such, is a ministerial officer, without authority to transact the business of the corporation upon his volition and judgment").

5. *Treasurer.* The apparent authority of the treasurer, under the case-law, is also close to nil. See, e.g., Ideal Foods, Inc. v. Action Leasing Corp., 413 So.2d 416 (Fla.App.1982).

6. *Closely Held Corporations.* In the context of closely held corporations, some cases hold that if the president has been exercising absolute authority over the corporation's affairs, and the board has

never questioned, altered, or rejected his decisions, the president will have extremely wide actual and apparent authority. See, e.g., Allen v. France Packing Co., 170 Pa.Super. 632, 90 A.2d 289 (1952); Blasingame v. American Materials, Inc., 654 S.W.2d 659 (Tenn.1983). More generally, it has been said that:

> Although the same broad principles of corporation and agency law determine the powers of officers in both close and publicly held corporations, the factual differences in the patterns of operation of the two kinds of corporations lead to wide disparities in the powers the courts actually recognize in corporate officers. In a close corporation, ownership and management normally coalesce; and the participants often conduct their enterprise internally much as if it were a partnership. The courts have seldom articulated a difference in the rules governing officers' powers in close and publicly held corporations; yet they appear in fact to have often cut through the technical legal form of close corporations to reach the results that would be reached if the enterprises were conducted as partnerships. In other words, the courts frequently, and perhaps usually, recognize in officers of a close corporation the same powers that are possessed by partners in a firm under the general rule of partnership law which makes each partner an agent of the firm for the purposes of its business and empowers each partner to bind the firm by acts apparently carried on to further the usual business of the partnership.

Zimmerman v. Hogg & Allen, 286 N.C. 24, 33, 209 S.E.2d 795, 801 (1974).

7. *Ratification.* Even if an officer lacks both actual and apparent authority, the corporation may be bound by the officer's act in entering into a contract or other transaction on its behalf, if the board later ratifies the officer's act. Ratification may occur where a corporation, knowing all of the facts, accepts and uses the proceeds of an unauthorized contract executed on its behalf. Western Life Ins. Co. v. Hicks, 135 Ga.App. 90, 217 S.E.2d 323 (1975).

8. *Terminology.* The terminology employed in the traditional rules concerning the apparent authority of a corporate officer has become somewhat archaic. When these rules were formulated, the top officer in the corporation had the title of president, the number-two officer had the title of executive vice-president, and the top financial officer had the title of treasurer.

Today, matters are much different. The title that signifies the top officer is not president, but chief executive officer, or CEO. (The CEO usually holds a second title, which may be either president, chairman of the board, or both.) The title that usually signifies the number-two officer is Chief Operating Officer, or COO. The title that signifies the top financial officer is Chief Financial Officer, or CFO.

It remains to be seen how the apparent authority of corporate officers will be adapted to this shift in terminology.

---

**SCHOONEJONGEN v. CURTISS WRIGHT CORP.**, 143 F.3d 120 (3d Cir.1998). "Beyond the board of directors, the corporation may validly act through its ... officers as authorized corporate agents. In general, an officer's powers stem from the organic law of the corporation, or a board delegation of authority which maybe express or implied.... Express authority to act on behalf of the corporation is usually manifested through a statute, the certificate of corporation, the by-laws, or a board or shareholder action.... Implied actual authority, which is express authority circumstantially proved, may be found through evidence as to the manner in which the business has operated in the past, the facts attending the transaction in question, circumstantial evidence of board declarations surrounding the given transaction, or the habitual usage or course of dealing common to the company.... Similarly, authority will be implied when it is reasonably necessary and proper to effectuate the purpose of the office or the main authority conferred."

# SECTION 6.   FORMALITIES REQUIRED FOR SHAREHOLDER ACTION

## DEL. GEN. CORP. LAW §§ 211, 213, 214, 216, 222, 228

[See Statutory Supplement]

## REV. MODEL BUS. CORP. ACT §§ 7.01, 7.02, 7.03–7.07, 7.21, 7.25–7.28

[See Statutory Supplement]

## NOTE ON FORMALITIES REQUIRED FOR SHAREHOLDER ACTION

1. *Meeting and Notice.* Notice of place, time, and date is required for the annual meeting of shareholders and for any special meeting. The notice of a *special* meeting must describe the purpose for which the meeting is called. Under most state statutes, the notice of an annual meeting must describe the matters to be acted upon only in certain cases—for example, when it is proposed to amend the certificate of incorporation, sell substantially all of the corporation's assets, engage in a merger, or dissolve. Some state statutes, and the federal Proxy Rules, also require a description of purpose in the notice of an annual meeting. However, the Proxy Rules apply to only a small fraction of all corporations.

Because the identity of the shareholders in a publicly held corporation constantly undergoes change, normally notice of a meeting is given to those persons who are shareholders of record on a designated record date prior to the meeting, not to those persons who are beneficial owners of stock on the date of the meeting. Correspondingly, only those persons who were record holders on the record date are entitled to vote at the meeting. The record date is normally fixed in the by-laws, or by the board, within prescribed statutory limits. If a record date is not fixed in this manner, the statutes usually provide that the record date will be the day of, or the business day preceding, the day on which the notice of meeting is sent. (Under an older, alternative procedure that is still sanctioned in many statutes, but is generally regarded as archaic, the corporation can close its share-transfer books as of a given date, and give notice only to those persons who were record holders at the time the transfer books were closed.)

2. *Quorum.* Under most of the statutes, a majority of the shares entitled to vote is necessary for a quorum, unless the certificate of incorporation sets a higher or lower figure. A substantial majority of the statutes provide that the certificate cannot set a quorum lower than one-third of the shares entitled to vote. Most of the remaining statutes set no minimum.

3. *Voting.* (i) *Ordinary matters.* Under most statutes, the affirmative vote of a majority of the shares represented at a meeting is required for shareholder action on ordinary matters. Under some statutes, however, only the affirmative vote of a majority of those voting is required. If a statute requires the affirmative vote of a majority of those present, an abstention effectively counts as a negative vote.

Virtually all the statutes permit the certificate of incorporation to set a higher vote than would otherwise be required. Under some of the statutes, a certificate amendment that adds a provision requiring a higher-than-normal vote may be adopted only by the same vote as that required under the amendment.

(ii) *Fundamental changes.* A group of actions known as *fundamental changes,* which includes amendment of the amendment, merger, sale of substantially all assets, and dissolution, usually require approval by a majority or two-thirds of the outstanding voting shares, rather than a majority of those present or voting at the meeting.

(iii) *Election of directors.* The election of directors requires only a plurality vote—that is, those candidates who receive the highest number of votes are elected, up to the maximum number to be chosen at the election, even if they receive less than a majority of the votes present at the meeting. Cumulative voting for directors is required by some states, and is sometimes voluntarily adopted even when not required. The mechanics of cumulative voting are described in the material that follows this Note.

(iv) *Written consent.* The statutes typically permit the shareholders to act by written consent in lieu of a meeting. Most of the statutes permit shareholder action by written consent only if the consent is unanimous.

## SECTION 7.   CUMULATIVE VOTING

---

### NOTE ON CUMULATIVE VOTING

1.   *Straight Voting and Cumulative Voting.* In the normal case—what is sometimes called a "straight" voting regime—a shareholder can cast, for each candidate for election to the board, a number of votes equal to her number of shares. For example, assume that shareholder S owns 100 shares in Blue Corporation, that Blue's board consists of seven directors, and that all seven directorship positions are up for election. Under straight voting, S can cast a total of 700 votes, but cannot cast more than 100 votes for any one candidate.

In contrast, under a cumulative-voting regime a shareholder can cast for any single candidate, or for two or more candidates, as she chooses, a number of votes equal to the number of shares she holds times the number of directors to be elected. Thus in the Blue corporation example, under cumulative voting S can cast 700 votes for one candidate, or 350 votes for each of two candidates, or 300 shares for each of two candidates and 100 shares for a third candidate, and so forth.

Under straight voting, a minority shareholder or faction can never elect a director to the board over the opposition of the majority. For example, suppose that Blue corporation has 300 shares, 100 of which are held by S, and 200 of which are held by T. Recall that Blue has seven directors, all of which are up for election. Under straight voting, S can cast no more than 100 votes for any of her candidates. Since T can cast 200 votes for each of his seven candidates, T can elect all the directors.

In contrast, if cumulative voting is in effect, S can distribute her 700 votes among one or more candidates. Similarly, T can cast a total of 1400 votes, which he can distribute among one or more candidates.

Suppose that S casts 350 votes for each of two candidates. If T distributes his 1400 votes among seven candidates, each of his candidates will receive 200 votes. Accordingly, S will elect her two candidates, because they will each receive more votes (350) than any of T's candidates (200). T will elect five candidates.

Suppose that T casts 351 votes for each of two candidates. In that case, T can cast only 698 votes for his other five candidates. Since some of T's candidates will therefore receive less than 350 votes, S will still elect her two candidates to the board.

2. *Mathematics*. Randall S. Thomas & Catherine T. Dixon's Aranow & Einhorn, Proxy Contests for Corporate Control 10.04[B] (3d ed. 1998) discusses the mathematics of cumulative voting, as follows:

The mathematics of cumulative voting cam become a very involved subject which we will not undertake to discuss in all its aspects. There are two basic formulas, both of which are relatively simple. The first formula is used to determine the minimum number of shares needed to elect a particular number of directors:

$$X = \frac{(S \times N)}{D + 1} + 1$$

X = minimum number of shares needed
S = total number of shares that will be voted at meeting
N = number of directors desired to elect
D = total number of directors to be elected

For example, assume there exists a corporation with 1,000 shares outstanding and seven directors to be elected. A minority stockholders' group wishes to elect two directors. It is estimated that 800 shares will be voted at the meeting. Applying these figures to the formula, the resulting calculation is:

$$\frac{(800 \times 2)}{7 + 1} + 1 = 201$$

The stockholders' group knows that it must have ownership or control of at least 201 shares in order to elect two directors.

The second formula can be used to determine how many directors can be elected by a group controlling a particular number of shares:

$$N = \frac{(X) \times (D + 1)}{S}$$

N = number of directors that can be elected
X = number of shares controlled
D = total number of directors to be elected
S = total number of shares that will be voted at meeting

In the example above, assume that the stockholders' group knows it will control 201 shares. Applying the figures to this formula, the resulting calculation is:

$$\frac{201 \times 8}{800} = 2.01$$

Thus, cumulation will result in the election of two directors. There are several other formulas that can be applied to more complicated questions.

Jesse Fried points out that:

The standard formula for determining the minimum number of shares necessary to elect a particular number of directors yields an easily interpretable result only when the expression $(S \times N)/(D + 1)$ is a whole number.

Suppose, as in the Aranow and Einhorn example, that there is a corporation with seven directors to be elected and a minority group wishes to elect two directors. However, 803 shares (rather than the 800 shares used in their example) will be voted at the meeting. The standard formula indicates that the number of shares needed to elect two directors is now:

$$[(803 \times 2)/(7 + 1)] + 1 = 201.75$$

If there are only whole shares, does this mean that the minority group needs 201 to elect two directors, or 202 shares? The answer is, surprisingly, 201—if the standard formula does not yield a whole number you must round down to determine the number of whole shares needed.

If there are fractional shares, then the standard formula yields the wrong result.

A more useful formula for determining the minimum number of shares needed (X), is $X > (S \times N)/(D + 1)$

If there are fractional shares, then any fraction greater than the righthandside expression will allow you to elect N directors. If there are whole shares, then you round up to the next whole number.

3. *Mandatory Cumulative Voting.* The percentage of stock that minority shareholders must hold to elect at least one director under cumulative voting varies inversely with the number of directors to be elected. Accordingly, a 12% minority (for example) can elect one director if nine directors are to be elected, but cannot elect any directors if three directors are to be elected. This can give rise to various problems when cumulative voting is mandatory.

One problem is whether, when cumulative voting is mandatory, a corporation can have a classified board, in which the directors are divided into classes and each class serves for a term of years. Where a board is classified the minority must hold more stock, to elect a single director, than if a board of the same size was unclassified. In Wolfson v. Avery, 6 Ill.2d 78, 126 N.E.2d 701 (1955), the Illinois court held that an Illinois constitutional requirement of cumulative voting prohibited classified boards. The Illinois Constitution was later amended to eliminate this requirement. In Bohannan v. Corporation Commission, 82 Ariz. 299, 313 P.2d 379 (1957), the Arizona court held to the contrary. (Subsequently, the Arizona legislature enacted a statutory provision that permitted classification if a board had nine or more directors.)

Still another issue concerns the removal of directors: Cumulative voting could be undercut if a director who is elected by a minority under cumulative voting could then be removed by majority. Accordingly, some statutes provide that under cumulative voting, a director cannot be removed if the number of shares voting against her removal would be sufficient to elect her. See, e.g., Cal.Corp. Code § 303(a)(1).

## SECTION 8. LIMITED LIABILITY

### DEL. GEN. CORP. LAW § 102(b)(6)

[See Statutory Supplement]

### REV. MODEL BUS. CORP. ACT § 6.22(b)

[See Statutory Supplement]

### INTRODUCTORY NOTE ON LIMITED LIABILITY

It is commonly said that shareholders have limited liability for corporation obligations. Actually, shareholders ordinarily have *no* liability for corporate obligations: Under modern statutes, a shareholder's risk is limited to her *investment*—that is, the most a shareholder stands to lose, even if the corporation fails, is the amount she paid for her shares.

Nevertheless, the term "limited liability" is universally used to refer to the no-liability rule, and it will therefore be used in this book as well.

It is sometimes said that shareholders are not liable for corporate obligations because corporations are separate legal entities. In fact, however, the entity status of corporations has almost nothing to do with shareholder limited liability. For example, English law conferred entity status on corporations long before shareholders were afforded limited liability. Similarly, the Revised Uniform Partnership Act (RUPA) confers entity status on partnerships, but also provides that the partners are individually liable for all partnership obligations once the partnership's assets are exhausted. Accordingly, although cases in which liability is imposed on shareholders are commonly said to involve "disregard of the corporate entity" or "piercing the corporate veil," really they involve only a conclusion that in a given case there are good reasons why the normal statutory rule of limited liability should not be applied.

It should also be borne in mind that corporate managers, as well as corporate shareholders, are ordinarily not liable for corporate obligations. Shareholders are not liable for corporate obligations by statute. In contrast, managers are not liable for corporate obligations on straightforward agency principles: In the case of a contract that is made by an agent within his authority, the agent is not liable as long as she purported to act in that capacity and the identity of her principal was disclosed. Similarly, in the case of a tort by a corporate employee, a manager will normally not be *vicariously* liable, even if the employee was a subordinate of the manager. (However, a corporate manager may be liable if he personally commits or directs the commission of the tortious action. The liability of corporate managers is considered in more detail in the Note on Civil Liabilities of Directors and Officers in Chapter 8, Section 1.)

--------

## Fletcher v. Atex, Inc.

United States Court of Appeals, Second Circuit, 1995.
68 F.3d 1451.

■ Before: KEARSE,, CALABRESI, and CABRANES, CIRCUIT JUDGES.

■ JOSE A. CABRANES, CIRCUIT JUDGE:

This is a consolidated appeal from a final judgment of the United States District Court for the Southern District of New York (Morris E. Lasker, Judge ), granting defendant-appellee Eastman Kodak Company's motion for summary judgment and dismissing all claims against it in two actions, Fletcher v. Atex, Inc., 92 Civ. 8758 and Hermanson v. 805 Middlesex Corp., Inc., 94 Civ. 1272. Fletcher v. Atex, Inc., 861 F.Supp. 242 (S.D.N.Y.1994). The plaintiffs-appellants filed suit against Atex, Inc. ("Atex") and its parent, Eastman Kodak Company ("Kodak"), to recover for repetitive stress injuries that they claim were caused by their use of computer keyboards manufactured by Atex.

Plaintiffs-appellants argue that the district court erred in granting summary judgment in favor of Kodak on the ground that Kodak could be held liable for the plaintiffs' alleged injuries. They contend that summary judgment was inappropriate because genuine issues of material fact existed regarding Kodak's liability as a defendant. . . .

### I.   BACKGROUND

The Fletcher and Hermanson plaintiffs filed their respective complaints on December 4, 1992, and February 25, 1994, seeking recovery from Atex and Kodak, among others, for repetitive stress injuries that they claim were caused by their use of Atex computer keyboards. From 1981 until December 1992, Atex was a wholly-owned subsidiary of Kodak. In 1987, Atex's name was changed to Electronic Pre–Press Systems, Inc., ("EPPS"), but its name was changed back to Atex in 1990. In December 1992, Atex sold substantially all of its assets to an independent third party and again changed its name to 805 Middlesex Corp., which holds the proceeds from the sale. Kodak continues to be the sole shareholder of 805 Middlesex Corp.

After extensive discovery, Kodak moved for summary judgment in Fletcher on April 21, 1994, and in Hermanson on April 28, 1994. The plaintiffs opposed Kodak's motion, arguing that genuine issues of material fact existed as to Kodak's liability under any number of theories, including (1) that Atex was merely Kodak's alter ego or instrumentality; (2) that Atex was Kodak's agent in the manufacture and marketing of the keyboards; (3) that Kodak was the "apparent manufacturer" of the Atex keyboards; and (4) that Kodak acted in tortious concert with Atex in manufacturing and marketing the allegedly defective keyboards.

In support of their first theory, the plaintiffs argued that Kodak "dominated and controlled" Atex by maintaining significant overlap between the boards of directors of the two companies, "siphoning" off funds from Atex through use of a cash management system, requiring Kodak's approval for major expenditures, stock sales, and real estate acquisitions, participating in negotiations involving the sale of Atex to a third party, and including references to Atex as a "division" of Kodak and to the "merger" between Atex and Kodak in Atex's promotional literature and Kodak's Annual Report....

On August 17, 1994, the district court rejected each of the plaintiffs' theories of Kodak's liability and granted Kodak's motion for summary judgment in both actions. In its opinion, the court referred to, but did not rely upon, an identical suit filed against Atex and Kodak in New York state court, King v. Eastman Kodak Co., No. 23439/92 (N.Y.Sup.Ct. June 9, 1994), in which Kodak's motion for summary judgment was granted on similar grounds. Fletcher, 861 F.Supp. at 243.

.... [T]he district court found that Kodak and Atex observed all corporate formalities and maintained separate corporate existences. It held that Atex's participation in Kodak's cash management system and Kodak's control over Atex's major expenditures and asset sales were insufficient to raise an issue of material fact regarding Kodak's liability under an alter ego theory. Id. at 244–45.... This appeal followed.

## II.  DISCUSSION ...

The plaintiffs claim that the district court erred in granting Kodak's motion for summary judgment on their alter ego theory of liability. The plaintiffs ... argue that ... genuine issues of material fact remain that preclude a grant of summary judgment in favor of Kodak.

The district court correctly noted that "[u]nder New York choice of law principles, '[t]he law of the state of incorporation determines when the corporate form will be disregarded and liability will be imposed on shareholders.' " Fletcher, 861 F.Supp. at 244 (quoting Kalb, Voorhis & Co. v. American Fin. Corp., 8 F.3d 130, 132 (2d Cir.1993)). Because Atex was a Delaware corporation, Delaware law determines whether the corporate veil can be pierced in this instance.

Delaware law permits a court to pierce the corporate veil of a company "where there is fraud or where [it] is in fact a mere instrumentality or alter ego of its owner." Geyer v. Ingersoll Publications Co., 621 A.2d 784, 793 (Del.Ch.1992). Although the Delaware

Supreme Court has never explicitly adopted an alter ego theory of parent liability for its subsidiaries, lower Delaware courts have applied the doctrine on several occasions, as has the United States District Court for the District of Delaware. See Geyer, 621 A.2d at 793; Mabon, Nugent & Co. v. Texas Am. Energy Corp., No. CIV.A. 8578, 1990 WL 44267, at *5, (Del.Ch. Apr.12, 1990); Harper v. Delaware Valley Broadcasters, Inc., 743 F.Supp. 1076, 1085 (D.Del.1990), aff'd, 932 F.2d 959 (3d Cir.1991). Thus, under an alter ego theory, there is no requirement of a showing of fraud. Id. at 1085. To prevail on an alter ego claim under Delaware law, a plaintiff must show (1) that the parent and the subsidiary "operated as a single economic entity" and (2) that an "overall element of injustice or unfairness ... [is] present." Id. (internal quotation marks omitted); see also Mabon, 1990 WL 44267, at *5; Harco Nat'l Ins. Co. v. Green Farms, Inc., No. CIV.A. 1331, 1989 WL 110537, at *5, (Del.Ch. Sept.19, 1989).

In the New York state action of King v. Eastman, the court granted Kodak's motion for summary judgment, relying on an erroneous interpretation of Delaware's alter ego doctrine. The court noted that although the plaintiffs had raised "ample questions of fact regarding the first element of the piercing theory—domination," they made "no showing that Kodak used whatever dominance it had over Atex to perpetrate a fraud or other wrong that proximately cause[d] injury to them." This was an error; under Delaware law, the alter ego theory of liability does not require any showing of fraud....

b.   Summary Judgment on the Alter Ego Theory

To prevail on an alter ego theory of liability, a plaintiff must show that the two corporations " 'operated as a single economic entity such that it would be inequitable ... to uphold a legal distinction between them.' " Harper, 743 F.Supp. at 1085 (quoting Mabon, 1990 WL 44267, at * 5). Among the factors to be considered in determining whether a subsidiary and parent operate as a "single economic entity" are:

> "[W]hether the corporation was adequately capitalized for the corporate undertaking; whether the corporation was solvent; whether dividends were paid, corporate records kept, officers and directors functioned properly, and other corporate formalities were observed; whether the dominant shareholder siphoned corporate funds; and whether, in general, the corporation simply functioned as a facade for the dominant shareholder."

Harco, 1989 WL 110537, at *4 (quoting United States v. Golden Acres, Inc., 702 F.Supp. 1097, 1104 (D.Del.1988)). As noted above, a showing of fraud or wrongdoing is not necessary under an alter ego theory, but the plaintiff must demonstrate an overall element of injustice or unfairness. Harco, 1989 WL 110537, at *5.

A plaintiff seeking to persuade a Delaware court to disregard the corporate structure faces "a difficult task." Harco, 1989 WL 110537, at *4. Courts have made it clear that "[t]he legal entity of a corporation will not be disturbed until sufficient reason appears." Id. Although the question of domination is generally one of fact, courts have granted motions to dismiss as well as motions for summary judgment in favor of defendant parent companies where there has been a lack of sufficient evidence to place the alter ego issue in dispute. See, e.g., Akzona, Inc. v. Du Pont, 607 F.Supp. 227, 237 (D.Del.1984) (rejecting plaintiffs' alter ego theory of liability on a motion to dismiss); Nelson v. International Paint Co., 734 F.2d 1084, 1092 (5th Cir.1984) ("[I]n the lack of sufficient evidence to place the alter ego issue in dispute, a corporate defendant may be entitled to summary judgment."); see also Japan Petroleum Co. (Nigeria) v. Ashland Oil Inc., 456 F.Supp. 831, 838, 846 (D.Del.1978) (finding that subsidiary was not instrumentality of parent on a motion for summary judgment).

Kodak has shown that Atex followed corporate formalities, and the plaintiffs have offered no evidence to the contrary. Significantly, the plaintiffs have not challenged Kodak's assertions that Atex's board of directors held regular meetings, that minutes from those meetings were routinely prepared and maintained in corporate minute books, that appropriate financial records and other files were maintained by Atex, that Atex filed its own tax returns and paid its own taxes, and that Atex had its own employees and management executives who were responsible for the corporation's day-to-day business. The plaintiffs' primary arguments regarding domination concern (1) the defendant's use of a cash management system; (2) Kodak's exertion of control over Atex's major expenditures, stock sales, and the sale of Atex's assets to a third party; (3) Kodak's "dominating presence" on Atex's board of directors; (4) descriptions of the relationship between Atex and Kodak in the corporations' advertising, promotional literature, and annual reports; and (5) Atex's assignment of one of its former officer's mortgage to Kodak in order to close Atex's asset-purchase agreement with a third party. The plaintiffs argue that each of these raises a genuine issue of material fact about Kodak's domination of Atex, and that the district court therefore erred in granting summary judgment to Kodak on the plaintiffs' alter ego theory. We find that the district court correctly held that, in light of the undisputed factors of independence cited by Kodak, "the elements identified by the plaintiffs ... [were] insufficient as a matter of law to establish the degree of domination necessary to disregard Atex's corporate identity." Fletcher, 861 F.Supp. at 245.

First, the district court correctly held that "Atex's participation in Kodak's cash management system is consistent with sound business practice and does not show undue domination or control." Id. at 244. The parties do not dispute the mechanics of Kodak's cash management system. Essentially, all of Kodak's domestic subsidiaries participate in the system and maintain zero-balance bank accounts. All funds transferred from the subsidiary accounts are recorded as credits to the subsidiary, and when a subsidiary is in need of funds, a transfer is made. At all times, a strict accounting is kept of each subsidiary's funds.

Courts have generally declined to find alter ego liability based on a parent corporation's use of a cash management system. See, e.g., In re Acushnet River & New Bedford Harbor Proceedings, 675 F.Supp. 22, 34 (D.Mass.1987) (Without "considerably more," "a centralized cash management system ... where the accounting records always reflect the indebtedness of one entity to another, is not the equivalent of intermingling funds" and is insufficient to justify disregarding the corporate form.); United States v. Bliss, 108 F.R.D. 127, 132 (E.D.Mo. 1985) (cash management system indicative of the "usual parent-subsidiary relationship"); Japan Petrol., 456 F.Supp. at 846 (finding segregation of subsidiary's accounts within parent's cash management system to be "a function of administrative convenience and economy, rather than a manifestation of control"). The plaintiffs offer no facts to support their speculation that Kodak's centralized cash management system was actually a "complete commingling" of funds or a means by which Kodak sought to "siphon[ ] all of Atex's revenues into its own account."

Second, the district court correctly concluded that it could find no domination based on the plaintiffs' evidence that Kodak's approval was required for Atex's real estate leases, major capital expenditures, negotiations for a sale of minority stock ownership to IBM, or the fact that Kodak played a significant role in the ultimate sale of Atex's assets to a third party. Again, the parties do not dispute that Kodak required Atex to seek its approval and/or participation for the above transactions. However, this evidence, viewed in the light most favorable to the plaintiffs, does not raise an issue of material fact about whether the two corporations constituted "a single economic entity." Indeed, this type of conduct is typical of a majority shareholder or parent corporation. See Phoenix Canada Oil Co. v. Texaco, 842 F.2d 1466, 1476 (3d Cir.1988) (declining to pierce the corporate veil where subsidiary required to secure approval from parent for "large investments and acquisitions or disposals of major assets"), cert. denied, 488 U.S. 908, 109 S.Ct. 259, 102 L.Ed.2d 247 (1988); *Akzona*, 607 F.Supp. at 237 (same, where parent approval required for expenditures exceeding $850,000); Japan Petrol., 456 F.Supp. at 843 (finding no parent liability where parent approval required for expenditures exceeding $250,000). In *Akzona*, the Delaware district court noted that a parent's "general executive responsibilities" for its subsidiary's operations included approval over major policy decisions and guaranteeing bank loans, and that that type of oversight was insufficient to demonstrate domination and control. *Akzona*, 607 F.Supp. at 238 (internal quotation marks omitted). Similarly, the district court in the instant case properly found that the presence of Kodak employees at periodic meetings with Atex's chief financial officer and comptroller to be "entirely appropriate." Fletcher, 861 F.Supp. at 245 (citing *Akzona*, 607 F.Supp. at 238); see *Acushnet*, 675 F.Supp. at 34 ("The quarterly and annual reports made [to the parent] do not represent an untoward intrusion by the owner into the corporate enterprise. The right of shareholders to remain informed is similarly recognized in many public and closely held corporations.").

The plaintiffs' third argument, that Kodak dominated the Atex board of directors, also fails. Although a number of Kodak employees have sat on the Atex board, it is undisputed that between 1981 and 1988, only one director of Atex was also a director of Kodak. Between 1989 and 1992, Atex and Kodak had no directors in common. Parents and subsidiaries frequently have overlapping boards of directors while maintaining separate business operations. In Japan Petroleum, the Delaware district court held that the fact that a parent and a subsidiary have common officers and directors does not necessarily demonstrate that the parent corporation dominates the activities of the subsidiary. 456 F.Supp. at 841; see Scott–Douglas Corp. v. Greyhound Corp., 304 A.2d 309, 314 (Del.Super.Ct.1973) (same). Since the overlap is negligible here, we find this evidence to be entirely insufficient to raise a question of fact on the issue of domination.

Fourth, the district court properly rejected the plaintiffs' argument that the descriptions of the relationship between Atex and Kodak and the presence of the Kodak logo in Atex's promotional literature justify piercing the corporate veil. Fletcher, 861 F.Supp. at 245. The plaintiffs point to several statements in both Kodak's and Atex's literature to evidence Kodak's domination of its subsidiary. For example, plaintiffs refer to (1) a promotional pamphlet produced by EPPS (a/k/a Atex) describing Atex as a business unit of EPPS and noting that EPPS was an "agent" of Kodak; (2) a document produced by Atex entitled "An Introduction to Atex Systems," which describes a "merger" between Kodak and Atex; (3) a statement in Kodak's 1985 and 1986 annual reports describing Atex as a "recent acquisition[ ]" and a "subsidiar[y] ... combined in a new division"; and (4) a statement in an Atex/EPPS document, "Setting Up TPE 6000 on the Sun 3 Workstation," describing Atex as "an unincorporated division of Electronic Pre–Press Systems, Inc., a Kodak company." They also refer generally to the fact that Atex's paperwork and packaging materials frequently displayed the Kodak logo.

It is clear from the record that Atex never merged with Kodak or operated as a Kodak division. The plaintiffs offer no evidence to the contrary, apart from these statements in Atex and Kodak documents that they claim are indicative of the true relationship between the two companies. Viewed in the light most favorable to the plaintiffs, these statements and the use of the Kodak logo are not evidence that the two companies operated as a "single economic entity." See Coleman v. Corning Glass Works, 619 F.Supp. 950, 956 (W.D.N.Y.1985) (upholding corporate form despite "loose language" in annual report about "merger" and parent's reference to subsidiary as a "division"), aff'd, 818 F.2d 874 (1987); Japan Petrol., 456 F.Supp. at 846 (noting that representations made by parent in its annual reports that subsidiary serves as an agent "may result from public relations motives or an attempt at simplification"); American Trading & Prod. Corp. v. Fischbach & Moore, Inc., 311 F.Supp. 412, 416 (N.D.Ill.1970) ("boastful" advertising and consideration of subsidiaries as "family" do not prove that corporate identities were ignored).

Fifth, the plaintiffs contend that Atex's assignment of its former CEO's mortgage to Kodak in order to close the sale of Atex's assets to a third party is evidence of Kodak's domination of Atex. We reject this argument as well. The evidence is undisputed that Kodak paid Atex the book value of the note and entered into a formal repayment agreement with the former CEO. Formal contracts were executed, and the two companies observed all corporate formalities.

Finally, even if the plaintiffs did raise a factual question about Kodak's domination of Atex, summary judgment would still be appropriate because the plaintiffs offer no evidence on the second prong of the alter ego analysis. The plaintiffs have failed to present evidence of an "overall element of injustice or unfairness" that would result from respecting the two companies' corporate separateness. See Harper, 743 F.Supp. at 1085 (holding that plaintiff cannot prevail on alter ego theory "because he has failed to allege any unfairness or injustice which would justify the court in disregarding the [companies'] separate legal existences"). In the instant case, the plaintiffs offer nothing more than the bare assertion that Kodak "exploited" Atex "to generate profits but not to safeguard safety." There is no indication that Kodak sought to defraud creditors and consumers or to siphon funds from its subsidiary. The plaintiffs' conclusory assertions, without more, are not evidence, see Quinn, 613 F.2d at 445, and are completely inadequate to support a finding that it would be unjust to respect Atex's corporate form.

For all of the foregoing reasons, the district court's order entering summary judgment on the plaintiffs' alter ego theory of liability is affirmed. . . .

[The court also granted summary judgment for Kodak on the plaintiffs' other theories.]

---

# Walkovszky v. Carlton

Court of Appeals of New York, 1966.
18 N.Y.2d 414, 276 N.Y.S.2d 585, 223 N.E.2d 6.

■ FULD, JUDGE. This case involves what appears to be a rather common practice in the taxicab industry of vesting the ownership of a taxi fleet in many corporations, each owning only one or two cabs.

The complaint alleges that the plaintiff was severely injured four years ago in New York City when he was run down by a taxicab owned by the defendant Seon Cab Corporation and negligently operated at the time by the defendant Marchese. The individual defendant, Carlton, is claimed to be a stockholder of 10 corporations, including Seon, each of which has but two cabs registered in its name, and it is implied that only the minimum automobile liability insurance required by law (in the amount of $10,000) is carried on any one cab. Although seemingly independent of one another, these corporations are alleged to be "operated . . . as a single entity, unit and enterprise" with regard to financing, supplies, repairs, employees and garaging, and all are named as defendants.[1] The plaintiff asserts that he is also entitled to hold their stockholders personally liable for the damages sought because the multiple corporate structure constitutes an unlawful attempt "to defraud members of the general public" who might be injured by the cabs.

The defendant Carlton has moved, pursuant to CPLR 3211(a)7, to dismiss the complaint on the ground that as to him it "fails to state a cause of action". The court at Special Term granted the motion but the Appellate Division, by a divided vote, reversed, holding that a valid cause of action was sufficiently stated. The defendant Carlton appeals to us, from the nonfinal order, by leave of the Appellate Division on a certified question.

The law permits the incorporation of a business for the very purpose of enabling its proprietors to escape personal liability (see, e.g., Bartle v. Home Owners Co-op., 309 N.Y. 103, 106, 127 N.E.2d 832, 833) but, manifestly, the privilege is not without its limits. Broadly speaking, the courts will disregard the corporate form, or, to use accepted terminology, "pierce the corporate veil", whenever necessary "to prevent fraud or to achieve equity". (International Aircraft Trading Co. v. Manufacturers Trust Co., 297 N.Y. 285, 292, 79 N.E.2d 249, 252.) In determining whether liability should be extended to reach assets beyond those belonging to the corporation, we are guided, as Judge Cardozo noted, by "general rules of agency". (Berkey v. Third Ave. Ry. Co., 244 N.Y. 84, 95, 155 N.E. 58, 61, 50 A.L.R. 599.) In other words, whenever anyone uses control of the corporation to further his own rather than the corporation's business, he will be liable for the corporation's acts "upon the principle of *respondeat superior* applicable even where the agent is a natural person".... Such liability, moreover, extends not only to the corporation's commercial dealings ... but to its negligent acts as well....

In [Mangan v. Terminal Transp. System, 247 App.Div. 853, 286 N.Y.S. 666, mot. for lv. to app. den. 286 N.Y.S. 666,] the plaintiff was injured as a result of the negligent operation of a cab owned and operated by one of four corporations affiliated with the defendant Terminal. Although the defendant was not a stockholder of any of the operating companies, both the defendant and the operating companies were owned, for the most part, by the same parties. The defendant's name (Terminal) was conspicuously displayed on the sides of all of the taxis used in the enterprise and, in point of fact, the defendant actually serviced, inspected, repaired and dispatched them. These facts were deemed to provide sufficient cause for piercing the corporate veil of the operating company—the nominal owner of the cab which injured the plaintiff—and holding the defendant liable. The operating companies were simply instrumentalities for carrying on the business of the defendant without imposing upon it financial and other liabilities incident to the actual ownership and operation of the cabs....

---

1.  The corporate owner of a garage is also included as a defendant.

In the case before us, the plaintiff has explicitly alleged that none of the corporations "had a separate existence of their own" and, as indicated above, all are named as defendants. However, it is one thing to assert that a corporation is a fragment of a larger corporate combine which actually conducts the business. (See Berle, The Theory of Enterprise Entity, 47 Col.L.Rev. 343, 348–350.) It is quite another to claim that the corporation is a "dummy" for its individual stockholders who are in reality carrying on the business in their personal capacities for purely personal rather than corporate ends. (See African Metals Corp. v. Bullowa, 288 N.Y. 78, 85, 41 N.E.2d 466, 469.) Either circumstance would justify treating the corporation as an agent and piercing the corporate veil to reach the principal but a different result would follow in each case. In the first, only a larger *corporate* entity would be held financially responsible ... while, in the other, the stockholder would be personally liable.... Either the stockholder is conducting the business in his individual capacity or he is not. If he is, he will be liable; if he is not, then it does not matter—insofar as his personal liability is concerned—that the enterprise is actually being carried on by a larger "enterprise entity". (See Berle, The Theory of Enterprise Entity, 47 Col.L.Rev. 343.)

At this stage in the present litigation, we are concerned only with the pleadings and, since CPLR 3014 permits causes of action to be stated "alternatively or hypothetically", it is possible for the plaintiff to allege both theories as the basis for his demand for judgment. In ascertaining whether he has done so, we must consider the entire pleading, educing therefrom " 'whatever can be imputed from its statements by fair and reasonable intendment.' " (Condon v. Associated Hosp. Serv., 287 N.Y. 411, 414, 40 N.E.2d 230, 231....) Reading the complaint in this case most favorably and liberally, we do not believe that there can be gathered from its averments the allegations required to spell out a valid cause of action against the defendant Carlton.

The individual defendant is charged with having "organized, managed, dominated and controlled" a fragmented corporate entity but there are no allegations that he was conducting business in his individual capacity. Had the taxicab fleet been owned by a single corporation, it would be readily apparent that the plaintiff would face formidable barriers in attempting to establish personal liability on the part of the corporation's stockholders. The fact that the fleet ownership has been deliberately split up among many corporations does not ease the plaintiff's burden in that respect. The corporate form may not be disregarded merely because the assets of the corporation, together with the mandatory insurance coverage of the vehicle which struck the plaintiff, are insufficient to assure him the recovery sought. If Carlton were to be held individually liable on those facts alone, the decision would apply equally to the thousands of cabs which are owned by their individual drivers who conduct their businesses through corporations organized pursuant to section 401 of the Business Corporation Law, Consol.Laws, c. 4 and carry the minimum insurance required by subdivision 1 (par. [a]) of section 370 of the Vehicle and Traffic Law,

Consol.Laws, c. 71. These taxi owner-operators are entitled to form such corporations (cf. Elenkrieg v. Siebrecht, 238 N.Y. 254, 144 N.E. 519, 34 A.L.R. 592), and we agree with the court at Special Term that, if the insurance coverage required by statute "is inadequate for the protection of the public, the remedy lies not with the courts but with the Legislature." It may very well be sound policy to require that certain corporations must take out liability insurance which will afford adequate compensation to their potential tort victims. However, the responsibility for imposing conditions on the privilege of incorporation has been committed by the Constitution to the Legislature (N.Y. Const., art. X, § 1) and it may not be fairly implied, from any statute, that the Legislature intended, without the slightest discussion or debate, to require of taxi corporations that they carry automobile liability insurance over and above that mandated by the Vehicle and Traffic Law.

This is not to say that it is impossible for the plaintiff to state a valid cause of action against the defendant Carlton. However, the simple fact is that the plaintiff has just not done so here. While the complaint alleges that the separate corporations were undercapitalized and that their assets have been intermingled, it is barren of any "sufficiently particular[ized] statements" (CPLR 3013; see 3 Weinstein–Korn–Miller, N.Y.Civ.Prac., par. 3013.01 et seq., pp. 30–142 et seq.) that the defendant Carlton and his associates are actually doing business in their individual capacities, shuttling their personal funds in and out of the corporations "without regard to formality and to suit their immediate convenience." (Weisser v. Mursam Shoe Corp., 2 Cir., 127 F.2d 344, 345, 145 A.L.R. 467, supra.) Such a "perversion of the privilege to do business in a corporate form" (Berkey v. Third Ave. Ry. Co., 244 N.Y. 84, 95, 155 N.E. 58, 61, 50 A.L.R. 599, supra) would justify imposing personal liability on the individual stockholders. (See African Metals Corp. v. Bullowa, 288 N.Y. 78, 41 N.E.2d 466, supra.) Nothing of the sort has in fact been charged, and it cannot reasonably or logically be inferred from the happenstance that the business of Seon Cab Corporation may actually be carried on by a larger corporate entity composed of many corporations which, under general principles of agency, would be liable to each other's creditors in contract and in tort.[2]

In point of fact, the principle relied upon in the complaint to sustain the imposition of personal liability is not agency but fraud. Such a cause of action cannot withstand analysis. If it is not fraudulent for the owner-operator of a single cab corporation to take out only the minimum required liability insurance, the enterprise does not become either illicit or fraudulent merely because it consists of many such

2. In his affidavit in opposition to the motion to dismiss, the plaintiff's counsel claimed that corporate assets had been "milked out" of, and "siphoned off" from the enterprise. Quite apart from the fact that these allegations are far too vague and conclusory, the charge is premature. If the plain-tiff succeeds in his action and becomes a judgment creditor of the corporation, he may then sue and attempt to hold the individual defendants accountable for any dividends and property that were wrongfully distributed (Business Corporation Law, §§ 510, 719, 720).

corporations. The plaintiff's injuries are the same regardless of whether the cab which strikes him is owned by a single corporation or part of a fleet with ownership fragmented among many corporations. Whatever rights he may be able to assert against parties other than the registered owner of the vehicle come into being not because he has been defrauded but because, under the principle of *respondeat superior,* he is entitled to hold the whole enterprise responsible for the acts of its agents.

In sum, then, the complaint falls short of adequately stating a cause of action against the defendant Carlton in his individual capacity.

The order of the Appellate Division should be reversed, with costs in this court and in the Appellate Division, the certified question answered in the negative and the order of the Supreme Court, Richmond County, reinstated, with leave to serve an amended complaint.

[The dissenting opinion of Judge Keating is omitted.]

■ Desmond, C.J., and Van Voorhis, Burke and Scileppi, JJ., concur with Fuld, J.

■ Keating, J., dissents and votes to affirm in an opinion in which Bergan, J., concurs.

Order reversed, etc.

---

## NOTE ON FURTHER PROCEEDINGS IN WALKOVSZKY v. CARLTON

Following the decision in *Walkovszky,* the plaintiff amended his complaint. The Appellate Division held that "the amended complaint sufficiently alleges a cause of action against appellant, i.e., that he and the other individual defendants were conducting the business of the taxicab fleet in their individual capacities." Walkovszky v. Carlton, 29 A.D.2d 763, 287 N.Y.S.2d 546 (1968). That decision was affirmed by the Court of Appeals, 23 N.Y.2d 714, 296 N.Y.S.2d 362, 244 N.E.2d 55 (1968), noting that the amended complaint "now meets the pleading requirements set forth in [our prior] opinion and states a valid cause of action." Neither opinion stated the particulars in which the amended complaint differed from the original.

---

## Minton v. Cavaney
Supreme Court of California, 1961.
56 Cal.2d 576, 15 Cal.Rptr. 641, 364 P.2d 473.

■ Traynor, Justice. The Seminole Hot Springs Corporation, hereinafter referred to as Seminole, was duly incorporated in California on March 8, 1954. It conducted a public swimming pool that it leased from its owner. On June 24, 1954 plaintiffs' daughter drowned in the pool, and plaintiffs recovered a judgment for $10,000 against Seminole for her wrongful death. The judgment remains unsatisfied.

On January 30, 1957, plaintiffs brought the present action to hold defendant Cavaney personally liable for the judgment against Seminole. Cavaney died on May 28, 1958 and his widow, the executrix of his estate, was substituted as defendant. The trial court entered judgment for plaintiffs for $10,000. Defendant appeals.

Plaintiffs introduced evidence that Cavaney was a director and secretary and treasurer of Seminole and that on November 15, 1954, about five months after the drowning, Cavaney as secretary of Seminole and Edwin A. Kraft as president of Seminole applied for permission to issue three shares of Seminole stock, one share to be issued to Kraft, another to F.J. Wettrick and the third to Cavaney. The commissioner of corporations refused permission to issue these shares unless additional information was furnished. The application was then abandoned and no shares were ever issued. There was also evidence that for a time Seminole used Cavaney's office to keep records and to receive mail. Before his death Cavaney answered certain interrogatories. He was asked if Seminole "ever had any assets?" He stated that "insofar as my own personal knowledge and belief is concerned said corporation did not have any assets." Cavaney also stated in the return to an attempted execution that "[I]nsofar as I know, this corporation had no assets of any kind or character. The corporation was duly organized but never functioned as a corporation."

Defendant introduced evidence that Cavaney was an attorney at law, that he was approached by Kraft and Wettrick to form Seminole, and that he was the attorney for Seminole. Plaintiffs introduced Cavaney's answer to several interrogatories that he held the post of secretary and treasurer and director in a temporary capacity and as an accommodation to his client.

Defendant contends that the evidence does not support the court's determination that Cavaney is personally liable for Seminole's debts and that the "alter ego" doctrine is inapplicable because plaintiffs failed to show that there was " '(1) . . . such unity of interest and ownership that the separate personalities of the corporation and the individual no longer exist and (2) that, if the acts are treated as those of the corporation alone, an inequitable result will follow.' " Riddle v. Leuschner, 51 Cal.2d 574, 580, 335 P.2d 107, 110; Automotriz Del Golfo De California S.A. De C.V. v. Resnick, 47 Cal.2d 792, 796, 306 P.2d 1, 63 A.L.R.2d 1042; Minifie v. Rowley, 187 Cal. 481, 487, 202 P. 673.

The figurative terminology "alter ego" and "disregard of the corporate entity" is generally used to refer to the various situations that are an abuse of the corporate privilege. . . . The equitable owners of a corporation, for example, are personally liable when they treat the assets of the corporation as their own and add or withdraw capital from the corporation at will . . .; when they hold themselves out as being personally liable for the debts of the corporation . . .; or when they provide inadequate capitalization and actively participate in the conduct of corporate affairs. . . .

In the instant case the evidence is undisputed that there was no attempt to provide adequate capitalization. Seminole never had any substantial assets. It leased the pool that it operated, and the lease was forfeited for failure to pay the rent. Its capital was " 'trifling compared with the business to be done and the risks of loss . . .' " Automotriz Del Golfo De California S.A. De C.V. v. Resnick, supra, 47 Cal.2d 792, 797, 306 P.2d 1, 4. The evidence is also undisputed that Cavaney was not only the secretary and treasurer of the corporation but was also a director. The evidence that Cavaney was to receive one-third of the shares to be issued supports an inference that he was an equitable owner (see Riddle v. Leuschner, supra, 51 Cal.2d 574, 580, 335 P.2d 107), and the evidence that for a time the records of the corporation were kept in Cavaney's office supports an inference that he actively participated in the conduct of the business. The trial court was not required to believe his statement that he was only a "temporary" director and officer "for accommodation." In any event it merely raised a conflict in the evidence that was resolved adversely to defendant. Moreover, section 800 of the Corporations Code provides that " . . . the business and affairs of every corporation shall be controlled by a board of not less than three directors." Defendant does not claim that Cavaney was a director with specialized duties (see 5 U.Chi.L.Rev. 668). It is immaterial whether or not he accepted the office of director as an "accommodation" with the understanding that he would not exercise any of the duties of a director. A person may not in this manner divorce the responsibilities of a director from the statutory duties and powers of that office. . . .

In this action to hold defendant personally liable upon the judgment against Seminole plaintiffs did not allege or present any evidence on the issue of Seminole's negligence or on the amount of damages sustained by plaintiffs. They relied solely on the judgment against Seminole. Defendant correctly contends that Cavaney or his estate cannot be held liable for the debts of Seminole without an opportunity to relitigate these issues. . . . Cavaney was not a party to the action against the corporation, and the judgment in that action is therefore not binding upon him unless he controlled the litigation leading to the judgment. . . .

The judgment is reversed.

■ Gibson, C.J., and Peters, White and Dooling, JJ., concur.

■ [The opinion of Justice Schauer, concurring and dissenting, is omitted. Justice McComb concurred without opinion.]

———

**ARNOLD v. BROWNE,** 27 Cal.App.3d 386, 396, 103 Cal.Rptr. 775, 783 (1972). "Evidence of inadequate capitalization is, at best, merely a factor to be considered by the trial court in deciding whether or not to pierce the corporate veil (Harris v. Curtis, 8 Cal.App.3d 837, 841, 87 Cal.Rptr. 614). To be sure, it is an important factor, but no case has been cited, nor have any been found, where it has been held that this factor alone *requires* invoking the equitable doctrine prayed for in the instant case."

--------

   **SLOTTOW v. FIDELITY FEDERAL BANK**, 10 F.3d 1355 (9th Cir.1993). "[T]he plaintiffs ... had an excellent argument under an alter ego theory for piercing the corporate veil. To begin with, [the] initial capitalization of $500,000 was woefully inadequate for a corporation that handled trust agreements of the magnitude involved here. The investors claimed damages [against the corporation] in the range of $10,000,000; the case settled for nearly half that. Under California law, inadequate capitalization of a subsidiary may alone be a basis for holding the parent corporation liable for acts of the subsidiary. See, e.g., Nilsson, Robbins, Dalgarn, Berliner, Carson & Wurst v. Louisiana Hydrolec, 854 F.2d 1538, 1544 (9th Cir.1988)...."

--------

   **RADASZEWSKI v. TELECOM CORP.**, 981 F.2d 305 (8th Cir. 1992). "... In order to pierce the corporate veil, a plaintiff must show, among other things, that the defendant's control of a subsidiary has

> been used by the defendant to commit fraud or wrong, to perpetrate the violation of a statutory or other positive legal duty, or dishonest and unjust act in contravention of plaintiff's legal rights....

Collet [v. American National Stores, Inc., 708 S.W.2d 273, 284 Mo.App. 1986]. To satisfy this ... element, plaintiff cites no direct evidence of improper motivation or violation of law on Telecom's part. He argues, instead, that Contrux was undercapitalized.

   "... [T]he creation of an undercapitalized subsidiary justifies an inference that the parent is either deliberately or recklessly creating a business that will not be able to pay its bills or satisfy judgments against it. This point has been made clear by the Supreme Court of Missouri....

   "Here, the District Court held, and we assume, that Contrux [the subsidiary] was undercapitalized in the accounting sense. Most of the money contributed to its operation by Telecom [the parent] was in the form of loans, not equity, and, when Contrux first went into business, Telecom did not pay for all of the stock that was issued to it.... Telecom in effect concedes that Contrux's balance sheet was anemic, and that, from the point of view of generally accepted accounting principles, Contrux was inadequately capitalized. Telecom says, however, that this doesn't matter, because Contrux had $11,000,000 worth of liability insurance available to pay judgments like the one that

Radaszewski hopes to obtain. No one can say, therefore, the argument runs, that Telecom was improperly motivated in setting up Contrux, in the sense of either knowingly or recklessly establishing it without the ability to pay tort judgments.

"In fact, Contrux did have $1,000,000 in basic liability coverage, plus $10,000,000 in excess coverage. This coverage was bound on March 1, 1984, about five and one-half months before the accident involving Radaszewski. Unhappily, Contrux's insurance carrier became insolvent two years after the accident and is now in receivership. . . .

"The District Court rejected this argument. Undercapitalization is undercapitalization, it reasoned, regardless of insurance. The Court said:

> The federal regulation does not speak to what constitutes a properly capitalized motor carrier company. Rather, the regulation speaks to what constitutes an appropriate level of *financial responsibility.*

. . . This distinction escapes us. The whole purpose of asking whether a subsidiary is "properly capitalized," is precisely to determine its "financial responsibility." If the subsidiary is financially responsible, whether by means of insurance or otherwise, the policy behind . . . the *Collet* test is met. Insurance meets this policy just as well, perhaps even better, than a healthy balance sheet."

--------

# Sea–Land Services, Inc. v. Pepper Source

United States Court of Appeals, Seventh Circuit, 1991.
941 F.2d 519.

■ Before BAUER, CHIEF JUDGE, WOOD, JR., and POSNER, CIRCUIT JUDGES.

■ BAUER, CHIEF JUDGE.

This spicy case finds its origin in several shipments of Jamaican sweet peppers. Appellee Sea–Land Services, Inc. ("Sea–Land"), an ocean carrier, shipped the peppers on behalf of The Pepper Source ("PS"), one of the appellants here. PS then stiffed Sea–Land on the freight bill, which was rather substantial. Sea–Land filed a federal diversity action for the money it was owed. On December 2, 1987, the district court entered a default judgment in favor of Sea–Land and against PS in the amount of $86,767.70. But PS was nowhere to be found; it had been "dissolved" in mid–1987 for failure to pay the annual state franchise tax. Worse yet for Sea–Land, even had it not been dissolved, PS apparently had no assets. With the well empty, Sea–Land could not recover its judgment against PS. Hence the instant lawsuit.

In June 1988, Sea–Land brought this action against Gerald J. Marchese and five business entities he owns: PS, Caribe Crown, Inc., Jamar Corp., Salescaster Distributors, Inc., and Marchese Fegan Associates. Marchese also was named individually. Sea–Land sought by this suit to pierce PS's corporate veil and render Marchese personally liable for the judgment owed to Sea–Land, and then "reverse pierce" Marchese's other corporations so that they, too, would be on the hook for the $87,000. Thus, Sea–Land alleged in its complaint that all of these corporations "are alter egos of each other and hide behind the veils of alleged separate corporate existence for the purpose of defrauding plaintiff and other creditors." Count I, ¶ 11. Not only are the corporations alter egos of each other, alleged Sea–Land, but also they are alter egos of Marchese, who should be held individually liable for the judgment because he created and manipulated these corporations and their assets for his own personal uses. Count III, ¶ ¶ 9–10. (Hot on the heels of the filing of Sea–Land's complaint, PS took the necessary steps to be reinstated as a corporation in Illinois.)

In early 1989, Sea–Land filed an amended complaint adding Tie–Net International, Inc., as a defendant. Unlike the other corporate defendants, Tie–Net is not owned solely by Marchese: he holds half of the stock, and an individual named George Andre owns the other half. Sea–Land alleged that, despite this shared ownership, Tie–Net is but another alter ego of Marchese and the other corporate defendants, and thus it also should be held liable for the judgment against PS.

... In December 1989, Sea–Land moved for summary judgment....

In an order dated June 22, 1990, the court granted Sea–Land's motion. The court discussed and applied the test for corporate veil-piercing explicated in *Van Dorn Co. v. Future Chemical and Oil Corp.,* 753 F.2d 565 (7th Cir.1985). Analyzing Illinois law, we held in *Van Dorn* that

a corporate entity will be disregarded and the veil of limited liability pierced when two requirements are met:

[F]irst, there must be such unity of interest and ownership that the separate personalities of the corporation and the individual [or other corporation] no longer exist; and second, circumstances must be such that adherence to the fiction of separate corporate existence would sanction a fraud or promote injustice.

753 F.2d at 569–70. As for determining whether a corporation is so controlled by another to justify disregarding their separate identities, the Illinois cases, as we summarized them in *Van Dorn,* focus on four factors: "(1) the failure to maintain adequate corporate records or to comply with corporate formalities, (2) the commingling of funds or assets, (3) undercapitalization, and (4) one corporation treating the assets of another corporation as its own." 753 F.2d at 570 (citations omitted). *See also Main Bank,* 427 N.E.2d at 102; *Pederson,* 214 Ill.App.3d at 820, 158 Ill.Dec. at 374, 574 N.E.2d at 168.

Following the lead of the parties, the district court in the instant case laid the template of *Van Dorn* over the facts of this case. Dist.Ct.Op. at 3–12. The court concluded that both halves and all features of the test had been satisfied, and, therefore, entered judgment in favor of Sea–Land and against PS, Caribe Crown, Jamar, Salescaster, Tie–Net, and Marchese individually. These defendants were held jointly liable for Sea–Land's $87,000 judgment, as well as for post-judgment interest under Illinois law. From that judgment Marchese and the other defendants brought a timely appeal....

The first and most striking feature that emerges from our examination of the record is that these corporate defendants are, indeed, little but Marchese's playthings. Marchese is the sole shareholder of PS, Caribe Crown, Jamar, and Salescaster. He is one of the two shareholders of Tie–Net. Except for Tie–Net, none of the corporations ever held a single corporate meeting. (At the handful of Tie–Net meetings held by Marchese and Andre, no minutes were taken.) During his deposition, Marchese did not remember any of these corporations ever passing articles of incorporation, bylaws, or other agreements. As for physical facilities, Marchese runs all of these corporations (including Tie–Net) out of the same, single office, with the same phone line, the same expense accounts, and the like. And how he does "run" the expense accounts! When he fancies to, Marchese "borrows" substantial sums of money from these corporations—interest free, of course. The corporations also "borrow" money from each other when need be, which left at least PS completely out of capital when the Sea–Land bills came due. What's more, Marchese has used the bank accounts of these corporations to pay all kinds of personal expenses, including alimony and child support payments to his ex-wife, education expenses for his children, maintenance of his personal automobiles, health care for his pet—the list goes on and on. Marchese did not even have a personal bank account! (With "corporate" accounts like these, who needs one?)

And Tie–Net is just as much a part of this as the other corporations. On appeal, Marchese makes much of the fact that he shares ownership of Tie–Net, and that Sea–Land has not been able to find an example of funds flowing from PS to Tie–Net to the detriment of Sea–Land and PS's other creditors. So what? The record reveals that, in all material senses, Marchese treated Tie–Net like his other corporations: he "borrowed" over $30,000 from Tie–Net; money and "loans" flowed freely between Tie–Net and the other corporations; and Marchese charged up various personal expenses (including $460 for a picture of himself with President Bush) on Tie–Net's credit card. Marchese was not deterred by the fact that he did not hold all of the stock of Tie–Net; why should his creditors be?[1]

In sum, we agree with the district court that [there] can be no doubt that the "shared control/unity of interest and ownership" part

1. We note that the record evidence in this case, if true, establishes that for years Marchese flagrantly has disregarded the tax code concerning the treatment of corporate funds. Yet, when we inquired at oral argument whether Marchese currently is under investigation by the IRS, his counsel informed us that to his knowledge he is not. Marchese also stated in his deposition that he never has been audited by the IRS. If these statements are true, and the IRS has so far shown absolutely no interest in Marchese's financial shenanigans with his "corporations," how and why that has occurred may be the biggest puzzles in this litigation.

of the *Van Dorn* test is met in this case: corporate records and formalities have not been maintained; funds and assets have been commingled with abandon; PS, the offending corporation, and perhaps others have been undercapitalized; and corporate assets have been moved and tapped and "borrowed" without regard to their source. Indeed, Marchese basically punted this part of the inquiry before the district court by coming forward with little or no evidence in response to Sea–Land's extensively supported argument on these points. That fact alone was enough to do him in; opponents to summary judgment motions cannot simply rest on their laurels, but must come forward with specific facts showing that there is a genuine issue for trial. Regarding the elements that make up the first half of the *Van Dorn* test, Marchese and the other defendants have not done so. Thus, Sea–Land is entitled to judgment on these points.

The second part of the *Van Dorn* test is more problematic, however. "Unity of interest and ownership" is not enough; Sea–Land also must show that honoring the separate corporate existences of the defendants "would sanction a fraud or promote injustice." *Van Dorn*, 753 F.2d at 570. This last phrase truly is disjunctive:

> Although an intent to defraud creditors would surely play a part if established, the Illinois test does not require proof of such intent. Once the first element of the test is established, *either* the sanctioning of a fraud (intentional wrongdoing) or the promotion of injustice, will satisfy the second element.

*Id.* (emphasis in original). Seizing on this, Sea–Land has abandoned the language in its two complaints that make repeated references to "fraud" by Marchese, and has chosen not to attempt to *prove* that PS and Marchese intended to defraud it—which would be quite difficult on summary judgment. Instead, Sea–Land has argued that honoring the defendants' separate identities would "promote injustice."

But what, exactly, does "promote injustice" mean, and how does one establish it on summary judgment? These are the critical, troublesome questions in this case. To start with, as the above passage from *Van Dorn* makes clear, "promote injustice" means something less than an affirmative showing of fraud—but how much less? In its one-sentence treatment of this point, the district court held that it was enough that "Sea–Land would be denied a judicially-imposed recovery." Dist.Ct.Op. at 11–12. Sea–Land defends this reasoning on appeal, arguing that "permitting the appellants to hide behind the shield of limited liability would clearly serve as an injustice against appellee" because it would "impermissibly deny appellee satisfaction." Appellee's Brief at 14–15. But that cannot be what is meant by "promote injustice." The prospect of an unsatisfied judgment looms in every veil-piercing action; why else would a plaintiff bring such an action? Thus, if an unsatisfied judgment is enough for the "promote injustice" feature of the test, then *every* plaintiff will pass on that score, and *Van Dorn* collapses into a one-step "unity of interest and ownership" test. . . .

Generalizing from [the Illinois] cases, we see that the courts that properly have pierced corporate veils to avoid "promoting injustice" have found that, unless [they] did so, some "wrong" beyond a creditor's inability to collect would result: the common sense rules of adverse possession would be undermined; former partners would be permitted to skirt the legal rules concerning monetary obligations; a party would be unjustly enriched; a parent corporation that caused a sub's liabilities and its inability to pay for them would escape those liabilities; or an intentional scheme to squirrel assets into a liability-free corporation while heaping liabilities upon an asset-free corporation would be successful. Sea–Land, although it alleged in its complaint the kind of intentional asset-and liability-shifting found in *Van Dorn,* has yet to come forward with evidence akin to the "wrongs" found in these cases. Apparently, it believed, as did the district court, that its unsatisfied judgment was enough. That belief was in error, and the entry of summary judgment premature. We, therefore, reverse the judgment and remand the case to the district court.

On remand, the court should require that Sea–Land produce, if it desires summary judgment, evidence and argument that would establish the kind of additional "wrong" present in the above cases. For example, perhaps Sea–Land could establish that Marchese, like Roth in *Van Dorn,* used these corporate facades to avoid its responsibilities to creditors; or that PS, Marchese, or one of the other corporations will be "unjustly enriched" unless liability is shared by all. Of course, Sea–Land is not required fully to prove intent to defraud, which it probably could not do on summary judgment anyway. But it is required to show the kind of injustice to merit the evocation of the court's essentially equitable power to prevent "injustice." It may well be that, after more of such evidence is adduced, no genuine issue of fact exists to prevent Sea–Land from reaching Marchese's other pet corporations for PS's debt. Or it may be that only a finder of fact will be able to determine whether fraud or "injustice" is involved here. In any event, the record as it currently stands is insufficient to uphold the entry of summary judgment.

Reversed and Remanded with instructions.

- - -

## Sea–Land Services, Inc. v. Pepper Source

United States Court of Appeals, Seventh Circuit, 1993.
993 F.2d 1309.

■ Before BAUER, CHIEF JUDGE, ROVNER, CIRCUIT JUDGE, and TIMBERS, SENIOR CIRCUIT JUDGE.[1]

■ TIMBERS, SENIOR CIRCUIT JUDGE.

Appellants appeal from a judgment entered after a bench trial in the Northern District of Illinois, James F. Holderman, *District Judge,*

---

1.  The Honorable William H. Timbers, Senior Circuit Judge, United States Court of   Appeals for the Second Circuit, sitting by designation.

piercing the corporate veil and awarding appellee $118,132.61 in damages. . . .

On remand, additional discovery was permitted. The issues raised by the second prong of *Van Dorn* were tried on July 6 and 7, 1992. On July 9, 1992, the [district] court entered judgment for Sea–Land, awarding it $118,132.61 in damages. The court concluded that Sea–Land satisfied the second prong of *Van Dorn* by establishing wrongs beyond its inability to collect on its judgment.

On the instant appeal, appellants contend that the evidence presented by Sea–Land at trial was insufficient to satisfy the second prong of *Van Dorn.* They also assert that the court misapplied Illinois law in reaching its decision. . . .

. . . Sea–Land adduced sufficient evidence at trial to establish additional wrongs to justify piercing the corporate veil. First, Sea–Land demonstrated that Marchese and his corporations were unjustly enriched. We have defined "unjust enrichment" as the receipt of money or its equivalent under circumstances that, in equity and good conscience, suggest that it ought not to be retained because it belongs to someone else. *Midcoast Aviation, Inc. v. General Elec. Credit Corp.,* 907 F.2d 732, 737 (7th Cir.1990). At trial, Sea–Land demonstrated that Marchese obtained countless benefits at the expense of not only Sea–Land, but the Internal Revenue Service (IRS) and other creditors as well. Indeed, Marchese used PS funds to pay his personal expenses as well as expenses incurred by his other corporations. As a result, PS was left without sufficient funds to satisfy Sea–Land or PS's other creditors. *American Trade Partners v. A–1 Int'l Importing Enter.,* 770 F.Supp. 273, 278 (E.D.Pa.1991) (corporate veil pierced on basis of unjust enrichment where managing shareholder, with knowledge of debt to creditor, used corporation's funds to pay personal expenses). Since Marchese was enriched unjustly by his intentional manipulation and diversion of funds from his corporate entities, to allow him to use these same entities to avoid liability "would be to sanction an injustice." *Gromer, Wittenstrom & Meyer, P.C. v. Strom,* 140 Ill.App.3d 349, 354, 489 N.E.2d 370, 374 (1986).

Sea–Land also satisfied the second prong of *Van Dorn* by demonstrating at trial that Marchese used his corporate entities as "playthings" to avoid his responsibilities to creditors. An accountant testified that Marchese's payment of personal expenses with corporate funds enabled those corporations to avoid their monetary obligations to vendors, creditors, and federal and state tax authorities. One example was Marchese's withdrawal of $19,000 as salary from Jamar Corporation. This withdrawal rendered Jamar insolvent and thus unable to satisfy liabilities in excess of $450,000. Marchese also frequently took "shareholder loans" from the corporations to pay personal expenses, leaving the corporations with insufficient funds to satisfy liabilities as they became due. Further, a tax accountant testified that Marchese's business practices were replete with illegal transactions. Indeed, as we previously recognized, "for years Marchese flagrantly has disregarded the tax code concerning the treatment of corporate funds." *Sea–Land, supra,* 941 F.2d at 522 n. 2.

Marchese's practice of avoiding liability to Sea–Land and other creditors by insuring that his corporations had insufficient funds with which to pay their debts, is ground for piercing the corporate veil. *Van Dorn, supra,* 753 F.2d at 572–73 (piercing of corporate veil allowed where subsidiary was stripped by parent corporation of its assets and rendered insolvent to the prejudice of creditor). Further, as the district court here properly recognized, Marchese was the "dominant force" behind all of the corporations and was responsible for the manipulation and diversion of corporate funds without regard for creditors or the law. *B. Kreisman & Co. v. First Arlington Nat'l Bank,* 91 Ill.App.3d 847, 415 N.E.2d 1070 (1980) (piercing corporate veil proper where defendant was the dominant force behind corporation). On the basis of the facts adduced at trial, the court properly concluded that Sea–Land satisfied the second-prong of *Van Dorn* and therefore was entitled to pierce the corporate veil. . . .

Appellants further assert that Sea–Land fails to satisfy the requirement that a nexus exist between its injuries and the fraud or injustice committed by appellants. *South Side Bank v. T.S.B. Corp.,* 94 Ill. App.3d 1006, 419 N.E.2d 477 (1981). This claim fails, however, in view of the fact that Marchese assured Sea–Land in 1987 that it would receive payment from PS as long as there were sufficient funds. The court's findings that Marchese knew at that time that he would manipulate the funds of PS so as to insure that Sea–Land would not be paid, and that he eventually did manipulate those funds, were not clearly erroneous. Since Marchese's intentional and improper financial maneuvering caused Sea–Land's inability to collect on its default judgment, the required nexus existed here. . . .

Affirmed.

———

**BERKEY v. THIRD AVE. RY. CO.,** 244 N.Y. 84, 155 N.E. 58 (1926) (Cardozo, J.). "The whole problem of the relation between parent and subsidiary corporations is one that is still enveloped in the mists of metaphor. Metaphors in law are to be narrowly watched, for starting as devices to liberate thought, they end often by enslaving it. We say at times that the corporate entity will be ignored when the parent corporation operates a business through a subsidiary which is characterized as an 'alias' or a 'dummy.' All this is well enough if the picturesqueness of the epithets does not lead us to forget that the essential term to be defined is the act of operation. Dominion may be so complete, interference so obtrusive, that by the general rules of agency the parent will be a principal and the subsidiary an agent. Where control is less than this, we are remitted to the tests of honesty and justice. Ballentine, Parent and Subsidiary Corporations, 14 Cal. Law Review, 12, 18, 19, 20. The logical consistency of a juridical conception will indeed be sacrificed at times, when the sacrifice is essential to the end that some accepted public policy may be defended or upheld. This is so, for illustration, though agency in any proper sense is lacking, where the attempted separation between parent and subsidiary will work a fraud upon the law. . . . At such times unity is ascribed to parts which, at least for many purposes, retain an independent life, for the reason that only thus can we overcome a perversion of the privilege to do business in a corporate form.''

### NOTE ON THE APPLICATION OF THE PIERCING–THE–VEIL DOCTRINE

Although the tests announced by the courts for piercing the corporate veil are often similar from state to state, the manner in which those tests are applied, and the occurrence of piercing, may vary considerably across jurisdictions. For example, Epperson & Canny examined the operation of the piercing doctrine in three neighboring jurisdictions—the District of Columbia, Maryland, and Virginia. Epperson & Canny, The Capital Shareholder's Ultimate Calamity: Pierced Corporate Veils and Shareholder Liability in the District of Columbia, Maryland, and Virginia, 37 Cath.U.L.Rev. 605 (1988). They concluded that in the District of Columbia, a disregard of corporate formalities, without more, may constitute prima facie evidence of unfairness or inequity. In contrast, Maryland courts accord the corporate entity "an extraordinary measure of deference, apparently relaxed only in instances of proven common law fraud." Virginia courts commonly resorted to a more fluid analysis which endeavors to take into account the "totality of the circumstances." Id. at 614–18, 621, 626.

### NOTE ON UNITED STATES v. BESTFOODS AND DIRECT LIABILITY

Closely related to piercing-the-veil cases, in a parent-subsidiary context, are cases in which a parent is sought to be held liable *without* piercing the subsidiary's veil, on the ground that the parent directed the subsidiary's operations, or some relevant portion of those operations, and is therefore *directly* liable as a primary wrongdoer for wrongs that were committed in the course of those operations. A leading exemplar of this kind of case is United States v. Bestfoods, 524 U.S. 51, 118 S.Ct. 1876, 141 L.Ed.2d 43 (1998). This case arose under the Comprehensive Environmental Response, Compensation, and Liability Act of 1980 (CERCLA). The question was whether CPC corporation was liable as an "owner or operator" of a plant owned by CPC's subsidiary, Ott II. The court said that a parent normally would not be considered the *owner* of its subsidiary's plant, but a parent could have direct liability for its own actions in *operating* a plant owned by its subsidiary. This might be the result, for example, where a person who was an officer and director of both the parent and the subsidiary departed so far from "the norms of parental influence exercised through dual officeholding as to serve the parent, even when ostensibly acting on behalf of the subsidiary in operating the facility.[13] Yet another possibility, suggested by the facts of this case, is that an agent of the parent with no hat to wear but the parent's hat might manage or direct activities at the facility."

Identifying such an occurrence calls for line drawing ... since the acts of direct operation that give rise to parental liability must necessarily be distinguished from the interference that stems from the normal relationship between parent and subsidiary. ... [N]orms of corporate behavior (undisturbed by any CERCLA provision) are crucial reference points. Just as we may look to such norms in identifying the limits of the presumption that a dual officeholder acts in his ostensible capacity, so here we may refer to them in distinguishing a parental officer's oversight of a subsidiary from such an officer's control over the operation of the subsidiary's facility. "[A]ctivities that involve the facility but which are consistent with the parent's investor status, such as monitoring of the subsidiary's performance, supervision of the subsidiary's finance and capital budget decisions, and articulation of general policies and procedures, should not give rise to direct liability." Oswald 282. The critical question is whether, in degree and detail, actions directed to the facility by an agent of the parent alone are eccentric under accepted norms of parental oversight of a subsidiary's facility.

There is, in fact, some evidence that CPC engaged in just this type and degree of activity at the Muskegon plant. The District Court's opinion speaks of an agent of CPC alone who played a conspicuous part in dealing with the toxic risks emanating from the operation of the plant. G.R.D. Williams worked only for CPC; he was not an employee, officer, or director of Ott II, see Tr. of Oral Arg. 7, and thus, his actions were of necessity taken only on behalf of CPC. The District Court found that "CPC became directly involved in environmental and regulatory matters through the work of ... Williams, CPC's governmental and environmental affairs director. Williams ... became heavily involved in environmental issues at Ott II." 777 F.Supp., at 561. He "actively participated in and exerted control over a variety of Ott II environmental matters," *ibid.*, and he "issued directives regarding Ott II's responses to regulatory inquiries," *id.*, at 575.

---

**13.** We do not attempt to recite the ways in which the Government could show that dual officers or directors were in fact acting on behalf of the parent. Here, it is prudent to say only that the presumption that an act is taken on behalf of the corporation for whom the officer claims to act is strongest when the act is perfectly consistent with the norms of corporate behavior, but wanes as the distance from those accepted norms approaches the point of action by a dual officer plainly contrary to the interests of the subsidiary yet nonetheless advantageous to the parent. [Footnote relocated by ed.]

We think that these findings are enough to raise an issue of CPC's operation of the facility through Williams's actions ...[14] (Emphasis added.)

## SECTION 9.   EQUITABLE SUBORDINATION OF SHAREHOLDER CLAIMS

### NOTE ON EQUITABLE SUBORDINATION OF SHAREHOLDER CLAIMS

1. *Equitable Subordination.* Under the doctrine of equitable subordination, when a corporation is in bankruptcy the claim of a controlling shareholder may be subordinated to the claims of others, including the claims of preferred shareholders, on various equitable grounds. The doctrine of equitable subordination is often referred to as the "Deep Rock" doctrine, named after a subsidiary in the seminal case of Taylor v. Standard Gas & Electric Co., 306 U.S. 307, 59 S.Ct. 543, 83 L.Ed. 669 (1939). The Court in that case subordinated the parent's claim, as a creditor of the subsidiary, to the claims of other creditors and of preferred stockholders, because of the parent's improper management of the subsidiary for the parent's benefit, and because the subsidiary had been inadequately capitalized. See also Pepper v. Litton, 308 U.S. 295, 310, 60 S.Ct. 238, 246, 84 L.Ed. 281 (1939); Hackney & Benson, Shareholder Liability for Inadequate Capital, 43 U.Pitt.L.Rev. 837 (1982).

2. *Comparison With Piercing.* Hackney & Benson comment that "As compared with denying to a shareholder his privilege of limited liability, the equitable remedy of subordination is much less drastic: it simply takes an investment already made, and denies it the status of a creditor's claim on a parity with outside creditors, whereas imposing liability for corporate debts undermines the essential premise of limited liability—that a shareholder's risk is limited to the amount of his investment. . . . It is logical, therefore, for the courts to have found it fair to subordinate a controlling person's claim based upon a lesser evidence of misuse of the corporate form than what is required to impose affirmative personal liability for all corporate obligations. Furthermore, if actual shareholder capital were so small as to result in treating a shareholder loan as equity, then the equity as supplemented by the subordinated loan may be deemed an adequate cushion to support limited liability. Accordingly, inadequate capitalization may result in subordination when it does not necessarily require imposition of affirmative liability." Hackney & Benson, supra, at 882.

14.   ... [T]he Government is, of course, [also] free on remand to point to any additional evidence ... that would tend to establish that Ott II's decisionmakers acted on specific orders from CPC.

## UNIFORM FRAUDULENT TRANSFER ACT § 4(a)

[See Statutory Supplement]

————

## BANKRUPTCY CODE § 548

[See Statutory Supplement]

————

## NOTE ON TRANSFERS MADE BY A CORPORATION WITHOUT AN EQUIVALENT EXCHANGE

Under the Bankruptcy Code a transfer by a corporation to its shareholders without an equivalent exchange—for example, a dividend—can be recovered on the corporation's behalf, even if the corporation was solvent at the time of the transfer, if the corporation "was engaged in business or a transaction, or was about to engage in business or a transaction, for which any property remaining with the debtor was an unreasonably small capital." Similarly, under the Uniform Fraudulent Transfer Act (UFTA) such a transfer can be recovered if the corporation "was engaged or was about to engage in a business or a transaction for which the remaining assets of the debtor were unreasonably small in relation to the business or transaction." The Reporter's Note to UFTA § 4 states that the term "assets," rather than the term "capital," was used in § 4 to avoid confusing the concept of working capital with the legal concept of capital under corporate law.

---

## SECTION 10.   THE CORPORATE ENTITY AND THE INTERPRETATION OF STATUTES AND CONTRACTS

The following two questions often arise: (1) Does a statute or contract that applies to a corporation also apply by implication to the corporation's shareholders? For example, if Corporation A agrees with X not to compete with X, may A's sole shareholder compete with X? (2) Does a statute or contract that applies to an individual also apply by implication to a corporation that the individual owns? For example, if a statute prohibits non-citizens from owning ships that ply the U.S. coastal trade, does it also prohibit corporations from owning ships if all of the corporation's stock is held by noncitizens?

These are not questions concerning whether individual liability should be imposed despite the general rule of limited liability. Rather, they are questions of interpretation. In making such interpretations, it must be borne in mind that on the one hand the law normally treats a corporation and its shareholders as distinct, but on the other hand the legislature or the contracting parties may not *intend* to treat a corporation and its shareholders as distinct for all purposes. Two of the leading cases in this area are United States v. Milwaukee Refrigerator

Transit Co., 142 Fed. 247, 255 (E.D.Wis.1905), and Anderson v. Abbott, 321 U.S. 349, 64 S.Ct. 531, 88 L.Ed. 793 (1944). In the *Milwaukee* case, a statute prohibited railroads from giving rebates to shippers. The statute was held applicable to a corporation that was not itself a shipper, but had been formed by a shipper's officers and principal shareholders for the purpose of obtaining what were in substance rebates. "[A] corporation will be looked upon as a legal entity as a general rule, and until sufficient reason to the contrary appears; but, when the notion of legal entity is used to defeat public convenience ... the law will regard the corporation as an association of persons." In the *Anderson* case, a statute made a shareholder in a national bank liable for the debts of the bank "to the amount of his stock therein, at the par value thereof in addition to the amount invested in such stock." The question was whether this statute applied to shareholders of a parent corporation with a national bank subsidiary, even though technically only the parent was a shareholder in the bank. The Supreme Court concluded that the parent's shareholders would be deemed shareholders of the bank for the purpose of the statute, on the ground that to hold otherwise would permit that purpose to be undercut:

> It has often been held that the interposition of a corporation will not be allowed to defeat a legislative policy, whether that was the aim or only the result of the arrangement. . . .

> To allow this holding company device to succeed would be to put the policy of double liability at the mercy of corporation finance.

321 U.S. at 362–63, 64 S.Ct. at 537–38. See also Reich v. Gateway Press, Inc., 13 F.3d 685 (3d Cir.1994); Kavanaugh v. Ford Motor Co., 353 F.2d 710, 716–17 (7th Cir.1965); Note, Efficacy of the Corporate Entity in Evasion of Statutes, 26 Iowa L.Rev. 350 (1941).

# CHAPTER V

# SHAREHOLDER INFORMATIONAL RIGHTS AND PROXY VOTING

## SECTION 1. SHAREHOLDER INFORMATIONAL RIGHTS UNDER STATE LAW

———

## (a) INSPECTION OF BOOKS AND RECORDS

———

### DEL. GEN. CORP. LAW §§ 219, 220

[See Statutory Supplement]

———

### REV. MODEL BUS. CORP. ACT §§ 7.20, 16.01–16.04

[See Statutory Supplement]

———

### CAL. CORP. CODE §§ 1600, 1601

[See Statutory Supplement]

———

### N.Y. BUS. CORP. LAW § 624

[See Statutory Supplement]

———

## Security First Corp. v. U.S. Die Casting and Development Co.

Supreme Court of Delaware, 1997.
687 A.2d 563.

■ Before VEASEY, C.J., HOLLAND, HARTNETT and BERGER, JJ., and RIDGELY,

PRESIDENT JUDGE,\* constituting the Court en Banc.

■ VEASEY, CHIEF JUSTICE.

In this appeal we hold that a stockholder may demonstrate a proper demand for the production of corporate books and records upon a showing, by the preponderance of the evidence, that there exists a credible basis to find probable corporate wrongdoing. The stockholder need not actually prove the wrongdoing itself by a preponderance of the evidence. Therefore, the trial judge's determination of that credible basis after considering the totality of the evidence is entitled to considerable deference.

The Section 220 demand for books and records under the Delaware General Corporation Law serves many salutary goals in the corporate governance landscape, but the burden on the plaintiff is not insubstantial. The statutory remedy is not an invitation to an indiscriminate fishing expedition. The plaintiff must not only show a credible basis to find probable wrongdoing, but must justify each category of the requested production. Accordingly, the trial court's order must be carefully tailored.

In this case, the judgment of the trial court on the entitlement to books and records is affirmed, but the scope of the judgment is reversed as overly broad on this record. The proceeding is remanded for a determination of a properly tailored order of inspection. In addition, the judgment of the Court of Chancery ordering a stock list is reversed, there being no proper basis on this record for the production of a stock list.

### *Facts*

The following factual background is summarized from the findings set forth in the trial court's opinion.

Defendant Security First Corporation ("Security First") is a Delaware corporation with its principal place of business in Mayfield Heights, Ohio. It serves as a bank holding company for Security First Federal Savings and Loan, an Ohio savings and loan. The stock of Security First is publicly traded on NASDAQ. Charles F. Valentine is the Chairman and Chief Executive Officer of Security First.

Plaintiff U.S. Die Casting and Development Corporation ("U.S. Die") is a closely-held Ohio corporation. It is the record holder of approximately five percent of the common stock of Security First. David Slyman is the President, Chief Executive Officer, and sole stockholder of U.S. Die.

On September 1, 1994, Security First entered into an Agreement and Plan of Merger ("Merger Agreement") with Mid Am, Inc. ("Mid Am"), a much larger regional bank holding company. Mid Am filed documents with the Securities and Exchange Commission by which

---

\* Sitting by designation pursuant to Del. Court Rules 2 and 4(a).
Const., Art. IV, §§ 12 and 38, and Supreme

the value of the merger was fixed at approximately $79 million. After the announcement of the merger, the fair market value of Security First's stock increased significantly.

The Merger Agreement enumerated specific terms by which the parties could terminate the merger. The relevant terms include:

**Section 9.01 Termination**. This AGREEMENT may be terminated at any time prior to the EFFECTIVE TIME, whether before or after approval by the shareholders of SECURITY and MID AM:

(a) By mutual consent of the Boards of Directors of SECURITY and MID AM;

(b) By the Board of Directors of either SECURITY or MID AM if:

(i) The MERGER shall not have been consummated on or before April 30, 1995 (unless the failure to consummate the MERGER by such date shall be due to the action or failure to act of the party seeking to terminate this AGREEMENT in breach of such party's obligation under this AGREEMENT); or

(ii) Any event occurs which, in the reasonable opinion of either Board, would preclude satisfaction of any of the conditions set forth in Section 7.01 of this AGREEMENT[.]

The Merger Agreement required Security First to pay a termination fee of $2 million, plus third-party expenses not to exceed $250,000, contingent on the occurrence of certain events within one year after termination:

**Section 9.05 Termination Fee**. In the event of the failure of the SECURITY shareholders to approve the MERGER and this AGREEMENT, provided at the time of the SECURITY shareholders' meeting to vote upon this MERGER either (a) there is outstanding an announced offer by a third-party to acquire SECURITY, by merger[,] consolidation, exchange offer or asset purchase, or a tender offer for at least fifty-one percent (51%) of the outstanding SECURITY common stock in either case providing a per share purchase valued at the time of its announcement of at least $14.79 to the SECURITY shareholders or (b) the Board of Directors of SECURITY fails to favorably recommend approval of the AGREEMENT, then in any such event, SECURITY shall pay Two Million Dollars ($2,000,000) to MID AM as an agreed upon termination fee plus the third-party expenses incurred by MID AM in connection with the transaction contemplated by this AGREEMENT but not to exceed Two Hundred Fifty Thousand Dollars ($250,000) upon the occurrence of any of the following events within one (1) year after termination of this AGREEMENT:

(i) any person or group of persons (other than MID AM and/or its affiliates) shall acquire more than fifty percent

(50%) of the outstanding SECURITY common stock at a per share purchase price equal to or greater than $14.79; or

(ii) upon the entry by SECURITY into a definitive agreement with a person or group of persons (other than MID AM and/or its affiliates) for such person or group of persons to acquire, merge, or consolidate with SECURITY or to acquire all or substantially all of SECURITY'S assets and wherein the per share purchase price at the time of the initial public announcement thereof equals or exceeds $14.79.

In December 1994, the merger fell through. Security First alleges that the breakdown resulted from "the realization that Mid Am's management philosophy and direction were fundamentally different from its own."

Without the occurrence of an event specified by Section 9.05 of the Merger Agreement, Security First and Mid Am entered into a Termination Agreement ("Termination Agreement") on December 28, 1994. Pursuant to the Termination Agreement, defendant paid Mid Am $275,000, and agreed to pay an additional $2 million contingent on the occurrence within one and a half years of the Termination Agreement of an event listed in Section 9.05, supra.

After the Termination Agreement was disclosed, the value of defendant's common stock dropped significantly, and has not rebounded. Defendant has increased dividend payments to its stockholders since the termination.

On January 12, 1995, plaintiff submitted a written demand to defendant pursuant to 8 *Del.C.* § 220 ("Section 220")[2] to inspect all of the defendant's and its subsidiaries' books and records related to the Mid Am merger and its termination. Defendant refused to comply.

On February 7, 1995, plaintiff initiated this action in the Court of Chancery. Trial of the matter was held on July 6, 1995. By order dated February 8, 1996, the Court of Chancery granted to plaintiff the relief it sought. From this decision, Security First appeals.

### *Proper Purpose: U.S. Die's Claim of Mismanagement*

Section 220 of the Delaware General Corporation Law permits a stockholder, who shows a specific proper purpose and who complies with the procedural requirements of the statute, to inspect specific books and records of a corporation.[3]

---

**2.** 8 *Del.C.* § 220, Inspection of books and records, provides in pertinent part:

(b) Any stockholder, in person or by attorney or other agent, shall, upon written demand under oath stating the purpose thereof, have the right during the usual hours for business to inspect for any proper purpose the corporation's stock ledger, a list of its stockholders, and its other books and records, and to make copies or extracts therefrom. A proper purpose shall mean a purpose reasonably related to such person's interest as a stockholder. . . .

**3.** This Court has encouraged the use of Section 220 as an "information-gathering tool in the derivative context," provided a proper purpose is shown. *Rales v. Blasband*, Del.Supr., 634 A.2d 927, 934–935 n. 10 (1993). *See also Grimes v. Donald*, Del.Supr., 673 A.2d 1207, 1216 (1996).

In the case *sub judice*, the Court of Chancery, after a trial which included live witnesses and documentary evidence, found that, "[a]ccording to the *Amended Complaint and Plaintiff's Trial Brief and Plaintiff's Post–Trial Reply Brief*, Plaintiff's purpose for requesting an inspection of Defendant's books and records is to investigate the possibility of corporate mismanagement." It is well established that investigation of mismanagement is a proper purpose for a Section 220 books and records inspection.[5] A stockholder's entitlement to inspection of corporate books and records depends on whether or not a credible basis to find probable wrongdoing on the part of corporate mismanagement has been established.[6] At the trial of a summary proceeding under Section 220(d), the plaintiff must show the credible basis by a preponderance of the evidence. The actual wrongdoing itself need not be proved in a Section 220 proceeding, however.

This Court reviews *de novo* the question of a "proper purpose" under Section 220(b).[7] Defendant's first contention is that the Court of Chancery erroneously relied upon plaintiff's "written proffer," *i.e.*, its Amended Complaint, Trial Brief, and Post–Trial Reply Brief. Defendant argues that the trial court should have relied instead on the trial testimony of David Slyman, the President, Chief Executive Officer, and sole stockholder of U.S. Die. Concerning the purpose for the inspection, Slyman testified:

> I would like to make my own decision as to why the merger was not completed. Telling me that it was a difference of philosophies didn't get me to understand why it was not completed. The philosophy was there prior to it....

Defendant argues that the purpose which Slyman articulated at trial was insufficient and that this insufficiency is fatal. This argument must fail. Slyman's testimony does call into question defendant's purported reason for abrogating the Merger Agreement—namely, that "the realization that Mid Am's management philosophy and direction were fundamentally different from its own."[8] The Court of Chancery found defendant's reason suspect. The Court stated that "[a] reasonable stockholder could conclude prudent management would have researched 'fundamental' similarities and dissimilarities of the merging company before entering the Merger Agreement."[9] ...

Defendant next contends that the Court of Chancery applied an incorrect legal standard, when it stated, "I accept Plaintiff's written proffer [that] this payment alone represents a specific transaction raising the *plausibility* of more than speculative, general mismanagement." This Court recently stated, "In order to meet that burden of proof, a stockholder must present some credible basis from which the

**5.** *Thomas & Betts Corp. v. Leviton Manufacturing Co.*, Del.Supr., 681 A.2d 1026, 1031 (1996).

**6.** *Id. See also Skouras v. Admiralty Enterprises, Inc.*, Del.Ch., 386 A.2d 674, 678 (1978).

**7.** *Thomas & Betts Corp.*, 681 A.2d at 1030.

**8.** *U.S. Die*, slip op. at 11.

**9.** *U.S. Die*, slip op. at 12.

court can infer that waste or mismanagement may have occurred,"[13] and cited with approval the following proposition:

> A mere statement of a purpose to investigate possible general mismanagement, without more, will not entitle a shareholder to broad § 220 inspection relief. There must be some evidence of *possible* mismanagement as would warrant further investigation of the matter.[14]

The difference between the Vice Chancellor's finding that "a specific transaction rais[ed] the *plausibility* of more than speculative, general mismanagement"[15] and the requirement that "[t]here must be some evidence of possible mismanagement as would warrant further investigation"[16] is merely semantic.

Finally, defendant maintains that plaintiff failed to produce any evidence of mismanagement. This argument misses the point. In a Section 220 action, a stockholder has the burden of proof to demonstrate a proper purpose,[17] but a stockholder is "not required to prove by a preponderance of the evidence that waste and [mis]management are actually occurring."[18] The threshold for a plaintiff in a Section 220 case is not insubstantial. Mere curiosity or a desire for a fishing expedition will not suffice. But the threshold may be satisfied by a credible showing, through documents, logic, testimony or otherwise, that there are legitimate issues of wrongdoing.

As specific instances of misconduct, plaintiff questions defendant's payment of $275,000 to Mid Am "when Defendant never broke the Merger Agreement." Plaintiff also questions defendant's failure to request documentation from Mid Am of its expenses to justify defendant's expenditure of $275,000, which was $25,000 more than the Merger Agreement stipulated for expenses. On their face, these issues raise questions. The effect of the Vice Chancellor's conclusion after trial is that the questions remain.

Defendant also agreed to pay Mid Am $2 million contingent on the certain occurrences within one and a half years of the Termination Agreement. Pursuant to the Merger Agreement, defendant previously had agreed to pay Mid Am $2 million contingent on the same occurrences within one year. As plaintiff's counsel, in a letter dated 1/19/95 to Security First's Chairman and CEO Charles Valentine, stated "This either takes the company 'out of play' or diminishes the amount payable to the stockholders if it is sold. In either event, the agreement seems inappropriate and destructive to stockholder values."

The Court of Chancery also viewed as evidence suggestive of misconduct the fact that, after the Termination Agreement was dis-

---

**13.** *Thomas & Betts Corp.*, 681 A.2d at 1031.

**14.** *Helmsman Management Servs.*, 525 A.2d at 166 (emphasis added).

**15.** *U.S. Die*, slip op. at 10.

**16.** *Helmsman Management Servs.*, 525 A.2d at 166.

**17.** 8 *Del.C.* § 220(c).

**18.** *Thomas & Betts Corp.*, 681 A.2d at 1031 ("In order to meet that burden of proof, a stockholder must present some credible basis from which the court can infer that waste or mismanagement may have occurred.").

closed, the value of defendant's common stock dropped significantly and has not rebounded. Moreover, defendant has increased dividend payments to its stockholders since the termination. According to the Court of Chancery, "A thoughtful stockholder might look at this dividend increase as an effort to ameliorate dismay about the Board of Directors' abandonment of a seemingly beneficial merger for Security First stockholders."[21]

In the instant case, the Court of Chancery found:

Contrary to Defendant's allegations, the evidentiary hearing produced testimony substantiating Plaintiff's claim. I listened to the trial testimony, observed the demeanor of the witnesses, and assessed their apparent frankness and the fairness of their testimony. I find Plaintiff's stated proper purpose convincing. Plaintiff's proper purpose is tied specifically to the point in time of Defendant's failure to consummate the Merger Agreement. . . .

The trial court's decision turned in part on the Vice Chancellor's determination that defendant's witnesses were not credible.[23] "When the determination of facts turns on a question of credibility and the acceptance or rejection of 'live' testimony by the trial judge, [the trial court's] findings will be approved upon review."[24] We hold that plaintiff has established a proper purpose for its request to inspect some books and records. The scope of that inspection is a separate issue on which plaintiff bears the burden of specific justification.

### The Scope of the Books and Records Inspection

Absent any apparent error of law, this Court reviews for abuse of discretion the decision of the trial court regarding the scope of a stockholder's inspection of books and records.[25] The plaintiff bears the burden of proving that each category of books and records is essential to the accomplishment of the stockholder's articulated purpose for the inspection.[26]

Section 220(c) provides that "[t]he Court may, in its discretion, prescribe any limitations or conditions with reference to the inspection." While the trial court has wide latitude in determining the proper scope of inspection, it is the responsibility of the trial court to tailor the inspection to the stockholder's stated purpose. "Undergirding this discretion is a recognition that the interests of the corporation must be harmonized with those of the inspecting stockholder."[27]

In the instant case, the Court of Chancery found that plaintiff's request to inspect books and records was "self-tailored." We disagree.

---

**21.** *U.S. Die*, slip op. at 11.

**23.** According to the Court of Chancery, defendant's Chief Executive Officer, Charles Valentine, "delivered patent sophistry from the witness stand. . . ." *U.S. Die*, slip op. at 11. Cf. *Thomas & Betts Corp.*, 681 A.2d at 1032.

**24.** *Levitt v. Bouvier*, Del.Supr., 287 A.2d 671, 673 (1972); *accord Thomas & Betts Corp.*, 681 A.2d at 1032.

**25.** 8 *Del.C.* § 220(c); *Thomas & Betts Corp.*, 681 A.2d at 1034–35.

**26.** *Thomas & Betts Corp.*, 681 A.2d at 1035.

**27.** *Id.*

Plaintiff sought, and the Court of Chancery granted, inspection of the following:

a.  The agreement by and between Security First and Mid Am reported to have been made on or about September 1, 1994, and any amendments and modifications thereof (hereinafter the "Agreement");

b.  All minutes, notes, records, memoranda, writings, correspondence, telephone messages or the like which in any way directly or indirectly deal with or discuss the Agreement;

c.  All press releases relative to the Agreement;

d.  Any and all documents or records discussing the relationship between the employees of Security First after the completion of the merger contemplated by the Agreement;

e.  Minutes of all proceedings of directors or committees of directors from January 1, 1994;

f.  All minutes, notes, records, memoranda, writings, correspondence, telephone calls or the like which in any way directly or indirectly deal with or discuss the payment of $275,000 to Mid Am and/or a penalty to be paid if Security First and/or its assets are sold to another in the future;

g.  Any and all bank or savings and loan regulatory applications and amendments thereto related to the Agreement;

h.  Any and all correspondence with federal and/or state bank or savings and loan regulatory agencies in connection with the Agreement; and

i.  The most recent list of stockholders.

We find that plaintiff has not met its burden of proof on this record to establish that each category of books and records requested is essential and sufficient to its stated purpose. For example, Paragraph 8(e) of the Amended Complaint requests "Minutes of all proceedings of directors or committees of directors from January 1, 1994." Security First did not enter into discussions with Mid Am until the Spring of 1994. While plaintiff argues that the pre-merger meeting minutes are reasonably related to its purpose, this determination is for the trial court to make.[29]

The scope of the production which the Court of Chancery ordered in this case is more akin to a comprehensive discovery order under Court of Chancery Rule 34 than a Section 220 order. The two procedures are not the same and should not be confused. A Section 220 proceeding should result in an order circumscribed with rifled precision. Rule 34 production orders may often be broader in keeping with the scope of discovery under Court of Chancery Rule 26(b).

---

**29.**  *See Thomas & Betts Corp.*, 681 A.2d at 1035; *Helmsman Management Servs.*,     525 A.2d at 167.

It may well be that upon remand a record will be developed to justify the breadth of all or a significant portion of the order before us in accordance with this standard. Accordingly, we remand this case to the Court of Chancery to determine whether the stockholder met its burden of showing, by a preponderance of the evidence, a proper purpose entitling the stockholder to an inspection of each category of the documents it seeks.

### *Inspection of Stockholder List*

Under Section 220(c), when a stockholder complies with the statutory requirements governing the form and manner of making a demand to obtain a stockholder list, the corporation bears the burden of proving that the demand is for an improper purpose.[30] This Court reviews *de novo* the question of proper purpose when a stockholder seeks to inspect a stockholder list.[31]

U.S. Die made a written demand for copies of defendant's most recent stockholder list "to communicate with the shareholders of Security with respect to Security's business, particularly the failed merger with Mid Am., Inc." In his deposition and at trial, however, Slyman admitted that he had no idea what he would do with such a list. It is a sufficient defense for a corporation to show that a stockholder list was sought from "idle curiosity."[32] We find that Security First has met its burden of proving that the plaintiff's demand to inspect the stockholder list was not for a proper purpose. Accordingly, we reverse the Court of Chancery's decision to grant plaintiff's request to inspect defendant's stockholder list.

We note, however, that U.S. Die is not precluded from making a new demand and, if necessary, filing a new proceeding to obtain the stockholder list. Neither the doctrine of *res judicata*[33] nor the principle of the law of the case has any application to a subsequent demand by U.S. Die to inspect the stockholder list. If U.S. Die has a *bona fide* purpose to inspect the list and if there has been a material change of circumstances since its February 1995 demand, U.S. Die may be able to establish its entitlement to inspect and copy the list of stockholders of Security First upon reasonable terms and conditions.

### *Conclusion*

Section 220 proceedings are an important part of the corporate governance landscape in Delaware. Stockholders have a right to at least a limited inquiry into books and records when they have established some credible basis to believe that there has been wrongdoing. In fact, a Section 220 proceeding may serve a salutary mission as a prelude to a derivative suit. Yet it would invite mischief to open

---

**30.**   8 *Del.C.* § 220(c); *Compaq Computer Corp. v. Horton,* Del.Supr., 631 A.2d 1, 3 (1993).

**31.**   *Western Air Lines, Inc. v. Kerkorian,* Del.Supr., 254 A.2d 240 (1969). *See also Compaq Computer Corp.,* 631 A.2d at 3.

**32.**   *Insuranshares Corporation of Delaware v. Kirchner,* Del.Supr., 5 A.2d 519, 521 (1939).

**33.**   *Hatleigh Corp. v. Lane Bryant, Inc.,* Del.Ch., 428 A.2d 350 (1981).

corporate management to indiscriminate fishing expeditions. The trial court must assure that a proper balance is struck.

The judgment of the Court of Chancery granting U.S. Die's entitlement to inspect books and records is **AFFIRMED**. The breadth of the order is **REVERSED** on this record, however. This case is **REMANDED** to the Court of Chancery to open the record and to consider whether the plaintiff has carried its burden of proving that each category of books and records is essential to the accomplishment of the stockholder's articulated purpose for the inspection. The judgment of the Court of Chancery granting U.S. Die's entitlement to inspect the list of Security First's stockholders is **REVERSED**.

Jurisdiction is not retained.

---

## NOTE ON SHAREHOLDERS' INSPECTION RIGHTS

1. *Common Law; Interpretation of the Statutes.* At common law, a shareholder "acting in good faith for the purpose of advancing the interests of the corporation and protecting his own interest as a stockholder" has a right to examine the corporate books and records at reasonable times. Albee v. Lamson & Hubbard Corp., 320 Mass. 421, 424, 69 N.E.2d 811, 813 (1946). The general rule is that the shareholder has the burden of alleging and proving good faith and proper purpose. Id. But see Bennett v. Mack's Supermarkets, Inc., 602 S.W.2d 143 (Ky.1979).

Many or most legislatures have now enacted statutes governing the right of inspection. Many of these statutes are more limited in their coverage than the common law rule. For example, a statute may apply only to certain kinds of shareholders (such as those who are record holders of at least 5% of the corporation's stock or who have been record holders for at least six months) or only to certain kinds of books and records. A common problem of interpretation is whether the statutes: (i) Preserve the common law rule that the shareholder must prove a proper purpose. (ii) Discard the proper-purpose test. (iii) Preserve the proper-purpose test, but place on the corporation the burden of proving that the shareholder's purpose is improper. Generally, the last interpretation is followed, at least if the language is ambiguous. See, e.g., Crane Co. v. Anaconda Co., 39 N.Y.2d 14, 382 N.Y.S.2d 707, 346 N.E.2d 507 (1976). A second common problem of interpretation is whether the statutes replace or supplement the common law. The general answer is that the statutes supplement the common law, so that a suit for inspection that does not fall within the relevant statute can still be brought under the common law. See, e.g., Bank of Heflin v. Miles, 294 Ala. 462, 318 So.2d 697 (1975).

2. *"Proper Purpose."* Among the purposes the courts have recognized as "proper," for purposes of exercising the shareholder's inspection right, are to determine the financial condition of the corporation and to ascertain the value of the petitioner's shares.

3. *Stockholder Lists*. As a practical matter, the courts are understandably much readier to grant access to stockholder lists and the like than to grant access to otherwise-confidential financial and business information, such as internal data and contracts. In the case of business and financial information, the shareholder will normally have to show the court a specific and plausible reason why the information is needed. In contrast, in the case of stockholder lists a statement by a shareholder that he wants the list to communicate with other shareholders will usually, although not always, suffice. This distinction is understandable. Requiring the production of a stockholder list is almost invariably a necessary step for shareholders to exercise their role in corporate governance, imposes only a minimum burden on the corporation, and usually cannot injure the business of the corporation. In contrast, other kinds of information may be costly to produce, may have the potential to injure the corporation's business if misused, and (depending on the information) may not be necessary for the normal exercise of the shareholder's role.

In some cases, the statutes themselves distinguish between different types of corporate books and records. See, e.g., Del.Gen.Corp.Law § 220; see also Model Act §§ 7.20(b), 16.02.

---

## NOTE ON RECORD OWNERSHIP AND THE RECORD DATE

The persons who are listed as shareholders on the corporation's records are known as *record owners*. For a variety of reasons, the persons who actually own shares—the *beneficial* owners—often differ from the record owners. For example, the stock of individual and even institutional shareholders is often held in "street name," that is, in the name of a broker or a bank. Brokers, banks, and others, in turn, often deposit the stock they hold in regional stock depositories (described below), which place the stock under still another name.

To promote certainty, in various contexts corporation law confers rights on record owners, rather than beneficial owners. One of these contexts is voting: normally, only record owners have the right to notice of a meeting and the right to vote.

When a corporation proposes to hold a meeting at which a shareholder vote will be taken, it must give notice of the meeting. To comply with the disclosure requirements of federal law, the notice frequently must be given a month or so before the meeting will take place. Because shares in publicly held corporations are constantly changing hands, the group of persons who are record owners on the date notice is given will differ from the persons who are record owners on the meeting date. Accordingly, if the shareholders entitled to vote at the meeting were the record holders as of the meeting date, then some shareholders entitled to vote would not have received notice of the meeting (because they purchased their shares after the notice was given), and the vote would be invalid.

To resolve this dilemma, the law permits corporations to set a *record date*—which is typically on or around the date that notice of the relevant meeting is given—for determining the shareholders who will be entitled to vote at the meeting. As a result, those persons, and only those persons, who are record shareholders on the record date are entitled to vote, even though the record date is a month or so before the meeting date, and many of the persons who were record holders on the record date are not record holders on the meeting date. (Under an older procedure, which is now little used, in lieu of setting a record date the corporation could close its transfer books, that is, could refuse to record transfers of stock between the time of the close of the books and the time of the meeting. As a result, all persons who were record holders when the transfer books were closed would still be record holders on the meeting date.)

---

## J. Heard & H. Sherman, Conflicts of Interest in the Proxy Voting System 74-78

(1987).

### The Owner Identification Problem ...

As many companies have discovered during their proxy solicitations, in today's securities markets it is difficult to identify just who a company's beneficial owners are, and even more difficult to determine who has voting authority for their shares. The problem of identifying beneficial owners exists because many individual shareholders, and most institutional investors, register their shares in so-called "street name" (... shares registered in the name of a bank or broker) or "nominee name" (registered in the name of a bank nominee account).

Stockholders register their shares in street name for a variety of reasons. Active traders do so to expedite stock transfers and subsequent reregistration. Individuals who do not want to store stock certificates themselves leave their shares with a broker, who usually registers the shares in the broker's name.... Other shareholders are required to register in street name. For example, individuals who purchase stock on margin must leave their shares with their broker, and since they do not truly own the shares until they are paid for in full, their brokers register the shares in street name....

Roughly 70 percent of all corporate stock is now held in street name. Of this amount, approximately 30 percent is held in broker name and 70 percent in bank nominee name.

Street name registration makes it difficult for companies to identify who their beneficial owners are. The identification problem is further complicated by the use of depositories. Shares registered in the name of a bank or broker rarely are held by the bank or broker any more. Instead, most banks and brokers hold their shares at one of the four regional depositories, the largest of which is the Depository Trust Co. in New York (nominee name Cede and Co.). When a bank or a broker holds its shares at a depository, the depository becomes the official holder of record for the shares. Thus, a company soliciting proxies is likely to find that "Cede and Co." and the other depositories are the registered owners of a majority of its shares.

One problem for companies soliciting proxy votes is that the depositories have no "beneficial interest" in the shares registered in their name; they are merely custodians of the physical securities. Companies wishing to identify who their beneficial owners are must obtain security listings from a depository telling them who "owns" the shares held at the depository. But this list only tells a company which banks and brokers hold shares registered in their name at the depository, not who the ultimate beneficial owners (the brokers' and banks' own customers) really are. . . .

. . . [T]he problem became critical in the early 1980s when some companies, unable to identify their beneficial owners and unable to guarantee that their proxy material was being received by owners in time to vote, if at all, were forced to postpone annual meetings because they failed to reach a quorum. To remedy the situation, the SEC passed its "NOBO" rules for brokers in 1985. Under the NOBO requirements, brokers must report to issuer companies the name, address and security position of clients holding the company's shares in broker name, as long as the client does not object (hence NOBO, for non-objecting beneficial owner).

**The Depositories**

. . . The holders of record for the majority of shares in the market today are the four major depositories: Depository Trust Co. [DTC] (nominee name—Cede and Co.), Midwest Securities Depository Trust Co. (Kray and Co.), Pacific Securities Depository Trust Co. (Pacific and Co.) and Philadelphia Depository Trust Co. (Philadep and Co.). Of the four, Depository Trust is by far the largest, followed by Midwest Depository. . . .

. . . The number of shares held by the four depositories combined represents more than 70 percent of all shares outstanding in the United States. . . .

———

## (b) REPORTING UNDER STATE LAW

———

### REV. MODEL BUS. CORP. ACT §§ 16.20

[See Statutory Supplement]

———

## CAL. CORP. CODE § 1501

[See Statutory Supplement]

———

## N.Y. BUS. CORP. LAW § 624(e)

[See Statutory Supplement]

———

### NOTE ON REPORTING UNDER STATE LAW

The inspection right requires a shareholder to take affirmative action and incur costs to obtain information, and may be defeated in litigation. In contrast, the Securities Exchange Act, which is applicable to corporations that have at least 500 record holders of a class of equity securities and meet certain other conditions, requires the corporation to report certain information to all shareholders without specific shareholder requests. However, a corporation that has less than 500 may be publicly held in the sense that its shareholders are scattered and not directly involved either in managing the corporation or in monitoring management, and its stock is traded on a market. Accordingly, there is a need to require corporations that have significant public ownership, but are not covered by the Securities Exchange Act, to report to their shareholders information on at least some subjects, such as financial results and material conflict-of-interest transactions.

The Revised Model Business Corporation Act partially address that need. For example, § 16.20 requires that every corporation must furnish to its shareholders annual financial statements, including a balance sheet and an income statement. The statements must be prepared on the basis of generally accepted accounting principles if the corporation prepares its financial statements on that basis. Many statutes, such as N.J.Stat.Ann. § 14A:5–28, simply provide that a corporation must furnish "its balance sheet as at the end of the preceding fiscal year, and its profit and loss and surplus statements for such fiscal year" upon a shareholder's written request. Some statutes, like that of Delaware, don't require corporations to furnish financial statements to shareholders even on written request.

---

## SECTION 2.   SHAREHOLDER INFORMATIONAL RIGHTS UNDER FEDERAL LAW AND STOCK EXCHANGE RULES

———

### INTRODUCTORY NOTE

Given the limitations on the shareholder's inspection right, and the limited obligations to report under state law, it was probably inevitable that corrective action would be taken to ensure that shareholders are provided with adequate information at the corporation's expense. Two major bodies of rules evolved to alleviate the deficiencies in the inspection right: the Securities Exchange Act of 1934 and the regulations promulgated thereunder, and the rules for listed companies promulgated by various stock exchanges. To put these rules in context, this Section will begin with overviews of the Securities Exchange Act and the stock markets.

——————

# (a) AN OVERVIEW OF THE STOCK MARKETS

——————

## S. Ross, R. Westerfield & B. Jordan, Fundamentals of Corporate Finance

Fifth ed. 2000.[*]

### Capital Markets and the Corporation

[Two] primary advantages of the corporate form of organization are that ownership can be transferred more quickly and easily than with other forms and that money can be raised more readily. Both of these advantages are significantly enhanced by the existence of financial markets and financial markets play an extremely important role in corporate finance. . . .

A financial market, like any market, is just a way of bringing buyers and sellers together. In financial markets, it is debt and equity securities that are bought and sold. Financial markets differ in detail, however. The most important differences concern the types of securities that are traded, how trading is conducted, and who the buyers and sellers are. Some of these differences are discussed next.

### Primary versus Secondary Markets

Financial markets function as both primary and secondary markets for debt and equity securities. The term *primary market* refers to the original sale of securities by governments and corporations. The *secondary markets* are those in which these securities are bought and sold after the original sale. Equities are, of course, issued solely by corporations. Debt securities are issued by both governments and corporations. In the discussion that follows, we focus on corporate securities only.

*Primary Markets.* In a primary market transaction, the corporation is the seller, and the transaction raises money for the corporation. Corporations engage in two types of primary market transactions: public offerings and private placements. A public offering, as the name suggests, involves selling securities to the general public, whereas a private placement is a negotiated sale involving a specific buyer.

By law, public offerings of debt and equity must be registered with the Securities and Exchange Commission (SEC). Registration requires the firm to disclose a great deal of information before selling any securities. The accounting, legal, and selling costs of public offerings can be considerable.

Partly to avoid the various regulatory requirements and the expense of public offerings, debt and equity are often sold privately to large financial institutions such as life insurance companies or mutual funds. Such private placements do not have to be registered with the SEC and do not require the involvement of underwriters (investment banks that specialize in selling securities to the public).

*Secondary Markets.* A secondary market transaction involves one owner or creditor selling to another. It is therefore the secondary markets that provide the means for transferring ownership of corporate securities. Although a corporation is only directly involved in a primary market transaction (when it sells securities to raise cash), the secondary markets are still critical to large corporations. The reason is that investors are much more willing to purchase securities in a primary market transaction when they know that those securities can later be resold if desired.

*Dealer versus Auction Markets.* There are two kinds of secondary markets: *auction* markets and *dealer* markets. Generally speaking. dealers buy and sell for themselves, at their own risk. A car dealer, for example. buys and sells automobiles. In contrast, brokers and agents match buyers and sellers, but they do not actually own the commodity that is bought or sold. A real estate agent, for example, does not normally buy and sell houses.

Dealer markets in stocks and long-term debt are called *over-the-counter* (OTC) markets. Most trading in debt securities takes place over the counter. The expression *over the counter* refers to days of old when securities were literally bought and sold at counters in offices around the country. Today, a significant fraction of the market for stocks and almost all of the market for long-term debt have no central location; the many dealers are connected electronically.

Auction markets differ from dealer markets in two ways. First, an auction market or exchange has a physical location (like Wall Street). Second, in a dealer market, most of the buying and selling is done by the dealer. The primary purpose of an auction market, on the other hand, is to match those who wish to sell with those who wish to buy. Dealers play a limited role.

*Trading in Corporate Securities.* The equity shares of most of the large firms in the United States trade in organized auction markets. The largest such market is the New York Stock Exchange (NYSE), which accounts for more than 85 percent of all the shares traded in auction markets. Other auction exchanges include the American Stock

Exchange (AMEX) and regional exchanges such as the Pacific Stock Exchange.

In addition to the stock exchanges, there is a large OTC market for stocks. In 1971, the National Association of Securities Dealers (NASD) made available to dealers and brokers an electronic quotation system called NASDAQ (NASD Automated Quotation system, pronounced "naz-dak" and now spelled "Nasdaq"). There are roughly three times as many companies on Nasdaq as there are on NYSE, but they tend to be much smaller in size and trade less actively. There are exceptions, of course. Both Microsoft and Intel trade OTC, for example. . . .

*Listing.* Stocks that trade on organized exchange are said to be *listed* on that exchange. In order to be listed, firms must meet certain minimum criteria concerning, for example, asset size and number of shareholders. These criteria differ for different exchanges.

NYSE has the most stringent requirements of the exchanges in the United States. For example, to be listed on NYSE, a company is expected to have a market value for its publicly held shares of at least $18 million and a total of at least 2,000 shareholders with at least 100 shares each. There are additional minimums on earnings, assets, and number of shares outstanding.

---

## (b) AN OVERVIEW OF THE SEC AND THE SECURITIES EXCHANGE ACT

---

## Securities and Exchange Commission, The Work of the SEC

(1997).

. . . The SEC's mission is to administer federal securities laws and issue rules and regulations to provide protection for investors and to ensure that the securities markets are fair and honest. This is accomplished primarily by promoting adequate and effective disclosure of information to the investing public. The laws administered by the Commission are the:

- Securities Act of 1933;
- Securities Exchange Act of 1934;
- Public Utility Holding Company Act of 1935;
- Trust Indenture Act of 1939;
- Investment Company Act of 1940; and
- Investment Advisers Act of 1940. . . .

The Commission is composed of five members appointed by the President, with the advice and consent of the Senate, for five-year terms. The Chairman is designated by the President. Terms are staggered; one expires on June 5th of every year. Not more than three members may be of the same political party.

Under the direction of the Commission, the staff ensures that publicly held companies, broker-dealers in securities, investment companies and advisers, and other participants in the securities markets comply with federal securities laws. (Ex. Among other things, the staff reviews registration statements and periodic reports, conducts examinations and inspections, makes rules and regulations, conducts investigations and brings enforcement actions against violators.) The SEC does not guarantee the value or merit of a particular investment. The Commission cannot bar the sale of securities of questionable value. The investor must make the ultimate judgment of the worth of securities offered for sale.

The SEC's staff is composed of lawyers, accountants, financial analysts and examiners, engineers, investigators, economists, and other professionals. The staff is divided into divisions and offices (including 11 regional and district offices), each directed by officials appointed by the Chairman.

The Commission's staff is composed of lawyers, accountants, financial analysts and examiners, engineers, investigators, and other professionals. The staff is divided into divisions and offices (including 11 regional and branch offices), each directed by officials appointed by the Chairman. . . .

By [The Securities Exchange Act of 1934], Congress extended the disclosure doctrine of investor protection to securities listed and registered for public trading on our national securities exchanges. Thirty years later, the Securities Act Amendments of 1964 extended disclosure and reporting provisions to equity securities in the over-the-counter market. This included hundreds of companies with . . . shareholders numbering 500 or more. Today, securities of thousands of companies are traded over-the-counter. The act seeks to ensure fair and orderly securities markets by prohibiting certain types of activities and by setting forth rules regarding the operation of the markets and participants. . . .

---

### SECURITIES EXCHANGE ACT § 12(a), (b), (g)

[See Statutory Supplement]

---

### SECURITIES EXCHANGE ACT RULE 12g–1

[See Statutory Supplement]

---

## (c) PERIODIC DISCLOSURE UNDER THE SECURITIES EXCHANGE ACT

---

### SECURITIES EXCHANGE ACT § 13(a)

[See Statutory Supplement]

---

### SECURITIES EXCHANGE ACT RULES 13a–1, 13a–11, 13a–13

---

### SECURITIES EXCHANGE ACT FORMS 8–K, 10–K, 10–Q

[See Statutory Supplement]

---

### NOTE ON PERIODIC REPORTING BY REGISTERED CORPORATIONS

The Securities Exchange Act addresses the informational deficiencies in state law by imposing periodic-reporting requirements on corporations with a security registered under section 12. Section 13 of the Act, and the rules promulgated thereunder, requires such corporations to file a Form 10–K annually, a Form 10–Q quarterly, and a Form 8–K within a specific number of days after the occurrence of certain specified events. The Form 10–K must include audited financial statements; management's discussion of the corporation's financial condition and results of operations; and disclosure concerning legal proceedings, developments in the corporation's business, executive compensation, conflict-of-interest transactions, and other specified issues. The Form 10–Q must include quarterly financial data prepared in accordance with generally accepted accounting principles; a management report; and disclosures concerning legal proceedings, defaults on senior securities, and other specified issues. Among the matters that trigger an 8–K Report are a change in control of the corporation, the acquisition or disposition of a significant amount of assets, and a change of accountants. Periodic reporting is also required under the Proxy Rules in connection with the corporation's annual meeting.

A limitation on the usefulness of the periodic reporting requirements under the Securities Exchange Act is that none of the required reports are both comprehensive and timely. The 8–K, which is the most timely form, need be filed in only very limited cases and may be filed as late as 15 days after the event. The 10–Q is also limited in its coverage, and need only be filed quarterly. The 10–K is comprehensive, but need only be filed annually. Periodic reporting under the Proxy Rules is also only made annually. Generally speaking, neither the Exchange Act nor the Securities Act require timely disclosure of material corporate developments, as such.

The disclosure required by the Securities Exchange Act's periodic reporting requirements is sometimes called *structured* disclosure, because what must be disclosed and how it must be disclosed is structured by the relevant SEC rules. Another example of structured disclosure is the disclosure required under the Securities Act when a corporation makes a public offering of securities.

Of course, a corporation may make voluntary timely disclosure of material corporate developments even if not required to do so by law. Furthermore, the rules of the major stock exchanges and of Nasdaq often require listed corporations to make timely disclosure of material developments.

———

## (d) Disclosure Under Stock Exchange Rules

———

### NEW YORK STOCK EXCHANGE, LISTED COMPANY MANUAL §§ 202.01, 202.03, 202.05, 202.06[1]

[See Statutory Supplement]

## Section 3.   The Proxy Rules (I): An Introduction

———

### NOTE ON TERMINOLOGY

This and the next two Sections concern the Proxy Rules, which are promulgated by the SEC. The following terms are important in considering these Rules:

*Proxy holder.* A person authorized to vote shares on a shareholder's behalf.

*Proxy,* or *form of proxy.* The written instrument in which such an authorization is embodied. (The term proxy is also sometimes used to mean a proxy holder, but for purposes of clarity that usage will be avoided in this Chapter.)

———

1. For similar rules, see American Stock Exchange, AMEX Company Guide, §§ 401–405 (Disclosure Policies), 2 CCH, American Stock Exchange Guide ¶ 10,121– 10,125; Nat'l Ass'n Sec. Dealers Manual (CCH) § 5, Schedule D, Part II, ¶ 1806A, at 1571–72.

*Proxy solicitation.* The process by which shareholders are asked to give their proxies.

*Proxy Statement.* A written statement sent to shareholders as a means of proxy solicitation.

*Proxy materials.* The proxy statement and form of proxy.

———

## SECURITIES EXCHANGE ACT § 14(a), (c)

———

## SECURITIES EXCHANGE ACT RULES 14a–1—14a–6, 14c–2, 14c–3, SCHEDULE 14A, SCHEDULE 14C

[See Statutory Supplement]

———

## NOTE—AN OVERVIEW OF THE PROXY RULES

1. *Background.* Proxy voting is the dominant mode of share-holder decisionmaking in publicly held corporations. There are a number of reasons for this. Shareholders in such corporations are often geographically dispersed, so that a given shareholder may not live near the site of the meeting. A given shareholding will normally represent only a small fraction of a shareholder's total wealth. Accordingly, physical attendance at a shareholders's meeting is normally an uneconomical use of a shareholder's time, when he can vote by proxy.

A natural outgrowth of the preference for proxy voting is proxy solicitation—the process of systematically contacting shareholders, and urging them to execute and return proxy forms that authorize named proxyholders to cast the shareholder's votes, either in a manner designated in the proxy form or according to the proxyholder's discretion.

Despite these developments, as of the 1930's state law hardly regulated proxy voting, except in the extreme case in which proxies had been fraudulently solicited. Abuses were notorious and wide-spread. Accordingly, Congress entered the field in 1934 through Section 14(a) of the Securities Exchange Act. In itself, Section 14(a) has no effect on private conduct: its only effect is to authorize the SEC to promulgate rules that will govern private conduct. Pursuant to Section 14(a), the SEC has promulgated a set of Proxy Rules that serve a variety of purposes.

2. *Coverage.* Rule 14a–2 provides that the Proxy Rules "apply to every solicitation of a proxy with respect to securities registered pursuant to section 12 of the Act," with certain exceptions such as "[a]ny solicitation made otherwise than on behalf of the registrant where the total number of persons solicited is not more than ten."

The definitions of "proxy" and "solicitation" are extremely broad. Under Rule 14a–1(f), the term "proxy" means "every proxy, consent, or authorization within the meaning of section 14(a) of the Act. The consent or authorization may take the form of failure to object or to dissent." Under Rule 14a–1($l$)(1), the term "solicitation" includes "(i) [a]ny request for a proxy . . .; (ii) [a]ny request to execute or not to execute, or to revoke, a proxy; or (iii) [t]he furnishing of a form of proxy or other communication to security holders under circumstances reasonably calculated to result in the procurement, withholding or revocation of a proxy." This language has been given a very expansive interpretation. For example, in Studebaker Corp. v. Gittlin, 360 F.2d 692 (2d Cir.1966), Gittlin, a shareholder in Studebaker, had solicited authorizations from other Studebaker shareholders to inspect Studebaker's stockholder list for the purpose of meeting the five percent test under the relevant New York inspection statute. Judge Friendly stated:

> . . . The assistant general counsel of the SEC . . . stated at the argument that the Commission believes § 14(a) should be construed, in all its literal breadth, to include authorizations to inspect stockholders lists, even in cases where obtaining the authorizations was not a step in a planned solicitation of proxies.
>
> We need not go that far to uphold the order of the district court. In SEC v. Okin, 132 F.2d 784 (2d Cir.1943), this court ruled that a letter which did not request the giving of any authorization was subject to the Proxy Rules if it was part of "a continuous plan" intended to end in solicitation and to prepare the way for success. This was the avowed purpose of Gittlin's demand for inspection of the stockholders list. . . .

Id. at 695–96.

3. *Transactional Disclosure.* One purpose of the Proxy Rules is to require full disclosure in connection with transactions that shareholders are being asked to approve, such as mergers, certificate amendments, or election of directors. This purpose is accomplished in the first instance by Rule 14a–3 and Schedule 14A. Rule 14a–3 provides that no solicitation of proxies that is subject to the Proxy Rules shall be made unless the person being solicited "is concurrently furnished or has previously been furnished with a written proxy statement containing the information specified in Schedule 14A." Schedule 14A, in turn, lists in detail the information that must be furnished when specified types of transactions are to be acted upon by the shareholders. Rule 14a–3 and Schedule 14A are backed up by Rule 14a–9, which provides that no solicitation subject to the Proxy Rules shall contain any statement that is false or misleading with respect to any material fact or omits a material fact.

4. *Periodic Disclosure.* The Proxy Rules also require certain forms of annual disclosure. Much of this disclosure is only very loosely related to any specific action the shareholders are asked to vote upon. For example, Rule 14a–3 provides that the proxy statement for an annual meeting at which directors are to be elected must be accompa-

nied by an annual report that includes audited balance sheets for each of the corporation's two most recent fiscal years, audited income statements for its three most recent fiscal years, and certain other information. Under Items 7 and 8 of Schedule 14A, the proxy statement for an annual meeting at which directors are being elected must disclose the compensation of the five most highly paid executives and the executive officers as a group (including not only salary, but bonuses, deferred compensation, stock options, and the like), and significant conflict-of-interest transactions during the corporation's last fiscal year involving, among others, directors, executive officers, and five percent beneficial owners. Under Item 7, the proxy statement for such a meeting must also disclose whether the corporation has audit, nominating, and compensation committees, and if so, the number of meetings each committee held during the last fiscal year and the functions it performs. And under Section 14(c), Regulation 14C, and Schedule 14C, a corporation that is registered under Section 12 must distribute, in connection with an annual meeting at which directors are to be elected, an annual report and certain other information (such as information relating to conflict-of-interest transactions and compensation), even if the corporation is *not* soliciting proxies.

5. *Proxy Contests.* Proxy Rule 14a–11 regulates proxy contests, in which insurgents try to oust incumbent directors. Basically, Rule 14a–11 is an adaptation of the salient concepts of other Proxy Rules to the special circumstances of a proxy fight. Its main bite is to require the filing of certain information by insurgents.

6. *Access to the Body of Shareholders.* Proxy Rules 14a–7 and 14a–8 provide mechanisms through which shareholders can communicate with each other. See Section 5, infra.

7. *Mechanics of Proxy Voting.* Still another purpose of the Proxy Rules is to regulate the mechanics of proxy voting itself. This is done, somewhat indirectly, through Rule 14a–4, which governs the form of proxy.

---

## FORM OF PROXY

[See Statutory Supplement]

---

## NOTE ON THE ANNUAL REPORT TO SHAREHOLDERS

When proxies for the election of directors are solicited on behalf of a corporation that is subject to the Proxy Rules, the corporation must send an Annual Report to its shareholders either in advance of or concurrently with the proxy statement. This Annual Report to Shareholders must be distinguished from the annual report on Form 10–K that the corporation must file with the SEC.

> [The] annual report to security holders is one of the most widely read disclosure documents, and potentially the best suited for communicating information in an informative, readable and understandable form to security holders and potential investors. The detailed disclosure required in annual reports on Form 10–K is of significant value to securities analysts. Many analysts have ready access to such reports and are able to analyze their contents. Form 10–K reports, however, are of little direct value to the average security holder who . . . [does] not have such access and may not have the necessary background and expertise to analyze the contents. The Commission believes that it is necessary to recognize the varying information[al] needs of different users of financial disclosure documents. The Commission considers it essential, therefore, that the annual report to security holders contain meaningful information about the company.

Notice of Proposed Amendments to Rules 14a–3 and 14c–3 Under the Securities Exchange Act of 1934, Exchange Act Release No. 10,59 (Jan. 10, 1974).

The contents of the Annual Report to Shareholders are governed by Rule 14a–3. The Report must include, among other things, the corporation's financial statements; selected financial data; and management's discussion and analysis of the registrant's financial condition and results of operations (MD & A). Either the Annual Report or the Proxy Statement must prominently feature an undertaking to furnish a copy of the Form 10–K to any shareholder, without charge, upon written request.

To encourage informality and directness in the Annual Report to Shareholders, Rule 146–3(c) provides that the Report is not to be deemed either soliciting material within the Proxy Rules or a "filing" under Securities Exchange Act § 18, which concerns express civil liabilities under that Act. (However, if the Annual Report to Shareholders contains a material misstatement or omission, it can serve as the basis for a suit under Rule 10b–5. See Chapter 10, infra.)

———

## SECTION 4. THE PROXY RULES (II): PRIVATE ACTIONS UNDER THE PROXY RULES

———

### SECURITIES EXCHANGE ACT RULE 14a–9

[See Statutory Supplement]

———

## NOTE ON J.I. CASE CO. v. BORAK

In J.I. Case Co. v. Borak, 377 U.S. 426, 84 S.Ct. 1555, 12 L.Ed.2d 423 (1964), the Supreme Court held that a shareholder could bring a private action for violation of the Proxy Rules, although neither the 1934 Act nor the Proxy Rules themselves explicitly provide for such an action. The rationale in *Borak* was as follows:

> . . . Private enforcement of the proxy rules provides a necessary supplement to Commission action. As in antitrust treble damage litigation, the possibility of civil damages or injunctive relief serves as a most effective weapon in the enforcement of the proxy requirements. The Commission advises that it examines over 2,000 proxy statements annually and each of them must necessarily be expedited. Time does not permit an independent examination of the facts set out in the proxy material and this results in the Commission's acceptance of the representations contained therein at their face value, unless contrary to other material on file with it. Indeed, on the allegations of respondent's complaint, the proxy material failed to disclose alleged unlawful market manipulation of the stock of ATC, and this unlawful manipulation would not have been apparent to the Commission until after the merger.

> We, therefore, believe that under the circumstances here it is the duty of the courts to be alert to provide such remedies as are necessary to make effective the congressional purpose.

Id. at 432–33, 84 S.Ct. at 1560.

---

**WYANDOTTE v. U.S.**, 389 U.S. 191, 202, 88 S.Ct. 379, 19 L.Ed.2d 407 (1967). "In [J.I. Case Co. v. Borak] we concluded that criminal liability was inadequate to ensure the full effectiveness of the statute which Congress had intended. Because the interest of the plaintiffs in those cases fell within the class that the statute was intended to protect, and because the harm that had occurred was of the type that the statute was intended to protect, and because the harm that had occurred was of the type that the statute was intended to forestall, we held that civil actions were proper. That conclusion was in accordance with a general rule of the law of torts. See Restatement (Second) of Torts § 286."

---

**CORT v. ASH**, 422 U.S. 66, 95 S.Ct. 2080, 45 L.Ed.2d 26 (1975). "In determining whether a private remedy is implicit in a statute not expressly providing one, several factors are relevant. First, is the plaintiff 'one of the class for whose *especial* benefit the statute was enacted,' Texas & Pacific R. Co. v. Rigsby, 241 U.S. 33, 39, 36 S.Ct. 482, 484, 60 L.Ed. 874 (1916) (emphasis supplied)—that is, does the statute create a federal right in favor of the plaintiff? Second, is there any indication of legislative intent, explicit or implicit, either to create such a remedy or to deny one? . . . Third, is it consistent with the underlying purposes of the legislative scheme to imply such a remedy for the plaintiff? . . . And finally, is the cause of action one traditionally relegated to state law, in an area basically the concern of the States, so that it would be inappropriate to infer a cause of action based solely on federal law?''

---

### NOTE ON MILLS v. ELECTRIC AUTO–LITE CO.

In Mills v. Electric Auto–Lite Co., 396 U.S. 375, 90 S.Ct. 616, 24 L.Ed.2d 593 (1970), the Supreme Court held that:

Where the misstatement or omission in a proxy statement has been shown to be "material," as it was found to be here, that determination itself indubitably embodies a conclusion that the defect was of such a character that it might have been considered important by a reasonable shareholder who was in the process of deciding how to vote. This requirement that the defect have a significant *propensity* to affect the voting process is found in the express terms of Rule 14a–9, and it adequately serves the purpose of ensuring that a cause of action cannot be established by proof of a defect so trivial, or so unrelated to the transaction for which approval is sought, that correction of the defect or imposition of liability would not further the interests protected by § 14(a).

There is no need to supplement this requirement, as did the Court of Appeals, with a requirement of proof of whether the defect actually had a decisive effect on the voting. Where there has been a finding of materiality, a shareholder has made a sufficient showing of causal relationship between the violation and the injury for which he seeks redress if, as here, he proves that the proxy solicitation itself, rather than the particular defect in the solicitation materials, was an essential link in the accomplishment of the transaction. This objective test will avoid the impracticalities of determining how many votes were affected, and, by resolving doubts in favor of those the statute is designed to protect, will effectuate the congressional policy of ensuring that the shareholders are able to make an informed choice when they are consulted on corporate transactions.

Mills v. Electric Auto–Lite Co. leaves no doubt that a materially false or misleading proxy statement must be deemed to be the cause of a shareholder vote the proxy statement solicits. Accordingly, where a shareholder seeks to set aside or enjoin a transaction approved by the shareholders on the ground that the approval was solicited by a proxy statement that involved misstatements or omissions, he need do nothing more to prove causation than to prove materiality. See Gaines v. Haughton, 645 F.2d 761, 773–74 (9th Cir.1981), cert. denied 454 U.S. 1145, 102 S.Ct. 1006, 71 L.Ed.2d 297 (1982); Weisberg v. Coastal

States Gas Corp., 609 F.2d 650, 653 (2d Cir.1979), cert. denied 445 U.S. 951, 100 S.Ct. 1600, 63 L.Ed.2d 786 (1980).

———

## NOTE ON TSC INDUSTRIES v. NORTHWAY, INC.

In TSC Industries, Inc. v. Northway, Inc., 426 U.S. 438, 96 S.Ct. 2126, 48 L.Ed.2d 757 (1976), the Supreme Court addressed the issue of how materiality was to be defined, as follows:

> ... [I]n *Mills,* .... we held that there was no need to demonstrate that the alleged defect in the proxy statement actually had a decisive effect on the voting. So long as the misstatement or omission was material, the causal relation between violation and injury is sufficiently established, we concluded, if "the proxy solicitation itself ... was an essential link in the accomplishment of the transaction." 396 U.S., at 385, 90 S.Ct., at 622. After *Mills,* then, the content given to the notion of materiality assumes heightened significance....

> The question of materiality, it is universally agreed, is an objective one, involving the significance of an omitted or misrepresented fact to a reasonable investor. Variations in the formulation of a general test of materiality occur in the articulation of just how significant a fact must be or, put another way, how certain it must be that the fact would affect a reasonable investor's judgment....

> The Court of Appeals in this case concluded that material facts include "all facts which a reasonable shareholder *might* consider important." 512 F.2d, at 330 (emphasis added). This formulation of the test of materiality has been explicitly rejected by at least two courts as setting too low a threshold for the imposition of liability under Rule 14a–9. Gerstle v. Gamble–Skogmo, Inc., 478 F.2d 1281, 1301–1302 (C.A.2 1973); Smallwood v. Pearl Brewing Co., 489 F.2d 579, 603–604 (C.A.5 1974)....

> ... [T]he disclosure policy embodied in the proxy regulations is not without limit. See id., at 384, 90 S.Ct., at 621. Some information is of such dubious significance that insistence on its disclosure may accomplish more harm than good. The potential liability for a Rule 14a–9 violation can be great indeed, and if the standard of materiality is unnecessarily low, not only may the corporation and its management be subjected to liability for insignificant omissions or misstatements, but also management's fear of exposing itself to substantial liability may cause it simply to bury the shareholder in an avalanche of trivial information—a result that is hardly conducive to informed decisionmaking. Precisely these dangers are presented, we think, by the definition of a material fact adopted by the Court of Appeals in this case—a fact which a reasonable shareholder *might* consider important. We agree with Judge Friendly, speaking for the Court of Appeals in

*Gerstle,* that the "might" formulation is "too suggestive of mere possibility, however unlikely." 478 F.2d, at 1302.

The general standard of materiality that we think best comports with the policies of Rule 14a–9 is as follows: an omitted fact is material if there is a substantial likelihood that a reasonable shareholder would consider it important in deciding how to vote. This standard is fully consistent with *Mills* general description of materiality as a requirement that "the defect have a significant *propensity* to affect the voting process." It does not require proof of a substantial likelihood that disclosure of the omitted fact would have caused the reasonable investor to change his vote. What the standard does contemplate is a showing of a substantial likelihood that, under all the circumstances, the omitted fact would have assumed actual significance in the deliberations of the reasonable shareholder. Put another way, there must be a substantial likelihood that the disclosure of the omitted fact would have been viewed by the reasonable investor as having significantly altered the "total mix" of information made available.

---

## Virginia Bankshares, Inc. v. Sandberg

Supreme Court of the United States, 1991.
501 U.S. 1083, 111 S.Ct. 2749, 115 L.Ed.2d 929.

■ . . . JUSTICE SOUTER delivered the opinion of the Court.

Section 14(a) of the Securities Exchange Act of 1934, 48 Stat. 895, 15 U.S.C. § 78n(a), authorizes the Securities and Exchange Commission to adopt rules for the solicitation of proxies, and prohibits their violation. In J.I. Case Co. v. Borak, 377 U.S. 426, 84 S.Ct. 1555, 12 L.Ed.2d 423 (1964), we first recognized an implied private right of action for the breach of § 14(a) as implemented by SEC Rule 14a–9, which prohibits the solicitation of proxies by means of materially false or misleading statements.[2]

The questions before us are whether a statement couched in conclusory or qualitative terms purporting to explain directors' reasons for recommending certain corporate action can be materially misleading within the meaning of Rule 14a–9, and whether causation of damages compensable under § 14(a) can be shown by a member of a class of minority shareholders whose votes are not required by law or corporate bylaw to authorize the corporate action subject to the proxy solicitation. We hold that knowingly false statements of reasons may be actionable even though conclusory in form, but that respondents have failed to demonstrate the equitable basis required to

---

**2.** . . .

The Federal Deposit Insurance Corporation (FDIC) administers and enforces the securities laws with respect to the activities of federally insured and regulated banks. See Section 12(i) of the Exchange Act, 15 U.S.C. § 78*l*(i). An FDIC rule also prohibits materially misleading statements in the solicitation of proxies, 12 CFR § 335.206 (1991), and is essentially identical to Rule 14a–9. See generally Brief for SEC et al. as Amici Curiae 4, n. 5.

extend the § 14(a) private action to such shareholders when any indication of congressional intent to do so is lacking.

I

In December 1986, First American Bankshares, Inc., (FABI), a bank holding company, began a "freeze-out" merger, in which the First American Bank of Virginia (Bank) eventually merged into Virginia Bankshares, Inc., (VBI), a wholly owned subsidiary of FABI. VBI owned 85% of the Bank's shares, the remaining 15% being in the hands of some 2,000 minority shareholders. FABI hired the investment banking firm of Keefe, Bruyette & Woods (KBW) to give an opinion on the appropriate price for shares of the minority holders, who would lose their interests in the Bank as a result of the merger. Based on market quotations and unverified information from FABI, KBW gave the Bank's executive committee an opinion that $42 a share would be a fair price for the minority stock. The executive committee approved the merger proposal at that price, and the full board followed suit.

Although Virginia law required only that such a merger proposal be submitted to a vote at a shareholders' meeting, and that the meeting be preceded by circulation of a statement of information to the shareholders, the directors nevertheless solicited proxies for voting on the proposal at the annual meeting set for April 21, 1987.[3] In their solicitation, the directors urged the proposal's adoption and stated they had approved the plan because of its opportunity for the minority shareholders to achieve a "high" value, which they elsewhere described as a "fair" price, for their stock.

Although most minority shareholders gave the proxies requested, respondent Sandberg did not, and after approval of the merger she sought damages in the United States District Court for the Eastern District of Virginia from VBI, FABI, and the directors of the Bank. She pleaded two counts, one for soliciting proxies in violation of § 14(a) and Rule 14a–9, and the other for breaching fiduciary duties owed to the minority shareholders under state law. Under the first count, Sandberg alleged, among other things, that the directors had not believed that the price offered was high or that the terms of the merger were fair, but had recommended the merger only because they believed they had no alternative if they wished to remain on the board. At trial, Sandberg invoked language from this Court's opinion in Mills v. Electric Auto–Lite Co., 396 U.S. 375, 385, 90 S.Ct. 616, 622, 24 L.Ed.2d 593 (1970), to obtain an instruction that the jury could find for her without a showing of her own reliance on the alleged misstatements, so long as they were material and the proxy solicitation was an "essential link" in the merger process.

The jury's verdicts were for Sandberg on both counts, after finding violations of Rule 14a–9 by all defendants and a breach of fiduciary duties by the Bank's directors. The jury awarded Sandberg

---

**3.** Had the directors chosen to issue a statement instead of a proxy solicitation, they would have been subject to an SEC antifraud provision analogous to Rule 14a–9. See 17 CFR 240.14c–6 (1990). See also 15 U.S.C. § 78n(c).

$18 a share, having found that she would have received $60 if her stock had been valued adequately. . . .

On appeal, the United States Court of Appeals for the Fourth Circuit affirmed . . ., holding that certain statements in the proxy solicitation were materially misleading for purposes of the Rule, and that respondents could maintain their action even though their votes had not been needed to effectuate the merger. 891 F.2d 1112 (1989).[4] We granted certiorari because of the importance of the issues presented. 495 U.S. 903, 110 S.Ct. 1921, 109 L.Ed.2d 285 (1990).

## II

The Court of Appeals affirmed petitioners' liability for two statements found to have been materially misleading in violation of § 14(a) of the Act, one of which was that "The Plan of Merger has been approved by the Board of Directors because it provides an opportunity for the Bank's public shareholders to achieve a high value for their shares." App. to Pet. for Cert. 53a. Petitioners argue that statements of opinion or belief incorporating indefinite and unverifiable expressions cannot be actionable as misstatements of material fact within the meaning of Rule 14a–9, and that such a declaration of opinion or belief should never be actionable when placed in a proxy solicitation incorporating statements of fact sufficient to enable readers to draw their own, independent conclusions.

## A

We consider first the actionability per se of statements of reasons, opinion or belief. Because such a statement by definition purports to express what is consciously on the speaker's mind, we interpret the jury verdict as finding that the directors' statements of belief and opinion were made with knowledge that the directors did not hold the beliefs or opinions expressed, and we confine our discussion to statements so made.[5] That such statements may be materially significant raises no serious question. The meaning of the materiality requirement for liability under § 14(a) was discussed at some length in TSC Industries, Inc. v. Northway, Inc., 426 U.S. 438, 96 S.Ct. 2126, 48 L.Ed.2d 757 (1976), where we held a fact to be material "if there is a substantial likelihood that a reasonable shareholder would consider it important in deciding how to vote." Id., at 449, 96 S.Ct., at 2132. We think there is no room to deny that a statement of belief by corporate directors about a recommended course of action, or an explanation of their reasons for recommending it, can take on just that importance. Shareholders know that directors usually have knowledge and expertness far exceeding the normal investor's resources, and the directors'

---

**4.** The Court of Appeals reversed the District Court, however, on its refusal to certify a class of all minority shareholders in Sandberg's action. Consequently, it ruled that petitioners were liable to all of the Bank's former minority shareholders for $18 per share. 891 F.2d, at 1119.

**5.** In TSC Industries, Inc. v. Northway, Inc., 426 U.S. 438, 444, n. 7, 96 S.Ct. 2126, 2130, n. 7, 48 L.Ed.2d 757 (1976), we reserved the question whether scienter was necessary for liability generally under § 14(a). We reserve it still.

perceived superiority is magnified even further by the common knowledge that state law customarily obliges them to exercise their judgment in the shareholders' interest. Cf. Day v. Avery, 179 U.S.App.D.C. 63, 71, 548 F.2d 1018, 1026 (1976) (action for misrepresentation). Naturally, then, the share owner faced with a proxy request will think it important to know the directors' beliefs about the course they recommend, and their specific reasons for urging the stockholders to embrace it.

B

1

But, assuming materiality, the question remains whether statements of reasons, opinions, or beliefs are statements "with respect to ... material fact[s]" so as to fall within the strictures of the Rule. Petitioners argue that we would invite wasteful litigation of amorphous issues outside the readily provable realm of fact if we were to recognize liability here on proof that the directors did not recommend the merger for the stated reason. . . .

Attacks on the truth of directors' statements of reasons or belief, however, need carry no such threats. Such statements are factual in two senses: as statements that the directors do act for the reasons given or hold the belief stated and as statements about the subject matter of the reason or belief expressed. In neither sense does the proof or disproof of such statements implicate the concerns expressed in Blue Chip Stamps [v. Manor Drug Stores, 421 U.S. 723, 95 S.Ct. 1917, 44 L.Ed. 539 (1975)]. The root of those concerns was a plaintiff's capacity to manufacture claims of hypothetical action, unconstrained by independent evidence. Reasons for directors' recommendations or statements of belief are, in contrast, characteristically matters of corporate record subject to documentation, to be supported or attacked by evidence of historical fact outside a plaintiff's control. Such evidence would include not only corporate minutes and other statements of the directors themselves, but circumstantial evidence bearing on the facts that would reasonably underlie the reasons claimed and the honesty of any statement that those reasons are the basis for a recommendation or other action, a point that becomes especially clear when the reasons or beliefs go to valuations in dollars and cents.

It is no answer to argue, as petitioners do, that the quoted statement on which liability was predicated did not express a reason in dollars and cents, but focused instead on the "indefinite and unverifiable" term, "high" value, much like the similar claim that the merger's terms were "fair" to shareholders. The objection ignores the fact that such conclusory terms in a commercial context are reasonably understood to rest on a factual basis that justifies them as accurate, the absence of which renders them misleading. Provable facts either furnish good reasons to make a conclusory commercial judgment, or they count against it, and expressions of such judgments can be uttered with knowledge of truth or falsity just like more definite statements, and defended or attacked through the orthodox evidentiary process that either substantiates their underlying justifications or tends to disprove their existence.... In this case, whether $42 was "high," and the proposal "fair" to the minority shareholders depended on whether provable facts about the Bank's assets, and about actual and potential levels of operation, substantiated a value that was above, below, or more or less at the $42 figure, when assessed in accordance with recognized methods of valuation.

Respondents adduced evidence for just such facts in proving that the statement was misleading about its subject matter and a false expression of the directors' reasons. Whereas the proxy statement described the $42 price as offering a premium above both book value and market price, the evidence indicated that a calculation of the book figure based on the appreciated value of the Bank's real estate holdings eliminated any such premium. The evidence on the significance of market price showed that KBW had conceded that the market was closed, thin and dominated by FABI, facts omitted from the statement. There was, indeed, evidence of a "going concern" value for the Bank in excess of $60 per share of common stock, another fact never disclosed. However conclusory the directors' statement may have been, then, it was open to attack by garden-variety evidence, subject neither to a plaintiff's control nor ready manufacture, and there was no undue risk of open-ended liability or uncontrollable litigation in allowing respondents the opportunity for recovery on the allegation that it was misleading to call $42 "high."

This analysis comports with the holding that marked our nearest prior approach to the issue faced here, in *TSC Industries,* 426 U.S., at 454–55, 96 S.Ct., at 2135. There, to be sure, we reversed summary judgment for a *Borak* plaintiff who had sued on a description of proposed compensation for minority shareholders as offering a "substantial premium over current market values." But we held only that on the case's undisputed facts the conclusory adjective "substantial" was not materially misleading as a necessary matter of law, and our remand for trial assumed that such a description could be both materially misleading within the meaning of Rule 14a–9 and actionable under § 14(a). See *TSC Industries,* supra, at 458–460, 463–464, 96 S.Ct., at 2136–2138, 2139.

2

Under § 14(a), then, a plaintiff is permitted to prove a specific statement of reason knowingly false or misleadingly incomplete, even when stated in conclusory terms. In reaching this conclusion we have considered statements of reasons of the sort exemplified here, which misstate the speaker's reasons and also mislead about the stated subject matter (e.g., the value of the shares). A statement of belief may be open to objection only in the former respect, however, solely as a misstatement of the psychological fact of the speaker's belief in what he says. In this case, for example, the Court of Appeals alluded to just such limited falsity in observing that "the jury was certainly justified in believing that the directors did not believe a merger at $42 per share was in the minority stockholders' interest but, rather, that they voted as they did for other reasons, e.g., retaining their seats on the board." 891 F.2d, at 1121.

The question arises, then, whether disbelief, or undisclosed belief or motivation, standing alone, should be a sufficient basis to sustain an action under § 14(a), absent proof by the sort of objective evidence described above that the statement also expressly or impliedly asserted something false or misleading about its subject matter. We think that proof of mere disbelief or belief undisclosed should not suffice for liability under § 14(a), and if nothing more had been required or proven in this case we would reverse for that reason.

On the one hand, it would be rare to find a case with evidence solely of disbelief or undisclosed motivation without further proof that the statement was defective as to its subject matter. While we certainly would not hold a director's naked admission of disbelief incompetent evidence of a proxy statement's false or misleading character, such an unusual admission will not very often stand alone, and we do not substantially narrow the cause of action by requiring a plaintiff to demonstrate something false or misleading in what the statement expressly or impliedly declared about its subject.

On the other hand, to recognize liability on mere disbelief or undisclosed motive without any demonstration that the proxy statement was false or misleading about its subject would authorize § 14(a) litigation confined solely to what one skeptical court spoke of as the "impurities" of a director's "unclean heart." Stedman v. Storer, 308 F.Supp. 881, 887 (S.D.N.Y.1969) (dealing with § 10(b)). This, we think, would cross the line that *Blue Chip Stamps* sought to draw. While it is true that the liability, if recognized, would rest on an actual, not hypothetical, psychological fact, the temptation to rest an otherwise nonexistent § 14(a) action on psychological enquiry alone would threaten just the sort of strike suits and attrition by discovery that *Blue Chip Stamps* sought to discourage. We therefore hold disbelief or undisclosed motivation, standing alone, insufficient to satisfy the element of fact that must be established under § 14(a).

## C

Petitioners' fall-back position assumes the same relationship between a conclusory judgment and its underlying facts that we described in Part II–B–1, supra. Thus, citing Radol v. Thomas, 534 F.Supp. 1302, 1315, 1316 (S.D.Ohio 1982), petitioners argue that even if conclusory statements of reason or belief can be actionable under § 14(a), we should confine liability to instances where the proxy material fails to disclose the offending statement's factual basis. There would be no justification for holding the shareholders entitled to judicial relief, that is, when they were given evidence that a stated reason for a proxy recommendation was misleading, and an opportunity to draw that conclusion themselves.

The answer to this argument rests on the difference between a merely misleading statement and one that is materially so. While a misleading statement will not always lose its deceptive edge simply by joinder with others that are true, the true statements may discredit the other one so obviously that the risk of real deception drops to nil. Since liability under § 14(a) must rest not only on deceptiveness but materiality as well (i.e., it has to be significant enough to be important to a reasonable investor deciding how to vote, see *TSC Industries*, 426 U.S., at 449, 96 S.Ct., at 2132), petitioners are on perfectly firm ground insofar as they argue that publishing accurate facts in a proxy statement can render a misleading proposition too unimportant to ground liability.

But not every mixture with the true will neutralize the deceptive. If it would take a financial analyst to spot the tension between the one and the other, whatever is misleading will remain materially so, and liability should follow. Gerstle v. Gamble–Skogmo, Inc., 478 F.2d 1281, 1297 (C.A.2 1973) ("[I]t is not sufficient that overtones might have been picked up by the sensitive antennae of investment analysts"). Cf. Milkovich v. Lorain Journal Co., ... 110 S.Ct. 2695, 2708, 111 L.Ed.2d 1 (1990) (a defamatory assessment of facts can be actionable even if the facts underlying the assessment are accurately presented). The point of a proxy statement, after all, should be to inform, not to challenge the reader's critical wits. Only when the inconsistency would exhaust the misleading conclusion's capacity to influence the reasonable shareholder would a § 14(a) action fail on the element of materiality.

Suffice it to say that the evidence invoked by petitioners in the instant case fell short of compelling the jury to find the facial materiality of the misleading statement neutralized. The directors claim, for example, to have made an explanatory disclosure of further reasons for their recommendation when they said they would keep their seats following the merger, but they failed to mention what at least one of them admitted in testimony, that they would have had no expectation of doing so without supporting the proposal, App. at 281–82. And although the proxy statement did speak factually about the merger price in describing it as higher than share prices in recent sales, it failed even to mention the closed market dominated by FABI. None of these disclosures that the directors point to was, then, anything more than a half-truth, and the record shows that another fact statement they invoke was arguably even worse. The claim that the merger price exceeded book value was controverted, as we have seen already, by evidence of a higher book value than the directors conceded, reflecting appreciation in the Bank's real estate portfolio. Finally, the solicitation omitted any mention of the Bank's value as a going concern at more than $60 a share, as against the merger price of $42. There was, in sum, no more of a compelling case for the statement's immateriality than for its accuracy.

### III

The second issue before us, left open in Mills v. Electric Auto–Lite Co., 396 U.S., at 385, n. 7, 90 S.Ct., at 622, n. 7, is whether causation of damages compensable through the implied private right of action under § 14(a) can be demonstrated by a member of a class of minority shareholders whose votes are not required by law or corporate bylaw to authorize the transaction giving rise to the claim.

[The Court held that the answer to this question was, no. The plaintiffs argued that such a claim could be supported by two theories: that the proxy statement was an essential link between the director's proposal and the merger (1) because VBI and FABI would have been unwilling to proceed with the merger unless the minority approved, and (2) because the vote of the minority was the means to satisfy a state statutory requirement of minority shareholder approval as a condition for saving the merger from voidability resulting from a conflict of interest. The court rejected the first theory on the ground that acceptance of the concept would give rise to speculative claims. As to the second theory, the court said:]

This case does not ... require us to decide whether § 14(a) provides a cause of action for lost state remedies, since there is no indication in the law or facts before us that the proxy solicitation resulted in any such loss. The contrary appears to be the case. Assuming the soundness of respondents' characterization of the proxy statement as materially misleading, the very terms of the Virginia statute indicate that a favorable minority vote induced by the solicitation would not suffice to render the merger invulnerable to later attack on the ground of the conflict. The statute bars a shareholder from seeking to avoid a transaction tainted by a director's conflict if, inter alia, the minority shareholders ratified the transaction following disclosure of the material facts of the transaction and the conflict. Va.Code § 13.1–691(A)(2) (1989). Assuming that the material facts about the merger and Beddow's interests were not accurately disclosed, the minority votes were inadequate to ratify the merger under state law, and there was no loss of state remedy to connect the proxy solicitation with harm to minority shareholders irredressable under state law. Nor is there a claim here that the statement misled respondents into entertaining a false belief that they had no chance to upset the merger, until the time for bringing suit had run out.[14]

### IV

The judgment of the Court of Appeals is reversed.

It is so ordered.

[Justice Scalia wrote a separate opinion in which he concurred in the judgment and joined in the opinion except for Part II. Justice Stevens, with whom Justice Marshall joined, wrote a separate opinion in which he agreed in substance with Parts I and II, but dissented from the reasoning in Part III. Justice Kennedy, with whom Justice Marshall, Justice Blackmun, and Justice Stevens joined, wrote a separate opinion

---

**14.** Respondents do not claim that any other application of a theory of lost state remedies would avail them here. It is clear, for example, that no state appraisal remedy was lost through a § 14(a) violation in this case....

which expressed general agreement with Parts I and II but dissented from Part III.]

---

## NOTE ON THE STANDARD OF FAULT IN PRIVATE ACTIONS UNDER THE PROXY RULES

Under *Borak* and *Mills,* shareholders have standing to bring an action under Rule 14a–9, which prohibits false or misleading proxy statements. Does a plaintiff-shareholder prevail if he shows that a proxy statement was false or misleading by virtue of a material misstatement or omission, or must he also show that the misstatement or omission resulted from the defendant's fault? If the plaintiff must show fault, does negligence suffice?

In the leading case of Gerstle v. Gamble–Skogmo, Inc., 478 F.2d 1281 (2d Cir.1973), the Second Circuit, in an opinion written by Judge Friendly, held that negligence sufficed to establish liability under Rule 14a–9:

> We thus hold that in a case like this, where the plaintiffs represent the very class who were asked to approve a merger on the basis of a misleading proxy statement and are seeking compensation from the beneficiary who is responsible for the preparation of the statement, they are not required to establish any evil motive or even reckless disregard of the facts. Whether in situations other than that here presented "the liability of the corporation issuing a materially false or misleading proxy statement is virtually absolute, as under Section 11 of the 1933 Act with respect to a registration statement," Jennings & Marsh, Securities Regulation: Cases and Materials 1358 (3d ed. 1972), we leave to another day. 478 F.2d at 1298–1301. Accord: Herskowitz v. Nutri/System, Inc., 857 F.2d 179 (3d Cir.1988), cert. denied 489 U.S. 1054, 109 S.Ct. 1315, 103 L.Ed.2d 584 (1989); Gould v. American–Hawaiian Steamship Co., 535 F.2d 761 (3d Cir.1976).

But see Adams v. Standard Knitting Mills, Inc., 623 F.2d 422 (6th Cir.1980), cert. denied 449 U.S. 1067, 101 S.Ct. 795, 66 L.Ed.2d 611. ("scienter should be an element of liability in private suits under the proxy provisions as they apply to outside accountants").

In Shidler v. All American Life & Financial Corp., 775 F.2d 917, 927 (8th Cir.1985), the Eighth Circuit addressed the issue that Judge Friendly left to another day in *Gerstle,* and held there was no liability without fault in an action under Section 14(a):

> The purpose of section 14(a) is "to prevent management or others from obtaining authorization for corporate action by means of deceptive or inadequate disclosure in proxy solicitation." J.I. Case Co. v. Borak, 377 U.S. 426, 431, 84 S.Ct. 1555, 1559, 12 L.Ed.2d 423 (1964). A strict liability rule would impose liability for fully innocent misstatements. It is too blunt a tool to ferret out

the kind of deceptive practices Congress sought to prevent in enacting section 14(a).

The Supreme Court has several times explicitly taken note of the position of *Gerstle* and other cases that scienter is not an element of liability under § 14(a), and has each time declined to address the issue. See Ernst & Ernst v. Hochfelder, 425 U.S. 185, 209 n. 28, 96 S.Ct. 1375, 1388 n. 28, 47 L.Ed.2d 668 (1976); TSC Indus., Inc. v. Northway, 426 U.S. 438, 444 n. 7, 96 S.Ct. 2126, 2130 n. 7, 48 L.Ed.2d 757 (1976); *Virginia Bankshares,* supra, at note 5.

———

## NOTE ON STATE LAW

Perhaps as a result of experience under the Proxy Rules, the standards applied by state courts today, in reviewing the adequacy of disclosure to shareholders under state law in connection with a matter proposed for a shareholder vote, is likely to be close to the standards under the Proxy Rules. See Chapter 10, Section 5, infra.

———

# SECTION 5.    THE PROXY RULES (III): SHAREHOLDER PROPOSALS

———

## SECURITIES EXCHANGE ACT RULE 14a–7

[See Statutory Supplement]

———

## SECURITIES EXCHANGE ACT RULE 14a–8

[See Statutory Supplement]

———

## NOTE ON NO–ACTION LETTERS INTERPRETING RULE 14a–8

Rule 14a–8 provides that if management believes a shareholder proposal can be excluded from the corporation's proxy statement under Rule 14a–8, it must submit to the SEC staff a statement of the reasons why it deems omission of the proposal to be proper. If the staff agrees with management's statement, it sends management a "no-action letter"—that is, a letter stating that if the shareholder proposal is omitted, no action will be taken by the SEC. If the staff disagrees with management's statement, it sends a letter stating why the proposal should be included. Such letters are also referred to as no-action letters, although in fact they are just the opposite—that is, they implicitly threaten legal proceedings if management omits the shareholder proposal. In such cases management may still omit the shareholder proposal and run the risk of legal proceedings by the SEC, but that option is seldom if ever exercised.

---

## Aon Corporation
[SEC NO–ACTION LETTER].
March 6, 1997.

The proposal requests that the board initiate a policy mandating no further purchases of tobacco equities and that the Company divest itself of all tobacco stocks by January 1, 1998.

The [SEC Division of Corporate Finance] is unable to concur in your view that the proposal may be omitted from the Company's proxy materials under Rule 14a–8(i)(5). That provision permits the omission of a proposal if it relates to operations which account for less than 5% of the registrant's total assets, net earnings and gross sales, and is not otherwise significantly related to the registrant's business. The staff is of the view that the proposal is "otherwise significantly related" to the Company's business. Accordingly, the Division does not believe the Company may rely on Rule 14a–8(i)(5) as a basis for omitting the proposal from its proxy materials.

The Division is unable to concur in your view that the proposal may be omitted from the Company's proxy materials under Rule 14a–8(i)(7) as a matter relating to ordinary business operations. Accordingly, the Division does not believe that the Company may rely on Rule 14a–8(i)(7) as a basis for omitting the proposal from its proxy materials. . . .

---

## Roosevelt v. E.I. Du Pont de Nemours & Co.
United States Court of Appeals, District of Columbia Circuit, 1992.
958 F.2d 416.

■ Before EDWARDS, RUTH BADER GINSBURG, and SENTELLE, CIRCUIT JUDGES.

■ Opinion for the Court filed by CIRCUIT JUDGE RUTH BADER GINSBURG.

■ RUTH BADER GINSBURG, CIRCUIT JUDGE.

Amelia Roosevelt appeals the district court's judgment that E.I. Du Pont de Nemours & Co. ("Du Pont") could omit her shareholder proposal from its proxy materials for the 1992 annual meeting. The district court concluded that Roosevelt's proposal "deals with a matter relating to the conduct of [Du Pont's] ordinary business operations," and is therefore excludable under Securities and Exchange Commission ("SEC") Rule 14a–8(c)(7), 17 C.F.R. § 240.14a–8(c)(7). We affirm the district court's judgment and deal first with a threshold question. Consistent with congressional intent and Supreme Court case law, we hold, a private right of action is properly implied from section 14(a) of the Securities Exchange Act of 1934 (the "Act"), 15 U.S.C. § 78n(a), to enforce a company's obligation to include shareholder proposals in annual meeting proxy materials. Reaching the merits, we uphold the district court's determination that Roosevelt's two-part proposal is excludable under Rule 14a–8(c)(7).

## I. Background

Prior to Du Pont's 1991 annual shareholder meeting, Friends of the Earth Oceanic Society ("Friends of the Earth") submitted a proposal, on behalf of Roosevelt, regarding: (1) the timing of Du Pont's phase out of the production of chlorofluorocarbons ("CFCs") and halons; and (2) the presentation to shareholders of a report detailing (a) research and development efforts to find environmentally sound substitutes, and (b) marketing plans to sell those substitutes.[1] Du Pont opposed inclusion of the proposal in its proxy materials; as required by SEC rule, see 17 C.F.R. § 240.14a–8(d), the company notified the SEC staff of its intention to omit the proposal and its reasons for believing the omission proper. Friends of the Earth filed with the staff a countersubmission on Roosevelt's behalf urging that the proposal was not excludable.

The SEC staff issued a "no-action letter"; citing the Rule 14a–8(c)(7) exception for matters "relating to the conduct of the [company's] ordinary business operations," the staff stated that it would not recommend Commission enforcement action against Du Pont if the company excluded the proposal. Du Pont, SEC No–Action Letter (available March 8, 1991). Roosevelt did not seek Commission review of the staff's disposition.

Instead, with the 1991 meeting weeks away, Roosevelt filed a complaint and a motion for a temporary restraining order in federal district court. Denying the motion, the motions judge stated preliminarily that "[t]he Supreme Court has recognized an implied private

---

1. Roosevelt's proposal consists of twelve "whereas" clauses followed by two resolutions. In relevant part, the proposal states:

Whereas, The international scientific community has determined that synthetic chemicals—including chlorofluorocarbons (CFCs), halons, carbon tetrachloride, methyl chloroform, and hydrochlorofluorocarbons (HCFCs)—are destroying the Earth's protective ozone layer at an alarming rate;

\* \* \*

Whereas, Many governments are taking action beyond the Montreal Protocol [the international ozone protection treaty, including an agreement to stop CFC production in the year 2000]; for example, Germany plans to stop CFC and halon production in 1995, and German CFC producers Hoechst AG and Kali–Chemie have announced they will stop making CFCs in 1995;

\* \* \*

Resolved, That the shareholders of the Du Pont Company, assembled in annual meeting in person and by proxy, request that the Board of Directors:

1. Rapidly accelerate plans to phase out CFC and halon production, surpassing our global competitors which have set a 1995 target date;

2. Present a report to shareholders within six months detailing (a) research and development program expenditures which dramatically increase efforts to find CFC and halon substitutes which do not harm the ozone layer or contribute significantly to global warning; and (b) a marketing plan to sell those environmentally safe alternatives to present customers.

right of action for alleged violations of Rule 14a–8." She found, however, that Roosevelt had not shown the requisite irreparable harm. If Du Pont mailed its proxy materials on March 18, as scheduled, without Roosevelt's proposal, the motions judge observed, a supplemental mailing containing the proposal could still be made in advance of the April 24 annual meeting date. C.A. No. 91–556, Memorandum Order (March 18, 1991) at 1, 3. The trial judge held an expedited trial on the morning of April 2, 1991; in a Memorandum Opinion filed two days later, he ruled that, based on the "ordinary business operations" exception in Rule 14a–8(c)(7), Du Point could omit Roosevelt's proposal. C.A. No. 91–556, Memorandum Opinion (April 4, 1991) ("Mem. Op.").

We expedited Roosevelt's appeal when she informed us that she sought inclusion of her proposal in the proxy materials for Du Pont's 1992 annual meeting. C.A. No. 91–5087, Order (April 9, 1991) (per curiam). Before the appeal was heard, Du Pont had again advised the SEC that it intended to exclude the proposal, and the SEC staff had issued a second no-action letter, once more concluding that "[t]here appears to be some basis for [Du Pont's] view that the proposal may be excluded ... pursuant to rule 14a–8(c)(7)." Du Pont, SEC No–Action Letter (available Sept. 11, 1991).[3] Neither Roosevelt nor the SEC staff requested the Commission's view on the applicability of the "ordinary business operations" exception to Roosevelt's proposal.

## II. The Implied Private Right of Action and Shareholder Proposals

Before reviewing the district court's application of Rule 14a–8(c)(7), we resolve a preliminary question: Does a shareholder have an implied right of action under section 14(a) of the Act and Commission Rule 14a–8 when a company refuses to include the shareholder's proposal in proxy materials? ...

[The court held that a shareholder did have such a right of action.]

## III. Roosevelt's Proposals and the Rule 14a–8(c)(7) Exception for "Ordinary Business Operations"

Reaching the merits, we restate the district court's ruling: "Roosevelt's proposal deals with matters relating to the conduct of the ordinary business operations of Du Pont. Therefore, [under Rule 14a–8(c)(7)], Du Pont properly omitted her proposal from its proxy statement." Mem.Op. at 1. In reviewing this ruling, we emphasize that Roosevelt's disagreement with Du Pont's current policy is not about whether to eliminate CFC production or even whether to do so at once. The former is an end to which Du Pont is committed, and immediate cessation, before environmentally safe alternatives are available, is not what Roosevelt proposes.

**3.** The staff reasoned in September 1991, as it had the previous March, that "the thrust of the proposal appears directed at those questions concerning the timing, research and marketing decisions that involve matters relating to the conduct of the Company's ordinary business operations." Id.

Roosevelt differs with Du Pont on a less fundamental matter—the rapidity with which the near-term phase out should occur. Roosevelt seeks a target no later than 1995 ("surpassing [Du Pont's] global competitors which have set a 1995 target date"). In contrast, when this litigation began, Du Pont had set a target of "as soon as possible, but at least by the year 2000." Mem.Op. at 4.

In recent months and days, the "at least by" year has moved ever closer to Roosevelt's target. Prior to oral argument, Roosevelt informed the court, pursuant to Fed.R.App.P. 28(j) and D.C.Cir.R. 11(h), that Du Pont had issued a press release reiterating its "as soon as possible" policy, but "advancing the end point to year-end 1994 for Halons and 1996 for CFCs." Du Pont Corporate News, Oct. 22, 1991, at 1 (citing "scientific data released today by the United Nations Environment Programme ... and World Meteorological Organization"). Following oral argument, Du Pont informed the court that, "[i]n response to an announcement issued by the White House today regarding an accelerated phaseout of CFCs and Halons," the company "will accelerate its CFC end date to no later than December 31, 1995 in developed countries." Du Pont Statement on Accelerated CFC Phaseout, Feb. 12, 1992.

Although the regulation necessary to give effect to the President's announcement has not yet been adopted, Du Pont immediately reported that it "supports the Administration's position," id., and that it will phase out CFC production by December 31, 1995. We accept that public statement as the company's current timetable. While the SEC staff and the district court considered Roosevelt's proposal with the company's year–2000 end point in view, we think it proper to take account of the current reality: Roosevelt's proposal would have Du Pont surpass its global competitors' target of 1995; Du Pont projects completion of the phase out "as soon as possible," but no later than year-end 1995.

Roosevelt has confirmed that the first, or phase-out portion of her proposal is the "core issue" and that, if necessary, she would withdraw the second, or report-to-shareholders portion, so that the first portion could be included in Du Pont's 1992 proxy materials. Plaintiff–Appellant's Reply to Brief of the Securities and Exchange Commission, Amicus Curiae, at 4–5. We therefore consider separately the two portions of Roosevelt's proposal.

Because both parts of Roosevelt's proposal must be measured against the Rule 14a-8(c)(7) "ordinary business operations" exception, we set out here the Commission's general understanding of that phrase. When the Commission adopted the current version of the "ordinary business operations" exception, it announced its intention to interpret the phrase both "more restrictive[ly]" and "more flexibly than in the past." *Adoption of Amendments Relating to Proposals by Security Holders,* Exchange Act Release No. 12,999, 41 Fed.Reg. 52,-994, 52,998 (Dec. 3, 1976) ("*1976 Rule 14a–8 Amendments*"). Specifically, the Commission explained:

[T]he term "ordinary business operations" has been deemed on occasion to include certain matters which have significant policy, economic or other implications inherent in them. For instance, a proposal that a utility company not construct a proposed nuclear power plant has in the past been considered excludable under [the predecessor of (c)(7)]. In retrospect, however, it seems apparent that the economic and safety considerations attendant to nuclear power plants are of such magnitude that a determination whether to construct one is not an "ordinary" business matter. Accordingly, proposals of that nature, as well as others that have major implications, will in the future be considered beyond the realm of an issuer's ordinary business operations. . . .

Id.; see *Grimes,* 909 F.2d at 531 (observing that, "[u]nfortunately, the phrase [ordinary business operations] has no precise definition"). The Commission contrasted with matters of such moment as a decision not to build a nuclear power plant, "matters . . . mundane in nature [that] do not involve any substantial policy . . . considerations." *1976 Rule 14a–8 Amendments,* 41 Fed.Reg. at 52,998. Proposals of that genre, the Commission said, may be safely omitted from proxy materials.

In its brief as amicus curiae, the SEC stated that it regarded the first portion of Roosevelt's proposal, on the timing of the CFC phase out, as not excludable under Rule 14a–8(c)(7), but the second part, on research and development programs and marketing plans, as fitting within the "ordinary business operations" exception. Brief of the Securities and Exchange Commission, Amicus Curiae, at 31. The Commission noted that "[its] staff, in contrast, viewed the timing of the phase-out as an ordinary business matter." Id. at 32 n. 23. We agree with the Commission on the second part of Roosevelt's proposal but not on the first.

### A. The Phase Out Target Date

It is not debated in this case that CFCs contribute intolerably to depletion of the ozone layer and that their manufacture has caused a grave environmental hazard. However, Roosevelt's proposal, we emphasize again, relates not to *whether* CFC production should be phased out, but *when* the phase out should be completed. Cf. Loews Corporation, SEC No–Action Letter (available Feb. 22, 1990) (shareholder proposal for eventual cessation of manufacture of tobacco products; company unsuccessfully urged that what products it makes is a matter of "ordinary business operations").

Timing questions no doubt reflect "significant policy" when large differences are at stake. That would be the case, for example, if Du Pont projected a phase-out period extending into the new century. On the other hand, were Roosevelt seeking to move up Du Pont's target date by barely a season, the matter would appear much more of an "ordinary" than an extraordinary business judgment. In evaluating the Commission's classification of the timing question here as extraordinary, *i.e.,* one involving "fundamental business strategy" or "long-term goals," see Brief of the Securities and Exchange Commission, Amicus

Curiae, at 31, we are mindful that the SEC focused on a five-year interval, see id. at 32 n. 25, not an interval cut down to one year. See supra pp. 425–26.[19]

We are furthermore mindful that we sit in this case as a court of review and owe respect to the findings made by the district court. The trial judge concluded from the record that "Du Pont's 'as soon as possible' policy," contrary to Roosevelt's argument, "does not lack definition." Mem.Op. at 5. The judge found the policy genuine based on evidence that Du Pont had already spent more than $240 million developing alternatives to CFCs and had just announced the shutdown of the facility that had been the largest CFC plant in the world. Id. Du Pont, the district court also observed, continues to work "toward a global policy of phasing out CFCs" and "with CFC consumers to phase out their use of CFCs." Id.

Stressing the undisputed need for the responsible development of safe substitutes, and the acknowledged irresponsibility of suddenly cutting off all CFC production, the trial judge highlighted the essential difference between this case and the nuclear power plant in the Commission's *1976 Rule 14a–8 Amendments* example. See supra p. 426. Phasing out CFC production is not a go/no go matter. Cf. *Medical Comm.*, 432 F.2d at 663 (proposal to halt immediately all production of napalm). The phase out takes work "day-to-day . . . with equipment manufacturers to help develop the technology needed for alternative compounds." Mem.Op. at 6. It takes careful planning "in sensitive areas, such as the storage of perishable food and medical products (like vaccines and transfusable blood)," and expertise "in technical fields, such as the sterilization of temperature-sensitive surgical instruments." Id.

We recognize that "ordinary business operations" ordinarily do not attract the interest of both the executive and legislative branches of the federal government. See supra notes 15, 18. But government regulation of the CFC phase out, even the President's headline-attracting decision to accelerate the schedule initially set by Congress, does not automatically elevate shareholder proposals on timing to the status of "significant policy." See supra p. 427. What the President and Congress have said about CFCs is not the subject of our closest look. Instead, Rule 14a–8(c)(7) requires us to home in on Roosevelt's proposal, to determine whether her request dominantly implicates ordinary business matters. The gap between her proposal and the company's schedule is now one year, not five. The steps to be taken to accomplish the phase out are complex; as the district court found, the company, having agreed on the essential policy, must carry it out safely, using "business and technical skills" day-to-day that are not meant for "shareholder debate and participation." Mem.Op. at 5, 6.

---

**19.** As Roosevelt correctly points out, the principle of deference described in Chevron U.S.A. Inc. v. NRDC, Inc., 467 U.S. 837, 104 S.Ct. 2778, 81 L.Ed.2d 694 (1984), is not applicable here, for neither the staff's no-action letter nor the Commission's brief ranks as an agency adjudication or rulemaking. See Reply Brief at 12–14. Nonetheless, we value the SEC's presentation; the Commission's brief has clarified several points and thereby aided our analysis considerably.

In sum, the parties agree that CFC production must be phased out, that substitutes must be developed, and that both should be achieved sooner rather than later. Du Pont has undertaken to eliminate the products in question by year-end 1995, and has pledged to do so sooner if "possible." The trial judge has found Du Pont's "as soon as possible" pledge credible. In these circumstances, we conclude that what is at stake is the "implementation of a policy," "the timing for an agreed-upon action," see Brief of the Securities and Exchange Commission, Amicus Curiae, at 31, and we therefore hold the target date for the phase out a matter excludable under Rule 14a–8(c)(7).

### B.  The Report to Shareholders

The second part of Roosevelt's proposal solicits a report from management within six months detailing research and development efforts on environmentally safe substitutes and a marketing plan to sell those substitutes. See supra note 1. This portion of the proposal, the SEC concluded in agreement with its staff, "requires detailed information about the company's day-to-day business operations [and] is subject to exclusion pursuant to [Rule 14a–8(c)(7)]." Brief of the Securities and Exchange Commission, Amicus Curiae, at 31. Roosevelt concedes that the report is not central to her proposal, see supra p. 426, and we find no cause to place the matter outside the "ordinary business operations" exception.

For a time, the Commission staff "ha[d] taken the position that proposals requesting issuers to prepare reports on specific aspects of their business or to form [study committees] would not be excludable under Rule 14a–8(c)(7)." *Amendments to Rule 14a–8 Under the Securities Exchange Act of 1934 Relating to Proposals by Security Holders,* Exchange Act Release No. 20,091, 48 Fed.Reg. 38,218, 38,221 (Aug. 23, 1983). The Commission has changed that position. Pointing out that the staff's interpretation "raise[d] form over substance," the Commission instructed the staff to "consider whether the subject matter of the [requested] report or [study] committee involves a matter of ordinary business: where it does, the proposal [is] excludable under Rule 14a–8(c)(7)." Id.

We need not linger over the report issue. The staff's no-action letters in this respect are unremarkable and entirely in keeping with current practice. See, e.g., Carolina Power & Light Co., SEC No–Action Letter (available Mar. 8, 1990) (shareholder proposal requesting preparation of a report on specific aspects of company's nuclear operations, covering, *inter alia,* safety, regulatory compliance, emissions problems, hazardous waste disposal and related cost information, may be omitted as relating to ordinary business operations).

Just as the Commission has clarified that requests for special reports or committee studies are not automatically includable in proxy materials, we caution that such requests are not inevitably excludable. But Roosevelt has not shown that the detailed research and development or marketing information she seeks implicates significant policy issues, and not merely implementation arrangements. She does not, for example, suggest that Du Pont is developing or planning to market hazardous substitutes. Cf. Lovenheim v. Iroquois Brands, Ltd., 618 F.Supp. 554, 556, 561 (D.D.C.1985) (in light of "ethical and social significance" of proposal, court granted preliminary injunction barring corporation from excluding from its proxy materials shareholder proposal that requested formation of committee to study, and submission of report to shareholders about, whether company's supplier produced pate de foie gras in a manner involving undue pain or suffering to animals and whether distribution of product should be discontinued pending development of a more humane method).

In agreement with the district judge, the Commission, and the staff, we hold that the second part of Roosevelt's proposal falls within the "ordinary business operations" exception.

### Conclusion

A private right of action is properly implied from section 14(a) of the Act, and Commission Rule 14a–8 thereunder, to enforce a registrant's obligation to include a shareholder's proposal in proxy materials mailed out in advance of the annual meeting. Roosevelt's proposal, however, may be excluded by Du Pont because, in both of its parts, the proposal falls within the exception furnished by Rule 14a–8(c)(7) for matters relating to "ordinary business operations." Accordingly, the judgment of the district court is

*Affirmed.*

---

## NOTE ON CORPORATE–GOVERNANCE SHAREHOLDER PROPOSALS

According to Kenneth Bertsch, Voting on Corporate Governance Shareholder Proposals—1998 (IRRC 1999), the following are the average votes cast in favor of shareholder resolutions on selected corporate-governance issues in 1998:

| Issue | Average Votes Cast in Favor |
|---|---|
| Confidential voting | 47.3 |
| Cumulative voting | 27.0 |
| Board inclusiveness | 14.4 |
| Golden parachutes | 23.9 |
| Indep. nominating committee | 22.9 |
| Majority independent directors | 23.8 |
| Pay directors in stock | 13.0 |
| Redeem or vote on poison pill | 58.1 |
| Repeal classified board | 47.9 |
| Restrict executive compensation | 9.6 |

---

## NOTE ON SHAREHOLDER SOCIAL-POLICY PROPOSALS

IRRC, Social Policy Shareholder Resolutions in 1998: Issues, Votes, and Views of Institutional Investors (1999) reports the following data for shareholder social-policy resolutions in 1998:

| Subject | Number of Resolutions | | | | | Average |
|---|---|---|---|---|---|---|
| | Proposed | Withdrawn | Omitted | Voted on | | Votes |
| | 1998 | 1998 | 1998 | 1997 | 1998 | 1998 |
| Board Diversity | 17 | 10 | 0 | 7 | 7 | 14.3 |
| Energy | 9 | 0 | 0 | 8 | 9 | 6.9 |
| Environment: Ceres | 30 | 17 | 0 | 10 | 13 | 8.4 |
| non-Ceres | 24 | 3 | 9 | 8 | 12 | 4.9 |
| Equal Employment | 22 | 5 | 14 | 8 | 3 | 13.7 |
| Executive Compensation | 24 | 7 | 5 | 11 | 11 | 4.6 |
| Human Rights | 13 | 0 | 2 | 8 | 11 | 5.9 |
| Global Labor/Env. Standards | 19 | 5 | 7 | 4 | 6 | 9.2 |
| Mexico | 4 | 2 | 2 | 3 | 0 | – |
| Military | 9 | 0 | 0 | 7 | 9 | 7.5 |
| Northern Ireland | 10 | 4 | 1 | 3 | 5 | 15.6 |
| Political Contributions/Ties | 22 | 2 | 5 | 13 | 14 | 6.6 |
| Tobacco | 21 | 3 | 6 | 18 | 12 | 7.3 |
| Other issues | 65 | 14 | 43 | 7 | 8 | NA |
| Total | 289 | 72 | 94 | 115 | 120 | 7.6 |

## SECTION 6. PROXY CONTESTS

---

## Rosenfeld v. Fairchild Engine and Airplane Corp.

Court of Appeals of New York, 1955.
309 N.Y. 168, 128 N.E.2d 291.

■ FROSSEL, JUDGE. In a stockholder's derivative action brought by plaintiff, an attorney, who owns 25 out of the company's over 2,300,000 shares, he seeks to compel the return of $261,522, paid out of the corporate treasury to reimburse both sides in a proxy contest for their expenses. The Appellate Division, 284 App.Div. 201, 132 N.Y.S.2d 273, has unanimously affirmed a judgment of an Official Referee, Sup., 116 N.Y.S.2d 840, dismissing plaintiff's complaint on the merits, and we agree. Exhaustive opinions were written by both courts below, and it will serve no useful purpose to review the facts again.

Of the amount in controversy $106,000 was spent out of corporate funds by the old board of directors while still in office in defense of their position in said contest; $28,000 [was] paid to the old board by the new board after the change of management following the proxy contest, to compensate the former directors for such of the remaining expenses of their unsuccessful defense as the new board found was fair and reasonable; payment of $127,000, representing reimbursement of expenses to members of the prevailing group, was expressly ratified by a 16 to 1 majority vote of the stockholders.

The essential facts are not in dispute, and, since the determinations below are amply supported by the evidence, we are bound by the findings affirmed by the Appellate Division. The Appellate Division found that the difference between plaintiff's group and the old board "went deep into the policies of the company", and that among these Ward's contract was one of the "main points of contention". The Official Referee found that the controversy "was based on an understandable difference in policy between the two groups, at the very bottom of which was the Ward employment contract".

By way of contrast with the findings here, in Lawyers' Advertising Co. v. Consolidated Ry., Lighting & Refrigerating Co., 187 N.Y. 395, at page 399, 80 N.E. 199, at page 200, which was an action to recover for the cost of publishing newspaper notices not authorized by the board of directors, it was expressly found that the proxy contest there involved was "by one faction in its contest with another for the control of the corporation ... a contest for the perpetuation of their offices and control." We there said by way of *dicta* that under *such* circumstances the publication of certain notices on behalf of the management faction was not a corporate expenditure which the directors had the power to authorize.

Other jurisdictions and our own lower courts have held that management may look to the corporate treasury for the reasonable expenses of soliciting proxies to defend its position in a bona fide policy contest. . . .

It should be noted that plaintiff does not argue that the aforementioned sums were fraudulently extracted from the corporation; indeed, his counsel conceded that "the charges were fair and reasonable", but denied "they were legal charges which may be reimbursed for". This is therefore not a case where a stockholder challenges specific items, which, on examination, the trial court may find unwarranted, excessive or otherwise improper. Had plaintiff made such objections here, the trial court would have been required to examine the items challenged.

If directors of a corporation may not in good faith incur reasonable and proper expenses in soliciting proxies in these days of giant corporations with vast numbers of stockholders, the corporate business might be seriously interfered with because of stockholder indifference and the difficulty of procuring a quorum, where there is no contest. In the event of a proxy contest, if the directors may not freely answer the challenges of outside groups and in good faith defend their actions with respect to corporate policy for the information of the stockholders, they and the corporation may be at the mercy of persons seeking to wrest control for their own purposes, so long as such persons have ample funds to conduct a proxy contest. The test is clear. When the directors act in good faith in a contest over policy, they have the right to incur reasonable and proper expenses for solicitation of proxies and in defense of their corporate policies, and are not obliged to sit idly by. The courts are entirely competent to pass upon their *bona fides* in any given case, as well as the nature of their expenditures when duly challenged.

It is also our view that the members of the so-called new group could be reimbursed by the corporation for their expenditures in this contest by affirmative vote of the stockholders. With regard to these ultimately successful contestants, as the Appellate Division below has noted, there was, of course, "no duty . . . to set forth the facts, with corresponding obligation of the corporation to pay for such expense". However, where a majority of the stockholders chose—in this case by a vote of 16 to 1—to reimburse the successful contestants for achieving the very end sought and voted for by them as owners of the corporation, we see no reason to deny the effect of their ratification nor to hold the corporate body powerless to determine how its own moneys shall be spent.

The rule then which we adopt is simply this: In a contest over policy, as compared to a purely personal power contest, corporate directors have the right to make reasonable and proper expenditures, subject to the scrutiny of the courts when duly challenged, from the corporate treasury for the purpose of persuading the stockholders of the correctness of their position and soliciting their support for policies which the directors believe, in all good faith, are in the best interests of the corporation. The stockholders, moreover, have the right to reimburse successful contestants for the reasonable and bona fide expenses incurred by them in any such policy contest, subject to like court scrutiny. That is not to say, however, that corporate directors can, under any circumstances, disport themselves in a proxy contest with the corporation's moneys to an unlimited extent. Where it is established that such moneys have been spent for personal power, individual gain or private advantage, and not in the belief that such expenditures are in the best interests of the stockholders and the corporation, or where the fairness and reasonableness of the amounts allegedly expended are duly and successfully challenged, the courts will not hesitate to disallow them.

The judgment of the Appellate Division should be affirmed, without costs.

■ DESMOND, JUDGE (concurring). We granted leave to appeal in an effort to pass, and in the expectation of passing, on this question, highly important in modern-day corporation law: is it lawful for a corporation, on consent of a majority of its stockholders, to pay, out of its funds, the expenses of a "proxy fight", incurred by competing candidates for election as directors? Now that the appeal has been argued, I doubt that the question is presented by this record. . . .

. . . The reason why that important question is, perhaps, not directly before us in this lawsuit is because, as the Appellate Division properly held, [284 App.Div. 201, 132 N.Y.S.2d 273] plaintiff failed "to urge liability as to specific expenditures". The cost of giving routinely necessary notice is, of course, chargeable to the corporation. It is just as clear, we think, that payment by a corporation of the expense of "proceedings by one faction in its contest with another for the control of the corporation" is *ultra vires,* and unlawful. Lawyers' Advertising Co. v. Consolidated Ry., Lighting & Refrigerating Co., 187 N.Y. 395, 399, 80 N.E. 199, 200. Approval by directors or by a majority stock vote could not validate such gratuitous expenditures. Continental Securities Co. v. Belmont, 206 N.Y. 7, 99 N.E. 138, 51 L.R.A.,N.S., 112. Some of the payments attacked in this suit were, on their face, for lawful purposes and apparently reasonable in amount but, as to others, the record simply does not contain evidentiary bases for a determination as to either lawfulness or reasonableness. Surely, the burden was on plaintiff to go forward to some extent with such particularization and proof. It failed to do so, and so failed to make out a prima facie case.

We are, therefore, reaching the same result as did the Appellate Division but on one only of the grounds listed by that court, that is, failure of proof. We think it not inappropriate, however, to state our general views on the question of law principally argued by the parties, that is, as to the validity of corporate payments for proxy solicitations and similar activities in addition to giving notice of the meeting, and of the questions to be voted on. For an answer to that problem we could not do better than quote from this court's opinion in the Lawyers' Advertising Co. case, 187 N.Y. 395, 399, 80 N.E. 199, 200, supra: "The remaining notices were not legally authorized and were not legitimately incidental to the meeting or necessary for the protection of the stockholders. They rather were proceedings by one faction in its contest with another for the control of the corporation, and the expense thereof, as such, is not properly chargeable to the latter. . . . [I]t would be altogether too dangerous a rule to permit directors in control of a corporation and engaged in a contest for the perpetuation of their offices and control, to impose upon the corporation the unusual expense of publishing advertisements or, by analogy, of dispatching special messengers for the purpose of procuring proxies in their behalf." . . .

The judgment should be affirmed, without costs.

■ Van Voorhis, Judge (dissenting). . . .

No resolution was passed by the stockholders approving payment to the management group. It has been recognized that not all of the $133,966 in obligations paid or incurred by the management group was designed merely for information of stockholders. This outlay included payment for all of the activities of a strenuous campaign to persuade and cajole in a hard-fought contest for control of this corporation. It included, for example, expenses for entertainment, chartered airplanes and limousines, public relations counsel and proxy solicitors. However legitimate such measures may be on behalf of stockholders themselves in such a controversy, most of them do not pertain to a corporate function but are part of the familiar apparatus of aggressive factions in corporate contests. . . .

The Appellate Division acknowledged in the instant case that "It is obvious that the management group here incurred a substantial amount of needless expense which was charged to the corporation," but this conclusion should have led to a direction that those defendants who were incumbent directors should be required to come forward with an explanation of their expenditures under the familiar rule that where it has been established that directors have expended corporate money for their own purposes, the burden of going forward with evidence of the propriety and reasonableness of specific items rests upon the directors.... The complaint should not have been dismissed as against incumbent directors due to failure of plaintiff to segregate the specific expenditures which are *ultra vires,* but, once plaintiff had proved facts from which an inference of impropriety might be drawn, the duty of making an explanation was laid upon the directors to explain and justify their conduct....

There is no doubt that the management was entitled and under a duty to take reasonable steps to acquaint the stockholders with essential facts concerning the management of the corporation, and it may well be that the existence of a contest warranted them in circularizing the stockholders with more than ordinarily detailed information....

What expenses of the incumbent group should be allowed and what should be disallowed should be remitted to the trial court to ascertain, after taking evidence, in accordance with the rule that the incumbent directors were required to assume the burden of going forward in the first instance with evidence explaining and justifying their expenditures. Only such as were reasonably related to informing the stockholders fully and fairly concerning the corporate affairs should be allowed. The concession by plaintiff that such expenditures as were made were reasonable in amount does not decide this question. By way of illustration, the costs of entertainment for stockholders may have been, and it is stipulated that they were, at the going rates for providing similar entertainment. That does not signify that entertaining stockholders is reasonably related to the purposes of the corporation. The Appellate Division, as above stated, found that the management group incurred a substantial amount of needless expense. That fact being established, it became the duty of the incumbent directors to unravel and explain these payments.

Regarding the $127,556 paid by the new management to the insurgent group for their campaign expenditures, the question immediately arises whether that was for a corporate purpose....

... The case most frequently cited and principally relied upon from among [the] Delaware decisions is Hall v. Trans–Lux Daylight Picture Screen Corp. [20 Del.Ch. 78]. There the English case was followed of Peel v. London & North Western Ry. Co. ... which distinguished between expenses merely for the purpose of maintaining control, and contests over policy questions of the corporation. In the Hall case the issues concerned a proposed merger, and a proposed sale of stock of a subsidiary corporation. These were held to be policy questions, and payment of the management campaign expenses was upheld.

In our view, the impracticability [of distinguishing between expenses incurred merely for the purpose of maintaining control, and expenses in contests over policy questions] is illustrated by the statement in the Hall case, supra, 20 Del.Ch. at page 85, 171 A. at page 229, that "It is impossible in many cases of intracorporate contests over directors, to sever questions of policy from those of persons". This circumstance is stressed in Judge Rifkind's opinion in [Steinberg v. Adams, 90 F.Supp. 604] at page 608: "The simple fact, of course, is that generally policy and personnel do not exist in separate compartments. A change in personnel is sometimes indispensable to a change of policy. A new board may be the symbol of the shift in policy as well as the means of obtaining it."

... [I]nasmuch as it is generally impossible to distinguish whether "policy" or "personnel" is the dominant factor, any averments must be accepted at their face value that questions of policy are dominant. Nowhere do these opinions mention that the converse is equally true and more pervasive, that neither the "ins" nor the "outs" ever say that they have no program to offer to the shareholders, but just want to acquire or to retain control, as the case may be. In common experience, this distinction is unreal....

The main question of "policy" in the instant corporate election, as is stated in the opinions below and frankly admitted, concerns the long-term contract with pension rights of a former officer and director, Mr. J. Carlton Ward, Jr. The insurgents' chief claim of benefit to the corporation from their victory consists in the termination of that agreement, resulting in an alleged actuarial saving of $350,000 to $825,000 to the corporation, and the reduction of other salaries and rent by more than $300,000 per year. The insurgents had contended in the proxy contest that these payments should be substantially reduced so that members of the incumbent group would not continue to profit personally at the expense of the corporation. If these charges were true, which appear to have been believed by a majority of the shareholders, then the disbursements by the management group in the proxy contest fall under the condemnation of the English and the Delaware rule.

These circumstances are mentioned primarily to illustrate how impossible it is to distinguish between "policy" and "personnel", ... but they also indicate that personal factors are deeply rooted in this contest. That is certainly true insofar as the former management group is concerned....

Some expenditures may concededly be made by a corporation represented by its management so as to inform the stockholders, but there is a clear distinction between such expenditures by management and by mere groups of stockholders. The latter are under no legal obligation to assume duties of managing the corporation. They may endeavor to supersede the management for any reason, regardless of whether it be advantageous or detrimental to the corporation but, if they succeed, that is not a determination that the company was previously mismanaged or that it may not be mismanaged in the future. A change in control is in no sense analogous to an adjudication that the former directors have been guilty of misconduct. The analogy of allowing expenses of suit to minority stockholders who have been successful in a derivative action based on misconduct of officers or directors, is entirely without foundation.

Insofar as a management group is concerned, it may charge the corporation with any expenses within reasonable limits incurred in giving widespread notice to stockholders of questions affecting the welfare of the corporation.... Expenditures in excess of these limits are *ultra vires*. The corporation lacks power to defray them. The corporation lacks power to defray the expenses of the insurgents in their entirety. The insurgents were not charged with responsibility for operating the company. No appellate court case is cited from any jurisdiction holding otherwise. No contention is made that such disbursements could be made, in any event, without stockholder ratification; they could not be ratified except by unanimous vote if they were *ultra vires*. ... If reimbursement of such items were permitted upon majority stockholder ratification, no court or other tribunal could pass upon which types of expenditures were "needless", to employ the characterization of the Appellate Division in this case. Whether the insurgents should be paid would be made to depend upon whether they win the stockholders election and obtain control of the corporation. It would be entirely irrelevant whether the corporation is "benefitted" by their efforts or by the outcome of such an election. The courts could not indulge in a speculative inquiry into that issue. That would truly be a matter of business judgment.... The way is open and will be kept open for stockholders and groups of stockholders to contest corporate elections, but if the promoters of such movements choose to employ the costly modern media of mass persuasion, they should look for reimbursement to themselves and to the stockholders who are aligned with them. If the law be that they can be recompensed by the corporation in case of success, and only in that event, it will operate as a powerful incentive to persons accustomed to taking calculated risks to increase this form of high-powered salesmanship to such a degree that, action provoking reaction, stockholders' meetings will be very costly. To the financial advantages promised by control of a prosperous corporation, would be added the knowledge that the winner takes all insofar as the campaign expenses are concerned. To the victor, indeed, would belong the spoils....

■ CONWAY, C.J., and BURKE, J., concur with FROESSEL, J.; DESMOND, J., concurs in part in a separate opinion; VAN VOORHIS, J., dissents in an opinion in which DYE and FULD JJ., concur.

Judgment affirmed.

_____

## J. Heard & H. Sherman Conflicts of Interest in the Proxy Voting System 84–85

(1987).

Very few contested elections are run without the aid of professional proxy solicitors. Because of their experience and personal contacts in the investment community and at proxy departments of brokerage houses and banks, professional solicitors usually are able to generate a higher vote turnout than issuer companies can do by themselves. For this reason, both management and the dissident side usually engage their own solicitors during contested elections. Even for uncontested elections, companies that are worried about not reaching a quorum count employ the services of a solicitor to guarantee a high turnout. Companies also use solicitors when they expect significant opposition to uncontested management proposals, such as antitakeover charter amendments or defensive recapitalizations.

The leading proxy solicitation firms include Georgeson and Co., the Carter Organization, D.F. King and Co., Morrow and Co. and the Kissel–Blake Organization.

By virtue of their years of experience in the business, solicitors often know how a particular shareholder, or a particular type of shareholder, will vote on different issues. For this reason, firms trying to pass proposals that they fear will be met with strong opposition often engage solicitors to determine whether or not the proposal should even be included on the ballot. For example, Georgeson and Co. prepares a best case/worst case voting scenario for clients on various types of proposals. If the likely outcome seems to be a defeat for management, based on Georgeson's analysis, the issuer company will often decide to exclude the proposal from its ballot. John Wilcox, a principal at Georgeson, told IRRC that this explains why so few antitakeover proposals are defeated. According to Wilcox, most antitakeover proposals that are likely to be defeated, based on Georgeson's or another solicitor's analysis, are never put on a ballot in the first place.

When engaged by management or a dissident during a contested election, a solicitor's services are invaluable. The solicitor handles all the physical requirements of the proxy campaign. It identifies beneficial owners, mails the proxy material to recordholders, makes sure that beneficial owners have received proxy material from the recordholder bank or broker, rounds up late votes with phone calls or follow-up mailings, and tabulates the vote for management or the dissident.

The first of these functions, identifying beneficial owners, is among the most important services a solicitor can offer.... [R]egistration in bank nominee name often enables a beneficial owner to hide its identity and security position from the issuer company. When votes come in to a solicitor from a bank client, the proxy is signed by the bank, and the owner is identified only by an account number assigned to the client by his bank. The owner's name does not appear on the proxy card. When such votes are cast against management or a dissident, the interested party has no way of knowing who is behind the shares being voted against him. But proxy solicitors have developed their own data bases over the years that match bank account numbers with the identity of their owners. This enables a solicitor to tell a client who is behind the bank votes being cast during the proxy campaign. When the proxy vote is going against the solicitor's client, this ability becomes very important, for it allows the solicitor or the solicitor's client to contact the shareowner and ask him to reconsider his vote.

During a proxy campaign, a solicitor keeps in close contact with the proxy clerks at brokerage firms and with appropriate bank officers to make sure that their client's proxy material is being forwarded to beneficial owners. A solicitor can therefore decide if a second mailing is necessary. Such contact also enables a solicitor to tell his client how the vote is progressing, since brokers and banks usually tally votes as they are received but wait until shortly before a meeting to submit their proxies. If a solicitor determines that the final voting results may go against its client, advance information gives the solicitor's client time to exert more pressure on important shareholders to influence their vote, to resolicit shareholders who may have voted against the client, or to redouble efforts to reach shareholders who have not responded.

When final proxies arrive, the solicitor checks them to make sure that they are valid proxies, that they have been signed correctly, that they represent the appropriate number of shares, and that they are not duplicate or replacement proxies. Once done, the solicitor usually also participates in the actual tabulation at the annual meeting. The solicitor's experience can save a company much time when counting the vote, since the solicitor knows which way of sorting and collating the proxies will be the most expedient. When proxy votes are challenged by the opposing side in a proxy contest, the solicitor's knowledge of the technical requirements of valid proxies can prove invaluable....

---

### NOTE ON PROXY CONTEST DATA

According to the SEC, there were 75 contested proxy solicitations in 1990, 65 in 1991, 58 in 1992, 35 in 1993, 42 in 1994, 59 in 1995, 62 in 1996, and 83 in 1997. SEC, Annual Reports (1994 & 1999). However, some of these contested solicitations may not have involved the election of directors.

Georgeson & Co., a leading proxy-solicitation firm, working from a different database (perhaps drawn only from its own files), reports significantly different numbers. For example, according to Georgeson there were only 3 contested proxy solicitations in 1993, 20–28 in each of the years 1996, 1997, and 1998, and 38 in 1999.

---

CHAPTER VI

# THE SPECIAL PROBLEMS OF CLOSE CORPORATIONS

---

## SECTION 1.   INTRODUCTION

---

## (a)   A BRIEF LOOK BACK AT PARTNERSHIP

### NOTE ON PARTNERSHIP LAW AND CORPORATE LAW

The title of this chapter refers to "close corporations." Exactly what constitutes a close corporation is a matter of theoretical dispute. Some authorities emphasize the number of shareholders, some emphasize the presence of owner-management, some emphasize the lack of a market for the corporation's stock, and some emphasize the existence of formal restrictions on the transferability of the corporation's shares. For present purposes, a close corporation can be regarded as one whose shares are held by a relatively small number of persons: given that element, the remaining incidents normally follow. Viewed from this perspective, the close corporation resembles the partnership, which is also typically characterized by a small number of owners, owner-management, and nontransferability of ownership interests. Indeed, certain aspects of partnership law form an important backdrop to the study of close corporations, because in recent years legislators and courts have increasingly looked to partnership-law norms in solving close-corporation-law problems.

1. *Basic Partnership–Law Norms.* The most striking aspect of partnership law is its heavily contractual nature. For many purposes, both the Uniform Partnership Act (the "UPA") and the Revised Uniform Partnership Act ("RUPA") operate only in the absence of an agreement by the partners on a given issue. The following is a highly generalized summary of the partnership-law rules most salient to the ongoing conduct of the firm:

a. *Internal governance.* As concerns internal governance, partnership law is facilitative rather than mandatory. Both the UPA and RUPA provide default rules to govern situations that the partners' arrangements fail to cover, but allow the owners to contract for different rules. The basic governance rules are:

(i) Absent contrary agreement, all partners have equal rights in the management and conduct of the partnership business.

(ii) Absent contrary agreement, differences among the partners "as to ordinary matters connected with the partnership business" are determined by a majority of the partners, but matters that are outside the scope of the partnership business, or that would be in conflict with the partnership agreement, require unanimous approval.

b.  *Authority.* Any partner has power to bind the partnership on a matter in the ordinary course of business. This is the case even if by virtue of the partnership's internal arrangements the partner lacks actual authority, unless the third party with whom the partner deals knows that the partner lacks actual authority.

c.  *Distributive shares.* Absent contrary agreement, partnership profits are shared per capita, and no partner is entitled to a salary.

d.  *Transferability.* Absent contrary agreement, no person can become a member of a partnership without the consent of all the partners.

e.  *Term.* Partnerships are normally created for a limited term— frequently a relatively short term—and dissolution is easy. If the partnership is not for a specified term (express or implied), any partner may cause dissolution at any time. If the partnership is for a specified term, dissolution occurs at the end of the term and under certain other circumstances.

f.  *Fiduciary duties.* Partners stand in a fiduciary relationship to each other.

g.  *Liability.* Partners in a general partnership are individually liable for the partnership's obligations.

2.  *Basic Corporation–Law Norms.* Traditionally, corporation-law norms were diametrically opposed to almost every one of these partnership-law norms:

a.  *Internal governance.* As to many aspects of internal governance, the traditional corporate statutes were mandatory. For example, under traditional corporate-law norms, shareholders, as such, have no right to participate in the management of the corporation's business.

b.  *Authority.* Because shareholders, as such, have no right to participate in the management of the corporation's business, they also have no apparent authority to bind the corporation.

c.  *Distributive shares.* Corporate distributions are not shared per capita, but in proportion to stock ownership.

d.  *Transferability.* Shares of stock, and the shareholder status they carry, are freely transferable.

e.  *Term.* Corporations are normally created for a perpetual term, and dissolution is relatively difficult.

f.  *Fiduciary duties.* The traditional view was that shareholders do not stand in a direct fiduciary relationship to each other, although that view has now changed in material respects. See chapters 9 and 10, infra.

g. *Liability.* Shareholders are not individually liable for a corporation's obligations.

Most of these basic corporate-laws norms were designed with an eye to the publicly held corporation. As will be seen in this Chapter, the application of these norms in the close-corporation context often leads to the frustration of legitimate expectations. As a result, under modern law, in close corporations many of these norms can be overridden by agreement.

———

## (b) AN INTRODUCTION TO THE CLOSE CORPORATION

## Donahue v. Rodd Electrotype Co.

Supreme Judicial Court of Massachusetts, 1975.
367 Mass. 578, 328 N.E.2d 505.

■ TAURO, CHIEF JUSTICE.

The plaintiff, Euphemia Donahue, a minority stockholder in the Rodd Electrotype Company of New England, Inc. (Rodd Electrotype), a Massachusetts corporation, brings this suit against the directors of Rodd Electrotype, Charles H. Rodd, Frederick I. Rodd and Mr. Harold E. Magnuson, against Harry C. Rodd, a former director, officer, and controlling stockholder of Rodd Electrotype and against Rodd Electrotype (hereinafter called defendants). The plaintiff seeks to rescind Rodd Electrotype's purchase of Harry Rodd's shares in Rodd Electrotype and to compel Harry Rodd "to repay to the corporation the purchase price of said shares; $36,000, together with interest from the date of purchase." The plaintiff alleges that the defendants caused the corporation to purchase the shares in violation of their fiduciary duty to her, a minority stockholder of Rodd Electrotype.[4]

The trial judge, after hearing oral testimony, dismissed the plaintiff's bill on the merits. He found that the purchase was without prejudice to the plaintiff and implicitly found that the transaction had been carried out in good faith and with inherent fairness. The Appeals Court affirmed with costs. Donahue v. Rodd Electrotype Co. of New England, Inc., 1 Mass.App. 876, 307 N.E.2d 8 (1974). The case is before us on the plaintiff's application for further appellate review....

[Briefly, the facts were as follows: In the mid–1930's Harry Rodd and Joseph Donahue had become employees of Royal Electrotype (the predecessor of Rodd Electrotype). Donahue's duties were confined to

---

**4.** In form, the plaintiff's bill of complaint presents, at least in part, a derivative action, brought on behalf of the corporation, and, in the words of the bill, "on behalf of ... [the] stockholders" of Rodd Electrotype. Yet ... the plaintiff's bill, in substance, was one seeking redress because of alleged breaches of the fiduciary duty owed *to her,* a minority stockholder, by the controlling stockholders.

We treat the bill of complaint (as have the parties) as presenting a proper cause of suit in the personal right of the plaintiff....

operational matters within the plants, and he never participated in the management aspect of the business. In contrast, Rodd's advancement within the company was rapid, and in 1946 he became general manager and treasurer. Subsequently Rodd acquired 200 of the corporation's 1000 shares and Donahue (at Rodd's suggestion) acquired 50 shares. In 1955 Rodd became president and general manager, and later that year Royal itself purchased the remaining 750 shares, so that Rodd and Donahue became Royal's sole shareholders, owning 80% and 20% of its stock, respectively. In 1960 the corporation was renamed Rodd Electrotype, and in the early 60's Harry Rodd's two sons, Charles and Frederick, took important positions with the company. In 1965 Charles succeeded his father as president and general manager.

In 1970 Harry Rodd was seventy-seven years old and not in good health, and his sons wished him to retire. Prior to 1967 Harry had distributed 117 of his 200 shares equally among his sons and his daughter, and had returned 2 shares to the corporate treasury. Harry insisted that as a condition to his retirement some financial arrangement be made with respect to his remaining 81 shares. Accordingly, Charles, acting on the corporation's behalf, negotiated for the purchase of 45 of Harry's shares for $800/share—a price which, Charles testified, reflected book and liquidating value. At a special board meeting in July 1970, the corporation's board (then consisting of Charles and Frederick Rodd and a lawyer) voted to have the corporation make the purchase at this price. Subsequently Harry Rodd sold 2 shares to each of his three children at $800/share, and gave each child 10 shares as a gift.[7] Meanwhile Donahue had died and his 50 shares had passed to his wife and son. When the Donahues learned that the corporation had purchased Harry Rodd's shares, they offered their shares to the corporation on the terms given to Harry but the offer was rejected.[10] This suit followed.]

In her argument before this court, the plaintiff has characterized the corporate purchase of Harry Rodd's shares as an unlawful distribution of corporate assets to controlling stockholders. She urges that the distribution constitutes a breach of the fiduciary duty owed by the Rodds, as controlling stockholders, to her, a minority stockholder in the enterprise, because the Rodds failed to accord her an equal opportunity to sell her shares to the corporation. The defendants reply that the stock purchase was within the powers of the corporation and met the requirements of good faith and inherent fairness imposed on a fiduciary in his dealings with the corporation. They assert that there is no right to equal opportunity in corporate stock purchases for the corporate treasury. For the reasons hereinafter noted, we agree with the plaintiff and reverse the decree of the Superior Court. However, we limit the applicability of our holding to "close corporations," as

**7.** An inference is permissible that the "gift" of these shares was a part of the "deal" for the stock purchase.

**10.** Between 1965 and 1969, the company offered to purchase the Donahue shares for amounts between $2,000 and $10,000 ($40 to $200 a share). The Donahues rejected these offers.

hereinafter defined. Whether the holding should apply to other corporations is left for decision in another case, on a proper record.

A. *Close Corporations.* In previous opinions, we have alluded to the distinctive nature of the close corporation ... but have never defined precisely what is meant by a close corporation. There is no single, generally accepted definition. Some commentators emphasize an "integration of ownership and management" (Note, Statutory Assistance for Closely Held Corporations, 71 Harv.L.Rev. 1498 [1958]), in which the stockholders occupy most management positions.... Others focus on the number of stockholders and the nature of the market for the stock. In this view, close corporations have few stockholders; there is little market for corporate stock. The Supreme Court of Illinois adopted this latter view in Galler v. Galler, 32 Ill.2d 16, 203 N.E.2d 577 (1964).... We accept aspects of both definitions. We deem a close corporation to be typified by: (1) a small number of stockholders; (2) no ready market for the corporate stock; and (3) substantial majority stockholder participation in the management, direction and operations of the corporation.

As thus defined, the close corporation bears striking resemblance to a partnership.... Just as in a partnership, the relationship among the stockholders must be one of trust, confidence and absolute loyalty if the enterprise is to succeed....

In Helms v. Duckworth, 101 U.S.App.D.C. 390, 249 F.2d 482 (1957) ... Judge Burger, now Chief Justice Burger, writing for the court, emphasized the resemblance of the two-man close corporation to a partnership: "In an intimate business venture such as this, stockholders of a close corporation occupy a position similar to that of joint adventurers and partners. While courts have sometimes declared stockholders 'do not bear toward each other that same relation of trust and confidence which prevails in partnerships,' this view ignores the practical realities of the organization and functioning of a small 'two-man' corporation organized to carry on a small business enterprise in which the stockholders, directors, and managers are the same persons" (footnotes omitted). Id. at 486.

Although the corporate form provides ... advantages for the stockholders (limited liability, perpetuity, and so forth), it also supplies an opportunity for the majority stockholders to oppress or disadvantage minority stockholders. The minority is vulnerable to a variety of oppressive devices, termed "freeze-outs," which the majority may employ.... An authoritative study of such "freeze-outs" enumerates some of the possibilities: "The squeezers ... may refuse to declare dividends; they may drain off the corporation's earnings in the form of exorbitant salaries and bonuses to the majority shareholder-officers and perhaps to their relatives, or in the form of high rent by the corporation for property leased from majority shareholders ...; they may deprive minority shareholders of corporate offices and of employment by the company...."

The minority can, of course, initiate suit against the majority and their directors. Self-serving conduct by directors is proscribed by the director's fiduciary obligation to the corporation.... However, in practice, the plaintiff will find difficulty in challenging dividend or employment policies. Such policies are considered to be within the judgment of the directors ... [G]enerally, plaintiffs who seek judicial assistance against corporate dividend or employment policies do not prevail....

Thus, when these types of "freeze-outs" are attempted by the majority stockholders, the minority stockholders, cut off from all corporation-related revenues, must either suffer their losses or seek a buyer for their shares. Many minority stockholders will be unwilling or unable to wait for an alteration in majority policy. Typically, the minority stockholder in a close corporation has a substantial percentage of his personal assets invested in the corporation. The stockholder may have anticipated that his salary from his position with the corporation would be his livelihood. Thus, he cannot afford to wait passively. He must liquidate his investment in the close corporation in order to reinvest the funds in income-producing enterprises.

At this point, the true plight of the minority stockholder in a close corporation becomes manifest. He cannot easily reclaim his capital. In a large public corporation, the oppressed or dissident minority stockholder could sell his stock in order to extricate some of his invested capital. By definition, this market is not available for shares in the close corporation. In a partnership, a partner who feels abused by his fellow partners may cause dissolution by his "express will ... at any time" ... and recover his share of partnership assets and accumulated profits.... By contrast, the stockholder in the close corporation or "incorporated partnership" may achieve dissolution and recovery of his share of the enterprise assets only by compliance with the rigorous terms of the applicable chapter of the General Laws....

Thus, in a close corporation, the minority stockholders may be trapped in a disadvantageous situation. No outsider would knowingly assume the position of the disadvantaged minority. The outsider would have the same difficulties. To cut losses, the minority stockholder may be compelled to deal with the majority. This is the capstone of the majority plan. Majority "freeze-out" schemes which withhold dividends are designed to compel the minority to relinquish stock at inadequate prices.... When the minority stockholder agrees to sell out at less than fair value, the majority has won.

Because of the fundamental resemblance of the close corporation to the partnership, the trust and confidence which are essential to this scale and manner of enterprise, and the inherent danger to minority interests in the close corporation, we hold that stockholders[17] in the close corporation owe one another substantially the same fiduciary duty in the operation of the enterprise[18] that partners owe to one

---

**17.** We do not limit our holding to majority stockholders. In the close corporation, the minority may do equal damage through unscrupulous and improper "sharp dealings" with an unsuspecting majority. See Helms v. Duckworth, 101 U.S.App.D.C. 390, 249 F.2d 482 (1957).

**18.** We stress that the strict fiduciary duty which we apply to stockholders in a close corporation in this opinion governs *only*

another. In our previous decisions, we have defined the standard of duty owed by partners to one another as the "utmost good faith and loyalty." Cardullo v. Landau, 329 Mass. 5, 8, 105 N.E.2d 843 (1952); DeCotis v. D'Antona, 350 Mass. 165, 168, 214 N.E.2d 21 (1966). Stockholders in close corporations must discharge their management and stockholder responsibilities in conformity with this strict good faith standard. They may not act out of avarice, expediency or self-interest in derogation of their duty of loyalty to the other stockholders and to the corporation.

We contrast this strict good faith standard with the somewhat less stringent standard of fiduciary duty to which directors and stockholders of all corporations must adhere in the discharge of their corporate responsibilities. Corporate directors are held to a good faith and inherent fairness standard of conduct (Winchell v. Plywood Corp., 324 Mass. 171, 177, 85 N.E.2d 313 [1949]) and are not "permitted to serve two masters whose interests are antagonistic." Spiegel v. Beacon Participations, 297 Mass. 398, 411, 8 N.E.2d 895, 904 (1937). "Their paramount duty is to the corporation, and their personal pecuniary interests are subordinate to that duty." Durfee v. Durfee & Canning, Inc., 323 Mass. 187, 196, 80 N.E.2d 522, 527 (1948).

The more rigorous duty of partners and participants in a joint adventure, here extended to stockholders in a close corporation, was described by then Chief Judge Cardozo of the New York Court of Appeals in Meinhard v. Salmon, 249 N.Y. 458, 164 N.E. 545 (1928): "Joint adventurers, like co-partners, owe to one another, while the enterprise continues, the duty of the finest loyalty. Many forms of conduct permissible in a workaday world for those acting at arm's length, are forbidden to those bound by fiduciary ties.... Not honesty alone, but the punctilio of an honor the most sensitive, is then the standard of behavior." Id. at 463–464, 164 N.E. at 546....

B. *Equal Opportunity in a Close Corporation.* Under settled Massachusetts law, a domestic corporation, unless forbidden by statute, has the power to purchase its own shares.... An agreement to reacquire stock "[is] enforceable, subject, at least, to the limitations that the purchase must be made in good faith and without prejudice to creditors and stockholders." ... When the corporation reacquiring its own stock is a close corporation, the purchase is subject to the additional requirement, in the light of our holding in this opinion, that the stockholders, who, as directors or controlling stockholders, caused the corporation to enter into the stock purchase agreement, must have acted with the utmost good faith and loyalty to the other stockholders.

To meet this test, if the stockholder whose shares were purchased was a member of the controlling group, the controlling stockholders

their actions relative to the operations of the enterprise and the effects of that operation on the rights and investments of other stockholders. We express no opinion as to the standard of duty applicable to transactions in the shares of the close corporation when the corporation is not a party to the transaction.

Cf. Andrews, The Stockholder's Right to Equal Opportunity in the Sale of Shares, 78 Harv.L.Rev. 505 (1965). Compare Perlman v. Feldmann, 219 F.2d 173 (2d Cir.), cert. den. 349 U.S. 952, 75 S.Ct. 880, 99 L.Ed. 1277 (1955) with Zahn v. Transamerica Corp., 162 F.2d 36 (3d Cir.1947).

must cause the corporation to offer each stockholder an equal opportunity to sell a ratable number of his shares to the corporation at an identical price. Purchase by the corporation confers substantial benefits on the members of the controlling group whose shares were purchased. These benefits are not available to the minority stockholders if the corporation does not also offer them an opportunity to sell their shares. The controlling group may not, consistent with its strict duty to the minority, utilize its control of the corporation to obtain special advantages and disproportionate benefit from its share ownership. See Jones v. H.F. Ahmanson & Co., 1 Cal.3d 93, 108, 81 Cal.Rptr. 592, 460 P.2d 464 (1969); Note, 83 Harv.L.Rev. 1904, 1908 (1970). Cf. Brudney and Chirelstein, Fair Shares in Corporate Mergers and Takeovers, 88 Harv.L.Rev. 297, 334 (1974).

The benefits conferred by the purchase are twofold: (1) provision of a market for shares; (2) access to corporate assets for personal use. By definition, there is no ready market for shares of a close corporation. The purchase creates a market for shares which previously had been unmarketable. It transforms a previously illiquid investment into a liquid one. If the close corporation purchases shares only from a member of the controlling group, the controlling stockholder can convert his shares into cash at a time when none of the other stockholders can. Consistent with its strict fiduciary duty, the controlling group may not utilize its control of the corporation to establish an exclusive market in previously unmarketable shares from which the minority stockholders are excluded. See Jones v. H.F. Ahmanson & Co. . . . .

The purchase also distributes corporate assets to the stockholder whose shares were purchased. Unless an equal opportunity is given to all stockholders, the purchase of shares from a member of the controlling group operates as a *preferential* distribution of assets. In exchange for his shares, he receives a percentage of the contributed capital and accumulated profits of the enterprise. The funds he so receives are available for his personal use. The other stockholders benefit from no such access to corporate property and cannot withdraw their shares of the corporate profits and capital in this manner unless the controlling group acquiesces. Although the purchase price for the controlling stockholder's shares may seem fair to the corporation and other stockholders under the tests established in the prior case law (see Spiegel v. Beacon Participations, 297 Mass. 398, 429, 8 N.E.2d 895 [1937]; Winchell v. Plywood Corp., 324 Mass. 171, 178, 85 N.E.2d 313 [1949]), the controlling stockholder whose stock has been purchased has still received a relative advantage over his fellow stockholders, inconsistent with his strict fiduciary duty—an opportunity to turn corporate funds to personal use.

The rule of equal opportunity in stock purchases by close corporations provides equal access to these benefits for all stockholders. We hold that, in any case in which the controlling stockholders have exercised their power over the corporation to deny the minority such equal opportunity, the minority shall be entitled to appropriate relief.

To the extent that language in Spiegel v. Beacon Participations, 297 Mass. 398, 431, 8 N.E.2d 895 (1937), and other cases suggests that there is no requirement of equal opportunity for minority stockholders when a close corporation purchases shares from a controlling stockholder, it is not to be followed.

C. *Application of the Law to this Case.* We turn now to the application of the learning set forth above to the facts of the instant case.

The strict standard of duty is plainly applicable to the stockholders in Rodd Electrotype. Rodd Electrotype is a close corporation [under the test set out above]. . . .

. . . In testing the stock purchase from Harry Rodd against the applicable strict fiduciary standard, we treat the Rodd family as a single controlling group. . . . From the evidence, it is clear that the Rodd family was a close-knit one with strong community of interest. . . .

Moreover, a strong motive of interest requires that the Rodds be considered a controlling group. When Charles Rodd and Frederick Rodd were called on to represent the corporation in its dealings with their father, they must have known that further advancement within the corporation and benefits would follow their father's retirement and the purchase of his stock. . . .

On its face, then, the purchase of Harry Rodd's shares by the corporation is a breach of the duty which the controlling stockholders, the Rodds, owed to the minority stockholders, the plaintiff and her son. The purchaser distributed a portion of the corporate assets to Harry Rodd, a member of the controlling group, in exchange for his shares. The plaintiff and her son were not offered an equal opportunity to sell their shares to the corporation. In fact, their efforts to obtain an equal opportunity were rebuffed by the corporate representative. As the trial judge found, they did not, in any manner, ratify the transaction with Harry Rodd.

Because of the foregoing, we hold that the plaintiff is entitled to relief. Two forms of suitable relief are set out hereinafter. The judge below is to enter an appropriate judgment. The judgment may require Harry Rodd to remit $36,000 with interest at the legal rate from July 15, 1970, to Rodd Electrotype in exchange for forty-five shares of Rodd Electrotype treasury stock. This, in substance, is the specific relief requested in the plaintiff's bill of complaint. Interest is manifestly appropriate. A stockholder, who, in violation of his fiduciary duty to the other stockholders, has obtained assets from his corporation and has had those assets available for his own use, must pay for that use. See Silversmith v. Sydeman, 305 Mass. 65, 74, 25 N.E.2d 215 (1940). Cf. Spiegel v. Beacon Participations, 297 Mass. 398, 420, 8 N.E.2d 895 (1937). In the alternative, the judgment may require Rodd Electrotype to purchase all of the plaintiff's shares for $36,000 without interest. In the circumstances of this case, we view this as the equal opportunity which the plaintiff should have received. Harry Rodd's retention of thirty-six shares, which were to be sold and given to his children within a year of the Rodd Electrotype purchase, cannot disguise the fact that the corporation acquired one hundred per cent of that portion of his holdings (forty-five shares) which he did not intend his children to own. The plaintiff is entitled to have one hundred per cent of her forty-five shares similarly purchased.[30]

The final decree, in so far as it dismissed the bill as to Harry C. Rodd, Frederick I. Rodd, Charles H. Rodd, Mr. Harold E. Magnuson and Rodd Electrotype Company of New England, Inc., and awarded costs, is reversed. The case is remanded to the Superior Court for entry of judgment in conformity with this opinion.

So ordered.*

■ WILKINS, JUSTICE (concurring).

I agree with much of what the Chief Justice says in support of granting relief to the plaintiff. However, I do not join in any implication (see, e.g., footnote 18 and the associated text) that the rule concerning a close corporation's purchase of a controlling stockholder's shares applies to all operations of the corporation as they affect minority stockholders. That broader issue, which is apt to arise in connection with salaries and dividend policy, is not involved in this case. The analogy to partnerships may not be a complete one.

---

## NOTE

One response to the kinds of problems described in Donahue v. Rodd Electrotype Co. is to plan around them in advance, by making special arrangements designed to suit the needs of the parties. In a partnership, this would be a relatively simple matter: as regards internal governance, partnership law is highly contractual in nature— that is, it gives the parties wide scope to determine the rules by which their relationship will be governed. In contrast, corporation law traditionally was not as attuned to contractualization, and in the corporate context there was often serious question whether such arrangements were deemed valid. Today, however courts and legislatures have shown themselves increasingly ready to enforce contractual arrangements in close corporations, leading to what might be called the contractualization of the close corporation.

Accordingly, the materials in Sections 2–5, infra, will be concerned to a large extent with the role of *advance planning* in the close corporation. Sections 8–10 will consider the remedies available when

**30.** If there has been a significant change in corporate circumstances since this case was argued, this is a matter which can be brought to the attention of the court below and may be considered by the judge in granting appropriate relief in the form of a judgment.

*See also Comolli v. Comolli, 241 Ga. 471, 246 S.E.2d 278 (1978); cf. Schwartz v. Marien, 37 N.Y.2d 487, 335 N.E.2d 334, 373 N.Y.S.2d 122 (1975). For additional cases and materials on the fiduciary obligations of shareholders in close corporations, see Section 7(a), infra. (Footnote by ed.)

advance planning has been inadequate or the problems are of a kind that resist advance solution.

————

## NOTE ON LEGISLATIVE STRATEGIES TOWARD THE CLOSE CORPORATION

Many of the problems raised by the early close-corporation case law reflects the fact that traditional statutory rules were drafted with publicly held corporations in mind. Accordingly, one of the major responses to these problems has been the enactment of new statutory provisions aimed primarily or exclusively at close corporations. The substantive content of such provisions will be considered throughout this chapter. The purpose of this Note is to lay the groundwork for that consideration, by examining several different legislative strategies toward the close corporation. The principal strategies to be examined are those exemplified by California, Delaware, New York, and the Model Act. Almost all other close-corporation legislation either derives from or closely parallels one of these statutes.

1. *Unified Strategies.* One legislative strategy is to make no special provision for close corporations as such, but to modify traditional statutory norms so that they will meet the needs of close corporations, although applicable to publicly held corporations as well.

2. *The New York and the Model Act Strategies.* A second strategy is to follow the unified approach up to a point, but to add one or two important provisions that are applicable only to those corporations with defined shareholding characteristics. Thus N.Y.Bus.Corp.Law § 620(c) authorizes certain kinds of certificate provisions "so long as no shares of the corporation are listed on a national securities exchange or regularly quoted in an over-the-counter market by one or more members of a national or affiliated securities association." Similarly, Model Act § 7.32 authorizes certain kinds of shareholder agreements in corporations that are not listed on a national securities exchange or traded in a market maintained by one or more members of a national securities association.

3. *Statutory Close Corporations.*

a. *Delaware.* Like the New York statute, the Delaware statute follows the unified approach up to a point, through various provisions that modify traditional statutory norms so that they will meet the needs of close corporations although applicable to publicly held corporations as well. However, the Delaware statute also contains, an integrated set of provisions, Subchapter XIV (§§ 341–356), which are explicitly made applicable *only* to corporations that both qualify for and formally elect statutory close-corporation status. In effect, therefore, the statute contemplates a special subclass of close corporations, which may be called *statutory close corporations*. Under Del. Gen.

Corp. Law § 342, a corporation can *qualify* for statutory close-corporation status if its certificate provides that:

(1) All of the corporation's issued stock of all classes, exclusive of treasury shares, shall be represented by certificates and shall be held of record by not more than a specified number of persons, not exceeding 30; and

(2) All of the issued stock of all classes shall be subject to 1 or more of the restrictions on transfer permitted by § 202 of this title; and

(3) The corporation shall make no offering of any of its stock of any class which would constitute a "public offering" within the meaning of the United States Securities Act of 1933. . . .

Under § 343, a corporation that qualifies for statutory close-corporation status can *elect* such status by adopting a heading in its certificate that states the name of the corporation and the fact that it is a close corporation.

Most of the substantive provisions of Del.Gen.Corp.Law Subchapter XIV are enabling—that is, most of the provisions do not regulate the conduct of the shareholders or managers of such corporations, but simply authorize shareholders in statutory close corporations to enter into arrangements that might otherwise be unenforceable or of doubtful validity. Subchapter XIV provides enormous flexibility—so much so, that for a well-advised corporation that elects to qualify under this Subchapter, many or most governance issues will turn on the lawyer's drafting, rather than on corporate law. At the same time, the remaining provisions of the Delaware statute are sufficiently flexible so that much the same may be true even for close corporations that do not qualify under Subchapter XIV.

b. *California.* The California strategy is comparable to that of Delaware—that is, it involves a combination of (i) unified provisions that are particularly useful for close corporations, but are not restricted to such corporations, and (ii) a systematic set of provisions applicable only to statutory close corporations. In contrast to the Delaware legislation, however, California's statutory-close-corporation provisions are scattered throughout the statute, rather than integrated in a single subchapter. In addition, there are important definitional differences. California does not require the articles of a statutory close corporation to either restrict stock transfers or prohibit public offerings. Instead, the articles of a statutory close corporation need only (1) provide that all of the corporation's issued shares shall be held of record by not more than a specified number of persons, not exceeding 35; (2) state that "This corporation is a close corporation"; and (3) include the words "corporation," "incorporated," or "limited" in the corporate name. See Cal. Corp. Code §§ 158(a), 202(a). As in Delaware, most of the California statutory close corporation provisions are enabling rather than regulatory.

c. *Significance of statutory close corporations.* The data shows that only a tiny fraction of newly formed corporations elect to become statutory closed corporations. 1 F.H. O'Neal & R. Thompson, O'Neal's Close Corporations § 1.19 (3d ed.). The result is that for practical purposes, statutory close corporation provisions are much ado about very little. For example, O'Neal & Thompson found that Wisconsin reported 5,101 statutory close corporations out of 98,602 total incorporations. Alabama reported 5,324 statutory close corporations out of 155,198 total corporations. Pennsylvania reported approximately 24,-000 statutory close corporations out of approximately 580,000 total corporations. The Kansas Secretary of State's office reported less than 5 percent statutory close corporations and "probably a lot less," adding that observations of attorneys and experienced people indicate that the number has been declining. Delaware reported 16,684 statutory close corporations in 1985. Four states enacting statutory close-corporation supplements most recently reported even smaller numbers—863 statutory close corporations out of 82,694 total corporations in Missouri; 828 statutory close corporations out of 97,009 total corporations in Montana; 742 statutory close corporations out of 63,172 in Nevada; and 753 statutory close corporations out of 12,422 total corporations in Wyoming. In Texas, about 6% of filing corporations elected close corporation status.

## NOTE ON NON–ELECTING CORPORATIONS

Recall that some statutes define a class of statutory close corporations and provide that only those corporations that explicitly opt in to certain provisions of statute are covered by those provisions. A difficult issue arises under such statutes concerning the effect of the statute on close corporations that do not opt in. This issue is especially important because so few close corporations elect statutory close-corporation status. One view is that the enactment of such statutes does not prohibit the courts from continuing to apply and develop corporate law in a way that is responsive to the special characteristics of close corporations. Instead, the special close-corporation statutes only provide a safe harbor under which close corporations do not have to rely on judicial understanding of their special needs, but can instead rely on specific statutory provisions. See Ramos v. Estrada, 8 Cal.App.4th 1070, 10 Cal.Rptr.2d 833 (1992). However, in Nixon v. Blackwell, 626 A.2d 1366 (1993) the Delaware Supreme Court took the contrary view:

> In 1967, when the Delaware General Corporation Law was significantly revised, a new Subchapter XIV entitled "Close Corporations; Special Provisions," became a part of that law for the first time. . . . [S]ubchapter XIV applies only to "close corporations," as defined in section 342. "Unless a corporation elects to become a close corporation under this subchapter in the manner prescribed in this subchapter, it shall be subject in all respects to this chapter, except this subchapter." 8 Del.C. § 341. The corporation

before the Court in this matter, is not a "close corporation." Therefore it is not governed by the provisions of Subchapter XIV.

One cannot read into the situation presented in the case at bar any special relief for the minority stockholders in this closely-held, but not statutory "close corporation" because the provisions of Subchapter XIV relating to close corporations and other statutory schemes preempt the field in their respective areas. It would run counter to the spirit of the doctrine of independent legal significance, and would be inappropriate judicial legislation for this Court to fashion a special judicially-created rule for minority investors when the entity does not fall within those statutes, or when there are no negotiated special provisions in the certificate of incorporation, by-laws, or stockholder agreements. The entire fairness test, correctly applied and articulated, is the proper judicial approach....

See also Sundberg v. Lampert Lumber Co., 390 N.W.2d 352 (Minn. App.1986).

---

## SECTION 2.   SPECIAL VOTING ARRANGEMENTS AT THE SHAREHOLDER LEVEL

———

## (a) VOTING AGREEMENTS

———

### DEL. GEN. CORP. LAW §§ 212(e), 218(c)

[See Statutory Supplement]

———

### REV. MODEL BUS. CORP. ACT §§ 7.22(d), 7.31

[See Statutory Supplement]

———

### CAL. CORP. CODE §§ 158(a), 705(e), 706

[See Statutory Supplement]

———

### N.Y. BUS. CORP. LAW §§ 609(f), 620

[See Statutory Supplement]

———

# Ringling Bros.–Barnum & Bailey Combined Shows v. Ringling

Supreme Court of Delaware, 1947.
29 Del.Ch. 610, 53 A.2d 441.

Suit by Edith Conway Ringling against Ringling Brothers–Barnum & Bailey Circus Combined Shows, Inc., and others to determine the right of individual defendants to hold office as directors or officers of the corporation and to determine the validity of election of directors at the 1946 annual stockholders' meeting. From a decree for complainant entered in conformity with opinion of the Vice Chancellor, 49 A.2d 603, the defendants appeal. . . .

■ Pearson, Judge.

The Court of Chancery was called upon to review an attempted election of directors at the 1946 annual stockholders meeting of the corporate defendant. The pivotal questions concern an agreement between two of the three present stockholders, and particularly the effect of this agreement with relation to the exercise of voting rights by these two stockholders. At the time of the meeting, the corporation had outstanding 1000 shares of capital stock held as follows: 315 by petitioner Edith Conway Ringling; 315 by defendant Aubrey B. Ringling Haley (individually or as executrix and legatee of a deceased husband); and 370 by defendant John Ringling North. The purpose of the meeting was to elect the entire board of seven directors. The shares could be voted cumulatively. Mrs. Ringling asserts that by virtue of the operation of an agreement between her and Mrs. Haley, the latter was bound to vote her shares for an adjournment of the meeting, or in the alternative, for a certain slate of directors. Mrs. Haley contends that she was not so bound for reason that the agreement was invalid, or at least revocable.

The two ladies entered into the agreement in 1941. It makes like provisions concerning stock of the corporate defendant and of another corporation, but in this case, we are concerned solely with the agreement as it affects the voting of stock of the corporate defendant. The agreement recites that each party was the owner "subject only to possible claims of creditors of the estates of Charles Ringling and Richard Ringling, respectively" (deceased husbands of the parties), of 300 shares of the capital stock of the defendant corporation; that in 1938 these shares had been deposited under a voting trust agreement which would terminate in 1947, or earlier, upon the elimination of certain liability of the corporation; that each party also owned 15 shares individually; that the parties had "entered into an agreement in April 1934 providing for joint action by them in matters affecting their ownership of stock and interest in" the corporate defendant; that the parties desired "to continue to act jointly in all matters relating to their stock ownership or interest in" the corporate defendant (and the other corporation). The agreement then provides as follows:

"Now, Therefore, in consideration of the mutual covenants and agreements hereinafter contained the parties hereto agree as follows:

"1. Neither party will sell any shares of stock or any voting trust certificates in either of said corporations to any other person whosoever, without first making a written offer to the other party hereto of all of the shares or voting trust certificates proposed to be sold, for the same price and upon the same terms and conditions as in such proposed sale, and allowing such other party a time of not less than 180 days from the date of such written offer within which to accept same.

"2. In exercising any voting rights to which either party may be entitled by virtue of ownership of stock or voting trust certificates held by them in either of said corporation, each party will consult and confer with the other and the parties will act jointly in exercising such voting rights in accordance with such agreement as they may reach with respect to any matter calling for the exercise of such voting rights.

"3. In the event the parties fail to agree with respect to any matter covered by paragraph 2 above, the question in disagreement shall be submitted for arbitration to Karl D. Loos, of Washington, D.C. as arbitrator and his decision thereon shall be binding upon the parties hereto. Such arbitration shall be exercised to the end of assuring for the respective corporations good management and such participation therein by the members of the Ringling family as the experience, capacity and ability of each may warrant. The parties may at any time by written agreement designate any other individual to act as arbitrator in lieu of said Loos.

"4. Each of the parties hereto will enter into and execute such voting trust agreement or agreements and such other instruments as, from time to time they may deem advisable and as they may be advised by counsel are appropriate to effectuate the purposes and objects of this agreement.

"5. This agreement shall be in effect from the date hereof and shall continue in effect for a period of ten years unless sooner terminated by mutual agreement in writing by the parties hereto.

"6. The agreement of April 1934 is hereby terminated.

"7. This agreement shall be binding upon and inure to the benefit of the heirs, executors, administrators and assigns of the parties hereto respectively."

The Mr. Loos mentioned in the agreement is an attorney and has represented both parties since 1937, and, before and after the voting trust was terminated in late 1942, advised them with respect to the exercise of their voting rights. At the annual meetings in 1943 and the two following years, the parties voted their shares in accordance with mutual understandings arrived at as a result of discussions. In each of these years, they elected five of the seven directors. Mrs. Ringling and Mrs. Haley each had sufficient votes, independently of the other, to elect two of the seven directors. By both voting for an additional candidate, they could be sure of his election regardless of how Mr.

North, the remaining stockholder, might vote.[1]

Some weeks before the 1946 meeting, they discussed with Mr. Loos the matter of voting for directors. They were in accord that Mrs. Ringling should cast sufficient votes to elect herself and her son; and that Mrs. Haley should elect herself and her husband; but they did not agree upon a fifth director. The day before the meeting, the discussions were continued, Mrs. Haley being represented by her husband since she could not be present because of illness. In a conversation with Mr. Loos, Mr. Haley indicated that he would make a motion for an adjournment of the meeting for sixty days, in order to give the ladies additional time to come to an agreement about their voting. On the morning of the meeting, however, he stated that because of something Mrs. Ringling had done, he would not consent to a postponement. Mrs. Ringling then made a demand upon Mr. Loos to act under the third paragraph of the agreement "to arbitrate the disagreement" between her and Mrs. Haley in connection with the manner in which the stock of the two ladies should be voted. At the opening of the meeting, Mr. Loos read the written demand and stated that he determined and directed that the stock of both ladies be voted for an adjournment of sixty days. Mrs. Ringling then made a motion for adjournment and voted for it. Mr. Haley, as proxy for his wife, and Mr. North voted against the motion. Mrs. Ringling (herself or through her attorney, it is immaterial which), objected to the voting of Mrs. Haley's stock in any manner other than in accordance with Mr. Loos' direction. The chairman ruled that the stock could not be voted contrary to such direction, and declared the motion for adjournment had carried. Nevertheless, the meeting proceeded to the election of directors. Mrs. Ringling stated that she would continue in the meeting "but without prejudice to her position with respect to the voting of the stock and the fact that adjournment had not been taken." Mr. Loos directed Mrs. Ringling to cast her votes 882 for Mrs. Ringling, 882 for her son, Robert, and 441 for a Mr. Dunn, who had been a member of the board for several years. She complied. Mr. Loos directed that Mrs. Haley's votes be cast 882 for Mrs. Haley, 882 for Mr. Haley, and 441 for Mr. Dunn. Instead of complying, Mr. Haley attempted to vote his wife's shares 1103 for Mrs. Haley, and 1102 for Mr. Haley. Mr. North voted his shares 864 for a Mr. Woods, 863 for a Mr. Griffin, and 863 for Mr. North. The chairman ruled that the five candidates proposed by Mr. Loos, together with Messrs. Woods and North, were elected. The Haley–North group disputed this ruling insofar as it declared the election of Mr. Dunn; and insisted that Mr. Griffin, instead, had been elected. A directors' meeting followed in which Mrs. Ringling partici-

---

**1.** Each lady was entitled to cast 2205 votes (since each had the cumulative voting rights of 315 shares, and there were 7 vacancies in the directorate). The sum of the votes of both is 4410, which is sufficient to allow 882 votes for each of 5 persons. Mr. North, holding 370 shares, was entitled to cast 2590 votes, which obviously cannot be divided so as to give to more than two candidates as many as 882 votes each. It will be observed that in order for Mrs. Ringling and Mrs. Haley to be sure to elect five directors (regardless of how Mr. North might vote) they must act together in the sense that their combined votes must be divided among five different candidates and at least one of the five must be voted for by both Mrs. Ringling and Mrs. Haley.

pated after stating that she would do so "without prejudice to her position that the stockholders' meeting had been adjourned and that the directors' meeting was not properly held." Mr. Dunn and Mr. Griffin, although each was challenged by an opposing faction, attempted to join in voting as directors for different slates of officers. Soon after the meeting, Mrs. Ringling instituted this proceeding.

The Vice Chancellor determined that the agreement to vote in accordance with the direction of Mr. Loos was valid as a "stock pooling agreement" with lawful objects and purposes, and that it was not in violation of any public policy of this state. He held that where the arbitrator acts under the agreement and one party refuses to comply with his direction, "the Agreement constitutes the willing party . . . an implied agent possessing the irrevocable proxy of the recalcitrant party for the purpose of casting the particular vote." It was ordered that a new election be held before a master, with the direction that the master should recognize and give effect to the agreement if its terms were properly invoked. [In reaching this result, Vice Chancellor Seitz stated, "Here an implied agency based on an irrevocable proxy is fully justified to implement the Agreement without doing violence to its terms. Moreover, the provisions of the Agreement make it clear that the proxy may be treated as one coupled with an interest so as to render it irrevocable under the circumstances. . . . Obviously, to deny specific performance here would be tantamount to declaring the Agreement invalid. Since petitioner's rights in this respect were properly preserved at the stockholders' meeting, the meeting was a nullity to the extent that it failed to give effect to the provisions of the Agreement here involved. However, I believe it preferable to hold a new election rather than attempt to reconstruct the contested meeting. In this way the parties will be acting with explicit knowledge of their rights."]

Before taking up defendants' objections to the agreement, let us analyze particularly what it attempts to provide with respect to voting, including what functions and powers it attempts to repose in Mr. Loos, the "arbitrator". The agreement recites that the parties desired "to continue to act jointly in all matters relating to their stock ownership or interest in" the corporation. The parties agreed to consult and confer with each other in exercising their voting rights and to act jointly—that is, concertedly; unitedly; towards unified courses of action—in accordance with such agreement as they might reach. Thus, so long as the parties agree for whom or for what their shares shall be voted, the agreement provides no function for the arbitrator. His role is limited to situations where the parties fail to agree upon a course of action. In such cases, the agreement directs that "the question in disagreement shall be submitted for arbitration" to Mr. Loos "as arbitrator and his decision thereon shall be binding upon the parties". These provisions are designed to operate in aid of what appears to be a primary purpose of the parties, "to act jointly" in exercising their voting rights, by providing a means for fixing a course of action whenever they themselves might reach a stalemate.

Should the agreement be interpreted as attempting to empower the arbitrator to carry his directions into effect? Certainly there is no express delegation or grant of power to do so, either by authorizing him to vote the shares or to compel either party to vote them in accordance with his directions. The agreement expresses no other function of the arbitrator than that of deciding questions in disagreement which prevent the effectuation of the purpose "to act jointly". The power to enforce a decision does not seem a necessary or usual incident of such a function. Mr. Loos is not a party to the agreement. It does not contemplate the transfer of any shares or interest in shares to him, or that he should undertake any duties which the parties might compel him to perform. They provided that they might designate any other individual to act instead of Mr. Loos. The agreement does not attempt to make the arbitrator a trustee of an express trust. What the arbitrator is to do is for the benefit of the parties, not for his own benefit. Whether the parties accept or reject his decision is no concern of his, so far as the agreement or the surrounding circumstances reveal. We think the parties sought to bind each other, but to be bound only to each other, and not to empower the arbitrator to enforce decisions he might make.

From this conclusion, it follows necessarily that no decision of the arbitrator could ever be enforced if both parties to the agreement were unwilling that it be enforced, for the obvious reason that there would be no one to enforce it. Under the agreement, something more is required after the arbitrator has given his decision in order that it should become compulsory: at least one of the parties must determine that such decision shall be carried into effect. Thus, any "control" of the voting of the shares, which is reposed in the arbitrator, is substantially limited in action under the agreement in that it is subject to the overriding power of the parties themselves.

The agreement does not describe the undertaking of each party with respect to a decision of the arbitrator other than to provide that it "shall be binding upon the parties". It seems to us that this language, considered with relation to its context and the situations to which it is applicable, means that each party promised the other to exercise her own voting rights in accordance with the arbitrator's decision. The agreement is silent about any exercise of the voting rights of one party by the other. The language with reference to situations where the parties arrive at an understanding as to voting plainly suggests "action" by each, and "exercising" voting rights by each, rather than by one for the other. There is no intimation that this method should be different where the arbitrator's decision is to be carried into effect.

Assuming that a power in each party to exercise the voting rights of the other might be a relatively more effective or convenient means of enforcing a decision of the arbitrator than would be available without the power, this would not justify implying a delegation of the power in the absence of some indication that the parties bargained for that means. The method of voting actually employed by the parties tends to show that they did not construe the agreement as creating powers to vote each other's shares; for at meetings prior to 1946 each party apparently exercised her own voting rights, and at the 1946 meeting, Mrs. Ringling, who wished to enforce the agreement, did not attempt to cast a ballot in exercise of any voting rights of Mrs. Haley. We do not find enough in the agreement or in the circumstances to justify a construction that either party was empowered to exercise voting rights of the other.

Having examined what the parties sought to provide by the agreement, we come now to defendants' contention that the voting provisions are illegal and revocable. They say that the courts of this state have definitely established the doctrine "that there can be no agreement, or any device whatsoever, by which the voting power of stock of a Delaware corporation may be irrevocably separated from the ownership of the stock, except by an agreement which complies with Section 18 of the Corporation Law [concerning voting trusts] and except by a proxy coupled with an interest. . . ."

[Section 18] authorizes, among other things, the deposit or transfer of stock in trust for a specified purpose, namely, "vesting" in the transferee "the right to vote thereon" for a limited period; and prescribes numerous requirements in this connection. Accordingly, it seems reasonable to infer that to establish the relationship and accomplish the purpose which the statute authorizes, its requirements must be complied with.

But the statute does not purport to deal with agreements whereby shareholders attempt to bind each other as to how they shall vote their shares. Various forms of such pooling agreements, as they are sometimes called, have been held valid and have been distinguished from voting trusts. . . . We think the particular agreement before us does not violate Section 18 or constitute an attempted evasion of its requirements, and is not illegal for any other reason.

Generally speaking, a shareholder may exercise wide liberality of judgment in the matter of voting, and it is not objectionable that his motives may be for personal profit, or determined by whims or caprice, so long as he violates no duty owed his fellow shareholders. Heil v. Standard G. & E. Co., 17 Del.Ch. 214, 151 A. 303. The ownership of voting stock imposes no legal duty to vote at all. A group of shareholders may, without impropriety, vote their respective shares so as to obtain advantages of concerted action. They may lawfully contract with each other to vote in the future in such way as they, or a majority of their group, from time to time determine.

Reasonable provisions for cases of failure of the group to reach a determination because of an even division in their ranks seem unobjectionable. The provision here for submission to the arbitrator is plainly designed as a deadlock-breaking measure, and the arbitrator's decision cannot be enforced unless at least one of the parties (entitled to cast one-half of their combined votes) is willing that it be enforced. We find the provision reasonable. It does not appear that the agreement enables the parties to take any unlawful advantage of the outside shareholder, or of any other person. It offends no rule of law or public policy of this state of which we are aware.

Legal consideration for the promises of each party is supplied by the mutual promises of the other party. The undertaking to vote in accordance with the arbitrator's decision is a valid contract. The good faith of the arbitrator's action has not been challenged and, indeed, the record indicates that no such challenge could be supported.

Accordingly, the failure of Mrs. Haley to exercise her voting rights in accordance with his decision was a breach of her contract. . . .

. . . The Court of Chancery may, in a review of an election, reject votes of a registered shareholder where his voting of them is found to be in violation of rights of another person. Compare: In re Giant Portland Cement Co., 26 Del.Ch. 32, 21 A.2d 697; In re Canal Construction Co., 21 Del.Ch. 155, 182 A. 545. It seems to us that upon the application of Mrs. Ringling, the injured party, the votes representing Mrs. Haley's shares should not be counted. Since no infirmity in Mr. North's voting has been demonstrated, his right to recognition of what he did at the meeting should be considered in granting any relief to Mrs. Ringling; for her rights arose under a contract to which Mr. North was not a party.

With this in mind, we have concluded that the election should not be declared invalid, but that effect should be given to a rejection of the votes representing Mrs. Haley's shares. No other relief seems appropriate in this proceeding. Mr. North's vote against the motion for adjournment was sufficient to defeat it. With respect to the election of directors, the return of the inspectors should be corrected to show a rejection of Mrs. Haley's votes, and to declare the election of the six persons for whom Mr. North and Mrs. Ringling voted.

This leaves one vacancy in the directorate. The question of what to do about such a vacancy was not considered by the court below and has not been argued here. For this reason, and because an election of directors at the 1947 annual meeting (which presumably will be held in the near future) may make a determination of the question unimportant, we shall not decide it on this appeal. If a decision of the point appears important to the parties, any of them may apply to raise it in the Court of Chancery, after the mandate of this court is received there.

An order should be entered directing a modification of the order of the Court of Chancery in accordance with this opinion.

———

## NOTE ON IRREVOCABLE PROXIES

Even if a proxy is expressly conferred in connection with a voting agreement, a further problem remains. Classically a proxy has been treated as an agency relationship, in which the shareholder is the principal and the proxyholder is the agent. It is a rule of agency law, however, that a principal can terminate an agent's authority at will, even if the termination is in breach of contract (although in such cases the principal may be liable to the agent in damages). See Restatement, Second, of Agency § 118. There is an exception to this rule in cases where the agent holds a "power coupled with an interest," or, as Restatement (Second) of Agency § 138 calls it, a "power given as security." See Restatement, Second, of Agency §§ 138, 139. Generally speaking, this exception is applicable to arrangements in which it is understood that the "agent" or power-holder has an interest in the subject-matter to which the power relates, and is therefore expected not to execute the power solely on the power-giver's behalf—the crux of the normal agency relationship—but on his own behalf as well. Accordingly, the safest way to insure that a proxy will be irrevocable is to confer it upon a proxyholder who has an "interest" in the shares to which the proxy relates. Relatively clear examples are cases where the proxyholder is a pledgee of the shares, or has agreed to purchase the shares. See N.Y.Bus.Corp.Law § 609(f)(1), (2).

Where a proxy is given pursuant to a voting agreement, however, normally the proxyholder is either an arbitrator, who has no proprietary interest in the shares or the corporation, or a shareholder, who has a proprietary interest in the corporation but not in the shares that are the subject-matter of the proxy. In In re Chilson, 19 Del.Ch. 398, 409, 168 A. 82, 86 (1933), the court held that where a proxyholder has only "an interest in the corporation generally," or "an interest in the bare voting power or the results to be accomplished by the use of" the proxy, the proxy is revocable. On the other hand, in Deibler v. Chas. H. Elliott Co., 368 Pa. 267, 81 A.2d 557 (1951), the Supreme Court of Pennsylvania, construing Delaware law, upheld the irrevocability of a proxy given to secure payment of the purchase price of stock in a Delaware corporation and the seller's continued employment by the corporation. This issue is now often addressed by the statutes. For example, Del. Gen. Corp. Law § 212(e) provide that "A proxy may be made irrevocable regardless of whether the interest with which it is coupled is an interest in the stock itself or an interest in the corporation generally."

## (b) VOTING TRUSTS

### DEL. GEN. CORP. LAW § 218

[See Statutory Supplement]

### REV. MODEL BUS. CORP. ACT § 7.30

[See Statutory Supplement]

## CAL. CORP. CODE § 706

[See Statutory Supplement]

———

## NOTE ON VOTING TRUSTS

1. *In General.* A voting trust is a device by which shareholders separate voting rights in, and legal title to, their shares from beneficial ownership, by conferring the voting rights and legal title on one or more voting trustees, while retaining the ultimate right to distributions and appreciation. Usually, two or more shareholders are involved, so that the voting trust is a type of pooling agreement. Sometimes, however, only one shareholder is involved—for example, where a sole shareholder creates a voting trust to satisfy creditors, or to vest control of his business in managers. The creation of a voting trust normally requires (i) the execution of a written trust agreement between participating shareholders and the voting trustees, and (ii) a transfer to the trustee, for a specified period, of the shareholders' stock certificates and the legal title to their stock. The voting trustee then registers the transfer on the corporation's books, so that during the term of the trust the trustee is the record owner of the shares, entitled to vote in the election of directors and often on other matters as well. Dividends are paid by the corporation to the trustee, but are almost invariably then paid over by the trustee to the beneficial owners. Several statutes require the trustee to issue certificates of beneficial interest to participating shareholders, and frequently such certificates are issued, even where not statutorily required, to facilitate trading in the beneficial interests.

Voting trusts are an effective and a moderately simple way to separate control and beneficial ownership for a limited period of time. The separation is self-executing, because the trustee is the legal owner and is registered as such on the corporation's books. The separation survives transfers by the beneficial owners, since they can transfer only their retained equitable interests (essentially, most ownership rights except the right to vote during the term of the trust). Upon termination of the voting trust, the beneficial owners receive stock certificates which reinstate them as complete owners, registered as such on the corporation's books.

2. *Validity.* Most states have statutes that both explicitly validate voting trusts and lay down certain requirements concerning their creation and their content. Among the most common limitations are a maximum time period (usually ten years), and a requirement that the voting-trust agreement be filed with the corporation and open to inspection.

3. *Overlap of Voting Trusts and Shareholders' Voting Agreements.* In the context of close corporations, voting trusts may sometimes be used, like voting agreements, to allocate voting control in other than a pro rata manner, or to preserve the solidarity of a faction

consisting of less than all the shareholders. Because voting trusts and voting agreements may have substantially overlapping purposes, the substantive legal rules applicable to one of these two legal forms have sometimes been applied to an arrangement that was nominally cast in the other form. Thus in Abercrombie v. Davies, 36 Del.Ch. 371, 130 A.2d 338 (1957), the Delaware Supreme Court held that an "Agent's Agreement" that was in form a voting agreement was in substance a voting trust, and was therefore unenforceable because it failed to comply with the requirements of the voting-trust statute.

## (c) CLASSIFIED STOCK AND WEIGHTED VOTING

### DEL. GEN. CORP. LAW §§ 102(a)(6), 212(a)
[See Statutory Supplement]

### REV. MODEL BUS. CORP. ACT §§ 6.01, 7.21, 8.04
[See Statutory Supplement]

### NOTE ON CLASSIFIED STOCK AND WEIGHTED VOTING

"One of the simplest and most effective ways of assuring that all the participants or that particular minority shareholders will have representation on the board of directors is to set up two or more classes of stock, provide that each class is to vote for and elect a specified number or a stated percentage of the directors, and then issue each class or a majority of shares in each class to a different shareholder or faction of shareholders. . . . Class A common stock might be given power, for instance, to elect three directors and Class B common stock power to elect two." 1 F.H. O'Neal & R. Thompson, O'Neal's Close Corporations § 3.19 (3d ed.). A few statutes validate this technique explicitly (e.g., N.Y.Bus.Corp.Law § 703), and most of the remaining statutes validate it implicitly by providing that a corporation may have one or more classes of stock with such voting powers as shall be stated in the certificate (e.g., Del.Gen.Corp.Law § 151(a)). In its simplest version, the use of classified common does not necessarily involve voting power for any class that is disproportionate to the investment made by that class. Often, however, separate classes carry voting power whose weight differs considerably from the relative investment made by their holders. At the extreme, a class of stock may have proprietary rights but no voting power, or voting power but no proprietary rights.

In Lehrman v. Cohen, 43 Del.Ch. 222, 222 A.2d 800 (1966), the Cohen and Lehrman families each owned equal quantities of the voting stock of Giant Food, Inc., designated Class AC and Class AL common stock, respectively. Each class of stock was entitled to elect two members of Giant Food's four-member board of directors. Over the years, there were differences of opinion between the Cohen and Lehrman families as to operating policies of the Company. At a certain point, an arrangement was made which provided for the establishment of a fifth directorship to obviate the risk of deadlock. Under the arrangement, Giant Food's certificate of incorporation was amended to create a third class of stock, designated Class AD common stock, consisting of one share of $10 par value stock. The Class AD stock had the right to elect one director, but essentially had no right to distributions and could be called for $10 by a vote of the other four directors. The share of the Class AD stock was issued to Food Giant's long-time counsel, Joseph Danzansky, who, by prearrangement, voted the share for himself as the fifth director.

Subsequently, the plaintiff, a member of the Lehrman family who at that point owned all the AL stock, claimed that the Class AD stock was illegal on the ground that in substance it was a voting trust and did not comply with the voting trust statute. The court rejected this argument:

> The criteria of a voting trust under our decisions have been summarized by this Court in Abercrombie v. Davies, 36 Del.Ch. 371, 130 A.2d 338 (1957). The tests there set forth, accepted by both sides of this cause as being applicable, are as follows: (1) the voting rights of the stock are separated from the other attributes of ownership; (2) the voting rights granted are intended to be irrevocable for a definite period of time; and (3) the principal purpose of the grant of voting rights is to acquire voting control of the corporation. . . .

> . . . The AD arrangement did not separate the voting rights of the AC or the AL stock from the other attributes of ownership of those classes of stock. Each AC and AL stockholder retains complete control over the voting of his stock; each can vote his stock directly; no AL or AC stockholder is divested of his right to vote his stock as he sees fit; no AL or AC stock can be voted against the shareholder's wishes; and the AL and AC stock continue to elect two directors each.

The court also held that it was not illegal to create a class of stock having voting rights but no proprietary rights.

## SECTION 3.  AGREEMENTS CONTROLLING MATTERS WITHIN THE BOARD'S DISCRETION

Voting arrangements of the kind discussed in Section 2, supra, control only those matters that are decided on a shareholder level. Typically, however, the issues that are most important to shareholders in a close corporation are determined on a board level—for example, managerial positions, managerial compensation, and dividends. If the shareholders attempt to also control these matters by agreement, the problem arises whether (or under what conditions) such an agreement is valid, in the face of the normal statutory provision that the business of the corporation shall be managed by or under the direction of the board. That question is addressed by the materials in this section.

---

## McQuade v. Stoneham

Court of Appeals of New York, 1934.
263 N.Y. 323, 189 N.E. 234.

Appeal, by permission of Court of Appeals, from judgment of Appellate Division, First Department, unanimously affirming judgment for plaintiff for $42,827.38 and other relief.

■ POUND, CH. J. The action is brought to compel specific performance of an agreement between the parties, entered into to secure the control of National Exhibition Company, also called the baseball club (New York Nationals or "Giants"). This was one of Stoneham's enterprises which used the New York Polo Grounds for its home games. McGraw was manager of the Giants. McQuade was, at the time the contract was entered into, a city magistrate. He resigned December 8, 1930.

Defendant Stoneham became the owner of 1,306 shares, or a majority of the stock of National Exhibition Company (there being then 2,500 shares outstanding). Plaintiff and defendant McGraw each purchased seventy shares of his stock. Plaintiff paid Stoneham $50,-338.10 for the stock he purchased. As a part of the transaction the agreement in question was entered into. It was dated May 21, 1919. Some of its pertinent provisions are:

"VIII. The parties hereto will use their best endeavors for the purpose of continuing as directors of said company and as officers thereof the following:

"Directors: Charles A. Stoneham, John J. McGraw, Francis X. McQuade, with right to the party of the first part (Stoneham) to name all additional directors as he sees fit.

"Officers: Charles A. Stoneham, president; John J. McGraw, vice-president; Francis X. McQuade, treasurer.

"IX. No salaries are to be paid to any of the above officers or directors, except as follows: President, $45,000; vice-president, $7,500; treasurer, $7,500.

"X. There shall be no change in said salaries, no change in the amount of capital, or the number of shares, no change or amendment of the by-laws of the corporation or any matters regarding the policy of the business of the corporation or any matters which may in anywise affect, endanger or interfere with the rights of minority stockholders, excepting upon the mutual and unanimous consent of all . . . of the parties hereto.

"XIV. This agreement shall continue and remain in force so long as the parties or any of them or the representative of any own the stock referred to in this agreement, to wit, the party of the first part, 1,166 shares, the party of the second part 70 shares and the party of the third part 70 shares, except as may otherwise appear by this agreement. . . ."

In pursuance of this contract Stoneham became president and McGraw vice-president of the corporation. McQuade became treasurer. In June, 1925, his salary was increased to $10,000 a year. He continued to act until May 2, 1928, when Leo J. Bondy was elected to succeed him. The board of directors consisted of seven men. The four outside of the parties hereto were selected by Stoneham and he had complete control over them. At the meeting of May 2, 1928, Stoneham and McGraw refrained from voting, McQuade voted for himself and the other four voted for Bondy. Defendants did not keep their agreement with McQuade to use their best efforts to continue him as treasurer. On the contrary, he was dropped with their entire acquiescence. At the next stockholders' meeting he was dropped as a director, although they might have elected him.

The courts below have refused to order the reinstatement of McQuade, but have given him damages for wrongful discharge, with a right to sue for future damages.

The cause for dropping McQuade was due to the falling out of friends. McQuade and Stoneham had disagreed. The trial court has found in substance that their numerous quarrels and disputes did not affect the orderly and efficient administration of the business of the corporation; that plaintiff was removed because he had antagonized the dominant Stoneham by persisting in challenging his power over the corporate treasury and for no misconduct on his part. The court also finds that plaintiff was removed by Stoneham for protecting the corporation and its minority stockholders. We will assume that Stoneham put him out when he might have retained him, merely in order to get rid of him.

Defendants say that the contract in suit was void because the directors held their office charged with the duty to act for the corporation according to their best judgment and that any contract which compels a director to vote to keep any particular person in office and at a stated salary is illegal. Directors are the exclusive executive representatives of the corporation, charged with administration of its internal affairs and the management and use of its assets. They manage the business of the corporation (Gen.Corp.Law, Cons. Laws, c. 23, sec. 27). "An agreement to continue a man as president is dependent upon his continued loyalty to the interests of the corporation" (Fells v. Katz, 256 N.Y. 67, 72, 175 N.E. 516, 517). So much is undisputed.

Plaintiff contends that the converse of this proposition is true and that an agreement among directors to continue a man as an officer of a corporation is not to be broken so long as such officer is loyal to the interests of the corporation and that, as plaintiff has been found loyal to the corporation, the agreement of defendants is enforceable.

Although it has been held that an agreement among stockholders whereby it is attempted to divest the directors of their power to discharge an unfaithful employee of the corporation is illegal as against public policy (Fells v. Katz, supra), it must be equally true that the stockholders may not, by agreement among themselves, control the directors in the exercise of the judgment vested in them by virtue of their office to elect officers and fix salaries. Their motives may not be questioned so long as their acts are legal. The bad faith or the improper motives of the parties does not change this rule (Manson v. Curtis, 223 N.Y. 313, 324, 119 N.E. 559). Directors may not by agreements entered into by stockholders abrogate their independent judgment (Creed v. Copps, 103 Vt. 164, 71 A.L.R.Ann. 1287).

Stockholders may, of course, combine to elect directors. That rule is well settled. As Holmes, Ch. J., pointedly said (Brightman v. Bates, 175 Mass. 105, 110, 55 N.E. 809, 811): "If stockholders want to make their power felt, they must unite. There is no reason why a majority should not agree to keep together." The power to unite is, however, limited to the election of directors and is not extended to contracts whereby limitations are placed on the power of directors to manage the business of the corporation by the selection of agents at defined salaries.

The minority shareholders whose interests McQuade says he has been punished for protecting, are not, aside from himself, complaining about his discharge. He is not acting for the corporation or for them in this action. It is impossible to see how the corporation has been injured by the substitution of Bondy as treasurer in place of McQuade. As McQuade represents himself in this action and seeks redress for his own wrongs, "we prefer to listen to [the corporation and the minority stockholders] before any decision as to their wrongs" (Faulds v. Yates, 57 Ill. 416).

It is urged that we should pay heed to the morals and manners of the market place to sustain this agreement, and that we should hold that its violation gives rise to a cause of action for damages, rather than base our decision on any outworn notions of public policy. Public policy is a dangerous guide in determining the validity of a contract, and courts should not interfere lightly with the freedom of competent parties to make their own contracts. We do not close our eyes to the fact that such agreements, tacitly or openly arrived at, are not uncommon, especially in close corporations where the stockholders are doing business for convenience under a corporate organization. We know that majority stockholders, united in voting trusts, effectively manage the business of a corporation by choosing trustworthy directors to reflect their policies in the corporate management. Nor are we unmindful that McQuade has, so the court has found, been shabbily treated as a purchaser of stock from Stoneham. We have said: "A trustee is held to something stricter than the morals of the market place" (Meinhard v. Salmon, 249 N.Y. 458, 464, 164 N.E. 545, 546), but Stoneham and McGraw were not trustees for McQuade as an individual. Their duty was to the corporation and its stockholders, to be exercised according to their unrestricted lawful judgment. They were under no legal obligation to deal righteously with McQuade if it was against public policy to do so.

The courts do not enforce mere moral obligations, nor legal ones either, unless someone seeks to establish rights which may be waived by custom and for convenience. We are constrained by authority to hold that a contract is illegal and void so far as it precludes the board of directors, at the risk of incurring legal liability, from changing officers, salaries or policies or retaining individuals in office, except by consent of the contracting parties. On the whole, such a holding is probably preferable to one which would open the courts to pass on the motives of directors in the lawful exercise of their trust. . . .

The judgment of the Appellate Division and that of the Trial Term should be reversed and the complaint dismissed, with costs in all courts.

[The court also held that the agreement violated the Inferior Criminal Courts Act, which provided that "[n]o city magistrate shall engage in any other business or profession . . . , but each of said justices and magistrates shall devote his whole time and capacity, so far as the public interest demands, to the duties of his office. . . ." At the date of the agreement McQuade was a city magistrate, and he did not resign his position until after commencement of the action.]

■ [The opinion of LEHMAN, J., concurring in the result, is omitted.]

## NOTE ON CLARK v. DODGE

In Clark v. Dodge, 269 N.Y. 410, 199 N.E. 641 (1936), two corporations manufactured medicinal preparations under secret formulas. Clark owned 25%, and Dodge owned 75%, of the stock of each corporation. Clark and Dodge entered into an agreement which provided that (1) Dodge would vote for Clark as a director. (2) Dodge, acting in his directorial capacity, would continue Clark as general manager as long as Clark proved faithful, efficient, and competent. (3) Clark would always receive as salary or dividends one-fourth of the corporation's net income. (4) No salaries to other officers would be unreasonable in amount or incommensurate with the services rendered by those officers. The court held that the agreement was valid:

> Except for the broad dicta in the *McQuade* opinion, we think there can be no doubt that the agreement here in question was legal and that the complaint states a cause of action. There was no attempt to sterilize the board of directors as in [*McQuade*]. . . .

If there was any invasion of the powers of the directorate under that agreement it is so slight as to be negligible; and certainly there is no damage suffered by or threatened to anybody. The broad statements in the *McQuade* opinion, applicable to the facts there, should be confined to those facts.

---

## Galler v. Galler

Supreme Court of Illinois, 1964, reh. denied 1964.
32 Ill.2d 16, 203 N.E.2d 577.

■ UNDERWOOD, JUSTICE. Plaintiff, Emma Galler, sued in equity for an accounting and for specific performance of an agreement made in July, 1955, between plaintiff and her husband, of one part, and defendants, Isadore A. Galler and his wife, Rose, of the other. Defendants appealed from a decree of the superior court of Cook County granting the relief prayed. The First District Appellate Court reversed the decree and denied specific performance, affirming in part the order for an accounting, and modifying the order awarding master's fees. (45 Ill. App.2d 452, 196 N.E.2d 5.) That decision is appealed here on a certificate of importance.

There is no substantial dispute as to the facts in this case. From 1919 to 1924, Benjamin and Isadore Galler, brothers, were equal partners in the Galler Drug Company, a wholesale drug concern. In 1924 the business was incorporated under the Illinois Business Corporation Act, each owning one half of the outstanding 220 shares of stock. In 1945 each contracted to sell 6 shares to an employee, Rosenberg, at a price of $10,500 for each block of 6 shares, payable within 10 years. They guaranteed to repurchase the shares if Rosenberg's employment were terminated, and further agreed that if they sold their shares, Rosenberg would receive the same price per share as that paid for the brothers' shares. Rosenberg was still indebted for the 12 shares in July, 1955, and continued to make payments on account even after Benjamin Galler died in 1957 and after the institution of this action by Emma Galler in 1959. Rosenberg was not involved in this litigation either as a party or as a witness, and in July of 1961, prior to the time that the master in chancery hearings were concluded, defendants Isadore and Rose Galler purchased the 12 shares from Rosenberg. A supplemental complaint was filed by the plaintiff, Emma Galler, asserting an equitable right to have 6 of the 12 shares transferred to her and offering to pay the defendants one half of the amount that the defendants paid Rosenberg. The parties have stipulated that pending disposition of the instant case, these shares will not be voted or transferred. For approximately one year prior to the entry of the decree by the chancellor in July of 1962, there were no outstanding minority shareholder interests.

In March, 1954, Benjamin and Isadore, on the advice of their accountant, decided to enter into an agreement for the financial protection of their immediate families and to assure their families, after the death of either brother, equal control of the corporation. [The agreement was executed in July 1955, after Benjamin had fallen ill. In September 1956, Emma agreed to permit Isadore's son Aaron to become president for one year and agreed that she would not interfere with the business during that year. In December 1957, Benjamin died.] The evidence is undisputed that defendants had decided prior to Benjamin's death they would not honor the agreement, but never disclosed their intention to plaintiff or her husband. . . .

Shortly after Benjamin's death, Emma went to the office and demanded the terms of the 1955 agreement be carried out. Isadore told her that anything she had to say could be said to Aaron, who then told her that his father would not abide by the agreement. He offered a modification of the agreement by proposing the salary continuation payment but without her becoming a director. When Emma refused to modify the agreement and sought enforcement of its terms, defendants refused and this suit followed.

During the last few years of Benjamin's life both brothers drew an annual salary of $42,000. Aaron, whose salary was $15,000 as manager of the warehouse prior to September, 1956, has since the time that Emma agreed to his acting as president drawn an annual salary of $20,000. In 1957, 1958, and 1959 a $40,000 annual dividend was paid. Plaintiff has received her proportionate share of the dividend.

The July, 1955, agreement in question here, entered into between Benjamin, Emma, Isadore and Rose, recites that Benjamin and Isadore each own 47½% of the issued and outstanding shares of the Galler Drug Company, an Illinois corporation, and that Benjamin and Isadore desired to provide income for the support and maintenance of their immediate families. No reference is made to the shares then being purchased by Rosenberg. The essential features of the contested portions of the agreement are substantially as set forth in the opinion of the Appellate Court: (2) that the bylaws of the corporation will be amended to provide for a board of four directors; that the necessary quorum shall be three directors; and that no directors' meeting shall be held without giving ten days notice to all directors. (3) The shareholders will cast their votes for the above named persons (Isadore, Rose, Benjamin and Emma) as directors at said special meeting and at any other meeting held for the purpose of electing directors. (4, 5) In the event of the death of either brother his wife shall have the right to nominate a director in place of the decedent. (6) Certain annual dividends will be declared by the corporation. The dividend shall be $50,000 payable out of the accumulated earned surplus in excess of $500,000. If 50% of the annual net profits after taxes exceeds the minimum $50,000 then the directors shall have discretion to declare a dividend up to 50% of the annual net profits. If the net profits are less than $50,000 nevertheless the minimum $50,000 annual dividend shall be declared, providing the $500,000 surplus is maintained. Earned surplus is defined. (9) The certificates evidencing the said shares of Benjamin Galler and Isadore Galler shall bear a legend that the shares are subject to the terms of this agreement. (10)

A salary continuation agreement shall be entered into by the corporation which shall authorize the corporation upon the death of Benjamin Galler or Isadore Galler, or both, to pay a sum equal to twice the salary of such officer, payable monthly over a five-year period. Said sum shall be paid to the widow during her widowhood, but should be paid to such widow's children if the widow remarries within the five-year period. (11, 12) The parties to this agreement further agree and hereby grant to the corporation the authority to purchase, in the event of the death of either Benjamin or Isadore, so much of the stock of Galler Drug Company held by the estate as is necessary to provide sufficient funds to pay the federal estate tax, the Illinois inheritance tax and other administrative expenses of the estate. If as a result of such purchase from the estate of the decedent the amount of dividends to be received by the heirs is reduced, the parties shall nevertheless vote for directors so as to give the estate and heirs the same representation as before (2 directors out of 4, even though they own less stock), and also that the corporation pay an additional benefit payment equal to the diminution of the dividends. In the event either Benjamin or Isadore decides to sell his shares he is required to offer them first to the remaining shareholders and then to the corporation at book value, according each six months to accept the offer.

The Appellate Court found the 1955 agreement void because "the undue duration, stated purpose and substantial disregard of the provisions of the Corporation Act outweigh any considerations which might call for divisibility" and held that "the public policy of this state demands voiding this entire agreement".

While the conduct of defendants towards plaintiff was clearly inequitable, the basically controlling factor is the absence of an objecting minority interest, together with the absence of public detriment. . . .

At this juncture it should be emphasized that we deal here with a so-called close corporation. . . . For our purposes, a close corporation is one in which the stock is held in a few hands, or in a few families, and wherein it is not at all, or only rarely, dealt in by buying or selling. (Brooks v. Willcuts, 8th Cir.1935, 78 F.2d 270, 273.) Moreover, it should be recognized that shareholder agreements similar to that in question here are often, as a practical consideration, quite necessary for the protection of those financially interested in the close corporation. While the shareholder of a public-issue corporation may readily sell his shares on the open market should management fail to use, in his opinion, sound business judgment, his counterpart of the close corporation often has a large total of his entire capital invested in the business and has no ready market for his shares should he desire to sell. He feels, understandably, that he is more than a mere investor and that his voice should be heard concerning all corporate activity. Without a shareholder agreement, specifically enforceable by the courts, insuring him a modicum of control, a large minority shareholder might find himself at the mercy of an oppressive or unknowledgeable majority. Moreover, as in the case at bar, the shareholders of a close corporation are often also the directors and officers thereof. With substantial shareholding interests abiding in each member of the board of directors, it is often quite impossible to secure, as in the large public-issue corporation, independent board judgment free from personal motivations concerning corporate policy. For these and other reasons too voluminous to enumerate here, often the only sound basis for protection is afforded by a lengthy, detailed shareholder agreement securing the rights and obligations of all concerned. For a discussion of these and other considerations, see Note, "A Plea for Separate Statutory Treatment of the Close Corporation", 33 N.Y.U.L.Rev. 700 (1958).

As the preceding review of the applicable decisions of this court points out, there has been a definite, albeit inarticulate, trend toward eventual judicial treatment of the close corporation as *sui generis.* Several shareholder-director agreements that have technically "violated" the letter of the Business Corporation Act have nevertheless been upheld in the light of the existing practical circumstances, i.e., no apparent public injury, the absence of a complaining minority interest, and no apparent prejudice to creditors. However, we have thus far not attempted to limit these decisions as applicable only to close corporations and have seemingly implied that general considerations regarding judicial supervision of all corporate behavior apply.

The practical result of this series of cases, while liberally giving legal efficacy to particular agreements in special circumstances notwithstanding literal "violations" of statutory corporate law, has been to inject much doubt and uncertainty into the thinking of the bench and corporate bar of Illinois concerning shareholder agreements. See e.g., Cary, "How Illinois Corporations May Enjoy Partnership Advantages: Planning for the Closely Held Firm." 48 N.W.U.L.Rev. 427; Note, "The Validity of Stockholders' Voting Agreements in Illinois," 3 U.Chi. L.Rev. 640.

It is therefore necessary, we feel, to discuss the instant case with the problems peculiar to the close corporation particularly in mind. . . .

This court has recognized, albeit *sub silentio,* the significant conceptual differences between the close corporation and its public-issue counterpart in, among other cases, Kantzler v. Benzinger, 214 Ill. 589, 73 N.E. 874, where an agreement quite similar to the one under attack here was upheld. Where, as in Kantzler and here, no complaining minority interest appears, no fraud or apparent injury to the public or creditors is present, and no clearly prohibitory statutory language is violated, we can see no valid reason for precluding the parties from reaching any arrangements concerning the management of the corporation which are agreeable to all. . . .

Since the question as to the duration of the agreement is a principal source of controversy, we shall consider it first. The parties provided no specific termination date, and while the agreement concludes with a paragraph that its terms "shall be binding upon and shall inure to the benefits of" the legal representatives, heirs and assigns of the parties, this clause is, we believe, intended to be operative only as long as one of the parties is living. It further provides that it shall be so construed as to carry out its purposes, and we believe these must be determined from a consideration of the agreement as a whole. Thus viewed, a fair construction is that its purposes were accomplished at the death of the survivor of the parties. While these life spans are not precisely ascertainable, and the Appellate Court noted Emma Galler's life expectancy at her husband's death was 26.9 years, we are aware of no statutory or public policy provision against stockholders' agreements which would invalidate this agreement on that ground.... While defendants argue that the public policy evinced by the legislative restrictions upon the duration of voting trust agreements (Ill.Rev.Stat.1963, chap. 32, par. 157.30a) should be applied here, this agreement is not a voting trust, but as pointed out by the dissenting justice in the Appellate Court, is a straight contractual voting control agreement which does not divorce voting rights from stock ownership. That the policy against agreements in which stock ownership and voting rights are separated, indicated in Luthy v. Ream, 270 Ill. 170, 110 N.E. 373, is inapplicable to voting control agreements was emphasized in Thompson wherein a control agreement was upheld as not attempting to separate ownership and voting power. While limiting voting trusts in 1947 to a maximum duration of 10 years, the legislature has indicated no similar policy regarding straight voting agreements although these have been common since prior to 1870. In view of the history of decisions of this court generally upholding, in the absence of fraud or prejudice to minority interests or public policy, the right of stockholders to agree among themselves as to the manner in which their stock will be voted, we do not regard the period of time within which this agreement may remain effective as rendering the agreement unenforceable.

The clause that provides for the election of certain persons to specified offices for a period of years likewise does not require invalidation. In Kantzler v. Bensinger, 214 Ill. 589, 73 N.E. 874, this court upheld an agreement entered into by all the stockholders providing that certain parties would be elected to the offices of the corporation for a fixed period. In Faulds v. Yates, 57 Ill. 416, we upheld a similar agreement among the majority stockholders of a corporation, notwithstanding the existence of a minority which was not before the court complaining thereof. See also Hornstein, "Judicial Tolerance of the Incorporated Partnership," 18 Law and Contemporary Problems 435 at page 444.

We turn next to a consideration of the effect of the stated purpose of the agreement upon its validity. The pertinent provision is: "The said Benjamin A. Galler and Isadore A. Galler desire to provide income for the support and maintenance of their immediate families." Obviously, there is no evil inherent in a contract entered into for the reason that the persons originating the terms desired to so arrange their property as to provide post-death support for those dependent upon them. Nor does the fact that the subject property is corporate stock alter the situation so long as there exists no detriment to minority stock interests, creditors or other public injury. It is, however, contended by defendants that the methods provided by the agreement for implementation of the stated purpose are, as a whole, violative of the Business Corporation Act (Ill.Rev.Stat.1963, chap. 32, pars. 157.28, 157.30a, 157.33, 157.34, 157.41) to such an extent as to render it void *in toto*.

The terms of the dividend agreement require a minimum annual dividend of $50,000, but this duty is limited by the subsequent provision that it shall be operative only so long as an earned surplus of $500,000 is maintained. It may be noted that in 1958, the year prior to commencement of this litigation, the corporation's net earnings after taxes amounted to $202,759 while its earned surplus was $1,543,270, and this was increased in 1958 to $1,680,079 while earnings were $172,964. The minimum earned surplus requirement is designed for the protection of the corporation and its creditors, and we take no exception to the contractual dividend requirements as thus restricted. Kantzler v. Bensinger, 214 Ill. 589, 73 N.E. 874.

The salary continuation agreement is a common feature, in one form or another, of corporate executive employment. It requires that the widow should receive a total benefit, payable monthly over a five-year period, aggregating twice the amount paid her deceased husband in one year. This requirement was likewise limited for the protection of the corporation by being contingent upon the payments being income tax-deductible by the corporation. The charge made in those cases which have considered the validity of payments to the widow of an officer and shareholder in a corporation is that a gift of its property by a noncharitable corporation is in violation of the rights of its shareholders and *ultra vires*. Since there are no shareholders here other than the parties to the contract, this objection is not here applicable, and its effect, as limited, upon the corporation is not so prejudicial as to require its invalidation.

Having concluded that the agreement, under the circumstances here present, is not vulnerable to the attack made on it, we must consider the accounting feature of this action. The trial court allowed the relief prayed, an action we deem proper except as to the master's fees which were modified by the Appellate Court. Since no question is here raised regarding them, we affirm the action of that court in this respect. The questions as to salary which the Appellate Court correctly held were improperly increased became ones of fact to be determined by the trial court.

We hold defendants must account for all monies received by them from the corporation since September 25, 1956, in excess of that theretofore authorized.

Accordingly, the judgment of the Appellate Court is reversed except insofar as it relates to fees, and is, as to them affirmed. The cause is remanded to the circuit court of Cook County with directions to proceed in accordance herewith.

Affirmed in part and reversed in part, and remanded with directions.

———

## NOTE ON FURTHER PROCEEDINGS IN GALLER v. GALLER

The decree in *Galler* became effective on February 11, 1965. It ordered Isadore and Rose to "account for all monies received by them from the company since September 25, 1956 [up to the time of the decree], in excess of that theretofore authorized," but provided that Isadore and Aaron be allowed "fair compensation ... for services rendered by them to the corporation during said period." On remand, defendants argued that the salaries of Aaron and Isadore during the relevant period represented the fair market value of their services, and in any event since Isadore's $42,000 salary after Benjamin's death was a continuation of his salary under the agreement, it had been "theretofore authorized" within the meaning of the decree. The Appellate Court rejected both arguments. As to the former issue the court adopted the findings of a master who valued Isadore's services at $10,000/year and Aaron's at $15,000/year. As to whether continuation of Isadore's $42,000 salary was authorized by the agreement, the court said

> ... Isadore's continued receipt of the same salary upon the death of Benjamin without the *quid pro quo* for his brother's family, is an alteration of the past arrangement, and was without authorization.

> Furthermore, the clear import of the 1955 shareholders' agreement is that the partnership-like arrangement was intended to remain after the death of either Benjamin or Isadore. While not specifically addressing itself to salaries, the agreement provides that upon the death of either Benjamin or Isadore, four directors are to be elected; two from Isadore's family and two from Benjamin's family. The officers and their salaries are voted upon by the directors. Dividends are required to be paid provided $500,000 earned surplus is maintained. It may be inferred that this agreement sought to replace a deceased brother's position as an officer with members of his family, thereby permitting them to share equally in the company's earnings, including salaries, a significant means of distributing the corporate profits. This inference is not negated by the fact that no provision in the 1955 agreement requires equality of salaries between the family branches.

For other disputes among the Gallers after the Supreme Court's decree, see Galler v. Galler, 69 Ill.App.2d 397, 217 N.E.2d 111 (1966); Galler v. Galler, 95 Ill.App.2d 340, 238 N.E.2d 274 (1968).

———

## DEL. GEN. CORP. LAW §§ 102(b)(1), 141(a), 142(b), 350, 351, 354

[See Statutory Supplement]

---

## REV. MODEL BUS. CORP. ACT §§ 2.02(b), 2.06, 7.32, 8.01(b)

---

## N.Y. BUS. CORP. LAW § 620

[See Statutory Supplement]

---

## CAL. CORP. CODE §§ 158, 186, 300, 312

[See Statutory Supplement]

---

**ADLER v. SVINGOS**, 80 A.D.2d 764, 436 N.Y.S.2d 719 (1981). Adler, Shaw, and Svingos each owned 33⅓% of the shares of 891 First Ave. Corp., a New York corporation that operated a restaurant. The corporation's certificate of incorporation was filed in November 1978. In December 1978, Adler, Shaw, and Svingos executed a Stockholders' Agreement. Paragraph 8 of the Agreement provided that all corporate operations, including changes in corporate structure, would require unanimous consent of the three signatories. Subsequently, when Adler and Shaw sought to sell the business, Svingos objected, relying upon the Stockholders' Agreement. Adler and Shaw then brought an action seeking to strike paragraph 8 of the Agreement as void under New York B.C.L. § 620(b), on the ground that under section 620(b) a provision that restricts the board in the management of the business of the corporation must be located in the certificate of incorporation. Svingos counterclaimed, and asked for reformation of the certificate of incorporation to reflect Paragraph 8 of the Stockholders' Agreement. The trial court granted summary judgement against Svingos: Reversed.

In Zion v. Kurtz (50 N.Y.2d 92), the Court of Appeals interpreted analogous provisions of the Delaware General Corporation Law and held enforceable, as between the parties to it, a provision of a shareholders' agreement between all the shareholders, proscribing corporate action without the consent of a minority shareholder, even though the disputed provision was not incorporated in the corporate charter as required by Delaware's statute. Speaking for the majority, Judge Meyer stated ... "Since there are no intervening rights of third persons, the agreement requires nothing that is not permitted by statute, and all of the stockholders of the corporation assented to it, the certificate of incorporation may be ordered reformed, by requiring Kurtz [whose position was analogous to that of plaintiffs Adler and Shaw] to file the appropriate amendments, or more directly he may be held estopped to rely upon the absence of those amendments from the corporate charter".

The principles set forth in *Zion* are controlling here. We conclude that it was error to grant partial summary judgment to plaintiffs and to dismiss defendant's first counterclaim. Indeed, the record warrants granting the defendant's motion for partial summary judgment reforming the certificate to reflect the unanimity of the stockholders' agreement.

---

## SECTION 4. SUPERMAJORITY VOTING AND QUORUM REQUIREMENTS AT THE SHAREHOLDER AND BOARD LEVELS

---

### Sutton v. Sutton

Court of Appeals of New York, 1994.
84 N.Y.2d 37, 637 N.E.2d 260, 614 N.Y.S.2d 369.

■ SIMONS, JUDGE.

In this CPLR article 78 proceeding, petitioners seek (1) a declaration that an amendment to the certificate of incorporation of Bag Bazaar, Ltd. is valid and (2) to compel respondent David S. Sutton, as a director of the corporation, to sign and deliver a certificate of amendment to petitioners for filing. Respondent has refused to execute the certificate, contending it is not valid because the amendment had the support of only 70% of the shareholders when the certificate of incorporation required unanimous approval. The appeal requires an interpretation of section 616(b) of the Business Corporation Law which states that supermajority provisions in a certificate of incorporation may be amended by a two-thirds vote unless the certificate "specifically" provides otherwise.

Petitioners contend that notwithstanding the general unanimity provision contained in Bag Bazaar's certificate, a two-thirds vote to amend is sufficient under this statute unless the certificate explicitly provides unanimous consent is required to amend the supermajority provision. As they see it, prior to a 1962 statutory amendment, which added the word "specifically", a general requirement of a unanimous vote for any amendment of the certificate—i.e., a provision like the one here—would be read to apply to the supermajority provision. Thus, they reason that the Legislature, by adding the word "specifically" in the 1962 amendment, intended to require an amendment provision explicitly directed at the procedure for changing a supermajority provision. The Appellate Division disagreed and held that the provision in Bag Bazaar's certificate of incorporation was sufficiently specific and that the amendment was not valid because it lacked unanimous shareholder approval (196 A.D.2d 411, 601 N.Y.S.2d 106). We now affirm.

In 1963, the certificate of incorporation of Bag Bazaar, Ltd. was amended to provide that "[t]he unanimous vote or consent of the holders of all the issued and outstanding shares of Common Stock of the corporation shall be necessary for the transaction of any business * * * of the corporation, including amendment to the certificate of incorporation". At that time the business was run by Abraham Sutton and none of the parties to this litigation was a shareholder. In 1971 Abraham's brother, respondent David S. Sutton, purchased 30 shares. Two years later Abraham's son, petitioner Solomon A. Sutton, joined the business and subsequently acquired 30 shares. On Abraham's death, in 1987, his widow, petitioner Yvette Sutton, inherited Abraham's remaining 40 shares. Thus, petitioners now own 70% of the outstanding shares of the corporation and respondent and his wife own 30 shares. Petitioner Solomon A. Sutton serves as one of the two directors of the company and respondent David S. Sutton as the other.

The corporation was run without incident for nearly 30 years under Abraham's leadership. After he relinquished control of the company, however, disputes arose between Solomon and David Sutton concerning the management of the corporation. These disputes culminated in an April 1992 shareholders' meeting, where petitioners voted their 70% of the shares in favor of a resolution to strike the unanimity provision, while respondent's 30% of the shares voted against the resolution.

Respondent, as a director of the corporation, refused to sign a certificate of amendment reflecting the deletion of the unanimity provision, thereby preventing the amendment from taking effect. Accordingly, petitioners commenced this proceeding and moved for judgment declaring the resolution valid and enforceable and compelling respondent to sign the certificate of amendment. Respondent cross-moved to dismiss the petition, for reformation of the certificate of incorporation and to compel arbitration of the dispute. Supreme Court granted the petition and denied the cross motion. The Appellate Division reversed and denied the petition.

To support their position on this appeal, petitioners contend that the Legislature added the word "specifically" to section 616(b) because it recognized that a unanimity provision gives minority shareholders the ability to deadlock any and all corporate action. The amendment was intended to minimize deadlocks by permitting a two-thirds majority of the shareholders to alter or delete the unanimity requirement unless the certificate of incorporation explicitly stated otherwise. Respondent maintains that "specifically" was added to the statute to clarify that if more than a two-thirds vote was required to amend a unanimity provision, the certificate should state exactly what greater percentage is needed. They maintain that this certificate satisfied that requirement by declaring that a unanimous vote was required for any amendment.

The history of Business Corporation Law § 616(b) begins with Benintendi v. Kenton Hotel, 294 N.Y. 112, 60 N.E.2d 829, where this Court invalidated a unanimity provision adopted by unanimous shareholder vote. We reasoned that such a provision was antithetical to the basic concept of corporate governance by majority rule and contrary to public policy (id., at 118–119, 60 N.E.2d 829). In 1948, the Legislature abrogated *Benintendi* by enacting section 9 of the Stock Corporation Law, which authorized unanimity provisions when approved by a unanimous vote (see, L.1948, ch. 862). The effect of section 9 was to require unanimous shareholder consent to either add or amend a unanimity provision (see, 3 White, New York Corporations ¶ 616.02, at 6–378 [13th ed.]). In 1951, this section was amended to allow adoption or change of a supermajority provision by a two-thirds or greater vote. A unanimous vote was still required, however, where the certificate called for a unanimous vote; where the unanimity provision itself required such a vote; or where the unanimity provision was adopted prior to the effective date of the 1951 amendment (see, L. 1951, ch. 717).

In 1961, the Business Corporation Law was adopted to replace the Stock Corporation Law, and section 9 was substantially reenacted as Business Corporation Law § 616(b) and § 709(b). However, in 1962, prior to the 1963 effective date of the Business Corporation Law, a series of changes were made, including the addition of the word "specifically" in section 616(b). As finally enacted, section 616(b) provides that "[a]n amendment of the certificate of incorporation which changes or strikes out a [supermajority] provision * * * shall be authorized at a meeting of shareholders by vote of the holders of two-thirds of all outstanding shares entitled to vote thereon, or of such greater proportion of shares * * * as may be provided specifically in the certificate of incorporation" (emphasis added). According to the Legislative Study Committee the word "specifically" was one of a number of "technical" amendments added to the chapter to clarify existing language and avoid minor inconsistencies. It was not intended to effect a substantive change in the law (Mem. of Joint Legis.Comm. To Study Revision of Corp. Laws, Bill Jacket, L.1962, ch. 834, at 86).

Thus, nothing in the legislative history or the statute itself suggests the necessity for a discrete paragraph addressed solely to the supermajority provision and explicitly declaring the vote required for its amendment. The history reveals that Stock Corporation Law § 9 stated that a provision in the certificate of incorporation requiring unanimous consent could only be amended by unanimous consent and this provision was substantially reenacted in the Business Corporation Law.* Inasmuch as the Legislature did not intend the "technical" revisions added before the effective date of the Business Corporation Law to change the existing law substantively, the present statute should be construed as section 9 of the Stock Corporation Law was.

---

* While the 1951 amendments to that section allowed a unanimity provision to be amended by a two-thirds vote in certain instances, petitioners acknowledge that the provision at issue here would have required unanimous shareholder consent to amend, despite the 1951 amendment. (Footnote by the court.)

Unanimity was required under the prior law to amend a unanimity provision, such as this one, and the addition of the word "specifically" merely provides that a two-thirds majority may now amend a unanimity provision unless the certificate requires a greater percentage.

The provision in Bag Bazaar's certificate is unambiguous: it requires unanimous shareholder consent for the transaction of "any business * * * including amendment to the certificate of incorporation." To read section 616(b) as requiring more to address amendment of the super-majority provision would be unnecessarily restrictive in light of the legislative history. The certificate need only clearly state what vote, if greater than two thirds, is required to amend a unanimity provision. The certificate of Bag Bazaar, Ltd. does so....

Finally, petitioners note that unless section 616(b) is read as requiring an explicit certificate provision governing the amendment of unanimity provisions, majority shareholders will be unable to conduct the business of a corporation in the face of opposition from the minority. But as respondent notes, there is nothing inherently unfair or improper about a voluntary organization's consensual decision to assure protection for minority shareholders, and shareholders are not without remedies where deadlocks do arise (see generally, Business Corporation Law § 1104).

Accordingly, the order of the Appellate Division should be affirmed, with costs.

■ Kaye, C.J., and Titone, Bellacosa, Smith, Levine and Ciparick, JJ., concur.

Order affirmed, with costs.

―――――

## N.Y. BUS. CORP. LAW §§ 616, 709

[See Statutory Supplement]

―――――

## DEL. GEN. CORP. LAW §§ 102(b)(4), 141(b), 216

[See Statutory Supplement]

―――――

## CAL. CORP. CODE §§ 204, 602

[See Statutory Supplement]

―――――

## REV. MODEL BUS. CORP. ACT §§ 7.27, 7.32, 8.24

[See Statutory Supplement]

―――――

## SECTION 5.   FIDUCIARY OBLIGATIONS OF SHAREHOLDERS IN CLOSE CORPORATIONS

### DONAHUE v. RODD ELECTROTYPE CO.
[See Section 1, supra.]

ROSENTHAL v. ROSENTHAL, 543 A.2d 348 (Me.1988). In this case, the trial court judge set out the following four specific fiduciary duties owed by the business associates in a close corporation to each other:

(1) To act with that degree of diligence, care and skill which ordinarily prudent persons would exercise under similar circumstances in like positions;

(2) To discharge the duties affecting their relationship in good faith with a view to furthering the interests of one another as to the matters within the scope of the relationship;

(3) To disclose and not withhold from one another relevant information affecting the status and affairs of the relationship;

(4) To not use their position, influence or knowledge respecting the affairs and organization that are subject to the relationship to gain any special privilege or advantage over the other person or persons involved in the relationship. . . .

On appeal, the Maine Supreme Court affirmed. "For the first time on appeal defendants object to the [trial judge's] definition of the scope of the [shareholders'] duties as including 'furthering the interests *of one another*,' rather than being restricted to furthering the interests of the business enterprise. We can find no clear error in that instruction, however, given the special nature of the [shareholders'] family business, which most closely resembles a single complex family partnership doing business through numerous entities of varied legal forms. . . . The duties owed in the circumstances here presented necessarily flowed to the other business associates, as well as to the [shareholders'] enterprise as a whole and the component entitles." (Emphasis by the court.)

## Wilkes v. Springside Nursing Home, Inc.
Supreme Judicial Court of Massachusetts, 1976.
370 Mass. 842, 353 N.E.2d 657.

■ HENNESSEY, CHIEF JUSTICE.

[The plaintiff (Wilkes) filed a bill in equity for declaratory judgment, naming as defendants T. Edward Quinn,[3] Leon L. Riche, the

---

**3.** T. Edward Quinn died while this action was sub judice. The executrix of his

executors of Lawrence R. Connor, and the Springside Nursing Home, Inc. Wilkes sought, among other forms of relief, damages in the amount of the salary he would have received had he continued as a director and officer of Springside subsequent to March, 1967. The court referred the suit to a master. The master's report was confirmed, a judgment was entered dismissing Wilkes's action on the merits, and the Massachusetts Supreme Court granted direct appellate review.] On appeal, Wilkes argued in the alternative that (1) he should recover damages for breach of the alleged partnership agreement; and (2) he should recover damages because the defendants, as majority stock-holders in Springside, breached their fiduciary duty to him as a minority stockholder by their action in February and March, 1967.

... [W]e reverse so much of the judgment as dismisses Wilkes's complaint and order the entry of a judgment substantially granting the relief sought by Wilkes under the second alternative set forth above.

A summary of the pertinent facts as found by the master is set out in the following pages. . . .

In 1951 Wilkes acquired an option to purchase a building and lot located on the corner of Springside Avenue and North Street in Pittsfield, Massachusetts, the building having previously housed the Hillcrest Hospital. Though Wilkes was principally engaged in the roofing and siding business, he had gained a reputation locally for profitable dealings in real estate. Riche, an acquaintance of Wilkes, learned of the option, and interested Quinn (who was known to Wilkes through membership on the draft board in Pittsfield) and Pipkin (an acquaintance of both Wilkes and Riche) in joining Wilkes in his investment. The four men met and decided to participate jointly in the purchase of the building and lot as a real estate investment which, they believed, had good profit potential on resale or rental.

The parties later determined that the property would have its greatest potential for profit if it were operated by them as a nursing home. Wilkes consulted his attorney, who advised him that if the four men were to operate the contemplated nursing home as planned, they would be partners and would be liable for any debts incurred by the partnership and by each other. On the attorney's suggestion, and after consultation among themselves, ownership of the property was vested in Springside, a corporation organized under Massachusetts law.

Each of the four men invested $1,000 and subscribed to ten shares of $100 par value stock in Springside.[6] At the time of incorporation it was understood by all of the parties that each would be a director of Springside and each would participate actively in the

estate has been substituted as a party-defendant. . . .

**6.** On May 2, 1955, and again on December 23, 1958, each of the four original investors paid for and was issued additional shares of $100 par value stock, eventually bringing the total number of shares owned by each to 115.

management and decision making involved in operating the corporation.[7] It was, further, the understanding and intention of all the parties
that, corporate resources permitting, each would receive money from
the corporation in equal amounts as long as each assumed an active
and ongoing responsibility for carrying a portion of the burdens
necessary to operate the business.

The work involved in establishing and operating a nursing home
was roughly apportioned, and each of the four men undertook his
respective tasks.[8] Initially, Riche was elected president of Springside,
Wilkes was elected treasurer, and Quinn was elected clerk.[9] Each of
the four was listed in the articles of organization as a director of the
corporation.

At some time in 1952, it became apparent that the operational
income and cash flow from the business were sufficient to permit the
four stockholders to draw money from the corporation on a regular
basis. Each of the four original parties initially received $35 a week
from the corporation. As time went on the weekly return to each was
increased until, in 1955, it totalled $100.

In 1959, after a long illness, Pipkin sold his shares in the corporation to Connor, who was known to Wilkes, Riche and Quinn through
past transactions with Springside in his capacity as president of the
First Agricultural National Bank of Berkshire County. Connor received
a weekly stipend from the corporation equal to that received by
Wilkes, Riche and Quinn. He was elected a director of the corporation
but never held any other office. He was assigned no specific area of
responsibility in the operation of the nursing home but did participate
in business discussions and decisions as a director and served additionally as financial adviser to the corporation.

In 1965 the stockholders decided to sell a portion of the corporate property to Quinn who, in addition to being a stockholder in
Springside, possessed an interest in another corporation which desired to operate a rest home on the property. Wilkes was successful in
prevailing on the other stockholders of Springside to procure a higher
sale price for the property than Quinn apparently anticipated paying
or desired to pay. After the sale was consummated, the relationship
between Quinn and Wilkes began to deteriorate.

**7.** Wilkes testified before the master
that, when the corporate officers were elected, all four men "were ... guaranteed directorships." Riche's understanding of the
parties' intentions was that they all wanted
to play a part in the management of the
corporation and wanted to have some "say"
in the risks involved; that, to this end, they
all would be directors; and that "unless you
[were] a director and officer you could not
participate in the decisions of [the] enterprise."

**8.** Wilkes took charge of the repair, up-
keep and maintenance of the physical plant
and grounds; Riche assumed supervision over
the kitchen facilities and dietary and food

aspects of the home; Pipkin was to make
himself available if and when medical problems arose; and Quinn dealt with the personnel and administrative aspects of the nursing
home, serving informally as a managing director. Quinn further coordinated the activities of the other parties and served as a
communication link among them when matters had to be discussed and decisions had to
be made without a formal meeting.

**9.** Riche held the office of president
from 1951 to 1963; Quinn served as president
from 1963 on, as clerk from 1951 to 1967,
and as treasurer from 1967 on; Wilkes was
treasurer from 1951 to 1967.

The bad blood between Quinn and Wilkes affected the attitudes of both Riche and Connor. As a consequence of the strained relations among the parties, Wilkes, in January of 1967, gave notice of his intention to sell his shares for an amount based on an appraisal of their value. In February of 1967 a directors' meeting was held and the board exercised its right to establish the salaries of its officers and employees.[10] A schedule of payments was established whereby Quinn was to receive a substantial weekly increase and Riche and Connor were to continue receiving $100 a week. Wilkes, however, was left off the list of those to whom a salary was to be paid. The directors also set the annual meeting of the stockholders for March, 1967.

At the annual meeting in March,[11] Wilkes was not reelected as a director, nor was he reelected as an officer of the corporation. He was further informed that neither his services nor his presence at the nursing home was wanted by his associates.

The meetings of the directors and stockholders in early 1967, the master found, were used as a vehicle to force Wilkes out of active participation in the management and operation of the corporation and to cut off all corporate payments to him. Though the board of directors had the power to dismiss any officers or employees for misconduct or neglect of duties, there was no indication in the minutes of the board of directors' meeting in February, 1967, that the failure to establish a salary for Wilkes was based on either ground. The severance of Wilkes from the payroll resulted not from misconduct or neglect of duties, but because of the personal desire of Quinn, Riche and Connor to prevent him from continuing to receive money from the corporation. Despite a continuing deterioration in his personal relationship with his associates, Wilkes had consistently endeavored to carry on his responsibilities to the corporation in the same satisfactory manner and with the same degree of competence he had previously shown. Wilkes was at all times willing to carry on his responsibilities and participation if permitted so to do and provided that he receive his weekly stipend.

1. We turn to Wilkes's claim for damages based on a breach of the fiduciary duty owed to him by the other participants in this venture. In light of the theory underlying this claim, we do not consider it vital to our approach to this case whether the claim is governed by partnership law or the law applicable to business corporations. This is so because, as all the parties agree, Springside was at all times relevant to this action, a close corporation as we have recently defined such an entity in Donahue v. Rodd Electrotype Co. of New England, Inc. . . . [where] we held that "stockholders in the close

---

**10.** The by-laws of the corporation provided that the directors, subject to the approval of the stockholders, had the power to fix the salaries of all officers and employees. This power, however, up until February, 1967, had not been exercised formally; all payments made to the four participants in the venture had resulted from the informal but unanimous approval of all the parties concerned.

**11.** Wilkes was unable to attend the meeting of the board of directors in February or the annual meeting of the stockholders in March, 1967. He was represented, however, at the annual meeting by his attorney, who held his proxy.

corporation owe one another substantially the same fiduciary duty in the operation of the enterprise that partners owe to one another." . . .

In the *Donahue* case we recognized that one peculiar aspect of close corporations was the opportunity afforded to majority stockholders to oppress, disadvantage or "freeze out" minority stockholders. . . .

. . . One . . . device which has proved to be particularly effective in accomplishing the purpose of the majority is to deprive minority stockholders of corporate offices and of employment with the corporation . . . This "freeze-out" technique has been successful because courts fairly consistently have been disinclined to interfere in those facets of internal corporate operations, such as the selection and retention or dismissal of officers, directors and employees, which essentially involve management decisions subject to the principle of majority control. . . .

The denial of employment to the minority at the hands of the majority is especially pernicious in some instances. A guaranty of employment with the corporation may have been one of the "basic reason[s] why a minority owner has invested capital in the firm." . . . The minority stockholder typically depends on his salary as the principal return on his investment, since the "earnings of a close corporation . . . are distributed in major part in salaries, bonuses, and retirement benefits." 1 F.H. O'Neal, Close Corporations § 1.07 (1971).[13] Other noneconomic interests of the minority stockholder are likewise injuriously affected by barring him from corporate office. See F.H. O'Neal, "Squeeze–Outs" of Minority Shareholders 79 (1975). Such action severely restricts his participation in the management of the enterprise, and he is relegated to enjoying those benefits incident to his status as a stockholder. See Symposium—The Close Corporation, 52 Nw.U.L.Rev. 345, 386 (1957). In sum, by terminating a minority stockholder's employment or by severing him from a position as an officer or director, the majority effectively frustrate the minority stockholder's purposes in entering on the corporate venture and also deny him an equal return on his investment.

The *Donahue* decision acknowledged, as a "natural outgrowth" of the case law of this Commonwealth, a strict obligation on the part of majority stockholders in a close corporation to deal with the minority with the utmost good faith and loyalty. On its face, this strict standard is applicable in the instant case. The distinction between the majority action in *Donahue* and the majority action in this case is more one of form than of substance. Nevertheless, we are concerned that untempered application of the strict good faith standard enunciated in *Donahue* to cases such as the one before us will result in the imposition of limitations on legitimate action by the controlling group in a close corporation which will unduly hamper its effectiveness in managing the corporation in the best interests of all concerned. The

---

**13.** We note here that the master found that Springside never declared or paid a dividend to its stockholders.

majority, concededly, have certain rights to what has been termed "selfish ownership" in the corporation which should be balanced against the concept of their fiduciary obligation to the minority. See Hill, The Sale of Controlling Shares, 70 Harv.L.Rev. 986, 1013–1015 (1957); Note, 44 Iowa L.Rev. 734, 740–741 (1959); Symposium—The Close Corporation, 52 Nw.U.L.Rev. 345, 395–396 (1957).

Therefore, when minority stockholders in a close corporation bring suit against the majority alleging a breach of the strict good faith duty owed to them by the majority, we must carefully analyze the action taken by the controlling stockholders in the individual case. It must be asked whether the controlling group can demonstrate a legitimate business purpose for its action. See Bryan v. Brock & Blevins Co., 343 F.Supp. 1062, 1068 (N.D.Ga.1972), aff'd, 490 F.2d 563, 570–571 (5th Cir.1974); Schwartz v. Marien, 37 N.Y.2d 487, 492, 373 N.Y.S.2d 122, 335 N.E.2d 334 (1975).... In asking this question, we acknowledge the fact that the controlling group in a close corporation must have some room to maneuver in establishing the business policy of the corporation. It must have a large measure of discretion, for example, in declaring or withholding dividends, deciding whether to merge or consolidate, establishing the salaries of corporate officers, dismissing directors with or without cause, and hiring and firing corporate employees.

When an asserted business purpose for their action is advanced by the majority, however, we think it is open to minority stockholders to demonstrate that the same legitimate objective could have been achieved through an alternative course of action less harmful to the minority's interest. See Schwartz v. Marien, supra.... If called on to settle a dispute, our courts must weigh the legitimate business purpose, if any, against the practicability of a less harmful alternative.

Applying this approach to the instant case it is apparent that the majority stockholders in Springside have not shown a legitimate business purpose for severing Wilkes from the payroll of the corporation or for refusing to reelect him as a salaried officer and director....

It is an inescapable conclusion from all the evidence that the action of the majority stockholders here was a designed "freeze out" for which no legitimate business purpose has been suggested. Furthermore, we may infer that a design to pressure Wilkes into selling his shares to the corporation at a price below their value well may have been at the heart of the majority's plan.[14]

In the context of this case, several factors bear directly on the duty owed to Wilkes by his associates. At a minimum, the duty of utmost good faith and loyalty would demand that the majority consider that their action was in disregard of a long-standing policy of the stockholders that each would be a director of the corporation and that

---

**14.** This inference arises from the fact that Connor, acting on behalf of the three controlling stockholders, offered to purchase Wilkes's shares for a price Connor admittedly would not have accepted for his own shares.

employment with the corporation would go hand in hand with stock ownership; that Wilkes was one of the four originators of the nursing home venture; and that Wilkes, like the others, had invested his capital and time for more than fifteen years with the expectation that he would continue to participate in corporate decisions. Most important is the plain fact that the cutting off of Wilkes's salary, together with the fact that the corporation never declared a dividend (see note 13 supra), assured that Wilkes would receive no return at all from the corporation.

2.   The question of Wilkes's damages at the hands of the majority has not been thoroughly explored on the record before us. Wilkes, in his original complaint, sought damages in the amount of the $100 a week he believed he was entitled to from the time his salary was terminated up until the time this action was commenced. However, the record shows that, after Wilkes was severed from the corporate payroll, the schedule of salaries and payments made to the other stockholders varied from time to time. In addition, the duties assumed by the other stockholders after Wilkes was deprived of his share of the corporate earnings appear to have changed in significant respects.[15] Any resolution of this question must take into account whether the corporation was dissolved during the pendency of this litigation.

Therefore our order is as follows: So much of the judgment as dismisses Wilkes's complaint and awards costs to the defendants is reversed.[16] The case is remanded . . . for further proceedings concerning the issue of damages. Thereafter a judgment shall be entered declaring that Quinn, Riche and Connor breached their fiduciary duty to Wilkes as a minority stockholder in Springside, and awarding money damages therefor. Wilkes shall be allowed to recover from Riche, the estate of T. Edward Quinn and the estate of Lawrence R. Connor, ratably, according to the inequitable enrichment of each, the salary he would have received had he remained an officer and director of Springside. In considering the issue of damages the judge on remand shall take into account the extent to which any remaining corporate funds of Springside may be diverted to satisfy Wilkes's claim.

———

**ZIMMERMAN v. BOGOFF,** 402 Mass. 650, 524 N.E.2d 849 (1988). "[T]he *Donahue* remedy is not intended to place a strait jacket on legitimate corporate activity. Where the alleged wrongdoer can demonstrate a legitimate business purpose for his action, no liability will result unless the wronged shareholder succeeds in showing that the

---

**15.**  In fairness to Wilkes, who, as the master found, was at all times ready and willing to work for the corporation, it should be noted that neither the other stockholders nor their representatives may be heard to say that Wilkes's duties were performed by them and that Wilkes's damages should, for that reason, be diminished.

**16.**  We do not disturb the judgment in so far as it dismissed a counterclaim by Springside against Wilkes arising from the payment of money by Quinn to Wilkes after the sale in 1965 of certain property of Springside to a corporation owned at that time by Quinn and his wife. . . .

proffered legitimate objective could have been achieved through a less harmful, reasonably practicable, alternative mode of action...."

———

**SMITH v. ATLANTIC PROPERTIES**, 12 Mass.App. 201, 422 N.E.2d 798 (1981). Wolfson, Smith, Zimble, and Burke each owned 25% of Atlantic Properties. Atlantic Properties owned 28 acres of land, on which stood about twenty buildings that required expensive and constant repairs. Wolfson wanted Atlantic's earnings devoted to repairs and possibly improvements. The other three shareholders wanted Atlantic's earnings distributed as dividends. Under the corporation's articles and by-laws, all acts of the board required an 80% vote. Because each of the shareholders owned 25% of the stock, each shareholder had a veto. Using his veto, Wolfson refused to vote for dividends. As a result, the Internal Revenue Service levied penalty taxes against Atlantic under a provision of the Internal Revenue Code prohibiting the corporations from unreasonably accumulating earnings. The trial court held that Wolfson was liable to the corporation for the amount of the penalties. Affirmed:

> In the *Donahue* case, ... the court recognized that cases may arise in which, in a close corporation, majority stockholders may ask protection from a minority stockholder. Such an instance arises in the present case because Dr. Wolfson has been able to exercise a veto concerning corporate action on dividends by the 80% provision (in Atlantic's articles [of] organization and by-law) already quoted. The 80% provision may have substantially the effect of reversing the usual roles of the majority and the minority shareholders. The minority, under that provision, becomes an ad hoc controlling interest.

> In the present case, Dr. Wolfson testified that he requested the inclusion of the 80% provision "in case the people [the other shareholders] whom I knew, but not very well, ganged up on me." The possibilities of shareholder disagreement on policy made the provision seem a sensible precaution. A question is presented, however, concerning the extent to which such a veto power possessed by a minority stockholder may be exercised as its holder may wish, without a violation of the "fiduciary duty" referred to in the *Donahue* case, ... as modified in the *Wilkes* case.

> The decided cases in Massachusetts do little to answer this question. The most pertinent guidance is probably found in the *Wilkes* case ... essentially to the effect that in any judicial intervention in such a situation there must be a weighing of the business interests advanced as reasons for their action (a) by the majority or controlling group and (b) by the rival persons or group....

> ... With respect to the past damage to Atlantic caused by Dr. Wolfson's refusal to vote in favor of any dividends, the trial judge was justified in finding that his conduct went beyond what was

reasonable. The other stockholders shared to some extent responsibility for what occurred by failing to accept Dr. Wolfson's proposals with much sympathy, but the inaction on dividends seems the principal cause of the tax penalties. Dr. Wolfson had been warned of the dangers of an assessment under the Internal Revenue Code, I.R.C. § 531 et seq. He had refused to vote dividends in any amount adequate to minimize that danger and had failed to bring forward, within the relevant taxable years, a convincing, definitive program of appropriate improvements which could withstand scrutiny by the Internal Revenue Service. Whatever may have been the reason for Dr. Wolfson's refusal to declare dividends (and even if in any particular year he may have gained slight, if any, tax advantage from withholding dividends) we think that he recklessly ran serious and unjustified risks of precisely the penalty taxes eventually assessed, risks which were inconsistent with any reasonable interpretation of a duty of "utmost good faith and loyalty." The trial judge (despite the fact that the other shareholders helped to create the voting deadlock and despite the novelty of the situation) was justified in charging Dr. Wolfson with the out-of-pocket expenditure incurred by Atlantic for the penalty taxes and related counsel fees of the tax cases.

## Merola v. Exergen Corp.

Supreme Judicial Court of Massachusetts, 1996.
423 Mass. 461, 668 N.E.2d 351.

■ Before LIACOS, C.J., and WILKINS, LYNCH, O'CONNOR and GREANEY, JJ.

■ LYNCH, JUSTICE.

The plaintiff, a former vice president of Exergen Corporation (Exergen) and a former minority stockholder of that corporation, brought suit in the Superior Court against Exergen and the president and majority stockholder, Francesco Pompei, because of his termination as an officer and employee of Exergen.... [The complaint] alleged that the corporation was a "close corporation," and that Pompei, as the majority stockholder, violated his fiduciary obligations to the plaintiff as a minority stockholder by terminating his employment without cause.

The trial judge ruled that ... she would make findings of fact and conclusions of law ... following the verdict of the jury. The jury rendered a verdict ... providing advisory answers....

... [T]he judge found that the corporation was a "close corporation" and that Pompei had breached his fiduciary obligations to the plaintiff by failing to give him an opportunity to become a major stockholder and by terminating his employment. She adopted the jury's advisory conclusion that he had been damaged only by the termination of employment to the extent of $50,000.

The Appeals Court affirmed the judgment as to Pompei, but modified it as to the corporation, holding that there was no basis for liability by Exergen to the plaintiff. 38 Mass.App.Ct. 462, 471–472 (1995). We granted the defendants' application for further appellate review and now reverse the judgment of the Superior Court.

We summarize the facts found by the judge. Exergen was formed in May, 1980, as a corporation in the business of developing and selling infrared heat detection devices. From Exergen's inception to the date of trial, Pompei, the founder, was the majority shareholder in the corporation, as well as its president, owning over sixty per cent of the shares issued. At all relevant times, Pompei actively participated in and controlled the management of Exergen and, as the majority shareholder, had power to elect and change Exergen's board of directors.

The plaintiff began working for Exergen on a part-time basis in late 1980 while he was also employed full-time by Analogic Corporation. In the course of conversations with Pompei in late 1981, and early 1982, the plaintiff was offered full-time employment with Exergen, and he understood that, if he came to work there and invested in Exergen stock, he would have the opportunity to become a major shareholder of Exergen and for continuing employment with Exergen.

As of March 1, 1982, the plaintiff resigned from Analogic and began working full time for Exergen. He also then began purchasing shares in Exergen when the company made periodic offerings to its employees. From March, 1982, through June, 1982, the plaintiff purchased 4,100 shares at $2.25 per share, for a total of $9,225. Exergen announced at the Exergen shareholders meeting in September, 1982, another option program to purchase shares at $5 per share within one year. By late 1983, the plaintiff had exercised his option to purchase an additional 1,200 shares. The plaintiff was not offered additional stock options after late 1983. ...

Principles of employment law permit the termination of employees at will, with or without cause excepting situations within a narrow public policy exception. *King v. Driscoll,* 418 Mass. 576, 581–582, 638 N.E.2d 488 (1994), and cases cited. However, the termination of a minority shareholder's employment may present a situation where the majority interest has breached its fiduciary duty to the minority interest. *Id.* at 586, 638 N.E.2d 488. *Wilkes v. Springside Nursing Home, Inc., supra* at 852–853, 353 N.E.2d 657. There the court concluded that the majority stockholders had attempted unfairly to "freeze out" a minority stockholder by terminating his employment, in part because their policy and practice was to divide the available resources of the corporation equally by way of salaries to the shareholders who all participated in the operation of the enterprise. *Id.* at 846, 353 N.E.2d 657. As the investment became more profitable, the salaries were increased. *Id.* The court recognized that "[t]he minority stockholder typically depends on his salary as the principal return on his investment, since the 'earnings of a close corporation . . . are distributed in major part in salaries, bonuses and retirement benefits.'" *Id.* at 850, 353 N.E.2d 657, quoting 1 F.H. O'Neal, Close Corporations § 1.07 (1971). Given those facts, this court concluded that the other shareholders did not show a legitimate business purpose for terminating the minority stockholder and that the other parties acted "in disregard of a longstanding policy of the stockholders that each would be a director of the corporation and that employment with the corporation would go hand in hand with stock ownership." *Id.* at 853, 353 N.E.2d 657.

Here, although the plaintiff invested in the stock of Exergen with the reasonable expectation of continued employment, there was no general policy regarding stock ownership and employment, and there was no evidence that any other stockholders had expectations of continuing employment because they purchased stock. The investment in the stock was an investment in the equity of the corporation which was not tied to employment in any formal way. The plaintiff acknowledged that he could have purchased 5,000 shares of stock while he was working part time before resigning from his position at Analogic Corporation and accepting full-time employment at Exergen. He testified that he was induced to work for Exergen with the promise that he could become a major stockholder. There was no testimony that he was ever required to buy stock as a condition of employment.

Unlike the *Wilkes* case, there was no evidence that the corporation distributed all profits to shareholders in the form of salaries. On the contrary, the perceived value of the stock increased during the time that the plaintiff was employed. The plaintiff first purchased his stock at $2.25 per share and, one year later, he purchased more for $5 per share. This indicated that there was some increase in value to the investment independent of the employment expectation. Neither was the plaintiff a founder of the business, his stock purchases were made after the business was established, and there was no suggestion that he had to purchase stock to keep his job.

The plaintiff testified that, when he sold his stock back to the corporation in 1991, he was paid $17 per share. This was a price that had been paid to other shareholders who sold their shares to the corporation at a previous date, and it is a price which, after consulting with his attorney, he concluded was a fair price. With this payment, the plaintiff realized a significant return on his capital investment independent of the salary he received as an employee.

We conclude that this is not a situation where the majority shareholder breached his fiduciary duty to a minority shareholder. "[T]he controlling group in a close corporation must have some room to maneuver in establishing the business policy of the corporation." *Wilkes v. Springside Nursing Home, Inc., supra* at 851, 353 N.E.2d 657. Although there was no legitimate business purpose for the termination of the plaintiff, neither was the termination for the financial gain of Pompei or contrary to established public policy. Not every discharge of an at-will employee of a close corporation who happens to own stock in the corporation gives rise to a successful breach of fiduciary duty claim. The plaintiff was terminated in accordance with his employment contract and fairly compensated for his stock. He failed to establish a sufficient basis for a breach of fiduciary duty claim under the principles of *Donahue v. Rodd Electrotype Co., supra.* . . .

*Judgment reversed.*

## SECTION 6.  VALUATION

Many issues of corporate law are intimately related to problems of valuation. That is particularly true of the issues raised in sections 7, 8, and 10, infra, concerning restrictions on the transferability of shares, mandatory sales of shares, and dissolution. Now is therefore an appropriate time to provide an introduction to the general problem of valuing a business, and the special problem of valuing a business in corporate form.

----

### NOTE ON THE DELAWARE BLOCK METHOD

For many years, and to some extent still today, corporate valuation in a judicial context centered on the so-called Delaware Block Method. Under that method, the court normally values a corporation by first determining the market value of the corporation's stock, the value of the corporation's net assets, and the corporation's "earnings value." Next, the court assigns weights to each of the values, depending on such factors as the comparative reliability of each factor in a particular case. Finally, the court sums the elements of value, as adjusted by their relative weights. In Piemonte v. New Boston Garden Corp., 377 Mass. 719, 387 N.E.2d 1145 (1979), the Massachusetts Supreme Court reviewed the decision of a trial court applying the Delaware Block Method to value a corporation, Garden Arena, that had engaged in a merger. In the course of its opinion, the court made the following observations about the market-value element of the Delaware Block Method in cases where a corporation's stock was only thinly traded:

> Market value may be a significant factor, even the dominant factor, in determining the "fair value" of shares of a particular corporation under G.L. c. 156B, § 92. Shares regularly traded on

a recognized stock exchange are particularly susceptible to valuation on the basis of their market price, although even in such cases the market value may well not be conclusive. See Martignette v. Sagamore Mfg. Co., 340 Mass. 136, 141–142, 163 N.E.2d 9 (1959). On the other hand, where there is no established market for a particular stock, actual market value cannot be used. In such cases, a judge might undertake to "reconstruct" market value, but he is not obliged to do so. Indeed, the process of the reconstruction of market value may actually be no more than a variation on the valuation of corporate assets and corporate earnings.

In this case, Garden Arena stock was traded on the Boston Stock Exchange, but rarely. Approximately ninety per cent of the company's stock was held by the controlling interests and not traded. Between January 1, 1968, and December 4, 1972, 16,741 shares were traded. During this period, an annual average of approximately 1.5% of the outstanding stock changed hands. In 1972, 4,372 shares were traded at prices ranging from $20.50 a share to $29 a share. The public announcement of the proposed merger was made on December 7, 1972. The last prior sale of 200 shares on December 4, 1972, was made at $26.50 a share. The judge accepted that sale price as the market price to be used in his determination of value.

The judge concluded that the volume of trading was sufficient to permit a determination of market value and expressed a preference for the actual sale price over any reconstruction of a market value, which he concluded would place "undue reliance on corporations, factors, and circumstances not applicable to Garden Arena stock." The decision to consider market value and the market value selected were within the judge's discretion.

(Based on the thin trading, the trial court assigned a weight of only 10% to the market-value element in *Piemonte*, and the Massachusetts Supreme Court affirmed this determination as within the trial court's discretion.)

The Massachusetts Supreme Court also made the following observations about earnings value under the Delaware Block Method:

The judge determined that the average per share earnings of Garden Arena for the five-fiscal-year period which ended June 30, 1973, was $5.26. To this amount he applied a factor, or multiplier, of 10 to arrive at $52.60 as the per share value based on earnings.

Each party objects to certain aspects of this process. We reject the plaintiffs' argument that the judge could not properly use any value based on earnings, and also reject the parties' various challenges to the judge's method of determining value based on earnings.

Delaware case law, which, as we have said, we regard as instructive but not binding, has established a method of computing value based on corporate earnings. The appraiser generally starts by computing the average earnings of the corporation for the past five years. Universal City Studios, Inc. v. Francis I. duPont & Co., 334 A.2d 216, 218 (Del.1975); Application of Del. Racing Ass'n, 213 A.2d 203, 212 (Del.1965). Extraordinary gains and losses are excluded from the average earnings calculation. Gibbons v. Schenley Indus., Inc., 339 A.2d 460, 468–470 (Del.Ch. 1975); Felder v. Anderson, Clayton & Co., 39 Del.Ch. 76, 86–87, 159 A.2d 278 (1960). The appraiser then selects a multiplier (to be applied to the average earnings) which reflects the prospective financial condition of the corporation and the risk factor inherent in the corporation and the industry. Universal City Studios, Inc. v. Francis I. duPont & Co., supra. In selecting a multiplier, the appraiser generally looks to other comparable corporations. Universal City Studios, Inc. v. Francis I. duPont & Co., supra at 219–221 (averaging price-earnings ratios of nine other motion picture companies as of date of merger); Gibbons v. Schenley Indus., Inc., supra at 471 (using Standard & Poor's Distiller's Index as of date of merger); Felder v. Anderson, Clayton & Co., supra, 39 Del.Ch. at 87, 159 A.2d 278 (averaging price-earnings ratios of representative stocks over previous five-year period because of recent boom in industry). The appraiser's choice of a multiplier is largely discretionary and will be upheld if it is "within the range of reason." Universal City Studios, Inc. v. Francis I. duPont & Co., supra at 219 (approving multiplier of 16.1); Application of Del. Racing Ass'n, supra at 213 (approving multiplier of 10); Swanton v. State Guar. Corp., 42 Del.Ch. 477, 483, 215 A.2d 242 (1965) (approving multiplier of 14).[9]

The Delaware Block Method has fallen out of favor. The trend is to use the valuation methodologies that are in use by the financial community at the relevant time. Indeed, the Delaware courts themselves normally use those methodologies today, although not absolutely precluding the use of the Delaware Block Method in appropriate cases. The newer financial methodologies are illustrated by the materials in the balance of this section.

––––––

# L. Solomon, D. Schwartz, J. Bauman & E. Weiss, The Old Man and the Tree: A Parable of Valuation, in Corporations—Law and Policy 206–212

4th ed. 1998.

Once there was a wise old man who owned an apple tree. The tree was a fine tree, and with little care it produced a crop of apples

----

**9.** Although Delaware courts have relied on, and continue to rely on, Professor Dewing's capitalization chart (see 1 A.S. Dewing, The Financial Policy of Corporations 390–391 [5th ed. 1953]), they have recognized that it is somewhat outdated and no longer the "be-all and end-all" on the subject of earnings value. See Universal City Studios, Inc. v. Francis I. duPont & Co., supra at 219; Swanton v. State Guar. Corp., 42 Del.Ch. 477, 483–484, 215 A.2d 242 (1965).

each year which he sold for $100. The man was getting old, wanted to retire to a different climate and he decided to sell the tree. He enjoyed teaching a good lesson, and he placed an advertisement in the Business Opportunities section of the Wall Street Journal in which he said he wanted to sell the tree for "the best offer."

The first person to respond to the ad offered to pay the $50 which, the offeror said, was what he would be able to get for selling the apple tree for firewood after he had cut it down. "You are a very foolish person," said the old man. "You are offering to pay only the salvage value of this tree. That might be a good price for a pine tree or perhaps even this tree if it had stopped bearing fruit or if the price of apple wood had gotten so high that the tree was more valuable as a source of wood than as a source of fruit. But my tree is worth much more than $50."

The next person to come to see the old man offered to pay $100 for the tree. "For that," said she, "is what I would be able to get for selling this year's crop of fruit which is about to mature."

"You are not quite so foolish as the first one," responded the old man. "At least you see that this tree has more value as a producer of apples than it would as a source of firewood. But $100 is not the right price. You are not considering the value of next year's crop of apples, nor that of the years after. Please take your $100 and go elsewhere."

The next person to come along was a young man who had just started business school. "I am going to major in marketing," he said. "I figure that the tree should live for at least another fifteen years. If I sell the apples for $100 a year, that will total $1,500. I offer you $1,500 for your tree."

"You, too, are foolish," said the man. "Surely the $100 you would earn by selling the apples from the tree fifteen years from now cannot be worth $100 to you today. In fact, if you placed $41.73 today in a bank account paying 6% interest, compounded annually, that small sum would grow to $100 at the end of fifteen years. Therefore the present value of $100 worth of apples fifteen years from now, assuming an interest rate of 6%, is only $41.73, not $100. Pray," said the old man, "take your $1,500 and invest it safely in high-grade corporate bonds until you have graduated from business school and know more about finance."

Before long, there came a wealthy physician, who said, "I don't know much about apple trees, but I know what I like. I'll pay the market price for it. The last fellow was willing to pay you $1,500 for the tree, and so it must be worth that."

"Doctor," advised the old man, "you should get yourself a knowledgeable investment adviser. If there were truly a market in which apple trees were traded with some regularity, the prices at which they were sold would be a good indication of their value. But there is no such market. And the isolated offer I just received tells very little about how much my tree is really worth—as you would surely realize if you had heard the other foolish offers I have heard today. Please take your money and buy a vacation home."

The next prospective purchaser to come along was an accounting student. When the old man asked "What price are you willing to give me?" the student first demanded to see the old man's books. The old man had kept careful records and gladly brought them out. After examining them the accounting student said, "Your books show that you paid $75 for this tree ten years ago. Furthermore, you have made no deductions for depreciation. I do not know if that conforms with generally accepted accounting principles, but assuming that it does, the book value of your tree is $75. I will pay that."

"Ah, you students know so much and yet so little," chided the old man. "It is true that the book value of my tree is $75, but any fool can see that it is worth far more than that. You had best go back to school and see if you can find some books that will show you how to use your numbers to better effect."

The next prospective purchaser was a young stockbroker who had recently graduated from business school. Eager to test her new skills she, too, asked to examine the books. After several hours she came back to the old man and said she was now prepared to make an offer that valued the tree on the basis of the capitalization of its earnings.

For the first time the old man's interest was piqued and he asked her to go on.

The young woman explained that while the apples were sold for $100 last year, that figure did not represent profits realized from the tree. There were expenses attendant to the tree, such as the cost of fertilizer, the expense of pruning the tree, the cost of the tools, expenses in connection with picking the apples, carting them into town and selling them. Somebody had to do these things, and a portion of the salaries paid to those persons ought to be charged against the revenues from the tree. Moreover, the purchase price, or cost, of the tree was an expense. A portion of the cost is taken into account each year of the tree's useful life. Finally, there were taxes. She concluded that the profit from the tree was $50 last year.

"Wow!" exclaimed the old man. "I thought I made $100 off that tree."

"That's because you failed to match expenses with revenues, in accordance with generally accepted accounting principles," she explained. "You don't actually have to write a check to be charged with what accountants consider to be your expenses. For example, you bought a station wagon some time ago and you used it part of the time to cart apples to market. The wagon will last a while and each year some of the original cost has to be matched against revenues. A portion of the amount has to be spread out over the next several years even though you expended it all at one time. Accountants call that depreciation. I'll bet you never figured that in your calculation of profits."

"I'll bet you're right," he replied. "Tell me more."

"I also went back into the books for a few years and I saw that in some years the tree produced fewer apples than in other years, the prices varied and the costs were not exactly the same each year. Taking an average of only the last three years, I came up with a figure of $45 as a fair sample of the tree's earnings. But that is only half of what we have to do so as to figure the value."

"What's the other half?" he asked.

"The tricky part," she told him. "We now have to figure the value to me of owning a tree that will produce average annual earnings of $45 a year. If I believed that the tree was a one year wonder, I would say 100% of its value—as a going business—was represented by one year's earnings. But if I believe, as both you and I do, that the tree is more like a corporation, in that it will continue to produce earnings year after year, then the key is to figure out an appropriate rate of return. In other words, I will be investing my capital in the tree, and I need to compute the value to me of an investment that will produce $45 a year in income. We can call that amount the capitalized value of the tree."

"Do you have something in mind?" he asked.

"I'm getting there. If this tree produced steady and predictable earnings each year, it would be like a U.S. Treasury bond. But its earnings are not guaranteed. So we have to take into account risk and uncertainty. If the risk of its ruin is high, I will insist that a single year's earnings represent a higher percentage of the value of the tree. After all, apples could become a glut on the market one day and you would have to cut the price and increase the costs of selling them. Or some doctor could discover a link between eating an apple a day and heart disease. A drought could cut the yield of the tree. Or, heaven forbid, the tree could become diseased and die. These are all risks. And of course we do not know what will happen to costs that we know we have to bear."

"You are a gloomy one," reflected the old man. "There are treatments, you know, that could be applied to increase the yield of the tree. This tree could help spawn a whole orchard."

"I am aware of that," she assured him. "We will include that in the calculus. The fact is, we are talking about risk, and investment analysis is a cold business. We don't know with certainty what's going to happen. You want your money now and I'm supposed to live with the risk. That's fine with me, but then I have to look through a cloudy crystal ball, and not with 20/20 hindsight. And my resources are limited. I have to choose between your tree and the strawberry patch down the road. I cannot do both and the purchase of your tree will deprive me of alternative investments. That means I have to compare the opportunities and the risks."

"To determine a proper rate of return," she continued, "I looked at investment opportunities that are comparable to the apple tree, particularly in the agribusiness industry, where these factors have been taken into account. I have concluded that 20% would be an appropriate rate of return. In other words, average earnings over the last three years (which seems to be a representative period) are indicative of the return I will receive, I am prepared to pay a price for the tree that will give me a 20% return on my investment. I am not willing to accept any lower rate of return because I don't have to; I can always buy the strawberry patch instead. Now, to figure the price, we simply divide 45 by .20."

"Long division was never my long suit. Is there a simpler way of doing the figuring?" he asked hopefully.

"There is," she assured him. "We can use an approach we Wall Street types prefer, called a price-earnings (or P–E) ratio. To compute the ratio, we divide 100 by the rate of return we are seeking. If I was willing to settle for an 8% return, I would use a P–E ratio of 12.5 to 1. But since I want to earn 20% on my investment, I divided 100 by 20 and came up with a P–E ratio of 5:1. In other words, I am willing to pay five times the tree's estimated annual earnings. Multiplying $45 by 5, I get a value of $225. That's my offer."

The old man sat back and said he greatly appreciated the lesson. He would have to think about her offer, and he asked if she could come by the next day.

When the young woman returned she found the old man emerging from a sea of work sheets, small print columns of numbers and a calculator. "Glad to see you," he said. "I think we can do some business."

"It's easy to see how you Wall Street smarties make so much money, buying people's property for a fraction of the value. I think my tree is worth more than you figured, and I think I can get you to agree to that."

"I'm open minded," she assured him.

"The number you worked so hard over my books to come up with was something you called profits, or earnings that I earned in the past. I'm not so sure it tells you anything that important."

"Of course it does," she protested. "Profits measure efficiency and economic utility."

"Maybe," he mused, "but it sure doesn't tell you how much money you've got. I looked in my safe yesterday after you left and I saw I had some stocks that hadn't ever paid much of a dividend to me. And I kept getting reports each year telling me how great the earnings were, but I sure couldn't spend them. It's just the opposite with the tree. You figured the earnings were lower because of some amounts I'll never have to spend. It seems to me these earnings are an idea worked up by the accountants. Now I'll grant you that ideas, or concepts as you call them, are important and give you lots of useful information, but you can't fold them up, and put them in your pocket."

Surprised, she asked, "What is important, then?"

"Cash flow," he answered. "I'm talking about dollars you can spend, or save or give to your children. This tree will go on for years yielding revenues after costs. And it is the future, not the past, that we're trying to figure out."

"Don't forget the risks," she reminded him. "And the uncertainties."

"Quite right," he observed. "I think we can deal with that. Chances are that you and I could agree, after a lot of thought, on the possible range of future revenues and costs. I suspect we would estimate that for the next five years, there is a 25% chance that the cash flow will be $40, a 50% chance it will be $50 and a 25% chance it will be $60. That makes $50 our best guess, if you average it out. Then let us figure that for ten years after that the average will be $40. And that's it. The tree doctor tells me it can't produce any longer than that. Now all we have to do is figure out what you pay today to get $50 a year from now, two years from now, and so on for the first five years until we figure what you would pay to get $40 a year for each of the ten years after that. Then, throw in the 20 bucks we can get for firewood at that time, and that's that."

"Simple," she said. "You want to discount to the present value of future receipts including salvage value. Of course you need to determine the rate at which you discount."

"Precisely," he noted. "That's what all these charts and the calculator are doing." She nodded knowingly as he showed her discount tables that revealed what a dollar received at a later time is worth today, under different assumptions of the discount rate. It showed, for example, that at an 8% discount rate, a dollar delivered a year from now is worth $.93 today, simply because $.93 today, invested at 8%, will produce $1 a year from now.

"You could put your money in a savings bank or a savings and loan association and receive 5% interest, insured. But you could also put your money into obligations of the United States Government and earn 8% interest. That looks like the risk free rate of interest to me.* Anywhere else you put your money deprives you of the opportunity to earn 8% risk free. Discounting by 8% will only compensate you for the time value of the money you invest in the tree rather than in government securities. But the cash flow from the apple tree is not riskless, sad to say, so we need to use a higher discount rate to compensate you for the risk in your investment. Let us agree that we discount the receipt of $50 a year from now by 15%, and so on with the other deferred receipts. That is about the rate that is applied to investments with this magnitude of risk. You can check that out with my cousin who just sold his strawberry patch yesterday. According to my figures, the present value of the anticipated annual net revenues is $268.05, and today's value of the firewood is $2.44, making a grand

_____

* These numbers will vary with prevail-     same.
ing interest rates. The principle remains the

total of $270.49. I'll take $270 even. You can see how much I'm allowing for risk because if I discounted the stream at 8%, it would come to $388.60."

After a few minutes reflection, the young woman said to the old man, "It was a bit foxy of you yesterday to let me appear to be teaching you something. Where did you learn so much about finance as an apple grower?"

"Don't be foolish, my young friend," he counseled her. "Wisdom comes from experience in many fields. Socrates taught us how to learn. I'll tell you a little secret; I spent a year in law school."

The young woman smiled at this last confession. "I have enjoyed this little exercise but let me tell you something that some of the financial whiz kids have told me. Whether we figure value on the basis of the discounted cash flow method or the capitalization of earnings, so long as we apply both methods perfectly we should come out at exactly the same point."

"Of course!" the old man exclaimed. "Some of the wunderkinds are catching on. But the clever ones are looking not at old earnings, but doing what managers are doing and projecting earnings into the future. The question is, however, which method is more likely to be misused. I prefer to calculate by my method because I don't have to monkey around with depreciation. You have to make these arbitrary assumptions about useful life and how fast you're going to depreciate. Obviously that's where you went wrong in your figuring."

"You are a crafty old devil," she rejoined. "There are plenty of places for your calculations to go off. It's easy to discount cash flows when they are nice and steady, but that doesn't help you when you've got some lumpy expenses that do not recur. For example, several years from now that tree will require some extensive pruning and spraying operations that simply do not show up in your flow. The labor and chemicals for that once-only occasion throw off the evenness of your calculations. But I'll tell you what, I'll offer you $250. My cold analysis tells me I'm overpaying, but I really like that tree. I think the psychic rewards of sitting in its shade must be worth something."

"It's a deal," said the old man. "I never said I was looking for the *perfect* offer, but only the *best* offer."

MORAL: There are several. Methods are useful as tools, but good judgment comes not from methods alone, but from experience. And experience comes from bad judgment.

Listen closely to the experts, and hear those things they don't tell you. Behind all the sweet sounds of their confident notes, there is a great deal of discordant uncertainty. One wrong assumption can carry you pretty far from the truth.

Finally, you are never too young to learn.

**LEBEAU v. N.C. BANCORPORATION, INC.**, 1998 WL 44993 (Del. Ch. 1998), aff'd in part, rev'd in part, 737 A.2d 513 (1999). This case concerned the valuation of a publicly held corporation, M.G. Bancorporation (MGB). MGB had two bank subsidiaries, Mount Greenwood Bank (Greenwood) and Worth Bancorp, Inc. (WBC). In the course of his opinion, Vice Chancellor Jacobs described the valuation techniques employed by David Clarke, an expert witness for the plaintiffs. Although Vice Chancellor Jacobs did not accept, in all respects, the manner in which Clarke applied the techniques to the case at hand, the techniques themselves nicely illustrate contemporary methods of valuation. The description of the valuation methods employed by Clarke follows:

> The Petitioners commenced this appraisal proceeding on March 15, 1994. At trial the Petitioners' expert witness, David Clarke ("Clarke"), testified that as of the Merger date the fair value of MGB common stock was at least $85 per share. In arriving at that conclusion, Clarke used three distinct methodologies to value MGB's two operating bank subsidiaries: (i) the comparative publicly-traded company approach, (ii) the discounted cash flow ("DCF") method, and (iii) the comparative acquisition technique. Clarke then added a control premium to the values of the two subsidiaries to reflect the value of the holding company's (MGB's) controlling interest in those subsidiaries. Lastly, Clarke then added the value of MGB's remaining assets to the sum of his valuations of the two subsidiaries, to arrive at an overall fair value of $85 per share for MGB.
>
> What follows is a more detailed description of how Clarke performed his valuation(s) of MGB.

### 1. Comparative Company Approach

> Clarke's comparative publicly-traded company approach involved five steps: (1) identifying an appropriate set of comparable companies, (2) identifying the multiples of earnings and book value at which the comparable companies traded, (3) comparing certain of MGB's financial fundamentals (e.g., return on assets and return on equity) to those of the comparable companies, (4) making certain adjustments to those financial fundamentals, and (5) adding an appropriate control premium. After completing the first four steps, Clarke arrived at a value for WBC of $33.059 million ($48.02 per share), and for Greenwood of $20.952 million ($30.44 per share). Clarke next determined that during the period January 1989 to June 1993, acquirors of controlling interests in publicly-traded companies had paid an average premium of at least 35%. On that basis, Clarke concluded that a 35% premium was appropriate, and applied that premium to the values he had determined for Greenwood and WBC, to arrive at fair values of $43.3 million ($62.90 per share) for WBC and $27.1 million ($39.37 per share) for Greenwood, respectively. Clarke then valued MGB's 75.5% controlling interest in WBC at $32.691 million

($47.49 per share), and MGB's 100% interest in Greenwood at $27.1 million ($39.37 per share), under his comparative company approach.

### 2.   *Discounted Cash Flow Approach*

Clarke's DCF valuation analysis involved four steps: (1) projecting the future net cash flows available to MGB's shareholders for ten years after the Merger date, (2) discounting those future cash flows to present value as of the Merger date by using a discount rate based on the weighted average cost of capital ("WACC"), (3) adding a terminal value that represented the present value of all future cash flows generated after the ten year projection period, and (4) applying a control premium to the sum of (2) and (3).

. . . [Clarke] concluded that it would require ten years for MGB's cash flows to stabilize. Based on a 1996 Ibbotson Associates ("Ibbotson") study of the banking industry, Clarke concluded that the appropriate . . . discount rate (WACC), was 1%, and that the appropriate discount rate (WACC) for MGB was 12%. Applying that 12% discount rate, Clarke calculated the present value of WBC's future cash flows to be $17.251 million, and WBC's terminal value to be $14 .824 million. Applying that same 12% discount rate, Clarke arrived at a present value of $10.937 million, and a terminal value of $9.138 million, for Greenwood.

Applying the same 35% control premium to those values of the two subsidiaries, Clarke calculated MGB's 75.5% interest in WBC at $33.824 million or $49.14 per share; and MGB's 100% interest in Greenwood at $28.3 million, or $41.11 per share.

### 3.   *Comparative Acquisition Approach*

Clarke's third valuation approach, the comparative acquisition method, focused upon multiples of MGB's last twelve months earnings and its tangible book value. Those multiples were determined by reference to the prices at which the stock of comparable companies had been sold in transactions involving the sale of control. Unlike the comparative company and DCF valuation approaches, this method did not require adding a control premium to the values of the subsidiaries because under that methodology, the parent holding company's controlling interest in the subsidiaries was already accounted for.

In valuing MGB under his third approach, Clarke identified three transactions involving community banks in the relevant geographic area that occurred within one year of the Merger. He also considered data published by The Chicago Corporation in its September 1993 issue of Midwest Bank & Thrift Survey.\*\*\* From these sources, Clarke determined that (i) control of WBC could be

\*\*\* That data reflected an analysis of 137     1989 to June 1, 1993.
bank acquisitions announced from January 1,

sold for a price between a multiple of 14 times WBC's last twelve months' earnings and 200% of WBC's tangible book value, and that (ii) control of Greenwood could be sold for a price between a multiple of 12 times Greenwood's last twelve months' earnings and 175% of its tangible book value. Giving equal weight to these two sets of values, Clarke valued MGB's 75.5% interest in WBC at $28.8 million (75.5% x $38.1 million) or $41.84 per share, and MGB's 100% interest in Greenwood, at $22.9 million, or $33.27 per share.

### 4. MGB's Remaining Assets

Having valued MGB's two subsidiaries, Clarke then determined the fair value of MGB's remaining net assets, which included (i) a $6.83 million note payable by Southwest, (ii) certain intangibles that Clarke did not include in his valuation, (iii) $78,000 in cash, and (iv) other assets worth $2000. These assets totaled $6.91 million, from which Clarke subtracted liabilities of $96,000 to arrive at a net asset value of $6.814 million ($9.90 per share) for MGB's remaining assets.

### 5. Fair Value Computation

Clarke then added the values he had determined under each of his valuation methodologies, for (i) MGB's 75.5% interest in WBC, (ii) MGB's 100% interest in Greenwood, and (iii) MGB's 100% interest in its remaining assets. Under his comparative publicly-traded method, Clarke concluded that MGB's value was $76.59 per share with no control premium, and $96.76 per share with a control premium. Under his DCF approach, Clarke determined that MGB's value was $74.75 per share with no control premium, and $100.15 per share with a control premium. And under his comparative acquisitions method, Clarke concluded that MGB's minimum fair value was $85 per share, which represented the median of the values described above.

The Chancery Court accepted the legitimacy of Clarke's valuation methods in principle, but concluded that there were various problems in the way that Clarke and the corporation's expert had actually applied most of the valuation methods they employed. However, the court accepted Clarke's valuation based on the comparative acquisition method, and concluded, largely on that basis, that the stock was worth $85/share. The Delaware Supreme Court affirmed on the valuation issue, but remanded on the issue whether compound or simple interest should be paid.

---

### NOTE

The *control* premium to which the *LeBeau* opinion refers is based on the principle that the market value of stock includes a minority discount—that is, a discount for the fact that shares traded on the market are not controlling shares. However, a minority discount, applicable to noncontrolling stock, is irrelevant when valuing the corporation. Therefore, if a given technique for valuing the *corporation* is based on the market price of *stock*, the minority discount applied to the stock must be reversed. The way to reverse the discount is to add back in a control premium, which should be the mirror image of, and identical to, the minority discount. See Rapid–American Corp. v. Harris, 603 A.2d 796 (Del.1992).

## SECTION 7.  RESTRICTIONS ON THE TRANSFERABILITY OF SHARES, AND MANDATORY-SALE PROVISIONS

———

### INTRODUCTORY NOTE

This Section concerns the extent to which restrictions on transferability can be imposed on the stock of close corporations. Central to this issue is the problem of valuation. In theory, a shareholder might object to a restriction on transferability simply because as a matter of principle he wants to be free to sell to whoever he wants, on whatever conditions he wants. In practice, however, problems with a restriction on transferability usually arise where the restriction precludes the shareholder from realizing the full value of his shares on a transfer. If a restriction on transferability is coupled with some mechanism that provides a shareholder who wants to transfer his shares with the same economic value he could have realized in the absence of the restriction, he would be unlikely to complain.

———

## Allen v. Biltmore Tissue Corp.

New York Court of Appeals, 1957.
2 N.Y.2d 534, 161 N.Y.S.2d 418, 141 N.E.2d 812.

■ FULD, JUDGE.

The by-laws of defendant corporation give it an option to purchase, in case of the death of a stockholder, his shares of the corporate stock. The enforceability of this option is one of the questions for decision.

Biltmore Tissue Corporation was organized under the Stock Corporation Law, Consol.Laws, c. 59, § 1 et seq., in 1932, with an authorized capitalization of 1,000 shares without par value, to manufacture and deal in paper and paper products. The by-laws, adopted by the incorporators-directors, contain provisions limiting the number of shares (originally 5, later 20) available to each stockholder (§ 28) and restricting stock transfers both during the life of the stockholder and in case of his death (§§ 29, 30). Whenever a stockholder desires to sell or transfer his shares, he must, according to one by-law (§ 29), give the corporation or other stockholders "an opportunity to repurchase the stock at the price that was paid for the same to the Corporation at the time the Corporation issued the stock"; if, however, the option is not exercised, "then, after the lapse of sixty days, the stock may be sold by the holder to such person and under such circumstances as he sees fit." The by-law, dealing with the transfer of stock upon the death of a stockholder (§ 30)—the provision with which we are here concerned—is almost identical. It recites that the corporation is to have the right to purchase its late stockholder's shares for the price it originally received for them:

> "Stock Transfer in Case of Death. In case of the death of any stockholder, the Corporation shall have the right to purchase the stock from the legal representative of the deceased for the same price that the Corporation received therefor originally. If the Corporation does not, or cannot, purchase such stock, the Board of Directors shall have the right to empower such of its existing stockholders as it sees fit to make such purchase from such legal representative at the same price. Should the option provided for in this section not be exercised, then, after the lapse of ninety days, the legal representative may dispose of said stock as he sees fit."

Harry Kaplan, a paper jobber, was one of Biltmore's customers and some months after its incorporation purchased 5 shares of stock from the corporation at $5 a share. In 1936, Kaplan received a stock dividend of 5 more shares, and two years later purchased an additional 10 shares for $100. On the face of each of the three certificates, running vertically along the left-hand margin, appeared the legend,

> "Issued subject to restrictions in sections 28, 29, and 30 of the By-laws."

On October 20, 1953, Kaplan wrote to the corporation stating that he was "interested in selling" his 20 shares of stock and requesting that he be given the "price" which the board of directors "will consider, so that I may come to a decision." He died five days later. Some months thereafter, in February, 1954, his son, who was also one of his executors, addressed a letter to Biltmore, inquiring whether it was "still interested in acquiring shares and at what price." By another letter, dated the same day, the attorney for the executors sent to the corporation the three stock certificates, representing the 20 shares, and requested that a new certificate be issued in the name of the estate or the executors. Within 30 days, on March 4, 1954, Biltmore's board of directors voted to exercise its option to purchase the stock, pursuant to section 30 of the by-laws, and about three weeks later the executors' attorney was advised of the corporation's action. He was also informed, that although the by-law provision permitted purchase at "the same price that the company received therefor from the stockholder originally," the corporation had, nevertheless, decided to pay $20 a share, "considerably more than the original purchase price", based on the prices at which it had acquired shares from other stockholders.

Kaplan's executors declined to sell to the corporation, insisting that the stock which had been in the decedent's name be transferred to them. When their demand was refused, they brought this action to compel Biltmore to accept surrender of the decedent's stock certificate and to issue a new certificate for 20 shares to them. They contended . . . that the by-law is void as an unreasonable restraint. The corporation interposed a counterclaim for specific performance based on the exercise of its option to purchase the shares under by-law section 30. The court at Special Term granted judgment to the corporation on its counterclaim and dismissed the complaint. The Appellate Division reversed, rendered judgment directing the transfer of the stock to the plaintiffs and dismissed the defendant's counterclaim upon the ground that the by-law in question is void.

Section 176 of the Personal Property Law, which is identical with section 15 of the Uniform Stock Transfer Act, provides that "there shall be no restriction upon the transfer of shares" represented by a stock certificate "by virtue of any by-law of such corporation, or otherwise, unless the . . . restriction is *stated* upon the certificate." (Emphasis supplied.) In order to comply with this statutory mandate, the corporation printed the words, "Issued subject to restrictions in sections 28, 29, and 30 of the By-laws," on the side of the certificate. . . .

Since . . . the legend on the certificate meets the statute's requirements, we turn to the validity of the by-law restriction.

The validity of qualifications on the ownership of corporate shares through restrictions on the right to transfer has long been a source of confusion in the law. The difficulties arise primarily from the clash between the concept of the shares as "creatures of the company's constitution and therefore . . . essentially contractual choses in action" (Gower, Some Contrasts between British and American Corporation Law, 69 Harv.L.Rev. 1369, 1377) and the concept of the shares as personal property represented so far as possible by the certificate itself and, therefore, subject to the time-honored rule that there be no unreasonable restraint upon alienation. While the courts of this state and of many other jurisdictions, as opposed to those of England and of Massachusetts (Gower, supra, 69 Harv.L.Rev. 1369, 1377–1378; O'Neal, Restrictions on Transfer of Stock in Closely Held Corporations, 65 Harv.L.Rev. 773, 778), have favored the "property" concept (see O'Neal, supra, 65 Harv.L.Rev. 773, 779), the tendency is, as section 176 of the Personal Property Law implies, to sustain a restriction imposed on the transfer of stock if "reasonable" and if the stockholder acquired such stock with requisite notice of the restriction.

The question posed, therefore, is whether the provision, according the corporation a right or first option to purchase the stock at the price which it originally received for it, amounts to an unreasonable restraint. In our judgment, it does not.

The courts have almost uniformly held valid and enforceable the first option provision, in charter or by-law, whereby a shareholder desirous of selling his stock is required to afford the corporation, his fellow stockholders or both an opportunity to buy it before he is free to offer it to outsiders.... The courts have often said that this first option provision is "in the nature of a contract" between the corporation and its stockholders and, as such, binding upon them. Hassel v. Pohle, ... 214 App.Div. 654, 658, 212 N.Y.S. 561, 565; see, also, 8 Fletcher, ... § 4194, p. 736. In Doss v. Yingling, ... 95 Ind.App. 494, 172 N.E. 801, a leading case on the subject and one frequently cited throughout the country, a by-law provision against transfer by any stockholder—there were three—of any shares until they had first been offered for sale to other stockholders at *book value,* was sustained as reasonable and valid, 95 Ind.App. at page 500, 172 N.E. at page 803: "The weight of authority is to the effect that a corporate by-law which requires the owner of the stock to give the other stockholders of the corporation ... *an option to purchase the same at an agreed price or the then-existing book value before offering the stock for sale to an outsider, is a valid and reasonable restriction* and binding upon the stockholders." (Emphasis supplied.) And in the Penthouse Properties case, ... 256 App.Div. 685, 690–691, 11 N.Y.S.2d 417, 422, the court declared that "The general rule that ownership of property cannot exist in one person and the right of alienation in another ... has in this State been frequently applied to shares of corporate stock ... and cognizance has been taken of the principle that 'the right of transfer is a right of property, and if another has the arbitrary power to forbid a transfer of property by the owner that amounts to annihilation of property'.... But restrictions against the sale of shares of stock, unless other stockholders or the corporation have first been accorded an opportunity to buy, are not repugnant to that principle.... The weight of authority elsewhere is to the same effect."**

As the cases thus make clear, what the law condemns is, not a *restriction* on transfer, a provision merely postponing sale during the option period, but an effective *prohibition* against transferability itself. Accordingly, if the by-law under consideration were to be construed as rendering the sale of the stock impossible to anyone except to the corporation at whatever price it wished to pay, we would, of course, strike it down as illegal. But that is not the meaning of the provision before us. The corporation had its option only for a 90–day period. If it did not exercise its privilege within that time, the deceased stockholder's legal representative was at liberty to "dispose of said stock as he [saw] fit" (§ 30), and, once so disposed of, it would thereafter be free of the restriction. In a very real sense, therefore, the primary purpose of the by-laws was to enable a particular party, the corporation, to buy the shares, not to prevent the other party, the stockhold-

---

** The court went further in the Penthouse Properties case than we are called upon to go here; in view of the special purposes of a corporation owning a cooperative apartment house, it sustained a restriction actually requiring the "consent" of the directors to a proposed transfer. 256 App.Div. 685, 689, 11 N.Y.S.2d 417, 420. The present case involves no such "consent" restriction.

er, from selling them. (See 3 Simes & Smith on Law of Future Interests [2d ed., 1956], § 1154, p. 61.)

The Appellate Division, however, was impressed with what it deemed the "unreasonableness," that is, "unfairness," of the price specified in the by-law, namely, a price at which the shares had originally been purchased from the corporation. Carried to its logical conclusion, such a rationale would permit, indeed, would encourage, expensive litigation in every case where the price specified in the restriction, or the formula for fixing the price, was other than a recognized and easily ascertainable fair market value. This would destroy part of the social utility of the first option type of restriction which, when imposed, is intended to operate *in futuro* and must, therefore, include some formula for future determination of the option price.

Generally speaking, these restrictions are employed by the so-called "close corporation" as part of the attempt to equate the corporate structure to a partnership by giving the original stockholders a sort of pre-emptive right through which they may if they choose, veto the admission of a new participant. . . . Obviously, the case where there is an easily ascertainable market value for the shares of a closely held corporate enterprise is the exception, not the rule, and, consequently, various methods or formulae for fixing the option price are employed in practice—e.g., book or appraisal value, often exclusive of good will . . . or a fixed price, Scruggs v. Cotterill . . . or the par value of the stock. . . .

In sum, then, the validity of the restriction on transfer does not rest on any abstract notion of intrinsic fairness of price. To be invalid, more than mere disparity between option price and current value of the stock must be shown. See Palmer v. Chamberlin, supra, 191 F.2d 532, 541, 27 A.L.R.2d 416. Since the parties have in effect agreed on a price formula which suited them, and provision is made freeing the stock for outside sale should the corporation not make, or provide for, the purchase, the restriction is reasonable and valid. . . .

The judgment of the Appellate Division dismissing the defendant's counterclaim and sustaining the plaintiff's complaint should be reversed, and that of Special Term reinstated, with costs in this court and in the Appellate Division.

■ CONWAY, C.J., and DESMOND, DYE, FROESSEL, VAN VOORHIS and BURKE, JJ., concur.

Judgment of Appellate Division reversed and that of Special Term reinstated, with costs in this court and in the Appellate Division.

———

**EVANGELISTA v. HOLLAND,** 27 Mass.App.Ct. 244, 537 N.E.2d 589 (1989). A shareholders' agreement allowed the corporation to buy out, for $75,000, the estate of any deceased shareholder. The corporation brought suit against the estate of a deceased shareholder to enforce the agreement. There was strong evidence that the decedent's stock was worth at least $191,000. Held, for the corporation:

> The executors suggest that to require them to part with their interest in the business for so much less than the [value of the stock] violates the duty of good faith and loyalty owed one another by stockholders in a closely held corporation.... Questions of good faith and loyalty do not arise when all the stockholders in advance enter into an agreement for the purchase of stock of a withdrawing or deceased stockholder.... That the price established by a stockholders' agreement may be less than the appraised or market value is unremarkable. Such agreements may have as their purpose: the payment of a price for a decedent's stock which will benefit the corporation or surviving stockholders by not unduly burdening them; the payment of a price tied to life insurance; or fixing a price which assures the beneficiaries of the deceased stockholder of a predetermined price for stock which might have little market value.... When the agreement was entered into in 1984, the order and time of death of stockholders was an unknown. There was a "mutuality of risk."

---

## DEL. GEN. CORP. LAW §§ 202, 342, 347, 349

[See Statutory Supplement]

---

## CAL. CORP. CODE §§ 204(a)(3), (b), 418

[See Statutory Supplement]

---

## REV. MODEL BUS. CORP. ACT § 6.27

---

## NOTE ON RESTRICTIONS ON TRANSFERABILITY AND MANDATORY SALES

1. *Restrictions on Alienability*. Although some of the earlier cases held that all restrictions on the transferability of shares constituted illegal restraints on alienation, the modern cases hold that "reasonable" restrictions are valid and enforceable. Three basic types of restrictions are commonly used in the context of the close corporation: (1) First refusals, which prohibit a sale of stock unless the shares have been first offered to the corporation, the other shareholders, or both, on the terms offered by the third party. (2) First options, which prohibit a transfer of stock unless the shares have been first offered to the corporation, the other shareholders, or both, at a price fixed under

the terms of the option. (3) *Consent restraints*, which prohibit a transfer of stock without the permission of the corporation's board of shareholders.

Of these three basic types, the *first refusal* is obviously least restrictive in its impact on a shareholder who wants to sell his stock, and such provisions are widely upheld. See, e.g., Groves v. Prickett, 420 F.2d 1119 (9th Cir.1970).

The restrictiveness of a *first option* depends largely on the relationship between the option price and a fair price at the time the option is triggered. As Allen v. Biltmore suggests, the courts have been giving increasing latitude to this type of provision. See, e.g., In re Mather's Estate, 410 Pa. 361, 189 A.2d 586 (1963) where an agreement setting a price of $1 per share was enforced although the actual value was $1,060 per share.

A *consent restraint* is obviously the most restrictive of the three basic types, and at one time such a restraint was almost certain to be deemed invalid. However, some recent statutes specifically contemplate the validity of such restraints (see, e.g., Del. § 202), and the courts have also begun to be more tolerant. Thus in Colbert v. Hennessey, 351 Mass. 131, 217 N.E.2d 914 (1966), three shareholders owning 55% of Bay State's stock agreed that none would transfer his stock without the others' consent. The court held that the agreement was valid. "The agreement was a means of securing corporate control of Bay State to those whose enterprise sponsored it and who contributed to the daily operation of the business. This was not a 'palpably unreasonable' purpose." The court cited Holmes's dictum, in Barrett v. King, 181 Mass. 476, 479, 63 N.E. 934, 935 (1902), that "there seems to be no greater objection to retaining the right of choosing one's associates in a corporation than in a firm."

In spite of the increasingly tolerant climate, however, the validity of consent restraints remains uncertain in the absence of statute or authoritative precedent. In Rafe v. Hindin, 29 A.D.2d 481, 288 N.Y.S.2d 662 (1968), P and D each owned 50% of the stock of Bil Cy Realty, which they had organized in 1963. A legend on each stock certificate made the stock nontransferable except to the other shareholder, and written permission from the other shareholder was required to record a transfer of the stock on Bil Cy's books. P brought an action for a declaratory judgment that the legend on the certificate was void, and that the stock was transferable without D's consent. The court so held:

> In New York certificates of stock are regarded as personal property and are subject to the rule that there be no unreasonable restraint on alienation. . . .

> The legend on the stock certificate at bar contains no provision that the individual defendant's consent may not be unreasonably withheld. Since the individual defendant is thus given the arbitrary power to forbid a transfer of the shares of stock by the plaintiff, the restriction amounts to annihilation of property. The

restriction is not only not reasonable, but it is against public policy and, therefore, illegal. It is an unwarrantable and unlawful restraint on the sale of personal property, the sale and interchange of which the law favors, and in restraint of trade.

2. *Mandatory Sales*. The three basic types of restraints discussed above limit the shareholders' power of transfer. Other types of arrangements go further, and give the corporation or the remaining shareholders an option to purchase a shareholder's stock upon the occurrence of designated contingencies, even if the shareholder wants to retain the stock. A common example is an arrangement under which the corporation is given an option to repurchase stock that it has issued to an employee, in the event the employment relationship is terminated. The courts have tended to enforce such an arrangement even when the option price is quite low in relation to the value of the stock at the time the buyback right is triggered. See, e.g., St. Louis Union Trust Co. v. Merrill Lynch, Pierce, Fenner & Smith Inc., 562 F.2d 1040 (8th Cir.1977), cert. denied 435 U.S. 925, 98 S.Ct. 1490, 55 L.Ed.2d 519 (1978). Another common example is the buy-sell or survivor-purchase agreement, which provides that on the death or retirement of a shareholder in a close corporation, his estate has an obligation to sell its shares to the corporation or the remaining shareholders at a price fixed under the agreement, and the corporation or the remaining shareholders have an obligation (rather than an option) to purchase the shares. A major purpose of such agreements is to provide liquidity to the seller or his estate: Because the corporation is by hypothesis closely held, any market for the shares is negligible. In the absence of the agreement, therefore, the retiring shareholder or his estate might be in a helpless bargaining position if more liquid or higher-yielding assets are needed to meet tax liabilities or other needs. The corporation's obligation is often "funded" in whole or in part by insurance on the shareholders' lives.

3. *Pricing Provisions*. Another kind of problem concerns the pricing clause in first-option, repurchase, or buy-sell arrangements. Where shares are closely held, price cannot realistically be set on the basis of market value. Some alternative pricing provision is therefore required.

a. *Book value*. One common approach is to use a pricing formula based on book value. Book value, however, may be an unreliable guide to a corporation's real worth: it reflects the historical cost of assets, rather than their present value, and usually ignores goodwill or going-concern value. The courts have tended to hold that a large disparity between book value and real value is not in itself sufficient to avoid the operation of a book-value pricing provision. Thus in Palmer v. Chamberlin, 191 F.2d 532 (5th Cir.1951), the court, quoting New England Trust Co. v. Abbott, 162 Mass. 148, 38 N.E. 432 (1894), stated, " '... specific performance of an agreement to convey will not be refused merely because the price is inadequate or excessive. The difference must be so great as to lead to a reasonable conclusion of fraud, mistake, or concealment in the nature of fraud, and to render it plainly inequitable and against conscience that the contract should be enforced.' " See also, e.g., In re Estate of Brown, 130 Ill.App.2d 514, 264 N.E.2d 287 (1970). Accordingly, a book-value formula may be disastrous where goodwill represents the most valuable component of the business—as is typical in non-capital-intensive enterprises, see, e.g., Jones v. Harris, 63 Wash.2d 559, 388 P.2d 539 (1964)—or where there is a significant disparity between historical costs and present values of tangible assets. See, e.g., S.C. Pohlman Co. v. Easterling, 211 Cal.App.2d 466, 27 Cal.Rptr. 450 (1962).

b. *Capitalized earnings*. A second common approach is to fix the price on the basis of capitalized earnings. This approach is less likely than a book-value formula to produce an unfair price, but involves a number of drafting or interpretation problems, such as (i) defining earnings, (ii) over what period, (iii) with or without salaries paid to shareholder-officers, and (iv) considering the possible impact of the transferor's withdrawal on the value of the business.

c. *Periodic revisions*. A third common approach is to agree on a dollar price when the provision is adopted, subject to periodic revision at agreed-upon intervals. This approach may lead to trouble when the parties fail to make periodic revisions through carelessness or inability to agree. In Helms v. Duckworth, 249 F.2d 482 (D.C.Cir. 1957), Easterday, age 70, and Duckworth, age 37, formed a corporation and agreed that when one died his stock would be sold to the other at $10 a share, which was then a fair price, "provided, however, that such sale and purchase price may, from time to time, be redetermined ... [annually] by an instrument in writing signed by the parties...." When Easterday died six years later, the price had never been adjusted, although the actual value of the stock had risen to $80 a share. Easterday's administratrix brought suit to declare the agreement void, and Duckworth submitted an affidavit in which he stated that it was never his intention to consent to any change in the price provision. The district court granted summary judgment to Duckworth, but the Court of Appeals reversed:

> ... Plainly [the agreement] implied a periodic bargaining or negotiating process in which each party must participate in good faith....

> ... We believe that the holders of closely held stock in a corporation such as shown here bear a fiduciary duty to deal fairly, honestly, and openly with their fellow stockholders and to make disclosure of all essential information.

> ... [T]he very nature of Duckworth's secret intent was such that it had to be kept secret and undisclosed or it would fail of its purpose.... [Duckworth's] failure to disclose to his corporate business "partner" his fixed intent never to alter the original price constitutes a flagrant breach of a fiduciary duty. Standing alone this warrants cancellation of the agreement by a court of equity.

d. *Appraisal*. A fourth approach is to provide for appraisal by a third party at the time the option is triggered. See, e.g., Ginsberg v.

Coating Products, Inc., 152 Conn. 592, 210 A.2d 667 (1965). This approach has the advantage of flexibility, but unless the shareholders are willing to give the appraiser free rein, it too may involve the use of an agreed-upon standard of valuation that can turn out to have unforeseen and undesired results.

---

## Gallagher v. Lambert

New York Court of Appeals, 1989.
74 N.Y.2d 562, 549 N.Y.S.2d 945, 549 N.E.2d 136.

### OPINION OF THE COURT

■ BELLACOSA, JUDGE.

Plaintiff Gallagher purchased stock in the defendant close corporation with which he was employed. The purchase of his 8.5% interest was subject to a mandatory buy-back provision: if the employment ended for any reason before January 31, 1985, the stock would return to the corporation for book value. The corporation fired plaintiff prior to the fulcrum date, after which the buy-back price would have been higher.

We must decide whether plaintiff's dismissed causes of action, seeking the higher repurchase price based on an alleged breach of a fiduciary duty, should be reinstated. We think not and affirm, concluding that the Appellate Division did not err in dismissing these causes of action by summary judgment because there was no cognizable breach of any fiduciary duty owed to plaintiff under the plain terms of the parties' repurchase agreement.

Gallagher was employed by defendant Eastdil Realty as a mortgage broker from 1968 to 1973. Three years later, in 1976, he returned to the company as a broker, officer and director, serving additionally as president and chief executive officer of defendant's wholly owned subsidiary, Eastdil Advisors, Inc. Gallagher was at all times an employee at will. Still later, in 1981, Eastdil offered all its executive employees an opportunity to purchase stock subject to a mandatory buy-back provision, which provided that upon "voluntary resignation or other termination" prior to January 31, 1985, an employee would be required to return the stock for book value. After that date, the formula for the buy-back price was keyed to the company's earnings. Plaintiff accepted the offer and its terms.

On January 10, 1985, Gallagher was fired by Eastdil Realty. He did not and does not now contest the firing. But he demanded payment for his shares calculated on the post-January 31, 1985 buy-back formula. Eastdil refused and Gallagher sued, asserting eight causes of action. Only three claims, based on an alleged breach of fiduciary duty of good faith and fair dealing, are before us. The trial court denied defendants' motion for summary judgment on these claims, stating that factual issues were raised relating to defendants' motive in firing plaintiff. The Appellate Division, by divided vote, reversed, dismissed those claims and ordered payment for the shares at book value. 143 A.D.2d 313, 532 N.Y.S.2d 255. That court then granted leave and certified the following question to us: "Was the order of this Court, which modified the order of the Supreme Court, properly made?"

The parties negotiated a written contract containing a common and plain buy-back provision. Plaintiff got what he bargained for— book value for his minority shares if his employment in the corporation ended before January 31, 1985. There being no basis presented for the courts to interfere with the operation and consequences of this agreement between the parties, the order of the Appellate Division granting summary judgment to defendants, dismissing the first three causes of action, should be affirmed and the certified question answered in the affirmative....

Accordingly, the order of the Appellate Division should be affirmed, with costs, and the certified question answered in the affirmative.

[The concurring opinion of Judge Hancock is omitted.]

■ KAYE, JUDGE (dissenting).

In summer 1984, Gallagher received 8.5% of Eastdil's stock, becoming the third largest shareholder, and he executed an amended stockholders' agreement. The agreement [provided] for mandatory repurchase at book value upon "voluntary resignation or other termination" of employment. But it also stipulated that after January 31, 1985, the buy-out price would be calculated by an escalating formula based on the company's earnings and the length of the shareholder's employment. According to Gallagher, the new buy-out price represented "golden handcuffs" designed to induce employees to remain on, at least until January 31, 1985.

On January 10, 1985—just 21 days before the new valuation formula became effective—Gallagher was fired and Eastdil invoked its right to repurchase his stock at book value. According to Gallagher, book value for the shares was $89,000; the price under the new valuation formula would have been around $3,000,000....

Gallagher alleges that defendants had no bona fide, business-related reason to terminate his employment when they did—assertions we must accept as true on this summary judgment motion. He charges that defendants fired him for the sole purpose of recapturing his shares at an unfairly low price and redistributing them among themselves....

If plaintiff were a minority shareholder, but not an employee, defendants would be barred from acting selfishly and opportunistically, for no corporate purpose, as he alleges they did. The controlling stockholders in a close corporation stand, in relation to minority owners, in the same fiduciary position as corporate directors generally, and are held "to the extreme measure of candor, unselfishness and good faith." (*Kavanaugh v. Kavanaugh Knitting Co.*, 226 N.Y. 185, 193, 123 N.E. 148.) Although, without more, the courts will not interfere when parties have set the repurchase price at book value

(*Allen v. Biltmore Tissue Corp.,* 2 N.Y.2d 534, 542–543, 161 N.Y.S.2d 418, 141 N.E.2d 812), here plaintiff asserts there was more. The corporation agreed, commencing January 31, 1985, to pay a higher price, said to be more reflective of the true value of defendant's shares. Defendants' invocation of the pre-January 31 repurchase price was adverse to plaintiff's interests as a minority stockholder, and therefore subject to a standard of good faith under the foregoing principles. . . .

Defendants' broad interpretation of the "other termination" language of the repurchase clause amounts to an assertion that plaintiff agreed to waive substantial rights he might otherwise have possessed as a minority shareholder. However, in the absence of evidence that plaintiff knowingly assented to such a waiver, I cannot agree that the general language of the clause unambiguously expresses an understanding that the option could be exploited for the sole personal gain of the controlling shareholders in derogation of their fiduciary obligations to minority shareholders. Notably, the repurchase clause contains no reference to plaintiff's at-will employment status and no reservation of defendant's right to discharge plaintiff for any reason at all.

Moreover, defendants' interpretation denies that defendants themselves had any duty of good faith in connection with the shareholders' agreement. We have said that "there is an implied covenant that neither party shall do anything which will have the effect of destroying or injuring the right of the other party to receive the fruits of the contract, which means that in every contract there exists an implied covenant of good faith and fair dealing." (*Kirke La Shelle Co. v. Paul Armstrong Co.,* 263 N.Y. 79, 87, 188 N.E. 163.) This general rule does not apply to at-will employment relationships, as "it would be incongruous to say that an inference may be drawn that the employer impliedly agreed to a provision which would be destructive of his right of termination." (*Murphy v. American Home Prods. Corp.,* 58 N.Y.2d 293, 304–305, 461 N.Y.S.2d 232, 448 N.E.2d 86.) It does not follow, however, that there can be no covenant of good faith implicit in the shareholders' agreement that gives rise to obligations surviving termination of the employment relationship.

Assuming plaintiff's claims about the purpose of the amendments to be true, the expectations and relationship of the parties, as structured by the shareholders' agreement, dictate an implied contractual obligation of good faith, notwithstanding that there is none in their employment relationship (*see, Wakefield v. Northern Telecom,* 769 F.2d 109 [2d Cir.]). A covenant of good faith is anomalous in the context of at-will employment because performance and entitlement to benefits are simultaneous. Termination even without cause does not operate to deprive the employee of the benefits promised in return for performance.

But the alleged "golden handcuffs" agreement is different. An implied covenant of good faith *is* necessary to enable the employee to receive the benefits promised for performance. As one court noted, "an unfettered right to avoid payment * * * creates incentives counterproductive to the purpose of the contract itself in that the better the performance by the employee, the greater the temptation to terminate." (*Wakefield v. Northern Telecom, supra,* at 112–113; Note, *Exercising Options to Repurchase Employee–Held Stock: A Question of Good Faith,* 68 Yale L.J. 773, 779 [1959].) ···

### IV.

Denial of summary judgment would deprive defendants of no legitimate expectation or right, contractual or otherwise. Under the law, they remain free to terminate plaintiff's employment as agreed; they remain free to buy back his stock at book value as agreed—so long as there is a corporate purpose for their conduct. What controlling shareholders cannot do to a minority shareholder is take action against him solely for the self-aggrandizing, opportunistic purpose of themselves acquiring his shares at the low price, and they cannot do this because in the law it means something to be a shareholder, particularly a minority shareholder....

■ SIMONS, ALEXANDER and TITONE, JJ., concur with BELLACOSA, J.

■HANCOCK, J., concurs in a separate opinion.

■KAYE, J., dissents and votes to reverse in another opinion in which WACHTLER, C.J., concurs.

Order affirmed, etc.

———

**JENSEN v. CHRISTENSEN & LEE INSURANCE, INC.,** 157 Wis.2d 758, 460 N.W.2d 441 (App.1990). In this case, the court held that a shareholder who was discharged from his corporate position did not have an action for wrongful discharge, as such, because in Wisconsin actions for wrongful discharge are limited to discharges that violate public policy. However, the court added, the shareholder's allegations that his discharge triggered a stock buyout at a low purchase price that redounded to the financial benefit of the remaining shareholder-directors stated a claim that those directors had breached their fiduciary duties by failing to deal fairly in a matter in which they had a material conflict of interest.

———

## SECTION 8.   DISSOLUTION FOR DEADLOCK

———

### DEL. GEN. CORP. LAW §§ 273, 355

[See Statutory Supplement]

———

## REV. MODEL BUS. CORP. ACT §§ 14.30, 14.34

[See Statutory Supplement]

---

## N.Y. BUS. CORP. LAW §§ 1002, 1104, 1111

[See Statutory Supplement]

---

## Wollman v. Littman

New York Supreme Court, Appellate Div., First Dept., 1970.
35 A.D.2d 935, 316 N.Y.S.2d 526.

■ PER CURIAM . . .

The stock of the corporation is held, fifty percent each, by two distinct groups, one of which, the Nierenberg sisters, are plaintiffs, and the other, the Littmans, defendants, each group having equal representation on the board of directors. The corporation's business is the selling of artificial fur fabrics to garment manufacturers. Defendants, the Littmans, allegedly had the idea for the business and developed a market for the fabrics among its manufacturing customers. Plaintiffs are the daughters of Louis Nierenberg, the main stockholder of Louis Nierenberg, Inc., who procures the fabrics and sells them to the corporation. The Littmans, in a separate action in which they are plaintiffs, charge the plaintiffs here (the Nierenberg sisters) and Louis Nierenberg Corporation with seeking to lure away the corporation's customers for Louis Nierenberg Corporation and with doing various acts to affect the corporation's business adversely. The Nierenberg faction countered with this suit, claiming that the bringing of the other action indicates that the corporate management is at such odds among themselves that effective management is impossible. Special Term agreed, but we do not. Irreconcilable differences even among an evenly divided board of directors do not in all cases mandate dissolution. . . . Here, two factors would require further exploration. The first is that the functions of the two disputing interests are distinct, one selling and the other procuring, and each can pursue its own without need for collaboration. The second is that a dissolution which will render nugatory the relief sought in the representative action would actually accomplish the wrongful purpose that defendants (Nierenberg) are charged with in that action. It would not only squeeze the Littmans out of the business but would require the receiver to dispose of the inventory with the Nierenbergs the only interested purchaser financially strong enough to take advantage of the situation. Such a result, if supported by the facts, would be intolerable to a court of equity. A trial of the issues is necessitated. On that trial it has been agreed by both counsel it would be advantageous to have the representative action and the action for dissolution tried together, though not consolidated (for a discussion of the distinction, see the comprehensive opinion in Padilla v. Greyhound Lines, 29 A.D.2d 495, 288 N.Y.S.2d 641), and it is so directed.

We affirm the appointment of a receiver. His function, however, should be limited to the necessities indicated, namely, to the orderly functioning of the regular course of business of the corporation until the further order of the court.

----

## NOTE ON DISSOLUTION FOR DEADLOCK

1.   A number of statutes provide for involuntary dissolution on a showing of deadlock. A few of the statutes define deadlock in terms of an "equally divided" board or body of shareholders, see, e.g., Mass. § 50; Cook v. Cook, 270 Mass. 534, 170 N.E. 455 (1930), but most are phrased broadly enough to include deadlock brought about by super-majority or veto arrangements.

2.   The deadlock statutes are generally interpreted to make dissolution discretionary even when deadlock is shown to exist, and the courts have often been reluctant to order the dissolution of a profitable corporation on deadlock grounds. However, profitability is not a *bar* to dissolution for deadlock. In Weiss v. Gordon, 32 A.D.2d 279, 301 N.Y.S.2d 839 (1969), the court stated, "The earlier thinking stressed the distinction between the corporation as an entity and the shareholders, and as long as the former could continue to function profitably the relationship between the shareholders was of no moment (cf. Matter of Radom & Neidorff, Inc., 307 N.Y. 1, 119 N.E.2d 563 (1954)). It is being increasingly realized that the relationship between the stockholders in a close corporation vis-a-vis each other in practice closely approximates the relationship between partners (see Mtr. of Surchin v. Approved Bus. Mach., 55 Misc.2d 888, 890, 286 N.Y.S.2d 580, 583 (1967)). As a consequence, when a point is reached where the shareholders who are actively conducting the business of the corporation cannot agree, it becomes in the best interests of those shareholders to order a dissolution. . . ."

----

# SECTION 9.   PROVISIONAL DIRECTORS, AND CUSTODIANS

----

## DEL. GEN. CORP. LAW §§ 226, 352, 353

[See Statutory Supplement]

----

## CAL. CORP. CODE §§ 308, 1802

[See Statutory Supplement]

----

**THOMPSON, THE SHAREHOLDER'S CAUSE OF ACTION FOR OPPRESSION,** 48 Bus.Law. 699, 723 (1993). "[More than half of the states have added to the remedies available in shareholder disputes by providing for the appointment of a custodian. About twenty states authorize a court to appoint a provisional director to help resolve shareholder disputes.] . . . Despite their widespread inclusion in statutes, these remedies are not used often. [The remedy is more important in states like Delaware, where it is the only effective remedy for shareholder dissension.] There is a cost to an additional layer of management, which would unduly burden a small enterprise, and the appointment of an outside party may not address the underlying differences among the participants."*

## SECTION 10. DISSOLUTION FOR OPPRESSION, AND MANDATORY BUY-OUT

## REV. MODEL BUS. CORP. ACT § 14.30, 14.34

[See Statutory Supplement]

## CAL. CORP. CODE §§ 1800, 1804, 2000

[See Statutory Supplement]

## N.Y. BUS. CORP. LAW §§ 1104–a, 1111, 1118

[See Statutory Supplement]

### NOTE ON HETHERINGTON AND DOOLEY

At one time, courts were extremely reluctant to order the involuntary dissolution of a profitable business, on the ground that it was bad social policy to break up such a business. In 1977, John Hetherington and Michael Dooley published a celebrated article on this problem, Illiquidity and Exploitation: A Proposed Statutory Solution to the Remaining Close Corporation Problem, 63 Va.L.Rev. 1 (1977). In this article, the authors pointed out that a judicial order to dissolve a corporation was unlikely to lead to the breakup of a profitable business: If it is advantageous to continue a business, then after

---

* The material in brackets has been by ed.) transposed from footnotes to text. (Footnote

dissolution is ordered, normally one or more of the shareholders, or a third party, would purchase and continue the business. Hetherington & Dooley backed up this point with empirical data by analyzing the fifty-four reported involuntary dissolution cases decided between 1960 and 1976. In half of the fifty-four cases, the plaintiff had been successful; in half, unsuccessful. Of the twenty-seven cases in which the plaintiff had been successful, the corporation was actually liquidated in only six. In seventeen of the twenty-seven cases one party bought out the other; in three of the cases, the business was sold to an outsider; and in one case there was no buyout or other change. (In fourteen of the twenty-seven cases in which plaintiff was unsuccessful, one party bought out the other. In two of the cases, the business was sold to a third party. In three of the cases, the business was liquidated. In six of the cases, there was no change in ownership. In two of the cases, the result was unknown.)

Furthermore, Hetherington & Dooley pointed out, dissolution, or something like it, was a central remedy for disaffected shareholders in close corporations because, given the limits of reasonable foreseeability, shareholders who organized such corporations could not possibly plan in advance to deal with all the interpersonal problems that might occur between them. Therefore, Hetherington & Dooley concluded, in the case of a close corporation a remedy comparable to dissolution— specifically, free exit through a mandatory buyout of the minority's interest—should be available on demand.

> The emphasis on contractual arrangements [in close corporations] reveals a fundamental misunderstanding of the nature of close corporations. Whether the parties adopt special contractual arrangements is much less important than their ability to sustain a close, harmonious relationship over time. The continuance of such a relationship is crucial because it reflects what is perhaps the fundamental assumption made by those who decide to invest in a close corporation: they expect that during the life of the firm the shareholders will be in substantial agreement as to its operation.

> Time and human nature may cause a divergence of interests and a breakdown in consensus, however. . . .

> Our thesis is that the problem of exploitation is uniquely related to liquidity and, for that reason, it is resistant to solution by ex ante contractual arrangements or by ex post judicial relief for breach of fiduciary duty. Accordingly, we [propose that the law should require] the majority to repurchase the minority's interest at the request of the latter and subject to appropriate safeguards.

The insights and empirical data in the Hetherington & Dooley article form a backdrop to the materials in this section.

———

# Matter of Kemp & Beatley, Inc.

Court of Appeals of New York, 1984.
64 N.Y.2d 63, 484 N.Y.S.2d 799, 473 N.E.2d 1173.

■ COOKE, CHIEF JUDGE. . . .

## I

The business concern of Kemp & Beatley, incorporated under the laws of New York, designs and manufactures table linens and sundry tabletop items. The company's stock consists of 1,500 outstanding shares held by eight shareholders. Petitioner Dissin had been employed by the company for 42 years when, in June 1979, he resigned. Prior to resignation, Dissin served as vice-president and a director of Kemp & Beatley. Over the course of his employment, Dissin had acquired stock in the company and currently owns 200 shares.

Petitioner Gardstein, like Dissin, had been a long-time employee of the company. Hired in 1944, Gardstein was for the next 35 years involved in various aspects of the business including material procurement, product design, and plant management. His employment was terminated by the company in December 1980. He currently owns 105 shares of Kemp & Beatley stock.

Apparent unhappiness surrounded petitioners' leaving the employ of the company. Of particular concern was that they no longer received any distribution of the company's earnings. Petitioners considered themselves to be "frozen out" of the company; whereas it had been their experience when with the company to receive a distribution of the company's earnings according to their stockholdings, in the form of either dividends or extra compensation, that distribution was no longer forthcoming.

Gardstein and Dissin, together holding 20.33% of the company's outstanding stock, commenced the instant proceeding in June 1981, seeking dissolution of Kemp & Beatley pursuant to section 1104–a of the Business Corporation Law. Their petition alleged "fraudulent and oppressive" conduct by the company's board of directors such as to render petitioners' stock "a virtually worthless asset." Supreme Court referred the matter for a hearing, which was held in March 1982.

Upon considering the testimony of petitioners and the principals of Kemp & Beatley, the referee concluded that "the corporate management has by its policies effectively rendered petitioners' shares worthless, and . . . the only way petitioners can expect any return is by dissolution". Petitioners were found to have invested capital in the company expecting, among other things, to receive dividends or "bonuses" based upon their stock holdings. Also found was the company's "established buyout policy" by which it would purchase the stock of employee shareholders upon their leaving its employ.

The involuntary-dissolution statute (Business Corporation Law, § 1104–a) permits dissolution when a corporation's controlling faction is found guilty of "oppressive action" toward the complaining shareholders. The referee considered oppression to arise when "those in control" of the corporation "have acted in such a manner as to defeat those expectations of the minority stockholders which formed the basis of [their] participation in the venture." The expectations of petitioners that they would not be arbitrarily excluded from gaining a return on their investment and that their stock would be purchased by the corporation upon termination of employment, were deemed defeated by prevailing corporate policies. Dissolution was recommended in the referee's report, subject to giving respondent corporation an opportunity to purchase petitioners' stock.

Supreme Court confirmed the referee's report. It, too, concluded that due to the corporation's new dividend policy petitioners had been prevented from receiving any return on their investments. Liquidation of the corporate assets was found the only means by which petitioners would receive a fair return. The court considered judicial dissolution of a corporation to be "a serious and severe remedy." Consequently, the order of dissolution was conditioned upon the corporation's being permitted to purchase petitioners' stock. The Appellate Division affirmed, without opinion. 99 A.D.2d 445, 471 N.Y.S.2d 245.

At issue in this appeal is the scope of section 1104–a of the Business Corporation Law. Specifically, this court must determine whether the provision for involuntary dissolution when the "directors or those in control of the corporation have been guilty of ... oppressive actions toward the complaining shareholders" was properly applied in the circumstances of this case. We hold that it was, and therefore affirm.

## II

Judicially ordered dissolution of a corporation at the behest of minority interests is a remedy of relatively recent vintage in New York. Historically, this State's courts were considered divested of equity jurisdiction to order dissolution, as statutory prescriptions were deemed exclusive (see Hitch v. Hawley, 132 N.Y. 212, 217, 30 N.E. 401)....

... [T]he Legislature has shown a special solicitude toward the rights of minority shareholders of closely held corporations by enacting section 1104–a of the Business Corporation Law. That statute provides a mechanism for the holders of at least 20% of the outstanding shares of a corporation whose stock is not traded on a securities market to petition for its dissolution "under special circumstances" (see Business Corporation Law, § 1104–a, subd. [a]). The circumstances that give rise to dissolution fall into two general classifications: mistreatment of complaining shareholders (subd. [a], par. [1]), or misappropriation of corporate assets (subd. [a], par. [2]) by controlling shareholders, directors or officers.

Section 1104–a (subd. [a], par. [1]) describes three types of proscribed activity: "illegal", "fraudulent", and "oppressive" conduct. The first two terms are familiar words that are commonly understood at law. The last, however, does not enjoy the same certainty gained through long usage. As no definition is provided by the statute, it falls upon the courts to provide guidance (see Goncalves v. Regent Int. Hotels, 58 N.Y.2d 206, 218, 460 N.Y.S.2d 750, 447 N.E.2d 693).

The statutory concept of "oppressive actions" can, perhaps, best be understood by examining the characteristics of close corporations and the Legislature's general purpose in creating this involuntary-dissolution statute. It is widely understood that, in addition to supplying capital to a contemplated or ongoing enterprise and expecting a fair and equal return, parties comprising the ownership of a close corporation may expect to be actively involved in its management and operation.... The small ownership cluster seeks to "contribute their capital, skills, experience and labor" toward the corporate enterprise....

As a leading commentator in the field has observed: "Unlike the typical shareholder in a publicly held corporation, who may be simply an investor or a speculator and cares nothing for the responsibilities of management, the shareholder in a close corporation is a co-owner of the business and wants the privileges and powers that go with ownership. His participation in that particular corporation is often his principal or sole source of income. As a matter of fact, providing employment for himself may have been the principal reason why he participated in organizing the corporation. He may or may not anticipate an ultimate profit from the sale of his interest, but he normally draws very little from the corporation as dividends. In his capacity as an officer or employee of the corporation, he looks to his salary for the principal return on his capital investment, because earnings of a close corporation, as is well known, are distributed in major part in salaries, bonuses and retirement benefits." (O'Neal, Close Corporations [2d ed.], § 1.07, at pp. 21–22 [n. omitted].)

Shareholders enjoy flexibility in memorializing these expectations through agreements setting forth each party's rights and obligations in corporate governance (see, generally, Kessler, Shareholder–Managed Close Corporation Under the New York Business Corporation Law, 43 Fordham L.Rev. 197; Davidian, op. cit., 56 St. John's L.Rev. 24, 29–30, and nn. 21–22). In the absence of such an agreement, however, ultimate decision-making power respecting corporate policy will be reposed in the holders of a majority interest in the corporation (see, e.g., Business Corporation Law, §§ 614, 708). A wielding of this power by any group controlling a corporation may serve to destroy a stockholder's vital interests and expectations.

As the stock of closely held corporations generally is not readily salable, a minority shareholder at odds with management policies may be without either a voice in protecting his or her interests or any reasonable means of withdrawing his or her investment. This predicament may fairly be considered the legislative concern underlying the provision at issue in this case; inclusion of the criteria that the corporation's stock not be traded on securities markets and that the complaining shareholder be subject to oppressive actions supports this conclusion.

Defining oppressive conduct as distinct from illegality in the present context has been considered in other forums. The question has been resolved by considering oppressive actions to refer to conduct that substantially defeats the "reasonable expectations" held by minority shareholders in committing their capital to the particular enterprise (see, e.g., Mardikos v. Arger, 116 Misc.2d 1028, 457 N.Y.S.2d 371; Matter of Barry One Hour Photo Process, 111 Misc.2d 559, 444 N.Y.S.2d 540....) This concept is consistent with the apparent purpose underlying the provision under review. A shareholder who reasonably expected that ownership in the corporation would entitle him or her to a job, a share of corporate earnings, a place in corporate management, or some other form of security, would be oppressed in a very real sense when others in the corporation seek to defeat those expectations and there exists no effective means of salvaging the investment.

Given the nature of close corporations and the remedial purpose of the statute, this court holds that utilizing a complaining shareholder's "reasonable expectations" as a means of identifying and measuring conduct alleged to be oppressive is appropriate. A court considering a petition alleging oppressive conduct must investigate what the majority shareholders knew, or should have known, to be the petitioner's expectations in entering the particular enterprise. Majority conduct should not be deemed oppressive simply because the petitioner's subjective hopes and desires in joining the venture are not fulfilled. Disappointment alone should not necessarily be equated with oppression.

Rather, oppression should be deemed to arise only when the majority conduct substantially defeats expectations that, objectively viewed, were both reasonable under the circumstances and were central to the petitioner's decision to join the venture. It would be inappropriate, however, for us in this case to delineate the contours of the courts' consideration in determining whether directors have been guilty of oppressive conduct. As in other areas of the law, much will depend on the circumstances in the individual case.

The appropriateness of an order of dissolution is in every case vested in the sound discretion of the court considering the application (see Business Corporation Law, § 1111, subd. [a]). Under the terms of this statute, courts are instructed to consider both whether "liquidation of the corporation is the only feasible means" to protect the complaining shareholder's expectation of a fair return on his or her investment and whether dissolution "is reasonably necessary" to protect "the rights or interests of any substantial number of shareholders" not limited to those complaining (Business Corporation Law, § 1104–a, subd. [b], pars. [1], [2]). Implicit in this direction is that once oppressive conduct is found, consideration must be given to the totality of circumstances surrounding the current state of corporate affairs and relations to determine whether some remedy short of or other than dissolution, constitutes a feasible means of satisfying both the petitioner's expectations and the rights and interests of any other substantial group of shareholders (see, also, Business Corporation Law, § 1111, subd. [b], par. [1]).

By invoking the statute, a petitioner has manifested his or her belief that dissolution may be the only appropriate remedy. Assuming the petitioner has set forth a prima facie case of oppressive conduct, it should be incumbent upon the parties seeking to forestall dissolution to demonstrate to the court the existence of an adequate, alternative remedy (cf. Baker v. Commercial Body Bldrs., 264 Or. 614, 507 P.2d 387, supra; White v. Perkins, 213 Va. 129, 189 S.E.2d 315). A court has broad latitude in fashioning alternative relief, but when fulfillment of the oppressed petitioner's expectations by these means is doubtful, such as when there has been a complete deterioration of relations between the parties, a court should not hesitate to order dissolution. Every order of dissolution, however, must be conditioned upon permitting any shareholder of the corporation to elect to purchase the complaining shareholder's stock at fair value (see Business Corporation Law, § 1118).

One further observation is in order. The purpose of this involuntary dissolution statute is to provide protection to the minority shareholder whose reasonable expectations in undertaking the venture have been frustrated and who has no adequate means of recovering his or her investment. It would be contrary to this remedial purpose to permit its use by minority shareholders as merely a coercive tool (see Davidian, op. cit., 56 St. John's L.Rev. 24, 59–60, and nn. 159–160). Therefore, the minority shareholder whose own acts, made in bad faith and undertaken with a view toward forcing an involuntary dissolution, give rise to the complained-of oppression should be given no quarter in the statutory protection (cf. Mardikos v. Arger, 116 Misc.2d 1028, 1032, 457 N.Y.S.2d 371, supra).

### III

There was sufficient evidence presented at the hearing to support the conclusion that Kemp & Beatley had a long-standing policy of awarding *de facto* dividends based on stock ownership in the form of "extra compensation bonuses." Petitioners, both of whom had extensive experience in the management of the company, testified to this effect. Moreover, both related that receipt of this compensation, whether as true dividends or disguised as "extra compensation", was a known incident to ownership of the company's stock understood by all of the company's principals. Finally, there was uncontroverted proof that this policy was changed either shortly before or shortly after petitioners' employment ended. Extra compensation was still awarded by the company. The only difference was that stock ownership was no longer a basis for the payments; it was asserted that the basis became services rendered to the corporation. It was not unreasonable for the fact finder to have determined that this change in policy amounted to nothing less than an attempt to exclude petitioners from gaining any return on their investment through the mere recharacterization of distributions of corporate income. Under the circumstances of this case, there was no error in determining that this conduct constituted oppressive action within the meaning of section 1104–a of the Business Corporation Law.

Nor may it be said that Supreme Court abused its discretion in ordering Kemp & Beatley's dissolution, subject to an opportunity for a buy-out of petitioners' shares. After the referee had found that the controlling faction of the company was, in effect, attempting to "squeeze-out" petitioners by offering them no return on their investment and increasing other executive compensation, respondents, in opposing the report's confirmation, attempted only to controvert the factual basis of the report. They suggested no feasible, alternative remedy to the forced dissolution. In light of an apparent deterioration in relations between petitioners and the governing shareholders of Kemp & Beatley, it was not unreasonable for the court to have determined that a forced buy-out of petitioners' shares or liquidation of the corporation's assets was the only means by which petitioners could be guaranteed a fair return on their investments.

Accordingly, the order of the Appellate Division should be modified, with costs to petitioners-respondents, by affirming the substantive determination of that court but extending the time for exercising the option to purchase petitioners-respondents' shares to 30 days following this court's determination.

■ JASEN, JONES, WACHTLER, MEYER and SIMONS, JJ., concur.

■ KAYE, J., taking no part.

Order modified, with costs to petitioners-respondents, in accordance with the opinion herein and, as so modified, affirmed.

———

**MEISELMAN v. MEISELMAN,** 309 N.C. 279, 307 S.E.2d 551 (1983). "Professor O'Neal, perhaps the foremost authority on close corporations, points out that many close corporations are companies based on personal relationships that give rise to certain 'reasonable expectations' on the part of those acquiring an interest in the close corporation. Those 'reasonable expectations' include, for example, the parties' expectation that they will participate in the management of the business or be employed by the company. O'Neal, *Close Corporations: Existing Legislation and Recommended Reform,* 33 Bus.Law 873, 885 (1978) . . . .

"Thus, when personal relations among the participants in a close corporation break down, the 'reasonable expectations' the participants had, for example, an expectation that their employment would be secure, or that they would enjoy meaningful participation in the management of the business—become difficult if not impossible to fulfill. In other words, when the personal relationships among the participants break down, the majority shareholder, because of his greater voting power, is in a position to terminate the minority shareholder's employment and to exclude him from participation in management decisions.

"Some may argue that the minority shareholder should have bargained for greater protection before agreeing to accept his minority shareholder position in a close corporation. However, the practical realities of this particular business situation oftentimes do not allow for such negotiations. . . .

"Apparently in response to these commentators' uniform calls for reform in this area of corporate law, many state legislatures have enacted statutes giving the tribunals in their states the power to grant relief to minority shareholders under more liberal circumstances. . . .

"In helping to establish this growing trend toward enactment of more liberal grounds under which dissolution will be granted to a complaining shareholder, the legislature in this State enacted in 1955 N.C.G.S. § 55–125(a)(4), the statute granting superior court judges the 'power to liquidate the assets and business of a corporation in an action by a shareholder when it is established' that '[l]iquidation is reasonably necessary for the protection of the rights or interests of the complaining shareholder.' . . .

"[B]efore it can be determined whether, in any given case, it has been 'established' that liquidation is 'reasonably necessary' to protect the complaining shareholder's 'rights or interest,' the particular 'rights or interests' of the complaining shareholder must be articulated. This is so because N.C.G.S. § 55–125(a)(4) refers to the 'rights or interests' of *the complaining shareholder';* the statute does not refer to the 'rights or interests' of shareholders generally. . . . [W]e hold that a complaining shareholder's 'rights or interests' in a close corporation include the 'reasonable expectations' the complaining shareholder has in the corporation. These 'reasonable expectations' are to be ascertained by examining the entire history of the participants' relationship. That history will include the 'reasonable expectations' created at the inception of the participants' relationship; those 'reasonable expectations' as altered over time; and the 'reasonable expectations' which develop as the participants engage in a course of dealing in conducting the affairs of the corporation. The interests and views of the other participants must be considered in determining 'reasonable expectations.' The key is *'reasonable.'* In order for plaintiff's expectations to be reasonable, they must be known to or assumed by the other shareholders and concurred in by them. Privately held expectations which are not made known to the other participants are not 'reasonable.' Only expectations embodied in understandings, express or implied, among the participants should be recognized by the court. . . .

"Defendants argue, however, that . . . [a shareholder] is only entitled to relief if his traditional shareholder rights have been infringed. They contend that those traditional shareholder rights include the right to notice of stockholders' meetings, the right to vote cumulatively, the right of access to the corporate offices and to corporate financial information, and the right to compel the payment of dividends. . . .

"While it may be true that a shareholder in, for example, a publicly held corporation may have 'rights or interests' defined as defendants argue, a shareholder's rights in a closely held corporation may not necessarily be so narrowly defined. . . ."

_____

## NOTE ON EVOLVING EXPECTATIONS

In *Meiselman*, the court stated that what constitutes a shareholder's reasonable expectations can change over time. An example is A.W. Chesterton Co. v. Chesterton, 128 F.3d 1 (1st Cir.1997). J.W. Chesterton Co. had been a closely held corporation since 1885. In 1985, all the shareholders, including Arthur Chesterton, agreed to change the corporation's tax status under the Internal Revenue Code from a C corporation to an S corporation. In the early 1990s, Arthur Chesterton proposed to transfer some of his stock to two shell corporations that he wholly owned. In order to qualify for S Corporation status, a corporation may not have any shareholders who are themselves corporations. Therefore, Arthur Chesterton's proposed transfer would have resulted in a loss of J.W. Chesterton's favorable tax treatment under IRC subchapter S. J.W. Chesterton Co. and its other shareholders sued Arthur Chesterton to enjoin him from making the proposed transfer. The First Circuit granted the injunction. "Under Massachusetts law, the expectations and understanding of the shareholders are relevant to a breach of fiduciary duty determination . . . The existence of the [1985] agreement . . . sheds light on the Company's and other shareholders' expectations. . . ." See also, e.g., Spurgeon Foster v. Foster Farms, 112 N.C.App. 700, 436 S.E.2d 843 (1993).

_____

**THOMPSON, THE SHAREHOLDER'S CAUSE OF ACTION FOR OPPRESSION,** 48 Bus.Law. 699, 709–12, 715–716 (1993). "Oppression as a ground for dissolution was included in the Illinois and Pennsylvania corporations acts in 1933, in the first Model Business Corporation Act in 1946, and in the English Companies Act of 1948. Thirty-seven American states now include oppression or a similar term in their corporations statutes. . . ."

_____

**HAYNSWORTH, THE EFFECTIVENESS OF INVOLUNTARY DISSOLUTION SUITS AS A REMEDY FOR CLOSE CORPORATION DISSENSION,** 35 Clev.St. L.Rev. 25 (1987). "In recent years courts have increasingly focused on developing the concept of oppression, and proof of oppressive conduct is rapidly becoming the most likely avenue for minority shareholder relief in close corporations. Three definitions of oppression have been used in the cases.

"The first, drawn from English case law is:

burdensome, harsh and wrongful conduct ... a lack of probity and fair dealing in the affairs of a company to the prejudice of some portion of its members; or a visual departure from the standards of fair dealing, and a violation of fair play on which every shareholder who entrusts his money to a company is entitled to rely.

Under this definition, oppression is basically a breach of the general fiduciary duty of good faith and fair dealing that majority shareholders in a corporation owe to the minority shareholders.

"The second definition, first enunciated in the now famous case of *Donahue v. Rodd Electrotype Company of New England, Inc.*, is conduct that constitutes a violation of the strict fiduciary duty of 'utmost good faith and loyalty' owed by partners *inter se.* This standard, which is based on the analogy of close corporation shareholders who are active in management to general partners in a partnership, is theoretically higher than the 'good faith and inherent fairness' standard normally applicable in a corporation.

"The third definition of oppression, initially derived from English case law, and long advocated by Dean F. Hodge O'Neal as well as other leading close corporation experts, is conduct which frustrates the reasonable expectations of the investors. The reasonable expectations doctrine has been gaining wide acceptance in the past few years. Decisions in at least eight states have explicitly adopted this concept, and decisions in at least nine additional states have implicitly recognized it. The approval of the reasonable expectations doctrine by the New York Court of Appeals in the 1984 case of *In re Kemp & Beatley, Inc.* is quite significant and will undoubtedly influence other courts."

----

## NOTE ON THE DUTY OF CARE AND THE DUTY OF LOYALTY IN THE CLOSELY HELD CORPORATION

Two major legal bulwarks for minority shareholders in publicly held corporations are the duty of care and the duty of loyalty imposed by law on corporate directors and officers. These duties are extremely complex in their details, and are the subject of Chapters 8–10. To oversimplify somewhat, the duty of care may render a director or officer liable for certain types of managerial negligence, and the duty of loyalty may render a director or officer liable for unfair self-interested transactions with the corporation. However, under the business judgment rule a decision by an officer or director will not subject her to liability for violation of the duty of care, even if the decision was unreasonable, if it was taken in good faith, there was no self-interest, the director or officer properly informed herself before making the decision, and the decision was not so unreasonable as to be irrational. Under the duty of loyalty, a self-interested transaction will not subject a director or officer to liability if she made full disclosure and the transaction was objectively fair.

The duties of care and loyalty protect minority shareholders in closely held as well as publicly held corporations, but in the closely held context they are often an insufficient protection. For example, the discharge of a minority shareholder from corporate office might qualify for protection under the business judgment rule, and a purchase of stock from majority shareholders might not violate the duty of loyalty if the price paid for the stock was fair. The real vice of such actions lies in the fact that they treat shareholders unequally, defeat legitimate expectations of a sort found in closely but not publicly held corporations, or both. Accordingly, the "reasonable expectations" analysis that is made explicit in cases like Meiselman v. Meiselman, that is implicit in cases like Donahue v. Rodd, and that in part underlies the concept of dissolution for oppression, fills a major gap in corporate law. It would be a mistake, however, to believe that analysis based on reasonable expectations can be separated from the concept of fairness. One way in which a court determines whether reasonable expectations of minority shareholders have been defeated by majority shareholders is by asking itself what similarly situated shareholders would have probably expected. Often the only way to answer that question is to ask what similarly situated shareholders would have regarded as fair.

---

## MICH. COMP. LAWS § 450.1489

[See Statutory Supplement]

---

## MINN. STAT. ANN. § 302A.751

[See Statutory Supplement]

---

# McCallum v. Rosen's Diversified, Inc.

United States Court of Appeals, Eighth Circuit, 1998.
153 F.3d 701.

■ Before BEAM, ROSS, and MAGILL, CIRCUIT JUDGES.

■ BEAM, CIRCUIT JUDGE.

William B. McCallum, a minority shareholder in Rosen's Diversified, Inc. (RDI), appeals from two adverse grants of summary judgment. McCallum seeks to have his shares in RDI redeemed for fair value pursuant to a court ordered buy-out. The district court held that McCallum failed to present evidence showing that RDI acted unfairly prejudicial toward him. We reverse and remand for a determination of the fair value of McCallum's shares.

## I.  BACKGROUND

This case involves a contentious dispute between the minority and controlling shareholders of a closely held Minnesota corporation. Two brothers, Elmer and Ludwig Rosen, founded RDI as a livestock trading business in the late 1940's. Today, RDI has grown into a thriving company, primarily engaged in meat packing and other agricultural businesses. In 1992, RDI had more than $400 million in sales. Members of the Rosen family own a majority of RDI's outstanding capital stock.

In January 1984, RDI hired McCallum, who had previously provided legal services to the company, as Executive Vice President and Chief Executive Officer (CEO). He was named a director in 1986. RDI performed well under McCallum's command. Accordingly, RDI rewarded McCallum—and three other key employees—with a bonus of $186,815 in cash and 12,000 shares of common stock in the company.[2] According to RDI, these payments were made because the key employees were almost entirely responsible for the financial success of the corporation, because the compensation package of the employees had been artificially low, and in order to maintain the unswerving loyalty of these employees. The parties did not enter into a shareholder's agreement or provide any mechanism for the transfer of those shares if circumstances changed.

By 1991, the amiable relationship between McCallum and RDI deteriorated, ultimately resulting in McCallum's termination and removal from the board. Subsequently, McCallum proposed that RDI redeem his shares for $5 million. RDI responded with an offer to redeem the shares for $600,000, which was at a small premium over the value determined by the annual valuation for RDI's Employee Stock Ownership Program (ESOP). The parties could not agree on a price and extensive litigation has followed.... The present case involves McCallum's 12,000 shares of RDI common stock which is not contained in the ESOP.

McCallum alleges that RDI's controlling shareholders have acted unfairly prejudicial toward him because they: (1) undermined his authority as CEO; (2) excluded him from important company decisions; (3) engaged in conduct directed at minimizing the value of the company; (4) terminated his employment; (5) offered to redeem his shares at an artificially low price; (6) denied him access to company books, records, and financial information; (7) engaged in self-dealing, usurped company opportunities, and commingled personal ventures with the affairs of the company.

---

**2.** During the course of his employment, McCallum also received approximately 3,300 shares of common stock in RDI through an Employee Stock Ownership Program (ESOP). McCallum's total ownership represented nearly 3% of the company's capital stock.

The district court dismissed many of McCallum's allegations as improperly pleaded derivative claims. The district court dismissed McCallum's request for a buyout of his stock on a subsequent motion for summary judgment. McCallum appeals.

## II.   DISCUSSION . . .

Concerned with the vulnerable position of minority shareholders in closely held corporations, the Minnesota legislature has provided the courts with broad equitable authority to protect the interests of minority shareholders. See Minn.Stat. § 302A.751 (amended 1994) (hereinafter "Section 751"). Section 751 provides for the buy-out of a minority shareholder's interest when "the directors or those in control of the corporation have acted in a manner unfairly prejudicial toward one or more shareholders in their capacities as shareholders or directors . . . or as officers or employees of a closely held corporation."

The phrase "unfairly prejudicial" is to be interpreted liberally. See *Pedro v. Pedro*, 463 N.W.2d 285, 288–89 (Minn.Ct.App.1990). One commentator, who helped draft certain revisions to the Minnesota Business Corporation Act and Section 751, stated that:

> The section is remedial in nature and should be liberally construed as an addition to the rights afforded non-controlling shareholders by law and the corporation's governing documents. The broad scope of Section 751 reflects the Legislature's trust in the ability of the judiciary to achieve equitable results on the facts appearing in individual cases.

See Joseph Edward Olson, Statutory Changes Improve Position of Minority Shareholders in Closely Held Corporations, *The Hennepin Lawyer*, Sept.-Oct.1983, at 11. In deciding whether to order a buy-out, the courts should consider "the reasonable expectations of the shareholders" with respect to each other and the corporation. See Minn. Stat. § 302A.751, subd. 3a (amended 1994). Oftentimes, a shareholder's reasonable expectations include a significant voice in management and an opportunity to work. See Olson at 23.

We find that the uncontested facts demonstrate that McCallum's reasonable expectations were defeated. RDI terminated McCallum's employment as CEO and subsequently offered to purchase his RDI shares at a small premium over the value determined by an annual valuation for RDI's ESOP. McCallum had received these shares as compensation for his outstanding service and as an inducement to remain at RDI, in order to foster its continued growth. Although the employment relationship later deteriorated, our focus is on McCallum's reasonable expectations at the inception of the relationship. See Minn.Stat. § 302A.751, subd. 3a.

On his termination, McCallum was divested of his primary expectations as a minority shareholder in RDI—an active role in the "management of the corporation and input as an employee." Pedro, 463 N.W.2d at 289. This expectation was particularly reasonable since

McCallum was CEO of RDI. We need not extend our holding as far as the Minnesota Court of Appeals, which held that controlling shareholders that terminate the employment of a minority shareholder must make a good-faith effort to buy out the shareholder at a fair price. See *Sawyer v. Curt & Co.*, 1991 WL 65320, at *2 (Minn.Ct.App. Feb.12, 1991) (publication order vacated). We simply hold that terminating the CEO—as opposed to an employee that did not have a significant role in management—and then offering to redeem his stock, which was issued partially to lure him to remain at the company, constituted conduct toward McCallum as a shareholder sufficient to invoke the requirements of the Minnesota Act. Accordingly, we remand the matter for a determination of the fair value of his stock.

On remand, the district court shall determine the fair value of McCallum's shares in accordance with Minn.Stat. § 302A.751, subd. 2 (amended 1994) and put an end to this pugnacious litigation. We express no opinion on the fair value of McCallum's shares or whether the ESOP valuation represents fair value.

## III.   CONCLUSION

For the foregoing reasons, we reverse the judgment of the district court and remand for further proceedings consistent with this opinion.

---

## Haynsworth, The Effectiveness of Involuntary Dissolution Suits as a Remedy for Close Corporation Dissension

35 Cleve.St.L.Rev. 25 (1987).

What results actually occur in close corporation involuntary dissolution suits? One way to answer this question is to examine existing published opinions. For the purposes of this article, the opinions published in 1984 and 1985 in which involuntary dissolution was one of the major causes of action were analyzed....

... [A] total of forty-seven cases ... qualified for the sample [but ten of the cases involved technical legal issues in which no decision on the type of relief, if any, had been made at the time the opinion was issued].

Of the remaining thirty-seven cases, a buy-out was the most frequent relief ordered by the court or elected by the defendants. This result occurred in twenty of the decisions (fifty-four percent). Dissolution was ordered in ten of the cases (twenty-seven percent). In four of the cases (eleven percent), no substantial relief was granted to the plaintiff on the merits. Finally, in the three other cases (eight percent) relief other than either dissolution or a buy-out was the exclusive remedy ordered....

What is somewhat surprising is the number of cases in which a court-supervised buy-out is the result of the involuntary dissolution suit. In a previous study of the fifty-four involuntary dissolution opinions decided between 1960–1976 conducted by [Hetherington and Dooley], a court-ordered or court supervised buy-out was involved in only three of the cases, whereas dissolution was ordered in sixteen of the twenty-seven cases in which some affirmative relief was granted [in the present sample]. . . .

––––––––

## NOTE ON DISSOLUTION

The evolution of the legal treatment of dissolution can, with some oversimplification, be divided into four stages.

1.  *First Stage: Dissolution Granted Only for Deadlock and Even Then Granted Very Sparingly.* In the first, original stage, which lasted until about the early 1960s, the courts typically granted dissolution only on the ground of deadlock. Furthermore, the courts were often reluctant to grant dissolution of a profitable corporation even on that ground, partly on the theory that there was a public interest in preserving economically viable businesses.

2.  *Second Stage: Dissolution on the Ground of the Majority's Fault.* In the second stage, courts became more willing to grant dissolution, even of profitable corporations, not only on the ground of deadlock but also on the ground of oppression.[1] This increased willingness resulted in part from a wave of dissolution-for-oppression statutes. It also resulted from the influence of scholarship like that of Hetherington & Dooley, and also of F. Hodge O'Neal, who wrote extensively to show that dissolution was often a highly desirable remedy to resolve the problems of minority shareholders.

3.  *Third Stage: Dissolution on the Ground of Defeat of the Minority's Reasonable Expectations.* In the third stage, the emphasis shifted from an inquiry into whether there was fault on the part of majority shareholders, to an inquiry into whether the reasonable expectations of the minority shareholders were being defeated. Often, this shift involved a reconstruction of the meaning of "oppression," as in *Kemp & Beatley, supra.*

4.  *Fourth Stage: Dissolution Converted into Mandatory Buy-Out.* In the fourth, present stage, there has been a marked tendency to grant relief even more freely to minority shareholders who petition for dissolution, but to cast that relief not in the form of dissolution, but in the form of a mandatory buy-out of the petitioner's shares at fair value. In many cases, the dissolution statutes give the majority a right to buy out the minority. In other cases, the courts order buy-out, rather than dissolution, as a matter of discretion.

----

**1.**  As stated in the Introduction to this Note, the evolution described in this Note is somewhat oversimplified. Even some very re- cent cases contain expressions of concern about the dissolution of profitable corporations.

At present, therefore, a petition by a minority shareholder for dissolution is commonly a trigger for requiring a mandatory buy-out of the minority shareholder's stock. To put this differently, the courts, with increasing frequency, hold that grounds for dissolution exist, but then substitute mandatory buy-out for dissolution as the appropriate remedy. This development has several implications.

*First*, because liquidation is not required under a mandatory buy-out, the power to order a mandatory buy-out serves to alleviate the persistent view of the courts that liquidation of a profitable corporation is against the public interest. As a result, the courts may now be more ready to find in favor of a minority shareholder in a dissolution proceeding, just because they know that such a finding will not necessarily result in a liquidation of the corporation's business.

*Second*, the power to order a mandatory buy-out in lieu of dissolution obviates a concern that freely granting dissolution may enable minority shareholders to opportunistically use a petition for dissolution (or the threat of such a petition) to put undue pressure on the majority shareholders by making them fear that they will lose control of the business, and thereby extort an unduly high settlement from the majority. This possibility is sometimes referred to as "oppression by the minority."

*Third*, the easier it is to convert a dissolution proceeding into mandatory buy-out, the less likely are the courts to require minority shareholders to satisfy a very high level of proof. In general, the less drastic is a remedy, the readier the courts will be to impose the remedy. This has been the trend of the law in the area of dissolution: as the remedy has been diluted from dissolution to buy-out, the standard for granting relief has also been diluted, and the frequency of relief to minority shareholders has increased.

*Fourth*, to the extent that petitions for dissolution have become triggering events for mandatory buy-outs, and the courts grant such petitions without a showing of fault by the majority, in effect the law is edging toward the position advocated by Hetherington and Dooley, that minority shareholders in close corporations should be allowed exit on demand. (This position also moves close corporation law toward partnership law, which already allows dissolution on very free terms.)

*Fifth*, properly conceived and administered, mandatory buy-out may have important advantages over dissolution. The minority shareholder can get just what he wants—the cash value of his stock and exit from a bad situation. At the same time, the majority shareholders are given the right to continue the business if they wish to do so.

---

## NOTE ON VALUATION OF THE MINORITY'S SHARES

To the extent that mandatory buy-out is substituted for dissolution, great pressure is put on the issue how the value of the minority's shares is determined, because the remedy of mandatory buy-out works properly only if the minority interest is properly valued. Indeed, from the perspective of valuation, dissolution has a major advantage over mandatory buy-out. In mandatory buy-out, the *court* must value the minority's interest. In contrast, in a dissolution there is a public sale of the corporation's business, so that the *market,* rather than the court, values the corporation and therefore the petitioner's shares. From a valuation perspective, therefore, dissolution may be preferable to mandatory buy-out on the ground that valuation by the market is more accurate than a valuation by the court.

Against this view, it can be argued that a mandatory sale of close corporation's business in the context of a dissolution proceeding may not in fact realize the fair value of the business. The problem with such a sale is that there may be no ready market for the corporation's business, especially if one or more of the shareholder-managers will not continue to participate, or if the only person who can realistically acquire the business is one of the shareholders, who might therefore be able to purchase the business at a public sale at an unduly low price. Professor Bahls has explained this problem especially well:

> . . . When corporations are liquidated, they usually sell their assets for cash. Frequently, when a receiver or court-appointed auctioneer sells a business, the sale does not yield the maximum value for any of the shareholders. Auction sales are fire sales. Rather than selling the entire business as a going concern, the business assets might be sold separately. If so, the sale does not yield the full value of a going concern. In addition, the business is not always operated between the appointment of the receiver or court-appointed auctioneer and the date of sale. During this interim, the customers of the business may develop relationships and preferences for other vendors, often dealing a fatal blow to the corporation's ability to operate profitably.

> Compounding the problem, auction sales or other court-supervised sales usually require payment of the purchase price immediately or within a short period of time. This requirement excludes potential purchasers from the market and may result in lower purchase prices offered by those not excluded. Finally, purchase prices are depressed because it is difficult to insure that the buyer will reap the benefit of the seller's goodwill. Business management, as well as nonmanagement employees, often develop important customer contracts and special expertise. To the extent that management expertise and customer relationships cannot be sold with the business, buyers do not receive the benefit of, nor are they willing to pay for, these important elements of goodwill. . . .

Bahls, Resolving Shareholder Dissension: Selection of the Appropriate Equitable Remedy, [1990] J.Corp.Law 285, 297 (1990).

On the other hand, mandatory buy-outs also raise severe problems of valuation. To begin with, the valuation of a business by a nonmarket mechanism, like a court, is always a very difficult and problematic enterprise. Furthermore, in the context of a mandatory buy-out two special problems are raised. For some valuation purposes, like estate-tax valuations, the value of shares is discounted from their pro rata share of the value of the business if the shares are minority shares or if they are not readily marketable. Discounts for these factors can run 25% or more. Some courts have applied minority or marketability discounts in the mandatory buy-out context as well. A distinction must be drawn, however, between the value of minority stock on the market and the value of minority stock to the majority shareholder. On the market, minority stock may be subject to a marketability discount, a minority discount, or both, because a third party who purchases minority stock will be in the same disadvantageous position as the selling minority shareholder. However, the majority shareholder will not be subject to these problems. Accordingly, the value of minority stock to a majority shareholder may be free of minority and marketability discounts. See Robblee v. Robblee, 68 Wash. App. 69, 78–81, 841 P.2d 1289, 1294–95 (1992):

In Charland v. Country View Golf Club, Inc., 588 A.2d 609 (R.I.1991), the court addressed these issues as follows:

> A minority discount has been described as a second-stage adjustment for valuing minority shares. *See* Note, *Rejecting the Minority Discount,* 1989 Duke L.J. 258, 260. That is, after a minority shareholder's stock is initially discounted for the minority percentage owned, the pro rata value is determined. Then an additional discount is applied to the pro rata value because the minority shareholder lacks corporate decisionmaking power. *Id.* This second calculation is called a minority discount. . . .

> Most courts that have considered this question have agreed that no minority discount should be applied when a corporation elects to buy out the shareholder who petitions for dissolution of the corporation. . . .

> [In *Brown v. Allied Corrugated Box Co.,* 91 Cal.App.3d 477, 154 Cal.Rptr. 170 (1979), the] court conceded that if the shares were placed on the open market, their minority status would substantially decrease their value. The court, however, went on to note that this devaluation has little validity when the shares are to be purchased by the corporation. When a corporation elects to buy out the shares of a dissenting shareholder, the fact that the shares are noncontrolling is irrelevant.

> In addition the court in *Brown* observed that had the plaintiffs proved their case and had the corporation been dissolved, each shareholder would have been entitled to the same amount per share. There would be no consideration given to whether the shares were controlling or noncontrolling. Furthermore an unscrupulous controlling shareholder could avoid a proportionate distribution under dissolution by buying out the shares, and the very misconduct and unfairness that incited the minority shareholders to seek dissolution could be used to oppress them

further. *Brown,* 91 Cal.App.3d at 486–87, 154 Cal.Rptr. at 176; *see also* Note, 1989 Duke L.J. at 269 n. 63.

We agree with the rationale of *Brown* and hereby adopt the rule that in circumstances in which a corporation elects to buy out a shareholder's stock pursuant to § 7–1.1–90.1, we shall not discount the shares solely because of their minority status.

A second and more difficult issue to resolve is whether a lack of marketability discount should be applied to Charland's shares. This discount is separate from and bears no relation to a minority discount. The courts that have addressed this question are divided.

The California courts have rejected a lack of marketability discount for the same reasons that they have rejected a minority discount. *See Brown,* 91 Cal.App.3d at 483, 154 Cal.Rptr. at 175. That is, no lack of marketability discount should be applied because the shares are not being sold on the open market; they are purchased by the corporation. The New York courts, however, have decided to apply a lack of marketability discount to shares in a closely held corporation when the corporation elects to buy out a minority shareholder in order to avoid dissolution. The reason for applying this discount is that shares of a closely held corporation cannot readily be sold on the public market. . . .

[A] lack of marketability discount is inapposite when a corporation elects to buy out a shareholder who has filed for dissolution of a corporation. As a recent law review article noted:

> "In dissolution cases, strong reasons support the use of pro rata value without a discount * * *. A minority shareholder seeking dissolution claims that majority shareholders have engaged in some unfair, possibly tortious, action. If the minority shareholder succeeds in having the company dissolved, all shareholders will receive their pro rata share of the assets, with no account given to the minority [or illiquidity] status of their shares. Minority shareholders should not receive less than this value if, instead of fighting the dissolution action, the majority decides to seek appraisal of minority shares in order to buy out the minority and reduce corporate discord." Note, 1989 Duke L.J. at 269 n. 63.

CHAPTER VII

# ALTERNATIVE FORMS OF BUSINESS ORGANIZATION: LIMITED PARTNERSHIPS, LIMITED LIABILITY COMPANIES, AND LIMITED LIABILITY PARTNERSHIPS

Although the different forms of business organization vary in a number of respects, traditionally the predominant considerations in selecting a form of organization have been taxation and liability. Owners want minimum taxation and maximum protection against individual liability. For many years, the major choice of prospective owners was between corporations and partnerships. Corporations offered maximum protection against liability; partnerships (for reasons to be explained in this Chapter) normally offered minimum taxation. In recent years, however, new, alternative forms of unincorporated business organization have emerged that offer both protection against liability and minimum taxation. Three of these forms will be considered in this Chapter, in the order in which they evolved: limited partnerships, limited liability companies, and limited liability partnerships.

## SECTION 1. LIMITED PARTNERSHIPS

Limited partnerships are not a new form of business organization. They are included in this chapter, rather than Chapter 2 (Partnership) for two reasons. First, recent changes in the administration of the Internal Revenue Code have affected several forms, including limited partnerships, in a way that makes it useful to consider these forms together. Second, although the limited partnership is an old form, in recent times there have been important changes in liability issues concerning limited partnerships. Both the liability and the tax developments will be considered in this section.

### (a) THE UNIFORM LIMITED PARTNERSHIP ACTS

Over the course of time, the Commissioners on Uniform State Laws have promulgated several uniform limited partnership acts.

In 1916, the Commissioners promulgated the original Uniform Limited Partnership Act. It was adopted in every state except Louisiana.

In 1976, the Commissioners promulgated a replacement for the Uniform Limited Partnership Act, called the Revised Uniform Partnership Act. The new Act modernized the prior Act and reflected the influence of the corporate model. It has been widely but not universally adopted.

In 1985, the Commissioners amended the Revised Uniform Limited Partnership Act in a number of important respects. The states are still in the process of adopting these amendments.

In the balance of this Section, the 1916 Act will be referred to as the ULPA, and the 1976 Act, as amended in 1985, will be referred to as RULPA.

## (b) FORMATION OF A LIMITED PARTNERSHIP

----

### REVISED UNIFORM LIMITED PARTNERSHIP
### ACT §§ 101, 201, 302, 403

[See Statutory Supplement]

----

**NOTE**

Unlike general partnerships, limited partnerships are basically creatures of statute, although they have nonstatutory historical antecedents. RULPA § 101 defines a limited partnership as "a partnership formed by two or more persons under the provisions of Section . . . having as members one or more general partners and one or more limited partners." RULPA § 201 provides that in order to form a limited partnership a certificate of limited partnership must be filed in the office of the Secretary of State. The certificate must state the name of the limited partnership, the name and business address of each general partner, the latest date upon which the limited partnership is to dissolve, and the name and address of the agent for service of process.

## (c) LIABILITY OF LIMITED PARTNERS

----

### REVISED UNIFORM LIMITED PARTNERSHIP ACT § 303

[See Statutory Supplement]

----

# Gateway Potato Sales v. G.B. Investment Co.

Court of Appeals of Arizona, 1991.
170 Ariz. 137, 822 P.2d 490.

■ TAYLOR, JUDGE.

Gateway Potato Sales (Gateway), a creditor of Sunworth Packing Limited Partnership (Sunworth Packing), brought suit to recover payment for goods it had supplied to the limited partnership. Gateway sought recovery from Sunworth Packing, from Sunworth Corporation as general partner, and from G.B. Investment Company (G.B. Investment) as a limited partner, pursuant to Arizona Revised Statutes Annotated (A.R.S.) § 29–319. Under § 29–319, a limited partner may become liable for the obligations of the limited partnership under certain circumstances in which the limited partner has taken part in the control of the business.

G.B. Investment moved for summary judgment, urging that there was no evidence that the circumstances described in A.R.S. § 29–319 had occurred in this case. It argued that, as a limited partner, it was not liable to the creditors of the limited partnership except to the extent of its investment. The trial court agreed, granting G.B. Investment's motion for summary judgment.

Gateway appeals from the judgment and the denial of its motion for reconsideration, arguing the existence of conflicting evidence of material facts relating to the participation of the limited partner in the control of the partnership business. We agree and reverse the grant of summary judgment.

## FACTS

On review from the trial court's order granting summary judgment, the facts are viewed in the light most favorable to the party against whom judgment is entered. Dolezal v. Carbrey, 161 Ariz. 365, 366, 778 P.2d 1261, 1262 (1989). Sunworth Corporation and G.B. Investment formed Sunworth Packing in November 1985 for the purpose of engaging in potato farming in Arizona. The limited partnership certificate and agreement of Sunworth Packing, filed with the office of the Arizona Secretary of State, specified Sunworth Corporation as the general partner and G.B. Investment Company as the limited partner. The agreement recited that the limited partner would not participate in the control of the business. The agreement further stated that the limited partner would not become liable to the creditors of the partnership, except to the extent of its initial contribution and any liability it may incur with an Arizona bank as a signatory party or guarantor of a loan and/or line of credit.

In late 1985, Robert C. Ellsworth, the president of Sunworth Corporation, called Robert Pribula, the owner of Gateway, located in Minnesota, to see if Gateway would supply Sunworth Packing with seed potatoes. Pribula hesitated to supply the seed potatoes without receiving assurance of payment because Pribula was aware that Ellsworth had previously undergone bankruptcy. Pribula, however, decided to sell the seed potatoes to Sunworth Packing after being assured by Ellsworth that he was in partnership with a large financial institution, G.B. Investment Company, and that G.B. Investment was providing the financing, was actively involved in the operation of the business, and had approved the purchase of the seed potatoes. Thereafter, from February 1986 through April 1986, Gateway sold substantial quantities of seed potatoes to Sunworth Packing.

While supplying the seed potatoes, Pribula believed that he was doing business with a general partnership (i.e., Sunworth Packing Company, formed by Sunworth Corporation and G.B. Investment Company). The sales documents used by the parties specified "Sunworth Packing Company" as the name of the partnership. Pribula was neither aware of the true name of the partnership nor that it was a limited partnership.

All of Gateway's dealings were with Ellsworth. Pribula neither contacted G.B. Investment prior to selling the seed potatoes to the limited partnership nor did he otherwise attempt to verify any of the statements Ellsworth had made about G.B. Investment's involvement. The only direct contact between G.B. Investment and Gateway occurred some time after the sale of the seed potatoes. It is, however, disputed whether G.B. Investment ever provided any assurance of payment to Gateway.

G.B. Investment's vice-president, Darl Anderson, testified in his affidavit that G.B. Investment had exerted no control over the daily management and operation of the limited partnership, Sunworth Packing. This testimony was contradicted, however, by the affidavit testimony of Ellsworth which was presented by Gateway in opposing G.B. Investment's motion for summary judgment. According to Ellsworth, G.B. Investment's employees, Darl Anderson and Thomas McHolm, controlled the day-to-day affairs of the limited partnership and made Ellsworth account to them for nearly everything he did. This day-to-day contact included but was not limited to approval of most of the significant operational decisions and expenditures and the use and management of partnership funds without Ellsworth's involvement.[1]

---

**1.** Ellsworth described with some specificity the ways in which G.B. Investment's control was exerted:

a. During the early months of the Partnership, Thomas McHolm and/or Darl Anderson were at the Partnership's offices on a daily basis directing the operation of the Partnership, and thereafter, they were at the Partnership's offices at least 2–3 times per week reviewing the operations of the business, directing changes in operations, and instructing me to make certain changes in operating the Partnership's affairs;

b. G.B. Investment Company was solely responsible for obtaining a $150,000.00 line-of-credit loan for the Partnership with Valley National Bank of Arizona,

and it also signed documents guaranteeing the repayment of the loan;

c. As the President of the general partner, I was not permitted to make any significant independent business decisions concerning the operations of the Partnership, but was directed to have all business decisions approved with Darl Anderson and/or Thomas McHolm, or was directed to carry out decisions made by Darl Anderson and/or Thomas McHolm. For example, instead of using Partnership funds to pay certain creditors and suppliers, I was directed by Darl Anderson and/or Thomas McHolm to use the Partnership funds to purchase additional machinery and equipment;

Ellsworth testified further that he had described G.B. Investment's control of the business operation to Pribula. Pribula confirmed that Ellsworth had informed him that G.B. Investment's employees, McHolm and Anderson, were at the partnership's office on a frequent basis, that Ellsworth reported directly to them, that daily operations of the partnership were reviewed by representatives of G.B. Investment, and that Ellsworth had to get their approval before making certain business decisions.

d. Prior to constructing improvements to the packaging facilities of the Partnership, Thomas McHolm and/or Darl Anderson had to approve all construction bids, individually selected some of the suppliers and subcontractors, and individually selected the equipment to be installed;

e. Thomas McHolm and/or Darl Anderson dictated the accounting procedures to be followed by the Partnership, reviewed the Partnership's books and accounts almost continually, dictated that the Partnership use the same accounting firm as that of G.B. Investment Company to do the Partnership accounting tasks, undertook the responsibility of having prepared all Partnership tax forms and returns, and I only signed tax returns after they had been prepared by G.B. Investment Company's accountants and reviewed by Darl Anderson or some other employee/agent of G.B. Investment Company;

f. During a great portion of the duration of the Partnership, Thomas McHolm and/or Darl Anderson oversaw the daily operations of the Partnership because I had to have all expenditures approved by Thomas McHolm and/or Darl Anderson and Darl Anderson had to approve and sign checks issued by the Partnership, including without limitation payroll checks and invoices for telephone charges, utilities, publications, interest payments, bank card charges, supplies, etc. Copies of a sampling of the invoices and the corresponding checks are attached hereto as Exhibit 2;

g. After it was decided to add a hydrocooler to the processing and packaging facilities of the Partnership, Thomas McHolm individually selected the refrigeration equipment and chose the contractor to install the refrigeration equipment on the hydrocooler, and even saw to it that G.B. Investment Company (not the Partnership) directly paid the contractor for all of his services;

h. Thomas McHolm insisted that the Partnership use a particular supplier, to-wit: Allied Packaging, to supply packaging materials to the Partnership, he further took an active role in reviewing and modifying the art work for use on the packaging items, and personally approved the bid submitted for the art work;

i. At least on two separate occasions, approximately in August, 1986 and again in November, 1986, Darl Anderson caused sums of monies (approximately $8,000 and $7,000 respectively) to be withdrawn from the Partnership account (No. 2270–8018) with Valley National Bank without the prior knowledge or consent of myself, as the President of the general partner of the Partnership. These monies were paid directly to G.B. Investment, and the withdrawals caused other checks of the Partnership to be dishonored due to insufficient funds and left the Partnership without sufficient funds to meet its payroll obligations;

j. Darl Anderson and/or Thomas McHolm caused certain expenses of the Partnership to be paid directly by G.B. Investment Company, to-wit: refrigeration equipment; and

k. After the Partnership defaulted on its loan payments to Valley National Bank, a loan which had been guaranteed by G.B. Investment Company, Darl Anderson, without my knowledge or consent, instructed the Valley National Bank to proceed with declaring the loan to be in default and to pursue its remedies under its Security Agreement with the Partnership, to-wit: to sell the equipment and machinery that it held as collateral at a foreclosure auction. At the foreclosure auction held on March 3, 1987, by Valley National Bank, Darl Anderson, on behalf of G.B. Investment Company, bought the equipment and machinery previously owned by Sunworth Corporation.

## DISCUSSION

Gateway argues that sufficient questions of fact exist which preclude the granting of summary judgment in favor of G.B. Investment. We will affirm the trial court's grant of summary judgment if there is no genuine issue of material fact in dispute and the moving party is entitled to judgment as a matter of law. *Orme School v. Reeves*, 166 Ariz. 301, 305, 802 P.2d 1000, 1004 (1990).

Subsection (a) of A.R.S. § 29–319 sets forth the general rule that a limited partner who is not also a general partner is not liable for the obligations of the limited partnership.

> [A] limited partner is not liable for the obligations of a limited partnership unless he is also a general partner or, in addition to the exercise of his rights and powers as a limited partner, he takes part in the control of the business. However, if the limited partner's participation in the control of the business is not substantially the same as the exercise of the powers of a general partner, he is liable only to persons who transact business with the limited partnership with actual knowledge of his participation in control.

In responding to the motion for summary judgment, Gateway urged the trial court to find that Gateway had presented a fact question of G.B. Investment's liability to it under A.R.S. § 29–319(a). Gateway argued that the statute imposes liability on a limited partner whose participation in the control of the business is substantially the same as the exercised power of a general partner. Gateway further argued that even if the person transacting business with the limited partnership did not know of the limited partner's participation in control, there is liability. Alternatively, Gateway argued that the statute imposes liability when the powers exercised in controlling the business might fall short of being "substantially the same as the exercise of powers of a general partner," but the person transacting business with the limited partnership had actual knowledge of the participation in control. Gateway asserted that the evidence it was presenting in response to the motion for summary judgment raised issues of material fact as to whether either of these situations had occurred. If either had occurred, Gateway argued, it would be entitled to recover from the limited partner, G.B. Investment.

In granting G.B. Investment's motion for summary judgment, the trial court gave two reasons for concluding that G.B. Investment could not be found liable under A.R.S. § 29–319(a) as a matter of law. First, as we interpret the trial court's comments, it read the statute as having a threshold requirement—that is, under all circumstances, a creditor of the limited partnership must have contact with the limited partner in order to impose liability on the limited partner. The evidence before the trial court showed that Gateway merely relied upon the statements made by Ellsworth, president of the general partner, and that Gateway did not contact G.B. Investment prior to transacting business with the limited partnership. Based upon these facts, the trial court concluded that liability could not be imposed upon G.B. Invest-ment. The trial court's minute entry states, in relevant part:

> [I]t is undisputed that the plaintiff contracted with and sold seed potatoes to the limited partnership, without any direct contact with the movant. In other words, at the time the sale with the limited partnership was consummated and completed—plaintiff can not by the posture of the evidence—be said to have been a person who, while transacting business with the limited partner-ship, did so with actual knowledge of defendant G.B. Investment Company's participation in control with the limited partnership or its general partner.

> Consequently, plaintiff fails to leap the first "hurdle"; and neither the court nor the trier-of-fact need review plaintiff's factual asser-tions regarding "safe harbor" excesses or violations, if any, under A.R.S. § 29–319(B). The only purported contact between plaintiff and defendant G.B. Investment Company occurred in the fall of 1986, well after the last of the seed potatoes were delivered by plaintiff to the limited partnership.

> Notwithstanding the representations made by Robert C. Ellsworth, as the president of the general partner, Sunworth Corporation, regarding the movant, plaintiff admits it never directly contacted the movant, to inquire into or verify Ellsworth's authority to bind the movant by such representations.

> The court finds, given the present record, that movant G.B. Investment has no liability to plaintiff arising from movant being a limited partner in Sunworth Packing Limited Partnership.

After reaching this conclusion, the trial court also found that no specific facts had been presented which would support the application of A.R.S. § 29–319 so as to impose liability on G.B. Investment. As the minute entry states:

> The court further finds that while the statutory protection extend-ed to limited partners is not absolute, there are no specific facts included within the plaintiff's response, supporting statement of facts, and supporting affidavits, which would support the applica-bility of A.R.S. § 29–319(A) so as to impose liability in favor of plaintiff and against the movant G.B. Investment.

To the extent that the trial court's ruling may have been based on a belief that a limited partner could never be liable under the statute unless the creditor had contact with the limited partner and learned directly from him of his participation and control of the business, we believe that ruling to be in error.

In A.R.S. § 29–319(a), the legislature stopped short of expressly stating that if the limited partner's participation in the control of the business is substantially the same as the exercise of the powers of a general partner, he is liable to persons who transact business with a limited partnership even though they have no knowledge of his participation and control. It has made this statement by implication, though, by stating to the opposite effect that "if the limited partner's participation in the control of the business is not substantially the same as the exercise of the powers of a general partner, he is liable only to persons who transact business with the limited partnership with actual knowledge of his participation in control." A.R.S. § 29–319(a).

We believe this interpretation is strengthened by an examination of the legislative history of Arizona's limited partnership statute. It is further strengthened by the legislature's refusal to modify this statute to correspond to the Revised Uniform Limited Partnership Act, as amended in 1985. Prior to 1982, Arizona's limited partnership statute was patterned after the Uniform Limited Partnership Act (ULPA), which was drafted in 1916. Section 7 of the ULPA provided that "[a] limited partner shall not become liable as a general partner unless, in addition to the exercise of his rights and powers as a limited partner, he takes part in the control of the business." Uniform Limited Partnership Act § 7, 6 U.L.A. 559 (1969).[3]

The Revised Uniform Limited Partnership Act (RULPA) was drafted in 1976. Revised Uniform Limited Partnership Act, 6 U.L.A. 239, 240 (Supp.1991). In 1982, the Arizona legislature adopted the RULPA after repealing its enactment of the ULPA. See 1982 Ariz.Sess.Laws, ch. 192, § 1 (effective July 24, 1982). Presently, A.R.S. § 29–319(a), dealing with a limited partner's liability to third parties, is very similar to the 1976 version of section 303(a) of the RULPA which stated:

> Except as provided in subsection (d), a limited partner is not liable for the obligations of a limited partnership unless he is also a general partner or, and in addition to the exercise of his rights and powers as a limited partner, he takes part in the control of the business. However, if the limited partner's participation in the control of the business is not substantially the same as the exercise of the powers of a general partner, he is liable only to persons who transact business with the limited partnership with actual knowledge of his participation in control.

Revised Uniform Limited Partnership Act § 303(a), 6 U.L.A. 239, 325 (Supp.1991). The drafters' comment to section 303 explained that limited partners exercising all of the powers of a general partner would not escape liability by avoiding direct dealings with third parties. The comment stated:

> Section 303 makes several important changes in Section 7 of the prior uniform law. The first sentence of Section 303(a) carries over the basic test from former Section 7 whether the limited partner "takes part in the control of the business" in order to ensure that judicial decisions under the prior uniform law remain applicable to the extent not expressly changed. The second sentence of Section 303(a) reflects a wholly new concept. Because of the difficulty of determining when the "control" line has been

---

**3.** The language of Arizona's then § 29–307 was taken verbatim from section 7 of the ULPA. For the text of Arizona's Uniform Limited Partnership Act, since repealed, see Uniform Limited Partnership Act, 1943 Ariz.Sess.Laws 124, reprinted in A.R.S. §§ 29–301 to–366 app. (1989) (as amended).

overstepped, it was thought it unfair to impose general partner's liability on a limited partner except to the extent that a third party had knowledge of his participation in control of the business. On the other hand, in order to avoid permitting a limited partner to exercise all of the powers of a general partner while avoiding any direct dealings with third parties, the "is not substantially the same as" test was introduced. . . .

Id. at 326 cmt.

In 1985, the drafters of the RULPA backtracked from the position taken in section 303(a) of the 1976 Act. The new amendments reflect a reluctance to hold a limited partner liable if the limited partner had no direct contact with the creditor. The 1985 revised RULPA section 303(a) was amended to provide as follows:

> Except as provided in Subsection (d), a limited partner is not liable for the obligations of a limited partnership unless he is also a general partner or, in addition to the exercise of his rights and powers as a limited partner, he participates in the control of the business. However, if the limited partner participates in the control of the business, he is liable only to persons who transact business with the limited partnership reasonably believing, based upon the limited partner's conduct, that the limited partner is a general partner.

Id. at 325 (emphasis added). The comment to section 303 was also revised to explain the reason for the amendment. The revised comment states:

> Section 303 makes several important changes in Section 7 of the 1916 Act. The first sentence of Section 303(a) differs from the text of Section 7 of the 1916 Act in that it speaks of participating (rather than taking part) in the control of the business; this was done for the sake of consistency with the second sentence of Section 303(a), not to change the meaning of the text. It is intended that judicial decisions interpreting the phrase "takes part in the control of the business" under the prior uniform law will remain applicable to the extent that a different result is not called for by other provisions of Section 303 and other provisions of the Act. The second sentence of Section 303(a) reflects a wholly new concept in the 1976 Act that has been further modified in the 1985 Act. It was adopted partly because of the difficulty of determining when the "control" line has been overstepped, but also (and more importantly) because of a determination that it is not sound public policy to hold a limited partner who is not also a general partner liable for the obligations of the partnership except to persons who have done business with the limited partnership reasonably believing, based on the limited partner's conduct, that he is a general partner. . . .

Id. at 326 cmt. (emphasis added).

The Arizona legislature, however, has not revised A.R.S. § 29–319(a) to correspond to the section 303 amendments. The Arizona statute continues to impose liability on a limited partner whenever the "substantially the same as" test is met, even though the creditor has no knowledge of the limited partner's control. It follows then that no contact between the creditor and the limited partner is required to impose liability.

Moreover, whereas section 303 of the RULPA states that the creditor's reasonable belief must be "based upon the limited partner's conduct," under A.R.S. § 29–319 the only requirement is that the creditor has had "actual knowledge of [the limited partner's] participation in control." The statute does not state that this knowledge must be based upon the limited partner's conduct. The comments to the original version of section 303 of the RULPA, from which Arizona's statute is taken, make it clear that only when the "substantially the same as" test is met is direct contact not a requirement. Conversely, if the "substantially the same as" test is not met, direct contact is required. Under the facts presented in this case, Gateway had no direct contact with G.B. Investment until after the sales were concluded. We conclude, therefore, that G.B. Investment would be liable only if the "substantially the same as" test was met.

Whether a limited partner has exercised the degree of control that will make him liable to a creditor has always been a factual question. This is so regardless of whether the particular statute involved is patterned after section 7 of the ULPA or after section 303 of the RULPA. E.g., Alzado v. Blinder, Robinson & Co., 752 P.2d 544 (Colo. 1988); Gast v. Petsinger, 228 Pa.Super. 394, 323 A.2d 371 (1974); Holzman v. DeEscamilla, 86 Cal.App.2d 858, 195 P.2d 833 (1948). Our current Arizona statute lists activities that a limited partner may undertake without participating in controlling the business. It also states that other activities may be excluded from the definition of such control. Where activities do not fall within the "safe harbor" of A.R.S. § 29–319(b), it is necessary for a trier-of-fact to determine whether such activities amount to "control." In the absence of actual knowledge of the limited partner's participation in the control of the partnership business, there must be evidence from which a trier-of-fact might find not only control, but control that is "substantially the same as the exercise of powers of a general partner."

We conclude that the evidence Gateway presented in this case should have allowed it to withstand summary judgment. The affidavit testimony of Ellsworth raises the issue whether he was merely a puppet for the limited partner, G.B. Investment. While a few of the activities Ellsworth listed may have fallen within the protected areas listed in A.R.S. § 29–319(b), others did not. Ellsworth's detailed statement raises substantial issues of material facts.

Viewing the facts in the light most favorable to Gateway, we cannot say as a matter of law that G.B. Investment was entitled to summary judgment. We conclude that Gateway is entitled to a determination by trial of the extent of control exercised by G.B. Investment over Sunworth Packing.

For the foregoing reasons, we reverse the judgment of the trial court and remand for further proceedings.

■ EHRLICH, P.J., and CLABORNE, J., concur.

————

## (d) CORPORATE GENERAL PARTNERS

————

### NOTE ON CORPORATE GENERAL PARTNERS

It seems likely that the plaintiff in *Gateway* sued the limited partner, rather than the general partner, because the sole general partner was a corporation with limited assets. Ordinarily, shareholders are not liable for their corporation's debts. Therefore, if both Gateway and the corporate general partner had insufficient assets to pay the debt to the plaintiff, the plaintiff would have been unable to collect on Gateway's debt unless the limited partner was liable.

RULPA §§ 303(b)(1) and 402(9) explicitly recognize that a corporation can be a general partner in a limited partnership. In addition, RULPA § 303(b) provides that "[a] limited partner does not participate in the control of the business . . . by . . . being an officer, director, or shareholder of a general partner that is a corporation. . . ."

Although a director or officer of a corporate general partner is not liable for the debts of a limited partnership merely because he participates in the control of the partnership's business in that capacity, he may become liable if the corporate officers fail to maintain their corporate-officer identity in conducting partnership affairs, or if corporate assets are intermingled with partnership assets, or if the corporation is not sufficiently capitalized. See Mursor Buildings, Inc. v. Crown Mountain Apartment Associates, 467 F.Supp. 1316 (D.Vi. 1978); Western Camps, Inc. v. Riverway Ranch Enterprises, 70 Cal.App.3d 714, 138 Cal.Rptr. 918 (1977). See generally Chapter 4, Section 6.

In Gonzalez v. Chalpin, 77 N.Y.2d 74, 564 N.Y.S.2d 702, 565 N.E.2d 1253 (1990), decided under the ULPA (the predecessor of RULPA), the court held that if a limited partner, who is also an officer and sole owner of the corporate general partner, takes part in the control of the limited partnership's business, she has the burden of proving "that any relevant actions taken were performed solely in the capacity as officer of the general partner." It is doubtful that this approach would be followed under RULPA.

————

As of 1996, there were 311,600 limited partnerships in the United States, with an average of 32 partners in each partnership. Alan Zempel, Partnership Returns, 1996, 18 Statistics of Income Bulletin No. 2, at 49–50 (1998).

————

## NOTE ON THE TAXATION OF UNINCORPORATED BUSINESS ORGANIZATIONS

Taxation is a major issue in the choice of business form. There are two basic patterns of business taxation under the Internal Revenue Code, which may be called firm taxation and flow-through taxation.

Under *firm taxation*, a business firm is taxable on its income. Accordingly, if the firm has income or expenses, or gains or losses, those items go into the firm's taxable income, not into the owners' taxable income. If the firm then makes distributions to its owners out of after-tax income, the owners ordinarily pay taxes on those distributions. This is sometimes referred to as "double taxation."

Under *flow-through* taxation, a firm is not subject to taxation. Instead, all of the firm's income and expenses, and gains and losses, are taxable directly to the firm's owners. Distributions are not taxed. There is no "double taxation" effect. If the firm has losses, the owners can utilize the losses to offset their income from other sources.

Whether firm taxation or flow-through taxation is preferable for the owners of an enterprise depends in any given case on corporate and individual tax rates, the owners' circumstances, and other variables. Generally speaking, under present tax rates, owners of an enterprise will ordinarily regard flow-through taxation as preferable to firm taxation.

Historically, a firm-taxation pattern applied more or less automatically to corporations, and a flow-through taxation pattern applied more or less automatically to partnerships. Until recently, however, it was often less clear which type of taxation would be applied to forms of business organization that are intermediate between general partnerships and corporations—forms such as the limited partnership.

This issue has now been resolved by the IRS's "check-the-box" Regulations. Under these Regulations, any domestic unincorporated business that constitutes an "eligible entity" can elect either flow-through taxation or firm (corporate) taxation. If an eligible entity has two or more owners, it will be taxed as a partnership—that is, it will be taxed under the partnership provisions of the Internal Revenue Code. If an eligible entity has only one owner, the entity will be disregarded for tax purposes—that is, all of the entity's income and expenses and gains and losses will be attributed to the owner.

Generally speaking, an eligible entity is any business entity other than a corporation or a business entity that is specifically made taxable as corporation under the Internal Revenue Code. The most important entity in the latter category is the *master limited partnership*. Essentially, a master limited partnership is a limited partnership whose limited-partnership interests are publicly traded—that is, traded on an established securities market, or readily tradeable on a secondary market. With certain exceptions, under the Internal Revenue Code publicly traded limited partnerships are taxed as corporations, and cannot elect partnership taxation.

There is another important respect in which the tax comparison of the traditional forms has been blurred. Just as publicly traded limited partnerships are now normally taxed like corporations, so the Internal Revenue Code provides a route through which partnership-tax treatment can be achieved by certain corporate enterprises. Subchapter S of the Code (I.R.C. §§ 1361–1379) permits the owners of qualifying corporations to elect a special tax status under which the corporation and its shareholders receive flow-though taxation that is comparable (although not identical) to partnership taxation, The taxable income of an S corporation is computed essentially as if the corporation were an individual. With some exceptions, items of income, loss, deduction, and credit, are passed through to the shareholders on a pro rata basis, and added to or subtracted from each shareholder's gross income.

Among the conditions for making and maintaining a Subchapter S election are the following: (1) The corporation may not have more than seventy-five shareholders. (2) The corporation may not have more than one class of stock. (3) All the shareholders must be individuals or qualified estates or trusts. (4) No shareholder may be a nonresident alien. The amount of the corporation's assets and income is immaterial under Subchapter S.

As of 1995, there were 4,474,000 corporations in the United States. Almost half—2,153,000—were S corporations. United States Bureau of the Census, Statistical Abstract of the United States (1998).

## SECTION 2.   LIMITED LIABILITY COMPANIES

### UNIFORM LIMITED LIABILITY COMPANY ACT §§ 101, 103, 201–203, 301–303, 404, 405, 408, 409

[See Statutory Supplement]

### DELAWARE LIMITED LIABILITY COMPANY ACT §§ 18–101, 18–107, 18–201, 18–206, 18–301, 18–303, 18–401, 18–402, 18–504

[See Statutory Supplement]

### NOTE ON LIMITED LIABILITY COMPANIES

Limited liability companies (LLCs) are noncorporate entities that are created under special statutes that combine elements of corporation and partnership law. As under corporation law, the owners (*members*) of LLCs have limited liability. As under partnership law, an

LLC has great freedom to structure its internal governance by agreement. Like a corporation, an LLC is an entity, so that it can, for example, hold property and sue and be sued in its own name. LLCs come in two flavors: member-managed LLCs, which are managed by their members, and manager-managed LLCs, which are managed by managers who may or may not be members.

The LLC is a relatively new form. As a result, the LLC statutes are still evolving and the case law is still sparse.

Moreover, unlike the limited partnership statutes of the various states, which tend to follow RULPA, the LLC statutes are highly variable. Part (although not all) of the reason for this variability is explained by tax issues. At the time LLCs first evolved, alternative forms of business organization (that is, alternative to general partnerships and corporations) were not automatically entitled to the benefits of partnership taxation. Instead, whether any given firm that was cast in an alternative unincorporated form, such as an LLC, qualified for partnership taxation, depended on whether or not the firm had a certain number of characteristics that were deemed by the Internal Revenue Service to be "critical corporate characteristics," such as continuity of life and transferability of ownership interests.

The original LLC statutes were partly shaped by this tax rule. Some of the statutes were highly flexible, and allowed each LLC to choose its own characteristics. Other statutes, however, made certain LLC characteristics mandatory, in an effort to ensure that LLCs created under the statute would be bulletproof against an attack based on the IRS's characteristic-counting test.

Under the new, check-the-box approach to the taxation of alternative forms of business organization, no special purpose is served by making a statute bulletproof, rather than flexible. It is therefore to be expected that bulletproof LLC statutes will converge with flexible LLC statutes.

This Note will describe the central characteristics of LLCs in terms of prevailing statutory patterns. Bear in mind that as to any given characteristic there will usually be some LLC statutes that fall outside the major patterns this Note describes.

1. *Formation; Articles of Organization; Powers.* An LLC is formed by filing articles of organization in a designated state office— usually, the office of the Secretary of State. (Some statutes use the term *certificate of organization* rather than the term *articles of organization.*) Most statutes allow LLCs to be formed by a single person. The articles must include the name of the LLC, the address of its principal place of business or registered office in the State, and the name and address of its agent for service of process. Many or most statutes also require the articles to state: (1) The purpose of the LLC. (2) If the LLC is to be manager-managed, the names of the initial managers. If the LLC is to be member-managed, the names of its initial members. (3) The duration of the LLC or the latest date on which it is to dissolve. Many statutes also require the articles to include various

kinds of additional information, the nature of which varies considerably.

Most statutes either (i) provide that LLCs have all powers necessary to effectuate their purposes or (ii) contain an exhaustive laundry list of an LLC's powers.

2. *Operating Agreements.* An LLC's articles of organization are usually very sketchy. In most LLCs, the critical foundational instrument document is the *operating agreement.* This is an agreement among the members concerning the LLC's affairs. (Some statutes use the term *limited liability agreement* rather than the term *operating agreement.*) The operating agreement typically provides for the governance of the LLC, its capitalization, the admission and withdrawal of members, and distributions. The statutes vary on whether an operating agreement must be in writing.

3. *Management.* Almost all of the LLC statutes provide as a default rule, which prevails unless agreed otherwise, that an LLC is to be managed by its members. A few statutes provide as a default rule that an LLC is to be managed by managers—who may but need not be members—unless otherwise agreed. Most of the statutes provide that the statutory default rule can be varied only by a provision in the LLC's articles of organization, but some provide that the statutory default rule can be varied in the operating agreement. One way to vary the statutory rule is to completely reverse it—either by providing for manager management in a state where the default rule is member management, or by providing for member management in a state where the default rule is manager management. Another way to vary the statutory default rule is to distribute management functions between members and managers.

4. *Voting by Members.* About half the statutes provide as a default rule that members vote per capita—that is, one vote per member—unless otherwise agreed. This is like the partnership default rule. About half provide that members vote pro rata, that is, by financial interest, unless otherwise agreed. This is the usual rule in corporations. Normally, members act by a majority vote, per capita or pro rata as the case may be. However, some of the statutes require a unanimous vote for certain designated actions.

5. *Agency Powers.*

a. *Member-managed LLCs.* Under a majority of the statutes, the apparent authority of a member of a member-managed LLC is comparable to the apparent authority of a partner—that is, each member has power to bind the LLC for any act that is for apparently carrying on the business of the LLC in the usual or ordinary way. Even if an action is not in the usual or ordinary way, the remaining members may confer on a given member actual authority to bind the LLC to an action or a type of action. Conversely, the remaining members may withdraw the actual authority of a member to take a certain kind of action that is in the ordinary or usual way. In that case, if the member takes such an action the LLC will be bound by virtue of the member's apparent authority, but the member may be obliged to indemnify the LLC for any loss that results from her contravention of the other members' decision.

b. *Manager-managed LLCs*. In manager-managed firms, the rules concerning authority are comparable to those in the corporations— that is, typically only the managers have apparent authority to bind the firm. Members of a manager-managed LLC have no apparent authority to bind the LLC, just as shareholders have no apparent authority to bind a corporation. Most of the statutes provide that a manager in a manager-managed LLC has partner-like apparent authority.

6. *Inspection of Books and Records*. The statutes generally provide that members are entitled to access to the LLC's books and records or to specified books and records. Some statutes include an explicit provision that the inspection must be for a proper purpose. Such a limitation might or might not be read into other statutes.

7. *Fiduciary Duties*. The fiduciary duties of managers and members of LLCs are largely unspecified by the LLC statutes, just as the fiduciary duties of directors, officers, and shareholders are largely unspecified by the corporate statutes. Presumably, the courts in deciding LLC cases involving fiduciary duties will borrow very heavily from the corporate and partnership case-law.

Despite the lack of extensive specification, the LLC statutes, like the corporate and partnership statutes, do include important provisions concerning particular issues of fiduciary duty. For example, most although not all of the statutes specify the elements of the duty of care. (Some statutes provide that a manager will be liable only for gross negligence, bad faith, recklessness, or equivalent conduct. Others require a manager to act as would a prudent person in similar circumstances.) Many of the LLC statutes, like most corporate statutes, also provide mechanisms for the authorization of self-interested transactions.

The most striking divergence between the LLC statutes and the corporate and partnership statutes is that some of the LLC statutes, at least on their face, permit the operating agreement to waive all fiduciary duties. There is support in both corporate law and partnership law for giving effect to the informed approval of specific self-interested transactions by the disinterested shareholders or partners. There is also support in corporate and partnership law for giving effect to contractual rules that allow a fiduciary to engage in specific types of conduct that would constitute a breach of the duty of loyalty in the absence of the rule. An example is a rule that allows the fiduciary to take certain kinds of corporate opportunities. In general, however, corporate law and partnership law do not permit an advance waiver of the entire duty of loyalty. How the courts will respond to waivers of the duty of loyalty in the LLC context—if any such waivers are actually adopted—remains to be seen.

Some of the statutes specifically provide that in a manager-managed LLC a member who is not also a manager owes no duties to the LLC or the other members solely by reason of being a member.

8. *Derivative Actions*. Most of the statutes explicitly permit members of LLCs to bring derivative actions on the LLC's behalf based on a breach of fiduciary duties. Even where the statute does not explicitly permit such actions, courts are highly likely to permit them, on analogy to corporation and limited-partnership law, and because a failure to do so might allow fiduciaries who were in control of an LLC to violate their fiduciary duties without any sanction.

9. *Distributions*. Most LLC statutes provide that in the absence of an agreement to the contrary, distributions to members are to be made pro rata according to the members' contributions, on analogy to corporation law, rather than per capita (the default rule in partnership law). Some of the statutes, however, provide that in the absence of agreement, distributions are to be on a per capita basis.

10. *Members' Interests*. A member of an LLC has financial rights, and may also have governance rights as a member—that is, apart from any governance rights she may have as a manager in a manager-managed LLC. A member's *financial* rights include her right to receive distributions. A member's governance rights include her right, if any, to participate in management, to vote on certain issues, and to be supplied with information. Some but not all statutes provide a list of actions that require member approval, at least in the absence of a contrary provision in the organic documents.

Most statutes define a member's *interest* in an LLC to consist of the member's financial rights. A few define a member's interest to include her governance rights.

Generally speaking, a member of an LLC can freely transfer her financial rights by transferring her interest in the LLC. Governance rights are treated differently. A number of statutes provide that a member can transfer her governance rights only with the unanimous consent of the other members. Some statutes provide that in the absence of an agreement to the contrary, a member can transfer her governance rights with the approval of a majority of the other members, or a majority of other members' financial interests, depending on the statute. Some statutes provide that a member can transfer governance rights, even without the unanimous or majority consent of the other members, if the articles of organization or operating agreement so provides.

It is clear that a member who assigns her interest normally cannot *assign* her governance rights, but it is not always clear whether an assigning member *retains* her governance rights. Some statutes provide that a member who assigns her membership interest loses her membership status. Some statutes provide that a member who assigns her membership interest loses her membership status if and when the assignee becomes a member. Some statutes provide that if a member assigns her membership interest, the remaining members can remove the assignor as a member. Some statutes don't speak to the issue.

If a member of an LLC assigns her interest in the LLC as a *pledge* to secure a debt, rather than in an outright sale, and if the creditor gets a judgment against the member, the creditor can get a charging order against the member's interest. A charging order gives the creditor the right to the member's share of any distributions.

11.   *Liability.* All of the LLC statutes provide that the members and managers of an LLC are not liable for the LLC's debts, obligations, and other liabilities. It is highly likely that the courts will develop a form of piercing-the-veil doctrine applicable to LLCs. See Hollowell v. Orleans Regional Hospital, infra.

12.   *Disassociation.* The LLC statutes vary considerably in their treatment of disassociation, that is, the termination of a member's interest in an LLC other than by the member's voluntary transfer of her interest. The statutes typically provide that the death, bankruptcy, or lawful expulsion of a member results in her disassociation. A number of statutes provide that a member either has (i) the right to withdraw (or "resign") at any time; (ii) the power although not necessarily the right to withdraw at any time; or (iii) the right to withdraw at any time unless otherwise provided in the operating agreement. However, a majority of the statutes do not explicitly provide a right or power to dissociate, although in some cases the right or power might be inferred from other statutory provisions.

———

As of 1996, there were 221,000 LLCs in the United States, with an average of 4 members in each LLC. The number of LLCs is growing rapidly. There were 17,000 LLCs in 1993, 48,000 LLCs in 1994, and 119,000 LLCs in 1995. Alan Zempel, Partnership Returns, 1996, 18 Statistics of Income Bulletin No. 2, at 49–50 (1998).

———

## Hollowell v. Orleans Regional Hospital

United States District Court, E.D. Louisiana 1998.
1998 WL 283298 (E.D.La.).

■ LEMMON, J. . . . .

### I.   BACKGROUND

#### A.   PROCEDURAL

Plaintiffs Lisa Hollowell, Terrence Pierce and Emma Chess filed this class action suit on behalf of themselves and others similarly situated against defendants Orleans Regional Hospital ("ORH"), Success Counseling Services, North Louisiana Regional Hospital ("NLRH"), Magnolia Health Systems ("MHS"), Precision Incorporated

Systems ("Precision"), ... New Orleans Rehabilitation Services ("NORS"), North Louisiana Regional Hospital Partnership ("NLRHP"), William C. Windham, John Turner, [and] Richard Williams.... Plaintiffs allege that they were laid off by the defendants without proper notice in violation of the provisions of the Worker Adjustment and Retraining Notification ("WARN") Act, 29 U.S.C. §§ 2101 to 2109.... United States District Judge Marcel Livaudais certified this case as a class action before transferring this case to this division.

Defendants filed a Motion for Summary Judgment and plaintiffs filed a Cross-Motion for Partial Summary Judgment....

## B.  FACTUAL

Plaintiffs allege the following facts. ORH was a Medicaid funded hospital in New Orleans which provided psychiatric and substance abuse treatment for children and adolescents. ORH was a limited liability company under Louisiana law whose members were NLRH, Precision, and NORS. ORH was operated by NLRHP, a partnership under Louisiana law consisting of NLRH and Precision. William Windham and John Turner were each fifty percent shareholders of NLRH and Richard Williams was the sole shareholder of Precision. MHS, another limited liability company under Louisiana law whose members consisted of NLRH and Precision, served as a management company for NLRH and ORH.

As Louisiana began implementing regulatory changes in its Medicaid reimbursement policies, ORH made several changes to its operating procedures, including providing outpatient services. These services were provided by Success Counseling Services, who "employed" a number of ORH employees. As regulatory changes began to affect admission and length of stay regulations in psychiatric hospitals, the patient census at ORH began to drop and consequently, ORH began discharging employees. Ultimately, ORH shut down its operations on November 3, 1995....

## II.  CROSS–MOTIONS FOR SUMMARY JUDGMENT

The WARN Act consists of Sections 2101 to 2109 of Title 29 of the United States Code. Section 2101(a) requires an "employer" to serve written notice to "employees" who suffer an "employment loss" as a result of a "plant closing" or "mass layoff" at least sixty-days prior to the "plant closing" or "mass layoff." In their Motion for Summary Judgment and in opposition to plaintiffs' Motion for Partial Summary Judgment, defendants argue that ... defendants Turner, Williams, Windham, as individuals, are not "employers" as that term is defined in Section 2101; that ORH is not an "employer" as that term is defined in Section 2101; [and] that all of the defendants did not constitute a "single business enterprise" within the meaning of the WARN Act.... In support of their Motion for Partial Summary Judgment and in opposition to defendants' Motion for Summary Judgment, plaintiffs argue that ... all of the defendants constitute a "single business enterprise"; and that defendants Turner, Williams, and Windham are directly liable in their individual capacities as "employers" as that term is defined in Section 2101, and are indirectly liable for ORH's WARN Act violations.

[The court held that an individual may not be held directly liable for WARN Act violations.]

Under Louisiana law, [however,] an individual may be held liable for the debts of a corporation under certain circumstances. Thus, while the WARN Act may not provide direct liability for individuals, under Louisiana law an individual may be held liable for damages sustained as a result of a corporation's unlawful acts, if the business entity is merely an "alter ego" of the individual. In United States v. Clinical Leasing Service, Inc. 982 F.2d 900 (5th Cir.1992), the Fifth Circuit noted that Louisiana courts focus on the following five elements in deciding whether in fact a corporation is merely an "alter ego" of an individual:

(1) commingling of corporate and shareholder funds;

(2) failure to follow statutory formalities for incorporation and the transaction of corporate affairs;

(3) undercapitalization of the corporation;

(4) failure to provide separate bank accounts and bookkeeping records; and

(5) failure to hold regular shareholder or director meetings.

Clinical Leasing Servs., 982 F.2d at 902.[11] In this manner, Louisiana law permits plaintiffs to hold individuals liable for the debts of a corporation. See generally Glenn G. Morris, Piercing the Corporate Veil in Louisiana, 52 LA.L.REV. 271 (1991). Louisiana law also permits plaintiffs to hold individual shareholders of a corporation liable for the debts of a corporation where the individuals act through the corporation to "commit fraud or deceit on a third party." McDonough Marine Servs. v. Doucet, 694 So.2d 305, 308 (La.Ct.App. 1st Cir.1996).

ORH is a limited liability company rather than a corporation. No case has yet explicitly held that the "veil" of protection from liability afforded by the limited liability company form of business in Louisiana may be "pierced" in the same manner as the "veil" of protection afforded Louisiana corporations. However, commentators throughout the nation appear to agree that the limited liability company "veil" may be "pierced" in the same manner as the corporate "veil."[8] More specifically, several commentators appear to assume that indeed a

---

**11.** Clinical Leasing Services did not involve a WARN Act claim.

**8.** See, e.g., See Karin Schwindt, Comment, Limited Liability Companies: Issues in Member Liability, 44 UCLA L. REV. 1541 (1997); Robert B. Thompson, The Limits of Liability in the New Limited Liability Entities, 32 WAKE FOREST L.REV. 1 (1997); Rachel Maizes, Limited Liability Companies: A Critique, 70 ST. JOHN'S L.REV. 575 (1996); Eric Fox, Note, Piercing the Veil of Limited Liability Companies, 62 GEO. WASH. L.REV. 1143 (1994); Wayne M. Gazur & Neil M. Goff, Assessing the Limited Liability Company, 41 CASE W. RES. L.REV. 387, 403 (1991); Robert R. Keatinge, et al. The Limited Liability Company: A Study of the Emerging Entity, 47 BUS. LAW. 375, 445 (1992); Curtis J. Braukmann, Comment, Limited Liability Companies, 39 KAN. L.REV. 967, 992 (1991).

Louisiana limited liability company's "veil" may be pierced.[9] As Professor Kalinka notes in her Louisiana Civil Law Treatise on Louisiana Limited Liability Companies and Partnerships, "[t]he same policy considerations in piercing the veil of a corporation apply to an LLC." Susan Kalinka, Louisiana Liability Companies & Partnerships: a Guide to Business and Tax Planning § 1.32, at 64 (1997), in 9 Louisiana Civil Law Treatise (1997). However, Professor Kalinka cautions that the analyses between corporate veil piercing and limited liability company veil piercing may not completely overlap, noting that "[b]ecause the Louisiana LLC law requires fewer formalities such as annual elections of directors, keeping minutes, or holding meetings, failure to follow these formalities should not serve as grounds for piercing the veil of an LLC." Id.

With this caveat in mind, this court holds that under Louisiana law the "veil" of protection afforded ORH by its Limited Liability Company form may be "pierced" if in fact ORH was operating as the "alter ego" of ORH's members or if ORH's members were committing fraud or deceit on third parties through ORH. Moreover, the veil provided by the corporate status of ORH's members may also be pierced in like fashion. These questions necessarily involve a fact-intensive review of the relationships among all of the members of ORH in order to make a determination of whether ORH was the "alter ego" of its members or, alternatively, whether ORH's members were using ORH to commit fraud. Accordingly, the court declines to grant summary judgment to any of the defendants, or in favor of the plaintiffs, on the plaintiffs' "veil piercing" claims.

## F.   "SINGLE BUSINESS ENTERPRISE"

In addition to holding the ORH's codefendants, including the individual defendants and ORH's members, liable for ORH's debts by "piercing" ORH's and/or its members' "veils," ORH's codefendants, but not the individual defendants, may be held directly liable for violating the WARN Act if they, along with ORH, are considered to be a single "business enterprise" within the meaning of the WARN Act. Section 639.3(a)(2) of Title 20 of the Code of Federal Regulations sets forth the factors to be considered in deciding whether to treat subsidiaries and parent companies as a single "business enterprise" under Section 2101(a)(1):

> Under existing legal rules, independent contractors and subsidiaries which are wholly or partially owned by a parent company are treated as separate employers or as part of the parent or

---

**9.** See J. William Callison & Maureen A. Sullivan, Limited Liability Companies: a State-by-state Guide to Law & Practice at § 15.28 (1996 & Supp.1997) ("[T]o the extent that the corporate law concept of 'piercing the corporate veil' applies to Louisiana LLCs, members can be liable to creditors who are able to pierce the corporate-type protection afforded by the LLC. Courts might pierce the LLC form and hold members personally lia-ble if respect for the LLC form would work injustice."); Susan Kalinka, The Louisiana Limited Liability Company After the "Check–The–Box", 57 LA. L.REV. 715, 794 (1997) ("a court may use a veil-piercing theory to hold members of an LLC liable for the LLC's obligations, especially if the LLC is thinly capitalized or under-insured. The limitations on a member's liability under the Louisiana LLC Law should be retained.").

contracting company depending upon the degree of their independence from the parent. Some of the factors to be considered in making this determination are (i) common ownership, (ii) common directors and/or officers, (iii) de facto exercise of control, (iv) unity of personnel policies emanating from a common source, and (v) the dependency of operations.

The Department of Labor has expounded on this regulation by stating:

> Several commenters raised questions about the definition of "[i]ndependent contractors and subsidiaries" in § 639.3(a)(2). Some of these commenters suggested that the definition should be simplified to treat subsidiaries as separate employers as long as they are "bona fide separate and distinct companies and hold themselves out to the public as such"; or to define as separate companies entities that have separate payroll functions. One commenter requested special treatment for the garment industry because of the peculiar relationship of jobbers and contractors within that industry. Another commenter suggested that the regulation also should recognize the doctrine of joint employer status, as that doctrine has been developed under the NLRA. A commenter suggested that the National Mediation Board should be recognized as the authority for determining whether companies covered by the Railway Labor Act (RLA) are separate. Another commenter stated that the rule on subsidiaries also should apply to operating divisions.

> The intent of the regulatory provision relating to independent contractors and subsidiaries is not to create a special definition of these terms for WARN purposes; the definition is intended only to summarize existing law that has developed under State Corporations laws and such statutes as the NLRA, the Fair Labor Standards Act (FLSA) and the Employee Retirement Income Security Act (ERISA). The Department does not believe that there is any reason to attempt to create new law in this area especially for WARN purposes when relevant concepts of State and federal law adequately cover the issue. Thus, no change has been made in the definition. Similarly, the regulation is not intended to foreclose any application of existing law or to identify the source of legal authority for making determinations of whether related entities are separate. To the extent that existing law recognizes the joint employer doctrine or the special situation of the garment industry, nothing in the regulation prevents application of that law. Nor does the regulation preclude recognition of the National Mediation Board as an authoritative decision maker for entities covered under the RLA. Neither does the regulation preclude treatment of operating divisions as separate entities if such divisions could be so defined under existing law.

54 Fed.Reg. 16045 (April 10, 1989) (alteration in original).

In determining whether several entities should be treated as a "single business enterprise" for purposes of WARN Act liability, courts have looked to state corporate law, other federal labor laws, and the above quoted regulations. See United Paperworkers v. Alden Corrugated Container, 901 F.Supp. 426, 437 (D.Mass.1995) (discussing the caselaw). Thus, the determination whether several entities are to be treated as a "single business enterprise" for purposes of WARN Act liability overlaps, in no small degree, the factors to be considered in determining whether ORH's "veil" may be "pierced." Therefore, for the same reasons that summary judgment is inappropriate on plaintiffs' "veil piercing" claims, summary judgment is also inappropriate on plaintiffs' WARN Act claims against the non-ORH defendants....

... Accordingly, the following issues remain for trial:

(1) Plaintiffs' damages;

(2) Whether any or all the non-ORH defendants,[10] excluding the individual defendants, and ORH operated a "single business enterprise" in light of the following factors:

(a) common ownership;

(b) common directors and/or officers;

(c) de facto exercise of control;

(d) unity of personnel policies emanating from a common source; and

(e) the dependency of operations.

(3) Whether ORH was the "alter ego" of any or all of the non-ORH defendants, including the individual defendants, and whether the members of ORH were the "alter egos" of their shareholders, in light of the following factors:

(a) commingling of funds;

(b) failure to follow statutory formalities for formation and the transaction affairs;

(c) undercapitalization;

(d) failure to provide separate bank accounts and book-keeping records; and

(e) failure to hold regular required meetings.

(4) Whether ORH's members acted through ORH to commit fraud or deceit, and whether the shareholders of ORH's members acted in similar fashion....

———

## McConnell v. Hunt Sports Enterprises

Court of Appeals of Ohio, 1999.
132 Ohio App.3d 657, 725 N.E.2d 1193.

On June 17, 1997, John H. McConnell and Wolfe Enterprises, Inc. filed a complaint for declaratory judgment in the Franklin County

---

**10.** The "non-ORH defendants" are Success Counseling Services, NLRH, MHS, Precision, NLRHP, William C. Windham, John Turner, and Richard Williams.

Court of Common Pleas against Hunt Sports Enterprises, Hunt Sports Enterprises, L.L.C., Hunt Sports Group, L.L.C. ("Hunt Sports Group") and Columbus Hockey Limited ("CHL"). CHL was a limited liability company formed under R.C. Chapter 1705. A brief background of the events leading up to the formation of CHL and the subsequent discord among certain of its members follows.

In 1996, the National Hockey League ("NHL") determined it would be accepting applications for new hockey franchises. In April 1996, Gregory S. Lashutka, the mayor of Columbus, received a phone call from an NHL representative inquiring as to Columbus's interest in a hockey team. As a result, Mayor Lashutka asked certain community leaders who had been involved in exploring professional sports in Columbus to pursue the possibility of applying for an NHL hockey franchise. Two of these persons were Ronald A. Pizzuti and McConnell.

Pizzuti began efforts to recruit investors in a possible franchise. Pizzuti approached Lamar Hunt, principal of Hunt Sports Group, as to Hunt's interest in investing in such a franchise for Columbus. Hunt was already the operating member of the Columbus Crew, a professional soccer team whose investors included Hunt Sports Group, Pizzuti, McConnell, and Wolfe Enterprises, Inc. Hunt expressed an interest in participating in a possible franchise. The deadline for applying for an NHL expansion franchise was November 1, 1996.

On October 31, 1996, CHL was formed when its articles of organization were filed with the secretary of state pursuant to R.C. 1705.04. The members of CHL were McConnell, Wolfe Enterprises, Inc., Hunt Sports Group, Pizzuti Sports Limited, and Buckeye Hockey, L.L.C.[1] Each member made an initial capital contribution of $25,000. CHL was subject to an operating agreement that set forth the terms between the members. Pursuant to section 2.1 of CHL's operating agreement, the general character of the business of CHL was to invest in and operate a franchise in the NHL.

On or about November 1, 1996, an application was filed with the NHL on behalf of the city of Columbus. In the application, the ownership group was identified as CHL, and the individuals in such group were listed as Pizzuti Sports Limited, McConnell, Wolfe Enterprises, Inc. and Hunt Sports Group. A $100,000 check from CHL was included as the application fee. Also included within the application package was Columbus's plan for an arena to house the hockey games. There was no facility at the time, and the proposal was to build a facility that would be financed, in large part, by a three-year countywide one-half percent sales tax. The sales tax issue would be on the May 1997 ballot.

---

[1]. In its answer and counterclaim, Hunt Sports Group averred that Ameritech was also a member of CHL. Ameritech's name does not appear on Schedule A of the operating agreement; however, the record re-flects that Ameritech contributed $25,000 to CHL and was considered a member of CHL. Ameritech's membership status is not an issue in this appeal.

On May 6, 1997, the sales tax issue failed. The day after, Mayor Lashutka met with Hunt, and other opportunities were discussed. The mayor also spoke with Gary Bettman, commissioner of the NHL, and they discussed whether an alternate plan for an arena was possible. Also on May 7, 1997, Dimon McPherson, chairman and chief executive officer of Nationwide Insurance Enterprise ("Nationwide"), met with Hunt, and they discussed the possibility of building the arena despite the failure of the sales tax issue. McPherson testified that he chose Hunt because: "[w]ell, he was the visible, obvious, only person that was involved in trying to bring NHL hockey to Columbus. There was really no one else to turn to." Hunt was interested, and Nationwide began working on an arena plan. On or about May 9, 1997, the mayor spoke with Bettman and let him know that alternate plans would be pursued, and Mr. Bettman gave Columbus until June 4, 1997 to come up with a plan.

By May 28, 1997, Nationwide had come up with a plan to finance an arena privately and on such date, Nationwide representatives met with representatives of Hunt Sports Group. Hunt Sports Group did not accept Nationwide's lease proposal. McPherson told Hunt that City Council would be meeting on Monday, June 2, 1997 to vote on an ordinance that, in general terms, included an authorization for the city to enter into an agreement with Nationwide to build a downtown arena. Nationwide informed Hunt Sports Group that it needed an answer by Friday, May 30, 1997 as to whether, in general terms, the lease proposal was acceptable. On May 29, 1997, Nationwide representatives again met with representatives of Hunt Sports Group. Again, Hunt Sports Group indicated that the lease proposal was unacceptable and that the NHL team would lose millions with this proposal. The June 4, 1997 NHL deadline was discussed. Hunt Sports Group stated that it would continue to evaluate the proposal, and it wanted the weekend to do so. Nationwide informed appellant that it needed an answer by close of business Friday, May 30.

On May 30, 1997, McPherson called McConnell and requested that they meet and discuss "where [they] were on the arena." McPherson "could see that the situation now was slipping away, and [he] just didn't want that to happen," so he went to see McConnell for advice and counsel. McConnell testified that the conversation was "totally out of the blue. [McPherson] said that Nationwide was going to finance and build an arena, and that he had offered the Hunt group the opportunity to pick up the lease and bring a franchise in. That was news to me. It was out of the blue." McPherson told McConnell about appellant's rejection of the lease proposal and discussed the NHL's June 4 deadline. McConnell stated that if Hunt would not step up and lease the arena and, therefore, get the franchise, McConnell would. Hunt Sports Group did not contact Nationwide on May 30, 1997.

On Saturday, May 31, McPherson told Nationwide's board of directors that there was not yet a lease commitment but that if Hunt Sports Group did not lease the arena, McConnell would. On Monday, June 2, 1997, City Council passed the resolution that set forth the terms for Nationwide to build an arena downtown. Also on June 2, 1997, McPherson met with Bettman and told him that Nationwide would be building an arena in downtown Columbus. McPherson also told Bettman that if need be, McConnell would purchase the franchise on his own. On or about Tuesday, June 3, McConnell was informed that appellant [Hunt] had not yet accepted the lease proposal. On June 3, Hunt spoke with Robert J. Woodward, Jr., executive vice-president and chief investment officer of Nationwide and asked him to fax a copy of the ordinance passed by City Council. On that same date, Hunt Sports Group told Nationwide that it still found the terms of the lease to be unacceptable. On June 3 or June 4, McConnell, in a conversation with the NHL, orally agreed to apply for a hockey franchise for Columbus. On June 4, McPherson returned a call from Hunt, and Hunt informed McPherson that he was still interested in pursuing an agreement with Nationwide.

On June 4, 1997, the NHL franchise expansion committee met. Bettman informed the committee that Nationwide would build an arena, and McConnell was prepared to go forward with the franchise even if he had to do it himself. The committee was told that Hunt Sports Group's involvement was an open issue, but McConnell as an owner was more than adequate. The expansion committee recommended Columbus to the NHL board of governors as one of four cities to be granted a franchise.

On June 5, 1997, the NHL sent Hunt a letter requesting that he let them know by Monday, June 9, 1997 whether he was going forward with his franchise application. In a June 6, 1997 letter to the NHL, Hunt responded that CHL intended to pursue the franchise application. Hunt informed the NHL that he had arranged a meeting with the members of CHL to be held on June 9, 1997. Hunt indicated that the application was contingent upon entering into an appropriate lease for a hockey facility.

On June 9, 1997, a meeting took place at Pizzuti's office. Those present at the meeting included: McConnell, Hunt, Pizzuti, John F. Wolfe, chairman of Wolfe Enterprises, Inc., and representatives of Buckeye Hockey, L.L.C. and Ameritech. The NHL required that the ownership group be identified and that such ownership group sign a lease term sheet by June 9, 1997. Brian Ellis, president and chief operating officer of Nationwide, presented the lease term sheet to those present at the meeting, left the meeting and went to a different room.

Hunt indicated the lease was unacceptable. Ameritech and Buckeye Hockey, L.L.C. indicated that if Hunt found it unacceptable then they too found it unacceptable. Pizzuti and Wolfe agreed to participate along with McConnell. John Christie, president of JMAC, Inc., the personal investment company of the McConnell family, left the meeting and joined Ellis. Christie informed Ellis that McConnell had accepted the term sheet and was signing it in his individual capacity. The term sheet contained a signature line for "Columbus Hockey Limited" as the franchise owner. Ellis phoned his secretary and had her omit the name "Columbus Hockey Limited" on her computer from under the signature line and fax the change to Ellis at Pizzuti's office. McConnell then signed the term sheet as the owner of the franchise. Christie faxed the signed lease term sheet to Bettman that day along with a cover letter and a description of the ownership group. Such ownership group was identified as: John H. McConnell, majority owner, Pizzuti Sports, L.L.C., John F. Wolfe and "[u]p to seven (7) other members." The cover letter indicated that the attached material signified an amendment to the November 1, 1996 application from the city.

On June 17, 1997, the NHL expansion committee recommended to the NHL board of governors that Columbus be awarded a franchise with McConnell's group as owner of the franchise. On the same date, the complaint in the case at bar was filed. On or about June 25, 1997, the NHL board of governors awarded Columbus a franchise with McConnell's group ["COLHOC"] as owner. Hunt Sports Group, Buckeye Hockey, L.L.C. and Ameritech have no ownership interest in the hockey franchise....

In their complaint, McConnell and Wolfe Enterprises, Inc. requested a declaration that section 3.3 of the CHL operating agreement allowed members of CHL to compete with CHL. Specifically, McConnell and Wolfe Enterprises, Inc. sought a declaration that under the operating agreement, they were permitted to participate in COLHOC and obtain the franchise....

On June 23, 1997, Hunt Sports Group filed an answer and counterclaim on its behalf and on behalf on CHL. The counterclaim was asserted against McConnell and alleged breach of contract, breach of fiduciary duty and interference with prospective business relationships.

On July 3, 1997, McConnell and Wolfe Enterprises, Inc. filed a motion for summary judgment as to count one of the first amended complaint (declaratory judgment as to section 3.3 of the operating agreement) and as to counts one through five of the counterclaim [which included breach of fiduciary duty and tortious interference with business relationships].... On October 31, 1997, the trial court rendered a decision, granting summary judgment in favor of McConnell and Wolfe Enterprises, Inc. on count one of the ... complaint and on [certain] counts.... of the counterclaim. Specifically, the trial court found that section 3.3 of the operating agreement was clear and unambiguous and allowed McConnell and Wolfe Enterprises, Inc. to compete against CHL and obtain the NHL franchise. In addition, the trial court found McConnell did not breach the operating agreement by competing against CHL. The claims that remained included ... breach of fiduciary duty and interference with prospective business relationships....

A jury trial was held in May 1998 on [certain counts of the] complaint.... On May 15, 1998, the trial court rendered a decision, granting McConnell and Wolfe Enterprises, Inc.'s motion for directed verdicts on counts three and four of the ... complaint....

Summary judgment is appropriate when, construing the evidence most strongly in favor of the nonmoving party, (1) there is no genuine issue of material fact, (2) the moving party is entitled to judgment as a matter of law, and (3) reasonable minds can come to but one conclusion, that conclusion being adverse to the nonmoving party. . . .

As indicated above, count one of the . . . complaint sought a declaration that section 3.3 of CHL's operating agreement allowed members to compete against CHL to obtain an NHL franchise. Appellees contend section 3.3 is plain and unambiguous and allows what occurred here—COLHOC competing for and obtaining the NHL franchise. Appellant asserts, in part, that the trial court's interpretation of section 3.3 was incorrect and that section 3.3 is ambiguous and subject to different interpretations. Therefore, appellant contends extrinsic evidence should have been considered, and such evidence would have shown the parties did not intend section 3.3 to mean members could compete against CHL and take away CHL's only purpose. . . .

Section 3.3 of the operating agreement states:

"Members May Compete. Members shall not in any way be prohibited from or restricted in engaging or owning an interest in any other business venture of any nature, including any venture which might be competitive with the business of the Company."

Appellant emphasizes the word "other" in the above language and states, in essence, that it means any business venture that is different from the business of the company. Appellant points out that under section 2.1 of the operating agreement, the general character of the business is "to invest in and operate a franchise in the National Hockey League." Hence, appellant contends that members may only engage in or own an interest in a venture that is not in the business of investing in and operating a franchise with the NHL.

Appellant's interpretation of section 3.3 goes beyond the plain language of the agreement and adds words or meanings not stated in the provision. Section 3.3, for example, does not state "[m]embers shall not be prohibited from or restricted in engaging or owning an interest in any other business venture that is different from the business of the company." Rather, section 3.3 states: "any other business venture of any nature." (Emphasis added.) It then adds to this statement: "including any venture which might be competitive with the business of the Company." The words "any nature" could not be broader, and the inclusion of the words "any venture which might be competitive with the business of the Company" makes it clear that members were not prohibited from engaging in a venture that was competitive with CHL's investing in and operating an NHL franchise. Contrary to appellant's contention, the word "other" simply means a business venture other than CHL. The word "other" does not limit the type of business venture in which members may engage.

Hence, section 3.3 did not prohibit appellees from engaging in activities that may have been competitive with CHL, including appellees' participation in COLHOC. Accordingly, summary judgment in favor of appellees was appropriate, and appellees were entitled to a declaration that section 3.3 of the operating agreement permitted appellees to request and obtain an NHL hockey franchise to the exclusion of CHL.

Appellant next contends that the trial court erred in granting summary judgment in favor of appellees on [count one] of appellant's counterclaim. Count one of the counterclaim alleged McConnell breached the operating agreement by forming COLHOC for the sole purpose of competing directly with CHL's application for an NHL franchise. . . .

. . . [T]here are no genuine issues of material fact, appellees are entitled to judgment as a matter of law and reasonable minds could only conclude that section 3.3 of the operating agreement allowed appellees to request and obtain an NHL franchise to the exclusion of CHL, McConnell did not breach the operating agreement by forming COLHOC and competing against CHL. . . . Therefore, summary judgment in favor of appellees on count one of the . . . complaint and on [count one] of appellant's counterclaim was appropriate. . . .

. . . [T]he trial court was correct in stating that it could not be considered a breach of fiduciary duty, in and of itself, to compete against CHL because the operating agreement allowed such competition. Contract provisions may affect the scope of fiduciary duties, and as such, the trial court was correct to indicate that the method of competing, not the competing itself, may constitute a breach of fiduciary duty. . . .

. . . In the case at bar, a limited liability company is involved which, like a partnership, involves a fiduciary relationship. Normally, the presence of such a relationship would preclude direct competition between members of the company. However, here we have an operating agreement that by its very terms allows members to compete with the business of the company. Hence, the question we are presented with is whether an operating agreement of a limited liability company may, in essence, limit or define the scope of the fiduciary duties imposed upon its members. We answer this question in the affirmative. . . .

Here, the injury complained of by appellant was, essentially, appellees competing with CHL and obtaining the NHL franchise. The operating agreement constitutes the undertaking of the parties herein. In becoming members of CHL, appellant and appellees agreed to abide by the terms of the operating agreement, and such agreement specifically allowed competition with the company by its members. As such, the duties created pursuant to such undertaking did not include a duty not to compete. Therefore, there was no duty on the part of appellees to refrain from subjecting appellant to the injury complained of herein. . . .

[The evidence also] does not show that appellees tortiously interfered with appellant's prospective business relationships with Nationwide and the NHL. The evidence does not show that appellees induced or otherwise purposely caused Nationwide and the NHL to not enter into or continue a business relationship with appellant. Indeed, and as indicated above, the evidence shows that McConnell stated he would lease the arena and obtain the franchise only if appellant did not. It was only after appellant rejected the lease proposal on several occasions that McConnell stepped in. Appellant had yet another opportunity on June 9, 1997 to participate in the Nationwide arena lease and the NHL franchise. Appellant again found the lease proposal unacceptable, and without a signed lease term sheet, there would have been no franchise from the NHL.

McPherson testified that Nationwide would accept a lease agreement with whomever the successful franchise applicant was. In addition, it is clear from Bettman's testimony that the NHL was still considering appellant as a potential franchise owner up until the last moment. Again, the evidence does not show that appellees' actions constituted an intentional interference with appellant's business relationships. It must be noted that appellees had the right to compete against CHL. However, even given such right, McConnell did not approach Nationwide or the NHL. Nationwide approached McConnell only after appellant indicated the lease terms were unacceptable. In short, it was appellant's actions that caused the termination of any relationship or potential relationship it had with Nationwide and the NHL.

In conclusion, there was not sufficient material evidence presented at trial so as to create a factual question for the jury on the issues of breach of fiduciary duty and tortious interference with business relationships. Therefore, a directed verdict in favor of appellees ... was appropriate. . . .

■ BOWMAN, J., concurs.

■ PEGGY L. BRYANT, J., concurs in part and dissents in part.*

---

# SECTION 3.   LIMITED LIABILITY PARTNERSHIPS

———

## UNIFORM PARTNERSHIP ACT §§ 101(5), 306(c), 1001

[See Statutory Supplement]

———

---

* Judge Bryant dissented on an issue concerning attorneys' fees. The majority's disposition of that issue is not included in the text. (Footnote by ed.).

## TEXAS LIMITED LIABILITY PARTNERSHIP ACT

[See Statutory Supplement]

---

## NOTE ON LIMITED LIABILITY PARTNERSHIPS

Another important new form of business organization is the limited liability partnership ("LLP"). Essentially, LLPs are general partnerships, with one core difference and several ancillary differences. The core difference is that, as the name indicates, the liability of general partners of a limited liability partnership is less extensive than the liability of a general partner. Although the statutes vary, generally speaking a partner in an LLP is not personally liable for *all* partnership obligations, but only for obligations arising from her own activities—with the exception, under some LLP statutes, that she is also liable for activities closely related to her, for contractual obligations, or both. This core idea is articulated differently under different statutes, and the precise liability of a partner in an LLP will depend on the statute.

Under the LLP statutes, the liability of a partner in an LLP is "limited" only in the sense that the partner is not personally liable for *all* of the LLP's obligations. A partner in an LLP *is* personally liable for certain obligations, and as to those obligations a partner's liability is unlimited—that is, a partner is personally liable for those obligations to the entire extent of her wealth.

An ancillary difference between ordinary general partnerships and LLPs is that under some LLP statutes there is a tradeoff for limited liability, in the form of a requirement of a minimum amount of liability insurance or segregated funds. Another ancillary difference between LLPs and ordinary general partnerships is that LLPs must be registered with the appropriate state office.

# CHAPTER VIII

# THE DUTY OF CARE AND THE DUTY TO ACT LAWFULLY

## SECTION 1. THE DUTY OF CARE

### (a) THE BASIC STANDARD OF CARE

### Francis v. United Jersey Bank

Supreme Court of New Jersey, 1981.
87 N.J. 15, 432 A.2d 814.

■ POLLOCK, J. The primary issue on this appeal is whether a corporate director is personally liable in negligence for the failure to prevent the misappropriation of trust funds by other directors who were also officers and shareholders of the corporation.

Plaintiffs are trustees in bankruptcy of Pritchard & Baird Intermediaries Corp. (Pritchard & Baird), a reinsurance broker or intermediary. Defendant Lillian P. Overcash is the daughter of Lillian G. Pritchard and the executrix of her estate. At the time of her death, Mrs. Pritchard was a director and the largest single shareholder of Pritchard & Baird. Because Mrs. Pritchard died after the institution of suit but before trial, her executrix was substituted as a defendant. United Jersey Bank is joined as the administrator of the estate of Charles Pritchard, Sr., who had been president, director and majority shareholder of Pritchard & Baird.

This litigation focuses on payments made by Pritchard & Baird to Charles Pritchard, Jr. and William Pritchard, who were sons of Mr. and Mrs. Charles Pritchard, Sr., as well as officers, directors and shareholders of the corporation. Claims against Charles, Jr. and William are being pursued in bankruptcy proceedings against them.

The trial court, sitting without a jury, characterized the payments as fraudulent conveyances within N.J.S.A. 25:2–10 and entered judgment of $10,355,736.91 plus interest against the estate of Mrs. Pritchard. 162 N.J.Super. 355, 392 A.2d 1233 (Law Div.1978). The judgment includes damages from her negligence in permitting payments from the corporation of $4,391,133.21 to Charles, Jr. and $5,483,799.02 to William. The trial court also entered judgment for payments of other

373

sums plus interest: (1) against the estate of Lillian Pritchard for $33,000 accepted by her during her lifetime; (2) against the estate of Charles Pritchard, Sr. for $189,194.17 paid to him during his lifetime and $168,454 for payment of taxes on his estate; and (3) against Lillian Overcash individually for $123,156.51 for payments to her.

The Appellate Division affirmed, but found that the payments were a conversion of trust funds, rather than fraudulent conveyances of the assets of the corporation. 171 N.J.Super. 34, 407 A.2d 1253 (1979). We granted certification limited to the issue of the liability of Lillian Pritchard as a director. 82 N.J. 285, 412 A.2d 791 (1980).

Although we accept the characterization of the payments as a conversion of trust funds, the critical question is not whether the misconduct of Charles, Jr. and William should be characterized as fraudulent conveyances or acts of conversion. Rather, the initial question is whether Mrs. Pritchard was negligent in not noticing and trying to prevent the misappropriation of funds held by the corporation in an implied trust. A further question is whether her negligence was the proximate cause of the plaintiffs' losses. Both lower courts found that she was liable in negligence for the losses caused by the wrongdoing of Charles, Jr. and William. We affirm.

### I

The matrix for our decision is the customs and practices of the reinsurance industry and the role of Pritchard & Baird as a reinsurance broker. Reinsurance involves a contract under which one insurer agrees to indemnify another for loss sustained under the latter's policy of insurance. Insurance companies that insure against losses arising out of fire or other casualty seek at times to minimize their exposure by sharing risks with other insurance companies. Thus, when the face amount of a policy is comparatively large, the company may enlist one or more insurers to participate in that risk. Similarly, an insurance company's loss potential and overall exposure may be reduced by reinsuring a part of an entire class of policies (e.g., 25% of all of its fire insurance policies). The selling insurance company is known as a ceding company. The entity that assumes the obligation is designated as the reinsurer.

The reinsurance broker arranges the contract between the ceding company and the reinsurer. In accordance with industry custom before the Pritchard & Baird bankruptcy, the reinsurance contract or treaty did not specify the rights and duties of the broker. Typically, the ceding company communicates to the broker the details concerning the risk. The broker negotiates the sale of portions of the risk to the reinsurers. In most instances, the ceding company and the reinsurer do not communicate with each other, but rely upon the reinsurance broker. The ceding company pays premiums due a reinsurer to the broker, who deducts his commission and transmits the balance to the appropriate reinsurer. When a loss occurs, a reinsurer pays money due a ceding company to the broker, who then transmits it to the ceding company.

The reinsurance business was described by an expert at trial as having "a magic aura around it of dignity and quality and integrity." A telephone call which might be confirmed by a handwritten memorandum is sufficient to create a reinsurance obligation. Though separate bank accounts are not maintained for each treaty, the industry practice is to segregate the insurance funds from the broker's general accounts. Thus, the insurance fund accounts would contain the identifiable amounts for transmittal to either the reinsurer or the ceder. The expert stated that in general three kinds of checks may be drawn on this account: checks payable to reinsurers as premiums, checks payable to ceders as loss payments and checks payable to the brokers as commissions.

Messrs. Pritchard and Baird initially operated as a partnership. Later they formed several corporate entities to carry on their brokerage activities. The proofs supporting the judgment relate only to one corporation, Pritchard & Baird Intermediaries Corp. (Pritchard & Baird), and we need consider only its activities. When incorporated under the laws of the State of New York in 1959, Pritchard & Baird had five directors: Charles Pritchard, Sr., his wife Lillian Pritchard, their son Charles Pritchard, Jr., George Baird and his wife Marjorie. William Pritchard, another son, became director in 1960. Upon its formation, Pritchard & Baird acquired all the assets and assumed all the liabilities of the Pritchard & Baird partnership. The corporation issued 200 shares of common stock. Charles Pritchard, Sr. acquired 120 shares, his sons Charles Pritchard, Jr., 15 and William 15; Mr. and Mrs. Baird owned the remaining 50. In June 1964, Baird and his wife resigned as directors and sold their stock to the corporation. From that time on the corporation operated as a close family corporation with Mr. and Mrs. Pritchard and their two sons as the only directors. After the death of Charles, Sr. in 1973, only the remaining three directors continued to operate as the board. Lillian Pritchard inherited 72 of her husband's 120 shares in Pritchard & Baird, thereby becoming the largest stockholder in the corporation with 48% of the stock.

The corporate minute books reflect only perfunctory activities by the directors, related almost exclusively to the election of officers and adoption of banking resolutions and a retirement plan. None of the minutes for any of the meetings contain a discussion of the loans to Charles, Jr. and William or of the financial condition of the corporation. Moreover, upon instructions of Charles, Jr. that financial statements were not to be circulated to anyone else, the company's statements for the fiscal years beginning February 1, 1970, were delivered only to him.

Charles Pritchard, Sr. was the chief executive and controlled the business in the years following Baird's withdrawal. Beginning in 1966, he gradually relinquished control over the operations of the corporation. In 1968, Charles, Jr. became president and William became executive vice president. Charles, Sr. apparently became ill in 1971 and during the last year and a half of his life was not involved in the affairs of the business. He continued, however, to serve as a director until his death on December 10, 1973. Notwithstanding the presence of Charles, Sr. on the board until his death in 1973, Charles, Jr. dominated the management of the corporation and the board from 1968 until the bankruptcy in 1975.

Contrary to the industry custom of segregating funds, Pritchard & Baird commingled the funds of reinsurers and ceding companies with its own funds. All monies (including commissions, premiums and loss monies) were deposited in a single account. Charles, Sr. began the practice of withdrawing funds from the commingled account in transactions identified on the corporate books as "loans." As long as Charles, Sr. controlled the corporation, the "loans" correlated with corporate profits and were repaid at the end of each year. Starting in 1970, however, Charles, Jr. and William begin to siphon ever-increasing sums from the corporation under the guise of loans. As of January 31, 1970, the "loans" to Charles, Jr. were $230,932 and to William were $207,329. At least by January 31, 1973, the annual increase in the loans exceeded annual corporate revenues. By October 1975, the year of bankruptcy, the "shareholders' loans" had metastasized to a total of $12,333,514.47.

The trial court rejected the characterization of the payments as "loans." 162 N.J.Super. at 365, 392 A.2d 1233. No corporate resolution authorized the "loans," and no note or other instrument evidenced the debt. Charles, Jr. and William paid no interest on the amounts received. The "loans" were not repaid or reduced from one year to the next; rather, they increased annually.

The designation of "shareholders' loans" on the balance sheet was an entry to account for the distribution of the premium and loss money to Charles, Sr., Charles, Jr. and William. As the trial court found, the entry was part of a "woefully inadequate and highly dangerous bookkeeping system." 162 N.J.Super. at 363, 392 A.2d 1233.

The "loans" to Charles, Jr. and William far exceeded their salaries and financial resources. If the payments to Charles, Jr. and William had been treated as dividends or compensation, then the balance sheets would have shown an excess of liabilities over assets. If the "loans" had been eliminated, the balance sheets would have depicted a corporation not only with a working capital deficit, but also with assets having a fair market value less than its liabilities. The balance sheets for 1970–1975, however, showed an excess of assets over liabilities. This result was achieved by designating the misappropriated funds as "shareholders' loans" and listing them as assets offsetting the deficits. Although the withdrawal of the funds resulted in an obligation of repayment to Pritchard & Baird, the more significant consideration is that the "loans" represented a massive misappropriation of money belonging to the clients of the corporation.

The "loans" were reflected on financial statements that were prepared annually as of January 31, the end of the corporate fiscal year. Although an outside certified public accountant prepared the 1970 financial statement, the corporation prepared only internal financial statements from 1971–1975. In all instances, the statements were simple documents, consisting of three or four 8½ × 11 inch sheets.

The statements of financial condition from 1970 forward demonstrated:

|  | **Working Capital Deficit** | **Shareholders' Loans** | **Net Brokerage Income** |
|---|---|---|---|
| 1970 | $   389,022 | $   509,941 | $   807,229 |
| 1971 | not available | not available | not available |
| 1972 | $ 1,684,289 | $ 1,825,911 | $1,546,263 |
| 1973 | $ 3,506,460 | $ 3,700,542 | $1,736,349 |
| 1974 | $ 6,939,007 | $ 7,080,629 | $   876,182 |
| 1975 | $10,176,419 | $10,298,039 | $   551,598. |

Those financial statements showed working capital deficits increasing annually in tandem with the amounts that Charles, Jr. and William withdrew as "shareholders' loans." In the last complete year of business (January 31, 1974, to January 31, 1975), "shareholders' loans" and the correlative working capital deficit increased by approximately $3,200,000.

The funding of the "loans" left the corporation with insufficient money to operate. Pritchard & Baird could defer payment on accounts payable because its clients allowed a grace period, generally 30 to 90 days, before the payment was due. During this period, Pritchard & Baird used the funds entrusted to it as a "float" to pay current accounts payable. By recourse to the funds of its clients, Pritchard & Baird not only paid its trade debts, but also funded the payments to Charles, Jr. and William. Thus, Pritchard & Baird was able to meet its obligations as they came due only through the use of clients' funds.

The pattern that emerges from these figures is the substantial increase in the monies appropriated by Charles Pritchard, Jr. and William Pritchard after their father's withdrawal from the business and the sharp decline in the profitability of the operation after his death. This led ultimately to the filing in December, 1975, of an involuntary petition in bankruptcy and the appointments of the plaintiffs as trustees in bankruptcy of Pritchard & Baird.

Mrs. Pritchard was not active in the business of Pritchard & Baird and knew virtually nothing of its corporate affairs. She briefly visited the corporate offices in Morristown on only one occasion, and she never read or obtained the annual financial statements. She was unfamiliar with the rudiments of reinsurance and made no effort to assure that the policies and practices of the corporation, particularly pertaining to the withdrawal of funds, complied with industry custom or relevant law. Although her husband had warned her that Charles, Jr. would "take the shirt off my back," Mrs. Pritchard did not pay any attention to her duties as a director or to the affairs of the corporation. 162 N.J.Super. at 370, 392 A.2d 1233.

After her husband died in December 1973, Mrs. Pritchard became incapacitated and was bedridden for a six-month period. She became listless at this time and started to drink rather heavily. Her physical condition deteriorated, and in 1978 she died. The trial court rejected testimony seeking to exonerate her because she "was old, was grief-stricken at the loss of her husband, sometimes consumed too much alcohol and was psychologically overborne by her sons." 162 N.J.Super. at 371, 392 A.2d 1233. That court found that she was competent to act and that the reason Mrs. Pritchard never knew what her sons "were doing was because she never made the slightest effort to discharge any of her responsibilities as a director of Pritchard & Baird." 162 N.J.Super. at 372, 392 A.2d 1233.

## II

A preliminary matter is the determination of whether New Jersey law should apply to this case. Although Pritchard & Baird was incorporated in New York, the trial court found that New Jersey had more significant relationships to the parties and the transactions than New York. The shareholder, officers and directors were New Jersey residents. The estates of Mr. and Mrs. Pritchard are being administered in New Jersey, and the bankruptcy proceedings involving Charles, Jr., William and Pritchard & Baird are pending in New Jersey. Virtually all transactions took place in New Jersey. Although many of the creditors are located outside the state, all had contacts with Pritchard & Baird in New Jersey. Consequently, the trial court applied New Jersey law. 162 N.J.Super. at 369, 392 A.2d 1233. The parties agree that New Jersey law should apply. We are in accord.

## III

Individual liability of a corporate director for acts of the corporation is a prickly problem. Generally directors are accorded broad immunity and are not insurers of corporate activities. The problem is particularly nettlesome when a third party asserts that a director, because of nonfeasance, is liable for losses caused by acts of insiders, who in this case were officers, directors and shareholders. Determination of the liability of Mrs. Pritchard requires findings that she had a duty to the clients of Pritchard & Baird, that she breached that duty and that her breach was a proximate cause of their losses.

The New Jersey Business Corporation Act, which took effect on January 1, 1969, was a comprehensive revision of the statutes relating to business corporations. One section, N.J.S.A. 14A:6–14, concerning a director's general obligation had no counterpart in the old Act. That section makes it incumbent upon directors to discharge their duties in good faith and with that degree of diligence, care and skill which ordinarily prudent men would exercise under similar circumstances in like positions. [N.J.S.A. 14A:6–14] ...

... [The principle underlying] N.J.S.A. 14A:6–14 is ... that directors must discharge their duties in good faith and act as ordinarily prudent persons would under similar circumstances in like positions. Although specific duties in a given case can be determined only after consideration of all of the circumstances, the standard of ordinary care is the wellspring from which those more specific duties flow.

As a general rule, a director should acquire at least a rudimentary understanding of the business of the corporation. Accordingly, a director should become familiar with the fundamentals of the business in which the corporation is engaged. [Campbell v. Watson, 62 N.J. Eq. 396, 50 A. 120 (Ch.1901)]. Because directors are bound to exercise ordinary care, they cannot set up as a defense lack of the knowledge needed to exercise the requisite degree of care. If one "feels that he has not had sufficient business experience to qualify him to perform the duties of a director, he should either acquire the knowledge by inquiry, or refuse to act." Ibid.

Directors are under a continuing obligation to keep informed about the activities of the corporation. Otherwise, they may not be able to participate in the overall management of corporate affairs. Barnes v. Andrews, 298 F. 614 (S.D.N.Y.1924).... Directors may not shut their eyes to corporate misconduct, and then claim that because they did not see the misconduct, they did not have a duty to look. The sentinel asleep at his post contributes nothing to the enterprise he is charged to protect. Wilkinson v. Dodd, 42 N.J. Eq. 234, 245, 7 A. 327 (Ch.1886), aff'd 42 N.J. Eq. 647, 9 A. 685 (E. & A.1887).

Directorial management does not require a detailed inspection of day-to-day activities, but rather a general monitoring of corporate affairs and policies. Williams v. McKay, [46 N.J. Eq. 25, 36, 18 A. 824 (Ch.1889)]. Accordingly, a director is well advised to attend board meetings regularly. Indeed, a director who is absent from a board meeting is presumed to concur in action taken on a corporate matter, unless he files a "dissent with the secretary of the corporation within a reasonable time after learning of such action." N.J.S.A. 14A:6–13 (Supp.1981–1982). Regular attendance does not mean that directors must attend every meeting, but that directors should attend meetings as a matter of practice. A director of a publicly held corporation might be expected to attend regular monthly meetings, but a director of a small, family corporation might be asked to attend only an annual meeting. The point is that one of the responsibilities of a director is to attend meetings of the board of which he or she is a member. That burden is lightened by N.J.S.A. 14A:6–7(2) (Supp.1981–1982), which permits board action without a meeting if all members of the board consent in writing.

While directors are not required to audit corporate books, they should maintain familiarity with the financial status of the corporation by a regular review of financial statements. *Campbell,* supra, 62 N.J.Eq. at 415, 50 A. 120; *Williams,* supra, 46 N.J.Eq. at 38–39, 18 A. 824; see Section of Corporation, Banking and Business Law, American Bar Association, "Corporate Director's Guidebook," 33 Bus.Law. 1595, 1608 (1978) (Guidebook).... In some circumstances, directors may be charged with assuring that bookkeeping methods conform to industry custom and usage. Lippitt v. Ashley, 89 Conn. 451, 464, 94 A. 995, 1000 (Sup.Ct.1915). The extent of review, as well as the nature and frequency of financial statements, depends not only on the customs of the industry, but also on the nature of the corporation and the business in which it is engaged. Financial statements of some small corporations may be prepared internally and only on an annual basis; in a large publicly held corporation, the statements may be produced monthly or at some other regular interval. Adequate financial review normally would be more informal in a private corporation than in a publicly held corporation.

Of some relevance in this case is the circumstance that the financial records disclose the "shareholders' loans". Generally directors are immune from liability if, in good faith,

> they rely upon the opinion of counsel for the corporation or upon written reports setting forth financial data concerning the corporation and prepared by an independent public accountant or certified public accountant or firm of such accountants or upon financial statements, books of account or reports of the corporation represented to them to be correct by the president, the officer of the corporation having charge of its books of account, or the person presiding at a meeting of the board. [N.J.S.A. 14A:6–14]

The review of financial statements, however, may give rise to a duty to inquire further into matters revealed by those statements. Corsicana Nat'l Bank v. Johnson, 251 U.S. 68, 71, 40 S.Ct. 82, 84, 64 L.Ed. 141 (1919). . . . Upon discovery of an illegal course of action, a director has a duty to object and, if the corporation does not correct the conduct, to resign. See Dodd v. Wilkinson, 42 N.J. Eq. 647, 651, 9 A. 685 (E. & A.1887); Williams v. Riley, 34 N.J. Eq. 398, 401 (Ch.1881).

In certain circumstances, the fulfillment of the duty of a director may call for more than mere objection and resignation. Sometimes a director may be required to seek the advice of counsel. *Guidebook*, supra, at 1631. One New Jersey case recognized the duty of a bank director to seek counsel where doubt existed about the meaning of the bank charter. Williams v. McKay, supra, 46 N.J. Eq. at 60, 18 A. 824. The duty to seek the assistance of counsel can extend to areas other than the interpretation of corporation instruments. Modern corporate practice recognizes that on occasion a director should seek outside advice. A director may require legal advice concerning the propriety of his or her own conduct, the conduct of other officers and directors or the conduct of the corporation. In appropriate circumstances, a director would be "well advised to consult with regular corporate counsel (or his own legal adviser) at any time in which he is doubtful regarding proposed action. . . ." *Guidebook*, supra, at 1618. Sometimes the duty of a director may require more than consulting with outside counsel. A director may have a duty to take reasonable means to prevent illegal conduct by co-directors; in an appropriate case, this may include threat of suit. See Selheimer v. Manganese Corp., 423 Pa. 563, 572, 584, 224 A.2d 634, 640, 646 (Sup.Ct.1966) (director exonerated when he objected, resigned, organized shareholder action group, and threatened suit).

A director is not an ornament, but an essential component of corporate governance. Consequently, a director cannot protect himself

behind a paper shield bearing the motto, "dummy director." ...
Thus, all directors are responsible for managing the business and
affairs of the corporation. N.J.S.A. 14A:6–1 (Supp.1981–1982); 1 G.
Hornstein, Corporation Law and Practice § 431 at 525 (1959).

The factors that impel expanded responsibility in the large, publicly held corporation may not be present in a small, close corporation. Nonetheless, a close corporation may, because of the nature of
its business, be affected with a public interest. For example, the stock
of a bank may be closely held, but because of the nature of banking
the directors would be subject to greater liability than those of another
close corporation. Even in a small corporation, a director is held to the
standard of that degree of care that an ordinarily prudent director
would use under the circumstances. M. Mace, The Board of Directors
of Small Corporations 83 (1948).

A director's duty of care does not exist in the abstract, but must
be considered in relation to specific obligees. In general, the relationship of a corporate director to the corporation and its stockholders is
that of a fiduciary. Whitfield v. Kern, 122 N.J. Eq. 332, 341, 192 A. 48
(E. & A.1937). Shareholders have a right to expect that directors will
exercise reasonable supervision and control over the policies and
practices of a corporation. The institutional integrity of a corporation
depends upon the proper discharge by directors of those duties.

While directors may owe a fiduciary duty to creditors also, that
obligation generally has not been recognized in the absence of insolvency. *Whitfield,* supra, 122 N.J.Eq. at 342, 345, 192 A. 48. With
certain corporations, however, directors are [deemed] to owe a duty
to creditors and other third parties even when the corporation is
solvent. Although depositors of a bank are considered in some respects to be creditors, courts have recognized that directors may owe
them a fiduciary duty. See *Campbell*, supra, 62 N.J.Eq. at 406–407, 50
A. 120. Directors of nonbanking corporations may owe a similar duty
when the corporation holds funds of others in trust. Cf. McGlynn v.
Schultz, 90 N.J.Super. 505, 218 A.2d 408 (Ch.Div.1966), aff'd 95
N.J.Super. 412, 231 A.2d 386 (App.Div.), certif. den. 50 N.J. 409, 235
A.2d 901 (1967) (directors who did not insist on segregating trust
funds held by corporation liable to the *cestuis que trust*).

Courts in other states have imposed liability on directors of
nonbanking corporations for the conversion of trust funds, even
though those directors did not participate in or know of the conversion.... The distinguishing circumstances in regard to banks and
other corporations holding trust funds is that the depositor or beneficiary can reasonably expect the director to act with ordinary prudence
concerning the funds held in a fiduciary capacity. Thus, recognition of
a duty of a director to those for whom a corporation holds funds in
trust may be viewed as another application of the general rule that a
director's duty is that of an ordinary prudent person under the
circumstances.

The most striking circumstances affecting Mrs. Pritchard's duty as
a director are the character of the reinsurance industry, the nature of

the misappropriated funds and the financial condition of Pritchard & Baird. The hallmark of the reinsurance industry has been the unqualified trust and confidence reposed by ceding companies and reinsurers in reinsurance brokers. Those companies entrust money to reinsurance intermediaries with the justifiable expectation that the funds will be transmitted to the appropriate parties. Consequently, the companies could have assumed rightfully that Mrs. Pritchard, as a director of a reinsurance brokerage corporation, would not sanction the commingling and the conversion of loss and premium funds for the personal use of the principals of Pritchard & Baird.

As a reinsurance broker, Pritchard & Baird received annually as a fiduciary millions of dollars of clients' money which it was under a duty to segregate.[6] To this extent, it resembled a bank rather than a small family business. Accordingly, Mrs. Pritchard's relationship to the clientele of Pritchard & Baird was akin to that of a director of a bank to its depositors. All parties agree that Pritchard & Baird held the misappropriated funds in an implied trust. That trust relationship gave rise to a fiduciary duty to guard the funds with fidelity and good faith. Ellsworth Dobbs, Inc. v. Johnson, 50 N.J. 528, 553, 236 A.2d 843 (1967); General Films, Inc. v. Sanco Gen. Mfg. Corp., supra, 153 N.J.Super. at 372–373, 379 A.2d 1042.

As a director of a substantial reinsurance brokerage corporation, she should have known that it received annually millions of dollars of loss and premium funds which it held in trust for ceding and reinsurance companies. Mrs. Pritchard should have obtained and read the annual statements of financial condition of Pritchard & Baird. Although she had a right to rely upon financial statements prepared in accordance with N.J.S.A. 14A:6–14, such reliance would not excuse her conduct. The reason is that those statements disclosed on their face the misappropriation of trust funds.

From those statements, she should have realized that, as of January 31, 1970, her sons were withdrawing substantial trust funds under the guise of "Shareholders' Loans." The financial statements for each fiscal year commencing with that of January 31, 1970, disclosed that the working capital deficits and the "loans" were escalating in tandem. Detecting a misappropriation of funds would not have required special expertise or extraordinary diligence; a cursory reading of the financial statements would have revealed the pillage. Thus, if Mrs. Pritchard had read the financial statements, she would have known that her sons were converting trust funds. When financial statements demonstrate that insiders are bleeding a corporation to death, a director should notice and try to stanch the flow of blood.

In summary, Mrs. Pritchard was charged with the obligation of basic knowledge and supervision of the business of Pritchard & Baird. Under the circumstances, this obligation included reading and under-

---

**6.** Following the Pritchard & Baird bankruptcy, New York, a reinsurance center, adopted legislation regulating reinsurance intermediaries. One statute codified the industry standard by prohibiting reinsurance intermediaries from commingling their funds with funds of their principals. N.Y.Ins.Law § 122–a(9) (McKinney Supp.1980–1981).

standing financial statements, and making reasonable attempts at detection and prevention of the illegal conduct of other officers and directors. She had a duty to protect the clients of Pritchard & Baird against policies and practices that would result in the misappropriation of money they had entrusted to the corporation. She breached that duty.

### IV

Nonetheless, the negligence of Mrs. Pritchard does not result in liability unless it is a proximate cause of the loss. . . .

Cases involving nonfeasance present a much more difficult causation question than those in which the director has committed an affirmative act of negligence leading to the loss. Analysis in cases of negligent omissions calls for determination of the reasonable steps a director should have taken and whether that course of action would have averted the loss.

Usually a director can absolve himself from liability by informing the other directors of the impropriety and voting for a proper course of action. Dyson, "The Director's Liability for Negligence," 40 Ind.L.J. 341, 365 (1965). . . .

Even accepting the hypothesis that Mrs. Pritchard might not be liable if she had objected and resigned, there are two significant reasons for holding her liable. First, she did not resign until just before the bankruptcy. Consequently, there is no factual basis for the speculation that the losses would have occurred even if she had objected and resigned. Indeed, the trial court reached the opposite conclusion: "The actions of the sons were so blatantly wrongful that it is hard to see how they could have resisted any moderately firm objection to what they were doing." 162 N.J.Super. at 372, 392 A.2d 1233. Second, the nature of the reinsurance business distinguishes it from most other commercial activities in that reinsurance brokers are encumbered by fiduciary duties owed to third parties. In other corporations, a director's duty normally does not extend beyond the shareholders to third parties.

In this case, the scope of Mrs. Pritchard's duties was determined by the precarious financial condition of Pritchard & Baird, its fiduciary relationship to its clients and the implied trust in which it held their funds. Thus viewed, the scope of her duties encompassed all reasonable action to stop the continuing conversion. Her duties extended beyond mere objection and resignation to reasonable attempts to prevent the misappropriation of the trust funds. *Campbell,* supra, 62 N.J.Eq. at 427, 50 A. 120. . . .

In assessing whether Mrs. Pritchard's conduct was a legal or proximate cause of the conversion, "[l]egal responsibility must be limited to those causes which are so closely connected with the result and of such significance that the law is justified in imposing liability." Prosser, supra, § 41 at 237. Such a judicial determination involves not only considerations of causation-in-fact and matters of policy, but also common sense and logic. Caputzal v. The Lindsay Co., 48 N.J. 69, 77–78 (1966). The act or the failure to act must be a substantial factor in producing the harm. Prosser, supra, § 41 at 240; Restatement (Second) of Torts, §§ 431, 432 (1965).

Within Pritchard & Baird, several factors contributed to the loss of the funds: comingling of corporate and client monies, conversion of funds by Charles, Jr. and William and dereliction of her duties by Mrs. Pritchard. The wrongdoing of her sons, although the immediate cause of the loss, should not excuse Mrs. Pritchard from her negligence which also was a substantial factor contributing to the loss. Restatement (Second) of Torts, supra, § 442B, comment b. Her sons knew that she, the only other director, was not reviewing their conduct; they spawned their fraud in the backwater of her neglect. Her neglect of duty contributed to the climate of corruption; her failure to act contributed to the continuation of that corruption.Consequently, her conduct was a substantial factor contributing to the loss.

Analysis of proximate cause is especially difficult in a corporate context where the allegation is that nonfeasance of a director is a proximate cause of damage to a third party. Where a case involves nonfeasance, no one can say "with absolute certainty what would have occurred if the defendant had acted otherwise." Prosser, supra, § 41 at 242. Nonetheless, where it is reasonable to conclude that the failure to act would produce a particular result and that result has followed, causation may be inferred. Ibid. We conclude that even if Mrs. Pritchard's mere objection had not stopped the depredations of her sons, her consultation with an attorney and the threat of suit would have deterred them. That conclusion flows as a matter of common sense and logic from the record. Whether in other situations a director has a duty to do more than protest and resign is best left to case-by-case determinations. In this case, we are satisfied that there was a duty to do more than object and resign. Consequently, we find that Mrs. Pritchard's negligence was a proximate cause of the misappropriations.

To conclude, by virtue of her office, Mrs. Pritchard had the power to prevent the losses sustained by the clients of Pritchard & Baird. With power comes responsibility. She had a duty to deter the depredation of the other insiders, her sons. She breached that duty and caused plaintiffs to sustain damages.

The judgment of the Appellate Division is affirmed.

■ For affirmance—JUSTICES SULLIVAN, PASHMAN, CLIFFORD, SCHREIBER, HANDLER and POLLOCK—6.

For reversal—none.

———

### REV. MODEL BUS. CORP. ACT §§ 8.30, 8.31

[See Statutory Supplement]

———

## CAL. CORP. CODE § 309

[See Statutory Supplement]

## NEW YORK BUS. CORP. LAW § 717

[See Statutory Supplement]

## ALI, PRINCIPLES OF CORPORATE GOVERNANCE
## §§ 4.01(a), (b), 4.02, 4.03

[See Statutory Supplement]

**ARONSON v. LEWIS,** 473 A.2d 805, 812 (Del.1984). "[D]irectors have a duty to inform themselves, prior to making a business decision, of all material information reasonably available to them. Having become so informed, they must then act with requisite care in the discharge of their duties. While the Delaware cases use a variety of terms to describe the applicable standard of care, our analysis satisfies us that under the business judgment rule director liability is predicated upon concepts of gross negligence."

**QUILLEN,** *TRANS UNION,* **BUSINESS JUDGMENT, AND NEUTRAL PRINCIPLES,** 10 Del.J.Corp.L. 465, 497–98 (1985). "Even if one assumes that negligence law is the proper pigeonhole for director liability—a most questionable assumption at least at the decisional level—the concept of 'gross negligence' has been expressly rejected by the better tort scholarship as practically meaningless. Therefore its recent adoption in corporate law would appear, in some respects, to be an analytical step backwards. . . .

"Perhaps we should say straight out that, on the threshold duty of care issue, the standard should be 'reasonable care under the circumstances' as some argued all along. If that flexible standard includes all factors, e.g., director expertise [and], time pressures, . . . as well as depth of inquiry, then one suspects the results probably would not radically change, but the judicial focus would be to a keener negligence standard and emphasis more on the qualitative nature of the varying circumstances."

## (b) THE BUSINESS JUDGMENT RULE

---

### Kamin v. American Express Co.

Supreme Court, Special Term, N.Y. County, Part 1, 1976.
86 Misc.2d 809, 383 N.Y.S.2d 807, aff'd on opinion below 54 A.D.2d 654, 387 N.Y.S.2d 993 (1st Dept.1976).

■ EDWARD J. GREENFIELD, JUSTICE:

In this stockholders' derivative action, the individual defendants, who are the directors of the American Express Company, move for an order dismissing the complaint for failure to state a cause of action pursuant to CPLR 3211(a)(7), and alternatively, for summary judgment pursuant to CPLR 3211(c).

The complaint is brought derivatively by two minority stockholders of the American Express Company, asking for a declaration that a certain dividend in kind is a waste of corporate assets, directing the defendants not to proceed with the distribution, or, in the alternative, for monetary damages. The motion to dismiss the complaint requires the Court to presuppose the truth of the allegations. It is the defendants' contention that, conceding everything in the complaint, no viable cause of action is made out.

After establishing the identity of the parties, the complaint alleges that in 1972 American Express acquired for investment 1,954,418 shares of common stock of Donaldson, Lufken and Jenrette, Inc. (hereafter DLJ), a publicly traded corporation, at a cost of $29.9 million. It is further alleged that the current market value of those shares is approximately $4.0 million. On July 28, 1975, it is alleged, the Board of Directors of American Express declared a special dividend to all stockholders of record pursuant to which the shares of DLJ would be distributed in kind. Plaintiffs contend further that if American Express were to sell the DLJ shares on the market, it would sustain a capital loss of $25 million, which could be offset against taxable capital gains on other investments. Such a sale, they allege, would result in tax savings to the company of approximately $8 million, which would not be available in the case of the distribution of DLJ shares to stockholders. It is alleged that on October 8, 1975 and October 16, 1975, plaintiffs demanded that the directors rescind the previously declared dividend in DLJ shares and take steps to preserve the capital loss which would result from selling the shares. This demand was rejected by the Board of Directors on October 17, 1975.

It is apparent that all the previously-mentioned allegations of the complaint go to the question of the exercise by the Board of Directors of business judgment in deciding how to deal with the DLJ shares. The crucial allegation which must be scrutinized to determine the legal sufficiency of the complaint is paragraph 19, which alleges:

"19. All of the defendant Directors engaged in or acquiesced in or negligently permitted the declaration and payment of the Dividend in violation of the fiduciary duty owed by them to Amex to care for and preserve Amex's assets in the same manner as a man of average prudence would care for his own property."

Plaintiffs never moved for temporary injunctive relief, and did nothing to bar the actual distribution of the DLJ shares. The dividend was in fact paid on October 31, 1975. Accordingly, that portion of the complaint seeking a direction not to distribute the shares is deemed to be moot, and the Court will deal only with the request for declaratory judgment or for damages.

Examination of the complaint reveals that there is no claim of fraud or self-dealing, and no contention that there was any bad faith or oppressive conduct. The law is quite clear as to what is necessary to ground a claim for actionable wrongdoing.

> "In actions by stockholders, which assail the acts of their directors or trustees, courts will not interfere unless the powers have been illegally or unconscientiously executed; or unless it be made to appear that the acts were fraudulent or collusive, and destructive of the rights of the stockholders. Mere errors of judgment are not sufficient as grounds for equity interference, for the powers of those entrusted with corporate management are largely discretionary." Leslie v. Lorillard, 110 N.Y. 519, 532, 18 N.E. 363, 365....

More specifically, the question of whether or not a dividend is to be declared or a distribution of some kind should be made is exclusively a matter of business judgment for the Board of Directors.

> " ... Courts will not interfere with such discretion unless it be first made to appear that the directors have acted or are about to act in bad faith and for a dishonest purpose. It is for the directors to say, acting in good faith of course, when and to what extent dividends shall be declared ... The statute confers upon the directors this power, and the minority stockholders are not in a position to question this right, so long as the directors are acting in good faith ... "

Thus, a complaint must be dismissed if all that is presented is a decision to pay dividends rather than pursuing some other course of conduct. Weinberger v. Quinn, 264 App.Div. 405, 35 N.Y.S.2d 567, affd. 290 N.Y. 635, 49 N.E.2d 131. A complaint which alleges merely that some course of action other than that pursued by the Board of Directors would have been more advantageous gives rise to no cognizable cause of action. Courts have more than enough to do in adjudicating legal rights and devising remedies for wrongs. The directors' room rather than the courtroom is the appropriate forum for thrashing out purely business questions which will have an impact on profits, market prices, competitive situations, or tax advantages. As stated by Cardozo, J., when sitting at Special Term, the substitution of someone else's business judgment for that of the directors "is no business for any court to follow." Holmes v. St. Joseph Lead Co., 84

Misc. 278, 283, 147 N.Y.S. 104, 107, quoting from Gamble v. Queens County Water Co., 123 N.Y. 91, 99, 25 N.E. 201, 208.

It is not enough to allege, as plaintiffs do here, that the directors made an imprudent decision, which did not capitalize on the possibility of using a potential capital loss to offset capital gains. More than imprudence or mistaken judgment must be shown.

> "Questions of policy of management, expediency of contracts or action, adequacy of consideration, lawful appropriation of corporate funds to advance corporate interests, are left solely to their honest and unselfish decision, for their powers therein are without limitation and free from restraint, and the exercise of them for the common and general interests of the corporation may not be questioned, although the results show that what they did was unwise or inexpedient." Pollitz v. Wabash Railroad Co., 207 N.Y. 113, 124, 100 N.E. 721, 724.

Section 720 of the Business Corporation Law permits an action against directors for "the neglect of, or failure to perform, or other violations of his duties in the management and disposition of corporate assets committed to his charge." This does not mean that a director is chargeable with ordinary negligence for having made an improper decision, or having acted imprudently. The "neglect" referred to in the statute is neglect of duties (i.e., malfeasance or nonfeasance) and not misjudgment. To allege that a director "negligently permitted the declaration and payment" of a dividend without alleging fraud, dishonesty or nonfeasance, is to state merely that a decision was taken with which one disagrees.

Nor does this appear to be a case in which a potentially valid cause of action is inartfully stated. . . . The affidavits of the defendants and the exhibits annexed thereto demonstrate that the objections raised by the plaintiffs to the proposed dividend action were carefully considered and unanimously rejected by the Board at a special meeting called precisely for that purpose at the plaintiffs' request. The minutes of the special meeting indicate that the defendants were fully aware that a sale rather than a distribution of the DLJ shares might result in the realization of a substantial income tax saving. Nevertheless, they concluded that there were countervailing considerations primarily with respect to the adverse effect such a sale, realizing a loss of $25 million, would have on the net income figures in the American Express financial statement. Such a reduction of net income would have a serious effect on the market value of the publicly traded American Express stock. This was not a situation in which the defendant directors totally overlooked facts called to their attention. They gave them consideration, and attempted to view the total picture in arriving at their decision. While plaintiffs contend that according to their accounting consultants the loss on the DLJ stock would still have to be charged against current earnings even if the stock were distributed, the defendants' accounting experts assert that the loss would be a charge against earnings only in the event of a sale, whereas in the event of distribution of the stock as a dividend, the proper accounting treatment would be to charge the loss only against surplus. While the chief accountant for the SEC raised some question as to the appropriate accounting treatment of this transaction, there was no basis for any action to be taken by the SEC with respect to the American Express financial statement.

The only hint of self-interest which is raised, not in the complaint but in the papers on the motion, is that four of the twenty directors were officers and employees of American Express and members of its Executive Incentive Compensation Plan. Hence, it is suggested, by virtue of the action taken earnings may have been overstated and their compensation affected thereby. Such a claim is highly speculative and standing alone can hardly be regarded as sufficient to support an inference of self-dealing. There is no claim or showing that the four company directors dominated and controlled the sixteen outside members of the Board. Certainly, every action taken by the Board has some impact on earnings and may therefore affect the compensation of those whose earnings are keyed to profits. That does not disqualify the inside directors, nor does it put every policy adopted by the Board in question. All directors have an obligation, using sound business judgment, to maximize income for the benefit of all persons having a stake in the welfare of the corporate entity. See, Amdur v. Meyer, 15 A.D.2d 425, 224 N.Y.S.2d 440, appeal dismissed 14 N.Y.2d 541, 248 N.Y.S.2d 639, 198 N.E.2d 30. What we have here as revealed both by the complaint and by the affidavits and exhibits, is that a disagreement exists between two minority stockholders and a unanimous Board of Directors as to the best way to handle a loss already incurred on an investment. The directors are entitled to exercise their honest business judgment on the information before them, and to act within their corporate powers. That they may be mistaken, that other courses of action might have differing consequences, or that their action might benefit some shareholders more than others presents no basis for the superimposition of judicial judgment, so long as it appears that the directors have been acting in good faith. The question of to what extent a dividend shall be declared and the manner in which it shall be paid is ordinarily subject only to the qualification that the dividend be paid out of surplus (Business Corporation Law Section 510, subd. b). The Court will not interfere unless a clear case is made out of fraud, oppression, arbitrary action, or breach of trust.

Courts should not shrink from the responsibility of dismissing complaints or granting summary judgment when no legal wrongdoing is set forth. . . .

In this case it clearly appears that the plaintiffs have failed as a matter of law to make out an actionable claim. Accordingly, the motion by the defendants for summary judgment and dismissal of the complaint is granted.

## ALI, PRINCIPLES OF CORPORATE GOVERNANCE § 4.01(c)

### [See Statutory Supplement]

---

### NOTE ON JOY v. NORTH

In Joy v. North, 692 F.2d 880 (2d Cir.1982), cert. denied, Citytrust v. Joy, 460 U.S. 1051, 103 S.Ct. 1498, 75 L.Ed.2d 930 (1983), the court, in discussing the duty of care, said:

> Consider the choice between two investments in an example adapted from Klein, Business Organization and Finance 147–49 (1980):

#### INVESTMENT A

| Estimated Probability of Outcome | Outcome Profit or Loss | Value |
|---|---|---|
| .4 | +15 | 6.0 |
| .4 | + 1 | .4 |
| .2 | −13 | −2.6 |
| 1.0 | | 3.8 |

#### INVESTMENT B

| Estimated Probability of Outcome | Outcome Profit or Loss | Value |
|---|---|---|
| .4 | +6 | 2.4 |
| .4 | +2 | .8 |
| .2 | +1 | .2 |
| 1.0 | | 3.4 |

> Although A is clearly "worth" more than B, it is riskier because it is more volatile. Diversification lessens the volatility by allowing investors to invest in 20 or 200 A's which will tend to guarantee a total result near the value. Shareholders are thus better off with the various firms selecting A over B, although after the fact they will complain in each case of the 2.6 loss. If the courts did not abide by the business judgment rule, they might well penalize the choice of A in each such case and thereby unknowingly injure shareholders generally by creating incentives for management always to choose B.

---

### NOTE ON THE DIVERGENCE OF STANDARDS OF CONDUCT AND STANDARDS OF REVIEW IN CORPORATE LAW, AND ON THE BUSINESS JUDGMENT RULE

A *standard of conduct* states how an actor should conduct a given activity or play a given role. A *standard of review* states the test a court should apply when it reviews an actor's conduct to determine whether to impose liability or grant injunctive relief. In many or most areas of law, standards of conduct and standards of review are identical. For example, the standard of conduct that governs an automobile driver is that he should drive carefully. Correspondingly, the standard of review in a liability claim against a driver is whether he drove carefully. The standard of conduct that governs an agent who engages in a transaction with his principal that involves the subject matter of the agency is that the agent must deal fairly. Correspondingly, the standard of review in a liability claim by the principal against an agent based on such a transaction is whether the agent dealt fairly.

An identity between standards of conduct and standards of review is so common that it is easy to overlook the fact that the two kinds of standards may diverge in any given area—that is, the standard of conduct that states how an actor should conduct himself may differ from the standard of review by which courts determine whether to impose liability on the basis of the actor's conduct. A divergence of standards of conduct and standards of review is particularly common in corporation law.

The duty of care is a leading example of this divergence. The general *standard of conduct* applicable to directors and officers in the performance of their functions, in relation to matters in which they are not interested, varies somewhat in its formulation, but the basic standard is set forth in Section 4.01(a) of the ALI's *Principles of Corporate Governance*. "A director or officer has a duty to the corporation to perform the director's or officer's functions in good faith, in a manner that he or she reasonably believes to be in the best interests of the corporation, and with the care that an ordinarily prudent person would reasonably be expected to exercise in a like position and under similar circumstances." The application of this standard of conduct to the functions of directors results in several distinct duties—in particular, the duty to monitor, the duty of inquiry, the duty to make prudent or reasonable decisions on matters that the board is obliged or chooses to act upon, and the duty to employ a reasonable process to make decisions.

Officers have comparable duties, although for most officers decisionmaking is likely to be more important than monitoring.

On their face, the duties of directors are fairly demanding, insofar as they are measured by reasonability. In practice, however, the standards of review applied to the performance of these duties are less stringent than the standards of conduct on which the duties are based. This is especially true when the quality of a decision—that is, the reasonableness of the decision, as opposed to the reasonableness of the decisionmaking process—is called into question. In such cases a much less demanding standard of review may apply, under the business judgment rule.

The business judgment rule consists of four conditions and, if the four conditions are satisfied, a special standard of review applicable to claims that are based on the quality of a decision.

The four conditions are as follows:

First, the director must have made a decision. So, for example, a director's failure to make due inquiry, or any other simple failure to take action (as opposed to a deliberative decision not to act), does not qualify for protection under the business judgment rule.

Second, the director must have informed himself with respect to the business judgment to the extent he reasonably believes appropriate under the circumstances—that is, he must have employed a reasonable decisionmaking process.

Third, the decision must have been made in good faith—a condition that is not satisfied if, among other things, the director knows that the decision violates the law.

Fourth, the director may not have a financial interest in the subject matter of the decision. For example, the business judgment rule is inapplicable to a director's decision to approve the corporation's purchase of his own property.

If the conditions of the business judgment rule are not satisfied, then the standard by which the quality of a decision is reviewed is comparable to the standard of conduct for making the decision—that is, the standard of review is based on entire fairness or reasonability. This is nicely illustrated by the Delaware Supreme Court's decision in Cede & Co. v. Technicolor, Inc., in 1993. Cede & Co. v. Technicolor, Inc., 634 A.2d 345 (Del.1993), modified, 636 A.2d 956 (Del.1994), on remand, Cinerama, Inc. v. Technicolor, Inc., 663 A.2d 1134 (Del.Ch. 1994), aff'd, 663 A.2d 1156 (Del.1995) appeal after remand, 684 A.2d 289 (Del.1996), on remand, 1999 WL 65042 (Del.Ch.) reconsideration denied 1999 WL 135242 (Del.Ch.).

In that case, Perelman, the CEO of MacAndrews & Forbes, Inc. ("MAF"), entered into negotiations with Kamerman, the CEO of Technicolor, with a view to an acquisition of Technicolor by MAF. Goldman Sachs, the investment banker, told Kamerman, on the basis of limited information, that a price of $20–22 per share was worth pursuing, that a $25 price might be feasible, and that Kamerman should consider other possible purchasers. Six days later, Kamerman and Perelman agreed on a price of $23. That evening, Kamerman called a special meeting of Technicolor's Board, to be held two days later. At the meeting, the board approved an agreement with Pantry Pride that reflected the $23 price, and recommended that Technicolor's shareholders accept that price.

At the trial, the Chancellor found that it was a matter of grave doubt whether Technicolor's board had exercised due care in making its decision for the following reasons, among others: (1) The agreement was not preceded by a prudent search of alternatives. (2) Given the terms of the merger and the circumstances, the directors had no reasonable basis to assume that a better offer from a third party could be expected once the agreement was signed. (3) Most of the directors had little or no knowledge of an impending sale of the company until they arrived at the meeting, and only a few of them had any knowledge of the terms of the sale.

On the basis of these conclusions, the Delaware Supreme Court held that Technicolor's board failed to reach an informed decision when it made its decision, so that the business judgment rule did not apply. As a result, the directors had the burden of showing that the transaction was entirely fair. If the $23 price was not entirely fair, the directors would be liable for damages. And, the court added, because the business judgment rule did not apply the directors had the burden of proving that the price was entirely fair.

In contrast, if the four conditions of the business judgment rule are satisfied, then the quality of a director's decision will be reviewed, not to determine whether the decision was reasonable, but only under a much more limited standard. There is some difference of opinion as to how that limited standard should be formulated. A few courts have stated that the standard is whether the director acted in good faith. See, e.g., In re RJR Nabisco, Inc. Shareholders Litig., [1988–89 Transfer Binder] Fed. Sec. L. Rep. (CCH) ¶ 94194, at 91,710 n.l3 (Del. Ch. Jan. 31, 1989). However, the prevalent formulation of the standard of review under the business judgment rule, if the four conditions of the rule have been satisfied, is that the decision must be rational, or must have a rational basis, or the like. See ALI, Principles of Corporate Governance § 4.01(c)(3). This standard of review may be referred to as the business-judgment standard.

An example of a decision that fails to satisfy the rationality standard is a decision that cannot be coherently explained. For example, in Selheimer v. Manganese Corp. of America, 224 A.2d 634 (Pa.1966), a corporation's managers poured the corporation's funds into the development of a single plant even though they knew that the plant could not be operated profitably for a number of reasons, including lack of a railroad siding and proper storage areas. The court imposed liability because the managers' conduct "defie[d] explanation; in fact, the defendants have failed to give any satisfactory explanation or advance any justification for [the] expenditures." (In contrast, a decision may be *unreasonable* if there are good reasons for and against the decision, but under the circumstances a person of sound judgment, giving appropriate weight to the reasons for and against, would not have made the decision. Accordingly, a decision may be unreasonable even though it was supported by some affirmative reasons and was therefore explicable, although on balance objectively undesirable.)

Although, as *Selheimer* shows, the rationality test has a bite, this standard of review is very much easier to satisfy than a reasonability standard. To see how exceptional a rationality standard is, we need only think about the judgments we make in everyday life. It is common to characterize a person's conduct as imprudent or unreasonable, but it is very uncommon to characterize a person's conduct as irrational.

Why should such a relatively undemanding standard of review, which differs so radically from the standard of conduct applicable to directors (and from the standards of both conduct and review applicable to persons who play most other life-roles) apply to the quality of decisions made by corporate directors? The answer to this question involves considerations of both fairness and policy.

To begin with, the application of a reasonableness standard of review to the quality of disinterested decisions by directors could result in the unfair imposition of liability. In paradigm negligence cases involving relatively simple decisions, such as automobile accidents, there is often little difference between decisions that turn out badly and bad decisions. In such cases, typically only one reasonable decision could have been made under a given set of circumstances, and decisions that turn out badly therefore almost inevitably turn out to have been bad decisions.

In contrast, in the case of business decisions it may often be difficult for fact-finders to distinguish between bad decisions and proper decisions that turn out badly. Business judgments are necessarily made on the basis of incomplete information and in the face of obvious risks, so that typically a range of decisions is reasonable. A decisionmaker faced with uncertainty must make a judgment concerning the relevant probability distribution and must act on that judgment. If the decisionmaker makes a reasonable assessment of the probability distribution, and the outcome falls on the unlucky tail, the decisionmaker has not made a bad decision, because in any normal probability distribution some outcomes will inevitably fall on the unlucky tail.

For example, a board faced with a promising but expensive and untried new technology may have to choose between investing in the technology or forgoing such an investment. Each alternative involves certain negative risks. If the board chooses one alternative and the associated negative risk materializes, the decision is "wrong" in the very restricted sense that if the board had it to do all over again it would make a different decision, but the decision is not for that reason a bad decision.

As a result of a systematic defect in cognition known as the hindsight bias, however, under a reasonableness standard of review fact-finders might too often erroneously treat decisions that turned out badly as bad decisions, and unfairly hold directors liable for such decisions. Experimental psychology has shown that in hindsight people consistently exaggerate the ease with which outcomes could have been anticipated in foresight. People view what has happened as relatively inevitable.[1] Accordingly, people who know that a bad *out-*

---

**1.** See Robyn M. Dawes, Rational Choice in an Uncertain World 119–20 (1988); Baruch Fischhoff, For Those Condemned to Study the Past: Heuristics and Biases in Hindsight, in Judgment Under Uncertainty: Heuristics and Biases 335, 341–43 (Daniel Kahneman et al. eds., 1982) [hereinafter Heuristics and Biases]. Baruch Fischhoff & Ruth Beyth, "I Knew It Would Happen"— Remembered Probabilities of Once–Future Things, 13 Organizational Behav. and Hum.

*come* resulted from a decision overestimate the extent to which the outcome was *predictable* and, therefore, the extent to which the decisionmaker was at fault for making the decision that led to the outcome.[2] Essentially, people find it difficult or even impossible to disregard information they possess about an outcome.[3] That information, in turn, renders the circumstances that pointed to the outcome more salient in their minds, because those circumstances can be integrated into a cohesive story that ends with the actual outcome, while circumstances pointing in other directions cannot.

The hindsight bias is nicely illustrated by an experiment in which 112 anesthesiologists reviewed the anesthesiological care in 21 paired cases that were based on actual files. Each of the anesthesiologists was presented with only one case from each pair. The patient and the treatments in each of the two paired cases were identical, and the results in all cases were as adverse. However, the files were edited so that in one case in each pair the adverse outcome was described as temporary, while in the other case the outcome was described as permanent. The reviewers were instructed to determine, in each of the 21 cases they reviewed, whether the anesthesiological care was less than appropriate, appropriate, or impossible to judge. When the adverse outcome was described as permanent rather than temporary, the overall distributions of the reviewers' judgments concerning the appropriateness of the care was shifted negatively by 30 percent.[4] Comparable results have been obtained in other experiments, even when the subjects have been explicitly instructed to disregard outcomes in evaluating fault.[5] The hindsight bias is also well-supported by survey evidence concerning the attribution of responsibility, and by casual empiricism.[6] The business judgment rule protects directors from the unfair imposition of liability as a result of the hindsight bias, by providing them with a large zone of protection when their decisions are attacked.

Furthermore, as a matter of policy the shareholders' own best interests may be served by conducting only a very limited review of the quality of directors' decisions. It is often in the interests of shareholders that directors choose the riskier of two alternative decisions,

Performance 1–16 (1975) [hereinafter Fischhoff & Beyth].

**2.** See Hal Arkes & Cindy Schipani, Medical Malpractice and the Business Judgment Rule, 73 Ore. L. Rev. 587 (1994) [hereinafter Arkes & Schipani, Medical Malpractice]; Jonathan D. Casper et al., Juror Decision Making, Attitudes, and the Hindsight Bias, 13 L. & Hum. Behav. 291 (1989) [hereinafter Casper, Juror Decision Making]; Raanan Lipshitz, "Either a Medal or a Corporal:" The Effects of Success and Failure on the Evaluation of Decision Making and Decision Makers, 44 Organizational Behav. & Hum. Decision Processes 380 (1989) [hereinafter Lipshitz, Success and Failure].

**3.** See Michael J. Saks & Robert F. Kidd, Human Information processing and Ad-

judication: Trial by Heuristics, 15 L. & Soc'y Rev. 123, 144 (1980).

**4.** Robert A. Caplan et al., Effect of Outcome on Physician Judgments of Appropriateness of Care, 265 J. Am. Med. Ass'n 1957 (1991). This experiment, as well as the hindsight bias, its application to the business judgment rule, and other hindsight experiments in the medical area, are discussed in a very illuminating way in Arkes & Schipani, Medical Malpractice, supra note 3.

**5.** See, e.g., Casper, Juror Decision Making, supra note 2.

**6.** See Lipshitz, Success and Failure, supra note 2, at 381–82.

because the expected value of the more risky decision may be greater than the expected value of the less risky decision. For example, suppose that Corporation C has $100 million in assets. C's board must choose between decision X and decision Y. Each decision requires an investment of $1 million. Decision X has a 75% likelihood of succeeding. If the decision succeeds, C will gain $2 million. If it fails, C will lose its $1 million investment. Decision Y has a 90% chance of succeeding. If the decision succeeds, C will gain $1 million. If it fails, C will recover its investment. It is in the interest of C's shareholders that the board make decision X, even though it is riskier, because the expected value of decision X is $1.25 million (75% times the $2 million potential gain, minus 25% times the $1 million loss), while the expected value of decision Y is only $900,000 (90% of the $1 million potential gain). If, however, the board was concerned about liability for making an unreasonable decision it might choose decision Y, because as a practical matter it is almost impossible for a plaintiff to win a duty of care action on the theory that a board should have taken greater risks than it did. A standard of review of the quality of decisions that impose liability on a director for unreasonable, as opposed to irrational, decisions might therefore have the perverse incentive effect of discouraging bold but desirable decisions. Putting this more generally, under such a standard of review directors might tend to be unduly risk-averse, because if a highly risky decision had a positive outcome the corporation but not the directors would gain, while if it had a negative outcome the directors might be required to make up the corporate loss. The business judgment rule helps to offset that tendency.

---------

## Smith v. Van Gorkom

Supreme Court of Delaware, 1985.
488 A.2d 858.

■ Before HERMANN, C.J., and MCNEILLY, HORSEY, MOORE and CHRISTIE, JJ., constituting the Court en banc.

■ HORSEY, JUSTICE (for the majority):

This appeal from the Court of Chancery involves a class action brought by shareholders of the defendant Trans Union Corporation ("Trans Union" or "the Company"), originally seeking rescission of a cash-out merger of Trans Union into the defendant New T Company ("New T"), a wholly-owned subsidiary of the defendant, Marmon Group, Inc. ("Marmon"). Alternate relief in the form of damages is sought against the defendant members of the Board of Directors of Trans Union, New T, and Jay A. Pritzker and Robert A. Pritzker, owners of Marmon.[1]

---

**1.**  The plaintiff, Alden Smith, originally sought to enjoin the merger; but, following extensive discovery, the Trial Court denied the plaintiff's motion for preliminary injunction by unreported letter opinion dated February 3, 1981. On February 10, 1981, the

Following trial, the former Chancellor granted judgment for the defendant directors by unreported letter opinion dated July 6, 1982.[2] Judgment was based on two findings: (1) that the Board of Directors had acted in an informed manner so as to be entitled to protection of the business judgment rule in approving the cash-out merger; and (2) that the shareholder vote approving the merger should not be set aside because the stockholders had been "fairly informed" by the Board of Directors before voting thereon. The plaintiffs appeal.

Speaking for the majority of the Court, we conclude that both rulings of the Court of Chancery are clearly erroneous. Therefore, we reverse and direct that judgment be entered in favor of the plaintiffs and against the defendant directors for the fair value of the plaintiffs' stockholdings in Trans Union. . . .

## I.

The nature of this case requires a detailed factual statement. The following facts are essentially uncontradicted. . . .

Trans Union was a publicly-traded, diversified holding company, the principal earnings of which were generated by its railcar leasing business. During the period here involved, the Company had a cash flow of hundreds of millions of dollars annually. However, the Company had difficulty in generating sufficient taxable income to offset increasingly large investment tax credits (ITCs). . . .

## B.

[Jerome Van Gorkom, Trans Union's Chairman and Chief Executive Officer, met with senior management on August 27, 1980, to discuss Trans Union's difficulty in producing sufficient taxable income to offset its increasing investment-tax credits and accelerated-depreciation deductions.] Donald Romans, Chief Financial Officer of Trans Union, stated that his department had done a "very brief bit of work on the possibility of a leveraged buy-out." . . . The work consisted of a "preliminary study" of the cash which could be generated by the Company if it participated in a leveraged buy-out. As Romans stated, this analysis "was very first and rough cut at seeing whether a cash flow would support what might be considered a high price for this type of transaction."

On September 5, at another Senior Management meeting which Van Gorkom attended, Romans again brought up the idea of a leveraged buy-out as a "possible strategic alternative" to the Compa-

---

proposed merger was approved by Trans Union's stockholders at a special meeting and the merger became effective on that date. Thereafter, John W. Gosselin was permitted to intervene as an additional plaintiff; and Smith and Gosselin were certified as representing a class consisting of all persons, other than defendants, who held shares of Trans Union common stock on all relevant dates. At the time of the merger, Smith owned 54,000 shares of Trans Union stock, Gosselin owned 23,600 shares, and members of Gosselin's family owned 20,000 shares.

**2.** Following trial, and before decision by the Trial Court, the parties stipulated to the dismissal, with prejudice, of the Messrs. Pritzker as parties defendant. However, all references to defendants hereinafter are to the defendant directors of Trans Union, unless otherwise noted.

ny's acquisition program. Romans and Bruce S. Chelberg, President and Chief Operating Officer of Trans Union, had been working on the matter in preparation for the meeting. According to Romans: They did not "come up" with a price for the Company. They merely "ran the numbers" at $50 a share and at $60 a share with the "rough form" of their cash figures at the time. Their "figures indicated that $50 would be very easy to do but $60 would be very difficult to do under those figures." This work did not purport to establish a fair price for either the Company or 100% of the stock. It was intended to determine the cash flow needed to service the debt that would "probably" be incurred in a leveraged buy-out, based on "rough calculations" without "any benefit of experts to identify what the limits were to that, and so forth." These computations were not considered extensive and no conclusion was reached.

At this meeting, Van Gorkom stated that he would be willing to take $55 per share for his own 75,000 shares. He vetoed the suggestion of a leveraged buy-out by Management, however, as involving a potential conflict of interest for Management. Van Gorkom, a certified public accountant and lawyer, had been an officer of Trans Union for 24 years, its Chief Executive Officer for more than 17 years, and Chairman of its Board for 2 years. It is noteworthy in this connection that he was then approaching 65 years of age and mandatory retirement.

For several days following the September 5 meeting, Van Gorkom pondered the idea of a sale. . . .

Van Gorkom decided to meet with Jay A. Pritzker, a well-known corporate takeover specialist and a social acquaintance. However, rather than approaching Pritzker simply to determine his interest in acquiring Trans Union, Van Gorkom assembled a proposed per share price for sale of the Company and a financing structure by which to accomplish the sale. Van Gorkom did so without consulting either his Board or any members of Senior Management except one: Carl Peterson, Trans Union's Controller. Telling Peterson that he wanted no other person on his staff to know what he was doing, but without telling him why, Van Gorkom directed Peterson to calculate the feasibility of a leveraged buy-out at an assumed price per share of $55. Apart from the Company's historic stock market price,[5] and Van Gorkom's long association with Trans Union, the record is devoid of any competent evidence that $55 represented the per share intrinsic value of the Company. . . .

Van Gorkom arranged a meeting with Pritzker at the latter's home on Saturday, September 13, 1980. Van Gorkom prefaced his presentation by stating to Pritzker: "Now as far as you are concerned, I can, I think, show how you can pay a substantial premium over the present

---

**5.** The common stock of Trans Union was traded on the New York Stock Exchange. Over the five year period from 1975 through 1979, Trans Union's stock had traded within a range of a high of $39½ and a low of $24¼. Its high and low range for 1980 through September 19 (the last trading day before announcement of the merger) was $38¼–$29½.

stock price and pay off most of the loan in the first five years. . . . If you could pay $55 for this Company, here is a way in which I think it can be financed."

Van Gorkom then reviewed with Pritzker his calculations based upon his proposed price of $55 per share. Although Pritzker mentioned $50 as a more attractive figure, no other price was mentioned. However, Van Gorkom stated that to be sure that $55 was the best price obtainable, Trans Union should be free to accept any better offer. Pritzker demurred, stating that his organization would serve as a "stalking horse" for an "auction contest" only if Trans Union would permit Pritzker to buy 1,750,000 shares of Trans Union stock at market price which Pritzker could then sell to any higher bidder. After further discussion on this point, Pritzker told Van Gorkom that he would give him a more definite reaction soon.

On Monday, September 15, Pritzker advised Van Gorkom that he was interested in the $55 cash-out merger proposal and requested more information on Trans Union. . . .

On Thursday, September 18, Van Gorkom met again with Pritzker. At that time, Van Gorkom knew that Pritzker intended to make a cash-out merger offer at Van Gorkom's proposed $55 per share. Pritzker instructed his attorney, a merger and acquisition specialist, to begin drafting merger documents. There was no further discussion of the $55 price. However, the number of shares of Trans Union's treasury stock to be offered to Pritzker was negotiated down to one million shares; the price was set at $38—75 cents above the per share price at the close of the market on September 19. At this point, Pritzker insisted that the Trans Union Board act on his merger proposal within the next three days, stating to Van Gorkom: "We have to have a decision by no later than Sunday [evening, September 21] before the opening of the English stock exchange on Monday morning." Pritzker's lawyer was then instructed to draft the merger documents, to be reviewed by Van Gorkom's lawyer, "sometimes with discussion and sometimes not, in the haste to get it finished."

On Friday, September 19, Van Gorkom, Chelberg, and Pritzker consulted with Trans Union's lead bank regarding the financing of Pritzker's purchase of Trans Union. The bank indicated that it could form a syndicate of banks that would finance the transaction. On the same day, Van Gorkom retained James Brennan, Esquire, to advise Trans Union on the legal aspects of the merger. Van Gorkom did not consult with William Browder, a Vice–President and director of Trans Union and former head of its legal department, or with William Moore, then the head of Trans Union's legal staff.

On Friday, September 19, Van Gorkom called a special meeting of the Trans Union Board for noon the following day. He also called a meeting of the Company's Senior Management to convene at 11:00 a.m., prior to the meeting of the Board. No one, except Chelberg and Peterson, was told the purpose of the meetings. Van Gorkom did not invite Trans Union's investment banker, Salomon Brothers or its Chicago-based partner, to attend.

Of those present at the Senior Management meeting on September 20, only Chelberg and Peterson had prior knowledge of Pritzker's offer. Van Gorkom disclosed the offer and described its terms, but he furnished no copies of the proposed Merger Agreement. Romans announced that his department had done a second study which showed that, for a leveraged buy-out, the price range for Trans Union stock was between $55 and $65 per share. Van Gorkom neither saw the study nor asked Romans to make it available for the Board meeting.

Senior Management's reaction to the Pritzker proposal was completely negative. No member of Management, except Chelberg and Peterson, supported the proposal. Romans objected to the price as being too low[6] . . . .

Ten directors served on the Trans Union Board, five inside (defendants Bonser, O'Boyle, Browder, Chelberg, and Van Gorkom) and five outside (defendants Wallis, Johnson, Lanterman, Morgan and Reneker). All directors were present at the meeting, except O'Boyle who was ill. Of the outside directors, four were corporate chief executive officers and one was the former Dean of the University of Chicago Business School. None was an investment banker or trained financial analyst. All members of the Board were well informed about the Company and its operations as a going concern. They were familiar with the current financial condition of the Company, as well as operating and earnings projections reported in the recent Five Year Forecast. The Board generally received regular and detailed reports and was kept abreast of the accumulated investment tax credit and accelerated depreciation problem.

Van Gorkom began the Special Meeting of the Board with a twenty-minute oral presentation. Copies of the proposed Merger Agreement were delivered too late for study before or during the meeting.[7] He reviewed the Company's ITC and depreciation problems and the efforts theretofore made to solve them. He discussed his initial meeting with Pritzker and his motivation in arranging that meeting. Van Gorkom did not disclose to the Board, however, the methodology by which he alone had arrived at the $55 figure, or the fact that he first proposed the $55 price in his negotiations with Pritzker.

Van Gorkom outlined the terms of the Pritzker offer as follows: Pritzker would pay $55 in cash for all outstanding shares of Trans Union stock upon completion of which Trans Union would be merged into New T Company, a subsidiary wholly-owned by Pritzker and

---

**6.** Van Gorkom asked Romans to express his opinion as to the $55 price. Romans stated that he "thought the price was too low in relation to what he could derive for the company in a cash sale, particularly one which enabled us to realize the values of certain subsidiaries and independent entities."

**7.** The record is not clear as to the terms of the Merger Agreement. The Agree-

ment, as originally presented to the Board on September 20, was never produced by defendants despite demands by the plaintiffs. Nor is it clear that the directors were given an opportunity to study the Merger Agreement before voting on it. All that can be said is that Brennan had the Agreement before him during the meeting.

formed to implement the merger; for a period of 90 days, Trans Union could receive, but could not actively solicit, competing offers; the offer had to be acted on by the next evening, Sunday, September 21; Trans Union could only furnish to competing bidders published information, and not proprietary information; the offer was subject to Pritzker obtaining the necessary financing by October 10, 1980; if the financing contingency were met or waived by Pritzker, Trans Union was required to sell to Pritzker one million newly-issued shares of Trans Union at $38 per share.

Van Gorkom took the position that putting Trans Union "up for auction" through a 90–day market test would validate a decision by the Board that $55 was a fair price. He told the Board that the "free market will have an opportunity to judge whether $55 is a fair price." Van Gorkom framed the decision before the Board not as whether $55 per share was the highest price that could be obtained, but as whether the $55 price was a fair price that the stockholders should be given the opportunity to accept or reject.[8]

Attorney Brennan advised the members of the Board that they might be sued if they failed to accept the offer and that a fairness opinion was not required as a matter of law.

Romans attended the meeting as chief financial officer of the Company. He told the Board that he had not been involved in the negotiations with Pritzker and knew nothing about the merger proposal until the morning of the meeting; that his studies did not indicate either a fair price for the stock or a valuation of the Company; that he did not see his role as directly addressing the fairness issue; and that he and his people "were trying to search for ways to justify a price in connection with such a [leveraged buy-out] transaction, rather than to say what the shares are worth." Romans testified:

> I told the Board that the study ran the numbers at 50 and 60, and then the subsequent study at 55 and 65, and that was not the same thing as saying that I have a valuation of the company at X dollars. But it was a way—a first step towards reaching that conclusion.

Romans told the Board that, in his opinion, $55 was "in the range of a fair price," but "at the beginning of the range." . . .

The Board meeting of September 20 lasted about two hours. Based solely upon Van Gorkom's oral presentation, Chelberg's supporting representations, Romans' oral statement, Brennan's legal advice, and their knowledge of the market history of the Company's stock, the directors approved the proposed Merger Agreement. However, the Board later claimed to have attached two conditions to its acceptance: (1) that Trans Union reserved the right to accept any better offer that was made during the market test period; and (2) that Trans Union could share its proprietary information with any other potential bidders. While the Board now claims to have reserved the

---

8. In Van Gorkom's words: The "real decision" is whether to "let the stockholders decide it" which is "all you are being asked to decide today."

right to accept any better offer received after the announcement of the Pritzker agreement (even though the minutes of the meeting do not reflect this), it is undisputed that the Board did not reserve the right to actively solicit alternate offers.

The Merger Agreement was executed by Van Gorkom during the evening of September 20 at a formal social event that he hosted for the opening of the Chicago Lyric Opera. Neither he nor any other director read the agreement prior to its signing and delivery to Pritzker. . . .

On Monday, September 22, the Company issued a press release announcing that Trans Union had entered into a "definitive" Merger Agreement with an affiliate of the Marmon Group, Inc., a Pritzker holding company. Within 10 days of the public announcement, dissent among Senior Management over the merger had become widespread. Faced with threatened resignations of key officers, Van Gorkom met with Pritzker who agreed to several modifications of the Agreement. Pritzker was willing to do so provided that Van Gorkom could persuade the dissidents to remain on the Company payroll for at least six months after consummation of the merger.

Van Gorkom reconvened the Board on October 8 and secured the directors' approval of the proposed amendments—sight unseen. The Board also authorized the employment of Salomon Brothers, its investment banker, to solicit other offers for Trans Union during the proposed "market test" period.

The next day, October 9, Trans Union issued a press release announcing: (1) that Pritzker had obtained "the financing commitments necessary to consummate" the merger with Trans Union; (2) that Pritzker had acquired one million shares of Trans Union common stock at $38 per share; (3) that Trans Union was now permitted to actively seek other offers and had retained Salomon Brothers for that purpose; and (4) that if a more favorable offer were not received before February 1, 1981, Trans Union's shareholders would thereafter meet to vote on the Pritzker proposal.

It was not until the following day, October 10, that the actual amendments to the Merger Agreement were prepared by Pritzker and delivered to Van Gorkom for execution. As will be seen, the amendments were considerably at variance with Van Gorkom's representations of the amendments to the Board on October 8; and the amendments placed serious constraints on Trans Union's ability to negotiate a better deal and withdraw from the Pritzker agreement. Nevertheless, Van Gorkom proceeded to execute what became the October 10 amendments to the Merger Agreement without conferring further with the Board members and apparently without comprehending the actual implications of the amendments. . . .

Salomon Brothers' efforts over a three-month period from October 21 to January 21 produced only one serious suitor for Trans Union—General Electric Credit Corporation ("GE Credit"), a subsidiary of the General Electric Company. However, GE Credit was unwilling to make an offer for Trans Union unless Trans Union first rescinded its Merger Agreement with Pritzker. When Pritzker refused, GE Credit terminated further discussions with Trans Union in early January.

In the meantime, in early December, the investment firm Kohlberg, Kravis, Roberts & Co. ("KKR"), the only other concern to make a firm offer for Trans Union, withdrew its offer under circumstances hereinafter detailed.

. . . On January 21, Management's Proxy Statement for the February 10 shareholder meeting was mailed to Trans Union's stockholders. On January 26, Trans Union's Board met and, after a lengthy meeting, voted to proceed with the Pritzker merger. . . .

On February 10, the stockholders of Trans Union approved the Pritzker merger proposal. Of the outstanding shares, 69.9% were voted in favor of the merger; 7.25% were voted against the merger; and 22.85% were not voted.

## II.

We turn to the issue of the application of the business judgment rule to the September 20 meeting of the Board.

The Court of Chancery concluded from the evidence that the Board of Directors' approval of the Pritzker merger proposal fell within the protection of the business judgment rule. The Court found that the Board had given sufficient time and attention to the transaction, since the directors had considered the Pritzker proposal on three different occasions, on September 20, and on October 8, 1980 and finally on January 26, 1981. On that basis, the Court reasoned that the Board had acquired, over the four-month period, sufficient information to reach an informed business judgment on the cash-out merger proposal. The Court ruled:

> . . . that given the market value of Trans Union's stock, the business acumen of the members of the board of Trans Union, the substantial premium over market offered by the Pritzkers and the ultimate effect on the merger price provided by the prospect of other bids for the stock in question, that the board of directors of Trans Union did not act recklessly or improvidently in determining on a course of action which they believed to be in the best interest of the stockholders of Trans Union.

The Court of Chancery made but one finding; i.e., that the Board's conduct over the entire period from September 20 through January 26, 1981 was not reckless or improvident, but informed. This ultimate conclusion was premised upon three subordinate findings, one explicit and two implied. The Court's explicit finding was that Trans Union's Board was "free to turn down the Pritzker proposal" not only on September 20 but also on October 8, 1980 and on January 26, 1981. The Court's implied, subordinate findings were: (1) that no legally binding agreement was reached by the parties until January 26; and (2) that if a higher offer were to be forthcoming, the market test would have produced it, and Trans Union would have been contractually free to accept such higher offer. However, the Court offered no factual basis or legal support for any of these findings; and the record compels contrary conclusions. . . .

Under Delaware law, the business judgment rule is the offspring of the fundamental principle, codified in 8 Del.C. § 141(a), that the business and affairs of a Delaware corporation are managed by or under its board of directors. . . . The rule itself "is a presumption that in making a business decision, the directors of a corporation acted on an informed basis, in good faith and in the honest belief that the action taken was in the best interests of the company." . . . [Aronson v. Lewis, 473 A.2d 805, 812 (Del.1984)]. Thus, the party attacking a board decision as uninformed must rebut the presumption that its business judgment was an informed one. Id.

The determination of whether a business judgment is an informed one turns on whether the directors have informed themselves "prior to making a business decision, of all material information reasonably available to them." Id.

Under the business judgment rule there is no protection for directors who have made "an unintelligent or unadvised judgment." Mitchell v. Highland–Western Glass, Del.Ch., 167 A. 831, 833 (1933). . . .

The standard of care applicable to a director's duty of care has also been recently restated by this Court. In *Aronson*, supra, we stated:

> While the Delaware cases use a variety of terms to describe the applicable standard of care, our analysis satisfies us that under the business judgment rule director liability is predicated upon concepts of gross negligence. (footnote omitted)

473 A.2d at 812.

We again confirm that view. We think the concept of gross negligence is also the proper standard for determining whether a business judgment reached by a board of directors was an informed one. . . .

It is against those standards that the conduct of the directors of Trans Union must be tested, as a matter of law and as a matter of fact, regarding their exercise of an informed business judgment in voting to approve the Pritzker merger proposal.

## III.   . . .

. . . [T]he question of whether the directors reached an informed business judgment in agreeing to sell the Company, pursuant to the terms of the September 20 Agreement presents, in reality, two questions: (A) whether the directors reached an informed business judgment on September 20, 1980; and (B) if they did not, whether the directors' actions taken subsequent to September 20 were adequate to cure any infirmity in their action taken on September 20. We first consider the directors' September 20 action in terms of their reaching an informed business judgment.

**–A–**

On the record before us, we must conclude that the Board of Directors did not reach an informed business judgment on September 20, 1980 in voting to "sell" the Company for $55 per share pursuant to the Pritzker cash-out merger proposal. Our reasons, in summary, are as follows:

The directors (1) did not adequately inform themselves as to Van Gorkom's role in forcing the "sale" of the Company and in establishing the per share purchase price; (2) were uninformed as to the intrinsic value of the Company; and (3) given these circumstances, at a minimum, were grossly negligent in approving the "sale" of the Company upon two hours' consideration, without prior notice, and without the exigency of a crisis or emergency.

As has been noted, the Board based its September 20 decision to approve the cash-out merger primarily on Van Gorkom's representations. None of the directors, other than Van Gorkom and Chelberg, had any prior knowledge that the purpose of the meeting was to propose a cash-out merger of Trans Union....

Without any documents before them concerning the proposed transaction, the members of the Board were required to rely entirely upon Van Gorkom's 20–minute oral presentation of the proposal. No written summary of the terms of the merger was presented; the directors were given no documentation to support the adequacy of $55 price per share for sale of the Company; and the Board had before it nothing more than Van Gorkom's statement of his understanding of the substance of an agreement which he admittedly had never read, nor which any member of the Board had ever seen.

Under 8 Del.C. § 141(e), "directors are fully protected in relying in good faith on reports made by officers." Michelson v. Duncan, 386 A.2d 1144, 1156 (Del.Ch. 1978); aff'd in part and rev'd in part on other grounds, Del.Supr., 407 A.2d 211 (1979). See also Graham v. Allis–Chalmers Mfg. Co., Del.Supr., 188 A.2d 125, 130 (1963); Prince v. Bensinger, Del.Ch., 244 A.2d 89, 94 (1968). The term "report" has been liberally construed to include reports of informal personal investigations by corporate officers, Cheff v. Mathes, Del.Supr., 199 A.2d 548, 556 (1964). However, there is no evidence that any "report," as defined under § 141(e), concerning the Pritzker proposal, was presented to the Board on September 20. Van Gorkom's oral presentation of his understanding of the terms of the proposed Merger Agreement, which he had not seen, and Romans' brief oral statement of his preliminary study regarding the feasibility of a leveraged buy-out of Trans Union do not qualify as § 141(e) "reports" for these reasons: The former lacked substance because Van Gorkom was basically uninformed as to the essential provisions of the very document about which he was talking. Romans' statement was irrelevant to the issues before the Board since it did not purport to be a valuation study. At a minimum for a report to enjoy the status conferred by § 141(e), it must be pertinent to the subject matter upon which a board is called to act, and otherwise be entitled to good faith, not blind, reliance.

Considering all of the surrounding circumstances—hastily calling the meeting without prior notice of its subject matter, the proposed sale of the Company without any prior consideration of the issue or necessity therefor, the urgent time constraints imposed by Pritzker, and the total absence of any documentation whatsoever—the directors were duty bound to make reasonable inquiry of Van Gorkom and Romans, and if they had done so, the inadequacy of that upon which they now claim to have relied would have been apparent.

The defendants rely on the following factors to sustain the Trial Court's finding that the Board's decision was an informed one: (1) the magnitude of the premium or spread between the $55 Pritzker offering price and Trans Union's current market price of $38 per share; (2) the amendment of the Agreement as submitted on September 20 to permit the Board to accept any better offer during the "market test" period; (3) the collective experience and expertise of the Board's "inside" and "outside" directors; and (4) their reliance on Brennan's legal advice that the directors might be sued if they rejected the Pritzker proposal. We discuss each of these grounds *seriatim:*

### (1)

A substantial premium may provide one reason to recommend a merger, but in the absence of other sound valuation information, the fact of a premium alone does not provide an adequate basis upon which to assess the fairness of an offering price. Here, the judgment reached as to the adequacy of the premium was based on a comparison between the historically depressed Trans Union market price and the amount of the Pritzker offer. Using market price as a basis for concluding that the premium adequately reflected the true value of the Company was a clearly faulty, indeed fallacious, premise. . . .

The record is clear that before September 20, Van Gorkom and other members of Trans Union's Board knew that the market had consistently undervalued the worth of Trans Union's stock. . . .

The parties do not dispute that a publicly-traded stock price is solely a measure of the value of a minority position and, thus, market price represents only the value of a single share. Nevertheless, on September 20, the Board assessed the adequacy of the premium over market, offered by Pritzker, solely by comparing it with Trans Union's current and historical stock price. . . .

Indeed, as of September 20, the Board had no other information on which to base a determination of the intrinsic value of Trans Union as a going concern. As of September 20, the Board had made no evaluation of the Company designed to value the entire enterprise, nor had the Board ever previously considered selling the Company or consenting to a buy-out merger. Thus, the adequacy of a premium is indeterminate unless it is assessed in terms of other competent and sound valuation information that reflects the value of the particular business.

Despite the foregoing facts and circumstances, there was no call by the Board, either on September 20 or thereafter, for any valuation study or documentation of the $55 price per share as a measure of the fair value of the Company in a cash-out context. It is undisputed that the major asset of Trans Union was its cash flow. Yet, at no time did the Board call for a valuation study taking into account that highly significant element of the Company's assets.

We do not imply that an outside valuation study is essential to support an informed business judgment; nor do we state that fairness opinions by independent investment bankers are required as a matter of law. Often insiders familiar with the business of a going concern are in a better position than are outsiders to gather relevant information; and under appropriate circumstances, such directors may be fully protected in relying in good faith upon the valuation reports of their management. See 8 Del.C. § 141(e)....

Here, the record establishes that the Board did not request its Chief Financial Officer, Romans, to make any valuation study or review of the proposal to determine the adequacy of $55 per share for sale of the Company. On the record before us: The Board rested on Romans' elicited response that the $55 figure was within a "fair price range" within the context of a leveraged buy-out. No director sought any further information from Romans. No director asked him why he put $55 at the bottom of his range. No director asked Romans for any details as to his study, the reason why it had been undertaken or its depth. No director asked to see the study; and no director asked Romans whether Trans Union's finance department could do a fairness study within the remaining 36-hour period available under the Pritzker offer....

Thus, the record compels the conclusion that on September 20 the Board lacked valuation information adequate to reach an informed business judgment as to the fairness of $55 per share for sale of the Company.

### (2)

This brings us to the post-September 20 "market test" upon which the defendants ultimately rely to confirm the reasonableness of their September 20 decision to accept the Pritzker proposal. In this connection, the directors present a two-part argument: (a) that by making a "market test" of Pritzker's $55 per share offer a condition of their September 20 decision to accept his offer, they cannot be found to have acted impulsively or in an uninformed manner on September 20; and (b) that the adequacy of the $17 premium for sale of the Company was conclusively established over the following 90 to 120 days by the most reliable evidence available—the marketplace. Thus, the defendants impliedly contend that the "market test" eliminated the need for the Board to perform any other form of fairness test either on September 20, or thereafter.

Again, the facts of record do not support the defendants' argument. There is no evidence: (a) that the Merger Agreement was effectively amended to give the Board freedom to put Trans Union up for auction sale to the highest bidder; or (b) that a public auction was in fact permitted to occur. The minutes of the Board meeting make no reference to any of this. Indeed, the record compels the conclusion that the directors had no rational basis for expecting that a market test was attainable, given the terms of the Agreement as executed during the evening of September 20. We rely upon the following facts which are essentially uncontradicted:

The Merger Agreement, specifically identified as that originally presented to the Board on September 20, has never been produced by the defendants, notwithstanding the plaintiffs' several demands for production before as well as during trial. No acceptable explanation of this failure to produce documents has been given to either the Trial Court or this Court. . . .

Van Gorkom states that the Agreement as submitted incorporated the ingredients for a market test by authorizing Trans Union to receive competing offers over the next 90–day period. However, he concedes that the Agreement barred Trans Union from actively soliciting such offers and from furnishing to interested parties any information about the Company other than that already in the public domain. Whether the original Agreement of September 20 went so far as to authorize Trans Union to receive competitive proposals is arguable. The defendants' unexplained failure to produce and identify the original Merger Agreement permits the logical inference that the instrument would not support their assertions in this regard. . . .

The defendant directors assert that they "insisted" upon including two amendments to the Agreement, thereby permitting a market test: (1) to give Trans Union the right to accept a better offer; and (2) to reserve to Trans Union the right to distribute proprietary information on the Company to alternative bidders. Yet, the defendants concede that they did not seek to amend the Agreement to permit Trans Union to solicit competing offers.

Several of Trans Union's outside directors resolutely maintained that the Agreement as submitted was approved on the understanding that, "if we got a better deal, we had a right to take it." Director Johnson so testified; but he then added, "And if they didn't put that in the agreement, then the management did not carry out the conclusion of the Board. And I just don't know whether they did or not." The only clause in the Agreement as finally executed to which the defendants can point as "keeping the door open" is the following underlined statement found in subparagraph (a) of section 2.03 of the Merger Agreement as executed:

The Board of Directors shall recommend to the stockholders of Trans Union that they approve and adopt the Merger Agreement ("the stockholders' approval") and to use its best efforts to obtain the requisite votes therefor. *GL acknowledges that Trans Union directors may have a competing fiduciary obligation to the shareholders under certain circumstances.*

Clearly, this language on its face cannot be construed as incorporating either of the two "conditions" described above: either the right to accept a better offer or the right to distribute proprietary information to third parties.... No reference to either of the so-called "conditions" or of Trans Union's reserved right to test the market appears in any notes of the Board meeting or in the Board Resolution accepting the Pritzker offer or in the Minutes of the meeting itself....

Thus, notwithstanding what several of the outside directors later claimed to have "thought" occurred at the meeting, the record compels the conclusion that Trans Union's Board had no rational basis to conclude on September 20 or in the days immediately following, that the Board's acceptance of Pritzker's offer was conditioned on (1) a "market test" of the offer; and (2) the Board's right to withdraw from the Pritzker Agreement and accept any higher offer received before the shareholder meeting.

### (3)

The directors' unfounded reliance on both the premium and the market test as the basis for accepting the Pritzker proposal undermines the defendants' remaining contention that the Board's collective experience and sophistication was a sufficient basis for finding that it reached its September 20 decision with informed, reasonable deliberation....

### (4) ...

We conclude that Trans Union's Board was grossly negligent in that it failed to act with informed reasonable deliberation in agreeing to the Pritzker merger proposal on September 20....

### –B–

We now examine the Board's post-September 20 conduct for the purpose of determining first, whether it was informed and not grossly negligent; and second, if informed, whether it was sufficient to legally rectify and cure the Board's derelictions of September 20.[23]

### (1)

First, as to the Board meeting of October 8....

The public announcement of the Pritzker merger resulted in an "en masse" revolt of Trans Union's Senior Management. The head of Trans Union's tank car operations (its most profitable division) informed Van Gorkom that unless the merger were called off, fifteen key personnel would resign.

Instead of reconvening the Board, Van Gorkom again privately met with Pritzker, informed him of the developments, and sought his advice. Pritzker then made the following suggestions for overcoming Management's dissatisfaction: (1) that the Agreement be amended to permit Trans Union to solicit, as well as receive, higher offers; and (2)

---

**23.** As will be seen, we do not reach the second question.

that the shareholder meeting be postponed from early January to February 10, 1981. In return, Pritzker asked Van Gorkom to obtain a commitment from Senior Management to remain at Trans Union for at least six months after the merger was consummated.

Van Gorkom then advised Senior Management that the Agreement would be amended to give Trans Union the right to solicit competing offers through January, 1981, if they would agree to remain with Trans Union. Senior Management was temporarily mollified; and Van Gorkom then called a special meeting of Trans Union's Board for October 8.

Thus, the primary purpose of the October 8 Board meeting was to amend the Merger Agreement, in a manner agreeable to Pritzker, to permit Trans Union to conduct a "market test." Van Gorkom understood that the proposed amendments were intended to give the Company an unfettered "right to openly solicit offers down through January 31." Van Gorkom presumably so represented the amendments to Trans Union's Board members on October 8. In a brief session, the directors approved Van Gorkom's oral presentation of the substance of the proposed amendments, the terms of which were not reduced to writing until October 10. But rather than waiting to review the amendments, the Board again approved them sight unseen and adjourned, giving Van Gorkom authority to execute the papers when he received them.[25] . . .

The next day, October 9, and before the Agreement was amended, Pritzker moved swiftly to off-set the proposed market test amendment. First, Pritzker informed Trans Union that he had completed arrangements for financing its acquisition and that the parties were thereby mutually bound to a firm purchase and sale arrangement. Second, Pritzker announced the exercise of his option to purchase one million shares of Trans Union's treasury stock at $38 per share—75 cents above the current market price. Trans Union's Management responded the same day by issuing a press release announcing: (1) that all financing arrangements for Pritzker's acquisition of Trans Union had been completed; and (2) Pritzker's purchase of one million shares of Trans Union's treasury stock at $38 per share.

The next day, October 10, Pritzker delivered to Trans Union the proposed amendments to the September 20 Merger Agreement. Van Gorkom promptly proceeded to countersign all the instruments on behalf of Trans Union without reviewing the instruments to determine if they were consistent with the authority previously granted him by the Board. The amending documents were apparently not approved by Trans Union's Board until a much later date, December 2. The

25. We do not suggest that a board must read *in haec verba* every contract or legal document which it approves, but if it is to successfully absolve itself from charges of the type made here, there must be some credible contemporary evidence demonstrating that the directors knew what they were doing, and ensured that their purported action was given effect. That is the consistent failure which cast this Board upon its unredeemable course.

record does not affirmatively establish that Trans Union's directors ever read the October 10 amendments.[26]

The October 10 amendments to the Merger Agreement did authorize Trans Union to solicit competing offers, but the amendments had more far-reaching effects. The most significant change was in the definition of the third-party "offer" available to Trans Union as a possible basis for withdrawal from its Merger Agreement with Pritzker. Under the October 10 amendments, a better *offer* was no longer sufficient to permit Trans Union's withdrawal. Trans Union was now permitted to terminate the Pritzker Agreement and abandon the merger only if, prior to February 10, 1981, Trans Union had either consummated a merger (or sale of assets) with a third party or had entered into a "definitive" merger agreement more favorable than Pritzker's and for a greater consideration—subject only to stockholder approval. Further, the "extension" of the market test period to February 10, 1981 was circumscribed by other amendments which required Trans Union to file its preliminary proxy statement on the Pritzker merger proposal by December 5, 1980 and use its best efforts to mail the statement to its shareholders by January 5, 1981. Thus, the market test period was effectively reduced, not extended. . . .

In our view, the record compels the conclusion that the directors' conduct on October 8 exhibited the same deficiencies as did their conduct on September 20. The Board permitted its Merger Agreement with Pritzker to be amended in a manner it had neither authorized nor intended. . . .

We conclude that the Board acted in a grossly negligent manner on October 8; and that Van Gorkom's representations on which the Board based its actions do not constitute "reports" under § 141(e) on which the directors could reasonably have relied. Further, the amended Merger Agreement imposed on Trans Union's acceptance of a third party offer conditions more onerous than those imposed on Trans Union's acceptance of Pritzker's offer on September 20. After October 10, Trans Union could accept from a third party a better offer only if it were incorporated in a definitive agreement between the parties, and not conditioned on financing or on any other contingency.

The October 9 press release, coupled with the October 10 amendments, had the clear effect of locking Trans Union's Board into the Pritzker Agreement. Pritzker had thereby foreclosed Trans Union's Board from negotiating any better "definitive" agreement over the remaining eight weeks before Trans Union was required to clear the Proxy Statement submitting the Pritzker proposal to its shareholders.

## (2)

[On December 2, KKR offered to buy Trans–Union for $60/share. Van Gorkom apparently was resistant to this offer, and KKR withdrew

---

**26.** There is no evidence of record that Trans Union's directors ever raised any objections, procedural or substantive, to the October 10 amendments or that any of them, including Van Gorkom, understood the opposite result of their intended effect—until it was too late.

it for reasons that were cloudy. In mid-January, GE Credit Corporation made a proposal which] was not in the form of an offer. Had there been time to do so, GE Credit was prepared to offer between $2 and $5 per share above the $55 per share price which Pritzker offered. But GE Credit needed an additional 60 to 90 days; and it was unwilling to make a formal offer without a concession from Pritzker extending the February 10 "deadline" for Trans Union's stockholder meeting. . . . Pritzker refused to grant such extension. . . .

Our review of the record compels a finding that confirmation of the appropriateness of the Pritzker offer by an unfettered or free market test was virtually meaningless in the face of the terms and time limitations of Trans Union's Merger Agreement with Pritzker as amended October 10, 1980.

. . . [W]e hold that the defendants' post-September conduct did not cure the deficiencies of their September 20 conduct; and that, accordingly, the Trial Court erred in according to the defendants the benefits of the business judgment rule. . . .

### V.

The defendants ultimately rely on the stockholder vote of February 10 for exoneration. The defendants contend that the stockholders' "overwhelming" vote approving the Pritzker Merger Agreement had the legal effect of curing any failure of the Board to reach an informed business judgment in its approval of the merger.

The parties tacitly agree that a discovered failure of the Board to reach an informed business judgment in approving the merger constitutes a voidable, rather than a void, act. Hence, the merger can be sustained, notwithstanding the infirmity of the Board's action, if its approval by majority vote of the shareholders is found to have been based on an informed electorate. . . . the disagreement between the parties arises over . . . the sufficiency of the evidence as to whether the Board satisfied that burden.

[The court rejected the shareholder-approval defense on the ground that Trans Union's stockholders were not fully informed of all facts material to their vote on the Pritzker Merger, and that the Trial Court's ruling to the contrary was clearly erroneous.] . . .

### VI.

. . . We hold, therefore, that the Trial Court committed reversible error in applying the business judgment rule in favor of the director defendants in this case.

On remand, the Court of Chancery shall conduct an evidentiary hearing to determine the fair value of the shares represented by the plaintiffs' class, based on the intrinsic value of Trans Union on September 20, 1980. Such valuation shall be made in accordance with Weinberger v. UOP, Inc., supra. . . . Thereafter, an award of damages may be entered to the extent that the fair value of Trans Union exceeds $55 per share.

Reversed and Remanded for proceedings consistent herewith.

■ McNEILLY, JUSTICE, dissenting . . .

I have no quarrel with the majority's analysis of the business judgment rule. It is the application of that rule to these facts which is wrong. An overview of the entire record, rather than the limited view of bits and pieces which the majority has exploded like popcorn, convinces me that the directors made an informed business judgment which was buttressed by their test of the market. . . .

At the time of the September 20 meeting the 10 members of Trans Union's Board of Directors were highly qualified and well informed about the affairs and prospects of Trans Union. These directors were acutely aware of the historical problems facing Trans Union which were caused by the tax laws. They had discussed these problems *ad nauseam*. In fact, within two months of the September 20 meeting the board had reviewed and discussed an outside study of the company done by The Boston Consulting Group and an internal five year forecast prepared by management. At the September 20 meeting Van Gorkom presented the Pritzker offer, and the board then heard from James Brennan, the company's counsel in this matter, who discussed the legal documents. Following this, the Board directed that certain changes be made in the merger documents. These changes made it clear that the Board was free to accept a better offer than Pritzker's if one was made. The above facts reveal that the Board did not act in a grossly negligent manner in informing themselves of the relevant and available facts before passing on the merger. To the contrary, this record reveals that the directors acted with the utmost care in informing themselves of the relevant and available facts before passing on the merger. . . .

[The dissenting opinion of Justice Christie is omitted.]

———

It is reported that after the decision of the Delaware Supreme Court, an agreement was reached to settle *Van Gorkom* by the payment of $23.5 million to the plaintiff class. Of that amount, $10 million, the policy limit, was provided by Trans Union's directors' and officers' liability-insurance carrier. Nearly all of the $13.5 million balance was paid by the Pritzker group on behalf of the Trans Union defendant directors, although the Pritzker group was not a defendant. See Manning, Reflections and Practical Tips on Life in the Boardroom After *Van Gorkom*, 41 Bus.Law. 1 (1985).

———

## NOTE ON SUBSTANCE AND PROCESS IN THE DUTY OF CARE

In many areas of law, a distinction is drawn between substance and process. The duty of care may be understood in that way too. In effect, the business judgment rule gives wide latitude to a substantive decision of a director or senior executive if the *process* elements of the duty of care are satisfied. Under this distinction, the process elements of the duty of care, which involve such matters as preparing to make a decision, general monitoring, and following up suspicious circumstances, are governed by a standard of reasonability. However, if the process by which a decision was made satisfies the reasonability standard, the substantive decision itself will be reviewed only under the much looser standard of rationality.

---

## (c) THE DUTY TO ENSURE THAT THE CORPORATION HAS EFFECTIVE INTERNAL CONTROLS

---

## In re Caremark International Inc. Derivative Litigation

Delaware Court of Chancery, 1996.
698 A.2d 959.

■ ALLEN, CHANCELLOR.

Pending is a motion pursuant to Chancery Rule 23.1 to approve as fair and reasonable a proposed settlement of a consolidated derivative action on behalf of Caremark International, Inc. ("Caremark"). The suit involves claims that the members of Caremark's board of directors (the "Board") breached their fiduciary duty of care to Caremark in connection with alleged violations by Caremark employees of federal and state laws and regulations applicable to health care providers. As a result of the alleged violations, Caremark was subject to an extensive four year investigation by the United States Department of Health and Human Services and the Department of Justice. In 1994 Caremark was charged in an indictment with multiple felonies. It thereafter entered into a number of agreements with the Department of Justice and others. Those agreements included a plea agreement in which Caremark pleaded guilty to a single felony of mail fraud and agreed to pay civil and criminal fines. Subsequently, Caremark agreed to make reimbursements to various private and public parties. In all, the payments that Caremark has been required to make total approximately $250 million.

This suit was filed in 1994, purporting to seek on behalf of the company recovery of these losses from the individual defendants who constitute the board of directors of Caremark.[1] The parties now propose that it be settled and, after notice to Caremark shareholders, a hearing on the fairness of the proposal was held on August 16, 1996.

A motion of this type requires the court to assess the strengths and weaknesses of the claims asserted in light of the discovery record

---

1. Thirteen of the Directors have been members of the Board since November 30, 1992. Nancy Brinker joined the Board in October 1993.

and to evaluate the fairness and adequacy of the consideration offered to the corporation in exchange for the release of all claims made or arising from the facts alleged. The ultimate issue then is whether the proposed settlement appears to be fair to the corporation and its absent shareholders. In this effort the court does not determine contested facts, but evaluates the claims and defenses on the discovery record to achieve a sense of the relative strengths of the parties' positions. Polk v. Good, Del.Supr., 507 A.2d 531, 536 (1986). In doing this, in most instances, the court is constrained by the absence of a truly adversarial process, since inevitably both sides support the settlement and legally assisted objectors are rare. . . .

Legally, evaluation of the central claim made entails consideration of the legal standard governing a board of directors' obligation to supervise or monitor corporate performance. For the reasons set forth below I conclude, in light of the discovery record, that there is a very low probability that it would be determined that the directors of Caremark breached any duty to appropriately monitor and supervise the enterprise. Indeed the record tends to show an active consideration by Caremark management and its Board of the Caremark structures and programs that ultimately led to the company's indictment and to the large financial losses incurred in the settlement of those claims. It does not tend to show knowing or intentional violation of law. Neither the fact that the Board, although advised by lawyers and accountants, did not accurately predict the severe consequences to the company that would ultimately follow from the deployment by the company of the strategies and practices that ultimately led to this liability, nor the scale of the liability, gives rise to an inference of breach of any duty imposed by corporation law upon the directors of Caremark.

## I.  BACKGROUND

For these purposes I regard the following facts, suggested by the discovery record, as material. Caremark, a Delaware corporation with its headquarters in Northbrook, Illinois, was created in November 1992 when it was spun-off from Baxter International, Inc. ("Baxter") and became a publicly held company listed on the New York Stock Exchange. The business practices that created the problem pre-dated the spin-off. During the relevant period Caremark was involved in two main health care business segments, providing patient care and managed care services. As part of its patient care business, which accounted for the majority of Caremark's revenues, Caremark provided alternative site health care services, including infusion therapy, growth hormone therapy, HIV/AIDS-related treatments and hemophilia therapy. Caremark's managed care services included prescription drug programs and the operation of multi-specialty group practices.

### A.  Events Prior to the Government Investigation

A substantial part of the revenues generated by Caremark's businesses is derived from third party payments, insurers, and Medicare and Medicaid reimbursement programs. The latter source of payments are subject to the terms of the Anti–Referral Payments Law ("ARPL") which prohibits health care providers from paying any form of remuneration to induce the referral of Medicare or Medicaid patients. From its inception, Caremark entered into a variety of agreements with hospitals, physicians, and health care providers for advice and services, as well as distribution agreements with drug manufacturers, as had its predecessor prior to 1992. Specifically, Caremark did have a practice of entering into contracts for services (e.g., consultation agreements and research grants) with physicians at least some of whom prescribed or recommended services or products that Caremark provided to Medicare recipients and other patients. Such contracts were not prohibited by the ARPL but they obviously raised a possibility of unlawful "kickbacks."

As early as 1989, Caremark's predecessor issued an internal "Guide to Contractual Relationships" ("Guide") to govern its employees in entering into contracts with physicians and hospitals. The Guide tended to be reviewed annually by lawyers and updated. Each version of the Guide stated as Caremark's and its predecessor's policy that no payments would be made in exchange for or to induce patient referrals. But what one might deem a prohibited quid pro quo was not always clear. Due to a scarcity of court decisions interpreting the ARPL, however, Caremark repeatedly publicly stated that there was uncertainty concerning Caremark's interpretation of the law.

To clarify the scope of the ARPL, the United States Department of Health and Human Services ("HHS") issued "safe harbor" regulations in July 1991 stating conditions under which financial relationships between health care service providers and patient referral sources, such as physicians, would not violate the ARPL. Caremark contends that the narrowly drawn regulations gave limited guidance as to the legality of many of the agreements used by Caremark that did not fall within the safe-harbor. Caremark's predecessor, however, amended many of its standard forms of agreement with health care providers and revised the Guide in an apparent attempt to comply with the new regulations.

### B. Government Investigation and Related Litigation

In August 1991, the HHS Office of the Inspector General ("OIG") initiated an investigation of Caremark's predecessor. Caremark's predecessor was served with a subpoena requiring the production of documents, including contracts between Caremark's predecessor and physicians (Quality Service Agreements ("QSAs")). Under the QSAs, Caremark's predecessor appears to have paid physicians fees for monitoring patients under Caremark's predecessor's care, including Medicare and Medicaid recipients. Sometimes apparently those monitoring patients were referring physicians, which raised ARPL concerns.

In March 1992, the Department of Justice ("DOJ") joined the OIG investigation and separate investigations were commenced by several additional federal and state agencies.[2]

### C.  Caremark's Response to the Investigation

During the relevant period, Caremark had approximately 7,000 employees and ninety branch operations. It had a decentralized management structure. By May 1991, however, Caremark asserts that it had begun making attempts to centralize its management structure in order to increase supervision over its branch operations.

The first action taken by management, as a result of the initiation of the OIG investigation, was an announcement that as of October 1, 1991, Caremark's predecessor would no longer pay management fees to physicians for services to Medicare and Medicaid patients. Despite this decision, Caremark asserts that its management, pursuant to advice, did not believe that such payments were illegal under the existing laws and regulations.

During this period, Caremark's Board took several additional steps consistent with an effort to assure compliance with company policies concerning the ARPL and the contractual forms in the Guide. In April 1992, Caremark published a fourth revised version of its Guide apparently designed to assure that its agreements either complied with the ARPL and regulations or excluded Medicare and Medicaid patients altogether. In addition, in September 1992, Caremark instituted a policy requiring its regional officers, Zone Presidents, to approve each contractual relationship entered into by Caremark with a physician.

Although there is evidence that inside and outside counsel had advised Caremark's directors that their contracts were in accord with the law, Caremark recognized that some uncertainty respecting the correct interpretation of the law existed. In its 1992 annual report, Caremark disclosed the ongoing government investigations, acknowledged that if penalties were imposed on the company they could have a material adverse effect on Caremark's business, and stated that no assurance could be given that its interpretation of the ARPL would prevail if challenged.

Throughout the period of the government investigations, Caremark had an internal audit plan designed to assure compliance with business and ethics policies. In addition, Caremark employed Price Waterhouse as its outside auditor. On February 8, 1993, the [Audit & ] Ethics Committee of Caremark's Board received and reviewed an outside auditors report by Price Waterhouse which concluded that there were no material weaknesses in Caremark's control structure.[3]

---

**2.** In addition to investigating whether Caremark's financial relationships with health care providers were intended to induce patient referrals, inquiries were made concerning Caremark's billing practices, activities which might lead to excessive and medically unnecessary treatments for patients, potentially improper waivers of pa-tient co-payment obligations, and the adequacy of records kept at Caremark pharmacies.

**3.** At that time, Price Waterhouse viewed the outcome of the OIG Investigation as uncertain. After further audits, however, on February 7, 1995, Price Waterhouse informed the Audit & Ethics Committee that it had not become aware of any irregularities or

Despite the positive findings of Price Waterhouse, however, on April 20, 1993, the Audit & Ethics Committee adopted a new internal audit charter requiring a comprehensive review of compliance policies and the compilation of an employee ethics handbook concerning such policies.[4]

The Board appears to have been informed about this project and other efforts to assure compliance with the law. For example, Caremark's management reported to the Board that Caremark's sales force was receiving an ongoing education regarding the ARPL and the proper use of Caremark's form contracts which had been approved by in-house counsel. On July 27, 1993, the new ethics manual, expressly prohibiting payments in exchange for referrals and requiring employees to report all illegal conduct to a toll free confidential ethics hotline, was approved and allegedly disseminated.[5] The record suggests that Caremark continued these policies in subsequent years, causing employees to be given revised versions of the ethics manual and requiring them to participate in training sessions concerning compliance with the law.

During 1993, Caremark took several additional steps which appear to have been aimed at increasing management supervision. These steps included new policies requiring local branch managers to secure home office approval for all disbursements under agreements with health care providers and to certify compliance with the ethics program. In addition, the chief financial officer was appointed to serve as Caremark's compliance officer. In 1994, a fifth revised Guide was published.

### D.  Federal Indictments Against Caremark and Officers

On August 4, 1994, a federal grand jury in Minnesota issued a 47 page indictment charging Caremark, two of its officers (not the firm's chief officer), an individual who had been a sales employee of Genentech, Inc., and David R. Brown, a physician practicing in Minneapolis, with violating the ARPL over a lengthy period. According to the indictment, over $1.1 million had been paid to Brown to induce him to distribute Protropin, a human growth hormone drug marketed by Caremark.[6] The substantial payments involved started, according to the allegations of the indictment, in 1986 and continued through 1993. Some payments were "in the guise of research grants", Ind. ¶ 20, and others were "consulting agreements", Ind. ¶ 19. The indictment

---

illegal acts in relation to the OIG investigation.

**4.**  Price Waterhouse worked in conjunction with the Internal Audit Department.

**5.**  Prior to the distribution of the new ethics manual, on March 12, 1993, Caremark's president had sent a letter to all senior, district, and branch managers restating Caremark's policies that no physician be paid for referrals, that the standard contract forms in the Guide were not to be modified, and that deviation from such policies would

result in the immediate termination of employment.

**6.**  In addition to prescribing Protropin, Dr. Brown had been receiving research grants from Caremark as well as payments for services under a consulting agreement for several years before and after the investigation. According to an undated document from an unknown source, Dr. Brown and six other researchers had been providing patient referrals to Caremark valued at $6.55 for each $1 of research money they received.

charged, for example, that Dr. Brown performed virtually none of the consulting functions described in his 1991 agreement with Caremark, but was nevertheless neither required to return the money he had received nor precluded from receiving future funding from Caremark. In addition the indictment charged that Brown received from Caremark payments of staff and office expenses, including telephone answering services and fax rental expenses. . . .

Subsequently, five stockholder derivative actions were filed in this court and consolidated into this action. The original complaint, dated August 5, 1994, alleged, in relevant part, that Caremark's directors breached their duty of care by failing adequately to supervise the conduct of Caremark employees, or institute corrective measures, thereby exposing Caremark to fines and liability. . . .

After each complaint was filed, defendants filed a motion to dismiss. According to defendants, if a settlement had not been reached in this action, the case would have been dismissed on two grounds. First, they contend that the complaints fail to allege particularized facts sufficient to excuse the demand requirement under Delaware Chancery Court Rule 23.1. Second, defendants assert that plaintiffs had failed to state a cause of action due to the fact that Caremark's charter eliminates directors' personal liability for money damages, to the extent permitted by law.

### E. Settlement Negotiations

In September, following the announcement of the Ohio indictment, Caremark publicly announced that as of January 1, 1995, it would terminate all remaining financial relationships with physicians in its home infusion, hemophilia, and growth hormone lines of business.[9] In addition, Caremark asserts that it extended its restrictive policies to all of its contractual relationships with physicians, rather than just those involving Medicare and Medicaid patients, and terminated its research grant program which had always involved some recipients who referred patients to Caremark.

Caremark began settlement negotiations with federal and state government entities in May 1995. In return for a guilty plea to a single count of mail fraud by the corporation, the payment of a criminal fine, the payment of substantial civil damages, and cooperation with further federal investigations on matters relating to the OIG investigation, the government entities agreed to negotiate a settlement that would permit Caremark to continue participating in Medicare and Medicaid programs. On June 15, 1995, the Board approved a settlement ("Government Settlement Agreement") with the DOJ, OIG, U.S. Veterans Administration, U.S. Federal Employee Health Benefits Program, federal Civilian Health and Medical Program of the Uniformed Services, and related state agencies in all fifty states and the District of Columbia.[10]

---

**9.** On June 1, 1993, Caremark had stopped entering into new contractual agreements in those business segments.

**10.** The agreement, covering allegations since 1986, required a Caremark subsidiary to enter a guilty plea to two counts of mail fraud, and required Caremark to pay

No senior officers or directors were charged with wrongdoing in the Government Settlement Agreement or in any of the prior indictments. In fact, as part of the sentencing in the Ohio action on June 19, 1995, the United States stipulated that no senior executive of Caremark participated in, condoned, or was willfully ignorant of wrongdoing in connection with the home infusion business practices.

The federal settlement included certain provisions in a "Corporate Integrity Agreement" designed to enhance future compliance with law. The parties have not discussed this agreement, except to say that the negotiated provisions of the settlement of this claim are not redundant of those in that agreement.

Settlement negotiations between the parties in this action commenced in May 1995 as well, based upon a letter proposal of the plaintiffs, dated May 16, 1995. These negotiations resulted in a memorandum of understanding ("MOU"), dated June 7, 1995, and the execution of the Stipulation and Agreement of Compromise and Settlement on June 28, 1995, which is the subject of this action.[13] The MOU, approved by the Board on June 15, 1995, required the Board to adopt several resolutions, discussed below, and to create a new compliance committee. The Compliance and Ethics Committee has been reporting to the Board in accord with its newly specified duties. . . .

### F. The Proposed Settlement of this Litigation

In relevant part the terms upon which these claims asserted are proposed to be settled are as follows:

1. That Caremark undertakes that it and its employees and agents not pay any form of compensation to a third party in exchange for the referral of a patient to a Caremark facility or service or the prescription of drugs marketed or distributed by Caremark for which reimbursement may be sought from Medicare, Medicaid, or a similar state reimbursement program;

2. That Caremark undertakes for itself and its employees, and agents not to pay to or split fees with physicians, joint ventures, any business combination in which Caremark maintains a direct financial interest, or other health care providers with whom Caremark has a financial relationship or interest, in exchange for the referral of a patient to a Caremark facility or service or the prescription of drugs marketed or distributed by Caremark for which reimbursement may be sought from Medicare, Medicaid, or a similar state reimbursement program;

---

$29 million in criminal fines, $129.9 million relating to civil claims concerning payment practices, $3.5 million for alleged violations of the Controlled Substances Act, and $2 million, in the form of a donation, to a grant program set up by the Ryan White Comprehensive AIDS Resources Emergency Act. Caremark also agreed to enter into a compliance agreement with the HHS.

**13.** Plaintiffs' initial proposal had both a monetary component, requiring Caremark's director-officers to relinquish stock options, and a remedial component, requiring management to adopt and implement several compliance related measures. The monetary component was subsequently eliminated.

3.  That the full Board shall discuss all relevant material changes in government health care regulations and their effect on relationships with health care providers on a semi-annual basis;

4.  That Caremark's officers will remove all personnel from health care facilities or hospitals who have been placed in such facility for the purpose of providing remuneration in exchange for a patient referral for which reimbursement may be sought from Medicare, Medicaid, or a similar state reimbursement program;

5.  That every patient will receive written disclosure of any financial relationship between Caremark and the health care professional or provider who made the referral;

6.  That the Board will establish a Compliance and Ethics Committee of four directors, two of which will be non-management directors, to meet at least four times a year to effectuate these policies and monitor business segment compliance with the ARPL, and to report to the Board semi-annually concerning compliance by each business segment; and

7.  That corporate officers responsible for business segments shall serve as compliance officers who must report semi-annually to the Compliance and Ethics Committee and, with the assistance of outside counsel, review existing contracts and get advance approval of any new contract forms.

## II.  LEGAL PRINCIPLES

### A.  Principles Governing Settlements of Derivative Claims

As noted at the outset of this opinion, this Court is now required to exercise an informed judgment whether the proposed settlement is fair and reasonable in the light of all relevant factors. Polk v. Good, Del.Supr., 507 A.2d 531 (1986). On an application of this kind, this Court attempts to protect the best interests of the corporation and its absent shareholders all of whom will be barred from future litigation on these claims if the settlement is approved. The parties proposing the settlement bear the burden of persuading the court that it is in fact fair and reasonable. Fins v. Pearlman, Del.Supr., 424 A.2d 305 (1980).

### B.  Directors' Duties To Monitor Corporate Operations

The complaint charges the director defendants with breach of their duty of attention or care in connection with the ongoing operation of the corporation's business. The claim is that the directors allowed a situation to develop and continue which exposed the corporation to enormous legal liability and that in so doing they violated a duty to be active monitors of corporate performance. The complaint thus does not charge either director self-dealing or the more difficult loyalty-type problems arising from cases of suspect director motivation, such as entrenchment or sale of control contexts.[14] The theory here advanced is possibly the most difficult theory

---

**14.**  See Weinberger v. UOP, Inc., Del. Supr., 457 A.2d 701, 711 (1983) (entire fair-ness test when financial conflict of interest involved); Unitrin, Inc. v. American General

in corporation law upon which a plaintiff might hope to win a judgment. . . .

1. *Potential liability for directoral decisions:* Director liability for a breach of the duty to exercise appropriate attention may, in theory, arise in two distinct contexts. First, such liability may be said to follow from a board decision that results in a loss because that decision was ill advised or "negligent". Second, liability to the corporation for a loss may be said to arise from an unconsidered failure of the board to act in circumstances in which due attention would, arguably, have prevented the loss. See generally Veasey & Seitz, The Business Judgment Rule in the Revised Model Act . . . 63 TEXAS L.REV. 1483 (1985). The first class of cases will typically be subject to review under the director-protective business judgment rule. . . . See Aronson v. Lewis, Del.Supr., 473 A.2d 805 (1984); Gagliardi v. TriFoods Int'l, Inc., Del.Ch. 683 A.2d 1049 (July 19, 1996) . . . .

2. *Liability for failure to monitor*: The second class of cases in which director liability for inattention is theoretically possible entail circumstances in which a loss eventuates not from a decision but, from unconsidered inaction. Most of the decisions that a corporation, acting through its human agents, makes are, of course, not the subject of director attention. Legally, the board itself will be required only to authorize the most significant corporate acts or transactions: mergers, changes in capital structure, fundamental changes in business, appointment and compensation of the CEO, etc. As the facts of this case graphically demonstrate, ordinary business decisions that are made by officers and employees deeper in the interior of the organization can, however, vitally affect the welfare of the corporation and its ability to achieve its various strategic and financial goals. If this case did not prove the point itself, recent business history would. Recall for example the displacement of senior management and much of the board of Salomon, Inc.;[18] the replacement of senior management of Kidder, Peabody following the discovery of large trading losses resulting from phantom trades by a highly compensated trader;[19] or the extensive financial loss and reputational injury suffered by Prudential Insurance as a result [of] its junior officers' misrepresentations in connection with the distribution of limited partnership interests. Financial and organizational disasters such as these raise the question, what is the board's responsibility with respect to the organization and monitoring of the enterprise to assure that the corporation functions within the law to achieve its purposes?

Modernly this question has been given special importance by an increasing tendency, especially under federal law, to employ the

Corp., Del.Supr., 651 A.2d 1361, 1372 (1995) (intermediate standard of review when "defensive" acts taken); Paramount Communications, Inc. v. QVC Network, Del.Supr., 637 A.2d 34, 45 (1994) (intermediate test when corporate control transferred).

**18.** See, e.g., Rotten at the Core, the Economist, August 17, 1991, at 69–70; The

Judgment of Salomon: An Anticlimax, Bus. Week, June 1, 1992, at 106.

**19.** See Terence P. Pare, Jack Welch's Nightmare on Wall Street, Fortune, Sept. 5, 1994, at 40–48.

criminal law to assure corporate compliance with external legal requirements, including environmental, financial, employee and product safety as well as assorted other health and safety regulations. In 1991, pursuant to the Sentencing Reform Act of 1984,[21] the United States Sentencing Commission adopted Organizational Sentencing Guidelines which impact importantly on the prospective effect these criminal sanctions might have on business corporations. The Guidelines set forth a uniform sentencing structure for organizations to be sentenced for violation of federal criminal statutes and provide for penalties that equal or often massively exceed those previously imposed on corporations.[22] The Guidelines offer powerful incentives for corporations today to have in place compliance programs to detect violations of law, promptly to report violations to appropriate public officials when discovered, and to take prompt, voluntary remedial efforts.

In 1963, the Delaware Supreme Court in Graham v. Allis–Chalmers Mfg. Co.,[23] addressed the question of potential liability of board members for losses experienced by the corporation as a result of the corporation having violated the anti-trust laws of the United States. There was no claim in that case that the directors knew about the behavior of subordinate employees of the corporation that had resulted in the liability. Rather, as in this case, the claim asserted was that the directors ought to have known of it and if they had known they would have been under a duty to bring the corporation into compliance with the law and thus save the corporation from the loss. The Delaware Supreme Court concluded that, under the facts as they appeared, there was no basis to find that the directors had breached a duty to be informed of the ongoing operations of the firm. In notably colorful terms, the court stated that "absent cause for suspicion there is no duty upon the directors to install and operate a corporate system of espionage to ferret out wrongdoing which they have no reason to suspect exists."[24] The Court found that there were no grounds for suspicion in that case and, thus, concluded that the directors were blamelessly unaware of the conduct leading to the corporate liability.[25]

How does one generalize this holding today? Can it be said today that, absent some ground giving rise to suspicion of violation of law, that corporate directors have no duty to assure that a corporate information gathering and reporting system exists which represents a good faith attempt to provide senior management and the Board with information respecting material acts, events or conditions within the corporation, including compliance with applicable statutes and regulations? I certainly do not believe so. I doubt that such a broad generalization of the Graham holding would have been accepted by the Supreme Court in 1963. The case can be more narrowly interpret-

---

**21.** See Sentencing Reform Act of 1984, Pub.L. 98–473, Title II, § 212(a)(2) (1984); 18 U.S.C.A. §§ 3331–4120.

**22.** See United States Sentencing Commission, Guidelines Manual, Chapter 8 (U.S. Government Printing Office November 1994).

**23.** Del.Supr., 188 A.2d 125 (1963).

**24.** Id. at 130.

**25.** Recently, the *Graham* standard was applied by the Delaware Chancery in a case involving Baxter. In re Baxter International, Inc. Shareholders Litig., Del.Ch., 654 A.2d 1268, 1270 (1995).

ed as standing for the proposition that, absent grounds to suspect deception, neither corporate boards nor senior officers can be charged with wrongdoing simply for assuming the integrity of employees and the honesty of their dealings on the company's behalf. See 188 A.2d at 130–31.

A broader interpretation of *Graham v. Allis–Chalmers*—that it means that a corporate board has no responsibility to assure that appropriate information and reporting systems are established by management—would not, in any event, be accepted by the Delaware Supreme Court in 1996, in my opinion. In stating the basis for this view, I start with the recognition that in recent years the Delaware Supreme Court has made it clear—especially in its jurisprudence concerning takeovers, from *Smith v. Van Gorkom* through *Paramount Communications v. QVC*[26]—the seriousness with which the corporation law views the role of the corporate board. Secondly, I note the elementary fact that relevant and timely information is an essential predicate for satisfaction of the board's supervisory and monitoring role under Section 141 of the Delaware General Corporation Law. Thirdly, I note the potential impact of the federal organizational sentencing guidelines on any business organization. Any rational person attempting in good faith to meet an organizational governance responsibility would be bound to take into account this development and the enhanced penalties and the opportunities for reduced sanctions that it offers.

In light of these developments, it would, in my opinion, be a mistake to conclude that our Supreme Court's statement in *Graham* concerning "espionage" means that corporate boards may satisfy their obligation to be reasonably informed concerning the corporation, without assuring themselves that information and reporting systems exist in the organization that are reasonably designed to provide to senior management and to the board itself timely, accurate information sufficient to allow management and the board, each within its scope, to reach informed judgments concerning both the corporation's compliance with law and its business performance.

Obviously the level of detail that is appropriate for such an information system is a question of business judgment. And obviously too, no rationally designed information and reporting system will remove the possibility that the corporation will violate laws or regulations, or that senior officers or directors may nevertheless sometimes be misled or otherwise fail reasonably to detect acts material to the corporation's compliance with the law. But it is important that the board exercise a good faith judgment that the corporation's information and reporting system is in concept and design adequate to assure the board that appropriate information will come to its attention in a timely manner as a matter of ordinary operations, so that it may satisfy its responsibility.

**26.** E.g., Smith v. Van Gorkom, Del. Supr., 488 A.2d 858 (1985); Paramount Communications v. QVC Network, Del.Supr., 637 A.2d 34 (1994).

Thus, I am of the view that a director's obligation includes a duty to attempt in good faith to assure that a corporate information and reporting system, which the board concludes is adequate, exists, and that failure to do so under some circumstances may, in theory at least, render a director liable for losses caused by non-compliance with applicable legal standards.[27] I now turn to an analysis of the claims asserted with this concept of the directors' duty of care, as a duty satisfied in part by assurance of adequate information flows to the board, in mind.

### III.  ANALYSIS OF THIRD AMENDED COMPLAINT AND SETTLEMENT

#### A.  The Claims

On balance, after reviewing an extensive record in this case, including numerous documents and three depositions, I conclude that this settlement is fair and reasonable. In light of the fact that the Caremark Board already has a functioning committee charged with overseeing corporate compliance, the changes in corporate practice that are presented as consideration for the settlement do not impress one as very significant. Nonetheless, that consideration appears fully adequate to support dismissal of the derivative claims of director fault asserted, because those claims find no substantial evidentiary support in the record and quite likely were susceptible to a motion to dismiss in all events.

In order to show that the Caremark directors breached their duty of care by failing adequately to control Caremark's employees, plaintiffs would have to show either (1) that the directors knew or (2) should have known that violations of law were occurring and, in either event, (3) that the directors took no steps in a good faith effort to prevent or remedy that situation, and (4) that such failure proximately resulted in the losses complained of, although under Cede & Co. v. Technicolor, Inc., Del.Supr., 636 A.2d 956 (1994) this last element may be thought to constitute an affirmative defense....

... I turn to a consideration of the [claim based on] ... director inattention or "negligence." Generally where a claim of directorial liability for corporate loss is predicated upon ignorance of liability creating activities within the corporation, as in *Graham* or in this case, in my opinion only a sustained or systematic failure of the board to exercise oversight—such as an utter failure to attempt to assure a reasonable information and reporting system exits—will establish the lack of good faith that is a necessary condition to liability. Such a test of liability—lack of good faith as evidenced by sustained or systematic

---

**27.** Any action seeking recover for losses would logically entail a judicial determination of proximate cause, since, for reasons that I take to be obvious, it could never be assumed that an adequate information system would be a system that would prevent all losses. I need not touch upon the burden allocation with respect to a proximate cause issue in such a suit. See Cede & Co. v. Technicolor, Inc., Del.Supr., 636 A.2d 956 (1994); Cinerama, Inc. v. Technicolor, Inc., Del.Ch., 663 A.2d 1134 (1994), aff'd., Del.Supr., 663 A.2d 1156 (1995). Moreover, questions of waiver of liability under certificate provisions authorized by 8 Del.C. § 102(b)(7) may also be faced.

failure of a director to exercise reasonable oversight—is quite high. But, a demanding test of liability in the oversight context is probably beneficial to corporate shareholders as a class, as it is in the board decision context, since it makes board service by qualified persons more likely, while continuing to act as a stimulus to good faith performance of duty by such directors.

Here the record supplies essentially no evidence that the director defendants were guilty of a sustained failure to exercise their oversight function. To the contrary, insofar as I am able to tell on this record, the corporation's information systems appear to have represented a good faith attempt to be informed of relevant facts. If the directors did not know the specifics of the activities that lead to the indictments, they cannot be faulted.

The liability that eventuated in this instance was huge. But the fact that it resulted from a violation of criminal law alone does not create a breach of fiduciary duty by directors. The record at this stage does not support the conclusion that the defendants either lacked good faith in the exercise of their monitoring responsibilities or conscientiously permitted a known violation of law by the corporation to occur. The claims asserted against them must be viewed at this stage as extremely weak.

### B. The Consideration For Release of Claim

The proposed settlement provides very modest benefits. Under the settlement agreement, plaintiffs have been given express assurances that Caremark will have a more centralized, active supervisory system in the future. Specifically, the settlement mandates duties to be performed by the newly named Compliance and Ethics Committee on an ongoing basis and increases the responsibility for monitoring compliance with the law at the lower levels of management. In adopting the resolutions required under the settlement, Caremark has further clarified its policies concerning the prohibition of providing remuneration for referrals. These appear to be positive consequences of the settlement of the claims brought by the plaintiffs, even if they are not highly significant. Nonetheless, given the weakness of the plaintiffs' claims the proposed settlement appears to be an adequate, reasonable, and beneficial outcome for all of the parties. Thus, the proposed settlement will be approved....

I am today entering an order consistent with the foregoing.

———

## (d) LIMITS ON LIABILITY; DIRECTORS' AND OFFICERS' LIABILITY INSURANCE

In assessing the duties of directors and officers to act with care, account must be taken of three elements that may serve to reduce or eliminate civil liability for breach of those duties: direct limits of liability, insurance, and indemnification. The first two elements are addressed in this Section. Indemnification is addressed in Chapter 11.

———

## (1) LIMITS ON LIABILITY

———

### VIRGINIA CORPORATIONS CODE § 13.1–690

[See Statutory Supplement]

———

### DEL. GEN. CORP. LAW § 102(b)(7)

[See Statutory Supplement]

———

### REV. MODEL BUSINESS CORP. ACT § 2.02(b)(4)

[See Statutory Supplement]

———

**EMERALD PARTNERS v. BERLIN**, (Del. 1999). "[T]he shield from liability provided by a certificate of incorporation provision adopted pursuant to 8 Del. C. § 102(b)(7) is in the nature of an affirmative defense.... Defendants seeking exculpation under such a provision will normally bear the burden of establishing each of its elements. Here, the Court of Chancery incorrectly ruled that Emerald Partners [the plaintiff] was required to establish at trial that the individual defendants acted in bad faith or in breach of their duty of loyalty. To the contrary, the burden of demonstrating good faith, however slight it might be in given circumstances, is upon the party seeking the protection of the statute. Nonetheless, where the factual basis for a claim solely implicates a violation of the duty of care, this Court has indicated that the protections of such a charter provision may properly be invoked and applied."

———

## (2) DIRECTORS' AND OFFICERS' LIABILITY INSURANCE

———

## FORM OF DIRECTORS' AND OFFICERS' LIABILITY INSURANCE

[See Statutory Supplement]

———

### NOTE ON DIRECTORS' AND OFFICERS' LIABILITY INSURANCE

1.   The liability and legal expenses of directors and officers who are the subject of claims based on a lack of due care, and for certain other wrongful acts, will often be covered by Directors' and Officers' ("D & O") insurance. Among approximately 1325 participants in the Towers Perrin 1999 Directors and Officers Liability Survey, D & O insurance was carried by 92% of those with $100–400 million in assets, 94% of those with $1–2 billion in assets, and 97% of those with over $10 billion in assets. (92% of respondents with under $50 million in assets carried D & O insurance.) D & O insurance is commonly referred to as—and often captioned—"liability" insurance, because it insures against liability and legal expenses. Technically, however, D & O is indemnification insurance, because it does not require the insurer to defend (although it does require the insurer to indemnify for losses, including defense costs), and the insurer's obligations do not accrue until the claim is settled or adjudicated. See J. Bishop, The Law of Corporate Officers and Directors—Indemnification and Insurance § 8.05 (G. O'Gradney rev. 1994).

2.   Typically, a D & O policy has two separate insurance agreements: (i) Corporate reimbursement, which insures the corporation against potential liability to officers and directors under the latters' right to indemnification from the corporation. (ii) Personal coverage, which insures the directors and officers themselves against losses based on claims against them for wrongful conduct, when they are not indemnified for the loss by the corporation. There are various reasons why a director or officer may not be indemnified for such a loss by the corporation. For example, the law may prohibit such indemnification, as where the director's or officer's loss consists of a judgment against him in a duty-of-care action. Or the corporation may be insolvent, or it may refuse to make indemnification in a case where indemnification is discretionary rather than required.

The precise scope of the personal coverage varies according to the policy form, but all policies would normally cover most liabilities arising in connection with claims based on a violation of the duty of care owed to the corporation, and many or most policies would normally cover liabilities for duties of care owed to the general public, barring either a specific exclusion in the insurance policy or a prohibition of public policy.

3.   D & O insurance does not render directors and officers completely risk-free with regard to claims based on the duty of care. To begin with, a variety of claims are excluded from coverage, and some kinds of duty-of-care claims may fall within an exclusion, particu-

larly claims owed to the public. Next, the policy limits in D & O insurance typically apply to the combined amount of liability and legal expenses, and in any given case the combination of the two may exceed the policy limit. See Helfand v. National Union Fire Ins. Co., 10 Cal.App.4th 869, 13 Cal.Rptr.2d 295 (1992). Furthermore, many D & O policies contain an "insured v. insured" exclusion, under which the insurer is not liable in connection with claims made against a director or officer by the corporation, except a claim made in a shareholder's derivative action (that is, a claim made by a shareholder on the corporation's behalf).

Another characteristic of D & O insurance that may be relevant to the protection afforded by such insurance is that such insurance is written on a "claims made" basis—that is, the insurance applies to, but only to, claims made while the policy is in force. To illustrate, suppose C Corporation procured a D & O policy from X Insurance Company for 1999. A claim that is based on events that occurred in 1997 may be covered by the policy even though X was not C's insurer in 1997. Conversely, however, a claim based on events that occurred in 1999 may not be covered by X's policy if the claim is not made before the policy expires or is canceled, unless a new claims-made policy is in effect.

The claims-made nature of D & O insurance is often modified by several features. First, a policy may contain a "retroactive date" provision, under which events occurring before a designated date will not be covered by the policy even if a claim based on the events is first made during the policy period. Second, a policy may include a right of "discovery," which allows an insured to extend the coverage for a claim made during a limited period after the policy has terminated, provided the claim is based on wrongful acts that occurred prior to termination of the policy. In addition, many policies permit an insured to present a notice of occurrence of a possible claim during the policy period, which has the same effect as an actual claim made against the insured. Subject to these exceptions, an effect of the claims-made nature of D & O insurance is that a director or executive cannot be positive that he will be covered for his present conduct if a claim arises in the future, after the policy has expired or has been canceled.

Another factor that affects the risk of a director or officer for duty-of-care liability is that D & O insurers often seem to be exceptionally ready to litigate claims brought against them by their insureds. Some of the litigation concerns the interpretation of the policy language, which is often less than crystal clear. In addition, partly because D & O insurance is on a claims-made basis, the corporation and the directors and officers who are to be covered under a D & O policy must fill out extensive application questionnaires, which include questions on such issues as whether the applicant has knowledge or information of any act, error, or omission that might give rise to a claim under the policy. It is often easy for an insurer to argue that the policy is unenforceable on the ground that the questionnaire was not answered accurately. Furthermore, unless the policy has a provision to the contrary, the failure of only one director or .officer to answer accurately may invalidate the coverage of all officers and directors. See, e.g., Bird v. Penn Central Co., 334 F.Supp. 255 (E.D.Pa.1971), 341 F.Supp. 291 (1972); Shapiro v. American Home Assurance Co., 584 F.Supp. 1245 (D.Mass.1984).

---

## SECTION 2.   THE DUTY TO ACT LAWFULLY

---

## Miller v. American Telephone & Telegraph Co.

United States Court of Appeals, Third Circuit, 1974.
507 F.2d 759.

■ Before SEITZ, CHIEF JUDGE, GIBBONS and GARTH, CIRCUIT JUDGES.

■ SEITZ, CHIEF JUDGE.

Plaintiffs, stockholders in American Telephone and Telegraph Company ("AT & T"), brought a stockholders' derivative action in the Eastern District of Pennsylvania against AT & T and all but one of its directors. The suit centered upon the failure of AT & T to collect an outstanding debt of some $1.5 million owed to the company by the Democratic National Committee ("DNC") for communications services provided by AT & T during the 1968 Democratic national convention. Federal diversity jurisdiction was invoked under 28 U.S.C. § 1332.

Plaintiffs' complaint alleged that "neither the officers or directors of AT & T have taken any action to recover the amount owed" from on or about August 20, 1968, when the debt was incurred, until May 31, 1972, the date plaintiffs' amended complaint was filed. The failure to collect was alleged to have involved a breach of the defendant directors' duty to exercise diligence in handling the affairs of the corporation, to have resulted in affording a preference to the DNC in collection procedures in violation of § 202(a) of the Communications Act of 1934, 47 U.S.C. § 202(a) (1970), and to have amounted to AT & T's making a "contribution" to the DNC in violation of a federal prohibition on corporate campaign spending, 18 U.S.C. § 610 (1970).

Plaintiffs sought permanent relief in the form of an injunction requiring AT & T to collect the debt, an injunction against providing further services to the DNC until the debt was paid in full, and a surcharge for the benefit of the corporation against the defendant directors in the amount of the debt plus interest from the due date. A request for a preliminary injunction against the provision of services to the 1972 Democratic convention was denied by the district court after an evidentiary hearing.

·On motion of the defendants, the district court dismissed the complaint for failure to state a claim upon which relief could be granted. 364 F.Supp. 648 (E.D.Pa.1973). The court stated that collection procedures were properly within the discretion of the directors whose determination would not be overturned by the court in the absence of an allegation that the conduct of the directors was "plainly illegal, unreasonable, or in breach of a fiduciary duty...." *Id.* at 651. Plaintiffs appeal from dismissal of their complaint.

In viewing the motion to dismiss, we must consider all facts alleged in the complaint and every inference fairly deductible therefrom in the light most favorable to the plaintiffs. A complaint should not be dismissed unless it appears that the plaintiffs would not be entitled to relief under any facts which they might prove in support of their claim. Judging plaintiffs' complaint by these standards, we feel that it does state a claim upon which relief can be granted for breach of fiduciary duty arising from the alleged violation of 18 U.S.C. § 610.

## I.

The pertinent law on the question of the defendant directors' fiduciary duties in this diversity action is that of New York, the state of AT & T's incorporation.... The sound business judgment rule, the basis of the district court's dismissal of plaintiffs' complaint, expresses the unanimous decision of American courts to eschew intervention in corporate decision-making if the judgment of directors and officers is uninfluenced by personal considerations and is exercised in good faith. Pollitz v. Wabash Railroad Co., 207 N.Y. 113, 100 N.E. 721 (1912); Bayer v. Beran, 49 N.Y.S.2d 2, 4–7 (Sup.Ct.1944); 3 Fletcher, Private Corporations § 1039 (perm. ed. rev. vol. 1965). Underlying the rule is the assumption that reasonable diligence has been used in reaching the decision which the rule is invoked to justify....

Had plaintiffs' complaint alleged only failure to pursue a corporate claim, application of the sound business judgment rule would support the district court's ruling that a shareholder could not attack the directors' decision. *See* United Copper Securities Co. v. Amalgamated Copper Co., 244 U.S. 261, 37 S.Ct. 509, 61 L.Ed. 1119 (1917); Clifford v. Metropolitan Life Insurance Co., 264 App.Div. 168, 34 N.Y.S.2d 693 (2d Dept.1942); 13 Fletcher, Private Corporations § 5822 (perm. ed. rev. vol. 1970). Where, however, the decision not to collect a debt owed the corporation is itself alleged to have been an illegal act, different rules apply. When New York law regarding such acts by directors is considered in conjunction with the underlying purposes of the particular statute involved here, we are convinced that the business judgment rule cannot insulate the defendant directors from liability if they did in fact breach 18 U.S.C. § 610, as plaintiffs have charged.

Roth v. Robertson, 64 Misc. 343, 118 N.Y.S. 351 (Sup.Ct.1909), illustrates the proposition that even though committed to benefit the corporation, illegal acts may amount to a breach of fiduciary duty in New York. In *Roth,* the managing director of an amusement park company had allegedly used corporate funds to purchase the silence of persons who threatened to complain about unlawful Sunday operation of the park. Recovery from the defendant director was sustained on the ground that the money was an illegal payment:

> For reasons of public policy, we are clearly of the opinion that payments of corporate funds for such purposes as those disclosed in this case must be condemned, and officers of a corporation making them held to a strict accountability, and be compelled to refund the amounts so wasted for the benefit of stockholders. . . . To hold any other rule would be establishing a dangerous precedent, tacitly countenancing the wasting of corporate funds for purposes of corrupting public morals. *Id.* at 346, 118 N.Y.S. at 353.

The plaintiffs' complaint in the instant case alleges a similar "waste" of $1.5 million through an illegal campaign contribution.

Abrams v. Allen, 297 N.Y. 52, 74 N.E.2d 305 (1947), reflects an affirmation by the New York Court of Appeals of the principle of *Roth* that directors must be restrained from engaging in activities which are against public policy. In *Abrams* the court held that a cause of action was stated by an allegation in a derivative complaint that the directors of Remington Rand, Inc., had relocated corporate plants and curtailed production solely for the purpose of intimidating and punishing employees for their involvement in a labor dispute. The Court of Appeals acknowledged that, "depending on the circumstances," proof of the allegations in the complaint might sustain recovery, *inter alia,* under the rule that directors are liable for corporate loss caused by the commission of an "unlawful or immoral act." *Id.* at 55, 74 N.E.2d at 306. In support of its holding, the court noted that the closing of factories for the purpose alleged was opposed to the public policy of the state and nation as embodied in the New York Labor Law and the National Labor Relations Act. *Id.* at 56, 74 N.E.2d at 307.[3]

The alleged violation of the federal prohibition against corporate political contributions not only involves the corporation in criminal activity but similarly contravenes a policy of Congress clearly enunciated in 18 U.S.C. § 610.[4] That statute and its predecessor reflect congressional efforts: (1) to destroy the influence of corporations over elections through financial contributions and (2) to check the practice of using corporate funds to benefit political parties without the consent of the stockholders. United States v. CIO, 335 U.S. 106, 113, 68 S.Ct. 1349, 92 L.Ed. 1849 (1948).

The fact that shareholders are within the class for whose protection the statute was enacted gives force to the argument that the

---

**3.** That violation of a federal statute is the basis of the breach of fiduciary duty and that therefore the court is required to interpret the federal statute has not deterred New York courts from entertaining such suits against directors. *See* Knopfler v. Bohen, 15 A.D.2d 922, 225 N.Y.S.2d 609 (2d Dept.1962); *cf.* Simon v. Socony–Vacuum Oil Co., 179 Misc. 202, 38 N.Y.S.2d 270 (Sup.Ct.1942).

**4.** We note that prior to June 1, 1974, corporate political contributions made "directly or indirectly" violated New York law. Law of July 20, 1965, ch. 1031, § 43, [1965]

N.Y.Laws 1783 (repealed 1974). Furthermore, apart from the statutory prohibition, political donations by corporations were apparently ultra vires acts in New York. *See* People ex rel. Perkins v. Moss, 187 N.Y. 410, 80 N.E. 383 (1907). Corporations or organizations financially supported by corporations doing business in the state are now permitted to make contributions up to $5,000 per year. N.Y. Election Law § 480 (McKinney's Consol.Laws, c. 17, Supp.1974).

alleged breach of that statute should give rise to a cause of action in those shareholders to force the return to the corporation of illegally contributed funds. Since political contributions by corporations can be checked and shareholder control over the political use of general corporate funds effectuated only if directors are restrained from causing the corporation to violate the statute, such a violation seems a particularly appropriate basis for finding breach of the defendant directors' fiduciary duty to the corporation. Under such circumstances, the directors cannot be insulated from liability on the ground that the contribution was made in the exercise of sound business judgment.

Since plaintiffs have alleged actual damage to the corporation from the transaction in the form of the loss of a $1.5 million increment to AT & T's treasury,[5] we conclude that the complaint does state a claim upon which relief can be granted sufficient to withstand a motion to dismiss.[6]

## II.

We have accepted plaintiffs' allegation of a violation of 18 U.S.C. § 610 as a shorthand designation of the elements necessary to establish a breach of that statute. This is consonant with the federal practice of notice pleading. *See* Conley v. Gibson, 355 U.S. 41, 47–48, 78 S.Ct. 99, 2 L.Ed.2d 80 (1957); Fed.R.Civ.P. 8(f). That such a designation is sufficient for pleading purposes does not, however, relieve plaintiffs of their ultimate obligation to prove the elements of the statutory violation as part of their proof of breach of fiduciary duty. At the appropriate time, plaintiffs will be required to produce evidence sufficient to establish three distinct elements comprising a violation of 18 U.S.C. § 610: that AT & T (1) made a contribution of money or anything of value to the DNC (2) in connection with a federal election (3) for the purpose of influencing the outcome of that election. *See* United States v. Boyle, 157 U.S.App.D.C. 166, 482 F.2d 755, cert. denied, 414 U.S. 1076, 94 S.Ct. 593, 38 L.Ed.2d 483 (1973); United States v. Lewis Food Co., Inc., 366 F.2d 710 (9th Cir.1966) . . . .[7]

The order of the district court will be reversed and the case remanded for further proceedings consistent with this opinion.

---

**5.** Under New York law, allegation of breach even of a federal statute is apparently insufficient to state a cause of action unless the breach caused independent damage to the corporation. *See* Diamond v. Davis, 263 App. Div. 68, 31 N.Y.S.2d 582 (1st Dept.1941); Borden v. Cohen, 231 N.Y.S.2d 902 (Sup.Ct. 1962). *But see* Runcie v. Bankers Trust Co., 6 N.Y.S.2d 623 (Sup.Ct.1938).

**6.** We express no opinion today on the question of whether plaintiffs' complaint may also state a cause of action for breach of fiduciary duty arising from the alleged violation of 47 U.S.C. § 202(a).

**7.** As amended by the Federal Election Campaign Act of 1971 (effective April 7, 1972), the definition of "contribution" for purposes of 18 U.S.C. § 610 is a gift of money or anything of value "made for the purpose of influencing the nomination for election, or election" of any person to federal office or for influencing the outcome of a primary or national nominating convention. 18 U.S.C. § 591 (1970), as amended (Supp.II 1972).

# CHAPTER IX

# THE DUTY OF LOYALTY

## SECTION 1. SELF-INTERESTED TRANSACTIONS

### Marsh, Are Directors Trustees?—Conflicts of Interest and Corporate Morality

22 Bus.Law. 35, 36–43 (1966).

a. *Prohibition.*

In 1880 it could have been stated with confidence that in the United States the general rule was that any contract between a director and his corporation was voidable at the instance of the corporation or its shareholders, without regard to the fairness or unfairness of the transaction. This rule was stated in powerful terms by a number of highly regarded courts and judges in cases which arose generally out of the railroad frauds of the 1860's and 1870's. . . .

Under this rule it mattered not the slightest that there was a majority of so-called disinterested directors who approved the contract. The courts stated that the corporation was entitled to the unprejudiced judgment and advice of all of its directors and therefore it did no good to say that the interested director did not participate in the making of the contract on behalf of the corporation. ". . . the very words in which he asserts his right declare his wrong; he ought to have participated. . . ."[1] Furthermore, the courts said that it was impossible to measure the influence which one director might have over his associates, even though ostensibly abstaining from participation in the discussion or vote. ". . . a corporation, in order to defeat a contract entered into by directors, in which one or more of them had a private interest, is not bound to show that the influence of the director or directors having the private interest determined the action of the board. The law cannot accurately measure the influence of a trustee with his associates, nor will it enter into the inquiry. . . ."[2]

Perhaps the strongest reason for this inflexibility of the law was given by the Maryland Supreme Court which stated that, when a contract is made with even one of the directors, "the remaining directors are placed in the embarrassing and invidious position of having to pass upon, scrutinize and check the transactions and ac-

---

**1.** Stewart v. Lehigh Valley R.R. Co., 38 N.J.Law 505, at 523 (Ct.Err. & App.1875).

**2.** Munson v. Syracuse, G. & C. Ry. Co., 103 N.Y. 58, at 74, 8 N.E. 355, at 358 (1886).

counts of one of their *own body, with* whom they are associated on terms of equality in the general management of all the affairs of the corporation."[3] Or, as Justice Davies of the New York Supreme Court expressed the same thought: "The moment the directors permit one or more of their number to deal with the property of the stockholders, they surrender their own independence and self control."[4]

This rule applied not only to individual contracts with directors, but also to the situation of interlocking directorates where even a minority of the boards were common to the two contracting corporations. Not only that, it was also applied to the situation where one corporation owned a majority of the stock of another and appointed its directors, even though they might not be the same men as sat on the board of the parent corporation. . . .

This principle, absolutely inhibiting contracts between a corporation and its directors or any of them, appeared to be impregnable in 1880. It was stated in ringing terms by virtually every decided case, with arguments which seemed irrefutable, and it was sanctioned by age. As Justice Davies stated:

> To hold otherwise, would be to overturn principles of equity which have been regarded as well settled since the days of Lord Keeper Bridgman, in the 22nd of Charles Second, to the present time—principles enunciated and enforced by Hardwicke, Thurlow, Loughborough, Eldon, Cranworth, Story and Kent, and which the highest courts in our country have declared to be founded on immutable truth and justice, and to stand upon our great moral obligation to refrain from placing ourselves in relations which excite a conflict between self interest and integrity.

Thirty years later this principle was dead.

b.   *Approval by a disinterested majority of the board.*

It could have been stated with reasonable confidence in 1910 that the general rule was that a contract between a director and his corporation was valid if it was approved by a disinterested majority of his fellow directors and was not found to be unfair or fraudulent by the court if challenged; but that a contract in which a majority of the board was interested was voidable at the instance of the corporation or its shareholders without regard to any question of fairness.

One searches in vain in the decided cases for a reasoned defense of this change in legal philosophy, or for the slightest attempt to refute the powerful arguments which had been made in support of the previous rule. Did the courts discover in the last quarter of the Nineteenth Century that greed was no longer a factor in human conduct? If so, they did not share the basis of this discovery with the public; nor did they humbly admit their error when confronted with

---

3. Cumberland Coal and Iron Co. v. Parish, 42 Md. 598, at 606 (1875).

4. Cumberland Coal and Iron Co. v. Sherman, 30 Barb. 553, at 573 (N.Y.Sup.Ct. 1859).

the next wave of corporate frauds arising out of the era of the formation of the "trusts" during the 1890's and early 1900's. . . .

The only explanation which seems to have been given for this change in position was the technical one that a trustee, while forbidden to deal with himself in connection with the trust property, could deal directly with the cestui que trust if he made full disclosure and took no unfair advantage; and that the case of a director who abstained from representing the corporation but dealt in his personal capacity with a majority of disinterested directors was properly analogized to a trustee dealing with the cestui que trust. As the Texas court said:[19]

> . . . we think it is not true that one who holds the position of director is incapable, under all circumstances, of divesting himself of his representative character in a particular transaction, and dealing with the corporation through others competent to represent it, as other trustees may deal directly with the beneficiaries. . . . [T]he company is represented by those who alone can act for it, and, if they are disinterested, he can, we think, deal with them as any other trustee can deal with the cestui que trust, if he makes a full disclosure of all facts known to him about the subject, takes no advantage of his position, deals honestly and openly, and concludes a contract fair and beneficial to the company.

But in no case is there any discussion or attempted refutation of the reasons previously given by the courts as to why it is impossible, in such a situation, for any director to be disinterested. Some courts seem simply to admit that the practice has grown too widespread for them to cope with. In *South Side Trust Co. v. Washington Tin Plate Co.* the Supreme Court of Pennsylvania said:[20] "The interests of corporations are sometimes so interwoven that it is desirable to have joint representatives in their respective managements, and at any rate it is a not uncommon and [therefore?] not unlawful practice." . . .

Under the rule that a disinterested majority of the directors must approve a transaction with one of their number, the question arose whether this meant a disinterested quorum (i.e., normally a majority of the whole board) or merely a disinterested majority of a quorum, so that the interested director or directors could be counted to make up the quorum. Virtually all of the cases held that the interested director could not be counted for quorum purposes. As the California court said, the interested director for this purpose was "as much a stranger to the board as if he had never been elected a director. . . ."[28]

c. *Judicial review of the fairness of the transaction.*

By 1960 it could be said with some assurance that the general rule was that no transaction of a corporation with any or all of its directors

---

**19.** Tenison v. Patton, 95 Tex. 284, at 292–93, 67 S.W. 92, at 95 (1902).

**20.** 252 Pa. 237 at 241, 97 A. 450 at 451 (1916).

**28.** Curtis v. Salmon River Hydraulic Gold–Mining & Dutch Co., . . . 10 Cal. at 349, 62 P. at 554.

was automatically voidable at the suit of a shareholder, whether there was a disinterested majority of the board or not; but that the courts would review such a contract and subject it to rigid and careful scrutiny, and would invalidate the contract if it was found to be unfair to the corporation. . . .

## Lewis v. S.L. & E., Inc.

United States Court of Appeals, Second Circuit, 1980.
629 F.2d 764.

■ Before TIMBERS and KEARSE, CIRCUIT JUDGES, and LASKER, DISTRICT JUDGE.

■ KEARSE, CIRCUIT JUDGE:

This case arises out of an intra-family dispute over the management of two closely-held affiliated corporations. Plaintiff Donald E. Lewis ("Donald"), a shareholder of S.L. & E., Inc. ("SLE"), appeals from judgments entered against him in the United States District Court for the Western District of New York, Harold P. Burke, Judge, after a bench trial of his derivative claim against directors of SLE, and of a claim asserted against him by the other corporation, Lewis General Tires, Inc. ("LGT"), which intervened in the suit. The defendants Alan E. Lewis ("Alan"), Leon E. Lewis, Jr. ("Leon, Jr."), and Richard E. Lewis ("Richard"), are the brothers of Donald; they were, at pertinent times herein, directors of SLE and officers, directors and shareholders of LGT. Donald charged that his brothers had wasted the assets of SLE by causing SLE to lease business premises to LGT from 1966 to 1972 at an unreasonably low rental. LGT was permitted to intervene in the action, and filed a complaint seeking specific performance of an agreement by Donald to sell his SLE stock to LGT in 1972. The district court held that Donald had failed to prove waste by the defendant directors, and entered judgment in their favor. The court also awarded attorneys' fees to the defendant directors and to SLE, and granted LGT specific performance of Donald's agreement to sell his SLE stock.

On appeal, Donald argues that the district court improperly allocated to him the burden of proving his claims of waste, and that since defendants failed to prove that the transactions in question were fair and reasonable, he was entitled to judgment. Donald also argues that the awards of attorneys' fees were improper. We agree with each of these contentions, and therefore reverse and remand.

### I

For many years Leon Lewis, Sr., the father of Donald and the defendant directors, was the principal shareholder of SLE and LGT. LGT, formed in 1933, operated a tire dealership in Rochester, New York. SLE, formed in 1943, owned the land and complex of buildings at 260 East Avenue in Rochester. This property was SLE's only significant asset. Prior to 1956 LGT occupied SLE's premises without benefit of a lease; the rent paid was initially $200 per month, and had increased over the years to $800 per month by 1956, when additional parcels were added. On February 28, 1956, SLE granted LGT a 10–year lease on the newly expanded property ("the Property"), for a rent of $1200 per month, or $14,400 per year. Under the terms of the lease, SLE was responsible for payment of real estate taxes on the Property, while all other current expenses were to be borne by the tenant, LGT.[1]

In 1962, Leon Lewis, Sr., transferred his SLE stock, 90 shares in all, to his six children (defendants Richard, Alan and Leon, Jr., plaintiff Donald, and two daughters, Margaret and Carol), giving 15 shares to each.[2] At that time Richard, Alan and Leon, Jr., were already shareholders, officers and directors of LGT. Contemporaneously with their receipt of SLE stock, all six of the children entered into a "shareholders' agreement" with LGT, under which each child who was not a shareholder of LGT on June 1, 1972 would be required to sell his or her SLE shares to LGT, within 30 days of that date, at a price equal to the book value of the SLE stock as of June 1, 1972.[3]

LGT's lease on the SLE property expired on February 28, 1966. At that time the directors of SLE were Richard, Alan, Leon, Jr., Leon, Sr., and Henry Etsberger; these five were also the directors of LGT. In 1966 Alan owned 44% of LGT, Richard owned 30%, Leon, Jr., owned 19%, and Leon, Sr., owned 7%. From 1967 to 1972 Richard owned 61% of LGT and Leon, Jr., owned the remaining 39%. When the lease expired in 1966, no new lease was entered into. LGT nonetheless continued to occupy the property and to pay SLE at the old rate, $14,400 per year. According to the defendants' testimony at trial, there was never any thought or discussion among the SLE directors of entering into a new lease or of increasing the rent. Richard testified: "We never gave consideration to a new lease." From all that appears, the defendant directors viewed SLE as existing purely for the benefit of LGT. Richard testified, for example, that although real estate taxes rose sharply during the period 1966–1971, from approximately $7,800 to more than $11,000, to be paid by SLE out of its constant $14,400 rental income, raising the rent was never mentioned. He testified that SLE was "only a shell to protect the operating company [LGT]." When this suit was commenced there had not been a formal meeting of either the shareholders or the directors of SLE since 1962. Richard, Alan and Leon, Jr., had largely ignored SLE's separate corporate existence[4] and disregarded the fact that SLE had shareholders who

---

1. It appears that SLE was also responsible for payments due on a mortgage on the Property. In addition, LGT charged SLE for the costs of certain capital improvements, such as the major structural repairs to the principal building's facade, carried out in 1969.

2. SLE had 150 shares outstanding, and each child thus received a ten percent interest. At the same time LGT purchased the remaining 60 outstanding shares from the elder Lewis's business partner, Henry Etsberger.

3. The agreement specified procedures by which the book value, and hence the price of the shares, would be determined.

4. For example, Richard's testimony includes the following statements:

Q Mr. Lewis, you have always looked at these two corporations as being one and the same, haven't you, Lewis General Tires and S.L. & E.?

A Yes.

\* \* \*

were not shareholders of LGT and who therefore could not profit from actions that used SLE solely for the benefit of LGT.

Neither Donald nor his sisters ever owned LGT stock. As the June 1972 date approached for the required sale of their SLE stock to LGT, Donald apparently came to believe that SLE's book value was lower than it should have been. He sought SLE financial information from Richard, who had been president of SLE since 1967.[5] Richard refused to provide information. Donald therefore refused to sell his SLE shares in 1972,[6] and commenced this shareholders' derivative action in the district court in August 1973, basing jurisdiction on diversity of citizenship. The sole claim raised in the complaint was that the defendant directors had wasted the assets of SLE by "grossly undercharging" LGT for the latter's occupancy and use of the Property. Although the complaint charged such mismanagement for the period 1962 to 1973, plaintiff subsequently limited this claim to the period between February 28, 1966, the date on which the lease expired,[9] and June 1, 1972, the date contractually set for valuation of the SLE shares which plaintiff had agreed to sell to LGT. LGT intervened and demanded specific performance of Donald's agreement to sell his SLE stock. Donald did not contest his ultimate obligation to sell, but took the position that since the book value of the shares would be increased if he prevailed on his derivative claim, specific performance should be granted only after adjudication of that claim.

There ensured an eight-day bench trial, at which plaintiff sought to prove, by the testimony of several expert witnesses, that the fair rental value of the Property was greater than the $14,400 per year that SLE had been paid by LGT. Defendants sought to show that the rental paid was reasonable, by offering evidence concerning the financial straits of LGT, the cost to LGT of operating the Property, the general economic decline of the East Avenue neighborhood, and rentals paid on two other properties in that neighborhood. LGT presented expert testimony that the value of plaintiff's stock as of June 1972, assuming a successful defense of the derivative claims, was $15,650.

The district court subsequently filed lengthy and detailed findings of fact and conclusions of law. Many of the court's findings went to the

---

I never really got into S.L. & E. at all. (Tr. 6/21/78, at 972–73.)

\* \* \*

I don't think I ever looked at an operating statement of S.L. & E. seriously. (*Id.* at 991.)

\* \* \*

I had very little to do with S.L. & E. (Tr. 7/28/78, at 80.)

Alan testified that at no time after 1964 did he participate in any discussions of any increase in rent for SLE. (*Id.* at 160, 164.)

And Leon, Jr., testified, "I didn't have anything to do with running S.L. & E ....." (*Id.* at 230.)

**5.** It does not appear that SLE paid salaries to any of its officers or directors.

**6.** Donald's sisters Carol and Margaret sold their SLE shares to LGT in 1972 and 1973 respectively. Alan, who had sold his LGT stock in 1967, sold his SLE stock to LGT in 1972.

**9.** Donald was not a shareholder of SLE in 1956 when the lease was entered into and hence had no standing to challenge its terms. BCL § 626(b); *Bernstein v. Polo Fashions, Inc.*, 55 A.D.2d 530, 389 N.Y.S.2d 368 (1st Dep't 1976).

validity and probative value of the testimony given by plaintiff's expert witnesses, and the court ultimately declined to credit that testimony. On this basis, the court held that Donald had failed to establish the rental value of the Property during the period at issue, and that defendants were therefore entitled to judgment on the derivative claims. Implicit in the district court's ruling, granting judgment for defendants upon plaintiff's failure to prove waste, was a determination that plaintiff bore the burden of proof on that issue. The court also ruled that LGT was entitled to specific performance of Donald's agreement to sell his SLE stock, and that Donald was not entitled to recover attorneys' fees from SLE, but that SLE and the individual defendants were entitled to attorneys' fees from Donald. This appeal followed.

## II

Turning first to the question of burden of proof, we conclude that the district court erred in placing upon plaintiff the burden of proving waste. Because the directors of SLE were also officers, directors and/or shareholders of LGT, the burden was on the defendant directors to demonstrate that the transactions between SLE and LGT were fair and reasonable. New York Business Corporation Law ("BCL") § 713(b) (McKinney Supp.1979) (eff. September 1, 1971); BCL § 713(a)(3) (McKinney 1963) (repealed as of September 1, 1971); *see Cohen v. Ayers,* 596 F.2d 733, 739–40 (7th Cir.1979) (construing current BCL § 713); *Remillard Brick Co. v. Remillard–Dandini Co.,* 109 Cal. App.2d 405, 241 P.2d 66, 75 (1952) (construing California Corporations Code § 820, upon which the prior BCL § 713 was patterned).

Under normal circumstances the directors of a corporation may determine, in the exercise of their business judgment, what contracts the corporation will enter into and what consideration is adequate, without review of the merits of their decisions by the courts. The business judgment rule places a heavy burden on shareholders who would attack corporate transactions. *Galef v. Alexander,* 615 F.2d 51, 57–58 (2d Cir.1980); *Auerbach v. Bennett,* 47 N.Y.2d 619, 629, 419 N.Y.S.2d 920, 926, 393 N.E.2d 994, 1000 (1979); 3A Fletcher, *Cyclopedia of the Law of Private Corporations* § 1039 (perm. ed. 1975). But the business judgment rule presupposes that the directors have no conflict of interest. When a shareholder attacks a transaction in which the directors have an interest other than as directors of the corporation, the directors may not escape review of the merits of the transaction. At common law such a transaction was voidable unless shown by its proponent to be fair, and reasonable to the corporation.[11] BCL § 713, in both its current and its prior versions, carries forward this common law principle, and provides special rules for scrutiny of a transaction between the corporation and an entity in which its di-

11. *E.g., Geddes v. Anaconda Copper Co.,* 254 U.S. 590, 599, 41 S.Ct. 209, 65 L.Ed. 425 (1921)....

rectors are directors or officers or have a substantial financial interest . . . .

The current version of § 713,* which became effective on September 1, 1971, and governs at least so much of the dealing between SLE and LGT as occurred after that date, expressly provides that a contract between a corporation and an entity in which its directors are interested may be set aside unless the proponent of the contract "shall establish affirmatively that the contract or transaction was fair and reasonable as to the corporation at the time it was approved by the board . . . ." § 713(b). Thus when the transaction is challenged in a derivative action against the interested directors, they have the burden of proving that the transaction was fair and reasonable to the corporation. *Cohen v. Ayers, supra.*

The same was true under the predecessor to § 713(b), former § 713(a)(3), which was in effect prior to September 1, 1971 . . . .

During the entire period 1966–1972, Richard, Alan and Leon, Jr., were directors of both SLE and LGT;[14] there were no SLE directors who were not also directors of LGT. Richard, Alan and Leon, Jr., were all shareholders of LGT in 1966, and from 1967 to 1972 Richard and Leon, Jr., were the sole shareholders of LGT. Under BCL § 713, therefore, Richard, Alan and Leon, Jr., had the burden of proving that $14,400 was a fair and reasonable annual rent for the SLE property for the period February 28, 1966 through June 1, 1972.

Our review of the record convinces us that defendants failed to carry their burden. At trial, there was no direct testimony as to what would have been a fair rental during the relevant period, *i.e.,* 1966 to 1972, and the evidence that was introduced fell far short of establishing that $14,400 was a fair annual rental value for those years.

Quite clearly Richard, Alan and Leon, Jr., had made no effort to determine contemporaneously what rental would be fair during the years 1966–1972. Their view was that the rent should simply cover expenses and that SLE existed for the benefit of LGT.[15] During this period no appraisals were made; no attempts were made to sell or rent the Property; no thought whatever was given to whether $14,400 was a fair and reasonable rent even when real estate taxes had risen to consume nearly all of that amount.

Defendants offered instead evidence of rents paid on other properties. Among their best evidence was the expert testimony of Harvey Rosenbloom, a real estate appraiser. Rosenbloom testified that two other East Avenue buildings, which the district court found to be comparable to the 260 East Avenue premises, were leased at lower per-square-foot rentals than was paid by LGT to SLE. However, as to one of these properties, Rosenbloom testified only to rent paid in

---

* See New York Bus.Corp.Law § 713 in the Statutory Supplement. (Footnote by ed.)

**14.** Alan ceased to be a director in November 1972; Leon, Jr., ceased to be a director in 1977. Richard remains a director.

**15.** *See* footnote 4 *supra,* and accompanying text.

1973 and 1974, and did not consider the 1966–1972 period. As to the other property, Rosenbloom described a fifteen year lease that was entered into in 1961. This testimony, while perhaps not wholly irrelevant to the issues in this suit, fell far short of demonstrating what rental the Property could have fetched in 1966, or in any other of the relevant years. Indeed, Rosenbloom himself testified that rental value could well be different for each year of the period. Thus, rentals that Rosenbloom testified were agreed to in 1961 or 1973 might well have been unfair in 1966 or 1967. This evidence thus could not support a finding that defendants acted fairly in maintaining an annual rental of $14,400 during the years from 1966 to 1972.[16]

Defendants also produced considerable evidence that over the relevant period, the East End neighborhood had been on an economic decline; that businesses had been leaving the area; that urban renewal projects and increased crime had depressed property values there; and that the area had, in general, become a less desirable place to do business. There was also evidence of specific developments that had an adverse effect on the Property: for example, the street running along one side of the Property was made a one-way street, thus limiting customers' access to LGT's premises. The district court credited all of this testimony, and it is fair to say that defendants proved that there was a general downward trend in the value of the Property. However, as noted above, defendants did not establish what was a fair rental value for the Property in 1966. Absent such a point of reference, a general downward trend in value is of no assistance in determining whether the rental actually paid was fair and reasonable during the ensuing years.

Moreover, working in reverse, some of defendants' own evidence as to the value of the Property at the end of the relevant period suggested that $14,400 was less than a fair rental in 1966, and that the figure of $38,099, estimated by plaintiff's expert, was perhaps not far off the mark.[17] First, there was a variety of evidence suggesting that in 1972 the Property was worth more than $200,000. An appraisal by defense witness Harold Grunert in 1972 set the fair market value of the Property as of June 30, 1972, at $220,000. In 1972 Leon, Jr., had offered personally to buy the Property for $200,000, an offer which Richard had rejected.[18] And in 1971, Richard had informed Donald that evaluations by another appraiser, Harold Galloway, had set the value of the Property at $200,000 and $236,000. Second, defendants' expert witness Rosenbloom, asked what he would consider a fair rent for the property, given Grunert's 1972 valuation of $220,000, stated that ten percent of the value would be inadequate and that fifteen to seventeen

---

**16.** Defendant Richard E. Lewis testified that defendants tried, without success, to sell the Property in 1975, listing it with a realtor for $200,000. In addition he testified that an effort was made to rent the Property in 1973, and that only one offer, for $700 per month, was forthcoming. Since these efforts were made in 1973 and 1975, this evidence, like the evidence as to rentals of other prop-erty, was too remote in time to establish a fair rental value, especially as to the earlier years of the 1966–1972 period.

**17.** Plaintiff's expert made his evaluation as of February 1973. He did not make any evaluation for the period 1966–1972.

**18.** Leon, Jr., had just been fired from LGT by Richard.

percent would be closer to adequate. Fifteen percent of $220,000 would have yielded a rent of $33,000 on the basis of the 1972 valuation. Grunert's own expert testimony was entirely consistent with this. While he had made no estimate as to the fair rental value of the property for 1966–1972, he opined that a fair rental as of June 30, 1972, would be $20–21,000 with the tenant paying all expenses including real estate taxes. According to Richard, SLE's real estate taxes in 1972 were about $12,000. Thus Grunert's testimony, too, suggests about $33,000 as the fair rental value in 1972. Finally, consistent with their view of the general downward economic trend, Richard and Alan conceded that, whatever the Property was worth in 1972, it was worth more in 1966.[19] Thus the evidence presented by defendants, far from carrying their burden of showing that $14,400 was a fair and reasonable annual rental in 1966–1972, suggested that the fair rental value of the Property throughout that period exceeded $33,000 per year.

The defendants argued, however, that LGT could not have afforded to pay SLE rent higher than $14,400. They produced evidence designed to show that LGT had made little profit; that this low profitability was due to the expenses of maintenance and upkeep of the 260 East Avenue property; and that LGT therefore would not have been able to pay a higher rent to SLE. The district court credited this evidence, finding that LGT had "experienced a number of years of very severe losses," that during the period from 1962–1973, LGT's overall profit was only $53,876, and that payment of rent at the rate of $39,099 per year during this period could have led to the "demise" of LGT. These findings have only a distorted relationship to this lawsuit.

The period in issue here is 1966–1972. The only "severe" losses shown, totaling nearly $83,000, occurred in 1963 and 1973. Their inclusion in the computation of what LGT could afford to pay in 1966–1972 was patently unfair. In fact LGT's only unprofitable year during the period in issue was 1969 when its loss was small: $1,168. LGT's after-tax profits in 1966–1972 in fact totaled $102,963, or an average of $14,709 per year. Thus, even on paper, LGT could have "afforded" to double its rent payments to SLE during the period in question.

Moreover, the proposition that LGT could not afford to pay as rent more than what its own books showed as profits ignores the fact that LGT was owned and managed by members of the Lewis family, some of whom were also employees of that corporation. It is entirely possible that these family members granted to themselves unusually high salaries or other perquisites, thus reducing LGT's paper profits. For example, in 1966 Richard's salary was approximately $21,000; Leon, Jr.'s compensation was $3,000 salary plus commissions. In 1967, LGT acquired all of Alan's LGT stock; and Richard and Leon, Jr., acquired all of the LGT stock of their father, agreeing to pay the purchase price over a ten-year period. Richard and Leon, Jr., thus became LGT's only shareholders, and their LGT salaries were immedi-

---

**19.** Leon, Jr., did not know whether the value had decreased from 1966 to 1972, but   did not believe it had risen.

ately increased by a total of $23,000 per year (Richard's salary went from $21,000 to $36,000; Leon, Jr.'s went from $3,000 to $11,000), to cover the cost of the LGT stock they had just acquired.[20] Defendants bore the burden of proof on the question of a fair and reasonable rental; if they would rely on the proposition that LGT was unable to pay more, it was incumbent on them to demonstrate the fairness of the management and the reasonableness of the conduct of LGT's affairs. It does not appear that they made any effort to do so.

Finally, even if we were to assume that LGT's financial records provided a fair basis for evaluating the SLE–LGT transactions, defendants would not have carried their burden of proof. Defendants did not demonstrate that SLE could not have found some other tenant, stronger financially than LGT, which would have been willing and able to pay a higher rental. Even given the general downward trend of the East Avenue neighborhood, it is entirely possible that at least during the early years of the 1966–1972 period, such a tenant might have been secured. No effort was made during that period to rent to anyone other than LGT.

We conclude, therefore, that defendants failed to prove that the rental paid by LGT to SLE for the years 1966–1972 was fair and reasonable. Thus, Donald is not required to sell his SLE shares to LGT without such upward adjustment in the June 1, 1972, book value of SLE as may be necessary to reflect the amount by which the fair rental value of the Property exceeded $14,400 in any of the years 1966–1972....

We remand to the district court (a) for the entry of judgment in favor of SLE against Richard, Alan and Leon, Jr., jointly and severally, in such amount as the district court shall determine to be equal to the amounts by which the annual fair rental value of the Property exceeded $14,400 in the period February 28, 1966–June 1, 1972, (b) for an accounting as to the value of Donald's SLE shares as of June 1, 1972, in light of such judgment, (c) for an order, following such accounting, of specific performance of the shareholders' agreement, and (d) for such other proceedings as are not inconsistent with this opinion.

---

## NOTE ON REMEDIES FOR VIOLATION OF THE DUTY OF LOYALTY

The traditional remedies for violation of the duty of loyalty are restitutionary in nature. For example, if a director has engaged in improper self-dealing with the corporation, normally the remedy is rescission—or, if rescission is not feasible, an accounting for the difference between the contract price and a fair price. Similarly, if an officer has improperly appropriated a corporate opportunity (see

---

**20.** Richard had no doubt he could have paid for his newly acquired shares without the increase in his LGT salary. Leon, Jr., apparently lacked other resources from which to pay for the LGT stock (at least after he was fired from LGT in 1972).

Section 4, infra), normally the remedy is to impose a constructive trust in the corporation's favor, conditioned on reimbursement by the corporation of the officer's outlay in acquiring the opportunity.

The result of this restitutionary theory of remedies is that as a practical matter, the legal sanctions for violation of the duty of loyalty are usually, although not invariably, much less severe than the legal sanctions for violation of the duty of care. If D, a director or officer, violates his duty of care, he must pay damages although he made no gain from his wrongful action. This leaves D much worse off than he was before the wrong. In contrast, if D violates his duty of fair dealing, under a restitutionary remedy he need only return a gain to which he was not entitled in the first place. This simply places D where he was before the wrong.

Indeed, putting aside important nonlegal remedies such as discharge and negative publicity, if D is totally immoral, he would conclude that under a strictly restitutionary regime it normally paid to engage in a course of wrongful self-interested transactions. Some of the transactions may remain undiscovered. Where D's wrongdoing is not discovered, he will retain his wrongful gains. Where D's wrongdoing is discovered, he will only be required to surrender his wrongful gains. If D engages in enough transactions, he will come out ahead.

In some cases, however, the remedies for violation of the duty of loyalty may make the director or officer worse off than he was before the wrong. For example:

(i) Where the director or officer sells property to the corporation at an unfairly high price, and the value of the property later drops below its fair value at the time of the transaction, rescission may leave him worse off than if he had sold the property to a third party. For example, suppose that in 1985, D sells property to his corporation at $110,000, when it had a fair value of $100,000. In 1986, the corporation discovers the wrong and rescinds. Meanwhile, the market has fallen and the property is only worth $70,000. If D had sold the property for $100,000 to a third party, the third party would not be able to rescind. Thus D is $30,000 worse off than if he had not engaged in wrongful self-dealing. A comparable result may obtain where D buys property from the corporation, the market rises, and the corporation rescinds.

(ii) A director or officer who violates the duty of fair dealing may be required to repay the corporation any salary he earned during the relevant period in addition to making restitution of his wrongful gain. This remedy was granted, for example, in American Timber & Trading Co. v. Niedermeyer, 276 Or. 1135, 558 P.2d 1211 (1976), a case in which the fiduciary had depleted the corporation's assets by a series of unfair deals. The court there said:

> The remedy of restoration of compensation is an equitable principle and its applicability is dependent upon the individual facts of each case.... The general rule, however, is that a corporate officer who engages in activities which constitute either

a breach of his duty of loyalty or a wilful breach of his contract of employment is not entitled to any compensation for services rendered during that period of time even though part of those services may have been properly performed. . . .

(iii) Courts have sometimes awarded punitive damages against directors or officers who have breached their duty of loyalty. See, e.g., Holden v. Construction Machinery Co., 202 N.W.2d 348 (Iowa 1972); Rowen v. Le Mars Mutual Insurance Co. of Iowa, 282 N.W.2d 639, 662 (Iowa 1979). In Goben v. Barry, 234 Kan. 721, 728, 676 P.2d 90, 97–98 (1984), the court said, "Punitive damages may be awarded in the trial court's discretion whenever there is proof of fraud. . . . Fraud itself is difficult to define, but it has been held [that] fraud 'in its general sense, is deemed to comprise anything calculated to deceive, including all acts, omissions, and concealments involving a breach of legal or equitable duty, trust, or confidence justly reposed, resulting in damage to another. . . .' Barry [the defendant] concealed his withdrawals [from the company], denied Goben [the plaintiff] had any interest in the company and ousted him, all to Goben's damage. That is sufficient evidence of fraud. The trial court did not err in awarding punitive damages."

(iv) ALI, Principles of Corporate Governance § 7.18(d) provides that a director or officer who violates the duty of fair dealing should normally be required to pay the counsel fees and other expenses incurred by the corporation in establishing the violation.

---

## Talbot v. James

Supreme Court of South Carolina, 1972.
259 S.C. 73, 190 S.E.2d 759.

■ Moss, Chief Justice:

This equitable action was brought by C.N. Talbot and Lula E. Talbot, appellants herein, against W.A. James, individually, and as President of Chicora Apartments, Inc., and Chicora Apartments, Inc., respondents herein, for an accounting. In the complaint it is alleged that W.A. James, as an officer and director of the Corporation, violated his fiduciary relationship to the Corporation and the appellants as stockholders thereof, by diverting specific funds to himself.

The respondents, by answer, denied the allegations of the complaint and alleged that W.A. James had received no funds from the Corporation except for the sums paid for the erection of Chicora Apartments, pursuant to a contract between Chicora Apartments, Inc., and the said W.A. James.

The case was referred to the Master in Equity for Horry County, who after taking the testimony, filed a report in which he found that W.A. James was not entitled to general overhead expense and profits arising out of the construction contract with Chicora Apartments, Inc., and recommended judgment in favor of Chicora Apartments, Inc., against him in the amount of $25,025.31.

The respondents timely appealed from the recommendations contained in the Report of the Master. The appeal was heard by the Honorable Dan F. Laney, Jr., presiding judge, and he issued his order reversing the findings of the Master and ordered judgment in favor of the respondents. This appeal followed.

This being an equity case and the Master and the Circuit Judge having disagreed and made contrary findings on the material issues in the case, this Court has jurisdiction to consider the evidence and make findings in accordance with our view of the preponderance or greater weight of the evidence. . . .

Lula E. Talbot owned a tract of land fronting on U.S. Highway 17, in Myrtle Beach, South Carolina. The title thereto was conveyed to her by her husband, C.N. Talbot. The appellants were approached by W.A. James with a proposal that the tract of land be used for the erection thereon of an apartment complex. After preliminary talks and negotiations, the parties on January 12, 1963, entered into a written agreement thereabout. Basically, the parties agreed to form a Corporation to construct and operate an apartment complex. Lula E. Talbot was to convey to said Corporation the tract of land owned by her and W.A. James agreed, as set forth in paragraph 5, of said contract,

"To promote the project aforementioned and shall be responsible for the planning, architectural work, construction, landscaping, legal fees, and loan processing of the entire project, same to contain at least fifty (50) one, two and three room air conditioned apartments for customer as approved by FHA appraisers."

It was further agreed that upon the formation of the Corporation that the appellants were to receive 50% of the stock of the Corporation in consideration for their transfer of the land to it. This was to be the absolute limit of the contribution of the appellants. W.A. James was to receive 50% of the stock of the Corporation in consideration of his efforts on its behalf.

It appears, that after the aforementioned contract was entered into, that W.A. James obtained the services of an architectural firm on a contingency basis and preliminary plans and sketches of the proposed apartment complex were made by such firm. James was also successful in obtaining commitments from the Federal Housing Administration and from an acceptable mortgagee with regard to financing. These commitments having been obtained, a corporation was formed to be known as Chicora Apartments, Inc., and a charter was duly issued by the Secretary of State on November 5, 1963.

Pursuant to the terms of the agreement dated January 12, 1963, 20 shares of no par value capital stock were issued, with W.A. James receiving 10 shares, C.N. Talbot one share and Lula E. Talbot 9 shares. At an organizational meeting of the corporation W.A. James was elected president, his wife, B.N. James, was elected secretary, C.N. Talbot was elected vice president, and Lula E. Talbot was elected treasurer. W.A. James and C.N. Talbot were elected as directors of the Corporation.

At a meeting of the Board of Directors held on November 5, 1963, a resolution was adopted accepting the offer of Lula E. Talbot to transfer the tract of land in question to Chicora Apartments, Inc., in exchange for 10 shares of the no par value capital stock thereof. In the said resolution, it was declared that the said property, to be so transferred, was of a value of $44,000.00. At the same meeting, a resolution was adopted accepting the offer of W.A. James to transfer to Chicora Apartments, Inc., in exchange for 10 shares of the no par value stock thereof, at a valuation of $44,000.00 the following:

"1. FHA Commitment issued pursuant to Title 2, Section 207 of the National Housing Act, whereby the FHA agrees to insure a mortgage loan in the amount of $850,700.00, on a parcel of land in Myrtle Beach, South Carolina, more particularly described in Schedule 'A' hereto attached, provided 66 apartment units are constructed thereon in accordance with plans and specifications as prepared by Lyles, Bissett, Carlisle & Wolff, Architects–Engineers, of Columbia, South Carolina.

"2. Commitment from United Mortgagee Servicing Corp. agreeing to make a mortgage loan on said property in the amount of $850,-700.00 and also commitment from said mortgagee to make an interim construction loan in an identical amount.

"3. Certain contracts and agreements which W.A. James over the past two years have worked out and developed in connection with the architectural and construction services required for said project.

"4. The use of the finances and credit of W.A. James during the past two years (and including the construction period) in order to make it possible to proceed with the project."

The day following the election of the officers and the issuance of the capital stock, the Board of Directors of Chicora Apartments, Inc., met in Columbia, South Carolina, and passed a resolution authorizing the Corporation to borrow from United Mortgagee Servicing Corporation of Norfolk, Virginia, the sum of $850,700.00, upon the terms stated, said loan to be insured with the Federal Housing Administration. It was further resolved:

"That the President of the corporation, W.A. James, be authorized, empowered and directed to make, execute and deliver such documents and instruments as are required by the F.H.A. and the lender, in order to close the loan transaction; said documents including but not limited to, note, mortgage, Building Loan Agreement, Construction Contract, Architect's Agreement, Mortgagor's Certificate, Regulatory Agreement, Mortgagor's Oath and Agreement and Certificate."

The record shows that on November 6, 1963, James Construction Company entered into a construction contract with Chicora Apartments, Inc. This contract was executed by W.A. James, as president, and attested by B.N. James, secretary, on behalf of Chicora Apartments, Inc., and by W.A. James, sole proprietor, for James Construction Company. The contract sum was to be the actual cost of construction plus a fee equal to $20,000.00 but in no event was the contract price, including the fee, to exceed $736,000.00. Attached to the contract was a "Trade Payment Breakdown" which made an allowance for overhead expenses in the amount of $31,589.00, but, this said sum was to be paid by means other than cash. The aforementioned loan was obtained and the apartment complex was constructed. All funds from the mortgage loan were received and disbursed by W.A. James and the renting of the apartments was begun, such being conducted by a resident manager, who was an employee of the Corporation.

It appears ... that in 1968, an accountant, who was employed by the corporation, advised James and C.N. Talbot that it was in financial straits. It was at this time that the appellants questioned the disbursement of the mortgage funds by W.A. James. Their demands to examine the corporate records were refused by James. Thereafter, an order was obtained from the Honorable James B. Morrison, Resident Judge of the Fifteenth Judicial Circuit, making available the corporate records to the appellants. This action was thereafter instituted.

The record in this case clearly shows that W.A. James personally received or there was paid for his benefit the sum of $25,025.31 from the proceeds of the mortgage loan. He received this directly or by payments of his own personal debts by the corporation. He contends that he was entitled to these funds and more under the construction contract which he had with Chicora Apartments, Inc. This raises the question of whether James, who was a stockholder, officer, and director of Chicora Apartments, Inc., could enter into a contract with himself as an individual and [make] a profit therefrom for himself.

The Master found that Chicora Apartments, Inc., through W.A. James as president thereof, entered into a contract with himself, as sole proprietor of James Construction Company, without disclosing his identity of interest to the other officers or stockholders of the corporation, and that such contract has not been acquiesced in or ratified by the other director, officers or stockholders. He further found that the initial agreement between the parties required W.A. James to perform the same duties that he later contracted with the corporation to perform and for which he now seeks to justify the payment to him from the mortgage funds of the corporation. It was also found that according to the initial agreement these services were to be performed and, in consideration of such performance, James was to receive one-half of the shares of the capital stock of Chicora Apartments, Inc. The trial judge, upon exceptions to the Master's Report, made contrary findings of fact and reversed the Master and entered judgment in favor of the respondents.

The first question for determination is whether the fiduciary relationship existing between W.A. James as a stockholder, officer and director of Chicora Apartments, Inc., prevented him from contracting with the said corporation for his profit without first having disclosed the terms of the contract to the disinterested officers and directors of the corporation.

The officers and directors of the corporation stand in a fiduciary relationship to the individual stockholders and in every instance must make a full disclosure of all relevant facts when entering into a contract with said corporation. *Jacobson v. Yaschik,* 249 S.C. 577, 155 S.E.(2d) 601. The object of this rule is to prevent directors from secretly using their fiduciary positions to their own advantage and to the detriment of the corporation and of the stockholders. . . .

. . . The testimony of C.N. Talbot is that he discussed with James as to who was going to construct the Chicora Apartments and was told that Dargan Construction Company was going to take the contract. He further testified that during the period of construction he saw Dargan Construction Company signs on the premises and also trucks bearing its name. This witness further testified that James never discussed with him or his wife the matter of his constructing the apartments. Talbot denied that he knew that James was to be the contractor.

James testified that he explained to C.N. Talbot that the only possible way that the apartments could be built without putting in money was that he be the building contractor. James further testified that the only way the project could survive and the only way that "we" could get the builder's equity was that he should be the builder. He says that everybody understood that because his attorney had explained it at a meeting of the directors.

Assuming that James revealed to Talbot that he was to be the building contractor for the Chicora Apartments complex, his testimony does not show that he disclosed his entitlement to a fee of $20,000.00 and an allowance for overhead expenses in the amount of $31,589.00. It is thus apparent that he did not make a full disclosure of the profits or monetary benefits that he was to receive under the terms of the contract. It was his duty to make such full disclosure and the burden of proof was upon him to show that such had been done.

We have carefully examined the minutes of the several meetings of the stockholders and directors of the corporation. We find from such examination that they reflect each and every detail and transaction looking toward the construction of the apartment complex but nowhere in said minutes is there any mention that James was to be the building contractor. The minutes reflect that there was a meeting of the directors of the corporation on November 6, 1963, and a resolution adopted at such meeting authorizing the borrowing of the sum of $850,700.00 from the United Mortgagee Servicing Corporation, and authorizing James, as president, to make, execute and deliver such documents and instruments as were required by the FHA and the lender. If James was to be the building contractor and such was discussed at this meeting, as he contends, the minutes should have reflected such, particularly in view of the fact that the building contract was being awarded to him when he was a director and president of the corporation. There is no explanation of why such a resolution or authorization was not considered or passed at this meeting of the Board of Directors.

The record shows that the appellants were stockholders and officers of the corporation. As such, they were entitled to inspect the books of the corporation at any and all times. Section 12–263 of the Code. When they demanded their right to exercise this privilege, such was refused by James and they only obtained the right to inspect the records and books of the corporation by an order of the court. James' only explanation was that the Talbots were not entitled to see the books. It is inferable from this action on the part of James that he did not want the appellants to discover how the funds of the corporation had been disbursed and see that he had received benefit in such disbursement.

It appears that at the meeting of the directors of the corporation held on November 6, 1963, W.A. James, as president, was authorized to execute and deliver several documents including a "construction contract." The respondents argue that this gave W.A. James the authority to make the construction contract here involved. It is true that he was authorized to sign a "construction contract" on behalf of the corporation but such resolution did not authorize him to sign one on behalf of the corporation in favor of himself individually.

The respondents contend and place great emphasis on the fact that the construction contract was approved by the Federal Housing Administration and the fees provided therein were allowed by it. This has no relevancy to the issue here.

Considering the entire record in this case, it is our conclusion that W.A. James, as president of Chicora Apartments, Inc., entered into a contract with himself as sole proprietor of James Construction Company without making full disclosure of his identity of interest to the other officers and stockholders of the corporation. In this conclusion, we agree with the findings of the Master. It follows that the Chicora Apartments, Inc., is entitled to judgment against the said W.A. James in the amount of $25,025.31, this being the amount of the corporate funds received by or paid in behalf of W.A. James.

The Master found that under the language in paragraph 5 of the pre-incorporation agreement, hereinbefore quoted, that W.A. James was to be responsible for overseeing, supervising and generally managing all aspects of the construction of the apartment complex. He found that W.A. James, as sole proprietor of James Construction Company, performed the contract obligations and for such he received one-half of the shares of the capital stock of Chicora Apartments, Inc. The trial judge reversed this finding of the Master. The appellants allege error.

James testified that he was the general contractor for the construction of the apartment complex. He testified further that the apartment complex was constructed by some eighteen to twenty subcontractors with whom he negotiated contracts. The record reveals that the only service that James rendered in connection with the construction of the apartment complex was supervisory. These duties were those contemplated by the pre-incorporation agreement of the parties. He was compensated for these services when he received one-half of the capital stock in the corporation. He was not entitled to any other compensation for the services rendered. We think the trial judge was in error in not so holding.

The order of the trial judge is reversed and this case remanded to the Court of Common Pleas for Horry County for an appropriate order to effectuate the views herein expressed.

Reversed and remanded.

■ LEWIS and LITTLEJOHN, JJ., concur.

■ BUSSEY and BRAILSFORD, JJ., dissent.

■ BUSSEY, JUSTICE (dissenting):

While admittedly there is some evidence tending to support the findings of fact by the master, adopted in the majority opinion, I have concluded after considerable study of the record and exhibits that the clear weight of the evidence preponderates in favor of the findings of fact by the circuit judge rather than those of the master. Being of this view, I am compelled to dissent.

The apartment complex was completed in July 1964, whereupon the plaintiff, C.N. Talbot, with the help of a resident manager, selected by him but approved by James, took charge of the management and operation of the apartment complex, all receipts being deposited by Talbot and all checks being written by Talbot. In 1968, after Talbot and his manager had been in charge of the apartment complex for nearly four years, the corporation was virtually insolvent and the recommendation of Talbot's auditor was that the project be surrendered to FHA as a failure. To this James did not agree; instead he took charge of the operation of the apartment complex himself for the corporation, and a little more than a year later the corporation had seventeen to eighteen thousand dollars in the bank with all current bills paid.

Talbot was obviously chagrined at this course of events and it was not until after he was ousted from management that he actively asserted any claim on behalf of the corporation against James. While he denied knowing that James Construction Company was the general contractor on the project, by his own testimony about January or February 1965 he knew that a check for more than fifteen thousand dollars had been drawn on the construction account for the benefit of James. There is no suggestion that he then made any issue thereabout; instead, he waited until nearly four years later and until after he had been ousted from the active management of the operation. . . .

The resolution of the Board of Directors at the meeting on November 5, 1963, unanimously confirmed by the meeting of the stockholders on the same date, as evidenced by their written signatures, clearly shows that all parties agreed that James' efforts over a two year period and the contracts and commitments thereby produced plus the continued use of the finances and credit of James during the actual construction period represented a value of $44,000, which was accepted in full payment for James' ten shares of stock. According to the literal terms of this resolution, nothing remained to be done by James to fully earn his ten shares except allow the use of his credit throughout the construction period. As president of the corporation, he would have been expected to at least reasonably supervise the construction of the project in the interest of the corporation, whether or not required to do so by either the resolution of November 5 or the pre-incorporation agreement between the parties. The general supervisory duties of a corporation president or a pre-incorporation promoter are a far cry from the arduous, time consuming and expensive duties of a general contractor.

Supervising a general contractor is one thing; while acting as a general contractor, engaging, supervising, and following up eighteen or twenty subcontractors is an entirely different thing. There is uncontradicted evidence of voluminous paper work, record keeping, reports, etc., on the part of James and his personnel in the performance of the general construction contract. The record leaves no doubt whatever, to my mind, that James Construction Company performed services to the corporation subsequent to November 5, 1963 far over and above the service contemplated by either the aforesaid resolution or the pre-incorporation agreement.

As mentioned in the majority opinion, the "Trade Payment Breakdown" attached to the approved FHA construction contract made an allowance for overhead expenses in the amount of $31,589, payable by means other than cash. Apparently from the evidence, this amount, otherwise drawable, as overhead by James, was to form a part of the equity of the corporation required for the FHA loan and, of course, not actually received by James. Aside, however, from this item, the record reflects that where, as here, there was an identity of interest between the contractor and the sponsor, FHA, within certain limitations, permitted the contractor to include in his certification of the actual cost of a project a reasonable allocation of his general overhead expense, *i.e.,* the proportion of his actual general overhead expense attributable to the particular contract job.

In his cost certification to FHA James showed the entire overhead of James Construction Company during the period that the apartment project was under construction, and represented that 88.98% thereof, or $22,817.34, was attributable to the construction of Chicora Apartments. Of this amount, FHA allowed only $21,231.90 (3% of other costs) as a portion of the actual cost of Chicora Apartments. James' figures as to his overhead and the portion thereof attributable to the construction of Chicora Apartments may or may not have been accurate, but he was not even cross-examined thereabout. Assuming the accuracy of his figures it follows that his net profit from this general construction contract was the sum of $25,025.31 less $22,817.34 overhead, or $2,207.97. Even Talbot had to frankly admit that he did not know of any loss suffered by the Talbots or the corporation as a result of the general contract being let to James. He tacitly, if not expressly, conceded that Dargan, or any other reputable contractor, would have cost the corporation some twenty-five or thirty thousand dollars more....

For the foregoing reasons, I would affirm the judgment of the lower court, but at the very least, if the corporation is to recover at all from James, its recovery should be limited to any profit actually received, as opposed to his overhead expense. If the judgment below be not affirmed, the cause should be remanded for the purpose of determining the amount of actual overhead which James should equitably be allowed to retain.

■ BRAILSFORD, J., concurs.

---

### NOTE ON THE DUTY OF LOYALTY

In the corporate context, fairness requires not only that the terms of a self-interested transaction be fair, but that entering into the transaction, even on fair terms, is in the corporation's interest. For example, in Fill Buildings, Inc. v. Alexander Hamilton Life Ins. Co. of America, 396 Mich. 453, 241 N.W.2d 466 (1976), Fill Buildings, Inc., which had leased premises to Wayne National Life Insurance Co., brought suit under the lease for past-due rent. Leon Fill was the principal shareholder and a director of Wayne National and the sole shareholder and president of Fill Buildings. Wayne's corporate successor sought to avoid liability under the lease, on the ground that the lease was unfair. The trial court held that Fill Buildings had not borne its burden of establishing that the lease was in the interests of Wayne National:

> Given an instance of alleged director enrichment at corporate expense such as in this case, the burden to establish fairness resting on the director requires not only a showing of "fair price" but also a showing of the fairness of the bargain to the interests of the corporation. Only when a convincing showing is made in both respects can "fairness" under the statute be said to have been established.

> We are inclined to agree with Fill Buildings' position that that corporation was entitled to make a profit on its lease and that a "fair price" for the leasehold agreement was established. The costs of extensive renovations and the thrust of expert testimony adduced at trial support this conclusion. The proofs respecting the showing that entry into the lease served the interests of Wayne National are, however, unconvincing. Evidence adduced at trial indicated that Wayne National was a corporation in trouble. The corporation had been warned against over-expansion. Yet here we have entry into a long-term lease (*i.e.*, expansion) at a time when the corporate future was in question. . . .

---

### ALI, PRINCIPLES OF CORPORATE GOVERNANCE
§§ 1.14, 1.25, 5.02, 5.07, 5.08

[See Statutory Supplement]

---

## SECTION 2.  STATUTORY APPROACHES

---

### CAL. CORP. CODE § 310

[See Statutory Supplement]

---

### DEL. GEN. CORP. LAW § 144

[See Statutory Supplement]

---

### REV. MODEL BUS. CORP. ACT §§ 8.60–8.63

[See Statutory Supplement]

---

### N.Y. BUS. CORP. LAW § 713

[See Statutory Supplement]

---

## Cookies Food Products v. Lakes Warehouse

Supreme Court of Iowa, 1988.
430 N.W.2d 447.

■ NEUMAN, JUSTICE.

This is a shareholders' derivative suit brought by the minority shareholders of a closely held Iowa corporation specializing in barbeque sauce, Cookies Food Products, Inc. (Cookies). The target of the lawsuit is the majority shareholder, Duane "Speed" Herrig and two of his family-owned corporations, Lakes Warehouse Distributing, Inc. (Lakes) and Speed's Automotive Co., Inc. (Speed's). Plaintiffs alleged that Herrig, by acquiring control of Cookies and executing self-dealing contracts, breached his fiduciary duty to the company and fraudulently misappropriated and converted corporate funds. Plaintiffs sought actual and punitive damages. Trial to the court resulted in a verdict for the defendants, the district court finding that Herrig's actions benefited, rather than harmed, Cookies. We affirm.

I.  *Background.*

We review decisions in shareholders' derivative suits de novo, deferring especially to district court findings where the credibility of witnesses is a factor in the outcome. *Midwest Management Corp. v. Stephens,* 353 N.W.2d 76, 78 (Iowa 1984). To better understand this dispute, and the issues this appeal presents, we shall begin by recounting in detail the facts surrounding the creation and growth of this corporation.

L.D. Cook of Storm Lake, Iowa, founded Cookies in 1975 to produce and distribute his original barbeque sauce. Searching for a plant site in a community that would provide financial backing, Cook met with business leaders in seventeen Iowa communities, outlining his plans to build a growth-oriented company. He selected Wall Lake, Iowa, persuading thirty-five members of that community, including Herrig and the plaintiffs, to purchase Cookies stock. All of the investors hoped Cookies would improve the local job market and tax base. The record reveals that it has done just that.

Early sales of the product, however, were dismal. After the first year's operation, Cookies was in dire financial straits. At that time, Herrig was one of thirty-five shareholders and held only two hundred shares. He was also the owner of an auto parts business, Speed's Automotive, and Lakes Warehouse Distributing, Inc., a company that distributed auto parts from Speed's. Cookies' board of directors approached Herrig with the idea of distributing the company's products. It authorized Herrig to purchase Cookies' sauce for twenty percent under wholesale price, which he could then resell at full wholesale price. Under this arrangement, Herrig began to market and distribute the sauce to his auto parts customers and to grocery outlets from Lakes' trucks as they traversed the regular delivery routes for Speed's Automotive.

In May 1977, Cookies formalized this arrangement by executing an exclusive distribution agreement with Lakes. Pursuant to this agreement, Cookies was responsible only for preparing the product; Lakes, for its part, assumed all costs of warehousing, marketing, sales, delivery, promotion, and advertising. Cookies retained the right to fix the sales price of its products and agreed to pay Lakes thirty percent of its gross sales for these services.

Cookies' sales have soared under the exclusive distributorship contract with Lakes. Gross sales in 1976, the year prior to the agreement, totaled only $20,000, less than half of Cookies' expenses that year. In 1977, however, sales jumped five-fold, then doubled in 1978, and have continued to show phenomenal growth every year thereafter. By 1985, when this suit was commenced, annual sales reached $2,400,000.

As sales increased, Cookies' board of directors amended and extended the original distributorship agreement. In 1979, the board amended the original agreement to give Lakes an additional two percent of gross sales to cover freight costs for the ever-expanding market for Cookies' sauce. In 1980, the board extended the amended agreement through 1984 to allow Herrig to make long-term advertising commitments. Recognizing the role that Herrig's personal strengths played in the success of their joint endeavor, the board also amended the agreement that year to allow Cookies to cancel the agreement with Lakes if Herrig died or disposed of the corporation's stock.

In 1981, L.D. Cook, the majority shareholder up to this time, decided to sell his interest in Cookies. He first offered the directors an opportunity to buy his stock, but the board declined to purchase any of his 8100 shares. Herrig then offered Cook and all other shareholders $10 per share for their stock, which was twice the original price. Because of the overwhelming response to these offers, Herrig had purchased enough Cookies stock by January 1982 to become the majority shareholder. His investment of $140,000 represented fifty-three percent of the 28,700 outstanding shares. Other shareholders had invested a total of $67,500 for the remaining forty-seven percent.

Shortly after Herrig acquired majority control he replaced four of the five members of the Cookies' board with members he selected. This restructuring of authority, following on the heels of an unsuccessful attempt by certain stockholders to prevent Herrig from acquiring majority status, solidified a division of opinion within the shareholder ranks. Subsequent changes made in the corporation under Herrig's leadership formed the basis for this lawsuit.

First, under Herrig's leadership, Cookies' board has extended the term of the exclusive distributorship agreement with Lakes and expanded the scope of services for which it compensates Herrig and his companies. In April 1982, when a sales increase of twenty-five percent over the previous year required Cookies to seek additional short-term storage for the peak summer season, the board accepted Herrig's proposal to compensate Lakes at the "going rate" for use of its nearby storage facilities. The board decided to use Lakes' storage facilities because building and staffing its own facilities would have been more expensive. Later, in July 1982, the new board approved an extension of the exclusive distributorship agreement. Notably, this agreement was identical to the 1980 extension that the former board had approved while four of the plaintiffs in this action were directors.

Second, Herrig moved from his role as director and distributor to take on an additional role in product development. This created a dispute over a royalty Herrig began to receive. Herrig's role in product development began in 1982 when Cookies diversified its product line to include taco sauce. Herrig developed the recipe because he recognized that taco sauce, while requiring many of the same ingredients needed in barbeque sauce, is less expensive to produce. Further, since consumer demand for taco sauce is more consistent throughout the year than the demand for barbeque sauce, this new product line proved to be a profitable method for increasing year-round utilization of production facilities and staff. In August 1982, Cookies' board approved a royalty fee to be paid to Herrig for this taco sauce recipe. This royalty plan was similar to royalties the board paid to L.D. Cook for the barbeque sauce recipe. That plan gives Cook three percent of the gross sales of barbeque sauce; Herrig receives a flat rate per case. Although Herrig's rate is equivalent to a sales percentage slightly higher than what Cook receives, it yields greater profit to Cookies because this new product line is cheaper to produce.

Third, since 1982 Cookies' board has twice approved additional compensation for Herrig. In January 1983, the board authorized payment of a $1000 per month "consultant fee" in lieu of salary, because accelerated sales required Herrig to spend extra time managing the company. Averaging eighty-hour work weeks, Herrig devoted approximately fifteen percent of his time to Cookies and eighty percent to Lakes business. In August, 1983, the board authorized another increase in Herrig's compensation. Further, at the suggestion of a Cookies director who also served as an accountant for Cookies, Lakes, and Speed's, the Cookies board amended the exclusive distributorship agreement to allow Lakes an additional two percent of gross sales as a promotion allowance to expand the market for Cookies products outside of Iowa. As a direct result of this action, by 1986 Cookies regularly shipped products to several states throughout the country.

As we have previously noted, however, Cookies' growth and success has not pleased all its shareholders. The discontent is motivated by two factors that have effectively precluded shareholders from sharing in Cookies' financial success: the fact that Cookies is a closely held corporation, and the fact that it has not paid dividends. Because Cookies' stock is not publicly traded, shareholders have no ready access to buyers for their stock at current values that reflect the company's success. Without dividends, the shareholders have no ready method of realizing a return on their investment in the company. This is not to say that Cookies has improperly refused to pay dividends. The evidence reveals that Cookies would have violated the terms of its loan with the Small Business Administration had it declared dividends before repaying that debt. That SBA loan was not repaid until the month before the plaintiffs filed this action.

Unsatisfied with the status quo, a group of minority shareholders commenced this equitable action in 1985. Based on the facts we have detailed, the plaintiffs claimed that the sums paid Herrig and his companies have grossly exceeded the value of the services rendered, thereby substantially reducing corporate profits and shareholder equity. Through the exclusive distributorship agreements, taco sauce royalty, warehousing fees, and consultant fee, plaintiffs claimed that Herrig breached his fiduciary duties to the corporation and its shareholders because he allegedly negotiated for these arrangements without fully disclosing the benefit he would gain. The plaintiffs sought recovery for lost profits, an accounting to determine the full extent of the damage, attorneys fees, punitive damages, appointment of a receiver to manage the company properly, removal of Herrig from control, and sale of the company in order to generate an appropriate return on their investment.

Having heard the evidence presented on these claims at trial, the district court filed a lengthy ruling that reflected careful attention to the testimony of the twenty-two witnesses and myriad of exhibits admitted. The court concluded that Herrig had breached no duties owed to Cookies or to its minority shareholders, and found that Herrig's compensation was fair and reasonable for each of the four challenged categories of service. In summary, the court found that: (1) the exclusive distributorship arrangement has been the "key to corporate growth and expansion" and the fees under the agreement were appropriate for the diverse services Lakes provided; (2) the warehousing agreement was fair because it allowed Cookies to store its goods at the "going rate" and the board had considered and rejected the idea of constructing its own warehouse as storage at the Lakes facility would be less expensive; (3) the taco sauce royalty agreement appropriately compensated Herrig for the value of his recipe; and (4) the consultant fee "is actually a management fee for services rendered seven days a week" and is "well within reason, considering the success of the business." Additionally, the district court found that Herrig had withheld no information from directors or other shareholders that he was obligated to provide. The court concluded its findings with the following observation:

> The Court believes that the plaintiffs' complaint is not that they have been damaged but that they have not been paid a profit for their investment yet. There is a vast difference. Plaintiffs have made a profit. That profit is in the form of increased value of their stocks rather than in the form of dividends because of the capital considerations of operating the company.

On appeal from this ruling, the plaintiffs challenge: (1) the district court's allocation of the burden of proof with regard to the four claims of self-dealing; (2) the standard employed by the court to determine whether Herrig's self-dealing was fair and reasonable to Cookies; (3) the finding that any self-dealing by Herrig was done in good faith, and with honesty and fairness; (4) the finding that Herrig breached no duty to disclose crucial facts to Cookies' board before it completed deliberations on Herrig's self-dealing transactions; and (5) the district court's denial of restitution and other equitable remedies as compensation for Herrig's alleged breach of his duty of loyalty. After a brief review of the nature and source of Herrig's fiduciary duties, we will address the appellants' challenges in turn.

## II. *Fiduciary Duties.*

Herrig, as an officer and director of Cookies, owes a fiduciary duty to the company and its shareholders. *See* Iowa Code § 496A.34 (1985) (director must serve in manner believed in good faith to be in best interest of corporation); *see also Schildberg Rock Prods. Co. v. Brooks,* 258 Iowa 759, 766–67, 140 N.W.2d 132, 136 (1966) (officers and directors occupy fiduciary relation to corporation and its stockholders). Herrig concedes that Iowa law imposed the same fiduciary responsibilities based on his status as majority stockholder. *See Des Moines Bank & Trust Co. v. George M. Bechtel & Co.,* 243 Iowa 1007, 1082–83, 51 N.W.2d 174, 217 (1952) (hereinafter *Bechtel*); *see also* 12B W. Fletcher, *Cyclopedia on the Law of Private Corporations*

§ 5810, at 149 (1986). Conversely, before acquiring majority control in February 1982, Herrig owed no fiduciary duty to Cookies or plaintiffs. *See* Fletcher § 5713, at 13 (stockholders not active in management of corporation owe duties radically different from director, and vote at shareholder's meetings merely for own benefit). Therefore, Herrig's conduct is subject to scrutiny only from the time he began to exercise control of Cookies....

Appellants ... claim that Herrig violated his duty of loyalty to Cookies. That duty derives from "the prohibition against self-dealing that inheres in the fiduciary relationship." *Norlin,* 744 F.2d at 264. As a fiduciary, one may not secure for oneself a business opportunity that "in fairness belongs to the corporation." *Rowen v. LeMars Mut. Ins. Co. of Iowa,* 282 N.W.2d 639, 660 (Iowa 1979). As we noted in *Bechtel:*

> Corporate directors and officers may under proper circumstances transact business with the corporation including the purchase or sale of property, but it must be done in the strictest good faith and with full disclosure of the facts to, and the consent of, all concerned. And the burden is upon them to establish their good faith, honesty and fairness. Such transactions are scanned by the courts with skepticism and the closest scrutiny, and may be nullified on slight grounds. It is the policy of the courts to put such fiduciaries beyond the reach of temptation and the enticement of illicit profit.

243 Iowa 1007, 1081, 51 N.W.2d 174, 216 (1952). We have repeatedly applied this standard, including the burden of proof and level of scrutiny, when a corporate director engages in self-dealing with another corporation for which he or she also serves as a director. *See Holden v. Construction Mach. Co.,* 202 N.W.2d 348, 356–57 (Iowa 1972).

Against this common law backdrop, the legislature enacted section 496A.34, quoted here in pertinent part, that establishes three sets of circumstances under which a director may engage in self-dealing without clearly violating the duty of loyalty:

> No contract or other transaction between a corporation and one or more of its directors or any other corporation, firm, association or entity in which one or more of its directors are directors or officers or are financially interested, shall be either void or voidable because of such relationship or interest ... if any of the following occur:
>
> 1. The fact of such relationship or interest is disclosed or known to the board of directors or committee which authorizes, approves, or ratifies the contract or transaction ... without counting the votes ... of such interested director.
>
> 2. The fact of such relationship or interest is disclosed or known to the shareholders entitled to vote [on the transaction] and they authorize ... such contract or transaction by vote or written consent.

3.   The contract or transaction is fair and reasonable to the corporation.

Some commentators have supported the view that satisfaction of any *one* of the foregoing statutory alternatives, in and of itself, would prove that a director has fully met the duty of loyalty. *See* Hansell, Austin, & Wilcox, *Director Liability Under Iowa Law—Duties and Protections,* 13 J.Corp.L. 369, 382. We are obliged, however, to interpret statutes in conformity with the common law wherever statutory language does not directly negate it. *See Hardwick v. Bublitz,* 253 Iowa 49, 59, 111 N.W.2d 309, 314 (1961); Iowa Code § 4.2 (1987). Because the common law and section 496A.34 require directors to show "good faith, honesty, and fairness" in self-dealing, we are persuaded that satisfaction of any one of these three alternatives under the statute would merely preclude us from rendering the transaction void or voidable *outright* solely on the basis "of such [director's] relationship or interest." Iowa Code § 496A.34; *see Bechtel,* 243 Iowa at 1081–82, 51 N.W.2d at 216. To the contrary, we are convinced that the legislature did not intend by this statute to enable a court, in a shareholder's derivative suit, to rubber stamp *any* transaction to which a board of directors or the shareholders of a corporation have consented. Such an interpretation would invite those who stand to gain from such transactions to engage in improprieties to obtain consent. We thus require directors who engage in self-dealing to establish the additional element that they have acted in good faith, honesty, and fairness. *Holi–Rest, Inc. v. Treloar,* 217 N.W.2d 517, 525 (Iowa 1974).

### III.   *Burden of Proof.*

[The court held that the district court had appropriately placed the burden of proof on Herrig.]

### IV.   *Standard of Law.*

Next, appellants claim the district court applied an inappropriate standard of law to determine whether Herrig's conduct was fair and reasonable to Cookies. Appellants correctly assert that self-dealing transactions must have the earmarks of arms-length transactions before a court can find them to be fair or reasonable. *See Bechtel,* 243 Iowa at 1023, 51 N.W.2d at 184. The crux of appellants' claim is that the court should have focused on the fair market value of Herrig's services to Cookies rather than on the success Cookies achieved as a result of Herrig's actions.

We agree with appellants' contention that corporate profitability should not be the sole criteria by which to test the fairness and reasonableness of Herrig's fees. In this connection, appellants cite authority from the Michigan Supreme Court that we find persuasive:

> Given an instance of alleged director enrichment at corporate expense ... the burden to establish fairness resting on the director requires not only a showing of "fair price" but also a showing of the fairness of the bargain to the interests of the corporation.

*Fill Bldgs., Inc. v. Alexander Hamilton Life Ins. Co.,* 396 Mich. 453, 241 N.W.2d 466, 469 (1976). Applying such reasoning to the record before us, however, we cannot agree with appellants' assertion that Herrig's services were either unfairly priced or inconsistent with Cookies corporate interest.

There can be no serious dispute that the four agreements in issue—for exclusive distributorship, taco sauce royalty, warehousing, and consulting fees—have all benefited Cookies, as demonstrated by its financial success. Even if we assume Cookies could have procured similar services from other vendors at lower costs, we are not convinced that Herrig's fees were therefore unreasonable or exorbitant. Like the district court, we are not persuaded by appellants' expert testimony that Cookies' sales and profits would have been the same under agreements with other vendors. As Cookies' board noted prior to Herrig's takeover, he was the driving force in the corporation's success. Even plaintiffs' expert acknowledged that Herrig has done the work of at least five people—production supervisor, advertising specialist, warehouseman, broker, and salesman. While eschewing the lack of internal control, for accounting purposes, that such centralized authority may produce, the expert conceded that Herrig may in fact be underpaid for all he has accomplished. We believe the board properly considered this source of Cookies' success when it entered these transactions, as did the district court when it reviewed them. . . .

## V.  *Denial of Equitable Relief.*

. . . [T]he record before us aptly demonstrates that all members of Cookies' board were well aware of Herrig's dual ownership in Lakes and Speed's. We are unaware of any authority supporting plaintiffs' contention that Herrig was obligated to disclose to Cookies' board or shareholders the extent of his profits resulting from these distribution and warehousing agreements; nevertheless, the exclusive distribution agreement with Lakes authorized the board to ascertain that information had it so desired. Appellants cannot reasonably claim that Herrig owed Cookies a duty to render such services at no profit to himself or his companies. Having found that the compensation he received from these agreements was fair and reasonable, we are convinced that Herrig furnished sufficient pertinent information to Cookies' board to enable it to make prudent decisions concerning the contracts. . . .

We concur in the trial court's assessment of the evidence presented and affirm its dismissal of plaintiffs' claims.

AFFIRMED.

All Justices concur except SCHULTZ, J., who dissents.

■ SCHULTZ, JUSTICE (dissenting) . . . .

Much of Herrig's evidence concerned the tremendous success of the company. I believe that the trial court and the majority opinion have been so enthralled by the success of the company that they have failed to examine whether these matters of self-dealing were fair to the stockholders. While much credit is due to Herrig for the success of the company, this does not mean that these transactions were fair to the company.

I believe that Herrig failed on his burden of proof by what he did not show. He did not produce evidence of the local going rate for distribution contracts or storage fees outside of a very limited amount of self-serving testimony. He simply did not show the fair market value of his services or expense for freight, advertising and storage cost. He did not show that his taco sauce royalty was fair. This was his burden. He cannot succeed on it by merely showing the success of the company.

The shareholders, on the other hand, produced testimony of what the fair market value of Herrig's services were. The majority discounts this testimony and chooses instead to focus on the success Cookies achieved as a result of Herrig's actions. They focus on the success of the company rather than whether his self-dealing actions were arms-length transactions that were fair and reasonable to the stockholders. The appellants have put forth convincing testimony that Herrig has been grossly over compensated for his services based on their fair market value. Appellant's expert witness, a CPA, performed an analysis to show what the company would have earned if it had hired a $65,000 a year executive officer, paid a marketing supervisor and an advertising agency a commission of five percent of the sales each, built a new warehouse and hired a warehouseman. It was compared with what the company actually did make under Herrig's management. The analysis basically shows what the operating cost of this company should be on the open market when hiring out the work to experts. In 1985 alone, the company's income would have doubled what it actually made were these changes made. The evidence clearly shows that the fair market value of those services is considerably less than what Herrig actually has been paid.

Similarly, appellant's food broker expert witness testified that for $110,865, what the CPA analysis stated was the fair market value for brokerage services, his company would have provided all of the services that Herrig had performed. The company actually paid $730,-637 for the services, a difference of $620,000 in one year.

In summary, I believe the majority was dazzled by the tales of Herrig's efforts and Cookies' success in these difficult economic times. In the process, however, it is forgotten that Herrig owes a fiduciary duty to the corporation to deal fairly and reasonably with it in his self-dealing transactions. Herrig is not entitled to skim off the majority of the profits through self-dealing transactions unless they are fair to the minority stockholders. At trial, he failed to prove how his charges were in line with what the company could have gotten on the open market. Because I cannot ignore this inequity to the company and its share-holders, I must respectfully dissent.

## NEW YORK STOCK EXCHANGE LISTED
## COMPANY MANUAL § 312.03(b)

[See Statutory Supplement]

---

## SECTION 3.   COMPENSATION, THE WASTE DOCTRINE, AND THE EFFECT OF SHAREHOLDER RATIFICATION

---

## DEL. GEN. CORP. LAW §§ 141(h), 157

[See Statutory Supplement]

---

## REV. MODEL BUS. CORP. ACT §§ 6.24, 8.11

[See Statutory Supplement]

---

## ALI, PRINCIPLES OF CORPORATE GOVERNANCE § 5.03

---

## Lewis v. Vogelstein

Court of Chancery of Delaware, 1997.
699 A.2d 327.

■ ALLEN, CHANCELLOR.

This shareholders' suit challenges a stock option compensation plan for the directors of Mattel, Inc., which was approved or ratified by the shareholders of the company at its 1996 Annual Meeting of Shareholders. Two claims are asserted.

First, and most interestingly, plaintiff asserts that the proxy statement that solicited shareholder proxies to vote in favor of the adoption of the 1996 Mattel Stock Option Plan ("1996 Plan" or "Plan") was materially incomplete and misleading, because it did not include an estimated present value of the stock option grants to which directors might become entitled under the Plan. Thus, the first claim asserts that the corporate directors had, in the circumstances presented, a duty to disclose the present value of future options as estimated by some option-pricing formula, such as the Black–Scholes option-pricing model.[1]

---

1.  See generally Stephen A. Ross, et al.,
Corporate Finance 629–631 (3d ed. 1993).

Second, it is asserted that the grants of options actually made under the 1996 Plan did not offer reasonable assurance to the corporation that it would receive adequate value in exchange for such grants, and that such grants represent excessively large compensation for the directors in relation to the value of their service to Mattel. For these reasons, the granting of the option is said to constitute a breach of fiduciary duty.

On this motion, this substantive liability theory is also pressed as an "entire fairness" claim. Plaintiff maintains that because the Plan constitutes a self-interested transaction by the incumbent directors, all of whom qualify for grants under the 1996 Plan, they must justify it as entirely fair in order to avoid liability for breach of loyalty, which it is said they cannot do. As shown below, this approach does not constitute a different claim than that stated above.

Pending is defendants' motion to dismiss the complaint for failure to state a claim upon which relief may be granted. A motion of this type may be granted only when it appears reasonably certain that plaintiff would not be entitled to the relief requested, even if all the facts as stated in the complaint are true and all inferences fairly inferable from those allegations are drawn in plaintiff's favor. Rabkin v. Philip A. Hunt Chem. Corp., Del.Supr., 498 A.2d 1099 (1985).

For the reasons set forth below I conclude that there is no legal obligation for corporate directors who seek shareholder ratification of a plan of officer or director option grants, to make and disclose an estimate of present value of future options under a plan of the type described in the complaint. There is, therefore, no basis to conclude that failure to set forth such estimate constitutes a violation of any board obligation to set forth all material facts in connection with a ratification vote. Second, I conclude that the allegations of the complaint are not necessarily inconsistent with a conclusion that the 1996 Plan constitutes a waste of corporate assets. Thus, the complaint may not be dismissed as failing to state a claim.

I.

The facts as they appear in the pleading are as follows. The Plan was adopted in 1996 and ratified by the company's shareholders at the 1996 annual meeting. It contemplates two forms of stock option grants to the company's directors: a one-time grant of options on a block of stock and subsequent, smaller annual grants of further options.

With respect to the one-time grant, the Plan provides that each outside director will qualify for a grant of options on 15,000 shares of Mattel common stock at the market price on the day such options are granted (the "one-time options"). The one-time options are alleged to be exercisable immediately upon being granted although they will achieve economic value, if ever, only with the passage of time. It is alleged that if not exercised, they remain valid for ten years.[2]

---

**2.** As to the term of the one-time options there exists a material dispute of relevant fact. The complaint alleges those options are valid for ten years. Defendants assert

With respect to the second type of option grant, the Plan qualifies each director for a grant of options upon his or her re-election to the board each year (the "Annual Options"). The maximum number of options grantable to a director pursuant to the annual options provision depends on the number of years the director has served on the Mattel board. Those outside directors with five or fewer years of service will qualify to receive options on no more than 5,000 shares, while those with more than five years service will qualify for options to purchase up to 10,000 shares.[3] Once granted, these options vest over a four year period, at a rate of 25% per year. When exercisable, they entitle the holder to buy stock at the market price on the day of the grant. According to the complaint, options granted pursuant to the annual options provision also expire ten years from their grant date, whether or not the holder has remained on the board.

When the shareholders were asked to ratify the adoption of the Plan, as is typically true, no estimated present value of options that were authorized to be granted under the Plan was stated in the proxy solicitation materials.

## II.

As the presence of valid shareholder ratification of executive or director compensation plans importantly affects the form of judicial review of such grants, it is logical to begin an analysis of the legal sufficiency of the complaint by analyzing the sufficiency of the attack on the disclosures made in connection with the ratification vote.

### A.   Disclosure Obligation:

I first note a preliminary point: The complaint's assertion is not simply that the ratification of the 1996 Plan by the Mattel shareholders was ineffective because it was defective. If that were the whole of plaintiff's theory, the effect of any defect in disclosure under it would be only to deny to the board the benefits that ratification bestows in such a case. See In re Wheelabrator Tech., Inc. Shareholders Litig., Del.Ch., 663 A.2d 1194 (1995). The thrust of the allegation, however, is that in seeking ratification and in, allegedly, failing fully to disclose material facts, the board has committed an independent wrong. Despite the fact that shareholder approval was not required for the authorization of this transaction and was sought only for its effect on the standard of judicial review, there is language in Delaware cases dealing with "fair process", suggesting that a misdisclosure may make

however that a reading of the Plan itself certainly establishes that in fact the options expire sixty days after an outside director ceases to be a member of Mattel's board or in ten years whichever occurs first. Thus, according to defendants, the value of the options only continues while the grantee is serving on the board and is, presumably, affected by their motivational effect. This fact if true would render these options very difficult to value under option pricing theory. The

procedural setting of the motion requires me to assume that plaintiff's allegation is correct.

**3.** From a corporation law perspective one might defend as rational the greater incentive for longer serving directors; from a corporate governance perspective, however, the wisdom of this structure, which creates greater incentives to remain on the board, could sustain debate.

available a remedy, even if the shareholder vote was not required to authorize the transaction and the transaction can substantively satisfy a fairness test. . . .

In all events, in this instance, the theory advanced is that the alleged non-disclosure itself breaches a duty of candor and gives rise to a remedy. The defect alleged is that the shareholders were not told the present value of the compensation to the outside directors that the Plan contemplated i.e., the present value of the options that were authorized. It is alleged that the present value of the one-time options was as much as $180,000 per director and that that "fact" would be material to a Mattel shareholder in voting whether or not to ratify the board's action in adopting the 1996 Plan. According to plaintiff, the shareholders needed to have a specific dollar valuation of the options in order to decide whether to ratify the 1996 Plan. Such a valuation could, plaintiff suggests, be determined by application of formulas such as the widely-used option-pricing model first devised by Professors Fischer Black and Myron Scholes.[6] Plaintiff urges that this court should hold that because no such valuation was provided to the shareholders, the proxy statement failed to disclose material matter and was, therefore, defective.

B.   Disclosure of Estimated Present Value of Options to be Granted:

As the terms of the options granted under the 1996 Plan demonstrate, option-pricing models, when applied to executive or director stock options, are subject to special problems. Significant doubt exists whether the Black-Scholes option-pricing formula, or other, similar option-pricing models, provide a sufficiently reliable estimate of the value of options with terms such as those granted to the outside directors of Mattel.[8]

First, the Black–Scholes formula assumes that the options being valued are issued and publicly traded. Publicly-traded options have certain common characteristics that are important in assessing their value. Steven Huddart & Mark Lang, Employee Stock Exercises: An Empirical Analysis, 21 J.Acct. & Econ. 1, 9 (1996). The options granted to the Mattel directors under the Plan include restrictive terms that are different from those of typical, publicly-traded options and which may effect their value. Importantly, for instance, the directors' options are not assignable.

**6.**   Fischer Black & Myron Scholes, The Pricing of Options and Corporate Liabilities, 81 J.POL.ECON. 637 (1973).

**8.**   For example, the term of such an option—a critical variable in estimating present value—is uncertain because it expires when exercised, at any time during its life, rather than at a fixed period at its maturity. See also footnote 2, regarding the dispute in this case concerning whether options terminate sixty days after any director to be employed by Mattel. Such a provision would also make calculation of a present value of the option grant difficult since the probability of a directors' termination at any (or every) point during the ten year term is impossible to know and very hard to responsibly estimate. Thus, one of the vital components of an option-pricing formula, the life of the option, appears quite problematic in instances of this sort.

Second, the Black–Scholes model overstates the value of options that can be exercised at any time during their term because it does not take into account the cost-reducing effect of early exercise. Huddart & Lang at 18. The Mattel directors' one-time options are not options that are exercisable on a set date. They can be exercised at any time after the grant for a period, according to plaintiff, of up to ten years.

Third, the value of publicly-traded options and restricted options responds very differently to increased volatility of the price of the underlying stock. The volatility of the stock price is one of the important variables in the Black–Scholes formula. Ross, et al., Corporate Finance 629–31 (3d ed. 1993). Publicly-traded options increase in value as the price volatility of the underlying stock increases. The value of options of the type granted to the Mattel directors, on the other hand, arguably decreases with increased volatility, because the holders are more likely to exercise the options early since they cannot be traded. Nalin Kulatilaka & Alan J. Marcus, Valuing Employee Stock Options, Fin.Analysts J. Nov.-Dec. 1994, at 46, 51.[9]

Plaintiff argues that option pricing techniques are sufficiently developed so that the Financial Accounting Standards Board ("FASB") requires that financial statements state a value of options granted to directors according to a stock-option pricing model. Thus, they assert, the same information should be given to shareholders by directors seeking ratification. There are salient differences, however, between financial statement disclosure of an estimated value of stock options under a plan and disclosure for the purpose of shareholder ratification of adoption of the plan. For instance, financial statements are compiled at the end of the fiscal year, when the value of the options granted can be assessed with greater certainty, than is possible at the time the option plan is authorized or ratified since the market price at time of issue is known at that later point.

More broadly, it may be the case that good public policy recommends the disclosure to shareholders of estimates of present value (determined by one technique or another) of options that may be granted as compensation to senior officers and directors, when feasible techniques produce reliable estimates. But while it is unquestionably the case that corporation law plays an important part in the development of public policy in the area of directors' legal relations to corporations and shareholders, including disclosure law, it does not follow that the fiduciary duty of corporate directors is the appropriate instrument to determine and implement sound public policy with respect to this technical issue.

---

**9.** Cf. Regulation S–K, Item 402(b) (mandating that companies report the value of compensation paid to executives in stock options, but not requiring that the value be arrived at by using an option-pricing formula). It should be noted that in this instance the utility of the Black–Scholes or a similar option-pricing formula would also be reduced if the outside directors' options do, in fact, expire sixty days after the directors terminate their employment with Mattel. Because the Plan has not been submitted to the court in a manner that permits its specific provisions to be interpreted, it is not possible at this point to conclude whether this would be another shortcoming of this method of pricing the options.

What makes good sense—good policy—in terms of mandated corporate disclosure concerning prospective option grants involves not simply the moral intuition that directors should be candid with shareholders with respect to relevant facts, but inescapably involves technical judgments concerning what is feasible and helpful in varying circumstances. Judgments concerning what disclosure, if any, of estimated present values of options should be mandated are best made at this stage of the science, not by a court under a very general materiality standard, but by an agency with finance expertise. An administrative agency—the Securities and Exchange Commission—has a technical staff, is able to hold public hearings, and can, thus, receive wide and expert input, and can specify forms of disclosure, if appropriate. It can propose rules for comment and can easily amend rules that do not work well in practice. As just one example, any option-pricing formula premised on the assumptions that underlie Professors Black and Scholes's model would be concerned with the expected volatility of the stock over the term of option. How that volatility is itself estimated would be a significant factor in any standardized disclosure regime. But this certainly is not the type of inquiry that the judicial process is designed optimally to address. Clearly, determining whether disclosure of estimates of the present value of options ought to be mandated, and how those values ought to be calculated, is not a subject that lends itself to the blunt instrument of duty of loyalty analysis.

In all events, for these reasons, I conclude that, given the tools currently used in financial analysis, a careful board or compensation committee may customarily be expected to consider whether expert estimates of the present value of option grants will be informative and reliable to itself or to shareholders. And if such estimates are deemed by the board, acting in good faith, to be reliable and helpful, the board may elect to disclose them to the shareholders, if it seeks ratification of its actions. But, such "soft information" estimates may be highly problematic and not helpful at all, as for example would likely be the case here, if the options terminate two months after the holder leaves Mattel's board, instead of continuing for ten years, as defendants assert. See supra note 2.

While generally the materiality of "facts" omitted from a proxy statement is a question of fact unsuitable for determination on a motion to dismiss, nevertheless, I conclude that the allegations of failure to disclose estimated present value calculations fails to state a claim upon which relief may be granted. Where shareholder ratification of a plan of option compensation is involved, the duty of disclosure is satisfied by the disclosure or fair summary of all of the relevant terms and conditions of the proposed plan of compensation, together with any material extrinsic fact within the board's knowledge bearing on the issue. The directors' fiduciary duty of disclosure does not mandate that the board disclose one or more estimates of present value of options that may be granted under the plan. Such estimates may be an appropriate subject of disclosure where they are generated competently, and disclosed in a good faith effort to inform shareholder action, but no case is cited in which disclosure of such estimates has been mandated in order to satisfy the directors' fiduciary duty and I lack sufficient confidence to break that fresh ground. Absent allegations of intentional manipulation, where shareholder ratification of a plan of stock option compensation is sought, what may constitute appropriate disclosure respecting estimated present (or other) values of such options grantable under the plan is a subject better left to the judgment of the Securities and Exchange Commission and, subject to that regulatory regime, the judgment of the board seeking such approval.

### III.

Thus, concluding that the complaint does not state a claim for breach of any duty to fully disclose material facts to shareholders in connection with the board's request that the shareholders ratify the board's act of creating a directors' stock option plan, I turn to the motion to dismiss the complaint's allegation to the effect that the Plan, or grants under it, constitute a breach of the directors' fiduciary duty of loyalty. As the Plan contemplates grants to the directors that approved the Plan and who recommended it to the shareholders, we start by observing that it constitutes self-dealing that would ordinarily require that the directors prove that the grants involved were, in the circumstances, entirely fair to the corporation. Weinberger v. U.O.P., Inc., Del.Supr., 457 A.2d 701 (1983). However, it is the case that the shareholders have ratified the directors' action. That ratification is attacked only on the ground just treated. Thus, for these purposes I assume that the ratification was effective. The question then becomes what is the effect of informed shareholder ratification on a transaction of this type (i.e., officer or director pay).

A.   Shareholder Ratification Under Delaware Law:

What is the effect under Delaware corporation law of shareholder ratification of an interested transaction? The answer to this apparently simple question appears less clear than one would hope or indeed expect. Four possible effects of shareholder ratification appear logically available: First, one might conclude that an effective shareholder ratification acts as a complete defense to any charge of breach of duty. Second, one might conclude that the effect of such ratification is to shift the substantive test on judicial review of the act from one of fairness that would otherwise be obtained (because the transaction is an interested one) to one of waste. Third, one might conclude that the ratification shifts the burden of proof of unfairness to plaintiff, but leaves that shareholder-protective test in place. Fourth, one might conclude (perhaps because of great respect for the collective action disabilities that attend shareholder action in public corporations) that shareholder ratification offers no assurance of assent of a character that deserves judicial recognition. Thus, under this approach, ratification on full information would be afforded no effect. Excepting the fourth of these effects, there are cases in this jurisdiction that reflect each of these approaches to the effect of shareholder voting to approve a transaction.[10]

---

10.  See, e.g., In re Wheelabrator Technologies, Inc., Shareholders Litig., Del.Ch., 663 A.2d 1194 (1995) (effect one: effective ratification eliminates any claim for breach of

In order to state my own understanding I first note that by shareholder ratification I do not refer to every instance in which shareholders vote affirmatively with respect to a question placed before them. I exclude from the question those instances in which shareholder votes are a necessary step in authorizing a transaction. Thus the law of ratification as here discussed has no direct bearing on shareholder action to amend a certificate of incorporation or bylaws, cf. Williams v. Geier, Del.Supr., 671 A.2d 1368 (1996); nor does that law bear on shareholder votes necessary to authorize a merger, a sale of substantially all the corporation's assets, or to dissolve the enterprise. For analytical purposes one can set such cases aside.

1.   Ratification generally: I start with principles broader than those of corporation law. Ratification is a concept deriving from the law of agency which contemplates the ex post conferring upon or confirming of the legal authority of an agent in circumstances in which the agent had no authority or arguably had no authority. Restatement (Second) of Agency § 82 (1958). To be effective, of course, the agent must fully disclose all relevant circumstances with respect to the transaction to the principal prior to the ratification. See, e.g., Breen Air Freight Ltd. v. Air Cargo, Inc., et al., 470 F.2d 767, 773 (2d Cir.1972); Restatement (Second) of Agency § 91 (1958). Beyond that, since the relationship between a principal and agent is fiduciary in character, the agent in seeking ratification must act not only with candor, but with loyalty. Thus an attempt to coerce the principal's consent improperly will invalidate the effectiveness of the ratification. Restatement (Second) of Agency § 100 (1958).

Assuming that a ratification by an agent is validly obtained, what is its effect? One way of conceptualizing that effect is that it provides, after the fact, the grant of authority that may have been wanting at the time of the agent's act. Another might be to view the ratification as consent or as an estoppel by the principal to deny a lack of authority. See Restatement (Second) of Agency § 103 (1958). In either event the effect of informed ratification is to validate or affirm the act of the agent as the act of the principal. Id. § 82.

Application of these general ratification principles to shareholder ratification is complicated by three other factors. First, most generally, in the case of shareholder ratification there is of course no single individual acting as principal, but rather a class or group of divergent individuals—the class of shareholders. This aggregate quality of the principal means that decisions to affirm or ratify an act will be subject to collective action disabilities ...; that some portion of the body doing the ratifying may in fact have conflicting interests in the transaction; and some dissenting members of the class may be able to assert more or less convincingly that the "will" of the principal is wrong, or

duty of care but only breach of care); Michelson v. Duncan, Del.Supr., 407 A.2d 211, 224 (1979) (effect two: effective ratification of director interested transaction triggers waste standard); Citron v. E.I. Du Pont de Nemours & Co., Del.Ch., 584 A.2d 490, 500–502 (1990), quoted with approval in Kahn v. Lynch Communication Systems, Inc., Del.Supr. 638 A.2d 1110 (1994) (effect three: effective ratification shifts burden of fairness to plaintiff).

even corrupt and ought not to be binding on the class. In the case of individual ratification these issues won't arise, assuming that the principal does not suffer from multiple personality disorder. Thus the collective nature of shareholder ratification makes it more likely that following a claimed shareholder ratification, nevertheless, there is a litigated claim on behalf of the principal that the agent lacked authority or breached its duty. The second, mildly complicating factor present in shareholder ratification is the fact that in corporation law the "ratification" that shareholders provide will often not be directed to lack of legal authority of an agent but will relate to the consistency of some authorized director action with the equitable duty of loyalty. Thus shareholder ratification sometimes acts not to confer legal authority—but as in this case—to affirm that action taken is consistent with shareholder interests. Third, when what is "ratified" is a director conflict transaction, the statutory law—in Delaware Section 144 of the Delaware General Corporation Law—may bear on the effect.[12]

2.   Shareholder ratification: These differences between shareholder ratification of director action and classic ratification by a single principal, do lead to a difference in the effect of a valid ratification in the shareholder context. The principal novelty added to ratification law generally by the shareholder context, is the idea—no doubt analogously present in other contexts in which common interests are held—that, in addition to a claim that ratification was defective because of incomplete information or coercion, shareholder ratification is subject to a claim by a member of the class that the ratification is ineffectual (1) because a majority of those affirming the transaction had a conflicting interest with respect to it or (2) because the transaction that is ratified constituted a corporate waste. As to the second of these, it has long been held that shareholders may not ratify a waste except by a unanimous vote. Saxe v. Brady, 40 Del.Ch., 184 A.2d 602, 605 (1962). The idea behind this rule is apparently that a transaction that satisfies the high standard of waste constitutes a gift of corporate property and no one should be forced against their will to make a gift of their property. In all events, informed, uncoerced, disinterested shareholder ratification of a transaction in which corporate directors have a material conflict of interest has the effect of protecting the transaction from judicial review except on the basis of

---

**12.** Most jurisdictions have enacted statutes that appear to offer a procedural technique for removing courts from a fairness evaluation of the terms of director conflict transactions. Generally courts have given them a very narrow interpretation, however. In Delaware that statute enacted in 1967—Act of July 3, 1967, Ch. 50, 56 Del.Laws 151, 170 (1967) amended in 1969—is Section 144 of the DGCL. Early on it was narrowly held that compliance with that section simply removed the automatic taint of a director conflict transaction, but nevertheless left the transaction subject to substantive judicial review for fairness. See Fliegler v. Lawrence, Del.Supr., 361 A.2d 218, 222 (1976) (involv-

ing claimed independent board action, not ratification by shareholders). This interpretation tended to be the general judicial response to these "safe-harbor" statutes. See Cookies Food Prod., Inc. v. Lakes Warehouse Distrib., Inc., 430 N.W.2d 447, 452–453 (Iowa 1988) (requiring directors who engage in self-dealing to prove that they have acted in good faith). See also Cohen v. Ayers, 596 F.2d 733, 740 (7th Cir.1979) (stating that under New York statutory law, in an unratified transaction involving interested directors the burden is on the directors to establish the fairness of the transaction, but where shareholder or disinterested-director ratification has occurred, the burden shifts to the challenger).

waste. Keenan v. Eshleman, Del.Supr., 2 A.2d 904 (1938); Gottlieb v. Heyden Chem. Corp., Del.Supr., 91 A.2d 57, 58 (1952); Steiner v. Meyerson, Del.Ch., C.A. No. 13139, 1995 WL 441999, Allen, C. (July 18, 1995).[13]

## B.   The Waste Standard:

The judicial standard for determination of corporate waste is well developed. Roughly, a waste entails an exchange of corporate assets for consideration so disproportionately small as to lie beyond the range at which any reasonable person might be willing to trade. See Saxe v. Brady, 184 A.2d 602, 610; Grobow v. Perot, Del.Supr., 539 A.2d 180, 189 (1988). Most often the claim is associated with a transfer of corporate assets that serves no corporate purpose; or for which no consideration at all is received. Such a transfer is in effect a gift. If, however, there is any substantial consideration received by the corporation, and if there is a good faith judgment that in the circumstances the transaction is worthwhile, there should be no finding of waste, even if the fact finder would conclude ex post that the transaction was unreasonably risky. Any other rule would deter corporate boards from the optimal rational acceptance of risk, for reasons explained elsewhere. See Gagliardi v. TriFoods Intern., Inc., Del.Ch., 683 A.2d 1049 (1996). Courts are ill-fitted to attempt to weigh the "adequacy" of consideration under the waste standard or, ex post, to judge appropriate degrees of business risk.

## C.   Ratification of Officer or Director Option Grants:

Let me turn now to the history of the Delaware law treating shareholder ratification of corporate plans that authorize the granting of stock options to corporate officers and directors. What is interesting about this law is that while it is consistent with the foregoing general treatment of shareholder ratification—i.e., it appears to hold that informed, non-coerced ratification validates any such plan or grant, unless the plan is wasteful[14]—in its earlier expressions, the waste standard used by the courts in fact was not a waste standard at all, but was a form of "reasonableness" or proportionality review.

1.   Development of Delaware law of option compensation: It is fair to say I think that Delaware law took a skeptical or suspicious stance towards the innovation of stock option compensation as it developed in a major way following World War II. See, e.g., Kerbs, et al. v. California Eastern Airways, Inc., Del.Supr., 90 A.2d 652 (1952); Gottlieb v. Heyden Chem. Corp., Del.Supr., 91 A.2d 57 (1952); Id., 90 A.2d 660 (1952); Id., Del.Ch., 99 A.2d 507 (1953). Such skepticism is a fairly natural consequence of the common law of director compensa-

---

**13.** Claims of breach of a duty of care seem difficult to relate to analysis under the waste standard. Duty of care analysis in this or other settings relate to deviations from ordinary care in the circumstances. Probably for this reason, it has been held, on authority, that ratification of a transaction that is thereafter made the subject of a breach of care claim is effective to defeat such a claim completely. See In re Wheelabrator Tech., Inc. Shareholders Litig., Del.Ch., 663 A.2d 1194, 1200 (1995).

**14.** See Michelson v. Duncan, Del. Supr., 407 A.2d 211 (1979); Beard v. Elster, Del.Supr., 160 A.2d 731 (1960).

tion[15] and of the experience that corporate law judges had over the decades with schemes to water stock or to divert investors funds into the hands of promoters or management.

The early Delaware cases on option compensation established that, even in the presence of informed ratification, in order for stock option grants to be valid a two part test had to be satisfied. First it was seen as necessary that the court conclude that the grant contemplates that the corporation will receive "sufficient consideration." E.g., Kerbs, at 90 A.2d 652, 656 (1952). "Sufficient consideration" as employed in the early cases does not seem like a waste standard: "Sufficient consideration to the corporation may be, inter alia, the retention of the services of an employee, or the gaining of the services of a new employee, provided there is a reasonable relationship between the value of the services . . . and the value of the options . . .". Kerbs at 656 (emphasis added).

Secondly it was held early on that, in addition, the plan or the circumstances of the grant must include "conditions or the existence of circumstances which may be expected to insure that the contemplated consideration will in fact pass to the corporation." Kerbs at 656 (emphasis added). Elsewhere the Supreme Court spoke of "circumstances which may reasonably be regarded as sufficient to insure that the corporation will receive that which it desires . . .". Id. at 657 (emphasis added).

This (1) weighing of the reasonableness of the relationship between the value of the consideration flowing both ways and (2) evaluating the sufficiency of the circumstances to insure receipt of the benefit sought, seem rather distant from the substance of a waste standard of judicial review. Indeed these tests seem to be a form of heightened scrutiny that is now sometimes referred to as an intermediate or proportionality review. Cf. Unocal Corp. v. Mesa Petroleum, Co., Del.Supr., 493 A.2d 946 (1985); Paramount Communications v. QVC Network, Del.Supr., 637 A.2d 34 (1994).

In all events, these tests were in fact operationally very problematic. Valuing an option grant (as part of a reasonable relationship test) is quite difficult, even under today's more highly developed techniques of financial analysis. This would be especially true where, as this case exemplifies, the options are tied to and conditioned upon a continued status as an officer or director. Even more problematic is valuing—or judicially reviewing a judgment of equivalency of value of—the future benefits that the corporation hopes to obtain from the option grant. There is no objective metric to gauge ex ante incentive effects of owning options by officers or directors.[17] Beyond this operational

---

**15.** See, e.g., Cahall v. Lofland, Del.Ch., 114 A. 224, aff'd, 118 A. 1 (1922) (directors serve without compensation unless it is explicitly authorized by its charter or by shareholders; director compensation where authorized is "scrutinized closely"; directors may not evaluate the value of their labor when it provides consideration for issuance of stock).

**17.** The benefits that Mattel contemplates receiving from the grant of options, according to its Proxy Statement, is to "attract, retain and reward . . . directors" and "to strengthen the mutuality of interests between [the option-recipients] and the . . . stockholders." Proxy Statement at 12.

problem, the approach of these early option cases may be thought to raise the question, why was it necessary for the court reviewing a stock option grant to conclude that the circumstances "insure" that the corporation will receive the benefits it seeks to achieve. In other contexts, even where interested transactions are involved, a fair (i.e., valid and enforceable) contract might contemplate payment in exchange for a probability of corporation benefit. A corporation, for example, certainly could acquire from an officer or director at a fair price a property interest that had only prospective commercial value.

In Beard v. Elster, Del.Supr., 160 A.2d 731 (1960), the Delaware Supreme Court relaxed slightly the general formulation of Kerbs, et al.,[19] and rejected the reading of Kerbs to the effect that the corporation had to have (or insure receipt of) legally cognizable consideration in order to make an option grant valid. The court also emphasized the effect that approval by an independent board or committee might have. It held that what was necessary to validate an officer or director stock option grant was a finding that a reasonable board could conclude from the circumstances that the corporation may reasonably expect to receive a proportionate benefit. A good faith determination by a disinterested board or committee to that effect, at least when ratified by a disinterested shareholder vote, entitled such a grant to business judgment protection (i.e., classic waste standard). See generally David A. Drexler, et al., Delaware Corporation Law & Practice § 14.03[2] (1997). After Beard, judicial review of officer and director option grants sensibly focused in practice less on attempting independently to assess whether the corporation in fact would receive proportionate value, and more on the procedures used to authorize and ratify such grants. But Beard addressed only a situation in which an independent committee of the board functioned on the question.

2.   Current law on ratification effect on option grants: A substantive question that remains however is whether in practice the waste standard that is utilized where informed shareholders ratify a grant of options adopted and recommended by a self-interested board is the classical waste test (i.e., no consideration; gift; no person of ordinary prudence could possibly agree, etc.) or whether, in fact, it is a species of intermediate review in which the court assesses reasonableness in relationship to perceived benefits.

The Supreme Court has not expressly deviated from the "proportionality" approach to waste of its earlier decision, although in recent decades it has had few occasions to address the subject. In Michelson v. Duncan, Del.Supr., 407 A.2d 211 (1979), a stock option case in which ratification had occurred, however, the court repeatedly referred to the relevant test where ratification had occurred as that of "gift or waste" and plainly meant by waste, the absence of any consideration (". . . when there are issues of fact as to the existence of

---

**19.** "All stock option plans must . . . contain conditions, or [the] surrounding circumstances [must be] such, that the corporation may reasonably expect to receive the contemplated benefit from the grant of options [, and] (2) there must be a reasonable relationship between the value of the benefit passing to the corporation and the value of the options granted." Beard v. Elster, 160 A.2d at 737 (1960). (emphasis added)

consideration, a full hearing is required regardless of shareholder ratification." 407 A.2d at 223). Issues of "sufficiency" of consideration or adequacy of assurance that a benefit or proportionate benefit would be achieved were not referenced.

The Court of Chancery has interpreted the waste standard in the ratified option context as invoking not a proportionality or reasonableness test a la *Kerbs* but the traditional waste standard referred to in *Michelson*. See, e.g., Steiner v. Meyerson, Del.Ch., C.A. No. 13139, 1995 WL 441999, Allen, C. (July 18, 1995); Zupnick v. Goizueta, Del.Ch., 698 A.2d 384, Jacobs, V.C. (1997) (both granting motions to dismiss shareholder claims that options grants constituted actionable waste).

In according substantial effect to shareholder ratification these more recent cases are not unmindful of the collective action problem faced by shareholders in public corporations. These problems do render the assent that ratification can afford very different in character from the assent that a single individual may give. In this age in which institutional shareholders have grown strong and can more easily communicate, however, that assent, is, I think, a more rational means to monitor compensation than judicial determinations of the "fairness," or sufficiency of consideration, which seems a useful technique principally, I suppose, to those unfamiliar with the limitations of courts and their litigation processes. In all events, the classic waste standard does afford some protection against egregious cases or "constructive fraud."

\* \* \*

Before ruling on the pending motion to dismiss the substantive claim of breach of fiduciary duty, under a waste standard, I should make one other observation. The standard for determination of motions to dismiss is of course well established and understood. Where under any state of facts consistent with the factual allegations of the complaint the plaintiff would be entitled to a judgment, the complaint may not be dismissed as legally defective. See, e.g., Rabkin v. Philip A. Hunt Chem. Corp., supra. It is also the case that in some instances "mere conclusions" may be held to be insufficient to withstand an otherwise well made motion. Since what is a "well pleaded" fact and what is a "mere conclusion" is not always clear, there is often and inevitably some small room for the exercise of informed judgment by courts in determining motions to dismiss under the appropriate test. Consider for example allegations that an arm's-length corporate transaction constitutes a waste of assets. Such an allegation is inherently factual and not easily amenable to determination on a motion to dismiss and indeed often not on a motion for summary judgment. See, e.g., Michelson v. Duncan, Del.Supr., 407 A.2d 211 (1979). Yet it cannot be the case that allegations of the facts of any (or every) transaction coupled with a statement that the transaction constitutes a waste of assets, necessarily states a claim upon which discovery may be had; such a rule would, in this area, constitute an undue encourage- ment to strike suits. Certainly some set of facts, if true, may be said as a matter of law not to constitute waste. For example, a claim that the grant of options on stock with a market price of say $5,000 to a corporate director, exercisable at a future time, if the optionee is still an officer or director of the issuer, constitutes a corporate waste, would in my opinion be subject to dismissal on motion, despite the contextual nature of judgments concerning waste. See Steiner v. Meyerson, Del.Ch., C.A. No. 13139, 1995 WL 441999, Allen, C. (July 18, 1995); Zupnick v. Goizueta, Del.Ch., 698 A.2d 384, Jacobs, V.C. (1997). In some instances the facts alleged, if true, will be so far from satisfying the waste standard that dismissal is appropriate.

This is not such a case in my opinion. Giving the pleader the presumptions to which he is entitled on this motion, I cannot conclude that no set of facts could be shown that would permit the court to conclude that the grant of these options, particularly focusing upon the one-time options, constituted an exchange to which no reasonable person not acting under compulsion and in good faith could agree. In so concluding, I do not mean to suggest a view that these grants are suspect, only that one time option grants to directors of this size seem at this point sufficiently unusual to require the court to refer to evidence before making an adjudication of their validity and consistency with fiduciary duty. Thus, for that reason the motion to dismiss will be denied. It is so Ordered.

----

## NOTE ON BLACK–SCHOLES

The Black–Scholes option-pricing model, referred to by Chancellor Allen, is a formula used to determine the price, or value, of an option. The model depends on five variables: (1) The risk-free rate of interest. (2) The market price of the underlying stock. (3) The volatility of the price of the underlying stock. (Volatility is the size of fluctuations of a stock's price.) (4) The exercise price of the option. (5) The length of the option's term. The value of an option will increase with increases in (i) the risk-free rate of interest; (ii) the excess (if any) of the market price of the stock over the exercise price of the option; (iii) the volatility of the underlying stock; and (iv) the length of the term of option.

All of these variables except volatility can be easily determined. Volatility is estimated in significant part on the basis of the stock's historical performance.

Certain factors that are not incorporated into the Black–Scholes option-pricing model may also affect the value of an option. For example, the model is designed to value a "European call option," which is exercisable only at the end of the option's term. If an option is an "American option," which permits the option holder to exercise the option at any time during the option's term, then the option's value will be higher. Variations of the Black–Scholes model take such factors into account.

---

## NOTE ON LEWIS v. VOGELSTEIN

Like all of Chancellor Allen's opinions, Lewis v. Vogelstein masterfully brings out the underlying problems in the issues raised by the case before him—here, compensation, waste, and the effect of shareholder ratification. In considering Lewis v. Vogelstein, however, it must be borne in mind that the courts only seldom overturn the compensation of senior executives in publicly held corporations if the compensation has been approved by disinterested directors. (In Lewis v. Vogelstein, the compensation at issue was payable to the directors themselves, so that approval by disinterested directors was not possible.)

For example, in Zupnick v. Goizueta, 698 A.2d 384 (Del.Ch.1997), Coca–Cola's board granted to Goizueta, Coca Cola's CEO, options to purchase 1 million shares. The options were based on Goizueta's past services, and were exercisable the day they were granted. The plaintiff, a shareholder in Coca Cola, claimed that the grant of options was waste. The court dismissed the complaint:

> ... To state a cognizable claim for waste where there is no contention that the directors were interested or that shareholder ratification was improperly obtained, the well-pleaded allegations of the complaint must support the conclusion that "no person of ordinary, sound business judgment would say that the consideration received for the options was a fair exchange for the options granted." ... That is "an extreme test, very rarely satisfied by a shareholder plaintiff," because "if under the circumstances any reasonable person might conclude that the deal made sense, then the judicial inquiry ends."

Steiner v. Meyerson, Del.Ch., C.A. No. 13139, Allen, C. (July 18, 1995), Mem. Op. at 2, 1995 WL 441999. As Chancellor Allen observed in Steiner, supra at p. 11:

> [T]he waste theory represents a theoretical exception to the statement very rarely encountered in the world of real transactions. There surely are cases of fraud; of unfair self dealing and, much more rarely negligence. But rarest of all—and indeed like Nessie, possibly non existent—would be the case of disinterested business people making non fraudulent deals (non-negligently) that meet the legal standard of waste!

The plaintiff's claim is that Coca Cola received no consideration because the options were issued to compensate Goizueta for his past performance. As the plaintiff alleges, the stock options granted to Goizueta in this case took the form of additional compensation (or a "bonus")for services previously performed. Plaintiff claims that such additional compensation was waste or a gift because Goizueta was already contractually obligated to perform those services and had been compensated for doing so. . . .

. . . In *Blish v. Thompson Automatic Arms Corporation*, Del.Supr., 64 A.2d 581 (1948), the Court [stated that retroactive compensation is permissible where the amount awarded is not unreasonable in view of the services rendered].

In this case, the pleaded facts establish (for present purposes) that reasonable, disinterested directors could have concluded—and in this instance did conclude—that Goizueta's past services were [unusual in character and that the resulting benefit to the corporation was of extraordinary magnitude]. This case, therefore, falls within a recognized exception to the common law rule that otherwise generally prohibits retroactive executive compensation. . . .

On the other hand, in Sanders v. Computer Associates, 1999 WL 1044880 (Del.Ch.1999), the board of Computer Associates (CA) had adopted, and the shareholders had approved, a Key Employee Stock Ownership Plan (KESOP). Section 3.1 of the Plan authorized the Compensation Committee to issue up to 6 million shares of common stock to Plan participants, contingent on the corporation's stock reaching specified price targets. Subsequently, the Compensation Committee issued 20.25 million shares, on the ground that the 6 million figure should be adjusted for three intervening stock splits. Plaintiff, a shareholder in Computer Associates, brought suit to set aside the award of the extra shares, and for damages. The defendants moved to dismiss on the ground that the grant of shares resulted from a valid exercise of business judgment. The court denied the motion, and held that the plaintiffs were entitled to equitable relief, although it postponed consideration of the damages claim:

. . . . As a practical matter, my rough calculations indicate that even under the strictest reading of the Plan, the three Participants will together still receive nearly $320 million. $320 million is no mere bagatelle. I find it remarkable that defendants would have me believe that CA's shareholders would consider that $320 million for three individuals failed to "encourage, recognize, and reward sustained outstanding individual performance by certain key employees." . . .

I find that the Committee awarded the 20.25 million shares in clear violation of § 3.1, and without any legal justification under the Plan. . . .

For a waste claim to survive a motion to dismiss, the plaintiff must allege facts sufficient to show that the corporation received no consideration for the transferred asset. The standard is stringent and requires that no person of ordinary business judgment would conclude that the deal was fair to the corporation. It is my view that the alleged acts, drawing all inferences in plaintiffs' favor, raise sufficient question about the appropriateness of the share grants to state a claim of breach of fiduciary duty and for this Court to deny the defendants' motion to dismiss. Decidedly, the characterization of the claim as one for "waste" or for unjust enrichment can not be the focus of analysis. Having concluded as a matter of law that the Board exceeded its authority, the alleged acts clearly call into question whether the transaction as consummated could have benefitted CA and whether the breach of fiduciary duty caused corporate officers to be unjustly enriched. . . .

It seems to me that just as in the corporate opportunity context, a share grant in excess of that authorized by a KESOP calls the mechanism of the constructive trust into play as an effective remedial measure. This case presents an interesting but complicating twist in that certain management executives, who also served in a fiduciary capacity, received a benefit wrongfully and unfairly conferred upon them by directors who also served as fiduciaries but who did not receive the benefit. At this stage of the proceedings, it is clear that plaintiffs are entitled to judgment on the pleadings that the directors wrongfully authorized the award and that the director executives who received the award must disgorge the benefit received in order to avoid being unjustly enriched.

In Brehm v. Eisner, 746 A.2d 244 (Del.2000), Michael Ovitz, who had been recently hired as the president of Walt Disney Co., came to a parting of the ways with Disney after only fourteen months. The board approved a severance payment of $140 million pursuant to the terms of Ovitz's employment contract. A shareholder brought suit challenging this payment. The Chancellor dismissed the complaint. On appeal, the Delaware Supreme Court commented:

> This is potentially a very troubling case on the merits. On the one hand, it appears from the Complaint that: (a) the compensation and termination payout for Ovitz were exceedingly lucrative, if not luxurious, compared to Ovitz' value to the Company; and (b) the processes of the boards of directors in dealing with the approval and termination of the Ovtiz Employment Agreement were casual, if not sloppy and perfunctory. On the other hand, the Complaint is so inartfully drafted that it was properly dismissed under our pleading standards for derivative suits. From what we can ferret out of this deficient pleading, the processes of the Old Board and the New Board were hardly paradigms of good corporate governance practices. Moreover, the sheer size of the payout to Ovitz, as alleged, pushes the envelope of judicial respect for the business judgment of directors in making compensation decisions. Therefore, both as to the processes of the two Boards and the waste test, this is a close case.

> But our concerns about lavish executive compensation and our institutional aspirations that boards of directors of Delaware corporations live up to the highest standards of good corporate practices do not translate into a holding that these plaintiffs have

set forth particularized facts excusing a pre-suit demand under our law and our pleading requirements.

The court gave the plaintiff leave to replead claims for breach of fiduciary duty and waste.

---

# SECTION 4.   THE CORPORATE OPPORTUNITY DOCTRINE

---

## Northeast Harbor Golf Club, Inc. v. Harris

Supreme Judicial Court of Maine, 1995.
661 A.2d 1146.

■ Before WATHEN, C.J., and ROBERTS, GLASSMAN, DANA, and LIPEZ, JJ.

■ ROBERTS, JUSTICE.

Northeast Harbor Golf Club, Inc., appeals from a judgment entered in the Superior Court (Hancock County, *Atwood, J.*) following a nonjury trial. The Club maintains that the trial court erred in finding that Nancy Harris did not breach her fiduciary duty as president of the Club by purchasing and developing property abutting the golf course. Because we today adopt principles different from those applied by the trial court in determining that Harris's activities did not constitute a breach of the corporate opportunity doctrine, we vacate the judgment.

### I.

#### The Facts

Nancy Harris was the president of the Northeast Harbor Golf Club, a Maine corporation, from 1971 until she was asked to resign in 1990. The Club also had a board of directors that was responsible for making or approving significant policy decisions. The Club's only major asset was a golf course in Mount Desert. During Harris's tenure as president, the board occasionally discussed the possibility of developing some of the Club's real estate in order to raise money. Although Harris was generally in favor of tasteful development, the board always "shied away" from that type of activity.

In 1979, Robert Suminsby informed Harris that he was the listing broker for the Gilpin property, which comprised three noncontiguous parcels located among the fairways of the golf course. The property included an unused right-of-way on which the Club's parking lot and clubhouse were located. It was also encumbered by an easement in favor of the Club allowing foot traffic from the green of one hole to the next tee. Suminsby testified that he contacted Harris because she was the president of the Club and he believed that the Club would be interested in buying the property in order to prevent development.

Harris immediately agreed to purchase the Gilpin property in her own name for the asking price of $45,000. She did not disclose her plans to purchase the property to the Club's board prior to the purchase. She informed the board at its annual August meeting that she had purchased the property, that she intended to hold it in her own name, and that the Club would be "protected." The board took no action in response to the Harris purchase. She testified that at the time of the purchase she had no plans to develop the property and that no such plans took shape until 1988.

In 1984, while playing golf with the postmaster of Northeast Harbor, Harris learned that a parcel of land owned by the heirs of the Smallidge family might be available for purchase. The Smallidge parcel was surrounded on three sides by the golf course and on the fourth side by a house lot. It had no access to the road. With the ultimate goal of acquiring the property, Harris instructed her lawyer to locate the Smallidge heirs. Harris testified that she told a number of individual board members about her attempt to acquire the Smallidge parcel. At a board meeting in August 1985, Harris formally disclosed to the board that she had purchased the Smallidge property.[1] The minutes of that meeting show that she told the board she had no present plans to develop the Smallidge parcel. Harris testified that at the time of the purchase of the Smallidge property she nonetheless thought it might be nice to have some houses there. Again, the board took no formal action as a result of Harris's purchase. Harris acquired the Smallidge property from ten heirs, paying a total of $60,000. In 1990, Harris paid $275,000 for the lot and building separating the Smallidge parcel from the road in order to gain access to the otherwise landlocked parcel.

The trial court expressly found that the Club would have been unable to purchase either the Gilpin or Smallidge properties for itself, relying on testimony that the Club continually experienced financial difficulties, operated annually at a deficit, and depended on contributions from the directors to pay its bills. On the other hand, there was evidence that the Club had occasionally engaged in successful fund-raising, including a two-year period shortly after the Gilpin purchase during which the Club raised $115,000. The Club had $90,000 in a capital investment fund at the time of the Smallidge purchase.

In 1987 or 1988, Harris divided the real estate into 41 small lots, 14 on the Smallidge property and 27 on the Gilpin property. Apparently as part of her estate plan, Harris conveyed noncontiguous lots among the 41 to her children and retained others for herself. In 1991, Harris and her children exchanged deeds to reassemble the small lots into larger parcels. At the time the Club filed this suit, the property was divided into 11 lots, some owned by Harris and others by her children who are also defendants in this case. Harris estimated the value of all the real estate at the time of the trial to be $1,550,000.

---

1. In fact, it appears that Harris did not take title to the property until October 26, 1985. She had only signed a purchase and sale agreement at the time of the August board meeting.

In 1988, Harris, who was still president of the Club, and her children began the process of obtaining approval for a five-lot subdivision known as Bushwood on the lower Gilpin property. Even when the board learned of the proposed subdivision, a majority failed to take any action. A group of directors formed a separate organization in order to oppose the subdivision on the basis that it violated the local zoning ordinance. After Harris's resignation as president, the Club also sought unsuccessfully to challenge the subdivision. *See Northeast Harbor Golf Club, Inc. v. Town of Mount Desert*, 618 A.2d 225 (Me.1992). Plans of Harris and her family for development of the other parcels are unclear, but the local zoning ordinance would permit construction of up to 11 houses on the land as currently divided.

After Harris's plans to develop Bushwood became apparent, the board grew increasingly divided concerning the propriety of development near the golf course. At least two directors, Henri Agnese and Nick Ludington, testified that they trusted Harris to act in the best interests of the Club and that they had no problem with the development plans for Bushwood. Other directors disagreed.

In particular, John Schafer, a Washington, D.C., lawyer and long-time member of the board, took issue with Harris's conduct. He testified that he had relied on Harris's representations at the time she acquired the properties that she would not develop them. According to Schafer, matters came to a head in August 1990 when a number of directors concluded that Harris's development plans irreconcilably conflicted with the Club's interests. As a result, Schafer and two other directors asked Harris to resign as president. In April 1991, after a substantial change in the board's membership, the board authorized the instant lawsuit against Harris for the breach of her fiduciary duty to act in the best interests of the corporation. The board simultaneously resolved that the proposed housing development was contrary to the best interests of the corporation.

The Club filed a complaint against Harris, her sons John and Shepard, and her daughter-in-law Melissa Harris. As amended, the complaint alleged that during her term as president Harris breached her fiduciary duty by purchasing the lots without providing notice and an opportunity for the Club to purchase the property and by subdividing the lots for future development. The Club sought an injunction to prevent development and also sought to impose a constructive trust on the property in question for the benefit of the Club.

The trial court found that Harris had not usurped a corporate opportunity because the acquisition of real estate was not in the Club's line of business. Moreover, it found that the corporation lacked the financial ability to purchase the real estate at issue. Finally, the court placed great emphasis on Harris's good faith. It noted her long and dedicated history of service to the Club, her personal oversight of the Club's growth, and her frequent financial contributions to the Club. The court found that her development activities were "generally ... compatible with the corporation's business." This appeal followed.

## II.

### The Corporate Opportunity Doctrine

Corporate officers and directors bear a duty of loyalty to the corporations they serve. As Justice Cardozo explained the fiduciary duty in *Meinhard v. Salmon,* 249 N.Y. 458, 164 N.E. 545, 546 (1928):

> A trustee is held to something stricter than the morals of the marketplace. Not honesty alone, but the punctilio of an honor the most sensitive, is then the standard of behavior. As to this there has developed a tradition that is unbending and inveterate.

Maine has embraced this "unbending and inveterate" tradition. Corporate fiduciaries in Maine must discharge their duties in good faith with a view toward furthering the interests of the corporation. They must disclose and not withhold relevant information concerning any potential conflict of interest with the corporation, and they must refrain from using their position, influence, or knowledge of the affairs of the corporation to gain personal advantage. *See Rosenthal v. Rosenthal,* 543 A.2d 348, 352 (Me.1988); 13–A M.R.S.A. § 716 (Supp. 1994).

Despite the general acceptance of the proposition that corporate fiduciaries owe a duty of loyalty to their corporations, there has been much confusion about the specific extent of that duty when, as here, it is contended that a fiduciary takes for herself a corporate opportunity. *See, e.g.,* Victor Brudney & Robert C. Clark, *A New Look at Corporate Opportunities,* 94 HARV.L.REV. 998, 998 (1981) ("Not only are the common formulations vague, but the courts have articulated no theory that would serve as a blueprint for constructing meaningful rules."). This case requires us for the first time to define the scope of the corporate opportunity doctrine in Maine.

Various courts have embraced different versions of the corporate opportunity doctrine. The test applied by the trial court and embraced by Harris is generally known as the "line of business" test. The seminal case applying the line of business test is *Guth v. Loft, Inc.,* 5 A.2d 503 (Del.1939). In *Guth,* the Delaware Supreme Court adopted an intensely factual test stated in general terms as follows:

> [I]f there is presented to a corporate officer or director a business opportunity which the corporation is financially able to undertake, is, from its nature, in the line of the corporation's business and is of practical advantage to it, is one in which the corporation has an interest or a reasonable expectancy, and, by embracing the opportunity, the self-interest of the officer or director will be brought into conflict with that of his corporation, the law will not permit him to seize the opportunity for himself.

*Id.* at 511. The "real issue" under this test is whether the opportunity "was so closely associated with the existing business activities . . . as to bring the transaction within that class of cases where the acquisition of the property would throw the corporate officer purchasing it into competition with his company." *Id.* at 513. The Delaware court described that inquiry as "a factual question to be decided by reasonable inferences from objective facts." *Id.*

The line of business test suffers from some significant weaknesses. First, the question whether a particular activity is within a corporation's line of business is conceptually difficult to answer. The facts of the instant case demonstrate that difficulty. The Club is in the business of running a golf course. It is not in the business of developing real estate. In the traditional sense, therefore, the trial court correctly observed that the opportunity in this case was not a corporate opportunity within the meaning of the *Guth* test. Nevertheless, the record would support a finding that the Club had made the policy judgment that development of surrounding real estate was detrimental to the best interests of the Club. The acquisition of land adjacent to the golf course for the purpose of preventing future development would have enhanced the ability of the Club to implement that policy. The record also shows that the Club had occasionally considered reversing that policy and expanding its operations to include the development of surrounding real estate. Harris's activities effectively foreclosed the Club from pursuing that option with respect to prime locations adjacent to the golf course.

Second, the *Guth* test includes as an element the financial ability of the corporation to take advantage of the opportunity. The court in this case relied on the Club's supposed financial incapacity as a basis for excusing Harris's conduct. Often, the injection of financial ability into the equation will unduly favor the inside director or executive who has command of the facts relating to the finances of the corporation. Reliance on financial ability will also act as a disincentive to corporate executives to solve corporate financing and other problems. In addition, the Club could have prevented development without spending $275,000 to acquire the property Harris needed to obtain access to the road.

The Massachusetts Supreme Judicial Court adopted a different test in *Durfee v. Durfee & Canning, Inc.*, 323 Mass. 187, 80 N.E.2d 522 (1948). The *Durfee* test has since come to be known as the "fairness test." According to *Durfee,* the

> true basis of governing doctrine rests on the unfairness in the particular circumstances of a director, whose relation to the corporation is fiduciary, taking advantage of an opportunity [for her personal profit] when the interest of the corporation justly call[s] for protection. This calls for application of ethical standards of what is fair and equitable . . . in particular sets of facts.

*Id.* at 529 (quoting *Ballantine on Corporations* 204–05 (rev. ed. 1946)). As with the *Guth* test, the *Durfee* test calls for a broad-ranging, intensely factual inquiry. The *Durfee* test suffers even more than the *Guth* test from a lack of principled content. It provides little or no practical guidance to the corporate officer or director seeking to measure her obligations.

The Minnesota Supreme Court elected "to combine the 'line of business' test with the 'fairness' test." *Miller v. Miller,* 301 Minn. 207, 222 N.W.2d 71, 81 (1974). It engaged in a two-step analysis, first determining whether a particular opportunity was within the corporation's line of business, then scrutinizing "the equitable considerations existing prior to, at the time of, and following the officer's acquisition."*Id.* The *Miller* court hoped by adopting this approach "to ameliorate the often-expressed criticism that the [corporate opportunity] doctrine is vague and subjects today's corporate management to the danger of unpredictable liability." *Id.* In fact, the test adopted in *Miller* merely piles the uncertainty and vagueness of the fairness test on top of the weaknesses in the line of business test.

Despite the weaknesses of each of these approaches to the corporate opportunity doctrine, they nonetheless rest on a single fundamental policy. At bottom, the corporate opportunity doctrine recognizes that a corporate fiduciary should not serve both corporate and personal interests at the same time. As we observed in *Camden Land Co. v. Lewis,* 101 Me. 78, 97, 63 A. 523, 531 (1905), corporate fiduciaries "owe their whole duty to the corporation, and they are not to be permitted to act when duty conflicts with interest. They cannot serve themselves and the corporation at the same time." The various formulations of the test are merely attempts to moderate the potentially harsh consequences of strict adherence to that policy. It is important to preserve some ability for corporate fiduciaries to pursue personal business interests that present no real threat to their duty of loyalty.

### III.

### The American Law Institute Approach

In an attempt to protect the duty of loyalty while at the same time providing long-needed clarity and guidance for corporate decisionmakers, the American Law Institute has offered the most recently developed version of the corporate opportunity doctrine. PRINCIPLES OF CORPORATE GOVERNANCE § 5.05 (May 13, 1992), provides as follows:

### § 5.05  Taking of Corporate Opportunities by Directors or Senior Executives

(a) *General Rule.* A director [§ 1.13] or senior executive [§ 1.33] may not take advantage of a corporate opportunity unless:

(1) The director or senior executive first offers the corporate opportunity to the corporation and makes disclosure concerning the conflict of interest [§ 1.14(a)] and the corporate opportunity [§ 1.14(b)];

(2) The corporate opportunity is rejected by the corporation; and

(3) Either:

(A) The rejection of the opportunity is fair to the corporation;

(B) The opportunity is rejected in advance, following such disclosure, by disinterested directors [§ 1.15], or, in the case of a senior executive who is not a director, by a disinterested superior, in a manner that satisfies the standards of the business judgment rule [§ 4.01(c)]; or

(C) The rejection is authorized in advance or ratified, following such disclosure, by disinterested shareholders [§ 1.16], and the rejection is not equivalent to a waste of corporate assets [§ 1.42].

(b) *Definition of a Corporate Opportunity.* For purposes of this Section, a corporate opportunity means:

(1) Any opportunity to engage in a business activity of which a director or senior executive becomes aware, either:

(A) In connection with the performance of functions as a director or senior executive, or under circumstances that should reasonably lead the director or senior executive to believe that the person offering the opportunity expects it to be offered to the corporation; or

(B) Through the use of corporate information or property, if the resulting opportunity is one that the director or senior executive should reasonably be expected to believe would be of interest to the corporation; or

(2) Any opportunity to engage in a business activity of which a senior executive becomes aware and knows is closely related to a business in which the corporation is engaged or expects to engage.

(c) *Burden of Proof.* A party who challenges the taking of a corporate opportunity has the burden of proof, except that if such party establishes that the requirements of Subsection (a)(3)(B) or (C) are not met, the director or the senior executive has the burden of proving that the rejection and the taking of the opportunity were fair to the corporation.

(d) *Ratification of Defective Disclosure.* A good faith but defective disclosure of the facts concerning the corporate opportunity may be cured if at any time (but no later than a reasonable time after suit is filed challenging the taking of the corporate opportunity) the original rejection of the corporate opportunity is ratified, following the required disclosure, by the board, the shareholders, or the corporate decisionmaker who initially approved the rejection of the corporate opportunity, or such decisionmaker's successor.

(e) *Special Rule Concerning Delayed Offering of Corporate Opportunities.* Relief based solely on failure to first offer an opportunity to the corporation under Subsection (a)(1) is not available if: (1) such failure resulted from a good faith belief that the business activity did not constitute a corporate opportunity, and (2) not later than a reasonable time after suit is filed challenging the taking of the corporate opportunity, the corporate opportunity is to the extent possible offered to the corporation and rejected in a manner that satisfies the standards of Subsection (a).

The central feature of the ALI test is the strict requirement of full disclosure prior to taking advantage of any corporate opportunity. *Id.*, § 5.05(a)(1). "If the opportunity is not offered to the corporation, the director or senior executive will not have satisfied § 5.05(a)." *Id.*, cmt. to § 5.05(a). The corporation must then formally reject the opportunity. *Id.*, § 505(a)(2). The ALI test is discussed at length and ultimately applied by the Oregon Supreme Court in *Klinicki v. Lundgren*, 298 Or. 662, 695 P.2d 906 (1985). As *Klinicki* describes the test, "full disclosure to the appropriate corporate body is ... an absolute condition precedent to the validity of any forthcoming rejection as well as to the availability to the director or principal senior executive of the defense of fairness." *Id.* at 920. A "good faith but defective disclosure" by the corporate officer may be ratified after the fact only by an affirmative vote of the disinterested directors or shareholders. PRINCIPLES OF CORPORATE GOVERNANCE § 5.05(d).

The ALI test defines "corporate opportunity" broadly. It includes opportunities "closely related to a business in which the corporation is engaged." *Id.*, § 5.05(b). It also encompasses any opportunities that accrue to the fiduciary as a result of her position within the corporation. *Id.* This concept is most clearly illustrated by the testimony of Suminsby, the listing broker for the Gilpin property, which, if believed by the factfinder, would support a finding that the Gilpin property was offered to Harris specifically in her capacity as president of the Club. If the factfinder reached that conclusion, then at least the opportunity to acquire the Gilpin property would be a corporate opportunity. The state of the record concerning the Smallidge purchase precludes us from intimating any opinion whether that too would be a corporate opportunity.

Under the ALI standard, once the Club shows that the opportunity is a corporate opportunity, it must show either that Harris did not offer the opportunity to the Club or that the Club did not reject it properly. If the Club shows that the board did not reject the opportunity by a vote of the disinterested directors after full disclosure, then Harris may defend her actions on the basis that the taking of the opportunity was fair to the corporation. *Id.*, § 5.05(c). If Harris failed to offer the opportunity at all, however, then she may not defend on the basis that the failure to offer the opportunity was fair. *Id.*, cmt. to § 5.05(c).

The *Klinicki* court viewed the ALI test as an opportunity to bring some clarity to a murky area of the law. *Klinicki*, 695 P.2d at 915. We agree, and today we follow the ALI test. The disclosure-oriented approach provides a clear procedure whereby a corporate officer may insulate herself through prompt and complete disclosure from the possibility of a legal challenge. The requirement of disclosure recognizes the paramount importance of the corporate fiduciary's duty of loyalty. At the same time it protects the fiduciary's ability pursuant to the proper procedure to pursue her own business ventures free from the possibility of a lawsuit.

The importance of disclosure is familiar to the law of corporations in Maine. Pursuant to 13–A M.R.S.A. § 717 (1981), a corporate officer or director may enter into a transaction with the corporation in which she has a personal or adverse interest only if she discloses her interest in the transaction and secures ratification by a majority of the disinterested directors or shareholders. Section 717 is part of the Model Business Corporations Act, adopted in Maine in 1971. P.L.1971, ch. 439, § 1. Like the ALI rule, section 717 was designed to "eliminate the inequities and uncertainties caused by the existing rules." MODEL BUSINESS CORP. ACT § 41, ¶ 2, at 844 (1971).

## IV.

### Conclusion

The question remains how our adoption of the rule affects the result in the instant case. The trial court made a number of factual findings based on an extensive record.[3] The court made those findings, however, in the light of legal principles that are different from the principles that we today announce. Similarly, the parties did not have the opportunity to develop the record in this case with knowledge of the applicable legal standard. In these circumstances, fairness requires that we remand the case for further proceedings. Those further proceedings may include, at the trial court's discretion, the taking of further evidence.

The entry is:

Judgment vacated.

Remanded for further proceedings consistent with the opinion herein.

All concurring.

––––––

## NOTE ON FURTHER PROCEEDINGS IN NORTHEAST HARBOR GOLF CLUB, INC. v. HARRIS

Following remand, the Superior Court entered judgment for the Club. On appeal, the Maine Supreme Court held that the Gilpin and Smallidge properties were both corporate opportunities, and that Harris breached her fiduciary obligations by not offering those opportunities to the Club's board:

The subject of this lawsuit is land surrounding the Club that Harris purchased in her own name, some in 1979, and more in

––––––

**3.** Harris raised the defense of laches and the statute of limitations but the court made no findings on those issues. We do not intimate what result the application of either doctrine would produce in this case....

1985. In 1979, in her capacity as Club president, Harris learned of an opportunity to purchase property owned by Lucy Gilpin. The Gilpin property adjoins Club property, including the driveway which provided access to the golf course, the clubhouse, and a portion of the Club's parking lot. Moreover, the Gilpin property is encumbered by an easement that allows golfers to travel from the green of one hole to the tee area of the next hole.

Harris purchased the Gilpin property in her own name for $45,000. She did not disclose her plans to the board prior to acquiring the property. . . .

In 1984, Harris, independent of her position with the Club,[2] learned of the availability of property owned by the Smallidge family. The property was surrounded on three sides by the Club and on the fourth side by a house. Harris contracted to purchase eight of the ten interests of the Smallidge heirs in February of 1985, another in March, and the last in June of 1985, for a total of $60,000.[3] Harris disclosed the purchase to the board of directors at the Club's annual meeting on August 28, 1985. . . .

Harris concedes that, because she learned of the opportunity to purchase the Gilpin property in her capacity as president of the Club, her purchase of that property in 1979 constituted the taking of a corporate opportunity. See Principles of Corporate Governance § 5.05(b)(1)(A) (American Law Institute, May 13, 1992). . . .

Even if the opportunity to engage in a business activity, in which the officer or director becomes involved, is not learned of through her connection to the business of the corporation, nevertheless, such an opportunity may be considered a corporate opportunity if the officer or director knows it "is closely related to a business in which the corporation is engaged or expects to engage." Principles of Corporate Governance § 5.50(b)(2).

"The central feature of the ALI test is the strict requirement of full disclosure prior to taking advantage of any corporate opportunity." Northeast Harbor Golf Club, 661 A.2d at 1151. This feature was designed to prevent individual directors and officers from substituting their own judgment for that of the corporation when determining whether it would be in the corporate interest, or whether the corporation is financially or otherwise able to take advantage of an opportunity. . . . Doubt about the financial capacity of a corporation to pursue an opportunity may affect the incentive of a director or officer to solve corporate financing problems, and evidence regarding the corporation's financial status is often controlled by the usurping corporate director or officer. See Victor Brudney & Robert Charles Clark, A New Look at Corporate Opportunities, 94 HARV. L. REV. 998, 1020–22 (1981).

---

**2.**  While playing golf with the postmaster of Northeast Harbor, Harris learned that property owned by the heirs of the Smallidge family might be available for purchase.

**3.**  In 1990, because the Smallidge property was landlocked, Harris purchased a house and property separating the Smallidge property from the road for $275,000.

The ALI approach recognizes the danger in allowing an individual director or officer to determine whether a corporation has the ability to take an opportunity, and accordingly disclosure to the corporation is required.

Full disclosure is likewise important to prevent individual directors and officers from using their own unfettered judgment to determine whether the business opportunity is related to the corporation's business, such that it would be in the corporate interest to take advantage of that opportunity. "The appropriate method to determine whether or not a corporate opportunity exists is to let the corporation decide at the time the opportunity is presented." 3 FLETCHER CYC. CORP. § 861.10, p. 285 (1994). This rule protects individual directors and officers because after disclosing the potential opportunity to the corporation, they can pursue their own business ventures free from the possibility of a lawsuit. If there is doubt as to whether a business opportunity is closely related to the business of the corporation, that doubt must be resolved in favor of the corporation so that the officer or director will have a strong incentive to disclose any business opportunity even remotely related to the business of the corporation.

In this case, the Club's normal business is maintaining and operating a golf course. That business is dependent on having sufficient land for the course itself and ensuring that the activity of golf is not hindered or affected by development of adjacent and surrounding property. The Club had frequently discussed developing some of its own land and on one occasion talked about the possibility of purchasing and developing adjacent land. The purchase of the Smallidge land, surrounded as it is on three sides by the Club's land and adjacent to three of its golf holes, land that could be developed, is, in the circumstances of this case, sufficiently related to the Club's business to constitute a corporate opportunity....

However, the court also concluded that the Club's action was barred by the statute of limitations.

_____

## ALI, PRINCIPLES OF CORPORATE GOVERNANCE §§ 5.05, 5.06

[See Statutory Supplement]

_____

## NOTE ON THE CORPORATE OPPORTUNITY DOCTRINE

1. *Tests.* A variety of tests have been formulated to determine whether a director or officer has wrongfully appropriated a corporate opportunity. Among these are three tests discussed in *Northeast Harbor*: (i) The line-of-business test, associated with Guth v. Loft, Inc.,

23 Del.Ch. 255, 5 A.2d 503 (1939). (ii) The fairness test, associated with Durfee v. Durfee & Canning, Inc., 323 Mass. 187, 80 N.E.2d 522 (1948). (iii) The two-step test, associated with Miller v. Miller, 301 Minn. 207, 222 N.W.2d 71 (1974). Under another test, associated with Lagarde v. Anniston Lime & Stone Co., 126 Ala. 496, 502, 28 So. 199, 201 (1900), the corporate opportunity doctrine applies only when the director or officer has acquired property in which "the corporation has an interest already existing or in which it has an expectancy growing out of an existing right," or his "interference will in some degree balk the corporation in effecting the purposes of its creation."

The application of the interest-or-expectancy branch of the *Lagarde* test is uncertain, because the terms "interest" and "expectancy" have no fixed meaning in this context. See, e.g., Abbott Redmont Thinlite Corp. v. Redmont, 475 F.2d 85, 88–89 (2d Cir.1973). In *Lagarde* itself, the court held that real estate in which the corporation was a tenant constituted a corporate expectancy, but real estate in which the corporation owned an undivided one-third interest did not.

The application of the interference-with-the-corporate-purpose branch of the *Lagarde* test is also uncertain. Presumably, it would cover cases in which the corporation's need for the property is very substantial. See, e.g., Harmony Way Bridge Co. v. Leathers, 353 Ill. 378, 187 N.E. 432 (1933) (a director purchased a right of way that was needed as an approach to the corporation's bridge); News–Journal Corp. v. Gore, 147 Fla. 217, 2 So.2d 741 (1941) (a director purchased a tract of land that the corporation leased for its building, and immediately increased the rent).

Insofar as the meaning of the *Lagarde* test can be determined, it is unduly narrow. Even the Alabama Supreme Court may now be seeking more leeway by broadening the second branch:

> The last restriction in *Lagarde,* that which prohibits "balking the corporate purpose," is really quite broad in its formulation, although the case has often been described as restrictive.... We think that *Lagarde* when properly read enforces responsibilities for the corporate officer or director comparable to those outlined in *Guth v. Loft, Inc.,* 23 Del.Ch. 255, 5 A.2d 503 (1939), where the Delaware Supreme Court employed the doctrine of corporate opportunity and observed that it
>
> "... demands of a corporate officer or director, peremptorily and inexorably, the most scrupulous observance of his duty, not only affirmatively to protect the interests of the corporation committed to his charge, but also to refrain from doing anything that would work injury to the corporation, or to deprive it of profit or advantage which his skill and ability might properly bring to it, or to enable it to make in the reasonable and lawful exercise of its powers...."

Morad v. Coupounas, 361 So.2d 6, 8–9 (Ala.1978).

2. *Data.* Pat K. Chew conducted a comprehensive analysis of corporate opportunity cases reported between April 1977 and April

1988. Chew, Competing Interests in the Corporate Opportunity Doctrine, 67 N. C. L. Rev. 436 (1989). She found that these disputes usually occur in close corporations, and that the opportunities were often directly competitive to the business of the corporation.

3. *Different Types of Corporate Opportunities.* Traditionally, the body of law governing corporate opportunities has lacked clarity in two important respects. To begin with, the corporate-opportunity cases have often tended to lump all corporate opportunities together. In fact, however, there are two very different kinds of reasons why an opportunity may be *a corporate* opportunity. Call an individual who is a director, officer, employee, or agent of a corporation, *A,* and call the Corporation *C.* One reason that an opportunity may be a corporate opportunity is that *A* became aware of the opportunity through the use of corporate property, corporate information, or *A*'s corporate position—that is, through the use of corporate assets. In such cases, the opportunity is Corporation *C*'s property. If *A* took such an opportunity for herself without offering it to Corporation *C,* she seems to be stealing it, just as much as if she had taken or used any other kind of corporate property for her own personal benefit.

A second, very different kind of reason why an opportunity can constitute a corporate opportunity is that it is closely related to the corporation's business. If that is the *only* reason why an opportunity constitutes a corporate opportunity, then by hypothesis *A* will have found the opportunity on her own, rather than through the use of corporate property, information, or position. If an opportunity that *A* finds on her own constitutes a corporate opportunity, it is not because the discovery of the opportunity is a product of the use of corporate assets—it isn't—but because for some other reason *A* owes Corporation *C* a duty to turn over the opportunity to it.

If *A* is an officer of Corporation *C,* the reason why she might owe *C* the duty to turn over an opportunity that she found on her own is based on her duties (i) not to interfere with, and (ii) to advance, *C*'s legitimate interests. Whether a given individual owes such duties may depend in part on the individual's position. The higher up in the corporate hierarchy the individual is, the more plausible it is that she owes such duties, and the more demanding the duties will normally be. Although a high-ranking executive can fairly be expected to turn over to the corporation any opportunity that is closely related to the corporation's business, solely because it is so related, the same expectation may not apply to a blue-collar or clerical employee.

In short, an opportunity that is discovered through the use of corporate property, information, or position should be a corporate opportunity, regardless of *A*'s position. In contrast, whether an opportunity that *A* discovers on her own is a corporate opportunity solely because it is closely related to the corporation's business, may partly depend on *A*'s position.

4. *Ability of the Corporation to take the Opportunity.* Another area in which the traditional law of corporate opportunities has lacked clarity concerns the issue whether and to what extent *A* can raise, as a

defense to a suit based on taking a corporate opportunity, that Corporation *C* was unable to take the opportunity. This issue usually, although not always, arises in the context of whether the corporation had the financial ability to take the relevant opportunity. The courts are all over the lot on this issue. At one extreme, some cases, such as Irving Trust Co. v. Deutsch, 73 F.2d 121 (2d Cir.1934), hold that the corporation's financial ability should be irrelevant, because it is too easy for executives who take a corporate opportunity to create a financial-inability excuse through manipulation of the corporation's financial picture. At the other extreme, some cases hold that not only is the corporation's financial ability relevant, but that a plaintiff who claims that a corporate opportunity has been taken has the burden of pleading and proving that the corporation had the financial ability to take the opportunity. See, e.g., Miller v. Miller, supra. Still other courts take some intermediate position between these two extremes. See, e.g., Klinicki v. Lundgren, 298 Or. 662, 695 P.2d 906 (1985) which allows financial inability to serve as a justification for the corporation's rejection of a corporate opportunity. Furthermore, there are a number of shadings on the issue how the corporation's financial ability should be measured in this context. See, e.g., Yiannatsis v. Stephanis, 653 A.2d 275 (Del.1995).

More importantly, the courts have failed to disentangle two very different scenarios in which a corporate-inability defense may play a role. In one scenario, *A* first offers the opportunity to Corporation *C*; *C* decides to reject the opportunity; and *A* then takes it for herself. A shareholder then brings a derivative action against *A*, and *A* raises as a defense that she did not take the opportunity until the corporation had rejected it. If, in such a case, the plaintiff puts into issue the fairness or reasonability of Corporation *C*'s rejection of the opportunity, *C*'s inability to take the opportunity is relevant, because it may justify the rejection.

In the second scenario, *A* takes an opportunity *without* having first offered it to Corporation *C*. When *A* is sued for taking the opportunity, she raises as a defense that *C* did not have the ability to take the opportunity. In this scenario, *C*'s inability to take the opportunity should not be a defense, because if an opportunity is a corporate opportunity, a fiduciary should always be obliged to offer the opportunity to the corporation in the first instance, and let the *corporation* decide whether it is, or can make itself, able to take the opportunity. Business enterprises can be very adaptable when faced with a profitable opportunity. For example, a corporation that doesn't have the cash to acquire an opportunity may find that if the opportunity is profitable, a bank will lend money on it. If *A* does not even offer the opportunity to the corporation, however, there is no way to tell whether the corporation would have been able to raise the money to acquire it, by bank financing or otherwise. That being so, it should be presumed, against *A*, that if she had offered the opportunity the corporation would have adopted as necessary to take advantage of it. This is essentially the position taken in ALI, Principles of Corporate Governance § 5.05.

## SECTION 5. DUTIES OF CONTROLLING SHAREHOLDERS

---

## ALI, PRINCIPLES OF CORPORATE GOVERNANCE §§ 5.10–5.12

---

## Sinclair Oil Corporation v. Levien

Supreme Court of Delaware, 1971.
280 A.2d 717.

■ WOLCOTT, CHIEF JUSTICE. This is an appeal by the defendant, Sinclair Oil Corporation (hereafter Sinclair), from an order of the Court of Chancery, 261 A.2d 911, in a derivative action requiring Sinclair to account for damages sustained by its subsidiary, Sinclair Venezuelan Oil Company (hereinafter Sinven), organized by Sinclair for the purpose of operating in Venezuela, as a result of dividends paid by Sinven, the denial to Sinven of industrial development, and a breach of contract between Sinclair's wholly-owned subsidiary, Sinclair International Oil Company, and Sinven.

Sinclair, operating primarily as a holding company, is in the business of exploring for oil and of producing and marketing crude oil and oil products. At all times relevant to this litigation, it owned about 97% of Sinven's stock. The plaintiff owns about 3000 of 120,000 publicly held shares of Sinven. Sinven, incorporated in 1922, has been engaged in petroleum operations primarily in Venezuela and since 1959 has operated exclusively in Venezuela.

Sinclair nominates all members of Sinven's board of directors. The Chancellor found as a fact that the directors were not independent of Sinclair. Almost without exception, they were officers, directors, or employees of corporations in the Sinclair complex. By reason of Sinclair's domination, it is clear that Sinclair owed Sinven a fiduciary duty. Getty Oil Company v. Skelly Oil Co., 267 A.2d 883 (Del. Supr.1970); Cottrell v. Pawcatuck Co., 35 Del.Ch. 309, 116 A.2d 787 (1955). Sinclair concedes this.

The Chancellor held that because of Sinclair's fiduciary duty and its control over Sinven, its relationship with Sinven must meet the test of intrinsic fairness. The standard of intrinsic fairness involves both a high degree of fairness and a shift in the burden of proof. Under this standard the burden is on Sinclair to prove, subject to careful judicial scrutiny, that its transactions with Sinven were objectively fair. Guth v. Loft, Inc., 23 Del.Ch. 255, 5 A.2d 503 (1939); Sterling v. Mayflower Hotel Corp., 33 Del.Ch. 293, 93 A.2d 107, 38 A.L.R.2d 425 (Del. Supr.1952); Getty Oil Co. v. Skelly Oil Co., supra.

Sinclair argues that the transactions between it and Sinven should be tested, not by the test of intrinsic fairness with the accompanying shift of the burden of proof, but by the business judgment rule under which a court will not interfere with the judgment of a board of directors unless there is a showing of gross and palpable overreaching. Meyerson v. El Paso Natural Gas Co., 246 A.2d 789 (Del.Ch.1967). A board of directors enjoys a presumption of sound business judgment, and its decisions will not be disturbed if they can be attributed to any rational business purpose. A court under such circumstances will not substitute its own notions of what is or is not sound business judgment.

We think, however, that Sinclair's argument in this respect is misconceived. When the situation involves a parent and a subsidiary, with the parent controlling the transaction and fixing the terms, the test of intrinsic fairness, with its resulting shifting of the burden of proof, is applied. Sterling v. Mayflower Hotel Corp., supra; David J. Greene & Co. v. Dunhill International, Inc., 249 A.2d 427 (Del.Ch. 1968); Bastian v. Bourns, Inc., 256 A.2d 680 (Del.Ch.1969) aff'd. Per Curiam (unreported) (Del.Supr.1970). The basic situation for the application of the rule is the one in which the parent has received a benefit to the exclusion and at the expense of the subsidiary.

Recently, this court dealt with the question of fairness in parent-subsidiary dealings in Getty Oil Co. v. Skelly Oil Co., supra. In that case, both parent and subsidiary were in the business of refining and marketing crude oil and crude oil products. The Oil Import Board ruled that the subsidiary, because it was controlled by the parent, was no longer entitled to a separate allocation of imported crude oil. The subsidiary then contended that it had a right to share the quota of crude oil allotted to the parent. We ruled that the business judgment standard should be applied to determine this contention. Although the subsidiary suffered a loss through the administration of the oil import quotas, the parent gained nothing. The parent's quota was derived solely from its own past use. The past use of the subsidiary did not cause an increase in the parent's quota. Nor did the parent usurp a quota of the subsidiary. Since the parent received nothing from the subsidiary to the exclusion of the minority stockholders of the subsidiary, there was no self-dealing. Therefore, the business judgment standard was properly applied.

A parent does indeed owe a fiduciary duty to its subsidiary when there are parent-subsidiary dealings. However, this alone will not evoke the intrinsic fairness standard. This standard will be applied only when the fiduciary duty is accompanied by self-dealing—the situation when a parent is on both sides of a transaction with its subsidiary. Self-dealing occurs when the parent, by virtue of its domination of the subsidiary causes the subsidiary to act in such a way that the parent receives something from the subsidiary to the exclusion of, and detriment to, the minority stockholders of the subsidiary.

We turn now to the facts. The plaintiff argues that, from 1960 through 1966, Sinclair caused Sinven to pay out such excessive dividends that the industrial development of Sinven was effectively prevented, and it became in reality a corporation in dissolution.

From 1960 through 1966, Sinven paid out $108,000,000 in dividends ($38,000,000 in excess of Sinven's earnings during the same period). The Chancellor held that Sinclair caused these dividends to be paid during a period when it had a need for large amounts of cash. Although the dividends paid exceeded earnings, the plaintiff concedes that the payments were made in compliance with 8 Del.C. § 170, authorizing payment of dividends out of surplus or net profits. However, the plaintiff attacks these dividends on the ground that they resulted from an improper motive—Sinclair's need for cash. The Chancellor, applying the intrinsic fairness standard, held that Sinclair did not sustain its burden of proving that these dividends were intrinsically fair to the minority stockholders of Sinven.

Since it is admitted that the dividends were paid in strict compliance with 8 Del.C. § 170, the alleged excessiveness of the payments alone would not state a cause of action. Nevertheless, compliance with the applicable statute may not, under all circumstances, justify all dividend payments. If a plaintiff can meet his burden of proving that a dividend cannot be grounded on any reasonable business objective, then the courts can and will interfere with the board's decision to pay the dividend.

Sinclair contends that it is improper to apply the intrinsic fairness standard to dividend payments even when the board which voted for the dividends is completely dominated. In support of this contention, Sinclair relies heavily on American District Telegraph Co. [ADT] v. Grinnell Corp., (N.Y.Sup.Ct.1969) aff'd. 33 A.D.2d 769, 306 N.Y.S.2d 209 (1969). Plaintiffs were minority stockholders of ADT, a subsidiary of Grinnell. The plaintiffs alleged that Grinnell, realizing that it would soon have to sell its ADT stock because of a pending anti-trust action, caused ADT to pay excessive dividends. Because the dividend payments conformed with applicable statutory law, and the plaintiffs could not prove an abuse of discretion, the court ruled that the complaint did not state a cause of action. Other decisions seem to support Sinclair's contention. In Metropolitan Casualty Ins. Co. v. First State Bank of Temple, 54 S.W.2d 358 (Tex.Civ.App.1932), rev'd. on other grounds, 79 S.W.2d 835 (Sup.Ct.1935), the court held that a majority of interested directors does not void a declaration of dividends because all directors, by necessity, are interested in and benefited by a dividend declaration. See, also, Schwartz v. Kahn, 183 Misc. 252, 50 N.Y.S.2d 931 (1944); Weinberger v. Quinn, 264 A.D. 405, 35 N.Y.S.2d 567 (1942).

We do not accept the argument that the intrinsic fairness test can never be applied to a dividend declaration by a dominated board, although a dividend declaration by a dominated board will not inevitably demand the application of the intrinsic fairness standard. Moskowitz v. Bantrell, 41 Del.Ch. 177, 190 A.2d 749 (Del.Supr.1963). If such a dividend is in essence self-dealing by the parent, then the intrinsic fairness standard is the proper standard. For example, suppose a parent dominates a subsidiary and its board of directors. The subsidiary has outstanding two classes of stock, X and Y. Class X is owned by the parent and Class Y is owned by minority stockholders of the subsidiary. If the subsidiary, at the direction of the parent, declares a dividend on its Class X stock only, this might well be self-dealing by the parent. It would be receiving something from the subsidiary to the exclusion of and detrimental to its minority stockholders. This self-dealing, coupled with the parent's fiduciary duty, would make intrinsic fairness the proper standard by which to evaluate the dividend payments.

Consequently it must be determined whether the dividend payments by Sinven were, in essence, self-dealing by Sinclair. The dividends resulted in great sums of money being transferred from Sinven to Sinclair. However, a proportionate share of this money was received by the minority shareholders of Sinven. Sinclair received nothing from Sinven to the exclusion of its minority stockholders. As such, these dividends were not self-dealing. We hold therefore that the Chancellor erred in applying the intrinsic fairness test as to these dividend payments. The business judgment standard should have been applied.

We conclude that the facts demonstrate that the dividend payments complied with the business judgment standard and with 8 Del.C. § 170. The motives for causing the declaration of dividends are immaterial unless the plaintiff can show that the dividend payments resulted from improper motives and amounted to waste. The plaintiff contends only that the dividend payments drained Sinven of cash to such an extent that it was prevented from expanding.

The plaintiff proved no business opportunities which came to Sinven independently and which Sinclair either took to itself or denied to Sinven. As a matter of fact, with two minor exceptions which resulted in losses, all of Sinven's operations have been conducted in Venezuela, and Sinclair had a policy of exploiting its oil properties located in different countries by subsidiaries located in the particular countries.

From 1960 to 1966 Sinclair purchased or developed oil fields in Alaska, Canada, Paraguay, and other places around the world. The plaintiff contends that these were all opportunities which could have been taken by Sinven. The Chancellor concluded that Sinclair had not proved that its denial of expansion opportunities to Sinven was intrinsically fair. He based this conclusion on the following findings of fact. Sinclair made no real effort to expand Sinven. The excessive dividends paid by Sinven resulted in so great a cash drain as to effectively deny to Sinven any ability to expand. During this same period Sinclair actively pursued a company-wide policy of developing through its subsidiaries new sources of revenue, but Sinven was not permitted to participate and was confined in its activities to Venezuela.

However, the plaintiff could point to no opportunities which came to Sinven. Therefore, Sinclair usurped no business opportunity belonging to Sinven. Since Sinclair received nothing from Sinven to the exclusion of and detriment to Sinven's minority stockholders, there was no self-dealing. Therefore, business judgment is the proper standard by which to evaluate Sinclair's expansion policies.

Since there is no proof of self-dealing on the part of Sinclair, it follows that the expansion policy of Sinclair and the methods used to achieve the desired result must, as far as Sinclair's treatment of Sinven is concerned, be tested by the standards of the business judgment rule. Accordingly, Sinclair's decision absent fraud or gross over-reaching, to achieve expansion through the medium of its subsidiaries, other than Sinven, must be upheld.

Even if Sinclair was wrong in developing these opportunities as it did, the question arises, with which subsidiaries should these opportunities have been shared? No evidence indicates a unique need or ability of Sinven to develop these opportunities. The decision of which subsidiaries would be used to implement Sinclair's expansion policy was one of business judgment with which a court will not interfere absent a showing of gross and palpable overreaching. Meyerson v. El Paso Natural Gas Co., 246 A.2d 789 (Del.Ch.1967). No such showing has been made here.

Next, Sinclair argues that the Chancellor committed error when he held it liable to Sinven for breach of contract.

In 1961 Sinclair created Sinclair International Oil Company (here-after International), a wholly owned subsidiary used for the purpose of coordinating all of Sinclair's foreign operations. All crude purchases by Sinclair were made thereafter through International.

On September 28, 1961, Sinclair caused Sinven to contract with International whereby Sinven agreed to sell all of its crude oil and refined products to International at specified prices. The contract provided for minimum and maximum quantities and prices. The plaintiff contends that Sinclair caused this contract to be breached in two respects. Although the contract called for payment on receipt, International's payments lagged as much as 30 days after receipt. Also, the contract required International to purchase at least a fixed mini-mum amount of crude and refined products from Sinven. International did not comply with this requirement.

Clearly, Sinclair's act of contracting with its dominated subsidiary was self-dealing. Under the contract Sinclair received the products produced by Sinven, and of course the minority shareholders of Sinven were not able to share in the receipt of these products. If the contract was breached, then Sinclair received these products to the detriment of Sinven's minority shareholders. We agree with the Chancellor's finding that the contract was breached by Sinclair, both as to the time of payments and the amounts purchased.

Although a parent need not bind itself by a contract with its dominated subsidiary, Sinclair chose to operate in this manner. As Sinclair has received the benefits of this contract, so must it comply with the contractual duties.

Under the intrinsic fairness standard, Sinclair must prove that its causing Sinven not to enforce the contract was intrinsically fair to the minority shareholders of Sinven. Sinclair has failed to meet this burden. Late payments were clearly breaches for which Sinven should have sought and received adequate damages. As to the quantities purchased, Sinclair argues that it purchased all the products produced by Sinven. This, however, does not satisfy the standard of intrinsic fairness. Sinclair has failed to prove that Sinven could not possibly have produced or some way have obtained the contract minimums. As such, Sinclair must account on this claim.

Finally, Sinclair argues that the Chancellor committed error in refusing to allow it a credit or setoff of all benefits provided by it to Sinven with respect to all the alleged damages. The Chancellor held that setoff should be allowed on specific transactions, e.g., benefits to Sinven under the contract with International, but denied an overall setoff against all damages claimed. We agree with the Chancellor, although the point may well be moot in view of our holding that Sinclair is not required to account for the alleged excessiveness of the dividend payments.

We will therefore reverse that part of the Chancellor's order that requires Sinclair to account to Sinven for damages sustained as a result of dividends paid between 1960 and 1966, and by reason of the denial to Sinven of expansion during that period. We will affirm the remaining portion of that order and remand the cause for further proceedings.

---

Accord: Ripley v. International Railways of Central America, 8 N.Y.2d 430, 209 N.Y.S.2d 289, 171 N.E.2d 443 (1960) (controlling shareholder of railroad was liable for the difference between (i) the transportation rates it paid for shipping commodities over the railroad and (ii) the fair and reasonable value of the transportation services).

---

## Kahn v. Tremont Corp.

Supreme Court of Delaware, 1997.
694 A.2d 422.

■ Before WALSH, HOLLAND, and BERGER, JJ. and RIDGELY, PRESIDENT JUDGE* and QUILLEN, JUDGE,* constituting the Court En Banc.

■ WALSH, JUSTICE.

This is an appeal by a plaintiff-shareholder, Alan R. Kahn ("Kahn"), from a decision of the Court of Chancery which approved the purchase by Tremont Corporation ("Tremont") of 7.8 million shares of the Common Stock of NL Industries, Inc. ("NL"). The shares, constituting 15% of NL's outstanding stock, were purchased from

---

* Appointed pursuant to Art. IV, § 12 of the Delaware Constitution and Supreme Court Rules 2 and 4.

Valhi, Inc. ("Valhi"), a corporation which was 90 percent owned by a trust for the family of Harold C. Simmons ("Simmons").[1] In turn, Valhi was the owner of a majority of NL's outstanding stock and controlled Tremont through the ownership of 44% of its outstanding shares.

Kahn alleges that Simmons effectively controlled the three related companies and through his influence, structured the purchase of NL shares in a manner which benefited himself at the expense of Tremont. Following a six day trial, the Court of Chancery concluded that due to [Simmons's] status as a controlling shareholder, the transaction must be evaluated under the entire fairness standard of review and not the more deferential business judgment rule. Nevertheless, the court found that Tremont's utilization of a Special Committee of disinterested directors was sufficient to shift the burden on the fairness issue to Kahn. With the burden shifted, the court concluded that both the price and the process were fair to Tremont.

Kahn has raised two contentions in this appeal: (i) that the court erred in its burden of proof allocation regarding the entire fairness of the transaction; and (ii) that the circumstances surrounding the purchase of NL shares indicate that the process was tainted and the price unfair to Tremont. After careful review of the record, we conclude that under the circumstances the Special Committee did not operate in an independent or informed manner and therefore, the Court of Chancery erred in shifting the burden of persuasion to Kahn. Accordingly, the judgment of the Court of Chancery is reversed and the matter remanded for a new fairness determination with the burden of proof upon the defendants.

## I

The lengthy presentation before the Court of Chancery requires a full exposition of the factual background of the dispute for analysis on appeal. Tremont is a Delaware corporation with its principal executive offices located in Denver, Colorado. Through its subsidiaries, Tremont produces titanium sponge, ingot and mill products. NL is a New Jersey corporation which derives a majority of its earnings from the manufacture and sale of titanium dioxide ("TiO2"), a chemical used to impart whiteness or opacity. NL conducts this business through its European subsidiary Krones, which, accounts for 85% to 90% of NL's total revenue. Valhi is also a Delaware corporation which, through subsidiary stock ownership, is engaged in a variety of businesses, including the production and sale of hardware, forest products, refined sugar, and the fast food restaurant business.

The individual defendants, collectively the board of directors of Tremont, are Susane E. Alderton, Richard J. Boushka, J. Landis Martin, Glenn R. Simmons, Harold C. Simmons, Michael A. Snetzer, Thomas P. Stafford and Avy H. Stein. Aside from their service on the Tremont board, several defendants hold influential positions with other Sim-

---

**1.** The Simmons Trusts did not control Valhi directly, but did so through its 100% ownership of the stock in Contran Corpora-tion ("Contran"), which, in turn, owned 90% of the outstanding stock of Valhi.

mons' controlled entities. Harold Simmons is chairman of the board of
Valhi, NL, and Contran, and the CEO of Contran and Valhi. J. Landis
Martin is both the president and CEO of NL and Tremont. Susan E.
Alderton serves as the vice president and treasurer of Tremont and NL.
Glenn R. Simmons is the vice chairman of the board of Valhi as well as
the vice chairman of the board and vice president of Contran. Michael
A. Snetzer is the president of Valhi and Contran and a director of NL
and Contran.

Kahn alleges that the defendants willingly participated in a series
of improper transactions, beginning in 1990, which were orchestrated
by Simmons for his own benefit. Specifically, he argues that the
purchase of NL shares by Tremont was the final step in a series of
transactions whereby Simmons was able to shift liquidity from several
of his controlled companies to Valhi. Under the theory advanced by
Kahn, two preceding transactions, a repurchase program and a "Dutch
auction," were initiated in order to artificially inflate the price of NL
shares. By increasing NL's per share price, Simmons was able to divest
himself, at the expense of Tremont, of the stock in a failing company
for above market prices.

In late 1990, NL's board believed that the current market price of
NL's stock, then selling between $10 and $11 per share, was significantly undervalued. Accordingly, on October 2, 1990, the board authorized a repurchase program in the open market for up to five million
shares. On the prior day NL stock had closed at $10.12 per share. Over
the first three months of the program, through January 10, 1991, NL
repurchased almost two million shares, at a total cost of over $22
million and an average price of approximately $11 per share.

Satisfied with this response, NL suspended its repurchases from
January through May of 1991. From May to July 1991, however, NL
resumed buying and purchased 733,700 shares on the open market
for a total cost of $10 million or approximately $13.50 a share. The
repurchase program was again suspended from August of 1991 to
September 11, 1991. Following this brief hiatus, NL once again reinstated its open-market repurchases and continued to repurchase
shares into early 1992. All told, NL repurchased over 3 million of its
own shares at an average price of $12 per share.

In June of 1991, NL shares were trading at or above $15 per
share. At this point NL, as the result of selling a large block of
Lockheed stock, was holding approximately $500 million in cash to be
used for investment purposes. In August 1991, with the market price
of the stock at $16, NL's management decided that it would be
advantageous for the company to buy additional NL shares beyond the
five million already authorized in the share repurchase program.
Accordingly, on August 6, 1991, the NL board voted to approve a
Dutch auction self-tender offer for 10 million shares of NL.

Under the Dutch auction mechanism, each shareholder of NL
would decide how many, if any, shares to tender and at what price
within a designated price range. After the expiration of the auction
period, NL would determine the lowest uniform price, within a preset

range of $14.50 to $17.50, that would enable it to purchase 10 million shares. All of the shares tendered at or below the sale price would be purchased at the sale price, subject to proration. In the event that more than 10 million shares were tendered at or below the sale price, NL had the option to purchase an additional 1.3 million shares.

On the date the Dutch auction was announced, Valhi owned approximately 68% of the 63.4 million outstanding shares of NL. Valhi tendered all of its shares, at $16, recognizing that with proration it would sell, at most, approximately 10 million shares. At the close of the Dutch auction, $16 per share proved to be the lowest price within the range at which NL could purchase the shares. On September 12, 1991, NL accepted for purchase 11,268,024 shares, 10,928,750 of which were acquired from Valhi. Shortly following the close of the Dutch auction, NL's stock price fell from $16 to around $13.50.

Upon completion of the Dutch auction, Valhi had sold 10.9 million shares of NL and had reduced its ownership interest in the company from 68% to 62%. If Valhi could sell an additional 7.8 million shares of NL and reduce its ownership interest to below 50%, it would be able to reap two significant benefits. First, it would receive a tax savings of approximately $11.8 million on its proceeds from the Dutch auction, a potential savings of $1.52 per share. Secondly, Valhi would be in a position to deconsolidate NL from its financial statements, thereby improving its access to capital markets. In order to obtain these benefits, however, Valhi needed to sell 7.8 million shares of NL, amounting to 15% of NL's outstanding stock, by the end of calendar year 1991.

To explore the prospect of a further sale of NL shares, Snetzer, Valhi's President, contacted two potential purchasers, RCM Capital and Keystone Inc. Although both maintained significant holdings of NL shares, neither was interested in further purchases. Snetzer also contacted Salomon Brothers and requested an opinion concerning the marketability of the stock. Snetzer was advised by Salomon Brothers that its equity syndicate groups in the U.S. and Europe as well as its private equity people, were in agreement that Valhi would incur an illiquidity discount of 20%, or greater, against NL's then market price in order to sell this unregistered stock in a series of private transactions. Snetzer did not retain Salomon to negotiate a sale because in his view Valhi was unwilling to sell the block of NL shares at that price.

Finding the alternatives unacceptable, Valhi decided to approach Tremont, which had $100 million in excess liquidity and was in the process of searching for a productive investment opportunity.[2] Snetzer

2. In October 1990, Tremont's corporate predecessor, Baroid Corp., divided itself into two parts, each to be publicly traded. As part of the spin-off, the new company contributed $100 million of capital to Tremont for acquisition purposes. Tremont had disclosed to its stockholders that the company intended to use this capital to attempt acquisitions, including "participation in the acqui- sition activities conducted by NL, Valhi and other companies that may be deemed to be controlled by Harold C. Simmons" and "could involve ... the acquisition of securities or other assets from such related parties." Prior to the purchase of the NL shares from Valhi, Tremont's excess capital had been invested temporarily in Treasury bills.

was of the opinion that an "all in the family" transaction would be more desirable since it had the potential to yield additional benefits for both companies. As a 44% owner of Tremont, Valhi would be more likely to accept an appropriate discount from market because it would still own an indirect 44% interest in the shares. In addition, a lower discount from market might be acceptable to Tremont because its management had access to better information concerning NL's business prospects than any unrelated buyers whom Salomon had considered. As a better informed purchaser, Tremont would be less susceptible to risk than would be a stranger and might be willing to pay a price closer to market. Based on this reasoning, on September 18, 1991, Snetzer wrote to Landis Martin, the President and CEO of Tremont, to propose the sale of 7.8 million shares of NL stock.

After speaking with Snetzer, Martin wrote to Tremont's three outside directors, Richard Boushka, Thomas Stafford, and Avy Stein, asking them to formulate an appropriate response to Valhi's offer. The three men were thereafter designated by the Tremont board as a Special Committee for the purpose of considering the proposal and recommending a course of action. Although the three men were deemed "independent" for purposes of this transaction, all had significant prior business relationships with Simmons or Simmons' controlled companies.

Stein, a lawyer, was affiliated with the law firm which represented Simmons on several of his corporate takeovers and had worked closely with Martin. In 1984 Stein left the law firm to organize and promote various business ventures. Over the next five years, Martin invested in projects which Stein was promoting despite their poor performance. In October of 1988, Stein's business ventures had all but dried up when Martin, then at NL, offered Stein a consulting position at $10,000 a month and bonuses to be paid at Martin's discretion. Stein remained in this position for one year, earning bonuses totaling $325,000, before taking a position with two subsidiaries of Continental Bank, N.A. Stafford was employed by NL in connection with Simmons' proxy contest to acquire control of Lockheed and received $300,000 in fees. Boushka was initially named to Simmons' slate of directors in connection with the Lockheed proxy contest and was paid a fee of $20,000.

Of the three Special Committee members, Stein was the most closely connected to management. Nevertheless, he assumed the role of chairman of the Special Committee and directed its operations. Stafford and Boushka deferred to Stein in the selection of both the financial and legal advisors for the Special Committee. The Court of Chancery noted that Stein's selection of advisors was not reassuring.

In choosing a financial advisor, the Special Committee considered several banking firms, both national and regional. In the end, at Stein's recommendation, the Special Committee retained Continental Partners ("Continental"), a company with whom Stein was affiliated. Continental is a wholly-owned subsidiary of Continental bank which, in prior years, had earned significant fee income from Simmons related companies. The record also reflects that Martin, not a member of the Special Committee, signed the retainer agreement with Continental Partners. The Special Committee's selection of a legal advisor also took an unusual form. David Garten, General Counsel for both Tremont and NL, recommended C. Neel Lemon of Thompson & Knight as the Special Committee's counsel. In addition, Garten assumed the responsibility for performing the conflicts check. Lemon had previously represented a Special Committee of NL in connection with a proposed merger between NL and Valhi and had also represented an underwriter in connection with a proposed convertible debt offering by Valhi.

On October 8, 1991, Boushka and Stein, along with their advisors, met with representatives of NL to receive a presentation on the business, operating results and prospects of NL. The following day, they met with representatives of Valhi for a presentation of the business purposes behind Valhi's proposal, specifically the tax benefits Valhi hoped to achieve by deconsolidating NL from its balance sheet. In the afternoon following each presentation, a second meeting was held so that the Special Committee members, Continental and the legal advisors could analyze the material presented in the morning sessions.

Stafford, who was in Europe on other business, was unable to attend any of the Special Committee meetings. He kept abreast of events through telephone conferences with the other two members. Boushka attended the morning sessions but did not attend the afternoon sessions. Of the three members of the Special Committee only Stein attended all four meetings and, more importantly, he was the only member who attended the review sessions with the Special Committee's advisors. In addition to the presentations, the Special Committee met twice, later in October, to consider the Valhi proposal prior to the final negotiations.

In considering the NL shares purchase, the Special Committee relied heavily upon the financial analysis performed by NL and its advisor Continental. During the October 8 meeting, NL provided information including its economic projections for the future price of TiO2, estimates of NL's earnings and the assumptions underlying these projections. With respect to the future price of TiO2, NL's projections assumed that an existing slump would end in late 1992 and higher prices and profits would return in the years 1993–1996.

The Special Committee requested Continental independently to assess the reasonableness of NL's projections. In performing a market analysis, Continental utilized five different methodologies to determine the value of the NL stock. These included a comparable company analysis, a comparable transaction analysis, a discounted cash flow analysis, an asset value/replacement cost analysis and a market value analysis. The results of this study were presented at the Special Committee's October 30 meeting. Continental determined that the intrinsic value of the NL shares was between $13 and $20 per share. In addition to this report, Boushka requested that an independent consultant provide a separate analysis concerning future TiO2 prices.

Although Boushka did not receive this report prior to the Special Committee's vote on October 30, the consultant appeared to support NL's projections for TiO2 prices.

In hindsight, the price of TiO2 would continue to be much more volatile than either NL's or Continental's predictions. During the late 1980's NL experienced record earnings when TiO2 was in short supply and prices were high. Beginning in 1990, however, prices began to fall as Europe entered into a recession and supply began to catch up with the demand. By year-end 1991, the price of TiO2 had dropped 20% from its high in 1989 and 15% from 1990. As a result, by the end of 1991 NL's profits had turned to losses and it was projected that 1992's operating results would be worse. In fact, in 1992, NL was forced to suspend its dividend as its year-end losses totaled $76.44 million. As of the time of the transaction, it was anticipated that world TiO2 prices would not begin to stabilize until 1995–1997.

Valhi's initial proposal to Tremont, made at the October 9 Special Committee meeting, was $14.50 per share, with no registration rights or other provisions to enhance the liquidity of the shares. On the previous day NL stock had closed at $13 per share. By the October 21 Special Committee meeting, Continental had developed a preliminary estimate of value in the $12.50 to $23 range. Following this meeting, Stein contacted Snetzer and informed him that some provision to afford liquidity to the buyer of the unregistered shares would be necessary. He also attempted to negotiate a per share price below the $14.50 offer. In response, Snetzer suggested Valhi might be willing to lower the asking price below $14 into the high $13 range. On that day NL stock closed slightly over $13 per share.

Stein and Snetzer also met in person to negotiate the non-price terms of the transaction. At the meeting the two discussed solutions to Tremont's liquidity concerns such as registration and co-sale rights, but did not broach the topic of a liquidity discount. Stein also told Snetzer that Tremont would not be willing to consummate a deal near the range suggested by Snetzer—the low to mid $13s. At its October 30 meeting the Special Committee decided to seek a transaction at or below $12 ⅝ per share. Continental indicated that it would be willing to deliver a fairness opinion supporting this price. Stein then met with Snetzer and offered to purchase the stock for $11.25. Eventually it was agreed that the price would be $11.75 per share with Valhi receiving a proration of NL's fourth quarter dividend, amounting to $800,000. In addition Tremont was to receive the registration and co-sale rights as protection for the limited liquidity of the investment. On this date NL stock closed at $12 ¾.

Stein presented the results of his negotiation with Snetzer to the entire Committee which, on October 30, 1991, agreed to recommend the transaction to the entire Tremont board. The Tremont board then met and approved the recommendation of the Special Committee, with the three most interested members of the board (H. Simmons, G. Simmons, and Snetzer) abstaining and the other two members (Martin and Alderton) voting with the Special Committee to provide a quorum.

## II

Kahn's attack on both the negotiating process and the resulting price must be evaluated under the standards of Delaware corporate law involving interested transactions by controlling shareholders. In discharging our appellate function, we view the factual findings of the Court of Chancery with considerable deference but exercise *de novo* review concerning the application of legal standards. See *Levitt v. Bouvier*, Del.Supr., 287 A.2d 671 (1972).

Ordinarily, in a challenged transaction involving self-dealing by a controlling shareholder, the substantive legal standard is that of entire fairness, with the burden of persuasion resting upon the defendants.[3] *Weinberger v. UOP, Inc.*, Del.Supr., 457 A.2d 701, 710 (1983); *See Rosenblatt v. Getty Oil Co.*, Del.Supr., 493 A.2d 929, 937 (1985). The burden, however, may be shifted from the defendants to the plaintiff through the use of a well functioning committee of independent directors. *Kahn v. Lynch Communication Sys.*, Del.Supr., 638 A.2d 1110, 1117 (1994). Regardless of where the burden lies, when a controlling shareholder stands on both sides of the transaction the conduct of the parties will be viewed under the more exacting standard of entire fairness as opposed to the more deferential business judgment standard. *Id.* at 1116.

Entire fairness remains applicable even when an independent committee is utilized because the underlying factors which raise the specter of impropriety can never be completely eradicated and still require careful judicial scrutiny. *Weinberger*, 457 A.2d at 710. This policy reflects the reality that in a transaction such as the one considered in this appeal, the controlling shareholder will continue to dominate the company regardless of the outcome of the transaction. *Citron v. E.I. Du Pont de Nemours & Co.*, Del. Ch., 584 A.2d 490, 502 (1990). The risk is thus created that those who pass upon the propriety of the transaction might perceive that disapproval may result in retaliation by the controlling shareholder. *Id.* Consequently, even when the transaction is negotiated by a special committee of independent directors, "no court could be certain whether the transaction fully approximate[d] what truly independent parties would have achieved in an arm's length negotiation." *Id.* Cognizant of this fact, we have chosen to apply the entire fairness standard to "interested transactions" in order to ensure that all parties to the transaction have fulfilled their fiduciary duties to the corporation and all its shareholders. *Kahn*, 638 A.2d at 1110.

Having established the appropriate legal standard by which the sale of NL stock will be reviewed, we turn to the issue of which party

---

**3.** The Court of Chancery determined that the sale of NL stock to Tremont was an "all in the family" transaction, with Simmons acting as the controlling shareholder of both the buyer and the seller. This ruling was not challenged by the defendants in this appeal.

bears the burden of proof. Delaware has long adhered to the principle that the controlling or dominant shareholder is initially allocated the burden of proving the transaction was entirely fair. *Id.* at 1117. In *Rosenblatt,* however, we stated that "approval of a [transaction], as here, by an informed vote of a majority of the minority shareholders, while not a legal prerequisite, shifts the burden of proving the unfairness of the transaction entirely to the plaintiffs." *Rosenblatt,* 493 A.2d at 937. To obtain the benefit of burden shifting, the controlling shareholder must do more than establish a perfunctory special committee of outside directors. *Rabkin v. Olin Corp.,* Del.Ch., C.A. No 7547 (Consolidated), Chandler, V.C., 1990; reprinted in 16 Del. J.Corp.L. 851, 861–62, 1990 WL 47648 (1990), aff'd, Del.Supr., 586 A.2d 1202 (1990). Rather, the committee must function in a manner which indicates that the controlling shareholder did not dictate the terms of the transaction and that the committee exercised real bargaining power "at an arms-length." *Id.*

Here, Tremont, with Valhi's approval, established a Special Committee consisting of three outside directors. In evaluating the composition of Tremont's Special Committee, the Court of Chancery confessed to "having reservations concerning the establishment of the Special Committee and the selection of its advisors." The court's reservations arose from two main concerns. First, Stein was the dominant member of the Special Committee and played a key role in the negotiations. The Chancellor questioned the Special Committee's decision to leave the bulk of the work in the hands of one "who had a long and personally beneficial relationship with Mr. Martin [and Simmons' controlled companies]."

The court's second concern was prompted by its recognition that in complicated financial transactions such as this, professional advisors have the ability to influence directors who are anxious to make the right decision but who are often [*in terra incognita*]. As the Chancellor noted, "the selection of professional advisors for the Special Committee doesn't give comfort; it raises questions." Notably, Tremont's General Counsel suggested the name of an appropriate legal counsel to the Special Committee, and that individual was promptly retained. The Special Committee chose as its financial advisor a bank which had lucrative past dealings with Simmons-related companies and had been affiliated with Stein through his employment with a connected bank.

Despite these reservations and the appearance of conflict, the Chancellor concluded that the Special Committee's advisors satisfied their professional obligations to the Special Committee. The Chancellor further concluded that the Special Committee had discharged its duties in an informed and independent manner. These findings were sufficient, in the Chancellor's view, to shift to the plaintiff the burden of proving that the transaction was unfair.

In our view, the Court of Chancery's determination that the Special Committee of Tremont's outside directors was fully informed, active and appropriately simulated an arms length transaction, is not supported by the record. It is clear that Boushka and Stafford abdicated their responsibility as committee members by permitting Stein, the member whose independence was most suspect, to perform the Special Committee's essential functions. In particular, Stafford's absence from all meetings with advisors or fellow committee members, rendered him ill-suited as a defender of the interests of minority shareholders in the dynamics of fast moving negotiations. Similarly, the circumstances surrounding the retaining of the Special Committee's advisors, as well as the advice given, cast serious doubt on the effectiveness of the Special Committee.

In our view, the Special Committee established to negotiate the purchase of the block of NL stock did not function independently. All three directors had previous affiliations with Simmons or companies which he controlled and, as a result, received significant financial compensation or influential positions on the boards of Simmons' controlled companies. Of the three directors, Stein was arguably the one most beholden to Simmons. In 1988 Stein was paid $10,000 a month as a consultant to NL and received over $325,000 in bonuses. The Special Committee's advisors did little to bolster the independence of the principals. The financial advisor, Continental Partners, was recommended by Stein and quickly retained by the full Special Committee. In the past, an affiliate bank of Continental had derived significant fees from Simmons controlled companies and at the time of the transaction was affiliated with Stein's current employer. In addition to being recommended by the General Counsel for NL and Tremont, the Special Committee's legal advisor had previously been retained by Valhi in connection with a convertible debt offering and by NL with respect to a proposed merger with Valhi.

From its inception, the Special Committee failed to operate in a manner which would create the appearance of objectivity in Tremont's decision to purchase the NL stock. As this Court has previously stated in defining director independence: "[i]t is the care, attention and sense of individual responsibility to the performance of one's duties ... that generally touches on independence." *Aronson v. Lewis*, Del.Supr., 473 A.2d 805, 816 (1984). The record amply demonstrates that neither Stafford nor Boushka possessed the "care, attention and sense of responsibility" necessary to afford them the status of independent directors. The result was that Stein, arguably the least detached member of the Special Committee, became, de facto, a single member committee—a tenuous role. Stein conducted all negotiations over price and ancillary terms of the proposed purchase with Martin, and did so without the participation of the remaining two directors. "If a single member committee is to be used, the member should, like Caesar's wife, be above reproach." *Lewis v. Fuqua*, Del.Ch., 502 A.2d 962, 967 (1985).

The record is replete with examples of how the lack of the Special Committee's independence fostered an atmosphere in which the directors were permitted to default on their obligation to remain fully informed. Most notable, was the failure of all three directors to attend the informational meetings with the Special Committee's advisors. These meetings were scheduled so that the Special Committee could explore, through the exchange of ideas with its advisors, the validity of the Valhi proposal and what terms the board should demand in order to make the purchase more beneficial to Tremont. Although Boushka had requested an independent analysis with respect to the future of the TiO2 market, and one was ordered, the report was not read prior to the Special Committee's October 30 vote on the purchase of the NL stock.[4] The failure of the individual directors to fully participate in an active process, severely limited the exchange of ideas and prevented the Special Committee as a whole from acquiring critical knowledge of essential aspects of the purchase. In sum, we conclude that the Special Committee did not operate in a manner which entitled the defendants to shift from themselves the burden which encumbers a controlled transaction. *Accord Kahn*, 638 A.2d at 1110.

### III

Although our invalidation of the role of the Independent Committee requires a remand for an entire fairness determination with the burden shifted, Kahn has asserted certain claims of "unfair dealing" which we address for the guidance of the parties and the Court of Chancery.

In *Weinberger* this Court stated that the test of fairness has two aspects: fair price and fair dealing. *Weinberger*, 457 A.2d at 711. *See also Cinerama v. Technicolor, Inc.*, Del.Supr., 663 A.2d 1156 (1995). The element of "fair dealing" focuses upon the conduct of the corporate fiduciaries in effectuating the transaction. These concerns include how the purchase was initiated, negotiated, structured and the manner in which director approval was obtained. *Mills Acquisition Co. v. Macmillan, Inc.*, Del.Supr., 559 A.2d 1261, 1280 (1989). The price element relates to the economic and financial considerations relied upon when valuing the proposed purchase including: assets, market values, future prospects, earnings, and other factors which effect the intrinsic value of the transaction. *Weinberger*, 457 A.2d at 711. This Court and the Court of Chancery have historically applied this heightened standard to ensure that individuals who purport to act as fiduciaries in the face of conflicting loyalties exercise their authority in light of what is best for all entities. *Id*.

Kahn alleges the Court of Chancery erred in several respects in its entire fairness analysis. As to the fair dealing component, Kahn argues that: (1) the initiation and the timing of the purchase were unfair; (2) the Special Committee's performance was deficient to an extent that it compromised the integrity of the negotiation process; and (3) Valhi failed to make material disclosures to Tremont. We address only the

---

**4.** This report takes on particular significance in light of the fact that Continental in evaluating Valhi's proposal, had relied upon NL's pricing forecast for TiO2. Without the benefit of this independent analysis, the directors, as buyers, relied solely on the projections of NL, the seller. Indeed, Stafford was not aware of the need for a third party analysis because he erroneously thought that Continental had made its own independent forecast.

initiation and timing claim and the disclosure claim as they may find application in any proceedings on remand.

### A.

In evaluating the fair dealing component of the transaction, the Court of Chancery determined that the initiation and timing of the purchase was not prejudicial to Tremont. Although the purchase was initiated and timed by Simmons-controlled Valhi, the court found this to be unimportant when considering the nature of the transaction, i.e., a straightforward purchase of a block of stock. Valhi's decision to offer the stock to Tremont was predicated on its desire to obtain over $11 million in tax benefits. This fact was fully disclosed and explained to the Special Committee which arguably bargained to share in those benefits. The record supports the Chancellor's conclusion that the Committee was afforded adequate time to fully consider Valhi's proposal and to assess its merits. Snetzer, Valhi's president, first proposed the transaction to Tremont in September of 1991 and indicated Valhi's need to conclude the purchase by the end of that calendar year. Although the Tremont board did not take advantage of the entire time period provided, under the terms of Valhi's offer they were afforded sufficient time to consider the proposal.

Initiation by the seller, standing alone, is not incompatible with the concept of fair dealing so long as the controlling shareholder does not gain financial advantage at the expense of the controlled company. *Kahn v. Lynch Communication Sys.*, Del.Supr., 669 A.2d 79, 85 (1995). While Valhi obtained a significant financial advantage in the timing of the purchase, it did not do so at the expense of Tremont. We conclude that there is ample support in the record for the Court of Chancery's finding that the initiation and timing of the transaction was not unfair to Tremont.

### B.

With respect to the disclosure issue, Kahn argues that Valhi was required to disclose that two previous companies had rejected an offer to purchase the block of NL stock and that Salomon Brothers had issued an informal opinion which opined that a 20% or greater illiquidity discount from market would be required in order to conclude a sale. In evaluating this claim the Court of Chancery correctly stated that "[a] controlling shareholder ... must disclose fully all material facts and circumstances surrounding the transaction." *Kahn*, 669 A.2d at 88. This standard of disclosure is not unlike that adopted by this Court in defining the level of disclosure necessary where shareholder action is implicated. "[A]n omitted fact is material if there is a substantial likelihood that, the omitted fact would have assumed actual significance in the deliberations of the reasonable shareholder." *Rosenblatt*, 493 A.2d at 944 (quoting *TSC Industries v. Northway*, 426 U.S. 438, 449, 96 S.Ct. 2126, 48 L.Ed.2d 757 (1976)).

Applying the materiality standard, the Court of Chancery determined that the decisions of RCM Capital and Keystone not to purchase the block of NL stock from Valhi were not material. The court noted that their reasons for not wanting to purchase the stock were simply the general concerns that any potential purchaser would have reason to know without specific disclosure; "namely, that the purchaser would own a minority share in a company that it did not control and that the market might react negatively when it learned that a principal stockholder (Valhi) was selling shares." Kahn's argument as to the materiality of this information is further undercut by the fact that Valhi never reached the stage of discussing price or terms with either of the potential buyers. Thus, disinterest of third parties was clearly not the type of information required to be disclosed. We find the Court of Chancery's analysis as to the disclosure of RCM Capitol's and Keystone's decisions not to pursue a purchase with Valhi to be supported by the record.

Kahn's second disclosure argument concerns Salomon Brother's advice to Valhi concerning an appropriate illiquidity discount. Although questioning the significance of this information, the Chancellor, for analysis purposes, assumed that the Salomon opinion would have been material to the Special Committee. The court went on to conclude, however, that, even if material, this information fell within a "narrow residual category of privileged information" which did not need to be disclosed. The Chancellor speculated that if the device of the independent committee is to effectively replicate an arms-length negotiation, this information cannot be required to be disclosed by a seller.

We do not adopt the court's conclusion that the Salomon opinion falls within a category of "privileged" information. We find no authority in Delaware or elsewhere, and counsel for defendants can point to none, which supports the Chancellor's decision to carve out a "privilege" exception to the materiality standard.[5] Under the facts here present, we find Valhi had no duty to disclose information which might be adverse to its interests because the normal standards of arms-length bargaining do not mandate a disclosure of weaknesses. The significance of the illiquidity discount to this transaction lies not in whether Valhi had a duty to disclose it but whether an informed independent committee had a duty to discover it.

## IV

Although the Chancellor made extensive findings incident to his fair price analysis he did so in a procedural construct which required Kahn to prove unfairness of price. In resolving issues of valuation the Court of Chancery undertakes a mixed determination of law and fact. *Kahn v. Household Acquisition Corp.*, Del.Supr., 591 A.2d 166, 175 (1991). We recognize the thoroughness of the Chancellor's fair price analysis and the considerable deference due his selection from among

---

**5.** If disclosure is required under the materiality test, information can be withheld only under a recognized claim of privilege. This Court has previously held the relationship between a corporation and its attorney to be such a recognized privilege. *Zirn v. VLI Corp.*, Del.Supr., 621 A.2d 773, 781 (1993) (citing Upjohn Co. v. United States, 449 U.S. 383, 101 S.Ct. 677, 66 L.Ed.2d 584 (1981)).

the various methodologies offered by competing experts. *Lynch Communication*, 669 A.2d at 87. But here, the process is so intertwined with price that under *Weinberger's* unitary standard a finding that the price negotiated by the Special Committee might have been fair does not save the result. *Cf. Lynch Communication Systems*, 669 A.2d 79.

Arguably, as the Chancellor found, the resulting price might be deemed to be at the lowest level in a broad range of fairness. But this does not satisfy the *Weinberger* test. Although often applied as a bifurcated or disjunctive test, the concept of entire fairness requires the court to examine all aspects of the transaction in an effort to determine whether the deal was entirely fair. *Weinberger*, 457 A.2d at 711. When assigned the burden of persuasion, this test obligates the directors, or their surrogates, to present evidence which demonstrates that the cumulative manner by which it discharged all of its fiduciary duties produced a fair transaction. *Cinerama*, 663 A.2d at 1163.

In our recent decision in *Kahn v. Lynch Communication*, we were confronted with a situation in which the actions of the majority shareholder dominated the negotiation process and stripped the independent committee of its ability to negotiate in an arms-length manner. After concluding that the Court of Chancery erred in shifting the burden of proof with regard to entire fairness to the controlling shareholder, we [remanded] the matter to the Court of Chancery for "a redetermination of the entire fairness ... with the burden of proof remaining on Alcatel, the dominant and interested shareholder." *Kahn*, 638 A.2d at 1122. A similar course is appropriate here. It is the responsibility of the Court of Chancery to make the requisite factual determinations under the appropriate standards, which underlie the concept of entire fairness. Whether the defendants, shouldering the burden of proof, will be able to demonstrate entire fairness is, in the first instance, a task committed to the Chancellor.

In the event, the Court of Chancery determines that the defendants have not demonstrated the entire fairness of the disputed transaction, we assume that it will grant appropriate relief within its broad equitable authority. *Weinberger*, 457 A.2d at 714. . . .

REVERSED and REMANDED.

■ QUILLEN, JUDGE, concurring.

With regard to the burden of proof on the issue of fairness, I concur in the decision reached by Justice Walsh in his excellent opinion. In my opinion, the burden of proof in the case *clearly* should *not* shift from the defendants to the plaintiff on the issue of fairness. Somewhat ironically, in reaching this conclusion, I do not find it necessary to go beyond the basic facts as found by the Chancellor. . . .

The Chancellor's opinion found: a parent-subsidiary transaction existed, "the context in which the greatest risk of undetectable bias may be present" (*Op. Below* 17–18); Committee member Avy H. Stein, who had prior profitable connections to Harold Simmons and his companies, played the lead Committee role (*Op. Below* 19, including n. 12); Mr. Stein suggested the selection of a financial adviser for the

Committee who had prior ties to both Mr. Stein and Mr. Simmons (*Op. Below* 9–10, including n. 5 and n. 6, and 19–20); the suggestion for the Committee's legal advisors came from Tremont's General Counsel (*Op. Below* 9–10, including n. 5 and n. 6, and 19–20); NL, in the thirteen months prior to the subject transaction, repurchased over 20% of its own shares, at least raising an issue of manipulated price inflation (*Op. Below* 5–7); this transaction by Valhi, probably not available in 1991 with a non-Simmons enterprise, was a multi-million dollar one for Valhi from a tax savings standpoint and had to be accomplished in the last quarter of 1991 (Op. Below 7–8); Valhi's chief negotiator knew that an illiquidity discount was appropriate and the block was in fact worth less than market (*Op. Below* 8, 24); in a very short period, NL's stock price fell from over $16 per share in late summer 1991 to $12.75 on the date of the purchase, October 30, 1991, at least raising the question of business viability (*Op. Below* 6–7, 12–24); the Committee relied heavily on regularly prepared projections of NL's management with incomplete help from its own consultant (*Op. Below* 11–12, 31–32); notwithstanding knowledge of the appropriateness of a discount, Valhi's first negotiating suggestion was a premium price and the results of the Committee's negotiations on other issues, splitting the fourth quarter dividend and registration and co-sale rights, are not self-verifying on the independence issue (*Op. Below* 1, 13–14 including n. 8); and the price, as finally negotiated, was found to be "as small a discount as could be accepted as fair," a finding that hardly forecloses questions as to independence (*Op. Below* 33).

In light of the above-enumerated factors, the independence of the Special Committee, integrity in a process sense, was clearly not substantial enough to shift the burden of persuasion to the plaintiff on the issue of fairness. To me, the case cries for Missouri skepticism; the burden should be on the control group to demonstrate entire fairness. While it can be of critical importance to the ultimate result whether or not the burden is shifted, failure to shift the burden is not necessarily outcome determinative. *Compare Nixon v. Blackwell*, Del.Supr., 626 A.2d 1366, 1376, 1381 (1993). Justice Walsh's decision appropriately remands the case to the Court of Chancery for the requisite factual determinations.

As to remedy, if any proves to be appropriate, I join Justice Walsh's opinion that all options are open to the Chancellor's discretion. *Lynch v. Vickers Energy Corp.*, Del.Supr., 429 A.2d 497, 507–08 (1981) (Quillen dissenting); *Weinberger*, 457 A.2d at 703–04.

■ Berger, Justice, with whom Ridgely, President Judge, joins dissenting.

The majority's thorough and well reasoned decision reverses the trial court's equally thorough and well reasoned decision. According to the majority, the Court of Chancery did not err in its legal analysis, but in its evaluation of the facts—particularly with respect to the Special Committee members' independence, level of knowledge and involvement in the negotiations. The trial court recognized these issues and was satisfied, after six days of trial, that the Special Committee members were "informed, active and loyal to the interests of Tremont." That finding is supported by the record and should be accorded deference. I respectfully dissent.

———

## Jones v. H.F. Ahmanson & Co.

Supreme Court of California, 1969.
1 Cal.3d 93, 81 Cal.Rptr. 592, 460 P.2d 464.

■ TRAYNOR, C.J.—June K. Jones, the owner of 25 shares of the capital stock of United Savings and Loan Association of California brings this action on behalf of herself individually and of all similarly situated minority stockholders of the Association. The defendants are United Financial Corporation of California, fifteen individuals, and four corporations, all of whom are present or former stockholders or officers of the Association. Plaintiff seeks damages and other relief for losses allegedly suffered by the minority stockholders of the Association because of claimed breaches of fiduciary responsibility by defendants in the creation and operation of United Financial, a Delaware holding company that owns 87 percent of the outstanding Association stock.

Plaintiff appeals from the judgment entered for defendants after an order sustaining defendants' general and special demurrers to her third amended complaint without leave to amend. Defendants have filed a protective cross-appeal. We have concluded that the allegations of the complaint and certain stipulated facts sufficiently state a cause of action and that the judgment must therefore be reversed.

The following facts appear from the allegations of the complaint and stipulation.

United Savings and Loan Association of California is a California chartered savings and loan association that first issued stock on April 5, 1956. Theretofore it had been owned by its depositors, who, with borrowing members, elected the board of directors. No one depositor had sufficient voting power to control the Association.

The Association issued 6,568 shares of stock on April 5, 1956. No additional stock has been issued. Of these shares, 987 (14.8 percent) were purchased by depositors pursuant to warrants issued in proportion to the amount of their deposits. Plaintiff was among these purchasers. The shares allocated to unexercised warrants were sold to the then chairman of the board of directors who later resold them to defendants and others. The stockholders have the right to elect a majority of the directors of the Association.

The Association has retained the major part of its earnings in tax-free reserves with the result that the book value of the outstanding shares has increased substantially.[2] The shares were not actively trad-

———

**2.** Between 1959 and 1966 the book value of each share increased from $1,131 to        $4,143.70.

ed. This inactivity is attributed to the high book value, the closely held nature of the Association,[3] and the failure of the management to provide investment information and assistance to shareholders, brokers, or the public. Transactions in the stock that did occur were primarily among existing stockholders. Fourteen of the nineteen defendants comprised 95 percent of the market for Association shares prior to 1959.

In 1958 investor interest in shares of savings and loan associations and holding companies increased. Savings and loan stocks that were publicly marketed enjoyed a steady increase in market price thereafter until June 1962, but the stock of United Savings and Loan Association was not among them. Defendants determined to create a mechanism by which they could participate in the profit taking by attracting investor interest in the Association. They did not, however, undertake to render the Association shares more readily marketable. Instead, the United Financial Corporation of California was incorporated in Delaware by all of the other defendants except defendant Thatcher on May 8, 1959. On May 14, 1959, pursuant to a prior agreement, certain Association stockholders who among them owned a majority of the Association stock exchanged their shares for those of United Financial, receiving a "derived block" of 250 United Financial shares for each Association share.[4]

After the exchange, United Financial held 85 percent of the outstanding Association stock. More than 85 percent of United Financial's consolidated earnings[5] and book value of its shares reflected its ownership of this Association stock. The former majority stockholders of the Association had become the majority shareholders of United Financial and continued to control the Association through the holding company. They did not offer the minority stockholders of the Association an opportunity to exchange their shares.

The first public offering of United Financial stock was made in June 1960. To attract investor interest, 60,000 units were offered, each of which comprised two shares of United Financial stock and one $100, 5 percent interest-bearing, subordinated, convertible debenture bond. The offering provided that of the $7,200,000 return from the sale of these units, $6,200,000 would be distributed immediately as a return of capital to the original shareholders of United Financial, *i.e.,* the former majority stockholders of the Association.[6] To obtain a permit from the California Corporations Commissioner for the sale, United Financial represented that the financial reserve requirement for debenture repayment established by Commissioner's Rules 480 subdi-

---

**3.** H.F. Ahmanson & Co. acquired a majority of the shares in May 1958. On May 14, 1959, the company owned 4,171 of the outstanding shares.

**4.** The number of shares in these derived blocks of United Financial stock was later modified by pro-rata surrenders and stock dividends in a series of transactions not pertinent here.

**5.** The balance reflected United Financial's ownership of three insurance agencies and stock in a fourth.

**6.** This distribution was equivalent to a $927.50 return of capital on each derived block of shares.

vision (a) and 486 would be met by causing the Association to liquidate or encumber its income producing assets for cash that the Association would then distribute to United Financial to service and retire the bonds.

In the Securities and Exchange Commission prospectus accompanying this first public offering, United Financial acknowledged that its prior earnings were not sufficient to service the debentures and noted that United Financial's direct earnings would have to be augmented by dividends from the Association.

A public offering of 50,000 additional shares by United Financial with a secondary offering of 600,000 shares of the derived stock by the original investors was made in February 1961 for a total price of $15,275,000. The defendants sold 568,190 shares of derived stock in this secondary offering. An underwriting syndicate of 70 brokerage firms participated. The resulting nationwide publicity stimulated trading in the stock until, in mid–1961, an average of 708.5 derived blocks were traded each month. Sales of Association shares decreased during this period from a rate of 170 shares per year before the formation of United Financial to half that number. United Financial acquired 90 percent of the Association shares that were sold.

Shortly after the first public offering of United Financial shares, defendants caused United Financial to offer to purchase up to 350 shares of Association stock for $1,100 per share. The book value of each of these shares was $1,411.57, and earnings were $301.15 per share. The derived blocks of United Financial shares then commanded an aggregate price of $3,700 per block exclusive of the $927.50 return of capital. United Financial acquired an additional 130 shares of Association stock as a result of this offer.

In 1959 and 1960 extra dividends of $75 and $57 per share had been paid by the Association, but in December 1960, after the foregoing offer had been made, defendants caused the Association's president to notify each minority stockholder by letter that no dividends other than the regular $4 per share annual dividend would be paid in the near future. The Association president, defendant M.D. Jameson, was then a director of both the Association and United Financial.

Defendants then proposed an exchange of United Financial shares for Association stock. Under this proposal each minority stockholder would have received approximately 51 United Financial shares of a total value of $2,400 for each Association share. When the application for a permit was filed with the California Corporations Commissioner on August 28, 1961, the value of the derived blocks of United Financial shares received by defendants in the initial exchange had risen to approximately $8,800.[9] The book value of the Association stock was in excess of $1,700 per share, and the shares were earning at an annual rate of $615 per share. Each block of 51 United Financial shares had a

---

**9.** The derived block sold for as much as $13,127.41 during 1960–1961. On January 30, 1962, the date upon which plaintiff com- menced this action, the mean value was $9,116.08.

book value of only $210 and earnings of $134 per year, 85 percent of which reflected Association earnings. At the hearings held on the application by the Commissioner, representatives of United Financial justified the higher valuation of United Financial shares on the ground that they were highly marketable, whereas Association stock was unmarketable and poor collateral for loans. Plaintiff and other minority stockholders objected to the proposed exchange, contending that the plan was not fair, just, and equitable. Defendants then asked the Commissioner to abandon the application without ruling on it.

Plaintiff contends that in following this course of conduct defendants breached the fiduciary duty owed by majority or controlling shareholders to minority shareholders. She alleges that they used their control of the Association for their own advantage to the detriment of the minority when they created United Financial, made a public market for its shares that rendered Association stock unmarketable except to United Financial, and then refused either to purchase plaintiff's Association stock at a fair price or exchange the stock on the same basis afforded to the majority. She further alleges that they also created a conflict of interest that might have been avoided had they offered all Association stockholders the opportunity to participate in the initial exchange of shares. Finally, plaintiff contends that the defendants' acts constituted a restraint of trade in violation of common law and statutory antitrust laws. . . .

## II

### *Majority Shareholders' Fiduciary Responsibility*

Defendants take the position that as shareholders they owe no fiduciary obligation to other shareholders, absent reliance on inside information, use of corporate assets, or fraud. This view has long been repudiated in California. The Courts of Appeal have often recognized that majority shareholders, either singly or acting in concert to accomplish a joint purpose, have a fiduciary responsibility to the minority and to the corporation to use their ability to control the corporation in a fair, just, and equitable manner. Majority shareholders may not use their power to control corporate activities to benefit themselves alone or in a manner detrimental to the minority. Any use to which they put the corporation or their power to control the corporation must benefit all shareholders proportionately and must not conflict with the proper conduct of the corporation's business. (*Brown v. Halbert*, 271 Cal. App.2d 252 [76 Cal.Rptr. 781]; *Burt v. Irvine Co.*, 237 Cal.App.2d 828 [47 Cal.Rptr. 392]; *Efron v. Kalmanovitz*, 226 Cal.App.2d 546 [38 Cal.Rptr. 148]; *Remillard Brick Co. v. Remillard–Dandini Co.*, 109 Cal.App.2d 405 [241 P.2d 66].)

The extensive reach of the duty of controlling shareholders and directors to the corporation and its other shareholders was described by the Court of Appeal in *Remillard Brick Co. v. Remillard–Dandini Co., supra*, 109 Cal.App.2d 405, where, quoting from the opinion of the United States Supreme Court in *Pepper v. Litton*, 308 U.S. 295 [84 L.Ed. 281, 60 S.Ct. 238], the court held: " 'A director is a fiduciary . . .

So is a dominant or controlling stockholder or group of stockholders ... Their powers are powers of trust ... Their dealings with the corporation are subjected to rigorous scrutiny and where any of their contracts or engagements with the corporation is challenged the burden is on the director or stockholder not only to prove the good faith of the transaction but also to show its inherent fairness from the viewpoint of the corporation and those interested therein ...' " ...

... The rule that has developed in California is a comprehensive rule of "inherent fairness from the viewpoint of the corporation and those interested therein." (*Remillard Brick Co. v. Remillard–Dandini Co., supra,* 109 Cal.App.2d 405, 420. See also, *In re Security Finance Co., supra,* 49 Cal.2d 370; *Brown v. Halbert, supra,* 271 Cal.App.2d 252; *Burt v. Irvine Co., supra,* 237 Cal.App.2d 828; *Efron v. Kalmanovitz, supra,* 226 Cal.App.2d 546.) The rule applies alike to officers, directors, and controlling shareholders in the exercise of powers that are theirs by virtue of their position and to transactions wherein controlling shareholders seek to gain an advantage in the sale or transfer or use of their controlling block of shares....

The increasingly complex transactions of the business and financial communities demonstrate the inadequacy of the traditional theories of fiduciary obligation as tests of majority shareholder responsibility to the minority. These theories have failed to afford adequate protection to minority shareholders and particularly to those in closely held corporations whose disadvantageous and often precarious position renders them particularly vulnerable to the vagaries of the majority. Although courts have recognized the potential for abuse or unfair advantage when a controlling shareholder sells his shares at a premium over investment value (*Perlman v. Feldmann,* 219 F.2d 173 [50 A.L.R.2d 1134] [premium paid for control over allocation of production in time of shortage]; *Gerdes v. Reynolds,* 28 N.Y.S.2d 622 [sale of control to looters or incompetents]; *Porter v. Healy,* 244 Pa. 427 [91 A. 428]; *Brown v. Halbert, supra,* 271 Cal.App.2d 252 [sale of only controlling shareholder's shares to purchaser offering to buy assets of corporation or all shares]) or in a controlling shareholder's use of control to avoid equitable distribution of corporate assets (*Zahn v. Transamerica Corp.* (3rd Cir.1947) 162 F.2d 36 [172 A.L.R. 495] [use of control to cause subsidiary to redeem stock prior to liquidation and distribution of assets]), no comprehensive rule has emerged in other jurisdictions. Nor have most commentators approached the problem from a perspective other than that of the advantage gained in the sale of control. Some have suggested that the price paid for control shares over their investment value be treated as an asset belonging to the corporation itself (Berle and Means, The Modern Corporation and Private Property (1932) p. 243), or as an asset that should be shared proportionately with all shareholders through a general offer (Jennings, *Trading in Corporate Control* (1956) 44 Cal.L.Rev. 1, 39), and another contends that the sale of control at a premium is always evil (Bayne, *The Sale-of-Control Premium: the Intrinsic Illegitimacy* (1969) 47 Texas L.Rev. 215).

The additional potential for injury to minority shareholders from majority dealings in its control power apart from sale has not gone unrecognized, however. The ramifications of defendants' actions here are not unlike those described by Professor Gower as occurring when control of one corporation is acquired by another through purchase of less than all of the shares of the latter: "The [acquired] company's existence is not affected, nor need its constitution be altered; all that occurs is that its shareholders change. From the legal viewpoint this methodological distinction is formidable, but commercially the two things may be almost identical. If . . . a controlling interest is acquired, the [acquired] company . . . will become a subsidiary of the acquiring company . . . and cease, in fact though not in law, to be an independent entity.

"This may produce the situation in which a small number of dissentient members are left as a minority in a company intended to be operated as a member of a group. As such, their position is likely to be unhappy, for the parent company will wish to operate the subsidiary for the benefit of the group as a whole and not necessarily for the benefit of that particular subsidiary." (Gower, The Principles of Modern Company Law (2d ed. 1957) p. 561.) Professor Eisenberg notes that as the purchasing corporation's proportionate interest in the acquired corporation approaches 100 percent, the market for the latter's stock disappears, a problem that is aggravated if the acquiring corporation for its own business purposes reduces or eliminates dividends. (Eisenberg, *The Legal Role of Shareholders and Management in Modern Corporate Decision–Making* (1969) 57 Cal.L.Rev. 1, 132. See also, O'Neal and Derwin, Expulsion or Oppression of Business Associates (1961) *passim;* Leech, *Transactions in Corporate Control* (1956) 104 U.Pa.L.Rev. 725, 728; Comment, *The Fiduciary Relation of the Dominant Shareholder to the Minority Shareholders* (1958) 9 Hastings L.J. 306, 314.) The case before us, in which no sale or transfer of actual control is directly involved, demonstrates that the injury anticipated by these authors can be inflicted with impunity under the traditional rules and supports our conclusion that the comprehensive rule of good faith and inherent fairness to the minority in any transaction where control of the corporation is material properly governs controlling shareholders in this state.

We turn now to defendants' conduct to ascertain whether this test is met.

### III

*Formation of United Financial and Marketing its Shares*

Defendants created United Financial during a period of unusual investor interest in the stock of savings and loan associations. They then owned a majority of the outstanding stock of the Association. This stock was not readily marketable owing to a high book value, lack of investor information and facilities, and the closely held nature of the Association. The management of the Association had made no effort to create a market for the stock or to split the shares and reduce their market price to a more attractive level. Two courses were available to defendants in their effort to exploit the bull market in savings and loan stock. Both were made possible by defendants' status as controlling stockholders. The first was either to cause the Association to effect a stock split (Corp.Code, § 1507) and create a market for the Association stock or to create a holding company for Association shares and permit all stockholders to exchange their shares before offering holding company shares to the public. All stockholders would have benefited alike had this been done, but in realizing their gain on the sale of their stock the majority stockholders would of necessity have had to relinquish some of their control shares. Because a public market would have been created, however, the minority stockholders would have been able to extricate themselves without sacrificing their investment had they elected not to remain with the new management.

The second course was that taken by defendants. A new corporation was formed whose major asset was to be the control block of Association stock owned by defendants, but from which minority shareholders were to be excluded. The unmarketable Association stock held by the majority was transferred to the newly formed corporation at an exchange rate equivalent to a 250 for 1 stock split. The new corporation thereupon set out to create a market for its own shares. Association stock constituted 85 percent of the holding company's assets and produced an equivalent proportion of its income. The same individuals controlled both corporations. It appears therefrom that the market created by defendants for United Financial shares was a market that would have been available for Association stock had defendants taken the first course of action.[13]

13. The situation of minority stockholders and the difficulties they faced in attempting to market their savings and loan stock were described in The Savings and Loan Industry in California, a report prepared by the Stanford Research Institute for the California Savings and Loan Commissioner, and published by the Commissioner in 1960. The attractiveness of the holding company as a device to enhance liquidity was recognized: "The majority and minority stockholders in the original associations often found that they had difficulties in selling their shares at a price approximating their book value. Their main difficulties arose from the fact that book values and prices of shares often ran into many thousands of dollars, a price not generally suitable for wide public sale. These shares were usually owned by a relatively small number of stockholders. When one of them, or his heirs, wished to sell his shares, he had to negotiate with a buyer in this small group or attempt to find an outside purchaser. Minority stockholders had a special problem, because they could not sell control with their stock.

"The holding company was regarded by many stockholders as an attractive device to solve the problem of the marketability of their shares. Through this method, the control of one, two, or several associations could be consolidated and offered to the investing public in a single large stock issue at relatively low prices, either over the counter or through a stock exchange. The wide public ownership of holding company shares would thus provide a more active market and more protection against large capital losses in the event the original owners or their heirs wished to sell their holding company stock.

" * * *

"Large capital gains on the sale of holding company stock to the public have been an important incentive and consequence of this form of organization. The issuance of holding company stock to the general public usually found an enthusiastic demand which made it possible to sell the stock for as much as two to three times book value. In many but not all cases the majority stockholders in the original associations have offered less than 50 percent of the holding company's stock to the public, thus retaining control of the association and the holding companies." (The Savings and Loan Industry in California (1960) pp. VI–6–VI–7.) Although defendants suggest that their transfer of the insurance busi-

After United Financial shares became available to the public it became a virtual certainty that no equivalent market could or would be created for Association stock. United Financial had become the controlling stockholder and neither it nor the other defendants would benefit from public trading in Association stock in competition with United Financial shares. Investors afforded an opportunity to acquire United Financial shares would not be likely to choose the less marketable and expensive Association stock in preference. Thus defendants chose a course of action in which they used their control of the Association to obtain an advantage not made available to all stockholders. They did so without regard to the resulting detriment to the minority stockholders and in the absence of any compelling business purpose. Such conduct is not consistent with their duty of good faith and inherent fairness to the minority stockholders. Had defendants afforded the minority an opportunity to exchange their stock on the same basis or offered to purchase them at a price arrived at by independent appraisal, their burden of establishing good faith and inherent fairness would have been much less. At the trial they may present evidence tending to show such good faith or compelling business purpose that would render their action fair under the circumstances. On appeal from the judgment of dismissal after the defendants' demurrer was sustained we decide only that the complaint states a cause of action entitling plaintiff to relief.

Defendants gained an additional advantage for themselves through their use of control of the Association when they pledged that control over the Association's assets and earnings to secure the holding company's debt, a debt that had been incurred for their own benefit. In so doing the defendants breached their fiduciary obligation to the minority once again and caused United Financial and its controlling shareholders to become inextricably wedded to a conflict of interest between the minority stockholders of each corporation. Alternatives were available to them that would have benefited all stockholders proportionately....

In so holding we do not suggest that the duties of corporate fiduciaries include in all cases an obligation to make a market for and to facilitate public trading in the stock of the corporation. But when, as here, no market exists, the controlling shareholders may not use their power to control the corporation for the purpose of promoting a marketing scheme that benefits themselves alone to the detriment of the minority. Nor do we suggest that a control block of shares may not be sold or transferred to a holding company. We decide only that the circumstances of any transfer of controlling shares will be subject to judicial scrutiny when it appears that the controlling shareholders may

nesses and the later acquisition of another savings and loan association by United Financial were necessary to the creation of a market for United Financial shares and that no market could be created for the shares of a single savings and loan association, the study does not support their claim. Whether defendants could have created a market for a holding company that controlled a single association or reasonably believed that they could not, goes to their good faith and to the existence of a proper business purpose for electing the course that they chose to follow. At the trial of the cause defendants can introduce evidence relevant to the necessity for inclusion of other businesses.

have breached their fiduciary obligation to the corporation or the remaining shareholders.

## IV

### *Damages* . . .

If, after the trial of the cause, plaintiff has established facts in conformity with the allegations of the complaint and stipulation, then upon tender of her Association stock to defendants she will be entitled to receive at her election either the appraised value of her shares on the date of the exchange, May 14, 1959, with interest at 7 percent a year from the date of this action, or a sum equivalent to the fair market value of a "derived block" of United Financial stock on the date of this action with interest thereon from that date, and the sum of $927.50 (the return of capital paid to the original United Financial shareholders) with interest thereon from the date United Financial first made such payments to its original shareholders, for each share tendered. The appraised or fair market value shall be reduced, however, by the amount by which dividends paid on Association shares during the period from May 14, 1959, to the present exceeds the dividends paid on a corresponding block of United Financial shares during the same period. . . .

The judgment appealed from by plaintiff is reversed. The trial court is directed to overrule the demurrer in conformity with this opinion. Defendants' appeal is dismissed.

■ PETERS, J., TOBRINER, J., BURKE, J., SULLIVAN, J., and COUGHLIN, J. pro tem., concurred.

■ . . . McCOMB, J., was of the opinion that the petition should be granted.

## SECTION 6.   SALE OF CONTROL

## Zetlin v. Hanson Holdings, Inc.

New York Court of Appeals, 1979.
48 N.Y.2d 684, 421 N.Y.S.2d 877, 397 N.E.2d 387.

MEMORANDUM.

The order of the Appellate Division should be affirmed, with costs.

Plaintiff Zetlin owned approximately 2% of the outstanding shares of Gable Industries, Inc., with defendants Hanson Holdings, Inc., and Sylvestri, together with members of the Sylvestri family, owning 44.4% of Gable's shares. The defendants sold their interests to Flintkote Co. for a premium price of $15 per share, at a time when Gable stock was selling on the open market for $7.38 per share. It is undisputed that the 44.4% acquired by Flintkote represented effective control of Gable.

Recognizing that those who invest the capital necessary to acquire a dominant position in the ownership of a corporation have the right of controlling that corporation, it has long been settled law that, absent looting of corporate assets, conversion of a corporate opportunity, fraud or other acts of bad faith, a controlling stockholder is free to sell, and a purchaser is free to buy, that controlling interest at a premium price (see *Barnes v. Brown*, 80 N.Y. 527; *Levy v. American Beverage Corp.*, 265 App.Div. 208; *Essex Universal Corp. v. Yates*, 305 F.2d 572).

Certainly, minority shareholders are entitled to protection against such abuse by controlling shareholders. They are not entitled, however, to inhibit the legitimate interests of the other stockholders. It is for this reason that control shares usually command a premium price. The premium is the added amount an investor is willing to pay for the privilege of directly influencing the corporation's affairs.

In this action plaintiff Zetlin contends that minority stockholders are entitled to an opportunity to share equally in any premium paid for a controlling interest in the corporation. This rule would profoundly affect the manner in which controlling stock interests are now transferred. It would require, essentially, that a controlling interest be transferred only by means of an offer to all stockholders, i.e., a tender offer. This would be contrary to existing law and if so radical a change is to be effected it would best be done by the Legislature.

■ CHIEF JUDGE COOKE and JUDGES JASEN, GABRIELLI, JONES, WACHTLER, FUCHSBERG and MEYER concur in memorandum.

Order affirmed.

———

## Andrews, The Stockholder's Right to Equal Opportunity in the Sale of Shares

78 Harv.L.Rev. 505, 515–22 (1965).

The rule to be considered can be stated thus: whenever a controlling stockholder sells his shares, every other holder of shares (of the same class) is entitled to have an equal opportunity to sell his shares, or a prorata part of them, on substantially the same terms. Or in terms of the correlative duty: before a controlling stockholder may sell his shares to an outsider he must assure his fellow stockholders an equal opportunity to sell their shares, or as high a proportion of theirs as he ultimately sells of his own. There are qualifications in the application of the rule, to which I will return; but for purposes of argument we can begin with this broad statement of it. . . .

[*Practical reasons for the proposed rule*] (*a*).—There is a substantial danger that following a transfer of controlling shares corporate affairs may be conducted in a manner detrimental to the interests of the stockholders who have not had an opportunity to sell their shares. The corporation may be looted; it may just be badly run. Or the sale of controlling shares may operate to destroy a favorable opportunity for corporate action. . . .

The equal opportunity rule does not deal directly with the problem of mismanagement, which may occur even after a transfer of control complying with the rule; but enforcement of the rule will remove much of the incentive a purchaser can offer a controlling stockholder to sell on profitable terms. Indeed, in the case of a purchasing looter there is nothing in it for the purchaser unless he can buy less than all the shares; there is no profit in stealing from a solvent corporation if the thief owns all the stock. But the controlling stockholder will be loath to sell only part of his shares (except at a price that compensates him for all of his shares) if he expects the purchaser to destroy the value of what he keeps. The rule forces the controlling stockholder to share equally with his fellow stockholders both the benefits of the price he receives for the shares he sells and the business risks incident to the shares he retains. This will tend strongly to discourage a sale of controlling shares when the risk of looting, or other harm to the corporation, is apparent; and it will provide the seller with a direct incentive to investigate and evaluate with care when the risks are not apparent, since his own financial interest continues to be at stake. . . .

Of course a transfer of control may have advantageous effects for a corporation and its stockholders—and these may be just as subtle as any adverse effects. Many sales of controlling shares come about because the selling stockholders are not doing as well with a business as a purchaser believes he can do; and the belief is often right. Often the sellers are members of a family that has simply run out of managerial talent or interest.

If the rule of equal opportunity would prevent sales in this sort of situation, that would be a high price to pay for the prevention of harm in other cases. . . . For my own part I do not believe the rule of equal opportunity would have much tendency to discourage beneficial transactions. After all, if the purchaser is optimistic—and can convince his bankers to share his optimism—he should be willing to buy out everyone. If the seller is optimistic about the consequences of the transfer, he should be willing to retain some of his shares. If minority stockholders are optimistic, they should be willing to hold their shares. If the financial community is optimistic (in the case of a publicly held corporation), the market itself should offer the minority stockholders a chance to sell at a price that satisfies the rule. Thus, on the face of it the rule would only operate to prevent a sale when all four of these—the seller, the purchaser, the minority stockholders, and the financial community—take a pessimistic view of the transfer. . . .

(b). . . . [A] purchaser attains control of the corporation's business and assets equally whether he purchases all the shares or a smaller controlling block. When a purchaser buys less than all the shares, he is acquiring a business worth more than what he pays in cash, and is financing the difference by leaving the minority shares outstanding. We think of mortgage debts that way; if a person buys property subject to a mortgage and leaves the mortgage outstanding, we recognize that the mortgage provides financing for the purchaser because it has the same effect, substantially, as a new loan with the proceeds of which the purchaser might have paid full value for the property. But stock provides financing just as much as a mortgage does. A purchaser who buys only part of the stock of an enterprise might have accomplished much the same net result by purchasing all the assets in the name of a newly organized corporation in which he takes only a part of the stock. The other stockholders in the new corporation would then be viewed as providing equity financing for the acquisition. The chief difference then between a sale of assets, or of all the stock, and a sale of a controlling block of shares only, is that in the latter case the purchaser has had his acquisition partially financed, perhaps unwillingly, by the stockholders from whom he does not buy. That is no reason to give the minority stockholders less protection than if the purchaser gave them an opportunity to sell, even at a lower price. . . .

(c).—A somewhat broader way of putting the argument is even simpler: each stockholder is entitled to share proportionately in the profits of the enterprise; from the stockholder's point of view a sale of stock is one very important way of realizing a profit on his investment; profits from stock sales ought to be regarded as profits of the enterprise subject to equal sharing among stockholders just as much as profits realized through corporate action.

A minority stockholder must invest largely on the strength of the expectation that decisions will tend to be made for his benefit because of the general identity of interest between him and those in control. This identity of interest is qualified when controlling stockholders have an opportunity to profit by entering into dealings with their corporation; this is permitted because such transactions may be mutually profitable, and there is no way to enforce equality of interest beyond allowing judicial scrutiny of such transactions for fairness. It would be impossible to insist, for example, that a publicly held corporation offer all its stockholders a proportionate opportunity to serve in an executive capacity. But when an opportunity arises for profit by selling shares, there is no such simple practical reason why it cannot be made equally available to all stockholders. . . .

———

## Javaras, Equal Opportunity in the Sale of Controlling Shares: A Reply to Professor Andrews

32 U.Chi.L.Rev. 420, 425–27 (1965).

I believe that the gravest defect in Professor Andrews' theory is a grievous underassessment of the costs of a preventive rule in restraining beneficial transactions. Such restraint would operate on the purchaser by imposing higher required investment—the price of all the shares of the corporation rather than only those owned by the controlling shareholder. Professor Andrews minimizes the effects of this factor on two grounds. First, the controlling shareholder under the rule of equal opportunity, when confronted with a purchaser who wants the controlling shares and no more, may be induced to retain some of his shares and share the sale ratably with the non-controlling shareholders. Admittedly, this requires faith in the management of the purchaser. Second, a beneficial purchaser should be willing to buy all the shares because, after all, the non-controlling shares have the same investment value as the controlling shares. All the purchaser would have to do, therefore, if he did not have the capital is to borrow it. If he could not, that would be a reflection either of superior knowledge in the financial community or dislocations in the capital market.

It is doubtful whether sufficient controlling sellers can be induced to retain their shares so as to eliminate the higher capital requirement. First, ... sales of securities are not dictated merely by an appraisal of investment value. Many sellers simply want immediate cash. Second, a controlling seller may not wish to hold, say twenty-five per cent as compared to his prior fifty per cent, because of the possibility of his views differing from those of the controlling purchaser in the future. This reticence would partly stem from ... the controlling sellers assessment of the change in risks when he is deprived of control. The loss of control would subject him to the risk of poor management, which might dictate a lesser investment in this corporation on the principle of risk diversification.

Likewise the purchaser himself might be unwilling that the seller retain some of his shares, particularly where working control (less than fifty per cent) is the subject of the offer. He might well be reluctant to have a large block of stock outstanding whose owners, under conditions of dissension, could mobilize the other shareholders and displace his control of the board of directors.

In effect then, the rule of equal treatment would impose higher capital requirements on beneficial purchasers in a substantial number of transactions. Professor Andrews inappropriately assumes, however, that the purchasers should be willing to meet these higher costs because the investment value of the additional shares is the same. He errs in that his reasoning is incomplete. It is true that the investment value is the same. But even if the capital market did function perfectly and the purchaser could arrange the financing, a rational businessman might not want to buy all the shares at a premium price justified by the investment potential. It might be sensible to decline to buy more than the bare amount necessary for control on the principles of diversification of risk and of opportunity. This might render the equal treatment rule ineffectual as a means of automatically distinguishing "good" and "bad" purchasers. I would think that the number of prospective beneficial purchasers prevented because of a desire to diversify will be much larger than those simply unable to raise the capital. Until empirical evidence is adduced to the contrary, I am predisposed to consider this cost of restraining beneficial transactions substantial when compared with the cases of detriment with which the present law is incompetent to deal. . . .

---

## NOTE ON HARRIS v. CARTER

In Harris v. Carter, 582 A.2d 222 (Del.Ch.1990) (Allen, Ch.), Donald Carter and others owned 52% of Atlas Corporation. The Carter Group sold its stock in Atlas, and transferred control of Atlas's board, to Frederic Mascolo and others. Plaintiff, a minority shareholder in Atlas, claimed that (i) the Mascolo group had looted Atlas by engaging in self-dealing transactions on unfair terms, and (ii) the Carter group was liable for the resulting losses to Atlas, because it had reason to suspect the integrity of the Mascolo group, but failed to conduct even a cursory investigation into any of several suspicious aspects of the transaction. The Carter defendants moved to dismiss for failure to state a claim upon which relief could be granted. Motion denied:

This motion raises novel questions of Delaware law. Stated generally the most basic of these questions is whether a controlling shareholder or group may under any circumstances owe a duty of care to the corporation in connection with the sale of a control block of stock. If such a duty may be said to exist under certain circumstances the questions in this case then become whether the facts alleged in the amended complaint would permit the finding that such a duty arose in connection with the sale to the Mascolo group and was breached. In this inquiry one applies the permissive standard appropriate for motions to dismiss: if on any state of facts that may reasonably be inferred from the pleaded facts plaintiff would be entitled to a judgment, a claim that will survive [such a motion] has been stated. . . .

A number of cases may be cited in support of the proposition that when transferring control of a corporation to another, a controlling shareholder may, in some circumstances, have a duty to investigate the bona fides of the buyer—that is, in those circumstances, to take such steps as a reasonable person would take to ascertain that the buyer does not intend or is unlikely to plan any depredations of the corporation. The circumstance to which these cases refer is the existence of facts that would give rise to suspicion by a reasonably prudent person. . . .

More generally, it does not follow from the proposition that ordinarily a shareholder has a right to sell her stock to whom and on such terms as she deems expedient, that no duty may arise from the particular circumstances to take care in the exercise of that right. It is established American legal doctrine that, unless privileged, each person owes a duty to those who may foreseeably be harmed by her action to take such steps as a reasonably prudent person would take in similar circumstances to avoid such harm to others.[16] While this principle arises from the law of torts and not the law of corporations

---

**16.** See Restatement of Torts Second § 281; Prosser & Keeton on Torts p. 284–290 (5th Ed.1984); Palsgraf v. Long Island Railroad Co., 248 N.Y. 339, 162 N.E. 99 (1928);

or of fiduciary duties, that distinction is not, I think, significant unless the law of corporations or of fiduciary duties somehow privileges a selling shareholder by exempting her from the reach of this principle. The principle itself is one of great generality and, if not negated by privilege, would apply to a controlling shareholder who negligently places others foreseeably in the path of injury.

That a shareholder may sell her stock (or that a director may resign his office) is a right that, with respect to the principle involved, is no different, for example, than the right that a licensed driver has to operate a motor vehicle upon a highway. The right exists, but it is not without conditions and limitations, some established by positive regulation, some by common-law. Thus, to continue the parallel, the driver owes a duty of care to her passengers because it is foreseeable that they may be injured if, through inattention or otherwise, the driver involves the car she is operating in a collision. In the typical instance a seller of corporate stock can be expected to have no similar apprehension of risks to others from her own inattention. But, in some circumstances, the seller of a control block of stock may or should reasonably foresee danger to other shareholders; with her sale of stock will also go control over the corporation and with it the opportunity to misuse that power to the injury of such other shareholders. Thus, the reason that a duty of care is recognized in any situation is fully present in this situation. I can find no universal privilege arising from the corporate form that exempts a controlling shareholder who sells corporate control from the wholesome reach of this common-law duty.[17] ...

Thus, I conclude that while a person who transfers corporate control to another is surely not a surety for his buyer, when the circumstances would alert a reasonably prudent person to a risk that his buyer is dishonest or in some material respect not truthful, a duty devolves upon the seller to make such inquiry as a reasonably prudent person would make, and generally to exercise care so that others who will be affected by his actions should not be injured by wrongful conduct....

------

## Perlman v. Feldmann

United States Court of Appeals, Second Circuit, 1955.
219 F.2d 173, cert. denied 349 U.S. 952, 75 S.Ct. 880, 99 L.Ed. 1277 (1955).

■ CLARK, CHIEF JUDGE. This is a derivative action brought by nority stockholders of Newport Steel Corporation to compel accounting for,

---

Delmarva Power & Light Company v. Burrows, Del.Supr., 435 A.2d 716, 718–20 (1981).

**17.** A privilege arguably does exist with respect to foreseeable risk of financial injury to share values that might arise from a risky though honest future business plan that the buyer may have in mind. Such a privilege would not be involved here when the thrust of the complaint is that Mascolo engaged in— and Carter defendants should have foreseen or at least investigated—dishonest transactions.

and restitution of, allegedly illegal gains which accrued to defendants as a result of the sale in August, 1950, of their controlling interest in the corporation. The principal defendant, C. Russell Feldmann, who represented and acted for the others, members of his family,[1] was at that time not only the dominant stockholder, but also the chairman of the board of directors and the president of the corporation. Newport, an Indiana corporation, operated mills for the production of steel sheets for sale to manufacturers of steel products, first at Newport, Kentucky, and later also at other places in Kentucky and Ohio. The buyers, a syndicate organized as Wilport Company, a Delaware corporation, consisted of end-users of steel who were interested in securing a source of supply in a market becoming ever tighter in the Korean War. Plaintiffs contend that the consideration paid for the stock included compensation for the sale of a corporate asset, a power held in trust for the corporation by Feldmann as its fiduciary. This power was the ability to control the allocation of the corporate product in a time of short supply, through control of the board of directors; and it was effectively transferred in this sale by having Feldmann procure the resignation of his own board and the election of Wilport's nominees immediately upon consummation of the sale.

The present action represents the consolidation of three pending stockholders' actions in which yet another stockholder has been permitted to intervene. Jurisdiction below was based upon the diverse citizenship of the parties. Plaintiffs argue here, as they did in the court below, that in the situation here disclosed the vendors must account to the nonparticipating minority stockholders for that share of their profit which is attributable to the sale of the corporate power. Judge Hincks denied the validity of the premise, holding that the rights involved in the sale were only those normally incident to the possession of a controlling block of shares, with which a dominant stockholder, in the absence of fraud or foreseeable looting, was entitled to deal according to his own best interests. Furthermore, he held that plaintiffs had failed to satisfy their burden of proving that the sales price was not a fair price for the stock per se. Plaintiffs appeal from these rulings of law which resulted in the dismissal of their complaint.

The essential facts found by the trial judge are not in dispute. Newport was a relative newcomer in the steel industry with predominantly old installations which were in the process of being supplemented by more modern facilities. Except in times of extreme shortage Newport was not in a position to compete profitably with other steel mills for customers not in its immediate geographical area. Wilport, the purchasing syndicate, consisted of geographically remote end-users of steel who were interested in buying more steel from Newport than they had been able to obtain during recent periods of tight supply. The price of $20 per share was found by Judge Hincks to be a

---

**1.** The stock was not held personally by Feldmann in his own name, but was held by the members of his family and by personal corporations. The aggregate of stock thus [held] amounted to 33% of the outstanding Newport stock and gave working control to the holder. The actual sale included 55,552 additional shares held by friends and associates of Feldmann, so that a total of 37% of the Newport stock was transferred.

fair one for a control block of stock, although the over-the-counter market price had not exceeded $12 and the book value per share was $17.03. But this finding was limited by Judge Hincks' statement that "[w]hat value the block would have had if shorn of its appurtenant power to control distribution of the corporate product, the evidence does not show." It was also conditioned by his earlier ruling that the burden was on plaintiffs to prove a lesser value for the stock.

Both as director and as dominant stockholder, Feldmann stood in a fiduciary relationship to the corporation and to the minority stockholders as beneficiaries thereof. Pepper v. Litton, 308 U.S. 295, 60 S.Ct. 238, 84 L.Ed. 281; Southern Pac. Co. v. Bogert, 250 U.S. 483, 39 S.Ct. 533, 63 L.Ed. 1099. His fiduciary obligation must in the first instance be measured by the law of Indiana, the state of incorporation of Newport. Rogers v. Guaranty Trust Co. of New York, 288 U.S. 123, 136, 53 S.Ct. 295, 77 L.Ed. 652; Mayflower Hotel Stockholders Protective Committee v. Mayflower Hotel Corp., 89 U.S.App.D.C. 171, 193 F.2d 666, 668. Although there is no Indiana case directly in point, the most closely analogous one emphasizes the close scrutiny to which Indiana subjects the conduct of fiduciaries when personal benefit may stand in the way of fulfillment of trust obligations. In Schemmel v. Hill, 91 Ind.App. 373, 169 N.E. 678, 682, 683, McMahan, J., said: "Directors of a business corporation act in a strictly fiduciary capacity. Their office is a trust. Stratis v. Andreson, 1926, 254 Mass. 536, 150 N.E. 832, 44 A.L.R. 567; Hill v. Nisbet, 1885, 100 Ind. 341, 353. When a director deals with his corporation, his acts will be closely scrutinized. Bossert v. Geis, 1914, 57 Ind.App. 384, 107 N.E. 95. Directors of a corporation are its agents, and they are governed by the rules of law applicable to other agents, and, as between themselves and their principal, the rules relating to honesty and fair dealing in the management of the affairs of their principal are applicable. They must not, in any degree, allow their official conduct to be swayed by their private interest, which must yield to official duty. Leader Publishing Co. v. Grant Trust Co., 1915, 182 Ind. 651, 108 N.E. 121. In a transaction between a director and his corporation, where he acts for himself and his principal at the same time in a matter connected with the relation between them, it is presumed, where he is thus potentially on both sides of the contract, that self-interest will overcome his fidelity to his principal, to his own benefit and to his principal's hurt." And the judge added: "Absolute and most scrupulous good faith is the very essence of a director's obligation to his corporation. The first principal duty arising from his official relation is to act in all things of trust wholly for the benefit of his corporation."

In Indiana, then, as elsewhere, the responsibility of the fiduciary is not limited to a proper regard for the tangible balance sheet assets of the corporation, but includes the dedication of his uncorrupted business judgment for the sole benefit of the corporation, in any dealings which may adversely affect it.... Although the Indiana case is particularly relevant to Feldmann as a director, the same rule should apply to his fiduciary duties as majority stockholder, for in that capacity he chooses and controls the directors, and thus is held to have assumed their liability. Pepper v. Litton, supra, 308 U.S. 295, 60 S.Ct. 238. This, therefore, is the standard to which Feldmann was by law required to conform in his activities here under scrutiny.

It is true, as defendants have been at pains to point out, that this is not the ordinary case of breach of fiduciary duty. We have here no fraud, no misuse of confidential information, no outright looting of a helpless corporation. But on the other hand, we do not find compliance with that high standard which we have just stated and which we and other courts have come to expect and demand of corporate fiduciaries. In the often-quoted words of Judge Cardozo: "Many forms of conduct permissible in a workaday world for those acting at arm's length, are forbidden to those bound by fiduciary ties. A trustee is held to something stricter than the morals of the market place. Not honesty alone, but the punctilio of an honor the most sensitive, is then the standard of behavior. As to this there has developed a tradition that is unbending and inveterate. Uncompromising rigidity has been the attitude of courts of equity when petitioned to undermine the rule of undivided loyalty by the 'disintegrating erosion' of particular exceptions." Meinhard v. Salmon, supra, 249 N.Y. 458, 464, 164 N.E. 545, 546, 62 A.L.R. 1. The actions of defendants in siphoning off for personal gain corporate advantages to be derived from a favorable market situation do not betoken the necessary undivided loyalty owed by the fiduciary to his principal.

The corporate opportunities of whose misappropriation the minority stockholders complain need not have been an absolute certainty in order to support this action against Feldmann. If there was possibility of corporate gain, they are entitled to recover. . . .

. . . In the past Newport had used and profited by its market leverage by operation of what the industry had come to call the "Feldmann Plan." This consisted of securing interest-free advances from prospective purchasers of steel in return for firm commitments to them from future production. The funds thus acquired were used to finance improvements in existing plants and to acquire new installations. In the summer of 1950 Newport had been negotiating for cold-rolling facilities which it needed for a more fully integrated operation and a more marketable product, and Feldmann plan funds might well have been used toward this end.

Further, as plaintiffs alternatively suggest, Newport might have used the period of short supply to build up patronage in the geographical area in which it could compete profitably even when steel was more abundant. Either of these opportunities was Newport's, to be used to its advantage only. Only if defendants had been able to negate completely any possibility of gain by Newport could they have prevailed. It is true that a trial court finding states: "Whether or not, in August, 1950, Newport's position was such that it could have entered into 'Feldmann Plan' type transactions to procure funds and financing for the further expansion and integration of its steel facilities and whether such expansion would have been desirable for Newport, the evidence does not show." This, however, cannot avail the defendants, who—contrary to the ruling below—had the burden of proof on this issue, since fiduciaries always have the burden of proof in establishing the fairness of their dealings with trust property. . . .

Defendants seek to categorize the corporate opportunities which might have accrued to Newport as too unethical to warrant further consideration. It is true that reputable steel producers were not participating in the gray market brought about by the Korean War and were refraining from advancing their prices, although to do so would not have been illegal. But Feldmann plan transactions were not considered within this self-imposed interdiction; the trial court found that around the time of the Feldmann sale Jones & Laughlin Steel Corporation, Republic Steel Company, and Pittsburgh Steel Corporation were all participating in such arrangements. In any event, it ill becomes the defendants to disparage as unethical the market advantages from which they themselves reaped rich benefits.

We do not mean to suggest that a majority stockholder cannot dispose of his controlling block of stock to outsiders without having to account to his corporation for profits or even never do this with impunity when the buyer is an interested customer, actual or potential, for the corporation's product. But when the sale necessarily results in a sacrifice of this element of corporate good will and consequent unusual profit to the fiduciary who has caused the sacrifice, he should account for his gains. So in a time of market shortage, where a call on a corporation's product commands an unusually large premium, in one form or another, we think it sound law that a fiduciary may not appropriate to himself the value of this premium. Such personal gain at the expense of his coventurers seems particularly reprehensible when made by the trusted president and director of his company. In this case the violation of duty seems to be all the clearer because of this triple role in which Feldmann appears, though we are unwilling to say, and are not to be understood as saying, that we should accept a lesser obligation for any one of his roles alone.

Hence to the extent that the price received by Feldmann and his codefendants included such a bonus, he is accountable to the minority stockholders who sue here. Restatement, Restitution §§ 190, 197 (1937); Seagrave Corp. v. Mount, supra, 6 Cir., 212 F.2d 389. And plaintiffs, as they contend, are entitled to a recovery in their own right, instead of in right of the corporation (as in the usual derivative actions), since neither Wilport nor their successors in interest should share in any judgment which may be rendered. See Southern Pacific Co. v. Bogert, 250 U.S. 483, 39 S.Ct. 533, 63 L.Ed. 1099. Defendants cannot well object to this form of recovery, since the only alternative, recovery for the corporation as a whole, would subject them to a greater total liability.

The case will therefore be remanded to the district court for a determination of the question expressly left open below, namely, the value of defendants' stock without the appurtenant control over the corporation's output of steel. We reiterate that on this issue, as on all others relating to a breach of fiduciary duty, the burden of proof must rest on the defendants. Bigelow v. RKO Radio Pictures, 327 U.S. 251, 265–266, 66 S.Ct. 574, 90 L.Ed. 652; Package Closure Corp. v. Sealright Co., 2 Cir., 141 F.2d 972, 979. Judgment should go to these plaintiffs and those whom they represent for any premium value so shown to the extent of their respective stock interests.

The judgment is therefore reversed and the action remanded for further proceedings pursuant to this opinion.

[The dissenting opinion of Judge Swan is omitted.]

---

### NOTE ON PERLMAN v. FELDMANN

On remand, the district court determined the enterprise value of the corporation, based upon its book value and earnings potential, to be $15,825,777, or $14.67 per share. This made the premium $5.33 a share, or $2,126,280. The complaining stockholders, owning sixty-three percent of the stock, were therefore entitled to judgment of $1,339,769, with interest of 6 percent from the sale date, plus costs. Perlman v. Feldmann, 154 F.Supp. 436 (D.Conn.1957).

---

### NOTE ON THE THEORY OF CORPORATE ACTION

If a prospective purchaser, P, wants to acquire complete control of the assets and business of a corporation, C, he has a choice of several means to do so: (1) He can try to acquire all of C's shares, and his first step would naturally be to approach those who hold the majority or at least large blocks of the shares, without which his efforts will fail. (2) He can try to induce holders of sufficient shares to make the requisite majority needed to vote for a merger with or a sale of all assets to a corporation he controls.

If P takes the first course, he deals with C's present holders individually. Each holder seems free to make his own terms of sale, and controlling shares may bring a better price than shares that do not give control. If P takes the second course, he is looking towards corporate action by C. If C's assets are sold, the consideration will pass into C's treasury. Usually the corporation will then be liquidated, and the net proceeds will be distributed pro rata to all C shares, so that each old C shareholder will receive the same amount per share. If C merges, the plan of conversion of C's shares for shares of the surviving corporation will normally provide for equal treatment of all shares of the same class. It may therefore be to the advantage of those who hold the majority, or at least large blocks, of shares of a corporation to have a purchaser like P take the first course.

If P originally proposes to take the second course, but is persuaded to take the first course, and the majority shareholders of C realize more per share for their holdings than the minority, the latter may assert that the difference in technique between the first and second courses of action is immaterial. This is the theory of "corporate action." It has been successfully employed in several cases where the buyer began on the second course and the controlling shareholders switched him to the first. See Commonwealth Title Ins. & Trust Co. v. Seltzer, 227 Pa. 410, 76 A. 77 (1910); Dunnett v. Arn, 71 F.2d 912 (10th Cir.1934); Roby v. Dunnett, 88 F.2d 68 (10th Cir.1937), cert. denied 301 U.S. 706, 57 S.Ct. 940, 81 L.Ed. 1360; American Trust Co. v. California Western States Life Ins. Co., 15 Cal.2d 42, 98 P.2d 497 (1940).

The problem with the theory of corporate action is that a controlling shareholder cannot be compelled to sell his shares at a price he does not accept. A knowledgeable seller therefore can avoid the application of the theory by simply voting down an offer to the corporation, and waiting for an offer to buy his shares. Accordingly, the theory of corporate action, although appealing, will operate only on sellers who are not well-counseled.

---

## Essex Universal Corp. v. Yates

United States Court of Appeals, Second Circuit, 1962.
305 F.2d 572.

■ Before LUMBARD, CHIEF JUDGE, and CLARK and FRIENDLY, CIRCUIT JUDGES.

■ LUMBARD, CHIEF JUDGE.

This appeal from the district court's summary judgment in favor of the defendant raises the question whether a contract for the sale of 28.3 per cent of the stock of a corporation is, under New York law, invalid as against public policy solely because it includes a clause giving the purchaser an option to require a majority of the existing directors to replace themselves, by a process of seriatim resignation, with a majority designated by the purchaser. Despite the disagreement evidenced by the diversity of our opinions, my brethren and I agree that such a provision does not on its face render the contract illegal and unenforceable, and thus that it was improper to grant summary judgment. Judge Friendly would reject the defense of illegality without further inquiry concerning the provision itself (as distinguished from any contention that control could not be safely transferred to the particular purchaser). Judge Clark and I are agreed that on remand, which must be had in any event to consider other defenses raised by the pleadings, further factual issues may be raised by the parties upon which the legality of the clause in question will depend; we disagree, however, on the nature of those factual issues, as our separate opinions reveal. Accordingly, the grant of summary judgment is reversed and the case is remanded for trial of the question of the legality of the contested provision and such further proceedings as may be proper on the other issues raised by the pleadings.

Since we are in agreement on certain preliminary questions, this opinion constitutes the opinion of the court up to the point where it is indicated that it thenceforth states only my individual views.

The defendant Herbert J. Yates, a resident of California, was president and chairman of the board of directors of Republic Pictures Corporation, a New York corporation which at the time relevant to this suit had 2,004,190 shares of common stock outstanding. Republic's stock was listed and traded on the New York Stock Exchange. In August 1957, Essex Universal Corporation, a Delaware corporation owning stock in various diversified businesses, learned of the possibility of purchasing from Yates an interest in Republic. Negotiations proceeded rapidly, and on August 28 Yates and Joseph Harris, the president of Essex, signed a contract in which Essex agreed to buy, and Yates agreed "to sell or cause to be sold" at least 500,000 and not more than 600,000 shares of Republic stock. The price was set at eight dollars a share, roughly two dollars above the then market price on the Exchange. Three dollars per share was to be paid at the closing on September 18, 1957 and the remainder in twenty-four equal monthly payments beginning January 31, 1958. The shares were to be transferred on the closing date, but Yates was to retain the certificates, endorsed in blank by Essex, as security for full payment. In addition to other provisions not relevant to the present motion, the contract contained the following paragraph:

"6. Resignations.

Upon and as a condition to the closing of this transaction if requested by Buyer at least ten (10) days prior to the date of the closing:

(a) Seller will deliver to Buyer the resignations of the majority of the directors of Republic.

(b) Seller will cause a special meeting of the board of directors of Republic to be held, legally convened pursuant to law and the by-laws of Republic, and simultaneously with the acceptance of the directors' resignations set forth in paragraph 6(a) immediately preceding will cause nominees of Buyer to be elected directors of Republic in place of the resigned directors."

Before the date of the closing, as provided in the contract, Yates notified Essex that he would deliver 566,223 shares, or 28.3 per cent of the Republic stock then outstanding, and Essex formally requested Yates to arrange for the replacement of a majority of Republic's directors with Essex nominees pursuant to paragraph 6 of the contract. This was to be accomplished by having eight of the fourteen directors resign seriatim, each in turn being replaced by an Essex nominee elected by the others; such a procedure was *in form* permissible under the charter and by-laws of Republic, which empowered the board to choose the successor of any of its members who might resign.

On September 18, the parties met as arranged for the closing at Republic's office in New York City. Essex tendered bank drafts and cashier's checks totalling $1,698,690, which was the 37½ per cent of the total price of $4,529,784 due at this time. The drafts and checks were payable to one Benjamin C. Cohen, who was Essex' banker and had arranged for the borrowing of the necessary funds. Although Cohen was prepared to endorse these to Yates, Yates upon advice of his lawyer rejected the tender as "unsatisfactory" and said, according to his deposition testimony, "Well, there can be no deal. We can't close it."

Essex began this action in the New York Supreme Court, and it was removed to the district court on account of diversity of citizenship. Essex seeks damages of $2,700,000, claiming that at the time of the aborted closing the stock was in actuality worth more than $12.75 a share.[1] Yates' answer raised a number of defenses, but the motion for summary judgment now before us was made and decided only on the theory that the provision in the contract for immediate transfer of control of the board of directors was illegal *per se* and tainted the entire contract. We have no doubt, and the parties agree, that New York law governs.

Appellant's contention that the provision for transfer of director control is separable from the rest of the contract can quickly be rejected. . . .

. . . [W]e hold the provision regarding directors inseparable from the sale of shares, and proceed to a consideration of its legality.

Up to this point my brethren and I are in agreement. The following analysis is my own, except insofar as the separate opinions of Judges Clark and Friendly may indicate agreement.

It is established beyond question under New York law that it is illegal to sell corporate office or management control by itself (that is, accompanied by no stock or insufficient stock to carry voting control). . . . The rationale of the rule is undisputable: persons enjoying management control hold it on behalf of the corporation's stockholders, and therefore may not regard it as their own personal property to dispose of as they wish.[3] Any other rule would violate the most fundamental principle of corporate democracy, that management must represent and be chosen by, or at least with the consent of, those who own the corporation.

Essex was, however, contracting with Yates for the purchase of a very substantial percentage of Republic stock. If, by virtue of the voting power carried by this stock, it could have elected a majority of the board of directors, then the contract was not a simple agreement for the sale of office to one having no ownership interest in the corporation, and the question of its legality would require further analysis. Such stock voting control would incontestably belong to the owner of

1. In 1959, while this action was pending, the stock was sold to another party for ten dollars a share.

3. The cases have made no distinction between contracts by directors or officers to resign and contracts by persons who in actuality control the actions of officers or directors to procure their resignations, and of course none should exist.

a majority of the voting stock, and it is commonly known that equivalent power usually accrues to the owner of 28.3% of the stock. For the purpose of this analysis, I shall assume that Essex was contracting to acquire a majority of the Republic stock, deferring consideration of the situation where, as here, only 28.3% is to be acquired.

Republic's board of directors at the time of the aborted closing had fourteen members divided into three classes, each class being "as nearly as may be" of the same size. Directors were elected for terms of three years, one class being elected at each annual shareholder meeting on the first Tuesday in April. Thus, absent the immediate replacement of directors provided for in this contract, Essex as the hypothetical new majority shareholder of the corporation could not have obtained managing control in the form of a majority of the board in the normal course of events until April 1959, some eighteen months after the sale of the stock. The first question before us then is whether an agreement to accelerate the transfer of management control, in a manner legal in form under the corporation's charter and by-laws, violates the public policy of New York.

There is no question of the right of a controlling shareholder under New York law normally to derive a premium from the sale of a controlling block of stock. In other words, there was no impropriety *per se* in the fact that Yates was to receive more per share than the generally prevailing market price for Republic stock. Levy v. American Beverage Corp., 265 App.Div. 208, 218, 38 N.Y.S.2d 517, 526 (1st Dept.1942); Stanton v. Schenck, 140 Misc. 621, 251 N.Y.S. 221 (N.Y.County Sup.Ct.1931); see Hill, supra, 70 Harv.L.Rev. at 991–92.

The next question is whether it is legal to give and receive payment for the immediate transfer of management control to one who has achieved majority share control but would not otherwise be able to convert that share control into operating control for some time. I think that it is.

Of course under some circumstances controlling shareholders transferring immediate control may be compelled to account to the corporation for that part of the consideration received by them which exceeds the fair value of the block of stock sold, as well as for the injury which they may cause to the corporation. . . . Gerdes v. Reynolds, 28 N.Y.S.2d 622 (N.Y.County Sup.Ct.1941). . . .

A fair generalization from [Perlman v. Feldmann and other] cases may be that a holder of corporate control will not, as a fiduciary, be permitted to profit from facilitating actions on the part of the purchasers of control which are detrimental to the interests of the corporation or the remaining shareholders. There is, however, no suggestion that the transfer of control over Republic to Essex carried any such threat to the interests of the corporation or its other shareholders.

Our examination of the New York cases . . . gives us no reason to regard as impaired the holding of the early case of Barnes v. Brown, 80 N.Y. 527 (1880), that a bargain for the sale of a majority stock interest is not made illegal by a plan for immediate transfer of management control by a program like that provided for in the Essex–Yates contract. Judge Earl wrote:

> "[The seller] had the right to sell out all his stock and interest in the corporation, ... and when he ceased to have any interest in the corporation, it was certainly legitimate and right that he should cease to control it ... It was simply the mode of transferring the control of the corporation to those who by the policy of the law ought to have it, and I am unable to see how any policy of the law was violated, or in what way, upon the evidence, any wrong was thereby done to anyone." 80 N.Y. at 537.

To be sure, in Barnes v. Brown no term of the contract of sale *required* the seller to effectuate the immediate replacement of directors, as did paragraph 6 of the Essex–Yates contract, but Judge Earl stated that "I shall assume that it was the understanding and a part of the scheme that he should do so." 80 N.Y. at 536. . . .

The easy and immediate transfer of corporate control to new interests is ordinarily beneficial to the economy and it seems inevitable that such transactions would be discouraged if the purchaser of a majority stock interest were required to wait some period before his purchase of control could become effective. Conversely it would greatly hamper the efforts of any existing majority group to dispose of its interest if it could not assure the purchaser of immediate control over corporation operations. I can see no reason why a purchaser of majority control should not ordinarily be permitted to make his control effective from the moment of the transfer of stock.

Thus if Essex had been contracting to purchase a majority of the stock of Republic, it would have been entirely proper for the contract to contain the provision for immediate replacement of directors. Although in the case at bar only 28.3 per cent of the stock was involved, it is commonly known that a person or group owning so large a percentage of the voting stock of a corporation which, like Republic, has at least the 1,500 shareholders normally requisite to listing on the New York Stock Exchange, is almost certain to have share control as a practical matter. If Essex was contracting to acquire what in reality would be equivalent to ownership of a majority of stock, i.e., if it would as a practical certainty have been guaranteed of the stock voting power to choose a majority of the directors of Republic in due course, there is no reason why the contract should not similarly be legal.[6] Whether Essex was thus to acquire the equivalent of majority stock control would, if the issue is properly raised by the defendants, be a factual issue to be determined by the district court on remand.

Because 28.3 per cent of the voting stock of a publicly owned corporation is usually tantamount to majority control, I would place

---

**6.** The fact that under the Essex–Yates contract only 37½% of the price of the stock was to be paid at the closing and the balance was not to be fully paid for twenty-eight months is irrelevant to this case. There is no indication that Essex did not have sound financial backing sufficient to discharge properly the obligation which had been incurred.

the burden of proof on this issue on Yates as the party attacking the legality of the transaction. Thus, unless on remand Yates chooses to raise the question whether the block of stock in question carried the equivalent of majority control, it is my view that the trial court should regard the contract as legal and proceed to consider the other issues raised by the pleadings. If Yates chooses to raise the issue, it will, on my view, be necessary for him to prove the existence of circumstances which would have prevented Essex from electing a majority of the Republic board of directors in due course. It will not be enough for Yates to raise merely hypothetical possibilities of opposition by the other Republic shareholders to Essex' assumption of management control. Rather, it will be necessary for him to show that, assuming neutrality on the part of the retiring management, there was at the time some concretely foreseeable reason why Essex' wishes would not have prevailed in shareholder voting held in due course. In other words, I would require him to show that there was at the time of the contract some other organized block of stock of sufficient size to outvote the block Essex was buying, or else some circumstance making it likely that enough of the holders of the remaining Republic stock would band together to keep Essex from control.

Reversed and remanded for further proceedings not inconsistent with the judgment of this court.

■ Friendly, Circuit Judge (concurring).

Chief Judge Lumbard's thoughtful opinion illustrates a difficulty, inherent in our dual judicial system, which has led at least one state to authorize its courts to answer questions about its law that a Federal court may ask. Here we are forced to decide a question of New York law, of enormous importance to all New York corporations and their stockholders, on which there is hardly enough New York authority for a really informed prediction what the New York Court of Appeals would decide on the facts here presented, see Cooper v. American Airlines, Inc., 149 F.2d 355, 359, 162 A.L.R. 318 (2 Cir., 1945); Pomerantz v. Clark, 101 F.Supp. 341 (D.Mass.1951); Corbin, The Laws of the Several States, 50 Yale L.J. 762, 775–776 (1941), yet too much for us to have the freedom used to good effect in Perlman v. Feldmann, 219 F.2d 173 (2 Cir.), cert. denied, 349 U.S. 952, 75 S.Ct. 880, 99 L.Ed. 1277 (1955).

I have no doubt that many contracts, drawn by competent and responsible counsel, for the purchase of blocks of stock from interests thought to "control" a corporation although owning less than a majority, have contained provisions like paragraph 6 of the contract *sub judice*. However, developments over the past decades seem to me to show that such a clause violates basic principles of corporate democracy. To be sure, stockholders who have allowed a set of directors to be placed in office, whether by their vote or their failure to vote, must recognize that death, incapacity or other hazard may prevent a director from serving a full term, and that they will have no voice as to his immediate successor. But the stockholders are entitled to expect that, in that event, the remaining directors will fill the vacancy in the exercise of their fiduciary responsibility. A mass seriatim resignation directed by a selling stockholder, and the filling of vacancies by his henchmen at the dictation of a purchaser and without any consideration of the character of the latter's nominees, are beyond what the stockholders contemplated or should have been expected to contemplate. This seems to me a wrong to the corporation and the other stockholders which the law ought not countenance, whether the selling stockholder has received a premium or not. Right in this Court we have seen many cases where sudden shifts of corporate control have caused serious injury; Pettit v. Doeskin Products, Inc., 270 F.2d 95 (2 Cir., 1959), cert. denied, 362 U.S. 910, 80 S.Ct. 660, 4 L.Ed.2d 618 (1960); United States v. Crosby, 294 F.2d 928 (2 Cir., 1961), cert. denied Mittelman v. United States, 368 U.S. 984, 82 S.Ct. 599, 7 L.Ed.2d 523 (1962); and Kirtley v. Abrams, 299 F.2d 341 (2 Cir., 1962), are a few recent examples. To hold the seller for delinquencies of the new directors only if he knew the purchaser was an intending looter is not a sufficient sanction. The difficulties of proof are formidable even if receipt of too high a premium creates a presumption of such knowledge, and, all too often, the doors are locked only after the horses have been stolen. Stronger medicines are needed—refusal to enforce a contract with such a clause, even though this confers an unwarranted benefit on a defaulter, and continuing responsibility of the former directors for negligence of the new ones until an election has been held. Such prophylactics are not contraindicated, as Judge Lumbard suggests, by the conceded desirability of preventing the dead hand of a former "controlling" group from continuing to dominate the board after a sale, or of protecting a would-be purchaser from finding himself without a majority of the board after he has spent his money. A special meeting of stockholders to replace a board may always be called, and there could be no objection to making the closing of a purchase contingent on the results of such an election. I perceive some of the difficulties of mechanics such a procedure presents, but I have enough confidence in the ingenuity of the corporate bar to believe these would be surmounted.

Hence, I am inclined to think that if I were sitting on the New York Court of Appeals, I would hold a provision like [paragraph] 6 violative of public policy save when it was entirely plain that a new election would be a mere formality—i.e., when the seller owned more than 50% of the stock. I put it thus tentatively because, before making such a decision, I would want the help of briefs, including those of *amici curiae,* dealing with the serious problems of corporate policy and practice more fully than did those here, which were primarily devoted to argument as to what the New York law has been rather than what it ought to be. Moreover, in view of the perhaps unexpected character of such a holding, I doubt that I would give it retrospective effect.

As a judge of this Court, my task is the more modest one of predicting how the judges of the New York Court of Appeals would rule, and I must make this prediction on the basis of legal materials rather than of personal acquaintance or hunch. Also, for obvious reasons, the prospective technique is unavailable when a Federal court is deciding an issue of state law. Although Barnes v. Brown, 80 N.Y. 527 (1880), dealt with the sale of a majority interest, I am unable to find any real indication that the doctrine there announced has been thus limited. True, there are New York cases saying that the sale of corporate offices is forbidden; but the New York decisions do not tell us what this means and I can find nothing, save perhaps one unexplained sentence in the opinion of a trial court in Ballantine v. Ferretti, 28 N.Y.S.2d 668, 682 (Sup.Ct.N.Y.Co.1941), to indicate that New York would not apply Barnes v. Brown to a case where a stockholder with much less than a majority conditioned a sale on his causing the resignation of a majority of the directors and the election of the purchaser's nominees.

Chief Judge Lumbard's proposal goes part of the way toward meeting the policy problem I have suggested. Doubtless proceeding from what, as it seems to me, is the only justification in principle for permitting even a majority stockholder to condition a sale on delivery of control of the board—namely that in such a case a vote of the stockholders would be a useless formality, he sets the allowable bounds at the line where there is "a practical certainty" that the buyer would be able to elect his nominees and, in this case, puts the burden of disproving that on the person claiming illegality.

Attractive as the proposal is in some respects, I find difficulties with it. One is that I discern no sufficient intimation of the distinction in the New York cases, or even in the writers, who either would go further in voiding such a clause, see Berle, "Control" in Corporate Law, 58 Colum.L.Rev. 1212, 1224 (1958); Leech, Transactions in Corporate Control, 104 U.Pa.L.Rev. 725, 809 (1956) [proposing legislation], or believe the courts have not yet gone that far, see Baker & Cary, Corporations: Cases and Materials (3d ed. unabr. 1959) 590. To strike down such a condition only in cases falling short of the suggested line accomplishes little to prevent what I consider the evil; in most instances a seller will not enter into a contract conditioned on his "delivering" a majority of the directors unless he has good reason to think he can do that. When an issue does arise, the "practical certainty" test is difficult to apply. The existence of such certainty will depend not merely on the proportion of the stock held by the seller but on many other factors—whether the other stock is widely or closely held, how much of it is in "street names," what success the corporation has experienced, how far its dividend policies have satisfied its stockholders, the identity of the purchasers, the presence or absence of cumulative voting, and many others. Often, unless the seller has nearly 50% of the stock, whether he has "working control" can be determined only by an election; groups who thought they had such control have experienced unpleasant surprises in recent years. Judge Lumbard correctly recognizes that, from a policy standpoint, the pertinent question must be the buyer's prospects of election, not the seller's—yet this inevitably requires the court to canvass the likely reaction of stockholders to a group of whom they know nothing and seems rather hard to reconcile with a position that it is "right" to insert such a condition if a seller has a larger proportion of the stock and "wrong" if he has a smaller. At the very least the problems and uncertainties arising from the proposed line of demarcation are great enough, and its advantages small enough, that in my view a Federal court would do better simply to overrule the defense here, thereby accomplishing what is obviously the "just" result in this particular case, and leave the development of doctrine in this area to the State, which has primary concern for it.

I would reverse the grant of summary judgment and remand for consideration of defenses other than a claim that the inclusion of paragraph 6 *ex mero motu* renders the contract void.

[The concurring opinion of Judge Clark is omitted.]

———

## NOTE ON ESSEX UNIVERSAL CORP. v. YATES

It is not at all clear that 28.3% will necessarily carry control of a publicly held corporation in and of itself, that is, unless coupled with control of the board. Consider Brannigan, Florida Businessman Seeks to Steer Bank Toward Sale, Wall Street Journal, Sept. 2, 1987, at 27, col. 1: "[Hugh F. Culverhouse] has launched a tender offer for 10% of Florida Commercial Banks Inc's shares, ... He already holds ... 39.9% of the bank's shares. Since 1984, Mr. Culverhouse has struggled unsuccessfully to win a seat on the company's board or to acquire control of the concern. As of earlier this year, 28.4% of the company's shares were controlled by a well-entrenched group of officers and directors that has opposed him...."

———

## SECURITIES EXCHANGE ACT RULE 14f–1

[See Statutory Supplement]

———

## ALI, PRINCIPLES OF CORPORATE GOVERNANCE § 5.16

[See Statutory Supplement]

# CHAPTER X

# INSIDER TRADING

## SECTION 1. THE COMMON LAW BACKGROUND

### Goodwin v. Agassiz

Massachusetts Supreme Judicial Court, 1933.
283 Mass. 358, 186 N.E. 659.

BILL IN EQUITY, filed in the Supreme Judicial Court for the county of Suffolk on September 17, 1928, described in the opinion....

RUGG, C.J. A stockholder in a corporation seeks in this suit relief for losses suffered by him in selling shares of stock in Cliff Mining Company by way of accounting, rescission of sales, or redelivery of shares. The named defendants are MacNaughton, a resident of Michigan not served or appearing, and Agassiz, a resident of this Commonwealth, the active party defendant.

The trial judge made findings of fact, rulings, and an order dismissing the bill. There is no report of the evidence. The case must be considered on the footing that the findings are true. The facts thus displayed are these: The defendants, in May, 1926, purchased through brokers on the Boston stock exchange seven hundred shares of stock of the Cliff Mining Company which up to that time the plaintiff had owned. Agassiz was president and director and MacNaughton a director and general manager of the company. They had certain knowledge, material as to the value of the stock, which the plaintiff did not have. The plaintiff contends that such purchase in all the circumstances without disclosure to him of that knowledge was a wrong against him. That knowledge was that an experienced geologist had formulated in writing in March, 1926, a theory as to the possible existence of copper deposits under conditions prevailing in the region where the property of the company was located. That region was known as the mineral belt in northern Michigan, where are located mines of several copper mining companies. Another such company, of which the defendants were officers, had made extensive geological surveys of its lands. In consequence of recommendations resulting from that survey, exploration was started on property of the Cliff Mining Company in 1925. That exploration was ended in May, 1926, because completed unsuccessfully, and the equipment was removed. The defendants discussed the geologist's theory shortly after it was formulated. Both felt that the theory had value and should be tested, but they agreed that, before starting to test it, options should be obtained by another copper company of which they were officers on land adjacent to or nearby in the copper belt, that if the geologist's theory were known to the owners of such other land there might be difficulty in securing options, and that that theory should not be communicated to any one unless it became absolutely necessary. Thereafter, options were secured which, if taken up, would involve a large expenditure by the other company. The defendants both thought, also, that, if there was any merit in the geologist's theory, the price of Cliff Mining Company stock in the market would go up. Its stock was quoted and bought and sold on the Boston stock exchange. Pursuant to agreement, they bought many shares of that stock through agents on joint account. The plaintiff first learned of the closing of exploratory operations on property of the Cliff Mining Company from an article in a paper on May 15, 1926, and immediately sold his shares of stock through brokers. It does not appear that the defendants were in any way responsible for the publication of that article. The plaintiff did not know that the purchase was made for the defendants and they did not know that his stock was being bought for them. There was no communication between them touching the subject. The plaintiff would not have sold his stock if he had known of the geologist's theory. The finding is express that the defendants were not guilty of fraud, that they committed no breach of duty owed by them to the Cliff Mining Company, and that that company was not harmed by the nondisclosure of the geologist's theory, or by their purchases of its stock, or by shutting down the exploratory operations.

The contention of the plaintiff is that the purchase of his stock in the company by the defendants without disclosing to him as a stockholder their knowledge of the geologist's theory, their belief that the theory had value, the keeping secret the existence of the theory, discontinuance by the defendants of exploratory operations begun in 1925 on property of the Cliff Mining Company and their plan ultimately to test the value of the theory, constitute actionable wrong for which he as stockholder can recover.

The trial judge ruled that conditions may exist which would make it the duty of an officer of a corporation purchasing its stock from a stockholder to inform him as to knowledge possessed by the buyer and not by the seller, but found, on all the circumstances developed by the trial and set out at some length by him in his decision, that there was no fiduciary relation requiring such disclosure by the defendants to the plaintiff before buying his stock in the manner in which they did.

The question presented is whether the decree dismissing the bill rightly was entered on the facts found.

The directors of a commercial corporation stand in a relation of trust to the corporation and are bound to exercise the strictest good faith in respect to its property and business. *Elliott v. Baker,* 194 Mass. 518, 523. *Beaudette v. Graham,* 267 Mass. 7. *L.E. Fosgate Co. v. Boston Market Terminal Co.,* 275 Mass. 99, 107. The contention that directors also occupy the position of trustee toward individual stockholders in the corporation is plainly contrary to repeated decisions of this court and cannot be supported. In *Smith v. Hurd,* 12 Met. 371, 384, it was said by Chief Justice Shaw: "There is no legal privity, relation, or immediate connection, between the holders of shares in a bank, in their individual capacity, on the one side, and the directors of the bank on the other. The directors are not the bailees, the factors, agents or trustees of such individual stockholders." In *Stewart v. Joyce,* 201 Mass. 301, 311, 312, and *Lee v. Fisk,* 222 Mass. 424, 426, the same principle was reiterated. In *Blabon v. Hay,* 269 Mass. 401, 407, occurs this language with reference to sale of stock in a corporation by a stockholder to two of its directors: "The fact that the defendants were directors created no fiduciary relation between them and the plaintiff in the matter of the sale of his stock."

The principle thus established is supported by an imposing weight of authority in other jurisdictions. *Steinfeld v. Nielsen,* 15 Ariz. 424. *Bawden v. Taylor,* 254 Ill. 464. *Tippecanoe County Commissioners v. Reynolds,* 44 Ind. 509. *Waller v. Hodge,* 214 Ky. 705. *Buckley v. Buckley,* 230 Mich. 504. *Dutton v. Barnes,* 162 Minn. 430. *Crowell v. Jackson,* 24 Vroom, 656. *Carpenter v. Danforth,* 52 Barb.S.C. 581. *Shaw v. Cole Mfg. Co.,* 132 Tenn. 210. *White v. Texas Co.,* 59 Utah, 180, 188. *Percival v. Wright,* [1902] 2 Ch.D. 421. *Tackey v. McBain,* [1912] A.C. 186. A rule holding that directors are trustees for individual stockholders with respect to their stock prevails in comparatively few States; but in view of our own adjudications it is not necessary to review decisions to that effect. See, for example, *Oliver v. Oliver,* 118 Ga. 362; *Dawson v. National Life Ins. Co. of United States,* 176 Iowa, 362; *Stewart v. Harris,* 69 Kans. 498. See, also, for collection of authorities, 14A C.J. § 1896; 27 Yale L.J. 731; 32 Yale L.J. 637.

While the general principle is as stated, circumstances may exist requiring that transactions between a director and a stockholder as to stock in the corporation be set aside. The knowledge naturally in the possession of a director as to the condition of a corporation places upon him a peculiar obligation to observe every requirement of fair dealing when directly buying or selling its stock. Mere silence does not usually amount to a breach of duty, but parties may stand in such relation to each other that an equitable responsibility arises to communicate facts. *Wellington v. Rugg,* 243 Mass. 30, 35. Purchases and sales of stock dealt in on the stock exchange are commonly impersonal affairs. An honest director would be in a difficult situation if he could neither buy nor sell on the stock exchange shares of stock in his corporation without first seeking out the other actual ultimate party to the transaction and disclosing to him everything which a court or jury might later find that he then knew affecting the real or speculative value of such shares. Business of that nature is a matter to be governed by practical rules. Fiduciary obligations of directors ought not to be made so onerous that men of experience and ability will be deterred from accepting such office. Law in its sanctions is not coextensive with morality. It cannot undertake to put all parties to every contract on an equality as to knowledge, experience, skill and shrewdness. It cannot undertake to relieve against hard bargains made between competent parties without fraud. On the other hand, directors cannot rightly be allowed to indulge with impunity in practices which do violence to prevailing standards of upright business men. Therefore, where a director personally seeks a stockholder for the purpose of buying his shares without making disclosure of material facts within his peculiar knowledge and not within reach of the stockholder, the transaction will be closely scrutinized and relief may be granted in appropriate instances. *Strong v. Repide,* 213 U.S. 419. *Allen v. Hyatt,* 30 T.L.R. 444. *Gammon v. Dain,* 238 Mich. 30. *George v. Ford,* 36 App.D.C. 315. See, also, *Old Dominion Copper Mining & Smelting Co. v. Bigelow,* 203 Mass. 159, 194–195. The applicable legal principles "have almost always been the fundamental ethical rules of right and wrong." *Robinson v. Mollett,* L.R. 7 H.L. 802, 817.

The precise question to be decided in the case at bar is whether on the facts found the defendants as directors had a right to buy stock of the plaintiff, a stockholder. Every element of actual fraud or misdoing by the defendants is negatived by the findings. Fraud cannot be presumed; it must be proved. *Brown v. Little, Brown & Co. (Inc.),* 269 Mass. 102, 117. The facts found afford no ground for inferring fraud or conspiracy. The only knowledge possessed by the defendants not open to the plaintiff was the existence of a theory formulated in a thesis by a geologist as to the possible existence of copper deposits where certain geological conditions existed common to the property of the Cliff Mining Company and that of other mining companies in its neighborhood. This thesis did not express an opinion that copper deposits would be found at any particular spot or on property of any specified owner. Whether that theory was sound or fallacious, no one knew, and so far as appears has never been demonstrated. The defendants made no representations to anybody about the theory. No facts found placed upon them any obligation to disclose the theory. A few days after the thesis expounding the theory was brought to the attention of the defendants, the annual report by the directors of the Cliff Mining Company for the calendar year 1925, signed by Agassiz for the directors, was issued. It did not cover the time when the theory was formulated. The report described the status of the operations under the exploration which had been begun in 1925. At the annual meeting of the stockholders of the company held early in April, 1926, no reference was made to the theory. It was then at most a hope, possibly an expectation. It had not passed the nebulous stage. No disclosure was made of it. The Cliff Mining Company was not harmed by the nondisclosure. There would have been no advantage to it, so far as appears, from a disclosure. The disclosure would have been detrimental to the interests of another mining corporation in which the defendants were directors. In the circumstances there was no duty on the part of the defendants to set forth to the stockholders at the annual meeting their faith, aspirations and plans for the future. Events as they developed might render advisable radical changes in such views. Disclosure of the theory, if it ultimately was proved to be erroneous or without foundation in fact, might involve the defendants in litigation with those who might act on the hypothesis that it was correct. The stock of the Cliff Mining Company was bought and sold on the stock exchange. The identity of buyers and seller of the stock in question in fact was not known to the parties and perhaps could not readily have been ascertained. The defendants caused the shares to be bought through brokers on the stock exchange. They said nothing to anybody as to the reasons actuating them. The plaintiff was no novice. He was a member of the Boston stock exchange and had kept a record of sales of Cliff Mining Company stock. He acted upon his own judgment in selling his stock. He made no inquiries of the defendants or of other officers of the company. The result is that the plaintiff cannot prevail.

*Decree dismissing bill affirmed with costs.*

---

### NOTE ON THE DUTIES OF DIRECTORS AND OFFICERS UNDER THE COMMON LAW WHEN TRADING IN THEIR CORPORATION'S STOCK

1. *Majority Rule.* The rule adopted in *Goodwin v. Agassiz* was the majority rule under the common law. Although the transactions in *Goodwin v. Agassiz* occurred in an impersonal market, there are cases in which the rule was applied to face-to-face transactions. See, e.g., Lank v. Steiner, 43 Del.Ch. 262, 224 A.2d 242 (1966); Gladstone v. Murray Co., 314 Mass. 584, 50 N.E.2d 958 (1943). However, there was a minority rule, sometimes known as the Kansas rule, which required full disclosure by a director or officer, at least in face-to-face transactions.

2. *"Special Facts."* Perhaps the most important exception to the majority rule was the "special facts" exception, adopted in Strong v. Repide, 213 U.S. 419, 29 S.Ct. 521, 53 L.Ed. 853 (1909) and later in many other cases. Repide was a director, the administrator general, and owner of nearly three-fourths of the shares of Philippine Sugar. Strong, who owned shares in Philippine Sugar, had given Jones a power of attorney to sell her shares. Philippine Sugar owned certain lands in the Philippines that the United States government wished to buy. The corporation was without funds, and the value of its shares was wholly dependent on making an advantageous sale of its properties to the government. Repide was in charge of the negotiations with the government, which dragged on for months, primarily because Repide was holding out for a higher price. While negotiations with the government were pending, Repide, knowing that a sale to the government was probable, used an intermediary to employ a broker to purchase Strong's shares from Jones. Jones was given no information as to the state of the negotiations with the government, and neither Strong nor Jones knew that Repide was the purchaser. The price paid to Strong was about one-tenth what the shares became worth less than three months later, when the sale of the corporation's property to the government was consummated.

The Supreme Court affirmed an award of damages to Strong, on the ground that even if a director has no general duty to disclose facts known to him before he purchases shares, "there are cases where, by reason of the special facts, such duty exists." Id. at 431, 29 S.Ct. at 525. Jones sold Strong's shares because the corporation was paying no dividends and the negotiations with the government had gone on for so long that he thought that there was no prospect that a sale of the corporation's property would be made in the near term. Repide was not only a director but, by reason of his ownership of three-fourths of the shares, his position as administrator general, and the acquiescence of the other shareholders, was in full charge of the negotiations and was able to come to an agreement with the government if and when he chose to do so. He concealed his identity as a purchaser and dealt in a roundabout fashion with Jones. In view of all these facts, "the law would indeed be impotent if the sale could not be set aside or [Repide] cast in damages for his fraud." Id. at 433, 29 S.Ct. at 526.

Since there was no meaningful way to differentiate those cases that involved "special facts" from those that didn't, the special-facts exception either ate up the majority rule or made the rule impossible to administer in a consistent fashion. At bottom, the exception was inconsistent with the majority rule, and was employed by the courts as a mechanism to escape from that rule while purporting to follow it.

3. *Atrophy.* The common law rule concerning disclosure in the sale of securities atrophied after the 1940's, due to the development of Rule 10b–5 under the Securities Exchange Act, which came to occupy most of the field. It is conceivable that if Rule 10b–5 had not been adopted, and the common law concerning the obligations of directors and officers in the purchase and sale of stock had continued to develop, the majority rule would have withered, because in the last fifty years the common law has evolved in the direction of requiring greater disclosure. For example, Restatement (Second) of Contracts § 161 (1979) provides that a "person's nondisclosure of a fact known to him is equivalent to an assertion that the fact does not exist . . . where the other person is entitled to know the fact because of a relation of trust and confidence between them."

# SECTION 2.  SECURITIES EXCHANGE ACT § 10(b) AND RULE 10b–5

---

## SECURITIES EXCHANGE ACT § 10(b)

[See Statutory Supplement]

---

## SECURITIES EXCHANGE ACT RULE 10b–5

[See Statutory Supplement]

———

**IN THE MATTER OF CADY, ROBERTS & CO.,** 40 S.E.C. 907, 911–12 (1961). "[Rule 10b–5 applies] to securities transactions by 'any person.' Misrepresentations will lie within [its] ambit, no matter who the speaker may be. An affirmative duty to disclose material information has been traditionally imposed on corporate 'insiders,' particularly officers, directors, or controlling stockholders. We, and the courts have consistently held that insiders must disclose material facts which are known to them by virtue of their position but which are not known to persons with whom they deal and which, if known, would affect their investment judgment. Failure to make disclosure in these circumstances constitutes a violation of the anti-fraud provisions. If, on the other hand, disclosure prior to effecting a purchase or sale would be improper or unrealistic under the circumstances, we believe the alternative is to forego the transaction. . . .

"We have already noted that the anti-fraud provisions are phrased in terms of 'any person' and that a special obligation has been traditionally required of corporate insiders, e.g., officers, directors and controlling stockholders. These three groups, however, do not exhaust the classes of persons upon whom there is such an obligation. Analytically, the obligation rests on two principal elements; first, the existence of a relationship giving access, directly or indirectly, to information intended to be available only for a corporate purpose and not for the personal benefit of anyone, and second, the inherent unfairness involved where a party takes advantage of such information knowing it is unavailable to those with whom he is dealing. In considering these elements under the broad language of the anti-fraud provisions we are not to be circumscribed by fine distinctions and rigid classifications. Thus our task here is to identify those persons who are in a special relationship with a company and privy to its internal affairs, and thereby suffer correlative duties in trading in its securities. Intimacy demands restraint lest the uninformed be exploited."

———

## Securities and Exchange Commission v. Texas Gulf Sulphur Co.

United States Court of Appeals, Second Circuit, 1968.
401 F.2d 833 (in banc), cert. denied 394 U.S. 976, 89 S.Ct. 1454, 22 L.Ed.2d 756 (1969).

■ WATERMAN, CIRCUIT JUDGE:

[This was an action brought by the S.E.C. against Texas Gulf Sulphur (TGS) based on the issuance of a misleading press release, and against certain officers and employees of TGS based on their trading and tipping. The case grew out of an important mineral discovery by TGS. Four of the individual defendants were members of the geological exploration group that made the discovery: Mollison, a vice-president and mining engineer who headed the exploration group; Holyk, TGS' chief geologist; Clayton, an electrical engineer and geophysicist, and Darke, a geologist. The other individual defendants included Stephens, who was TGS's President; Fogarty, its Executive Vice–President; Kline, its Vice–President and General Counsel; and Coates, a director.

[Those portions of the opinion dealing with the liability of TGS for the misleading press release and the liability of individual defendants for tipping have been omitted, because the discussion of those issues has been largely superseded by later Supreme Court cases, set out below.]

This action derives from the exploratory activities of TGS begun in 1957 on the Canadian Shield in eastern Canada. In March of 1959, aerial geophysical surveys were conducted over more than 15,000 square miles of this area by a group led by defendant Mollison, a mining engineer and a Vice President of TGS. The group included defendant Holyk, TGS's chief geologist, defendant Clayton, an electrical engineer and geophysicist, and defendant Darke, a geologist. These operations resulted in the detection of numerous anomalies, i.e., extraordinary variations in the conductivity of rocks, one of which was on the Kidd 55 segment of land located near Timmins, Ontario.

On October 29 and 30, 1963, Clayton conducted a ground geophysical survey on the northeast portion of the Kidd 55 segment which confirmed the presence of an anomaly and indicated the necessity of diamond core drilling for further evaluation. Drilling of the initial hole, K–55–1, at the strongest part of the anomaly was commenced on November 8 and terminated on November 12 at a depth of 655 feet. Visual estimates by Holyk of the core of K–55–1 indicated an average copper content of 1.15% and an average zinc content of 8.64% over a length of 599 feet. This visual estimate convinced TGS that it was desirable to acquire the remainder of the Kidd 55 segment, and in order to facilitate this acquisition TGS President Stephens instructed the exploration group to keep the results of K–55–1 confidential and undisclosed even as to other officers, directors, and employees of TGS. The hole was concealed and a barren core was intentionally drilled off the anomaly. Meanwhile, the core of K–55–1 had been shipped to Utah for chemical assay which, when received in early December, revealed an average mineral content of 1.18% copper, 8.26% zinc, and 3.94% ounces of silver per ton over a length of 602 feet. These results were so remarkable that neither Clayton, an experienced geophysicist, nor four other TGS expert witnesses, had ever seen or heard of a comparable initial exploratory drill hole in a base metal deposit. So, the trial court concluded, "There is no doubt that the drill core of K–55–1 was unusually good and that it excited the interest and speculation of those who knew about it." Id. at 282. By March 27, 1964, TGS decided that the land acquisition program had advanced to such a point that the company might well resume drilling, and drilling was resumed on March 31.

During this period, from November 12, 1963 when K–55–1 was completed, to March 31, 1964 when drilling was resumed certain of the individual defendants ... and persons ... said to have received "tips" from them, purchased TGS stock or calls thereon. Prior to these transactions these persons had owned 1135 shares of TGS stock and possessed no calls; thereafter they owned a total of 8235 shares and possessed 12,300 calls.

On February 20, 1964, also during this period, TGS issued stock options to 26 of its officers and employees whose salaries exceeded a specified amount, five of whom were the individual defendants Stephens, Fogarty, Mollison, Holyk, and Kline. Of these, only Kline was unaware of the detailed results of K–55–1, but he, too, knew that a hole containing favorable bodies of copper and zinc ore had been drilled in Timmins. At this time, neither the TGS Stock Option Committee nor its Board of Directors had been informed of the results of K–55–1, presumably because of the pending land acquisition program which required confidentiality. All of the foregoing defendants accepted the options granted them.

When drilling was resumed on March 31, hole K–55–3 was commenced 510 feet west of K–55–1 and was drilled easterly at a 45° angle so as to cross K–55–1 in a vertical plane. Daily progress reports of the drilling of this hole K–55–3 and of all subsequently drilled holes were sent to defendants Stephens and Fogarty (President and Executive Vice President of TGS) by Holyk and Mollison. Visual estimates of K–55–3 revealed an average mineral content of 1.12% copper and 7.93% zinc over 641 of the hole's 876–foot length. On April 7, drilling of a third hole, K–55–4, 200 feet south of and parallel to K–55–1 and westerly at a 45° angle, was commenced and mineralization was encountered over 366 of its 579–foot length. Visual estimates indicated an average content of 1.14% copper and 8.24% zinc. Like K–55–1, both K–55–3 and K–55–4 established substantial copper mineralization on the eastern edge of the anomaly. On the basis of these findings relative to the foregoing drilling results, the trial court concluded that the vertical plane created by the intersection of K–55–1 and K–55–3, which measured at least 350 feet wide by 500 feet deep extended southward 200 feet to its intersection with K–55–4, and that "There was real evidence that a body of commercially mineable ore might exist." Id. at 281–82.

On April 8 TGS began with a second drill rig to drill another hole, K–55–6, 300 feet easterly of K–55–1. This hole was drilled westerly at an angle of 60° and was intended to explore mineralization beneath K–55–1. While no visual estimates of its core were immediately available, it was readily apparent by the evening of April 10 that substantial copper mineralization had been encountered over the last 127 feet of the hole's 569–foot length. On April 10, a third drill rig commenced drilling yet another hole, K–55–5, 200 feet north of K–55–1, parallel to the prior holes, and slanted westerly at a 45° angle. By the evening of

April 10 in this hole, too, substantial copper mineralization had been encountered over the last 42 feet of its 97–foot length.

Meanwhile, rumors that a major ore strike was in the making had been circulating throughout Canada. On the morning of Saturday, April 11, Stephens at his home in Greenwich, Conn. read in the New York Herald Tribune and in the New York Times unauthorized reports of the TGS drilling which seemed to infer a rich strike from the fact that the drill cores had been flown to the United States for chemical assay. Stephens immediately contacted Fogarty at his home in Rye, N.Y., who in turn telephoned and later that day visited Mollison at Mollison's home in Greenwich to obtain a current report and evaluation of the drilling progress.[7] The following morning, Sunday, Fogarty again telephoned Mollison, inquiring whether Mollison had any further information and told him to return to Timmins with Holyk, the TGS Chief Geologist, as soon as possible "to move things along." With the aid of one Carroll, a public relations consultant, Fogarty drafted a press release designed to quell the rumors, which release, after having been channeled through Stephens and Huntington, a TGS attorney, was issued at 3:00 P.M. on Sunday, April 12, and which appeared in the morning newspapers of general circulation on Monday, April 13. It read in pertinent part as follows:

New York, April 12—The following statement was made today by Dr. Charles F. Fogarty, executive vice president of Texas Gulf Sulphur Company, in regard to the company's drilling operations near Timmins, Ontario, Canada. Dr. Fogarty said:

"During the past few days, the exploration activities of Texas Gulf Sulphur in the area of Timmins, Ontario, have been widely reported in the press, coupled with rumors of a substantial copper discovery there. These reports exaggerate the scale of operations, and mention plans and statistics of size and grade of ore that are without factual basis and have evidently originated by speculation of people not connected with TGS.

"The facts are as follows. TGS has been exploring in the Timmins area for six years as part of its overall search in Canada and elsewhere for various minerals—lead, copper, zinc, etc. During the course of this work, in Timmins as well as in Eastern Canada, TGS has conducted exploration entirely on its own, without the participation by others. Numerous prospects have been investigated by geophysical means and a large number of selected ones have been core-drilled. These cores are sent to the United States for assay and detailed examination as a matter of routine and on advice of expert Canadian legal counsel. No inferences as to grade can be drawn from this procedure.

---

**7.** Mollison had returned to the United States for the weekend. Friday morning April 10, he had been on the Kidd tract "and had been advised by defendant Holyk as to the drilling results to 7:00 p.m. on April 10. At that time drill holes K–55–1, K–55–3 and K–55–4 had been completed; drilling of K–55–5 had started on Section 2200 S and had been drilled to 97 feet, encountering mineralization on the last 42 feet; and drilling of K–55–6 had been started on Section 2400 S and had been drilled to 569 feet, encountering mineralization over the last 127 feet." Id. at 294.

"Most of the areas drilled in Eastern Canada have revealed either barren pyrite or graphite without value; a few have resulted in discoveries of small or marginal sulphide ore bodies.

"Recent drilling on one property near Timmins has led to preliminary indications that more drilling would be required for proper evaluation of this prospect. The drilling done to date has not been conclusive, but the statements made by many outside quarters are unreliable and include information and figures that are not available to TGS.

"The work done to date has not been sufficient to reach definite conclusions and any statement as to size and grade of ore would be premature and possibly misleading. When we have progressed to the point where reasonable and logical conclusions can be made, TGS will issue a definite statement to its stockholders and to the public in order to clarify the Timmins project."

* * *

The release purported to give the Timmins drilling results as of the release date, April 12. From Mollison Fogarty had been told of the developments through 7:00 P.M. on April 10, and of the remarkable discoveries made up to that time, detailed supra, which discoveries, according to the calculations of the experts who testified for the SEC at the hearing, demonstrated that TGS had already discovered 6.2 to 8.3 million tons of proven ore having gross assay values from $26 to $29 per ton. TGS experts, on the other hand, denied at the hearing that proven or probable ore could have been calculated on April 11 or 12 because there was then no assurance of continuity in the mineralized zone.

The evidence as to the effect of this release on the investing public was equivocal and less than abundant. On April 13 the New York Herald Tribune in an article head-noted "Copper Rumor Deflated" quoted from the TGS release of April 12 and backtracked from its original April 11 report of a major strike but nevertheless inferred from the TGS release that "recent mineral exploratory activity near Timmins, Ontario, has provided preliminary favorable results, sufficient at least to require a step-up in drilling operations." Some witnesses who testified at the hearing stated that they found the release encouraging. On the other hand, a Canadian mining security specialist, Roche, stated that "earlier in the week [before April 16] we had a Dow Jones saying that they [TGS] didn't have anything basically" and a TGS stock specialist for the Midwest Stock Exchange became concerned about his long position in the stock after reading the release. The trial court stated only that "While, in retrospect, the press release may appear gloomy or incomplete, this does not make it misleading or deceptive on the basis of the facts then known." Id. at 296.

Meanwhile, drilling operations continued. . . .

While drilling activity ensued to completion, TGS officials were taking steps toward ultimate disclosure of the discovery. On April 13, a previously-invited reporter for The Northern Miner, a Canadian mining industry journal, visited the drillsite, interviewed Mollison, Holyk and Darke, and prepared an article which confirmed a 10 million ton ore strike. This report, after having been submitted to Mollison and returned to the reported unamended on April 15, was published in the April 16 issue. A statement relative to the extent of the discovery, in substantial part drafted by Mollison, was given to the Ontario Minister of Mines for release to the Canadian media. Mollison and Holyk expected it to be released over the airways at 11 P.M. on April 15th, but, for undisclosed reasons, it was not released until 9:40 A.M. on the 16th. An official detailed statement, announcing a strike of at least 25 million tons of ore, based on the drilling data set forth above, was read to representatives of American financial media from 10:00 A.M. to 10:10 or 10:15 A.M. on April 16, and appeared over Merrill Lynch's private wire at 10:29 A.M. and, somewhat later than expected, over the Dow Jones ticker tape at 10:54 A.M.

Between the time the first press release was issued on April 12 and the dissemination of the TGS official announcement on the morning of April 16, the only defendants before us on appeal who engaged in market activity were Clayton and Crawford and TGS director Coates. Clayton ordered 200 shares of TGS stock through his Canadian broker on April 15 and another 300 shares at 8:30 A.M. the next day, and these orders were executed over the Midwest Exchange in Chicago at its opening on April 16. Coates left the TGS press conference and called his broker son-in-law Haemisegger shortly before 10:20 A.M. on the 16th and ordered 2,000 shares of TGS for family trust accounts of which Coates was a trustee but not a beneficiary; Haemisegger executed this order over the New York and Midwest Exchanges, and he and his customers purchased 1500 additional shares.

During the period of drilling in Timmins, the market price of TGS stock fluctuated but steadily gained overall. On Friday, November 8, when the drilling began, the stock closed at $17\frac{3}{8}$; on Friday, November 15, after K–55–1 had been completed, it closed at 18. After a slight decline to $16\frac{3}{8}$ by Friday, November 22, the price rose to $20\frac{7}{8}$ by December 13, when the chemical assay results of K–55–1 were received, and closed at a high of $24\frac{1}{8}$ on February 21, the day after the stock options had been issued. It had reached a price of 26 by March 31, after the land acquisition program had been completed and drilling had been resumed, and continued to ascend to $30\frac{1}{8}$ by the close of trading on April 10, at which time the drilling progress up to then was evaluated for the April 12th press release. On April 13, the day on which the April 12 release was disseminated, TGS opened at $30\frac{1}{8}$, rose immediately to a high of 32 and gradually tapered off to close at $30\frac{7}{8}$. It closed at $30\frac{1}{4}$ the next day, and at $29\frac{3}{8}$ on April 15. On April 16, the day of the official announcement of the Timmins discovery, the price climbed to a high of 37 and closed at 36⅜. By May 15, TGS stock was selling at 58¼. . . .*

## I. The Individual Defendants

### A. *Introductory*

. . . Whether predicated on traditional fiduciary concepts, see, e.g., Hotchkiss v. Fischer, 136 Kan. 530, 16 P.2d 531 (Kan.1932), or on the "special facts" doctrine, see, e.g., Strong v. Repide, 213 U.S. 419, 29 S.Ct. 521, 53 L.Ed. 853 (1909), . . . Rule [10b–5] is based in policy on the justifiable expectation of the securities marketplace that all

* The purchases by the parties during this period were:

| Purchase Date | Purchaser | Shares Number | Shares Price | Calls Number | Calls Price |
|---|---|---|---|---|---|
| Hole K–55–1 Completed November 12, 1963 | | | | | |
| 1963 | | | | | |
| Nov. 12 | Fogarty | 300 | 17¾–18 | | |
| 15 | Clayton | 200 | 17¾ | | |
| 15 | Fogarty | 700 | 17⅝–17⅞ | | |
| 15 | Mollison | 100 | 17⅞ | | |
| 19 | Fogarty | 500 | 18⅛ | | |
| 26 | Fogarty | 200 | 17¾ | | |
| 29 | Holyk (Mrs.) | 50 | 18 | | |
| Chemical Assays of Drill Core of K–55–1 Received December 9–13, 1963 | | | | | |
| Dec. 10 | Holyk (Mrs.) | 100 | 20⅜ | | |
| 12 | Holyk (or wife) | | | 200 | 21 |
| 13 | Mollison | 100 | 21⅛ | | |
| 30 | Fogarty | 200 | 22 | | |
| 31 | Fogarty | 100 | 23¼ | | |
| 1964 | | | | | |
| Jan. 6 | Holyk (or wife) | | | 100 | 23⅝ |
| 8 | Murray | | | 400 | 23¼ |
| 24 | Holyk (or wife) | | | 200 | 22¼–22⅜ |
| Feb. 10 | Fogarty | 300 | 22⅛–22¼ | | |
| 20 | Darke | 300 | 24⅛ | | |
| 24 | Clayton | 400 | 23⅞ | | |
| 24 | Holyk (or wife) | | | 200 | 24⅛ |
| 26 | Holyk (or wife) | | | 200 | 23⅜ |
| 26 | Huntington | 50 | 23¼ | | |
| 27 | Darke (Moran as nominee) | | | 1000 | 22⅝–22¾ |
| Mar. 2 | Holyk (Mrs.) | 200 | 22⅜ | | |
| 3 | Clayton | 100 | 22¼ | | |
| 16 | Huntington | | | 100 | 22⅜ |
| 16 | Holyk (or wife) | | | 300 | 23¼ |
| 17 | Holyk (Mrs.) | 100 | 23⅞ | | |
| 23 | Darke | | | 1000 | 24¾ |
| 26 | Clayton | 200 | 25 | | |
| Land Acquisition Completed March 27, 1964 | | | | | |
| Mar. 30 | Darke | | | 100 | 25½ |
| 30 | Holyk (Mrs.) | 100 | 25⅞ | | |
| Core Drilling of Kidd Segment Resumed March 31, 1964 | | | | | |
| April 1 | Clayton | 60 | 26½ | | |
| 1 | Fogarty | 400 | 26½ | | |
| 2 | Clayton | 100 | 26⅞ | | |
| 6 | Fogarty | 400 | 28⅛–28⅞ | | |
| 8 | Mollison (Mrs.) | 100 | 28⅛ | | |
| First Press Release Issued April 12, 1964 | | | | | |
| April 15 | Clayton | 200 | 29⅜ | | |
| 16 | Crawford (and wife) | 600 | 30⅛–30¼ | | |
| Second Press Release Issued 10:00–10:10 or 10:15 A.M., April 16, 1964 . . . | | | | | |
| 1963 | | | | | |
| April 16 | (app. 10:20 A.M.) | | | | |
| | Coates (for family trusts) | 2000 | 31–31⅝ | | |

[Footnote by the court; relocated by the editor.]

investors trading on impersonal exchanges have relatively equal access to material information, see Cary, Insider Trading in Stocks, 21 Bus. Law. 1009, 1010 (1966), Fleischer, Securities Trading and Corporation Information Practices: The Implications of the Texas Gulf Sulphur Proceeding, 51 Va.L.Rev. 1271, 1278–80 (1965). The essence of the Rule is that anyone who, trading for his own account in the securities of a corporation has "access, directly or indirectly, to information intended to be available only for a corporate purpose and not for the personal benefit of anyone" may not take "advantage of such information knowing it is unavailable to those with whom he is dealing," i.e., the investing public. Matter of Cady, Roberts & Co., 40 SEC 907, 912 (1961). Insiders, as directors or management officers are, of course, by this Rule, precluded from so unfairly dealing, but the Rule is also applicable to one possessing the information who may not be strictly termed an "insider" within the meaning of Sec. 16(b) of the Act. Cady, Roberts, supra. Thus, anyone in possession of material inside information must either disclose it to the investing public, or, if he is disabled from disclosing it in order to protect a corporate confidence, or he chooses not to do so, must abstain from trading in or recommending the securities concerned while such inside information remains undisclosed. So, it is here no justification for insider activity that disclosure was forbidden by the legitimate corporate objective of acquiring options to purchase the land surrounding the exploration site; if the information was, as the SEC contends, material, its possessors should have kept out of the market until disclosure was accomplished. Cady, Roberts, supra at 911.

## B.   *Material Inside Information*

An insider is not, of course, always foreclosed from investing in his own company merely because he may be more familiar with company operations than are outside investors. An insider's duty to disclose information or his duty to abstain from dealing in his company's securities arises only in "those situations which are essentially extraordinary in nature and which are reasonably certain to have a substantial effect on the market price of the security if [the extraordinary situation is] disclosed." Fleischer, Securities Trading and Corporate Information Practices: The Implications of the Texas Gulf Sulphur Proceeding, 51 Va.L.Rev. 1271, 1289.

Nor is an insider obligated to confer upon outside investors the benefit of his superior financial or other expert analysis by disclosing his educated guesses or predictions. 3 Loss, op. cit. supra at 1463. The only regulatory objective is that access to material information be enjoyed equally, but this objective requires nothing more than the disclosure of basic facts so that outsiders may draw upon their own evaluative expertise in reaching their own investment decisions with knowledge equal to that of the insiders.

This is not to suggest, however, as did the trial court, that "the test of materiality must necessarily be a conservative one, particularly since many actions under Section 10(b) are brought on the basis of hindsight," 258 F.Supp. 262 at 280, in the sense that the materiality of facts is to be assessed solely by measuring the effect the knowledge of the facts would have upon prudent or conservative investors. As we stated in List v. Fashion Park, Inc., 340 F.2d 457, 462, "The basic test of materiality ... is whether a *reasonable* man would attach importance ... in determining his choice of action in the transaction in question. Restatement, Torts § 538(2)(a); accord Prosser, Torts 554–55; I Harper & James, Torts 565–66." (Emphasis supplied.) ... [M]aterial facts include not only information disclosing the earnings and distributions of a company but also those facts which affect the probable future of the company and those which may affect the desire of investors to buy, sell, or hold the company's securities.

In each case, then, whether facts are material within Rule 10b–5 when the facts relate to a particular event and are undisclosed by those persons who are knowledgeable thereof will depend at any given time upon a balancing of both the indicated probability that the event will occur and the anticipated magnitude of the event in light of the totality of the company activity. Here, notwithstanding the trial court's conclusion that the results of the first drill core, K–55–1, were "too 'remote' ... to have had any significant impact on the market, i.e., to be deemed material," 258 F.Supp. at 283, knowledge of the possibility, which surely was more than marginal, of the existence of a mine of the vast magnitude indicated by the remarkably rich drill core located rather close to the surface (suggesting mineability by the less expensive open pit method) within the confines of a large anomaly (suggesting an extensive region of mineralization) might well have affected the price of TGS stock and would certainly have been an important fact to a reasonable, if speculative, investor in deciding whether he should buy, sell, or hold. After all, this first drill core was "unusually good and ... excited the interest and speculation of those who knew about it." 258 F.Supp. at 282.

... Our survey of the facts found below conclusively establishes that knowledge of the results of the discovery hole, K–55–1, would have been important to a reasonable investor and might have affected the price of the stock.[2] On April 16, The Northern Miner, a trade publication in wide circulation among mining stock specialists, called K–55–1, the discovery hole, "one of the most impressive drill holes completed in modern times." Roche, a Canadian broker whose firm specialized in mining securities, characterized the importance to investors of the results of K–55–1. He stated that the completion of "the first drill hole" with "a 600 foot drill core is very very significant ... anything over 200 feet is considered very significant and 600 feet is

---

**2.** We do not suggest that material facts must be disclosed immediately; the timing of disclosure is a matter for the business judgment of the corporate officers entrusted with the management of the corporation within the affirmative disclosure requirements promulgated by the exchanges and by the SEC. Here, a valuable corporate purpose was served by delaying the publication of the K–55–1 discovery. We do intend to convey, however, that where a corporate purpose is thus served by withholding the news of a material fact, those persons who are thus quite properly true to their corporate trust must not during the period of non-disclosure deal personally in the corporation's securities or give to outsiders confidential information not generally available to all the corporations' stockholders and to the public at large.

just beyond your wildest imagination." He added, however, that it "is a natural thing to buy more stock once they give you the first drill hole." Additional testimony revealed that the prices of stocks of other companies, albeit less diversified, smaller firms, had increased substantially solely on the basis of the discovery of good anomalies or even because of the proximity of their lands to the situs of a potentially major strike.

Finally, a major factor in determining whether the K–55–1 discovery was a material fact is the importance attached to the drilling results by those who knew about it. In view of other unrelated recent developments favorably affecting TGS, participation by an informed person in a regular stock-purchase program, or even sporadic trading by an informed person, might lend only nominal support to the inference of the materiality of the K–55–1 discovery; nevertheless, the timing by those who knew of it of their stock purchases and their purchases of *short-term* calls—purchases in some cases by individuals who had never before purchased calls or even TGS stock—virtually compels the inference that the insiders were influenced by the drilling results. This insider trading activity, which surely constitutes highly pertinent evidence and the only truly objective evidence of the materiality of the K–55–1 discovery, was apparently disregarded by the court below in favor of the testimony of defendants' expert witnesses, all of whom "agreed that one drill core does not establish an ore body, much less a mine," 258 F.Supp. at 282–283. Significantly, however, the court below, while relying upon what these defense experts said the defendant insiders *ought* to have thought about the worth to TGS of the K–55–1 discovery, and finding that from November 12, 1963 to April 6, 1964 Fogarty, Murray, Holyk and Darke spent more than $100,000 in purchasing TGS stock and calls on that stock, made no finding that the insiders were motivated by any factor other than the extraordinary K–55–1 discovery when they bought their stock and their calls. No reason appears why outside investors, perhaps better acquainted with speculative modes of investment and with, in many cases, perhaps more capital at their disposal for intelligent speculation, would have been less influenced, and would not have been similarly motivated to invest if they had known what the insider investors knew about the K–55–1 discovery.

Our decision to expand the limited protection afforded outside investors by the trial court's narrow definition of materiality is not at all shaken by fears that the elimination of insider trading benefits will deplete the ranks of capable corporate managers by taking away an incentive to accept such employment. Such benefits, in essence, are forms of secret corporate compensation, see Cary, Corporate Standards and Legal Rules, 50 Calif.L.Rev. 408, 409–10 (1962), derived at the expense of the uninformed investing public and not at the expense of the corporation which receives the sole benefit from insider incentives. Moreover, adequate incentives for corporate officers may be provided by properly administered stock options and employee purchase plans of which there are many in existence. In any event, the normal motivation induced by stock ownership, i.e., the identification of an individual with corporate progress, is ill-promoted by condoning the sort of speculative insider activity which occurred here; for example, some of the corporation's stock was sold at market in order to purchase short-term calls upon that stock, calls which would never be exercised to increase a stockholder equity in TGS unless the market price of that stock rose sharply.

The core of Rule 10b–5 is the implementation of the Congressional purpose that all investors should have equal access to the rewards of participation in securities transactions. It was the intent of Congress that all members of the investing public should be subject to identical market risks,—which market risks include, of course the risk that one's evaluative capacity or one's capital available to put at risk may exceed another's capacity or capital. The insiders here were not trading on an equal footing with the outside investors. They alone were in a position to evaluate the probability and magnitude of what seemed from the outset to be a major ore strike; they alone could invest safely, secure in the expectation that the price of TGS stock would rise substantially in the event such a major strike should materialize, but would decline little, if at all, in the event of failure, for the public, ignorant at the outset of the favorable probabilities would likewise be unaware of the unproductive exploration, and the additional exploration costs would not significantly affect TGS market prices. Such inequities based upon unequal access to knowledge should not be shrugged off as inevitable in our way of life, or, in view of the congressional concern in the area, remain uncorrected.

We hold, therefore, that all transactions in TGS stock or calls by individuals apprised of the drilling results[14] of K–55–1 were made in violation of Rule 10b–5.[15] Inasmuch as the visual evaluation of that drill core (a generally reliable estimate though less accurate than a chemical assay) constituted material information, those advised of the results of the visual evaluation as well as those informed of the chemical assay traded in violation of law. The geologist Darke possessed undisclosed material information and traded in TGS securities. Therefore we reverse the dismissal of the action as to him and his personal transactions. . . .

With reference to Huntington, the trial court found that he "had no detailed knowledge as to the work" on the Kidd–55 segment, 258 F.Supp. 281. Nevertheless, the evidence shows that he knew about and participated in TGS's land acquisition program which followed the receipt of the K–55–1 drilling results, and that on February 26, 1964 he purchased 50 shares of TGS stock. Later, on March 16, he helped prepare a letter for Dr. Holyk's signature in which TGS made a

---

**14.** The trial court found that defendant Murray "had no detailed knowledge as to the work" on the Kidd–55 segment. There is no evidence in the record suggesting that Murray purchased his stock on January 8, 1964, on the basis of material undisclosed information, and the disposition below is undisturbed as to him.

**15.** Even if insiders were in fact ignorant of the broad scope of the Rule and acted pursuant to a mistaken belief as to the applicable law such an ignorance does not insulate them from the consequences of their acts. Tager v. SEC, 344 F.2d 5, 8 (2 Cir.1965).

substantial offer for lands near K–55–1, and on the same day he, who had never before purchased calls on any stock, purchased a call on 100 shares of TGS stock. We are satisfied that these purchases in February and March, coupled with his readily inferable and probably reliable, understanding of the highly favorable nature of preliminary operations on the Kidd segment, demonstrate that Huntington possessed material inside information such as to make his purchase violative of the Rule and the Act.

### C.   *When May Insiders Act?*

Appellant Crawford, who ordered[17] the purchase of TGS stock shortly before the TGS April 16 official announcement, and defendant Coates, who placed orders with and communicated the news to his broker immediately after the official announcement was read at the TGS-called press conference, concede that they were in possession of material information. They contend, however, that their purchases were not proscribed purchases for the news had already been effectively disclosed. We disagree.

Crawford telephoned his orders to his Chicago broker about midnight on April 15 and again at 8:30 in the morning of the 16th, with instructions to buy at the opening of the Midwest Stock Exchange that morning. The trial court's finding that "he sought to, and did, 'beat the news,' " 258 F.Supp. at 287, is well documented by the record. The rumors of a major ore strike which had been circulated in Canada and, to a lesser extent, in New York, had been disclaimed by the TGS press release of April 12, which significantly promised the public an official detailed announcement when possibilities had ripened into actualities. The abbreviated announcement to the Canadian press at 9:40 A.M. on the 16th by the Ontario Minister of Mines and the report carried by The Northern Miner, parts of which had sporadically reached New York on the morning of the 16th through reports from Canadian affiliates to a few New York investment firms, are assuredly not the equivalent of the official 10–15 minute announcement which was not released to the American financial press until after 10:00 A.M. Crawford's orders had been placed before that. Before insiders may act upon material information, such information must have been effectively disclosed in a manner sufficient to insure its availability to the investing public. Particularly here, where a formal announcement to the entire financial news media had been promised in a prior official release known to the media, all insider activity must await dissemination of the promised official announcement.

---

**17.** The effective protection of the public from insider exploitation of advance notice of material information requires that the time that an insider places an order, rather than the time of its ultimate execution, be determinative for Rule 10b–5 purposes. Otherwise, insiders would be able to "beat the news," cf. Fleischer, supra, 51 Va.L.Rev. at 1291, by requesting in advance that their orders be executed immediately after the dissemination of a major news release but before outsiders could act on the release. Thus it is immaterial whether Crawford's orders were executed before or after the announcement was made in Canada (9:40 A.M., April 16) or in the United States (10:00 A.M.) or whether Coates's order was executed before or after the news appeared over the Merrill Lynch (10:29 A.M.) or Dow Jones (10:54 A.M.) wires.

Coates was absolved by the court below because his telephone order was placed shortly before 10:20 A.M. on April 16, which was after the announcement had been made even though the news could not be considered already a matter of public information. 258 F.Supp. at 288. This result seems to have been predicated upon a misinterpretation of dicta in *Cady, Roberts,* where the SEC instructed insiders to "keep out of the market until the established procedures for public release of the information are *carried out* instead of hastening to execute transactions in advance of, and in frustration of, the objectives of the release," 40 SEC at 915 (emphasis supplied). The reading of a news release, which prompted Coates into action, is merely the first step in the process of dissemination required for compliance with the regulatory objective of providing all investors with an equal opportunity to make informed investment judgments. Assuming that the contents of the official release could instantaneously be acted upon,[18] at the minimum Coates should have waited until the news could reasonably have been expected to appear over the media of widest circulation, the Dow Jones broad tape, rather than hastening to insure an advantage to himself and his broker son-in-law.[19] . . .

### E. *May Insiders Accept Stock Options Without Disclosing Material Information to the Issuer?*

On February 20, 1964, defendants Stephens, Fogarty, Mollison, Holyk and Kline accepted stock options issued to them and a number of other top officers of TGS, although not one of them had informed the Stock Option Committee of the Board of Directors or the Board of the results of K–55–1, which information we have held was then material. The SEC sought rescission of these options. The trial court, in addition to finding the knowledge of the results of the K–55 discovery to be immaterial, held that Kline had no detailed knowledge of the drilling progress and that Holyk and Mollison could reasonably assume that their superiors, Stephens and Fogarty, who were directors of the corporation, would report the results if that was advisable; indeed all employees had been instructed not to divulge this information pending completion of the land acquisition program, 258 F.Supp. at 291. Therefore, the court below concluded that only directors

---

**18.** Although the only insider who acted after the news appeared over the Dow Jones broad tape is not an appellant and therefore we need not discuss the necessity of considering the advisability of a "reasonable waiting period" during which outsiders may absorb and evaluate disclosures, we note in passing that, where the news is of a sort which is not readily translatable into investment action, insiders may not take advantage of their advance opportunity to evaluate the information by acting immediately upon dissemination. In any event, the permissible timing of insider transactions after disclosures of various sorts is one of the many areas of expertise for appropriate exercise of the SEC's rule-making power, which we hope will be utilized in the future to provide some predictability of certainty for the business community.

**19.** The record reveals that news usually appears on the Dow Jones broad tape 2–3 minutes after the reporter completes dictation. Here, assuming that the Dow Jones reporter left the press conference as early as possible, 10:10 A.M., the 10–15 minute release (which took at least that long to dictate) could not have appeared on the wire before 10:22, and for other reasons unknown to us did not appear until 10:54. Indeed, even the abbreviated version of the release reported by Merrill Lynch over its private wire did not appear until 10:29. Coates, however, placed his call no later than 10:20.

Stephens and Fogarty, of the top management, would have violated the Rule by accepting stock options without disclosure, but it also found that they had not acted improperly as the information in their possession was not material. 258 F.Supp. at 292. In view of our conclusion as to materiality we hold that Stephens and Fogarty violated the Rule by accepting them. However, as they have surrendered the options and the corporation has canceled them, supra at 292, n. 17, we find it unnecessary to order that the injunctions prayed for be actually issued. We point out, nevertheless, that the surrender of these options after the SEC commenced the case is not a satisfaction of the SEC claim, and a determination as to whether the issuance of injunctions against Stephens and Fogarty is advisable in order to prevent or deter future violations of regulatory provisions is remanded for the exercise of discretion by the trial court.

Contrary to the belief of the trial court that Kline had no duty to disclose his knowledge of the Kidd project before accepting the stock option offered him, we believe that he, a vice president, who had become the general counsel of TGS in January 1964, but who had been secretary of the corporation since January 1961, and was present in that capacity when the options were granted, and who was in charge of the mechanics of issuance and acceptance of the options, was a member of top management and under a duty before accepting his option to disclose any material information he may have possessed, and, as he did not disclose such information to the Option Committee we direct rescission of the option he received.[24] As to Holyk and Mollison, the SEC has not appealed the holding below that they, not being then members of top management (although Mollison was a vice president) had no duty to disclose their knowledge of the drilling before accepting their options. Therefore, the issue of whether, by accepting, they violated the Act, is not before us, and the holding below is undisturbed....

---

**24.** The options granted on February 20, 1964 to Mollison, Holyk, and Kline were ratified by the Texas Gulf directors on July 15, 1965 after there had been, of course, a full disclosure and after this action had been commenced. However, the ratification is irrelevant here, for we would hold with the district court that a member of top management, as was Kline, is required, before accepting a stock option, to disclose material inside information which, if disclosed, might affect the price of the stock during the period when the accepted option could be exercised. Kline had known since November 1962 that K–55–1 had been drilled, that the drilling had intersected a sulphide body containing copper and zinc, and that TGS desired to acquire adjacent property.

Of course, if any of the five knowledgeable defendants had rejected his option there might well have been speculation as to the reason for the rejection. Therefore, in a case where disclosure to the grantors of an option would seriously jeopardize corporate security, it could well be desirable, in order to protect a corporation from selling securities to insiders who are in a position to appreciate their true worth at a price which may not accurately reflect the true value of the securities and at the same time to preserve when necessary the secrecy of corporate activity, not to require that an insider possessed of undisclosed material information reject the offer of a stock option, but only to require that he abstain from exercising it until such time as there shall have been a full disclosure and, after the full disclosure, a ratification such as was voted here. However, as this suggestion was not presented to us, we do not consider it or make any determination with reference to it.

■ FRIENDLY, CIRCUIT JUDGE (concurring):

Agreeing with the result reached by the majority and with most of Judge Waterman's searching opinion, I take a rather different approach to two facets of the case.

## I.

The first is a situation that will not often arise, involving as it does the acceptance of stock options during a period when inside information likely to produce a rapid and substantial increase in the price of the stock was known to some of the grantees but unknown to those in charge of the granting. I suppose it would be clear, under Ruckle v. Roto American Corp., 339 F.2d 24 (2 Cir.1964), that if a corporate officer having such knowledge persuaded an unknowing board of directors to grant him an option at a price approximating the current market, the option would be rescindable in an action under Rule 10b–5. It would seem, by the same token, that if, to make the pill easier to swallow, he urged the directors to include others lacking the knowledge he possessed, he would be liable for all the resulting damage. The novel problem in the instant case is to define the responsibility of officers when a directors' committee administering a stock option plan proposes of its own initiative to make options available to them and others at a time when they know that the option price, geared to the market value of the stock, did not reflect a substantial increment likely to be realized in short order and was therefore unfair to the corporation.

A rule requiring a minor officer to reject an option so tendered would not comport with the realities either of human nature or of corporate life. If the SEC had appealed the ruling dismissing this portion of the complaint as to Holyk and Mollison, I would have upheld the dismissal quite apart from the special circumstance that a refusal on their part could well have broken the wall of secrecy it was important for TGS to preserve. Whatever they knew or didn't know about Timmins, they were entitled to believe their superiors had reported the facts to the Option Committee unless they had information to the contrary. Stephens, Fogarty and Kline stand on an altogether different basis; as senior officers they had an obligation to inform the Committee that this was not the right time to grant options at 95% of the current price. Silence, when there is a duty to speak, can itself be a fraud. I am unimpressed with the argument that Stephens, Fogarty and Kline could not perform this duty on the peculiar facts of this case, because of the corporate need for secrecy during the land acquisition program. Non-management directors would not normally challenge a recommendation for postponement of an option plan from the President, the Executive Vice President, and the Vice President and General Counsel. Moreover, it should be possible for officers to communicate with directors, of all people, without fearing a breach of confidence. Hence, as one of the foregoing hypotheticals suggests, I am not at all sure that a company in the position of TGS might not have a claim against top officers who breached their duty of disclosure for the entire damage suffered as a result of the untimely issuance of options, rather than merely one for rescission of the options issued to them.[2] Since that issue is not before us, I merely make the reservation of my position clear. . . .

[The opinions of Judges Kaufman and Anderson (concurring), Judge Hays (concurring in part and dissenting in part), and Judges Moore and Lumbard (dissenting) are omitted.]

———

**SEC v. TEXAS GULF SULPHUR CO.**, 446 F.2d 1301, 1307–08 (2d Cir.1971). "[On remand, the] district court required Holyk, Huntington, Clayton, and Darke to pay to TGS the profits they had derived (and, in Darke's case, also the profits which his tippees had derived) from their TGS stock between their respective purchase dates and April 17, 1964, when the ore strike was fully known to the public. The payments are to be held in escrow in an interest-bearing account for a period of five years, subject to disposition in such manner as the court might direct upon application by the SEC or other interested person, or on the court's own motion. At the end of five years any money remaining undisposed of would become the property of TGS. To protect the appellants against double liability, any private judgments against these appellants arising out of the events of this case are to be paid from this fund. . . .

"Appellants, of course, contend that the required restitution is . . . a penalty assessment. . . . [However, restitution] of the profits on these transactions merely deprives the appellants of the gains of their wrongful conduct. . . .

"Finally, appellants contend that the order is punitive because it contains no element of compensation to those who have been damaged. However, as the New York Court of Appeals in Diamond v. Oreamuno, 24 N.Y.2d 494, 499, 301 N.Y.S.2d 78, 81–82, 248 N.E.2d 910, 912–913 (1969), recognized, a corporate enterprise may well suffer harm 'when officers and directors abuse their position to obtain personal profits' since 'the effect may be to cast a cloud on the corporation's name, injure stockholder relations and undermine public regard for the corporation's securities.' Although the sellers of TGS stock who sold before April 17, 1964, may have a higher equity than TGS to recover from appellants the wrongful profits appellants obtained, this fact does not preclude conditional compensation to TGS."

———

**2.** Though the Board of Directors of TGS ratified the issuance of the options after the Timmins discovery had been fully publicized, it obviously was of the belief that Kline had committed no serious wrong in remaining silent. Throughout this litigation TGS has supported the legality of the actions of all the defendants—the company's counsel having represented, among others, Stephens, Fogarty and Kline. Consequently, I agree with the majority in giving the Board's action no weight here. If a fraud of this kind may ever be cured by ratification, compare Continental Securities Co. v. Belmont, 206 N.Y. 7, 99 N.E. 138, 51 L.R.A., N.S., 112 (1912), with Claman v. Robertson, 164 Ohio St. 61, 128 N.E.2d 429 (1955); cf. Wilko v. Swan, 346 U.S. 427, 74 S.Ct. 182, 98 L.Ed. 168 (1953), that cannot be done without an appreciation of the illegality of the conduct proposed to be excused, cf. United Hotels Co. v. Mealey, 147 F.2d 816, 819 (2 Cir.1945).

## American Bar Association, Committee on Federal Regulation of Securities, Report of the Task Force on Regulation of Insider Trading, Part I: Regulation under the Antifraud Provisions of the Securities Exchange Act of 1934

41 Bus.Law. 223 (1985).

### THE POLICY BASIS FOR INSIDER TRADING REGULATION

The task force first considered whether, in today's market and legal environment, a sound policy basis remains for prohibiting the use of nonpublic information by one trader to gain advantage over others. . . .

In today's securities markets, where vast amounts of information are quickly available about corporate issuers (at least widely followed ones) and electronic communication is instantaneous, some respected scholars have argued that the markets themselves provide an adequate corrective for temporary informational advantage by promptly reporting the trading that occurs. They argue that the economic incentive of allowing a trader to use nonpublic information is of social value because it encourages and rewards analytic research and initiative. But other scholars see valid policy bases for continued regulation of unfair informational advantage even in today's impersonal, high-speed securities markets. The task force has considered these policy arguments and is persuaded that there are still valid and persuasive reasons for continuing insider trading regulation.

In our society, we traditionally abhor those who refuse to play by the rules, that is, the cheaters and the sneaks. A spitball pitcher, or a card shark with an ace up his sleeve, may win the game but not our respect. And if we know such a person is in the game, chances are we won't play. These commonsense observations suggest that two of the traditional bases for prohibitions against insider trading are still sound: the "fair play" and "integrity of the markets" arguments. The first relies on the basic policy that cheating is wrong and on the traditional sympathy for the victim of the cheat. The second rests on the oft-repeated argument that people will not entrust their resources to a marketplace they don't believe is fair, any more than a card player will put his chips on the table in a poker game that may be fixed. Although the task force knows of no empirical research that directly demonstrates that concerns about integrity affect market activity, both authoritative commentators[8] and common sense tell us that if investors do not anticipate fair treatment, they will avoid investing in securities. As a result, capital formation through securities offerings will become less attractive and more difficult. . . .

---

**8.** *See, e.g.,* comments of Arthur Levitt, Jr., Chairman of the American Stock Exchange, *quoted in* Business Week, April 29, 1985, at 79 ("If the investor thinks he's not getting a fair share, he's not going to invest and that is going to hurt capital formation in the long run").

Several other forceful policy arguments favor insider trading prohibitions. When the nonpublic information originates within the corporation—as in the case of a new product discovery or an unannounced earnings increase or decrease—the information itself is corporate property until publicly released. Those who "take" it for their own advantage rather than the corporate good may be sued for their "misappropriation" of it.

If there were no penalty for personal use of such nonpublic information to gain a market profit, then officers, employees, and even directors of a corporation might keep such information to themselves for a time and trade upon it, rather than act in the corporate interest by promptly communicating the information through appropriate corporate channels. The flow of information from its corporate source to officers, directors, and other decision makers and to the investing public could thus be impeded by the incentive to delay long enough to speculate on a stock market profit. Some have argued that such profits are an appropriate reward for corporate entrepreneurs. The task force disagrees. Unbridled insider trading would distort the intended impact of corporate compensation programs approved by directors and shareholders and based on business performance. Both the beneficiaries and the amount of benefit would be unpredictable and not subject to corporate control; the random rewards would be unrelated to overall corporate performance or to specific compensation objectives.

These corporate structure arguments certainly provide support for prohibiting trading on nonpublic, *inside* information, that is, information originating from within the corporation. But these arguments provide less support for prohibiting trading on *market* information, that is, information that comes from outside the issuer but may affect the value of its securities, such as advance news of an impending tender offer, a favorable newspaper article, or an announcement of a major governmental decision.

We continue to believe, however, that a "disclose or abstain" rule should be applied even when only *market* information is involved. The traditional fairness and market integrity bases for regulating insider trading are still important to uphold when market information is involved. Moreover, one can posit that, if those having material, nonpublic market information could trade on it without fear of liability, the incentive to promptly move such information into the marketplace would be greatly reduced. Rather, those "in the know" would keep secret, and accumulate or liquidate a position on the basis of, the information for as long as possible to maximize their gain or minimize their loss. The task force believes the result of such behavior would be a less informed (not to mention less attractive) marketplace. The task force believes that fairness, information efficiency, and market integrity are served by laws that discourage retaining material market information for personal advantage.

Although it has been argued that insider trading activity affects the market quickly, so that the economic value of the undisclosed information is reflected in market prices even before the information is announced, at a minimum this involves some fundamental, and potentially costly, unfairness to the uninformed traders on the other side of the initial trades by the insiders and their tippees.

In the judgment of the task force, these policy bases provide persuasive support for prohibitions against trading on the basis of material, nonpublic "inside information." They also support extending the prohibitions beyond corporate insiders to others who may, through improper means, obtain or abuse selective access to either material "inside information" or material "market information."

In a federal system like ours, another question should be considered: to what extent are the above policies the concern of federal as opposed to state law? If insider trading prohibitions are to be imposed because of a concern for market integrity and market information efficiency, the interests would clearly be federal since the securities markets are an integral part of interstate commerce. Although the corporate structure and the misappropriation of business property are not traditional areas of federal interest, because the securities markets are national—even international—in scope, the task force believes that exclusive reliance on state regulation would be both impractical and unwise. Federal standards are required.

----

**UNITED STATES v. CHESTMAN,** 947 F.2d 551 (2d Cir.1991), cert. denied 503 U.S. 1004, 112 S.Ct. 1759, 118 L.Ed.2d 422 (1992). (Winter, J., dissenting). "One commentator has attempted to explain the Supreme Court [insider-trading] decisions in terms of [a] business-property rationale.... See Easterbrook, [Insider Trading, Secret Agents, Evidentiary Privileges, and the Production of Information, 1981 Sup.Ct.Rev. 309,] at 309–39. That rationale may be summarized as follows. Information is perhaps the most precious commodity in commercial markets. It is expensive to produce, and, because it involves facts and ideas that can be easily photocopied or carried in one's head, there is a ubiquitous risk that those who pay to produce information will see others reap the profit from it. Where the profit from an activity is likely to be diverted, investment in that activity will decline. If the law fails to protect property rights in commercial information, therefore, less will be invested in generating such information. Id. at 313.

"For example, mining companies whose investments in geological surveys have revealed valuable deposits do not want word of the strike to get out until they have secured rights to the land.[3] If word does get out, the price of the land not only will go up, but other mining companies may also secure the rights. In either case, the mining company that invested in geological surveys (including the inevitably

----

**3.** Although [*Texas Gulf Sulphur*] stressed the unfairness of insider trading to those who deal with the trader, the reason for the nondisclosure that allowed insider trading in TGS stock was the company's insider trading in real estate.

sizeable number of unsuccessful drillings) will see profits from that investment enjoyed by others. If mining companies are unable to keep the results of such surveys confidential, less will be invested in them.

"Similarly, firms that invest money in generating information about other companies with a view to some form of combination will maintain secrecy about their efforts, and if secrecy cannot be maintained, less will be invested in acquiring such information. Hostile acquirers will want to keep such information secret lest the target mount defensive actions or speculators purchase the target's stock. Even when friendly negotiations with the other company are undertaken, the acquirer will often require the target corporation to maintain secrecy about negotiations, lest the very fact of negotiation tip off others on the important fact that the two firms think a combination might be valuable.... In the instant matter, A & P made secrecy a condition of its acquisition of Waldbaum's.

"Insider trading may reduce the return on information in two ways. First, it creates incentives for insiders to generate or disclose information that may disregard the welfare of the corporation. Easterbrook, supra, at 332–33. That risk is not implicated by the facts in the present case, and no further discussion is presently required.

"Second, insider trading creates a risk that information will be prematurely disclosed by such trading, and the corporation will lose part or all of its property in that information. Id. at 331. Although trades by an insider may rarely affect market price, others who know of the insider's trading may notice that a trader is unusually successful, or simply perceive unusual activity in a stock and guess the information and/or make piggyback trades. Id. at 336. A broker who executes a trade for a geologist or for a financial printer may well draw relevant conclusions. Or, as in the instant matter, the trader ... may tell his or her broker about the inside information, who may then trade on his or her account, on clients' accounts, or may tell friends and relatives. One inside trader has publicly attributed his exposure in part to the fact that the bank through which he made trades piggybacked on the trades, as did the broker who made the trades for the bank. See Levine, The Inside Story of An Inside Trader, Fortune, May 21, 1990, at 80. Once activity in a stock reaches an unusual stage, others may guess the reason for the trading—the corporate secret. Insider trading thus increases the risk that confidential information acquired at a cost may be disclosed. If so, the owner of the information may lose its investment."

---

### NOTE ON BLUE CHIP STAMPS v. MANOR DRUG STORES, ERNST & ERNST v. HOCHFELDER, AND SANTA FE INDUSTRIES, INC. v. GREEN

It was early established that private actions could be brought under Rule 10b–5. Although *Texas Gulf Sulphur* was a government action, it helped give impetus to an explosion of private actions. Three important Supreme Court cases decided between 1975 and 1977 placed important limits on private actions under Rule 10b–5, but by and large the law that emerged from these cases was more important in setting outer boundaries on Rule 10b–5 than in curbing the Rule's central vitality.

1. *Blue Chip*. In the first of these cases, Blue Chip Stamps v. Manor Drug Stores, 421 U.S. 723, 95 S.Ct. 1917, 44 L.Ed.2d 539 (1975), the plaintiff alleged that defendants' misrepresentations had caused him to refrain from purchasing stock, to his loss. The Court rejected this claim, approving a rule (previously adopted by several Court of Appeal cases) that only a person who had actually bought or sold securities—only a buyer or a seller—could bring a private action under rule 10b–5.

Although some nexus between a violation of Rule 10b–5 and a purchase or sale is required under *Blue Chip*, "[t]he courts have interpreted [the term 'in connection with'] broadly. Any statement that is reasonably calculated to affect the investment decision of a reasonable investor will satisfy the 'in connection with' requirement." 2 T. Hazen, Securities Regulation 108 (2d ed. 1990). Accordingly, it is well established that although the *plaintiff* in a private action under Rule 10b–5 must be a buyer or a seller, the *defendants* need not be. An action can be brought on the basis of a statement or omission that influences trading but is made by a person who did not himself trade or tip.

2. *Ernst & Ernst*. In the second case, Ernst & Ernst v. Hochfelder, 425 U.S. 185, 96 S.Ct. 1375, 47 L.Ed.2d 668 (1976), the Supreme Court held that *scienter* was a necessary element of a Rule 10b–5 damage action, so that conduct by a defendant that was deceptive merely as a result of the defendant's negligence did not give rise to damages liability under the Rule. *Ernst & Ernst* left open whether recklessness was sufficient to satisfy the scienter requirement. Subsequent decisions by the Courts of Appeals have unanimously held that recklessness satisfies the scienter requirement. See, e.g., Rolf v. Blyth, Eastman Dillon & Co., Inc., 570 F.2d 38, 44–47 (2d Cir.1978), cert. denied 439 U.S. 1039, 99 S.Ct. 642, 58 L.Ed.2d 698.)

What constitutes recklessness for purposes of Rule 10b–5 is less clear. Prior to 1995, several courts adopted, or cited with approval, observations in Sundstrand Corp. v. Sun Chemical Corp., 553 F.2d 1033 (7th Cir.1977), cert. denied 434 U.S. 875, 98 S.Ct. 224, 54 L.Ed.2d 155:

> [R]eckless conduct may be defined as [highly unreasonable conduct], involving not merely simple, or even inexcusable negligence, but an extreme departure from the standards of ordinary care, and which presents a danger of misleading buyers or sellers that is either known to the defendant or is so obvious that the actor must have been aware of it.

Section 21E of the Securities Exchange Act, added by the Private Litigation Securities Reform Act of 1995, provided that a plaintiff under the Act whose claim is based on an allegedly fraudulent *forward-looking* statement must establish that the misstatement was made with "actual knowledge." Accordingly, the Act eliminated recklessness as sufficient scienter under Rule 10b–5 for forward-looking statements, although it did not affect omissions or statements that purport to concern historical or existing facts.

The 1995 Act also provided that a plaintiff alleging securities fraud must plead as follows with respect to the defendant's state of mind:

> In any private action arising under this title in which the plaintiff may recover money damages only on the proof that the defendant acted with a particular state of mind, the complaint shall, with respect to each act or omission alleged to violate this chapter, state with particularity facts giving rise to a strong inference that the defendant acted with the required state of mind.

Securities Exchange Act § 21D(b)(2).

Prior to the 1995 Act, the pleading requirements in a securities fraud case were governed by Federal Rules of Civil Procedure 9(b), which requires plaintiffs to plead fraud with "particularity." The 1995 Act was intended to strengthen the Rule 9(b) pleading requirements, on the ground that Rule 9(b) had not effectively prevented abusive securities fraud cases and had been applied inconsistently by the different circuits.

The Second Circuit had established the most stringent pleading requirement prior to the 1995 Act. It required the plaintiff to state with particularity facts that gave rise to a "strong inference" of the defendant's intent. However, under the Second Circuit standard the plaintiff could establish this strong inference by alleging facts that showed either direct evidence of scienter, circumstantial evidence of conscious misbehavior or recklessness, or the defendant's motive and opportunity to commit fraud. The Conference Report for the 1995 Act stated that 1995 Act pleading requirement was based in part on the pleading standard that had been established by the Second Circuit, but that the Act did "not intend into codify the Second Circuit's case law interpreting this pleading standard." It isn't clear whether the Report disapproved of the Second Circuit's tests, or was simply unwilling to codify what tests could be used to establish a "strong inference."

The Securities Litigation Uniform Standards Act of 1998, and its Conference Report, add to the confusion. The Report states that Congress intended the 1995 Act to establish a "heightened uniform Federal standard on pleading requirements based upon the pleading standard applied by the Second Circuit." The Report also states that neither the 1995 Act nor the 1998 Act attempted to define the defendant's state of mind.

Two primary issues remain outstanding after the passage of the 1998 Act. First, can a plaintiff meet the 1995 Act's pleading requirements by merely alleging that the defendant had the "motive and opportunity to commit fraud," as previously established by the Second

Circuit? Second, did Congress intend to strengthen the substantive definition of scienter, thus invalidating the nearly universal pre–1995 Act interpretation that scienter included recklessness?

A number of circuits have addressed these two questions, with varying results. On the pleading issue, for example, the Second and Third Circuits have concluded that the 1995 Act's pleading requirement could be met through the Second Circuit's "motive and opportunity" test. Press v. Chemical Investment Services Corp., 166 F.3d 529 (2 Cir.1999); In Re Advanta Corp. Securities Litigation, 180 F.3d 525 (3 Cir., 1999). The First, Sixth, and Eleventh Circuits have concluded that alleging the defendant's motive and opportunity to commit fraud is not sufficient, and that although motive and opportunity are relevant factors to consider, the plaintiff must allege facts with particularity that demonstrate scienter. Greebel v. FTP Software, Inc., 194 F.3d 185 (1 Cir. 1999); In Re Comshare, Inc. Securities Litigation, 183 F.3d 542 (6 Cir.1999); Bryant v. Avado Brands, Inc., 187 F.3d 1271 (11 Cir. 1999). The Ninth Circuit has concluded that motive and opportunity cannot be used to plead scienter, and that the 1995 Act requires stronger facts. In Re Silicon Graphics Inc. Securities Litigation, 183 F.3d 970 (9 Cir.1999).

On the scienter issue, a number of circuits have concluded that the 1995 Act did not alter the substantive definition of scienter. These courts opted to retain their pre–1995 Act definitions of recklessness. However, the Ninth Circuit has concluded that the 1995 Act increased the substantive requirements of scienter, and has strengthened its definition of scienter from "recklessness" to "deliberate recklessness."In Re Silicon Graphics Inc. Securities Litigation , supra.

3. *Santa Fe*. In Santa Fe Industries, Inc. v. Green, 430 U.S. 462, 97 S.Ct. 1292, 51 L.Ed.2d 480 (1977), minority shareholders who were being involuntarily cashed out through a short-form merger alleged that the price to be paid for their shares was unfairly low, and that the merger therefore violated Rule 10b–5. The underlying facts concerning the value of the minority's shares had been disclosed to the minority shareholders. Furthermore, under state law any minority shareholder could have turned down the merger price, and chosen instead to be paid the fair value of his shares as determined by a court. The Supreme Court rejected the plaintiffs' claim, adopting the rule that Rule 10b–5 requires deception or manipulation, so that conduct that is fully disclosed at the time it occurs will not give rise to a Rule 10b–5 action.

Although the language of the majority opinion in *Santa Fe* indicated a reluctance to extend Rule 10b–5 into the province of state law regarding corporate mismanagement. *Santa Fe* does not carry quite that far. For example, if D, a director of Corporation C, persuades C's board, by fraud, to sell him stock, C can sue D under Rule 10b–5 even though it can also sue D for breach of fiduciary duty. Similarly, if C's board doesn't sue D, a shareholder could sue D under Rule 10b–5 in a derivative action.

Suppose that a controlling shareholder causes a corporation to issue stock to him at an unfair price with the approval of a majority of the directors, when material facts are not disclosed to the minority shareholders.

In Schoenbaum v. Firstbrook, 405 F.2d 215 (2d Cir.1968) (en banc), cert. denied 395 U.S. 906, 89 S.Ct. 1747, 23 L.Ed.2d 219 (1969), decided before *Santa Fe,* Aquitaine was a majority shareholder of Banff Oil Ltd. and had appointed three of its eight directors. It was alleged that Aquitaine used its controlling influence to cause Banff to sell Banff shares to Aquitaine for wholly inadequate consideration. The Second Circuit held that a Banff minority shareholder could bring a derivative action on Banff's behalf under Rule 10b–5:

> . . . [I]t is alleged that Aquitaine exercised a controlling influence over the issuance to it of treasury stock of Banff for a wholly inadequate consideration. If it is established that the transaction took place as alleged, it constituted a violation of Rule 10b–5, subdivision (3), because Aquitaine engaged in an "act, practice or course of business which operates or would operate as a fraud or deceit upon any person, in connection with the purchase or sale of any security." Moreover, Aquitaine and the directors of Banff were guilty of deceiving the stockholders of Banff (other than Aquitaine).

In Goldberg v. Meridor, 567 F.2d 209 (2d Cir.1977), cert. denied 434 U.S. 1069, 98 S.Ct. 1249, 55 L.Ed.2d 771 (1978), decided shortly after *Santa Fe,* UGO Corporation was controlled by Maritimecor, which in turn was controlled by Maritime Fruit. An UGO shareholder alleged that Maritimecor, Maritime Fruit, and directors of the various companies had caused UGO to acquire Maritimecor's assets in exchange for UGO stock, and that the agreement "was fraudulent and unfair in that the assets of Maritimecor were overpriced." Id. at 211. Press releases that described the agreement failed to disclose certain material facts concerning the value of Maritimecor's assets. The Second Circuit, in an opinion by Judge Friendly, held that *Schoenbaum* had survived *Santa Fe.* A derivative action could be brought under Rule 10b–5 on the basis of an unfair transaction between a corporation and a controlling shareholder if (1) the transaction involved stock and (2) material facts concerning the transaction had not been disclosed to all shareholders:

> *Schoenbaum* . . . can rest solidly on the now widely recognized ground that there is deception of the corporation (in effect, of its minority shareholders) when the corporation is influenced by its controlling shareholder to engage in a transaction adverse to the corporation's interests (in effect, the minority shareholders' interests) and there is nondisclosure or misleading disclosures as to the material facts of the transaction. . . .
>
> Here the complaint alleged "deceit . . . upon UGO's minority shareholders". . . . The nub of the matter is that the conduct attacked in *[Santa Fe]* did not violate the " 'fundamental purpose' of the Act as implementing a 'philosophy of full disclosure' ", . . . [T]he conduct here attacked does. . . .

Id. at 217–18.

Goldberg v. Meridor has been widely followed. See, e.g., Kas v. Financial General Bankshares, Inc., 796 F.2d 508, 512 (D.C.Cir.1986). But see Isquith v. Caremark International, 136 F.3d 531 (7th Cir. 1998).

---

## Basic Inc. v. Levinson

Supreme Court of the United States, 1988.
485 U.S. 224, 108 S.Ct. 978, 99 L.Ed.2d 194.

■ JUSTICE BLACKMUN delivered the opinion of the Court.

This case requires us to apply the materiality requirement of § 10(b) of the Securities Exchange Act of 1934, 48 Stat. 881, as amended, 15 U.S.C. § 78a *et seq.* (1934 Act), and the Securities and Exchange Commission's Rule 10b–5, promulgated thereunder, see 17 CFR § 240.10b–5 (1987), in the context of preliminary corporate merger discussions. We must also determine whether a person who traded a corporation's shares on a securities exchange after the issuance of a materially misleading statement by the corporation may invoke a rebuttable presumption that, in trading, he relied on the integrity of the price set by the market.

I

Prior to December 20, 1978, Basic Incorporated was a publicly traded company primarily engaged in the business of manufacturing chemical refractories for the steel industry. As early as 1965 or 1966, Combustion Engineering, Inc., a company producing mostly alumina-based refractories, expressed some interest in acquiring Basic, but was deterred from pursuing this inclination seriously because of antitrust concerns it then entertained. See App. 81–83. In 1976, however, regulatory action opened the way to a renewal of Combustion's interest. The "Strategic Plan," dated October 25, 1976, for Combustion's Industrial Products Group included the objective: "Acquire Basic Inc. $30 million." App. 337.

Beginning in September 1976, Combustion representatives had meetings and telephone conversations with Basic officers and directors, including petitioners here,[2] concerning the possibility of a merger. During 1977 and 1978, Basic made three public statements denying that it was engaged in merger negotiations.[4] On December 18,

---

**2.** In addition to Basic itself, petitioners are individuals who had been members of its board of directors prior to 1979; Anthony M. Caito, Samuel Eells, Jr., John A. Gelbach, Harley C. Lee, Max Muller, H. Chapman Rose, Edmund Q. Sylvester, and John C. Wilson, Jr. Another former director, Mathew J. Ludwig, was a party to the proceedings below but died on July 17, 1986, and is not a petitioner here. See Brief for Petitioners ii.

**4.** On October 21, 1977, after heavy trading and a new high in Basic stock, the following news item appeared in the Cleveland Plain Dealer:

"[Basic] President Max Muller said the company knew no reason for the stock's activity and that no negotiations

1978, Basic asked the New York Stock Exchange to suspend trading in its shares and issued a release stating that it had been "approached" by another company concerning a merger. *Id.,* at 413. On December 19, Basic's board endorsed Combustion's offer of $46 per share for its common stock, *id.,* at 335, 414–416, and on the following day publicly announced its approval of Combustion's tender offer for all outstanding shares.

Respondents are former Basic shareholders who sold their stock after Basic's first public statement of October 21, 1977, and before the suspension of trading in December 1978. Respondents brought a class action against Basic and its directors, asserting that the defendants issued three false or misleading public statements and thereby were in violation of § 10(b) of the 1934 Act and of Rule 10b–5. Respondents alleged that they were injured by selling Basic shares at artificially depressed prices in a market affected by petitioners' misleading statements and in reliance thereon.

The District Court adopted a presumption of reliance by members of the plaintiff class upon petitioners' public statements that enabled the court to conclude that common questions of fact or law predominated over particular questions pertaining to individual plaintiffs. See Fed.Rule Civ.Proc. 23(b)(3). The District Court therefore certified respondents' class. On the merits, however, the District Court granted summary judgment for the defendants. It held that, as a matter of law, any misstatements were immaterial: there were no negotiations ongoing at the time of the first statement, and although negotiations were taking place when the second and third statements were issued, those negotiations were not "destined, with reasonable certainty, to become a merger agreement in principle." App. to Pet. for Cert. 103a.

The United States Court of Appeals for the Sixth Circuit affirmed the class certification, but reversed the District Court's summary judgment, and remanded the case. 786 F.2d 741 (1986). The court reasoned that while petitioners were under no general duty to disclose their discussions with Combustion, any statement the company voluntarily released could not be " 'so incomplete as to mislead.' " *Id.,* at 746, quoting SEC v. Texas Gulf Sulphur Co., 401 F.2d 833, 862 (C.A.2 1968) (en banc), cert. denied *sub nom.* Coates v. SEC, 394 U.S. 976 (1969). In the Court of Appeals' view, Basic's statements that no negotiations were taking place, and that it knew of no corporate

were under way with any company for a merger. He said Flintkote recently denied Wall Street rumors that it would make a tender offer of $25 a share for control of the Cleveland-based maker of refractories for the steel industry." App. 363.

On September 25, 1978, in reply to an inquiry from the New York Stock Exchange, Basic issued a release concerning increased activity in its stock and stated that

"management is unaware of any present or pending company development that would result in the abnormally heavy trading activity and price fluctuation in company shares that have been experienced in the past few days." *Id.,* at 401.

On November 6, 1978, Basic issued to its shareholders a "Nine Months Report 1978." This Report stated:

"With regard to the stock market activity in the Company's shares we remain unaware of any present or pending developments which would account for the high volume of trading and price fluctuations in recent months." *Id.,* at 403.

developments to account for the heavy trading activity, were misleading. With respect to materiality, the court rejected the argument that
preliminary merger discussions are immaterial as a matter of law, and
held that "once a statement is made denying the existence of any
discussions, even discussions that might not have been material in
absence of the denial are material because they make the statement
made untrue." 786 F.2d, at 749.

The Court of Appeals joined a number of other circuits in
accepting the "fraud-on-the-market theory" to create a rebuttable
presumption that respondents relied on petitioners' material misrepresentations, noting that without the presumption it would be impractical to certify a class under Fed.Rule Civ.Proc. 23(b)(3). See 786 F.2d, at
750–751.

We granted certiorari, 479 U.S. 1083 (1987), to resolve the split,
see Part III, *infra,* among the Courts of Appeals as to the standard of
materiality applicable to preliminary merger discussions, and to determine whether the courts below properly applied a presumption of
reliance in certifying the class, rather than requiring each class member to show direct reliance on Basic's statements.

## II.   . .

. . . The Court also explicitly has defined a standard of materiality
under the securities laws, see *TSC Industries, Inc. v. Northway, Inc.,*
426 U.S. 438 (1976), concluding in the proxy-solicitation context that
"[a]n omitted fact is material if there is a substantial likelihood that a
reasonable shareholder would consider it important in deciding how
to vote." *Id.,* at 449.[7] Acknowledging that certain information concerning corporate developments could well be of "dubious significance,"
*id.,* at 448, the Court was careful not to set too low a standard of
materiality; it was concerned that a minimal standard might bring an
overabundance of information within its reach, and lead management
"simply to bury the shareholders in an avalanche of trivial information—a result that is hardly conducive to informed decisionmaking."
*Id.,* at 448–449. It further explained that to fulfill the materiality
requirement "there must be a substantial likelihood that the disclosure
of the omitted fact would have been viewed by the reasonable investor
as having significantly altered the 'total mix' of information made
available." *Id.,* at 449. We now expressly adopt the *TSC Industries*
standard of materiality for the § 10(b) and Rule 10b–5 context.

## III

The application of this materiality standard to preliminary merger
discussions is not self-evident. Where the impact of the corporate
development on the target's fortune is certain and clear, the *TSC
Industries* materiality definition admits straightforward application.
Where, on the other hand, the event is contingent or speculative in
nature, it is difficult to ascertain whether the "reasonable investor"

**7.** *TSC Industries* arose under § 14(a), § 78n(a), and Rule 14a–9, 17 CFR § 240.14a–
as amended, of the 1934 Act, 15 U.S.C.   9 (1975).

would have considered the omitted information significant at the time. Merger negotiations, because of the ever-present possibility that the contemplated transaction will not be effectuated, fall into the latter category. . . .

Petitioners urge upon us a Third Circuit test for resolving this difficulty. See Brief for Petitioners 20–22. Under this approach, preliminary merger discussions do not become material until "agreement-in-principle" as to the price and structure of the transaction has been reached between the would-be merger partners. See *Greenfield v. Heublein, Inc.,* 742 F.2d 751, 757 (C.A.3 1984), cert. denied, 469 U.S. 1215 (1985). By definition, then, information concerning any negotiations not yet at the agreement-in-principle stage could be withheld or even misrepresented without a violation of Rule 10b–5.

[The Court rejected the "agreement in principle" test, concluding that "We . . . find no valid justification for artificially excluding from the definition of materiality information concerning merger discussions, which would otherwise be considered significant to the trading decision of a reasonable investor, merely because agreement-in-principle as to price and structure has not yet been reached by the parties or their representatives.]" . . .

Even before this Court's decision in *TSC Industries,* the Second Circuit had explained the role of the materiality requirement of Rule 10b–5, with respect to contingent or speculative information or events, in a manner that gave that term meaning that is independent of the other provisions of the Rule. Under such circumstances, materiality "will depend at any given time upon a balancing of both the indicated probability that the event will occur and the anticipated magnitude of the event in light of the totality of the company activity." *SEC v. Texas Gulf Sulphur Co.,* 401 F.2d, at 849. Interestingly, neither the Third Circuit decision adopting the agreement-in-principle test nor petitioners here take issue with this general standard. Rather, they suggest that with respect to preliminary merger discussions, there are good reasons to draw a line at agreement on price and structure.

In a subsequent decision, the late Judge Friendly, writing for a Second Circuit panel, applied the *Texas Gulf Sulphur* probability/magnitude approach in the specific context of preliminary merger negotiations. After acknowledging that materiality is something to be determined on the basis of the particular facts of each case, he stated:

> "Since a merger in which it is bought out is the most important event that can occur in a small corporation's life, to wit, its death, we think that inside information, as regards a merger of this sort, can become material at an earlier stage than would be the case as regards lesser transactions—and this even though the mortality rate of mergers in such formative stages is doubtless high."

*SEC v. Geon Industries, Inc.,* 531 F.2d 39, 47–48 (C.A.2 1976). We agree with that analysis.

Whether merger discussions in any particular case are material therefore depends on the facts. Generally, in order to assess the probability that the event will occur, a factfinder will need to look to indicia of interest in the transaction at the highest corporate levels. Without attempting to catalog all such possible factors, we note by way of example that board resolutions, instructions to investment bankers, and actual negotiations between principals or their intermediaries may serve as indicia of interest. To assess the magnitude of the transaction to the issuer of the securities allegedly manipulated, a factfinder will need to consider such facts as the size of the two corporate entities and of the potential premiums over market value. No particular event or factor short of closing the transaction need be either necessary or sufficient by itself to render merger discussions material.

As we clarify today, materiality depends on the significance the reasonable investor would place on the withheld or misrepresented information. The fact-specific inquiry we endorse here is consistent with the approach a number of courts have taken in assessing the materiality of merger negotiations. Because the standard of materiality we have adopted differs from that used by both courts below, we remand the case for reconsideration of the question whether a grant of summary judgment is appropriate on this record.

IV

A

We turn to the question of reliance and the fraud-on-the-market theory. Succinctly put:

> "The fraud on the market theory is based on the hypothesis that, in an open and developed securities market, the price of a company's stock is determined by the available material information regarding the company and its business.... Misleading statements will therefore defraud purchasers of stock even if the purchasers do not directly rely on the misstatements.... The causal connection between the defendants' fraud and the plaintiffs' purchase of stock in such a case is no less significant than in a case of direct reliance on misrepresentations." *Peil v. Speiser*, 806 F.2d 1154, 1160–61 (C.A.3 1986).

Our task, of course, is not to assess the general validity of the theory, but to consider whether it was proper for the courts below to apply a rebuttable presumption of reliance, supported in part by the fraud-on-the-market theory.

This case required resolution of several common questions of law and fact concerning the falsity or misleading nature of the three public statements made by Basic, the presence or absence of scienter, and the materiality of the misrepresentations, if any. In their amended complaint, the named plaintiffs alleged that in reliance on Basic's statements they sold their shares of Basic stock in the depressed market created by petitioners. See Amended Complaint in No. C79–1220 (ND Ohio) ¶¶ 27, 29, 35, 40; see also *id.*, at ¶ 33 (alleging effect on market price of Basic's statements). Requiring proof of individualized reliance from each member of the proposed plaintiff class effectively would have prevented respondents from proceeding with a class action, since individual issues then would have overwhelmed the common ones. The District Court found that the presumption of reliance created by the fraud-on-the-market theory provided "a practical resolution to the problem of balancing the substantive requirement of proof of reliance in securities cases against the procedural requisites of [Fed.Rule Civ.Proc.] 23." The District Court thus concluded that with reference to each public statement and its impact upon the open market for Basic shares, common questions predominated over individual questions, as required by Fed.Rule Civ.Proc. 23(a)(2) and (b)(3).

Petitioners and their *amici* complain that the fraud-on-the-market theory effectively eliminates the requirement that a plaintiff asserting a claim under Rule 10b–5 prove reliance. They note that reliance is and long has been an element of common-law fraud, see *e.g.,* Restatement (Second) of Torts § 525 (1977); Prosser and Keeton on The Law of Torts § 108 (5th ed. 1984), and argue that because the analogous express right of action includes a reliance requirement, see, *e.g.,* § 18(a) of the 1934 Act, as amended, 15 U.S.C. § 78r(a), so too must an action implied under § 10(b).

We agree that reliance is an element of a Rule 10b–5 cause of action. See *Ernst & Ernst v. Hochfelder,* 425 U.S., at 206 (quoting Senate Report). Reliance provides the requisite causal connection between a defendant's misrepresentation and a plaintiff's injury. See, *e.g., Wilson v. Comtech Telecommunications Corp.,* 648 F.2d 88, 92 (C.A.2 1981); *List v. Fashion Park, Inc.,* 340 F.2d 457, 462 (CA2), cert. denied *sub nom. List v. Lerner,* 382 U.S. 811 (1965). There is, however, more than one way to demonstrate the causal connection. Indeed, we previously have dispensed with a requirement of positive proof of reliance, where a duty to disclose material information had been breached, concluding that the necessary nexus between the plaintiffs' injury and the defendant's wrongful conduct had been established. See *Affiliated Ute Citizens v. United States,* 406 U.S., at 153–154. Similarly, we did not require proof that material omissions or misstatements in a proxy statement decisively affected voting, because the proxy solicitation itself, rather than the defect in the solicitation materials, served as an essential link in the transaction. See *Mills v. Electric Auto–Lite Co.,* 396 U.S. 375, 384–385 (1970).

The modern securities markets, literally involving millions of shares changing hands daily, differ from the face-to-face transactions contemplated by early fraud cases, and our understanding of Rule 10b–5's reliance requirement must encompass these differences.

> "In face-to-face transactions, the inquiry into an investor's reliance upon information is into the subjective pricing of that information by that investor. With the presence of a market, the market is interposed between seller and buyer and, ideally, transmits information to the investor in the processed form of a market price. Thus the market is performing a substantial part of the valuation process performed by the investor in a face-to-face transaction. The market is acting as the unpaid agent of the investor, inform-

ing him that given all the information available to it, the value of the stock is worth the market price." *In re LTV Securities Litigation,* 88 F.R.D. 134, 143 (N.D.Tex.1980).

Accord, *e.g., Peil v. Speiser,* 806 F.2d, at 1161 ("In an open and developed market, the dissemination of material misrepresentations or withholding of material information typically affects the price of the stock, and purchasers generally rely on the price of the stock as a reflection of its value"); *Blackie v. Barrack,* 524 F.2d 891, 908 (C.A.9 1975) ("the same causal nexus can be adequately established indirectly, by proof of materiality coupled with the common sense that a stock purchaser does not ordinarily seek to purchase a loss in the form of artificially inflated stock"), cert. denied, 429 U.S. 816 (1976).

### B

Presumptions typically serve to assist courts in managing circumstances in which direct proof, for one reason or another, is rendered difficult. See, *e.g.,* D. Louisell & C. Mueller, Federal Evidence 541–542 (1977). The courts below accepted a presumption, created by the fraud-on-the-market theory and subject to rebuttal by petitioners, that persons who had traded Basic shares had done so in reliance on the integrity of the price set by the market, but because of petitioners' material misrepresentations that price had been fraudulently depressed. Requiring a plaintiff to show a speculative state of facts, *i.e.,* how he would have acted if omitted material information had been disclosed, see *Affiliated Ute Citizens v. United States,* 406 U.S., at 153– 154, or if the misrepresentation had not been made, see *Sharp v. Coopers & Lybrand,* 649 F.2d 175, 188 (C.A.3 1981), cert. denied, 455 U.S. 938 (1982), would place an unnecessarily unrealistic evidentiary burden on the Rule 10b–5 plaintiff who has traded on an impersonal market. Cf. *Mills v. Electric Auto–Lite Co.,* 396 U.S., at 385.

Arising out of considerations of fairness, public policy, and probability, as well as judicial economy, presumptions are also useful devices for allocating the burdens of proof between parties. See E. Cleary, McCormick on Evidence 968–969 (3rd ed. 1984); see also Fed.Rule Evid. 301 and notes. The presumption of reliance employed in this case is consistent with, and, by facilitating Rule 10b–5 litigation, supports, the congressional policy embodied in the 1934 Act. In drafting that Act, Congress expressly relied on the premise that securities markets are affected by information, and enacted legislation to facilitate an investor's reliance on the integrity of those markets....

The presumption is also supported by common sense and probability. Recent empirical studies have tended to confirm Congress' premise that the market price of shares traded on well-developed markets reflects all publicly available information, and, hence, any material misrepresentations. It has been noted that "it is hard to imagine that there ever is a buyer or seller who does not rely on market integrity. Who would knowingly roll the dice in a crooked crap game?" *Schlanger v. Four–Phase Systems, Inc.,* 555 F.Supp. 535, 538 (S.D.N.Y.1982). Indeed, nearly every court that has considered the proposition has concluded that where materially misleading statements have been disseminated into an impersonal, well-developed market for securities, the reliance of individual plaintiffs on the integrity of the market price may be presumed. Commentators generally have applauded the adoption of one variation or another of the fraud-on-the-market theory. An investor who buys or sells stock at the price set by the market does so in reliance on the integrity of that price. Because most publicly available information is reflected in market price, an investor's reliance on any public material misrepresentations, therefore, may be presumed for purposes of a Rule 10b–5 action.

C

The Court of Appeals found that petitioners "made public, material misrepresentations and [respondents] sold Basic stock in an impersonal, efficient market. Thus the class, as defined by the district court, has established the threshold facts for proving their loss." 786 F.2d, at 751. The court acknowledged that petitioners may rebut proof of the elements giving rise to the presumption, or show that the misrepresentation in fact did not lead to a distortion of price or that an individual plaintiff traded or would have traded despite his knowing the statement was false. *Id.*, at 750, n. 6.

Any showing that severs the link between the alleged misrepresentation and either the price received (or paid) by the plaintiff, or his decision to trade at a fair market price, will be sufficient to rebut the presumption of reliance. For example, if petitioners could show that the "market makers" were privy to the truth about the merger discussions here with Combustion, and thus that the market price would not have been affected by their misrepresentations, the causal connection could be broken: the basis for finding that the fraud had been transmitted through market price would be gone. Similarly, if, despite petitioners' allegedly fraudulent attempt to manipulate market price, news of the merger discussions credibly entered the market and dissipated the effects of the misstatements, those who traded Basic shares after the corrective statements would have no direct or indirect connection with the fraud. Petitioners also could rebut the presumption of reliance as to plaintiffs who would have divested themselves of their Basic shares without relying on the integrity of the market. For example, a plaintiff who believed that Basic's statements were false and that Basic was indeed engaged in merger discussions, and who consequently believed that Basic stock was artificially underpriced, but sold his shares nevertheless because of other unrelated concerns, *e.g.*, potential antitrust problems, or political pressures to divest from shares of certain businesses, could not be said to have relied on the integrity of a price he knew had been manipulated.

V

In summary:

1.   We specifically adopt, for the § 10(b) and Rule 10b–5 context, the standard of materiality set forth in *TSC Industries, Inc. v. Northway, Inc.,* 426 U.S., at 449.

2.   We reject "agreement-in-principle as to price and structure" as the bright-line rule for materiality. . . .

4.   Materiality in the merger context depends on the probability that the transaction will be consummated, and its significance to the issuer of the securities. Materiality depends on the facts and thus is to be determined on a case-by-case basis.

5.   It is not inappropriate to apply a presumption of reliance supported by the fraud-on-the-market theory.

6.   That presumption, however, is rebuttable.

7.   The District Court's certification of the class here was appropriate when made but is subject on remand to such adjustment, if any, as developing circumstances demand.

The judgment of the Court of Appeals is vacated and the case is remanded to that court for further proceedings consistent with this opinion.

*It is so ordered.*

■ THE CHIEF JUSTICE, JUSTICE SCALIA, and JUSTICE KENNEDY took no part in the consideration or decision of this case.

■ JUSTICE WHITE, with whom JUSTICE O'CONNOR joins, concurring in part and dissenting in part.

I join Parts I–III of the Court's opinion, as I agree that the standard of materiality we set forth in *TSC Industries, Inc. v. Northway, Inc.,* 426 U.S. 438, 449, 96 S.Ct. 2126, 48 L.Ed.2d 757 (1976), should be applied to actions under § 10(b) and Rule 10b–5. But I dissent from the remainder of the Court's holding because I do not agree that the "fraud-on-the-market" theory should be applied in this case. . . .

At the bottom of the Court's conclusion that the fraud-on-the-market theory sustains a presumption of reliance is the assumption that individuals rely "on the integrity of the market price" when buying or selling stock in "impersonal, well-developed market[s] for securities." *Ante,* at 21–22. Even if I was prepared to accept (as a matter of common sense or general understanding) the assumption that most persons buying or selling stock do so in response to the market price, the fraud-on-the-market theory goes further. For in adopting a "presumption of reliance," the Court *also* assumes that buyers and sellers rely—not just on the market price—but on the *"integrity"* of that price. It is this aspect of the fraud-on-the-market hypothesis which most mystifies me.

To define the term "integrity of the market price," the majority quotes approvingly from cases which suggest that investors are entitled to " 'rely on the price of a stock as a reflection of its value.' " But the meaning of this phrase eludes me, for it implicitly suggests that stocks have some "true value" that is measurable by a standard other than their market price. While the Scholastics of Medieval times professed a means to make such a valuation of a commodity's "worth," I doubt that the federal courts of our day are similarly equipped. . . .

———

## SECURITIES ACT § 27A
## SECURITIES EXCHANGE ACT § 21E

[See Statutory Supplement]

———

## SECURITIES ACT RULE 175

## SECURITIES EXCHANGE ACT RULE 3b–6

[See Statutory Supplement]

———

## NOTE ON "FORWARD–LOOKING STATEMENTS" AND THE "BESPEAKS CAUTION" DOCTRINE

1. *Forward-Looking Statements.* The securities acts, and the rules thereunder, now provide special protection for "forward-looking statements"—that is, statements about the future (for example, predictions of earnings). Section 21E(i) of the Securities Exchange Act defines a forward-looking statement to mean:

(A) a statement containing a projection of revenues, income (including income loss), earnings (including earnings loss) per share, capital expenditures, dividends, capital structure, or other financial items;

(B) a statement of the plans and objectives of management for future operations, including plans or objectives relating to the products or services of the issuer;

(C) a statement of future economic performance, including any such statement contained in a discussion and analysis of financial condition by the management or in the results of operations included pursuant to the rules and regulations of the Commission;

(D) any statement of the assumptions underlying or relating to any statement described in subparagraph (A), (B), or (C);

(E) any report issued by an outside reviewer retained by an issuer, to the extent that the report assesses a forward-looking statement made by the issuer; or

(F) a statement containing a projection or estimate of such other items as may be specified by rule or regulation of the Commission.

Section 21E(c)(1) provides a safe harbor against civil liability for oral or written forward-looking statements, as defined. Under that section, subject to a number of important exceptions, a person who makes a forward-looking statement, whether written or oral, is protected from liability if and to the extent that:

(A) the forward-looking statement is—

(i) identified as a forward-looking statement, and is accompanied by meaningful cautionary statements identifying important factors that could cause actual results to differ materially from those in the forward-looking statement; or

(ii) immaterial; or

(B) the plaintiff fails to prove that the forward-looking statement—

(i) if made by a natural person, was made with actual knowledge by that person that the statement was false or misleading; or

(ii) if made by a business entity; was—

(I) made by or with the approval of an executive officer of that entity; and

(II) made or approved by such officer with actual knowledge by that officer that the statement was false or misleading.

Section 21E(c)(2) provides special additional safe harbor applicable only to oral statements.

2. *"Bespeaks Caution."* Under a doctrine known as "bespeaks caution," a forward-looking statement does not give rise to liability, even though it is misleading, if the document in which the statement is contained includes sufficient cautionary language. See, e.g., In re Donald J. Trump Casino Securities Litigation—Taj Mahal Litigation (Kaufman v. Trump's Castle Funding), 7 F.3d 357 (3d Cir.1993), *cert. denied* Gollomp v. Trump, 510 U.S. 1178, 114 S.Ct. 1219, 127 L.Ed.2d 565 (1994); Saltzberg v. TM Sterling/Austin Associates, Ltd., 45 F.3d 399 (11th Cir.1995).

———

## Richard A. Brealey & Steward C. Myers, Principles of Corporate Finance

Sixth ed., 2000.

### WHAT IS AN EFFICIENT MARKET?

#### A *Startling Discovery: Price Changes Are Random*

As is so often the case with important ideas, the concept of efficient capital markets stemmed from a chance discovery. In 1953

Maurice Kendall, a British statistician, presented a controversial paper to the Royal Statistical Society on the behavior of stock and commodity prices. Kendall had expected to find regular price cycles, but to his surprise they did not seem to exist. Each series appeared to be "a 'wandering' one, almost as if once a week the Demon of Chance drew a random number . . . and added it to the current price to determine the next week's price." In other words, the prices of stocks and commodities seemed to follow a random walk.

When Maurice Kendall suggested that stock prices follow a random walk, he was implying that the price changes are independent of one another . . .

### Three Forms of Market Efficiency

You should see . . . why prices in competitive markets must follow a random walk. If past price changes could be used to predict future price changes, investors could make easy profits. But in competitive markets easy profits don't last. As investors try to take advantage of the information in past prices, prices adjust immediately until the superior profits from studying past price movements disappear. As a result, all the information in past prices will be reflected in today's stock price, not tomorrow's. Patterns in prices will no longer exist and price changes in one period will be independent of changes in the next. In other words, the share price will follow a random walk.

In competitive markets today's stock price must already reflect the information in past prices. But why stop there? If markets are competitive, shouldn't today's stock price reflect all the information that is available to investors? If so, securities will be fairly priced and security returns will be unpredictable, whatever information you consider.

Economists often define three levels of market efficiency, which are distinguished by the degree of information reflected in security prices. In the first level, prices reflect the information contained in the record of past prices. This is called the weak form of efficiency. If markets are efficient in the weak sense, then it is impossible to make consistently superior profits by studying past returns. Prices will follow a random walk.

The second level of efficiency requires that prices reflect not just past prices but all other published information, such as you might get from reading the financial press. This is known as the semistrong form of market efficiency. If markets are efficient in this sense, then prices will adjust immediately to public information such as the announcement of the last quarter's earnings, a new issue of stock, a proposal to merge two companies, and so on.

Finally, we might envisage a strong form of efficiency, in which prices reflect all the information that can be acquired by painstaking analysis of the company and the economy. In such a market we would observe lucky and unlucky investors, but we wouldn't find any superior investment managers who can consistently beat the market.

Two types of investment analysts help to make markets efficient. Many analysts study the company's business and try to uncover information about its profitability that will shed new light on the value of the stock. These analysts are called fundamental analysts. Competition in fundamental research will tend to ensure that prices reflect all relevant information and that price changes are unpredictable. The other analysts study the past price record and look for trends or cycles. These analysts are called technical analysts. Competition in technical research will tend to ensure that current prices reflect all information in the past sequence of prices and that future price changes cannot be predicted from past prices. . . .

### PUZZLES AND ANOMALIES . . .

Almost without exception, early researchers concluded that the efficient market hypothesis was a remarkably good description of reality. So powerful was the evidence that any dissenting research was regarded with suspicion. But eventually the readers of finance journals grew weary of hearing the same message. The interesting articles became those that turned up some puzzle. Soon the journals were packed with evidence of anomalies that investors have apparently failed to exploit. . . .

### *The Crash of 1987*

On Monday, October 19, 1987, the Dow Jones Industrial Average (the Dow) fell 23 percent in one day. Immediately after the crash, everybody started to ask . . . "Do prices reflect fundamental values?" . . .

. . . [W]hy did prices fall so sharply? There was no obvious, new fundamental information to justify such a sharp and widespread decline in share values. For this reason, the idea that the market price is the best estimate of intrinsic value seems less compelling than before the crash. It appears that either prices were irrationally high before Black Monday or irrationally low afterward. Could the theory of efficient markets be another casualty of the crash?

The events of October 1987 remind us how exceptionally difficult it is to value common stocks from scratch. . . .

The extreme difficulty of valuing common stocks from scratch has two important consequences. First, investors almost always price a common stock relative to yesterday's price or relative to today's price of comparable securities. In other words, they generally take yesterday's price as correct, adjusting upward or downward on the basis of today's information. If information arrives smoothly, then as time passes, investors become more and more confident that today's market level is correct. However, when investors lose confidence in the benchmark of yesterday's price, there may be a period of confused trading and volatile prices before a new benchmark is established.

Second, the hypothesis that stock price always equals intrinsic value is nearly impossible to test, precisely because it's so difficult to calculate intrinsic value without referring to prices. Thus the crash didn't conclusively disprove the hypothesis, but many people now find it less plausible.

However, the crash does not undermine the evidence for market efficiency, with respect to relative prices. Take for example, Quaker Oats, which sold for $53 per share in June 1998. Could we prove that true intrinsic value is $53? No, but we could be more confident that the price of Quaker Oats should be close to that of Heinz ($52) since the two companies had almost the same earnings per share, paid a similar dividend, and had similar prospects. Moreover, if either company announced unexpectedly higher earnings, we could be quite confident that its share price would respond instantly and without bias. In other words, the subsequent price would be set correctly relative to the prior price. The most important lessons of market efficiency for the corporate financial manager are concerned with relative efficiency. . . .

## THE SIX LESSONS OF MARKET EFFICIENCY

### Lesson 1: Markets Have No Memory

The weak form of the efficient-market hypothesis states that the sequence of past price changes contains no information about future changes. Economists express the same idea more concisely when they say that the market has no memory. . . .

### Lesson 2: Trust Market Prices

In an efficient market you can trust prices, for they impound all available information about the value of each security. This means that in an efficient market, there is no way for most investors to achieve consistently superior rates of return. To do so, you not only need to know more than anyone else, but you also need to know more than everyone else. . . .

### Lesson 3: Read the Entrails

If the market is efficient, prices impound all available information. Therefore, if we can only learn to read the entrails, security prices can tell us a lot about the future. For example, . . . if the company's bonds are offering a much higher yield than the average, you can deduce that the firm is probably in trouble. . . .

### Lesson 4: There Are No Financial Illusions

In an efficient market there are no financial illusions. Investors are unromantically concerned with the firm's cash flows and the portion of those cash flows to which they are entitled. . . .

### Lesson 5: The Do–It–Yourself Alternative

In an efficient market investors will not pay others for what they can do equally well themselves. . . . [M]any of the controversies in corporate financing center on how well individuals can replicate corporate financial decisions. For example, companies often justify mergers on the grounds that they produce a more diversified and hence more stable firm. But if investors can hold the stocks of both companies why should they thank the companies for diversifying? It is much easier and cheaper for them to diversify than it is for the firm....

*Lesson 6: Seen One Stock, Seen Them All*

The elasticity of demand for any article measures the percentage change in the quantity demanded for each percentage addition to the price. If the article has close substitutes, the elasticity will be strongly negative; if not, it will be near zero. For example, coffee, which is a staple commodity, has a demand elasticity of about −.2. This means that a 5 percent increase in the price of coffee changes sales by −.2 × .05 = −.01; in other words, it reduces demand by only 1 percent. Consumers are likely to regard different brands of coffee as much closer substitutes for each other. Therefore, the demand elasticity for a particular brand could be in the region of, say, −2.0. A 5 percent increase in the price of Maxwell House relative to that of Folgers would in this case reduce demand by 10 percent.

Investors don't buy a stock for its unique qualities; they buy it because it offers the prospect of a fair return for its risk. This means that stocks should be like very similar brands of coffee, almost perfect substitutes. Therefore, the demand for a company's stock should be highly elastic. If its prospective return is too low relative to its risk, nobody will want to hold that stock. If the reverse is true, everybody will scramble to buy.

Suppose that you want to sell a large block of stock. Since demand is elastic, you naturally conclude that you need only to cut the offering price very slightly to sell your stock. Unfortunately, that doesn't necessarily follow. When you come to sell your stock, other investors may suspect that you want to get rid of it because you know something they don't. Therefore, they will revise their assessment of the stock's value downward. Demand is still elastic, but the whole demand curve moves down. Elastic demand does not imply that stock prices never change when a large sale or purchase occurs; it does imply that you can sell large blocks of stock at close to the market price as long as you can convince other investors that you have no private information....

———

**DAINES & HANSON, THE CORPORATE LAW PARADOX: THE CASE FOR RESTRUCTURING CORPORATE LAW,** 103 Yale L.J. 577, 614–15 (1992). "Beginning in the mid–1980's, doubts regarding the ECMH emerged first in the financial economics literature, and then began to trickle into the legal literature. But what began as a trickle has more recently become a deluge. Legal scholars familiar with current financial economics literature agree that there is now reason to doubt the efficiency of markets. Professors Macey, Miller, Mitchell and Netter summarize the current research as follows: '[W]e can at a minimum conclude that substantial disagreement exists among financial economists about what conclusions empirical tests of market efficiency support.' Indeed, 'substantial disagreement exists about to what degree markets are efficient, how to test for efficiency, and even the definition of efficiency.' Similarly, Professor Langevoort concludes from his review of the current financial economics literature that 'what is important for present purposes seems beyond debate: strong claims of efficiency are debatable.'

"To understand the source of the new doubts, it is helpful to recognize that the ECMH makes *two* general efficiency claims—namely, that the stock market is both informationally efficient and fundamentally efficient: The market is 'informationally efficient' if all public information is immediately incorporated into the stock price; it is 'fundamentally efficient' if stock prices accurately reflect only information relating to the net present value of the corporation's future profits. A growing body of work in financial economics now suggests, first, that informational efficiency—for which there *is* substantial empirical support—does not imply fundamental efficiency, and, second, that both the empirical and theoretical bases for the belief that markets are fundamentally efficient are suspect."

---

## NOTE ON CAUSATION AND RELIANCE

In principle, it is well-established that causation and reliance are required elements of a private action under Rule 10b–5. In practice, however, those requirements have sometimes proved to be elusive or even illusory.

1.  *Causation.* In the area of causation, the case-law under Rule 10b–5 has distinguished between "transaction causation" and "loss causation." *Transaction causation* means that there must be a causal connection between the defendant's violation of Rule 10b–5 and the plaintiff's purchase or sale. This connection may be simply a requirement that but for the violation the plaintiff's purchase or sale would not have occurred, or it may be a requirement that the violation was a proximate cause of the purchase or sale. What constitutes proximate cause in this context? Loss & Seligman state:

> At most a plaintiff is required to prove that defendant's misstatement or misconduct was a "substantial factor" in causing a loss. "In other words a plaintiff must demonstrate that the defendant's fraudulent conduct 'touches upon the reasons for the investment's decline in value.'" Alternatively the element has been framed in terms of whether a misstatement *affected* an investment decision.

9 L. Loss & J. Seligman 4407 (3d ed. 1992).

The meaning of *loss causation* is harder to pin down. The best interpretation of this concept is that the defendant's wrongful act not only must have caused the plaintiff to buy or sell a security (transaction causation); it must also have been the cause of the plaintiff's *loss* on the security. Essentially, "loss causation" is simply a fancy and confusing name for the concept that even if an investment is induced by a violation of Rule 10b–5, the investor's loss may have been the result of an investment risk that was independent of the violation. "[W]hen an investor makes any investment he or she assumes certain investment risks. It may be too harsh a rule under rule 10b–5 that would place the wrongdoer in the position of insurer against those market risks. Otherwise, for example, a seller who fraudulently induced a purchase of securities in early October, 1987 would be an insurer against the precipitous price decline caused in large part by the market crash on October 19." 2 T. Hazen, *Securities Regulation 104* (2d ed. 1990).

Both the meaning of the loss-causation concept and the difficulty that can arise in applying the concept are exemplified by a pair of cases, Huddleston v. Herman & MacLean, 640 F.2d 534, 549 n. 25 (5th Cir.1981), *aff'd in part, rev'd in part on other grounds* 459 U.S. 375, 103 S.Ct. 683, 74 L.Ed.2d 548 (1983), and *In re* Washington Public Power Supply System, 650 F.Supp. 1346, 1354 (W.D.Wash.1986). In *Huddleston*, the Fifth Circuit court used the following example to explain loss causation:

> [Assume that a vessel is described in a prospectus as having] a certain capacity when in fact it had less capacity than was represented in the prospectus. However, the prospectus does disclose truthfully that the vessel will not be insured. One week after the investment the vessel sinks as a result of a casualty and the stock becomes worthless. In such circumstances, a fact-finder might conclude that the misrepresentation was material and relied upon by the investor but that it did not cause the loss.

In *Washington Public Power*, the court criticized this example:

> By misrepresenting the capacity of the ship, the investor was induced to pay a certain price for stock in the venture. As a result of the misrepresentation, the investor paid more for the stock than it was worth. When the ship sank, the entire investment was lost. The investor, however, was injured by more than the true value of the investment because he paid an inflated price for the stock. His damages thus consist of two components: the value lost due to the casualty and the amount lost because he overpaid for the stock. This latter component of damages is related directly to the initial misrepresentation. Hence, this amount should be recoverable in an action for securities fraud.

2. *Reliance.* At one time, it seemed that the rule that reliance is an element of a private action would require the plaintiff to prove that he actually and specifically relied on the defendant's wrongful statement or omission. Later, however, the requirement of reliance became radically transformed. The reasons for the transformation differed somewhat as to (i) omissions and (ii) affirmative misstatements.

(i) *Omissions*. Reliance on an omission is an illogical concept. We can say that *A* acted—bought or sold—at a given price in reliance on what *B* told him, but we can seldom say that *A* acted—bought or sold at a given price—in reliance on *B*'s silence. What we *can* say in the latter case is that a reasonable investor who knew the omitted fact probably would or would not have bought or sold at the given price. In TSC Industries v. Northway, Inc., a major foundation for *Basic,* the Supreme Court held that the standard of *materiality* in an omissions case is satisfied by "a showing of a substantial likelihood that, under all the circumstances, the omitted fact would have assumed actual significance in the deliberations of the reasonable shareholder." 426 U.S. 438, 449, 96 S.Ct. 2126, 2132, 48 L.Ed.2d 757 (1976). This standard is so close to what must be shown to prove causation in an omissions case that for all intents and purposes, causation in such a case collapses into materiality. Thus in Affiliated Ute Citizens of Utah v. United States, 406 U.S. 128, 92 S.Ct. 1456, 31 L.Ed.2d 741 (1972), a bank purchased stock from a group of unsophisticated investors without disclosing that the stock was selling at a higher price on a secondary market made by the bank. The Tenth Circuit denied recovery because the record failed to show that the plaintiffs relied on any misstatements made by the bank. The Supreme Court reversed:

> Under the circumstances of this case, involving primarily a failure to disclose, positive proof of reliance is not a prerequisite to recovery. All that is necessary is that the facts withheld be material in the sense that a reasonable investor might have considered them important in the making of this decision.

406 U.S. at 153–54, 92 S.Ct. at 1472.

On its face, *Ute* seemed to eliminate any requirement of reliance in a case of nondisclosure. In general, however, the cases have held that *Ute* "merely established a presumption that made it possible for the plaintiffs to meet their burden." Shores v. Sklar, 647 F.2d 462, 468 (5th Cir.1981) (en banc), cert. denied 459 U.S. 1102, 103 S.Ct. 722, 74 L.Ed.2d 949 (1983). The defendant can rebut this presumption "by showing that the ... plaintiff would have have followed the same course of conduct even with full and honest disclosure, [so that] the defendant's action (or lack thereof) cannot be said to have caused plaintiff's loss." Id. The defendant might carry this burden by showing, for example, that the plaintiff learned the omitted fact from an independent source before making his investment decision, so that the decision could not have been caused by the defendant's nondisclosure. Although the cases continue to use the language of "reliance" in the omissions context, the real question is causation. When the question is properly framed in causation terms, once the plaintiff has shown that defendant omitted to disclose a material fact he was obliged to disclose, the burden is on the defendant to prove that the plaintiff would have made the same investment decision even if disclosure had been made.[1]

---

1.   A few cases have held that *Affiliated*   *Ute* doesn't apply unless the relationship be-

(ii) *Misrepresentations*. In the case of a face-to-face misrepresentation, reliance is a meaningful concept. For example, the defendant might be able to show that the plaintiff did not rely on a misrepresentation because he knew from other sources that the misrepresentation was false. In face-to-face misrepresentation cases, therefore, reliance continues to be an element of plaintiff's case. However, although a lack of reliance in such cases is possible, it is extremely unlikely. People who trade soon after material misrepresentations have been made to them will have almost always have relied on the misrepresentations. Accordingly, once the plaintiff shows that a material misrepresentation was made to him, and that he traded soon thereafter, as a practical matter reliance will normally be presumed, and the burden will shift to the defendant to show that the plaintiff did not rely on the misrepresentation. In the end, therefore, the misrepresentation case is similar to the omission case—that is, once the plaintiff makes a showing of materiality, the burden shifts to the defendant to show that reliance did not occur.

---

### NOTE ON THE USE TEST UNDER RULE 10b–5

In 1998, the Ninth and Eleventh Circuits held that Rule 10b–5 is not violated unless the defendant not only *possessed* material inside information when she traded, but actually *used* the information in deciding to buy or sell. These decisions were rested on the theory that having inside information in one's possession when trading does not wrongfully cause harm; only using such information wrongfully causes harm. SEC v. Adler, 137 F.3d 1325 (11th Cir.1998); United States v. Smith, 155 F.3d 1051 (9th Cir.1998).

This esoteric distinction between possession and use of inside information had been rejected by the Second Circuit in 1993, in United States v. Teicher, 987 F.2d 112. There the court said:

A number of factors weigh in favor of a "knowing possession" standard. First, as the government points out, both § 10(b) and Rule 10b–5 require only that a deceptive practice be conducted "in connection with the purchase or sale of a security." We have previously stated that the "in connection with" clause must be "construed . . . flexibly to include deceptive practices 'touching' the sale of securities, a relationship which has been described as 'very tenuous indeed.'" *United States v. Newman*, 664 F.2d 12, 18 (2d Cir.1981), cert. denied, 464 U.S. 863, 104 S.Ct. 193, 78 L.Ed.2d 170 (1983). . . .

In addition, a "knowing possession" standard comports with the oft-quoted maxim that one with a fiduciary or similar duty to

tween the plaintiff and the defendant preceded the omission. See Fridrich v. Bradford, 542 F.2d 307, 318–20 (6th Cir.1976), cert. denied 429 U.S. 1053, 97 S.Ct. 767, 50 L.Ed.2d 769 (1977); Cavalier Carpets, Inc. v. Caylor, 746 F.2d 749 (11th Cir.1984). Since the concept of reliance in an omissions case is illogical, it's hard to find the logic in cases like *Cavalier* and *Fridrich*.

hold material nonpublic information in confidence must either "disclose or abstain" with regard to trading. See Chiarella v. United States, 445 U.S. 222, 227, 100 S.Ct. 1108, 1114, 63 L.Ed.2d 348 (1980) . . .

Finally, a "knowing possession" standard has the attribute of simplicity. It recognizes that one who trades while knowingly possessing material inside information has an informational advantage over other traders. Because the advantage is in the form of information, it exists in the mind of the trader. Unlike a loaded weapon which may stand ready but unused, material information can not lay idle in the human brain. The individual with such information may decide to trade upon that information, to alter a previously decided-upon transaction, to continue with a previously planned transaction even though publicly available information would now suggest otherwise, or simply to do nothing. In our increasingly sophisticated securities markets, where subtle shifts in strategy can produce dramatic results, it would be a mistake to think of such decisions as merely binary choices—to buy or to sell. . . .

In SEC. v. Adler, supra, the Eleventh Circuit rejected this reasoning and adopted a use test. The court said:

We believe that the use test best comports with precedent and Congressional intent, and that mere knowing possession—i.e., proof that an insider traded while in possession of material nonpublic information—is not a per se violation. However, when an insider trades while in possession of material nonpublic information, a strong inference arises that such information was used by the insider in trading. The insider can attempt to rebut the inference by adducing evidence that there was no causal connection between the information and the trade—i.e., that the information was not used. The factfinder would then weigh all of the evidence and make a finding of fact as to whether the inside information was used.

We adopt this test for the following reasons. First, of the several arguments in support of the knowing possession test, the strongest is the fact that it often would be difficult for the SEC to prove that an alleged violator actually used the material nonpublic information; the motivations for the trader's decision to trade are difficult to prove and peculiarly within the trader's knowledge. However, we believe that the inference of use, which arises from the fact that the insider traded while in knowing possession of material nonpublic information, alleviates the SEC's problem. The inference allows the SEC to make out its prima facie case without having to prove the causal connection with more direct evidence.

In United States v. Smith, supra, the Ninth Circuit also adopted a use test.

It's hard to resist the conclusion that the courts in *Adler* and *Smith* were operating under highly questionable assumptions about human psychology. If *A* has inside information that's relevant to an action she takes, the information must be a cause in fact of her action, because every action a person takes is based on all the information she then has that is relevant to the action. Even the trader can't really know if she would have traded in the absence of the information, unless she was contractually committed to trade before she obtained the information.

---

## NOTE ON AIDING AND ABETTING LIABILITY UNDER RULE 10b–5

In Central Bank of Denver v. First Interstate Bank of Denver, 511 U.S. 164, 114 S.Ct. 1439, 128 L.Ed.2d 119 (1994), the Supreme Court held that liability cannot be imposed on a person under Rule 10b–5 solely because that person aided and abetted a violation of the Rule. Prior to *Central Bank,* issues concerning aiding-and-abetting liability under Rule 10b–5 usually arose in the context of a suit against a primary violator, in which the plaintiff joined as defendants such secondary actors as lawyers, accountants, or banks who had somehow furthered the primary violator's course of conduct. The *Central Bank* opinion held that such secondary actors could not be sued on an aiding-and-abetting theory, but left open the possibility of suing such actors as primary violators:

> . . . The absence of § 10(b) aiding and abetting liability does not mean that secondary actors in the securities markets are always free from liability under the securities Acts. Any person or entity, including a lawyer, accountant, or bank, who employs a manipulative device or makes a material misstatement (or omission) on which a purchaser or seller of securities relies may be liable as a primary violator under 10b–5, assuming *all* of the requirements for primary liability under Rule 10b–5 are met. . . . In any complex securities fraud, moreover, there are likely to be multiple violators; in this case, for example, respondents named four defendants as primary violators. (Emphasis by the Court.)

---

## Chiarella v. United States

United States Supreme Court, 1980.
445 U.S. 222, 100 S.Ct. 1108, 63 L.Ed.2d 348.

■ MR. JUSTICE POWELL, delivered the opinion of the Court.

The question in this case is whether a person who learns from the confidential documents of one corporation that it is planning an attempt to secure control of a second corporation violates § 10(b) of the Securities Exchange Act of 1934 if he fails to disclose the impending takeover before trading in the target company's securities.

## I

Petitioner is a printer by trade. In 1975 and 1976, he worked as a "markup man" in the New York composing room of Pandick Press, a financial printer. Among documents that petitioner handled were five announcements of corporate takeover bids. When these documents were delivered to the printer, the identities of the acquiring and target corporations were concealed by blank spaces or false names. The true names were sent to the printer on the night of the final printing.

The petitioner, however, was able to deduce the names of the target companies before the final printing from other information contained in the documents. Without disclosing his knowledge, petitioner purchased stock in the target companies and sold the shares immediately after the takeover attempts were made public. By this method, petitioner realized a gain of slightly more than $30,000 in the course of 14 months. Subsequently, the Securities and Exchange Commission (Commission or SEC) began an investigation of his trading activities. In May 1977, petitioner entered into a consent decree with the Commission in which he agreed to return his profits to the sellers of the shares. On the same day, he was discharged by Pandick Press.

In January 1978, petitioner was indicted on 17 counts of violating § 10(b) of the Securities Exchange Act of 1934 (1934 Act) and SEC Rule 10b-5. After petitioner unsuccessfully moved to dismiss the indictment, he was brought to trial and convicted on all counts.

The Court of Appeals for the Second Circuit affirmed petitioner's conviction. 588 F.2d 1358 (2d Cir.1978). We granted certiorari, 441 U.S. 942, 99 S.Ct. 2158, 60 L.Ed.2d 1043 (1979), and we now reverse.

## II . . .

This case concerns the legal effect of the petitioner's silence. The District Court's charge permitted the jury to convict the petitioner if it found that he willfully failed to inform sellers of target company securities that he knew of a forthcoming takeover bid that would make their shares more valuable. In order to decide whether silence in such circumstances violates § 10(b), it is necessary to review the language and legislative history of that statute as well as its interpretation by the Commission and the federal courts.

Although the starting point of our inquiry is the language of the statute, *Ernst & Ernst v. Hochfelder,* 425 U.S. 185, 197, 96 S.Ct. 1375, 47 L.Ed.2d 668 (1976), § 10(b) does not state whether silence may constitute a manipulative or deceptive device. Section 10(b) was designed as a catchall clause to prevent fraudulent practices. 425 U.S., at 202, 206. But neither the legislative history nor the statute itself affords specific guidance for the resolution of this case. When Rule 10b-5 was promulgated in 1942, the SEC did not discuss the possibility that failure to provide information might run afoul of § 10(b).

The SEC took an important step in the development of § 10(b) when it held that a broker-dealer and his firm violated that section by selling securities on the basis of undisclosed information obtained from a director of the issuer corporation who was also a registered representative of the brokerage firm. In *Cady, Roberts & Co.,* 40 S.E.C. 907 (1961), the Commission decided that a corporate insider must abstain from trading in the shares of his corporation unless he has first disclosed all material inside information known to him. The obligation to disclose or abstain derives from

> "[a]n affirmative duty to disclose material information[, which] has been traditionally imposed on corporate 'insiders,' particularly officers, directors, or controlling stockholders. We, and the courts have consistently held that insiders must disclose material facts which are known to them by virtue of their position but which are not known to persons with whom they deal and which, if known, would affect their investment judgment." *Id.,* at 911.

The Commission emphasized that the duty arose from (i) the existence of a relationship affording access to inside information intended to be available only for a corporate purpose, and (ii) the unfairness of allowing a corporate insider to take advantage of that information by trading without disclosure. *Id.,* at 912, and n. 15.[8]

That the relationship between a corporate insider and the stockholders of his corporation gives rise to a disclosure obligation is not a novel twist of the law. At common law, misrepresentation made for the purpose of inducing reliance upon the false statement is fraudulent. But one who fails to disclose material information prior to the consummation of a transaction commits fraud only when he is under a duty to do so. And the duty to disclose arises when one party has information "that the other [party] is entitled to know because of a fiduciary or other similar relation of trust and confidence between them."[9] In its *Cady, Roberts* decision, the Commission recognized a relationship of trust and confidence between the shareholders of a corporation and those insiders who have obtained confidential information by reason of their position with that corporation. This relationship gives rise to a duty to disclose because of the "necessity of preventing a corporate insider from ... tak[ing] unfair advantage of the uninformed minority stockholders." *Speed v. Transamerica Corp.,* 99 F.Supp. 808, 829 (Del.1951).

The federal courts have found violations of § 10(b) where corporate insiders used undisclosed information for their own benefit. *E.g.,*

---

**8.** ... The transaction in *Cady, Roberts* involved sale of stock to persons who previously may not have been shareholders in the corporation. 40 S.E.C., at 913, and n. 21. The Commission embraced the reasoning of Judge Learned Hand that "the director or officer assumed a fiduciary relation to the buyer by the very sale; for it would be a sorry distinction to allow him to use the advantage of his position to induce the buyer into the position of a beneficiary although he was forbidden to do so once the buyer had become one." *Id.,* at 914, n. 23, quoting *Gratz v. Claughton,* 187 F.2d 46, 49 (CA2), cert. denied, 341 U.S. 920, 71 S.Ct. 741, 95 L.Ed. 1353 (1951).

**9.** Restatement (Second) of Torts § 551(2)(a) (1976). See James & Gray, Misrepresentation—Part II, 37 Md.L.Rev. 488, 523–527 (1978). As regards securities transactions, the American Law Institute recognizes that "silence when there is a duty to ... speak may be a fraudulent act." ALI, Federal Securities Code § 262(b) (Prop.Off. Draft 1978).

*SEC v. Texas Gulf Sulphur Co.,* 401 F.2d 833 (C.A.2 1968), cert. denied, 404 U.S. 1005 (1971). The cases also have emphasized, in accordance with the common-law rule, that "[t]he party charged with failing to disclose market information must be under a duty to disclose it." *Frigitemp Corp. v. Financial Dynamics Fund, Inc.,* 524 F.2d 275, 282 (C.A.2 1975). Accordingly, a purchaser of stock who has no duty to a prospective seller because he is neither an insider nor a fiduciary has been held to have no obligation to reveal material facts. See *General Time Corp. v. Talley Industries, Inc.,* 403 F.2d 159, 164 (C.A.2 1968), cert. denied, 393 U.S. 1026, 89 S.Ct. 631, 21 L.Ed.2d 570 (1969)....

Thus, administrative and judicial interpretations have established that silence in connection with the purchase or sale of securities may operate as a fraud actionable under § 10(b) despite the absence of statutory language or legislative history specifically addressing the legality of nondisclosure. But such liability is premised upon a duty to disclose arising from a relationship of trust and confidence between parties to a transaction. Application of a duty to disclose prior to trading guarantees that corporate insiders, who have an obligation to place the shareholder's welfare before their own, will not benefit personally through fraudulent use of material, nonpublic information.[12]

### III

In this case, the petitioner was convicted of violating § 10(b) although he was not a corporate insider and he received no confidential information from the target company. Moreover, the "market information" upon which he relied did not concern the earning power or operations of the target company, but only the plans of the acquiring company. Petitioner's use of that information was not a fraud under § 10(b) unless he was subject to an affirmative duty to disclose it before trading. In this case, the jury instructions failed to specify any such duty. In effect, the trial court instructed the jury that petitioner owed a duty to everyone; to all sellers, indeed, to the market as a whole. The jury simply was told to decide whether petitioner used material, nonpublic information at a time when "he knew other people trading in the securities market did not have access to the same information." Record 677.

The Court of Appeals affirmed the conviction by holding that "[*a* ]*nyone*—corporate insider or not—who regularly receives material nonpublic information may not use that information to trade in securities without incurring an affirmative duty to disclose." 588 F.2d, at 1365 (emphasis in original). Although the court said that its test would include only persons who regularly receive material, nonpublic

---

**12.** "Tippees" of corporate insiders have been held liable under § 10(b) because they have a duty not to profit from the use of inside information that they know is confidential and know or should know came from a corporate insider, *Shapiro v. Merrill Lynch,* *Pierce, Fenner & Smith, Inc.,* 495 F.2d 228, 237–238 (C.A.2 1974). The tippee's obligation has been viewed as arising from his role as a participant after the fact in the insider's breach of a fiduciary duty....

information, *id.,* at 1366, its rationale for that limitation is unrelated to the existence of a duty to disclose.[14] The Court of Appeals, like the trial court, failed to identify a relationship between petitioner and the sellers that could give rise to a duty. Its decision thus rested solely upon its belief that the federal securities laws have "created a system providing equal access to information necessary for reasoned and intelligent investment decisions." *Id.,* at 1362. The use by anyone of material information not generally available is fraudulent, this theory suggests, because such information gives certain buyers or sellers an unfair advantage over less informed buyers and sellers.

This reasoning suffers from two defects. First, not every instance of financial unfairness constitutes fraudulent activity under § 10(b). See *Santa Fe Industries, Inc. v. Green,* 430 U.S. 462, 474–477, 97 S.Ct. 1292, 51 L.Ed.2d 480 (1977). Second, the element required to make silence fraudulent—a duty to disclose—is absent in this case. No duty could arise from petitioner's relationship with the sellers of the target company's securities, for petitioner had no prior dealings with them. He was not their agent, he was not a fiduciary, he was not a person in whom the sellers had placed their trust and confidence. He was, in fact, a complete stranger who dealt with the sellers only through impersonal market transactions.

We cannot affirm petitioner's conviction without recognizing a general duty between all participants in market transactions to forgo actions based on material, nonpublic information. Formulation of such a broad duty, which departs radically from the established doctrine that duty arises from a specific relationship between two parties, see n. 9, *supra,* should not be undertaken absent some explicit evidence of congressional intent.

As we have seen, no such evidence emerges from the language or legislative history of § 10(b). Moreover, neither the Congress nor the Commission ever has adopted a parity-of-information rule. Instead the problems caused by misuse of market information have been addressed by detailed and sophisticated regulation that recognizes when use of market information may not harm operation of the securities markets. For example, the Williams Act[15] limits but does not completely prohibit a tender offeror's purchases of target corporation stock before public announcement of the offer. Congress' careful action in this and other areas contrasts, and is in some tension, with the broad rule of liability we are asked to adopt in this case....

... As we have emphasized before, the 1934 Act cannot be read " 'more broadly than its language and the statutory scheme reasonably permit.' " *Touche Ross & Co. v. Redington,* 442 U.S. 560, 578, 99 S.Ct.

**14.** The Court of Appeals said that its "regular access to market information" test would create a workable rule embracing "those who occupy ... strategic places in the market mechanism." 588 F.2d, at 1365. These considerations are insufficient to support a duty to disclose. A duty arises from the relationship between parties, see nn. 9 and 10, *supra,* and accompanying text, and not merely from one's ability to acquire information because of his position in the market....

**15.** Title 15 U.S.C. § 78m(d)(1) (1976 ed., Supp. II) permits a tender offeror to purchase 5% of the target company's stock prior to disclosure of its plan for acquisition.

2479, 61 L.Ed.2d 82 (1979), quoting *SEC v. Sloan,* 436 U.S. 103, 116, 98 S.Ct. 1702, 56 L.Ed.2d 148 (1978). Section 10(b) is aptly described as a catchall provision, but what it catches must be fraud. When an allegation of fraud is based upon nondisclosure, there can be no fraud absent a duty to speak. We hold that a duty to disclose under § 10(b) does not arise from the mere possession of nonpublic market information. The contrary result is without support in the legislative history of § 10(b) and would be inconsistent with the careful plan that Congress has enacted for regulation of the securities markets. Cf. *Santa Fe Industries, Inc. v. Green,* 430 U.S., at 479.[20]

## IV

In its brief to this Court, the United States offers an alternative theory to support petitioner's conviction. It argues that petitioner breached a duty to the acquiring corporation when he acted upon information that he obtained by virtue of his position as an employee of a printer employed by the corporation. The breach of this duty is said to support a conviction under § 10(b) for fraud perpetrated upon both the acquiring corporation and the sellers.

We need not decide whether this theory has merit for it was not submitted to the jury. . . .

The jury instructions demonstrate that petitioner was convicted merely because of his failure to disclose material, nonpublic information to sellers from whom he bought the stock of target corporations. The jury was not instructed on the nature or elements of a duty owed by petitioner to anyone other than the sellers. Because we cannot affirm a criminal conviction on the basis of a theory not presented to the jury, *Rewis v. United States,* 401 U.S. 808, 814, 91 S.Ct. 1056, 28 L.Ed.2d 493 (1971), see *Dunn v. United States,* 442 U.S. 100, 106, 99 S.Ct. 2190, 60 L.Ed.2d 743 (1979), we will not speculate upon whether such a duty exists, whether it has been breached, or whether such a breach constitutes a violation of § 10(b).

The judgment of the Court of Appeals is

*Reversed.*

[The concurring opinions of Justices Stevens and Brennan are omitted.]

■ Mr. Chief Justice Burger, dissenting.

I believe that the jury instructions in this case properly charged a violation of § 10(b) and Rule 10b–5, and I would affirm the conviction.

## I

As a general rule, neither party to an arm's-length business transaction has an obligation to disclose information to the other

---

**20.** . . . It is worth noting that this is apparently the first case in which criminal liability has been imposed upon a purchaser for § 10(b) nondisclosure. Petitioner was sentenced to a year in prison, suspended except for one month, and a 5-year term of probation. 588 F.2d, at 1373, 1378 (Meskill, J., dissenting).

unless the parties stand in some confidential or fiduciary relation. See W. Prosser, Law of Torts § 106 (2d ed. 1955). This rule permits a businessman to capitalize on his experience and skill in securing and evaluating relevant information; it provides incentive for hard work, careful analysis, and astute forecasting. But the policies that underlie the rule also should limit its scope. In particular, the rule should give way when an informational advantage is obtained, not by superior experience, foresight, or industry, but by some unlawful means. One commentator has written:

> "[T]he way in which the buyer acquires the information which he conceals from the vendor should be a material circumstance. The information might have been acquired as the result of his bringing to bear a superior knowledge, intelligence, skill or technical judgment; it might have been acquired by mere chance; or it might have been acquired by means of some tortious action on his part. . . . *Any time information is acquired by an illegal act it would seem that there should be a duty to disclose that information.*" Keeton, Fraud—Concealment and Non–Disclosure, 15 Texas L.Rev. 1, 25–26 (1936) (emphasis added).

I would read § 10(b) and Rule 10b–5 to encompass and build on this principle: to mean that a person who has misappropriated nonpublic information has an absolute duty to disclose that information or to refrain from trading.

The language of § 10(b) and of Rule 10b–5 plainly supports such a reading. By their terms, these provisions reach *any* person engaged in *any* fraudulent scheme. This broad language negates the suggestion that congressional concern was limited to trading by "corporate insiders" or to deceptive practices related to "corporate information."[1] Just as surely Congress cannot have intended one standard of fair dealing for "white collar" insiders and another for the "blue collar" level. The very language of § 10(b) and Rule 10b–5 "by repeated use of the word 'any' [was] obviously meant to be inclusive." *Affiliated Ute Citizens v. United States,* 406 U.S. 128, 151, 92 S.Ct. 1456, 31 L.Ed.2d 741 (1972).

The history of the statute and of the Rule also supports this reading. The antifraud provisions were designed in large measure "to assure that dealing in securities is fair and without undue preferences or advantages among investors." H.R.Conf.Rep. No. 94–229, p. 91 (1975). These provisions prohibit "those manipulative and deceptive practices which have been demonstrated to fulfill no useful function." S.Rep. No. 792, 73d Cong., 2d Sess., 6 (1934). An investor who purchases securities on the basis of misappropriated nonpublic infor-

---

**1.** Academic writing in recent years has distinguished between "corporate information"—information which comes from within the corporation and reflects on expected earnings or assets—and "market information." See, *e.g.,* Fleischer, Mundheim, & Murphy, An Initial Inquiry into the Responsibility to Disclose Market Information, 121 U.Pa. L.Rev. 798, 799 (1973). It is clear that § 10(b) and Rule 10b–5 by their terms and by their history make no such distinction. See Brudney, Insiders, Outsiders, and Informational Advantages Under the Federal Securities Laws, 93 Harv.L.Rev. 322, 329–333 (1979).

mation possesses just such an "undue" trading advantage; his conduct quite clearly serves no useful function except his own enrichment at the expense of others.

This interpretation of § 10(b) and Rule 10b–5 is in no sense novel. It follows naturally from legal principles enunciated by the Securities and Exchange Commission in its seminal *Cady, Roberts* decision. 40 S.E.C. 907 (1961). There, the Commission relied upon two factors to impose a duty to disclose on corporate insiders: (1) "... access ... to information intended to be available only for a corporate purpose *and not for the personal benefit of anyone*"(emphasis added); and (2) the unfairness inherent in trading on such information when it is inaccessible to those with whom one is dealing. Both of these factors are present whenever a party gains an informational advantage by unlawful means. Indeed, in *In re Blyth & Co.,* 43 S.E.C. 1037 (1969), the Commission applied its *Cady, Roberts* decision in just such a context. In that case a broker-dealer had traded in Government securities on the basis of confidential Treasury Department information which it received from a Federal Reserve Bank employee. The Commission ruled that the trading was "improper use of inside information" in violation of § 10(b) and Rule 10b–5. 43 S.E.C., at 1040. It did not hesitate to extend *Cady, Roberts* to reach a "tippee" of a Government insider.

Finally, it bears emphasis that this reading of § 10b and Rule 10b–5 would not threaten legitimate business practices. So read, the antifraud provisions would not impose a duty on a tender offeror to disclose its acquisition plans during the period in which it "tests the water" prior to purchasing a full 5% of the target company's stock. Nor would it proscribe "warehousing." See generally SEC, Institutional Investor Study Report, H.R.Doc. No. 92–64, pt. 4, p. 2273 (1971). Likewise, market specialists would not be subject to a disclose-or-refrain requirement in the performance of their everyday market functions. In each of these instances, trading is accomplished on the basis of material, nonpublic information, but the information has not been unlawfully converted for personal gain.

## II

The Court's opinion, as I read it, leaves open the question whether § 10(b) and Rule 10b–5 prohibit trading on misappropriated nonpublic information.[4] Instead, the Court apparently concludes that this theory of the case was not submitted to the jury. In the Court's view, the instructions given the jury were premised on the erroneous notion that the mere failure to disclose nonpublic information, however acquired, is a deceptive practice. . . .

---

**4.** There is some language in the Court's opinion to suggest that only "a relationship between petitioner and the sellers ... could give rise to a duty [to disclose]." ... The Court's holding, however, is much more limited, namely, that mere possession of material, nonpublic information is insufficient to create a duty to disclose or to refrain from trading. . . . Accordingly, it is my understanding that the Court has not rejected the view, advanced above, that an absolute duty to disclose or refrain arises from the very act of misappropriating nonpublic information.

The Court's reading of the District Court's charge is unduly restrictive. Fairly read as a whole and in the context of the trial, the instructions required the jury to find that Chiarella obtained his trading advantage by misappropriating the property of his employer's customers. . . .

In sum, the evidence shows beyond all doubt that Chiarella, working literally in the shadows of the warning signs in the printshop, misappropriated—stole to put it bluntly—valuable nonpublic information entrusted to him in the utmost confidence. He then exploited his ill-gotten informational advantage by purchasing securities in the market. In my view, such conduct plainly violates § 10(b) and Rule 10b–5. Accordingly, I would affirm the judgment of the Court of Appeals.

■ [The dissenting opinions of Justices Blackman and Marshall are omitted.]

---

## SECURITIES EXCHANGE ACT § 14(e) AND RULE 14e(3)

[See Statutory Supplement]

---

# Dirks v. Securities and Exchange Commission

Supreme Court of the United States, 1983.
463 U.S. 646, 103 S.Ct. 3255, 77 L.Ed.2d 911.

■ Justice Powell delivered the opinion of the Court.

Petitioner Raymond Dirks received material nonpublic information from "insiders" of a corporation with which he had no connection. He disclosed this information to investors who relied on it in trading in the shares of the corporation. The question is whether Dirks violated the antifraud provisions of the federal securities laws by this disclosure.

### I

In 1973, Dirks was an officer of a New York broker-dealer firm who specialized in providing investment analysis of insurance company securities to institutional investors. On March 6, Dirks received information from Ronald Secrist, a former officer of Equity Funding of America. Secrist alleged that the assets of Equity Funding, a diversified corporation primarily engaged in selling life insurance and mutual funds, were vastly overstated as the result of fraudulent corporate practices. Secrist also stated that various regulatory agencies had failed to act on similar charges made by Equity Funding employees. He urged Dirks to verify the fraud and disclose it publicly.

Dirks decided to investigate the allegations. He visited Equity Funding's headquarters in Los Angeles and interviewed several officers and employees of the corporation. The senior management denied any wrongdoing, but certain corporation employees corroborated the charges of fraud. Neither Dirks nor his firm owned or traded any Equity Funding stock, but throughout his investigation he openly discussed the information he had obtained with a number of clients and investors. Some of these persons sold their holdings of Equity Funding securities, including five investment advisers who liquidated holdings of more than $16 million.[2]

While Dirks was in Los Angeles, he was in touch regularly with William Blundell, the Wall Street Journal's Los Angeles bureau chief. Dirks urged Blundell to write a story on the fraud allegations. Blundell did not believe, however, that such a massive fraud could go undetected and declined to write the story. He feared that publishing such damaging hearsay might be libelous.

During the two-week period in which Dirks pursued his investigation and spread word of Secrist's charges, the price of Equity Funding stock fell from $26 per share to less than $15 per share. This led the New York Stock Exchange to halt trading on March 27. Shortly thereafter California insurance authorities impounded Equity Funding's records and uncovered evidence of the fraud. Only then did the Securities and Exchange Commission (SEC) file a complaint against Equity Funding[3] and only then, on April 2, did the Wall Street Journal publish a front-page story based largely on information assembled by Dirks. Equity Funding immediately went into receivership.[4]

The SEC began an investigation into Dirks' role in the exposure of the fraud. After a hearing by an administrative law judge, the SEC found that Dirks had aided and abetted violations of § 17(a) of the Securities Act of 1933, 15 U.S.C. § 77q(a), § 10(b) of the Securities Exchange Act of 1934, 15 U.S.C. § 78j(b), and SEC Rule 10b–5, 17 CFR § 240.10b–5 (1982), by repeating the allegations of fraud to members of the investment community who later sold their Equity Funding stock. The SEC concluded: "Where 'tippees'—regardless of their motivation or occupation—come into possession of material 'information that they know is confidential and know or should know came from a corporate insider,' they must either publicly disclose that information

---

**2.** Dirks received from his firm a salary plus a commission for securities transactions above a certain amount that his clients directed through his firm. See 21 S.E.C. Docket, at 1402, n. 3. But "[i]t is not clear how many of those with whom Dirks spoke promised to direct some brokerage business through [Dirks' firm] to compensate Dirks, or how many actually did so." 220 U.S.App. D.C., at 316, 681 F.2d, at 831. The Boston Company Institutional Investors, Inc., promised Dirks about $25,000 in commissions, but it is unclear whether Boston actually generated any brokerage business for his firm. See App. 199, 204–205; 21 S.E.C. Docket, at 1404, n. 10; 220 U.S.App.D.C., at 316, n. 5, 681 F.2d, at 831, n. 5.

**3.** As early as 1971, the SEC had received allegations of fraudulent accounting practices at Equity Funding. Moreover, on March 9, 1973, an official of the California Insurance Department informed the SEC's regional office in Los Angeles of Secrist's charges of fraud. Dirks himself voluntarily presented his information at the SEC's regional office beginning on March 27.

**4.** A federal grand jury in Los Angeles subsequently returned a 105–count indictment against 22 persons, including many of Equity Funding's officers and directors. All defendants were found guilty of one or more counts, either by a plea of guilty or a conviction after trial. See Brief for Petitioner 15; App. 149–153.

or refrain from trading." 21 S.E.C. Docket 1401, 1407 (1981) (footnote omitted) (quoting Chiarella v. United States, 445 U.S. 222, 230 n. 12, 100 S.Ct. 1108, 1115 n. 12, 63 L.Ed.2d 348 (1980)). Recognizing, however, that Dirks "played an important role in bringing [Equity Funding's] massive fraud to light," 21 S.E.C. Docket, at 1412, the SEC only censured him.

Dirks sought review in the Court of Appeals for the District of Columbia Circuit. The court entered judgment against Dirks....

In view of the importance to the SEC and to the securities industry of the question presented by this case, we granted a writ of certiorari. 459 U.S. 1014, 103 S.Ct. 371, 74 L.Ed.2d 506 (1982). We now reverse.

## II

In the seminal case of In re Cady, Roberts & Co., 40 S.E.C. 907 (1961), the SEC recognized that the common law in some jurisdictions imposes on "corporate 'insiders,' particularly officers, directors, or controlling stockholders" an "affirmative duty of disclosure ... when dealing in securities." Id., at 911, and n. 13.[10] The SEC found that not only did breach of this common-law duty also establish the elements of a Rule 10b–5 violation, but that individuals other than corporate insiders could be obligated either to disclose material non-public information before trading or to abstain from trading altogether. Id., at 912. In *Chiarella*, we accepted the two elements set out in *Cady, Roberts* for establishing a Rule 10b–5 violation: "(i) the existence of a relationship affording access to inside information intended to be available only for a corporate purpose, and (ii) the unfairness of allowing a corporate insider to take advantage of that information by trading without disclosure." 445 U.S., at 227, 100 S.Ct. at 1114. In examining whether Chiarella had an obligation to disclose or abstain, the Court found that there is no general duty to disclose before trading on material nonpublic information, and held that "a duty to disclose under § 10(b) does not arise from the mere possession of nonpublic market information." Id., at 235, 100 S.Ct., at 1118. Such a duty arises rather from the existence of a fiduciary relationship. See id., at 227–235, 100 S.Ct., at 1114–1118.

Not "all breaches of fiduciary duty in connection with a securities transaction," however, come within the ambit ofRule 10b–5. Santa Fe Industries, Inc. v. Green, 430 U.S. 462, 472, 97 S.Ct. 1292, 1300, 51 L.Ed.2d 480 (1977). There must also be "manipulation or deception." Id., at 473, 97 S.Ct., at 1300. In an inside-trading case this fraud

**10.** The duty that insiders owe to the corporation's shareholders not to trade on inside information differs from the common-law duty that officers and directors also have to the corporation itself not to mismanage corporate assets, of which confidential information is one. See 3 Fletcher Cyclopedia of the Laws of Private Corporations §§ 848, 900 (1975 ed. and Supp.1982); 3A Fletcher §§ 1168.1, 1168.2. In holding that breaches of this duty to shareholders violated the Securities Exchange Act, the *Cady, Roberts* Commission recognized, and we agree, that "[a] significant purpose of the Exchange Act was to eliminate the idea that use of inside information for personal advantage was a normal emolument of corporate office." See 40 S.E.C., at 912, n. 15.

derives from the "inherent unfairness involved where one takes advantage" of "information intended to be available only for a corporate purpose and not for the personal benefit of anyone." In re Merrill Lynch, Pierce, Fenner & Smith, Inc., 43 S.E.C. 933, 936 (1968). Thus, an insider will be liable under Rule 10b–5 for inside trading only where he fails to disclose material nonpublic information before trading on it and thus makes "secret profits." *Cady, Roberts,* 40 S.E.C., at 916, n. 31.

## III

We were explicit in *Chiarella* in saying that there can be no duty to disclose where the person who has traded on inside information "was not [the corporation's] agent, . . . was not a fiduciary, [or] was not a person in whom the sellers [of the securities] had placed their trust and confidence." 445 U.S., at 232, 100 S.Ct., at 1116. Not to require such a fiduciary relationship, we recognized, would "depar[t] radically from the established doctrine that duty arises from a specific relationship between two parties" and would amount to "recognizing a general duty between all participants in market transactions to forgo actions based on material, nonpublic information." Id., at 232, 233, 100 S.Ct., at 1116, 1117. This requirement of a specific relationship between the shareholders and the individual trading on inside information has created analytical difficulties for the SEC and courts in policing tippees who trade on inside information. Unlike insiders who have independent fiduciary duties to both the corporation and its shareholders, the typical tippee has no such relationships.[14] In view of this absence, it has been unclear how a tippee acquires the *Cady, Roberts* duty to refrain from trading on inside information. . . .

## A

The SEC's position, as stated in its opinion in this case, is that a tippee "inherits" the *Cady, Roberts* obligation to shareholders whenever he receives inside information from an insider . . .

. . . This [position] conflicts with the principle set forth in *Chiarella* that only some persons, under some circumstances, will be barred from trading while in possession of material nonpublic information. . . . See *Chiarella,* 445 U.S., at 235, n. 20, 100 S.Ct., at 1118, n.

---

**14.** Under certain circumstances, such as where corporate information is revealed legitimately to an underwriter, accountant, lawyer, or consultant working for the corporation, these outsiders may become fiduciaries of the shareholders. The basis for recognizing this fiduciary duty is not simply that such persons acquired nonpublic corporate information, but rather that they have entered into a special confidential relationship in the conduct of the business of the enterprise and are given access to information solely for corporate purposes. See SEC v. Monarch Fund, 608 F.2d 938, 942 (C.A.2 1979); In re Investors Management Co., 44 S.E.C. 633, 645 (1971); In re Van Alystne, Noel & Co., 43 S.E.C. 1080, 1084–1085 (1969); In re Merrill Lynch, Pierce, Fenner & Smith, Inc., 43 S.E.C. 933, 937 (1968); *Cady, Roberts,* 40 S.E.C., at 912. When such a person breaches his fiduciary relationship, he may be treated more properly as a tipper than a tippee. See Shapiro v. Merrill Lynch, Pierce, Fenner & Smith, Inc., 495 F.2d 228, 237 (C.A.2 1974) (investment banker had access to material information when working on a proposed public offering for the corporation). For such a duty to be imposed, however, the corporation must expect the outsider to keep the disclosed nonpublic information confidential, and the relationship at least must imply such a duty.

20. We reaffirm today that "[a] duty [to disclose] arises from the relationship between parties . . . and not merely from one's ability to acquire information because of his position in the market." [Chiarella,] 445 U.S., at 232–233, n. 14, 100 S.Ct., at 1116–1117, n. 14.

Imposing a duty to disclose or abstain solely because a person knowingly receives material nonpublic information from an insider and trades on it could have an inhibiting influence on the role of market analysts, which the SEC itself recognizes is necessary to the preservation of a healthy market. It is commonplace for analysts to "ferret out and analyze information," 21 S.E.C., at 1406,[18] and this often is done by meeting with and questioning corporate officers and others who are insiders. And information that the analysts obtain normally may be the basis for judgments as to the market worth of a corporation's securities. The analyst's judgment in this respect is made available in market letters or otherwise to clients of the firm. It is the nature of this type of information, and indeed of the markets themselves, that such information cannot be made simultaneously available to all of the corporation's stockholders or the public generally.

### B

The conclusion that recipients of inside information do not invariably acquire a duty to disclose or abstain does not mean that such tippees always are free to trade on the information. The need for a ban on some tippee trading is clear. Not only are insiders forbidden by their fiduciary relationship from personally using undisclosed corporate information to their advantage, but they may not give such information to an outsider for the same improper purpose of exploiting the information for their personal gain. See 15 U.S.C. § 78t(b) (making it unlawful to do indirectly "by means of any other person" any act made unlawful by the federal securities laws). Similarly, the transactions of those who knowingly participate with the fiduciary in such a breach are "as forbidden" as transactions "on behalf of the trustee himself." Mosser v. Darrow, 341 U.S. 267, 272, 71 S.Ct. 680, 683, 95 L.Ed. 927 (1951). See Jackson v. Smith, 254 U.S. 586, 589, 41 S.Ct. 200, 202, 65 L.Ed. 418 (1921); Jackson v. Ludeling, 21 Wall. 616, 88 U.S. 616, 631–632, 22 L.Ed. 492 (1874). As the Court explained in *Mosser,* a contrary rule "would open up opportunities for devious dealings in the name of the others that the trustee could not conduct in his own." 341 U.S., at 271, 71 S.Ct., at 682. See SEC v. Texas Gulf

---

**18.** On its facts, this case is the unusual one. Dirks is an analyst in a broker-dealer firm, and he did interview management in the course of his investigation. He uncovered, however, startling information that required no analysis or exercise of judgment as to its market relevance. Nonetheless, the principle at issue here extends beyond these facts. The SEC's rule—applicable without regard to any breach by an insider—could have serious ramifications on reporting by analysts of investment views.

Despite the unusualness of Dirks' "find," the central role that he played in uncovering the fraud at Equity Funding, and that analysts in general can play in revealing information that corporations may have reason to withhold from the public, is an important one. Dirks' careful investigation brought to light a massive fraud at the corporation. And until the Equity Funding fraud was exposed, the information in the trading market was grossly inaccurate. But for Dirks' efforts, the fraud might well have gone undetected longer. See n. 8, supra.

Sulphur Co., 446 F.2d 1301, 1308 (CA2), cert. denied, 404 U.S. 1005, 92 S.Ct. 561, 30 L.Ed.2d 558 (1971). Thus, the tippee's duty to disclose or abstain is derivative from that of the insider's duty. See Tr. of Oral Arg. 38. Cf. *Chiarella*, 445 U.S., at 246, n. 1, 100 S.Ct., at 1122, n. 1 (Blackmun, J., dissenting). As we noted in *Chiarella*, "[t]he tippee's obligation has been viewed as arising from his role as a participant after the fact in the insider's breach of a fiduciary duty." 445 U.S., at 230, n. 12, 100 S.Ct., at 1115, n. 12.

Thus, some tippees must assume an insider's duty to the shareholders not because they receive inside information, but rather because it has been made available to them *improperly*. And for Rule 10b–5 purposes, the insider's disclosure is improper only where it would violate his *Cady, Roberts* duty. Thus, a tippee assumes a fiduciary duty to the shareholders of a corporation not to trade on material nonpublic information only when the insider has breached his fiduciary duty to the shareholders by disclosing the information to the tippee and the tippee knows or should know that there has been a breach. As Commissioner Smith perceptively observed in *Investors Management Co.*: "[T]ippee responsibility must be related back to insider responsibility by a necessary finding that the tippee knew the information was given to him in breach of a duty by a person having a special relationship to the issuer not to disclose the information...." 44 S.E.C., at 651 (concurring in the result). Tipping thus properly is viewed only as a means of indirectly violating the *Cady, Roberts* disclose-or-abstain rule.

C

In determining whether a tippee is under an obligation to disclose or abstain, it thus is necessary to determine whether the insider's "tip" constituted a breach of the insider's fiduciary duty. All disclosures of confidential corporate information are not inconsistent with the duty insiders owe to shareholders. In contrast to the extraordinary facts of this case, the more typical situation in which there will be a question whether disclosure violates the insider's *Cady, Roberts* duty is when insiders disclose information to analysts. See n. 16, supra. In some situations, the insider will act consistently with his fiduciary duty to shareholders, and yet release of the information may affect the market. For example, it may not be clear—either to the corporate insider or to the recipient analyst—whether the information will be viewed as material nonpublic information. Corporate officials may mistakenly think the information already has been disclosed or that it is not material enough to affect the market. Whether disclosure is a breach of duty therefore depends in large part on the purpose of the disclosure. This standard was identified by the SEC itself in *Cady, Roberts*: a purpose of the securities laws was to eliminate "use of inside information for personal advantage." 40 S.E.C., at 912, n. 15. See n. 10, supra. Thus, the test is whether the insider personally will benefit, directly or indirectly, from his disclosure. Absent some personal gain, there has been no breach of duty to stockholders. And absent a breach by the insider, there is no derivative breach. As Commissioner Smith stated in

*Investors Management Co.* "It is important in this type of case to focus on policing insiders and what they do ... rather than on policing information *per se* and its possession...." 44 S.E.C., at 648 (concurring in the result).

The SEC argues that, if inside-trading liability does not exist when the information is transmitted for a proper purpose but is used for trading, it would be a rare situation when the parties could not fabricate some ostensibly legitimate business justification for transmitting the information. We think the SEC is unduly concerned. In determining whether the insider's purpose in making a particular disclosure is fraudulent, the SEC and the courts are not required to read the parties' minds. Scienter in some cases is relevant in determining whether the tipper has violated his *Cady, Roberts* duty. But to determine whether the disclosure itself "deceive[s], manipulate[s], or defraud[s]" shareholders, Aaron v. SEC, 446 U.S. 680, 686, 100 S.Ct. 1945, 1950, 64 L.Ed.2d 611 (1980), the initial inquiry is whether there has been a breach of duty by the insider. This requires courts to focus on objective criteria, i.e., whether the insider receives a direct or indirect personal benefit from the disclosure, such as a pecuniary gain or a reputational benefit that will translate into future earnings. Cf. 40 S.E.C., at 912, n. 15; Brudney, Insiders, Outsiders, and Informational Advantages Under the Federal Securities Laws, 93 Harv.L.Rev. 324, 348 (1979) ("The theory ... is that the insider, by giving the information out selectively, is in effect selling the information to its recipient for cash, reciprocal information, or other things of value for himself ... "). There are objective facts and circumstances that often justify such an inference. For example, there may be a relationship between the insider and the recipient that suggests a *quid pro quo* from the latter, or an intention to benefit the particular recipient. The elements of fiduciary duty and exploitation of nonpublic information also exist when an insider makes a gift of confidential information to a trading relative or friend. The tip and trade resemble trading by the insider himself followed by a gift of the profits to the recipient.

Determining whether an insider personally benefits from a particular disclosure, a question of fact, will not always be easy for courts. But it is essential, we think, to have a guiding principle for those whose daily activities must be limited and instructed by the SEC's inside-trading rules, and we believe that there must be a breach of the insider's fiduciary duty before the tippee inherits the duty to disclose or abstain. In contrast, the rule adopted by the SEC in this case would have no limiting principle.

### IV

Under the inside-trading and tipping rules set forth above, we find that there was no actionable violation by Dirks. It is undisputed that Dirks himself was a stranger to Equity Funding, with no pre-existing fiduciary duty to its shareholders. He took no action, directly or indirectly, that induced the shareholders or officers of Equity Funding to repose trust or confidence in him. There was no expectation by

Dirks' sources that he would keep their information in confidence. Nor did Dirks misappropriate or illegally obtain the information about Equity Funding. Unless the insiders breached their *Cady, Roberts* duty to shareholders in disclosing the nonpublic information to Dirks, he breached no duty when he passed it on to investors as well as to the Wall Street Journal.

It is clear that neither Secrist nor the other Equity Funding employees violated their *Cady, Roberts* duty to the corporation's shareholders by providing information to Dirks. The tippers received no monetary or personal benefit for revealing Equity Funding's secrets, nor was their purpose to make a gift of valuable information to Dirks. As the facts of this case clearly indicate, the tippers were motivated by a desire to expose the fraud. . . . In the absence of a breach of duty to shareholders by the insiders, there was no derivative breach by Dirks. See n. 20, supra. Dirks therefore could not have been "a participant after the fact in [an] insider's breach of a fiduciary duty." *Chiarella,* 445 U.S., at 230, n. 12, 100 S.Ct., at 1115, n. 12.

### V

We conclude that Dirks, in the circumstances of this case, had no duty to abstain from use of the inside information that he obtained. The judgment of the Court of Appeals therefore is reversed.

[The dissenting opinion of Justice Blackmun, in which Justice Brennan and Justice Marshall concurred, is omitted.]

-----

## United States v. O'Hagan

United States Supreme Court, 1997.
521 U.S. 642, 117 S.Ct. 2199, 138 L.Ed.2d 724.

■ JUSTICE GINSBURG delivered the opinion of the Court.

This case concerns the interpretation and enforcement of § 10(b) and § 14(e) of the Securities Exchange Act of 1934, and rules made by the Securities and Exchange Commission pursuant to these provisions, Rule 10b–5 and Rule 14e–3(a). Two prime questions are presented. The first relates to the misappropriation of material, nonpublic information for securities trading; the second concerns fraudulent practices in the tender offer setting. In particular, we address and resolve these issues: (1) Is a person who trades in securities for personal profit, using confidential information misappropriated in breach of a fiduciary duty to the source of the information, guilty of violating § 10(b) and Rule 10b–5? (2) Did the Commission exceed its rulemaking authority by adopting Rule 14e–3(a), which proscribes trading on undisclosed information in the tender offer setting, even in the absence of a duty to disclose? Our answer to the first question is yes, and to the second question, viewed in the context of this case, no.

I

Respondent James Herman O'Hagan was a partner in the law firm of Dorsey & Whitney in Minneapolis, Minnesota. In July 1988, Grand Metropolitan PLC (Grand Met), a company based in London, England, retained Dorsey & Whitney as local counsel to represent Grand Met regarding a potential tender offer for the common stock of the Pillsbury Company, headquartered in Minneapolis. Both Grand Met and Dorsey & Whitney took precautions to protect the confidentiality of Grand Met's tender offer plans. O'Hagan did no work on the Grand Met representation. Dorsey & Whitney withdrew from representing Grand Met on September 9, 1988. Less than a month later, on October 4, 1988, Grand Met publicly announced its tender offer for Pillsbury stock.

On August 18, 1988, while Dorsey & Whitney was still representing Grand Met, O'Hagan began purchasing call options for Pillsbury stock. Each option gave him the right to purchase 100 shares of Pillsbury stock by a specified date in September 1988. Later in August and in September, O'Hagan made additional purchases of Pillsbury call options. By the end of September, he owned 2,500 unexpired Pillsbury options, apparently more than any other individual investor. See App. 85, 148. O'Hagan also purchased, in September 1988, some 5,000 shares of Pillsbury common stock, at a price just under $39 per share. When Grand Met announced its tender offer in October, the price of Pillsbury stock rose to nearly $60 per share. O'Hagan then sold his Pillsbury call options and common stock, making a profit of more than $4.3 million.

The Securities and Exchange Commission (SEC or Commission) initiated an investigation into O'Hagan's transactions, culminating in a 57–count indictment. The indictment alleged that O'Hagan defrauded his law firm and its client, Grand Met, by using for his own trading purposes material, nonpublic information regarding Grand Met's planned tender offer. Id., at 8. According to the indictment, O'Hagan used the profits he gained through this trading to conceal his previous embezzlement and conversion of unrelated client trust funds. Id., at 10.[2] O'Hagan was charged with 20 counts of mail fraud, in violation of 18 U.S.C. § 1341; 17 counts of securities fraud, in violation of § 10(b) of the Securities Exchange Act of 1934 (Exchange Act), 48 Stat. 891, 15 U.S.C. § 78j(b), and SEC Rule 10b–5, 17 CFR § 240.10b–5 (1996); 17 counts of fraudulent trading in connection with a tender offer, in violation of § 14(e) of the Exchange Act, 15 U.S.C. § 78n(e), and SEC Rule 14e–3(a), 17 CFR § 240.14e–3(a) (1996); and 3 counts of violating federal money laundering statutes, 18 U.S.C. §§ 1956(a)(1)(B)(i), 1957. See App. 13–24. A jury convicted O'Hagan on all 57 counts, and he was sentenced to a 41–month term of imprisonment.

**2.** O'Hagan was convicted of theft in state court, sentenced to 30 months' imprisonment, and fined. See State v. O'Hagan, 474 N.W.2d 613, 615, 623 (Minn.App.1991). The Supreme Court of Minnesota disbarred O'Hagan from the practice of law. See In re O'Hagan, 450 N.W.2d 571 (Minn.1990).

A divided panel of the Court of Appeals for the Eighth Circuit reversed all of O'Hagan's convictions. 92 F.3d 612 (1996). Liability under § 10(b) and Rule 10b–5, the Eighth Circuit held, may not be grounded on the "misappropriation theory" of securities fraud on which the prosecution relied. Id., at 622. The Court of Appeals also held that Rule 14e–3(a)—which prohibits trading while in possession of material, nonpublic information relating to a tender offer—exceeds the SEC's § 14(e) rulemaking authority because the rule contains no breach of fiduciary duty requirement. Id., at 627. The Eighth Circuit further concluded that O'Hagan's mail fraud and money laundering convictions rested on violations of the securities laws, and therefore could not stand once the securities fraud convictions were reversed. Id., at 627–628. Judge Fagg, dissenting, stated that he would recognize and enforce the misappropriation theory, and would hold that the SEC did not exceed its rulemaking authority when it adopted Rule 14e–3(a) without requiring proof of a breach of fiduciary duty. Id., at 628.

Decisions of the Courts of Appeals are in conflict on the propriety of the misappropriation theory under § 10(b) and Rule 10b–5, see infra this page and n. 3, and on the legitimacy of Rule 14e–3(a) under § 14(e), see infra, at 25. We granted certiorari, 519 U.S. __ (1997), and now reverse the Eighth Circuit's judgment.

## II

We address first the Court of Appeals' reversal of O'Hagan's convictions under § 10(b) and Rule 10b–5. Following the Fourth Circuit's lead, see United States v. Bryan, 58 F.3d 933, 943–959 (1995), the Eighth Circuit rejected the misappropriation theory as a basis for § 10(b) liability. We hold, in accord with several other Courts of Appeals, that criminal liability under § 10(b) may be predicated on the misappropriation theory.[4]

## A . . .

[Section] 10(b) of the Exchange Act proscribes (1) using any deceptive device (2) in connection with the purchase or sale of securities, in contravention of rules prescribed by the Commission. The provision, as written, does not confine its coverage to deception of a purchaser or seller of securities, see United States v. Newman, 664 F.2d 12, 17 (C.A.2 1981); rather, the statute reaches any deceptive device used "in connection with the purchase or sale of any security."

---

**4.** Twice before we have been presented with the question whether criminal liability for violation of § 10(b) may be based on a misappropriation theory. In Chiarella v. United States, 445 U.S. 222, 235–237 (1980), the jury had received no misappropriation theory instructions, so we declined to address the question.... In Carpenter v. United States, 484 U.S. 19, 24 (1987), the Court divided evenly on whether, under the circumstances of that case, convictions resting on the misappropriation theory should be affirmed. See Aldave, The Misappropriation Theory: Carpenter and Its Aftermath, 49 Ohio St. L.J. 373, 375 (1988) (observing that "Carpenter was, by any reckoning, an unusual case," for the information there misappropriated belonged not to a company preparing to engage in securities transactions, e.g., a bidder in a corporate acquisition, but to the Wall Street Journal).

Pursuant to its § 10(b) rulemaking authority, the Commission has adopted Rule 10b–5. . . .

Under the "traditional" or "classical theory" of insider trading liability, § 10(b) and Rule 10b–5 are violated when a corporate insider trades in the securities of his corporation on the basis of material, nonpublic information. Trading on such information qualifies as a "deceptive device" under § 10(b), we have affirmed, because "a relationship of trust and confidence [exists] between the shareholders of a corporation and those insiders who have obtained confidential information by reason of their position with that corporation." Chiarella v. United States, 445 U.S. 222, 228 (1980). That relationship, we recognized, "gives rise to a duty to disclose [or to abstain from trading] because of the 'necessity of preventing a corporate insider from . . . taking unfair advantage of . . . uninformed . . . stockholders.' " Id., at 228–229 (citation omitted). The classical theory applies not only to officers, directors, and other permanent insiders of a corporation, but also to attorneys, accountants, consultants, and others who temporarily become fiduciaries of a corporation. See Dirks v. SEC, 463 U.S. 646, 655, n. 14 (1983).

The "misappropriation theory" holds that a person commits fraud "in connection with" a securities transaction, and thereby violates § 10(b) and Rule 10b–5, when he misappropriates confidential information for securities trading purposes, in breach of a duty owed to the source of the information. See Brief for United States 14. Under this theory, a fiduciary's undisclosed, self-serving use of a principal's information to purchase or sell securities, in breach of a duty of loyalty and confidentiality, defrauds the principal of the exclusive use of that information. In lieu of premising liability on a fiduciary relationship between company insider and purchaser or seller of the company's stock, the misappropriation theory premises liability on a fiduciary-turned-trader's deception of those who entrusted him with access to confidential information.

The two theories are complementary, each addressing efforts to capitalize on nonpublic information through the purchase or sale of securities. The classical theory targets a corporate insider's breach of duty to shareholders with whom the insider transacts; the misappropriation theory outlaws trading on the basis of nonpublic information by a corporate "outsider" in breach of a duty owed not to a trading party, but to the source of the information. The misappropriation theory is thus designed to "protect the integrity of the securities markets against abuses by 'outsiders' to a corporation who have access to confidential information that will affect the corporation's security price when revealed, but who owe no fiduciary or other duty to that corporation's shareholders." Ibid.

In this case, the indictment alleged that O'Hagan, in breach of a duty of trust and confidence he owed to his law firm, Dorsey & Whitney, and to its client, Grand Met, traded on the basis of nonpublic information regarding Grand Met's planned tender offer for Pillsbury common stock. App. 16. This conduct, the Government charged, constituted a fraudulent device in connection with the purchase and sale of securities.[5]

## B

We agree with the Government that misappropriation, as just defined, satisfies § 10(b)'s requirement that chargeable conduct involve a "deceptive device or contrivance" used "in connection with" the purchase or sale of securities. We observe, first, that misappropriators, as the Government describes them, deal in deception. A fiduciary who "[pretends] loyalty to the principal while secretly converting the principal's information for personal gain," Brief for United States 17, "dupes" or defrauds the principal. See Aldave, Misappropriation: A General Theory of Liability for Trading on Nonpublic Information, 13 Hofstra L.Rev. 101, 119 (1984).

We addressed fraud of the same species in Carpenter v. United States, 484 U.S. 19 (1987), which involved the mail fraud statute's proscription of "any scheme or artifice to defraud," 18 U.S.C. § 1341. Affirming convictions under that statute, we said in Carpenter that an employee's undertaking not to reveal his employer's confidential information "became a sham" when the employee provided the information to his co-conspirators in a scheme to obtain trading profits. 484 U.S. at 27. A company's confidential information, we recognized in Carpenter, qualifies as property to which the company has a right of exclusive use. Id., at 25–27. The undisclosed misappropriation of such information, in violation of a fiduciary duty, the Court said in Carpenter, constitutes fraud akin to embezzlement—" 'the fraudulent appropriation to one's own use of the money or goods entrusted to one's care by another.' " Id., at 27 (quoting Grin v. Shine, 187 U.S. 181, 189 (1902)); see Aldave, 13 Hofstra L.Rev., at 119. Carpenter's discussion of the fraudulent misuse of confidential information, the Government notes, "is a particularly apt source of guidance here, because [the mail fraud statute] (like Section 10(b)) has long been held to require deception, not merely the breach of a fiduciary duty." Brief for United States 18, n. 9 (citation omitted).

Deception through nondisclosure is central to the theory of liability for which the Government seeks recognition. As counsel for the Government stated in explanation of the theory at oral argument: "To satisfy the common law rule that a trustee may not use the property that [has] been entrusted [to] him, there would have to be consent. To satisfy the requirement of the Securities Act that there be no deception, there would only have to be disclosure." Tr. of Oral Arg. 12; see generally Restatement (Second) of Agency §§ 390, 395 (1958)

---

**5.** The Government could not have prosecuted O'Hagan under the classical theory, for O'Hagan was not an "insider" of Pillsbury, the corporation in whose stock he traded. Although an "outsider" with respect to Pillsbury, O'Hagan had an intimate association with, and was found to have traded on confidential information from Dorsey & Whitney, counsel to tender offeror Grand Met. Under the misappropriation theory, O'Hagan's securities trading does not escape Exchange Act sanction, as it would under the dissent's reasoning, simply because he was associated with, and gained nonpublic information from, the bidder, rather than the target.

(agent's disclosure obligation regarding use of confidential information).[6]

... [F]ull disclosure forecloses liability under the misappropriation theory: Because the deception essential to the misappropriation theory involves feigning fidelity to the source of information, if the fiduciary discloses to the source that he plans to trade on the nonpublic information, there is no "deceptive device" and thus no § 10(b) violation—although the fiduciary-turned-trader may remain liable under state law for breach of a duty of loyalty.[7]

We turn next to the § 10(b) requirement that the misappropriator's deceptive use of information be "in connection with the purchase or sale of [a] security." This element is satisfied because the fiduciary's fraud is consummated, not when the fiduciary gains the confidential information, but when, without disclosure to his principal, he uses the information to purchase or sell securities. The securities transaction and the breach of duty thus coincide. This is so even though the person or entity defrauded is not the other party to the trade, but is, instead, the source of the nonpublic information. See Aldave, 13 Hofstra L.Rev., at 120 ("a fraud or deceit can be practiced on one person, with resultant harm to another person or group of persons"). A misappropriator who trades on the basis of material, nonpublic information, in short, gains his advantageous market position through deception; he deceives the source of the information and simultaneously harms members of the investing public. See id., at 120–121, and n. 107.

The misappropriation theory targets information of a sort that misappropriators ordinarily capitalize upon to gain no-risk profits through the purchase or sale of securities. Should a misappropriator put such information to other use, the statute's prohibition would not be implicated. The theory does not catch all conceivable forms of fraud involving confidential information; rather, it catches fraudulent means of capitalizing on such information through securities transactions.

The Government notes another limitation on the forms of fraud § 10(b) reaches: "The misappropriation theory would not ... apply to a case in which a person defrauded a bank into giving him a loan or embezzled cash from another, and then used the proceeds of the misdeed to purchase securities." Brief for United States 24, n. 13. In such a case, the Government states, "the proceeds would have value to the malefactor apart from their use in a securities transaction, and

---

**6.** Under the misappropriation theory urged in this case, the disclosure obligation runs to the source of the information, here, Dorsey & Whitney and Grand Met. Chief Justice Burger, dissenting in Chiarella, advanced a broader reading of § 10(b) and Rule 10b–5; the disclosure obligation, as he envisioned it, ran to those with whom the misappropriator trades. 445 U.S., at 240 ("a person who has misappropriated nonpublic information has an absolute duty to disclose that information or to refrain from trading"); see also id., at 243, n. 4. The Government does not propose that we adopt a misappropriation theory of that breadth.

**7.** Where, however, a person trading on the basis of material, nonpublic information owes a duty of loyalty and confidentiality to two entities or persons—for example, a law firm and its client—but makes disclosure to only one, the trader may still be liable under the misappropriation theory.

the fraud would be complete as soon as the money was obtained." Ibid. In other words, money can buy, if not anything, then at least many things; its misappropriation may thus be viewed as sufficiently detached from a subsequent securities transaction that § 10(b)'s "in connection with" requirement would not be met. Ibid. . . .

The misappropriation theory comports with § 10(b)'s language, which requires deception "in connection with the purchase or sale of any security," not deception of an identifiable purchaser or seller. The theory is also well-tuned to an animating purpose of the Exchange Act: to insure honest securities markets and thereby promote investor confidence. See 45 Fed.Reg. 60412 (1980) (trading on misappropriated information "undermines the integrity of, and investor confidence in, the securities markets"). Although informational disparity is inevitable in the securities markets, investors likely would hesitate to venture their capital in a market where trading based on misappropriated nonpublic information is unchecked by law. An investor's informational disadvantage vis-a-vis a misappropriator with material, nonpublic information stems from contrivance, not luck; it is a disadvantage that cannot be overcome with research or skill. See Brudney, Insiders, Outsiders, and Informational Advantages Under the Federal Securities Laws, 93 Harv.L.Rev. 322, 356 (1979) ("If the market is thought to be systematically populated with . . . transactors [trading on the basis of misappropriated information] some investors will refrain from dealing altogether, and others will incur costs to avoid dealing with such transactors or corruptly to overcome their unerodable informational advantages."); Aldave, 13 Hofstra L.Rev., at 122–123.

In sum, considering the inhibiting impact on market participation of trading on misappropriated information, and the congressional purposes underlying § 10(b), it makes scant sense to hold a lawyer like O'Hagan a § 10(b) violator if he works for a law firm representing the target of a tender offer, but not if he works for a law firm representing the bidder. The text of the statute requires no such result.[9] The misappropriation at issue here was properly made the subject of a § 10(b) charge because it meets the statutory requirement that there be "deceptive" conduct "in connection with" securities transactions.

## C

. . . [T]he misappropriation theory, as we have examined and explained it in this opinion, is both consistent with the statute and

---

**9.** As noted earlier, however, see supra, at 9–10, the textual requirement of deception precludes § 10(b) liability when a person trading on the basis of nonpublic information has disclosed his trading plans to, or obtained authorization from, the principal—even though such conduct may affect the securities markets in the same manner as the conduct reached by the misappropriation theory. . . . [T]he fact that § 10(b) is only a partial antidote to the problems it was designed to allevi-ate does not call into question its prohibition of conduct that falls within its textual proscription. Moreover, once a disloyal agent discloses his imminent breach of duty, his principal may seek appropriate equitable relief under state law. Furthermore, in the context of a tender offer, the principal who authorizes an agent's trading on confidential information may, in the Commission's view, incur liability for an Exchange Act violation under Rule 14e–3(a).

with our precedent.[11] ...

The Eighth Circuit erred in holding that the misappropriation theory is inconsistent with § 10(b). The Court of Appeals may address on remand O'Hagan's other challenges to his convictions under § 10(b) and Rule 10b–5.

... [T]he misappropriation theory, as we have examined and explained it in this opinion, is both consistent with the statute and with our precedent.[11] ...

## III

We consider next the ground on which the Court of Appeals reversed O'Hagan's convictions for fraudulent trading in connection with a tender offer, in violation of § 14(e) of the Exchange Act and SEC Rule 14e–3(a). A sole question is before us as to these convictions: Did the Commission, as the Court of Appeals held, exceed its rulemaking authority under § 14(e) when it adopted Rule 14e–3(a) without requiring a showing that the trading at issue entailed a breach of fiduciary duty? We hold that the Commission, in this regard and to the extent relevant to this case, did not exceed its authority....

... [W]e agree with the United States that Rule 14e–3(a), as applied to cases of this genre, qualifies under § 14(e) as a "means reasonably designed to prevent" fraudulent trading on material, non-public information in the tender offer context. A prophylactic measure, because its mission is to prevent, typically encompasses more than the core activity prohibited.... [Section] 14(e)'s rulemaking authorization gives the Commission "latitude," even in the context of a term of art

---

**11.** The United States additionally argues that Congress confirmed the validity of the misappropriation theory in the Insider Trading and Securities Fraud Enforcement Act of 1988 (ITSFEA), § 2(1), 102 Stat. 4677, note following 15 U.S.C. § 78u–1. See Brief for United States 32–35. ITSFEA declares that "the rules and regulations of the Securities and Exchange Commission under the Securities Exchange Act of 1934 ... governing trading while in possession of material, nonpublic information are, as required by such Act, necessary and appropriate in the public interest and for the protection of investors." Note following 15 U.S.C. § 78u–1. ITSFEA also includes a new § 20A(a) of the Exchange Act expressly providing a private cause of action against persons who violate the Exchange Act "by purchasing or selling a security while in possession of material, nonpublic information", such an action may be brought by "any person who, contemporaneously with the purchase or sale of securities that is the subject of such violation, has purchased ... or sold ... securities of the same class." 15 U.S.C. § 78r–1(a). Because we uphold the misappropriation theory on the basis of § 10(b) itself, we do not address ITSFEA's significance for cases of this genre.

like "manipulative," "to regulate nondeceptive activities as a 'reasonably designed' means of preventing manipulative acts, without suggesting any change in the meaning of the term 'manipulative' itself." 472 U.S., at 11, n. 11. We hold, accordingly, that under § 14(e), the Commission may prohibit acts, not themselves fraudulent under the common law or § 10(b), if the prohibition is "reasonably designed to prevent . . . acts and practices [that] are fraudulent." 15 U.S.C. § 78n(c). . . .

As an alternate ground for affirming the Eighth Circuit's judgment, O'Hagan urges that Rule 14e–3(a) is invalid because it prohibits trading in advance of a tender offer—when "a substantial step . . . to commence" such an offer has been taken—while § 14(e) prohibits fraudulent acts "in connection with any tender offer." See Brief for Respondent 41–42. O'Hagan further contends that, by covering pre-offer conduct, Rule 14e–3(a) "fails to comport with due process on two levels": The rule does not "give fair notice as to when, in advance of a tender offer, a violation of § 14(e) occurs," id., at 42; and it "disposes of any scienter requirement," id., at 43. The Court of Appeals did not address these arguments, and O'Hagan did not raise the due process points in his briefs before that court. We decline to consider these contentions in the first instance.[23] The Court of Appeals may address on remand any arguments O'Hagan has preserved.

## IV

Based on its dispositions of the securities fraud convictions, the Court of Appeals also reversed O'Hagan's convictions, under 18 U.S.C. § 1341, for mail fraud. See 92 F.3d, at 627–628. Reversal of the securities convictions, the Court of Appeals recognized, "did not as a matter of law require that the mail fraud convictions likewise be reversed." Id., at 627 (citing Carpenter, 484 U.S., at 24, in which this Court unanimously affirmed mail and wire fraud convictions based on the same conduct that evenly divided the Court on the defendants' securities fraud convictions). But in this case, the Court of Appeals said, the indictment was so structured that the mail fraud charges could not be disassociated from the securities fraud charges, and absent any securities fraud, "there was no fraud upon which to base the mail fraud charges." 92 F.3d, at 627–628.[24]

. . . We need not linger over this matter, for our rulings on the securities fraud issues require that we reverse the Court of Appeals judgment on the mail fraud counts as well.[25] . . .

**23.** As to O'Hagan's scienter argument, . . . 15 U.S.C. § 78ff(a) requires the Government to prove "willful violation" of the securities laws, and that lack of knowledge of the relevant rule is an affirmative defense to a sentence of imprisonment. . . .

**24.** The Court of Appeals reversed respondent's money laundering convictions on similar reasoning. See 92 F.3d, at 628. Because the United States did not seek review

of that ruling, we leave undisturbed that portion of the Court of Appeals' judgment.

**25.** The dissent finds O'Hagan's convictions on the mail fraud counts, but not on the securities fraud counts, sustainable. . . . Under the dissent's view, securities traders like O'Hagan would escape SEC civil actions and federal prosecutions under legislation targeting securities fraud, only to be caught for their trading activities in the broad mail

The judgment of the Court of Appeals for the Eighth Circuit is reversed, and the case is remanded for further proceedings consistent with this opinion.

It is so ordered.

■ DISSENT: JUSTICE SCALIA, concurring in part and dissenting in part.

I join Parts I, III, and IV of the Court's opinion. I do not agree, however, with Part II of the Court's opinion, containing its analysis of respondent's convictions under § 10(b) and Rule 10b–5....

While the Court's explanation of the scope of § 10(b) and Rule 10b–5 would be entirely reasonable in some other context, it does not seem to accord with the principle of lenity we apply to criminal statutes....

In light of that principle, it seems to me that the unelaborated statutory language: "to use or employ in connection with the purchase or sale of any security ... any manipulative or deceptive device or contrivance," § 10(b), must be construed to require the manipulation or deception of a party to a securities transaction.

[The opinion of Justice Thomas, concurring with the majority on the Mail Fraud Act issue, but dissenting on the Rule 10b–5 and Rule 14e–3(a) issues, is omitted. Chief Justice Rehnquist concurred in Justice Thomas's opinion.]

---

### NOTE ON THE OBLIGATIONS OF A NONTRADING CORPORATION UNDER RULE 10b–5

Most private actions under Rule 10b–5 are brought against persons who have traded or tipped, but as *Basic* shows, a corporation that makes *misstatements* may be liable under Rule 10b–5 even if it does not trade. The imposition of Rule 10b–5 liability on a nontrading corporation for *nondisclosure* is much less usual. In *Texas Gulf Sulphur Co.,* the court stated that "the timing of the disclosure [of material facts] is a matter for the business judgment of the corporate officers entrusted with the management of the corporation within the affirmative disclosure requirements promulgated by the exchanges and by the SEC." Id. at 850 n. 12. This is still the general rule. See, e.g., Staffin v. Greenberg, 672 F.2d 1196, 1204 (3d Cir.1982). There are, however, several exceptions to this rule.

1. If the corporation makes a statement that is misleading (inaccurate) when made, even though not intentionally or recklessly so, and the corporation later learns that the statement was misleading, it is under a duty to *correct* the statement if the statement is still "alive,"

---

fraud net. If misappropriation theory cases could proceed only under the federal mail and wire fraud statutes, practical consequences for individual defendants might not be large, see Aldave, 49 Ohio St. L.J., at 381, and n. 60; however, "proportionally more persons accused of insider trading [might] be pursued by a U.S. Attorney, and proportionally fewer by the SEC," id., at 382. Our decision, of course, does not rest on such enforcement policy considerations.

rather than "stale"—that is, if the statement would still be likely to be material to investors. See, e.g., Backman v. Polaroid Corp., 910 F.2d 10 (1st Cir.1990) (en banc).

2.   Several courts have held that if a corporation makes a public statement that is correct when made, but that becomes materially misleading in light of subsequent events, the corporation may have a duty to *update* the statement. In the leading case, Greenfield v. Heublein, Inc., 742 F.2d 751, 758 (3d Cir.1984), cert. denied 469 U.S. 1215, 105 S.Ct. 1189, 84 L.Ed.2d 336 (1985), the court said, "[a]l-though a corporation may be under no duty to disclose ..., if a corporation voluntarily makes a public statement that is correct when issued, [the corporation] has a duty to update the statement if it becomes materially misleading in light of subsequent events." See also In re Time Warner Inc. Securities Litigation, 9 F.3d 259, 167 (2d Cir.1993), cert. denied 511 U.S. 1017, 114 S.Ct. 1397, 128 L.Ed.2d 70 (1994) ("a duty to update opinions and projections may arise if the original opinions or projections have become misleading as the result of intervening events.")

In Backman v. Polaroid Corp., supra, the First Circuit qualified this position by taking the view that the duty to update applies only to forward-looking statements:

> Obviously, if a disclosure is in fact misleading when made, and the speaker thereafter learns of this, there is a duty correct it.... In Greenfield v. Heublien, Inc. ... the court called for disclosure if a prior disclosure "becomes materially misleading in light of subse-quent events".... We may agree that, in special circumstances, a statement, correct at the time, may have a forward intent and connotation upon which parties may be expected to rely. If this is a clear meaning, and there is a change, correction, more exactly, further disclosure may be called for....

The scope of the duty to update has been brought into question by the safe harbor provisions of the Private Securities Litigation Reform Act of 1995 (1995 Act). Subject to certain exceptions, the safe harbor provisions provide that a defendant will not be liable with respect a statutorily defined "forward-looking statement" if the statement is accompanied by meaningful cautionary statements identifying impor-tant factors that could cause actual results to differ materially from those in the forward-looking statement, the statement is immaterial, or the plaintiff fails to prove that the statement was made with actual knowledge that the statement was false or misleading. Section 27A(c)(1) and Section 21E(c)(1). The 1995 Act also provides that "nothing in this section shall impose a duty to update a forward-looking statement." Section 27A(d) and Section 21E(d).

3.   A corporation may so involve itself in the preparation of statements about the corporation by outsiders—such as analysts' re-ports or earnings projections—that it assumes a duty to correct material errors in those statements. Such a duty "may occur when officials of the company have, by their activity, made an implied representation that the information they have reviewed is true or at

least in accordance with the company's views." Elkind v. Liggett & Myers, Inc., 635 F.2d 156, 163 (2d Cir.1980).

4. A corporation may be under a duty to correct erroneous rumors resulting from leaks by the corporation or its agents. See, e.g., State Teachers Retirement Board v. Fluor Corp., 654 F.2d 843, 850 (2d Cir.1981) (dictum).

It is sometimes suggested, in dictum or by inference, that nondisclosure by a corporation may violate Rule 10b–5 if no valid corporate purpose requires nondisclosure. It is not easy to see why this should be so, and no corporation seems to have been held liable under this theory.

## SECTION 3. LIABILITY FOR SHORT-SWING TRADING UNDER § 16(b) OF THE SECURITIES EXCHANGE ACT

### SECURITIES EXCHANGE ACT § 16

[See Statutory Supplement]

### SECURITIES EXCHANGE ACT RULES 3a–11–1, 3b–2, 16a–1, 16a–2, 16a–3, 16a–10, 16b–3, 16b–5, 16b–6, 16b–7, 16b–9; FORM 3; FORM 4; FORM 5

[See Statutory Supplement]

**FELDMAN & TEBERG, BENEFICIAL OWNERSHIP UNDER SECTION 16 OF THE SECURITIES EXCHANGE ACT OF 1934,** 17 Western Res.L.Rev. 1054, 1063–65 (1966). "The juxtaposition of section 16(a) and 16(b), plus the fact that both operate with respect to the same persons, has led many to erroneously conclude that section 16(a) was enacted only to reveal transactions within the scope of section 16(b). That section 16(a) is not confined to transactions within the scope of section 16(b) is clear not only from the fact that section 16(a) pre-existed section 16(b) [as a matter of legislative history], but also from the different language of the two subsections. For while section 16(b) speaks of purchases and sales within six months of each other, section 16(a) speaks of changes in beneficial ownership, a much broader concept. . . .

"Since the terms of section 16(a) require insiders to disclose any changes in their beneficial ownership of securities, it provides a means for bringing to light possible violations of . . . Rule 10b–5, as well as a 'purchase and sale' within the scope of section 16(b). However, two other functions of the section 16(a) reports are equally important to the efficacious operations of the Exchange Act's scheme to banish investors' ignorance and upgrade the ethics of corporate managers. Its second function is to reveal information which may be used in evaluating the securities of the issuer. This is a pure disclosure device in which the conclusions to be drawn from the reports and the weight to be attached thereto are left to the judgment of the individual investor. The information contained in the reports may be used (1) as a guide to the insiders' current confidence or lack thereof in the company's fortunes or (2) to detect an evolving change in control in the company. Undoubtedly this investment information function of the section largely explains why the Commission's monthly summary of transactions reported under section 16(a) has become a perennial best seller. Finally, section 16(a) is itself a deterrent to the misuse of inside information through the publicity which attaches to the reports, apart from any other statutory prohibition or liability. This is a standard by-product or goal of any disclosure provision, since presumably people are likely to refrain from improper acts, or acts which may appear improper, if they know such acts will be exposed to public scrutiny."

---

## NOTE ON GOLLUST v. MENDELL

In Gollust v. Mendell, 501 U.S. 115, 111 S.Ct. 2173, 115 L.Ed.2d 109 (1991), the Supreme Court made the following observations on the procedural aspects of § 16(b):

> To enforce this strict liability rule on insider trading, Congress chose to rely solely on the issuers of stock and their security holders. Unlike most of the federal securities laws, § 16(b) does not confer enforcement authority on the Securities and Exchange Commission. It is, rather, the security holders of an issuer who have the ultimate authority to sue for enforcement of § 16(b). If the issuer declines to bring a § 16(b) action within 60 days of a demand by a security holder, or fails to prosecute the action "diligently" ... then the security holder may "institut[e]" an action to recover insider shortswing profits for the issuer....

> Although plaintiffs seeking to sue under the statute must own a "security," § 16(b) places no significant restriction on the type of security adequate to confer standing. "[A]ny security" will suffice, ... the statutory definition being broad enough to include stock, notes, warrants, bonds, debentures, puts, calls, and a variety of other financial instruments; it expressly excludes only "currency or any note, draft, bill of exchange, or banker's acceptance which has a maturity at the time of issuance of not exceeding nine months...."

---

## Report of the Task Force on Regulation of Insider Trading, Part II: Reform of Section 16

42 Bus.Law. 1087, 1091–92 (1987).

In recent years, a number of commentators have suggested that section 16(b) causes more harm than good and that it should be repealed. It has been argued that section 16(b) is ineffectual in preventing insider trading and does not even address all of the ways in which insider trades can be perpetrated, while it imposes punitive liability on the innocent, the naive, and the unaware corporate officers who unwittingly sell in violation of, for example, the labyrinthine restrictions of rule 16b–3. These commentators raise the question: Given the development of the insider trading doctrine under rule 10b–5, the substantial limitations of section 16(b) in preventing insider trading, and the hardships that it imposes, is the statute needed?

The task force believes that it is. Section 16(b) has a different legislative focus than the prohibition of trading on inside information. Indeed, it is the only provision of the 1934 Act that specifically regulates insider trading. It is aimed at three specific types of insider trading abuses, only one of which involves abuse of inside information.

First, section 16(b) was intended to remove the temptation for corporation executives to profit from short-term stock price fluctuations at the expense of the long-term financial health of their companies. It prevents insiders from being obsessed with trading in their companies' securities to the detriment of their managerial and fiduciary responsibilities. In this regard, based on the testimony of insider abuses presented at the hearings, it was Congress's judgment that short-swing trading by corporate executives is not good for their companies or the American capital markets.

Second, the section was intended to penalize the unfair use of inside information by insiders. This includes both trading on inside information in violation of rule 10b–5 and the use of "softer" information of the type that insiders often have but that members of the investing public do not: the ability to make better informed guesses as to the success of new products, the likely results of negotiations, and the real risks of contingencies and other uncertainties, the underlying facts of which have been publicly disclosed.

Third, section 16(b) was designed to eliminate the temptation for insiders to manipulate corporate events so as to maximize their own short-term trading profits. Before the enactment of section 16(b), insiders had been able to make quick profits from short-term price swings by such practices as the announcement of generous (but imprudent) dividend programs followed by postinsider trading dividend reductions. Thus, the section provides a minimum standard of fiduciary conduct for corporate insiders.

The task force thus concludes that section 16 remains a useful tool for preventing speculative abuses by insiders and for focusing their attention on their fiduciary duty and on long-term corporate health, rather than on short-term trading profits.

———

## Gratz v. Claughton

United States Court of Appeals, Second Circuit, 1951.
187 F.2d 46, cert. denied 341 U.S. 920, 71 S.Ct. 741, 95 L.Ed. 1353 (1951).

■ Before L. HAND, CHIEF JUDGE, and SWAN and AUGUSTUS N. HAND, CIRCUIT JUDGES.

■ L. HAND, CHIEF JUDGE.

This is an appeal by the defendant, Claughton, from a judgment against him, entered upon the report of a master, in an action by a shareholder of the Missouri–Kansas–Texas Railroad Company under § 16(b) of the Securities Exchange Act of 1934.... The court first granted a summary judgment as to all the issues except the amount of the profits made by the defendant, which it referred to a master, on whose report it entered final judgment. The defendant does not dispute the propriety of a summary disposition of all the issues except that referred, but he does dispute the propriety of the judgment in law. First, he argues that the venue was wrong because he was domiciled in Florida, and the summons was served upon him in that state. Second, he disputes the rule adopted by the master in computing his profits. Third, he challenges the constitutionality of the statute which imposes the liability, and of the provisions for venue. We shall take up the first and third in sequence, reserving the second for the last.

[The court held that venue was proper.] . . .

The challenge to the constitutionality of § 16(b) we have answered twice before. For many years a grave omission in our corporation law had been its indifference to dealings of directors or other corporate officers in the shares of their companies. When they bought shares, they came literally within the conventional prohibitions of the law of trusts; yet the decisions were strangely slack in so deciding. When they sold shares, it could indeed be argued that they were not dealing with a beneficiary, but with one whom his purchase made a beneficiary. That should not, however, have obscured the fact that the director or officer assumed a fiduciary relation to the buyer by the very sale; for it would be a sorry distinction to allow him to use the advantage of his position to induce the buyer into the position of a beneficiary, although he was forbidden to do so, once the buyer had become one. Certainly this is true, when the buyer knows he is buying of a director or officer, for he expects to become the seller's *cestui que* trust. If the buyer does not know, he is entitled to assume that if his seller in fact is already a director or officer, he will remain so after the sale. Nor was it necessary to confine this disability to directors or other officers of the corporation. The reason for the doctrine was that a director or officer may have information not accessible to a shareholder, actual or prospective, and that advantage is not confined to them. We take judicial notice that an effective control over the affairs of a corporation often does not require anything approaching a majority of the shares; and this is particularly true in the case of those corporations whose shares are dealt in upon national exchanges. Nor is it common for the control so obtained to be in the hands of one individual; more often a number share it, who are all in a position to gain a more intimate acquaintance with the enterprise and its prospects than the shareholders at large. It is of course true that the ownership of ten per cent of the shares does not always put the owner among those who do control; but neither Congress, nor any other legislature, is obliged to limit the means which it chooses so exactly to its ends that the correspondence is exact. If only those persons were liable, who could be proved to have a bargaining advantage, the execution of the statute would be so encumbered as to defeat its whole purpose. We do not mean that the interest, of which a statute deprives an individual, may never be so vital that he must not be given a trial of his personal guilt; but that is not so when all that is at stake is a director's, officer's or "beneficial owner's" privilege to add to, or subtract from, his holdings for a period of six months. In such situations it is well settled that a statute may provide any means which can reasonably be thought necessary to deal with the evil, even though they may cover instances where it is not present. . . .

There remains the question of the computation of profits, which we dealt with in Smolowe v. Delendo Corporation. . . .[8] Section 16(b) declares that "any profit realized . . . from any purchase and sale, or any sale and purchase . . . within any period of less than six months . . . shall inure to and be recoverable by the issuer": the corporation. It is plain that this presupposes some matching of (1) purchases against sales, or of (2) sales against purchases, and that there must therefore be some principle upon which both the minuend—the sale price—and the subtrahend—the purchase price—can be determined. At first blush it might seem that the statute limited the recovery to profits derived from transactions in the same shares; as, for example, that a dealer's profit upon the sale of any given number of shares was to be measured by subtracting what he paid for those shares from what he got upon a sale of the same certificate. However, as we observed in Smolowe v. Delendo Corporation, supra, that would allow an easy avoidance of the statute; in order to speculate freely an officer, director, or "beneficial owner" need only hold a substantial block of shares for more than six months. If, for example, on January 1st, he had 10,000 shares which he had bought before October 1st, he could buy 1,000 shares on February 1st and sell 1,000 shares at a profit on April 1st, making delivery out of certificates from the 10,000 shares purchased before October 1st. After the two transactions his position would be what it had been on January 1st save that in two months he had made a profitable turn in 1,000 shares—exactly the evil against which the statute is directed. Moreover, there is an added reason for

---

**8.**   2 Cir., 136 F.2d 231, 148 A.L.R. 300.

this interpretation, if one be needed. In the case of a sale followed by a purchase it is impossible to identify any purchase with any previous sale; one would have to confine such transactions to the practically non-existent occasions when the proceeds of the sale were used to purchase. Thus it appears, regardless of anything said during the passage of the bill through Congress and of the different forms it took, that the Act does not demand—that the same shares should be sold which were bought. This accords with the fungible nature of shares of stock. Indeed, if we translate the transaction into sales and purchases, or purchases and sales, of gallons of oil in a single tank, or of bushels of wheat in a single bin, it at once appears that the ascertainment of the particular shares bought or sold must be wholly irrelevant.

Although for these reasons it appears that the transactions—sales and purchases, or purchases and sales—are not to be matched by identifying the shares dealt in, we are no nearer than before to finding an answer as to how transactions shall be matched; all that so far appeared, is that the matching is to be between contracts of sale and contracts of purchase, or vice versa. On the other hand it is manifest that the intent of the fiduciary cannot be the test; first, because he generally has no ascertainable intent; and second, because that would open the door even more widely to the evil in question. The statute does not allow the fiduciary to minimize his profits, any more than to set off his losses against them. We can therefore find no principle by which to select any two transactions which are to be matched; and, so far as we can see, we are forced to one of two alternatives: to match any given sale taken as minuend, against any given purchase, taken as subtrahend, in such a way as to reduce profits to their lowest possible amount, or in such a way as to increase them to the greatest possible amount. The master adopted the second course, following what he supposed to be the doctrine of Smolowe v. Delendo Corporation, supra. We think that he was right for the following reasons.

The question is in substance the same as when a trustee's account is to be surcharged, for, as we have said, the statute makes the fiduciary a constructive trustee for any profits he may make. It is true that on the beneficiary in an accounting rests the burden of proof of a surcharge,[9] although the fiduciary has the burden of establishing any credits.[10] Since the plaintiff was seeking to surcharge the defendant we will therefore assume that it rested upon her to show how the transactions are to be matched; and, that, if there were nothing more, since she cannot do so, she must be content to have them matched in the way that shows the least profit. Obviously that cannot be the right answer, for the reasons we have given; and perhaps the fact that it cannot be, is reason enough for adopting the alternative. But there is another ground for reaching the same result. As we have said, the statute makes all such dealings unlawful, and makes the fiduciary accountable to the corporation. Although it is impossible in the case at bar to compute the defendant's profits, except that they must fall

---

**9.** Ewen v. Peoria & Eastern Ry., D.C., 78 F.Supp. 312, 334.

**10.** Wootton Land and Fuel Co. v. Ownbey, 8 Cir., 265 F. 91.

between two limits—the minimum and the maximum—the cause of this uncertainty is the number of transactions within six months: that is, the number of defendant's derelictions. The situation falls within the doctrine which has been law since the days of the "Chimney Sweeper's Jewel Case,"[11] that when damages are at some unascertainable amount below an upper limit and when the uncertainty arises from the defendant's wrong, the upper limit will be taken as the proper amount.[12]

This results in looking for six months both before and after any sale, and not for three months only, as the defendant insists. If one is seeking an equation of purchase and sale, one may take any sale as the minuend and look back for six months for a purchase at less price to match against it. On the other hand, if one is looking for an equation of sale and purchase, one may take the same sale and look forward for six months for any purchase at a lower price. Although obviously no transaction can figure in more than one equation, with that exception we can see no escape from what we have just said. It is true that this means that no director, officer, or "beneficial owner" may safely buy and sell, or sell and buy, shares of stock in the company except at intervals of six months. Whether that is too drastic a means of meeting the evil, we have not to decide; it is enough that we can find no other way to administer the statute. Therefore, not only will we follow Smolowe v. Delendo Corporation, supra, as a precedent; but as *res integra* and after independent analysis we reassert its doctrine. The defendant concedes that, except for carrying the transactions backward and forward for six months, instead of for three, the master followed the rule laid down in that decision; and the plaintiff has not appealed, so that she is not entitled to any more than she has recovered. On this account we have not examined the master's computations in detail and are not to be understood to have passed upon them. The crushing liabilities which § 16(b) may impose are apparent from this action in which the judgment was for over $300,000; it should certainly serve as a warning, and may prove a deterrent.[1]

Judgment affirmed.

---

## NOTE ON THE COMPUTATION OF PROFITS UNDER § 16(b)

1.   In Smolowe v. Delendo Corporation, 136 F.2d 231 (2d Cir. 1943), cert. denied 320 U.S. 751, 64 S.Ct. 56, 88 L.Ed. 446, which was cited and relied upon in Gratz v. Claughton, the court considered and

**11.**  Armory v. Delamirie, 1722, 1 Strange 505.

**12.**  ... Story Parchment Co. v. Paterson Parchment Paper Co., 282 U.S. 555, 563–565, 51 S.Ct. 248, 75 L.Ed. 544; Bigelow v. RKO Radio Pictures, Inc., 327 U.S. 251, 264, 265, 66 S.Ct. 574, 90 L.Ed. 652....

**1.**  In Adler v. Klawans, 267 F.2d 840, 848 (2d Cir.1959), it is reported that "during the pertinent periods, [Gratz] suffered a net loss of $400,000 on trading in the stock for which he was charged under section 16(b)." (Footnote by ed.)

rejected several formulas for computing profits under § 16(b) other than those analyzed in *Gratz:*

> Once the principle of [measuring damages based on the identification of the stock certificates involved] is rejected, its corollary, the first-in, first-out rule, is left at loose ends.... Its rationalization is the same as that for the identification rule, for which it operates as a presumptive principle; and it has no other support. If we reject one, we reject the other and for like reasons. Its application would render the large stockholder with a backlog of stock not immediately devoted to trading immune from the Act. Further, we should note that it does not fit the broad statutory language; a purchase followed immediately by a sale, albeit a transaction within the exact statutory language, would often be held immune from the statutory penalty because the purchase would be deemed by arbitrary rule to have been made at an earlier date; while a sale followed by purchase would never even be within the terms of the rule....

> Another possibility might be the striking of an average purchase price and an average sale price during the period, and using these as bases of computation. What this rule would do in concrete effect is to allow as offsets all losses made by such trading. This in effect the district court first planned to do.... But it corrected this in its supplemental opinion, properly pointing out that the statute provided for the recovery of "any" profit realized and obviously precluded a setting off of losses. Even had the statutory language been more uncertain, this rule seems one not to be favored in the light of the statutory purpose. Compared to other possible rules, it tends to stimulate more active trading by reducing the chance of penalty.... Its application to a case where trading continued more than six months might be most uncertain, depending upon how the beginning of each six months' period was ascertained. It is not a clear-cut taking of "any profit" for the corporation, and we agree with the district court in rejecting it.

2. The formula adopted in *Smolowe* and *Gratz* has been generally approved by the courts. It is often referred to the "lowest purchase price, highest sale price" method. See, e.g., Whittaker v. Whittaker Corp., 639 F.2d 516, 530 (9th Cir.1981). Here are three illustrations of this method:

(i) D is a director of C Corporation, whose stock is traded on a national securities exchange. On January 2, D purchases 1,000 shares of C at $10. On April 1, D sells 1,000 shares of C at $15. This is a short-swing "purchase and sale," and D is liable under § 16(b) for his profit of $5,000.

(ii) On January 2, D purchases 1,000 shares of C at $10. On August 1, D sells 1,000 shares at $15. On November 1, D purchases 1,000 shares at $10. D has no § 16(b) liability on the basis of the January–August swing, because the two ends of the swing did not occur within six months. However, the August and November transactions constitute a short-swing "sale and purchase," and D would be liable under § 16(b) for a profit of $5,000 on these two transactions. Why has D made a $5,000 "profit"? Because after D's November 1 purchase, his position in C Corporation's stock is exactly as it was just before August 1 (that is, he owns 1,000 C shares) but he has also added $5,000 cash to his bank account. D may have accomplished this result by using inside information. The sale at $15 may have been made on the basis of undisclosed bad news. The purchase at $10 may have been made on the basis of undisclosed good news.

(iii)  D engages in the following pattern of activity:

| Date | Action | Amount | Price |
|------|--------|--------|-------|
| 2/1 | Purchase | 1,000 | $30 |
| 3/1 | Sale | 1,000 | $25 |
| 4/1 | Purchase | 1,000 | $20 |
| 5/1 | Sale | 1,000 | $15 |

Under the *Smolowe/Gratz* formula, D has a profit of $5,000, because the purchase at $20 on 4/1 can be matched with the sale at $25 on 3/1. At first glance, this looks counterintuitive: it seems that D has a $10,000 loss in his total trading, not a $5,000 profit. But it may be that except for inside information, D would not have sold on 3/1, and instead would have ridden the C stock all the way down from $30 to $15, for a loss of $15,000. Accordingly, there is a possibility (which is all that § 16(b) requires) that D has profited by $5,000 by holding his loss to $10,000 through the use of inside information.[1]

---

## NOTE ON SECTION 16(b)

Section 16(b) is often criticized on the ground that it can result in liability in cases where there has been no insider trading, and in cases where there has been no real profit. As the Report of the ABA Task Force makes clear, however, this criticism has failed to strike a responsive chord among most members of the corporate bar. The ABA Task Force Report addresses these kinds of criticisms by giving affirmative justifications for the operation of § 16(b). See also Fox, Insider Trading Deterrence versus Managerial Incentives: A Unified Theory of Section 16(b), 92 Mich.L.Rev. 2088.

Furthermore, it's hard to see that § 16(b) has any significant capacity for harm. It's often thought to be desirable to encourage directors and executives to become shareholders, so as to tie their fortunes more closely to those of the corporation's owners. However, it is seldom thought to be desirable to discourage directors and executives from engaging in short-term in-and-out trading. In the overwhelming majority of cases, that's all that § 16(b) does. Moreover, if we put aside exotic scenarios that could occur in theory, but almost

---

1. For a hypothetical in which a finding of profits under the *Smolowe/Gratz* formula does seem counterintuitive, see Lowenfels, Section 16(b): A New Trend in Regulating Insider Trading, 54 Cornell L.Rev. 45, 46–47 n. 6 (1968).

never occur in practice, the sanction of § 16(b) is exceptionally mild, because normally all § 16(b) does is put the director or executive back where she was before she engaged in the relevant transactions.

---

## NOTE ON THE INTERPRETATION OF § 16(b)

The courts have tended to use two somewhat different approaches in cases in which the applicability of § 16(b) is contestable. Until the early 1960s, the predominant theory of interpreting § 16(b) was that the section should be construed to cover all transactions within its literal reach. "[T]he statute was intended to be thoroughgoing, to squeeze all possible profits out of stock transactions, and thus to establish a standard so high as to prevent any conflict between the selfish interest of [an insider] and the faithful performance of his duty." Smolowe v. Delendo Corp., 136 F.2d 231, 239 (2d Cir.1943), cert. denied 320 U.S. 751, 64 S.Ct. 56, 88 L.Ed. 446. This theory of interpreting § 16(b) was known as the "objective" approach, although it has been aptly suggested that "automatic" would be more descriptive. Blau v. Lamb, 363 F.2d 507, 520 (2d Cir.1966), cert. denied 385 U.S. 1002, 87 S.Ct. 707, 17 L.Ed.2d 542 (1967).

Beginning in the mid–1960s, § 16(b) came to be perceived by some as overly harsh, because it operates without regard to fault. A different theory of interpretation, known as the "subjective" or "pragmatic" approach, then set in. Under this approach, in borderline cases—particularly cases involving an "unorthodox" transaction, rather than a garden-variety purchase or sale—the statute would be interpreted to impose liability only if the insider actually had access to inside information, or the transaction was of a type that carries a potential for insider abuse. See Whittaker v. Whittaker Corp., 639 F.2d 516, 522 (9th Cir.1981), cert. denied, 454 U.S. 1031, 102 S.Ct. 566, 70 L.Ed.2d 473; Lowenfels, Section 16(b): A New Trend in Regulating Insider Trading, 54 Cornell L.Rev. 45 (1968).

The names given to these two approaches are misleading. The "subjective" approach does not turn, as its name suggests, on the defendant's subjective intent to use inside information. Conversely, the "objective" approach can be just as pragmatic as the "pragmatic" approach. If the names of the two approaches are put aside, the conflict is between an approach that treats § 16(b) as a prophylactic rule of thumb, whose purpose would be defeated if defendants could escape liability on the ground that in their particular case no abuse could have occurred, and an approach that treats § 16(b) as inviting an inquiry into the possibility of abuse, at least in borderline cases. To a certain extent, which approach is adopted in a given case may depend on whether the court perceives § 16(b) as a good idea or a bad idea.

It should be emphasized that although the tension between the approaches to the interpretation of § 16(b) is real and important, it is a tension only at the margins. In the great bulk of potential cases, the application of § 16(b) is relatively straightforward. As pointed out in *Whittaker,* supra:

> [T]he pragmatic approach has not ousted the objective view. Rather, the pragmatic approach is used to determine the boundaries of the statute's definitional scope in borderline situations, especially unorthodox transactions. . . . For a garden-variety transaction which cannot be regarded as unorthodox, the pragmatic approach is not applicable. . . . In such cases, if the situation is within the requirements established by Congress for § 16, then the mechanical, "objective," operation of the statute imposes liability.

___

### NOTE ON "UNORTHODOX" TRANSACTIONS

One of the major interpretive problems under Section 16(b) is the application of that Section to a transaction that is not a "garden-variety" sale, but is instead an "exotic" or "unorthodox" transaction that seems to offer no possibility for speculative abuse because the disposition of shares by the defendant is involuntary and the defendant apparently had no access to inside information. One such case is a disposition of shares by a more-than–10%-shareholder as part of a merger over which the shareholder had no control and as to which she had no special information.

In Kern County Land Co. v. Occidental Petroleum Corp., 411 U.S. 582, 93 S.Ct. 1736, 36 L.Ed.2d 503 (1973), the Supreme Court held that Section 16(b) was inapplicable to an unorthodox transaction by Occidental, a more-than–10%-shareholder. Occidental was an unsuccessful tender offeror who had no access to inside information, and disposed of its shares in connection with a defensive merger undertaken by the target company for the very purpose of defeating Occidental's tender offer.

The result reached in *Kern County* may seem appealing on the facts. However, the premise of Section 16(b) is that every more-than–10%-shareholder should be deemed an insider. *Kern County* rests on part on the assumption that this premise is incorrect. That assumption may well be true as a matter of fact, but it seems inconsistent with the statute.

___

**NOTE, SHORT–SWING PROFITS IN FAILED TAKEOVER BIDS— THE ROLE OF SECTION 16(b),** 59 Wash.L.Rev. 895 (1984). "Although the *Kern* decision did not state the threshold requirement for application of the pragmatic approach, subsequent courts have generally held that an involuntary transaction is necessary. To prove that a particular transaction is involuntary, the insider must apparently show that it had no control over the timing of the transaction. If the insider fails to make this showing, liability attaches automatically. If the insider does make this showing, however, courts will regard the transaction as unorthodox and will then ask whether the defendant had access to inside information. This inquiry, though secondary, is critical. One with access to inside information can speculate profitably by relying on an imminent 'involuntary' transaction. A finding of involuntariness, therefore, does not guarantee exoneration. . . ."

## NOTE ON ATTRIBUTION OF OWNERSHIP UNDER SECTIONS 16(a) AND (b)

Sections 16(a) and (b) use the term or the concept of "beneficial ownership" for several different purposes.

Under § 16(a), a person who is either "a beneficial owner of more than 10 per centum of any class of equity security" (hereafter, a "10 percent owner"), or an officer or director, must report the amount of all equity securities of the issuer "of which he is the beneficial owner."

Under § 16(b), a director, officer, or 10 percent owner is liable for short-swing profits "realized by him from any purchase and sale, or any sale and purchase, of any equity security" of the issuer. Given both the purpose of the statute and the context, § 16(b) seems generally intended to cover the purchase or sale of those equity securities of which a person is a beneficial owner for purposes of § 16(a).

If a person is the record owner of an equity security and also has a pecuniary interest in the security, he is undoubtedly a beneficial owner for all purposes under § 16. Problems of interpretation arise, however, if a person is a record owner of shares but has no pecuniary interest; or if a person has a pecuniary interest but is not the record owner; or if a person is neither the record owner nor has a pecuniary interest, but there is nevertheless an important relationship between the person and the security, such as the right to control the security. For most although not all practical purposes, the problem can be stated as follows: when should an equity security that is not legally owned by a person in the conventional sense nevertheless be *attributed* to the person under § 16, so that either (i) the security counts toward determining whether the person's ownership crosses the 10–percent-beneficial-ownership line, (ii) the person's transactions in the security must be reported under § 16(a), or (iii) the person's transactions in the security may subject him to liability under § 16(b)?

These problems are addressed in detail by the rules under § 16. Those rules draw a distinction between what constitutes beneficial ownership for purposes of determining whether a person is a 10 percent owner, and what constitutes beneficial ownership for purposes of determining whether a person who *is* a 10 percent owner, or a director or officer, must report under § 16(a) and may be liable for short-swing profits under § 16(b).

As to the first problem (whether a person is a 10 percent owner), Rule 16a–1(a)(1) provides that, with certain exceptions, "*solely for purposes of determining whether a person is a beneficial owner of more than ten percent of* any class of equity securities registered pursuant to § 12 of the Act, the term 'beneficial owner' shall mean any person who is deemed a beneficial owner pursuant to § 13(d) of the Act and the rules thereunder...." (emphasis added). Rule 13d–3, in turn, provides that a beneficial owner of a security includes "any person who, directly or indirectly, through any contract, arrangement, understanding, relationship, or otherwise has or shares: (1) Voting power which includes the power to vote, or to direct the voting of, such security; and/or, (2) Investment power which includes the power to dispose, or to direct the disposition of, such security." In short, in determining whether a person is a 10 percent owner of stock, the emphasis under Rule 16a–1 is on the person's *control* over the stock.

As to the second problem (what constitutes beneficial ownership for reporting and liability purposes) Rule 16a–1(a)(2) provides that as a general principle, with certain exceptions and elaborations, "*other than for purposes of determining whether a person is a beneficial owner of more than ten percent of any class of equity securities* registered under § 12 of the Act, the term 'beneficial owner' shall mean any person who, directly or indirectly, through any contract, arrangement, understanding, relationship or otherwise, has or shares a direct or indirect pecuniary interest in the equity securities...."; and that "[t]he term 'pecuniary interest' in any class of equity securities shall mean the opportunity, directly or indirectly, to profit or share in any profit derived from a transaction in the subject securities." (emphasis added) In short, unlike Rule 16a–1(a)(1), which emphasizes *control* for purposes of determining who is a 10 percent owner, Rule 16a–1(a)(2) emphasizes *pecuniary interest* for purposes of determining what transactions in equity securities must be reported and may give rise to liability.

After stating the pecuniary-interest test as a general principle to govern the determination of beneficial ownership for reporting and liability purposes, Rule 16a–1(a)(2) then goes on to deal with certain recurring cases in which problems of attribution based on a pecuniary interest may arise.

*Family members.* Rule 16a–1(a)(2)(ii)(A) provides that "[t]he term 'indirect pecuniary interest' [under Rule 16a–2] in any class of equity securities shall include, but not be limited to ... securities held by members of a person's immediate family sharing the same household; *provided, however,* that the presumption of such beneficial ownership may be rebutted...." Rule 16a–1(e) then provides that "[t]he term 'immediate family', shall mean any child, stepchild, grandchild, parent, stepparent, grandparent, spouse, sibling, mother-in-law, father-in-law, son-in-law, daughter-in-law, brother-in-law, or sister-in-law, and shall include adoptive relationships."

*Partnerships.* Rule 16a–1(a)(2)(ii)(B) provides that the term "indirect pecuniary interest" [under Rule 16a–1(a)(2)] includes "a general partner's proportionate interest in the portfolio securities held by a general or limited partnership."

*Corporations.* Rule 16a–1(a)(2)(iii) provides that "[a] shareholder shall not be deemed to have a pecuniary interest in the portfolio securities held by a corporation or similar entity in which the person owns securities if the shareholder is not a controlling shareholder of the entity and does not have or share investment control over the entity's portfolio. . . ." Note that this Rule does not specify a general principle for determining when a corporation's portfolio securities will be attributed to shareholders in the corporation, but only provides a safe harbor in the cases that the rule specified.

The Rules under § 16 also contain elaborate provisions dealing with such matters as when a trustee is a beneficial owner for reporting and liability purposes, and when the ownership of a derivative security makes a person the beneficial owner of the derivative security.

––––––––

## NOTE ON WHO IS AN "OFFICER" UNDER § 16(b)

The battle between "objective" and "subjective" approaches to the interpretations of Section 16(b) has played a dramatic role in the question who is an "officer" for purposes of that Section. Under the objective view, an officer *title* would give rise to § 16(b) liability. Under the subjective view, liability would depend on whether the person had access to inside information by virtue of her position. An intermediate view is that liability should turn on a person's corporate role or function (rather than her title), but that the issue is whether the function is "officer-like," not whether the person's corporate function gives her access to inside information.

After much back-and-forth, the SEC adopted a definition of "officer" that is essentially function-based. Rule 16a–1(f) provides that:

[T]he term "officer" shall mean an issuer's president, principal financial officer, or principal accounting officer (or, if there is no such accounting officer, the controller), any vice-president of the issuer in charge of a principal business unit, division or function (such as sales, administration or finance), any other officer who performs a policy-making function, or any other person who performs similar policy-making functions for the issuer.

In a note to Rule 16a–1(f), the SEC states that the term "policy-making function" is not intended to include policy-making functions that are not significant.

The Chairman of the SEC, in his opening remarks at the meeting at which the new rule was adopted, stated that:

The definition of officer . . . [makes] clear that a person's functions and not simply title will determine the applicability of Section 16. The definition . . . is intended to make clear that individuals with executive functions do not avoid liability under

Section 16 simply by foregoing title, and those with a title but no significant executive responsibilities are not subject to the automatic short-swing profit liability of Section 16(b). Thus, for example, a vice-president of a bank, who has no policy-making responsibility would not have to be concerned with possible liability under Section 16(b), if because of an unexpected family emergency, he needed to sell securities.

Barron, Control and Restricted Securities, 19 Sec.Reg.L.J. 292, 294–95 (1991).

––––––

### NOTE ON DEPUTIZATION

Closely related to the theory of attribution under § 16(b) is the theory of deputization. In Blau v. Lehman, 368 U.S. 403, 82 S.Ct. 451, 7 L.Ed.2d 403 (1962), the Supreme Court held that one enterprise, A, could be a "director" of second enterprise, B, within the meaning of § 16(b), if one of B's directors had been deputized by A to act on its behalf. In *Blau*, Thomas, a partner in Lehman Brothers (Enterprise A) sat on the board of Tide Water (Enterprise B), and Lehman profited from short-swing trading in Tide Water stock. The Court said:

> No doubt Lehman Brothers, though a partnership, could for purposes of § 16 be a "director" of Tide Water and function through a deputy, since § 3(a)(9) of the Act provides that " 'person' means ... partnership" and § 3(a)(7) that " 'director' means any director of a corporation or any person performing similar functions with respect to any organization, whether incorporated or unincorporated." Consequently, Lehman Brothers would be a "director" of Tide Water, if as petitioner's complaint charged Lehman actually functioned as a director through Thomas, who had been deputized by Lehman to perform a director's duties not for himself but for Lehman.

Id. at 409. However, the courts below had made findings that the Supreme Court believed precluded the conclusion that deputization had actually occurred, and Lehman Brothers was therefore not held liable. (Thomas himself was held liable below for his pro rata share of the short-swing profits made by Lehman, and this aspect of the case was not appealed.)

Deputization was found to be present in Feder v. Martin Marietta Corp., 406 F.2d 260 (2d Cir.1969), cert. denied 396 U.S. 1036, 90 S.Ct. 678, 24 L.Ed.2d 681 (1970). Bunker, the president of Martin Marietta (Enterprise A), had become a director of Sperry (Enterprise B), in which Martin Marietta held substantial stock. Bunker was ultimately responsible for the total operation of Martin Marietta, and personally approved all of the firm's financial investments—in particular, its purchase of the Sperry stock. Bunker's control over Martin Marietta, coupled with his membership on Sperry's Board, placed him in a position in which he could acquire inside information concerning

Sperry and could utilize such information for Martin. Further, Bunker admitted discussing Sperry's affairs with two officials at Martin Marietta and participating in sessions when Martin Marietta's investment in Sperry was reviewed, and Bunker's ultimate letter of resignation to Martin Marietta's president stated that "When I became a member of the [Sperry] board ... it appeared to your associates that the Martin Marietta ownership of a substantial number of shares of Sperry Rand should have representation on your Board." On these facts, the Second Circuit concluded that "The control possessed by Bunker, his letter of resignation, the approval by the Martin Board of Bunker's directorship with Sperry and the functional similarity between Bunker's acts as a Sperry director and the acts of Martin's representatives on other boards ... are all definite and concrete indicatives that Bunker, in fact, was a Martin deputy." Martin Marietta was therefore held liable, as a director, for its short-swing profits in Sperry stock.

## SECTION 4.   THE COMMON LAW REVISITED

### Diamond v. Oreamuno

New York Court of Appeals, 1969.
24 N.Y.2d 494, 301 N.Y.S.2d 78, 248 N.E.2d 910.

■ CHIEF JUDGE FULD. Upon this appeal from an order denying a motion to dismiss the complaint as insufficient on its face, the question presented—one of first impression in this court—is whether officers and directors may be held accountable to their corporation for gains realized by them from transactions in the company's stock as a result of their use of material inside information.

The complaint was filed by a shareholder of Management Assistance, Inc. (MAI) asserting a derivative action against a number of its officers and directors to compel an accounting for profits allegedly acquired as a result of a breach of fiduciary duty. It charges that two of the defendants—Oreamuno, chairman of the board of directors, and Gonzalez, its president—had used inside information, acquired by them solely by virtue of their positions, in order to reap large personal profits from the sale of MAI shares and that these profits rightfully belong to the corporation. Other officers and directors were joined as defendants on the ground that they acquiesced in or ratified the assertedly wrongful transactions.

MAI is in the business of financing computer installations through sale and lease back arrangements with various commercial and industrial users. Under its lease provisions, MAI was required to maintain and repair the computers but, at the time of this suit, it lacked the capacity to perform this function itself and was forced to engage the manufacturer of the computers, International Business Machines (IBM), to service the machines. As a result of a sharp increase by IBM of its charges for such service, MAI's expenses for August of 1966 rose considerably and its net earnings declined from $262,253 in July to $66,233 in August, a decrease of about 75%. This information, although earlier known to the defendants, was not made public until October of 1966. Prior to the release of the information, however, Oreamuno and Gonzalez sold off a total of 56,500 shares of their MAI stock at the then current market price of $28 a share.

After the information concerning the drop in earnings was made available to the public, the value of a share of MAI stock immediately fell from the $28 realized by the defendants to $11. Thus, the plaintiff alleges, by taking advantage of their privileged position and their access to confidential information, Oreamuno and Gonzalez were able to realize $800,000 more for their securities than they would have had this inside information not been available to them. Stating that the defendants were "forbidden to use [such] information . . . for their own personal profit or gain", the plaintiff brought this derivative action seeking to have the defendants account to the corporation for this difference. A motion by the defendants to dismiss the complaint— pursuant to CPLR 3211 (subd. [a], par. 7)—for failure to state a cause of action was granted by the court at Special Term. The Appellate Division, with one dissent, modified Special Term's order by reinstating the complaint as to the defendants Oreamuno and Gonzalez. The appeal is before us on a certified question.

In reaching a decision in this case, we are, of course, passing only upon the sufficiency of the complaint and we necessarily accept the charges contained in that pleading as true.

It is well established, as a general proposition, that a person who acquires special knowledge or information by virtue of a confidential or fiduciary relationship with another is not free to exploit that knowledge or information for his own personal benefit but must account to his principal for any profits derived therefrom. (See, e.g., *Byrne v. Barrett,* 268 N.Y. 199.) This, in turn, is merely a corollary of the broader principle, inherent in the nature of the fiduciary relationship, that prohibits a trustee or agent from extracting secret profits from his position of trust.

In support of their claim that the complaint fails to state a cause of action, the defendants take the position that, although it is admittedly wrong for an officer or director to use his position to obtain trading profits for himself in the stock of his corporation, the action ascribed to them did not injure or damage MAI in any way. Accordingly, the defendants continue, the corporation should not be permitted to recover the proceeds. They acknowledge that, by virtue of the exclusive access which officers and directors have to inside information, they possess an unfair advantage over other shareholders and, particularly, the persons who had purchased the stock from them but, they contend, the corporation itself was unaffected and, for that reason, a derivative action is an inappropriate remedy.

It is true that the complaint before us does not contain any allegation of damages to the corporation but this has never been considered to be an essential requirement for a cause of action founded on a breach of fiduciary duty. (See, e.g., *Matter of People* [*Bond & Mtge. Guar. Co.*], 303 N.Y. 423, 431; *Wendt v. Fischer*, 243 N.Y. 439, 443; *Dutton v. Willner*, 52 N.Y. 312, 319.) This is because the function of such an action, unlike an ordinary tort or contract case, is not merely to *compensate* the plaintiff for wrongs committed by the defendant but, as this court declared many years ago (*Dutton v. Willner*, 52 N.Y. 312, 319, *supra*), "to *prevent* them, by removing from agents and trustees all inducement to attempt dealing for their own benefit in matters which they have undertaken for others, or to which their agency or trust relates." (Emphasis supplied.)

Just as a trustee has no right to retain for himself the profits yielded by property placed in his possession but must account to his beneficiaries, a corporate fiduciary, who is entrusted with potentially valuable information, may not appropriate that asset for his own use even though, in so doing, he causes no injury to the corporation. The primary concern, in a case such as this, is not to determine whether the corporation has been damaged but to decide, as between the corporation and the defendants, who has a higher claim to the proceeds derived from the exploitation of the information. In our opinion, there can be no justification for permitting officers and directors, such as the defendants, to retain for themselves profits which, it is alleged, they derived solely from exploiting information gained by virtue of their inside position as corporate officials.

In addition, it is pertinent to observe that, despite the lack of any specific allegation of damage, it may well be inferred that the defendants' actions might have caused some harm to the enterprise. Although the corporation may have little concern with the day-to-day transactions in its shares, it has a great interest in maintaining a reputation of integrity, an image of probity, for its management and in insuring the continued public acceptance and marketability of its stock. When officers and directors abuse their position in order to gain personal profits, the effect may be to cast a cloud on the corporation's name, injure stockholder relations and undermine public regard for the corporation's securities. As Presiding Justice BOTEIN aptly put it, in the course of his opinion for the Appellate Division, "[t]he prestige and good will of a corporation, so vital to its prosperity, may be undermined by the revelation that its chief officers had been making personal profits out of corporate events which they had not disclosed to the community of stockholders." (29 A.D.2d, at p. 287.)

The defendants maintain that extending the prohibition against personal exploitation of a fiduciary relationship to officers and directors of a corporation will discourage such officials from maintaining a stake in the success of the corporate venture through share ownership, which, they urge, is an important incentive to proper performance of their duties. There is, however, a considerable difference between corporate officers who assume the same risks and obtain the same benefits as other shareholders and those who use their privileged position to gain special advantages not available to others. The sale of shares by the defendants for the reasons charged was not merely a wise investment decision which any prudent investor might have made. Rather, they were assertedly able in this case to profit solely because they had information which was not available to any one else—including the other shareholders whose interests they, as corporate fiduciaries, were bound to protect.

Although no appellate court in this State has had occasion to pass upon the precise question before us, the concept underlying the present cause of action is hardly a new one. (See, e.g., Securities Exchange Act of 1934 [48 U.S.Stat. 881], § 16[b]; U.S.Code, tit. 15, § 78p, subd. [b]; *Brophy v. Cities Serv. Co.,* 31 Del.Ch. 241; Restatement, 2d, Agency, § 388, comment *c*; Israels, A New Look at Corporate Directorship, 24 Business Lawyer 727, 732 *et seq.;* Note, 54 Cornell L.Rev. 306, 309–312.) Under Federal law (Securities Exchange Act of 1934, § 16[b]), for example, it is conclusively presumed that, when a director, officer or 10% shareholder buys and sells securities of his corporation within a six-month period, he is trading on inside information. The remedy which the Federal statute provides in that situation is precisely the same as that sought in the present case under State law, namely, an action brought by the corporation or on its behalf to recover all profits derived from the transactions.

In providing this remedy, Congress accomplished a dual purpose. It not only provided for an efficient and effective method of accomplishing its primary goal—the protection of the investing public from unfair treatment at the hands of corporate insiders—but extended to the corporation the right to secure for itself benefits derived by those insiders from their exploitation of their privileged position. The United States Court of Appeals for the Second Circuit has stated the policy behind section 16(b) in the following terms (*Adler v. Klawans,* 267 F.2d 840, 844):

> "The undoubted congressional intent in the enactment of § 16(b) was to discourage what was reasonably thought to be a widespread abuse of a fiduciary relationship—specifically to discourage if not prevent three classes of persons from making private and gainful use of information acquired by them by virtue of their official relationship to a corporation."

Although the provisions of section 16(b) may not apply to all cases of trading on inside information, it demonstrates that a derivative action can be an effective method for dealing with such abuses which may be used to accomplish a similar purpose in cases not specifically covered by the statute. In *Brophy v. Cities Serv. Co.* (31 Del.Ch. 241, *supra*), for example, the Chancery Court of Delaware allowed a similar remedy in a situation not covered by the Federal legislation. One of the defendants in that case was an employee who had acquired inside information that the corporate plaintiff was about to enter the market and purchase its own shares. On the basis of this confidential information, the employee, who was not an officer and, hence, not liable under Federal law, bought a large block of shares and, after the corporation's purchases had caused the price to rise, resold them at a profit. The court sustained the complaint in a derivative action brought for an accounting, stating that "[p]ublic policy will not permit an employee occupying a position of trust and confidence toward his employer to abuse that relation to his own profit, regardless of whether his employer suffers a loss" (31 Del.Ch., at p. 246). And a similar view has been expressed in the Restatement, 2d, Agency (§ 388, comment *c*):

> "*c. Use of confidential information.* An agent who acquires confidential information in the course of his employment or in violation of his duties has a duty ... to account for any profits made by the use of such information, although this does not harm the principal.... So, if [a corporate officer] has 'inside' information that the corporation is about to purchase or sell securities, or to declare or to pass a dividend, profits made by him in stock transactions undertaken because of his knowledge are held in constructive trust for the principal."

In the present case, the defendants may be able to avoid liability to the corporation under section 16(b) of the Federal law since they had held the MAI shares for more than six months prior to the sales. Nevertheless, the alleged use of the inside information to dispose of their stock at a price considerably higher than its known value constituted the same sort of "abuse of a fiduciary relationship" as is condemned by the Federal law. Sitting as we are in this case as a court of equity, we should not hesitate to permit an action to prevent any unjust enrichment realized by the defendants from their allegedly wrongful act.

The defendants recognize that the conduct charged against them directly contravened the policy embodied in the Securities Exchange Act but, they maintain, the Federal legislation constitutes a comprehensive and carefully wrought plan for dealing with the abuse of inside information and that allowing a derivative action to be maintained under State law would interfere with the Federal scheme. Moreover, they urge, the existence of dual Federal and State remedies for the same act would create the possibility of double liability.

An examination of the Federal regulatory scheme refutes the contention that it was designed to establish any particular remedy as exclusive. In addition to the specific provisions of section 16(b), the Securities and Exchange Act contains a general anti-fraud provision in section 10(b), (U.S.Code, tit. 15, § 78j, subd. [b]) which, as implemented by rule 10b–5 (Code of Fed.Reg., tit. 17, § 240.10b–5) under that section, renders it unlawful to engage in a variety of acts considered to be fraudulent. In interpreting this rule, the Securities and Exchange Commission and the Federal courts have extended the common-law definition of fraud to include not only affirmative misrepresentations, relied upon by the purchaser or seller, but also a failure to disclose material information which might have affected the transaction. (See, e.g., *Securities & Exch. Comm. v. Texas Gulf Sulphur Co.,* 401 F.2d 833, 847–848; *Myzel v. Fields,* 386 F.2d 718, 733–735.)

Accepting the truth of the complaint's allegations, there is no question but that the defendants were guilty of withholding material information from the purchasers of the shares and, indeed, the defendants acknowledge that the facts asserted constitute a violation of rule 10b–5. The remedies which the Federal law provides for such violation, however, are rather limited. An action could be brought, in an exceptional case, by the SEC for injunctive relief. This, in fact, is what happened in the *Texas Gulf Sulphur* case (401 F.2d 833, *supra*). The purpose of such an action, however, would appear to be more to establish a principle than to provide a regular method of enforcement. A class action under the Federal rule might be a more effective remedy but the mechanics of such an action have, as far as we have been able to ascertain, not yet been worked out by the Federal courts and several questions relating thereto have never been resolved. These include the definition of the class entitled to bring such an action, the measure of damages, the administration of the fund which would be recovered and its distribution to the members of the class. (See Note, 54 Cornell L.Rev. 306, 309, *supra*.) Of course, any individual purchaser, who could prove his own injury as a result of a rule 10b–5 violation can bring an action for rescission but we have not been referred to a single case in which such an action has been successfully prosecuted where the public sale of securities is involved. The reason for this is that sales of securities, whether through a stock exchange or over-the-counter, are characteristically anonymous transactions, usually handled through brokers, and the matching of the ultimate buyer with the ultimate seller presents virtually insurmountable obstacles. Thus, unless a section 16(b) violation is also present, the Federal law does not yet provide a really effective remedy.

In view of the practical difficulties inherent in an action under the Federal law, the desirability of creating an effective common-law remedy is manifest. "Dishonest directors should not find absolution from retributive justice", Ballantine observed in his work on Corporations ( [rev. ed., 1946], p. 216), "by concealing their identity from their victims under the mask of the stock exchange." There is ample room in a situation such as is here presented for a "private Attorney General" to come forward and enforce proper behavior on the part of corporate officials through the medium of the derivative action brought in the name of the corporation. (See, e.g., *Associated Ind. v. Ickes,* 134 F.2d 694, 704; *Cherner v. Transitron Electronic Corp.,* 201 F.Supp. 934, 936.) Only by sanctioning such a cause of action will there be any effective method to prevent the type of abuse of corporate office complained of in this case.

There is nothing in the Federal law which indicates that it was intended to limit the power of the States to fashion additional remedies to effectuate similar purposes. Although the impact of Federal securities regulation has on occasion been said to have created a "Federal corporation law," in fact, its effect on the duties and obligations of directors and officers and their relation to the corporation and its shareholders is only occasional and peripheral. The primary source of the law in this area ever remains that of the State which created the corporation. Indeed, Congress expressly provided against any implication that it intended to pre-empt the field by declaring, in section 28(a) of the Securities Exchange Act of 1934 (48 U.S.Code 903), that "[t]he rights and remedies provided by this title shall be in addition to any and all other rights and remedies that may exist at law or in equity".

Nor should we be deterred, in formulating a State remedy, by the defendants' claim of possible double liability. Certainly, as already indicated, if the sales in question were publicly made, the likelihood that a suit will be brought by purchasers of the shares is quite remote. But, even if it were not, the mere possibility of such a suit is not a defense nor does it render the complaint insufficient. It is not unusual for an action to be brought to recover a fund which may be subject to a superior claim by a third party. If that be the situation, a defendant should not be permitted to retain the fund for his own use on the chance that such a party may eventually appear. A defendant's course, if he wishes to protect himself against double liability, is to interplead any and all possible claimants and bind them to the judgment (CPLR 1006, subd. [b]).

In any event, though, no suggestion has been made either in brief or on oral argument that any purchaser has come forward with a claim against the defendants or even that anyone is in a position to advance such a claim.[1] As we have stated, the defendants' assertion that such a party may come forward at some future date is not a basis for permitting them to retain for their own benefit the fruits of their allegedly wrongful acts. For all that appears, the present derivative action is the only effective remedy now available against the abuse by these defendants of their privileged position.

As we have previously indicated, what we have written must be read in the light of the charges contained in the complaint, and it must be borne in mind that "it will be incumbent upon the plaintiff, if he is to succeed, to prove upon the trial the truth and correctness of his allegations." (*Walkovszky v. Carlton,* 23 N.Y.2d 714, 715.)

The order appealed from should be affirmed, with costs, and the question certified answered in the affirmative.

◼ JUDGES BURKE, SCILEPPI, BERGAN, KEATING, BREITEL and JASEN concur.

Order affirmed, etc.

———

Accord: Brophy v. Cities Service Co., 31 Del.Ch. 241, 70 A.2d 5 (1949). See also Carpenter v. United States, 484 U.S. 19, 108 S.Ct. 316, 98 L.Ed.2d 275 (1987), supra, p. 919; Thomas v. Roblin Indus., Inc., 520 F.2d 1393, 1397 (3d Cir.1975); In re ORFA Securities Litigation,

---

1. In the absence of any such appearance by adverse claimants, we need not now decide whether the corporation's recovery would be affected by any amounts which might have to be refunded by the defendant to the injured purchasers.

654 F.Supp. 1449 (D.N.J.1987). Contra: Freeman v. Decio, 584 F.2d 186 (7th Cir.1978); Schein v. Chasen, 313 So.2d 739 (Fla.1975).

---

## Malone v. Brincat

Supreme Court of Delaware, 1998.
722 A.2d 5.

■ Before Veasey, Chief Justice, Walsh, Holland, Hartnett and Berger, Justices (constituting the Court en Banc).

■ Holland, Justice:

Doran Malone, Joseph P. Danielle, and Adrienne M. Danielle, the plaintiffs-appellants, filed this individual and class action in the Court of Chancery. The complaint alleged that the directors of Mercury Finance Company ("Mercury"), a Delaware corporation, breached their fiduciary duty of disclosure. The individual defendant-appellee directors are John N. Brincat, Dennis H. Chookaszian, William C. Croft, Clifford R. Johnson, Andrew McNally, IV, Bruce I. McPhee, Fred G. Steingraber, and Phillip J. Wicklander. The complaint also alleged that the defendant-appellee, KPMG Peat Marwick LLP ("KPMG") aided and abetted the Mercury directors' breaches of fiduciary duty. The Court of Chancery dismissed the complaint with prejudice pursuant to Chancery Rule 12(b)(6) for failure to state a claim upon which relief may be granted.

The complaint alleged that the director defendants intentionally overstated the financial condition of Mercury on repeated occasions throughout a four-year period in disclosures to Mercury's shareholders. Plaintiffs contend that the complaint states a claim upon which relief can be granted for a breach of the fiduciary duty of disclosure. Plaintiffs also contend that, because the director defendants breached their fiduciary duty of disclosure to the Mercury shareholders, the Court of Chancery erroneously dismissed the aiding and abetting claim against KPMG.

This Court has concluded that the Court of Chancery properly granted the defendants' motions to dismiss the complaint. That dismissal, however, should have been without prejudice. Plaintiffs are entitled to file an amended complaint. Therefore, the judgment of the Court of Chancery is affirmed in part, reversed in part, and remanded for further proceedings consistent with this opinion.

### Facts

Mercury is a publicly-traded company engaged primarily in purchasing installment sales contracts from automobile dealers and providing short-term installment loans directly to consumers. This action was filed on behalf of the named plaintiffs and all persons (excluding defendants) who owned common stock of Mercury from 1993 through the present and their successors in interest, heirs and assigns (the "putative class"). The complaint alleged that the directors "knowingly and intentionally breached their fiduciary duty of disclosure because the SEC filings made by the directors and every communication from the company to the shareholders since 1994 was materially false" and that "as a direct result of the false disclosures ... the Company has lost all or virtually an of its value (about $2 billion)." The complaint also alleged that KPMG knowingly participated in the directors' breaches of their fiduciary duty of disclosure.

According to plaintiffs, since 1994, the director defendants caused Mercury to disseminate information containing overstatements of Mercury's earnings, financial performance and shareholders' equity. Mercury's earnings for 1996 were actually only $56.7 million, or $33 a share, rather than the $120.7 million, or $.70 a share, as reported by the director defendants. Mercury's earnings in 1995 were actually $76.9 million, or $.44 a share, rather than $98.9 million, or $.57 a share, as reported by the director defendants. Mercury's earnings for 1994 were $83 million, or $.47 a share, rather than $86.5 million, or $.49 a share, as reported by the director defendants. Mercury's earnings for 1993 were $64.2 million, rather than $64.9 million, as reported by the director defendants. Shareholders' equity on December 31, 1996 was disclosed by the director defendants as $353 million, but was only $263 million or less. The complaint alleged that all of the foregoing inaccurate information was included or referenced in virtually every filing Mercury made with the SEC and every communication Mercury's directors made to the shareholders during this period of time.

Having alleged these violations of fiduciary duty, which (if true) are egregious, plaintiffs alleged that as "a direct result of [these] false disclosures ... the company has lost all or virtually all its value (about $2 billion)," and seeks class action status to pursue damages against the directors and KPMG for the individual plaintiffs and common stockholders. The individual director defendants filed a motion to dismiss, contending that they owed no fiduciary duty of disclosure under the circumstances alleged in the complaint. KPMG also filed a motion to dismiss the aiding and abetting claim asserted against it.

After briefing and oral argument, the Court of Chancery granted both of the motions to dismiss with prejudice. The Court of Chancery held that directors have no fiduciary duty of disclosure under Delaware law in the absence of a request for shareholder action. In so holding, the Court stated:

> The federal securities laws ensure the timely release of accurate information into the marketplace. The federal power to regulate should not be duplicated or impliedly usurped by Delaware. When a shareholder is damaged merely as a result of the release of inaccurate information into the marketplace, unconnected with any Delaware corporate governance issue, that shareholder must seek a remedy under federal law.

We disagree, and although we hold that the Complaint as drafted should have been dismissed, our rationale is different.

## Standard of Review

A motion to dismiss a complaint presents the trial court with a question of law and is subject to de novo review by this Court on appeal. This Court and the trial court must accept all well-pleaded allegations of fact as true. A complaint should be dismissed for failure to state a claim only when it appears "with a reasonable certainty that a plaintiff would not be entitled to the relief sought under any set of facts which could be proven to support the action."

## Issue On Appeal

This Court has held that. a board of directors is under a fiduciary duty to disclose material information when seeking shareholder action:

> It is well-established that the duty of disclosure "represents nothing more than the well-recognized proposition that directors of Delaware corporations are under a fiduciary duty to disclose fully and fairly all material information within the board's control when it seeks shareholder action."[1]

The majority of opinions from the Court of Chancery have held that there may be a cause of action for disclosure violations only where directors seek shareholder action.[2] The present appeal requires this Court to decide whether a director's fiduciary duty arising out of misdisclosure is implicated in the absence of a request for shareholder action. We hold that directors who knowingly disseminate false information that results in corporate injury or damage to an individual stockholder violate their fiduciary duty, and may be held accountable in a manner appropriate to the circumstances.

## Fiduciary Duty
## Delaware Corporate Directors

An underlying premise for the imposition of fiduciary duties is a separation of legal control from beneficial ownership. Equitable principles act in those circumstances to protect the beneficiaries who are not in a position to protect themselves. One of the fundamental tenets of Delaware corporate law provides for a separation of control and ownership. The board of directors has the legal responsibility to manage the business of a corporation for the benefit of its shareholder owners. Accordingly, fiduciary duties are imposed on the directors of Delaware corporations to regulate their conduct when they discharge that function.

The directors of Delaware corporations stand in a fiduciary relationship not only to the stockholders but-also to the corporations

---

**1.** Zirn v. VLI Corp., Del.Supr., 681 A.2d 1050, 1056 (1996) quoting *Stroud v. Grace*, 606 A.2d at 84 (emphasis added). [Editor's Note: A number of the footnotes in this opinion have been deleted. The balance have been renumbered.]

**2.** *Kahn v. Roberts*, Del.Supr., 679 A.2d 460, 467 (1996) (collecting cases). *Cf. Ciro, Inc. v. Gold*, D. Del. 816 F.Supp. 253, 267 (1993).

upon whose boards they serve.[3] The director's fiduciary duty to both the corporation and its shareholders has been characterized by this Court as a triad: due care, good faith, and loyalty.[4] That triparte fiduciary duty does not operate intermittently but is the constant compass by which all director actions for the corporation and interactions with its shareholders must be guided.

Although the fiduciary duty of a Delaware director is unremitting, the exact course of conduct that must be charted to properly discharge that responsibility will change in the specific context of the action the director is taking with regard to either the corporation or its shareholders. This Court has endeavored to provide the directors with clear signal beacons and brightly lined-channel markers as they navigate with due care, good faith, and loyalty on behalf of a Delaware corporation and its shareholders. This Court has also endeavored to mark the safe harbors clearly.

### Director Communications
### Shareholder Reliance Justified

The shareholder constituents of a Delaware corporation are entitled to rely upon their elected directors to discharge their fiduciary duties at all times. Whenever directors communicate publicly or directly with shareholders about the corporation's affairs, with or without a request for shareholder action, directors have a fiduciary duty to shareholders to exercise due care, good faith and loyalty. It follows a fortiori that when directors communicate publicly or directly with shareholders about corporate matters the sine qua non of directors' fiduciary duty to shareholders is honesty.[5]

According to the appellants, the focus of the fiduciary duty of disclosure is to protect shareholders as the "beneficiaries" of all material information disseminated by the directors. The duty of disclosure is, and always has been, a specific application of the general fiduciary duty owed by directors. The duty of disclosure obligates directors to provide the stockholders with accurate and complete information material to a transaction or other corporate event that is being presented to them for action.

The issue in this case is not whether Mercury's directors breached their duty of disclosure. It is whether they breached their more general fiduciary duty of loyalty and good faith by knowingly disseminating to the stockholders false information about the financial condition of the company. The directors' fiduciary duties include the duty to deal with their stockholders honestly.

**3.** *Guth v. Loft*, Del.Supr., 5 A.2d 503, 510 (1939). *See David A. Drexler et al.*, Delaware Corporation Law § 15.02 (Matthew Bender 1998).

**4.** *Cede & Co. v. Technicolor, Inc.*, Del. Supr., 734 A.2d 345, 361 (1993).

**5.** *Marhart, Inc. v. Calmat Co.*, Del. Ch., CA No. 11820, Berger, V.C., 1992 WL 212587 (Apr. 22, 1992), slip op. At 6 (reported in 18 Del. J. Corp. L. 330 (1992)) ("Delaware directors are fiduciaries and are held to a high standard of conduct.... It is entirely consistent with this settled principle of law that fiduciaries who undertake the responsibility of informing shareholders about corporate affairs, be required to do so honestly.").

Shareholders are entitled to rely upon the truthfulness of all information disseminated to them by the directors they elect to manage the corporate enterprise. Delaware directors disseminate information in at least three contexts: public statements made to the market, including shareholders; statements informing shareholders about the affairs of the corporation without a request for shareholder action; and, statements to shareholders in conjunction with a request for shareholder action. Inaccurate information in these contexts may be the result of violation of the fiduciary duties of care, loyalty or good faith. We will examine the remedies that are available to shareholders for misrepresentations in each of these three contexts by the directors of a Delaware corporation.

### State Fiduciary Disclosure Duty
### Shareholder Remedy In Action–Requested Context

In the absence of a request for stockholder action, the Delaware General Corporation Law does not require directors to provide shareholders with information concerning the finances or affairs of the corporation. Even when shareholder action is sought, the provisions in the General Corporation Law requiring notice to the shareholders of the proposed action do not require the directors to convey substantive information beyond a statutory minimum.[6] Consequently, in the context of a request for shareholder action, the protection afforded by Delaware law is a judicially recognized equitable cause of action by shareholders against directors.

The fiduciary duty of directors in connection with disclosure violations in Delaware jurisprudence was restated in Lynch v. Vickers Energy Corp., Del.Supr., 383 A.2d 278 (1977). In *Lynch*, this Court held that, in making a tender offer to acquire the stock of the minority stockholders, a majority stockholder "owed a fiduciary duty ... which required 'complete candor' in disclosing fully 'all the facts and circumstances surrounding the' tender offer.[7] In *Stroud v. Grace,* we noted that the language of our jurisprudence should be clarified to the extent that 'candor' requires no more than the duty to disclose all material facts when seeking stockholder action.[8] An article by Professor Lawrence Hamermesh[9] includes an excellent historical summary of the content, context, and parameters of the law of disclosure, as it has been developed in a series of decisions during the last two decades."

**6.**  *See Stroud v. Grace*, 606 A.2d at 85 (discussing 8 Del. C. § 222(a) and 242(b)(1)).

**7.**  *Lynch v. Vickers Energy Corp.*, Del. Supr., 383 A.2d 278, 279 (1977) quoting *Lynch v. Vickers Energy Corp.*, Del. Ch., 351 A.2d 570, 573 (1976); *accord Shell Petroleum, Inc. v. Smith*, Del. Supr., 606 A.2d 112, 114–15 (1992) (majority stockholder bears burden of showing full disclosure of all facts within its knowledge that are material to stockholder action). The fiduciary duty of disclosure is also applicable to directors of a Delaware corporation, *In re Anderson, Clayton Share-*holders Litig., Del. Ch., 519 A.2d 680, 688–90 (1986); *Smith v. Van Gorkom*, Del. Supr., 488 A.2d 858, 890 (1985) and to less-than-majority shareholders who control or affirmatively attempt to mandate the destiny of the corporation. *In re Tri–Star Pictures, Inc. Litig.*, 634 A.2d at 328–29.

**8.**  *Stroud v. Grace*, 606 A.2d at 84.

**9.**  Lawrence A. Hamermesh, Calling Off the Lynch Mob: A Corporate Director's Fiduciary Disclosure Duty, 49 Vand. L. Rev. 1087, 1174 n.394 (1996).

The duty of directors to observe proper disclosure requirements derives from the combination of the fiduciary duties of care, loyalty and good faith.[10] The plaintiffs contend that, because directors fiduciary responsibilities are not "intermittent duties," there is no reason why the duty of disclosure should not be implicated in every public communication by a corporate board of directors. The directors of a Delaware corporation are required to disclose fully and fairly all material information within the board's control when it seeks shareholder action. When the directors disseminate information to stockholders when no stockholder action is sought, the fiduciary duties of care, loyalty and good faith apply. Dissemination of false information could violate one or more of those duties.

An action for a breach of fiduciary duty arising out of disclosure violations in connection with a request for stockholder action does not include the elements of reliance, causation and actual quantifiable monetary damages.[11] Instead, such actions require the challenged disclosure to have a connection to the request for shareholder action. The essential inquiry in such an action is whether the alleged omission or misrepresentation is material. Materiality is determined with respect to the shareholder action being sought.

The directors' duty to disclose all available material information in connection with a request for shareholder action must be balanced against its concomitant duty to protect the corporate enterprise, in particular, by keeping certain financial information confidential. Directors are required to provide shareholders with all information that is material to the action being requested and to provide a balanced, truthful account of all matters disclosed in the communications with shareholders.[12] Accordingly, directors have definitive guidance in discharging their fiduciary duty by an analysis of the factual circumstances relating to the specific shareholder action being requested and an inquiry into the potential for deception or misinformation.[13]

### Fraud On Market Regulated by Federal Law

When corporate directors impart information they must comport with the obligations imposed by both the Delaware law and the federal statutes and regulations of the United States Securities and Exchange

---

**10.** *See Cinerama, Inc. v. Technicolor, Inc.,* Del.Supr, 663 A.2d 1156, 1160 (1995); *Zirn v. VLI Corp.,* 621 A.2d at 778.

**11.** *See Cinerama, Inc. v. Technicolor, Inc.,* Del.Supr, 663 A.2d at 1163; *In re Tri-Star Pictures, Inc. Litig.,* 634 A.2d at 327 n.10 and 333. *Loudon v. Archer–Daniels–Midland Co.,* 700 A.2d at 142 ("where directors have breached their disclosure duties in a corporate transaction ... there must at least be an award of nominal damages.").

**12.** *Zirn v. VLI Corp.,* 681 A.2d at 1056. In *Zirn II,* this Court held, "in addition to the traditional duty to disclose all facts material to the proffered transaction, directors are under a fiduciary obligation to avoid mislead-

ing partial disclosures. The law of partial disclosure is likewise clear: Once defendants travel down the road of partial disclosure they have an obligation to provide the stockholders with an accurate, full and fair characterization of those historic events." (Internal quotations omitted).

**13.** *See Zirn v. VLI Corp.,* 681 A.2d at 1062 ("a good faith erroneous judgment as to the proper scope or content of required disclosure implicates the duty of care rather than the duty of loyalty."); *Arnold v. Society for Savings Bancorp,* 650 A.2d at 1287–88 & no. 36.

Commission ("SEC"). Historically, federal law has regulated disclosures by corporate directors into the general interstate market. This Court has noted that "in observing its congressional mandate the SEC has adopted a 'basic philosophy of disclosure.' "[14] Accordingly, this Court has held that there is "no legitimate basis to create a new cause of action which would replicate, by state decisional law, the provisions of ... the 1934 Act."[15] In deference to the panoply of federal protections that are available to investors in connection with the purchase or sale of securities of Delaware corporations, this Court has decided not to recognize a state common law cause of action against the directors of Delaware corporations for "fraud on the market."[16] Here, it is to be noted, the claim appears to be made by those who did not sell and, therefore, would not implicate federal securities laws which relate to the purchase or sale of securities.

The historic roles played by state and federal law in regulating corporate disclosures have been not only compatible but complementary.[17] That symbiotic relationship has been perpetuated by the recently enacted federal Securities Litigation Uniform Standards Act of 1998.[18] Although that statute by its terms does not apply to this case, the new statute will require securities class actions involving the purchase or sale of nationally traded securities, based upon false or misleading statements, to be brought exclusively in federal court under federal law. The 1998 Act, however, contains two important exceptions:[19] the first provides that an "exclusively derivative action

**14.** *Stroud v. Grace*, Del.Supr. 606 A.2d 75, 86 (1992). *See, e.g.*, Randall S. Thomas & Catherine T. Dixon, Aranow & Einhorn on *Proxy Contents for Corporation Control*, § 21.02 (3d ed. 1998).

**15.** *Arnold v. Society for Savings Bankcorp, Inc.*, Del.Supr., 678 A.2d 533, 539 (1996).

**16.** *Gaffin v. Teledyne, Inc.*, Del.Supr., 611 A.2d 467, 471 (1992). *See Basic Incorporated v. Levinson*, 485 U.S. 224, 241–42, 108 S.Ct. 978, 99 L.Ed.2d 194 (1988) (discussing the theory of fraud on the market.)

**17.** *See Santa Fe Industries, Inc. v. Green*, 430 U.S. 462, 474–80, 97 S.Ct. 1292, 51 L.Ed.2d 480 (1977) (discussing state corporation law and the purpose of disclosure in federal securities law). *Cf.* Roberta Romano, Empowering Investors: A Market Approach to Securities Regulation 107 Yale L.J. 2359 (1998) ("Advocating fundamental reform of the current strategy toward securities regulation by implementing a regulatory approach of competitive federalism.").

**18.** Securities Litigation Uniform Standards Act of 1998, Pub.L. No. 105–353, 112 Stat. 3227 (1998).

**19.** Section 16(d) of the Act provides:

(d) Preservation of Certain Actions.—

(1) Actions under state law of state of incorporation.—

(A) Actions preserved.—Notwithstanding subsection (b) or (c), a covered class action described in subparagraph (B) of this paragraph that is based upon the statutory or common law of the State in which the issuer is incorporated (in the case of a corporation) or organized (in the case of any other entity) may be maintained in a State or Federal court by a private party.

(B) Permissible actions.—A covered class action is described in this subparagraph if it involves—

(i) the purchase or sale of securities by the issuer or an affiliate of the issuer exclusively from or to holders of equity securities of the issuer; or

(ii) any recommendation, position, or other communication with respect to the sale of securities of the issuer securities by the issuer or an affiliate

that—

(I) is made by or on behalf of the issuer or an affiliate of the issuer to holders of equity securities of the issuer; and

(II) concerns decisions of those equity holders with respect to voting

brought by one or more shareholders on behalf of a corporation" is not preempted; the second preserves the availability of state court class actions, where state law already provides that corporate directors have fiduciary disclosure obligations to shareholders.[20] These exceptions have become known as the "Delaware carve-outs."[21]

We need not decide at this time, however, whether this new Act will have any effect on this litigation if plaintiffs elect to replead. See Section (c) of the Act:

> (c) Applicability.—The amendments made by this section shall not affect or apply to any action commenced before and pending on the date of enactment of this Act.

## State Common Law
## Shareholder Remedy In Nonaction Context

Delaware law also protects shareholders who receive false communications from directors even in the absence of a request for shareholder action. When the directors are not seeking shareholder action, but are deliberately misinforming shareholders about the business of the corporation, either directly or by a public statement, there is a violation of fiduciary duty. That violation may result in a derivative claim on behalf of the corporation or a cause of action for damages. There may also be a basis for equitable relief to remedy the violation.

## Complaint Properly Dismissed
## No Shareholder Action Requested

Here the complaint alleges (if true) an egregious violation of fiduciary duty by the directors in knowingly disseminating materially false information. Then it alleges that the corporation lost about $2 billion in value as a result. Then it merely claims that the action is brought on behalf of the named plaintiffs and the putative class. It is a non sequitur rather than a syllogism.

The allegation in paragraph 3 that the false disclosures resulted in the corporation losing virtually all its equity seems obliquely to claim an injury to the corporation. The plaintiffs, however, never expressly assert a derivative claim on behalf of the corporation or allege compliance with Court of Chancery Rule 23.1, which requires pre-suit demand or cognizable and particularized allegations that demand is

their securities, acting in response to a tender or exchange offer, or exercising dissenters' or appraisal rights.

**20.** See, e.g., Zirn v. VLI Corp., 621 A.2d 773; Zirn v. VLI Corp., 681 A.2d at 1060–61. See also Michael A. Perino, Fraud and Federalism: Preempting Private State Securities Fraud Causes of Action, 50 Stan. L.Rev. 273 (1998).

**21.** The Senate Committee Report on the Act is instructive. It states, in part:

The Committee is keenly aware of the importance of state corporate law, specifically those states that have laws that establish a fiduciary duty of disclosure. It is not the intent of the Committee in adopting this legislation to interfere with state law regarding the duties and performance of an issuer's directors or officers in connection with a purchase or sale of securities by the issuer or an affiliate from current shareholders or communicating with existing shareholders with respect to voting their shares, acting in response to a tender or exchange offer, or exercising dissenters' or appraisal rights.

S. Rep. No. 105–182, at 11–12 (May 4, 1998).

excused.[22] If the plaintiffs intend to assert a derivative claim,[23] they should be permitted to replead to assert such a claim and any damage or equitable remedy sought on behalf of the corporation.[24] Likewise, the plaintiffs should have the opportunity to replead to assert any individual cause of action and articulate a remedy that is appropriate on behalf of the named plaintiffs individually, or a properly recognizable class consistent with Court of Chancery Rule 23, and our decision in Gaffin.[25]

The Court of Chancery properly dismissed the complaint before it against the individual director defendants, in the absence of well-pleaded allegations stating a derivative, class or individual cause of action and properly assertable remedy. Without a well-pleaded allegation in the complaint for a breach of fiduciary duty, there can be no claim for aiding and abetting such a breach. Accordingly, the plaintiffs' aiding and abetting claim against KPMG was also properly dismissed.

Nevertheless, we disagree with the Court of Chancery's holding that such a claim cannot be articulated on these facts. The plaintiffs should have been permitted to amend their complaint, if possible, to state a properly cognizable cause of action against the individual defendants and KPMG. Consequently, the Court of Chancery should have dismissed the complaint *without* prejudice.

### Conclusion

The judgment of the Court of Chancery to dismiss the complaint is affirmed. The judgment to dismiss the complaint with prejudice is reversed. This matter is remanded for further proceedings in accordance with this opinion.

---

**22.** It seems that plaintiffs have attempted to allege the basis for demand excusal by the very nature of the central claim that the directors knowingly misstated the company's financial condition, thus seemingly taking this case out of the business judgment rule because all the directors are alleged to be implicated in the wrongdoing.

**23.** This will require an articulation of the classic "direct v. derivative" theory. *See Grimes v. Donald*, Del.Supr., 673 A.2d 1207 (1996) (distinguishing individual and derivative actions).

**24.** We express no opinion whether equitable remedies such as injunctive relief, judicial removal of directors or disqualification from directorship could be asserted here. No such equitable relief has been sought in the current complaint. *See* Randall S. Thomas & Catherine T. Dixon, Aranow & Einhorn on Proxy Contests for Corporate Control, § 19.01 (3d ed. 1998).

**25.** *Gaffin v. Teledyne, Inc.*, 611 A.2d 467, 474 (1992) ("A class action may not be maintained in a purely common law or equitable fraud case since individual questions of law or fact, particularly as to the element of justifiable reliance, will inevitably predominate over common questions of law or fact."). . . .

# CHAPTER XI

# SHAREHOLDER SUITS

## SECTION 1. INTRODUCTION

### BACKGROUND NOTE

If the fiduciary duties owed by directors, officers, and controlling shareholders could be enforced only in suits by the corporation, many wrongs would never be remedied. If a controlling shareholder breaches its duty, it will normally cause the corporation to not institute litigation to remedy the wrong. Similarly, directors will only seldom bring suit against one of their colleagues or top executives for such a breach. To overcome these obstacles, and hold wrongdoing managers and controlling shareholders to account, the law permits shareholders to bring suit for breach of fiduciary duty on the corporation's behalf.

In Ross v. Bernhard, 396 U.S. 531, 534–35, 90 S.Ct. 733, 735–6, 24 L.Ed.2d 729 (1970), the Supreme Court sketched the background and nature of such suits in the following terms:

> The common law refused ... to permit stockholders to call corporate managers to account in actions at law. The possibilities for abuse, thus presented, were not ignored by corporate officers and directors. Early in the 19th century, equity provided relief both in this country and in England. Without detailing these developments, it suffices to say that the remedy in this country, first dealt with by this Court in Dodge v. Woolsey, 59 U.S. 331, 18 How. 331, 15 L.Ed. 401 (1855), provided redress ... against faithless officers and directors.... The remedy made available in equity was the derivative suit, viewed in this country as a suit to enforce a *corporate* cause of action against officers, directors, and third parties. As elaborated in the cases, one precondition for the suit was a valid claim on which the corporation could have sued; another was that the corporation itself had refused to proceed after suitable demand, unless excused by extraordinary conditions. Thus the dual nature of the stockholder's action: first, the plaintiff's right to sue on behalf of the corporation and, second, the merits of the corporation's claim itself.

This type of suit is commonly known as a *derivative action*, since the shareholder's right to bring the suit derives from the corporation.

Two features of the derivative action warrant highlighting at the outset. First is the extraordinary procedural complexity inherent in such actions—complexity involving, for example, proper parties and

**651**

their alignment, jurisdiction, demand on the board, demand on the shareholders, right to sue, intervention, settlement, and dismissal. Second is the difficult problem of social policy raised by such actions, particularly in the publicly held corporation. Through the derivative action, a shareholder with a tiny investment can force an expenditure by the corporation of a large amount of funds and executive time. The question is whether the overall benefits of such actions justify their overall costs, which are, in effect, borne involuntarily by the noncomplaining shareholders.

Where the corporation is publicly held the plaintiff-shareholder's gain is not only indirect, but usually very small and often infinitesimal. For example, the defendants' briefs in Hornstein v. Paramount Pictures, Inc., 37 N.Y.S.2d 404 (Sup.Ct. 1942), aff'd, 266 App.Div. 659, 41 N.Y.S.2d 210 (1943), aff'd 292 N.Y. 468, 55 N.E.2d 740 (1944), asserted that the five plaintiffs in that case stood to gain $3.57, $.41, $2.41, $.17 and $.65, respectively. In another well-known case, Winkelman v. General Motors Corp., 44 F.Supp. 960 (S.D.N.Y.1942), the three plaintiffs gained 8¢/share for the eighty shares held between them. In contrast, the plaintiff's lawyer stands to be awarded a very substantial fee out of the proceeds of any judgment or settlement—a fee that often runs into many hundreds of thousands, or even millions, of dollars. Furthermore, defendants in derivative actions are sometimes able to make settlements involving the illicit use of corporate funds to discharge their own liabilities. As a result of these elements, substantial concern exists that unscrupulous lawyers will exploit either the nuisance value of a nonmeritorious claim, or management's desire to cover up its own wrongdoing, through the institution of suits essentially brought to extract an exorbitant attorneys' fee.

Many or most of the issues to be considered in this chapter, although couched in technical terms, reflect an underlying tension between a concern that managers be held accountable for their wrongdoing, on the one hand, and a concern with the abusive or *strike suit* potential of derivative actions, on the other. Emphasis on the former element leads to liberality in permitting derivative actions; emphasis on the latter leads to rules that restrict such actions. In weighing these concerns, it should be borne in mind that the derivative action and the disclosure requirements of the securities acts constitute the two major legal bulwarks against managerial self-dealing. In considering the various rules taken up in this chapter, it is therefore critical to evaluate the extent to which each rule cuts into the effectiveness of the derivative action, and whether the benefits of the rule justify that cost.

It should also be kept in mind, while considering the problems raised in this chapter, that significant substantive consequences often turn on the success of a motion to dismiss a derivative action on procedural grounds. If the plaintiff can survive such a motion, the facts that he already knows together with the material that he can develop through discovery will often lead to a quick and substantial settlement. If the defendant can get the case dismissed on procedural grounds, however, no other plaintiff may come forward—either because no other shareholder who would bring suit knows all the relevant facts, or because the statute of limitations has run. Accordingly, for practical purposes many derivative actions will be won or lost on the basis of procedural issues that do not go to the merits of the case.

--------

## FEDERAL RULES OF CIVIL PROCEDURE, RULE 11

[See Statutory Supplement]

--------

## AMERICAN LAW INSTITUTE, PRINCIPLES OF CORPORATE GOVERNANCE §§ 7.04(a)(1), (b), (d)

[See Statutory Supplement]

--------

## NOTE ON WHO CAN BRING A DERIVATIVE ACTION

1. *Shareholder Status.* It is generally agreed that the plaintiff in a derivative action must be a shareholder at the time the action is begun, e.g., Vista Fund v. Garis, 277 N.W.2d 19 (Minn.1979), and must remain a shareholder during the pendency of the action, see, e.g., Schilling v. Belcher, 582 F.2d 995 (5th Cir.1978). What constitutes shareholdership for derivative-action purposes? In a few states, a statute or rule speaks to the issue directly. For example, N.Y.Bus.Corp. Law § 626(a) provides that the plaintiff in a derivative suit must be "a holder of shares or of voting trust certificates ... or of a beneficial interest in such shares or certificates."

Where the statute is silent, courts normally define shareholdership in a very expansive manner. First, record ownership is generally not required; an unregistered shareholder will qualify. See, e.g., Rosenthal v. Burry Biscuit Corp., 30 Del.Ch. 299, 60 A.2d 106 (Del.Ch. 1948). Second, legal ownership is not required—equitable ownership suffices. The latter category has been held to include, among others, an owner of stock held by a broker in a margin account in the broker's street name, a pledgee, the beneficiary of a trust, a legatee, a surviving widow with a community interest in stock held in her husband's name, and a person who has contracted to purchase stock.

It is also established that in an appropriate case a shareholder in a parent corporation can bring a derivative action on behalf of a subsidiary, despite the fact that he is not a shareholder in the subsidiary. See Painter, Double Derivative Suits and Other Remedies With Regard to Damaged Subsidiaries, 36 Ind.L.J. 143, 147–49 (1961).

2. *Creditors.* An implication from the rule that the plaintiff in a derivative action must be a shareholder at the time he brings suit is

that a creditor (including a bondholder) ordinarily has no right to bring a derivative action. See, e.g., Harff v. Kerkorian, 324 A.2d 215 (Del.Ch.1974), aff'd in pertinent part 347 A.2d 133 (Del.1975). However, if a corporation is insolvent in fact, the directors owe fiduciary duties to the creditors, whether or not there has been a statutory filing under bankruptcy law. See Geyer v. Ingersoll Publications Co., 621 A.2d 784 (Del.Ch.1992). Presumably, therefore, creditors could bring an action against directors for violation of those duties. Moreover, in Credit Lyonnais Bank Nederland, N.V. v. Pathe Communications Corp., 1991 WL 277613 (Del.Ch.1991), Chancellor Allen stated that "At least where a corporation is operating *in the vicinity* of bankruptcy, a board of directors is not merely the agent of the [shareholders], but owes its duty to the corporate enterprise." (Emphasis added.) And in Francis v. United Jersey Bank, Chapter 8, supra, the court stated that in the case of certain kinds of corporations and creditors—such as banks and bank depositors—directors owe a duty to creditors even while the corporation is solvent.

3. *Directors*. Occasionally a statute gives an officer or director the right to bring a derivative action. See N.Y.Bus.Corp.Law § 720(b).

---

### NOTE ON THE CORPORATION AS AN INDISPENSABLE PARTY

It is well established that the corporation is an indispensable party to a derivative action, and therefore must be joined in the suit:

> If the defendants account, it must be to the corporation and not to the shareholders. As to the defendants charged with defrauding it, the corporation is an indispensable party.... Furthermore, the decree must protect the defendants against any further suit by the corporation, and this will not be true unless it properly be made a party to the action.... The usual American practice is to name the beneficiary corporation as a party defendant, although in substance it is a party plaintiff; the flexibility of equity procedure permits an affirmative judgment to be entered in favor of one defendant against other defendants.

Dean v. Kellogg, 294 Mich. 200, 207–08, 292 N.W. 704, 707–08 (1940).

---

## SECTION 2. THE NATURE OF THE DERIVATIVE ACTION

---

### Sax v. World Wide Press, Inc.

United States Court of Appeals, Ninth Circuit, 1987.
809 F.2d 610.

■ Before NELSON, HALL and KOZINSKI, CIRCUIT JUDGES.

■ NELSON, CIRCUIT JUDGE:

Arnold J. Sax appeals the district court's dismissal of his amended complaint in a diversity action. The district court concluded that Sax's claims for damages stated a derivative cause of action under Montana law and that he had failed to comply with Fed.R.Civ.P. 23.1.... Sax contends that the counts seeking damages state grounds for a direct shareholder action because they allege conduct by the defendants that injured Sax personally.... We disagree. Accordingly, we affirm the district court's dismissal of Sax's amended complaint.

## FACTS

World Wide, a Montana corporation, manufactures and markets punchboards and other gambling supplies and equipment. The individual defendants own more than half of the stock of World Wide. In 1972, World Wide hired Sax as its general manager for the purpose of creating a plant at Great Falls, Montana. The oral employment agreement gave Sax an option to purchase up to 75,000 shares of stock in World Wide. After Sax successfully started the business and had acquired approximately 5% of World Wide's outstanding stock, World Wide allegedly breached the option agreement by refusing to sell him further stock. Sax terminated his employment on June 30, 1976.

After he terminated his employment, Sax alleges that the individual defendants conspired to deplete World Wide's assets and depreciate the value of his stock, which "deprived [him] of income consisting of the going rate of interest of the value of his stock." He claims that the members of the conspiracy illegally sold punchboards and kept inadequate records of inventory. He also alleges that the conspirators diverted World Wide's assets to their own use by selling punchboards to their corporation, Instant Ticket Factory, Inc., at less than fair market value, by causing World Wide to make unsecured loans to themselves, and by using World Wide assets to secure personal investments. Furthermore, Sax claims that the conspirators published false and fraudulent annual statements concealing their personal interests and conflicts of interest.

On December 3, 1983, Sax filed a complaint as an individual shareholder seeking compensation for actual and punitive damages caused by the alleged wrongful conduct of the conspiracy.... In response to the defendants' motions, the district court struck Sax's claims for actual and punitive damages under Fed.R.Civ.P. 12(f)....

Sax filed an amended complaint in an attempt to comply with the district court's opinion and order. On July 19, 1985, the district court withdrew its earlier opinion and dismissed the counts seeking damages in the amended complaint on the ground that the claims stated a derivative cause of action and that Sax had failed to comply with Fed.R.Civ.P. 23.1. It reasoned that the alleged wrongful acts of the defendants did not injure Sax personally but rather damaged World Wide and that therefore the action must be brought derivatively.... Accordingly, the district court dismissed Sax's complaint.

## DISCUSSION

### I. *Standard of Review*

We review de novo a dismissal for failure to state a claim pursuant to Fed.R.Civ.P. 12(b)(6).[1] . . .

### II. *The Claims for Damages*

In diversity actions, the characterization of an action as derivative or direct is a question of state law. C. Wright, A. Miller & M. Kane, *Federal Practice and Procedure* § 1821 (2d ed. 1986); *see Lewis v. Chiles*, 719 F.2d 1044, 1048–49 (9th Cir.1983) (citing state law in diversity action to determine the nature of the appropriate cause of action). Once state law characterizes the action as either derivative or direct, the applicable procedural rules are determined by federal law. *Gadd v. Pearson*, 351 F.Supp. 895, 900 (M.D.Fla.1972); *see Hanna v. Plumer*, 380 U.S. 460, 464–74, 85 S.Ct. 1136, 1140–45, 14 L.Ed.2d 8 (1965). . . . In federal courts, derivative suits are subject to the procedural requirements of Fed.R.Civ.P. 23.1. . . . Rule 23.1 governs derivative actions " 'to enforce a right of a corporation' when the corporation itself 'failed to enforce a right which may properly be asserted by it' in court." *Daily Income Fund, Inc. v. Fox*, 464 U.S. 523, 533–34, 104 S.Ct. 831, 836–37, 78 L.Ed.2d 645 (1984) (quoting Fed.R.Civ.P. 23.1).

Under Montana law, a shareholder can enforce a corporate right in a derivative action if certain conditions are met. Mont.R.Civ.P. 23.1; *see S–W Co. v. John Wight, Inc.*, 179 Mont. 392, 402–03, 587 P.2d 348, 354 (1978). As a general rule, an action enforces a corporate right "if the gravamen of the complaint is injury to the corporation, or to the whole body of its stock or property without any severance or distribution among individual holders." 12B W. Fletcher, *Cyclopedia of the Law of Private Corporations,* § 5911 (rev. perm. ed. 1984). . . . Therefore, if the corporate wrong decreases the value of the corporation's stock, it does not necessarily create a direct cause of action for shareholders. *Lewis*, 719 F.2d at 1049 (applying Oregon law); W. Fletcher, *supra,* § 5913; Annot., 167 A.L.R. 279, 280 (1947). The general rule that a shareholder cannot enforce corporate rights in a direct action applies to actions arising out of either contract or tort law. *Schaffer v. Universal Rundle Corp.*, 397 F.2d 893, 896 (5th Cir.1968) (applying Texas law). A direct action can be brought either when there is a special duty, such as a contractual duty, between the wrongdoer and the shareholder, or when the shareholder suffers injury separate and distinct from that suffered by other shareholders. W. Fletcher, *supra,* § 5911; *see Schaffer*, 397 F.2d at 896.

Sax argues that the district court improperly dismissed the damage counts of his amended complaint. He contends that he has an individual cause of action to which Rule 23.1 does not apply because

---

1. The district court dismissed Sax's complaint for failure to comply with Fed. R.Civ.P. 23.1. We interpret this decision as a dismissal for failure to state a claim under Fed.R.Civ.P. 12(b)(6).

he "gave up his prior job in Indiana, moved to Montana, successfully started World Wide, was refused his contractual right to purchase additional stock and therefore resigned," and because he was unable to sell his stock as a result of the defendants' actions. He cites *Jones v. H.F. Ahmanson & Co.,* 1 Cal.3d 93, 460 P.2d 464, 81 Cal.Rptr. 592 (1969) and *Davis v. Ben O'Callaghan Co.,* 238 Ga. 218, 232 S.E.2d 53 (1977), as support for the argument that he has stated grounds for a direct action. We disagree. The damages sought by Sax for the loss of interest income on his stock investment are incidental to injuries to World Wide and, therefore, are not injuries to Sax personally. *See* W. Fletcher, *supra* p. 6, at § 5913; Annot., 167 A.L.R. 279, 280 (1947).

Sax alleges that the conspiracy depleted World Wide's assets through corporate mismanagement and diversion of corporate assets. These actions are injuries to the corporation. *See* W. Fletcher, *supra* p. 6, at § 5913. Even if the defendants depleted World Wide's assets with the sole purpose of decreasing the value of Sax's stock and destroying his return on his investment, the action would nonetheless be derivative. *See id.*

Sax attempts to invoke the exception to the general rule that actions to redress corporate injuries must be brought derivatively by establishing that his employment contract with World Wide created a special duty between himself and the defendants. However, the employment relationship is irrelevant to the gravamen of Sax's complaint. The acts that allegedly caused Sax's damages occurred after Sax terminated his employment with World Wide and are unrelated to the defendants' breach of the employment agreement. Indeed, Sax does not request damages for World Wide's refusal to sell him the promised stock; rather, the alleged damages are based on the unmarketability of his stock as a result of the defendants' actions. This is an injury suffered by all of World Wide's shareholders and not by Sax alone. Therefore, the injury is incidental to injuries to World Wide and is not an injury to Sax personally. . . .

Sax cites *Jones v. H.F. Ahmanson & Co.* as support for his contention that he can bring a direct action under Montana law. This case is distinguishable. In *Jones,* the majority shareholders of a closely held corporation contributed their shares to a new corporation in exchange for stock. They sold a portion of their shares in the new corporation for a considerable profit. As a result, the value of the minority shareholders' stock in the close corporation fell. The California Supreme Court permitted the class of minority shareholders to bring a direct action. Unlike the present case, however, the minority shareholders in *Jones* were excluded from participating in the new corporation and, therefore, were uniquely injured by the acts of the majority shareholders. Moreover, because the majority shareholders were merely selling their stock at a profit, they probably breached no fiduciary duty to the corporation. Therefore, unlike the present case, it is questionable whether the corporation could have collected damages in a derivative suit.

Sax also argues that he should be permitted to bring a direct action on the grounds that the defendants control the corporation and that a derivative action would place any judgment into the corporate treasury and therefore under the defendants' control. *See Davis,* 238 Ga. at 222, 232 S.E.2d at 56; *Thomas v. Dickson,* 162 Ga.App. 569, 571, 291 S.E.2d 747, 749 (1982), *aff'd,* 250 Ga. 772, 301 S.E.2d 49 (1983); W. Fletcher, *supra* p. 6, at § 5911. Although some jurisdictions recognize this exception, it is an undecided question in Montana courts. However, the official comment in the annotations to Mont. Code Ann. § 35–1–514 states that "[t]he need for the derivative remedy is *best* illustrated when those in control of the corporation are the alleged wrongdoers." (emphasis added). Moreover, we believe that the strong policy in favor of preventing unnecessary litigation countenances against recognizing such an exception in the case of suits brought individually by shareholders.[2] Otherwise, there would be as many suits as there were shareholders in the corporation. *See* 4 D. Dowling, Mont.Code Annotated (Annotations) 66–67 (1986) ("Redress in the form of a separate suit by each individual shareholder whenever the value of his shares is impaired by a wrong to the corporation would result in unnecessary multiplicity of actions."). Therefore, we refrain from recognizing this exception under the facts of this case. Accordingly, we affirm the district court's dismissal of the damage counts of Sax's complaint because they state a derivative cause of action and Sax failed to comply with the requirements of Fed.R.Civ.P. 23.1. . . .

For the reasons above, the district court's dismissal of Sax's complaint is AFFIRMED.

––––––––

**GRIMES v. DONALD,** 673 A.2d 1207 (Del.1996). DSC Communications Corp. entered into an Employment Agreement with James Donald, its CEO. Under the Agreement, Donald was entitled to very substantial severance payments if in his good faith judgment there was "substantial interference . . . by the Board . . . in [Donald's] carrying out" the general management and affairs of DSC. Grimes, a shareholder in DSC, brought an action seeking a declaration that the Agreement was invalid on the ground that the board had breached its fiduciary duties by abdicating its authority to Grimes. Held, the action was direct, not derivative:

As the Court of Chancery has noted: "Although the tests have been articulated many times, it is often difficult to distinguish between a derivative and an individual action." In re Rexene Corp. Shareholders Litig., Del.Ch., 17 Del.J.Corp.L. 342, 348 (1991); see also Abelow v. Symonds, 38 Del.Ch. 572, 156 A.2d 416, 420 (1959) ("line of distinction . . . is often a narrow one

––––––––

**2.** In a direct action brought by injured shareholders as a class, there would be no unnecessary litigation and this policy concern would not arise. However, we need not decide whether this exception would have applied had Sax brought the suit as a class action.

... "). The distinction depends upon " 'the nature of the wrong alleged' and the relief, if any, which could result if plaintiff were to prevail." Kramer v. Western Pacific, 546 A.2d at 352 (quoting Elster v. American Airlines, Inc., 34 Del.Ch. 94, 100 A.2d 219, 221–223 (1953)). To pursue a direct action, the stockholder-plaintiff "must allege more than an injury resulting from a wrong to the corporation." Id. at 351. The plaintiff must state a claim for " 'an injury which is separate and distinct from that suffered by other shareholders,' ... or a wrong involving a contractual right of a shareholder ... which exists independently of any right of the corporation." Moran v. Household Int'l, Inc., 490 A.2d 1059, 1070, aff'd, Del.Supr., 500 A.2d 1346 (1985) (quoting 12B Fletcher Cyclopedia Corps., § 5291 (Perm.Ed.1984)).

The American Law Institute ("ALI") Principles of Corporate Governance: Analysis and Recommendations (1992) ("Principles") is helpful in this instance. Section 7.01 of the Principles undertakes to state the common law with respect to the distinction between direct and derivative actions. Id. § 7.01, cmt. a. The Comment also discusses a situation relevant to the case sub judice:

> In some instances, actions that essentially involve the structural relationship of the shareholder to the corporation ... may also give rise to a derivative action when the corporation suffers or is threatened with a loss. One example would be a case in which a corporate official knowingly acts in a manner that the certificate of incorporation [or the Delaware General Corporation Law] denied the official authority to do, thereby violating both specific restraints imposed by the shareholders [or the GCL] and the official's duty of care.

Id., cmt. c. The Comment further notes that, "courts have been more prepared to permit the plaintiff to characterize the action as direct when the plaintiff is seeking only injunctive or prospective relief." Id., cmt. d.

With respect to the abdication claim, Grimes seeks only a declaration of the invalidity of the Agreements. Monetary recovery will not accrue to the corporation as a result. Chancellor Seitz illustrated this distinction in *Bennett*. The Court of Chancery there allowed the plaintiff-stockholder to proceed individually on his claim that stock was issued for an improper purpose and entrenchment; he proceeded derivatively on his claim that the stock was issued for an insufficient price. 99 A.2d at 241. . . .

Since the abdication claim is direct, not derivative, a motion to dismiss such a claim pursuant to Chancery Rule 12(b)(6) implicates the pleading standard of Chancery Rule 8(a). Solomon v. Pathe Communications Corp., 672 A.2d 35 (Del.Supr.1996), slip op. at 9, Hartnett, J. (Jan. 4, 1996). Neither the pleading standard of Chancery Rule 9(b) ("circumstances constituting fraud or mistake shall be stated with particularity") nor that of Chancery Rule 23.1 which requires, with respect to derivative claims, that a plaintiff plead "with particularity the efforts, if any . . . to obtain the action the plaintiff desires . . . and the reasons for the . . . failure to obtain the action or for not making the effort," is implicated. . . .

---

**BARTH v. BARTH,** 659 N.E.2d 559 (1995). "While we affirm the general rule requiring a shareholder to bring a derivative rather than direct action when seeking redress for injury to the corporation, we nevertheless observe two reasons why this rule will not always apply in the case of closely-held corporations. First, shareholders in a close corporation stand in a fiduciary relationship to each other, and as such, must deal fairly, honestly, and openly with the corporation and with their fellow shareholders. *W & W Equipment Co.*, 568 N.E.2d at 570; *Krukemeier v. Krukemeier Machine and Tool Co., Inc.* (Ind.App. 1990), 551 N.E.2d 885; *Garbe v. Excel Mold, Inc.* (Ind.App.1979), 397 N.E.2d 296. Second, shareholder litigation in the closely-held corporation context will often not implicate the policies that mandate requiring derivative litigation when more widely-held corporations are involved. . . .

"Because shareholders of closely-held corporations have very direct obligations to one another and because shareholder litigation in the closely-held corporation context will often not implicate the principles which gave rise to the rule requiring derivative litigation, courts in many cases are permitting direct suits by shareholders of closely-held corporations where the complaint is one that in a public corporation would have to be brought as a derivative action. See F. Hodge O'Neal & Robert B. Thompson, O'Neal's Close Corporations § 8.16 n. 32 (3d ed. & 1995 Cum.Supp.) (collecting cases); American Law Institute, Principles of Corporate Governance: Analysis and Recommendations § 7.01, reporter's n. 4 (1994) (collecting cases). However, it is important to keep in mind that the principles which gave rise to the rule requiring derivative actions will sometimes be present even in litigation involving closely-held corporations. For example, because a corporate recovery in a derivative action will benefit creditors while a direct recovery by a shareholder will not, the protection of creditors principle could well be implicated in a shareholder suit against a closely-held corporation with debt. . . ."

---

**BAGDON v. BRIDGESTONE/FIRESTONE, INC.,** 916 F.2d 379 (7th Cir.1990), cert. denied 500 U.S. 952, 111 S.Ct. 2257, 114 L.Ed.2d 710 (1991). "Ohio, like a few other states, has expanded the 'special injury' doctrine into a general exception for closely held corporations, treating them as if they were partnerships. *Crosby [v. Beam]* follows *Donahue v. Rodd Electrotype Co.*, 367 Mass. 578, 328 N.E.2d 505 (1975), and *Jones v. H.F. Ahmanson & Co.*, 1 Cal.3d 93, 460 P.2d 464, 81 Cal.Rptr. 592 (1969). The American Law Institute recommends that other states do the same. *Principles of Corporate Governance* § 7.01(d) and pp. 22–25 (comment), 30–36 (reporter's note). The premise of this extension may be questioned. Corporations are *not* partnerships. Whether to incorporate entails a choice of many formalities. Commercial rules should be predictable; this objective is best served by treating corporations as what they are, allowing the investors and other participants to vary the rules by contract if they think deviations are warranted. So it is understandable that not all states have joined the parade.

"Delaware, for one, has not. ... When the owner of 95% of a closely held firm's stock proposed to liquidate the corporation at what the minority thought was an inadequate price, Delaware again required the minority to bring the objection derivatively. *Abelow v. Symonds,* 38 Del.Ch. 572, 156 A.2d 416 (1959). In neither case did the Chancellor think it important that the wrong alleged involved the controlling stockholder enriching itself at corporate expense, or that the corporation was closely held. ... The Reporter of the ALI's corporate governance project disapproves, *Principles of Corporate Governance* at 36, but *Abelow* is the law of Delaware today. ... "

--------

## NOTE ON THE DISTINCTION BETWEEN DERIVATIVE AND DIRECT ACTIONS

1. *The Impact of a Determination that an Action is Derivative.* What's the difference whether a shareholder's action is properly characterized as derivative or direct? The answer is that, as shown in the balance of this Chapter, a number of special procedural rules apply to—and set hurdles to—derivative actions, but not to direct actions. A shareholder who is concerned whether she can satisfy one or more of these rules will therefore prefer that her action is characterized as direct.

2. *Reasons for Distinguishing Between Direct and Derivative Actions.* Two kinds of reasons are commonly advanced for distinguishing between a *derivative* action, which is brought on the corporation's behalf against either corporate fiduciaries or third persons, and a *direct* action, which is brought on a shareholder's own behalf against either corporate fiduciaries or the corporation itself. The first kind of reason is theoretical: Since a corporation is a legal person separate from its shareholders, an injury to the corporation is not an injury to its shareholders. This proposition is somewhat dubious, because every injury to a corporation must also have an impact, however slight, on the shareholders as well. The second kind of reason is pragmatic: "(1) To avoid a multiplicity of suits by each injured shareholder, (2) to protect the corporate creditors, and (3) to protect all the stockholders since a corporate recovery benefits all equally." Watson v. Button, 235 F.2d 235 (9th Cir.1956).

3. *Easy Cases.* Some principles concerning the distinction between derivative and direct actions are relatively well-established. At

one end of the spectrum, a wrongful act that depletes or destroys corporate assets, and affects the shareholder only by reducing the value of his stock, gives rise only to an action on the corporation's behalf. At the other end of the spectrum, a wrongful act that does not deplete or divert corporate assets, and interferes with rights that are traditionally viewed as either incident to the ownership of stock or inhering in the shares themselves (such as voting or pre-emptive rights), gives rise only to a direct action by the injured shareholders. Thus in Reifsnyder v. Pittsburgh Outdoor Advertising Co., 405 Pa. 142, 173 A.2d 319 (1961), Reifsnyder had brought suit attacking a transaction in which Pittsburgh Outdoor Advertising, acting pursuant to a shareholder resolution, had purchased all the Pittsburgh stock owned by General (Pittsburgh's largest shareholder), and had increased its indebtedness to finance the purchase. Reifsnyder's theories were: (i) The transaction was accomplished only by the vote of General, acting in its shareholder capacity, and General's shares were not entitled to vote on the resolution because of its self-interest. (ii) The price paid by Pittsburgh for General's shares was excessive. The court held the suit was direct, not derivative. If the complaint had been limited to the excessive-price theory, the court said, the action may have been deemed derivative. However, the gravamen of the complaint concerned the right of a majority shareholder to vote on a resolution in which it had a personal pecuniary interest, and this theory gave rise to a direct action. "If it should become a rule of law that a shareholder cannot vote on matters in which he has an interest, an aggrieved shareholder would necessarily be permitted to bring an action to enjoin the voting of 'interested' shares or to require the corporate officers to rescind action taken in reliance upon the votes of such shares. The aggrieved shareholder in those instances would, in essence, be preventing the dilution of his own votes by challenging and disqualifying improper votes. The right to vote is basic and fundamental to most shares of stock and is independent of any right that the corporate entity possesses and the shareholder could enforce and protect such rights by bringing a direct action."[1]

4. *Harder Cases.* Many kinds of cases fall between the two ends of the spectrum described in the preceding paragraph. In some of these cases, the rules are relatively clear; in others, rules are just beginning to emerge. For example, it is relatively clear that a direct action will lie based on the issuance of stock for the wrongful purpose of perpetuating or shifting control (e.g., Sheppard v. Wilcox, 210 Cal.App.2d 53, 26 Cal.Rptr. 412 (1962)), or to enjoin a threatened ultra vires act (e.g., Alexander v. Atlanta & West Point R.R., 113 Ga. 193, 38 S.E. 772 (1901)). A rule permitting a direct action seems to be

---

**1.** In Knapp v. Bankers Securities Corp., 230 F.2d 717, 721 (3d Cir.1956), the Third Circuit held that as a matter of Pennsylvania law "[t]he right to dividends is an incident of the ownership of stock," so that a suit to compel the declaration of dividends lies as a direct action. The New York Court of Appeals had earlier reached a different result in Gordon v. Elliman, 306 N.Y. 456, 119 N.E.2d 331 (1954), but as the opinion in *Flying Tiger* points out, that decision was widely criticized and the rule it handed down was eventually reversed by the New York legislature. See also Bokat v. Getty Oil Co., 262 A.2d 246 (Del.1970).

emerging in suits based on wrongs by controlling against noncontrolling shareholders, e.g., Jones v. H.F. Ahmanson & Co., Chapter 9, supra. Suits to enjoin improperly authorized corporate actions are also commonly treated as direct actions, either implicitly (that is, without discussion of the issue), or explicitly, but the authorities are in conflict on this type of case.

5.   *Actions that can be Characterized as Either Direct or Derivative.* In many cases a wrongful act both depletes corporate assets *and* interferes with rights traditionally viewed as inhering in shares. The general principle governing such cases is that a direct action is not precluded simply because the same facts could also give rise to a derivative action. An illustration is Snyder v. Epstein, 290 F.Supp. 652, 655 (E.D.Wis.1968), where the court held that "[t]he sale of a corporate office gives rise to a cause of action for breach ... of the fiduciary duties owed to both the corporation and the stockholders." Similarly, in Bennett v. Breuil Petroleum Corp., 34 Del.Ch. 6, 99 A.2d 236 (1953), the plaintiff claimed that the controlling shareholders had caused the corporation to issue stock for an improper purpose (impairing his interest and forcing him out on management's terms), and at a grossly inadequate consideration. The court held that the first claim stated a direct and the second a derivative cause of action.[2]

Another important kind of case in which suit may be either direct or derivative is that involving proxy-rule violations. Insofar as such a violation interferes with the individual shareholder's voting right, suit can be regarded as direct; insofar as it involves a breach of management's fiduciary obligations, suit can be regarded as derivative.

————

## AMERICAN LAW INSTITUTE, PRINCIPLES OF CORPORATE GOVERNANCE § 7.01

### [See Statutory Supplement]

2.   See also, e.g., Buschmann v. Professional Men's Ass'n, 405 F.2d 659 (7th Cir. 1969). In General Rubber Co. v. Benedict, 215 N.Y. 18, 109 N.E. 96 (1915), a parent corporation sued one of its directors for acquiescing in the looting of a subsidiary, thereby injuring the parent by reducing the value of its shares in the subsidiary. The court held that the complaint stated a good cause of action. In answer to the argument that recovery would subject the defendant to double liability, the court said: (1) the subsidiary might not have a cause of action, since the defendant was not its director and would be liable to it only if he participated in—rather than merely failed to prevent—the wrong; and (2) the possibility that the subsidiary had an enforceable cause of action should be taken into consideration in determining the extent to which the value of the parent's shares had been depreciated. Cf. In re Auditore's Will, 249 N.Y.S. 335, 164 N.E. 242 (1928).

---

## SECTION 3. INDIVIDUAL RECOVERY IN DERIVATIVE ACTIONS

---

### Glenn v. Hoteltron Systems, Inc.

Court of Appeals of New York, 1989.
74 N.Y.2d 386, 547 N.Y.S.2d 816, 547 N.E.2d 71.

■ WACHTLER, CHIEF JUDGE. . . .

The dispute here is between Jacob Schachter and Herbert Kulik, the founders of Ketek Electric Corporation. Schachter and Kulik each own 50% of the corporation's shares and serve as the corporation's only officers. . . . [T]he Appellate Division, on [a] prior appeal, found Schachter liable for diverting Ketek assets and opportunities to Hoteltron Systems, Inc., a corporation wholly owned by Schachter.

Following the trial on damages, Supreme Court concluded that Hoteltron had earned profits of $362,242.84 from Schachter's usurpation of Ketek assets and opportunities. . . .

On Schachter's appeal, the Appellate Division . . . concluded that the Hoteltron profits should be awarded to the injured corporation, Ketek, rather than the innocent shareholder Kulik. . . .

It is the general rule that, because a shareholders' derivative suit seeks to vindicate a wrong done to the corporation through enforcement of a corporate cause of action, any recovery obtained is for the benefit of the injured corporation. . . .

Kulik argues that this result is inequitable because Schachter, as a shareholder of Ketek, will ultimately share in the proceeds of the damage award. But that prospect exists in any successful derivative action in which the wrongdoer is a shareholder of the injured corporation. An exception based on that fact alone would effectively nullify the general rule that damages for a corporate injury should be awarded to the corporation.

It is true that this anomaly is magnified in cases involving closely held corporations, because the errant fiduciary is likely to own a large share of the corporation—as Schachter owns 50% of Ketek—and will share proportionately in the restitution to the corporation generated by a successful suit against him. Thus, it may be argued that in such circumstances an award of damages to the corporation does not provide a sufficient deterrent to the potential wrongdoer. We conclude, however, that this consideration does not require a different damage rule for close corporations.

While awarding damages directly to the innocent shareholder may seem equitable with respect to the parties before the court, other interests, particularly those of the corporation's creditors, should not be overlooked. The fruits of a diverted corporate opportunity are properly a corporate asset. Awarding that asset directly to a shareholder could impair the rights of creditors whose claims may be superior to that of the innocent shareholder. . . .

Thus, while we do not rule out the possibility that an award to innocent shareholders rather than to the corporation would be appropriate in some circumstances, we find no need to invoke such an exception here.

Accordingly, the order of the Appellate Division should be affirmed, without costs.

■ Simons, Kaye, Alexander, Titone, Hancock and Bellacosa, JJ., concur.

Order affirmed, without costs.

———

## PERLMAN v. FELDMANN
[Chapter 9, supra.]

———

## NOTE ON INDIVIDUAL RECOVERY IN DERIVATIVE ACTIONS

1. *The Basic Principle.* Pro-rata recovery cases involve derivative actions that take a sudden turn at the remedy stage. Normally, in a derivative action the recovery goes to the corporation, in whose name the action is brought. When pro rata recovery is granted, however, the recovery goes directly to the shareholders—more accurately, to certain shareholders. Each shareholder who is entitled to participate in a pro rata recovery gets a share of the recovery equal to her percentage ownership of stock. For example, suppose A owns 20% of Azure Corporation's stock, B owns 20%, and C owns 60%. A brings a derivative action against C on Azure's behalf. The court awards damages of $1 million against C, in favor of Azure. In a normal derivative action, the $1 million would go to Azure. If pro rata recovery is granted to A and B, A will get $200,000 (20% of $1 million), B will get $200,000 (same), C will get nothing, and Azure will got nothing.

Pro rata recovery is a useful tool to achieve justice in a variety of cases that are properly characterized as derivative actions. Although pro rata recovery results in direct payments by the defendants to shareholders, rather than a payment solely to the corporation, pro rata recovery is consistent with characterizing an action as derivative rather than as direct, for two reasons. First, the plaintiff in such an action must satisfy all the relevant requirements for bringing a derivative action. Second, the amount of damages is measured by the injury to the corporation—although once that measurement is made, a portion of the amount is distributed directly to certain shareholders.

2. *Preventing Wrongdoers from Sharing in the Recovery.* It is frequently said that pro rata recovery may be decreed to prevent the wrongdoers from sharing in the recovery. See, e.g., Atkinson v. Marquart, 112 Ariz. 304, 541 P.2d 556 (1975). However, in most derivative actions the defendants own stock in the corporation, and this in itself seldom leads to pro rata recovery. Nor should it, in the typical case. For example, suppose D, the owner of forty percent of Blue Corporation, is found liable in a derivative suit in the amount of $1 million. If corporate recovery is decreed, D must pay Blue $1 million. Since D "shares" in the recovery, his net output is only $600,000 (assuming that he can recover the balance through a dividend or appreciation in

the value of his stock). But if pro rata recovery is decreed, D's output will also be $600,000. Indeed, for reasons of liquidity D may very well prefer the pro rata alternative. The fact that D "shares" in a corporate recovery is therefore not sufficient in itself to justify pro rata relief.

3. *Wrongdoers are Still in Control.* Similarly, it is sometimes said that pro rata recovery is appropriate where the wrongdoers are still in control of the corporation, and therefore would control any corporate recovery. See Backus v. Finkelstein, 23 F.2d 357, 366 (D.C.Minn.1927); Note, 69 Harv.L.Rev. 1314, at 1314–16 (1956). However, derivative actions in situations where the wrongdoers still control the corporation are legion, and pro rata recovery will normally not be decreed on this ground alone.

4. *Most of the Shareholders are Subject to Personal Defenses.* The cases suggest that pro rata relief will be decreed where the great bulk of the corporation's shares are held by persons who could not themselves have brought suit because they are subject to a personal defense. For example, in Young v. Columbia Oil Co., 110 W.Va. 364, 158 S.E. 678 (1931), pro rata recovery was decreed where thirteen of sixteen shareholders were barred by laches or acquiescence, and the remaining three shareholders owned only 145 of the corporation's 5000 outstanding shares. In Joyce v. Congdon, 114 Wash. 239, 195 P. 29 (1921), pro rata recovery was decreed where 423 out of the corporation's 429 shares were owned by either the wrongdoers, persons alleged by the plaintiff to be in collusion with the wrongdoers, or persons who had acquired their stock from the wrongdoers. In Chounis v. Laing, 125 W.Va. 275, 23 S.E.2d 628 (1942), more than ninety-five percent of the shareholders had either ratified or participated in the defendant's wrongful actions. The court held that the ratification was not effective as against innocent minority shareholders, but decreed pro rata relief, excluding all those shareholders who had either participated or ratified. See also, e.g., May v. Midwest Refining Co., 121 F.2d 431 (1st Cir.1941), cert. denied 314 U.S. 668, 62 S.Ct. 129, 86 L.Ed. 534, noted, 30 Calif.L.Rev. 338 (1942).

---

## SECTION 4.   THE CONTEMPORANEOUS–OWNERSHIP RULE

---

### FEDERAL RULES OF CIVIL PROCEDURE, RULE 23.1
[See Statutory Supplement]

---

### DELAWARE GEN. CORP. LAW § 327
[See Statutory Supplement]

---

## REV. MODEL BUS. CORP. ACT § 7.41

[See Statutory Supplement]

## CAL. CORP. CODE § 800(b)(1)

[See Statutory Supplement]

## ALI, PRINCIPLES OF CORPORATE GOVERNANCE § 7.02(a)

[See Statutory Supplement]

# Bangor Punta Operations, Inc. v. Bangor & Aroostook R.R.

Supreme Court of the United States, 1974.
417 U.S. 703, 94 S.Ct. 2578, 41 L.Ed.2d 418.

■ MR. JUSTICE POWELL delivered the opinion of the Court. . . .

### I

[Prior to October 1964, Bangor & Aroostook Corporation ("B & A") held 98.3% of the stock of the Bangor & Aroostook Railroad Company ("BAR"), a Maine corporation. In October 1964, B & A sold its BAR stock to Bangor Punta, a Delaware corporation. Bangor Punta held the stock for five years, and then sold it in October 1969 to Amoskeag Co. for $5 million. Amoskeag later acquired additional shares which gave it ownership of more than 99% (but less than 100%) of BAR.]*

In 1971, BAR ... filed the present action against Bangor Punta ... in the United States District Court for the District of Maine. The complaint specified 13 counts of alleged mismanagement, misappropriation, and waste of BAR's corporate assets occurring during the period from 1960 through 1967 when B & A and then Bangor Punta controlled BAR.[1] Damages were sought in the amount of $7,000,000 for violations of both federal and state laws. The federal statutes and regulations alleged to have been violated included § 10 of the Clayton Act, 15 U.S.C.A. § 20; § 10(b) of the Securities Exchange Act of 1934,

---

* In the interests of clarity, the statement of facts eliminates subsidiaries that do not figure in the opinion. (Footnote by ed.)

1. Several of the alleged acts of corporate mismanagement occurred between 1960 and 1964 when B & A ... was in control of the railroad. Liability for these acts was nevertheless sought to be imposed on Bangor Punta, even though it had no interest in either BAR or B & A during this period. The apparent basis for liability was the 1964 purchase agreement between B & A and Bangor Punta. The complaint in the instant case alleged that under the agreement Bangor Punta, through its subsidiary, assumed "all ... debts, obligations, contracts and liabilities" of B & A.

15 U.S.C.A. § 78j(b); and Rule 10b–5.... The state claims were grounded on § 104 of the Maine Public Utilities Act, Maine Rev.Stat. Ann., Tit. 35, § 104 (1965), and the common law of Maine.

The complaint focused on four intercompany transactions which allegedly resulted in injury to BAR. Counts I and II averred that B & A, and later Bangor Punta, overcharged BAR for various legal, accounting, printing, and other services. Counts III, IV, V, and VI averred that B & A improperly acquired the stock of the St. Croix Paper Co. which BAR owned through its subsidiary. Counts VII, VIII, IX, and X charged that B & A and Bangor Punta improperly caused BAR to declare special dividends to its stockholders, including B & A and Bangor Punta, and also caused BAR's subsidiary to borrow in order to pay regular dividends. Counts XI, XII, and XIII charged that B & A improperly caused BAR to excuse payment by B & A and Bangor Punta of the interest due on a loan made by BAR to B & A. In sum, the complaint alleged that during the period of their control of BAR, Bangor Punta, and its predecessor in interest B & A, "exploited it solely for their own purposes" and "calculatedly drained the resources of BAR in violation of law for their own benefit."

The District Court granted petitioners' motion for summary judgment and dismissed the action. 353 F.Supp. 724 (1972). The court first observed that although the suit purported to be a primary action brought in the name of the corporation, the real party in interest and hence the actual beneficiary of any recovery, was Amoskeag, the present owner of more than 99% of the outstanding stock of BAR. The court then noted that Amoskeag had acquired all of its BAR stock long after the alleged wrongs occurred and that Amoskeag did not contend that it had not received full value for its purchase price, or that the purchase transaction was tainted by fraud or deceit. Thus, any recovery on Amoskeag's part would constitute a windfall because it had sustained no injury. With this in mind, the court then addressed the claims based on federal law and determined that Amoskeag would have been barred from maintaining a shareholder derivative action because of its failure to satisfy the "contemporaneous ownership" requirement of Fed.Rule Civ.Proc. 23.1(1).[3] Finding that equitable principles prevented the use of the corporate fiction to evade the proscription of Rule 23.1, the court concluded that Amoskeag's efforts to recover under the Securities Exchange Act and the Clayton Act must fail. Turning to the claims based on state law, the court recognized that the applicability of Rule 23.1(1) has been questioned where federal jurisdiction is based on diversity of citizenship.[4] The court

---

**3.** Rule 23.1(1), which specifies the requirements applicable to shareholder derivative actions, states that the complaint shall aver that "the plaintiff was a shareholder or member at the time of the transaction of which he complains...." This provision is known as the "contemporaneous ownership" requirement. See 3B J. Moore, Federal Practice ¶ 23.1 et seq. (2d ed. 1974).

**4.** The "contemporaneous ownership" requirement in shareholder derivative actions was first announced in Hawes v. Oakland, 104 U.S. 450, 26 L.Ed. 827 (1881), and soon thereafter adopted as Equity Rule 97. This provision was later incorporated in Equity Rule 27 and finally in the present Rule 23.1. After the decision in Erie R. Co. v. Tompkins, 304 U.S. 64, 58 S.Ct. 817, 82 L.Ed. 1188 (1938), the question arose whether the confound it unnecessary to resolve this issue, however, since its examination of state law indicated that Maine probably followed the "prevailing rule" requiring contemporaneous ownership in order to maintain a shareholder derivative action. Thus, whether the federal rule or state substantive law applied, the present action could not be maintained.

The United States Court of Appeals for the First Circuit reversed. . . .

We granted petitioners' application for certiorari. 414 U.S. 1127 (1974). We now reverse.

## II

### A

We first turn to the question whether respondent corporations* may maintain the present action under § 10 of the Clayton Act, 15 U.S.C.A. § 20, and § 10(b) of the Securities Exchange Act of 1934, 15 U.S.C.A. § 78j(b), and Rule 10b–5, 17 CFR § 240.10b–5. The resolution of this issue depends upon the applicability of the settled principle of equity that a shareholder may not complain of acts of corporate mismanagement if he acquired his shares from those who participated or acquiesced in the allegedly wrongful transactions. See, e.g., Bloodworth v. Bloodworth, 225 Ga. 379, 387, 169 S.E.2d 150, 156–157 (1969). . . .[5] This principle has been invoked with special force where a shareholder purchases all or substantially all the shares of a corporation from a vendor at a fair price, and then seeks to have the corporation recover against that vendor for prior corporate mismanagement. See, e.g., Matthews v. Headley Chocolate Co., 130 Md. 523, 532–535, 100 A. 645, 650–651 (1917); Home Fire Insurance Co. v. Barber, 67 Neb. 644, 661–662, 93 N.W. 1024, 1030–1031 (1903). See also Amen v. Black, 234 F.2d 12, 23 (C.A.10 1956). The equitable considerations precluding recovery in such cases were explicated long ago by Dean (then Commissioner) Roscoe Pound in Home Fire Insurance Co. v. Barber, supra. Dean Pound, writing for the Supreme Court of Nebraska, observed that the shareholders of the plaintiff corporation in that case had sustained no injury since they had acquired their shares from the alleged wrongdoers after the disputed transactions occurred and had received full value for their purchase price. Thus, any recovery on their part would constitute a windfall, for it would enable them to obtain funds to which they had no just title or claim. Moreover, it would in effect allow the shareholders to recoup a large part of the price they agreed to pay for their shares, notwithstanding the fact that they received all they had bargained for. Finally,

temporaneous-ownership requirement was one of procedure or substantive law. If the requirement were substantive, then under the regime of *Erie* it could not be validly applied in federal diversity cases where state law permitted a noncontemporaneous shareholder to maintain a derivative action. See 3B J. Moore, Federal Practice ¶ ¶ 23.1.01– 23.1.15[2] (2d ed. 1974). Although most cases

treat the requirement as one of procedure, this Court has never resolved the issue. Ibid.

* The respondents were BAR and a wholly owned subsidiary. (Footnote by ed.)

**5.** This principle obtains in the great majority of jurisdictions. See, e.g., Russell v. Louis Melind Co., 331 Ill.App. 182, 72 N.E.2d 869 (1947).

it would permit the shareholders to reap a profit from wrongs done to others, thus encouraging further such speculation. Dean Pound stated that these consequences rendered any recovery highly inequitable and mandated dismissal of the suit.

The considerations supporting the *Home Fire* principle are especially pertinent in the present case. As the District Court pointed out, Amoskeag, the present owner of more than 99% of the BAR shares, would be the principal beneficiary of any recovery obtained by BAR. Amoskeag, however, acquired 98.3% of the outstanding shares of BAR from petitioner Bangor Punta in 1969, well after the alleged wrongs were said to have occurred. Amoskeag does not contend that the purchase transaction was tainted by fraud or deceit, or that it received less than full value for its money. Indeed, it does not assert that it has sustained any injury at all. Nor does it appear that the alleged acts of prior mismanagement have had any continuing effect on the corporations involved or the value of their shares.[6] Nevertheless, by causing the present action to be brought in the name of respondent corporations, Amoskeag seeks to recover indirectly an amount equal to the $5,000,000 it paid for its stock, plus an additional $2,000,000. All this would be in the form of damages for wrongs petitioner Bangor Punta is said to have inflicted, not upon Amoskeag, but upon respondent corporations during the period in which Bangor Punta owned 98.3% of the BAR shares. In other words, Amoskeag seeks to recover for wrongs Bangor Punta did to *itself* as owner of the railroad.[7] At the same time it reaps this windfall, Amoskeag desires to retain all its BAR stock. Under *Home Fire,* it is evident that Amoskeag would have no standing in equity to maintain the present action.[8]

We are met with the argument, however, that since the present action is brought in the name of respondent corporations, we may not look behind the corporate entity to the true substance of the claims

**6.** In *Home Fire,* Dean Pound suggested that equitable principles might not prevent recovery where the effects of the wrongful acts continued and resulted in injury to present shareholders. 67 Neb. 644, 662, 93 N.W. 1024, 1031. In their complaint in the instant case, respondents alleged that "[t]he injury to BAR is a continuing one surviving the aforesaid sale [from petitioner BPO] to Amoskeag." The District Court noted that respondents alleged no facts to support this contention and therefore found any such exception inapplicable. 353 F.Supp. 724, 727 n. 1 (1972). Respondents apparently did not renew this contention on appeal.

**7.** Similarly, as to the period before October 1964, Amoskeag seeks to recover for wrongs B & A and its shareholders did to *themselves* as owners of the railroad.

**8.** Conceding the lack of equity in any recovery by Amoskeag, the dissent argues that the present action can nevertheless be maintained because there are 20 minority

shareholders, holding less than 1% of the BAR stock, who owned their shares "during the period from 1960 through 1967 when the transactions underlying the railroad's complaint took place, and who still owned that stock in 1971 when the complaint was filed." ... The dissent would conclude that the existence of these innocent minority shareholders entitled BAR, and hence Amoskeag, to recover the entire $7,000,000 amount of alleged damages.

Aside from the illogic of such an approach, the dissent's position is at war with the precedents, for the *Home Fire* principle has long been applied to preclude full recovery by a corporation even where there are innocent minority shareholders who acquired their shares prior to the alleged wrongs. See cases cited at n. 5, supra, and accompanying text. The dissent also mistakes the factual posture of this case, since the respondent corporations did not institute this action for the benefit of the minority shareholders. See discussion at n. 15, infra.

and the actual beneficiaries. The established law is to the contrary. Although a corporation and its shareholders are deemed separate entities for most purposes, the corporate form may be disregarded in the interests of justice where it is used to defeat an overriding public policy. New Colonial Ice Co. v. Helvering, 292 U.S. 435, 442, 54 S.Ct. 788, 78 L.Ed. 1348 (1934); Chicago, M. & St. P.R. Co. v. Minneapolis Civic Assn., 247 U.S. 490, 501, 38 S.Ct. 553, 62 L.Ed. 1229 (1918). In such cases, courts of equity, piercing all fictions and disguises, will deal with the substance of the action and not blindly adhere to the corporate form. Thus, where equity would preclude the shareholders from maintaining an action in their own right, the corporation would also be precluded. Amen v. Black, supra; Capitol Wine & Spirit Corp. v. Pokrass, 277 App.Div. 184, 98 N.Y.S.2d 291 (1950), aff'd, 302 N.Y. 734, 98 N.E.2d 704 (1951); Matthews v. Headley Chocolate Co., supra; Home Fire Insurance Co. v. Barber, supra. It follows that Amoskeag, the principal beneficiary of any recovery and itself estopped from complaining of petitioners' alleged wrongs, cannot avoid the command of equity through the guise of proceeding in the name of respondent corporations which it owns and controls.

### B

Respondents fare no better in their efforts to maintain the present actions under state law, specifically § 104 of the Maine Public Utilities Act, Maine Rev.Stat.Ann., Tit. 35, § 104 (1965), and the common law of Maine. In Forbes v. Wells Beach Casino, Inc., 307 A.2d 210, 223 n. 10 (1973), the Maine Supreme Judicial Court recently declared that it had long accepted the equitable principle that a "stockholder has no standing if either he or his vendor participated or acquiesced in the wrong...." See Hyams v. Old Dominion Co., 113 Me. 294, 302, 93 A. 747, 750 (1915).[9] ...

### III

In reaching the contrary conclusion, the Court of Appeals stated that it could not accept the proposition that Amoskeag would be the "sole beneficiary" of any recovery by BAR. 482 F.2d, at 868. The court noted that in view of the railroad's status as a "quasi-public" corporation and the essential nature of the services it provides, the public had an identifiable interest in BAR's financial health. Thus, any recovery by BAR would accrue to the benefit of the public through the improvement in BAR's economic position and the quality of its services. The court thought that this factor rendered any windfall to Amoskeag irrelevant.

**9.** In addition, the new Maine Business Corporation Act adopts the contemporaneous-ownership requirement for shareholder derivative actions. See Maine Rev.Stat.Ann., Tit. 13-A, § 627.1.A (1974). This provision apparently became effective two days after the present action was filed. As the District Court noted, it is an open question whether Maine in fact had a contemporaneous-ownership requirement prior to that time. 353 F.Supp., at 727. See R. Field, V. McKusick & L. Wroth, Maine Civil Practice § 23.2, p. 393 (2d ed. 1970). In the absence of any indication that Maine would not have followed the "prevailing view," the District Court determined that the contemporaneous-ownership requirement of Fed.Rule Civ.Proc. 23.1 applied.

At the outset, we note that the Court of Appeals' assumption that any recovery would necessarily benefit the public is unwarranted. As that court explicitly recognized, any recovery by BAR could be diverted to its shareholders, namely Amoskeag, rather than re-invested in the railroad for the benefit of the public. . . .

The Court of Appeals' position also appears to overlook the fact that Amoskeag, the actual beneficiary of any recovery through its ownership of more than 99% of the BAR shares, would be unjustly enriched since it has sustained no injury. . . .

The Court of Appeals further stated that it was important to insure that petitioners would not be immune from liability for their wrongful conduct and noted that BAR's recovery would provide a needed deterrent to mismanagement of railroads. Our difficulty with this argument is that it proves too much. If deterrence were the only objective, then in logic any plaintiff willing to file a complaint would suffice. No injury or violation of a legal duty to the particular plaintiff would have to be alleged. The only prerequisite would be that the plaintiff agree to accept the recovery, lest the supposed wrongdoer be allowed to escape a reckoning. Suffice it to say that we have been referred to no authority which would support so novel a result, and we decline to adopt it.

We therefore conclude that respondent corporations may not maintain the present action.[15] The judgment of the Court of Appeals is reversed.

■ MR. JUSTICE MARSHALL, with whom MR. JUSTICE DOUGLAS, MR. JUSTICE BRENNAN, and MR. JUSTICE WHITE join, dissenting. . . .

The majority places primary reliance on Dean Pound's decision in Home Fire Insurance Co. v. Barber, supra. In that case, *all* of the shares of the plaintiff corporation had been acquired from the alleged wrongdoers after the transactions giving rise to the causes of action stated in the complaint. Since none of the corporation's shareholders held stock at the time of the alleged wrongful transactions, none had been injured thereby. Dean Pound therefore held that equity barred

---

**15.** Our decision rests on the conclusion that equitable principles preclude recovery by Amoskeag, the present owner of more than 99% of the BAR shares. The record does not reveal whether the minority shareholders who hold the remaining fraction of 1% of the BAR shares stand in the same position as Amoskeag. Some courts have adopted the concept of a pro-rata recovery where there are innocent minority shareholders. Under this procedure, damages are distributed to the minority shareholders individually on a proportional basis, even though the action is brought in the name of the corporation to enforce primary rights. See, e.g., Matthews v. Headley Chocolate Co., 130 Md. 523, 536–540, 100 A. 645, 650–652 (1917). In the present case, respondents have expressly disavowed any intent to obtain a pro-rata recovery on behalf of the 1% minority shareholders of BAR. We therefore do not reach the question whether such recovery would be appropriate.

The dissent asserts that the alleged acts of corporate mismanagement have placed BAR "close to the brink of bankruptcy" and that the present action is maintained for the benefit of BAR's creditors. . . . With all respect, it appears that the dissent has sought to redraft respondents' complaint. As the District Court noted, respondents have not brought this action on behalf of any creditors. 353 F.Supp., at 726. Indeed, they have never so contended. Moreover, respondents have conceded that the financial health of the railroad is excellent. Tr. of Oral Arg. 18.

the corporation from pursuing a claim where none of its shareholders could complain of injury.

Dean Pound thought it clear, however, that the opposite result would obtain if *any* of the present shareholders

> "are entitled to complain of the acts of the defendant and of his past management of the company; for if any of them are so entitled, there can be no doubt of the right and duty of the corporation to maintain this suit. It would be maintainable in such a case even though the wrongdoers continued to be stock-holders and would share in the proceeds." 67 Neb., at 655, 93 N.W., at 1028.

Cf. Capitol Wine & Spirit Corp. v. Pokrass, 277 App.Div. 184, 186, 98 N.Y.S.2d 291, 293 (1950), aff'd, 302 N.Y. 734, 98 N.E.2d 704 (1951).

The rationale for the distinction drawn by Dean Pound is simple enough. The sole shareholder who defrauds or mismanages his own corporation hurts only himself. For the corporation to sue him for his wrongs is simply to take money out of his right pocket and put it in his left. It is therefore appropriate for equity to intervene to pierce the corporate veil. But where there are minority shareholders, misappropriation and conversion of corporate assets injure their interests as well as the interest of the majority shareholder. The law imposes upon the directors of a corporation a fiduciary obligation to all of the corporation's shareholders, and part of that obligation is to use due care to ensure that the corporation seek redress where a majority shareholder has drained the corporation's resources for his own benefit and to the detriment of minority shareholders.[1] . . .

---

## Rifkin v. Steele Platt

Colorado Court of Appeals, 1991.
824 P.2d 32.

■ Opinion by JUDGE PLANK.

Defendants, Steele Platt and Fas–Wok, Inc. (sellers), appeal the judgment of the trial court in favor of the corporate plaintiff, The Boiler Room, Inc. (the corporation). Plaintiffs cross-appeal the award of damages. We affirm in part and remand for further proceedings consistent with this opinion.

This matter involves the sale of the controlling shares of the corporation, which owns a restaurant of the same name located in the Tivoli Shopping Center in Denver, Colorado. Plaintiffs include the corporation and its present principal shareholders, Robert C. Rifkin,

---

[1]. Under a separate rule, the plaintiff must be a shareholder at the time the action is brought. See Note on Who Can Bring a Derivative Action, Section 1, supra. The two rules are bridged by a third rule requiring that the plaintiff's ownership between the time of the wrong and the time of the suit must be uninterrupted. Vista Fund v. Garis, 277 N.W.2d 19 (Minn.1979); Gresov v. Shattuck Denn Mining Corp., 40 Misc.2d 569, 243 N.Y.S.2d 760 (1963).

Gerald N. Kernis, and Gary G. Kortz (buyers). Sellers are the former controlling shareholders.

Buyers and sellers executed a Stock Purchase Agreement to effectuate the sale of the corporation. After the closing, the buyers discovered inaccuracies in financial representations made in the agreement. Consequently, they filed suit against the sellers asserting claims of breach of contract, breach of good faith, breach of fiduciary duty, and unjust enrichment.

The complaint alleged, in part, that Platt, as officer and director of the corporation, had misappropriated funds from it and that certain assets on the balance sheet were actually owned by Platt or other entities that he controlled. Sellers counterclaimed seeking rescission of the agreement.

After a trial to the court, judgment was entered in favor of the buyers on the breach of contract claim and the corporation on the breach of fiduciary duty claim. The court also awarded attorney fees pursuant to the agreement. Sellers do not appeal that part of the judgment concerning the breach of contract claim. . . .

Sellers . . . contend that the trial court erred in awarding the corporation damages for breach of fiduciary duty for conduct which occurred prior to buyers' acquisition of stock. They cite *Bangor Punta Operations, Inc. v. Bangor & Aroostook R. Co.,* 417 U.S. 703, 94 S.Ct. 2578, 41 L.Ed.2d 418 (1974) in support of this argument. We agree that *Bangor Punta* raises issues which must be resolved in this matter.

In *Bangor Punta,* the new shareholders of the corporation, in the name of the corporation, sought damages from the former shareholders for violations of state and federal law which occurred before the sale. The United States Supreme Court held that the corporation could not maintain the action for wrongs that occurred before the new shareholders' acquisition of the shares. The court reasoned that the real parties that would gain from a successful lawsuit would be the new shareholders. It presumed that the purchase price that they paid reflected the prior wrongdoings. Thus, the shareholders would improperly receive a windfall if allowed to recover damages.

Here, it is undisputed that the acts which constituted Platt's breach of fiduciary duty occurred prior to the buyers' acquisition of stock in The Boiler Room. However, the parties dispute whether the purchase price reflected the prior wrongdoings. The trial court did not make a finding on this issue. Therefore, we remand it to the trial court for further findings. *See El Dorado Bancshares v. Martin,* 701 F.Supp. 1515 (D.Kan.1988).

If on review the court finds that the price, in fact, reflected Platt's wrongdoings, it must dismiss the breach of fiduciary duty claim. If, on the other hand, it finds that the purchase price of the shares did not reflect the wrongdoings, then the corporation's previous damage award may stand. . . .

■ HUME and NEY, JJ., concur.

––––––––––

## NOTE ON THE CONTEMPORANEOUS–OWNERSHIP RULE

At common law, the cases were divided on whether a shareholder was barred from bringing a derivative action if he was not a "contemporaneous shareholder"—that is, if he did not hold his shares when the wrong occurred. 2 Model Bus.Corp.Act Ann. § 49, ¶ 4.11 (1971). Today, however, most jurisdictions have adopted some version of the contemporaneous-ownership rule by either case-law, statute, or court rule. The rule is subject to several important exceptions:

1. *Devolution by Operation of Law.* A non-contemporaneous shareholder is normally allowed to bring a derivative action if his shares devolved upon him "by operation of law"—for example, by inheritance. (This exception is sometimes made applicable only where the shares have devolved from a person who was a shareholder at the time of the wrong.)

2. *Continuing–Wrong Theory.* Under the continuing-wrong theory, a plaintiff can bring an action to challenge a wrong that began before he acquired his shares, but continued thereafter. In principle this may not seem to be an exception at all, since the plaintiff is only complaining about what happened after he became a shareholder. In practice, however, it is often difficult to distinguish between a wrongful continuing course of conduct, on the one hand, and the continued effect of a completed wrongful transaction, on the other. Therefore, while the continuing-wrong exception is widely accepted in principle, in practice there is considerable divergence in the way it is applied, and different cases often seem to come out differently on virtually the same facts.

For example, in Forbes v. Wells Beach Casino, Inc., 307 A.2d 210 (Me.1973), the plaintiff was allowed to sue under the continuing-wrong theory where he had purchased his stock after a fiduciary had wrongfully taken possession of corporate property, but while the fiduciary continued to hold it. In contrast, in Weinhaus v. Gale, 237 F.2d 197 (7th Cir.1956), the continuing-wrong theory was deemed inapplicable where plaintiff had purchased after stock had been sold by a subsidiary to its parent at a price alleged to be unfairly low, but before the parent had resold the stock. In Palmer v. Morris, 316 F.2d 649 (5th Cir.1963), the plaintiff was allowed to sue under the continuing-wrong theory where he had purchased his stock after an allegedly wrongful deal was made, but while payments under the deal continued. In contrast, in Chaft v. Kass, 19 A.D.2d 610, 241 N.Y.S.2d 284 (1963), the theory was deemed inapplicable where plaintiff purchased his stock after the corporation had entered into an allegedly invalid contract, but while payments under the contract were still being made.

Several statutes provide that the plaintiff must allege that he was a shareholder at the time of the transaction "or any part thereof." E.g.,

Cal. § 800(b)(1); Wis. § 180.405. Where there is a close question whether the continuing-wrong theory applies to a given case, such a statute might tip the scale in the plaintiff's favor.

## SECTION 5.   THE RIGHT TO TRIAL BY JURY IN DERIVATIVE ACTIONS

---

### NOTE ON THE RIGHT TO TRIAL BY JURY IN DERIVATIVE ACTIONS

Since a derivative action has traditionally been conceived as an equitable remedy, until recently it did not carry the right to a trial by jury. In 1970, however, the Supreme Court held in Ross v. Bernhard, 396 U.S. 531, 90 S.Ct. 733, 24 L.Ed.2d 729 that in a derivative action brought in federal court the parties have a right to a jury where the action would be triable to a jury if it had been brought by the corporation itself rather than by a shareholder:

> We have noted that the derivative suit has dual aspects: first, the stockholder's right to sue on behalf of the corporation, historically an equitable matter; second, the claim of the corporation against directors or third parties on which, if the corporation had sued and the claim presented legal issues, the company could demand a jury trial. . . . [L]egal claims are not magically converted into equitable issues by their presentation to a court of equity in a derivative suit. The claim pressed by the stockholder against directors or third parties "is not his own but the corporation's." . . . The heart of the action is the corporate claim. If it presents a legal issue, one entitling the corporation to a jury trial under the Seventh Amendment, the right to a jury is not forfeited merely because the stockholder's right to sue must first be adjudicated as an equitable issue triable to the court.[1]

The Seventh Amendment applies only to federal proceedings. State-court decisions vary. Compare Rankin v. Frebank Co., 47 Cal. App.3d 75, 121 Cal.Rptr. 348 (1975) (under the California Constitution there is no right to a jury in derivative actions), and Pelfrey v. Bank of Greer, 270 S.C. 691, 244 S.E.2d 315 (1978) (same result under South Carolina statute) with Finance, Investment & Rediscount Co. v. Wells, 409 So.2d 1341 (Ala.1981) (there is a right to a jury trial under Alabama law), and Fedoryszyn v. Weiss, 62 Misc.2d 889, 310 N.Y.S.2d 55 (1970) (same under New York law).

---

**1.**  Id. at 538–39, 90 S.Ct. at 738. It is reported that after Ross v. Bernhard was decided, several cases were settled in which the defendants would have gone to trial had the case been triable to the judge. Rosenfeld, Plaintiff's Strategy in Prosecuting and Defending Stockholders Suits 241, 250 (S. Wechsler ed. 1972).

## SECTION 6.   DEMAND ON THE BOARD AND TERMINATION OF DERIVATIVE ACTIONS ON THE RECOMMENDATION OF THE BOARD OR A COMMITTEE

————

### CAL. CORP. CODE § 800(b)(2)

[See Statutory Supplement]

————

### FEDERAL RULES OF CIVIL PROCEDURE RULE 23.1

[See Statutory Supplement]

————

### INTRODUCTORY NOTE

Until about the 1970s, it was well settled that before bringing a derivative action a shareholder was required to make a demand on the board, unless demand was excused. Two related issues, however, were much less settled. The first issue was, when was demand excused? The general rule was that demand was excused if it was futile. The most important application of this rule was that demand was excused if a majority of the directors were interested. It was not clear, however, what constituted *interest* for these matters. For example, it was not clear whether a director was interested merely because he or she was named as a defendant, and if not, how much more had to be shown.

The second unsettled issue was the consequence of *not* making demand. In most of the reported cases, demand had not been made and the corporation moved to dismiss the action on the ground that demand was required. The courts in such cases often simply held that demand was or was not required, without getting into what consequences would follow if a required demand was made and rejected—although some courts did say or hold that if demand was required and rejected, and the rejection was by disinterested directors who constituted a majority of the board, a derivative action could not proceed unless in rejecting demand the board violated the business judgment rule.

The picture was complicated further in the 1970s, when a series of cases held that even when a majority of directors were interested, so that demand was not required, the board could appoint a committee to consider whether the derivative action was in the best interests of the corporation. If the committee concluded that the action was not in the corporation's best interests, and the committee had engaged in an adequate investigation, the court could dismiss the action on the committee's motion, subject to a designated standard of review. If the board was disinterested, the board itself could conduct the investigation and make the motion.

In short, as of the 1970s a cluster of related issues were raised concerning the role and power of the board in derivative actions. When was demand on the board excused? What were the consequences if demand was required, made, and denied? What, if anything, could a board do if demand was excused?

It was against this background that the cases in this Section were decided.

---

## Marx v. Akers

New York Court of Appeals, 1996.
88 N.Y.2d 189, 644 N.Y.S.2d 121, 666 N.E.2d 1034.

■ JUDGES: Opinion by JUDGE SMITH. CHIEF JUDGE KAYE and JUDGES SIMONS, TITONE, LEVINE and CIPARICK concur. JUDGE BELLACOSA took no part.

■ SMITH, J.:

Plaintiff commenced this shareholder derivative action against International Business Machines Corporation (IBM) and IBM's board of directors without first demanding that the board initiate a lawsuit. The amended complaint (complaint) alleges that the board wasted corporate assets by awarding excessive compensation to IBM's executives and outside directors. The issues raised on this appeal are whether the Appellate Division abused its discretion by dismissing plaintiff's complaint for failure to make a demand and whether plaintiff's complaint fails to state a cause of action. We affirm the order of the Appellate Division because we conclude that plaintiff was not excused from making a demand with respect to the executive compensation claim and that plaintiff has failed to state a cause of action for corporate waste in connection with the allegations concerning payments to IBM's outside directors.

### Facts and Procedural History

The complaint alleges that during a period of declining profitability at IBM the director defendants engaged in self-dealing by awarding excessive compensation to the 15 outside directors on the 18–member board. Although the complaint identifies only one of the three inside directors as an IBM executive (defendant Akers is identified as a former chief executive officer of IBM), plaintiff also appears to allege that the director defendants violated their fiduciary duties to IBM by voting for unreasonably high compensation for IBM executives.[2]

---

**2.** Executives at IBM are compensated through a fixed salary and performance incentives. Payouts on the performance incentives are based on IBM's earnings per share, return on equity and cash flow. Plaintiff's complaint criticizes only the performance incentive component of executive compensation as excessive because of certain accounting practices which plaintiff alleges artificially inflate earnings, return on equity and cash flow.

Defendants moved to dismiss the complaint for (1) failure to state a cause of action, and (2) failure to serve a demand on IBM's board to initiate a lawsuit based on the complaint's allegations. The Supreme Court dismissed, holding that plaintiff failed to establish the futility of a demand. Supreme Court concluded that excusing a demand here would render Business Corporation Law § 626(c) "virtually meaningless in any shareholders' derivative action in which all members of a corporate board are named as defendants." Having decided the demand issue in favor of defendants, the court did not reach the issue of whether plaintiff's complaint stated a cause of action. The Appellate Division affirmed the dismissal, concluding that the complaint did not contain any details from which the futility of a demand could be inferred. The Appellate Division found that plaintiff's objections to the level of compensation were not stated with sufficient particularity in light of statutory authority permitting directors to set their own compensation.

### *Background*

A shareholder's derivative action is an action "brought in the right of a domestic or foreign corporation to procure a judgment in its favor, by a holder of shares or of voting trust certificates of the corporation or of a beneficial interest in such shares or certificates" (Business Corporation Law § 626[a]). "Derivative claims against corporate directors belong to the corporation itself" (Auerbach v. Bennett, 47 N.Y. 2d 619, 631).

> "The remedy sought is for wrong done to the corporation; the primary cause of action belongs to the corporation; recovery must enure to the benefit of the corporation. The stockholder brings the action, in behalf of others similarly situated, to vindicate the corporate rights and a judgment on the merits is a binding adjudication of these rights (citations omitted)" (Isaac v. Marcus, 258 N.Y. 257, 264).

... Business Corporation Law § 626(c) provides that in any shareholders' derivative action, "the complaint shall set forth with particularity the efforts of the plaintiff to secure the initiation of such action by the board or the reasons for not making such effort." Enacted in 1961 (L 1961, ch 855), section 626(c) codified a rule of equity developed in early shareholder derivative actions requiring plaintiffs to demand that the corporation initiate an action, unless such demand was futile, before commencing an action on the corporation's behalf (Barr v. Wackman, 36 N.Y. 2d 371, 377). The purposes of the demand requirement are to (1) relieve courts from deciding matters of internal corporate governance by providing corporate directors with opportunities to correct alleged abuses, (2) provide corporate boards with reasonable protection from harassment by litigation on matters clearly within the discretion of directors, and (3) discourage "strike suits" commenced by shareholders for personal gain rather than for the benefit of the corporation (Barr, 36 NY2d at

378). "The demand is generally designed to weed out unnecessary or illegitimate shareholder derivative suits" (id.).

By their very nature, shareholder derivative actions infringe upon the managerial discretion of corporate boards. "As with other questions of corporate policy and management, the decision whether and to what extent to explore and prosecute such [derivative] claims lies within the judgment and control of the corporation's board of directors" (Auerbach, supra, 47 NY2d at 631). Consequently, we have historically been reluctant to permit shareholder derivative suits, noting that the power of courts to direct the management of a corporation's affairs should be "exercised with restraint" (Gordon v. Elliman, 306 N.Y. 456, 462).

In permitting a shareholder derivative action to proceed because a demand on the corporation's directors would be futile,

> "the object is for the court to chart the course for the corporation which the directors should have selected, and which it is presumed that they would have chosen if they had not been actuated by fraud or bad faith. Due to their misconduct, the court substitutes its judgment ad hoc for that of the directors in the conduct of its business" (id. at 462).

Achieving a balance between preserving the discretion of directors to manage a corporation without undue interference, through the demand requirement, and permitting shareholders to bring claims on behalf of the corporation when it is evident that directors will wrongfully refuse to bring such claims, through the demand futility exception, has been accomplished by various jurisdictions in different ways. One widely cited approach to demand futility which attempts to balance these competing concerns has been developed by Delaware courts and applies a two-pronged test to each case to determine whether a failure to serve a demand is justified. At the other end of the spectrum is a universal demand requirement which would abandon particularized determinations in favor of requiring a demand in every case before a shareholder derivative suit may be filed.

### The Delaware Approach

Delaware's demand requirement, codified in Delaware Chancery Court Rule 23.1, provides, in relevant part,

> "In a derivative action brought by 1 or more shareholders or members to enforce a right of a corporation * * * [the complaint shall allege] with particularity the efforts, if any, made by the plaintiff to obtain the action the plaintiff desires from the directors or comparable authority and the reasons for the plaintiff's failure to obtain the action or for not making the effort."

Interpreting Rule 23.1, the Delaware Supreme Court in Aronson v. Lewis (473 A.2d 805) developed a two-prong test for determining the futility of a demand. Plaintiffs must allege particularized facts which create a reasonable doubt that,

"(1) the directors are disinterested and independent and (2) the challenged transaction was otherwise the product of a valid exercise of business judgment. Hence, the Court of Chancery must make two inquiries, one into the independence and disinterestedness of the directors and the other into the substantive nature of the challenged transaction and the board's approval thereof" (473 A2d at 814).

The two branches of the *Aronson* test are disjunctive (see, Levine v. Smith, 591 A.2d 194, 205). Once director interest has been established, the business judgment rule becomes inapplicable and the demand excused without further inquiry (*Aronson,* 473 A2d at 814). Similarly, a director whose independence is compromised by undue influence exerted by an interested party cannot properly exercise business judgment and the loss of independence also justifies the excusal of a demand without further inquiry (see, Levine, supra, 591 A2d at 205–206). Whether a board has validly exercised its business judgment must be evaluated by determining whether the directors exercised procedural (informed decision) and substantive (terms of the transaction) due care (Grobow v. Perot, 539 A.2d 180, 189).

The reasonable doubt threshold of Delaware's two-fold approach to demand futility has been criticized. The use of a standard of proof which is the heart of a jury's determination in a criminal case has raised questions concerning its applicability in the corporate context (see, Starrels v. First Natl. Bank, 870 F.2d 1168, 1175 (7th Cir.)) [Easterbrook, J, concurring]. The reasonable doubt standard has also been criticized as overly subjective, thereby permitting a wide variance in the application of Delaware law to similar facts (2 American Law Institute, Principles of Corporate Governance: Analysis and Recommendations § 7.03, Comment d at 57 [1992]).

### Universal Demand

A universal demand requirement would dispense with the necessity of making case-specific determinations and impose an easily applied bright line rule. The Business Law Section of the American Bar Association has proposed requiring a demand in all cases, without exception, and permits the commencement of a derivative proceeding within 90 days of the demand unless the demand is rejected earlier (Model Business Corporation Act § 7.42[1] [1995 Supplement]). However, plaintiffs may file suit before the expiration of 90 days, even if their demand has not been rejected, if the corporation would suffer irreparable injury as a result (Model Business Corporation Act § 7.42[2]).

The American Law Institute (ALI) has also proposed a "universal" demand. Section 7.03 of ALI's Principles of Corporate Governance would require shareholder derivative action plaintiffs to serve a written demand on the corporation unless a demand is excused because "the plaintiff makes a specific showing that irreparable injury to the corporation would otherwise result" (2 American Law Institute, Principles of Corporate Governance: Analysis and Recommendations,

§ 7.03[b] at 53–54, [1992]). Once a demand has been made and rejected, however, the ALI would subject the board's decision to "an elaborate set of standards that calibrates the deference afforded the decision of the directors to the character of the claim being asserted" (Kamen v. Kemper Financial Services, Inc., 500 U.S. 90, 104).

At least 11 states have adopted, by statute, the universal demand requirement proposed in the Model Business Corporation Act. Georgia, Michigan, Wisconsin, Montana, Virginia, New Hampshire, Mississippi, Connecticut, Nebraska and North Carolina require shareholders to wait 90 days after serving a demand before filing a derivative suit unless the demand is rejected before the expiration of the 90 days, or irreparable injury to the corporation would result. . . . Arizona additionally permits shareholders to file suit before the expiration of 90 days if the statute of limitations would expire during the 90 day period. . . . Florida also appears to have adopted a universal demand requirement, although the statutory language does not track the Model Business Corporation Act. Florida's statute provides, "A complaint in a proceeding brought in the right of a corporation must be verified and allege with particularity the demand made to obtain action by the board of directors and that the demand was refused or ignored (emphasis added)". . . .

New York State has also considered and continues to consider implementing a universal demand requirement. However, even though bills to adopt a universal demand have been presented over three legislative sessions, the Legislature has yet to enact a universal demand requirement. . . .

### New York's Approach to Demand Futility

Although instructive, neither the universal demand requirement nor the Delaware approach to demand futility is adopted here. Since New York's demand requirement is codified in Business Corporation Law § 626(c), a universal demand can only be adopted by the Legislature. Delaware's approach, which resembles New York law in some respects, incorporates a "reasonable doubt" standard which, as we have already pointed out, has provoked criticism as confusing and overly subjective. An analysis of the *Barr* decision compels the conclusion that in New York, a demand would be futile if a complaint alleges with particularity that (1) a majority of the directors are interested in the transaction, or (2) the directors failed to inform themselves to a degree reasonably necessary about the transaction, or (3) the directors failed to exercise their business judgment in approving the transaction.

In Barr v. Wackman (36 N.Y. 2d 371, supra), we considered whether the plaintiff was excused from making a demand where the board of Talcott National Corporation (Talcott), consisting of 13 outside directors, a director affiliated with a related company and four interested inside directors, rejected a merger proposal involving Gulf & Western Industries (Gulf & Western) in favor of another proposal on allegedly less favorable terms for Talcott and its shareholders. The merger proposal, memorialized in a board-approved "agreement in principle," proposed exchanging one share of Talcott common stock for approximately $24.00 consisting of $17.00 in cash and 0.6 of a warrant to purchase Gulf & Western stock, worth approximately $7.00. This proposal was abandoned in favor of a cash tender offer for Talcott shares by Associated First Capital Corporation (a Gulf & Western subsidiary) at $20.00 per share—four dollars less than proposed for the merger.

The plaintiff in *Barr* alleged that Talcott's board discarded the merger proposal after the four "controlling" inside directors received pecuniary and personal benefits from Gulf & Western in exchange for ceding control of Talcott on terms less favorable to Talcott's shareholders. As alleged in the complaint, these benefits included new and favorable employment contracts for nine Talcott officers, including five-year employment contracts for three of the controlling directors. In addition to his annual salary of $125,000 with Talcott, defendant Silverman (a controlling director) would allegedly receive $60,000 a year under a five year employment contract with Associated First Capital, and an aggregate of $275,000 for the next five years in an arrangement with Associated First Capital to serve as a consultant. This additional compensation would be awarded to Silverman after control of Talcott passed to Associated First Capital and Gulf & Western. Plaintiff also alleged that Gulf & Western and Associated First Capital paid an excessive "finder's fee" of $340,000 to a company where Silverman's son was an executive vice president. In addition to alleging that the controlling defendants obtained personal benefits, the complaint also alleged that Talcott's board agreed to sell a Talcott subsidiary at a net loss of $6,100,000 solely to accommodate Gulf & Western.

In *Barr*, we held that insofar as the complaint attacked the controlling directors' acts in causing the corporation to enter into a transaction for their own financial benefit, demand was excused because of the self-dealing, or self-interest of those directors in the challenged transaction. Specifically, we pointed to the allegation that the controlling directors "breached their fiduciary obligations to Talcott in return for personal benefits" (id., at 376).

We also held in *Barr*, however, that as to the disinterested outside directors, demand could be excused even in the absence of their receiving any financial benefit from the transaction. That was because the complaint alleged that, by approving the terms of the less advantageous offer, those directors were guilty of a "breach of their duties of due care and diligence to the corporation" (id., at 380). Their performance of the duty of care would have "put them on notice of the claimed self-dealing of the affiliated directors" (id.). The complaint charged that the outside directors failed "to do more than passively rubber stamp the decisions of the active managers" (id., at 381) resulting in corporate detriment. These allegations, the *Barr* Court concluded, also excused demand as to the charges against the disinterested directors.

*Barr* also makes clear that "it is not sufficient * * * merely to name a majority of the directors as parties defendant with the conclusory allegation of wrongdoing or control by wrongdoers" (id., at 379) to justify failure to make a demand. Thus, *Barr* reflects the statutory requirement that the complaint "must set forth with particularity the * * * reasons for not making such effort" (Business Corporation Law § 626[c]).

Unfortunately, various courts have overlooked the explicit warning that conclusory allegations of wrongdoing against each member of the board are not sufficient to excuse demand and have misinterpreted *Barr* as excusing demand whenever a majority of the board members who approved the transaction are named as defendants (see, Miller v. Schreyer, 200 A.D. 2d 492; Curreri v. Verni, 156 A.D. 2d 420; MacKay v. Pierce, 86 A.D. 2d 655; Joseph v. Amrep Corp., 59 A.D. 2d 841; see also, Allison Publications Incorporated v. Mutual Benefit Life Insurance, 197 A.D. 2d 463). As stated most recently, "the rule is clear in this State that no demand is necessary 'if the complaint alleges acts for which a majority of the directors may be liable and plaintiff reasonably concluded that the board would not be responsive to a demand'" (Miller v Schreyer, supra, at 494 [quoting from *Barr,* supra, 36 N.Y.2d at 371]; but see, Lewis v. Welch, 126 A.D. 2d 519, 521). The problem with such an approach is that it permits plaintiffs to frame their complaint in such a way as to automatically excuse demand, thereby allowing the exception to swallow the rule.

We thus deem it necessary to offer the following elaboration of *Barr's* demand/futility standard. (1) Demand is excused because of futility when a complaint alleges with particularity that a majority of the board of directors is interested in the challenged transaction. Director interest may either be self-interest in the transaction at issue (see, Barr v Wackman, supra, at 376 [receipt of "personal benefits"]), or a loss of independence because a director with no direct interest in a transaction is "controlled" by a self-interested director. (2) Demand is excused because of futility when a complaint alleges with particularity that the board of directors did not fully inform themselves about the challenged transaction to the extent reasonably appropriate under the circumstances (see, *Barr,* supra, at 380, 368 N.Y.S.2d 497, 329 N.E.2d 180). The "long-standing rule" is that a director "does not exempt himself from liability by failing to do more than passively rubber-stamp the decisions of the active managers" (id., at 381). (3) Demand is excused because of futility when a complaint alleges with particularity that the challenged transaction was so egregious on its face that it could not have been the product of sound business judgment of the directors.

### The Current Appeal

Plaintiff argues that the demand requirement was excused both because the outside directors awarded themselves generous compensation packages and because of the acquiescence of the disinterested directors in the executive compensation schemes. The complaint states:

> "Plaintiff has made no demand upon the directors of IBM to institute this lawsuit because such demand would be futile. As set forth above, each of the directors authorized, approved, participated and/or acquiesced in the acts and transactions complained of herein and are liable therefor. Further, each of the Non–Employee [outside] Directors has received and retained the benefit of his excessive compensation and each of the other directors has received and retained the benefit of the incentive compensation described above. The defendants cannot be expected to vote to prosecute an action against themselves. Demand upon the company to bring action (sic) to redress the wrongs herein is therefore unnecessary."

Defendants argue that neither the Supreme Court nor the Appellate Division abused its discretion in holding that plaintiff's complaint did not set forth the futility of a demand with particularity.

As in *Barr*, we look to the complaint here to determine whether the allegations are sufficient and establish with particularity that demand would have been futile. Here, the plaintiff alleges that the compensation awarded to IBM's outside directors and certain IBM executives was excessive.

Defendant's motion to dismiss for failure to make a demand as to the allegations concerning the compensation paid to IBM's executive officers was properly granted. A board is not interested "in voting compensation for one of its members as an executive or in some other nondirectorial capacity, such as a consultant to the corporation," although "so-called 'back-scratching' arrangements, pursuant to which all directors vote to approve each other's compensation as officers or employees, do not constitute disinterested directors' action" (1 ALI, supra, at 250). Since only three directors are alleged to have received the benefit of the executive compensation scheme, plaintiff has failed to allege that a majority of the board was interested in setting executive compensation. Nor do the allegations that the board used faulty accounting procedures to calculate executive compensation levels move beyond "conclusory allegations of wrongdoing" (Barr v Wackman, supra, at 379) which are insufficient to excuse demand. The complaint does not allege particular facts in contending that the board failed to deliberate or exercise its business judgment in setting those levels. Consequently, the failure to make a demand regarding the fixing of executive compensation was fatal to [the] portion of the complaint challenging that transaction.

However, a review of the complaint indicates that plaintiff also alleged that a majority of the board was self-interested in setting the compensation of outside directors because the outside directors comprised a majority of the board.

Directors are self-interested in a challenged transaction where they will receive a direct financial benefit from the transaction which is different from the benefit to shareholders generally (see, Rales v. Blasband, 634 A.2d 927, 936 [Del Sup Ct]; Bergstein v. Texas Intern. Co., 453 A.2d 467, 472–473 [Del Ch]; ALI, Principles of Corporate Governance § 1.23, at 25; 13 Fletcher, Cyclopedia Corporations § 5965, at 138). A director who votes him or herself a raise in directors' compensation is always "interested" because that person will receive a personal financial benefit from the transaction not shared in by stockholders (see, 1 ALI Principles of Corporate Governance § 5.03, comment g, at 250 ["if the board votes directorial compensation for itself, the board is interested"]; see also, Steiner v. Meyerson, [1995 Transfer Binder] , Fed. Sec. L. Rep. P 98857 [Del Ch], 1995 WL 441999, at 12 ["As the outside directors comprise a majority of the Telxon board and are personally interested in their compensation levels, demand upon them to challenge or decrease their own compensation is excused"]). Consequently, a demand was excused as to plaintiff's allegations that the compensation set for outside directors was excessive.

## Corporate Waste

Our conclusion that demand should have been excused as to the part of the complaint challenging the fixing of directors' compensation does not end our inquiry, however. We must also determine whether plaintiff has stated a cause of action regarding that transaction, i.e., some wrong to the corporation. We conclude that plaintiff has not, and thus dismiss the complaint in its entirety.

Historically, directors did not receive any compensation for their work as directors (see, Fletcher, Cyclopedia Corporations, § 2109). Thus, a bare allegation that corporate directors voted themselves excessive compensation was sufficient to state a cause of action (e.g., Walsh v. Van Ameringen–Haebler, Inc., 257 N.Y. 478, 480; Jacobson v. Brooklyn Lumber Co., 184 N.Y. 152, 162). Many jurisdictions, including New York, have since changed the common law rule by statute providing that a corporation's board of directors has the authority to fix director compensation unless the corporation's charter or bylaws provides otherwise. Thus, the allegation that directors have voted themselves compensation is clearly no longer an allegation which gives rise to a cause of action, as the directors are statutorily entitled to set those levels. Nor does a conclusory allegation that the compensation directors have set for themselves is excessive give rise to a cause of action.

> The courts will not undertake to review the fairness of the official salaries, at the suit of a shareholder attacking them as excessive, unless wrongdoing and oppression or possible abuse of a fiduciary position are shown. However, the courts will take a hand in the matter at the instance of the corporation or of shareholders in extreme cases. A case of fraud is presented where directors increase their collective salaries so as to use up nearly the entire earnings of a company; where directors or officers appropriate the income so as to deprive shareholders of reasonable dividends, or

perhaps so reduce to assets as to threaten the corporation with insolvency * * * (Fletcher, Cyclopedia Corporations, § 2122, at 46–47).

Thus, a complaint challenging the excessiveness of director compensation must—to survive a dismissal motion—allege compensation rates excessive on their face or other facts which call into question whether the compensation was fair to the corporation when approved, the good faith of the directors setting those rates, or that the decision to set the compensation could not have been a product of valid business judgment.[3]

Applying the foregoing principles to plaintiff's complaint, it is clear that it must be dismissed. The complaint alleges that the directors increased their compensation rates from a base of $20,000 plus $500 for each meeting attended to a retainer of $55,000 plus 100 shares of IBM stock over a five-year period. The complaint also alleges that "this compensation bears little relation to the part-time services rendered by the Non–Employee Directors or to the profitability of IBM. The board's responsibilities have not increased, its performance, measured by the company's earnings and stock price, has been poor yet its compensation has increased far in excess of the cost of living."

These conclusory allegations do not state a cause of action. There are no factually-based allegations of wrongdoing or waste which would, if true, sustain a verdict in plaintiff's favor. Plaintiff's bare allegations that the compensation set lacked a relationship to duties performed or to the cost of living are insufficient as a matter of law to state a cause of action.

Accordingly, the order of the Appellate Division should be affirmed, with costs.

——————

## Auerbach v. Bennett

Court of Appeals of New York, 1979.
47 N.Y.2d 619, 419 N.Y.S.2d 920, 393 N.E.2d 994.

■ JONES, JUDGE.

While the substantive aspects of a decision to terminate a shareholders' derivative action against defendant corporate directors made by a committee of disinterested directors appointed by the corporation's board of directors are beyond judicial inquiry under the business judgment doctrine, the court may inquire as to the disinterested independence of the members of that committee and as to the

---

**3.** There is general agreement that the allocation of the burden of proof differs depending on whether the compensation was approved by disinterested directors or shareholders, or by interested directors. Plaintiffs must prove wrongdoing or waste as to compensation arrangements regarding disinterested directors or shareholders, but directors who approve their own compensation bear the burden of proving that the transaction was fair to the corporation (see, Block, et al, The Business Judgment Rule, at 149 [4th ed.]; Fletcher, supra, § 514.1, 632; ALI, supra, § 5.03). However, at the pleading stage we are not concerned with burdens of proof.

appropriateness and sufficiency of the investigative procedures chosen and pursued by the committee. In this instance, however, no basis is shown to warrant either inquiry by the court. Accordingly we hold that it was error to reverse the lower court's dismissal of the shareholders' derivative action.

In the summer of 1975 the management of General Telephone & Electronics Corporation, in response to reports that numerous other multinational companies had made questionable payments to public officials or political parties in foreign countries, directed that an internal preliminary investigation be made to ascertain whether that corporation had engaged in similar transactions. On the basis of the report of this survey, received in October, 1975, management brought the issue to the attention of the corporation's board of directors. At a meeting held on November 6 of that year the board referred the matter to the board's audit committee. The audit committee retained as its special counsel the Washington, D.C., law firm of Wilmer, Cutler & Pickering which had not previously acted as counsel to the corporation. With the assistance of such special counsel and Arthur Andersen & Co., the corporation's outside auditors, the audit committee engaged in an investigation into the corporation's worldwide operations, focusing on whether, in the period January 1, 1971 to December 31, 1975, corporate funds had been (1) paid directly or indirectly to any political party or person or to any officer, employee, shareholder or director of any governmental or private customer, or (2) used to reimburse any officer of the corporation or other person for such payments.

On March 4, 1976 the audit committee released its report which was filed with the Securities and Exchange Commission and disclosed to the corporation's shareholders in a proxy statement prior to the annual meeting of shareholders held in April, 1976. The audit committee reported that it had found evidence that in the period from 1971 to 1975 the corporation or its subsidiaries had made payments abroad and in the United States constituting bribes and kickbacks in amounts perhaps totaling more than 11 million dollars and that some of the individual defendant directors had been personally involved in certain of the transactions.

Almost immediately Auerbach, a shareholder in the corporation, instituted the present shareholders' derivative action on behalf of the corporation against the corporation's directors, Arthur Andersen & Co. and the corporation. The complaint alleged that in connection with the transactions reported by the audit committee defendants, present and former members of the corporation's board of directors and Arthur Andersen & Co., are liable to the corporation for breach of their duties to the corporation and should be made to account for payments made in those transactions.

On April 21, 1976 the board of directors of the corporation adopted a resolution creating a special litigation committee "for the purpose of establishing a point of contact between the Board of Directors and the Corporation's General Counsel concerning the position to be taken by the Corporation in certain litigation involving shareholder derivative claims on behalf of the Corporation against certain of its directors and officers" and authorizing that committee "to take such steps from time to time as it deems necessary to pursue its objectives including the retention of special outside counsel." The special committee comprised three disinterested directors who had joined the board after the challenged transactions had occurred. The board subsequently additionally vested in the committee "all of the authority of the Board of Directors to determine, on behalf of the Board, the position that the Corporation shall take with respect to the derivative claims alleged on its behalf" in the present and similar shareholder derivative actions.

The special litigation committee reported under date of November 22, 1976. It found that defendant Arthur Andersen & Co. had conducted its examination of the corporation's affairs in accordance with generally accepted auditing standards and in good faith and concluded that no proper interest of the corporation or its shareholders would be served by the continued assertion of a claim against it. The committee also concluded that none of the individual defendants had violated the New York State statutory standard of care, that none had profited personally or gained in any way, that the claims asserted in the present action are without merit, that if the action were allowed to proceed the time and talents of the corporation's senior management would be wasted on lengthy pretrial and trial proceedings, that litigation costs would be inordinately high in view of the unlikelihood of success, and that the continuing publicity could be damaging to the corporation's business. The committee determined that it would not be in the best interests of the corporation for the present derivative action to proceed, and, exercising the authority delegated to it, directed the corporation's general counsel to take that position in the present litigation as well as in pending comparable shareholders' derivative actions.

On December 17, 1976 the corporation and the four individual defendants who had been served moved for an order pursuant to CPLR 3211 (subd. [a], pars. [3], [7]) dismissing the complaint or in the alternative for an order pursuant to CPLR 3211 (subd. [c]) for summary judgment. On January 7, 1977 Arthur Andersen & Co. made a similar motion. On May 13, 1977 Supreme Court, Special Term, granted the motions of all defendants and dismissed the complaint on the merits. . . .

As all parties and both courts below recognize, the disposition of this case on the merits turns on the proper application of the business judgment doctrine, in particular to the decision of a specially appointed committee of disinterested directors acting on behalf of the board to terminate a shareholders' derivative action. That doctrine bars judicial inquiry into actions of corporate directors taken in good faith and in the exercise of honest judgment in the lawful and legitimate furtherance of corporate purposes. "Questions of policy of management, expediency of contracts or action, adequacy of consideration, lawful appropriation of corporate funds to advance corporate interests, are left solely to their honest and unselfish decision, for their powers therein are without limitation and free from restraint, and the exercise of them for the common and general interests of the corporation may not be questioned, although the results show that what they did was unwise or inexpedient." (Pollitz v. Wabash, R.R. Co., 207 N.Y. 113, 124, 100 N.E. 721, 724.)

In this instance our inquiry, to the limited extent to which it may be pursued, has a two-tiered aspect. The complaint initially asserted liability on the part of defendants based on the payments made to foreign governmental customers and privately owned customers, some unspecified portions of which were allegedly passed on to officials of the customers, i.e., the focus was on first-tier bribes and kickbacks. Then subsequent to the service of the complaint there came the report of a special litigation committee, particularly appointed by the corporation's board of directors to consider the merits of the present and similar shareholders' derivative actions, and its determination that it would not be in the best interests of the corporation to press claims against defendants based on their possible first-tier liability. The motions for summary judgment were predicated principally on the report and determination of the special litigation committee and on the contention that this second-tier corporate action insulated the first-tier transactions from judicial inquiry and was itself subject to the shelter of the business judgment doctrine. The disposition at Special Term was predicated on this analysis; its decision focused on the actions of the special litigation committee, and the motions for summary judgment were granted on the ground that the business judgment doctrine precluded the courts from going back of the decision of the special litigation committee on behalf of the corporation not to pursue the claims alleged in the complaint. Similarly the reversal at the Appellate Division was based on that court's perception of the proper application of the business judgment rule to the actions and determination of the special litigation committee. We proceed on the same analysis, concluding, however, on the record before us, at variance with the Appellate Division, that the determination of the special litigation committee forecloses further judicial inquiry in this case.

It appears to us that the business judgment doctrine, at least in part, is grounded in the prudent recognition that courts are ill equipped and infrequently called on to evaluate what are and must be essentially business judgments. The authority and responsibilities vested in corporate directors both by statute and decisional law proceed on the assumption that inescapably there can be no available objective standard by which the correctness of every corporate decision may be measured, by the courts or otherwise. Even if that were not the case, by definition the responsibility for business judgments must rest with the corporate directors; their individual capabilities and experience peculiarly qualify them for the discharge of that responsibility. Thus, absent evidence of bad faith or fraud (of which there is none here) the courts must and properly should respect their determinations.

Derivative claims against corporate directors belong to the corporation itself. As with other questions of corporate policy and management, the decision whether and to what extent to explore and prosecute such claims lies within the judgment and control of the corporation's board of directors. Necessarily such decision must be predicated on the weighing and balancing of a variety of disparate considerations to reach a considered conclusion as to what course of action or inaction is best calculated to protect and advance the interests of the corporation. This is the essence of the responsibility and role of the board of directors, and courts may not intrude to interfere.

In the present case we confront a special instance of the application of the business judgment rule and inquire whether it applies in its full vigor to shield from judicial scrutiny the decision of a three-person minority committee of the board acting on behalf of the full board not to prosecute a shareholder's derivative action. The record in this case reveals that the board is a 15–member board, and that the derivative suit was brought against four of the directors. Nothing suggests that any of the other directors participated in any of the challenged first-tier transactions. Indeed the report of the audit committee on which the complaint is based specifically found that no other directors had any prior knowledge of or were in any way involved in any of these transactions. Other directors had, however, been members of the board in the period during which the transactions occurred. Each of the three director members of the special litigation committee joined the board thereafter.

The business judgment rule does not foreclose inquiry by the courts into the disinterested independence of those members of the board chosen by it to make the corporate decision on its behalf—here the members of the special litigation committee. Indeed the rule shields the deliberations and conclusions of the chosen representatives of the board only if they possess a disinterested independence and do not stand in a dual relation which prevents an unprejudicial exercise of judgment. (Cf. Koral v. Savory, Inc., 276 N.Y. 215, 11 N.E.2d 883.)

We examine then the proof submitted by defendants. It is not disputed that the members of the special litigation committee were not members of the corporation's board of directors at the time of the first-tier transactions in question. Howard Blauvelt, chairman of the board of Continental Oil Company, had been elected to the corporation's board of directors on October 9, 1975. Dr. John T. Dunlop, Lamont University professor at the Graduate School of Business Administration of Harvard University had been elected to the board on April 21, 1976. James R. Barker, chairman of the board and chief executive officer of Moore McCormack Resources, Inc., was added as the third member of the committee when he was elected to the board on July 19, 1976. None of the three had had any prior affiliation with the corporation. Notwithstanding the vigorous and imaginative hypothesizing and innuendo of counsel there is nothing in this record to raise a triable issue of fact as to the independence and disinterested status of these three directors.

The contention of Wallenstein that any committee authorized by the board of which defendant directors were members must be held to be legally infirm and may not be delegated power to terminate a derivative action must be rejected. In the very nature of the corporate organization it was only the existing board of directors which had authority on behalf of the corporation to direct the investigation and to assure the cooperation of corporate employees, and it is only that same board by its own action—or as here pursuant to authority duly delegated by it—which had authority to decide whether to prosecute the claims against defendant directors. The board in this instance, with slight adaptation, followed prudent practice in observing the general policy that when individual members of a board of directors prove to have personal interests which may conflict with the interests of the corporation, such interested directors must be excluded while the remaining members of the board proceed to consideration and action. (Cf. Business Corporation Law, § 713, which contemplates such situations and provides that the interested directors may nonetheless be included in the quorum count.) Courts have consistently held that the business judgment rule applies where some directors are charged with wrongdoing, so long as the remaining directors making the decision are disinterested and independent. (Swanson v. Traer, 249 F.2d 854, 858–859; Gall v. Exxon Corp., 418 F.Supp. 508, supplemented 75 Civ. 3582 [U.S.Dist.Ct., S.D.N.Y., Jan. 17, 1977]; Issner v. Aldrich, 254 F.Supp. 696, 701–702; Republic Nat. Life Ins. Co. v. Beasley, 73 F.R.D. 658, 668–669; Gilbert v. Curtiss–Wright Corp., 179 Misc. 641, 645, 38 N.Y.S.2d 548, 552.)

To accept the assertions of the intervenor and to disqualify the entire board would be to render the corporation powerless to make an effective business judgment with respect to prosecution of the derivative action. The possible risk of hesitancy on the part of the members of any committee, even if composed of outside, independent, disinterested directors, to investigate the activities of fellow members of the board where personal liability is at stake is an inherent, inescapable, given aspect of the corporation's predicament. To assign responsibility of the dimension here involved to individuals wholly separate and apart from the board of directors would, except in the most extraordinary circumstances, itself be an act of default and breach of the nondelegable fiduciary duty owed by the members of the board to the corporation and to its shareholders, employees and creditors. For the courts to preside over such determinations would similarly work an ouster of the board's fundamental responsibility and authority for corporate management.

We turn then to the action of the special litigation committee itself which comprised two components. First, there was the selection of procedures appropriate to the pursuit of its charge, and second, there was the ultimate substantive decision; predicated on the procedures chosen and the data produced thereby, not to pursue the claims advanced in the shareholders' derivative actions. The latter, substantive decision falls squarely within the embrace of the business judgment doctrine, involving as it did the weighing and balancing of legal, ethical, commercial, promotional, public relations, fiscal and other factors familiar to the resolution of many if not most corporate problems. To this extent the conclusion reached by the special litigation committee is outside the scope of our review. Thus, the courts cannot inquire as to which factors were considered by that committee or the relative weight accorded them in reaching that substantive decision—"the reasons for the payments, the advantages or disadvantages accruing to the corporation by reason of the transactions, the extent of the participation or profit by the respondent directors and the loss, if any, of public confidence in the corporation which might be incurred" (64 A.D.2d, at p. 107, 408 N.Y.S.2d at pp. 87–88). Inquiry into such matters would go to the very core of the business judgment made by the committee. To permit judicial probing of such issues would be to emasculate the business judgment doctrine as applied to the actions and determinations of the special litigation committee. Its substantive evaluation of the problems posed and its judgment in their resolution are beyond our reach.

As to the other component of the committee's activities, however, the situation is different, and here we agree with the Appellate Division. As to the methodologies and procedures best suited to the conduct of an investigation of facts and the determination of legal liability, the courts are well equipped by long and continuing experience and practice to make determinations. In fact they are better qualified in this regard than are corporate directors in general. Nor do the determinations to be made in the adoption of procedures partake of the nuances or special perceptions or comprehensions of business judgment or corporate activities or interests. The question is solely how appropriately to set about to gather the pertinent data.

While the court may properly inquire as to the adequacy and appropriateness of the committee's investigative procedures and methodologies, it may not under the guise of consideration of such factors trespass in the domain of business judgment. At the same time those responsible for the procedures by which the business judgment is reached may reasonably be required to show that they have pursued their chosen investigative methods in good faith. What evidentiary proof may be required to this end will, of course, depend on the nature of the particular investigation, and the proper reach of disclosure at the instance of the shareholders will in turn relate inversely to the showing made by the corporate representatives themselves. The latter may be expected to show that the areas and subjects to be examined are reasonably complete and that there has been a good-faith pursuit of inquiry into such areas and subjects. What has been uncovered and the relative weight accorded in evaluating and balancing the several factors and considerations are beyond the scope of judicial concern. Proof, however, that the investigation has been so restricted in scope, so shallow in execution, or otherwise so *pro forma* or halfhearted as to constitute a pretext or sham, consistent with the principles underlying the application of the business judgment doctrine, would raise questions of good faith or conceivably fraud which would never be shielded by that doctrine.

In addition to the issue of the disinterested independence of the special litigation committee, addressed above, the disposition of the present appeal turns, then, on whether on defendants' motions for summary judgment predicated on the investigation and determination of the special litigation committee, Wallenstein by tender of evidentiary proof in admissible form has shown facts sufficient to require a trial of any material issue of fact as to the adequacy or appropriateness of the *modus operandi* of that committee or has demonstrated acceptable excuse for failure to make such tender. (Friends of Animals v. Associated Fur Mfrs., 46 N.Y.2d 1065, 416 N.Y.S.2d 790, 390 N.E.2d 298; CPLR 3212, subd. [b].) We conclude that the requisite showing has not been made on this record. . . .

On the submissions made by defendants in support of their motions, we do not find either insufficiency or infirmity as to the procedures and methodologies chosen and pursued by the special litigation committee. That committee promptly engaged eminent special counsel to guide its deliberations and to advise it. The committee reviewed the prior work of the audit committee, testing its completeness, accuracy and thoroughness by interviewing representatives of Wilmer, Cutler & Pickering, reviewing transcripts of the testimony of 10 corporate officers and employees before the Securities and Exchange Commission, and studying documents collected by and work papers of the Washington law firm. Individual interviews were conducted with the directors found to have participated in any way in the questioned payments, and with representatives of Arthur Andersen & Co. Questionnaires were sent to and answered by each of the corporation's nonmanagement directors. At the conclusion of its investigation the special litigation committee sought and obtained pertinent legal advice from its special counsel. The selection of appropriate investigative methods must always turn on the nature and characteristics of the particular subject being investigated, but we find nothing in this record that requires a trial of any material issue of fact concerning the sufficiency or appropriateness of the procedures chosen by this special litigation committee. Nor is there anything in this record to raise a triable issue of fact as to the good-faith pursuit of its examination by that committee.

Finally, there should be a word as to the contention advanced by the intervenor that summary judgment should at least be withheld until there has been opportunity for disclosure. We note preliminarily as a matter of procedure that there was no application at Special Term for any such relief nor is there in the record any opposing affidavit from which it appears that essential facts may exist which could be obtained by disclosure (CPLR 3212, subd. [f]). It is also significant that neither in his brief nor on oral argument did Wallenstein identify any particulars as to which he desires discovery relating to the disinterestedness of the members of the special litigation committee or to the procedures followed by that committee. To speculate that something might be caught on a fishing expedition provides no basis to postpone decision on the summary judgment motions under the authority of CPLR 3212 (subd. [f]). The disclosure proposed and described by Wallenstein on oral argument would go only to particulars as to the results of the committee's investigation and work, the factors bearing on its substantive decision not to prosecute the derivative actions and the factual aspects of the underlying first-tier activities of defendants— all matters falling within the ambit of the business judgment doctrine and thus excluded from judicial scrutiny.

For the reasons stated the order of the Appellate Division should be modified, with costs to defendants, by reversing so much thereof as reversed the order of Supreme Court, and, as so modified, affirmed.

[The dissenting opinion of Chief Judge Cooke is omitted.]

■ JASEN, WACHTLER, FUCHSBERG and MEYER, JJ., concur with JONES, J.

■ COOKE, C.J., dissents and votes to affirm in a separate opinion.

■ GABRIELLI, J., taking no part.

Order modified, with costs to defendants, in accordance with the opinion herein and, as so modified, affirmed. Question certified answered in the negative.

————

## Zapata Corp. v. Maldonado

Supreme Court of Delaware, 1981.
430 A.2d 779.

■ Before DUFFY, QUILLEN and HORSEY, JJ.

[The claims on which this case was apparently based are stated as follows in Maldonado v. Flynn, 597 F.2d 789 (2d Cir.1979): A stock-option plan had been adopted by the board of Zapata Corporation in 1970 and approved by Zapata's shareholders in 1971. The board was authorized to amend the plan freely. The options were exercisable in five equal installments; the last exercise date was July 14, 1970. Flynn, the chief executive officer and a director of Zapata, as well as other senior officers of Zapata, were granted options under the plan to purchase Zapata stock at $12.15 per share.

[In 1974, Flynn and the board had decided Zapata should make a cash tender offer for its own stock at $25–$30 per share. Since Zapata stock was then trading at only $19 per share, the announcement of the tender offer would trigger a sharp rise in the price of Zapata stock. The tender offer was to be publicly announced on July 2, 1974. Early that day, trading in Zapata stock on the New York Stock Exchange was suspended at the request of Zapata's management, pending the announcement. Before trading resumed, the board accelerated the final exercise date for the options held by Flynn and the other senior officers from July 14, 1974 to July 2, 1974. The board also modified the plan to authorize Zapata to make interest-free loans to Flynn and the other senior officers in the amount of (i) the purchase price of the options they exercised and (ii) the tax liability they would incur by exercising the options. The purpose and effect of these amendments were to permit Flynn and the other senior officers to benefit at Zapata's expense. Under applicable federal tax laws, on the exercise of the option Flynn and the other senior officers would realize ordinary income in the amount of the spread between the option price and the fair market price of the stock at the time the option was exercised. Correspondingly, Zapata could deduct the amount of that spread as a business expense. By accelerating the last exercise date, and allowing Flynn and the other senior officers to exercise their options before the market price of the stock rose as a result of the tender offer, the board permitted the optionees to save a considerable amount of taxes but prevented Zapata from enjoying a correspondingly higher tax deduction.]

■ QUILLEN, JUSTICE. This is an interlocutory appeal from an order entered on April 9, 1980, by the Court of Chancery denying appellant-defendant Zapata Corporation's (Zapata) alternative motions to dismiss the complaint or for summary judgment. The issue to be addressed has reached this Court by way of a rather convoluted path.

In June, 1975, William Maldonado, a stockholder of Zapata, instituted a derivative action in the Court of Chancery on behalf of Zapata against ten officers and/or directors of Zapata, alleging, essentially, breaches of fiduciary duty. Maldonado did not first demand that the board bring this action, stating instead such demand's futility because all directors were named as defendants and allegedly participated in the acts specified.[1] In June, 1977, Maldonado commenced an action in the United States District Court for the Southern District of New York against the same defendants, save one, alleging federal security law violations as well as the same common law claims made previously in the Court of Chancery.

By June, 1979, four of the defendant-directors were no longer on the board, and the remaining directors appointed two new outside directors to the board. The board then created an "Independent Investigation Committee" (Committee), composed solely of the two new directors, to investigate Maldonado's actions . . . and to determine whether the corporation should continue any or all of the litigation. The Committee's determination was stated to be "final, . . . not . . . subject to review by the Board of Directors and . . . in all respects . . . binding upon the Corporation."

Following an investigation, the Committee concluded, in September, 1979, that each action should "be dismissed forthwith as their continued maintenance is inimical to the Company's best interests. . . ." Consequently, Zapata moved for dismissal or summary judgment. . . .

---

1. Court of Chancery Rule 23.1 states in part: "The complaint shall also allege with particularity the efforts, if any, made by the plaintiff to obtain the action he desires from the directors or comparable authority and the reasons for his failure to obtain the action or for not making the effort."

On March 18, 1980, the Court of Chancery, in a reported opinion, the basis for the order of April 9, 1980, denied Zapata's motions, holding that Delaware law does not sanction this means of dismissal. . . .

[T]he focus in this case is on the power to speak for the corporation as to whether the lawsuit should be continued or terminated. As we see it, this issue in the current appellate posture of this case . . . [concerns] the corporate power under Delaware law of an authorized board committee to cause dismissal of litigation instituted for the benefit of the corporation; and the role of the Court of Chancery in resolving conflicts between the stockholder and the committee. . . .

Consistent with the purpose of requiring a demand, a board decision to cause a derivative suit to be dismissed as detrimental to the company, after demand has been made and refused, will be respected unless it was wrongful.[10] . . . A claim of a wrongful decision not to sue is thus the first exception and the first context of dispute. Absent a wrongful refusal, the stockholder in such a situation simply lacks legal managerial power. . . .

But it cannot be implied that, absent a wrongful board refusal, a stockholder can never have an individual right to initiate an action. For, as is stated in *[McKee]*, a "well settled" exception exists to the general rule.

> "[A] stockholder may sue in equity in his derivative right to assert a cause of action in behalf of the corporation, *without prior demand* upon the directors to sue, when it is apparent that a demand would be futile, that the officers are under an influence that sterilizes discretion and could not be proper persons to conduct the litigation."

156 A. at 193 (emphasis added). . . .[11]

These comments in *McKee* . . . make obvious sense. A demand, when required and refused (if not wrongful), terminates a stockholder's legal ability to initiate a derivative action. But where demand is properly excused, the stockholder does possess the ability to initiate the action on his corporation's behalf.

These conclusions, however, do not determine the question before us. Rather, they merely bring us to the question to be decided. . . .

The question to be decided becomes: When, if at all, should an authorized board committee be permitted to cause litigation, properly initiated by a derivative stockholder in his own right, to be dismissed?

---

**10.** In other words, when stockholders, after making demand and having their suit rejected, attack the board's decision as improper, the board's decision falls under the "business judgment" rule and will be respected if the requirements of the rule are met. . . . That situation should be distinguished from the instant case, where demand was not made, and the *power* of the board to seek a dismissal, due to disqualification, presents a threshold issue. . . .

**11.** These statements are consistent with Rule 23.1's "reasons for . . . failure" to make demand. . . .

As noted above, a board has the power to choose not to pursue litigation when demand is made upon it, so long as the decision is not wrongful. If the board determines that a suit would be detrimental to the company, the board's determination prevails. Even when demand is excusable, circumstances may arise when continuation of the litigation would not be in the corporation's best interests. Our inquiry is whether, under such circumstances, there is a permissible procedure under § 141(a) by which a corporation can rid itself of detrimental litigation. If there is not, a single stockholder in an extreme case might control the destiny of the entire corporation. This concern was bluntly expressed by the Ninth Circuit in Lewis v. Anderson, 9th Cir., 615 F.2d 778, 783 (1979), cert. denied, 449 U.S. 869, 101 S.Ct. 206, 66 L.Ed.2d 89 (1980): "To allow one shareholder to incapacitate an entire board of directors merely by leveling charges against them gives too much leverage to dissident shareholders." But, when examining the means, including the committee mechanism examined in this case, potentials for abuse must be recognized. This takes us to the second and third aspects of the issue on appeal. . . .

The corporate power inquiry then focuses on whether the board, tainted by the self-interest of a majority of its members, can legally delegate its authority to a committee of two disinterested directors. We find our statute clearly requires an affirmative answer to this question. As has been noted, under an express provision of the statute, § 141(c), a committee can exercise all of the authority of the board to the extent provided in the resolution of the board. Moreover, at least by analogy to our statutory section on interested directors, 8 Del.C. § 141, it seems clear that the Delaware statute is designed to permit disinterested directors to act for the board.[14] Compare Puma v. Marriott, Del.Ch., 283 A.2d 693, 695–96 (1971).

We do not think that the interest taint of the board majority is per se a legal bar to the delegation of the board's power to an independent committee composed of disinterested board members. The committee can properly act for the corporation to move to dismiss derivative litigation that is believed to be detrimental to the corporation's best interest.

Our focus now switches to the Court of Chancery which is faced with a stockholder assertion that a derivative suit, properly instituted, should continue for the benefit of the corporation and a corporate assertion, properly made by a board committee acting with board authority, that the same derivative suit should be dismissed as inimical to the best interests of the corporation.

At the risk of stating the obvious, the problem is relatively simple. If, on the one hand, corporations can consistently wrest bona fide derivative actions away from well-meaning derivative plaintiffs through the use of the committee mechanism, the derivative suit will lose much, if not all, of its generally-recognized effectiveness as an intra-corporate means of policing boards of directors. See Dent, [supra note

---

**14.**   [The court quoted Del. § 144.]

5,] 75 Nw.U.L.Rev. at 96 & n. 3, 144 & n. 241. If, on the other hand, corporations are unable to rid themselves of meritless or harmful litigation and strike suits, the derivative action, created to benefit the corporation, will produce the opposite, unintended result. . . . It thus appears desirable to us to find a balancing point where bona fide stockholder power to bring corporation causes of action cannot be unfairly trampled on by the board of directors, but the corporation can rid itself of detrimental litigation.

[T]he question has been treated by other courts as one of the "business judgment" of the board committee. If a "committee, composed of independent and disinterested directors, conducted a proper review of the matters before it, considered a variety of factors and reached, in good faith, a business judgment that [the] action was not in the best interest of [the corporation]", the action must be dismissed. See, e.g., Maldonado v. Flynn, . . . 485 F.Supp. at 282, 286. The issues become solely independence, good faith, and reasonable investigation. The ultimate conclusion of the committee, under that view, is not subject to judicial review.

We are not satisfied, however, that acceptance of the "business judgment" rationale at this stage of derivative litigation is a proper balancing point. While we admit an analogy with a normal case respecting board judgment, it seems to us that there is sufficient risk in the realities of a situation like the one presented in this case to justify caution beyond adherence to the theory of business judgment.

The context here is a suit against directors where demand on the board is excused. We think some tribute must be paid to the fact that the lawsuit was properly initiated. It is not a board refusal case. Moreover, this complaint was filed in June of 1975 and, while the parties undoubtedly would take differing views on the degree of litigation activity, we have to be concerned about the creation of an "Independent Investigation Committee" four years later, after the election of two new outside directors. Situations could develop where such motions could be filed after years of vigorous litigation for reasons unconnected with the merits of the lawsuit.

Moreover, notwithstanding our conviction that Delaware law entrusts the corporate power to a properly authorized committee, we must be mindful that directors are passing judgment on fellow directors in the same corporation and fellow directors, in this instance, who designated them to serve both as directors and committee members. The question naturally arises whether a "there but for the grace of God go I" empathy might not play a role. And the further question arises whether inquiry as to independence, good faith and reasonable investigation is sufficient safeguard against abuse, perhaps subconscious abuse.

There is another line of exploration besides the factual context of this litigation which we find helpful. The nature of this motion finds no ready pigeonhole, as perhaps illustrated by its being set forth in the alternative. It is perhaps best considered as a hybrid summary judgment motion for dismissal because the stockholder plaintiff's standing to maintain the suit has been lost. But it does not fit neatly into a category described in Rule 12(b) of the Court of Chancery Rules nor does it correspond directly with Rule 56 since the question of genuine issues of fact on the merits of the stockholder's claim are not reached.

It seems to us that there are two other procedural analogies that are helpful in addition to reference to Rules 12 and 56. There is some analogy to a settlement in that there is a request to terminate litigation without a judicial determination of the merits. See Perrine v. Pennroad Corp., Del.Super., 47 A.2d 479, 487 (1946). "In determining whether or not to approve a proposed settlement of a derivative stockholders' action [when directors are on both sides of the transaction], the Court of Chancery is called upon to exercise its own business judgment." Neponsit Investment Co. v. Abramson, Del.Super., 405 A.2d 97, 100 (1979) and cases therein cited. In this case, the litigating stockholder plaintiff facing dismissal of a lawsuit properly commenced ought, in our judgment, to have sufficient status for strict Court review.

Finally, if the committee is in effect given status to speak for the corporation as the plaintiff in interest, then it seems to us there is an analogy to Court of Chancery Rule 41(a)(2) where the plaintiff seeks a dismissal after an answer. Certainly, the position of record of the litigating stockholder is adverse to the position advocated by the corporation in the motion to dismiss. Accordingly, there is perhaps some wisdom to be gained by the direction in Rule 41(a)(2) that "an action shall not be dismissed at the plaintiff's instance save upon order of the Court and upon such terms and conditions as the Court deems proper."

Whether the Court of Chancery will be persuaded by the exercise of a committee power resulting in a summary motion for dismissal of a derivative action, where a demand has not been initially made, should rest, in our judgment, in the independent discretion of the Court of Chancery. We thus steer a middle course between those cases which yield to the independent business judgment of a board committee and this case as determined below which would yield to unbridled plaintiff stockholder control. In pursuit of the course, we recognize that "[t]he final substantive judgment whether a particular lawsuit should be maintained requires a balance of many factors—ethical, commercial, promotional, public relations, employee relations, fiscal as well as legal." Maldonado v. Flynn, [supra,] 485 F.Supp. at 285. But we are content that such factors are not "beyond the judicial reach" of the Court of Chancery which regularly and competently deals with fiduciary relationships, disposition of trust property, approval of settlements and scores of similar problems. We recognize the danger of judicial overreaching but the alternatives seem to us to be outweighed by the fresh view of a judicial outsider. Moreover, if we failed to balance all the interests involved, we would in the name of practicality and judicial economy foreclose a judicial decision on the merits. At this point, we are not convinced that is necessary or desirable.

After an objective and thorough investigation of a derivative suit, an independent committee may cause its corporation to file a pretrial motion to dismiss in the Court of Chancery. The basis of the motion is the best interests of the corporation, as determined by the committee. The motion should include a thorough written record of the investigation and its findings and recommendations. Under appropriate court supervision, akin to proceedings on summary judgment, each side should have an opportunity to make a record on the motion. As to the limited issues presented by the motion noted below, the moving party should be prepared to meet the normal burden under Rule 56 that there is no genuine issue as to any material fact and that the moving party is entitled to dismiss as a matter of law.[15] The Court should apply a two-step test to the motion.

First, the Court should inquire into the independence and good faith of the committee and the bases supporting its conclusions. Limited discovery may be ordered to facilitate such inquiries. The corporation should have the burden of proving independence, good faith and a reasonable investigation, rather than presuming independence, good faith and reasonableness.[17] If the Court determines that the committee is not independent or has not shown reasonable bases for its conclusions, or, if the Court is not satisfied for other reasons relating to the process, including but not limited to the good faith of the committee, the Court shall deny the corporation's motion. If, however, the Court is satisfied under Rule 56 standards that the committee was independent and showed reasonable bases for good faith findings and recommendations, the Court may proceed, in its discretion, to the next step.

The second step provides, we believe, the essential key in striking the balance between legitimate corporate claims as expressed in a derivative stockholder suit and a corporation's best interests as expressed by an independent investigating committee. The Court should determine, applying its own independent business judgment, whether the motion should be granted.[18] This means, of course, that instances could arise where a committee can establish its independence and sound bases for its good faith decisions and still have the corporation's motion denied. The second step is intended to thwart instances where corporate actions meet the criteria of step one, but the result does not appear to satisfy its spirit, or where corporate actions would simply prematurely terminate a stockholder grievance deserving of further consideration in the corporation's interest. The Court of Chancery of course must carefully consider and weigh how compelling the corpo-

**15.** We do not foreclose a discretionary trial of factual issues but that issue is not presented in this appeal. See Lewis v. Anderson, supra, 615 F.2d at 780. Nor do we foreclose the possibility that other motions may proceed or be joined with such a pretrial summary judgment motion to dismiss, e.g., a partial motion for summary judgment on the merits.

**17.** Compare Auerbach v. Bennett, 47 N.Y.2d 619, 419 N.Y.S.2d 920, 928–29, 393 N.E.2d 994 (1979). Our approach here is analogous to and consistent with the Dela-

ware approach to "interested director" transactions, where the directors, once the transaction is attacked, have the burden of establishing its "intrinsic fairness" to a court's careful scrutiny. See, e.g., Sterling v. Mayflower Hotel Corp., Del.Supr., 93 A.2d 107 (1952).

**18.** This step shares some of the same spirit and philosophy of the statement by the Vice Chancellor: "Under our system of law, courts and not litigants should decide the merits of litigation." 413 A.2d at 1263.

rate interest in dismissal is when faced with a nonfrivolous lawsuit. The Court of Chancery should, when appropriate, give special consideration to matters of law and public policy in addition to the corporation's best interests.

If the Court's independent business judgment is satisfied, the Court may proceed to grant the motion, subject, of course, to any equitable terms or conditions the Court finds necessary or desirable.

The interlocutory order of the Court of Chancery is reversed and the cause is remanded for further proceedings consistent with this opinion.

————

**ARONSON v. LEWIS,** 473 A.2d 805 (Del.1984). "The gap in our law, which we address today, arises from this Court's decision in Zapata Corp. v. Maldonado. There, the Court defined the limits of a board's managerial power granted by Section 141(a) and restricted application of the business judgment rule in a factual context similar to this action. . . .

"After *Zapata* numerous derivative suits were filed without prior demand upon boards of directors. The complaints in such actions all alleged that demand was excused because of board interest, approval or acquiescence in the wrongdoing. In any event, the *Zapata* demand-excused/demand-refused bifurcation, has left a crucial issue unanswered: when is demand futile and, therefore, excused?

"Delaware courts have addressed the issue of demand futility on several earlier occasions. . . . The rule emerging from these decisions is that where officers and directors are under an influence which sterilizes their discretion, they cannot be considered proper persons to conduct litigation on behalf of the corporation. Thus, demand would be futile. See e.g., McKee v. Rogers, Del.Ch., 156 A. 191, 192 (1931) (holding that where a defendant controlled the board of directors, '[i]t is manifest then that there can be no expectation that the corporation would sue him, and if it did, it can hardly be said that the prosecution of the suit would be entrusted to proper hands') . . . .

"However, those cases cannot be taken to mean that any board approval of a challenged transaction automatically connotes 'hostile interest' and 'guilty participation' by directors, or some other form of sterilizing influence upon them. Were that so, the demand requirements of our law would be meaningless, leaving the clear mandate of Chancery Rule 23.1 devoid of its purpose and substance. . . .

"Our view is that in determining demand futility the Court of Chancery in the proper exercise of its discretion must decide whether, under the particularized facts alleged, a reasonable doubt is created that: (1) the directors are disinterested and independent and (2) the challenged transaction was otherwise the product of a valid exercise of business judgment. Hence, the Court of Chancery must make two inquiries, one into the independence and disinterestedness of the directors and the other into the substantive nature of the challenged transaction and the board's approval thereof. As to the latter inquiry the court does not assume that the transaction is a wrong to the corporation requiring corrective steps by the board. Rather, the alleged wrong is substantively reviewed against the factual background alleged in the complaint. As to the former inquiry, directorial independence and disinterestedness, the court reviews the factual allegations to decide whether they raise a reasonable doubt, as a threshold matter, that the protections of the business judgment rule are available to the board. Certainly, if this is an 'interested' director transaction, such that the business judgment rule is inapplicable to the board majority approving the transaction, then the inquiry ceases. In that event futility of demand has been established by any objective or subjective standard.[8] See, e.g., Bergstein v. Texas International Co., Del.Ch., 453 A.2d 467, 471 (1982) (because five of nine directors approved stock appreciation rights plan likely to benefit them, board was interested for demand purposes and demand held futile). This includes situations involving self-dealing directors. . . .

"However, the mere threat of personal liability for approving a questioned transaction, standing alone, is insufficient to challenge either the independence or disinterestedness of directors, although in rare cases a transaction may be so egregious on its face that board approval cannot meet the test of business judgment, and a substantial likelihood of director liability therefore exists. . . . In sum the entire review is factual in nature. The Court of Chancery in the exercise of its sound discretion must be satisfied that a plaintiff has alleged facts with particularity which, taken as true, support a reasonable doubt that the challenged transaction was the product of a valid exercise of business judgment. Only in that context is demand excused."

---

**GROBOW v. PEROT**, 539 A.2d 180 (Del.1988). "[G]iven the highly factual nature of the inquiry presented to the Trial Court by a Rule 23.1 defense, we conclude that it would be neither practicable nor wise to attempt to formulate a criterion of general application for determining reasonable doubt [under *Aronson v. Lewis*]. The facts necessary to support a finding of reasonable doubt either of director disinterest or independence, or whether proper business judgment was exercised in the transaction will vary with each case. Reasonable doubt must be decided by the trial court on a case-by-case basis employing an objective analysis. Were we to adopt a standard criterion for resolving a motion to dismiss based on Rule 23.1, the test for

---

**8.** We recognize that drawing the line at a majority of the board may be an arguably arbitrary dividing point. Critics will charge that we are ignoring the structural bias common to corporate boards throughout America, as well as the other unseen socialization processes cutting against independent discussion and decisionmaking in the board- room. The difficulty with structural bias in a demand futile case is simply one of establishing it in the complaint for purposes of Rule 23.1. We are satisfied that discretionary review by the Court of Chancery of complaints alleging specific facts pointing to bias on a particular board will be sufficient for determining demand futility.

demand excusal would, in all likelihood, become rote and inelastic. . . .

"We think it sufficient simply to say that the Court of Chancery must weigh the presumption of the business judgment rule that attaches to a board of directors' decision against the well-pleaded facts alleged in a plaintiff's demand-futility complaint."

See also Levine v. Smith, 591 A.2d 194 (Del.Supr.1991).

————

### NOTE ON CUKER v. MIKALAUSKAS

In Cuker v. Mikalauskas, 547 Pa. 600, 692 A.2d 1042 (Pa. 1997), PECO Energy Co. filed a motion for summary judgment seeking termination of minority shareholder derivative actions. The motion was filed on behalf of the board, which had adopted the report of a special litigation committee that proceeding with the actions would not be in the corporation's best interests. The trial court rejected PECO's motion for summary judgment. The Pennsylvania Supreme Court reversed and remanded, with the following instructions:

We specifically adopt §§ 7.02–7.10, and § 7.13 of the *ALI Principles*.[5] In doing so we have weighed many considerations. First, the opinion of the trial court, the questions certified to the Superior Court, and the inability of PECO to obtain a definitive ruling from the lower courts all demonstrate the need for specific guidance from this court on how such litigation should be managed; the ALI principles provide such guidance in specific terms which will simplify this litigation. Second, we have often found ALI guidance helpful in the past, most frequently in adopting or citing sections of various Restatements; the scholarship reflected in work of the American Law Institute has been consistently reliable and useful. Third, the principles set forth by the ALI are generally consistent with Pennsylvania precedent. Fourth, although the *ALI Principles* incorporate much of the law of New York and Delaware, other states with extensive corporate jurisprudence, the ALI Principles better serve the needs of Pennsylvania. Although New York law parallels Pennsylvania law in many respects, it does not set forth any procedures to govern the review of corporate decisions relating to derivative litigation, and this omission would fail to satisfy the needs evident in this case. Delaware law permits a court in some cases ("demand excused" cases) to apply its own business judgment in the review process

**5.** Our adoption of these sections is not a rejection of other sections not cited. We have identified and studied the sections which apply to this case and have adopted those which appear most relevant.

The entire publication, all seven parts, is a comprehensive, cohesive work more than a decade in preparation. Additional sections of the publication, particularly procedural ones due to their interlocking character, may be adopted in the future. Issues in future cases or, perhaps, further proceedings in this case might implicate additional sections of the *ALI Principles*. Courts of the Commonwealth are free to consider other parts of the work and utilize them if they are helpful and appear to be consistent with Pennsylvania law.

when deciding to honor the directors' decision to terminate derivative litigation. In our view, this is a defect which could eviscerate the business judgment rule and contradict a long line of Pennsylvania precedents. Delaware law also fails to provide a procedural framework for judicial review of corporate decisions under the business judgment rule.

In an Appendix to its opinion, the court set out Principles of Corporate Governance §§ 7.02–7.10 and 7.13 in full.

---

## REVISED MODEL BUSINESS CORPORATION ACT §§ 7.42–7.44

[See Statutory Supplement]

---

## AMERICAN LAW INSTITUTE, PRINCIPLES OF CORPORATE GOVERNANCE §§ 7.03, 7.04, 7.08–7.13

[See Statutory Supplement]

---

## SECTION 7.  DEMAND ON THE SHAREHOLDERS

---

### NOTE ON DEMAND ON SHAREHOLDERS

The rules governing demand on the shareholders vary widely.

1. *Demand Not Required.* Under the law of many jurisdictions, demand on shareholders is not required. For example, the California and New York statutory counterparts to FRCP 23.1 omit any reference to demand on the shareholders, and it is clear that this omission was deliberate. See Syracuse Television, Inc. v. Channel 9, Syracuse, Inc., 51 Misc.2d 188, 273 N.Y.S.2d 16 (1966).

2. *Demand Required; Exceptions.* In a number of jurisdictions demand on the shareholders is required unless excused, but there is considerable divergence concerning what constitutes an acceptable excuse.

a. *Wrongdoers hold a majority of the stock.* All courts agree that demand on shareholders is excused when the alleged wrongdoers hold a majority of the stock. See, e.g., Heilbrunn v. Hanover Equities Corp., 259 F.Supp. 936 (S.D.N.Y.1966). Most courts would probably come to the same result where the wrongdoers hold a controlling but less-than-majority interest. See Gottesman v. General Motors Corp.,

268 F.2d 194 (2d Cir.1959). But see Levitan v. Stout, 97 F.Supp. 105 (W.D.Ky.1951).

b. *Demand futile*. All courts would probably agree that demand on shareholders is also excused when it is futile for other reasons, although there might be considerable divergence as to whether a given state of facts constitutes futility. See, e.g., Pioche Mines Consolidated, Inc. v. Dolman, 333 F.2d 257, 264–65 (9th Cir.1964), cert. denied 380 U.S. 956, 85 S.Ct. 1081, 13 L.Ed.2d 972 (1965) (demand excused where only one shareholders' meeting had been held for many years, and management had ignored earlier demands that such meetings be held).

c. *Large number of shareholders*. The cases are split on whether demand on shareholders is excused because the corporation has a large number of shareholders, compare Weiss v. Sunasco Inc., 316 F.Supp. 1197 (E.D.Pa.1970) (demand excused), with Quirke v. St. Louis–San Francisco Ry., 277 F.2d 705 (8th Cir.1960), cert. denied 363 U.S. 845, 80 S.Ct. 1615, 4 L.Ed.2d 1728 (contra); or because management has refused to supply plaintiff with a shareholders' list, compare Escoett v. Aldecress Country Club, 16 N.J. 438, 109 A.2d 277 (1954) (demand excused), with Bell v. Arnold, 175 Colo. 277, 487 P.2d 545 (1971) (plaintiffs alleged that the corporation had 26,000 shareholders, but this allegation was apparently made as part of the argument that access to the shareholder list had been unreasonably restricted. The court stated, "[s]ince the number of shareholders ... was not pled as an excuse, nor was it accompanied by any allegation regarding unreasonable costs of making the demand, we do not, on this writ of error, determine whether 26,000 shareholders did, or did not, formulate a valid basis for an excuse in making demand on them").

d. *Nonratifiable wrong*. The cases are also split on whether demand on shareholders is excused where the alleged wrong could not be ratified. The majority rule, reflected in Mayer v. Adams, 37 Del.Ch. 298, 141 A.2d 458 (1958) is that nonratifiability excuses demand. However, there is a very strong minority view. For example, in Bell v. Arnold, supra, the court stated:

> One reason set forth in the complaint for not making a demand on the shareholders is that they could not ratify the alleged wrongs because of the illegal nature of the wrongs. We hold this is not an acceptable reason or a valid excuse for not making a demand on the shareholders here. The purpose of making demand on the shareholders is to inform them of the alleged nonratifiable wrongs; to seek their participation in available courses of action, such as, the removal of the involved directors and the election of new directors who will seek the redress required in the circumstances; or to secure shareholder approval of an action for damages to the corporation caused by the alleged wrongdoing directors.

See also Claman v. Robertson, 164 Ohio St. 61, 128 N.E.2d 429 (1955).

3. *Two Distinctions.* A distinction must be drawn between the question whether a plaintiff must make a demand on shareholders and the question whether shareholder ratification has a substantive effect. A further distinction is drawn by some courts (most notably Massachusetts), which hold that the shareholders have power to preclude suit even where they do not have power to ratify. The leading case is S. Solomont & Sons Trust v. New England Theatres Operating Corp., 326 Mass. 99, 111–12, 93 N.E.2d 241, 247–48 (1950).

# SECTION 8.   PLAINTIFF'S COUNSEL FEES

---

## Sugarland Industries, Inc. v. Thomas

Supreme Court of Delaware, 1980.
420 A.2d 142.*

■ Before DUFFY, QUILLEN and HORSEY, JJ.

■ DUFFY, JUSTICE:

This is an appeal from an order of the Court of Chancery awarding $3.5 million in attorney fees. Counsel's efforts in the case are separable into two phases, and the appeal places both of them in issue, that is, a Phase I award of $3 million and a Phase II award of $500,000. Plaintiffs have cross-appealed as to the orders governing interest on the awards.

I

The relevant facts are as follows:

In January 1973, Sugarland Industries, Inc., a Delaware corporation (defendant) controlled by the Kempner family,[1] owned 7,500 acres of land in Texas south of Houston which it was attempting to sell. Lyda Ann Q. Thomas and her husband, J. Redmond Thomas (plaintiffs), who are members of the Kempner family and shareholders in Sugarland, were concerned about a proposed sale of the so-called South Tract (which is the major part of the property and includes some 5,900 acres) to White and Hill, a Texas partnership involved in real estate development, for $23,800,000. Plaintiffs considered the price to be inadequate and retained Brantly Harris, a Houston lawyer and a partner in the firm of Prappas, Caldwell & Moncure (now, Prappas, Moncure, Harris & Termini) to represent their interest in the proposed sale. Shortly thereafter, and at least partially as a result of Mr. Harris' efforts, a syndicate known as R–S–C was formed and it offered to buy the South Tract for $27,000,000, or $3.2 million more than White and Hill had offered.

---

* On appeal after remand, 431 A.2d 1271 (Del.1981) (footnote by ed.)

**1.** All members of the Board of Directors of Sugarland are members of the Kempner family, with one exception.

Ignoring the higher bid by R–S–C, Sugarland's directors continued to favor White and Hill and gave notice that a special meeting of stockholders would be held on March 7, 1973, to consider and accept the $23.8 million proposal. After being informed of such a meeting, the Prappas firm, concerned that the Sugarland directors had excluded the possibility of selling the property to anyone other than White and Hill, consulted counsel in Delaware about litigation to block the sale. Prappas had suggested to R–S–C that it would be helpful if R–S–C, which would benefit if plaintiffs prevailed in such litigation, advanced $10,000 as a retainer for Delaware counsel; under this plan, plaintiffs would pay any fees in excess of the $10,000. Both R–S–C and plaintiffs agreed to that arrangement.

Shortly thereafter, on March 6, plaintiffs filed a stockholders' derivative action in the Court of Chancery to enjoin the proposed sale of the South Tract to White and Hill. On March 9, Mr. Prappas wrote a letter to the Thomases confirming their fee arrangement with his firm. . . .

[The court held that the fee agreement entered into by the plaintiffs' lawyers did not preclude their application to the court for attorneys' fees on a basis other than hourly rates.]

On March 22, the Chancellor filed an opinion in which he ruled that Sugarland would be enjoined from accepting the White and Hill proposal and ordered competitive bidding for the Sugarland properties. The opinion was implemented by order dated April 10. Because this created a conflict between the Thomases who, as Sugarland shareholders, wanted the sale to bring top dollar, and R–S–C, which wanted the property at the lowest possible price, the Prappas firm (by letter dated April 6, 1973) withdrew from its representation of R–S–C.

Thereafter, Sugarland conducted a sale by sealed bids, and on April 30, the Gerald D. Hines Interests submitted the highest bid, an offer of $37,229,069 for the South Tract. Hines later negotiated for Sugarland's North Tract and on July 3 entered into a contract for both the North and South Tracts. Hines' bid on the North Tract similarly exceeded the next highest bid on that tract by about $1,243,139. The total price for both properties was about $44,000,000. (The closing was held on December 14, 1973.)

On July 25, after Hines had contracted to buy both Tracts, the Prappas firm wrote to the Thomases "releasing" them from the fee agreement. . . .

Meanwhile, on April 30, a second action on behalf of the same plaintiffs by the same attorneys against the same defendants had been filed in the Court of Chancery; on November 12, a supplemental complaint was filed, thereby beginning the "damage" or Phase II of this controversy. That action was essentially a claim for damages against the Sugarland directors. Unlike the first or injunctive phase which was swiftly concluded, the second phase remained unresolved over the next three years and consumed some 13,000 hours on the part of lawyers (and their respective staffs) representing plaintiffs.

On November 10, 1977, a settlement of the Phase II litigation was finally made and approved by the Court of Chancery. While the complaint addressed to the second phase had alleged wrongdoing involving Sugarland, the terms of settlement did not directly affect the corporation; they centered, rather, on a reorganization of the management of various other business entities owned by the Kempner family.

After the settlement had been approved, plaintiffs' attorneys filed an application in the Court of Chancery seeking a combined fee of approximately $6 million for their services as to Phases I and II of the litigation.

The United States National Bank of Galveston, Trustee (intervenor) owns some 47,500 shares (about 23%) of Sugarland stock. It entered the litigation as an objector to the fee application.

On January 26, 1979, the Chancellor awarded plaintiffs' counsel[2] a fee of $3,500,000 computed as follows: (a) as to Phase I, a fee equal to 20% of the benefit created by their efforts, with a cap of $3 million, and (b) as to Phase II, the sum of $500,000 for time expended in achieving the settlement. An order implementing the opinion was entered on May 11, 1979. It directed that $1,376,130 be paid within the month, and required that the remainder be paid "if, as, and when" Sugarland received additional monies in the future from Hines. It also provided that petitioners would be entitled to 6% interest on any late payments made by Sugarland.

Defendant and the intervenor have docketed this appeal. . . .

## II

We consider, first, the arguments made by the United States National Bank of Galveston, Trustee. . . . [The Bank contends that] Sugarland did not benefit from the Phase II efforts of counsel and, therefore, should not be obliged to pay for them. . . .

The Phase II settlement did not result in the creation of a fund or transfer of a tangible benefit to Sugarland. The Bank concedes, tacitly at least, that the case was settled in the interest of "family harmony" by effecting a reorganization of the personnel of the boards or management of the various Kempner entities.

In his opinion, the Chancellor described in some detail the changes in management effected by the settlement agreement, and it is unnecessary to repeat them here. It is enough to say that they were numerous and relatively complex; they involved some eight or nine separate entities and a seemingly endless series of personnel changes and power balancing. As we see it, the result was accurately summarized in the Chancellor's opinion, thus:

"... As to the second phase application, I am satisfied that petitioners are entitled to be compensated on the non-pecuniary

---

**2.** For convenience, we will hereafter refer to the attorneys whose compensation is in issue as "petitioners." They include, of course, both the Delaware and Texas firms.

All parties tacitly concede that whatever fee arrangements plaintiffs made with Prappas are equally applicable to Delaware counsel.

results of their effort to bring harmony to the Kempner family although such benefit does not inure directly to the benefit of Sugarland Industries and its stockholders....

Petitioners will be allowed the amount of $500,000 for the time expended and effort exerted by them during the second phase of this case, which resulted in a settlement which promises to terminate the feud which has split the Kempner family in recent years, thus indirectly benefiting Sugarland Industries and its stockholders...."

It is undisputed that the settlement agreement was the culmination of long and intensive efforts by counsel over many years. Sugarland was not a direct beneficiary of the "family harmony" which, legally speaking at least, resulted from the settlement. But it was very much involved in both lawsuits and it was a party to the settlement of both of them. Indeed, the purpose of the settlement agreement was to "settle all claims" in both actions[5] and thus to put an end to the controversy and the issues in litigation. A hearing was held and the settlement was approved on the basis of Sugarland participation in it. Prior thereto, notice as to the agreement, the stipulation of settlement, the other pertinent documents and the date of hearing was sent to all Sugarland stockholders, including the Bank. The Bank elected not to appear nor to challenge the settlement. It arrived only after the *fait accompli* to challenge the right of the settling corporation to pay counsel fees.

In the stipulation of settlement, Sugarland reserved the right "to object to any application for allowance of fees and expenses of plaintiffs and their attorneys," but the stipulation also provides that "Sugarland has determined that this settlement is beneficial to it and in the best interests of Sugarland and its stockholders." Given that representation by Sugarland to the Court before the settlement was approved, Sugarland's reservations as to fees might well be construed as going to the amount of any allowance, not to whether it had, in principle, any duty to pay an allowance.

In any event, we are satisfied that the Chancellor properly invoked his power to order Sugarland to pay fees to petitioners for Phase II services. In saying this, we note that most of the stockholders of Sugarland are also (in the same proportion) stockholders in or beneficial owners of other Kempner enterprises, and that Sugarland was in liquidation. Compare *Mills v. Electric Auto–Lite Co.,* 396 U.S. 375, 90

---

**5.** The agreement provides in part, as follows:

"I. 1. The purpose of this agreement is to settle all claims remaining in the above litigation, and the agreement and actions contemplated in Section II hereof are the direct result of the assertion and prosecution of such claims, derivatively by plaintiffs for the benefit of defendant Sugarland Industries, Inc. ('Sugarland').

2. Section II of this agreement and the actions that it contemplates provide a substantial, real benefit to the body of stockholders of Sugarland, constituting a proper basis and appropriate, commensurate consideration for the settlement of the remaining claims of Sugarland, which is itself in the course of liquidation.

3. The parties will each support the settlement and will each promptly seek the required judicial approval for it."

S.Ct. 616, 24 L.Ed.2d 593 (1970); *Richman v. DeVal Aerodynamics, Inc.,* Del.Ch., 185 A.2d 884 (1962).

### III

We now consider Sugarland's argument that the fee awarded for Phase I is grossly excessive under any standard. The thrust of the argument is that petitioners had expended only $122,881 worth of time, at their regular hourly rates, and that the percentage approach adopted by the Chancellor was arbitrary under the circumstances.

The standard of review of an award of attorney fees in Chancery is well settled under Delaware case law: the test is abuse of discretion. *Chrysler Corporation v. Dann,* Del.Supr., 223 A.2d 384 (1966). . . .

As to the amount of the fee, Sugarland observes that there is no real dispute between the parties as to the "elements of the Delaware standard" governing fees. It argues that the "results achieved" by counsel plus the following factors stated by the Chancellor are pertinent:

> ". . . the amount of time and effort applied to a case by counsel for plaintiff, the relative complexities of the litigation, the skills applied to their resolution by counsel, as well as any contingency factor and the standing and ability of petitioning counsel are, of course, considered in the award of fees in an appropriate case. . . ."

Sugarland invites our attention to *Lindy I* [Lindy Bros. Buildings, Inc. v. American Radiator & Standard Sanitary Corp., 487 F.2d 161 (1973)], an opinion authored by Chief Judge Seitz, who served as Chancellor of Delaware (and before then as Vice Chancellor) for some twenty years during which he ruled on many applications for counsel fees. Sugarland argues that Delaware should adopt the *Lindy I* guidelines as other jurisdictions have done.[8]

The evolution of *Lindy I* has not been limited to jurisdictions other than the Third Circuit. Indeed, the case has its own progeny in *Lindy II,* an *en banc* ruling by the Third Circuit [540 F.2d 102 (1976)]; see also *Baughman v. Wilson Freight Forwarding Co.,* 3 Cir., 583 F.2d 1208 (1978).

As we understand Sugarland's contention, *Lindy I's* principal significance for Phase I purposes is its emphasis on the "time factor" and because petitioners' entire fee was not "at risk."

Under *Lindy I,* the Court's analysis must begin with a calculation of the number of hours to be credited to the attorney seeking compensation. The total hours multiplied by the approved hourly rate is the "lodestar" in the Third Circuit's formulation. It has, indeed, been said that the time approach is virtually the sole consideration in making a fee ruling under *Lindy I.* Be that as it may, we conclude that

---

**8.** See, for example, *City of Detroit v. Grinnell Corporation,* 2 Cir., 495 F.2d 448 (1974); *Grunin v. International House of Pancakes,* 8 Cir., 513 F.2d 114 (1975), *cert. denied* 423 U.S. 864, 96 S.Ct. 124, 46 L.Ed.2d 93 (1975); *National Treasury Employees Union v. Nixon,* D.C.Cir., 521 F.2d 317 (1975).

our Chancery Judges should not be obliged to make the kind of elaborate analyses called for by the several opinions in *Lindy I* and *Lindy II.* To put it another way, while *Lindy's* careful craftsmanship has much to commend it, we are not persuaded that our case law governing fee applications is an inadequate criterion for a fair judgment in this case, nor that new guidelines are needed for the Court of Chancery.

It is undisputed that the White and Hill offer was $23,800,000, so, in one sense, petitioners are entitled to "some" credit for any amount received by Sugarland in excess of that sum.

The Chancellor determined that petitioners are entitled to a fair percentage of the benefit inuring to Sugarland and its stockholders from the sale of both Tracts to the Hines group; he computed the monetary benefit to Sugarland, as a result of petitioners' efforts, to be about $21,812,000. That figure gives petitioners full credit for all of the additional cash received or to be received, including principal and interest, from the sale of both tracts. The Chancellor held that petitioners are entitled to 20% of the fund thus created through their efforts, but subject to a $3,000,000 cap. Petitioners say that with that limitation, the award computes to about 14% of the benefit conferred.

We agree with substantially all of the Chancellor's findings and most of his conclusions, but we are unable to agree with him on one significant element in his formulations: in measuring benefit, he credited petitioners with all amounts received or to be received by Sugarland in excess of the White and Hill offer of $23,800,000. In our view of the case, petitioners' services and the nature of the benefits separate into two distinct parts and the R–S–C offer is at the dividing line between them.

It is crystal clear from the record that the services of petitioners benefited Sugarland to the extent of the difference between the White and Hill offer of $23,800,000 and the $27,000,000 which was submitted by R–S–C. But how one should view the amount received by Sugarland in excess of the $27,000,000 is not so clear. Petitioners had sought the best price obtainable and but for their initiative (and success) at the injunctive stage, Sugarland might not have received anything over the White and Hill offer. Thus, there is, as we have noted, "some" cause and effect between what petitioners did and the ultimate price received. But petitioners are attorneys seeking compensation for services rendered in litigation. They are not brokers or real estate agents seeking a commission or a percentage of sale price for having produced a buyer. And how much anyone would pay, at least in excess of the $27,000,000 offered by R–S–C, was a circumstance neither caused nor influenced by petitioners. The highest offer eventually made has in it something in the nature of [a] "windfall".... [P]etitioners here cannot take full credit for the price which Hines was willing to pay for both tracts.

There is also another factor which relates to the amount of compensation.... [The Prappas firm's contract] did assure *some* compensation for services, at least through the restraining order phrase, and thus petitioners were not providing services entirely on a contingent basis.

Sugarland has taken the position that if the Court reduces the fee award, we should, in the interest of justice and judicial economy, determine the appropriate fee. We conclude that it is appropriate for us to do so in this case.

In making the award, the Chancellor used a 20%–of–benefit factor and that seems reasonable to us when applied to the difference between the respective offers. But for the reasons we have discussed, it is unreasonable when applied to the amounts paid by the buyer in excess of the $27,000,000. We have held that petitioners are entitled to some credit for the benefit received in excess of that sum and, in view of the circumstances, any percentage is arguably fair or not, depending on one's point of view. In our judgment, based on the various factors we have noted, compensation at the rate of 5% of the benefit achieved is fair and should be applied to the additional benefits Sugarland received from the sale of both the North and South Tracts. Given the fee which that percentage generates (about $573,609 in all), we conclude that it is reasonable (and perhaps generous) compensation for the significant skills and expertise which petitioners demonstrated in identifying an inadequate price for the Tracts, in stimulating the competitive offer from R–S–C, in quickly initiating the litigation, in successfully carrying it to a conclusion against highly competent counsel and thus opening the door for entry by the Hines Interests with their offers.

The total amount to be allowed to petitioners as compensation for Phase I services (on an "if, as and when" received basis) is computed as follows:

| South Tract | |
|---|---|
| R–S–C Offer | $27,000,000 |
| White and Hill Offer | 23,800,000 |
| | $ 3,200,000 |
| | |
| Hines Purchase Price | $37,229,069 |
| R–S–C Offer | 27,000,000 |
| | $10,229,069 |
| | |
| North Tract | |
| Additional Benefit (Cash) | $ 1,243,139 |
| | |
| Computation of the Fee | |
| 20% × $ 3,200,000 | $   640,000 |
| 5% × 10,229,069 | 511,453 |
| 5% × 1,243,139 | 62,156 |
| Total | $ 1,213,609 |

It is difficult to test this allowance on an hourly rate basis because that was not determined by the Chancellor and, indeed, was not crucial to the awards he made. And the allocation of hours is a matter of dispute in this Court. For present purposes, we note only that

Sugarland agreed that the total time given to both phases of the litigation by petitioners and their staffs totals 15,110.8 hours. Petitioners say that it amounts to more than that, including about 2,800[10] hours in 1973 for the Phase I representation. In our view of the appeal, we need not resolve the time controversy.

### IV

Turning now to Phase II, Sugarland also argues that the $500,000 allowed by the Chancellor is grossly excessive, under any standard.

It is apparent that the Chancellor based the award for this phase largely on a "time and effort" basis. Specifically, he said:

> "As to the second phase application, I am satisfied that petitioners are entitled to be compensated on the nonpecuniary results of their efforts to bring harmony to the Kempner family although such benefit does not inure directly to the benefit of Sugarland Industries and its stockholders.

> \* \* \*

> Petitioners will be allowed the amount of $500,000 for the time expended and effort exerted by them during the second phase of this case...."

Given the extraordinary difficulties involved in this phase and the central purpose accomplished (family peace by litigation settlement), we conclude that the Chancellor did not abuse his discretion in making the award. Tested on an hourly rate basis, the $500,000 computes to $50 per hour, if only 10,000 of the agreed 15,110.8 hours were assigned to this phase. And that is a modest rate....

Affirmed in part and reversed in part with directions to enter judgment in accordance herewith.

[A motion by the petitioners for reargument was denied. 420 A.2d 142, 146.]

----

### ALI, PRINCIPLES OF CORPORATE GOVERNANCE § 7.17

[See Statutory Supplement]

----

### BACKGROUND NOTE ON THE AWARD OF COUNSEL FEES TO SUCCESSFUL DERIVATIVE–ACTION PLAINTIFFS

1. *Rationale.* The derivative action constitutes a major legal bulwark against managerial self-dealing. As a practical matter this

----

**10.** All of Phase I was completed in 1973. Accepting petitioners' representations that they gave 2,800 hours to that Phase, then the allowance made herein computes to about $433 per hour.

means that the rules governing plaintiffs' legal fees are critical to the operation of the corporate system: Because very few shareholders would pay an attorney's fee out of their own pockets to finance a suit that is brought on the corporation's behalf and normally holds only a slight and indirect benefit for the plaintiff, very few derivative actions would be brought if the law did not allow the plaintiff's attorney to be compensated by a contingent fee payable out of the corporate recovery.

As a conceptual matter, the award of counsel fees to successful plaintiffs in derivative actions has been justified by several overlapping rationales, none of which is unique to derivative actions. The most important of these is the "common fund" theory, under which a plaintiff who has successfully established a fund under the control of the court, from which many besides himself will benefit, may recover his counsel fees out of that fund. As stated in the seminal case of Trustees v. Greenough, 105 U.S. (15 Otto) 527, 532, 26 L.Ed. 1157 (1881), to deny an allowance for fees in such circumstances "would not only be unjust to [plaintiff], but ... would give to the other parties entitled to participate in the benefits of the fund an unfair advantage." This theory was later elaborated, under the heading of the "substantial benefit" or "common benefit" theory, to cover cases where the plaintiff had not brought a fund into the court's control but had established a right to a fund from which others would benefit. See Sprague v. Ticonic Nat. Bank, 307 U.S. 161, 59 S.Ct. 777, 83 L.Ed. 1184 (1939). Eventually, the common-benefit theory was extended to cover cases involving the establishment of nonpecuniary benefits.

Another basic rationale for the award of attorneys' fees to successful plaintiffs in derivative actions is the "private attorney-general" doctrine—that plaintiff's counsel fees should be awarded in appropriate cases to encourage the initiation of private actions that vindicate important legal policies. See Newman v. Piggie Park Enterprises, Inc., 390 U.S. 400, 402, 88 S.Ct. 964, 966, 19 L.Ed.2d 1263 (1968).

In the corporate area, this doctrine is important chiefly as a reinforcement to the common-fund or common-benefit theory, particularly where the benefit is not pecuniary. For example, in Mills v. Electric Auto–Lite Co., 396 U.S. 375, 90 S.Ct. 616, 24 L.Ed.2d 593 (1970), plaintiffs, who were former Auto–Lite shareholders, alleged that defendants had violated the Proxy Rules in connection with a merger of Auto–Lite into Mergenthaler. The Court held that plaintiffs were entitled to summary judgment on the merits. It then went on to award interim counsel fees, although it recognized that if on remand the merger were found to be fair, there might be no feasible way to remedy the violation, and therefore no economically measurable benefit to either Auto–Lite or its shareholders. The opinion began by attempting to bring the case within the common benefit rule: "In many suits under § 14(a) ... it may be impossible to assign monetary value to the benefit. Nevertheless, the stress placed by Congress on the importance of fair and informed corporate suffrage leads to the conclusion that, in vindicating the statutory policy, petitioners have rendered a substantial service to the corporation and its shareholders." However, the Court then seemed to shift rationales by stressing that the action conferred a benefit on a subsector of the public, that is, shareholders as a class.

In Alyeska Pipeline Service Co. v. Wilderness Society, 421 U.S. 240, 95 S.Ct. 1612, 44 L.Ed.2d 141 (1975), the Supreme Court held that in the absence of statutory authorization, attorney's fees may not be awarded on the private-attorney-general theory in suits brought under federal statutes. While the opinion left the common-fund theory (and its derivative, the common-benefit theory) undisturbed, and cited *Sprague* and *Mills* with approval, it is open to question whether the Court would again go as far as it did in *Mills* in determining what constitutes a benefit for these purposes.

2.   *Criteria.* In Goodrich v. E.F. Hutton Group, 681 A.2d 1039 (Del.1996), the court summarized current federal law as follows: "In the 1970s, courts began to use the 'lodestar' approach to calculate fee awards in common fund cases. *Lindy Bros. Builders, Inc. of Phila. v. American Radiator & Standard Sanitary Corp.*, 487 F.2d 161, 167–68 (3d Cir.1973). *See* Report of the Third Circuit Task Force, *Court Awarded Attorney Fees*, 108 F.R.D. 237, 242 (1985). That method requires a court to calculate the product of an attorney's reasonable hours expended on the litigation and reasonable hourly rate to arrive at the 'lodestar.' *Swedish Hosp. Corp. v. Shalala*, 1 F.3d at 1266. That lodestar calculation can then be adjusted, through application of a 'multiplier' or fee enhancer, to account for additional factors, *e.g.,* the contingent nature of the case and the quality of an attorney's work. *Lindy Bros. Builders, Inc. of Phila. v. American Radiator & Standard Sanitary Corp.*, 540 F.2d 102, 112 (3d Cir.1976); *Swedish Hosp. Corp. v. Shalala*, 1 F.3d at 1266. During the 1970s, the 'lodestar/multiplier' method of awarding fees was frequently invoked in common fund cases, instead of determining a reasonable percentage of recovery from the fund, based upon a multifactor analysis. *Johnson v. Georgia Highway Express, Inc.*, 488 F.2d 714, 716–19 (5th Cir.1974) ('*Johnson*' factors); *Lindy Bros. Builders, Inc. v. American Radiator & Standard Sanitary Corp.*, 487 F.2d at 164–69 ('*Lindy*' factors)....

"[However, in 1985 a report was issued] by a Task Force the Third Circuit had appointed to evaluate the practical effectiveness of the lodestar method in making attorney fee awards. *See* Report of the Third Circuit Task Force, *Court Awarded Attorney Fees*, 108 F.R.D. 237 (1985). The Task Force recommended continued use of the lodestar technique in statutory fee-shifting cases. *Id. See also City of Burlington v. Dague*, 505 U.S. at 562, 112 S.Ct. at 2641 (acknowledging, in the statutory fee-shifting context, 'a strong presumption that the lodestar represents the reasonable fee'). The Task Force concluded, however, that all attorney fee awards in common fund cases should be structured as a percentage of the fund. Report of the Third Circuit Task Force, *Court Awarded Attorney Fees*, 108 F.R.D. at 255.

"At the present time, the majority of federal courts use a reasonable percentage of the fund method when making attorney fee awards in common fund cases. *See Swedish Hosp. Corp. v. Shalala,* 1 F.3d at 1266 (chronicling history of the methodologies). *See also* FEDERAL JUDICIAL CENTER, AWARDING ATTORNEYS' FEES AND MANAGING FEE LITIGATION 63–64 (1994) (canvassing case law.) The Third Circuit has recently held that the percentage of the fund is generally the preferable method for awarding fees in common fund cases, but noted that a lodestar analysis might be used to cross check the propriety of the award (a 'hybrid' approach). *See In re General Motors Corp. Pick–Up Truck Fuel Tank Products Liability Litigation,* 55 F.3d at 821. Ultimately, however, the Third Circuit permits the trial court to exercise its discretion in choosing *either* the percentage method *or* the lodestar method, *or* some combination or hybrid, as the circumstances warrant, in making common fund fee awards. *Id."*

3. *Awards.* In a widely cited decision, In re Activision Securities Litigation, 723 F.Supp. 1373 (N.D.Cal.1989), the court determined, on the basis of a review of recent reported cases, that in nearly all common fund cases the attorney's fee award ranges around 30% of the fund, even if the fee is purportedly calculated under the lodestar or related methods. The court observed that "[m]ost of these cases achieve this result after lengthy motion practice, volumes of discovery, and hence, the accumulation of extensive attorney time on behalf of all parties." Id. at 1377. Accordingly, the court concluded that the better practice in common fund cases is to set a percentage fee, and that the percentage should be 30%, absent extraordinary circumstances. Other courts have mentioned other benchmark percentages. For example, in Paul, Johnson, Alston & Hunt v. Graulty, 886 F.2d 268 (9th Cir.1989), the court noted with approval a benchmark fee of 25%. In In re Warner Communications Securities Litigation, 618 F.Supp. 735, 750 (S.D.N.Y.1985), aff'd 798 F.2d 35 (2d Cir.1986), the court concluded that fee awards had averaged 20%–30% in the Second Circuit.

4. *Absence of a judgment.* While *success* is a prerequisite to an award of counsel fees, a *judgment* is not. Counsel fees may be awarded even if a case is settled or the defendants or the corporation takes a unilateral act that renders the plaintiff's demand or complaint moot. See, e.g., Bird v. Lida, Inc., 681 A.2d 399 (Allen, Ch.1996). In the latter kind of case, the plaintiff must show that his course of action was a significant cause of the act. Normally, however, the plaintiff is allowed to prove causation indirectly, by showing that his claim or demand was meritorious and that corrective action followed. It has been said that "[a] claim is meritorious within the meaning of the rule if it can withstand a motion to dismiss on the pleadings [and] if, at the same time, the plaintiff possesses knowledge of provable facts which hold out some reasonable likelihood of ultimate success. It is not necessary that factually there be absolute assurance of ultimate success, but only that there be some reasonable hope." Chrysler Corp. v. Dann, 43 Del.Ch. 252, 256–57, 223 A.2d 384, 387 (1966). Although a few cases suggest that meritoriousness is the only relevant issue in such cases, the rule seems to be that the plaintiff has the burden of showing meritoriousness, and once that showing is made the burden

shifts to defendants to show that their actions did not result from plaintiff's course of action. See, e.g., Baron v. Allied Artists Pictures Corp., 395 A.2d 375 (Del.Ch.1978).

5. *Nonmonetary benefits.* The rule that attorneys' fees can be awarded to a plaintiff on the basis of a common but nonmonetary benefit, such as the corporation's agreement to change its governance structure, as opposed to the creation of a common fund, has two important implications in derivative actions.

First, it is often very difficult to attribute any realistic value to nonmonetary benefits. As a result, in such cases attorney's fees usually must be, and are, measured under the lodestar method, even by courts that employ the percentage-of-the-benefit test in common-fund cases.

Second, the rule that a plaintiff's attorney is entitled to a fee based for producing a nonmonetary benefit opens the door to the possibility of collusive settlements in which the real defendants in a derivative action (the directors or officers) pay little or nothing; the corporation agrees to a change that is largely cosmetic; plaintiff's attorney and the corporation join hands to inflate the importance of the change; and plaintiff's attorney is then paid a fee that is supposed to be justified by that importance, but is really a bribe to drop the case. The real defendants are happy, because they get a release although they have paid little or nothing. Plaintiff's counsel is happy, because she gets a very nice fee. The shareholders aren't unhappy, because they don't realize what happened. If they did realize what happened, they would be very unhappy.

This doesn't mean that every settlement involving only a nonmonetary benefit is collusive. Nevertheless, the possibility that settlements involving only nonmonetary benefits may be collusive suggests that the courts should be especially cautious in reviewing such settlements.

---

## Kaplan v. Rand

United States Court of Appeals, Second Circuit, 1999.
192 F.3d 60.

■ Before: KEARSE, MINER and McLAUGHLIN, CIRCUIT JUDGES,

■ MINER, CIRCUIT JUDGE:

Appellant–Objector William C. Rand, Esq. appeals from a judgment entered in the United States District Court for the Southern District of New York (Brieant, J.) awarding to counsel for plaintiffs-appellees Nathan Kaplan, Edith Citron and Martin H. Philip $1 million for legal fees and disbursements in connection with services rendered in a stockholders' derivative action. Kaplan, Citron and Philip, stockholders of Texaco, Inc., brought this action on behalf of Texaco against the various officers, directors and employees of the corporation named as defendants in the caption. In their consolidated amended complaint, they sought various forms of relief against the defendants for breach of fiduciary duties and contractual obligations. Over stockholder objections, the district court ultimately approved a proposed Stipulation of Settlement that required Texaco to make certain reports available to stockholders and to insert a non-discrimination statement in its vendor contracts. The settlement afforded the plaintiff stockholders no relief of any kind against the defendant officers and employees.

The district court deemed the settlement fair and reasonable, found that counsel for the plaintiffs had conferred a benefit upon the corporation, and referred to a Special Master for hearing and report the application of plaintiffs' counsel for fees and disbursements for services rendered in the prosecution and settlement of the derivative action. The report of the Special Master recommended an award of $1 million, computed by applying a multiplier to the lodestar figure and adding expenses. Several stockholders, including Rand, who is an attorney, filed objections to that report. However, the district court adopted the report in toto and entered judgment accordingly. Rand, although not a party, appeals only the award of counsel fees. For the reasons that follow, we reject the contention of counsel for the stockholders that we lack jurisdiction to consider this appeal on account of Rand's non-party status and reverse the judgment of the district court with directions for the entry of judgment denying any award to counsel.

## BACKGROUND

The foundation for the action giving rise to this appeal was laid in an earlier action in the district court entitled Roberts v. Texaco, Inc. The individual plaintiffs in the earlier case sued on behalf of themselves and a putative plaintiff class, alleging in their complaint that Texaco had engaged in a pattern and practice of discrimination against them in violation of the Civil Rights Act of 1871, 42 U.S.C. § 1981, and the New York Human Rights Law, N.Y. Exec. Law § 296. Thereafter, a first amended complaint was filed to add claims on behalf of other individual plaintiffs. It included allegations that all of the plaintiffs, as well as the putative class, were disadvantaged by Texaco's violations of Title VII of the Civil Rights Law of 1964, 42 U.S.C. §§ 2000e et seq. The amended complaint accused Texaco of violating the rights of its African–American salaried employees by engaging in prohibited conduct that had a disparate impact upon them. According to the amended complaint, this conduct consisted of discrimination in compensation, promotion and other terms and conditions of employment, including training and job assignments.

Following various proceedings in the course of the litigation, see Roberts v. Texaco, Inc., 979 F.Supp. 185, 189–191 (S.D.N.Y.1997), the parties on November 15, 1996 entered into an Agreement in Principle for settlement of the action. Concluding, after a fairness hearing, that the settlement was beneficial to the class, the district court approved the agreement by order dated March 21, 1997.

The approved settlement had several components. First, Texaco created a $115 million settlement fund to pay (i) monetary claims arising out the settlement, (ii) costs, including reasonable attorneys' fees for plaintiffs' counsel, experts, and consultants, (iii) costs associated with administration of the settlement, (iv) other obligations that Texaco might have in connection with the settlement, and (v) the expenses of any other court ordered remediation. The settlement provided that Texaco would not object to the payment of reasonable attorneys' fees and expenses to be approved by the district court. Second, Texaco agreed to increase the annual base salary of each plaintiff-employee by 11.34%. Third, Texaco formed and funded the Task Force on Equality and Fairness (the "Task Force") which, during its five-year term, was charged with "initiating and determining the effectiveness of improvements and additions to Texaco's human resources programs and helping to monitor the progress made in such programs toward creating opportunity for African-Americans, diversity in the Texaco workforce and equal opportunity for all Texaco employees." Id. at 192.

The district court would oversee the Task Force by monitoring biannual reports by the Task Force to Texaco's Chairman and its Board of Directors and an annual report by the Task Force to the court. These reports were to detail the "impact of the settlement." Id. Any objections by Texaco to the determinations of the Task Force would be resolved by the district court. Pursuant to the settlement, Texaco also agreed to fund reasonable compensation of the staff, consultants, statisticians and other experts of the Task Force.

The district court had referred for review the application of plaintiffs' counsel for legal fees and expenses and the application of the individual plaintiffs for incentive awards to a Special Master. By order dated September 11, 1997, the district court adopted the Report of the Special Master and authorized payment in accordance with the Report. Id. at 189.

On November 6, 1996, two years after the commencement of the Roberts action and less than two weeks before the execution of the Agreement in Principle approved by the district court, plaintiff-appellee Nathan Kaplan initiated the derivative action that was later consolidated with another derivative action brought by plaintiffs-appellees Edith Citron and Martin H. Philip. It is the award of counsel fees following the settlement of that consolidated action that we examine here. The consolidated amended complaint invoked the diversity jurisdiction of the district court and included the following allegations:

> Plaintiffs bring this action derivatively in the right of and for the benefit of Texaco to redress injuries suffered and to be suffered by the Company as a direct result of the violations of law and breaches of fiduciary duty, corporate mismanagement, waste of corporate assets, and abuse of control by the Individual Defendants.

. . . .

This action is brought to remedy violations of applicable state common law, fiduciary duty and contractual obligations.

In the consolidated complaint, the individual defendants were charged with responsibility for the illegal discriminatory employment practices of Texaco and therefore with the financial losses and other detriments sustained by the corporation as a result of those practices. The Roberts settlement was reviewed in some detail in the amended complaint, and it was alleged that the settlement in that case resulted in a cost to Texaco of some $176.1 million dollars, all brought about as the result of the wrongful acts of the officers, directors and employees named as defendants. The complaint listed additional losses in the following allegation:

Despite the settlement in the Roberts Action, Defendants' wrongdoing has caused and will cause Texaco to be subjected to substantial negative and detrimental publicity; the alienation of past, present and potential employees, customers and other persons and entities with whom it does business; the potential loss of substantial revenues and earnings; the loss of hundreds of millions of dollars in market capitalization; the payment of a large settlement award; the possible imposition of criminal and civil fines, penalties and court sanctions; the incurrence of millions of dollars of legal fees and expenses; and other costs and damages.

The relief sought against the defendants was comprehensive:

WHEREFORE, plaintiffs request judgment as follows:

A. declaring that the directors and officers and employees named as Individual Defendants herein have committed breaches of trust and have breached their fiduciary duties and contractual obligations as alleged herein;

B. against the Individual Defendants, jointly and severally, requiring them to pay to Texaco the amounts by which it has been damaged or will be damaged by reason of the conduct complained of herein;

C. requiring the Individual Defendants to remit to the Company all of their salaries and other compensation received for the periods when they breached their duties;

D. ordering that the Individual Defendants and those under their supervision and control refrain from any further such unlawful activities as are alleged herein and implement corrective measures, including a system of internal controls and procedures sufficient to prevent the repetition of the acts complained of herein, which will rectify all such wrongs as have been committed and prevent their recurrence;

E. awarding plaintiffs reasonable attorneys' fees, expert fees and other reasonable costs and expenses; and

F. granting such other and further relief as this Court may deem just and proper.

Following the oral argument of motions to dismiss the complaint on various grounds, the attorneys for the parties commenced settlement discussions. An agreement in principle for settlement was reached on September 26, 1997, and the district court thereafter denied the pending motions to dismiss without prejudice and with leave to renew if the settlement was not consummated. A proposed Stipulation of Settlement was filed on December 31, 1997, and the parties agreed to submit it for court review as soon as practicable. Other than six pages relating to releases of all concerned in the litigation from every known and unknown claim (except claims by and against Texaco with respect to three individual defendants who were not past or present directors of the corporation), the Stipulation contains only the two following substantive provisions:

a.   A statement will be included in Texaco's Annual Report to shareholders for the year 1997 stating that shareholders may receive a copy of the public portion of the Equality and Fairness Task Force's Annual Report to the Court, prepared pursuant to the Settlement of the Roberts Action, by writing to, sending an e-mail to, or calling a toll-free number at, Texaco and requesting a copy. This obligation will continue for so long as the Task Force remains in existence. Any portion of the Task Force's report that is not made public by the Task Force or that is sealed by the Court need not be provided to shareholders.

b.   The following "Statement of Equality and Tolerance Objectives" will be made a part of all new contracts entered into by Texaco with outside vendors:

Texaco, Inc. is affirmatively committed to the fullest extent to an environment of inclusion; to eradicate all forms of prejudice within the company; to promote and foster complete equality of job opportunities within the company to all applicants and employees regardless of race, gender, religion, age, national origin and disability; and to ensure tolerance, respect and dignity for all people.

Texaco will take reasonable steps to enforce the principles set forth in this Statement. The affirmative commitment in this Paragraph shall not apply to existing contracts, and shall not apply in any jurisdiction if and to the extent that it is or becomes inconsistent with any law of that jurisdiction. Any failure by Texaco to act in accordance with this obligation will not give rise to any cause of action or third party beneficiary right in favor of any person or entity other than Texaco.

According to the Stipulation, counsel for plaintiffs would seek fees and expenses not to exceed $1.4 million in the event of approval of the Settlement by the district court, and "[d]efendants will not oppose this application."

The district court approved the settlement by Memorandum and Order dated April 15, 1998. The approval followed a settlement hearing held pursuant to notice duly given and was issued over stockholder objections to the settlement as well as to the award of counsel fees. Finding that the settlement terms were "essentially institutional," the court concluded "that the non-pecuniary so-called therapeutic benefits to the corporation" formed a sufficient basis for settlement of the derivative claims. Accordingly, the settlement was designated "fair and reasonable." The court observed that "it is obvious that the settlement, which brings no monetary benefit to the company, is far less than was envisioned." Nevertheless, the court recognized that there were certain obstacles to plaintiffs' original claims and ultimately determined the plaintiffs "to be prevailing parties and to have conferred a benefit on the corporation."

As to the issue of attorneys' fees, the court entered an Order on April 23, 1998 appointing a Special Master. According to the docket entry of April 23, 1998, the Special Master was to "inquir[e] into the application for legal fees pending in the above entitled litigation, to take the arguments and proofs and otherwise consider the matter and report as to a reasonable fee to be awarded under the totality of the circumstances found to be present in the case." The Special Master sent a notice of hearing to all counsel and objectors and received oral and written submissions both supporting and opposing a fee award. The Special Master filed his Report on July 6, 1998.

In his Report, the Special Master noted that the law firms representing plaintiffs were seeking a total of approximately $1.4 million dollars. See In re Texaco, Inc. Shareholder Litig., 20 F.Supp.2d 577, 587 (S.D.N.Y.1998) (appending report of Special Master). This sum was computed by applying a multiplier of 2.15 to the total hourly charges and adding expenses of approximately $34,000. In support of this application, counsel for plaintiffs cited the litigation risks, the contingent nature of the fees, the quality of the opposition and the benefit achieved. The objectors variously contended that the settlement provided no more than a minimal additional benefit to the benefits achieved in the Roberts action, that the total fees claimed were excessive, and that the hours billed were exaggerated. See id. at 588. Counsel for Texaco, in accordance with the Settlement Agreement, raised no opposition to the fee requested. The Special Master observed that Texaco's counsel did provide a post-hearing submission responding to the objectors' contention that, despite the fact that any attorneys' fees awarded would be paid by Texaco's directors' and officers' liability insurer, the corporation ultimately would pay in the form of increased future insurance premiums. The response was that the insurance policy subsequently had been renewed without an increase in premiums. Id.

Following a discussion of the need to establish a substantial benefit to the corporation as a condition precedent to the award of attorneys' fees in a stockholders' derivative action, and of the nature of the benefit here as simply therapeutic, the Special Master turned to the rules governing the computation of fees. After reviewing the lodestar method of computation (hours reasonably expended times reasonable hourly rate), the Special Master determined that the hours and rates put forward by plaintiffs' counsel were reasonable in all respects, "considering the issues and challenges presented and the vigor with which skilled and highly experienced plaintiffs' counsel proceeded and equally skilled and experienced defense counsel pressed an aggressive defense strategy." Id. at 591.

In connection with the application of counsel to apply a 2.15 multiplier to the lodestar calculation, the Special Master noted that the use of a multiplier has been subject to stringent requirements in cases where no common fund has been created. With respect to counsel's argument in favor of the enhancement on the basis of litigation risks, contingent nature of the fee, quality of opposition and benefit achieved, the Special Master recognized the countervailing arguments of the objectors that there was no monetary benefit to the corporation and that both the lodestar and the enhancement should be reduced or disallowed altogether for lack of success. Observing that a risk of success multiplier is "problematic" in this circuit, and that there is no "decision precisely on point in the context of an equitable fund/substantial benefit case," the Special Master nevertheless found a multiplier justified by the "quantum of benefit" provided by the settlement. Id. at 593–94. The Special Master concluded that the benefit was "substantial for the stockholders, but not enough to justify the fee enhancement requested." Id. at 595. In recommending an aggregate fee of $1 million, representing total fees and expenses to be allowed, the Special Master granted what he described as "a multiplier on the order of 1.5 (as contrasted with a requested total award of $1.4 million based on a multiplier of 2.15)." Id. at 596.

By Memorandum and Order filed on September 15, 1998, the district court approved the Report of the Special Master in all respects, rejecting various objections to the Report filed by certain shareholders as well as by plaintiffs' counsel. With respect to one shareholder's objection, the district court rejected the contention that the wide availability of the Annual Report of the Task Force on the Internet detracted from the advantage gained by making that Report available on request by telephone or correspondence. See id. at 579. In further justification of the fee, the court rejected the contention that nothing was gained by the vendor non-discrimination contract clause by noting that counsel for Texaco opined that failure to police the clause could give rise to (another) stockholders' derivative action. See id. at 579–80.

The district court next addressed objections by plaintiffs' counsel to the reduction of their requested fee. The district court did not accept the contention that the settlement came at no cost to Texaco because there was no increase in the directors' and officers' insurance premiums. See id. at 581. The court observed (a) that counsel improperly relied upon "the unfounded assumption that Texaco's insurance premiums would not have been reduced absent this lawsuit" and (b) that insurance payments generate "an economic and social cost, imposed upon and spread across the entire economy." Id. In any event, the district court found that plaintiffs "prevailed" by securing wide access to the Task Force Report and by causing the placing and policing of the anti-discrimination clause in Texaco's vendor contracts. Id. Under the circumstances, the district court deemed the lodestar fee and its enhancement, as recommended by the Special Master, "entirely reasonable." Id.

## DISCUSSION ...

A stockholders' derivative action has been described as "an action brought by one or more stockholders of a corporation to enforce a corporate right or remedy a wrong to the corporation in cases where the corporation, because it is controlled by the wrongdoers or for other reasons, fails and refuses to take appropriate action for its own protection." 19 Am.Jur.2d Corporations § 2250, at 151 (1986) (footnotes omitted). It has long been the rule that the plaintiffs in such an action may recover attorneys' fees out of any common fund created as the result of their successful efforts on behalf of the corporation. See Mills v. Electric Auto–Lite Co., 396 U.S. 375, 392, 90 S.Ct. 616, 24 L.Ed.2d 593 (1970). It is by now also well established that an award of counsel fees [in a nonmonetary-benefit case] is only justified where the derivative action results in a substantial non-monetary benefit to a corporation. See id. at 395, 90 S.Ct. 616. The Mills Court quoted with approval a decision of the Supreme Court of Minnesota defining "substantial benefit" as "something more than technical in its consequence and ... one that accomplishes a result which corrects or prevents an abuse which would be prejudicial to the rights and interests of the corporation or affect the enjoyment or protection of an essential right to the stockholder's interest." Id. at 396, 90 S.Ct. 616 (quoting Bosch v. Meeker Coop. Light & Power Ass'n., 257 Minn. 362, 366–67, 101 N.W.2d 423 (1960)).

In *Mills*, minority stockholders bringing the derivative action successfully established their claim that a proxy statement pertaining to an upcoming merger was materially misleading and violative of § 14(a) of the Securities Exchange Act of 1934 and Rule 14a–9 adopted thereunder. See 396 U.S. at 386, 90 S.Ct. 616. Despite the fact that no monetary fund was created (or sought to be created), the Court held that the plaintiffs had "rendered a substantial service to the corporation and its shareholders," id. at 396, 90 S.Ct. 616, and that the award of attorneys' fees to the successful plaintiffs therefore would be proper. The Court concluded that, "regardless of the relief granted, private stockholders' actions of this sort 'involve corporate therapeutics,' and furnish a benefit to all shareholders by providing an important means of enforcement of the proxy statute." Id. (footnote omitted)....

Along similar lines, we were confronted in Kopet v. Esquire Realty Co., 523 F.2d 1005 (2d Cir.1975), with the issue of attorneys' fees in a class action involving claims of violations of the Securities Act of 1933 for failure to file a registration statement relating to the refinancing of property by a limited partnership. Citing *Mills*, we determined "that appellant rendered a service to the partnership by vindicating the statutory policy against unregistered offerings." Id. at 1008. In remanding for the award of counsel fees, we observed that the partnership had "received substantial benefits from appellant's efforts in the litigation before it, including the production of certified financial statements." Id. at 1009. In Kopet we also noted precedent cases holding that "federal courts may award counsel fees based on benefits resulting from litigation efforts even where adjudication on the merits is never reached, e.g., after a settlement." Id. at 1008. . . .

But the action that gives rise to this appeal is not grounded in the Securities Exchange Act or any other federal statute. It is a diversity action grounded in state law claims of breach of fiduciary duty, corporate waste and mismanagement and violation of contractual obligations. Accordingly, state law governs the issue of counsel fee availability. See Lewis v. S.L. & E., Inc., 629 F.2d 764, 773 n. 21 (2d Cir.1980). Our determination in the case before us therefore must be bottomed on New York law. Attorneys' fees may be awarded under New York law to an attorney for a successful derivative plaintiff out of a recovery obtained on behalf of the corporation from the defendants. See N.Y. Bus. Corp. Law § 626(e) (McKinney 1986). Attorneys' fees may also be paid from corporate funds under New York law where benefits to the corporation arising from the derivative action are therapeutic in nature. See Seinfeld v. Robinson, 246 A.D.2d 291, 676 N.Y.S.2d 579, 582 (1st Dep't 1998).

*Seinfeld* was a derivative action brought by certain shareholders of American Express Co. for redress of misconduct on the part of officers, directors and employees of the corporation. The action had its genesis in the purchase by American Express of the Geneva-based Trade Development Bank from Edmond J. Safra. See id. at 580. The corporation merged the Bank into its international banking arm, and Safra continued as its Chairman. After a brief period, Safra resigned on account of conflicts with James Robinson, the Chairman and CEO of American Express, and agreed not to start a new bank for four years. When the four-year period ended, American Express became concerned that Safra would return to the banking business and regain his former customers. An executive in the American Express public relations department was assigned to investigate Safra, with the object of finding evidence that could be used to prevent the issuance of a new Swiss banking license. To assist in this effort, the public relations executive hired one Greco, a private detective with a criminal past. See id.

After Safra was issued the Swiss license and opened a new bank in Geneva, scandalous articles about him appeared in the press. These articles charged various acts of misconduct, including money-laundering, drug trafficking, organized crime associations and the like. After a great deal of effort, Safra was able to identify Greco and the public relations executive as the people who placed the false stories. Rather than proceed with any claims relating to the wrongs perpetrated against him, Safra settled for a public apology by Robinson on behalf of American Express and an agreement by the corporation to donate $8 million to charities designated by Safra. See id. at 581.

Eight American Express shareholders joined in a derivative action seeking various forms of relief, including money damages and attorneys' fees, against the officers and employees of the corporation said to be responsible for the malignment of Safra. That action was settled by a stipulation requiring approval by the general counsel of American Express of any contract to hire outside investigators at a cost of more than $150,000 and a confirmation by any such investigator that he has read the corporate "Code of Conduct." The stipulation also provided that the corporation would not acquire more than fifty percent of any investment banking business for four years without the approval of a majority of its outside directors. The trial court found that no substantial benefit was achieved in the derivative action and denied attorneys' fees to the plaintiffs. See id. at 581.

In reversing, the state appellate court applied the "substantial benefit" standard, although it noted that certain federal decisions in the Southern District of New York apparently had applied more lenient standards. See id. at 583. The court adopted the rule in Mills and cited with approval the Kopet and Koppel holdings of this Court. Remanding for computation of counsel fees, the state appellate court determined that the benefits gained by the Seinfeld plaintiffs "are precisely the type of 'corporate therapeutics' the Supreme Court deemed a substantial benefit in Mills." Id. at 584. Characterizing the clandestine activities of American Express as a deceit upon the shareholders of the corporation, the Court stated that "in implementing procedures that will prevent the exact sequence of events from reoccurring, petitioners have furnished a benefit to all shareholders." Id.

The parties before us agree, as did the parties in *Seinfeld*, that the plaintiffs in a derivative action are entitled to counsel fees upon a settlement of the action only when the non-monetary, therapeutic benefits obtained are substantial in nature. Even under the most liberal definition of "substantial benefit," the settlement in the case before us does not meet the test. The action was commenced with a worthy goal—to require the officers, directors and employees responsible for Texaco's discriminatory policies to reimburse the corporation for the millions of dollars expended as a result of the necessary settlement of the Roberts litigation. This action was of course "piggy-backed" on the Roberts action, in which the settlement involved extensive provisions for the remedy of past discrimination and for the setting of a course for a non-discriminatory future as well as for substantial monetary relief. This is not a case like the earlier cases in this Circuit that were instituted to remedy securities violations and resulted in relief that accomplished their goals. Nor is this a case like *Seinfeld*, where the settlement devised a plan to prevent a sequence of misconduct from reoccurring. Indeed, the relief sought by the plaintiffs in this case never was achieved.

Far from providing a remedy for clearly identified past misconduct, the settlement in this case strives to provide therapeutic "benefits" that can only be characterized as illusory. As to the first "benefit," the inclusion of a statement in the 1997 Annual Report to Shareholders that the public portion of the annual report of the Fairness Task Force is available on request, there never was any claim that the report was not available to stockholders on request. The report is a public document, available to all persons from the court. Presumably, the report is also available (as are most public documents of this kind) on the Internet. Publishing a notice to the shareholders of the availability of the report therefore adds nothing of value to the Roberts settlement, pursuant to which the Task Force was created. The Task Force was established with a five-year duration, and the fact that the notice is to be published in only one Annual Report to shareholders is indicative of the cosmetic nature of this provision. See Mokhiber v. Cohn, 608 F.Supp. 616, 628 (S.D.N.Y.1985) ("We do not believe that equity should authorize compensating a stockholder or his attorney for bringing about . . . purely 'cosmetic' and ephemeral changes."), aff'd, 783 F.2d 26 (2d Cir.1986).

The second substantive provision of the settlement, the inclusion of a non-discrimination statement in all contracts entered into between Texaco and outside vendors, also fails to serve as a remedy for past misconduct. There never was any claim, either in Roberts or in the case at bar, that Texaco discriminated in its relations with its vendors. The law prohibits such discrimination in any event, see 42 U.S.C. § 1981, and there is no reason to believe that a contractual non-discrimination provision adds anything to the rights of vendors. Interpreting the insertion of the "Statement of Equity and Tolerance Objectives" in vendor contracts as a requirement that vendors not discriminate, there has been no showing, or even allegation, of discriminatory conduct on the part of any of Texaco's vendors either. The fact that counsel for Texaco assured the Special Master, in response to an inquiry from the Special Master, that the directors and officers could be subject to another derivative suit if they failed to police the vendors adds nothing but an additional and especially burdensome layer to existing remedies.[11] Those who are subject to discrimination by Texaco's vendors are perfectly capable of suing on their own behalf. The provision in question can only be characterized as "ephemeral." Mokhiber, 608 F.Supp. at 628.

In an effort to justify an award of fees, counsel for plaintiffs point to the great obstacles they faced in bringing the derivative action to a successful conclusion. These included the protections afforded the directors by the business judgment rule, the limited liability provisions of Texaco's corporate charter, and the failure of plaintiffs to make the demand for remedial action prior to suit required by Fed.R.Civ.P. 23.1. Rather than providing a reason to allow fees to counsel for their superficial accomplishments in this case, these arguments raise questions about counsel's compliance with Fed.R.Civ.P. 11. That rule specifies that counsel's signature on a pleading certifies that "the

---

**11.** This assurance of counsel was given despite the following limitation in the contractual non-discrimination provision: "Any failure by Texaco to act in accordance with this obligation will not give rise to any cause of action or third-party beneficiary right in favor of any person or entity other than Texaco."

claims ... and other legal contentions therein are warranted by existing law or by a nonfrivolous argument for the extension, modification, or reversal of existing law or the establishment of new law." Fed.R.Civ.P. 11(b)(2).

As far as can be ascertained, no argument has been made for the extension of current law or the establishment of new law with regard to stockholders' derivative actions. An argument therefore could be made, on the basis of the contentions now advanced by plaintiffs' counsel, that the extensive claims originally made in this case had no chance of success and, accordingly, were made for the improper purpose of early settlement and the allowance of substantial counsel fees. See Ralph K. Winter, Paying Lawyers, Empowering Prosecutors, and Protecting Managers: Raising the Cost of Capital in America, 42 Duke L.J. 945, 948–53 (1993) (noting that a large percentage of stockholders' derivative actions are brought solely to collect attorneys' fees).

It is sufficient for our purposes here to say that the settlement of this particular derivative action provided no substantial benefit to the corporation or its shareholders and that attorneys' fees are not justified under the circumstances. We therefore find it unnecessary to review the appellant's objection to the computation of the fees, including the use of a multiplier.

## CONCLUSION

We reverse the judgment of the district court and remand for the entry of judgment denying counsel fees.

## SECTION 9. SECURITY FOR EXPENSES

### N.Y. BUS. CORP. LAW § 627

[See Statutory Supplement]

### CAL. CORP. CODE § 800(c)–(f)

[See Statutory Supplement]

### SECURITIES ACT § 11(e), 27(c)

[See Statutory Supplement]

**SECURITIES EXCHANGE ACT § 21D(c)**

---

## Alcott v. M.E.V. Corp.

California Court of Appeal, Sixth District, 1987.
193 Cal.App.3d 797, 238 Cal.Rptr. 520.

■ BRAUER, J.—This stockholder derivative action collapsed after all defendants had prevailed in pretrial skirmishes: one defendant obtained dismissal for failure to serve summons in time, and the others secured either summary judgment or judgment upon demurrer sustained without leave to amend. Thereafter defendants filed cost bills containing demands for attorneys' fees. This appeal is taken from an order awarding defendants their attorneys' fees. ... Plaintiffs also challenge the amount of the fees awarded, an issue we do not reach in view of our conclusion that no attorneys' fees are recoverable here. . . .

The action was commenced in 1980 under authority of Corporations Code section 800. . . .

No security was ever sought or posted. The attorneys' fees clause in section 800, subdivision (d) is the only statutory basis for the trial court's ruling.

Section 800 is susceptible of two constructions: (1) Attorneys' fees are recoverable only out of the security, if posted; (2) Prevailing defendants are entitled to their attorneys' fees. . . .

In *Freeman v. Goldberg* (1961) 55 Cal.2d 622 [12 Cal.Rptr. 668, 361 P.2d 244], a derivative suit was dismissed after plaintiffs failed to post the security demanded. Thereafter the prevailing defendants filed a cost bill including attorneys' fees. [The Supreme Court unanimously held] that the statute "contains no provision for an award of attorney's fees where, as here, security is not furnished. . . ." (*Id.*, at p. 626.) The court was interpreting section 834, the predecessor to section 800, which was identical in all relevant respects to section 800 as it read in 1980. . . .

Judgment reversed. Costs on appeal to appellants.

■ AGLIANO, P.J., and CAPACCIOLI, J., concurred.

---

### BACKGROUND NOTE ON SECURITY–FOR–EXPENSES STATUTES

Security-for-expenses statutes must be considered against the background of the general American rule that the losing party in a lawsuit does not have to pay the winner's expenses, except for "taxable costs," such as clerk's, witness, docket, and transcript fees. Security-for-expenses statutes are normally not interpreted to impose *individual* liability on the plaintiff for expenses—that is, liability beyond the amount of his bond.

A shareholder who wants to bring a derivative action in a state that has a security-for-expenses statute is under heavy pressure to find some way to bring suit without posting security. Since the statutes are normally interpreted to be inapplicable to direct (as opposed to derivative) actions, one alternative is to frame the suit as a direct action. A second alternative is to bring the action under some provision of federal law, such as the Proxy Rules or Rule 10b–5. The security-for-expenses requirement may also be avoided in certain types of cases by petitioning for dissolution or the appointment of a receiver. See Leibert v. Clapp, 13 N.Y.2d 313, 247 N.Y.S.2d 102, 196 N.E.2d 540 (1963).

Even where these alternatives are infeasible, two judicial practices tend to soften the impact of the security-for-expenses statutes. The first practice is to stay the effectiveness of an order to post security, so that the plaintiff can find intervenors to help qualify under a statutory exemption based on the percentage or dollar value of complaining shares. See Baker v. MacFadden Publications, 300 N.Y. 325, 90 N.E.2d 876 (1950).

A second judicial practice, which builds on the first, is to order a corporation that moves for the posting of security to produce a shareholders' list, so that during the period of the stay the plaintiff can solicit other shareholders to join the action. A study based on interviews with knowledgeable plaintiffs' and defense attorneys in New York concluded that the courts have been extremely permissive in granting these motions. The study continues:

> [Thus if] the motion for security for expenses were to be made, it is likely that the plaintiff would request and obtain a 60–day stay and access to the corporate stocklist. By granting the plaintiff access to the list, defendants have hurt themselves in several ways. The motion involves additional expense in corporate time and effort in furnishing a stockholders' list to the plaintiff. Moreover, circularization by the plaintiff apprises stockholders and the press that a lawsuit involving management is pending. "Most if not all directors don't like to have their deeds or misdeeds advertised. They are sensitive to public opinion, particularly when a proxy fight is involved or imminent." Further, the plaintiffs' counsel now has a list of potential plaintiffs which may be used against the corporation in future litigation. Finally, there is a risk that a motion for security may cause the plaintiff to discontinue the original action and start another in a sister-state having no security-for-expenses statute. . . .

As a result, it is not uncommon for defendants in New York cases to refrain from moving for security. Note, Security for Expenses in Shareholders' Derivative Suits: 23 Years' Experience, 4 Colum.J.L. & Soc.Prob. 50, 62–65 (1968).

---

## SECTION 10. INDEMNIFICATION AND INSURANCE

---

## (a) INDEMNIFICATION

---

### DEL. GEN. CORP. LAW § 145

[See Statutory Supplement]

---

### REV. MODEL BUS. CORP. ACT §§ 8.50–8.59

[See Statutory Supplement]

---

### N.Y. BUS. CORP. LAW §§ 721–726

[See Statutory Supplement]

---

### CAL. CORP. CODE § 317

[See Statutory Supplement]

---

### ALI, PRINCIPLES OF CORPORATE GOVERNANCE § 7.20

[See Statutory Supplement]

---

## Waltuch v. Conticommodity Services, Inc.

United States Court of Appeals, Second Circuit, 1996.
88 F.3d 87.

■ Before: Van Graafeiland, Jacobs and Parker, Circuit Judges.

■ Jacobs, Circuit Judge:

Famed silver trader Norton Waltuch spent $2.2 million in unreimbursed legal fees to defend himself against numerous civil lawsuits and an enforcement proceeding brought by the Commodity Futures Trading Commission (CFTC). In this action under Delaware law, Waltuch seeks indemnification of his legal expenses from his former employer. The district court denied any indemnity, and Waltuch appeals.

As vice-president and chief metals trader for Conticommodity Services, Inc., Waltuch traded silver for the firm's clients, as well as for his own account. In late 1979 and early 1980, the silver price spiked upward as the then-billionaire Hunt brothers and several of Waltuch's foreign clients bought huge quantities of silver futures contracts. Just as rapidly, the price fell until (on a day remembered in trading circles as "Silver Thursday") the silver market crashed. Between 1981 and 1985, angry silver speculators filed numerous lawsuits against Waltuch and Conticommodity, alleging fraud, market manipulation, and anti-trust violations. All of the suits eventually settled and were dismissed with prejudice, pursuant to settlements in which Conticommodity paid over $35 million to the various suitors. Waltuch himself was dismissed from the suits with no settlement contribution. His unreimbursed legal expenses in these actions total approximately $1.2 million.

Waltuch was also the subject of an enforcement proceeding brought by the CFTC, charging him with fraud and market manipulation. The proceeding was settled, with Waltuch agreeing to a penalty that included a $100,000 fine and a six-month ban on buying or selling futures contracts from any exchange floor. Waltuch spent $1 million in unreimbursed legal fees in the CFTC proceeding.[1]

Waltuch brought suit in the United States District Court for the Southern District of New York (Lasker, J.) against Conticommodity and its parent company, Continental Grain Co. (together "Conti"), for indemnification of his unreimbursed expenses.[2] Only two of Waltuch's claims reach us on appeal.

Waltuch first claims that Article Ninth of Conticommodity's articles of incorporation requires Conti to indemnify him for his expenses in both the private and CFTC actions. Conti responds that this claim is barred by subsection (a) of § 145 of Delaware's General Corporation Law, which permits indemnification only if the corporate officer acted "in good faith," something that Waltuch has not established. Waltuch counters that subsection (f) of the same statute permits a corporation to grant indemnification rights outside the limits of subsection (a), and that Conticommodity did so with Article Ninth (which has no stated good-faith limitation). The district court held that, notwithstanding § 145(f), Waltuch could recover under Article Ninth only if Waltuch met the "good faith" requirement of § 145(a).[3] 833 F.Supp. 302, 308–

---

1. The parties have stipulated that Waltuch's "reasonable attorney's fees and costs" for the private lawsuits totaled $1,228,586.67, and that the comparable expenses for the CFTC proceeding are an even $1 million.

2. Conticommodity and Continental Grain are incorporated in Delaware and have their principal places of business in New York; Waltuch is a New Jersey citizen. We therefore have diversity jurisdiction under 28 U.S.C. § 1332. All parties agree that Delaware law governs.

3. A Special Committee of Continental Grain Co.'s Board of Directors reached the same conclusion in November 1991. Waltuch filed his complaint two months later. In the district court, Conti argued that under the business judgment rule, the Special Committee's decision was immune from challenge, an argument the district court rejected. 833 F.Supp. at 305. Although the parties signed a stipulation preserving Conti's right to contest the district court's ruling on this issue, Conti

09 (S.D.N.Y.1993). On the factual issue of whether Waltuch had acted "in good faith," the court denied Conti's summary judgment motion and cleared the way for trial. Id. at 313. The parties then stipulated that they would forgo trial on the issue of Waltuch's "good faith," agree to an entry of final judgment against Waltuch on his claim under Article Ninth and § 145(f), and allow Waltuch to take an immediate appeal of the judgment to this Court. Thus, as to Waltuch's first claim, the only question left is how to interpret §§ 145(a) and 145(f), assuming Waltuch acted with less than "good faith." As we explain in part I below, we affirm the district court's judgment as to this claim and hold that § 145(f) does not permit a corporation to bypass the "good faith" requirement of § 145(a).

Waltuch's second claim is that subsection (c) of § 145 requires Conti to indemnify him because he was "successful on the merits or otherwise" in the private lawsuits.[4] The district court ruled for Conti on this claim as well. The court explained that, even though all the suits against Waltuch were dismissed without his making any payment, he was not "successful on the merits or otherwise," because Conti's settlement payments to the plaintiffs were partially on Waltuch's behalf. Id. at 311. For the reasons stated in part II below, we reverse this portion of the district court's ruling, and hold that Conti must indemnify Waltuch under § 145(c) for the $1.2 million in unreimbursed legal fees he spent in defending the private lawsuits.

I

Article Ninth, on which Waltuch bases his first claim, is categorical and contains no requirement of "good faith":

> The Corporation shall indemnify and hold harmless each of its incumbent or former directors, officers, employees and agents ... against expenses actually and necessarily incurred by him in connection with the defense of any action, suit or proceeding threatened, pending or completed, in which he is made a party, by reason of his serving in or having held such position or capacity, except in relation to matters as to which he shall be adjudged in such action, suit or proceeding to be liable for negligence or misconduct in the performance of duty.[5]

Conti argues that § 145(a) of Delaware's General Corporation Law, which does contain a "good faith" requirement, fixes the outer limits of a corporation's power to indemnify; Article Ninth is thus invalid under Delaware law, says Conti, to the extent that it requires indemnification of officers who have acted in bad faith. The affirmative grant of power in § 145(a) is as follows:

has abandoned its business judgment rule argument on appeal.

**4.** The district court held that Waltuch was not successful "on the merits or otherwise" in the CFTC proceeding. 833 F.Supp. at 311. Waltuch does not appeal this aspect of the court's ruling.

**5.** Because the private suits and the CFTC proceeding were settled, it is undisputed that Waltuch was not "adjudged ... to be liable for negligence or misconduct in the performance of duty."

*A corporation shall have power to indemnify* any person who was or is a party or is threatened to be made a party to any threatened, pending or completed action, suit or proceeding, whether civil, criminal, administrative or investigative (other than an action by or in the right of the corporation) by reason of the fact that he is or was a director, officer, employee or agent of the corporation, or is or was serving at the request of the corporation as a director, officer, employee or agent of another corporation, partnership, joint venture, trust or other enterprise, against expenses (including attorneys' fees), judgments, fines and amounts paid in settlement actually and reasonably incurred by him in connection with such action, suit or proceeding *if he acted in good faith and in a manner he reasonably believed to be in or not opposed to the best interests of the corporation,* and, with respect to any criminal action or proceeding, had no reasonable cause to believe his conduct was unlawful.

56 Del.Laws 50, § 1 at 170–71 (1967) (emphasis added) (rewriting Delaware's General Corporation Law, title 8, chapter 1 of the Delaware Code), *codified at* 8 Del.Code Ann. tit. 8, § 145(a) (Michie 1991). Key language in the Delaware Code Annotated's version of this subsection is in error, as explained in the margin.[6]

In order to escape the "good faith" clause of § 145(a), Waltuch argues that § 145(a) is not an *exclusive* grant of indemnification power, because § 145(f) expressly allows corporations to indemnify officers in a manner broader than that set out in § 145(a). The "nonexclusivity" language of § 145(f) provides:

The indemnification and advancement of expenses provided by, or granted pursuant to, the other subsections of this section *shall not be deemed exclusive of any other rights* to which those

---

**6.** There is some confusion about whether this subsection begins, "A corporation *shall have power* to indemnify ..." or "A corporation *may* indemnify ...". As originally enacted, § 145(a) contained the phrase "shall have power". 56 Del.Laws 50, § 1 at 170 (1967). According to the annotations in the *Delaware Code Annotated* (and confirmed by a review of the legislative records since 1967), § 145(a) has never been amended. *See* 8 Del.Code Ann. tit. 8, § 145(a) (1991 & 1995 Supp.).

Nevertheless, the *Delaware Code Annotated,* a private compilation by the Michie Company of all Delaware legislative acts, at some point began using the phrase "may" in place of "shall have power". *See* 8 Del.Code Ann. tit. 8, § 145(a) (1974). We have not been able to explain this non-legislative change in statutory language. The *Delaware Corporation Law Annotated,* published by the Corporation Trust Company, continues to use the phrase "shall have power". Del.Corp. L.Ann. § 145(a) (20th ed. Corp.Trust Co.1991).

One treatise uses the phrase "shall have power", *see* Ernest L. Folk, III, et al., *Folk on the Delaware General Corporation Law* at 145:1 (3d ed. 1994), while another uses "may". *See* 5 R. Franklin Balotti & Jesse A. Finkelstein, *The Delaware Law of Corporations and Business Organizations* at 100 (1990 & 1993 Supp.) ("Balotti & Finkelstein"). The parties to this appeal perpetuate the confusion: their joint appendix contains a version of § 145(a) that says "shall have power", but one of the briefs quotes a version that says "may".

When there is a conflict between an original enactment of the Delaware Legislature and the codification of the law, the original enactment controls. *Elliott v. Blue Cross & Blue Shield,* 407 A.2d 524, 528 (Del.1979); *Kimmey v. Farmers Bank,* 373 A.2d 569, 570 (Del.1977). We therefore employ the Legislature's version of § 145(a), which says "shall have power".

We are indebted to Lesley Lawrence and the staff at the Third Circuit library in Wilmington for their assistance on this issue.

seeking indemnification or advancement of expenses may be entitled under any bylaw, agreement, vote of stockholders or disinterested directors or otherwise, both as to action in his official capacity and as to action in another capacity while holding such office.

56 Del.Laws 50, § 1 at 172 (emphasis added), *as amended and codified* at 8 Del.Code Ann. tit. 8, § 145(f). Waltuch contends that the "nonexclusivity" language in § 145(f) is a separate grant of indemnification power, not limited by the good faith clause that governs the power granted in § 145(a). Conti on the other hand contends that § 145(f) must be limited by "public policies," one of which is that a corporation may indemnify its officers only if they act in "good faith."

In a thorough and scholarly opinion, Judge Lasker agreed with Conti's reading of § 145(f), writing that "it has been generally agreed that there are public policy limits on indemnification under Section 145(f)," although it was "difficult . . . to define precisely what limitations on indemnification public policy imposes." 833 F.Supp. at 307, 308. After reviewing cases from Delaware and elsewhere and finding that they provided no authoritative guidance, Judge Lasker surveyed the numerous commentators on this issue and found that they generally agreed with Conti's position. *Id.* at 308–09. He also found that Waltuch's reading of § 145(f) failed to make sense of the statute as a whole:

> [T]here would be no point to the carefully crafted provisions of Section 145 spelling out the permissible scope of indemnification under Delaware law if subsection (f) allowed indemnification in additional circumstances without regard to these limits. The exception would swallow the rule.

*Id.* at 309. The fact that § 145(f) was limited by § 145(a) did not make § 145(f) meaningless, wrote Judge Lasker, because § 145(f) "still 'may authorize the adoption of various procedures and presumptions to make the process of indemnification more favorable to the indemnitee without violating the statute.'" *Id.* at 309 (quoting 1 Balotti & Finkelstein § 4.16 at 4–321). As will be evident from the discussion below, we adopt much of Judge Lasker's analysis.

### A.   Delaware Cases

No Delaware court has decided the very issue presented here; but the applicable cases tend to support the proposition that a corporation's grant of indemnification rights cannot be *inconsistent* with the substantive statutory provisions of § 145, notwithstanding § 145(f). We draw this rule of "consistency" primarily from our reading of the Delaware Supreme Court's opinion in *Hibbert v. Hollywood Park, Inc.*, 457 A.2d 339 (Del.1983). In that case, Hibbert and certain other directors sued the corporation and the remaining directors, and then demanded indemnification for their expenses and fees related to the litigation. The company refused indemnification on the ground that directors were entitled to indemnification only as *defendants* in legal proceedings. The court reversed the trial court and held that Hibbert was entitled to indemnification under the plain terms of a company bylaw that did not draw an express distinction between plaintiff directors and defendant directors. *Id.* at 343. The court then proceeded to test the bylaw for consistency with § 145(a):

> Furthermore, *indemnification here is consistent with current Delaware law.* Under 8 Del.C. § 145(a) ..., "a corporation may indemnify any person who was or is a party or is threatened to be made a party to any threatened, pending or completed" derivative or third-party action. By this language, indemnity is *not limited to* only those who stand as a defendant in the main action. The corporation can also grant indemnification rights beyond those provided by statute. 8 Del.C. § 145(f).

*Id.* at 344 (emphasis added and citations omitted). *See supra* note 6 (explaining the error in the *Delaware Code Annotated*'s use of the phrase "may indemnify" in § 145(a)). This passage contains two complementary propositions. Under § 145(f), a corporation may provide indemnification rights that go "beyond" the rights provided by § 145(a) and the other substantive subsections of § 145. At the same time, any such indemnification rights provided by a corporation must be "consistent with" the substantive provisions of § 145, including § 145(a). In *Hibbert,* the corporate bylaw was "consistent with" § 145(a), because this subsection was "not limited to" suits in which directors were defendants. *Hibbert*'s holding may support an inverse corollary that illuminates our case: if § 145(a) had been expressly limited to directors who were named as defendants, the bylaw could not have stood, regardless of § 145(f), because the bylaw would not have been "consistent with" the substantive statutory provision.[7] ...

### B. Statutory Reading

The "consistency" rule suggested by [the] Delaware cases is reinforced by our reading of § 145 as a whole. Subsections (a) (indemnification for third-party actions) and (b) (similar indemnification for derivative suits) expressly grant a corporation the power to indemnify directors, officers, and others, if they "acted in good faith and in a manner reasonably believed to be in or not opposed to the best interest of the corporation." These provisions thus limit the scope

---

**7.** The *Hibbert* court cites to a 1978 article by Samuel Arsht, chairman of the committee of experts that drafted Delaware's General Corporation Law in 1967, *id.,* which supports our conclusion that indemnification rights permitted under § 145(f) must be consistent with the other substantive provisions of § 145. At the pages cited by the court, Arsht writes:

> The question most frequently asked by practicing lawyers is what subsection (f), the nonexclusive clause, means.... The question which subsection (f) invariably raises is whether a corporation can adopt a by-law or make a contract with its directors providing that they will be in-demnified for whatever they may have to pay if they are sued and lose or settle. The answer to this question is "no." Subsection (f) ... permits additional rights to be created, but *it is not a blanket authorization to indemnify directors* against all expenses, fines, or settlements of whatever nature and *regardless of the directors' conduct.* The statutory language is circumscribed by limits of public policy....

S. Samuel Arsht, *Indemnification Under Section 145 of Delaware General Corporation Law,* 3 Del.J.Corp.L. 176, 176–77 (1978) (emphasis added).

of the power that they confer. They are permissive in the sense that a corporation may exercise less than its full power to grant the indemnification rights set out in these provisions. *See Essential Enter. Corp. v. Dorsey Corp.,* 182 A.2d 647, 653 (Del.Ch.1962). By the same token, subsection (f) permits the corporation to grant additional rights: the rights provided in the rest of § 145 "shall not be deemed exclusive of any other rights to which those seeking indemnification may be entitled." But crucially, subsection (f) merely acknowledges that one seeking indemnification may be entitled to "other rights" (of indemnification or otherwise); it does not speak in terms of corporate power, and therefore cannot be read to free a corporation from the "good faith" limit explicitly imposed in subsections (a) and (b).

An alternative construction of these provisions would effectively force us to ignore certain explicit terms of the statute. Section 145(a) gives Conti the power to indemnify Waltuch "*if* he acted in good faith and in a manner reasonably believed to be in or not opposed to the best interest of the corporation." 56 Del.Laws 50, § 1 at 171 (emphasis added). This statutory limit must mean that there is *no power* to indemnify Waltuch if he did not act in good faith. Otherwise, as Judge Lasker pointed out, § 145(a)—and its good faith clause—would have no meaning: a corporation could indemnify whomever and however it wished regardless of the good faith clause or anything else the Delaware Legislature wrote into § 145(a).

When the Legislature intended a subsection of § 145 to augment the powers limited in subsection (a), it set out the additional powers expressly. Thus subsection (g) explicitly allows a corporation to circumvent the "good faith" clause of subsection (a) by purchasing a directors and officers liability insurance policy. Significantly, that subsection is framed as a grant of corporate power:

> A corporation shall have power to purchase and maintain insurance on behalf of any person who is or was a director, officer, employee or agent of the corporation ... against any liability asserted against him and incurred by him in any such capacity, or arising out of his status as such, *whether or not the corporation would have the power to indemnify him against such liability under this section.*

56 Del.Laws 50, § 1 at 172 (1967) (emphasis added), *codified at* 8 Del.Code Ann. tit. 8, § 145(g) (Michie 1991). The italicized passage reflects the principle that corporations have the power under § 145 to indemnify in some situations and not in others. Since § 145(f) is neither a grant of corporate power nor a limitation on such power, subsection (g) must be referring to the limitations set out in § 145(a) and the other provisions of § 145 that describe corporate power. If § 145 (through subsection (f) or another part of the statute) gave corporations unlimited power to indemnify directors and officers, then the final clause of subsection (g) would be unnecessary: that is, its grant of "power to purchase and maintain insurance" (exercisable regardless of whether the corporation itself would have the power to indemnify the loss directly) is meaningful only because, in some

insurable situations, the corporation simply lacks the power to indemnify its directors and officers directly.

A contemporaneous account from the principal drafter of Delaware's General Corporation Law confirms what an integral reading of § 145 demonstrates: the statute's affirmative grants of power also impose limitations on the corporation's power to indemnify. Specifically, the good faith clause (unchanged since the Law's original enactment in 1967) was included in subsections (a) and (b) as a carefully calculated improvement on the prior indemnification provision and as an explicit limit on a corporation's power to indemnify:

> During the three years of the Revision Committee's study, no subject was more discussed among members of the corporate bar than the subject of indemnification of officers and directors. As far as Delaware law was concerned, the existing statutory provision on the subject had been found inadequate. Numerous by-laws and charter provisions had been adopted clarifying and extending its terms, but *uncertainty existed in many instances as to whether such provisions transgressed the limits* which the courts had indicated they would establish based on public policy.

> . . . .

> It was ... apparent that revision was appropriate with respect to *the limitations which must necessarily be placed on the power to indemnify* in order to prevent the statute from undermining the substantive provisions of the criminal law and corporation law....

> [There was a] need for a ... provision to protect the corporation law's requirement of loyalty to the corporation.... Ultimately, it was decided that *the power to indemnify should not be granted unless* it appeared that the person seeking indemnification had "acted in good faith and in a manner reasonably believed to be in or not opposed to the best interest of the corporation."

S. Samuel Arsht & Walter K. Stapleton, *Delaware's New General Corporation Law: Substantive Changes,* 23 Bus.Law. 75, 77–78 (1967).[8] This passage supports *Hibbert*'s rule of "consistency" and makes clear that a corporation has no power to transgress the indemnification limits set out in the substantive provisions of § 145.

Waltuch argues at length that reading § 145(a) to bar the indemnification of officers who acted in bad faith would render § 145(f) meaningless. This argument misreads § 145(f). That subsection refers to "any other rights to which those seeking indemnification or advancement of expenses may be entitled." Delaware commentators have identified various indemnification rights that are "beyond those

---

**8.** Delaware commentators consider this article to be part of (if not all of) "[t]he legislative history of Section 145." A. Gilchrist Sparks, III, et al., *Indemnification, Directors and Officers Liability Insurance and* *Limitations of Director Liability Pursuant to Statutory Authorization: The Legal Framework Under Delaware Law,* 696 PLI/Corp. 941 (1990) (at page 10 out of 123 on WESTLAW). . . .

provided by statute," *Hibbert*, 457 A.2d at 344, and that are at the same time consistent with the statute:

> [S]ubsection (f) provides general authorization for the adoption of various procedures and presumptions making the process of indemnification more favorable to the indemnitee. For example, indemnification agreements or by-laws could provide for: (i) mandatory indemnification unless prohibited by statute; (ii) mandatory advancement of expenses, which the indemnitee can, in many instances, obtain on demand; (iii) accelerated procedures for the "determination" required by section 145(d) to be made in the "specific case"; (iv) litigation "appeal" rights of the indemnitee in the event of an unfavorable determination; (v) procedures under which a favorable determination will be deemed to have been made under circumstances where the board fails or refuses to act; [and] (vi) reasonable funding mechanisms.

E. Norman Veasey, et al., *Delaware Supports Directors With a Three-Legged Stool of Limited Liability, Indemnification, and Insurance*, 42 Bus.Law. 399, 415 (1987).[9] Moreover, subsection (f) may reference nonindemnification rights, such as advancement rights or rights to other payments from the corporation that do not qualify as indemnification.

We need not decide in this case the precise scope of those "other rights" adverted to in § 145(f). We simply conclude that § 145(f) is not rendered meaningless or inoperative by the conclusion that a Delaware corporation lacks power to indemnify an officer or director "unless [he] 'acted in good faith and in a manner reasonably believed to be in or not opposed to the best interest of the corporation.' " *See* Arsht & Stapleton, 23 Bus.Law. at 78. As a result, we hold that Conti's Article Ninth, which would require indemnification of Waltuch even if he acted in bad faith, is inconsistent with § 145(a) and thus exceeds the scope of a Delaware corporation's power to indemnify. Since Waltuch has agreed to forgo his opportunity to prove at trial that he acted in good faith, he is not entitled to indemnification under Article Ninth for the $2.2 million he spent in connection with the private lawsuits and the CFTC proceeding. We therefore affirm the district court on this issue.

## II

Unlike § 145(a), which grants a discretionary indemnification power, § 145(c) affirmatively *requires* corporations to indemnify its officers and directors for the "successful" defense of certain claims:

> To the extent that a director, officer, employee or agent of a corporation has been successful on the merits or otherwise in defense of any action, suit or proceeding referred to in subsections (a) and (b) of this section, or in defense of any claim, issue

---

**9.** Veasey is now Chief Justice of the Delaware Supreme Court. *See also* 1 Balotti & Finkelstein § 4.16 at 4–321, which makes the same suggestions. Other suggestions are made in Joseph F. Johnston, Jr., *Corporate Indemnification and Liability Insurance for Directors and Officers*, 33 Bus.Law. 1993, 1996, 2009–10 (1978).

or matter therein, he shall be indemnified against expenses (including attorneys' fees) actually and reasonably incurred by him in connection therewith.

56 Del.Laws 50, § 1 at 171 (1967), *codified at* 8 Del.Code Ann. tit. 8, § 145(c) (Michie 1991). Waltuch argues that he was "successful on the merits or otherwise" in the private lawsuits, because they were dismissed with prejudice without any payment or assumption of liability by him. Conti argues that the claims against Waltuch were dismissed only because of Conti's $35 million settlement payments, and that this payment was contributed, in part, "on behalf of Waltuch."[10]

The district court agreed with Conti that "the successful settlements cannot be credited to Waltuch but are attributable solely to Conti's settlement payments. It was not Waltuch who was successful, but Conti who was successful for him." 833 F.Supp. at 311. The district court held that § 145(c) mandates indemnification when the director or officer "is vindicated," but that there was no vindication here:

> Vindication is also ordinarily associated with a dismissal with prejudice without any payment. However, a director or officer is not vindicated when the reason he did not have to make a settlement payment is because someone else assumed that liability. Being bailed out is not the same thing as being vindicated.

*Id.* We believe that this understanding and application of the "vindication" concept is overly broad and is inconsistent with a proper interpretation of § 145(c).

No Delaware court has applied § 145(c) in the context of indemnification stemming from the settlement of civil litigation. One lower court, however, has applied that subsection to an analogous case in the criminal context, and has illuminated the link between "vindication" and the statutory phrase, "successful on the merits or otherwise." In *Merritt–Chapman & Scott Corp. v. Wolfson,* 321 A.2d 138 (Del.Super.Ct.1974), the corporation's agents were charged with several counts of criminal conduct. A jury found them guilty on some counts, but deadlocked on the others. The agents entered into a "settlement" with the prosecutor's office by pleading nolo contendere to one of the counts in exchange for the dropping of the rest. *Id.* at 140. The agents claimed entitlement to mandatory indemnification under § 145(c) as to the counts that were dismissed. In opposition, the corporation raised an argument similar to the argument raised by Conti:

> [The corporation] argues that the statute and sound public policy require indemnification only where there has been vindication by a finding or concession of innocence. *It contends that the charges against [the agents] were dropped for practical reasons,* not because of their innocence....

---

**10.** Although this is not essential to our holding, we note that Conti points to no evidence in support of its contention that the plaintiffs would have continued to pursue their suits as to Waltuch if Conti had paid some lesser amount.

The statute requires indemnification to the extent that the claimant "has been successful on the merits or otherwise." *Success is vindication.* In a criminal action, any result other than conviction must be considered success. *Going behind the result,* as [the corporation] attempts, is neither authorized by subsection (c) nor consistent with the presumption of innocence.

*Id.* at 141 (emphasis added).

Although the underlying proceeding in *Merritt* was criminal, the court's analysis is instructive here. The agents in *Merritt* rendered consideration—their guilty plea on one count—to achieve the dismissal of the other counts. The court considered these dismissals both "success" and (therefore) "vindication," and refused to "go[ ] behind the result" or to appraise the reason for the success. In equating "success" with "vindication," the court thus rejected the more expansive view of vindication urged by the corporation. Under *Merritt*'s holding, then, vindication, when used as a synonym for "success" under § 145(c), does not mean moral exoneration. Escape from an adverse judgment or other detriment, for whatever reason, is determinative. According to *Merritt,* the only question a court may ask is what the result was, not why it was.[12]

Conti's contention that, because of its $35 million settlement payments, Waltuch's settlement without payment should not really count as settlement without payment, is inconsistent with the rule in *Merritt.* Here, Waltuch was sued, and the suit was dismissed without his having paid a settlement. Under the approach taken in *Merritt,* it is not our business to ask why this result was reached. Once Waltuch achieved his settlement gratis, he achieved success "on the merits or otherwise." And, as we know from *Merritt,* success is sufficient to constitute vindication (at least for the purposes of § 145(c)). Waltuch's settlement thus vindicated him.

The concept of "vindication" pressed by Conti is also inconsistent with the fact that a director or officer who is able to defeat an adversary's claim by asserting a technical defense is entitled to indemnification under § 145(c). *See* 1 Balotti & Finkelstein, § 4.13 at 4–302. In such cases, the indemnitee has been "successful" in the palpable sense that he has won, and the suit has been dismissed, whether or

---

**12.** Our adoption of *Merritt*'s interpretation of the statutory term "successful" does not necessarily signal our endorsement of the result in that case. The *Merritt* court sliced the case into individual counts, with indemnification pegged to each count independently of the others. We are not faced with a case in which the corporate officer claims to have been "successful" on some parts of the case but was clearly "unsuccessful" on others, and therefore take no position on this feature of the *Merritt* holding.

We also do not mean our discussion of *Merritt* to suggest that the line between success and failure in a criminal case may be drawn in the same way in the civil context. In a criminal case, conviction on a particular count is obvious failure, and dismissal of the charge is obvious success. In a civil suit for damages, however, there is a monetary continuum between complete success (dismissal of the suit without any payment) and complete failure (payment of the full amount of damages requested by the plaintiff). Because Waltuch made no payment in connection with the dismissal of the suits against him, we need not decide whether a defendant's settlement payment automatically renders that defendant "unsuccessful" under § 145(c).

not the victory is deserved in merits terms. If a technical defense is deemed "vindication" under Delaware law, it cannot matter why Waltuch emerged unscathed, or whether Conti "bailed [him] out", or whether his success was deserved. Under § 145(c), mere success is vindication enough.

This conclusion comports with the reality that civil judgments and settlements are ordinarily expressed in terms of cash rather than moral victory. No doubt, it would make sense for Conti to buy the dismissal of the claims against Waltuch along with its own discharge from the case, perhaps to avoid further expense or participation as a non-party, potential cross-claims, or negative publicity. But Waltuch apparently did not accede to that arrangement, and Delaware law cannot allow an indemnifying corporation to escape the mandatory indemnification of subsection (c) by paying a sum in settlement on behalf of an unwilling indemnitee.

... In *Wisener v. Air Express Int'l Corp.*, 583 F.2d 579 (2d Cir.1978), we construed an Illinois indemnification statute that was intentionally enacted as a copy of Delaware's § 145. *See id.* at 582 n. 3; 1 Balotti & Finkelstein, § 4.12 at 4–296 n. 1048 (§ 145 was the "prototype" for Illinois's indemnification statute). Our holding in that case is perfectly applicable here:

> It is contended that [the director] was not "successful" in the litigation, since the third-party claims against him never proceeded to trial. The statute, however, refers to success "on the merits or otherwise," which surely is broad enough to cover a termination of claims by agreement without any payment or assumption of liability.

583 F.2d at 583. It is undisputed that the private lawsuits against Conti and Waltuch were dismissed with prejudice, "without any payment of assumption of liability" by Waltuch. Applying the analysis of *Wisener,* Conti must indemnify Waltuch for his expenses in connection with the private lawsuits.

... [T]he extent of Waltuch's success] is not lessened by Conti's payments, even if it is true (as it stands to reason) that his success was achieved because Conti was willing to pay. Whatever the impetus for the plaintiffs' dismissal of their claims against Waltuch, he still walked away without liability and without making a payment. This constitutes a success that is untarnished by the process that achieved it.

For all of these reasons, we agree with Waltuch that he is entitled to indemnification under § 145(c) for his expenses pertaining to the private lawsuits.

### III

The judgment of the district court is affirmed in part and reversed in part. This case is remanded to the district court so that judgment may be entered in favor of Waltuch on his claim for $1,228,586.67, representing the unreimbursed expenses from the private lawsuits. *See supra* note 1.

---

**IN RE LANDMARK LAND CO.**, 76 F.3d 553. "An agent who has intentionally participated in illegal activity or wrongful conduct against third persons cannot be said to have acted in good faith, even if the conduct benefits the corporation. *Plate [v. Sun–Diamond Growers], 275 Cal.Rptr. at 672.*" For example, corporate executives who participate in a deliberate price-fixing conspiracy with competing firms could not be found to have acted in good faith, even though they may have reasonably believed that a deliberate flouting of the antitrust laws would increase the profits of the corporation. "1 Harold Marsh, Jr. and R. Roy Finkle, Marsh's California Corporation Law (3d ed.) § 10.43, at 751; see *Plate, 275 Cal.Rptr. at 672* (citing same language from second edition). We recognize that the Directors did not break any law by filing the bankruptcy petitions, and that the OTS has not filed criminal charges against the Directors. Nonetheless, we find that a deliberate attempt to undermine the regulatory authority of a government agency cannot constitute good faith conduct, even if such actions benefit the corporation."

---

### NOTE ON ADVANCES

In Advanced Mining Systems, Inc. v. Fricke, 623 A.2d 82 (Del.Ch. 1992), the Delaware court held that indemnification rights and advancement rights stand apart as two "distinct types of legal rights," so that a bylaw provision that required a corporation to "indemnify . . . to the extent permitted" under Delaware law did not wrest from a corporation the ability to refuse advance payments. See also Rev. Model Bus. Corp. Act § 8.58(a) and Official Comment.

---

### (b) INSURANCE

[See Chapter 8.]

---

## SECTION 11.   SETTLEMENT OF DERIVATIVE ACTIONS

---

### KAPLAN v. RAND
[See Section 8, supra]

---

### FEDERAL RULES OF CIVIL PROCEDURE, RULE 23.1
[See Statutory Supplement]

---

### REVISED MODEL BUSINESS CORPORATION ACT § 7.45
[See Statutory Supplement]

---

### NEW YORK BUS. CORP. LAW § 626(d), (e)
[See Statutory Supplement]

---

### IN RE CAREMARK, INTERNATIONAL, INC. DERIVATIVE LITIGATION
[Chapter 8, supra]

---

### ALI, PRINCIPLES OF CORPORATE GOVERNANCE §§ 7.14–7.16
[See Statutory Supplement]

---

**DESIMONE v. INDUSTRIAL BIO–TEST LABORATORIES,INC.,** 83 F.R.D. 615 (S.D.N.Y.1979). "The court will approve a proposed settlement of a class action if the proposal is fair, reasonable and adequate. This determination requires three levels of analysis. First, the proponents have the burden of proving that (1) the settlement is not collusive but was reached after arm's length negotiation; (2) the proponents are counsel experienced in similar cases; (3) there has been sufficient discovery to enable counsel to act intelligently and (4) the number of objectants or their relative interest is small. If the proponents establish these propositions, the burden of attacking the settlement then shifts to the objectants, if any. Finally, the court must approve the settlement only after finding it to be reasonable in light of the plaintiffs' ultimate probability of success in the lawsuit....

"In determining reasonableness, the courts in this circuit have not applied any single, inflexible test. Instead, they have considered the amount of the settlement in light of all the circumstances, including such factors as: (1) the best possible recovery; (2) the likely recovery if the claims were fully litigated; (3) the complexity, expense and probable duration of continued litigation; (4) the risk of establishing liability; (5) the risk of establishing damages; (6) the risk of maintaining the class action throughout trial; (7) the reaction of the class to the settlement; (8) the stage of the proceedings and (9) the ability of the defendants to withstand a greater judgment." . . .

---

## Macey & Miller, The Plaintiffs' Attorneys' Role in Class Actions and Derivative Litigation: Economic Analysis and Recommendations for Reform

58 U.Chi.L.Rev. 1, 44–48 (1991).

Most class action and derivative litigation is settled prior to judgment. When such litigation is settled, the problem of agency costs appears in a particularly problematic form. As already discussed, the plaintiffs' attorney often faces a severe conflict of interest in settling class and derivative litigation. In common fund cases where the attorney earns a percentage of the judgment, the attorney has an incentive to settle early at a relatively low figure in order to maximize her profit. In common fund cases in which the attorney is compensated according to the lodestar formula, the attorney has an incentive to delay reaching a settlement in order to increase the hours upon which the compensation is calculated. The attorney may also agree to an inappropriately low settlement on the merits in exchange for the defendant's implicit or explicit promise to allow the attorney to expend additional risk-free hours in order to build up a fee. In common benefit and fee-shifting cases the attorney has an incentive both to delay settlement and to agree to inappropriately low settlements in exchange for generous negotiated attorney's fees. . . .

The regulatory response to these conflicts is to require judicial scrutiny of proposed settlements. Unfortunately, judicial approval appears to be highly imperfect as a protection for the plaintiffs' interests, for several reasons. First, and most important, the judge herself has a powerful interest in approving the settlement. Judges' calendars are crowded with cases, and despite various reform efforts, the workload only seems to increase. If the judge approves the settlement, the result will be to remove a potentially complex and time-consuming case from the judge's calendar; if she rejects it she faces a substantial probability of further litigation. A judge faces virtually no prospect of reversal for approving a settlement, whereas a decision rejecting a settlement might well be appealed. Moreover, trial judges are heavily conditioned by the ethos of their jobs to view settlements as desirable; they routinely encourage settlement in other contexts. It would be unrealistic to expect trial judges to shift gears suddenly and view settlements with suspicion rather than approbation when they arise in the class action or derivative contexts.

Second, trial courts may simply lack information to make an informed evaluation of the fairness of the settlement. Typically, when a case is settled well in advance of trial, the only information available to the judge is found in papers filed in court—pleadings, briefs, and supporting materials filed on motions—and materials submitted to the judge in connection with the settlement hearing. Such evidence is likely to be highly incomplete and, in the case of materials submitted to support the proposed settlement, biased in favor of the settlement. The matters on which the judge must rule are also highly subjective and imprecise. Even if the judge had adequate information on which to decide, it would be difficult to make reliable estimates of the settlement value of a case.

Third, settlement hearings are typically pep rallies jointly orchestrated by plaintiffs' counsel and defense counsel. Because both parties desire that the settlement be approved, they have every incentive to present it as entirely fair. Objectors to the settlement, on the other hand, are uncommon; those who do object are often either disgruntled plaintiffs' attorneys who have fallen out with others in the plaintiffs' consortium, or naive class members who demonstrate their ignorance of the issues in dispute. The deck is heavily stacked toward approval of the settlement.

Trial courts happily play along with the camaraderie. In approving settlement, courts often engage in paeans of praise for counsel or lambaste anyone rash enough to object to the settlement. Not surprisingly, it is uncommon to find cases where trial courts reject settlements that are presented to them by defense counsel and plaintiffs' attorneys. Given that settlements are nearly always approved, one might well question the efficacy of judicial review of class action and derivative settlements.

---

## ALI, PRINCIPLES OF CORPORATE GOVERNANCE § 7.15

[See Statutory Supplement]

CHAPTER XII

# STRUCTURAL CHANGES: CORPORATE COMBINATIONS AND TENDER OFFERS

---

## SECTION 1. CORPORATE COMBINATIONS

---

### (a) SALE OF SUBSTANTIALLY ALL ASSETS

---

#### DEL. GEN. CORP. LAW § 271
[See Statutory Supplement]

---

#### REV. MODEL BUS. CORP. ACT §§ 12.01, 12.02, 13.02(3)
[See Statutory Supplement]

---

### Katz v. Bregman
Court of Chancery of Delaware, 1981.
431 A.2d 1274, appeal ref'd sub nom.
Plant Indus., Inc. v. Katz, 435 A.2d 1044 (Del.1981).

■ MARVEL, CHANCELLOR:

The complaint herein seeks the entry of an order preliminarily enjoining the proposed sale of the Canadian assets of Plant Industries, Inc. to Vulcan Industrial Packaging, Ltd., the plaintiff Hyman Katz allegedly being the owner of approximately 170,000 shares of common stock of the defendant Plant Industries, Inc., on whose behalf he has brought this action, suing not only for his own benefit as a stockholder but for the alleged benefit of all other record owners of common stock of the defendant Plant Industries, Inc. . . . Significantly, at common law, a sale of all or substantially all of the assets of a corporation required the unanimous vote of the stockholders, Folk, The Delaware General Corporation Law, p. 400.

748

The complaint alleges that during the last six months of 1980 the board of directors of Plant Industries, Inc., under the guidance of the individual defendant Robert B. Bregman, the present chief executive officer of such corporation, embarked on a course of action which resulted in the disposal of several unprofitable subsidiaries of the corporate defendant located in the United States, namely Louisiana Foliage Inc., a horticultural business, Sunaid Food Products, Inc., a Florida packaging business, and Plant Industries (Texas), Inc., a business concerned with the manufacture of woven synthetic cloth. As a result of these sales Plant Industries, Inc. by the end of 1980 had disposed of a significant part of its unprofitable assets.

According to the complaint, Mr. Bregman thereupon proceeded on a course of action designed to dispose of a subsidiary of the corporate defendant known as Plant National (Quebec) Ltd., a business which constitutes Plant Industries, Inc.'s entire business operation in Canada and has allegedly constituted Plant's only income producing facility during the past four years. The professed principal purpose of such proposed sale is to raise needed cash and thus improve Plant's balance sheets. And while interest in purchasing the corporate defendant's Canadian plant was thereafter evinced not only by Vulcan Industrial Packaging, Ltd. but also by Universal Drum Reconditioning Co., which latter corporation originally undertook to match or approximate and recently to top Vulcan's bid, a formal contract was entered into between Plant Industries, Inc. and Vulcan on April 2, 1981 for the purchase and sale of Plant National (Quebec) despite the constantly increasing bids for the same property being made by Universal. One reason advanced by Plant's management for declining to negotiate with Universal is that a firm undertaking having been entered into with Vulcan that the board of directors of Plant may not legally or ethically negotiate with Universal. But see *Thomas v. Kempner,* C.A. 4138, March 22, 1973.

In seeking injunctive relief, as prayed for, plaintiff relies on two principles, one that found in 8 Del.C. § 271 to the effect that a decision of a Delaware corporation to sell "... all or substantially all of its property and assets ..." requires not only the approval of such corporation's board of directors but also a resolution adopted by a majority of the outstanding stockholders of the corporation entitled to vote thereon at a meeting duly called upon at least twenty days' notice.

Support for the other principle relied on by plaintiff for the relief sought, namely an alleged breach of fiduciary duty on the part of the board of directors of Plant Industries, Inc. is allegedly found in such board's studied refusal to consider a potentially higher bid for the assets in question which is being advanced by Universal, *Thomas v. Kempner,* supra.

Turning to the possible application of 8 Del.C. § 271 to the proposed sale of substantial corporate assets of National to Vulcan, it is stated in *Gimbel v. Signal Companies, Inc.,* Del.Ch., 316 A.2d 599 (1974) as follows:

"If the sale is of assets quantitatively vital to the operation of the corporation and is out of the ordinary [course] and substantially affects the existence and purpose of the corporation then it is beyond the power of the Board of Directors."

According to Plant's 1980 10K form, it appears that at the end of 1980, Plant's Canadian operations represented 51% of Plant's remaining assets. Defendants also concede that National represents 44.9% of Plant's sales' revenues and 52.4% of its pretax net operating income. Furthermore, such report by Plant discloses, in rough figures, that while National made a profit in 1978 of $2,900,000, the profit from the United States businesses in that year was only $770,000. In 1979, the Canadian business profit was $3,500,000 while the loss of the United States businesses was $344,000. Furthermore, in 1980, while the Canadian business profit was $5,300,000, the corporate loss in the United States was $4,500,000. And while these figures may be somewhat distorted by the allocation of overhead expenses and taxes, they are significant. In any event, defendants concede that ". . . National accounted for 34.9% of Plant's pretax income in 1976, 36.9% in 1977, 42% in 1978, 51% in 1979 and 52.4% in 1980."

While in the case of *Philadelphia National Bank v. B.S.F. Co.,* Del.Ch., 199 A.2d 557 (1964), rev'd on other grounds, Del.Supr., 204 A.2d 746 (1964), the question of whether or not there had been a proposed sale of substantially all corporate assets was tested by provisions of an indenture agreement covering subordinated debentures, the result was the same as if the provisions of 8 Del.C. § 271 had been applicable, the trial Court stating:

"While no pertinent Pennsylvania case is cited, the critical factor in determining the character of a sale of assets is generally considered not the amount of property sold but whether the sale is in fact an unusual transaction or one made in the regular course of business of the seller * * * ".

Furthermore, in the case of *Wingate v. Bercut* (C.A.9) 146 F.2d 725 (1944), in which the Court declined to apply the provisions of 8 Del.C. § 271, it was noted that the transfer of shares of stock there involved, being a dealing in securities, constituted an ordinary business transaction.

In the case at bar, I am first of all satisfied that historically the principal business of Plant Industries, Inc. has not been to buy and sell industrial facilities but rather to manufacture steel drums for use in bulk shipping as well as for the storage of petroleum products, chemicals, food, paint, adhesives and cleaning agents, a business which has been profitably performed by National of Quebec. Furthermore, the proposal, after the sale of National, to embark on the manufacture of plastic drums represents a radical departure from Plant's historically successful line of business, namely steel drums. I therefore conclude that the proposed sale of Plant's Canadian operations, which constitute over 51% of Plant's total assets and in which are generated approximately 45% of Plant's 1980 net sales, would, if consummated, constitute a sale of substantially all of Plant's assets. By way of contrast, the proposed sale of Signal Oil in *Gimbel v. Signal Companies, Inc.,* supra, represented only about 26% of the total assets of Signal Companies, Inc. And while Signal Oil represented 41% of Signal Companies, Inc. total net worth, it generated only about 15% of Signal Companies, Inc. revenue and earnings.

I conclude that because the proposed sale of Plant National (Quebec) Ltd. would, if consummated, constitute a sale of substantially all of the assets of Plant Industries, Inc., as presently constituted, that an injunction should issue preventing the consummation of such sale at least until it has been approved by a majority of the outstanding stockholders of Plant Industries, Inc., entitled to vote at a meeting duly called on at least twenty days' notice. Compare *Robinson v. Pittsburg Oil Refining Company,* Del.Ch., 126 A. 46 (1924).

In light of this conclusion it will be unnecessary to consider whether or not the sale here under attack, as proposed to be made, is for such an inadequate consideration, viewed in light of the competing bid of Universal, as to constitute a breach of trust on the part of the directors of Plant Industries, Inc., *Robinson v. Pittsburg Oil Refining Company,* supra.

Being persuaded for the reasons stated that plaintiff has demonstrated a reasonable probability of ultimate success on final hearing in the absence of stockholder approval of the proposed sale of the corporate assets here in issue to Vulcan, a preliminary injunction against the consummation of such transaction, at least until stockholder approval is obtained, will be granted.

On notice, an appropriate form of order in conformity with the above may be submitted.

———

## NOTE ON SALE OF SUBSTANTIALLY ALL ASSETS

At common law, a sale of substantially all assets required unanimous shareholder approval, on the theory that it breached an implied contract among the shareholders to further the corporate enterprise. See, e.g., Fontaine v. Brown County Motors Co., 251 Wis. 433, 437, 29 N.W.2d 744, 746–47 (1947). The statutory sale-of-substantially-all-assets provisions were enacted against this backdrop. It has been held that under those statutes a sale of substantially all assets in the ordinary course of business does not require shareholder approval. See Jeppi v. Brockman Holding Co., 34 Cal.2d 11, 206 P.2d 847 (1949). The theory is that because such a sale does not prevent furtherance of the corporate enterprise, it would not have required unanimous shareholder approval at common law, and the statutory sale-of-substantially-all-assets provisions were not intended to change that result.

———

**THORP v. CERBCO**, 676 A.2d 436 (Del.1996). CERBCO was a holding company with voting control of three subsidiaries. Only one of these subsidiaries, Insituform East, Inc., was profitable. The issue arose whether a sale of East would constitute a sale of substantially all of CERBCO's assets and would therefore require the approval of CERBCO's shareholders. Held, yes:

The standard for determining whether shareholder approval is required under § 271 was set forth in Oberly v. Kirby, Del. Supr., 592 A.2d 445, 464 (1991):

[T]he rule announced in Gimbel v. Signal Cos., Del.Ch., 316 A.2d 599, aff'd, Del.Supr., 316 A.2d 619 (1974), makes it clear that the need for shareholder ... approval is to be measured not by the size of a sale alone, but also by its qualitative effect upon the corporation. Thus, it is relevant to ask whether a transaction "is out of the ordinary and substantially affects the existence and purpose of the corporation." [Gimbel, 316 A.2d] at 606.

In the opinion below, the Chancellor determined that the sale of East would constitute a radical transformation of CERBCO. In addition, CERBCO's East stock accounted for 68% of CERBCO's assets in 1990 and this stock was its primary income generating asset. We therefore affirm the decision that East stock constituted "substantially all" of CERBCO's assets as consistent with Delaware law.

————

## (b) THE APPRAISAL REMEDY

————

### DEL. GEN. CORP. LAW § 262

[See Statutory Supplement]

————

### REV. MODEL BUS. CORP. ACT §§ 13.01–13.03, 13.20–13.26, 13.30–13.31

[See Statutory Supplement]

————

### ALI, PRINCIPLES OF CORPORATE GOVERNANCE §§ 7.21–7.23

[See Statutory Supplement]

————

### CAL. CORP. CODE § 1300, 1311

[See Statutory Supplement]

———

## BACKGROUND NOTE ON APPRAISAL RIGHTS

The value and function of the appraisal right are intimately related to the way in which the value of dissenting shares is determined. The most common statutory formula instructs the courts to determine the "fair value" of such shares. This formula obviously leaves considerable room for elaboration. Unfortunately, there is often a very substantial difference between the elements of valuation applied by the courts in appraisal cases under the Delaware Block Method and the elements of valuation in the real world. Many aspects of the approach taken under the block method are highly questionable, and the result may be a gross undervaluation as compared to real-world values. This in turn diminishes the usefulness of the appraisal right and opens up the possibility of manipulation, by those in control, to freeze out the minority at unfairly low prices.

In Weinberger v. UOP, 457 A.2d 701 (1983), the Delaware Supreme Court overturned the traditional Delaware Block Method of valuation:

> Turning to the matter of price, plaintiff also challenges its fairness. His evidence was that on the date the merger was approved the stock was worth at least $26 per share. In support, he offered the testimony of a chartered investment analyst who used two basic approaches to valuation: a comparative analysis of the premium paid over market in ten other tender offer-merger combinations, and a discounted cash flow analysis.

> In this breach of fiduciary duty case, the Chancellor perceived that the approach to valuation was the same as that in an appraisal proceeding. Consistent with precedent, he rejected plaintiff's method of proof and accepted defendants' evidence of value as being in accord with practice under prior case law. This means that the so-called "Delaware block" or weighted average method was employed wherein the elements of value, i.e., assets, market price, earnings, etc., were assigned a particular weight and the resulting amounts added to determine the value per share. This procedure has been in use for decades. . . . However, to the extent it excludes other generally accepted techniques used in the financial community and the courts, it is now clearly outmoded. It is time we recognize this in appraisal and other stock valuation proceedings and bring our law current on the subject.

> . . . Accordingly, the standard "Delaware block" or weighted average method of valuation, formerly employed in appraisal and other stock valuation cases, shall no longer exclusively control such proceedings. We believe that a more liberal approach must include proof of value by any techniques or methods which are

generally considered acceptable in the financial community and otherwise admissible in court, subject only to our interpretation of 8 Del.C. § 262(h), infra . . . . . This will obviate the very structured and mechanistic procedure that has heretofore governed such matters. . . .

It is significant that section 262 now mandates the determination of "fair" value based upon "all relevant factors". Only the speculative elements of value that may arise from the "accomplishment or expectation" of the merger are excluded. We take this to be a very narrow exception to the appraisal process, designed to eliminate use of *pro forma* data and projections of a speculative variety relating to the completion of a merger. But elements of future value, including the nature of the enterprise, which are known or susceptible of proof as of the date of the merger and not the product of speculation, may be considered. When the trial court deems it appropriate, fair value also includes any damages, resulting from the taking, which the stockholders sustain as a class. If that was not the case, then the obligation to consider "all relevant factors" in the valuation process would be eroded.

———

## NEW YORK BUS. CORP. LAW § 623(h)(4)

[See Statutory Supplement]

———

## (c) STATUTORY MERGERS

———

## (1) CLASSICAL MERGERS

———

## DEL. GEN. CORP. LAW §§ 251(a)–(e), 259–261

[See Statutory Supplement]

———

## REV. MODEL BUS. CORP. ACT §§ 11.01, 11.02, 11.04, 11.06, 11.07

[See Statutory Supplement]

———

## NOTE ON CLASSICAL MERGERS

1. *Statutory Mergers*. Del.Gen.Corp.Law §§ 251(a)–(e), 259–61 and Rev.Model Bus.Corp.Act §§ 11.01, 11.03 authorize a type of transaction commonly referred to as a statutory merger. Although the term *merger* is often used by nonlawyers to describe any form of combination, to a lawyer a merger is a combination involving the fusion of two constituent corporations pursuant to a formal agreement executed with reference to specific statutory merger provisions under which one corporation (the survivor) succeeds to the assets and liabilities of the other corporation by operation of law.

While details vary from state to state, generally the first formal step in such a merger, after negotiations have been completed, is a preliminary agreement (often embodied in a "letter of intent") signed by representatives of the constituent corporations. If the merger is approved by the board and shareholders of each constituent corporation, then: (1) Articles of merger are filed with the secretary of state; and (2) Stock or other consideration issued by the surviving corporation is exchanged for the stock and other securities of the disappearing corporation, which is fused into the survivor and loses its identity. In general, no deeds, bills of sale, or other instruments of conveyance, are necessary to pass title from the "disappearing" or nonsurviving corporation to the survivor: By operation of law, the survivor acquires all the rights, privileges, franchises, and assets of both constituents, and assumes all of their liabilities.

2. *Consolidations*. A statutory *consolidation* is identical to a statutory merger, except for the fact that in a merger one constituent fuses into another, while in a consolidation two (or more) constituents fuse to form a new corporation. Because the consolidation technique is seldom employed, and when employed is treated almost identically to a merger, no separate attention will be given in this Chapter to statutory consolidations.

3. *Short-Form and Small-Scale Mergers*. At one time, virtually all statutory mergers required approval by a majority or two-thirds vote of the outstanding shares of each constituent, and also triggered appraisal rights for the shareholders of each constituent. Many statutes now carve out exceptions to these requirements in the case of "short-form" and "small-scale" mergers. These types of merger will be considered in the next two sections.

---

## (2) SMALL–SCALE MERGERS

---

### DEL. GEN. CORP. LAW § 251(f)

[See Statutory Supplement]

---

**REV. MODEL BUS. CORP. ACT § 11.04(g)**

[See Statutory Supplement]

———

## R. Ward, E. Welch & A. Turezyn, Folk on the Delaware General Corporation Law § 251.2.1.1

(4th ed. 1999).

(1) [The requirement of Del. § 251(f) that the survivor's certificate of incorporation not be amended] is designed to assure that the merger technique cannot be used to deprive stockholders of the voting rights that they would enjoy if the certificate were being amended under section 242. . . .

(2) The theory underlying the . . . 20 percent limitation on increasing the number of common shares—is that a merger that involves less than 20 percent of the survivor's shares is not such a major change as to require a stockholder vote, and is really no more than an enlargement of the business that could be achieved by other means without triggering voting rights. For instance, a corporation purchasing assets need not secure approval of its stockholders to issue already authorized shares to the seller. Nor would voting rights exist if a corporation offered its own authorized shares in exchange for the shares of another corporation and thereby gained control, or if the corporation were to sell its authorized shares for cash and then use the proceeds of the sale to purchase assets. When business needs demand that the acquisition take the form of a merger rather than a purchase of assets or shares, the premise of the statute is that the merger should not require a stockholder vote when other procedures with nearly identical economic consequences do not require a stockholder vote. Stated otherwise, [§ 251(f)] puts mergers more on a parity with acquisition of assets or shares so far as the legal requirements are concerned.

———

## (3) SHORT–FORM MERGERS

———

**DEL. GEN. CORP. LAW § 253**

[See Statutory Supplement]

———

**REV. MODEL BUS. CORP. ACT § 11.05**

[See Statutory Supplement]

———

## NOTE ON SHORT–FORM MERGERS

Most of the major corporate statutes now include provisions authorizing the so-called short-form merger, under which certain parent-subsidiary mergers can be effected simply by vote of the parent's board—that is, without a vote of the parent's or the subsidiary's shareholders, without appraisal rights in the parent's shareholders, and frequently without a vote of the subsidiary's board. Most of the early short-form statutes were applicable only to mergers involving a parent and its 100–percent–owned subsidiary, and were probably conceived as procedural in nature, designed to simplify the mechanics of mergers. Today, however, the reach of short-form merger provisions has been substantively extended in two important ways. First, many such provisions are now applicable to mergers between parents and less–than–100–percent–owned subsidiaries: typically, although not invariably, the floor is set at 90 percent. Second, it has been held that the purpose of these statutes is to provide the parent corporation with a means of eliminating the minority shareholder's interest in the enterprise by issuing cash rather than stock to the minority. See e.g., Beloff v. Consolidated Edison Co., 300 N.Y. 11, 87 N.E.2d 561 (1949). To the extent this view is followed, these statutory provisions operate as *cash-out* rather than *merger* statutes. Furthermore, they are cash-out statutes that run in one direction only: the parent can force the minority to sell at any time, but the minority cannot force the parent to buy.

---

## (d) TAX AND ACCOUNTING ASPECTS OF CORPORATE COMBINATIONS

---

## NOTE ON THE TAX AND ACCOUNTING TREATMENT OF CORPORATE COMBINATIONS

1. *Tax Treatment.* Much is made of taxation as a principal motive for corporate combinations, but this factor, while significant, can be exaggerated. Whatever its role as a motive, however, taxation is often critical in determining *how* a combination will be effected. The principal issue is whether the combination will be tax-free—which means, essentially, that taxes on the transferor's gain will be postponed, that the basis in the stock or property received will remain the same, and that past operating losses of both companies can generally be carried over to apply against future earnings. See IRC §§ 354(a)(1), 358, 361(a), 381, 382.

In general, the Code provides three basic routes by which a tax-free combination—or, in tax parlance, a "reorganization"—can be achieved. These routes are popularly known as Type A, B, and C reorganizations, and are the tax counterparts of statutory mergers, stock-for-stock combinations, and stock-for-assets combinations, respectively.

a. A "Type A" reorganization—covered by IRC § 368(a)(1)(A)—is defined as a statutory merger or consolidation.

b. A "Type B" reorganization—covered by § 368(a)(1)(B)—is defined as the acquisition by one corporation, in exchange solely for all or part of its voting stock (or the voting stock of a parent corporation) of stock of another corporation, if the acquiring corporation has control of the acquired corporation immediately after the acquisition. Control is defined by § 368(c) as the ownership of stock possessing at least 80 percent of total combined voting power, plus at least 80 percent of the total number of shares of all other classes of stock.

c. A "Type C" reorganization—covered by § 368(a)(1)(C)—is defined as the acquisition by one corporation, in exchange for all or part of its voting stock (or the voting stock of a parent corporation), of substantially all the properties of another corporation.

In a Type B reorganization the consideration given by the acquiring corporation must consist solely of voting stock. In a Type C reorganization the consideration must consist primarily of voting stock, but the use of money or other property is permitted if at least 80 percent of the fair market value of all the property of the transferor corporation is acquired for voting stock.[1] Section 368(a)(1)(A), which covers Type A reorganizations, does not explicitly restrict the consideration issued by the survivor to voting stock, or indeed to stock. Thus the survivor in a statutory merger can use consideration other than voting stock—including bonds, nonvoting stock, short-term notes, and cash. However, if property other than "stock or securities" is permissibly issued to the transferor or its shareholders under a Type A or Type C reorganization, gain will be recognized in an amount not exceeding the value of this property or "boot." IRC § 356. Furthermore, under the "continuity of interest" doctrine, in a statutory merger the transferor's shareholders must receive a significant equity interest in the survivor if the merger is to qualify as a tax-free reorganization. See Treas.Reg. § 1.368–1(b), (c). In Helvering v. Minnesota Tea Co., 296 U.S. 378, 56 S.Ct. 269, 80 L.Ed. 284 (1935), the Supreme Court held that under this doctrine the equity issued to the transferor must represent a "substantial part of the value of the [transferred assets]" and that 56 percent was sufficient under this standard. See also May B. Kass, 60 T.C. 218, 1973 WL 2497 (1973) (16 percent insufficient); Yoc Heating Corp., 61 T.C. 168, 1973 WL 2680 (1973) (15 percent insufficient); Miller v. Commissioner, 84 F.2d 415 (6th Cir.1936) (25% sufficient). To ensure that a proposed transaction meets the continuity of interest requirement, the parties can describe the transaction to the Internal Revenue Service, and request the Service to issue a private letter ruling stating that the transaction qualifies as a tax-free reorgani-

---

**1.** IRC § 368(a)(2)(B). The survivor's assumption of the transferor's liabilities is not treated as money paid for the transferor's property unless the survivor uses consideration other than voting stock. Id.

zation. The Service will issue such a ruling if the transferor's share-holders will receive at least 50% of their consideration in the form of equity. Rev.Proc. 77–37, 1977–2 C.B. 568, § 3.02.

2. *Accounting Aspects.* Although in theory accounting statements should simply report the results of business decisions, in practice business decisions are frequently controlled by the manner in which they will be accounted for. This is nowhere more true than in the area of business combinations.

There are two basic methods of accounting for business combinations—purchase, and pooling of interests. Under the *purchase* method, a combination is accounted for as an acquisition by one corporation (herein called A) of another (herein called B). Accordingly, A records B's assets and liabilities at A's cost—i.e., the price A paid to effect the combination. If that price differs from the fair value of B's tangible assets minus B's liabilities, the difference is recorded as "goodwill." Under the *pooling of interests* method, a combination is accounted for as a uniting of ownership interests. Accordingly, A records B's assets at B's costs, and the assets, liabilities, and equity accounts of A and B are then carried forward at their combined historical or book values.

The two methods can be illustrated by the following example. Suppose A engages in a combination with B involving the issuance by A of $4000 in A common stock (with a par value of $400), in exchange for all of B's assets and the assumption by A of B's liabilities of $1000, i.e., a total price of $5000. A's business has a fair market value of $7000. B's business, if sold as a going concern, has a fair market value of $5000, and its physical assets have a fair market value of $3800 ($3300 plant and $500 inventory). The results under the pooling and purchase methods are as follows:

| | A's Pre–Combination Balance Sheet | B's Pre–Combination Balance Sheet | A's Post–Combination Balance Sheet Under Pooling Accounting | A's Post–Combination Balance Sheet Under Purchase Accounting |
|---|---|---|---|---|
| Plant | $800 | $2,000 | $2,800 | $4,100 |
| Inventory | $200 | $ 500 | $ 700 | $ 700 |
| Goodwill | — | — | — | $1,200 |
| Liabilities | $ 0 | $1,000 | $1,000 | $1,000 |
| Stated Capital | $500 | $ 700 | $ 900 (1) | $ 900 (1) |
| Capital Surplus | $300 | $ 0 | $ 600 (2) | $3,900 (4) |
| Earned Surplus | $200 | $ 800 | $1,000 (3) | $ 200 (5) |

Notes: (1) Under either purchase or pooling accounting, A adds to its stated capital the par value of the shares it issues to effect the combination.

(2) Under pooling accounting, A adds to its capital surplus the amount of B's equity ($1500), minus the increases in A's stated capital ($400) and earned surplus ($800).

(3) Under pooling accounting, A adds to its earned surplus the amount of B's earned surplus.

(4) Under purchase accounting, A adds to its capital surplus the value of the consideration received for its stock ($4000), minus the amount of that consideration allocated to stated capital ($400).

(5) Under purchase accounting, A's earned surplus is not increased by B's, since the transaction is treated as if A was acquiring assets, rather than combining.

Whether a business combination is treated under the purchase or pooling-of-interest method depends on the characteristics of the combining companies and the structure of the combination. Under Accounting Principles Board Opinion No. 16, the pooling method must be used if certain conditions are met. Among the most important of these conditions are the following: (1) The independent ownership interests of the combining companies must be combined in their entirety to continue previously separate operations. (2) The combination must be effected through the issuance of voting common stock in a manner that preserves all shareholders' equity interest in the combined company. (3) The combining companies must not plan to enter into any post-combination transactions that would be inconsistent with the objective of combining the common stockholders' entire existing interests. If a combination does not meet all three of these conditions, it must be accounted for under the purchase method.

———

## (e) THE STOCK MODES AND THE DE FACTO MERGER THEORY

We now pass to a consideration of two newer modes of corporate combination: stock-for-assets combinations and stock-for-stock combinations. In a *stock-for-assets* combination, Corporation A issues shares of its own stock to Corporation B in exchange for substantially all of B's assets. Often, in such a combination, A agrees to assume B's liabilities. In some cases, however, A may assume B's liabilities on only a selective basis. (Indeed, one reason for using this mode in preference to a statutory merger may be A's desire to avoid assuming all of B's liabilities.) Usually, B agrees that upon completion of the exchange it will dissolve and distribute its stock in A to its own shareholders. (The major reason for this is that A does not want a large block of its stock concentrated in a single holder.) Frequently, it is also agreed or understood that some or all of B's officers and directors will join A's management.

In a *stock-for-stock* combination, Corporation A issues shares of its own stock directly to the shareholders of Corporation B in exchange for an amount of B stock—normally at least a majority—sufficient to carry control. By virtue of such a combination the shareholder groups of the two corporations are combined to a substantial extent, and B becomes a subsidiary of A. Frequently B is then liquidated or merged into A, but whether or not this occurs, B's assets will be under A's control. Such a combination does not require approval by B's management (since corporate action by B is not required). Often, however, the terms of the exchange of stock are worked out beforehand by the managements of both corporations, and often too, it is agreed or understood that some or all of B's management will stay on with B in its new role as a subsidiary, or will join Corporation A itself.

There has been a sharp division of opinion on the issue, how to characterize such combinations. Take, for example, a stock-for-assets combination in which A acquires substantially all of the assets of B in exchange for A's common stock; A assumes all of B's liabilities; and B agrees to dissolve, and to distribute to its shareholders the A common stock it receives.

One possible way to view such a combination is as a de facto merger. This is the position taken in Farris v. Glen Alden Corp., infra. If the combination is viewed as a de facto merger, then in the normal case (that is, in the absence of some special exception) it requires a vote of A's shareholders and B's shareholders, and triggers appraisal rights in A's shareholders and B's shareholders.

Alternatively, the transaction could be characterized as a purchase by A and a sale of substantially all assets by B. That is the position taken in Hariton v. Arco Electronics Corp., infra. Under the corporate statutes, a purchase does not require shareholder approval and does not trigger appraisal rights. Therefore, if the combination is treated as a purchase by A, it neither requires a vote of A's shareholders nor triggers appraisal rights for those shareholders—although it would have required a shareholder vote, and triggered appraisal rights, if it had been characterized as a merger.

Now turn to B's shareholders. Under the corporate statutes, a sale of substantially all assets, unlike a purchase, does require shareholder approval. Therefore, unlike the case with A, the combination will require the approval of B's shareholders. Furthermore, most statutes provide that if a corporation sells substantially all of its assets, the transaction triggers appraisal rights in the corporation's shareholders. Therefore, B's shareholders, unlike A's shareholders, will usually have appraisal rights. Howsoever, under some statutes, most notably the Delaware statute, a sale of substantially all assets does not trigger appraisal rights. Under such statutes, if a stock-for-assets combination is treated as a purchase by A and a sale by B, rather than as a merger of A and B, B's shareholders will not have appraisal rights, although they would have had appraisal rights if the transaction had been characterized as a merger.

---

# Hariton v. Arco Electronics, Inc.

Supreme Court of Delaware, 1963.
41 Del.Ch. 74, 188 A.2d 123.

■ SOUTHERLAND, CHIEF JUSTICE: This case involves a sale of assets under § 271 of the corporation law, 8 Del.C. It presents for decision the question presented, but not decided, in Heilbrunn v. Sun Chemical Corporation, 38 Del.Ch. 321, 150 A.2d 755. It may be stated as follows:

A sale of assets is effected under § 271 in consideration of shares of stock of the purchasing corporation. The agreement of sale embodies also a plan to dissolve the selling corporation and distribute the shares so received to the stockholders of the seller, so as to accomplish the same result as would be accomplished by a merger of the seller into the purchaser. Is the sale legal?

The facts are these:

The defendant Arco and Loral Electronics Corporation, a New York corporation, are both engaged, in somewhat different forms, in the electronic equipment business. In the summer of 1961 they negotiated for an amalgamation of the companies. As of October 27, 1961, they entered into a "Reorganization Agreement and Plan." The provisions of this Plan pertinent here are in substance as follows:

1.   Arco agrees to sell all its assets to Loral in consideration (*inter alia*) of the issuance to it of 283,000 shares of Loral.

2.   Arco agrees to call a stockholders meeting for the purpose of approving the Plan and the voluntary dissolution.

3.   Arco agrees to distribute to its stockholders all the Loral shares received by it as a part of the complete liquidation of Arco.*

At the Arco meeting all the stockholders voting (about 80%) approved the Plan. It was thereafter consummated.

Plaintiff, a stockholder who did not vote at the meeting, sued to enjoin the consummation of the Plan on the grounds (1) that it was illegal, and (2) that it was unfair. The second ground was abandoned. Affidavits and documentary evidence were filed, and defendant moved for summary judgment and dismissal of the complaint. The Vice Chancellor granted the motion and plaintiff appeals.

The question before us we have stated above. Plaintiff's argument that the sale is illegal runs as follows:

The several steps taken here accomplish the same result as a merger of Arco into Loral. In a "true" sale of assets, the stockholder of the seller retains the right to elect whether the selling company shall continue as a holding company. Moreover, the stockholder of the selling company is forced to accept an investment in a new enterprise without the right of appraisal granted under the merger statute. § 271 cannot therefore be legally combined with a dissolution proceeding under § 275 and a consequent distribution of the purchaser's stock. Such a proceeding is a misuse of the power granted under § 271, and a *de facto* merger results.

---

* According to the Vice Chancellor's opinion below, 40 Del.Ch. 326, 182 A.2d 22 (1962), the agreement also provided that Loral would assume and pay all of Arco's debts and liabilities, and that after the closing date Arco would not engage in any business or activity except as might be required to complete the liquidation and dissolution of Arco. (Footnote by ed.)

The foregoing is a brief summary of plaintiff's contention.

Plaintiff's contention that this sale has achieved the same result as a merger is plainly correct. The same contention was made to us in Heilbrunn v. Sun Chemical Corporation, 38 Del.Ch. 321, 150 A.2d 755. Accepting it as correct, we noted that this result is made possible by the overlapping scope of the merger statute and section 271, mentioned in Sterling v. Mayflower Hotel Corporation, 33 Del.Ch. 293, 93 A.2d 107, 38 A.L.R.2d 425. We also adverted to the increased use, in connection with corporate reorganization plans, of § 271 instead of the merger statute. Further, we observed that no Delaware case has held such procedure to be improper, and that two cases appear to assume its legality. Finch v. Warrior Cement Corporation, 16 Del.Ch. 44, 141 A. 54, and Argenbright v. Phoenix Finance Co., 21 Del.Ch. 288, 187 A. 124. But we were not required in the *Heilbrunn* case to decide the point.

We now hold that the reorganization here accomplished through § 271 and a mandatory plan of dissolution and distribution is legal. This is so because the sale-of-assets statute and the merger statute are independent of each other. They are, so to speak, of equal dignity, and the framers of a reorganization plan may resort to either type of corporate mechanics to achieve the desired end. This is not an anomalous result in our corporation law. As the Vice Chancellor pointed out, the elimination of accrued dividends, though forbidden under a charter amendment (Keller v. Wilson & Co., 21 Del.Ch. 391, 190 A. 115) may be accomplished by a merger. Federal United Corporation v. Havender, 24 Del.Ch. 318, 11 A.2d 331.

In Langfelder v. Universal Laboratories, D.C., 68 F.Supp. 209, Judge Leahy commented upon "the general theory of the Delaware Corporation Law that action taken pursuant to the authority of the various sections of that law constitute acts of independent legal significance and their validity is not dependent on other sections of the Act." 68 F.Supp. 211, footnote.

In support of his contentions of a *de facto* merger plaintiff cites Finch v. Warrior Cement Corporation, 16 Del.Ch. 44, 141 A. 54, and Drug Inc. v. Hunt, 5 W.W.Harr. 339, 35 Del. 339, 168 A. 87. They are patently inapplicable. Each involved a disregard of the statutory provisions governing sales of assets. Here it is admitted that the provisions of the statute were fully complied with.

Plaintiff concedes, as we read his brief, that if the several steps taken in this case had been taken separately they would have been legal. That is, he concedes that a sale of assets, followed by a separate proceeding to dissolve and distribute, would be legal, even though the same result would follow. This concession exposes the weakness of his contention. To attempt to make any such distinction between sales under § 271 would be to create uncertainty in the law and invite litigation.

We are in accord with the Vice Chancellor's ruling, and the judgment below is affirmed.

———

## Farris v. Glen Alden Corp.

Supreme Court of Pennsylvania, 1958.
393 Pa. 427, 143 A.2d 25.

■ COHEN, JUSTICE. We are required to determine on this appeal whether, as a result of a "Reorganization Agreement" executed by the officers of Glen Alden Corporation and List Industries Corporation, and approved by the shareholders of the former company, the rights and remedies of a dissenting shareholder accrue to the plaintiff.

Glen Alden is a Pennsylvania corporation engaged principally in the mining of anthracite coal and lately in the manufacture of air conditioning units and fire-fighting equipment. In recent years the company's operating revenue has declined substantially, and in fact, its coal operations have resulted in tax loss carryovers of approximately $14,000,000. In October 1957, List, a Delaware holding company owning interests in motion picture theaters, textile companies and real estate, and to a lesser extent, in oil and gas operations, warehouses and aluminum piston manufacturing, purchased through a wholly owned subsidiary 38.5% of Glen Alden's outstanding stock.[1] This acquisition enabled List to place three of its directors on the Glen Alden board.

On March 20, 1958, the two corporations entered into a "reorganization agreement," subject to stockholder approval, which contemplated the following actions:

1.   Glen Alden is to acquire all of the assets of List, excepting a small amount of cash reserved for the payment of List's expenses in connection with the transaction. These assets include over $8,000,000 in cash held chiefly in the treasuries of List's wholly owned subsidiaries.

2.   In consideration of the transfer, Glen Alden is to issue 3,621,-703 shares of stock to List. List in turn is to distribute the stock to its shareholders at a ratio of five shares of Glen Alden stock for each six shares of List stock. In order to accomplish the necessary distribution, Glen Alden is to increase the authorized number of its shares of capital stock from 2,500,000 shares to 7,500,000 shares without according preemptive rights to the present shareholders upon the issuance of any such shares.

3.   Further, Glen Alden is to assume all of List's liabilities including a $5,000,000 note incurred by List in order to purchase Glen Alden stock in 1957, outstanding stock options, incentive stock options plans, and pension obligations.

_____

1.   Of the purchase price of $8,719,109,
$5,000,000 was borrowed.

4.   Glen Alden is to change its corporate name from Glen Alden Corporation to List Alden Corporation.

5.   The present directors of both corporations are to become directors of List Alden.

6.   List is to be dissolved and List Alden is to then carry on the operations of both former corporations.

Two days after the agreement was executed notice of the annual meeting of Glen Alden to be held on April 11, 1958, was mailed to the shareholders together with a proxy statement analyzing the reorganization agreement and recommending its approval as well as approval of certain amendments to Glen Alden's articles of incorporation and bylaws necessary to implement the agreement. At this meeting the holders of a majority of the outstanding shares, (not including those owned by List), voted in favor of a resolution approving the reorganization agreement.

On the day of the shareholders' meeting, plaintiff, a shareholder of Glen Alden, filed a complaint in equity against the corporation and its officers seeking to enjoin them temporarily until final hearing, and perpetually thereafter, from executing and carrying out the agreement.

The gravamen of the complaint was that the notice of the annual shareholders' meeting did not conform to the requirements of the Business Corporation Law, 15 P.S. § 2852–1 et seq., in three respects: (1) It did not give notice to the shareholders that the true intent and purpose of the meeting was to effect a merger or consolidation of Glen Alden and List; (2) It failed to give notice to the shareholders of their right to dissent to the plan of merger or consolidation and claim fair value for their shares, and (3) It did not contain copies of the text of certain sections of the Business Corporation Law as required.[3]

By reason of these omissions, plaintiff contended that the approval of the reorganization agreement by the shareholders at the annual meeting was invalid and unless the carrying out of the plan were enjoined, he would suffer irreparable loss by being deprived of substantial property rights.

The defendants answered admitting the material allegations of fact in the complaint but denying that they gave rise to a cause of action because the transaction complained of was a purchase of corporate assets as to which shareholders had no rights of dissent or appraisal. For these reasons the defendants then moved for judgment on the pleadings.[4]

**3.**  The proxy statement included the following declaration: "Appraisal Rights.

"In the opinion of counsel, the shareholders of neither Glen Alden nor List Industries will have any rights of appraisal or similar rights of dissenters with respect to any matter to be acted upon at their respective meetings."

**4.**  Counsel for the defendants concedes that if the corporation is required to pay the dissenting shareholders the appraised fair value of their shares, the resultant drain of cash would prevent Glen Alden from carrying out the agreement. On the other hand, plaintiff contends that if the shareholders had been told of their rights as dissenters, rather than specifically advised that they had no such rights, the resolution approving the reorganization agreement would have been defeated.

The court below concluded that the reorganization agreement entered into between the two corporations was a plan for a *de facto* merger, and that therefore the failure of the notice of the annual meeting to conform to the pertinent requirements of the merger provisions of the Business Corporation Law rendered the notice defective and all proceedings in furtherance of the agreement void. Wherefore, the court entered a final decree denying defendants' motion for judgment on the pleadings, entering judgment upon plaintiff's complaint and granting the injunctive relief therein sought. This appeal followed.

When use of the corporate form of business organization first became widespread, it was relatively easy for courts to define a "merger" or a "sale of assets" and to label a particular transaction as one or the other. See, e.g., 15 Fletcher, Corporations §§ 7040–7045 (rev. vol. 1938); In re Buist's Estate, 1929, 297 Pa. 537, 541, 147 A. 606; Koehler v. St. Mary's Brewing Co., 1910, 228 Pa. 648, 653–654, 77 A. 1016. But prompted by the desire to avoid the impact of adverse, and to obtain the benefits of favorable, government regulations, particularly federal tax laws, new accounting and legal techniques were developed by lawyers and accountants which interwove the elements characteristic of each, thereby creating hybrid forms of corporate amalgamation. Thus, it is no longer helpful to consider an individual transaction in the abstract and solely by reference to the various elements therein determine whether it is a "merger" or a "sale". Instead, to determine properly the nature of a corporate transaction, we must refer not only to all the provisions of the agreement, but also to the consequences of the transaction and to the purposes of the provisions of the corporation law said to be applicable. We shall apply this principle to the instant case.

Section 908, subd. A of the Pennsylvania Business Corporation Law provides: "If any shareholder of a domestic corporation which becomes a party to a plan of merger or consolidation shall object to such plan of merger or consolidation . . . such shareholder shall be entitled to . . . [the fair value of his shares upon surrender of the share certificate or certificates representing his shares]." Act of May 5, 1933, P.L. 364, as amended, 15 P.S. § 2852–908, subd. A.[5]

This provision had its origin in the early decision of this Court in Lauman v. Lebanon Valley R.R. Co., 1858, 30 Pa. 42. There a shareholder who objected to the consolidation of his company with another was held to have a right in the absence of statute to treat the consolidation as a dissolution of his company and to receive the value of his shares upon their surrender.

---

**5.** Furthermore, section 902, subd. B provides that notice of the proposed merger and of the right to dissent thereto must be given the shareholders. "There shall be included in, or enclosed with . . . notice [of meeting of shareholders to vote on plan of merger] a copy or a summary of the plan of merger or plan of consolidation, as the case may be, and . . . a copy of subsection A of section 908 and of subsections B, C and D of section 515 of this act." Act of May 5, 1933, P.L. 364, § 902, subd. B, as amended, 15 P.S. § 2852–902, subd. B.

The rationale of the Lauman case, and of the present section of the Business Corporation Law based thereon, is that when a corporation combines with another so as to lose its essential nature and alter the original fundamental relationships of the shareholders among themselves and to the corporation, a shareholder who does not wish to continue his membership therein may treat his membership in the original corporation as terminated and have the value of his shares paid to him. See Lauman v. Lebanon Vally R.R. Co., supra, 30 Pa. at pages 46–47. See also Bloch v. Baldwin Locomotive Works, C.P., Del.1950, 75 Pa.Dist. & Co.R. 24, 35–38.

Does the combination outlined in the present "reorganization" agreement so fundamentally change the corporate character of Glen Alden and the interest of the plaintiff as a shareholder therein, that to refuse him the rights and remedies of a dissenting shareholder would in reality force him to give up his stock in one corporation and against his will accept shares in another? If so, the combination is a merger within the meaning of section 908, subd. A of the corporation law. See Bloch v. Baldwin Locomotive Works, supra. Cf. Marks v. Autocar Co., E.D.Pa.1954, 153 F.Supp. 768. See also Troupiansky v. Henry Disston & Sons, E.D.Pa.1957, 151 F.Supp. 609.

If the reorganization agreement were consummated plaintiff would find that the "List Alden" resulting from the amalgamation would be quite a different corporation than the "Glen Alden" in which he is now a shareholder. Instead of continuing primarily as a coal mining company, Glen Alden would be transformed, after amendment of its articles of incorporation, into a diversified holding company whose interests would range from motion picture theaters to textile companies. Plaintiff would find himself a member of a company with assets of $169,000,000 and a long-term debt of $38,000,000 in lieu of a company one-half that size and with but one-seventh the long-term debt.

While the administration of the operations, and properties of Glen Alden as well as List would be in the hands of management common to both companies, since all executives of List would be retained in List Alden, the control of Glen Alden would pass to the directors of List; for List would hold eleven of the seventeen directorships on the new board of directors.

As an aftermath of the transaction plaintiff's proportionate interest in Glen Alden would have been reduced to only two-fifths of what it presently is because of the issuance of an additional 3,621,703 shares to List which would not be subject to pre-emptive rights. In fact, ownership of Glen Alden would pass to the stockholders of List who would hold 76.5% of the outstanding shares as compared with but 23.5% retained by the present Glen Alden shareholders.

Perhaps the most important consequence to the plaintiff, if he were denied the right to have his shares redeemed at their fair value, would be the serious financial loss suffered upon consummation of the agreement. While the present book value of his stock is $38 a share after combination it would be worth only $21 a share. In contrast, the shareholders of List who presently hold stock with a total book value of $33,000,000 or $7.50 a share, would receive stock with a book value of $76,000,000 or $21 a share.

Under these circumstances it may well be said that if the proposed combination is allowed to take place without right of dissent, plaintiff would have his stock in Glen Alden taken away from him and the stock of a new company thrust upon him in its place. He would be projected against his will into a new enterprise under terms not of his own choosing. It was to protect dissident shareholders against just such a result that this Court one hundred years ago in the *Lauman* case, and the legislature thereafter in section 908, subd. A, granted the right of dissent. And it is to accord that protection to the plaintiff that we conclude that the combination proposed in the case at hand is a merger within the intendment of section 908, subd. A.

Nevertheless, defendants contend that the 1957 amendments to sections 311 and 908 of the corporation law preclude us from reaching this result and require the entry of judgment in their favor. Subsection F of section 311 dealing with the voluntary transfer of corporate assets provides: "The shareholders of a business corporation which acquires by sale, lease or exchange all or substantially all of the property of another corporation by the issuance of stock, securities or otherwise shall not be entitled to the rights and remedies of dissenting shareholders...." Act of July 11, 1957, P.L. 711, § 1, 15 P.S. § 2852–311, subd. F.

And the amendment to section 908 reads as follows: "The right of dissenting shareholders ... shall not apply to the purchase by a corporation of assets whether or not the consideration therefor be money or property, real or personal, including shares of bonds or other evidences of indebtedness of such corporation. The shareholders of such corporation shall have no right to dissent from any such purchase." Act of July 11, 1957, P.L. 711, § 1, 15 P.S. § 2852–908, subd. C.

Defendants view these amendments as abridging the right of shareholders to dissent to a transaction between two corporations which involves a transfer of assets for a consideration even though the transfer has all the legal incidents of a merger. They claim that only if the merger is accomplished in accordance with the prescribed statutory procedure does the right of dissent accrue. In support of this position they cite to us the comment on the amendments by the Committee on Corporation Law of the Pennsylvania Bar Association, the committee which originally drafted these provisions. The comment states that the provisions were intended to overrule cases which granted shareholders the right to dissent to a sale of assets when accompanied by the legal incidents of a merger. See 61 Ann.Rep.Pa.Bar Ass'n. 277, 284 (1957). Whatever may have been the intent of the *committee,* there is no evidence to indicate that the *legislature* intended the 1957 amendments to have the effect contended for. But furthermore, the language of these two provisions does not support the opinion of the committee and is inept to achieve any such purpose. The amendments of 1957 do not provide that a transaction between two corporations which has the effect of a merger but which includes a transfer of assets for consideration is to be exempt from the protective provisions of sections 908, subd. A and 515. They provide only that the shareholders of a corporation which acquires the property or purchases the assets of another corporation, *without more,* are not entitled to the right to dissent from the transaction. So, as in the present case, when as part of a transaction between two corporations, one corporation dissolves, its liabilities are assumed by the survivor, its executives and directors take over the management and control of the survivor, and, as consideration for the transfer, its stockholders acquire a majority of the shares of stock of the survivor, then the transaction is no longer simply a purchase of assets or acquisition of property to which sections 311, subd. F and 908, subd. C apply, but a merger governed by section 908, subd. A of the corporation law. To divest shareholders of their right of dissent under such circumstances would require express language which is absent from the 1957 amendments.

Even were we to assume that the combination provided for in the reorganization agreement is a "sale of assets" to which section 908, subd. A does not apply, it would avail the defendants nothing; we will not blind our eyes to the realities of the transaction. Despite the designation of the parties and the form employed, Glen Alden does not in fact acquire List, rather, List acquires Glen Alden, cf. Metropolitan Edison Co. v. Commissioner, 3 Cir., 1938, 98 F.2d 807, affirmed sub nom., Helvering v. Metropolitan Edison Co., 1939, 306 U.S. 522, 59 S.Ct. 634, 83 L.Ed. 957, and under section 311, subd. D[8] the right of dissent would remain with the shareholders of Glen Alden.

We hold that the combination contemplated by the reorganization agreement, although consummated by contract rather than in accordance with the statutory procedure, is a merger within the protective purview of sections 908, subd. A and 515 of the corporation law. The shareholders of Glen Alden should have been notified accordingly and advised of their statutory rights of dissent and appraisal. The failure of the corporate officers to take these steps renders the stockholder approval of the agreement at the 1958 shareholders' meeting invalid. The lower court did not err in enjoining the officers and directors of Glen Alden from carrying out this agreement.

Decree affirmed at appellants' costs.

--------

**8.** "If any shareholder of a business corporation which sells, leases or exchanges all or substantially all of its property and assets otherwise than (1) in the usual and regular course of its business, (2) for the purpose of relocating its business, or (3) in connection with its dissolution and liquidation, shall object to such sale, lease or exchange and comply with the provisions of section 515 of this act, such shareholder shall be entitled to the rights and remedies of dissenting shareholders as therein provided."
. . .

## NOTE ON FARRIS

1. *Reasons for the Form in Which the Transaction was Cast.* It is clear that a major reason for structuring the transaction in *Farris* as a stock-for-assets combination, rather than as a statutory merger, was to avoid conferring appraisal rights on the Glen Alden shareholders. But given the stock-for-assets mode, why did the parties also use an upside-down format, in which the smaller corporation nominally purchased the larger corporation's assets? Why didn't the parties arrange the transaction in a more natural way, by having the larger corporation, List, issue shares for assets of the smaller corporation, Glen Alden?

Again, one reason had to do with appraisal rights. List was a Delaware corporation. Under Delaware law, in a purchase and sale of assets neither the purchaser's shareholders nor the seller's shareholders had appraisal rights. Under Pennsylvania law, however, a seller's shareholders did have appraisal rights, while a purchaser's did not—or so counsel thought. Therefore, by making List the nominal seller and Glen Alden the nominal purchaser, the parties hoped to avoid giving appraisal rights to the shareholders of either corporation.

A second reason for the upside-down format may have been a desire to keep alive Glen Alden's tax loss carryover. While the rules governing the survival of such carryovers were complex, in general survival was more likely if the entity of the carryover corporation was left intact.

A third reason is given in the Supplemental Brief for Appellee: "In answer to the question of Mr. Justice Bell as to why List did not purchase the assets of Glen Alden, Mr. Littleton answered that the one percent Pennsylvania realty tax on the transfer of [the huge coal-mining] holdings of Glen Alden would make such a sale prohibitive."

Following the decision in Farris v. Glen Alden, the two corporations were combined pursuant to a statutory merger. Probably for some of the reasons just given, Glen Alden was the surviving corporation. The List shareholders received one Glen Alden share for each List share, and the Glen Alden shareholders ended up with five Glen Alden shares for each four they had previously held. New York Times, March 7, 1959; Moody's Industrial Manual 954 (1972).

2. *Subsequent Legislation.* After the decision in *Farris*, Pa. §§ 311(F) and 908(B) were amended, and now read as follows:

§ [311]. Voluntary Transfer of Corporate Assets . . .

F. The shareholders of a business corporation which acquires by purchase, lease or exchange all or substantially all of the property of another corporation by the issuance of shares, evidences of indebtedness or otherwise, with or without assuming the liabilities of such other corporation, shall be entitled to the rights and remedies of dissenting shareholders provided in . . . this act, if any, if, but only if, such acquisition shall have been accomplished by the issuance of voting shares of such corporation to be outstanding immediately after the acquisition sufficient to elect a majority of the directors of the corporation.

§ [908]. Rights of Dissenting Shareholders . . .

B.   Where a corporation acquires assets by purchase, lease or exchange, by the issuance of shares, evidences of indebtedness or otherwise, with or without assuming liabilities other than by the procedure for merger or consolidation prescribed in this Article IX, the rights, if any, of dissenting shareholders shall be governed by section [1311] and not by this section.

---

### NEW YORK STOCK EXCHANGE, LISTED COMPANY MANUAL § 312.00

[See Statutory Supplement]

---

### CAL. CORP. CODE §§ 152, 160, 168, 181, 187, 194.5, 1001, 1101, 1200, 1201, 1300

[See Statutory Supplement]

---

### REV. MODEL BUS. CORP. ACT § 6.21(f)

[See Statutory Supplement]

---

## (f) TRIANGULAR MERGERS AND SHARE EXCHANGES

---

## Terry v. Penn Central Corp.

United States Court of Appeals, Third Circuit, 1981.
668 F.2d 188.

■ Before ADAMS, MARIS and HIGGINBOTHAM, CIRCUIT JUDGES. . . .

■ ADAMS, CIRCUIT JUDGE.

The Penn Central Corporation ("Penn Central"), an appellee in this case, has sought to acquire Colt Industries Inc. ("Colt"), also an appellee, by merging Colt with PCC Holdings, Inc. ("Holdings"), a wholly-owned subsidiary of Penn Central. Howard L. Terry and W.H. Hunt, the appellants, are shareholders of Penn Central who objected to the transaction. In a diversity action before the United States District Court for the Eastern District of Pennsylvania, appellants sought injunctive and declaratory relief to enforce voting and dissenters' rights to which appellants asserted they were entitled. Appellants further sought to enjoin Holdings from proceeding with the proposed merger, and in particular moved to enjoin a vote on the transaction, scheduled for October 29, 1981, by the shareholders of Penn Central. In an opinion issued on October 22, 1981, Judge Pollak denied appellants' requests. Appellants thereupon filed an appeal in this Court, and then petitioned for a temporary injunction against the proposed shareholder vote until the appeal on the merits of the district court order could be heard. On October 27, following oral argument, we entered an order denying the petition for temporary injunction, stating that appellants had failed to demonstrate a sufficient likelihood of prevailing on the merits. C.A. No. 81–3955. The shareholders of Penn Central voted, as scheduled, on October 29. Pursuant to an expedited hearing schedule, the appeal from the district court's denial of injunctive and declaratory relief was submitted to this Court following oral argument on November 5.

After argument on appeal, the shareholders disapproved of the merger, and the corporations thereafter publicly announced their abandonment of this particular merger. Penn Central, however, has not abandoned its proposed series of acquisitions, of which the Colt acquisition was merely one instance.

## I.

Penn Central is the successor to the Penn Central Transportation Corporation, which underwent a reorganization under the bankruptcy laws that was completed in 1978. No longer involved in the railroading business, Penn Central, since 1978, has had the advantage, for tax purposes, of a large loss carry-forward. In order to put that loss carry-forward to its best use, Penn Central has embarked on a program of acquiring corporations whose profits could be sheltered. To this end Penn Central created Holdings, a wholly-owned subsidiary which was to acquire the businesses that Penn Central desired. The first acquisition under the plan was Marathon Manufacturing Company ("Marathon"), in 1979. In the Marathon acquisition, a class of preferred Penn Central stock was created, and 30 million shares of "First Series Preference Stock" was issued to the owners of Marathon stock. Appellants were shareholders of Marathon who thereby obtained shares of this First Series Preference Stock. Terry was promptly elected to the Penn Central board of directors.

In 1981, Penn Central decided upon another acquisition: Colt. The management and directors of Colt and Penn Central agreed upon a merger of Colt into Holdings, compensated for by issuance of a second series of Penn Central preference stock to Colt shareholders. Terry opposed the merger at the directors' meeting, and sought to preclude the consummation of the transaction.

. . . [A]ppellants argue that under Pennsylvania's corporate law, they are entitled to dissent and appraisal rights if the merger is adopted over their opposition.[2] . . .

Because Colt and Penn Central have now announced their abandonment of the proposed merger, the request for injunctive relief considered by the district court is now conceded by all parties to be moot. However, the appellants' request for declaratory relief, which the appellants now contend is moot as well, involves legal questions that go to Penn Central's plan of acquisitions, rather than to the Colt transaction alone, and these questions appear likely to recur in future disputes between the parties here. . . . In a case such as this, a voluntary termination by the parties of the specific activity challenged in the lawsuit—here, the proposed treatment of the dissenting preferred shareholders in the Colt–Holdings plan—does not render the action moot because there is "a reasonable likelihood that the parties or those in privity with them will be involved in a suit on the same issues in the future." American Bible Society v. Blount, 446 F.2d 588, 595 (3d Cir.1971) . . . .

### III.

Terry and Hunt contend that under Pennsylvania law they are entitled to dissent and appraisal rights if a merger is approved by the Penn Central shareholders. As the district court concluded, this assertion is unsupported by Pennsylvania statute or caselaw. Sitting as a court in diversity, we are not at liberty to diverge from the outcome that the Pennsylvania legislature and the Pennsylvania courts prescribe. Briefly, appellants' argument is that the proposed merger between Holdings and Colt constitutes a *de facto* merger between Colt and Penn Central, and that the Penn Central shareholders are therefore entitled to the protections for dissenting shareholders that Pennsylvania corporate law provides for shareholders of parties to a merger. Although this reasoning, with its emphasis on the substance of the transaction rather than its formal trappings, may be attractive as a matter of policy, see, e.g., Note, Three–Party Mergers: The Fourth Form of Corporate Acquisition, 57 Va.L.Rev. 1242 (1971), it contravenes the language employed by the Pennsylvania legislature in setting out the rights of shareholders.

Section 908 of the Pennsylvania Business Corporation Law (PBCL), 15 P.S. § 1908, provides that shareholders of corporations that are parties to a plan of merger are entitled to dissent and appraisal rights, but adds that for an acquisition other than such a merger, the only rights are those provided for in Section 311 of the PBCL, 15 P.S. § 1311 (Purdon 1967 & Supp.1981–82). Section 311, in turn, provides for dissent and appraisal rights only when an acquisi-

---

**2.** In addition, appellants claim a right under Pennsylvania law to require approval of an absolute majority vote of the shares outstanding on the proposed merger, relying on § 902(B) of the Pennsylvania Business Corporation Law (PBCL), 15 P.S. § 1902(B) (Purdon Supp.1981–82). For the reasons discussed in Part III of this opinion, we conclude that Penn Central is not a "party" to the merger, within the technical meaning of the term under that section and the related Section 908 of the PBCL, 15 P.S. § 1908 (Purdon Supp.1981–82). Accordingly, section 902 does not apply to the Penn Central vote on the merger.

tion has been accomplished by "the issuance of voting shares of such corporation to be outstanding immediately after the acquisition sufficient to elect a majority of the directors of the corporation." In this case the shares of Penn Central stock to be issued in the Colt transaction do not exceed the number of shares already existing, and thus the transaction is not covered by Section 311. Any statutory dissent and appraisal rights for Penn Central shareholders are therefore contingent upon Penn Central's status as a party to the merger within the meaning of Section 908. And as the district court points out, the PBCL describes the parties to a merger as those entities that are *actually* combined into a single corporation. Section 907, 15 P.S. § 1907 (Purdon Supp.1981–82), states that:

> Upon the merger or consolidation becoming effective, the several corporations parties to the plan of merger or consolidation shall be a single corporation which, in the case of a merger, shall be that corporation designated in the plan of merger as the surviving corporation. . . .

At the consummation of the proposed merger plan here, both Holdings and Penn Central would survive as separate entities, and it would therefore appear that Penn Central is not a party within the meaning of ... Section 907. We can discern no reason to infer that the legislature intended the word "party" to have different meanings in Sections 907 and 908, and accordingly conclude that Penn Central is not a party to the merger.

Appellants argue that Penn Central is nevertheless brought into the amalgamation by the *de facto* merger doctrine as set out in Pennsylvania law in Farris v. Glen Alden Corp., 393 Pa. 427, 143 A.2d 25 (1958). *Farris* was the penultimate step in a *pas de deux* involving the Pennsylvania courts and the Pennsylvania legislature regarding the proper treatment for transactions that reached the same practical result as a merger but avoided the legal form of merger and the concomitant legal obligations. In the 1950s the Pennsylvania courts advanced the doctrine that a transaction having the effect of an amalgamation would be treated as a *de facto* merger. See, e.g., Bloch v. The Baldwin Locomotive Works, 75 Pa.D. & C. 24 (1951). The legislature responded with efforts to constrict the *de facto* merger doctrine. *Farris,* addressing those efforts, held that the doctrine still covered a reorganization agreement that had the effect of merging a large corporation into a smaller corporation. In a 1959 response to *Farris,* the legislature made explicit its objection to earlier cases that found certain transactions to be *de facto* mergers. The legislature enacted a law, modifying *inter alia* Sections 311 and 908, entitled in part:

> An Act ... changing the law as to ... the acquisition or transfer of corporate assets, the rights of dissenting shareholders, ... abolishing the doctrine of de facto mergers or consolidation and reversing the rules laid down in *Bloch v. Baldwin Locomotive Works,* 75 Pa. D. & C. 24, and *Marks v. The Autocar Co.,* 153 F.Supp. 768, . . . .

Act of November 10, 1959 (P.L. 1406, No. 502).

Following this explicit statement, the *de facto* merger doctrine has rarely been invoked by the Pennsylvania courts. Only once has the Pennsylvania Supreme Court made reference to it, in In re Jones & Laughlin Steel Corp., 488 Pa. 524, 412 A.2d 1099 (1980). Even there, the Court's reference was oblique. It merely cited *Farris* for the proposition that shareholders have the right to enjoin "proposed unfair or fraudulent corporate actions." 488 Pa. at 533, 412 A.2d at 1104. This Court, sitting in diversity in Knapp v. North American Rockwell Corp., 506 F.2d 361 (3d Cir.1974), cert. denied, 421 U.S. 965, 95 S.Ct. 1955, 44 L.Ed.2d 452 (1975), made reference to the *de facto* merger doctrine to hold that a transaction structured as a sale of assets could nevertheless be deemed a merger for purposes of requiring the merging corporation to assume the acquired corporation's liability for damages to a worker who was injured by a faulty piece of equipment manufactured by the acquired company....

None of [the] cases persuades us that a Pennsylvania court would apply the *de facto* merger doctrine to the situation before us. Although *Jones & Laughlin Steel* suggests that dissent and appraisal rights might be available if fraud or fundamental unfairness were shown, we are not faced with such a situation. No allegation of fraud has been advanced, and the only allegation of fundamental unfairness is that the appellants will, if the merger is consummated, be forced into what they consider a poor investment on the part of Penn Central without the opportunity to receive an appraised value for their stock. Even if appellants' evaluation of the merits of the proposed merger is accurate, poor business judgment on the part of management would not be enough to constitute unfairness cognizable by a court. And the denial of appraisal rights to dissenters cannot constitute fundamental unfairness, or the *de facto* merger doctrine would apply in every instance in which dissenters' rights were sought and the 1959 amendments by the legislature would be rendered nugatory.[7] ...

In the absence of any explicit guidance to the contrary by the Pennsylvania courts, we conclude that the language of the legislature in 1959 precludes a decision that the transaction in this case constitutes a *de facto* merger sufficient to entitle Penn Central shareholders to dissent and appraisal rights. We therefore hold that appellants do not possess such rights if a transaction such as the one involved here is consummated....

---

## NOTE ON TRIANGULAR MERGERS AND SHARE EXCHANGES

1. *Triangular Mergers.* A statutory merger is often preferable to either a stock-for-assets or a stock-for-stock combination. To begin

---

7. A different result might be reached if here, as in *Farris*, the acquiring corporation were significantly smaller than the acquired corporation such that the acquisition greatly transformed the nature of the successor corporation. But in this situation we do not have such a case; after the merger Penn Central would remain a major, diversified corporation, and would continue on the course of acquiring other corporations.

with, the Internal Revenue Code provides greater liberality as to the type of consideration that can be given in an A reorganization (a statutory merger) than in a B reorganization (a stock-for-stock combination), or a C reorganization (a stock-for-assets combination). See Section 1(e), supra. Furthermore, a stock-for-assets combination may involve sales taxes, while a statutory merger ordinarily will not. A stock-for-assets combination also ordinarily involves a great amount of paperwork, in the form of deeds and assignments of the transferor's property and (in some cases) notice to creditors in compliance with the applicable bulk sales law. In contrast, in a statutory merger the survivor succeeds to the transferor's assets by operation of law, so that neither individual documents of title nor compliance with the bulk sales law is ordinarily required.

On the other hand, a statutory merger normally triggers voting and appraisal rights in the shareholders of both constituents. In contrast, other forms of combination may require a vote only by the shareholders of one constituent, and may not trigger appraisal rights. Accordingly, the management of a corporation that proposes to engage in a corporate combination may prefer to use the statutory-merger form, except for the voting and appraisal rights entailed by that form. The triangular merger is a technique designed to give management the best of both possible worlds: the form of a merger, but without voting or appraisal rights in the survivor's shareholders.

A conventional or foreward triangular merger works this way: Assume that Corporations S and T want to engage in a merger in which S will be the survivor and T's shareholders will end up with 100,000 shares of S. In a normal merger this would be accomplished by having S issue 100,000 shares of its own stock to T's shareholders. In a conventional triangular merger, however, S instead begins by creating a new subsidiary, S/Sub, and then transfers 100,000 shares of its own stock to S/Sub in exchange for all of S/Sub's stock. S/Sub and T then engage in a statutory merger, but instead of issuing its *own* stock to T's shareholders, S/Sub issues its 100,000 shares of S stock. The net result is that T's business is owned by S's wholly owned subsidiary (rather than by S itself, as in a normal merger), and T's shareholders own 100,000 shares of S stock. By use of this technique, S may therefore achieve the advantages of a statutory merger while insulating itself from direct responsibility for T's liabilities.[1]

Such a transaction would probably not have been permissible under the traditional statutory merger provisions, because those provisions usually contemplated that the surviving corporation would issue its *own* shares or securities. However, the merger statutes of most corporate jurisdictions have now been amended to permit the survivor to issue shares or securities of *any* corporation. (See, e.g., Del. § 251(b)(4).) In tandem with this development, the Internal Revenue Code was amended by adding § 368(a)(2)(D), which permits a conventional triangular merger to qualify as a tax-free A reorganization, if

---

[1]. However, a court might impose these liabilities on S under the de facto merger doctrine, on the theory that in effect S itself is a constituent to the merger.

(i) substantially all of T's properties are acquired by S/Sub; (ii) the merger would have qualified as an A reorganization if T had merged directly into S; and (iii) no stock of S/Sub is used in the transaction.

A *reverse* triangular merger proceeds like a conventional triangular merger, except that instead of merging T into S/Sub, S/Sub is merged into T. The merger agreement provides that all previously outstanding T shares are automatically converted into the 100,000 shares of S held by S/Sub, and that all shares in S/Sub (which are held by S) are automatically converted into shares in T. When all the shooting is over, therefore, S/Sub will have disappeared, T will be a wholly owned subsidiary of S, and T's shareholders will own 100,000 shares of S stock. By use of this technique S may therefore achieve the advantages of a statutory merger while preserving T's legal status, which could be important where T has valuable rights under contracts, leases, licenses, or franchises. Under IRC § 368(a)(2)(E), a reverse triangular merger will qualify as a tax-free A reorganization, if (i) T ends up with substantially all of the properties of both S/Sub and T, and (ii) S voting stock is exchanged for at least 80% of T's voting and nonvoting stock. (The balance of T's stock can be acquired for other types of consideration.)

An important problem raised by triangular mergers is that they may allow subversion of shareholder voting and appraisal rights, since it can be argued that voting and appraisal rights on the survivor's side are vested in S (as the sole shareholder of S/Sub) rather than in S's shareholders. This argument was rejected in Terry v. Penn Central Corp., supra, but that case was at least partly controlled by the unusual Pennsylvania legislative history. Ideally, this problem should be dealt with by statute. For example, under Cal. §§ 1200(d), 1201, a merger reorganization must be approved by the shareholders of a corporation which is "in control of any constituent . . . corporation . . . and whose equity securities are issued or transferred in the reorganization." Even where a statute does not deal with the problem explicitly, it can be argued that a triangular merger triggers voting and appraisal rights in S's shareholders on the theory that S should be deemed a constituent to the merger, or alternatively that such a result is necessary to prevent subversion of the merger statutes.

2. *Share Exchanges.* Another new mode of combination, inspired by the triangular merger, is known as the share exchange. In a share exchange, the shareholders of the acquired corporation vote on whether to engage in the exchange. If the proposed transaction is approved by a majority of that corporation's outstanding shares, all of the shares must be surrendered—including those of nonconsenting shareholders (unless they exercise appraisal rights).

## (g) EXCLUSIVITY OF THE APPRAISAL REMEDY

### REV. MODEL BUS. CORP. ACT § 13.02(d)
[See Statutory Supplement]

### ALI, PRINCIPLES OF CORPORATE GOVERNANCE §§ 7.24, 7.25
[See Statutory Supplement]

### NOTE ON EXCLUSIVITY OF THE APPRAISAL REMEDY

The question frequently arises whether the appraisal right is intended by the legislature as an exclusive remedy, so that the availability of appraisal precludes shareholders from seeking equitable relief such as injunction or rescission. This question does not always admit of a hard-and-fast answer.

In some cases the issue is specifically addressed by language in the appraisal statute itself. In the absence of explicit statutory language, it is clear that the availability of appraisal rights normally does not preclude an attack based on any of the following grounds:

(a) That the transaction is illegal under corporation law in that it is not authorized by the statute. See, e.g., Eisenberg v. Central Zone Property Corp., 306 N.Y. 58, 115 N.E.2d 652 (1953).

(b) That the transaction is illegal under corporation law in that the procedural steps required to authorize the transaction were not properly taken. See, e.g., Johnson v. Spartanburg County Fair Ass'n, 210 S.C. 56, 41 S.E.2d 599 (1947) (required number of votes not validly cast).

(c) That shareholder approval of the transaction was improperly obtained, as through fraudulent misrepresentation or violation of the Proxy Rules. See, e.g., Victor Broadcasting Co. v. Mahurin, 236 Ark. 196, 365 S.W.2d 265 (1963).

At least in the past, it has also been clear that the availability of appraisal rights normally *does* preclude a shareholder from seeking to recover the money value of his shares under a nonstatutory remedy in connection with transactions for which appraisal rights are given. See, e.g., Adams v. United States Distributing Corp., 184 Va. 134, 34 S.E.2d 244 (1945).

Beyond this, the matter is less clear. A few cases have suggested or implied that even in the absence of explicit statutory language, the availability of appraisal rights precludes an attack based on any ground other than illegality or fraudulent misrepresentation. The general rule, however, is that the mere availability of appraisal rights does not preclude shareholders from seeking injunctive relief or rescission for fraud, using that term in the broad sense to include unfair self-dealing by fiduciaries. See, e.g., Pupecki v. James Madison & Corp., 376 Mass.

212, 382 N.E.2d 1030 (1978). The net result is that, in the absence of explicit statutory language, the availability of appraisal rights may preclude a shareholder from attacking an *arm's-length* transaction on the ground of unfairness, but will usually not insulate *self-interested* transactions from an attack on that ground—although in the latter case it may lead the court to impose a somewhat less rigorous standard of fairness than would otherwise prevail. See Vorenberg, Exclusiveness of the Dissenting Stockholder's Appraisal Right, 77 Harv.L.Rev. 1189, 1214–15 (1964).

———

## CAL. CORP. CODE § 1312

[See Statutory Supplement]

———

## (h) FREEZEOUTS

———

## NOTE ON FREEZEOUT TECHNIQUES

A freezeout is a corporate transaction whose principal purpose is to reconstitute the corporation's ownership by involuntarily eliminating the equity interest of minority shareholders. Until twenty-five or thirty years ago, freezeouts tended to take one of three forms, all of which met with only indifferent success at the hands of the courts.

1. *Dissolution Freezeouts.* Assume that S (who may be an individual, a group, or a corporation) owns 70% of C Corporation, and wishes to eliminate C's minority shareholders.In a dissolution freezeout, S causes C to dissolve under a plan of dissolution which provides that C's productive assets will be distributed to S (or to an entity S controls), while cash or notes will be distributed to C's minority shareholders. This technique has been held illegal in a number of cases, most of which stress that such a plan of dissolution violates a corporate norm of equal treatment among all shareholders of the same class. See e.g., In re San Joaquin Light & Power Corp., 52 Cal.App.2d 814, 127 P.2d 29 (1942).

2. *Sale-of-Assets Freezeouts.* In a sale-of-assets freezeout, C's controlling shareholder, S, organizes a new corporation, T, all of whose stock S owns. S then causes C to sell its assets to T for cash or notes. Result: S owns C's business through T, while the equity interest of C's minority shareholders in C's business is involuntarily terminated. (C is then normally dissolved, although a freezeout will be effected even without dissolution.) Such a procedure has been disapproved in several cases. See, e.g., Theis v. Spokane Falls Gaslight Co., 34 Wash. 23, 74 P. 1004 (1904).

*3. Debt or Redeemable-Preferred Mergers.* A debt or redeemable-preferred merger begins like a sale-of-assets freezeout, with the organization by S of a new corporation, T. S then causes C to merge with T, but instead of issuing common stock, T issues either short-term debentures or redeemable preferred stock. Accordingly, the interest of C's minority shareholders in T either terminates automatically after a period of years (in the case of debentures) or is terminable at T's election (in the case of redeemable preferred).

*4. Cashout Mergers.* Modern freezeouts commonly employ still a fourth technique. Many states have amended their regular merger statutes to allow the survivor in a regular merger to issue cash as well as stock or securities. This opened the door to the possibility of cash mergers, which resemble debt or redeemable stock mergers except that the survivor issues cash rather than stock or securities. Under this technique, the freezeout possibilities of the short-form merger are extended to cases where the parent does not own the percentage of stock requisite for a short-form merger.

A recurrent issue in the freezeout area is whether such a transaction is permissible if it is effected with no business purpose other than to increase the controlling shareholders' portion of the pie. That issue is addressed in the materials that follow.

---

## Weinberger v. UOP, Inc.

Supreme Court of Delaware, 1983.
457 A.2d 701.

■ Before HERMANN, C.J., McNEILLY, QUILLEN, HORSEY and MOORE, JJ., constituting the Court en Banc.

■ MOORE, JUSTICE:

This post-trial appeal was reheard en banc from a decision of the Court of Chancery. It was brought by the class action plaintiff below, a former shareholder of UOP, Inc., who challenged the elimination of UOP's minority shareholders by a cash-out merger between UOP and its majority owner, The Signal Companies, Inc. [T]he defendants in this action are Signal, UOP, [and] certain officers and directors of those companies.... The present Chancellor held that the terms of the merger were fair to the plaintiff and the other minority shareholders of UOP. Accordingly, he entered judgment in favor of the defendants.

Numerous points were raised by the parties, but we address only the following questions presented by the trial court's opinion:

(1) The plaintiff's duty to plead sufficient facts demonstrating the unfairness of the challenged merger;

(2) The burden of proof upon the parties where the merger has been approved by the purportedly informed vote of a majority of the minority shareholders;

(3) The fairness of the merger in terms of adequacy of the defendants' disclosures to the minority shareholders;

(4) The fairness of the merger in terms of adequacy of the price paid for the minority shares and the remedy appropriate to that issue; and

(5) The continued force and effect of Singer v. Magnavox Co., Del.Supr., 380 A.2d 969, 980 (1977), and its progeny.

In ruling for the defendants, the Chancellor re-stated his earlier conclusion that the plaintiff in a suit challenging a cash-out merger must allege specific acts of fraud, misrepresentation, or other items of misconduct to demonstrate the unfairness of the merger terms to the minority. We approve this rule and affirm it.

The Chancellor also held that even though the ultimate burden of proof is on the majority shareholder to show by a preponderance of the evidence that the transaction is fair, it is first the burden of the plaintiff attacking the merger to demonstrate some basis for invoking the fairness obligation. We agree with that principle. However, where corporate action has been approved by an informed vote of a majority of the minority shareholders, we conclude that the burden entirely shifts to the plaintiff to show that the transaction was unfair to the minority. See, e.g., Michelson v. Duncan, Del.Supr., 407 A.2d 211, 224 (1979). But in all this, the burden clearly remains on those relying on the vote to show that they completely disclosed all material facts relevant to the transaction.

Here, the record does not support a conclusion that the minority stockholder vote was an informed one. Material information, necessary to acquaint those shareholders with the bargaining positions of Signal and UOP, was withheld under circumstances amounting to a breach of fiduciary duty. We therefore conclude that this merger does not meet the test of fairness, at least as we address that concept, and no burden thus shifted to the plaintiff by reason of the minority shareholder vote. Accordingly, we reverse and remand for further proceedings consistent herewith.

In considering the nature of the remedy available under our law to minority shareholders in a cash-out merger, we believe that it is, and hereafter should be, an appraisal under 8 Del.C. § 262 as hereinafter construed. We therefore overrule Lynch v. Vickers Energy Corp., Del.Supr., 429 A.2d 497 (1981) (*Lynch II*) to the extent that it purports to limit a stockholder's monetary relief to a specific damage formula. See *Lynch II*. 429 A.2d at 507–08 (McNeilly & Quillen, JJ., dissenting). But to give full effect to section 262 within the framework of the General Corporation Law we adopt a more liberal, less rigid and stylized, approach to the valuation process than has heretofore been permitted by our courts. While the present state of these proceedings does not admit the plaintiff to the appraisal remedy per se, the practical effect of the remedy we do grant him will be co-extensive with the liberalized valuation and appraisal methods we herein approve for cases coming after this decision.

Our treatment of these matters has necessarily led us to a reconsideration of the business purpose rule announced in the trilogy of Singer v. Magnavox Co., supra; Tanzer v. International General Industries, Inc., Del.Supr., 379 A.2d 1121 (1977); and Roland International Corp. v. Najjar, Del.Supr., 407 A.2d 1032 (1979). For the reasons hereafter set forth we consider that the business purpose requirement of these cases is no longer the law of Delaware.

## I.

The facts found by the trial court, pertinent to the issues before us, are supported by the record, and we draw from them as set out in the Chancellor's opinion.

Signal is a diversified, technically based company operating through various subsidiaries. Its stock is publicly traded on the New York, Philadelphia and Pacific Stock Exchanges. UOP, formerly known as Universal Oil Products Company, was a diversified industrial company engaged in various lines of business, including petroleum and petro-chemical services and related products, construction, fabricated metal products, transportation equipment products, chemicals and plastics, and other products and services including land development, lumber products and waste disposal. Its stock was publicly held and listed on the New York Stock Exchange.

In 1974 Signal sold one of its wholly-owned subsidiaries for $420,000,000 in cash. See Gimbel v. Signal Companies, Inc., Del.Ch., 316 A.2d 599, aff'd, Del.Supr., 316 A.2d 619 (1974). While looking to invest this cash surplus, Signal became interested in UOP as a possible acquisition. Friendly negotiations ensued, and Signal proposed to acquire a controlling interest in UOP at a price of $19 per share. UOP's representatives sought $25 per share. In the arm's length bargaining that followed, an understanding was reached whereby Signal agreed to purchase from UOP 1,500,000 shares of UOP's authorized but unissued stock at $21 per share.

This purchase was contingent upon Signal making a successful cash tender offer for 4,300,000 publicly held shares of UOP, also at a price of $21 per share. This combined method of acquisition permitted Signal to acquire 5,800,000 shares of stock, representing 50.5% of UOP's outstanding shares. The UOP board of directors advised the company's shareholders that it had no objection to Signal's tender offer at that price. Immediately before the announcement of the tender offer, UOP's common stock had been trading on the New York Stock Exchange at a fraction under $14 per share.

The negotiations between Signal and UOP occurred during April 1975, and the resulting tender offer was greatly oversubscribed. However, Signal limited its total purchase of the tendered shares so that, when coupled with the stock bought from UOP, it had achieved its goal of becoming a 50.5% shareholder of UOP.

Although UOP's board consisted of thirteen directors, Signal nominated and elected only six. Of these, five were either directors or employees of Signal. The sixth, a partner in the banking firm of Lazard Freres & Co., had been one of Signal's representatives in the negotiations and bargaining with UOP concerning the tender offer and purchase price of the UOP shares.

However, the president and chief executive officer of UOP retired during 1975, and Signal caused him to be replaced by James V. Crawford, a long-time employee and senior executive vice president of one of Signal's wholly-owned subsidiaries. Crawford succeeded his predecessor on UOP's board of directors and also was made a director of Signal.

By the end of 1977 Signal basically was unsuccessful in finding other suitable investment candidates for its excess cash, and by February 1978 considered that it had no other realistic acquisitions available to it on a friendly basis. Once again its attention turned to UOP.

The trial court found that at the instigation of certain Signal management personnel, including William W. Walkup, its board chairman, and Forrest N. Shumway, its president, a feasibility study was made concerning the possible acquisition of the balance of UOP's outstanding shares. This study was performed by two Signal officers, Charles S. Arledge, vice president (director of planning), and Andrew J. Chitiea, senior vice president (chief financial officer). Messrs. Walkup, Shumway, Arledge and Chitiea were all directors of UOP in addition to their membership on the Signal board.

Arledge and Chitiea concluded that it would be a good investment for Signal to acquire the remaining 49.5% of UOP shares at any price up to $24 each. Their report was discussed between Walkup and Shumway who, along with Arledge, Chitiea and Brewster L. Arms, internal counsel for Signal, constituted Signal's senior management. In particular, they talked about the proper price to be paid if the acquisition was pursued, purportedly keeping in mind that as UOP's majority shareholder, Signal owed a fiduciary responsibility to both its own stockholders as well as to UOP's minority. It was ultimately agreed that a meeting of Signal's Executive Committee would be called to propose that Signal acquire the remaining outstanding stock of UOP through a cash-out merger in the range of $20 to $21 per share.

The Executive Committee meeting was set for February 28, 1978. As a courtesy, UOP's President, Crawford, was invited to attend, although he was not a member of Signal's executive committee. On his arrival, and prior to the meeting, Crawford was asked to meet privately with Walkup and Shumway. He was then told of Signal's plan to acquire full ownership of UOP and was asked for his reaction to the proposed price range of $20 to $21 per share. Crawford said he thought such a price would be "generous", and that it was certainly one which should be submitted to UOP's minority shareholders for their ultimate consideration. He stated, however, that Signal's 100% ownership could cause internal problems at UOP. He believed that employees would have to be given some assurance of their future place in a fully-owned Signal subsidiary. Otherwise, he feared the departure of essential personnel. Also, many of UOP's key employees had stock option incentive programs which would be wiped out by a merger. Crawford therefore urged that some adjustment would have to be made, such as providing a comparable incentive in Signals' shares, if after the merger he was to maintain his quality of personnel and efficiency at UOP.

Thus, Crawford voiced no objection to the $20 to $21 price range, nor did he suggest that Signal should consider paying more than $21 per share for the minority interests. Later, at the Executive Committee meeting the same factors were discussed, with Crawford repeating the position he earlier took with Walkup and Shumway. Also considered was the 1975 tender offer and the fact that it had been greatly oversubscribed at $21 per share. For many reasons, Signal's management concluded that the acquisition of UOP's minority shares provided the solution to a number of its business problems.

Thus, it was the consensus that a price of $20 to $21 per share would be fair to both Signal and the minority shareholders of UOP. Signal's executive committee authorized its management "to negotiate" with UOP "for a cash acquisition of the minority ownership in UOP, Inc., with the intention of presenting a proposal to [Signal's] board of directors ... on March 6, 1978". Immediately after this February 28, 1978 meeting, Signal issued a press release stating:

> The Signal Companies, Inc. and UOP, Inc. are conducting negotiations for the acquisition for cash by Signal of the 49.5 per cent of UOP which it does not presently own, announced Forrest N. Shumway, president and chief executive officer of Signal, and James V. Crawford, UOP president.
>
> Price and other terms of the proposed transaction have not yet been finalized and would be subject to approval of the boards of directors of Signal and UOP, scheduled to meet early next week, the stockholders of UOP and certain federal agencies.

The announcement also referred to the fact that the closing price of UOP's common stock on that day was $14.50 per share.

Two days later, on March 2, 1978, Signal issued a second press release stating that its management would recommend a price in the range of $20 to $21 per share for UOP's 49.5% minority interest. This announcement referred to Signal's earlier statement that "negotiations" were being conducted for the acquisition of the minority shares.

Between Tuesday, February 28, 1978 and Monday, March 6, 1978, a total of four business days, Crawford spoke by telephone with all of UOP's non-Signal, i.e., outside, directors. Also during that period, Crawford retained Lehman Brothers to render a fairness opinion as to the price offered the minority for its stock. He gave two reasons for this choice. First, the time schedule between the announcement and the board meetings was short (by then only three business days) and since Lehman Brothers had been acting as UOP's investment banker for many years, Crawford felt that it would be in the best position to respond on such brief notice. Second, James W. Glanville, a long-time director of UOP and a partner in Lehman Brothers, had acted as a financial advisor to UOP for many years. Crawford believed that Glanville's familiarity with UOP, as a member of its board, would also be of assistance in enabling Lehman Brothers to render a fairness opinion within the existing time constraints.

Crawford telephoned Glanville, who gave his assurance that Lehman Brothers had no conflicts that would prevent it from accepting the task. Glanville's immediate personal reaction was that a price of $20 to $21 would certainly be fair, since it represented almost a 50% premium over UOP's market price. Glanville sought a $250,000 fee for Lehman Brothers' services, but Crawford thought this too much. After further discussions Glanville finally agreed that Lehman Brothers would render its fairness opinion for $150,000.

During this period Crawford also had several telephone contacts with Signal officials. In only one of them, however, was the price of the shares discussed. In a conversation with Walkup, Crawford advised that as a result of his communications with UOP's non-Signal directors, it was his feeling that the price would have to be the top of the proposed range, or $21 per share, if the approval of UOP's outside directors was to be obtained. But again, he did not seek any price higher than $21.

Glanville assembled a three-man Lehman Brothers team to do the work on the fairness opinion. These persons examined relevant documents and information concerning UOP, including its annual reports and its Securities and Exchange Commission filings from 1973 through 1976, as well as its audited financial statements for 1977, its interim reports to shareholders, and its recent and historical market prices and trading volumes. In addition, on Friday, March 3, 1978, two members of the Lehman Brothers team flew to UOP's headquarters in Des Plaines, Illinois, to perform a "due diligence" visit, during the course of which they interviewed Crawford as well as UOP's general counsel, its chief financial officer, and other key executives and personnel.

As a result, the Lehman Brothers team concluded that "the price of either $20 or $21 would be a fair price for the remaining shares of UOP". They telephoned this impression to Glanville, who was spending the weekend in Vermont.

On Monday morning, March 6, 1978, Glanville and the senior member of the Lehman Brothers team flew to Des Plaines to attend the scheduled UOP directors meeting. Glanville looked over the assembled information during the flight. The two had with them the draft of a "fairness opinion letter" in which the price had been left blank. Either during or immediately prior to the directors' meeting, the two-page "fairness opinion letter" was typed in final form and the price of $21 per share was inserted.

On March 6, 1978, both the Signal and UOP boards were convened to consider the proposed merger. Telephone communications were maintained between the two meetings. Walkup, Signal's board chairman, and also a UOP director, attended UOP's meeting with Crawford in order to present Signal's position and answer any questions that UOP's non-Signal directors might have. Arledge and Chitiea, along with Signal's other designees on UOP's board, participated by conference telephone. All of UOP's outside directors attended the meeting either in person or by conference telephone.

First, Signal's board unanimously adopted a resolution authorizing Signal to proposed to UOP a cash merger of $21 per share as outlined in a certain merger agreement and other supporting documents. This proposal required that the merger be approved by a majority of UOP's outstanding minority shares voting at the stockholders meeting at which the merger would be considered, and that the minority shares voting in favor of the merger, when coupled with Signal's 50.5% interest would have to comprise at least two-thirds of all UOP shares. Otherwise the proposed merger would be deemed disapproved.

UOP's board then considered the proposal. Copies of the agreement were delivered to the directors in attendance, and other copies had been forwarded earlier to the directors participating by telephone. They also had before them UOP financial data for 1974–1977, UOP's most recent financial statements, market price information, and budget projections for 1978. In addition they had Lehman Brothers' hurriedly prepared fairness opinion letter finding the price of $21 to be fair. Glanville, the Lehman Brothers partner, and UOP director, commented on the information that had gone into preparation of the letter.

Signal also suggests that the Arledge–Chitiea feasibility study, indicating that a price of up to $24 per share would be a "good investment" for Signal, was discussed at the UOP directors' meeting. The Chancellor made no such finding, and our independent review of the record, detailed infra, satisfies us by a preponderance of the evidence that there was no discussion of this document at UOP's board meeting. Furthermore, it is clear beyond peradventure that nothing in that report was ever disclosed to UOP's minority shareholders prior to their approval of the merger.

After consideration of Signal's proposal, Walkup and Crawford left the meeting to permit a free and uninhibited exchange between UOP's non-Signal directors. Upon their return a resolution to accept Signal's offer was then proposed and adopted. While Signal's men on UOP's board participated in various aspects of the meeting they abstained from voting. However, the minutes show that each of them "if voting would have voted yes".

On March 7, 1978, UOP sent a letter to its shareholders advising them of the action taken by UOP's board with respect to Signal's offer. This document pointed out, among other things, that on February 28, 1978 "both companies had announced negotiations were being conducted."

Despite the swift board action of the two companies, the merger was not submitted to UOP's shareholders until their annual meeting on May 26, 1978. In the notice of that meeting and proxy statement sent to shareholders in May, UOP's management and board urged that the merger be approved. The proxy statement also advised:

> The price was determined after *discussions* between James V. Crawford, a director of Signal and Chief Executive Officer of UOP, and officers of Signal which took place during meetings on February 28, 1978, and in the course of several subsequent telephone conversations. (Emphasis added.)

In the original draft of the proxy statement the word "negotiations" had been used rather than "discussions". However, when the Securities and Exchange Commission sought details of the "negotiations" as part of its review of these materials, the term was deleted and the word "discussions" was substituted. The proxy statement indicated that the vote of UOP's board in approving the merger had been unanimous. It also advised the shareholders that Lehman Brothers had given its opinion that the merger price of $21 per share was fair to UOP's minority. However, it did not disclose the hurried method by which this conclusion was reached.

As of the record date for UOP's annual meeting, there were 11,488,302 shares of UOP common stock outstanding, 5,688,302 of which were owned by the minority. At the meeting only 56%, or 3,208,652, of the minority shares were voted. Of these, 2,953,812, or 51.9% of the total minority, voted for the merger, and 254,840 voted against it. When Signal's stock was added to the minority shares voting in favor, a total of 76.2% of UOP's outstanding shares approved the merger while only 2.2% opposed it.

By its terms the merger became effective on May 26, 1978, and each share of UOP's stock held by the minority was automatically converted into a right to receive $21 cash.

II.

A.

A primary issue mandating reversal is the preparation by two UOP directors, Arledge and Chitiea, of their feasibility study for the exclusive use and benefit of Signal. This document was of obvious significance to both Signal and UOP. Using UOP data, it described the advantages to Signal of ousting the minority at a price range of $21–$24 per share. Mr. Arledge, one of the authors, outlined the benefits to Signal:*

*Purpose of the Merger*

(1) Provides an outstanding investment opportunity for Signal—(Better than any recent acquisition we have seen.)

(2) Increases Signal's earnings.

---

\* The parentheses indicate certain hand-written comments of Mr. Arledge.

(3) Facilitates the flow of resources between Signal and its subsidiaries—(Big factor—works both ways.)

(4) Provides cost savings potential for Signal and UOP.

(5) Improves the percentage of Signal's 'operating earnings' as opposed to 'holding company earnings'.

(6) Simplifies the understanding of Signal.

(7) Facilitates technological exchange among Signal's subsidiaries.

(8) Eliminates potential conflicts of interest.

Having written those words, solely for the use of Signal, it is clear from the record that neither Arledge nor Chitiea shared this report with their fellow directors of UOP. We are satisfied that no one else did either. This conduct hardly meets the fiduciary standards applicable to such a transaction. While Mr. Walkup, Signal's chairman of the board and a UOP director, attended the March 6, 1978 UOP board meeting and testified at trial that he had discussed the Arledge–Chitiea report with the UOP directors at this meeting, the record does not support this assertion. Perhaps it is the result of some confusion on Mr. Walkup's part. In any event Mr. Shumway, Signal's president, testified that he made sure the Signal outside directors had this report prior to the March 6, 1978 Signal board meeting, but he did not testify that the Arledge–Chitiea report was also sent to UOP's outside directors.

Mr. Crawford, UOP's president, could not recall that any documents, other than a draft of the merger agreement, were sent to UOP's directors before the March 6, 1978 UOP meeting. Mr. Chitiea, an author of the report, testified that it was made available to Signal's directors, but to his knowledge it was not circulated to the outside directors of UOP. He specifically testified that he "didn't share" that information with the outside directors of UOP with whom he served.

None of UOP's outside directors who testified stated that they had seen this document. The minutes of the UOP board meeting do not identify the Arledge–Chitiea report as having been delivered to UOP's outside directors. This is particularly significant since the minutes describe in considerable detail the materials that actually were distributed. While these minutes recite Mr. Walkup's presentation of the Signal offer, they do not mention the Arledge–Chitiea report or any disclosure that Signal considered a price of up to $24 to be a good investment. If Mr. Walkup had in fact provided such important information to UOP's outside directors, it is logical to assume that these carefully drafted minutes would disclose it. The post-trial briefs of Signal and UOP contain a thorough description of the documents purportedly available to their boards at the March 6, 1978, meetings. Although the Arledge–Chitiea report is specifically identified as being available to the Signal directors, there is no mention of it being among the documents submitted to the UOP board. Even when queried at a prior oral argument before this Court, counsel for Signal did not claim that the Arledge–Chitiea report had been disclosed to UOP's outside directors. Instead, he chose to belittle its contents. This was the same approach taken before us at the last oral argument.

Actually, it appears that a three-page summary of figures was given to all UOP directors. Its first page is identical to one page of the Arledge–Chitiea report, but this dealt with nothing more than a justification of the $21 price. Significantly, the contents of this three-page summary are what the minutes reflect Mr. Walkup told the UOP board. However, nothing contained in either the minutes or this three-page summary reflects Signal's study regarding the $24 price.

The Arledge–Chitiea report speaks for itself in supporting the Chancellor's finding that a price of up to $24 was a "good investment" for Signal. It shows that a return on the investment at $21 would be 15.7% versus 15.5% at $24 per share. This was a difference of only two-tenths of one percent, while it meant over $17,000,000 to the minority. Under such circumstances, paying UOP's minority shareholders $24 would have had relatively little long-term effect on Signal, and the Chancellor's findings concerning the benefit to Signal, even at a price of $24, were obviously correct. Levitt v. Bouvier, Del.Supr., 287 A.2d 671, 673 (1972).

Certainly, this was a matter of material significance to UOP and its shareholders. Since the study was prepared by two UOP directors, using UOP information for the exclusive benefit of Signal, and nothing whatever was done to disclose it to the outside UOP directors or the minority shareholders, a question of breach of fiduciary duty arises. This problem occurs because there were common Signal–UOP directors participating, at least to some extent, in the UOP board's decision-making processes without full disclosure of the conflicts they faced.[7]

### B.

In assessing this situation, the Court of Chancery was required to:

examine what information defendants had and to measure it against what they gave to the minority stockholders, in a context in which "complete candor" is required. In other words, the limited function of the Court was to determine whether defendants had disclosed all information in their possession germane to the transaction in issue. And by "germane" we mean, for present

7. Although perfection is not possible, or expected, the result here could have been entirely different if UOP had appointed an independent negotiating committee of its outside directors to deal with Signal at arm's length. See, e.g., Harriman v. E.I. du Pont De Nemours & Co., 411 F.Supp. 133 (D.Del. 1975). Since fairness in this context can be equated to conduct by a theoretical, wholly independent, board of directors acting upon the matter before them, it is unfortunate that this course apparently was neither considered nor pursued. Johnston v. Greene, Del.Supr., 121 A.2d 919, 925 (1956). Particularly in a parent-subsidiary context, a showing that the action taken was as though each of the contending parties had in fact exerted its bargaining power against the other at arm's length is strong evidence that the transaction meets the test of fairness. Getty Oil Co. v. Skelly Oil Co., Del.Supr., 267 A.2d 883, 886 (1970); Puma v. Marriott, Del.Ch., 283 A.2d 693, 696 (1971).

purposes, information such as a reasonable shareholder would consider important in deciding whether to sell or retain stock.

\* \* \*

. . . Completeness, not adequacy, is both the norm and the mandate under present circumstances.

Lynch v. Vickers Energy Corp., Del.Supr., 383 A.2d 278, 281 (1977) (*Lynch I*). This is merely stating in another way the long-existing principle of Delaware law that these Signal designated directors on UOP's board still owed UOP and its shareholders an uncompromising duty of loyalty. The classic language of Guth v.Loft, Inc., Del.Supr., 5 A.2d 503, 510 (1939), requires no embellishment:

> A public policy, existing through the years, and derived from a profound knowledge of human characteristics and motives, has established a rule that demands of a corporate officer or director, peremptorily and inexorably, the most scrupulous observance of his duty, not only affirmatively to protect the interests of the corporation committed to his charge, but also to refrain from doing anything that would work injury to the corporation, or to deprive it of profit or advantage which his skill and ability might properly bring to it, or to enable it to make in the reasonable and lawful exercise of its powers. The rule that requires an undivided and unselfish loyalty to the corporation demands that there shall be no conflict between duty and self-interest.

Given the absence of any attempt to structure this transaction on an arm's length basis, Signal cannot escape the effects of the conflicts it faced, particularly when its designees on UOP's board did not totally abstain from participation in the matter. There is no "safe harbor" for such divided loyalties in Delaware. When directors of a Delaware corporation are on both sides of a transaction, they are required to demonstrate their utmost good faith and the most scrupulous inherent fairness of the bargain. Gottlieb v. Heyden Chemical Corp., Del.Supr., 91 A.2d 57, 57–58 (1952). The requirement of fairness is unflinching in its demand that where one stands on both sides of a transaction, he has the burden of establishing its entire fairness, sufficient to pass the test of careful scrutiny by the courts. Sterling v. Mayflower Hotel Corp., Del.Supr., 93 A.2d 107, 110 (1952); Bastian v. Bourns, Inc., Del.Ch., 256 A.2d 680, 681 (1969), aff'd, Del.Supr., 278 A.2d 467 (1970); David J. Greene & Co. v. Dunhill International Inc., Del.Ch., 249 A.2d 427, 431 (1968).

There is no dilution of this obligation where one holds dual or multiple directorships, as in a parent-subsidiary context. Levien v. Sinclair Oil Corp., Del.Ch., 261 A.2d 911, 915 (1969). Thus, individuals who act in a dual capacity as directors of two corporations, one of whom is parent and the other subsidiary, owe the same duty of good management to both corporations, and in the absence of an independent negotiating structure (see note 7, supra), or the directors' total abstention from any participation in the matter, this duty is to be exercised in light of what is best for both companies. Warshaw v.

Calhoun, Del.Supr., 221 A.2d 487, 492 (1966). The record demonstrates that Signal has not met this obligation.

### C.

The concept of fairness has two basic aspects: fair dealing and fair price. The former embraces questions of when the transaction was timed, how it was initiated, structured, negotiated, disclosed to the directors, and how the approvals of the directors and the stockholders were obtained. The latter aspect of fairness relates to the economic and financial considerations of the proposed merger, including all relevant factors: assets, market value, earnings, future prospects, and any other elements that affect the intrinsic or inherent value of a company's stock. Moore, The "Interested" Director or Officer Transaction, 4 Del.J.Corp.L. 674, 676 (1979); Nathan & Shapiro, Legal Standard of Fairness of Merger Terms Under Delaware Law, 2 Del.J.Corp.L. 44, 46–47 (1977). See Tri–Continental Corp. v. Battye, Del.Supr., 74 A.2d 71, 72 (1950); 8 Del.C. § 262(h). However, the test for fairness is not a bifurcated one as between fair dealing and price. All aspects of the issue must be examined as a whole since the question is one of entire fairness. However, in a non-fraudulent transaction we recognize that price may be the preponderant consideration outweighing other features of the merger. Here, we address the two basic aspects of fairness separately because we find reversible error as to both.

### D.

Part of fair dealing is the obvious duty of candor required by *Lynch I,* supra. Moreover, one possessing superior knowledge may not mislead any stockholder by use of corporate information to which the latter is not privy. Lank v. Steiner, Del.Supr., 224 A.2d 242, 244 (1966). Delaware has long imposed this duty even upon persons who are not corporate officers or directors, but who nonetheless are privy to matters of interest or significance to their company. Brophy v. Cities Service Co., Del.Ch., 70 A.2d 5, 7 (1949). With the well-established Delaware law on the subject, and the Court of Chancery's findings of fact here, it is inevitable that the obvious conflicts posed by Arledge and Chitiea's preparation of their "feasibility study", derived from UOP information, for the sole use and benefit of Signal, cannot pass muster.

The Arledge–Chitiea report is but one aspect of the element of fair dealing. How did this merger evolve? It is clear that it was entirely initiated by Signal. The serious time constraints under which the principals acted were all set by Signal. It had not found a suitable outlet for its excess cash and considered UOP a desirable investment, particularly since it was now in a position to acquire the whole company for itself. For whatever reasons, and they were only Signal's, the entire transaction was presented to and approved by UOP's board within four business days. Standing alone, this is not necessarily indicative of any lack of fairness by a majority shareholder. It was what occurred, or more properly, what did not occur, during this brief period that makes the time constraints imposed by Signal relevant to the issue of fairness.

The structure of the transaction, again, was Signal's doing. So far as negotiations were concerned, it is clear that they were modest at best. Crawford, Signal's man at UOP, never really talked price with Signal, except to accede to its management's statements on the subject, and to convey to Signal the UOP outside directors' view that as between the $20–$21 range under consideration, it would have to be $21. The latter is not a surprising outcome, but hardly arm's length negotiations. Only the protection of benefits for UOP's key employees and the issue of Lehman Brothers' fee approached any concept of bargaining.

As we have noted, the matter of disclosure to the UOP directors was wholly flawed by the conflicts of interest raised by the Arledge–Chitiea report. All of those conflicts were resolved by Signal in its own favor without divulging any aspect of them to UOP.

This cannot but undermine a conclusion that this merger meets any reasonable test of fairness. The outside UOP directors lacked one material piece of information generated by two of their colleagues, but shared only with Signal. True, the UOP board had the Lehman Brothers' fairness opinion, but that firm has been blamed by the plaintiff for the hurried task it performed, when more properly the responsibility for this lies with Signal. There was no disclosure of the circumstances surrounding the rather cursory preparation of the Lehman Brothers' fairness opinion. Instead, the impression was given UOP's minority that a careful study had been made, when in fact speed was the hallmark, and Mr. Glanville, Lehman's partner in charge of the matter, and also a UOP director, having spent the weekend in Vermont, brought a draft of the "fairness opinion letter" to the UOP directors' meeting on March 6, 1978 with the price left blank. We can only conclude from the record that the rush imposed on Lehman Brothers by Signal's timetable contributed to the difficulties under which this investment banking firm attempted to perform its responsibilities. Yet, none of this was disclosed to UOP's minority.

Finally, the minority stockholders were denied the critical information that Signal considered a price of $24 to be a good investment. Since this would have meant over $17,000,000 more to the minority, we cannot conclude that the shareholder vote was an informed one. Under the circumstances, an approval by a majority of the minority was meaningless. *Lynch I,* 383 A.2d at 279, 281; Cahall v. Lofland, Del.Ch., 114 A. 224 (1921).

Given these particulars and the Delaware law on the subject, the record does not establish that this transaction satisfies any reasonable concept of fair dealing, and the Chancellor's findings in that regard must be reversed.

### E.

Turning to the matter of price, plaintiff also challenges its fairness. His evidence was that on the date the merger was approved the stock was worth at least $26 per share. In support, he offered the testimony of a chartered investment analyst who used two basic approaches to valuation: a comparative analysis of the premium paid over market in ten other tender offer-merger combinations, and a discounted cash flow analysis.

In this breach of fiduciary duty case, the Chancellor perceived that the approach to valuation was the same as that in an appraisal proceeding. Consistent with precedent, he rejected plaintiff's method of proof and accepted defendants' evidence of value as being in accord with practice under prior case law. This means that the so-called "Delaware block" or weighted average method was employed wherein the elements of value, i.e., assets, market price, earnings, etc., were assigned a particular weight and the resulting amounts added to determine the value per share.

[The court held that the use of this valuation technique was in error. See Chapter 6, supra.]

Although the Chancellor received the plaintiff's evidence, his opinion indicates that the use of it was precluded because of past Delaware practice. While we do not suggest a monetary result one way or the other, we do think the plaintiff's evidence should be part of the factual mix and weighed as such. Until the $21 price is measured on remand by the valuation standards mandated by Delaware law, there can be no finding at the present stage of these proceedings that the price is fair. Given the lack of any candid disclosure of the material facts surrounding establishment of the $21 price, the majority of the minority vote, approving the merger, is meaningless.

The plaintiff has not sought an appraisal, but rescissory damages of the type contemplated by Lynch v. Vickers Energy Corp., Del.Supr., 429 A.2d 497, 505–06 (1981) (*Lynch II*). In view of the approach to valuation that we announce today, we see no basis in our law for *Lynch II's* exclusive monetary formula for relief. On remand the plaintiff will be permitted to test the fairness of the $21 price by the standards we herein establish, in conformity with the principle applicable to an appraisal—that fair value be determined by taking "into account all relevant factors" [see 8 Del.C. § 262(h), supra]. In our view this includes the elements of rescissory damages if the Chancellor considers them susceptible of proof and a remedy appropriate to all the issues of fairness before him. To the extent that *Lynch II,* 429 A.2d at 505–06, purports to limit the Chancellor's discretion to a single remedial formula for monetary damages in a cash-out merger, it is overruled.

While a plaintiff's monetary remedy ordinarily should be confined to the more liberalized appraisal proceeding herein established, we do not intend any limitation on the historic powers of the Chancellor to grant such other relief as the facts of a particular case may dictate. The appraisal remedy we approve may not be adequate in certain cases, particularly where fraud, misrepresentation, self-dealing, deliberate waste of corporate assets, or gross and palpable overreaching are involved. Cole v. National Cash Credit Association, Del.Ch., 156 A.

183, 187 (1931). Under such circumstances, the Chancellor's powers are complete to fashion any form of equitable and monetary relief as may be appropriate, including rescissory damages. Since it is apparent that this long completed transaction is too involved to undo, and in view of the Chancellor's discretion, the award, if any, should be in the form of monetary damages based upon entire fairness standards, i.e., fair dealing and fair price.

Obviously, there are other litigants, like the plaintiff, who abjured an appraisal and whose rights to challenge the element of fair value must be preserved.[8] Accordingly, the quasi-appraisal remedy we grant the plaintiff here will apply only to: (1) this case; (2) any case now pending on appeal to this Court; (3) any case now pending in the Court of Chancery which has not yet been appealed but which may be eligible for direct appeal to this Court; (4) any case challenging a cash-out merger, the effective date of which is on or before February 1, 1983; and (5) any proposed merger to be presented at a shareholders' meeting, the notification of which is mailed to the stockholders on or before February 23, 1983. Thereafter, the provisions of 8 Del.C. § 262, as herein construed, respecting the scope of an appraisal and the means for perfecting the same, shall govern the financial remedy available to minority shareholders in a cash-out merger. Thus, we return to the well established principles of Stauffer v. Standard Brands, Inc., Del.Supr., 187 A.2d 78 (1962) and David J. Greene & Co. v. Schenley Industries, Inc., Del.Ch., 281 A.2d 30 (1971), mandating a stockholder's recourse to the basic remedy of an appraisal.

### III.

Finally, we address the matter of business purpose. The defendants contend that the purpose of this merger was not a proper subject of inquiry by the trial court. The plaintiff says that no valid purpose existed—the entire transaction was a mere subterfuge designed to eliminate the minority. The Chancellor ruled otherwise, but in so doing he clearly circumscribed the thrust and effect of *Singer*. Weinberger v. UOP, 426 A.2d at 1342–43, 1348–50. This has led to the thoroughly sound observation that the business purpose test "may be ... virtually interpreted out of existence, as it was in *Weinberger*".[9]

The requirement of a business purpose is new to our law of mergers and was a departure from prior case law. See Stauffer v. Standard Brands, Inc., supra; David J. Greene & Co. v. Schenley Industries, Inc., supra.

In view of the fairness test which has long been applicable to parent-subsidiary mergers, Sterling v. Mayflower Hotel Corp., Del. Supr., 93 A.2d 107, 109–10 (1952), the expanded appraisal remedy now available to shareholders, and the broad discretion of the Chancellor to fashion such relief as the facts of a given case may dictate we

---

**8.** Under 8 Del.C. § 262(a), (d) & (e), a stockholder is required to act within certain time periods to perfect the right to an appraisal.

**9.** Weiss, The Law of Take Out Mergers: A Historical Perspective, 56 N.Y.U.L.Rev. 624, 671, n. 300 (1981).

do not believe that any additional meaningful protection is afforded minority shareholders by the business purpose requirement of the trilogy of *Singer, Tanzer,*[10] *Najjar,*[11] and their progeny. Accordingly, such requirement shall no longer be of any force or effect.

The judgment of the Court of Chancery, finding both the circumstances of the merger and the price paid the minority shareholders to be fair, is reversed. The matter is remanded for further proceedings consistent herewith. Upon remand the plaintiff's post-trial motion to enlarge the class should be granted.

\* \* \*

Reversed and Remanded.

---

## KAHN v. LYNCH COMMUNICATION SYSTEMS

Chapter 9, supra

---

**COGGINS v. NEW ENGLAND PATRIOTS FOOTBALL CLUB, INC.,** 397 Mass. 525, 492 N.E.2d 1112 (1986). "Unlike the Delaware court . . . we believe that the 'business-purpose' test is an additional useful means under our statutes and case law for examining a transaction in which a controlling stockholder eliminates the minority interest in a corporation. . . . This concept of fair dealing is not limited to close corporations but applies to judicial review of cash freeze-out mergers. . . .

"The defendants argue that judicial review of a merger cannot be invoked by disgruntled stockholders, absent illegal or fraudulent conduct. They rely on G.L. c. 156B, § 98 (1984 ed.).[1] In the defendants' view, 'the Superior Court's finding of liability was premised solely on the claimed inadequacy of the offering price.' Any dispute over offering price, they urge, must be resolved solely through the statutory remedy of appraisal. . . .

"We have held in regard to so called 'close corporations' that the statute does not divest the courts of their equitable jurisdiction to assure that the conduct of controlling stockholders does not violate the fiduciary principles governing the relationship between majority and minority stockholders. *Pupecki v. James Madison Corp.,* 376 Mass. 212, 216–217, 382 N.E.2d 1030 (1978) (when controlling stockholder fails to assure that corporation receives adequate consideration for its

---

**10.** Tanzer v. International General Industries, Inc., Del.Supr., 379 A.2d 1121, 1124–25 (1977).

**11.** Roland International Corp. v. Najjar, Del.Supr., 407 A.2d 1032, 1036 (1979).

**1.** "The enforcement by a stockholder of his right to receive payment for his shares in the manner provided in this chapter shall be an exclusive remedy except that this chapter shall not exclude the right of such stockholder to bring or maintain an appropriate proceeding to obtain relief on the ground that such corporate action will be or is illegal or fraudulent as to him." G.L. c. 156B, § 98. [Footnote renumbered by editor.]

assets, transaction is illegal or fraudulent, and G.L. c. 156B, § 98, does not foreclose review). 'Where the director's duty of loyalty to the corporation is in conflict with his self-interest the court will vigorously scrutinize the situation.' *American Discount Corp. v. Kaitz*, 348 Mass. 706, 711, 206 N.E.2d 156 (1965). The court is justified in exercising its equitable power when a violation of fiduciary duty is claimed.

"The dangers of self-dealing and abuse of fiduciary duty are greatest in freeze-out situations like the Patriots merger, where a controlling stockholder and corporate director chooses to eliminate public ownership. It is in these cases that a judge should examine with closest scrutiny the motives and the behavior of the controlling stockholder. A showing of compliance with statutory procedures is an insufficient substitute for the inquiry of the courts when a minority stockholder claims that the corporate action 'will be or is illegal or fraudulent as to him.' G.L. c. 156B, § 98. *Leader v. Hycor, Inc.*, 395 Mass. 215, 221, 479 N.E.2d 173 (1985) (judicial review may be had of claims of breach of fiduciary duty and unfairness).

"Judicial scrutiny should begin with recognition of the basic principle that the duty of a corporate director must be to further the legitimate goals of the corporation. The result of a freeze-out merger is the elimination of public ownership in the corporation. The controlling faction increases its equity from a majority to 100%, using corporate processes and corporate assets. The corporate directors who benefit from this transfer of ownership must demonstrate how the legitimate goals of the corporation are furthered. A director of a corporation violates his fiduciary duty when he uses the corporation for his or his family's personal benefit in a manner detrimental to the corporation. *Widett & Widett v. Snyder*, 392 Mass. 778, 785–786, 467 N.E.2d 1312 (1984). See *Buckman v. Elm Hill Realty Co. of Peabody*, 312 Mass. 10, 15, 42 N.E.2d 814 (1942). Because the danger of abuse of fiduciary duty is especially great in a freeze-out merger, the court must be satisfied that the freeze-out was for the advancement of a legitimate corporate purpose. If satisfied that elimination of public ownership is in furtherance of a business purpose, the court should then proceed to determine if the transaction was fair by examining the totality of the circumstances...."

---

**ALPERT v. 28 WILLIAMS ST. CORP.**, 63 N.Y.2d 557, 483 N.Y.S.2d 667, 473 N.E.2d 19 (1984). "In the context of a freeze-out merger, variant treatment of the minority shareholders—i.e., causing their removal—will be justified when related to the advancement of a general corporate interest. The benefit need not be great, but it must be for the corporation. For example, if the sole purpose of the merger is reduction of the number of profit sharers—in contrast to increasing the corporation's capital or profits, or improving its management structure—there will exist no 'independent corporate interest' (see *Schwartz v. Marien*, 37 N.Y.2d 487, 492, 373 N.Y.S.2d 122, 335 N.E.2d

334, supra). All of these purposes ultimately seek to increase the individual wealth of the remaining shareholders. What distinguishes a proper corporate purpose from an improper one is that, with the former, removal of the minority shareholders furthers the objective of conferring some general gain upon the corporation. Only then will the fiduciary duty of good and prudent management of the corporation serve to override the concurrent duty to treat all shareholders fairly (see Klurfeld v. Equity Enterprises, 79 A.D.2d 124, 136, 436 N.Y.S.2d 303, supra). We further note that a finding that there was an independent corporate purpose for the action taken by the majority will not be defeated merely by the fact that the corporate objective could have been accomplished in another way, or by the fact that the action chosen was not the best way to achieve the bona fide business objective.''

See also Grimes v. Donaldson, Lufkin & Jenrette, Inc., 392 F.Supp. 1393 (N.D.Fla.1974), aff'd without opinion 521 F.2d 812 (5th Cir. 1975).

---

## CAL. CORP. CODE § 407

[See Statutory Supplement]

---

## ALI, PRINCIPLES OF CORPORATE GOVERNANCE §§ 5.15, 7.25

[See Statutory Supplement]

---

## (i) GOING PRIVATE

"Going private" involves the conversion of a corporation that is publicly held into one that is privately held—or, more particularly, the conversion of a corporation whose stock is registered under the 1934 Act, and listed on a Stock Exchange or actively traded over the counter, into one whose stock is unregistered, unlisted, and traded thinly if at all. While going private is often accomplished through a freezeout, the two categories are not entirely coextensive: going private, unlike freezeouts, does not necessarily involve *legal* compulsion, since it may be accomplished through purchase of the minority's shares. On the other hand, as the following material shows, such purchases, while apparently involving voluntary action on the minority's part, may in fact involve very little meaningful choice, and are often accomplished in part by the implicit or explicit threat that those who do not sell voluntarily will be made to sell involuntarily through use of a cashout merger or other freezeout device.

---

## SECURITIES EXCHANGE ACT RULE 13e–3 AND SCHEDULE 13E–3

[See Statutory Supplement]

---

# SECTION 2. TENDER OFFERS

---

## SECURITIES EXCHANGE ACT §§ 13(d), (e), 14(d), (e)

[See Statutory Supplement]

---

## SECURITIES EXCHANGE ACT RULES 13d–1, 13d–3, 13d–5, 13e–1, 13e–4, 14d–1 to 14d–4, 14d–6 to 14d–10, 14e–1 to 14e–3, 14e–5

[See Statutory Supplement]

---

## SCHEDULES 13D, TO 14D–9

[See Statutory Supplement]

---

## HART–SCOTT–RODINO ACT

[See Statutory Supplement]

---

## NOTE ON TERMINOLOGY

The legal profession has developed a rich terminology in connection with tender offers. The terms are too numerous and change too quickly to permit a comprehensive glossary, and some of the terms are fairly well defined in the cases that follow. This Note defines a few of the more important terms that are not defined in those cases.

*Crown jewels.* To defeat or discourage a takeover bid by a disfavored bidder, the target's management may sell or (more usually) give to a white knight a lock-up option that covers the target's most desirable business or, at least, the business most coveted by the disfavored bidder—its *crown jewels.*

*Fair-price provisions.* A *fair-price provision* requires that a super-majority (usually eighty percent) of the voting power of a corporation must approve any merger or similar combination with an acquiror who owns a specified interest in the corporation (usually twenty percent of the voting power). The supermajority vote is not required under certain conditions—most notably, if the transaction is approved by a majority of those directors who are not affiliated with the acquiror and were directors at the time the acquiror reached the specified level of ownership of the company, or if certain minimum-price criteria and procedural requirements are satisfied. A fair-price provision discourages purchasers whose objective is to seek control of a corporation at a relatively cheap price, and discourages accumulations of large blocks, since it reduces the options an acquiror has once it reaches the specified level of shares. M. Lipton & E. Steinberger, Takeovers & Freezeouts § 6.03[2] (1987).

*Junk bonds.* A *junk bond* is a bond that has an unusually high risk of default (and is therefore below investment grade), but, correspondingly, carries an unusually high yield. (The theory is that by diversification—that is, by holding a portfolio of junk bonds—investors in junk bonds can insulate themselves from catastrophic loss if any one bond issue goes under.) Because an LBO is so highly leveraged, much or most of the debt issued to finance an LBO usually consists of junk bonds.

*Leveraged buyout.* A leveraged buyout is a combination of a management buyout and a high degree of leverage. A *management buyout* (MBO) is the acquisition for cash or non-convertible senior securities of the business of a public corporation, by a newly organized corporation in which members of the former management of the public corporation will have a significant equity interest, pursuant to a merger or other form of combination. See Lowenstein, Management Buyouts, 85 Colum.L.Rev. 730, 732 (1985). *Leverage* involves the use of debt to increase the return on equity. The extent of leverage is measured by the ratio of debt to equity. The higher the ratio, the greater the leverage (or, to put it differently, the more highly leveraged the corporation is). A *leveraged buyout* (LBO) is an MBO that is highly leveraged—that is, in which the newly organized acquiring corporation has a very high amount of debt in relation to its equity. Characteristically, an LBO is arranged by a firm that specializes in such transactions, can find investors (or will itself invest) along with senior management in the new firm's securities, and can arrange for (or help arrange for) placement of the massive amount of debt that the new corporation must issue to finance the acquisition of the old corporation's business.

*Lock-up.* A *lock-up* is a device that is designed to protect one bidder (normally, a friendly bidder) against competition by other bidders (deemed less friendly). The favored bidder is given an option to acquire selected assets or a given amount of shares of the target at a favorable price under designated conditions. These conditions usually involve either defeat of the favored bidder's attempt to acquire the corporation, or the occurrence of events that would make that defeat likely.

*No-shop clauses.* A board of a corporation that enters into an agreement for a merger or other corporate combination (whether with a white knight or otherwise) may agree that it will recommend the combination to the shareholders, that it will not shop around for a more attractive deal, or both. The courts have divided on the question whether such provisions are unenforceable on the ground that they conflict with the director's fiduciary obligation to maximize the shareholders' best interests. Compare Jewel Companies, Inc. v. Pay Less Drug Stores Northwest, Inc., 741 F.2d 1555 (9th Cir.1984) (no-shop clause enforceable) with Great Western Producers Co–Operative v. Great Western United Corporation, 200 Colo. 180, 613 P.2d 873 (1980) (agreement to recommend transaction to the shareholders not effectively enforceable).

*Poison pills.* In essence, a *poison pill* (also known as a *Rights Plan* or a *Shareholder Rights Plan*) is a plan under which the board of directors creates Rights that are distributed or distributable to shareholders. Under the Rights, upon the occurrence of certain events shareholders *other than a tender-offer bidder or prospective bidder* have the right to purchase stock in the corporation, or under certain circumstances in an acquiror, at a deep discount—normally, half-price. Because the potential exercise of the Rights would dramatically dilute the value of the target stock that the bidder proposes to acquire, the mere potential that the Rights will be exercised may serve as a deterrent to making a bid in the first place (although for reasons that will be explored in the materials that follow, the pill is usually not a complete show-stopper).

The actual mechanics of pills are highly complex, and have evolved over time. Here is a description of a fairly standard modern version of the pill, taken from Carmody v. Toll Brothers, Inc., 723 A.2d 1180 (Del.Ch.1998). The corporation whose pill is described was named Toll Brothers:

> The Rights Plan would operate as follows: there would be a dividend distribution of one preferred stock purchase right (a "Right") for each outstanding share of common stock as of July 11, 1997. Initially the Rights would attach to the company's outstanding common shares, and each Right would initially entitle the holder to purchase one thousandth of a share of a newly registered series Junior A Preferred Stock for $100. The Rights would become exercisable, and would trade separately from the common shares, after the "Distribution Date," which is defined as the earlier of (a) ten business days following a public announcement that an acquiror has acquired, or obtained the right to acquire, beneficial ownership of 15% or more of the company's outstanding common shares (the "Stock Acquisition Date"), or (b) ten business days after the commencement of a tender offer or exchange offer that would result in a person or group beneficially owning 15% or more of the company's outstanding common shares. Once exercisable, the Rights remain exercisable until their Final Expiration Date (June 12, 2007, ten years after the adoption

of the Plan), unless the Rights are earlier redeemed by the company.

The dilutive mechanism of the Rights is "triggered" by certain defined events. One such event is the acquisition of 15% or more of Toll Brothers' stock by any person or group of affiliated or associated persons. Should that occur, each Rights holder (except the acquiror and its affiliates and associates) becomes entitled to buy two shares of Toll Brothers common stock or other securities at half price. That is, the value of the stock received when the Right is exercised is equal to two times the exercise price of the Right. In that manner, this so-called "flip in" feature of the Rights Plan would massively dilute the value of the holdings of the unwanted acquiror. . . .

The "flip-in" feature of a rights plan is triggered when the acquiror crosses the specified ownership threshold, regardless of the acquiror's intentions with respect to the use of the shares. At that point, rights vest in all shareholders other than the acquiror, and as a result, those holders become entitled to acquire additional shares of voting stock at a substantially discounted price, usually 50% of the market price. Commonly, rights plans also contain a "flip-over" feature entitling target company shareholders (again, other than the acquiror) to purchase shares of the acquiring company at a reduced price. That feature is activated when, after a "flip-in" triggering event, the acquiror initiates a triggering event, such as a merger, self-dealing transaction, or sale of assets. . . .

The Rights [in the case at bar] have a standard "flip over" feature, which is triggered if after the Stock Acquisition Date, the company is made a party to a merger in which Toll Brothers is not the surviving corporation, or in which it is the surviving corporation and its common stock is changed or exchanged. In either event, each Rights holder becomes entitled to purchase common stock of the acquiring company, again at half-price, thereby impairing the acquiror's capital structure and drastically diluting the interest of the acquiror's other stockholders.

Id. at 1183–84 & n.5.

A flip-over pill is normally triggered only by a corporate combination between the bidder and the target following the initial tender offer. The effect of a flip-over pill may therefore be moderated where the bidder's business plan allows it to forgo such a merger. A flip-in pill is much more wide-ranging in its applicability, but usually the Rights issued under such a pill can be redeemed by the target's board for a nominal consideration at any time before a triggering event and, often, for a brief period thereafter.

*Raider.* The term *raider* refers to a person (normally, although not necessarily, a corporation) that makes a tender offer. The term is invidious; a more accurate term is *bidder.*

*Standstill.* A target may seek an accommodation with a shareholder who has acquired a significant amount of stock, under which the shareholder agrees to limit his stock purchases—hence, *standstill.* In the typical standstill agreement, the shareholder makes one or more commitments: (i) it will not increase its shareholdings above designated limits for a specified period of time; (ii) it will not sell its shares without giving the corporation a right of first refusal; (iii) it will not engage in a proxy contest; and (iv) it will vote its stock in a designated manner in the election of directors, and perhaps on other issues. In return, the corporation typically agrees to give the shareholder board representation, to register the shareholder's stock under the Securities Act on demand, and not to oppose the shareholder's acquisition of stock up to the specified limit.

*Target.* The corporation whose shares the raider or bidder seeks to acquire is referred to as the *target.*

*White knight.* Often the management of a target realizes that it will be taken over, but prefers a takeover by someone (sometimes, anyone) other than the original bidder. The management therefore solicits competing tender offers from other corporations. These more friendly corporations are known as *white knights.*

———

## NOTE ON THE WILLIAMS ACT

Tender offers, and the toehold share acquisitions that often precede them, are regulated in a great number of respects by the Williams Act, which added 13(d) and (e), and 14(d), (e), and (f), to the Securities Exchange Act. Section 14(d), and Rule 14d thereunder, apply to tender offers for more than 5% of any class of equity security that is registered under Section 12 of the Act. Section 14(e), and Rule 14e thereunder, apply to any tender offer for any class of security. Accordingly, in theory section 14(e) and Rule 14e cover more tender offers than section 14(d) and Rule 14d. In practice, however, most tender offers will be covered by both sections and both rules. For ease of exposition, in the balance of this Note all references to tender offers will mean tender offers that are covered by the relevant sections and rules, unless otherwise stated.

1. *Toehold Acquisitions.* Under section 13(d) of the Securities Exchange Act, a person who has acquired beneficial ownership of more than 5% of any class of equity securities registered under section 12 of the Act must file a Schedule 13D within 10 days of the acquisition. The Schedule 13D must include the purchaser's identity and background; the amount and sources of the funds for the purchase; the purpose of the purchase; any plans with respect to extraordinary corporate transactions involving the corporation whose stock has been acquired; and any contracts, arrangements, or understandings with other persons regarding the corporation's securities. Under Rule 13d–2, any material changes in the information disclosed in a Schedule 13D must be promptly updated, and any further acquisitions

of an additional 1% or more of the corporation's stock will be deemed material. Even further acquisitions of less than 1% of the corporation's stock may be deemed material, depending on the circumstances.

Furthermore, under section 13(d)(3) of the Securities Exchange Act, as implemented by Rule 13d–5(b), when two or more persons agree to act together for the purpose of acquiring, holding, voting, or disposing of an issuer's equity securities, the group formed by the agreement is deemed to have acquired ownership of all securities of that issuer owned by any member of the group for purposes of section 13(d). Even acting in concert may create a group for these purposes.

Wholly aside from the Williams Act, the Hart–Scott–Rodino Antitrust Improvements Act requires notification of acquisitions of stock in medium-size and large publicly held companies, if the acquisition will result in the acquiror's owning voting stock in the corporation in excess of $15 million. For most corporations that are likely to be made subject to a tender offer, $15 million of the corporation's stock will be substantially less than 5% of its stock. Thus Hart–Scott–Rodino effectively lowers the reporting threshold for most toehold acquisitions.

2. *What Constitutes a Tender Offer.* What constitutes a "tender offer" within the meaning of the Williams Act is not completely settled. Purchases made anonymously on the open market almost certainly do not constitute a tender offer within the meaning of the Act. Kennecott Copper Corp. v. Curtiss–Wright Corp., 584 F.2d 1195 (2d Cir.1978); Calumet Industries, Inc. v. MacClure, 464 F.Supp. 19 (N.D.Ill.1978). As a practical matter, therefore, the problem arises when an offer is made to a limited number of potential sellers, rather than to all the shareholders as in a conventional tender offer. Some courts have adopted an eight-factor test to determine whether an offer to buy stock is a tender offer under the Act. These factors are: (i) Whether the purchasers engage in active and widespread solicitation of public shareholders. (ii) Whether the solicitation is made for a substantial percentage of the issuer's stock. (iii) Whether the offer to purchase is made at a premium over the prevailing market price. (iv) Whether the terms of the offer are firm rather than negotiable. (v) Whether the offer is contingent on the tender of a fixed number of shares. (vi) Whether the offer is open only for a limited person of time. (vii) Whether the offerees are under pressure to sell their stock. (viii) Whether public announcements of a purchasing program preceded or accompanied a rapid accumulation of large amounts of the target's securities. Wellman v. Dickinson, 475 F.Supp. 783 (S.D.N.Y.1979), aff'd on other grounds 682 F.2d 355 (2d Cir.1982), cert. denied 460 U.S. 1069, 103 S.Ct. 1522, 75 L.Ed.2d 946 (1983); SEC v. Carter Hawley Hale Stores, Inc., 760 F.2d 945 (9th Cir.1985).

In Hanson Trust PLC v. SCM Corp., 774 F.2d 47 (2d Cir.1985), the Second Circuit rejected the eight-factor test, and held instead that whether an offer to buy stock constitutes a tender offer under the Williams Act turns on whether there appears to be a likelihood that unless the Act's rules are followed, there will be a substantial risk that solicited shareholders will lack information needed to make a carefully considered appraisal of the proposal put before them. Applying that standard, the Second Circuit held in *Hanson* that the transaction before it was not a tender offer. The target had 22,800 shareholders and offers were made to only six. At least five of the sellers were highly sophisticated professionals, knowledgeable in the market place and well aware of the essential facts needed to exercise their professional skills and to appraise the offer. The sellers were not pressured to sell their shares by any conduct that the Williams Act was designed to alleviate, but only by the forces of the market place. There was no active or widespread advance publicity or public solicitation. The price received by the six sellers was not at a premium over the then-market price. The purchases were not made contingent upon acquiring a fixed minimum number or percentage of the target's outstanding shares. There was no time limit within which the buyer would purchase the target's stock.

3. *Schedule 14D.* Section 14(d) of the Securities Exchange Act requires any person who makes a tender offer for a class of registered equity securities that would result in that person owning more than 5% of the class to file a Schedule 14D. The Schedule 14D must contain extensive disclosure of such matters as the offer; the identity of the bidder; past dealings between the bidder and the target corporation; the bidder's source of funds; the bidder's purposes and plans concerning the target; the bidder's contracts and understandings or relationships with respect to securities of the target; financial statements of the bidder, if they are material and the bidder is not an individual; and arrangements between the bidder and persons holding important positions with the target.

4. *Regulation of the Terms of Tender Offers.* Section 14(d) of the Securities Exchange Act, and Rules 14d and 14e, regulate the terms of tender offers. These provisions impose the following requirements, among others:

(i) *Minimum duration.* Under Rule 14e–1, a tender offer must be held open for at least twenty business days.

(ii) *All-holders rule.* Rule 14d–10 provides that a bidder may not make a tender offer for a class of securities unless the offer is open, at the same price and on the same terms, to all holders of the class. Under the Supremacy Clause, this rule, called the "all holders rule," displaces the outcome of the *Unocal* case, infra, which held that under Delaware law a corporation can make an exclusionary self-tender— that is, a tender offer that excludes certain shares of the class for which the offer is made.

(iii) *Best-price rule.* Rule 14d–10 also provides that the price paid to any security holder pursuant to a tender offer must equal the highest price that the bidder pays to any other security holder during the tender offer. See Epstein v. MCA, Inc., 47 F.3d 1175 (9th Cir.1995), rev'd on other grounds sub nom. Matsushita Electrical Industrial Corp. v. Epstein, 516 U.S. 367, 116 S.Ct. 873, 134 L.Ed.2d 6 (1996), reaffirmed on remand, 126 F.2d 1235 (9th Cir. 1997). Under this rule, if, as frequently occurs, the bidder increases the bid price during a tender offer, the new, higher price must be made retroactively available to all holders who tendered before the increase. In addition, Rule 10b–13 provides that during the pendency of tender offer, the bidder cannot purchase securities that are subject to the tender offer except under the tender offer—that is, the bidder cannot make private purchases for the duration of the tender offer.

(iv) *Withdrawal rights.* Under section 14(d)(5) of the Williams Act, a tendering shareholder can withdraw at any time after sixty days from the date the offer was disseminated as to shares that have not yet been accepted. Under Rule 14d–7, a tendering shareholder can withdraw the tendered shares during the entire duration of the offer and any extension of the offer.

(v) *Proration.* Under Rule 14d–8, if a bidder makes a partial tender offer—that is, an offer for less than 100% of the target's securities—and more securities are tendered during the duration of the tender offer than the bidder has offered to accept, the bidder must accept all tendered securities, up to the stated percentage, on a pro rata basis.

5. *Obligations of the Target's Management.* Rule 14e–2 requires the target corporation (really, the target's board), no later than ten business days from the date the tender offer is first published, to give its shareholders a statement disclosing that the target either: (A) Recommends acceptance of the tender offer. (B) Recommends rejection of the tender offer. (C) Expresses no opinion and is remaining neutral toward the tender offer. (D) Is unable to take a position with respect to the tender offer. The statement must also describe the reasons for target's position.

Furthermore, under Rule 14d–9 any person who solicits or makes a recommendation to shareholders in respect of a tender offer (as opposed to making a tender offer) must file a Schedule 14D–9. This Schedule requires disclosure of, among other things, the nature of and the reasons for the solicitation or recommendation, conflicts of interest of the person filing the statement, and any negotiation or transaction that is being undertaken that relates to an extraordinary transaction (such as a merger) involving the target, a purchase or sale of a material amount of assets by the target, an acquisition of securities by the target, or a material change in the target's capitalization or in its dividend policy. Under Rule 14d–9(f), the statement that management is required to make concerning its position on the tender offer is a solicitation or recommendation to shareholders within the meaning of Rule 14d–9. Accordingly, as a practical matter the management of a corporation for whom a tender offer is made must make the disclosures required in Schedule 14D–9.

6. *Tender Offers by Issuers.* Under section 13(e) of the Securities Exchange Act and Rule 13e, corporations that tender for their own stock ("issuer" or "self" tenders) are subject to obligations similar to those imposed on outside bidders under rules 14d and 14e.

7.  *Anti-Fraud Provision.* Section 14(e) of the Securities Exchange Act prohibits material misstatements, misleading omissions, and fraudulent or manipulative acts, in connection with a tender offer or any solicitation in favor of or in opposition to a tender offer. Section 14(e) is closely comparable to Rule 10b–5, except that it does not contain the limiting language, "in connection with the purchase or sale" of securities, found in Rule 10b–5. It has been held that a plaintiff who brings suit for damages under section 14(e) must establish scienter. See Connecticut National Bank v. Fluor Corp., 808 F.2d 957 (2d Cir.1987).

8.  *Standing.* A bidder does not have standing to sue for damages under the Williams Act, on the theory that the purpose of the Act is to protect the target's shareholders. Piper v. Chris–Craft Industries, Inc., 430 U.S. 1, 97 S.Ct. 926, 51 L.Ed.2d 124 (1977). The target's shareholders have standing to sue for damages and, in appropriate cases, injunctive relief. The target can also sue for an injunction against the bidder for violation of section 14(e), because such an injunction will protect the interests of the target's shareholders. Gearhart Industries, Inc. v. Smith International, Inc., 741 F.2d 707 (5th Cir.1984). Even a nontendering shareholder may be able to bring suit for damages under the anti-fraud provision, section 14(e), if she can show causation, because section 14(e) does not contain the purchaser-or-seller requirement of Rule 10b–5.

--------

# Unocal Corp. v. Mesa Petroleum Co.

Supreme Court of Delaware, 1985.
493 A.2d 946.

■ Before McNEILLY and MOORE, JJ., and TAYLOR, JUDGE (Sitting by designation pursuant to Del.Const. Art. 4, § 12.)

■ MOORE, JUSTICE.

We confront an issue of first impression in Delaware—the validity of a corporation's self-tender for its own shares which excludes from participation a stockholder making a hostile tender offer for the company's stock.

The Court of Chancery granted a preliminary injunction to the plaintiffs, Mesa Petroleum Co., Mesa Asset Co., Mesa Partners II, and Mesa Eastern, Inc. (collectively "Mesa")[1], enjoining an exchange offer of the defendant, Unocal Corporation (Unocal) for its own stock. The trial court concluded that a selective exchange offer, excluding Mesa, was legally impermissible. We cannot agree with such a blanket rule. The factual findings of the Vice Chancellor, fully supported by the record, establish that Unocal's board, consisting of a majority of independent directors, acted in good faith, and after reasonable investigation found that Mesa's tender offer was both inadequate and

---

1.  T. Boone Pickens, Jr., is President and Chairman of the Board of Mesa Petroleum and President of Mesa Asset and controls the related Mesa entities.

coercive. Under the circumstances the board had both the power and duty to oppose a bid it perceived to be harmful to the corporate enterprise. On this record we are satisfied that the device Unocal adopted is reasonable in relation to the threat posed, and that the board acted in the proper exercise of sound business judgment. We will not substitute our views for those of the board if the latter's decision can be "attributed to any rational business purpose." Sinclair Oil Corp. v. Levien, Del.Supr., 280 A.2d 717, 720 (1971). Accordingly, we reverse the decision of the Court of Chancery and order the preliminary injunction vacated.

## I.

The factual background of this matter bears a significant relationship to its ultimate outcome.

On April 8, 1985, Mesa, the owner of approximately 13% of Unocal's stock, commenced a two-tier "front loaded" cash tender offer for 64 million shares, or approximately 37%, of Unocal's outstanding stock at a price of $54 per share. The "back-end" was designed to eliminate the remaining publicly held shares by an exchange of securities purportedly worth $54 per share. However, pursuant to an order entered by the United States District Court for the Central District of California on April 26, 1985, Mesa issued a supplemental proxy statement to Unocal's stockholders disclosing that the securities offered in the second-step merger would be highly subordinated, and that Unocal's capitalization would differ significantly from its present structure. Unocal has rather aptly termed such securities "junk bonds".[2]

Unocal's board consists of eight independent outside directors and six insiders. It met on April 13, 1985, to consider the Mesa tender offer. Thirteen directors were present, and the meeting lasted nine and one-half hours. The directors were given no agenda or written materials prior to the session. However, detailed presentations were made by legal counsel regarding the board's obligations under both

---

**2.** Mesa's May 3, 1985 supplement to its proxy statement states:

(i) following the Offer, the Purchasers would seek to effect a merger of Unocal and Mesa Eastern or an affiliate of Mesa Eastern (the "Merger") in which the remaining Shares would be acquired for a combination of subordinated debt securities and preferred stock; (ii) the securities to be received by Unocal shareholders in the Merger would be subordinated to $2,400 million of debt securities of Mesa Eastern, indebtedness incurred to refinance up to $1,000 million of bank debt which was incurred by affiliates of Mesa Partners II to purchase Shares and to pay related interest and expenses and all then-existing debt of Unocal; (iii) the corporation surviving the Merger would be responsible for the payment of all securities of Mesa Eastern (including any

such securities issued pursuant to the Merger) and the indebtedness referred to in item (ii) above, and such securities and indebtedness would be repaid out of funds generated by the operations of Unocal; (iv) the indebtedness incurred in the Offer and the Merger would result in Unocal being much more highly leveraged, and the capitalization of the corporation surviving the Merger would differ significantly from that of Unocal at present; and (v) in their analyses of cash flows provided by operations of Unocal which would be available to service and repay securities and other obligations of the corporation surviving the Merger, the Purchasers assumed that the capital expenditures and expenditures for exploration of such corporation would be significantly reduced.

Delaware corporate law and the federal securities laws. The board then received a presentation from Peter Sachs on behalf of Goldman Sachs & Co. (Goldman Sachs) and Dillon, Read & Co. (Dillon Read) discussing the bases for their opinions that the Mesa proposal was wholly inadequate. Mr. Sachs opined that the minimum cash value that could be expected from a sale or orderly liquidation for 100% of Unocal's stock was in excess of $60 per share. In making his presentation, Mr. Sachs showed slides outlining the valuation techniques used by the financial advisors, and others, depicting recent business combinations in the oil and gas industry. The Court of Chancery found that the Sachs presentation was designed to apprise the directors of the scope of the analyses performed rather than the facts and numbers used in reaching the conclusion that Mesa's tender offer price was inadequate.

Mr. Sachs also presented various defensive strategies available to the board if it concluded that Mesa's two-step tender offer was inadequate and should be opposed. One of the devices outlined was a self-tender by Unocal for its own stock with a reasonable price range of $70 to $75 per share. The cost of such a proposal would cause the company to incur $6.1–6.5 billion of additional debt, and a presentation was made informing the board of Unocal's ability to handle it. The directors were told that the primary effect of this obligation would be to reduce exploratory drilling, but that the company would nonetheless remain a viable entity.

The eight outside directors, comprising a clear majority of the thirteen members present, then met separately with Unocal's financial advisors and attorneys. Thereafter, they unanimously agreed to advise the board that it should reject Mesa's tender offer as inadequate, and that Unocal should pursue a self-tender to provide the stockholders with a fairly priced alternative to the Mesa proposal. The board then reconvened and unanimously adopted a resolution rejecting as grossly inadequate Mesa's tender offer. Despite the nine and one-half hour length of the meeting, no formal decision was made on the proposed defensive self-tender.

On April 15, the board met again with four of the directors present by telephone and one member still absent. This session lasted two hours. Unocal's Vice President of Finance and its Assistant General Counsel made a detailed presentation of the proposed terms of the exchange offer. A price range between $70 and $80 per share was considered, and ultimately the directors agreed upon $72. The board was also advised about the debt securities that would be issued, and the necessity of placing restrictive covenants upon certain corporate activities until the obligations were paid. The board's decisions were made in reliance on the advice of its investment bankers, including the terms and conditions upon which the securities were to be issued. Based upon this advice, and the board's own deliberations, the directors unanimously approved the exchange offer. Their resolution provided that if Mesa acquired 64 million shares of Unocal stock through its own offer (the Mesa Purchase Condition), Unocal would buy the remaining 49% outstanding for an exchange of debt securities having an aggregate par value of $72 per share. The board resolution also stated that the offer would be subject to other conditions that had been described to the board at the meeting, or which were deemed necessary by Unocal's officers, including the exclusion of Mesa from the proposal (the Mesa exclusion). Any such conditions were required to be in accordance with the "purport and intent" of the offer.

Unocal's exchange offer was commenced on April 17, 1985, and Mesa promptly challenged it by filing this suit in the Court of Chancery. On April 22, the Unocal board met again and was advised by Goldman Sachs and Dillon Read to waive the Mesa Purchase Condition as to 50 million shares. This recommendation was in response to a perceived concern of the shareholders that, if shares were tendered to Unocal, no shares would be purchased by either offeror. The directors were also advised that they should tender their own Unocal stock into the exchange offer as a mark of their confidence in it.

Another focus of the board was the Mesa exclusion. Legal counsel advised that under Delaware law Mesa could only be excluded for what the directors reasonably believed to be a valid corporate purpose. The directors' discussion centered on the objective of adequately compensating shareholders at the "back-end" of Mesa's proposal, which the latter would finance with "junk bonds". To include Mesa would defeat that goal, because under the proration aspect of the exchange offer (49%) every Mesa share accepted by Unocal would displace one held by another stockholder. Further, if Mesa were permitted to tender to Unocal, the latter would in effect be financing Mesa's own inadequate proposal.

On April 24, 1985 Unocal issued a supplement to the exchange offer describing the partial waiver of the Mesa Purchase Condition. On May 1, 1985, in another supplement, Unocal extended the withdrawal, proration and expiration dates of its exchange offer to May 17, 1985.

Meanwhile, on April 22, 1985, Mesa amended its complaint in this action to challenge the Mesa exclusion. . . .

. . . [H]he Vice Chancellor granted Mesa a preliminary injunction. . . .

On May 13, 1985 the Court of Chancery certified this interlocutory appeal to us as a question of first impression, and we accepted it on May 14. The entire matter was scheduled on an expedited basis.

II.

The issues we address involve these fundamental questions: Did the Unocal board have the power and duty to oppose a takeover threat it reasonably perceived to be harmful to the corporate enterprise, and if so, is its action here entitled to the protection of the business judgment rule?

Mesa contends that the discriminatory exchange offer violates the fiduciary duties Unocal owes it. Mesa argues that because of the Mesa exclusion the business judgment rule is inapplicable, because the directors by tendering their own shares will derive a financial benefit that is not available to *all* Unocal stockholders. Thus, it is Mesa's ultimate contention that Unocal cannot establish that the exchange offer is fair to *all* shareholders, and argues that the Court of Chancery was correct in concluding that Unocal was unable to meet this burden.

Unocal answers that it does not owe a duty of "fairness" to Mesa, given the facts here. Specifically, Unocal contends that its board of directors reasonably and in good faith concluded that Mesa's $54 two-tier tender offer was coercive and inadequate, and that Mesa sought selective treatment for itself. Furthermore, Unocal argues that the board's approval of the exchange offer was made in good faith, on an informed basis, and in the exercise of due care. Under these circumstances, Unocal contends that its directors properly employed this device to protect the company and its stockholders from Mesa's harmful tactics.

## III.

We begin with the basic issue of the power of a board of directors of a Delaware corporation to adopt a defensive measure of this type. Absent such authority, all other questions are moot. Neither issues of fairness nor business judgment are pertinent without the basic underpinning of a board's legal power to act.

The board has a large reservoir of authority upon which to draw. Its duties and responsibilities proceed from the inherent powers conferred by 8 Del.C. § 141(a), respecting management of the corporation's "business and affairs". Additionally, the powers here being exercised derive from 8 Del.C. § 160(a), conferring broad authority upon a corporation to deal in its own stock. From this it is now well established that in the acquisition of its shares a Delaware corporation may deal selectively with its stockholders, provided the directors have not acted out of a sole or primary purpose to entrench themselves in office. Cheff v. Mathes, Del.Supr., 199 A.2d 548, 554 (1964); Bennett v. Propp, Del.Supr., 187 A.2d 405, 408 (1962); Martin v. American Potash & Chemical Corporation, Del.Supr., 92 A.2d 295, 302 (1952); Kaplan v. Goldsamt, Del.Ch., 380 A.2d 556, 568–569 (1977); Kors v. Carey, Del.Ch., 158 A.2d 136, 140–141 (1960).

Finally, the board's power to act derives from its fundamental duty and obligation to protect the corporate enterprise, which includes stockholders, from harm reasonably perceived, irrespective of its source. See e.g.... Cheff v. Mathes, 199 A.2d at 556; Martin v. American Potash & Chemical Corp., 92 A.2d at 302; Kaplan v. Goldsamt, 380 A.2d at 568–69; Kors v. Carey, 158 A.2d at 141 ... Thus, we are satisfied that in the broad context of corporate governance, including issues of fundamental corporate change, a board of directors is not a passive instrumentality.[8]

Given the foregoing principles, we turn to the standards by which director action is to be measured. In Pogostin v. Rice, Del.Supr., 480

---

**8.** Even in the traditional areas of fundamental corporate change, i.e., charter amendments [8 Del.C. § 242(b)], mergers [8 Del.C. §§ 251(b), 252(c), 253(a), and 254(d)], sale of assets [8 Del.C. § 271(a)], and dissolution [8 Del.C. § 275(a)], director action is a prerequisite to the ultimate disposition of

A.2d 619 (1984), we held that the business judgment rule, including the standards by which director conduct is judged, is applicable in the context of a takeover. Id. at 627. The business judgment rule is a "presumption that in making a business decision the directors of a corporation acted on an informed basis, in good faith and in the honest belief that the action taken was in the best interests of the company." Aronson v. Lewis, Del.Supr., 473 A.2d 805, 812 (1984) (citations omitted). A hallmark of the business judgment rule is that a court will not substitute its judgment for that of the board if the latter's decision can be "attributed to any rational business purpose." Sinclair Oil Corp. v. Levien, Del.Supr., 280 A.2d 717, 720 (1971).

When a board addresses a pending takeover bid it has an obligation to determine whether the offer is in the best interests of the corporation and its shareholders. In that respect a board's duty is no different from any other responsibility it shoulders, and its decision should be no less entitled to the respect they otherwise would be accorded in the realm of business judgment. See also Johnson v. Trueblood, 629 F.2d 287, 292–293 (3d Cir.1980). There are, however, certain caveats to a proper exercise of this function. Because of the omnipresent specter that a board may be acting primarily in its own interests,rather than those of the corporation and its shareholders, there is an enhanced duty which calls for judicial examination at the threshold before the protections of the business judgment rule may be conferred.

This Court has long recognized that:

> We must bear in mind the inherent danger in the purchase of shares with corporate funds to remove a threat to corporate policy when a threat to control is involved. The directors are of necessity confronted with a conflict of interest, and an objective decision is difficult.

Bennett v. Propp, Del.Supr., 187 A.2d 405, 409 (1962). In the face of this inherent conflict directors must show that they had reasonable grounds for believing that a danger to corporate policy and effectiveness existed because of another person's stock ownership. Cheff v. Mathes, 199 A.2d at 554–55. However, they satisfy that burden "by showing good faith and reasonable investigation...." Id. at 555. Furthermore, such proof is materially enhanced, as here, by the approval of a board comprised of a majority of outside independent directors who have acted in accordance with the foregoing standards. See Aronson v. Lewis, 473 A.2d at 812, 815; Puma v. Marriott, Del.Ch., 283 A.2d 693, 695 (1971); Panter v. Marshall Field & Co., 646 F.2d 271, 295 (7th Cir.1981).

### IV.

#### A.

In the board's exercise of corporate power to forestall a takeover bid our analysis begins with the basic principle that corporate di-

---

such matters. See also, Smith v. Van Gor-      kom, Del.Supr., 488 A.2d 858, 888 (1985).

rectors have a fiduciary duty to act in the best interests of the corporation's stockholders. Guth v. Loft, Inc., Del.Supr., 5 A.2d 503, 510 (1939). As we have noted, their duty of care extends to protecting the corporation and its owners from perceived harm whether a threat originates from third parties or other shareholders. But such powers are not absolute. A corporation does not have unbridled discretion to defeat any perceived threat by any Draconian means available.

The restriction placed upon a selective stock repurchase is that the directors may not have acted solely or primarily out of a desire to perpetuate themselves in office. See Cheff v. Mathes, 199 A.2d at 556; Kors v. Carey, 158 A.2d at 140. Of course, to this is added the further caveat that inequitable action may not be taken under the guise of law. Schnell v. Chris–Craft Industries, Inc., Del.Supr. 285 A.2d 437, 439 (1971). The standard of proof established in Cheff v. Mathes ... is designed to ensure that a defensive measure to thwart or impede a takeover is indeed motivated by a good faith concern for the welfare of the corporation and its stockholders, which in all circumstances must be free of any fraud or other misconduct. Cheff v. Mathes, 199 A.2d at 554–55. However, this does not end the inquiry.

### B.

A further aspect is the element of balance. If a defensive measure is to come within the ambit of the business judgment rule, it must be reasonable in relation to the threat posed. This entails an analysis by the directors of the nature of the takeover bid and its effect on the corporate enterprise. Examples of such concerns may include: inadequacy of the price offered, nature and timing of the offer, questions of illegality, the impact on "constituencies" other than shareholders (i.e., creditors, customers, employees, and perhaps even the community generally), the risk of nonconsummation, and the quality of securities being offered in the exchange. See Lipton and Brownstein, Takeover Responses and Directors' Responsibilities: An Update, p. 7, ABA National Institute on the Dynamics of Corporate Control (December 8, 1983). While not a controlling factor, it also seems to us that a board may reasonably consider the basic stockholder interests at stake, including those of short term speculators, whose actions may have fueled the coercive aspect of the offer at the expense of the long term investor.[9] Here, the threat posed was viewed by the Unocal board as a

---

**9.** There has been much debate respecting such stockholder interests. One rather impressive study indicates that the stock of over 50 percent of target companies, who resisted hostile takeovers, later traded at higher market prices than the rejected offer price, or were acquired after the tender offer was defeated by another company at a price higher than the offer price. See Lipton, supra 35 Bus.Law. at 106–109, 132–133. Moreover, an update by Kidder Peabody & Company of this study, involving the stock prices of target companies that have defeated hostile tender offers during the period from 1973 to 1982 demonstrates that in a majority of cases the target's shareholders benefited from the defeat. The stock of 81% of the targets studied has, since the tender offer, sold at prices higher than the tender offer price. When adjusted for the time value of money, the figure is 64%. See Lipton & Brownstein, supra ABA Institute at 10. The thesis being that this strongly supports application of the business judgment rule in response to takeover threats. There is, however, a rather vehement contrary view. See Easterbrook & Fischel, supra 36 Bus.Law. at 1739–1745.

grossly inadequate two-tier coercive tender offer coupled with the threat of greenmail.

Specifically, the Unocal directors had concluded that the value of Unocal was substantially above the $54 per share offered in cash at the front end. Furthermore, they determined that the subordinated securities to be exchanged in Mesa's announced squeeze out of the remaining shareholders in the "back-end" merger were "junk bonds" worth far less than $54. It is now well recognized that such offers are a classic coercive measure designed to stampede shareholders into tendering at the first tier, even if the price is inadequate, out of fear of what they will receive at the back end of the transaction. Wholly beyond the coercive aspect of an inadequate two-tier tender offer, the threat was posed by a corporate raider with a national reputation as a "greenmailer".[13]

In adopting the selective exchange offer, the board stated that its objective was either to defeat the inadequate Mesa offer or, should the offer still succeed, provide the 49% of its stockholders, who would otherwise be forced to accept "junk bonds", with $72 worth of senior debt. We find that both purposes are valid.

However, such efforts would have been thwarted by Mesa's participation in the exchange offer. First, if Mesa could tender its shares, Unocal would effectively be subsidizing the former's continuing effort to buy Unocal stock at $54 per share. Second, Mesa could not, by definition, fit within the class of shareholders being protected from its own coercive and inadequate tender offer.

Thus, we are satisfied that the selective exchange offer is reasonably related to the threats posed. It is consistent with the principle that "the minority stockholder shall receive the substantial equivalent in value of what he had before." Sterling v. Mayflower Hotel Corp., Del.Supr., 93 A.2d 107, 114 (1952). See also Rosenblatt v. Getty Oil Co., Del.Supr., 493 A.2d 929, 940 (1985). This concept of fairness, while stated in the merger context, is also relevant in the area of tender offer law. Thus, the board's decision to offer what it determined to be the fair value of the corporation to the 49% of its shareholders, who would otherwise be forced to accept highly subordinated "junk bonds", is reasonable and consistent with the directors' duty to ensure that the minority stockholders receive equal value for their shares.

## V.

Mesa contends that it is unlawful, and the trial court agreed, for a corporation to discriminate in this fashion against one shareholder. It argues correctly that no case has ever sanctioned a device that pre-

---

**13.** The term "greenmail" refers to the practice of buying out a takeover bidder's stock at a premium that is not available to other shareholders in order to prevent the takeover. The Chancery Court noted that "Mesa has made tremendous profits from its takeover activities although in the past few years it has not been successful in acquiring any of the target companies on an unfriendly basis." Moreover, the trial court specifically found that the actions of the Unocal board were taken in good faith to eliminate both the inadequacies of the tender offer and to forestall the payment of "greenmail".

cludes a raider from sharing in a benefit available to all other stockholders. However, as we have noted earlier, the principle of selective stock repurchases by a Delaware corporation is neither unknown nor unauthorized. Cheff v. Mathes, 199 A.2d at 554; Bennett v. Propp, 187 A.2d at 408; Martin v. American Potash & Chemical Corporation, 92 A.2d at 302; Kaplan v. Goldsamt, 380 A.2d 556–569; Kors v. Carey, 158 A.2d at 140–141; 8 Del.C. § 160. The only difference is that heretofore the approved transaction was the payment of "greenmail" to a raider or dissident posing a threat to the corporate enterprise. All other stockholders were denied such favored treatment, and given Mesa's past history of greenmail, its claims here are rather ironic.

However, our corporate law is not static. It must grow and develop in response to, indeed in anticipation of, evolving concepts and needs. Merely because the General Corporation Law is silent as to a specific matter does not mean that it is prohibited. See Providence & Worcester Co. v. Baker, Del.Supr., 378 A.2d 121, 123–124 (1977). In the days when *Cheff, Bennett, Martin* and *Kors* were decided, the tender offer, while not an unknown device, was virtually unused, and little was known of such methods as two-tier "front-end" loaded offers with their coercive effects. Then, the favored attack of a raider was stock acquisition followed by a proxy contest. Various defensive tactics, which provided no benefit whatever to the raider, evolved. Thus, the use of corporate funds by management to counter a proxy battle was approved. Hall v. Trans–Lux Daylight Picture Screen Corp., Del. Supr., 171 A. 226 (1934); Hibbert v. Hollywood Park, Inc., Del.Supr., 457 A.2d 339 (1983). Litigation, supported by corporate funds, aimed at the raider has long been a popular device.

More recently, as the sophistication of both raiders and targets has developed, a host of other defensive measures to counter such ever mounting threats has evolved and received judicial sanction. These include defensive charter amendments and other devices bearing some rather exotic, but apt, names: Crown Jewel, White Knight, Pac Man, and Golden Parachute. Each has highly selective features, the object of which is to deter or defeat the raider.

Thus, while the exchange offer is a form of selective treatment, given the nature of the threat posed here the response is neither unlawful nor unreasonable. If the board of directors is disinterested, has acted in good faith and with due care, its decision in the absence of an abuse of discretion will be upheld as a proper exercise of business judgment.

To this Mesa responds that the board is not disinterested, because the directors are receiving a benefit from the tender of their own shares, which because of the Mesa exclusion, does not devolve upon *all* stockholders equally. See Aronson v. Lewis, Del.Supr., 473 A.2d 805, 812 (1984). However, Mesa concedes that if the exclusion is valid, then the directors and all other stockholders share the same benefit. The answer of course is that the exclusion is valid, and the directors' participation in the exchange offer does not rise to the level of a disqualifying interest. . . .

Nor does this become an "interested" director transaction merely because certain board members are large stockholders. As this Court has previously noted, that fact alone does not create a disqualifying "personal pecuniary interest" to defeat the operation of the business judgment rule. Cheff v. Mathes, 199 A.2d at 554.

Mesa also argues that the exclusion permits the directors to abdicate the fiduciary duties they owe it. However, that is not so. The board continues to owe Mesa the duties of due care and loyalty. But in the face of the destructive threat Mesa's tender offer was perceived to pose, the board had a supervening duty to protect the corporate enterprise, which includes the other shareholders, from threatened harm.

Mesa contends that the basis of this action is punitive, and solely in response to the exercise of its rights of corporate democracy. Nothing precludes Mesa, as a stockholder, from acting in its own self-interest. See e.g., DuPont v. DuPont, 251 Fed. 937 (D.Del.1918), aff'd 256 Fed. 129 (3d Cir.1919); Ringling Bros.–Barnum & Bailey Combined Shows, Inc. v. Ringling, Del.Supr., 53 A.2d 441, 447 (1947); Heil v. Standard Gas & Electric Co., Del.Ch., 151 A. 303, 304 (1930). But see, Allied Chemical & Dye Corp. v. Steel & Tube Co. of America, Del.Ch., 120 A. 486, 491 (1923) (majority shareholder owes a fiduciary duty to the minority shareholders). However, Mesa, while pursuing its own interests, has acted in a manner which a board consisting of a majority of independent directors has reasonably determined to be contrary to the best interests of Unocal and its other shareholders. In this situation, there is no support in Delaware law for the proposition that, when responding to a perceived harm, a corporation must guarantee a benefit to a stockholder who is deliberately provoking the danger being addressed. There is no obligation of self-sacrifice by a corporation and its shareholders in the face of such a challenge.

Here, the Court of Chancery specifically found that the "directors' decision [to oppose the Mesa tender offer] was made in the good faith belief that the Mesa tender offer is inadequate." Given our standard of review under Levitt v. Bouvier, Del.Supr., 287 A.2d 671, 673 (1972), and Application of Delaware Racing Association, Del.Supr., 213 A.2d 203, 207 (1965), we are satisfied that Unocal's board has met its burden of proof. Cheff v. Mathes, 199 A.2d at 555.

### VI.

In conclusion, there was directorial power to oppose the Mesa tender offer, and to undertake a selective stock exchange made in good faith and upon a reasonable investigation pursuant to a clear duty to protect the corporate enterprise. Further, the selective stock repurchase plan chosen by Unocal is reasonable in relation to the threat that the board rationally and reasonably believed was posed by Mesa's inadequate and coercive two-tier tender offer. Under those circumstances the board's action is entitled to be measured by the standards of the business judgment rule. Thus, unless it is shown by a preponderance of the evidence that the directors' decisions were primarily based on perpetuating themselves in office, or some other breach of fiduciary duty such as fraud, overreaching, lack of good faith, or being uninformed, a Court will not substitute its judgment for that of the board.

In this case that protection is not lost merely because Unocal's directors have tendered their shares in the exchange offer. Given the validity of the Mesa exclusion, they are receiving a benefit shared generally by all other stockholders except Mesa. In this circumstance the test of Aronson v. Lewis, 473 A.2d at 812, is satisfied. See also Cheff v. Mathes, 199 A.2d at 554. If the stockholders are displeased with the action of their elected representatives, the powers of corporate democracy are at their disposal to turn the board out. Aronson v. Lewis, Del.Supr., 473 A.2d 805, 811 (1984). See also 8 Del.C. §§ 141(k) and 211(b).

With the Court of Chancery's findings that the exchange offer was based on the board's good faith belief that the Mesa offer was inadequate, that the board's action was informed and taken with due care, that Mesa's prior activities justify a reasonable inference that its principle objective was greenmail, and implicitly, that the substance of the offer itself was reasonable and fair to the corporation and its stockholders if Mesa were included, we cannot say that the Unocal directors have acted in such a manner as to have passed an "unintelligent and unadvised judgment". Mitchell v. Highland–Western Glass Co., Del.Ch., 167 A. 831, 833 (1933). The decision of the Court of Chancery is therefore REVERSED, and the preliminary injunction is VACATED.

---

### NOTE ON UNOCAL

The specific outcome in *Unocal*, allowing an exclusionary (discriminatory) tender offer, has been superseded by the all-holders rule under the Williams Act, which ousts Delaware law under the Supremacy Clause of the Constitution. However, the basic standard of review of defensive tactics adopted in the *Unocal* decision has survived, with some glosses, as the central rule governing takeovers under Delaware law.

---

### ALI, PRINCIPLES OF CORPORATE GOVERNANCE § 6.02

[See Statutory Supplement]

---

### FORM OF SHAREHOLDERS' RIGHTS PLAN

[See Statutory Supplement]

---

## NOTE ON MORAN AND REVLON

*Unocal* was one of a famous trilogy of cases on takeovers decided by the Delaware Supreme Court in 1985. The other two cases in the trilogy were Moran v. Household International, Inc., 500 A.2d 1346 (Del. 1985) and Revlon, Inc. v. MacAndrews & Forbes Holdings, Inc., 506 A.2d 173 (Del.1985).

1. *Moran.* In *Moran*, the Delaware Supreme Court held that a corporation could validly adopt a "shareholders' rights plan"—more colloquially, a poison pill. (See Note on Terminology, supra.) A shareholders' rights plan or poison pill is the most effective weapon that a corporation can employ against takeovers, especially when coupled with ancillary measures, such as staggered boards. However, *Moran* left open a variety of issues concerning poison pills, and also explicitly left some room for limits on the use of a pill:

> [T]he Rights Plan is not absolute. When the Household Board of Directors is faced with a tender offer and a request to redeem the Rights, they will not be able to arbitrarily reject the offer. They will be held to the same fiduciary standards any other board of directors would be held to in deciding to adopt a defensive mechanism, the same standard as they were held to in originally approving the Rights Plan. See *Unocal*, 493 A.2d at 954–55, 958.

Some of the questions concerning poison pills that were left open by *Moran* were resolved by two more recent Delaware cases, Carmody v. Toll Brothers, Inc. and Quickturn Design Systems, Inc. v. Shapiro. Those cases will be considered at the end of this Chapter.

2. *Revlon.* In *Revlon*, the Delaware Supreme Court held that when the board of a corporation decided that the corporation was for sale, the duty of the board changed

> from the preservation of [the company] as a corporate entity to the maximization of the company's value at a sale for the stockholders' benefit. This significantly altered the board's responsibilities under the *Unocal* standards. It no longer faced threats to corporate policy and effectiveness, or to the stockholders' interests, from a grossly inadequate bid. The whole question of defensive measures became moot. The directors' role changed from defenders of the corporate bastion to auctioneers charged with getting the best price for the stockholders at a sale of the company.

The meaning and applicability of *Revlon* has been much debated. In Barkan v. Amsted Industries, Inc., 567 A.2d 1279 (Del.1989), the Delaware court said:

> This Court has found that certain fact patterns demand certain responses from the directors. Notably, in *Revlon* we held that when several suitors are actively bidding for control of a corporation, the directors may not use defensive tactics that destroy the auction process. *Revlon,* 506 A.2d at 182–85. When it becomes clear that the auction will result in a change of corporate

control, the board must act in a neutral manner to encourage the highest possible price for shareholders. *Id.* However, *Revlon* does not demand that every change in the control of a Delaware corporation be preceded by a heated bidding contest. *Revlon* is merely one of an unbroken line of cases that seek to prevent the conflicts of interest that arise in the field of mergers and acquisitions by demanding that directors act with scrupulous concern for fairness to shareholders. When multiple bidders are competing for control, this concern for fairness forbids directors from using defensive mechanisms to thwart an auction or to favor one bidder over another. *Id.* When the board is considering a single offer and has no reliable grounds upon which to judge its adequacy, this concern for fairness demands a canvas of the market to determine if higher bids may be elicited. *In re Fort Howard Corp. Shareholders Litig.*, C.A. No. 9991, 1988 WL 83147 (Del.Ch.1988). When, however, the directors possess a body of reliable evidence with which to evaluate the fairness of a transaction, they may approve that transaction without conducting an active survey of the market. As the Chancellor recognized, the circumstances in which this passive approach is acceptable are limited. "A decent respect for reality forces one to admit that ... advice [of an investment banker] is frequently a pale substitute for the dependable information that a canvas of the relevant market can provide." *In re Amsted Indus. Litig.*, letter op. at 19–20. The need for adequate information is central to the enlightened evaluation of a transaction that a board must make. Nevertheless, there is no single method that a board must employ to acquire such information. Here, the Chancellor found that the advice of the Special Committee's investment bankers, when coupled with the special circumstances surrounding the negotiation and consummation of the MBO, supported a finding that Amsted's directors had acted in good faith to arrange the best possible transaction for shareholders. Our own review of the record leads us to rule that the Chancellor's finding was well within the scope of his discretion.

------

## Paramount Communications, Inc. v. Time Inc.

Supreme Court of Delaware, 1989.
571 A.2d 1140.

■ Horsey, Justice:

Paramount Communications, Inc. ("Paramount") and two other groups of plaintiffs[1] ("Shareholder Plaintiffs"), shareholders of Time Incorporated ("Time"), a Delaware corporation, separately filed suits

------

1. Plaintiffs in these three consolidated appeals are: (i) Paramount Communications, Inc. and KDS Acquisition Corp. (collectively "Paramount"); (ii) Literary Partners L.P., Cablevision Media Partners, L.P., and A. Jerrold Perenchio (collectively "Literary Partners"), suing individually; and (iii) certain other shareholder plaintiffs, suing individually and as an uncertified class.

in the Delaware Court of Chancery seeking a preliminary injunction to halt Time's tender offer for 51% of Warner Communication, Inc.'s ("Warner") outstanding shares at $70 cash per share. The court below consolidated the cases and, following the development of an extensive record, after discovery and an evidentiary hearing, denied plaintiffs' motion. In a 50–page unreported opinion and order entered July 14, 1989, the Chancellor refused to enjoin Time's consummation of its tender offer, concluding that the plaintiffs were unlikely to prevail on the merits. In re Time Incorporated Shareholder Litigation, Del.Ch., C.A. No. 10670, Allen, C. (July 14, 1989).

[Plaintiffs filed an interlocutory appeal.]

The principal ground for reversal, asserted by all plaintiffs, is that Paramount's June 7, 1989 uninvited all-cash, all-shares, "fully negotiable" (though conditional) tender offer for Time triggered duties under Unocal Corp. v. Mesa Petroleum Co., Del.Supr., 493 A.2d 946 (1985), and that Time's board of directors, in responding to Paramount's offer, breached those duties. As a consequence, plaintiffs argue that in our review of the Time board's decision of June 16, 1989 to enter into a revised merger agreement with Warner, Time is not entitled to the benefit and protection of the business judgment rule.

Shareholder Plaintiffs also assert a claim based on Revlon v. MacAndrews & Forbes Holdings, Inc., Del.Supr., 506 A.2d 173 (1985). They argue that the original Time–Warner merger agreement of March 4, 1989 resulted in a change of control which effectively put Time up for sale, thereby triggering *Revlon* duties. Those plaintiffs argue that Time's board breached its *Revlon* duties by failing, in the face of the change of control, to maximize shareholder value in the immediate term.

Applying our standard of review, we affirm the Chancellor's ultimate finding and conclusion under *Unocal.* We find that Paramount's tender offer was reasonably perceived by Time's board to pose a threat to Time and that the Time board's "response" to that threat was, under the circumstances, reasonable and proportionate. Applying *Unocal,* we reject the argument that the only corporate threat posed by an all-shares, all-cash tender offer is the possibility of inadequate value.

We also find that Time's board did not by entering into its initial merger agreement with Warner come under a *Revlon* duty either to auction the company or to maximize short-term shareholder value, notwithstanding the unequal share exchange. Therefore, the Time board's original plan of merger with Warner was subject only to a business judgment rule analysis. See Smith v. Van Gorkom, Del.Supr., 488 A.2d 858, 873–74 (1985).

I

Time is a Delaware corporation with its principal offices in New York City. Time's traditional business is publication of magazines and books; however, Time also provides pay television programming through its Home Box Office, Inc. and Cinemax subsidiaries. In addition, Time owns and operates cable television franchises through its subsidiary, American Television and Communication Corporation. During the relevant time period, Time's board consisted of sixteen directors. Twelve of the directors were "outside," nonemployee directors. Four of the directors were also officers of the company. The outside directors included: James F. Bere, chairman of the board and CEO of Borg–Warner Corporation (Time director since 1979); Clifford J. Grum, president and CEO of Temple–Inland, Inc. (Time director since 1980); Henry C. Goodwin, former chairman of Sonat, Inc. (Time directors since 1978); Matina S. Horner, then president of Radcliffe College (Time director since 1975); David T. Kearns, chairman and CEO of Xerox Corporation (Time director since 1978); Donald S. Perkins, former chairman and CEO of Jewel Companies, Inc. (Time director since 1979); Michael D. Dingman, chairman and CEO of The Henley Group, Inc. (Time director since 1978); Edward S. Finkelstein, chairman and CEO of Macy's Inc. (Time director since 1984); John R. Opel, former chairman and CEO of IBM Corporation (Time director since 1984); Arthur Temple, chairman of Temple–Inland, Inc. (Time director since 1983); Clifton R. Wharton, Jr., chairman and CEO of The Henley Group, Inc. (Time director since 1978); and Henry R. Luce III, president of The Henry Luce Foundation, Inc. (Time director since 1967). Mr. Luce, the son of the founder of Time, individually and in a representative capacity controlled 4.2% of the outstanding Time stock. The inside officer directors were: J. Richard Munro, Time's chairman and CEO since 1980; N.J. Nicholas, Jr., president and chief operating officer of the company since 1986; Gerald M. Levin, vice chairman of the board; and Jason D. McManus, editor-in-chief of *Time* magazine and a board member since 1988.[3]

As early as 1983 and 1984, Time's executive board began considering expanding Time's operations into the entertainment industry. In 1987, Time established a special committee of executives to consider and propose corporate strategies for the 1990s. The consensus of the committee was that Time should move ahead in the area of ownership and creation of video programming. This expansion, as the Chancellor noted, was predicated upon two considerations: first, Time's desire to have greater control, in terms of quality and price, over the film products delivered by way of its cable network and franchises; and second, Time's concern over the increasing globalization of the world economy. Some of Time's outside directors, especially Luce and Temple, had opposed this move as a threat to the editorial integrity and journalistic focus of Time.[4] Despite this concern, the board saw

**3.** Four directors, Arthur Temple, Henry C. Goodrich, Clifton R. Wharton, and Clifford J. Grum, have since resigned from Time's board. The Chancellor found, with the exception of Temple, their resignations to reflect more a willingness to step down than disagreement or dissension over the Time–Warner merger. Temple did not choose to continue to be associated with a corporation that was expanding into the entertainment field. Under the board of the combined Time–Warner corporation, the number of Time directors, as well as Warner directors, was limited to twelve each.

**4.** The primary concern of Time's outside directors was the preservation of the "Time Culture." They believed that Time

the advantages of a vertically integrated video enterprise to complement Time's existing HBO and cable networks would enable it to compete on a global basis.

In late spring of 1987, a meeting took place between Steve Ross, CEO of Warner Brothers, and Nicholas of Time. Ross and Nicholas discussed the possibility of a joint venture between the two companies through the creation of a jointly-owned cable company. Time would contribute its cable system and HBO. Warner would contribute its cable system and provide access to Warner Brothers Studio. The resulting venture would be a larger, more efficient cable network, able to produce and distribute its own movies on a worldwide basis. Ultimately the parties abandoned this plan, determining that it was impractical for several reasons, chief among them being tax considerations.

On August 11, 1987, Gerald M. Levin, Time's vice chairman and chief strategist, wrote J. Richard Munro a confidential memorandum in which he strongly recommended a strategic consolidation with Warner. In June 1988, Nicholas and Munro sent to each outside director a copy of the "comprehensive long-term planning document" prepared by the committee of Time executives that had been examining strategies for the 1990s. The memo included reference to and a description of Warner as a potential acquisition candidate.

Thereafter, Munro and Nicholas held meetings with Time's outside directors to discuss, generally, long-term strategies for Time and, specifically, a combination with Warner. Nearly a year later, Time's board reached the point of serious discussion of the "nuts and bolts" of a consolidation with an entertainment company. On July 21, 1988, Time's board met, with all outside directors present. The meeting's purpose was to consider Time's expansion into the entertainment industry on a global scale. Management presented the board with a profile of various entertainment companies in addition to Warner, including Disney, 20th Century Fox, Universal, and Paramount.

Without any definitive decision on choice of a company, the board approved in principle a strategic plan for Time's expansion. The board gave management the "go-ahead" to continue discussions with Warner concerning the possibility of a merger. With the exception of Temple and Luce, most of the outside directors agreed that a merger involving expansion into the entertainment field promised great growth opportunity for Time. Temple and Luce remained unenthusiastic about Time's entry into the entertainment field. See supra note [3].

The board's consensus was that a merger of Time and Warner was feasible, but only if Time controlled the board of the resulting corporation and thereby preserved a management committed to Time's journalistic integrity. To accomplish this goal, the board stressed the

had become recognized in this country as an institution built upon a foundation of journalistic integrity. Time's management made a studious effort to refrain from involvement in Time's editorial policy. Several of Time's outside directors feared that a merger with an entertainment company would divert Time's focus from news journalism and threaten the Time Culture.

importance of carefully defining in advance the corporate governance provisions that would control the resulting entity. Some board members expressed concern over whether such a business combination would place Time *"in play."* The board discussed the wisdom of adopting further defensive measures to lessen such a possibility.[5]

Of a wide range of companies considered by Time's board as possible merger candidates, Warner Brothers, Paramount, Columbia, M.C.A., Fox, MGM, Disney, and Orion, the board, in July 1988, concluded that Warner was the superior candidate for a consolidation. Warner stood out on a number of counts. Warner had just acquired Lorimar and its film studios. Time–Warner could make movies and television shows for use on HBO. Warner had an international distribution system, which Time could use to sell films, videos, books and magazines. Warner was a giant in the music and recording business, an area into which Time wanted to expand. None of the other companies considered had the musical clout of Warner. Time and Warner's cable systems were compatible and could be easily integrated; none of the other companies considered presented such a compatible cable partner. Together, Time and Warner would control half of New York City's cable system; Warner had cable systems in Brooklyn and Queens; and Time controlled cable systems in Manhattan and Queens. Warner's publishing company would integrate well with Time's established publishing company. Time sells hardcover books and magazines, and Warner sells softcover books and comics.[6] Time–Warner could sell all of these publications and Warner's videos by using Time's direct mailing network and Warner's international distribution system. Time's network could be used to promote and merchandise Warner's movies.

In August 1988, Levin, Nicholas, and Munro, acting on instructions from Time's board, continued to explore a business combination with Warner. By letter dated August 4, 1988, management informed the outside directors of proposed corporate governance provisions to be discussed with Warner. The provisions incorporated the recommendations of several of Time's outside directors.

From the outset, Time's board favored an all-cash or cash and securities acquisition of Warner as the basis for consolidation. Bruce Wasserstein, Time's financial advisor, also favored an outright purchase of Warner. However, Steve Ross, Warner's CEO, was adamant that a business combination was only practicable on a stock-for-stock basis. Warner insisted on a stock swap in order to preserve its shareholders' equity in the resulting corporation. Time's officers, on the other hand, made it abundantly clear that Time would be the

---

**5.** Time had in place a panoply of defensive devices, including a staggered board, a "poison pill" preferred stock rights plan triggered by an acquisition of 15% of the company, a fifty-day notice period for shareholder motions, and restrictions on shareholders' ability to call a meeting or act by consent.

**6.** In contrast, Paramount's publishing endeavors were in the areas of professional volumes and text books. Time's board did not find Paramount's publishing as compatible as Warner's publishing efforts.

acquiring corporation and that Time would control the resulting board. Time refused to permit itself to be cast as the "acquired" company.

Eventually Time acquiesced in Warner's insistence on a stock-for-stock deal, but talks broke down over corporate governance issues. Time wanted Ross' position as a co-CEO to be temporary and wanted Ross to retire in five years. Ross, however, refused to set a time for his retirement and viewed Time's proposal as indicating a lack of confidence in his leadership. Warner considered it vital that their executives and creative staff not perceive Warner as selling out to Time. Time's request of a guarantee that Time would dominate the CEO succession was objected to as inconsistent with the concept of a Time–Warner merger "of equals." Negotiations ended when the parties reached an impasse. Time's board refused to compromise on its position on corporate governance. Time, and particularly its outside directors, viewed the corporate governance provisions as critical for preserving the "Time Culture" through a pro-Time management at the top. See supra note 4.

Throughout the fall of 1988 Time pursued its plan of expansion into the entertainment field; Time held informal discussions with several companies, including Paramount. Capital Cities/ABC approached Time to propose a merger. Talks terminated, however, when Capital Cities/ABC suggested that it was interested in purchasing Time or in controlling the resulting board. Time steadfastly maintained it was not placing itself up for sale.

Warner and Time resumed negotiations in January 1989. The catalyst for the resumption of talks was a private dinner between Steve Ross and Time outside director, Michael Dingman. Dingman was able to convince Ross that the transitional nature of the proposed co–CEO arrangement did not reflect a lack of confidence in Ross. Ross agreed that this course was best for the company and a meeting between Ross and Munro resulted. Ross agreed to retire in five years and let Nicholas succeed him. Negotiations resumed and many of the details of the original stock-for-stock exchange agreement remained intact. In addition, Time's senior management agreed to long-term contracts.

Time insider directors Levin and Nicholas met with Warner's financial advisors to decide upon a stock exchange ratio. Time's board had recognized the potential need to pay a premium in the stock ratio in exchange for dictating the governing arrangement of the new Time–Warner. Levin and outside director Finkelstein were the primary proponents of paying a premium to protect the "Time Culture." The board discussed premium rates of 10%, 15% and 20%. Wasserstein also suggested paying a premium for Warner due to Warner's rapid growth rate. The market exchange ratio of Time stock for Warner stock was .38 in favor of Warner. Warner's financial advisors informed the board that any exchange rate over .400 was a fair deal and any exchange rate over .450 was "one hell of a deal." The parties ultimately agreed upon an exchange rate favoring Warner of .465. On that basis, Warner stockholders would own slightly over 62%[7] of the common stock of Time–Warner.

On March 3, 1989, Time's board, with all but one director in attendance, met and unanimously approved the stock-for-stock merger with Warner. Warner's board likewise approved the merger. The agreement called for Warner to be merged into a wholly-owned Time subsidiary with Warner becoming the surviving corporation. The common stock of Warner would then be converted into common stock of Time at the agreed upon ratio. Thereafter, the name of Time would be changed to Time–Warner, Inc.

The rules of the New York Stock Exchange required that Time's issuance of shares to effectuate the merger be approved by a vote of Time's stockholders. The Delaware General Corporation Law required approval of the merger by a majority of the Warner stockholders. Delaware law did not require any vote by Time stockholders. The Chancellor concluded that the agreement was the product of "an arms-length negotiation between two parties seeking individual advantage through mutual action."

The resulting company would have a 24–member board, with 12 members representing each corporation. The company would have co–CEO's, at first Ross and Munro, then Ross and Nicholas, and finally, after Ross' retirement, . . . Nicholas alone. The board would create an editorial committee with a majority of members representing Time. A similar entertainment committee would be controlled by Warner board members. A two-thirds supermajority vote was required to alter CEO successions but an earlier proposal to have supermajority protection for the editorial committee was abandoned. Warner's board suggested raising the compensation levels for Time's senior management under the new corporation. Warner's management, as with most entertainment executives, received higher salaries than comparable executives in news journalism. Time's board, however, rejected Warner's proposal to equalize the salaries of the two management teams.

At its March 3, 1989 meeting, Time's board adopted several defensive tactics. Time entered an automatic share exchange agreement with Warner. Time would receive 17,292,747 shares of Warner's outstanding common stock (9.4%) and Warner would receive 7,080,-016 shares of Time's outstanding common stock (11.1%). Either party could trigger the exchange. Time sought out and paid for "confidence" letters from various banks with which they did business. In these letters, the banks promised not to finance any third-party attempt to acquire Time. Time argues these agreements served only to preserve the confidential relationship between itself and the banks. The Chancellor found these agreements to be inconsequential and futile attempts to "dry up" money for a hostile takeover. Time also agreed to a "no-shop" clause, preventing Time from considering any other consolidation proposal, thus relinquishing its power to consider

---

**7.** As was noted in the briefs and at oral argument, this figure is somewhat misleading because it does not take into consid-eration the number of individuals who owned stock in both companies.

other proposals, regardless of their merits. Time did so at Warner's insistence. Warner did not want to be left "on the auction block" for an unfriendly suitor, if Time were to withdraw from the deal.

Time's board simultaneously established a special committee of outside directors, Finkelstein, Kearns, and Opel, to oversee the merger. The committee's assignment was to resolve any impediments that might arise in the course of working out the details of the merger and its consummation.

Time representatives lauded the lack of debt to the United States Senate and to the President of the United States. Public reaction to the announcement of the merger was positive. Time–Warner would be a media colossus with international scope. The board scheduled the stockholder vote for June 23; and a May 1 record date was set. On May 24, 1989, Time sent out extensive proxy statements to the stockholders regarding the approval vote on the merger. In the meantime, with the merger proceeding without impediment, the special committee had concluded, shortly after its creation, that it was not necessary either to retain independent consultants, legal or financial, or even to meet. Time's board was unanimously in favor of the proposed merger with Warner; and, by the end of May, the Time–Warner merger appeared to be an accomplished fact.

On June 7, 1989, these wishful assumptions were shattered by Paramount's surprising announcement of its all-cash offer to purchase all outstanding shares of Time for $175 per share. The following day, June 8, the trading price of Time's stock rose from $126 to $170 per share. Paramount's offer was said to be "fully negotiable."[8]

Time found Paramount's "fully negotiable" offer to be in fact subject to at least three conditions. First, Time had to terminate its merger agreement and stock exchange agreement with Warner, and remove certain other of its defensive devices, including the redemption of Time's shareholder rights. Second, Paramount had to obtain the required cable franchise transfers from Time in a fashion acceptable to Paramount in its sole discretion. Finally, the offer depended upon a judicial determination that section 203 of the General Corporate Law of Delaware (The Delaware Anti–Takeover Statute) was inapplicable to any Time–Paramount merger. While Paramount's board had been privately advised that it could take months, perhaps over a year, to forge and consummate the deal, Paramount's board publicly proclaimed its ability to close the offer by July 5, 1989. Paramount executives later conceded that none of its directors believed that July 5th was a realistic date to close the transaction.

On June 8, 1989, Time formally responded to Paramount's offer. Time's chairman and CEO, J. Richard Munro, sent an aggressively worded letter to Paramount's CEO, Martin Davis. Munro's letter attacked Davis' personal integrity and called Paramount's offer "smoke

---

**8.** Subsequently, it was established that Paramount's board had decided as early as March 1989 to move to acquire Time. However, Paramount management intentionally delayed publicizing its proposal until Time had mailed to its stockholders its Time–Warner merger proposal along with the required proxy statements.

and mirrors.'' Time's nonmanagement directors were not shown the letter before it was sent. However, at a board meeting that same day, all members endorsed management's response as well as the letter's content.

Over the following eight days, Time's board met three times to discuss Paramount's $175 offer. The board viewed Paramount's offer as inadequate and concluded that its proposed merger with Warner was the better course of action. Therefore, the board declined to open any negotiations with Paramount and held steady its course toward a merger with Warner.

In June, Time's board of directors met several times. During the course of their June meetings, Time's outside directors met frequently without management, officers or directors being present. At the request of the outside directors, corporate counsel was present during the board meetings and, from time to time, the management directors were asked to leave the board sessions. During the course of these meetings, Time's financial advisors informed the board that, on an auction basis, Time's per share value was materially higher than Warner's $175 per share offer.[9] On this basis, the board concluded that Paramount's $175 offer was inadequate.

At these June meetings, certain Time directors expressed their concern that Time stockholders would not comprehend the long-term benefits of the Warner merger. Large quantities of Time shares were held by institutional investors. The board feared that even though there appeared to be wide support for the Warner transaction, Paramount's cash premium would be a tempting prospect to these investors. In mid-June, Time sought permission from the New York Stock Exchange to alter its rules and allow the Time–Warner merger to proceed without stockholder approval. Time did so at Warner's insistence. The New York Stock Exchange rejected Time's request on June 15; and on that day, the value of Time stock reached $182 per share.

The following day, June 16, Time's board met to take up Paramount's offer. The board's prevailing belief was that Paramount's bid presented a threat to Time's control of its own destiny and retention of the "Time Culture." Even after Time's financial advisors made another presentation of Paramount and its business attributes, Time's board maintained its position that a combination within Warner presented greater potential for Time. Warner presented Time with a much desired production capability and an established international marketing chain. Time's advisors presented the board with various options, including defensive measures. The board considered and rejected the idea of purchasing Paramount in a "Pac Man" defense.[10] The board considered other defenses as well, including a recapitalization, the acquisition of another company, and a material change in the present capitalization structure or dividend policy. The board determined to

---

**9.** Time's advisors estimated the value of Time in a control premium situation to be significantly higher than the value of Time in other than a sale situation.

**10.** In a "Pac Man" defense, Time would launch a tender offer for the stock of Paramount, thus consuming its rival....

retain its same advisors even in light of the changed circumstances. The board rescinded its agreement to pay its advisors a bonus based on the consummation of the Time–Warner merger and agreed to pay a flat fee for any advice the advisors rendered. Finally, Time's board formally rejected Paramount's offer.[11]

At the same meeting, Time's board decided to recast its consolidation with Warner into an outright cash and securities acquisition of Warner by Time; and Time so informed Warner. Time accordingly restructured its proposal to acquire Warner as follows: Time would make an immediate all-cash offer for 51% of Warner's outstanding stock at $70 per share. The remaining 49% would be purchased at some later date for a mixture of cash and securities worth $70 per share. To provide the funds required for its outright acquisition of Warner, Time would assume 7–10 billion dollars worth of debt, thus eliminating one of the principal transaction-related benefits of the original merger agreement. Nine billion dollars of the total purchase price would be allocated to the purchase of Warner's goodwill.

Warner agreed but insisted on certain terms. Warner sought a control premium and guarantees that the governance provisions found in the original merger agreement would remain intact. Warner further sought agreements that Time would not employ its poison pill against Warner and that, unless enjoined, Time would be legally bound to complete the transaction. Time's board agreed to these last measures only at the insistence of Warner. For its part, Time was assured of its ability to extend its efforts into production arenas and international markets, all the while maintaining the Time identity and culture. The Chancellor found the initial Time–Warner transaction to have been negotiated at arms length and the restructured Time–Warner transaction to have resulted from Paramount's offer and its expected effect on a Time shareholder vote.

On June 23, 1989, Paramount raised its all-cash offer to buy Time's outstanding stock to $200 per share. Paramount still professed that all aspects of the offer were negotiable. Time's board met on June 26, 1989 and formally rejected Paramount's $200 per share second offer. The board reiterated its belief that, despite the $25 increase, the offer was still inadequate. The Time board maintained that the Warner transaction offered a greater long-term value for the stockholders and, unlike Paramount, did not pose a threat to Time's survival and its "culture." Paramount then filed this action in the Court of Chancery.

## II

The Shareholder Plaintiffs first assert a *Revlon* claim. They contend that the March 4 Time–Warner agreement effectively put Time up for sale, triggering *Revlon* duties, requiring Time's board to enhance short-term shareholder value and to treat all other interested acquirors on an equal basis. The Shareholder Plaintiffs base this argument on

**11.** Meanwhile, Time had already begun erecting impediments to Paramount's offer. Time encouraged local cable franchises to sue Paramount to prevent it from easily obtaining the franchises.

two facts: (i) the ultimate Time–Warner exchange ratio of .465 favoring Warner, resulting in Warner shareholders' receipt of 62% of the combined company; and (ii) the subjective intent of Time's directors as evidenced in their statements that the market might perceive the Time–Warner merger as putting Time up "for sale" and their adoption of various defensive measures.

The Shareholder Plaintiffs further contend that Time's directors, in structuring the original merger transaction to be "takeover-proof," triggered *Revlon* duties by foreclosing their shareholders from any prospect of obtaining a control premium. In short, plaintiffs argue that Time's board's decision to merge with Warner imposed a fiduciary duty to maximize immediate share value and not erect unreasonable barriers to further bids. Therefore, they argue, the Chancellor erred in finding: that Paramount's bid for Time did not place Time "for sale"; that Time's transaction with Warner did not result in any transfer of control; and that the combined Time–Warner was not so large as to preclude the possibility of the stockholders of Time–Warner receiving a future control premium.

Paramount asserts only a *Unocal* claim in which the shareholder plaintiffs join. Paramount contends that the Chancellor, in applying the first part of the *Unocal* test, erred in finding that Time's board had reasonable grounds to believe that Paramount posed both a legally cognizable threat to Time shareholders and a danger to Time's corporate policy and effectiveness. Paramount also contests the court's finding that Time's board made a reasonable and objective investigation of Paramount's offer so as to be informed before rejecting it. Paramount further claims that the court erred in applying *Unocal*'s second part in finding Time's response to be "reasonable." Paramount points primarily to the preclusive effect of the revised agreement which denied Time shareholders the opportunity both to vote on the agreement and to respond to Paramount's tender offer. Paramount argues that the underlying motivation of Time's board in adopting these defensive measures was management's desire to perpetuate itself in office.

The Court of Chancery posed the pivotal question presented by this case to be: Under what circumstances must a board of directors abandon an in-place plan of corporate development in order to provide its shareholders with the option to elect and realize an immediate control premium? As applied to this case, the question becomes: Did Time's board, having developed a strategic plan of global expansion to be launched through a business combination with Warner, come under a fiduciary duty to jettison its plan and put the corporation's future in the hands of its shareholders?

While we affirm the result reached by the Chancellor, we think it unwise to place undue emphasis upon long-term versus short-term corporate strategy. Two key predicates underpin our analysis. First, Delaware law imposes on a board of directors the duty to manage the business and affairs of the corporation. 8 Del.C. § 141(a). This broad mandate includes a conferred authority to set a corporate course of action, including time frame, designed to enhance corporate profitability. Thus, the question of "long-term" versus "short-term" values is largely irrelevant because directors, generally, are obliged to charter a course for a corporation which is in its best interests without regard to a fixed investment horizon. Second, absent a limited set of circumstances as defined under *Revlon,* a board of directors, while always required to act in an informed manner, is not under any *per se* duty to maximize shareholder value in the short term, even in the context of a takeover.[12] In our view, the pivotal question presented by this case is: "Did Time, by entering into the proposed merger with Warner, put itself up for sale?" A resolution of that issue through application of *Revlon* has a significant bearing upon the resolution of the derivative *Unocal* issue.

### A.

We first take up plaintiffs' principal *Revlon* argument, summarized above. In rejecting this argument, the Chancellor found the original Time–Warner merger agreement not to constitute a "change of control" and concluded that the transaction did not trigger *Revlon* duties. The Chancellor's conclusion is premised on a finding that "[b]efore the merger agreement was signed, control of the corporation existed in a fluid aggregation of unaffiliated shareholders representing a voting majority—in other words, in the market." The Chancellor's findings of fact are supported by the record and his conclusion is correct as a matter of law. However, we premise our rejection of plaintiffs' *Revlon* claim on different grounds, namely, the absence of any substantial evidence to conclude that Time's board, in negotiating with Warner, made the dissolution or breakup of the corporate entity inevitable, as was the case in *Revlon.*

Under Delaware law there are, generally speaking and without excluding other possibilities, two circumstances which may implicate *Revlon* duties. The first, and clearer one, is when a corporation initiates an active bidding process seeking to sell itself or to effect a business reorganization involving a clear break-up of the company. See, e.g., Mills Acquisition Co. v. Macmillan, Inc., Del.Supr., 559 A.2d 1261 (1989). However, *Revlon* duties may also be triggered where, in response to a bidder's offer, a target abandons its long-term strategy and seeks an alternative transaction also involving the breakup of the company.[13] Thus, in *Revlon,* when the board responded to Pantry Pride's offer by contemplating a "bust-up" sale of assets in a leveraged acquisition, we imposed upon the board a duty to maximize immedi-

---

**12.** Thus, we endorse the Chancellor's conclusion that it is not a breach of faith for directors to determine that the present stock market price of shares is not representative of true value or that there may indeed be several market values for any corporation's stock. We have so held in another context. See *Van Gorkom,* 488 A.2d at 876.

**13.** As we stated in *Revlon,* in both such cases, "[t]he duty of the board [has]

changed from the preservation of ... [the] corporate entity to the maximization of the company's value at a sale for the stockholder's benefit.... [The board] no longer face[s] threats to corporate policy and effectiveness, or to the stockholders' interests, from a grossly inadequate bid." Revlon v. MacAndrews & Forbes Holdings, Inc., Del.Supr., 506 A.2d 173, 182 (1985).

ate shareholder value and an obligation to auction the company fairly. If, however, the board's reaction to a hostile tender offer is found to constitute only a defensive response and not an abandonment of the corporation's continued existence, *Revlon* duties are not triggered, though *Unocal* duties attach.[14] See, e.g., Ivanhoe Partners v. Newmont Mining Corp., Del.Supr., 535 A.2d 1334, 1345 (1987).

The plaintiffs insist that even though the original Time–Warner agreement may not have worked "an objective change of control," the transaction made a "sale" of Time inevitable. Plaintiffs rely on the subjective intent of Time's board of directors and principally upon certain board members' expressions of concern that the Warner trans-action *might* be viewed as effectively putting Time up for sale. Plain-tiffs argue that the use of a lock-up agreement, a no-shop clause, and so-called "dry-up" agreements prevented shareholders from obtaining a control premium in the immediate future and thus violated *Revlon.*

We agree with the Chancellor that such evidence is entirely insufficient to invoke *Revlon* duties; and we decline to extend *Revlon's* application to corporate transactions simply because they might be construed as putting a corporation either "in play" or "up for sale." See Citron v. Fairchild Camera, Del.Supr., 569 A.2d 53 (1989); *Macmillan,* 559 A.2d at 1285 n. 35. The adoption of structural safety devices alone does not trigger *Revlon.*[15] Rather, as the Chancellor stated, such devices are properly subject to a *Unocal* analysis.

Finally, we do not find in Time's recasting of its merger agree-ment with Warner from a share exchange to a share purchase a basis to conclude that Time had either abandoned its strategic plan or made a sale of Time inevitable. The Chancellor found that although the merged Time–Warner company would be large (with a value ap-proaching approximately $30 billion), recent takeover cases have proven that acquisition of the combined company might nonetheless be possible. In re Time Incorporated Shareholder Litigation, Del.Ch., C.A. No. 10670, Allen, C. (July 14, 1989), slip op. at 56. The legal consequence is that *Unocal* alone applies to determine whether the business judgment rule attaches to the revised agreement. . . .

**14.** Within the auction process, any ac-tion taken by the board must be reasonably related to the threat posed or reasonable in relation to the advantage sought, see Mills Acquisition Co. v. Macmillan, Inc., Del.Supr., 559 A.2d 1261, 1288 (1989). Thus, a *Unocal* analysis may be appropriate when a corpora-tion is in a *Revlon* situation and *Revlon* duties may be triggered by a defensive action taken in response to a hostile offer. Since *Revlon,* we have stated that differing treat-ment of various bidders is not actionable when such action reasonably relates to achieving the best price available for the stockholders. *Macmillan,* 559 A.2d at 1286–87.

**15.** Although the legality of the various safety devices adopted to protect the original agreement is not a central issue, there is substantial evidence to support each of the trial court's related conclusions. Thus, the court found that the concept of the Share Exchange Agreement predated any takeover threat by Paramount and had been adopted for a rational business purpose: to deter Time and Warner from being "put in play" by their March 4 Agreement. The court fur-ther found that Time had adopted the "no-shop" clause at Warner's insistence and for Warner's protection. Finally, although cer-tain aspects of the "dry-up" agreements were suspect on their face, we concur in the Chan-cellor's view that in this case they were in-consequential.

## B.

We turn now to plaintiffs' *Unocal* claim. We begin by noting, as did the Chancellor, that our decision does not require us to pass on the wisdom of the board's decision to enter into the original Time–Warner agreement. That is not a court's task. Our task is simply to review the record to determine whether there is sufficient evidence to support the Chancellor's conclusion that the initial Time–Warner agreement was the product of a proper exercise of business judgment. *Macmillan*, 559 A.2d at 1288.

We have purposely detailed the evidence of the Time board's deliberative approach, beginning in 1983–84, to expand itself. Time's decision in 1988 to combine with Warner was made only after what could be fairly characterized as an exhaustive appraisal of Time's future as a corporation. After concluding in 1983–84 that the corporation must expand to survive, and beyond journalism into entertainment, the board combed the field of available entertainment companies. By 1987 Time had focused upon Warner; by late July 1988 Time's board was convinced that Warner would provide the best "fit" for Time to achieve its strategic objectives. The record attests to the zealousness of Time's executives, fully supported by their directors, in seeing to the preservation of Time's "culture," i.e., its perceived editorial integrity in journalism. We find ample evidence in the record to support the Chancellor's conclusion that the Time board's decision to expand the business of the company through its March 3 merger with Warner was entitled to the protection of the business judgment rule. See Aronson v. Lewis, Del.Supr., 473 A.2d 805, 812 (1984).

The Chancellor reached a different conclusion in addressing the Time–Warner transaction as revised three months later. He found that the revised agreement was defense-motivated and designed to avoid the potentially disruptive effect that Paramount's offer would have had on consummation of the proposed merger were it put to a shareholder vote. Thus, the court declined to apply the traditional business judgment rule to the revised transaction and instead analyzed the Time board's June 16 decision under *Unocal*. The court ruled that *Unocal* applied to all director actions taken, following receipt of Paramount's hostile tender offer, that were reasonably determined to be defensive. Clearly that was a correct ruling and no party disputes that ruling.

In *Unocal*, we held that before the business judgment rule is applied to a board's adoption of a defensive measure, the burden will lie with the board to prove (a) reasonable grounds for believing that a danger to corporate policy and effectiveness existed; and (b) that the defensive measure adopted was reasonable in relation to the threat posed. *Unocal*, 493 A.2d 946. Directors satisfy the first part of the *Unocal* test by demonstrating good faith and reasonable investigation. We have repeatedly stated that the refusal to entertain an offer may comport with a valid exercise of a board's business judgment. See, e.g., *MacMillan*, 559 A.2d at 1285 n. 35; *Van Gorkom*, 488 A.2d at 881; Pogostin v. Rice, Del.Supr., 480 A.2d 619, 627 (1984).

*Unocal* involved a two-tier, highly coercive tender offer. In such a case, the threat is obvious: shareholders may be compelled to tender to avoid being treated adversely in the second stage of the transaction. Accord *Ivanhoe,* 535 at 1344. In subsequent cases, the Court of Chancery has suggested that an all-cash, all-shares offer, falling within a range of values that a shareholder might reasonably prefer, cannot constitute a legally recognized "threat" to shareholder interests sufficient to withstand a *Unocal* analysis. AC Acquisitions Corp. v. Anderson, Clayton & Co., Del.Ch., 519 A.2d 103 (1986); see Grand Metropolitan, PLC v. Pillsbury Co., Del.Ch., 558 A.2d 1049 (1988); City Capital Associates v. Interco Inc., Del.Ch., 551 A.2d 787 (1988). In those cases, the Court of Chancery determined that whatever threat existed related only to the shareholders and only to price and not to the corporation.

From those decisions by our Court of Chancery, Paramount and the individual plaintiffs extrapolate a rule of law that an all-cash, all-shares offer with values reasonably in the range of acceptable price cannot pose any objective threat to a corporation or its shareholders. Thus, Paramount would have us hold that only if the value of Paramount's offer were determined to be clearly inferior to the value created by management's plan to merge with Warner could the offer be viewed—objectively—as a threat.

Implicit in the plaintiffs' argument is the view that a hostile tender offer can pose only two types of threats: the threat of coercion that results from a two-tier offer promising unequal treatment for nontendering shareholders, and the threat of inadequate value from an all-shares, all-cash offer at a price below what a target board in good faith deems to be the present value of its shares. See, e.g., *Interco,* 551 A.2d at 797; *see also* BNS, Inc. v. Koppers, D.Del., 683 F.Supp. 458 (1988). Since Paramount's offer was all-cash, the only conceivable "threat, plaintiffs argue, was inadequate value. We disapprove of such a narrow and rigid construction of *Unocal,* for the reasons which follow.

Plaintiffs' position represents a fundamental misconception of our standard of review under *Unocal* principally because it would involve the court in substituting its judgment for what is a "better" deal for that of a corporation's board of directors. To the extent that the Court of Chancery has recently done so in certain of its opinions, we hereby reject such approach as not in keeping with a proper *Unocal* analysis. See, e.g., *Interco,* 551 A.2d 787, and its progeny; but see TW Services, Inc. v. SWT Acquisition Corp., Del.Ch., C.A. No. 10427, Allen, C. 1989 WL 20290 (March 2, 1989).

The usefulness of *Unocal* as an analytical tool is precisely its flexibility in the face of a variety of fact scenarios. *Unocal* is not intended as an abstract standard; neither is it a structured and mechanistic procedure of appraisal. Thus, we have said that directors may consider, when evaluating the threat posed by a takeover bid, the "inadequacy of the price offered, nature and timing of the offer, questions of illegality, the impact on [constituencies] other than shareholders, the risk of nonconsummation and the quality of securities being offered in the exchange." 493 A.2d at 955. The open-ended analysis mandated by *Unocal* is not intended to lead to a simple mathematical exercise: that is, of comparing the discounted value of Time–Warner's expected trading price at some future date with Paramount's offer and determining which is the higher. Indeed, in our view, precepts underlying the business judgment rule mitigate against a court's engaging in the process of attempting to appraise and evaluate the relative merits of a long-term versus a short-term investment goal for shareholders. To engage in such an exercise is a distortion of the *Unocal* process and, in particular, the application of the second part of *Unocal's* test, discussed below.

In this case, the Time board reasonably determined that inadequate value was not the only legally cognizable threat that Paramount's all-cash, all-shares offer could present. Time's board concluded that Paramount's eleventh hour offer posed other threats. One concern was that Time shareholders might elect to tender into Paramount's cash offer in ignorance or a mistaken belief of the strategic benefit which a business combination with Warner might produce. Moreover, Time viewed the conditions attached to Paramount's offer as introducing a degree of uncertainty that skewed a comparative analysis. Further, the timing of Paramount's offer to follow issuance of Time's proxy notice was viewed as arguably designed to upset, if not confuse, the Time stockholders' vote. Given this record evidence, we cannot conclude that the Time board's decision of June 6 that Paramount's offer posed a threat to corporate policy and effectiveness was lacking in good faith or dominated by motives of either entrenchment or self-interest.

Paramount also contends that the Time board had not duly investigated Paramount's offer. Therefore, Paramount argues, Time was unable to make an informed decision that the offer posed a threat to Time's corporate policy. Although the Chancellor did not address this issue directly, his findings of fact do detail Time's exploration of the available entertainment companies, including Paramount, before determining that Warner provided the best strategic "fit." In addition, the court found that Time's board rejected Paramount's offer because Paramount did not serve Time's objectives or meet Time's needs. Thus, the record does, in our judgment, demonstrate that Time's board was adequately informed of the potential benefits of a transaction with Paramount. We agree with the Chancellor that the Time board's lengthy pre-June investigation of potential merger candidates, including Paramount, mooted any obligation on Time's part to halt its merger process with Warner to reconsider Paramount. Time's board was under no obligation to negotiate with Paramount. *Unocal,* 493 A.2d at 954–55; see also *Macmillan,* 559 A.2d at 1285 n. 35. Time's failure to negotiate cannot be fairly found to have been uninformed. The evidence supporting this finding is materially enhanced by the fact that twelve of Time's sixteen board members were outside independent directors. *Unocal,* 493 A.2d at 955; Moran v. Household Intern., Inc., Del.Supr., 500 A.2d 1346, 1356 (1985).

We turn to the second part of the *Unocal* analysis. The obvious requisite to determining the reasonableness of a defensive action is a clear identification of the nature of the threat. As the Chancellor correctly noted, this "requires an evaluation of the importance of the corporate objective threatened; alternative methods of protecting that objective; impacts of the 'defensive' action, and other relevant factors." In Re: Time Incorporated Shareholder Litigation, Del.Ch., 565 A.2d 281 (1989). It is not until both parts of the *Unocal* inquiry have been satisfied that the business judgment rule attaches to defensive actions of a board of directors. *Unocal,* 493 A.2d at 954.[16] As applied to the facts of this case, the question is whether the record evidence supports the Court of Chancery's conclusion that the restructuring of the Time–Warner transaction, including the adoption of several preclusive defensive measures, was a *reasonable response* in relation to a perceived threat.

Paramount argues that, assuming its tender offer posed a threat, Time's response was unreasonable in precluding Time's shareholders from accepting the tender offer or receiving a control premium in the immediately foreseeable future. Once again, the contention stems, we believe, from a fundamental misunderstanding of where the power of corporate governance lies. Delaware law confers the management of the corporate enterprise to the stockholders' duly elected board representatives. 8 Del.C. § 141(a). The fiduciary duty to manage a corporate enterprise includes the selection of a time frame for achievement of corporate goals. That duty may not be delegated to the stockholders. *Van Gorkom,* 488 A.2d at 873. Directors are not obliged to abandon a deliberately conceived corporate plan for a short-term shareholder profit unless there is clearly no basis to sustain the corporate strategy. See, e.g., *Revlon,* 506 A.2d 173.

Although the Chancellor blurred somewhat the discrete analyses required under *Unocal,* he did conclude that Time's board reasonably perceived Paramount's offer to be a significant threat to the planned Time–Warner merger and that Time's response was not "overly broad." We have found that even in light of a valid threat, management actions that are coercive in nature or force upon shareholders a management-sponsored alternative to a hostile offer may be struck down as unreasonable and nonproportionate responses. *Macmillan,* 559 A.2d 1261; *AC Acquisitions Corp.,* 519 A.2d 103.

Here, on the record facts, the Chancellor found that Time's responsive action to Paramount's tender offer was not aimed at "cramming down" on its shareholders a management-sponsored alternative, but rather had as its goal the carrying forward of a pre-existing transaction in an altered form. Thus, the response was reasonably related to the threat. The Chancellor noted that the revised agreement and its accompanying safety devices did not preclude Paramount from

---

**16.** Some commentators have criticized *Unocal* by arguing that once the board's deliberative process has been analyzed and found not to be wanting in objectivity, good faith or deliberateness, the so-called "enhanced" business judgment rule has been satisfied and no further inquiry is undertaken. See generally Johnson, Siegel, *Corporate Mergers: Redefining the Role of Target Directors,* 136 U.Pa.L.Rev. 315 (1987). We reject such views.

making an offer for the combined Time–Warner company or from changing the conditions of its offer so as not to make the offer dependent upon the nullification of the Time–Warner agreement. Thus, the response was proportionate. We affirm the Chancellor's rulings as clearly supported by the record. Finally, we note that although Time was required, as a result of Paramount's hostile offer, to incur a heavy debt to finance its acquisition of Warner, that fact alone does not render the board's decision unreasonable so long as the directors could reasonably perceive the debt load not to be so injurious to the corporation as to jeopardize its well being.

### C.

### *Conclusion*

Applying the test for grant or denial of preliminary injunctive relief, we find plaintiffs failed to establish a reasonable likelihood of ultimate success on the merits. Therefore, we affirm.

———

# Paramount Communications Inc. v. QVC Network

Supreme Court of Delaware, 1994.
637 A.2d 34.

■ Before VEASEY, CHIEF JUSTICE, MOORE and HOLLAND, JUSTICES.

Upon appeal from the Court of Chancery. AFFIRMED.

■ VEASEY, CHIEF JUSTICE.

In this appeal we review an order of the Court of Chancery dated November 24, 1993 (the "November 24 Order"), preliminarily enjoining certain defensive measures designed to facilitate a so-called strategic alliance between Viacom Inc. ("Viacom") and Paramount Communications Inc. ("Paramount") approved by the board of directors of Paramount (the "Paramount Board" or the "Paramount directors") and to thwart an unsolicited, more valuable, tender offer by QVC Network Inc. ("QVC"). In affirming, we hold that the sale of control in this case, which is at the heart of the proposed strategic alliance, implicates enhanced judicial scrutiny of the conduct of the Paramount Board under Unocal Corp. v. Mesa Petroleum Co., Del.Supr., 493 A.2d 946 (1985), and Revlon, Inc. v. MacAndrews & Forbes Holdings, Inc., Del.Supr., 506 A.2d 173 (1985). We further hold that the conduct of the Paramount Board was not reasonable as to process or result.

QVC and certain stockholders of Paramount commenced separate actions (later consolidated) in the Court of Chancery seeking preliminary and permanent injunctive relief against Paramount, certain members of the Paramount Board, and Viacom. This action arises out of a proposed acquisition of Paramount by Viacom through a tender offer followed by a second-step merger (the "Paramount–Viacom transaction"), and a competing unsolicited tender offer by QVC. The Court of Chancery granted a preliminary injunction. QVC Network, Inc. v. Paramount Communications Inc., Del.Ch., 635 A.2d 1245, Jacobs, V.C.

(1993) (the "Court of Chancery Opinion"). We affirmed by order dated December 9, 1993, Paramount Communications Inc. v. QVC Network Inc., Del.Supr., Nos. 427 and 428, 1993, 637 A.2d 828, Veasey, C.J. (Dec. 9, 1993) (the "December 9 Order").

The Court of Chancery found that the Paramount directors violated their fiduciary duties by favoring the Paramount–Viacom transaction over the more valuable unsolicited offer of QVC. The Court of Chancery preliminarily enjoined Paramount and the individual defendants (the "Paramount defendants") from amending or modifying Paramount's stockholder rights agreement (the "Rights Agreement"), including the redemption of the Rights, or taking other action to facilitate the consummation of the pending tender offer by Viacom or any proposed second-step merger, including the Merger Agreement between Paramount and Viacom dated September 12, 1993 (the "Original Merger Agreement"), as amended on October 24, 1993 (the "Amended Merger Agreement"). Viacom and the Paramount defendants were enjoined from taking any action to exercise any provision of the Stock Option Agreement between Paramount and Viacom dated September 12, 1993 (the "Stock Option Agreement"), as amended on October 24, 1993. The Court of Chancery did not grant preliminary injunctive relief as to the termination fee provided for the benefit of Viacom in Section 8.05 of the Original Merger Agreement and the Amended Merger Agreement (the "Termination Fee").

Under the circumstances of this case, the pending sale of control implicated in the Paramount–Viacom transaction required the Paramount Board to act on an informed basis to secure the best value reasonably available to the stockholders. Since we agree with the Court of Chancery that the Paramount directors violated their fiduciary duties, we have AFFIRMED the entry of the order of the Vice Chancellor granting the preliminary injunction and have REMANDED these proceedings to the Court of Chancery for proceedings consistent herewith....

## I.  FACTS ...

Paramount is a Delaware corporation with its principal offices in New York City. Approximately 118 million shares of Paramount's common stock are outstanding and traded on the New York Stock Exchange. The majority of Paramount's stock is publicly held by numerous unaffiliated investors. Paramount owns and operates a diverse group of entertainment businesses, including motion picture and television studios, book publishers, professional sports teams, and amusement parks.

There are 15 persons serving on the Paramount Board. Four directors are officer-employees of Paramount: Martin S. Davis ("Davis"), Paramount's Chairman and Chief Executive Officer since 1983; Donald Oresman ("Oresman"), Executive Vice–President, Chief Administrative Officer, and General Counsel; Stanley R. Jaffe, President and Chief Operating Officer; and Ronald L. Nelson, Executive Vice President and Chief Financial Officer. Paramount's 11 outside directors are distinguished and experienced business persons who are present or former senior executives of public corporations or financial institutions.

Viacom is a Delaware corporation with its headquarters in Massachusetts. Viacom is controlled by Sumner M. Redstone ("Redstone"), its Chairman and Chief Executive Officer, who owns indirectly approximately 85.2 percent of Viacom's voting Class A stock and approximately 69.2 percent of Viacom's nonvoting Class B stock through National Amusements, Inc. ("NAI"), an entity 91.7 percent owned by Redstone. Viacom has a wide range of entertainment operations, including a number of well-known cable television channels such as MTV, Nickelodeon, Showtime, and The Movie Channel. Viacom's equity co-investors in the Paramount–Viacom transaction include NYNEX Corporation and Blockbuster Entertainment Corporation.

QVC is a Delaware corporation with its headquarters in West Chester, Pennsylvania. QVC has several large stockholders, including Liberty Media Corporation, Comcast Corporation, Advance Publications, Inc., and Cox Enterprises Inc. Barry Diller ("Diller"), the Chairman and Chief Executive Officer of QVC, is also a substantial stockholder. QVC sells a variety of merchandise through a televised shopping channel. QVC has several equity co-investors in its proposed combination with Paramount including BellSouth Corporation and Comcast Corporation.

Beginning in the late 1980s, Paramount investigated the possibility of acquiring or merging with other companies in the entertainment, media, or communications industry. Paramount considered such transactions to be desirable, and perhaps necessary, in order to keep pace with competitors in the rapidly evolving field of entertainment and communications. Consistent with its goal of strategic expansion, Paramount made a tender offer for Time Inc. in 1989, but was ultimately unsuccessful. See Paramount Communications, Inc. v. Time Inc., Del. Supr., 571 A.2d 1140 (1989) (*"Time–Warner"*).

Although Paramount had considered a possible combination of Paramount and Viacom as early as 1990, recent efforts to explore such a transaction began at a dinner meeting between Redstone and Davis on April 20, 1993. Robert Greenhill ("Greenhill"), Chairman of Smith Barney Shearson Inc. ("Smith Barney"), attended and helped facilitate this meeting. After several more meetings between Redstone and Davis, serious negotiations began taking place in early July.

It was tentatively agreed that Davis would be the chief executive officer and Redstone would be the controlling stockholder of the combined company, but the parties could not reach agreement on the merger price and the terms of a stock option to be granted to Viacom. With respect to price, Viacom offered a package of cash and stock (primarily Viacom Class B nonvoting stock) with a market value of approximately $61 per share, but Paramount wanted at least $70 per share.

Shortly after negotiations broke down in July 1993, two notable events occurred. First, Davis apparently learned of QVC's potential interest in Paramount, and told Diller over lunch on July 21, 1993, that Paramount was not for sale. Second, the market value of Viacom's Class B nonvoting stock increased from $46.875 on July 6 to $57.25 on August 20. QVC claims (and Viacom disputes) that this price increase was caused by open market purchases of such stock by Redstone or entities controlled by him.

On August 20, 1993, discussions between Paramount and Viacom resumed when Greenhill arranged another meeting between Davis and Redstone. After a short hiatus, the parties negotiated in earnest in early September, and performed due diligence with the assistance of their financial advisors, Lazard Freres & Co. ("Lazard") for Paramount and Smith Barney for Viacom. On September 9, 1993, the Paramount Board was informed about the status of the negotiations and was provided information by Lazard, including an analysis of the proposed transaction.

On September 12, 1993, the Paramount Board met again and unanimously approved the Original Merger Agreement whereby Paramount would merge with and into Viacom. The terms of the merger provided that each share of Paramount common stock would be converted into 0.10 shares of Viacom Class A voting stock, 0.90 shares of Viacom Class B nonvoting stock, and $9.10 in cash. In addition, the Paramount Board agreed to amend its "poison pill" Rights Agreement to exempt the proposed merger with Viacom. The Original Merger Agreement also contained several provisions designed to make it more difficult for a potential competing bid to succeed. We focus, as did the Court of Chancery, on three of these defensive provisions: a "no-shop" provision (the "No–Shop Provision"), the Termination Fee, and the Stock Option Agreement.

First, under the No–Shop Provision, the Paramount Board agreed that Paramount would not solicit, encourage, discuss, negotiate, or endorse any competing transaction unless: (a) a third party "makes an unsolicited written, bona fide proposal, which is not subject to any material contingencies relating to financing"; and (b) the Paramount Board determines that discussions or negotiations with the third party are necessary for the Paramount Board to comply with its fiduciary duties.

Second, under the Termination Fee provision, Viacom would receive a $100 million termination fee if: (a) Paramount terminated the Original Merger Agreement because of a competing transaction; (b) Paramount's stockholders did not approve the merger; or (c) the Paramount Board recommended a competing transaction.

The third and most significant deterrent device was the Stock Option Agreement, which granted to Viacom an option to purchase approximately 19.9 percent (23,699,000 shares) of Paramount's outstanding common stock at $69.14 per share if any of the triggering events for the Termination Fee occurred. In addition to the customary terms that are normally associated with a stock option, the Stock

Option Agreement contained two provisions that were both unusual and highly beneficial to Viacom: (a) Viacom was permitted to pay for the shares with a senior subordinated note of questionable marketability instead of cash, thereby avoiding the need to raise the $1.6 billion purchase price (the "Note Feature"); and (b) Viacom could elect to require Paramount to pay Viacom in cash a sum equal to the difference between the purchase price and the market price of Paramount's stock (the "Put Feature"). Because the Stock Option Agreement was not "capped" to limit its maximum dollar value, it had the potential to reach (and in this case did reach) unreasonable levels.

After the execution of the Original Merger Agreement and the Stock Option Agreement on September 12, 1993, Paramount and Viacom announced their proposed merger. In a number of public statements, the parties indicated that the pending transaction was a virtual certainty. Redstone described it as a "marriage" that would "never be torn asunder" and stated that only a "nuclear attack" could break the deal. Redstone also called Diller and John Malone of Tele–Communications Inc., a major stockholder of QVC, to dissuade them from making a competing bid.

Despite these attempts to discourage a competing bid, Diller sent a letter to Davis on September 20, 1993, proposing a merger in which QVC would acquire Paramount for approximately $80 per share, consisting of 0.893 shares of QVC common stock and $30 in cash. QVC also expressed its eagerness to meet with Paramount to negotiate the details of a transaction. When the Paramount Board met on September 27, it was advised by Davis that the Original Merger Agreement prohibited Paramount from having discussions with QVC (or anyone else) unless certain conditions were satisfied. In particular, QVC had to supply evidence that its proposal was not subject to financing contingencies. The Paramount Board was also provided information from Lazard describing QVC and its proposal.

On October 5, 1993, QVC provided Paramount with evidence of QVC's financing. The Paramount Board then held another meeting on October 11, and decided to authorize management to meet with QVC. Davis also informed the Paramount Board that Booz–Allen & Hamilton ("Booz–Allen"), a management consulting firm, had been retained to assess, *inter alia,* the incremental earnings potential from a Paramount–Viacom merger and a Paramount–QVC merger. Discussions proceeded slowly, however, due to a delay in Paramount signing a confidentiality agreement. In response to Paramount's request for information, QVC provided two binders of documents to Paramount on October 20.

On October 21, 1993, QVC filed this action and publicly announced an $80 cash tender offer for 51 percent of Paramount's outstanding shares (the "QVC tender offer"). Each remaining share of Paramount common stock would be converted into 1.42857 shares of QVC common stock in a second-step merger. The tender offer was conditioned on, among other things, the invalidation of the Stock

Option Agreement, which was worth over $200 million by that point.[5] QVC contends that it had to commence a tender offer because of the slow pace of the merger discussions and the need to begin seeking clearance under federal antitrust laws.

Confronted by QVC's hostile bid, which on its face offered over $10 per share more than the consideration provided by the Original Merger Agreement, Viacom realized that it would need to raise its bid in order to remain competitive. Within hours after QVC's tender offer was announced, Viacom entered into discussions with Paramount concerning a revised transaction. These discussions led to serious negotiations concerning a comprehensive amendment to the original Paramount–Viacom transaction. In effect, the opportunity for a "new deal" with Viacom was at hand for the Paramount Board. With the QVC hostile bid offering greater value to the Paramount stockholders, the Paramount Board had considerable leverage with Viacom.

At a special meeting on October 24, 1993, the Paramount Board approved the Amended Merger Agreement and an amendment to the Stock Option Agreement. The Amended Merger Agreement was, however, essentially the same as the Original Merger Agreement, except that it included a few new provisions. One provision related to an $80 per share cash tender offer by Viacom for 51 percent of Paramount's stock, and another changed the merger consideration so that each share of Paramount would be converted into 0.20408 shares of Viacom Class A voting stock, 1.08317 shares of Viacom Class B nonvoting stock, and 0.20408 shares of a new series of Viacom convertible preferred stock. The Amended Merger Agreement also added a provision giving Paramount the right not to amend its Rights Agreement to exempt Viacom if the Paramount Board determined that such an amendment would be inconsistent with its fiduciary duties because another offer constituted a "better alternative."[6] Finally, the Paramount Board was given the power to terminate the Amended Merger Agreement if it withdrew its recommendation of the Viacom transaction or recommended a competing transaction.

Although the Amended Merger Agreement offered more consideration to the Paramount stockholders and somewhat more flexibility to the Paramount Board than did the Original Merger Agreement, the defensive measures designed to make a competing bid more difficult were not removed or modified. In particular, there is no evidence in the record that Paramount sought to use its newly-acquired leverage to eliminate or modify the No–Shop Provision, the Termination Fee, or the Stock Option Agreement when the subject of amending the Original Merger Agreement was on the table.

---

**5.** By November 15, 1993, the value of the Stock Option Agreement had increased to nearly $500 million based on the $90 QVC bid. See Court of Chancery Opinion, 635 A.2d 1245, 1271.

**6.** Under the Amended Merger Agreement and the Paramount Board's resolutions approving it, no further action of the Paramount Board would be required in order for Paramount's Rights Agreement to be amended. As a result, the proper officers of the company were authorized to implement the amendment unless they were instructed otherwise by the Paramount Board.

Viacom's tender offer commenced on October 25, 1993, and QVC's tender offer was formally launched on October 27, 1993. Diller sent a letter to the Paramount Board on October 28 requesting an opportunity to negotiate with Paramount, and Oresman responded the following day by agreeing to meet. The meeting, held on November 1, was not very fruitful, however, after QVC's proposed guidelines for a "fair bidding process" were rejected by Paramount on the ground that "auction procedures" were inappropriate and contrary to Paramount's contractual obligations to Viacom.

On November 6, 1993, Viacom unilaterally raised its tender offer price to $85 per share in cash and offered a comparable increase in the value of the securities being proposed in the second-step merger. At a telephonic meeting held later that day, the Paramount Board agreed to recommend Viacom's higher bid to Paramount's stockholders.

QVC responded to Viacom's higher bid on November 12 by increasing its tender offer to $90 per share and by increasing the securities for its second-step merger by a similar amount. In response to QVC's latest offer, the Paramount Board scheduled a meeting for November 15, 1993. Prior to the meeting, Oresman sent the members of the Paramount Board a document summarizing the "conditions and uncertainties" of QVC's offer. One director testified that this document gave him a very negative impression of the QVC bid.

At its meeting on November 15, 1993, the Paramount Board determined that the new QVC offer was not in the best interests of the stockholders. The purported basis for this conclusion was that QVC's bid was excessively conditional. The Paramount Board did not communicate with QVC regarding the status of the conditions because it believed that the No–Shop Provision prevented such communication in the absence of firm financing. Several Paramount directors also testified that they believed the Viacom transaction would be more advantageous to Paramount's future business prospects than a QVC transaction.[7] Although a number of materials were distributed to the Paramount Board describing the Viacom and QVC transactions, the only quantitative analysis of the consideration to be received by the stockholders under each proposal was based on then-current market prices of the securities involved, not on the anticipated value of such securities at the time when the stockholders would receive them.[8]

The preliminary injunction hearing in this case took place on November 16, 1993. On November 19, Diller wrote to the Paramount Board to inform it that QVC had obtained financing commitments for

---

**7.** This belief may have been based on a report prepared by Booz–Allen and distributed to the Paramount Board at its October 24 meeting. The report, which relied on public information regarding QVC, concluded that the synergies of a Paramount–Viacom merger were significantly superior to those of a Paramount–QVC merger. QVC has labelled the Booz–Allen report as a "joke."

**8.** The market prices of Viacom's and QVC's stock were poor measures of their actual values because such prices constantly fluctuated depending upon which company was perceived to be the more likely to acquire Paramount.

its tender offer and that there was no antitrust obstacle to the offer. On November 24, 1993, the Court of Chancery issued its decision granting a preliminary injunction in favor of QVC and the plaintiff stockholders. This appeal followed.

## II. APPLICABLE PRINCIPLES OF ESTABLISHED DELAWARE LAW

The General Corporation Law of the State of Delaware (the "General Corporation Law") and the decisions of this Court have repeatedly recognized the fundamental principle that the management of the business and affairs of a Delaware corporation is entrusted to its directors, who are the duly elected and authorized representatives of the stockholders. 8 Del.C. § 141(a); Aronson v. Lewis, Del.Supr., 473 A.2d 805, 811–12 (1984); Pogostin v. Rice, Del.Supr., 480 A.2d 619, 624 (1984). Under normal circumstances, neither the courts nor the stockholders should interfere with the managerial decisions of the directors. The business judgment rule embodies the deference to which such decisions are entitled. *Aronson,* 473 A.2d at 812.

Nevertheless, there are rare situations which mandate that a court take a more direct and active role in overseeing the decisions made and actions taken by directors. In these situations, a court subjects the directors' conduct to enhanced scrutiny to ensure that it is reasonable.[9] The decisions of this Court have clearly established the circumstances where such enhanced scrutiny will be applied. E.g., *Unocal,* 493 A.2d 946; Moran v. Household Int'l, Inc., Del.Supr., 500 A.2d 1346 (1985); *Revlon,* 506 A.2d 173. . . . The case at bar implicates two such circumstances: (1) the approval of a transaction resulting in a sale of control, and (2) the adoption of defensive measures in response to a threat to corporate control.

### A. The Significance of a Sale or Change[10] of Control

When a majority of a corporation's voting shares are acquired by a single person or entity, or by a cohesive group acting together, there is a significant diminution in the voting power of those who thereby become minority stockholders. Under the statutory framework of the General Corporation Law, many of the most fundamental corporate changes can be implemented only if they are approved by a majority vote of the stockholders. Such actions include elections of directors, amendments to the certificate of incorporation, mergers, consolidations, sales of all or substantially all of the assets of the corporation, and dissolution. 8 Del.C. §§ 211, 242, 251–258, 263, 271, 275. Because of the overriding importance of voting rights, this Court and the

---

**9.** Where actual self-interest is present and affects a majority of the directors approving a transaction, a court will apply even more exacting scrutiny to determine whether the transaction is entirely fair to the stockholders. E.g., Weinberger v. UOP, Inc., Del. Supr., 457 A.2d 701, 710–11 (1983); Nixon v. Blackwell, Del.Supr., 626 A.2d 1366, 1376 (1993).

**10.** For purposes of our December 9 Order and this Opinion, we have used the terms "sale of control" and "change of control" interchangeably without intending any doctrinal distinction.

Court of Chancery have consistently acted to protect stockholders from unwarranted interference with such rights.[11]

In the absence of devices protecting the minority stockholders,[12] stockholder votes are likely to become mere formalities where there is a majority stockholder. For example, minority stockholders can be deprived of a continuing equity interest in their corporation by means of a cash-out merger. *Weinberger,* 457 A.2d at 703. Absent effective protective provisions, minority stockholders must rely for protection solely on the fiduciary duties owed to them by the directors and the majority stockholder, since the minority stockholders have lost the power to influence corporate direction through the ballot. The acquisition of majority status and the consequent privilege of exerting the powers of majority ownership come at a price. That price is usually a control premium which recognizes not only the value of a control block of shares, but also compensates the minority stockholders for their resulting loss of voting power.

In the case before us, the public stockholders (in the aggregate) currently own a majority of Paramount's voting stock. Control of the corporation is not vested in a single person, entity, or group, but vested in the fluid aggregation of unaffiliated stockholders. In the event the Paramount–Viacom transaction is consummated, the public stockholders will receive cash and a minority equity voting position in the surviving corporation. Following such consummation, there will be a controlling stockholder who will have the voting power to: (a) elect directors; (b) cause a break-up of the corporation; (c) merge it with another company; (d) cash-out the public stockholders; (e) amend the certificate of incorporation; (f) sell all or substantially all of the corporate assets; or (g) otherwise alter materially the nature of the corporation and the public stockholders' interests. Irrespective of the present Paramount Board's vision of a long-term strategic alliance with Viacom, the proposed sale of control would provide the new controlling stockholder with the power to alter that vision.

Because of the intended sale of control, the Paramount–Viacom transaction has economic consequences of considerable significance to

**11.** See Schnell v. Chris–Craft Industries Inc., Del.Supr., 285 A.2d 437, 439 (1971) (holding that actions taken by management to manipulate corporate machinery "for the purpose of obstructing the legitimate efforts of dissident stockholders in the exercise of their rights to undertake a proxy contest against management" were "contrary to established principles of corporate democracy" and therefore invalid); Giuricich v. Emtrol Corp., Del.Supr., 449 A.2d 232, 239 (1982) (holding that "careful judicial scrutiny will be given in a situation in which the right to vote for the election of successor directors has been effectively frustrated"); ... Stroud v. Grace, Del.Supr., 606 A.2d 75, 84 (1992) (directors' duty of disclosure is premised on the importance of stockholders being fully informed when voting on a specific matter);

Blasius Indus., Inc. v. Atlas Corp., Del.Ch., 564 A.2d 651, 659 n. 2 (1988) ("Delaware courts have long exercised a most sensitive and protective regard for the free and effective exercise of voting rights.").

**12.** Examples of such protective provisions are supermajority voting provisions, majority of the minority requirements, etc. Although we express no opinion on what effect the inclusion of any such stockholder protective devices would have had in this case, we note that this Court has upheld, under different circumstances, the reasonableness of a standstill agreement which limited a 49.9 percent stockholder to 40 percent board representation. *Ivanhoe,* 535 A.2d at 1343.

the Paramount stockholders. Once control has shifted, the current Paramount stockholders will have no leverage in the future to demand another control premium. As a result, the Paramount stockholders are entitled to receive, and should receive, a control premium and/or protective devices of significant value. There being no such protective provisions in the Viacom–Paramount transaction, the Paramount directors had an obligation to take the maximum advantage of the current opportunity to realize for the stockholders the best value reasonably available.

### B.  The Obligations of Directors in a Sale or Change of Control Transaction

The consequences of a sale of control impose special obligations on the directors of a corporation. In particular, they have the obligation of acting reasonably to seek the transaction offering the best value reasonably available to the stockholders. The courts will apply enhanced scrutiny to ensure that the directors have acted reasonably. The obligations of the directors and the enhanced scrutiny of the courts are well-established by the decisions of this Court. The directors' fiduciary duties in a sale of control context are those which generally attach. In short, "the directors must act in accordance with their fundamental duties of care and loyalty." Barkan v. Amsted Indus., Inc., Del.Supr., 567 A.2d 1279, 1286 (1989). As we held in *Macmillan:*

> It is basic to our law that the board of directors has the ultimate responsibility for managing the business and affairs of a corporation. In discharging this function, the directors owe fiduciary duties of care and loyalty to the corporation and its shareholders. **This unremitting obligation extends equally to board conduct in a sale of corporate control.**

559 A.2d at 1280 (emphasis supplied) (citations omitted).

In the sale of control context, the directors must focus on one primary objective—to secure the transaction offering the best value reasonably available for the stockholders—and they must exercise their fiduciary duties to further that end. The decisions of this Court have consistently emphasized this goal. *Revlon,* 506 A.2d at 182 ("The duty of the board ... [is] the maximization of the company's value at a sale for the stockholders' benefit.") . . . .

In pursuing this objective, the directors must be especially diligent. See Citron v. Fairchild Camera and Instrument Corp., Del.Supr., 569 A.2d 53, 66 (1989) (discussing "a board's active and direct role in the sale process"). In particular, this Court has stressed the importance of the board being adequately informed in negotiating a sale of control: "The need for adequate information is central to the enlightened evaluation of a transaction that a board must make." *Barkan,* 567 A.2d at 1287. This requirement is consistent with the general principle that "directors have a duty to inform themselves, prior to making a business decision, of all material information reasonably available to them." *Aronson,* 473 A.2d at 812. See also Cede & Co. v. Technicolor, Inc., Del.Supr., 634 A.2d 345, 367 (1993); Smith v. Van

Gorkom, Del.Supr., 488 A.2d 858, 872 (1985). Moreover, the role of outside, independent directors becomes particularly important because of the magnitude of a sale of control transaction and the possibility, in certain cases, that management may not necessarily be impartial. See *Macmillan,* 559 A.2d at 1285 (requiring "the intense scrutiny and participation of the independent directors").

*Barkan* teaches some of the methods by which a board can fulfill its obligation to seek the best value reasonably available to the stockholders. 567 A.2d at 1286–87. These methods are designed to determine the existence and viability of possible alternatives. They include conducting an auction, canvassing the market, etc. Delaware law recognizes that there is "no single blueprint" that directors must follow. Id. at 1286–87; *Citron,* 569 A.2d at 68; *Macmillan,* 559 A.2d at 1287.

In determining which alternative provides the best value for the stockholders, a board of directors is not limited to considering only the amount of cash involved, and is not required to ignore totally its view of the future value of a strategic alliance. See *Macmillan,* 559 A.2d at 1282 n. 29. Instead, the directors should analyze the entire situation and evaluate in a disciplined manner the consideration being offered. Where stock or other non-cash consideration is involved, the board should try to quantify its value, if feasible, to achieve an objective comparison of the alternatives.[13] In addition, the board may assess a variety of practical considerations relating to each alternative, including:

> [an offer's] fairness and feasibility; the proposed or actual financing for the offer, and the consequences of that financing; questions of illegality; . . . the risk of non-consum[m]ation; . . . the bidder's identity, prior background and other business venture experiences; and the bidder's business plans for the corporation and their effects on stockholder interests.

*Macmillan,* 559 A.2d at 1282 n. 29. These considerations are important because the selection of one alternative may permanently foreclose other opportunities. While the assessment of these factors may be complex, the board's goal is straightforward: having informed themselves of all material information reasonably available, the directors must decide which alternative is most likely to offer the best value reasonably available to the stockholders.

### C. Enhanced Judicial Scrutiny of a Sale or Change of Control Transaction

Board action in the circumstances presented here is subject to enhanced scrutiny. Such scrutiny is mandated by: (a) the threatened

---

**13.** When assessing the value of non-cash consideration, a board should focus on its value as of the date it will be received by the stockholders. Normally, such value will be determined with the assistance of experts using generally accepted methods of valuation. See In re RJR Nabisco, Inc. Shareholders Litig., Del.Ch., C.A. No. 10389, Allen, C. (Jan. 31, 1989), reprinted at 14 Del.J.Corp.L. 1132, 1161.

diminution of the current stockholders' voting power; (b) the fact that an asset belonging to public stockholders (a control premium) is being sold and may never be available again; and (c) the traditional concern of Delaware courts for actions which impair or impede stockholder voting rights (see supra note 11). In *Macmillan,* this Court held:

> When *Revlon* duties devolve upon directors, this Court will continue to exact an enhanced judicial scrutiny at the threshold, as in *Unocal,* before the normal presumptions of the business judgment rule will apply.[14]

559 A.2d at 1288. The *Macmillan* decision articulates a specific two-part test for analyzing board action where competing bidders are not treated equally:[15]

> In the face of disparate treatment, the trial court must first examine whether the directors properly perceived that shareholder interests were enhanced. In any event the board's action must be reasonable in relation to the advantage sought to be achieved, or conversely, to the threat which a particular bid allegedly poses to stockholder interests.

Id. See also Roberts v. General Instrument Corp., Del.Ch., C.A. No. 11639, Allen, C. (Aug. 13, 1990), reprinted at 16 Del.J.Corp.L. 1540, 1554 ("This enhanced test requires a judicial judgment of reasonableness in the circumstances.").

The key features of an enhanced scrutiny test are: (a) a judicial determination regarding the adequacy of the decisionmaking process employed by the directors, including the information on which the directors based their decision; and (b) a judicial examination of the reasonableness of the directors' action in light of the circumstances then existing. The directors have the burden of proving that they were adequately informed and acted reasonably.

Although an enhanced scrutiny test involves a review of the reasonableness of the substantive merits of a board's actions,[16] a court should not ignore the complexity of the directors' task in a sale of control. There are many business and financial considerations implicated in investigating and selecting the best value reasonably available. The board of directors is the corporate decisionmaking body best equipped to make these judgments. Accordingly, a court applying enhanced judicial scrutiny should be deciding whether the directors

---

**14.** Because the Paramount Board acted unreasonably as to process and result in this sale of control situation, the business judgment rule did not become operative.

**15.** Before this test is invoked, "the plaintiff must show, and the trial court must find, that the directors of the target company treated one or more of the respective bidders on unequal terms." *Macmillan,* 559 A.2d at 1288.

**16.** It is to be remembered that, in cases where the traditional business judgment rule is applicable and the board acted with due care, in good faith, and in the honest belief that they are acting in the best interests of the stockholders (which is not this case), the Court gives great deference to the substance of the directors' decision and will not invalidate the decision, will not examine its reasonableness, and "will not substitute our views for those of the board if the latter's decision can be 'attributed to any rational business purpose.'" *Unocal,* 493 A.2d at 949 (quoting Sinclair Oil Corp. v. Levien, Del.Supr., 280 A.2d 717, 720 (1971)). See *Aronson,* 473 A.2d at 812.

made a **reasonable** decision, not a **perfect** decision. If a board selected one of several reasonable alternatives, a court should not second-guess that choice even though it might have decided otherwise or subsequent events may have cast doubt on the board's determination. Thus, courts will not substitute their business judgment for that of the directors, but will determine if the directors' decision was, on balance, within a range of reasonableness. See *Unocal*, 493 A.2d at 955–56; *Macmillan*, 559 A.2d at 1288; Nixon, 626 A.2d at 1378.

### D.  *Revlon* and *Time–Warner* Distinguished

The Paramount defendants and Viacom assert that the fiduciary obligations and the enhanced judicial scrutiny discussed above are not implicated in this case in the absence of a "break-up" of the corporation, and that the order granting the preliminary injunction should be reversed. This argument is based on their erroneous interpretation of our decisions in *Revlon* and *Time–Warner*.

In *Revlon*, we reviewed the actions of the board of directors of Revlon, Inc. ("Revlon"), which had rebuffed the overtures of Pantry Pride, Inc. and had instead entered into an agreement with Forstmann Little & Co. ("Forstmann") providing for the acquisition of 100 percent of Revlon's outstanding stock by Forstmann and the subsequent breakup of Revlon. Based on the facts and circumstances present in *Revlon*, we held that "[t]he directors' role changed from defenders of the corporate bastion to auctioneers charged with getting the best price for the stockholders at a sale of the company." 506 A.2d at 182. We further held that "when a board ends an intense bidding contest on an insubstantial basis, ... [that] action cannot withstand the enhanced scrutiny which *Unocal* requires of director conduct." Id. at 184.

It is true that one of the circumstances bearing on these holdings was the fact that "the break-up of the company ... had become a reality which even the directors embraced." Id. at 182. It does not follow, however, that a "break-up" must be present and "inevitable" before directors are subject to enhanced judicial scrutiny and are required to pursue a transaction that is calculated to produce the best value reasonably available to the stockholders. In fact, we stated in *Revlon* that "when bidders make relatively similar offers, or dissolution of the company becomes inevitable, the directors cannot fulfill their enhanced *Unocal* duties by playing favorites with the contending factions." Id. at 184 (emphasis added). *Revlon* thus does not hold that an inevitable dissolution or "break-up" is necessary.

The decisions of this Court following *Revlon* reinforced the applicability of enhanced scrutiny and the directors' obligation to seek the best value reasonably available for the stockholders where there is a pending sale of control, regardless of whether or not there is to be a break-up of the corporation. In *Macmillan*, this Court held:

> We stated in *Revlon*, and again here, that **in a sale of corporate control** the responsibility of the directors is to get the highest value reasonably attainable for the shareholders.

559 A.2d at 1288 (emphasis added). In *Barkan,* we observed further:

> We believe that the general principles announced in *Revlon,* in Unocal Corp. v. Mesa Petroleum Co., Del.Supr., 493 A.2d 946 (1985), and in Moran v. Household International, Inc., Del.Supr., 500 A.2d 1346 (1985) govern this case and every case in which a **fundamental change of corporate control** occurs or is contemplated.

567 A.2d at 1286 (emphasis added).

Although *Macmillan* and *Barkan* are clear in holding that a change of control imposes on directors the obligation to obtain the best value reasonably available to the stockholders, the Paramount defendants have interpreted our decision in *Time–Warner* as requiring a corporate break-up in order for that obligation to apply. The facts in *Time–Warner,* however, were quite different from the facts of this case, and refute Paramount's position here. In *Time–Warner,* the Chancellor held that there was no change of control in the original stock-for-stock merger between Time and Warner because Time would be owned by a fluid aggregation of unaffiliated stockholders both before and after the merger:

> If the appropriate inquiry is whether a change in control is contemplated, the answer must be sought in the specific circumstances surrounding the transaction. Surely under some circumstances a stock for stock merger could reflect a transfer of corporate control. That would, for example, plainly be the case here if Warner were a private company. But where, as here, the shares of both constituent corporations are widely held, corporate control can be expected to remain unaffected by a stock for stock merger. This in my judgment was the situation with respect to the original merger agreement. When the specifics of that situation are reviewed, it is seen that, aside from legal technicalities and aside from arrangements thought to enhance the prospect for the ultimate succession of [Nicholas J. Nicholas, Jr., president of Time], neither corporation could be said to be acquiring the other. **Control of both remained in a large, fluid, changeable and changing market.**
>
> The existence of a control block of stock in the hands of a single shareholder or a group with loyalty to each other does have real consequences to the financial value of "minority" stock. The law offers some protection to such shares through the imposition of a fiduciary duty upon controlling shareholders. **But here, effectuation of the merger would not have subjected Time shareholders to the risks and consequences of holders of minority shares. This is a reflection of the fact that no control passed to anyone in the transaction contemplated.** The shareholders of Time would have "suffered" dilution, of course, but they would suffer the same type of dilution upon the public distribution of new stock.

Paramount Communications, Inc. v. Time Inc., Del.Ch., No. 10866, Allen, C. (July 17, 1989), reprinted at 15 Del.J.Corp.L. 700, 739 (emphasis added). Moreover, the transaction actually consummated in *Time–Warner* was not a merger, as originally planned, but a sale of Warner's stock to Time.

In our affirmance of the Court of Chancery's well-reasoned decision, this Court held that "The Chancellor's findings of fact are supported by the record and **his conclusion is correct as a matter of law.**" 571 A.2d at 1150 (emphasis added). Nevertheless, the Paramount defendants here have argued that a break-up is a requirement and have focused on the following language in our *Time–Warner* decision:

> However, we premise our rejection of plaintiffs' *Revlon* claim on different grounds, namely, the absence of any substantial evidence to conclude that Time's board, in negotiating with Warner, made the dissolution or break-up of the corporate entity inevitable, as was the case in *Revlon*.
>
> Under Delaware law there are, generally speaking and **without excluding other possibilities,** two circumstances which may implicate *Revlon* duties. The first, and clearer one, is when a corporation **initiates an active bidding process seeking to sell itself** or to effect a business reorganization involving a clear break-up of the company. However, *Revlon* duties may also be triggered where, in response to a bidder's offer, a target abandons its long-term strategy and seeks an alternative transaction involving the breakup of the company.

Id. at 1150 (emphasis added) (citation and footnote omitted).

The Paramount defendants have misread the holding of *Time–Warner*. Contrary to their argument, our decision in *Time–Warner* expressly states that the two general scenarios discussed in the above-quoted paragraph are not the only instances where "*Revlon* duties" may be implicated. The Paramount defendants' argument totally ignores the phrase "without excluding other possibilities." Moreover, the instant case is clearly within the first general scenario set forth in *Time–Warner*. The Paramount Board, albeit unintentionally, had "initiate[d] an active bidding process seeking to sell itself" by agreeing to sell control of the corporation to Viacom in circumstances where another potential acquiror (QVC) was equally interested in being a bidder.

The Paramount defendants' position that both a change of control and a break-up are required must be rejected. Such a holding would unduly restrict the application of *Revlon*, is inconsistent with this Court's decisions in *Barkan* and *Macmillan*, and has no basis in policy. There are few events that have a more significant impact on the stockholders than a sale of control or a corporate break-up. Each event represents a fundamental (and perhaps irrevocable) change in the nature of the corporate enterprise from a practical standpoint. It is the significance of **each** of these events that justifies: (a) focusing on the directors' obligation to seek the best value reasonably available to the stockholders; and (b) requiring a close scrutiny of board action which could be contrary to the stockholders' interests.

Accordingly, when a corporation undertakes a transaction which will cause: (a) a change in corporate control; or (b) a break-up of the corporate entity, the directors' obligation is to seek the best value reasonably available to the stockholders. This obligation arises because the effect of the Viacom–Paramount transaction, if consummated, is to shift control of Paramount from the public stockholders to a controlling stockholder, Viacom. Neither *Time–Warner* nor any other decision of this Court holds that a "break-up" of the company is essential to give rise to this obligation where there is a sale of control.

## III.   BREACH OF FIDUCIARY DUTIES BY PARAMOUNT BOARD

We now turn to duties of the Paramount Board under the facts of this case and our conclusions as to the breaches of those duties which warrant injunctive relief.

### A.   The Specific Obligations of the Paramount Board

Under the facts of this case, the Paramount directors had the obligation: (a) to be diligent and vigilant in examining critically the Paramount–Viacom transaction and the QVC tender offers; (b) to act in good faith; (c) to obtain, and act with due care on, all material information reasonably available, including information necessary to compare the two offers to determine which of these transactions, or an alternative course of action, would provide the best value reasonably available to the stockholders; and (d) to negotiate actively and in good faith with both Viacom and QVC to that end.

Having decided to sell control of the corporation, the Paramount directors were required to evaluate critically whether or not all material aspects of the Paramount–Viacom transaction (separately and in the aggregate) were reasonable and in the best interests of the Paramount stockholders in light of current circumstances, including: the change of control premium, the Stock Option Agreement, the Termination Fee, the coercive nature of both the Viacom and QVC tender offers,[17] the No–Shop Provision, and the proposed disparate use of the Rights Agreement as to the Viacom and QVC tender offers, respectively.

These obligations necessarily implicated various issues, including the questions of whether or not those provisions and other aspects of the Paramount–Viacom transaction (separately and in the aggregate): (a) adversely affected the value provided to the Paramount stockholders; (b) inhibited or encouraged alternative bids; (c) were enforceable contractual obligations in light of the directors' fiduciary duties; and

---

17. Both the Viacom and the QVC tender offers were for 51 percent cash and a "back-end" of various securities, the value of each of which depended on the fluctuating value of Viacom and QVC stock at any given time. Thus, both tender offers were two-ti- ered, front-end loaded, and coercive. Such coercive offers are inherently problematic and should be expected to receive particularly careful analysis by a target board. See *Unocal*, 493 A.2d at 956.

(d) in the end would advance or retard the Paramount directors' obligation to secure for the Paramount stockholders the best value reasonably available under the circumstances.

The Paramount defendants contend that they were precluded by certain contractual provisions, including the No–Shop Provision, from negotiating with QVC or seeking alternatives. Such provisions, whether or not they are presumptively valid in the abstract, may not, validly define or limit the directors' fiduciary duties under Delaware law or prevent the Paramount directors from carrying out their fiduciary duties under Delaware law. To the extent such provisions are inconsistent with those duties, they are invalid and unenforceable. See *Revlon,* 506 A.2d at 184–85.

Since the Paramount directors had already decided to sell control, they had an obligation to continue their search for the best value reasonably available to the stockholders. This continuing obligation included the responsibility, at the October 24 board meeting and thereafter, to evaluate critically both the QVC tender offers and the Paramount–Viacom transaction to determine if: (a) the QVC tender offer was, or would continue to be, conditional; (b) the QVC tender offer could be improved; (c) the Viacom tender offer or other aspects of the Paramount–Viacom transaction could be improved; (d) each of the respective offers would be reasonably likely to come to closure, and under what circumstances; (e) other material information was reasonably available for consideration by the Paramount directors; (f) there were viable and realistic alternative courses of action; and (g) the timing constraints could be managed so the directors could consider these matters carefully and deliberately.

## B. The Breaches of Fiduciary Duty by the Paramount Board

The Paramount directors made the decision on September 12, 1993, that, in their judgment, a strategic merger with Viacom on the economic terms of the Original Merger Agreement was in the best interests of Paramount and its stockholders. Those terms provided a modest change of control premium to the stockholders. The directors also decided at that time that it was appropriate to agree to certain defensive measures (the Stock Option Agreement, the Termination Fee, and the No–Shop Provision) insisted upon by Viacom as part of that economic transaction. Those defensive measures, coupled with the sale of control and subsequent disparate treatment of competing bidders, implicated the judicial scrutiny of *Unocal, Revlon, Macmillan,* and their progeny. We conclude that the Paramount directors' process was not reasonable, and the result achieved for the stockholders was not reasonable under the circumstances.

When entering into the Original Merger Agreement, and thereafter, the Paramount Board clearly gave insufficient attention to the potential consequences of the defensive measures demanded by Viacom. The Stock Option Agreement had a number of unusual and potentially "draconian"[18] provisions, including the Note Feature and the Put Feature. Furthermore, the Termination Fee, whether or not unreasonable by itself, clearly made Paramount less attractive to other bidders, when coupled with the Stock Option Agreement. Finally, the No–Shop Provision inhibited the Paramount Board's ability to negotiate with other potential bidders, particularly QVC which had already expressed an interest in Paramount.[19]

Throughout the applicable time period, and especially from the first QVC merger proposal on September 20 through the Paramount Board meeting on November 15, QVC's interest in Paramount provided the **opportunity** for the Paramount Board to seek significantly higher value for the Paramount stockholders than that being offered by Viacom. QVC persistently demonstrated its intention to meet and exceed the Viacom offers, and frequently expressed its willingness to negotiate possible further increases.

The Paramount directors had the opportunity in the October 23–24 time frame, when the Original Merger Agreement was renegotiated, to take appropriate action to modify the improper defensive measures as well as to improve the economic terms of the Paramount–Viacom transaction. Under the circumstances existing at that time, it should have been clear to the Paramount Board that the Stock Option Agreement, coupled with the Termination Fee and the No–Shop Clause, were impeding the realization of the best value reasonably available to the Paramount stockholders. Nevertheless, the Paramount Board made no effort to eliminate or modify these counterproductive devices, and instead continued to cling to its vision of a strategic alliance with Viacom. Moreover, based on advice from the Paramount management, the Paramount directors considered the QVC offer to be "conditional" and asserted that they were precluded by the No–Shop Provision from seeking more information from, or negotiating with, QVC.

By November 12, 1993, the value of the revised QVC offer on its face exceeded that of the Viacom offer by over $1 billion at then current values. This significant disparity of value cannot be justified on

---

**18.** The Vice Chancellor so characterized the Stock Option Agreement. Court of Chancery Opinion, 635 A.2d 1245, 1272. We express no opinion whether a stock option agreement of essentially this magnitude, but with a reasonable "cap" and without the Note and Put Features, would be valid or invalid under other circumstances. See Hecco Ventures v. Sea–Land Corp., Del.Ch., C.A. No. 8486, Jacobs, V.C. (May 19, 1986) (21.7 percent stock option); In re Vitalink Communications Corp. Shareholders Litig., Del.Ch., C.A. No. 12085, Chandler, V.C. (May 16, 1990) (19.9 percent stock option).

**19.** We express no opinion whether certain aspects of the No–Shop Provision here could be valid in another context. Whether or not it could validly have operated here at an early stage solely to prevent Paramount from

actively "shopping" the company, it could not prevent the Paramount directors from carrying out their fiduciary duties in considering unsolicited bids or in negotiating for the best value reasonably available to the stockholders. *Macmillan,* 559 A.2d at 1287. As we said in *Barkan:* "Where a board has no reasonable basis upon which to judge the adequacy of a contemplated transaction, a no-shop restriction gives rise to the inference that the board seeks to forestall competing bids." 567 A.2d at 1288. See also *Revlon,* 506 A.2d at 184 (holding that "[t]he no-shop provision, like the lock-up option, while not *per se* illegal, is impermissible under the *Unocal* standards when a board's primary duty becomes that of an auctioneer responsible for selling the company to the highest bidder").

the basis of the directors' vision of future strategy, primarily because the change of control would supplant the authority of the current Paramount Board to continue to hold and implement their strategic vision in any meaningful way. Moreover, their uninformed process had deprived their strategic vision of much of its credibility. See *Van Gorkom*, 488 A.2d at 872; Cede v. Technicolor, 634 A.2d at 367; Hanson Trust PLC v. ML SCM Acquisition Inc., 2d Cir., 781 F.2d 264, 274 (1986).

When the Paramount directors met on November 15 to consider QVC's increased tender offer, they remained prisoners of their own misconceptions and missed opportunities to eliminate the restrictions they had imposed on themselves. Yet, it was not "too late" to reconsider negotiating with QVC. The circumstances existing on November 15 made it clear that the defensive measures, taken as a whole, were problematic: (a) the No–Shop Provision could not define or limit their fiduciary duties; (b) the Stock Option Agreement had become "draconian"; and (c) the Termination Fee, in context with all the circumstances, was similarly deterring the realization of possibly higher bids. Nevertheless, the Paramount directors remained paralyzed by their uninformed belief that the QVC offer was "illusory." This final opportunity to negotiate on the stockholders' behalf and to fulfill their obligation to seek the best value reasonably available was thereby squandered.[20]

## IV.  VIACOM'S CLAIM OF VESTED CONTRACT RIGHTS

Viacom argues that it had certain "vested" contract rights with respect to the No–Shop Provision and the Stock Option Agreement.[21] In effect, Viacom's argument is that the Paramount directors could enter into an agreement in violation of their fiduciary duties and then render Paramount, and ultimately its stockholders, liable for failing to carry out an agreement in violation of those duties. Viacom's protestations about vested rights are without merit. This Court has found that those defensive measures were improperly designed to deter potential bidders, and that such measures do not meet the reasonableness test to which they must be subjected. They are consequently invalid and unenforceable under the facts of this case.

The No–Shop Provision could not validly define or limit the fiduciary duties of the Paramount directors. To the extent that a

---

**20.** The Paramount defendants argue that the Court of Chancery erred by assuming that the Rights Agreement was "pulled" at the November 15 meeting of the Paramount Board. The problem with this argument is that, under the Amended Merger Agreement and the resolutions of the Paramount Board related thereto, Viacom would be exempted from the Rights Agreement in the absence of further action of the Paramount Board and no further meeting had been scheduled or even contemplated prior to the closing of the Viacom tender offer. This failure to schedule and hold a meeting short-

ly before the closing date in order to make a final decision, based on all of the information and circumstances then existing, whether to exempt Viacom from the Rights Agreement was inconsistent with the Paramount Board's responsibilities and does not provide a basis to challenge the Court of Chancery's decision.

**21.** Presumably this argument would have included the Termination Fee had the Vice Chancellor invalidated that provision or if appellees had cross-appealed from the Vice Chancellor's refusal to invalidate that provision.

contract, or a provision thereof, purports to require a board to act or not act in such a fashion as to limit the exercise of fiduciary duties, it is invalid and unenforceable. Cf. Wilmington Trust v. Coulter, 200 A.2d at 452–54. Despite the arguments of Paramount and Viacom to the contrary, the Paramount directors could not contract away their fiduciary obligations. Since the No–Shop Provision was invalid, Viacom never had any vested contract rights in the provision.

As discussed previously, the Stock Option Agreement contained several "draconian" aspects, including the Note Feature and the Put Feature. While we have held that lock-up options are not *per se* illegal, see *Revlon*, 506 A.2d at 183, no options with similar features have ever been upheld by this Court. Under the circumstances of this case, the Stock Option Agreement clearly is invalid. Accordingly, Viacom never had any vested contract rights in that Agreement.

Viacom, a sophisticated party with experienced legal and financial advisors, knew of (and in fact demanded) the unreasonable features of the Stock Option Agreement. It cannot be now heard to argue that it obtained vested contract rights by negotiating and obtaining contractual provisions from a board acting in violation of its fiduciary duties. As the Nebraska Supreme Court said in rejecting a similar argument in ConAgra, Inc. v. Cargill, Inc., Neb.Supr., 382 N.W.2d 576, 587–88 (1986), "To so hold, it would seem, would be to get the shareholders coming and going." Likewise, we reject Viacom's arguments and hold that its fate must rise and fall, and in this instance fall, with the determination that the actions of the Paramount Board were invalid.

## V.  CONCLUSION

The realization of the best value reasonably available to the stockholders became the Paramount directors' primary obligation under these facts in light of the change of control. That obligation was not satisfied, and the Paramount Board's process was deficient. The directors' initial hope and expectation for a strategic alliance with Viacom was allowed to dominate their decisionmaking process to the point where the arsenal of defensive measures established at the outset was perpetuated (not modified or eliminated) when the situation was dramatically altered. QVC's unsolicited bid presented the opportunity for significantly greater value for the stockholders and enhanced negotiating leverage for the directors. Rather than seizing those opportunities, the Paramount directors chose to wall themselves off from material information which was reasonably available and to hide behind the defensive measures as a rationalization for refusing to negotiate with QVC or seeking other alternatives. Their view of the strategic alliance likewise became an empty rationalization as the opportunities for higher value for the stockholders continued to develop.

It is the nature of the judicial process that we decide only the case before us—a case which, on its facts, is clearly controlled by established Delaware law. Here, the proposed change of control and the implications thereof were crystal clear. In other cases they may be less clear. The holding of this case on its facts, coupled with the holdings of the principal cases discussed herein where the issue of sale of control is implicated, should provide a workable precedent against which to measure future cases.

For the reasons set forth herein, the November 24, 1993, Order of the Court of Chancery has been AFFIRMED, and this matter has been REMANDED for proceedings consistent herewith, as set forth in the December 9, 1993, Order of this Court.

---

### NOTE ON UNITRIN, INC. v. AMERICAN GENERAL CORP.

In Unitrin, Inc. v. American General Corp., 651 A.2d 1361 (1995), American General Corporation announced a tender offer to purchase all of the stock of Unitrin, Inc. at $50⅜ per share. Unitrin's board responded by taking several defensive measures, including the adoption of a poison pill and a program to repurchase up to 10 million of Unitrin's 51.8 million shares on the open market at $50⅜. Unitrin's certificate of incorporation provided that a business combination with a more–than–15% shareholder had to be approved by a majority of continuing directors or by a 75% shareholder vote. Unitrin's directors collectively held 23% of Unitrin's stock prior to adoption of the repurchase program. The directors did not intend to sell their stock to Unitrin under the repurchase program.

American General brought an action in Delaware Chancery court to enjoin Unitrin from completing its repurchase program. The Chancery court issued a preliminary injunction against Unitrin, at a point when Unitrin had purchased nearly 5 million shares of its stock, partly on the ground that since the director-shareholders were not selling their stock the effect of the repurchase program would be to increase their stock ownership from 23% to over 25%, thereby giving them a veto under the 75% supermajority voting provision. The Delaware Supreme Court reversed, and remanded for a decision by Chancery under the standards it set out. The Supreme Court's opinion provides a gloss on *Unocal* as read in light of subsequent cases:

> . . . [T]he Court of Chancery erred in applying the proportionality review *Unocal* requires by focusing upon whether the Repurchase Program was an "unnecessary" defensive response. See Paramount Communications, Inc. v. QVC Network, Inc., 637 A.2d at 45–46. The Court of Chancery should have directed its enhanced scrutiny: first, upon whether the Repurchase Program the Unitrin Board implemented was draconian, by being either preclusive or coercive and; second, if it was not draconian, upon whether it was within a range of reasonable responses to the threat American General's Offer posed. Consequently, the interlocutory preliminary injunctive judgment of the Court of Chancery is reversed. . . .

The first aspect of the *Unocal* burden, the reasonableness test, required the Unitrin Board to demonstrate that, after a reasonable investigation, it determined in good faith, that American General's Offer presented a threat to Unitrin that warranted a defensive response. . . .

. . . The Court of Chancery determined . . . that the Board reasonably believed that the American General Offer was inadequate and also reasonably concluded that the Offer was a threat to Unitrin's uninformed stockholders. . . .

The second aspect or proportionality test of the initial *Unocal* burden required the Unitrin Board to demonstrate the proportionality of its response to the threat American General's Offer posed. . . .

This Court has been and remains assiduous in its concern about defensive actions designed to thwart the essence of corporate democracy by disenfranchising shareholders. . . .

Nevertheless, this Court has upheld the propriety of adopting poison pills in given defensive circumstances. Keeping a poison pill in place may be inappropriate, however, when those circumstances change dramatically. . . .

The Court of Chancery and all parties agree that proxy contests do not generate 100% shareholder participation. The shareholder plaintiffs argue that 80–85% may be a usual turnout. Therefore, *without* the Repurchase Program, the director shareholders' absolute voting power of 23% would already constitute *actual voting power greater than* 25% in a proxy contest with normal shareholder participation below 100%. . . .

This Court has recognized "the prerogative of a board of directors to resist a third party's unsolicited acquisition proposal or offer." *Paramount Communications, Inc. v. QVC Network, Inc.,* Del.Supr., 637 A.2d 34, 43 n. 13 (1994). The Unitrin Board did not have unlimited discretion to defeat the threat it perceived from the American General Offer by any draconian means available. *See Unocal,* 493 A.2d at 955. Pursuant to the *Unocal* proportionality test, the nature of the threat associated with a particular hostile offer sets the parameters for the range of permissible defensive tactics. Accordingly, the purpose of enhanced judicial scrutiny is to determine whether the Board acted reasonably in "relation . . . to the threat which a particular bid allegedly poses to stockholder interests." *Mills Acquisition Co. v. Macmillan, Inc.,* Del.Supr., 559 A.2d 1261, 1288 (1989).

. . . Courts, commentators and litigators have attempted to catalogue the threats posed by hostile tender offers. . . . Commentators have categorized three types of threats:

(i) *opportunity loss* . . . [where] a hostile offer might deprive target shareholders of the opportunity to select a superior alternative offered by target management [or, we would add, offered by another bidder]; (ii) *structural coercion,* . . . the risk that disparate treatment of non-tendering shareholders might distort shareholders' tender decisions; and (iii) *substantive coercion*, ... the risk that shareholders will mistakenly accept an underpriced offer because they disbelieve management's representations of intrinsic value....*

The record reflects that the Unitrin Board perceived the threat from American General's Offer to be a form of substantive coercion....

The record appears to support Unitrin's argument that the Board's justification for adopting the Repurchase Program was its reasonably perceived risk of substantive coercion, *i.e.*, that Unitrin's shareholders might accept American General's inadequate Offer because of "ignorance or mistaken belief" regarding the Board's assessment of the long-term value of Unitrin's stock. *See Shamrock Holdings, Inc. v. Polaroid Corp.*, Del.Ch., 559 A.2d 278, 290 (1989).... The adoption of the Repurchase Program also appears to be consistent with this Court's holding that economic inadequacy is not the only threat presented by an all cash for all shares hostile bid, because the threat of such a hostile bid could be exacerbated by shareholder "ignorance or ... mistaken belief." *Paramount Communications, Inc. v. Time, Inc.*, 571 A.2d at 1153....

An examination of the cases applying *Unocal* reveals a direct correlation between findings of proportionality or disproportionality and the judicial determination of whether a defensive response was draconian because it was either coercive or preclusive in character. In *Time,* for example, this Court concluded that the Time board's defensive response was reasonable and proportionate since it was not aimed at "cramming down" on its shareholders a management-sponsored alternative, *i.e.*, was not coercive, and because it did not preclude Paramount from making an offer for the combined Time–Warner company, *i.e.*, was not preclusive....

... As common law applications of *Unocal's* proportionality standard have evolved, at least two characteristics of draconian defensive measures taken by a board of directors in responding to a threat have been brought into focus through enhanced judicial scrutiny. In the modern takeover lexicon, it is now clear that since *Unocal,* this Court has consistently recognized that defensive measures which are either preclusive or coercive are included within the common law definition of draconian.

If a defensive measure is not draconian, however, because it is not either coercive or preclusive, the *Unocal* proportionality test requires the focus of enhanced judicial scrutiny to shift to "the range of reasonableness." *Paramount Communications, Inc.*

* See Paramount Communications, Inc. v. Time Inc., n. 17, pp. 1270–1271, supra.  (Footnote by ed.)

*v. QVC Network, Inc.,* Del.Supr., 637 A.2d 34, 45–46 (1994). Proper and proportionate defensive responses are intended and permitted to thwart perceived threats. When a corporation is not for sale, the board of directors is the defender of the metaphorical medieval corporate bastion and the protector of the corporation's shareholders. The fact that a defensive action must not be coercive or preclusive does not prevent a board from responding defensively before a bidder is at the corporate bastion's gate. . . .

The Court of Chancery found that the Unitrin Board reasonably believed that American General's Offer was inadequate. . . . Upon remand, in applying the correct legal standard to the factual circumstances of this case, the Court of Chancery may conclude that the implementation of the limited Repurchase Program was also within a range of reasonable additional defensive responses available to the Unitrin Board. In considering whether the Repurchase Program was within a range of reasonableness the Court of Chancery should take into consideration whether: (1) it is a statutorily authorized form of business decision which a board of directors may routinely make in a non-takeover context; (2) as a defensive response to American General's Offer it was limited and corresponded in degree or magnitude to the degree or magnitude of the threat, (*i.e.,* assuming the threat was relatively "mild," was the response relatively "mild"?); (3) with the Repurchase Program, the Unitrin Board properly recognized that all shareholders are not alike, and provided immediate liquidity to those shareholders who wanted it. . . .

———

## NOTE ON CARMODY v. TOLL BROTHERS, INC.

The facts of the next principal case, *Quickturn Design Systems, Inc. v. Shapiro,* decided by the Delaware Supreme Court, can best be understood against the background of an earlier case decided by the Delaware Chancery Court, Carmody v. Toll Brothers, Inc., 723 A.2d 1180 (Del.Ch.1998). *Carmody* concerned the validity of a "dead hand" poison pill adopted by Toll Brothers, Inc. As described by Vice Chancellor Jacobs:

A "dead hand" rights plan is one that cannot be redeemed except by the incumbent directors who adopted the plan or their designated successors.

In substance, the "dead hand" provision operates to prevent any directors of Toll Brothers, except those who were in office as of the date of the Rights Plan's adoption (June 12, 1997) or their designated successors, from redeeming the Rights until they expire on June 12, 2007. That consequence flows directly from the Rights Agreement's [provision that] only "Continuing Directors" could redeem the Rights, and from its definition of a "Continuing Director," which is:

(i) any member of the Board of Directors of the Company, while such person is a member of the Board, who is not an Acquiring Person, or an Affiliate [as defined] or Associate [as defined] of an Acquiring Person, or a representative or nominee of an Acquiring Person or of any such Affiliate or Associate, and was a member of the Board prior to the date of this agreement, or (ii) any Person who subsequently becomes a member of the Board, while such Person is a member of the Board, who is not an Acquiring Person, or an Affiliate [as defined] or Associate [as defined] of an Acquiring Person, or a representative or nominee of an Acquiring Person or of any such Affiliate or Associate, if such Person's nomination for election or election to the Board is recommended or approved by a majority of the Continuing Directors.

Vice Chancellor Jacobs explained the genesis of dead hand pills as follows:

For our purposes, the relevant history begins in the early 1980s with the advent of the "poison pill" as an antitakeover measure. That innovation generated litigation focused upon the issue of whether any poison pill rights plan could validly be adopted under state corporation law. The seminal case, Moran v. Household International, Inc., answered that question in the affirmative.

In *Moran*, this Court and the Supreme Court upheld the "flip over" rights plan in issue there based on three distinct factual findings. The first was that the poison pill would not erode fundamental shareholder rights, because the target board would not have unfettered discretion arbitrarily to reject a hostile offer or to refuse to redeem the pill. Rather, the board's judgment not to redeem the pill would be subject to judicially enforceable fiduciary standards. The second finding was that even if the board refused to redeem the pill (thereby preventing the shareholders from receiving the unsolicited offer), that would not preclude the acquiror from gaining control of the target company, because the offeror could "form a group of up to 19.9% and solicit proxies for consents to remove the Board and redeem the Rights." Third, even if the hostile offer was precluded, the target company's stockholders could always exercise their ultimate prerogative— wage a proxy contest to remove the board. On this basis, the Supreme Court concluded that "the Rights Plan will not have a severe impact upon proxy contests and it will not preclude all hostile acquisitions of Household."

It being settled that a corporate board could permissibly adopt a poison pill, the next litigated question became: under what circumstances would the directors' fiduciary duties require the board to redeem the rights in the face of a hostile takeover proposal? That issue was litigated, in Delaware and elsewhere, during the second half of the 1980s. The lesson taught by that experience was that courts were extremely reluctant to order the redemption of poison pills on fiduciary grounds. The reason was the prudent deployment of the pill proved to be largely beneficial to shareholder interests: it often resulted in a bidding contest that culminated in an acquisition on terms superior to the initial hostile offer.

Once it became clear that the prospects were unlikely for obtaining judicial relief mandating a redemption of the poison pill, a different response to the pill was needed. That response, which echoed the Supreme Court's suggestion in *Moran*, was the foreseeable next step in the evolution of takeover strategy: a tender offer coupled with a solicitation for shareholder proxies to remove and replace the incumbent board with the acquiror's nominees who, upon assuming office, would redeem the pill. Because that strategy, if unopposed, would enable hostile offerors to effect an "end run" around the poison pill, it again was predictable and only a matter of time that target company boards would develop counter-strategies. With one exception—the "dead hand" pill—these counter-strategies proved "successful" only in cases where the purpose was to delay the process to enable the board to develop alternatives to the hostile offer. The counter-strategies were largely unsuccessful, however, where the goal was to stop the proxy contest (and as a consequence, the hostile offer) altogether.

For example, in cases where the target board's response was either to (i) amend the by-laws to delay a shareholders meeting to elect directors, or (ii) delay an annual meeting to a later date permitted under the bylaws, so that the board and management would be able to explore alternatives to the hostile offer (but not entrench themselves), those responses were upheld. On the other hand, where the target board's response to a proxy contest (coupled with a hostile offer) was (i) to move the shareholders meeting to a later date to enable the incumbent board to solicit revocations of proxies to defeat the apparently victorious dissident group, or (ii) to expand the size of the board, and then fill the newly created positions so the incumbents would retain control of the board irrespective of the outcome of the proxy contest, those responses were declared invalid.

This litigation experience taught that a target board, facing a proxy contest joined with a hostile tender offer, could, in good faith, employ non-preclusive defensive measures to give the board time to explore transactional alternatives. The target board could not, however, erect defenses that would either preclude a proxy contest altogether or improperly bend the rules to favor the board's continued incumbency.

In this environment, the only defensive measure that promised to be a "show stopper" (i.e., had the potential to deter a proxy contest altogether) was a poison pill with a "dead hand" feature. The reason is that if only the incumbent directors or their designated successors could redeem the pill, it would make little sense for shareholders or the hostile bidder to wage a proxy contest to replace the incumbent board. Doing that would eliminate from the scene the only group of persons having the power to give the hostile bidder and target company shareholders what they desired: control of the target company (in the case of the hostile bidder) and the opportunity to obtain an attractive price for their shares (in the case of the target company stockholders). It is against that backdrop that the legal issues presented here, which concern the validity of the "dead hand" feature, attain significance.

Vice Chancellor Jacobs concluded that the plaintiff's complaint stated a legally cognizable claim that a dead hand plan is invalid, on several grounds:

First, a dead hand pill violates the Delaware statute by impermissibly creating voting-power distinctions among directors without authorization in the certificate of incorporation, and by interfering with the directors' statutory power to manage the business and affairs of the corporation.

Second, a dead hand pill is unlawful under *Blasius* (See Chapter 4, supra), because it purposefully interferes with the shareholder voting franchise without any compelling justification.

Third, a dead hand pill is a "disproportionate" defensive measure under *Unocal/Unitrin*, because it either precludes or materially abridges the shareholders' rights to receive tender offers and to wage a proxy contest to replace the board.

In contrast to *Carmody*, a dead hand pill was upheld by a federal district court under Georgia law in *Invacare Corp. v. Healthdyne Technologies, Inc.*, 968 F.Supp. 1578 (N.D.Ga.1997), although the result in that case was driven at least in part by an interpretation of language in the Georgia statute.

---

## Quickturn Design Systems, Inc. v. Shapiro

Supreme Court of Delaware, 1998.
721 A.2d 1281.

■ Before WALSH, HOLLAND and HARTNETT, JUSTICES.

■ HOLLAND, JUSTICE:

The Quickturn case is an expedited appeal from a final judgment entered by the Court of Chancery. The dispute arises out of an ongoing effort by Mentor Graphics Corporation ("Mentor"), a hostile bidder, to acquire Quickturn Design Systems, Inc. ("Quickturn"), the target company. The plaintiffs-appellees are Mentor and an unaffiliated stockholder of Quickturn. The named defendants-appellants are Quickturn and its directors.

In response to Mentor's tender offer and proxy contest to replace the Quickturn board of directors, as part of Mentor's effort to acquire

Quickturn, the Quickturn board enacted two defensive measures. First, it amended the Quickturn shareholder rights plan ("Rights Plan") by adopting a "no hand" feature of limited duration (the "Delayed Redemption Provision" or "DRP"). Second, the Quickturn board amended the corporation's by-laws to delay the holding of any special stockholders meeting requested by stockholders for 90 to 100 days after the validity of the request is determined (the "Amendment" or "By–Law Amendment").

Mentor filed actions for declarative and injunctive relief in the Court of Chancery challenging the legality of both defensive responses by Quickturn's board. The Court of Chancery conducted a trial on the merits. It determined that the By–Law Amendment is valid. It also concluded, however, that the DRP is invalid on fiduciary duty grounds.

In this appeal, Quickturn argues that the Court of Chancery erred in finding that Quickturn's directors breached their fiduciary duty by adopting the Delayed Redemption Provision. We have concluded that, as a matter of Delaware law, the Delayed Redemption Provision was invalid. Therefore, on that alternative basis, the judgment of the Court of Chancery is affirmed.

## STATEMENT OF FACTS

### The Parties

Mentor (the hostile bidder) is an Oregon corporation, headquartered in Wilsonville, Oregon, whose shares are publicly traded on the NASDAQ national market system. Mentor manufactures, markets, and supports electronic design automation ("EDA") software and hardware. It also provides related services that enable engineers to design, analyze, simulate, model, implement, and verify the components of electronic systems. Mentor markets its products primarily for large firms in the communications, computer, semiconductor, consumer electronics, aerospace, and transportation industries.

Quickturn, the target company, is a Delaware corporation, headquartered in San Jose, California. Quickturn has 17,922,518 outstanding shares of common stock that are publicly traded on the NASDAQ national market system. Quickturn invented, and was the first company to successfully market, logic emulation technology, which is used to verify the design of complex silicon chips and electronics systems. Quickturn is currently the market leader in the emulation business, controlling an estimated 60% of the worldwide emulation market and an even higher percentage of the United States market. Quickturn maintains the largest intellectual property portfolio in the industry, which includes approximately twenty-nine logic emulation patents issued in the United States, and numerous other patents issued in foreign jurisdictions. Quickturn's customers include the world's leading technology companies, among them Intel, IBM, Sun Microsystems, Texas Instruments, Hitachi, Fujitsu, Siemens, and NEC.

Quickturn's board of directors consists of eight members, all but one of whom are outside, independent directors.[4] All have distin-

---

**4.** The Quickturn board includes Messrs. Glen Antle (President and Chairman of Quickturn's board of directors); Michael D'Amour (Quickturn's founding CEO and

guished careers and significant technological experience. Collectively, the board has more than 30 years of experience in the EDA industry and owns one million shares (about 5%) of Quickturn's common stock.

Since 1989, Quickturn has historically been a growth company, having experienced increases in earnings and revenues during the past seven years. Those favorable trends were reflected in Quickturn's stock prices, which reached a high of $15.75 during the first quarter of 1998, and generally traded in the $15.875 to $21.25 range during the year preceding Mentor's hostile bid.

Since the spring of 1998, Quickturn's earnings, revenue growth, and stock price levels have declined, largely because of the downturn in the semiconductor industry and more specifically in the Asian semiconductor market. Historically, 30%–35% of Quickturn's annual sales (approximately $35 million) had come from Asia, but in 1998, Quickturn's Asian sales declined dramatically with the downturn of the Asian market.[5] Management has projected that the negative impact of the Asian market upon Quickturn's sales should begin reversing itself sometime between the second half of 1998 and early 1999.

### Quickturn–Mentor Patent Litigation

Since 1996, Mentor and Quickturn have been engaged in patent litigation that has resulted in Mentor being barred from competing in the United States emulation market. Because its products have been adjudicated to infringe upon Quickturn's patents, Mentor currently stands enjoined from selling, manufacturing, or marketing its emulation products in the United States. Thus, Mentor is excluded from an unquestionably significant market for emulation products.

The origin of the patent controversy was Mentor's sale of its hardware emulation assets, including its patents, to Quickturn in 1992. Later, Mentor reentered the emulation business when it acquired a French company called Meta Systems ("Meta") and began to market Meta's products in the United States in December 1995. Quickturn

chairman through 1993, and Executive Vice President for research and development and head of international sales until he left Quickturn management in 1995); Dean William A. Hasler (a former Vice Chairman and partner of KPMG Peat Marwick; a former Dean of the Haas Graduate School of Business at the University of California, Berkeley, a position he held until 1998; and currently a technology and business advisor); Keith Lobo (Quickturn's President and CEO); Charles D. Kissner (currently CEO and Chairman of the Board of Digital Microwave Corporation, a telecommunications company, and a former President, CEO, and director for Aristacom International, Inc.; also a former AT & T executive); Richard Alberding (a management consultant for high technology companies; and who currently serves on the board of directors of several technology companies); Dr. David Lam (former Vice President at Wyse Technology, former President and CEO of Expert Edge, Inc., and currently a technology and business advisor in the semiconductor equipment industry and Chairman of the David Lam Group); Dr. Yen–Son (Paul) Huang (a co-founder and President of PiE and, following PiE's merger with Quickturn in 1993, Executive Vice President of Quickturn until June 1997. Since then, Dr. Huang has served Quickturn only as a director).

5. By the summer of 1998, Quickturn's stock price had declined to $6 per share. On August 11, 1998, the closing price was $8.00 It was in this "trough" period that Mentor, which had designs upon Quickturn since the fall of 1997, saw an opportunity to acquire Quickturn for an advantageous price.

reacted by commencing a proceeding before the International Trade Commission ("ITC") claiming that Meta and Mentor were infringing Quickturn's patents. In August 1996, the ITC issued an order prohibiting Mentor from importing, selling, distributing, advertising, or soliciting in the United States, any products manufactured by Meta. That preliminary order was affirmed by the Federal Circuit Court of Appeals in August 1997. In December 1997, the ITC issued a Permanent Exclusion Order prohibiting Mentor from importing, selling, marketing, advertising, or soliciting in the United States, until at least April 28, 2009, any of the emulation products manufactured by Meta outside the United States.

At present, the only remaining patent litigation is pending in the Oregon Federal District Court. Quickturn is asserting a patent infringement damage claim that, Quickturn contends, is worth approximately $225 million. Mentor contends that Quickturn's claim is worth only $5.2 million or even less.

### Mentor's Interest in Acquiring Quickturn

Mentor began exploring the possibility of acquiring Quickturn. If Mentor owned Quickturn, it would also own the patents, and would be in a position to "unenforce" them by seeking to vacate Quickturn's injunctive orders against Mentor in the patent litigation. The exploration process began when Mr. Bernd Braune, a Mentor senior executive, retained Arthur Andersen ("Andersen") to advise Mentor how it could successfully compete in the emulation market. The result was a report Andersen issued in October 1997, entitled "PROJECT VELOCITY" and "Strategic Alternatives Analysis." The Andersen report identified several advantages and benefits Mentor would enjoy if it acquired Quickturn.[10]

In December 1997, Mentor retained Salomon Smith Barney ("Salomon") to act as its financial advisor in connection with a possible acquisition of Quickturn. Salomon prepared an extensive study which it reviewed with Mentor's senior executives in early 1998. The Salomon study concluded that although a Quickturn acquisition could provide substantial value for Mentor, Mentor could not afford to acquire Quickturn at the then-prevailing market price levels. Ultimately, Mentor decided not to attempt an acquisition of Quickturn during the first half of 1998.

After Quickturn's stock price began to decline in May 1998, however, Gregory Hinckley, Mentor's Executive Vice President, told Dr. Walden Rhines, Mentor's Chairman, that "the market outlook being very weak due to the Asian crisis made it a good opportunity" to try acquiring Quickturn for a cheap price. Mr. Hinckley then assembled Mentor's financial and legal advisors, proxy solicitors, and others,

**10.** These included: (i) eliminating the time and expense associated with litigation; (ii) creating synergy from combining two companies with complementary core competencies; (iii) reducing customer confusion over product availability, which in turn would accelerate sales; and (iv) eliminating the threat of a large competitor moving into the emulation market. Mentor has utilized these reasons in public statements in which it attempted to explain why its bid made sense.

and began a three month process that culminated in Mentor's August 12, 1998 tender offer.

### Mentor Tender Offer and Proxy Contest

On August 12, 1998, Mentor announced an unsolicited cash tender offer for all outstanding common shares of Quickturn at $12.125 per share, a price representing an approximate 50% premium over Quickturn's immediate pre-offer price, and a 20% discount from Quickturn's February 1998 stock price levels. Mentor's tender offer, once consummated, would be followed by a second step merger in which Quickturn's nontendering stockholders would receive, in cash, the same $12.125 per share tender offer price.

Mentor also announced its intent to solicit proxies to replace the board at a special meeting. Relying upon Quickturn's then-applicable by-law provision governing the call of special stockholders meetings, Mentor began soliciting agent designations from Quickturn stockholders to satisfy the by-law's stock ownership requirements to call such a meeting.[11]

### Quickturn Board Meetings

Under the Williams Act, Quickturn was required to inform its shareholders of its response to Mentor's offer no later than ten business days after the offer was commenced. During that ten day period, the Quickturn board met three times, on August 13, 17, and 21, 1998. During each of those meetings, it considered Mentor's offer and ultimately decided how to respond.

The Quickturn board first met on August 13, 1998, the day after Mentor publicly announced its bid. All board members attended the meeting, for the purpose of evaluating Mentor's tender offer. The meeting lasted for several hours. Before or during the meeting, each board member received a package that included (i) Mentor's press release announcing the unsolicited offer; (ii) Quickturn's press release announcing its board's review of Mentor's offer; (iii) Dr. Rhines's August 11 letter to Mr. Antle [Quickturn's president]; (iv) ... complaints filed by Mentor against Quickturn and its directors; and (v) copies of Quickturn's then-current Rights Plan and by-laws.

The Quickturn board first discussed retaining a team of financial advisors to assist it in evaluating Mentor's offer and the company's strategic alternatives. The board discussed the importance of selecting a qualified investment bank, and considered several investment banking firms. Aside from Hambrecht & Quist ("H & Q"), Quickturn's long-time investment banker, other firms that the board considered included Goldman Sachs & Co. and Morgan Stanley Dean Witter.

---

**11.** The applicable by-law (Article II, § 2.3) authorized a call of a special stockholders meeting by shareholders holding at least 10% of Quickturn's shares. In their agent solicitation, Mentor informed Quickturn stockholders that Mentor intended to call a special meeting approximately 45 days after it received sufficient agent designations to satisfy the 10% requirement under the original by-law. The solicitation also disclosed Mentor's intent to set the date for the special meeting, and to set the record date and give formal notice of that meeting.

Ultimately, the board selected H & Q, because the board believed that H & Q had the most experience with the EDA industry in general and with Quickturn in particular.[12]

During the balance of the meeting, the board discussed for approximately one or two hours (a) the status, terms, and conditions of Mentor's offer; (b) the status of Quickturn's patent litigation with Mentor; (c) the applicable rules and regulations that would govern the board's response to the offer required by the Securities Exchange Act of 1934 (the "34 Act"); (d) the board's fiduciary duties to Quickturn and its shareholders in a tender offer context; (e) the scope of defensive measures available to the corporation if the board decided that the offer was not in the best interests of the company or its stockholders; (f) Quickturn's then-current Rights Plan and special stockholders meeting by-law provisions; (g) the need for a federal antitrust filing; and (h) the potential effect of Mentor's offer on Quickturn's employees. The board also instructed management and H & Q to prepare analyses to assist the directors in evaluating Mentor's offer, and scheduled two board meetings, August 17, and August 21, 1998.

The Quickturn board next met on August 17, 1998. That meeting centered around financial presentations by management and by H & Q. Mr. Keith Lobo, Quickturn's President and CEO, presented a Medium Term Strategic Plan, which was a "top down" estimate detailing the economic outlook and the company's future sales, income prospects and future plans (the "Medium Term Plan"). The Medium Term Plan contained an optimistic (30%) revenue growth projection for the period 1998–2000.[13] After management made its presentation, H & Q supplied its valuation of Quickturn, which relied upon a "base case" that assumed management's 30% revenue growth projection. On that basis, H & Q presented various "standalone" valuations based on various techniques, including a discounted cash flow ("DCF") analysis. Finally, the directors discussed possible defensive measures, but took no action at that time.

The Quickturn board held its third and final meeting in response to Mentor's offer on August 21, 1998. Again, the directors received extensive materials and a further detailed analysis performed by H & Q. The focal point of that analysis was a chart entitled "Summary of Implied Valuation." That chart compared Mentor's tender offer price to the Quickturn valuation ranges generated by H & Q's application of five different methodologies.[14] The chart showed that Quickturn's

---

**12.** Apparently, the board had already decided to retain Quickturn's outside counsel, Wilson, Sonsini, Goodrich & Rosati, as its legal advisors. Larry Sonsini, Esquire, a senior partner of that firm, is shown on the minutes of all three board meetings as "Secretary of the Meeting," and appears to have authored those minutes in that capacity.

**13.** The Court of Chancery concluded that the Quickturn board had grounds to anticipate that the company could "turn around" in a year and perform at the projected revenue levels.

**14.** The five methodologies and the respective price ranges were: Historical Trading Range ($6.13–$21.63); Comparable Public Companies ($2.55–$15.61); Comparable M & A Transactions ($6.00–$31.36); Comparable Premiums Paid ($9.54–$10.72); and Discounted Cash Flow Analysis ($11.88–$57.87).

value under all but one of those methodologies was higher than Mentor's $12.125 tender offer price.

### Quickturn's Board Rejects Mentor's Offer as Inadequate

After hearing the presentations, the Quickturn board concluded that Mentor's offer was inadequate, and decided to recommend that Quickturn shareholders reject Mentor's offer. The directors based their decision upon: (a) H & Q's report; (b) the fact that Quickturn was experiencing a temporary trough in its business, which was reflected in its stock price; (c) the company's leadership in technology and patents and resulting market share; (d) the likely growth in Quickturn's markets (most notably, the Asian market) and the strength of Quickturn's new products (specifically, its Mercury product); (e) the potential value of the patent litigation with Mentor; and (f) the problems for Quickturn's customers, employees, and technology if the two companies were combined as the result of a hostile takeover.

### Quickturn's Defensive Measures

At the August 21 board meeting, the Quickturn board adopted two defensive measures in response to Mentor's hostile takeover bid. First, the board amended Article II, § 2.3 of Quickturn's by-laws, which permitted stockholders holding 10% or more of Quickturn's stock to call a special stockholders meeting. The By–Law Amendment provides that if any such special meeting is requested by shareholders, the corporation (Quickturn) would fix the record date for, and determine the time and place of, that special meeting, which must take place not less than 90 days nor more than 100 days after the receipt and determination of the validity of the shareholders' request.

Second, the board amended Quickturn's shareholder Rights Plan by eliminating its "dead hand" feature and replacing it with the Deferred Redemption Provision, under which no newly elected board could redeem the Rights Plan for six months after taking office, if the purpose or effect of the redemption would be to facilitate a transaction with an "Interested Person" (one who proposed, nominated or financially supported the election of the new directors to the board).[15] Mentor would be an Interested Person.

The effect of the By–Law Amendment would be to delay a shareholder-called special meeting for at least three months. The effect of the DRP would be to delay the ability of a newly-elected, Mentor-

---

**15.** The amended Rights Plan pertinently provides that: "[I]n the event that a majority of the Board of Directors of the Company is elected by stockholder action at an annual or special meeting of stockholders, then until the 180th day following the effectiveness of such election (including any postponement or adjournment thereof), the Rights shall not be redeemed if such redemption is reasonably likely to have the purpose or effect of facilitating a Transaction with an Interested Person."

An "Interested Person" is defined under the amended Rights Plan as "any Person who (i) is or will become an Acquiring Person if such Transaction were to be consummated or an Affiliate or Associate of such a Person, and (ii) is, or directly or indirectly proposed, nominated or financially supported, a director of [Quickturn] in office at the time of consideration of such Transaction who was elected at an annual or special meeting of stockholders."

nominated board to redeem the Rights Plan or "poison pill" for six months, in any transaction with an Interested Person. Thus, the combined effect of the two defensive measures would be to delay any acquisition of Quickturn by Mentor for at least nine months.

## PROCEDURAL HISTORY

Mentor filed this action in the Court of Chancery on August 12, 1998, seeking a declaratory judgment that Quickturn's newly adopted takeover defenses are invalid and an injunction requiring the Quickturn board to dismantle those defenses. After expedited briefing and oral argument, the Court of Chancery denied Quickturn's case dispositive pre-trial motion on October 9, 1998. A trial was held on October 19, 20, 23, 26 and 28, 1998. Thereafter, the parties submitted post-trial briefs on an expedited schedule.

During the course of the litigation in the Court of Chancery, the Quickturn board, relying upon the By–Law Amendment, noticed the special meeting requested by Mentor for January 8, 1999—71 days after the October 1, 1998 meeting date originally noticed by Mentor.[17] After the trial, Mentor announced in Amendments to its Schedule 14A–1 that were filed with the Securities and Exchange Commission, that it had received tenders of Quickturn shares which, together with the shares that Mentor already owned, represented over 51% of Quickturn's outstanding stock.

## QUICKTURN BY–LAW AMENDMENT

At the time Mentor commenced its tender offer and proxy contest, Quickturn's by-laws authorized shareholders holding at least 10% of Quickturn's voting stock to call a special meeting of stockholders. The then-applicable by-law, Article II, § 2.3, read thusly:

A special meeting of the stockholders may be called at any time by (i) the board of directors, (ii) the chairman of the board, (iii) the president, (iv) the chief executive officer or (v) one or more shareholders holding shares in the aggregate entitled to cast not less than ten percent (10%) of the votes at that meeting.

At the August 21, 1998 board meeting, the Quickturn board amended § 2.3 in response to the Mentor bid, to read as follows:

A special meeting of the stockholders may be called at any time by (i) the board of directors, (ii) the chairman of the board, (iii) the president, (iv) the chief executive officer or (v) subject to the procedures set forth in this Section 2.3, one or more stockholders holding shares in the aggregate entitled to cast not less than ten percent (10%) of the votes at that meeting.

---

**17.** Mentor later renoticed the special meeting date to November 24, 1998, anticipating that the Court of Chancery would issue its decision before that time. After the Court of Chancery informed the parties that it would be unable to issue a decision by November 24, Mentor agreed that its meeting would be convened and then immediately adjourned to a later date.

Upon request in writing sent by registered mail to the president or chief executive officer by any stockholder or stockholders entitled to call a special meeting of stockholders pursuant to this Section 2.3, the board of directors shall determine a place and time for such meeting, which time shall be not less than ninety (90) nor more than one hundred (100) days after the receipt and determination of the validity of such request, and a record date for the determination of stockholders entitled to vote at such meeting in the manner set forth in Section 2.12 hereof. Following such receipt and determination, it shall be the duty of the secretary to cause notice to be given to the stockholders entitled to vote at such meeting, in the manner set forth in Section 2.4 hereof, that a meeting will be held at the time and place so determined.

The Court of Chancery found that the Quickturn board amended the By–Law because (i) the original § 2.3 was incomplete: it did not explicitly state who would be responsible for determining the time, place, and record date for the meeting and (ii) the original by-law language arguably would have allowed a hostile bidder holding the requisite percentage of shares to call a special stockholders meeting on minimal notice and stampede the shareholders into making a decision without time to become adequately informed.

The Court of Chancery concluded that the By–Law Amendment responded to those concerns by explicitly making the Quickturn board responsible for fixing the time, place, record date and notice of the special meeting and by mandating a 90 to 100 day period of delay for holding the meeting after the validity of the shareholder's meeting request is determined. That specific delay period was chosen to make § 2.3 parallel to, and congruent with, Quickturn's "advance notice" by-law, which contained a similar 90 to 100 day minimum advance notice period.

The only By–Law Amendment-related issue that the Court of Chancery decided was whether the Amendment, standing alone, fell outside any range of potentially reasonable responses and, therefore, constituted a disproportionate response to the threat posed by the Mentor tender offer and proxy contest. Among the factors the Court of Chancery considered were whether the challenged defensive response "is a statutorily authorized form of business decision that a board of directors may routinely make in a non-takeover context,"[18] and whether the response "was limited and corresponded in degree or magnitude to the degree or magnitude of the threat."[19]

The Court of Chancery concluded that the Quickturn board's adoption of the By–Law Amendment did not violate the fiduciary principles embodied in Unocal and its progeny. Although the Delayed

---

**18.** Unitrin, Inc. v. American General Corp., Del.Supr., 651 A.2d 1361, 1389 (1995); Unocal Corp. v. Mesa Petroleum Co., Del. Supr., 493 A.2d 946, 958 (1985); Cheff v. Mathes, Del.Supr., 199 A.2d 548, 554 (1964).

**19.** Unitrin, Inc. v. American General Corp., 651 A.2d at 1389.

Redemption Provision and the By–Law Amendment were enacted as a concerted defensive response to Mentor's hostile takeover efforts, Mentor did not file a cross-appeal challenging the Court of Chancery's decision upholding the validity of Quickturn's amendment to its by-laws. Consequently, the Court of Chancery's ruling on the By–Law Amendment is not at issue in this appeal and has become final.

## QUICKTURN'S DELAYED REDEMPTION PROVISION

At the time Mentor commenced its bid, Quickturn had in place a Rights Plan that contained a so-called "dead hand" provision. That provision had a limited "continuing director" feature that became operative only if an insurgent that owned more than 15% of Quickturn's common stock successfully waged a proxy contest to replace a majority of the board. In that event, only the "continuing directors" (those directors in office at the time the poison pill was adopted) could redeem the rights.

During the same August 21, 1998 meeting at which it amended the special meeting by-law, the Quickturn board also amended the Rights Plan to eliminate its "continuing director" feature, and to substitute a "no hand" or "delayed redemption provision" into its Rights Plan. The Delayed Redemption Provision provides that, if a majority of the directors are replaced by stockholder action, the newly elected board cannot redeem the rights for six months if the purpose or effect of the redemption would be to facilitate a transaction with an "Interested Person."[21]

It is undisputed that the DRP would prevent Mentor's slate, if elected as the new board majority, from redeeming the Rights Plan for six months following their election, because a redemption would be "reasonably likely to have the purpose or effect of facilitating a Transaction" with Mentor, a party that "directly or indirectly proposed, nominated or financially supported" the election of the new board. Consequently, by adopting the DRP, the Quickturn board built into the process a six month delay period in addition to the 90 to 100 day delay mandated by the By–Law Amendment.

## COURT OF CHANCERY INVALIDATES DELAYED REDEMPTION PROVISION

When the board of a Delaware corporation takes action to resist a hostile bid for control, the board of directors' defensive actions are subjected to "enhanced" judicial scrutiny.[22] For a target board's ac-

---

**21.** The "no hand" or Delayed Redemption Provision is found in a new Section 23(b) of the Rights Plan, which states: (b) Notwithstanding the provisions of Section 23(a), in the event that a majority of the Board of Directors of the Company is elected by stockholder action at an annual or special meeting of stockholders, then until the 180th day following the effectiveness of such election (including any postponement or adjournment thereof), the Rights shall not be redeemed if

such redemption is reasonably likely to have the purpose or effect of facilitating a Transaction with an Interested Person.

Substantially similar provisions were added to Sections 24 ("Exchange") and 27 ("Supplements and Amendments") of the Rights Plan.

**22.** Unocal Corp. v. Mesa Petroleum Co., Del.Supr., 493 A.2d 946, 955 (1985).

tions to be entitled to business judgment rule protection, the target board must first establish that it had reasonable grounds to believe that the hostile bid constituted a threat to corporate policy and effectiveness; and second, that the defensive measures adopted were "proportionate," that is, reasonable in relation to the threat that the board reasonably perceived. The Delayed Redemption Provision was reviewed by the Court of Chancery pursuant to that standard.

The Court of Chancery found: "the evidence, viewed as a whole, shows that the perceived threat that led the Quickturn board to adopt the DRP, was the concern that Quickturn shareholders might mistakenly, in ignorance of Quickturn's true value, accept Mentor's inadequate offer, and elect a new board that would prematurely sell the company before the new board could adequately inform itself of Quickturn's fair value and before the shareholders could consider other options." The Court of Chancery concluded that Mentor's combined tender offer and proxy contest amounted to substantive coercion.[25] Having concluded that the Quickturn board reasonably perceived a cognizable threat, the Court of Chancery then examined whether the board's response—the Delayed Redemption Provision—was proportionate in relation to that threat.

In assessing a challenge to defensive measures taken by a target board in response to an attempted hostile takeover, enhanced judicial scrutiny requires an evaluation of the board's justification for each contested defensive measure and its concomitant results. The Court of Chancery found that the Quickturn board's "justification or rationale for adopting the Delayed Redemption Provision was to force any newly elected board to take sufficient time to become familiar with Quickturn and its value, and to provide shareholders the opportunity to consider alternatives, before selling Quickturn to any acquiror." The Court of Chancery concluded that the Delayed Redemption Provision could not pass the proportionality test. Therefore, the Court of Chancery held that "the DRP cannot survive scrutiny under Unocal and must be declared invalid."

### DELAYED REDEMPTION PROVISION VIOLATES FUNDAMENTAL DELAWARE LAW

In this appeal, Mentor argues that the judgment of the Court of Chancery should be affirmed because the Delayed Redemption Provision is invalid as a matter of Delaware law. According to Mentor, the Delayed Redemption Provision, like the "dead hand" feature in the Rights Plan that was held to be invalid in *Toll Brothers*,[29] will imper-

**25.** Unitrin, Inc. v. American General Corp., 651 A.2d at 1387.

**29.** Carmody v. Toll Brothers, Inc., Del. Ch., C.A. No. 15983, Jacobs, V.C., 1998 WL 418896 (July 24, 1998) ("Toll Brothers"). See Bank of New York Co., Inc. v. Irving Bank Corp., N.Y.Sup.Ct., 139 Misc.2d 665, 528 N.Y.S.2d 482 (1988). See also Shawn C. Lese, Note: Preventing Control From the Grave: A Proposal for Judicial Treatment of Dead Hand Provisions in Poison Pills, 96 Colum.L.Rev. 2175 (1996); Jeffrey N. Gordon, "Just Say Never?" Poison Pills, Dead Hand Pills, and Shareholder Adopted By–Laws: An Essay for Warren Buffett, 19 Cardozo L.Rev. 511 (1997). Cf. Invacare Corp. v. Healthdyne Technologies, Inc., N.D.Ga., 968 F.Supp. 1578 (1997) (applying Georgia law).

missibly deprive any newly elected board of both its statutory authority to manage the corporation under 8 Del.C. § 141(a) and its concomitant fiduciary duty pursuant to that statutory mandate. We agree.

Our analysis of the Delayed Redemption Provision in the Quickturn Rights Plan is guided by the prior precedents of this Court with regard to a board of directors authority to adopt a Rights Plan or "poison pill." In *Moran*, this Court held that the "inherent powers of the Board conferred by 8 Del.C. § 141(a) concerning the management of the corporation's 'business and affairs' provides the Board additional authority upon which to enact the Rights Plan."[30] Consequently, this Court upheld the adoption of the Rights Plan in *Moran* as a legitimate exercise of business judgment by the board of directors. In doing so, however, this Court also held "the rights plan is not absolute":

In *Moran*, this Court held that the "ultimate response to an actual takeover bid must be judged by the Directors' actions at the time and nothing we say relieves them of their fundamental duties to the corporation and its shareholders." Consequently, we concluded that the use of the Rights Plan would be evaluated when and if the issue arises.

One of the most basic tenets of Delaware corporate law is that the board of directors has the ultimate responsibility for managing the business and affairs of a corporation.[36] Section 141(a) requires that any limitation on the board's authority be set out in the certificate of incorporation.[37] The Quickturn certificate of incorporation contains no provision purporting to limit the authority of the board in any way. The Delayed Redemption Provision, however, would prevent a newly elected board of directors from completely discharging its fundamental management duties to the corporation and its stockholders for six months. While the Delayed Redemption Provision limits the board of directors' authority in only one respect, the suspension of the Rights Plan, it nonetheless restricts the board's power in an area of fundamental importance to the shareholders—negotiating a possible sale of the corporation. Therefore, we hold that the Delayed Redemption Provision is invalid under Section 141(a), which confers upon any newly elected board of directors full power to manage and direct the business and affairs of a Delaware corporation.

**30.** Moran v. Household International, Inc., Del.Supr., 500 A.2d 1346, 1353 (1985), citing Unocal Corp. v. Mesa Petroleum Co., Del.Supr., 493 A.2d 946, 953 (1985).

When the Household Board of Directors is faced with a tender offer and a request to redeem the Rights [Plan], they will not be able to arbitrarily reject the offer. They will be held to the same fiduciary standards any other board of directors would be held to in deciding to adopt a defensive mechanism, the same standards as they were held to in originally approving the Rights Plan.

**36.** 8 Del.C. § 141(a). See Mills Acquisition Co. v. Macmillan, Inc., Del.Supr., 559 A.2d 1261, 1280 (1989).

**37.** 8 Del.C. § 141(a) states: "The business and affairs of every corporation organized under this chapter shall be managed by or under the direction of a board of directors, except as may be otherwise provided in this chapter or in its certificate of incorporation. If any such provision is made in the certificate of incorporation, the powers and duties conferred or imposed upon the board of directors by this chapter shall be exercised or performed to such extent and by such person or persons as shall be provided in the certificate of incorporation."

In discharging the statutory mandate of Section 141(a), the directors have a fiduciary duty to the corporation and its shareholders. This unremitting obligation extends equally to board conduct in a contest for corporate control. The Delayed Redemption Provision prevents a newly elected board of directors from completely discharging its fiduciary duties to protect fully the interests of Quickturn and its stockholders.[41]

This Court has recently observed that "although the fiduciary duty of a Delaware director is unremitting, the exact course of conduct that must be charted to properly discharge that responsibility will change in the specific context of the action the director is taking with regard to either the corporation or its shareholders."[42] This Court has held "[t]o the extent that a contract, or a provision thereof, purports to require a board to act or not act in such a fashion as to limit the exercise of fiduciary duties, it is invalid and unenforceable."[43] The Delayed Redemption Provision "tends to limit in a substantial way the freedom of [newly elected] directors' decisions on matters of management policy."[44] Therefore, "it violates the duty of each [newly elected] director to exercise his own best judgment on matters coming before the board."[45]

In this case, the Quickturn board was confronted by a determined bidder that sought to acquire the company at a price the Quickturn board concluded was inadequate. Such situations are common in corporate takeover efforts.[46] In *Revlon*, this Court held that no defensive measure can be sustained when it represents a breach of the directors' fiduciary duty. A fortiori, no defensive measure can be sustained which would require a new board of directors to breach its fiduciary duty. In that regard, we note Mentor has properly acknowledged that in the event its slate of directors are elected, those newly elected directors will be required to discharge their unremitting fiduciary duty to manage the corporation for the benefit of Quickturn and its stockholders.[47]

## Conclusion

The Delayed Redemption Provision would prevent a new Quickturn board of directors from managing the corporation by redeeming the Rights Plan to facilitate a transaction that would serve the stock-

**41.** See Moran v. Household International, Inc., 500 A.2d at 1354.

**42.** Malone v. Brincat, Del.Supr., 722 A.2d 5 (1998).

**43.** See Paramount Communications, Inc. v. QVC Network, Inc., 637 A.2d at 51 (emphasis added). See, e.g., Mills Acquisition Co. v. Macmillan, Inc., 559 A.2d at 1281 (holding that a "board of directors ... may not avoid its active and direct duty of oversight in a matter as significant as the sale of corporate control"); Grimes v. Donald, Del. Ch., C.A. No. 13358, slip op. at 17, Allen, C., 1995 WL 54441 (Jan. 11, 1995, revised Jan. 19, 1995), aff'd, Del.Supr., 673 A.2d 1207 (1996) ("[t]he board may not either formally or effectively abdicate its statutory power and its fiduciary duty to manage or direct the management of the business and affairs of this corporation").

**44.** Abercrombie v. Davies, Del.Ch., 123 A.2d 893, 899 (1956), rev'd on other grounds, Del.Supr., 130 A.2d 338 (1957).

**45.** Id.

**46.** Revlon, Inc. v. MacAndrews & Forbes Holdings, Inc., 506 A.2d at 185.

**47.** Malone v. Brincat, Del.Supr., 722 A.2d 5 (1998).

holders' best interests, even under circumstances where the board would be required to do so because of its fiduciary duty to the Quickturn stockholders. Because the Delayed Redemption Provision impermissibly circumscribes the board's statutory power under Section 141(a) and the directors' ability to fulfill their concomitant fiduciary duties, we hold that the Delayed Redemption Provision is invalid. On that alternative basis, the judgment of the Court of Chancery is AFFIRMED.

---

## NOTE ON STATE TAKEOVER STATUTES

Most states now have statutes regulating takeover bids. These statutes tend to fall into several patterns, although they are highly variable within those patterns. This Note will canvass the major patterns, generally by discussing one statute within each pattern. However, it should be borne in mind that even statutes that fall into a given pattern often diverge in material respects. Because the statutes are highly complex, only their main features will be discussed.

State takeover statutes have evolved over time. Conventionally, they are categorized as first-, second-, and third-generation statutes.

1. *First-Generation Statutes.* The *first-generation* statutes tended to impose very stringent requirements on takeover bids, including fairness reviews by state agencies. Moreover, generally speaking the application of the statutes was not limited to corporations incorporated in the relevant state. In Edgar v. MITE Corp., 457 U.S. 624, 102 S.Ct. 2629, 73 L.Ed.2d 269 (1982), the Supreme Court held one such statute, the Illinois Takeover Act, unconstitutional. Six justices addressed the merits of the case. Three held that the Illinois statute was unconstitutional under the Supremacy Clause, on the ground that a major objective of the Williams Act was maintaining a neutral balance between management and the bidder, and the Illinois Act violated this balance. All of the six Justices held that the Illinois Act violated the Commerce Clause by: (1) Regulating commerce taking place across state lines, because the Act applied to prevent an offeror from making an offer even to non-Illinois shareholders; and (2) Imposing an excessive burden on interstate commerce, because the Act permitted the Illinois secretary of state to block a nationwide tender offer.

2. *Second-Generation Statutes.* After the decision in Edgar v. MITE Corp., a number of states adopted *second-generation takeover statutes*. These statutes fall into two major patterns: control share acquisition statutes and fair price statutes.

a. *Control share acquisition statutes. Control share acquisition statutes* provide that if an acquiring shareholder crosses a designated stock-ownership threshold, the shareholder is prohibited from voting the acquired shares unless he obtains approval to do so by vote of a majority of the corporation's shareholders, other than the acquiring shareholder and the corporation's management.

In CTS Corp. v. Dynamics Corp. of America, 481 U.S. 69, 107 S.Ct. 1637, 95 L.Ed.2d 67 (1987), the Supreme Court upheld Indiana's control share acquisition statute. That statute applied whenever a person acquired shares that, but for the operation of the statute, would bring the person's voting power in the corporation to or above any of three thresholds: 20%, 33 1/3%, or 50%. An acquiror that crossed such a threshold could not vote the acquired stock unless its voting rights were approved by a majority of all disinterested shareholders voting at the next regularly scheduled meeting of the shareholders or at a specially scheduled meeting. The statute was limited to targets incorporated in Indiana.

The Supreme Court held that the statute was not preempted by the Williams Act. The Court contrasted the Indiana statute with the Illinois statute found unconstitutional in *MITE*.

First, the Illinois statute provided for a twenty-day precommencement period. During this time, management could disseminate its views on the upcoming tender offer to shareholders, but bidders could not publish their offers. This conflicted with the Williams Act, because Congress had deleted precommencement-notice provisions from the Williams Act. In contrast, the Indiana statute did not give either management or the acquiring person an advantage in communicating with shareholders about an impending tender offer.

Second, the Illinois statute provided for a state-agency hearing on a tender offer. Because no deadline was set for the hearing, management could indefinitely stymie a takeover. This conflicted with the Williams Act, because Congress anticipated that bidders would be free to go forward without unreasonable delay. In contrast, the Indiana statute did not impose an indefinite delay on tender offers. Nothing in the statute prohibited an offeror from consummating an offer on the twentieth business day, the earliest day permitted under federal law, and full voting rights would be vested or denied within fifty days after commencement of the tender offer.

Third, the Illinois statute provided for a review of the fairness of tender offers by the Illinois Secretary of State. This conflicted with the Williams Act, because Congress intended shareholders to be free to make their own decisions. In contrast, the Indiana statute did not allow the state government to interpose its views of fairness between willing buyers and sellers of shares of the target company. Rather, the statute allowed shareholders to collectively evaluate the fairness of the offer.

The Court in *CTS* also concluded that the Indiana statute did not violate the Commerce Clause, because it did not discriminate against interstate commerce and did not subject activities to inconsistent regulation. The statute applied only to Indiana corporations, and a state has authority to regulate domestic corporations, including the authority to define the voting rights of shareholders.

b. *Fair price statutes*. *Fair price statutes* essentially require a winning bidder who makes a two-tier tender offer to pay nontendering shareholders the highest price it has paid for shares of the target within a specified recent period (typically, two years) if, after having acquired control of the target, the bidder seeks to engage in a business combination or one of certain other defined transactions with the target. There is an exception if the transaction is approved by (typically) 80 percent of all shares and two-thirds of the shares not owned by the bidder.

3.   *Third-Generation Statutes.*

a.   *Waiting-period statutes.* Many of the third-generation statutes prohibit a corporation, B, who acquires more than a specific percentage of another corporation, T, from merging with T, or engaging in certain other transactions with T, for a designated waiting period, unless certain conditions are satisfied.

The idea is that in many cases a prospective bidder (B) expects to finance a tender offer for the stock of the target (T) partly by using T's assets as collateral. If B cannot expect to merge with T shortly after the tender offer succeeds, that kind of financing will be difficult or impossible to obtain. In addition, B may have various business reasons for wanting to merge with T after a tender offer, rather than running T as a partly owned subsidiary. These purposes are also frustrated by waiting-period statutes.

The New York statute, N.Y. Bus.Corp.Law § 912, provides for a five-year delay in effecting specified transactions, even if the transaction is not self-interested, unless the transaction is approved by T's board of directors prior to B's acquisition of the designated percentage of T's stock. The less stringent Delaware statute, Del.G.C.L. § 203, prohibits business combinations and other designated transactions between B and T for a period of three years, unless B acquires 85% of T's shares in the initial tender offer, or the transaction is approved by 85% of T's shares other than the shares held by B.

b.   *Amanda.* In Amanda Acquisition Corp. v. Universal Foods Corp., 877 F.2d 496, cert. denied, 493 U.S. 955, 110 S.Ct. 367, 107 L.Ed.2d 353 (1989), the Seventh Circuit held that the Wisconsin waiting-period statute was constitutional:

> [Arguments against state anti-takeover statutes based on pre-emption have] not won easy acceptance among the Justices for several reasons. First there is § 28(a) of the '34 Act, 14 U.S.C. § 78bb(a), which provides that "[n]othing in this chapter shall affect the jurisdiction of the securities commission ... of any State over any security or any person insofar as it does not conflict with the provisions of this chapter or the rules and regulations thereunder." ... [T]he SEC has not drafted regulations concerning mergers with controlling shareholders, and the Act itself does not address the subject....
>
> ... [T]he best argument for preemption is the Williams Act's "neutrality" between bidder and management, a balance designed to leave investors free to choose. This is not a confident jumping-off point, though....

There is a big difference between what congress *enacts* and what it *supposes* will ensue. Expectations about the consequences of a law are not themselves law. To say that Congress wanted to be neutral between bidder and target . . . is not to say that it also forbade the states to favor one of these sides. . . .

Any bidder complying with federal law is free to acquire shares of Wisconsin firms on schedule. Delay in completing a second-stage merger may make the target less attractive, and thus depress the price offered or even lead to an absence of bids; it does not, however, alter any of the procedures governed by federal regulation. . . .

. . . It is not attractive [under the statute] to put bids on the table for Wisconsin corporations, but because Wisconsin leaves the process alone once a bidder appears, its law may co-exist with the Williams Act. . . .

The Commerce Clause, Art. I, § 8 cl. 3 of the Constitution, grants Congress the power "[t]o regulate Commerce . . . among the several States". . . .

When state law discriminates against interstate commerce expressly—for example, when Wisconsin closes its border to butter from Minnesota—the [anti-discrimination aspect of the] Commerce Clause steps in. The law before us is not of this type; it is neutral between inter-state and intra-state commerce. Amanda therefore presses on us the broader, all-weather, be-reasonable vision of the Constitution. Wisconsin has passed a law that unreasonably injures investors, most of whom live outside of Wisconsin, and therefore it has to be unconstitutional, as Amanda sees things. . . . [However, the Supreme] Court has looked for discrimination rather than for baleful effects. . . .

. . . The Commerce clause does not demand that states leave bidders a "meaningful opportunity for success".

c. *Other third-generation statutes. Amanda*, and perhaps other factors, emboldened some states to adopt other, extremely exotic, and in some cases extremely draconian, third-generation statutes. For example, the Pennsylvania statute provides, among many other things, that persons who own, offer to acquire, or publicly announce an intention to acquire, 20% of the stock of a publicly traded Pennsylvania corporation must disgorge any profits they realize from the disposition of that corporation's stock within a defined period. The Massachusetts statute requires every publicly held Massachusetts corporation to have a classified board.

d. *Constituency statutes*. A number of states have also adopted *constituency statutes*, which allow a board to consider the interests of groups ("constituencies") other than shareholders in making decisions, including decisions to resist takeovers. These statutes give the board increased leeway to resist a takeover because often these other constituencies—for example, labor and the local community—are opposed to takeovers.

CHAPTER XIII

# DISTRIBUTIONS TO SHAREHOLDERS

INTRODUCTION

Corporations normally can distribute funds to shareholders in one of four ways:

(1) As dividends, that is, by making pro rata distributions of cash, securities, or interests in other kinds of property.

(2) By repurchasing shares.

(3) By paying shareholder-employees inflated salaries. This technique is most commonly used in close corporations, for tax reasons: In calculating taxable income, a corporation can deduct salaries, but cannot deduct dividends.

(4) On liquidation, by paying each shareholder her pro rata share of corporate assets remaining after the claim of creditors have been satisfied or provided for.

This Chapter will concern the first two kinds of distributions—dividends and stock repurchases. Inflated salaries are considered in Chapters 6 (Close Corporations) and 9 (Duty of Loyalty), supra. Distributions in liquidation only infrequently raise difficult legal problems, if creditors have been either paid or provided for.

## SECTION 1. DIVIDEND POLICY

### (a) THE ELEMENTS OF DIVIDEND POLICY

### Richard A. Brealey & Steward C. Myers, Principles of Corporate Finance

Sixth ed., 2000.

In the mid–1950s John Lintner conducted a classic series of interviews with corporate managers about their dividend policies. His description of how dividends are determined can be summarized in four "stylized facts":

1. Firms have long-run target dividend payout ratios. Mature companies with stable earnings generally pay out a high proportion of earnings; growth companies have low payouts.

2.   Managers focus more on dividend changes than on absolute levels. Thus, paying a $2.00 dividend is an important financial decision if last year's dividend was $1.00, but no big deal if last year's dividend was $2.00.

3.   Dividend changes follow shifts in long-run, sustainable earnings. Managers "smooth" dividends. Transitory earnings changes are unlikely to affect dividend payouts.

4.   Managers are reluctant to make dividend changes that might have to be reversed. They are particularly worried about having to rescind a dividend increase. . . .

Lintner's simple model [of dividend decisions] suggests that the dividend depends in part on the firm's current earnings and in part on the dividend for the previous year, which in turn depends on that year's earnings and the dividend in the year before. Therefore if Lintner is correct, we should be able to describe dividends in terms of a weighted average of current and past earnings. The probability of an increase in the dividend rate should be greatest when *current* earnings have increased; it should be somewhat less when only the earnings from the previous year have increased; and so on. An extensive study by Fama and Babiak confirmed this hypothesis. Their tests of Lintner's model suggest that it provides a fairly good explanation of how companies decide on the dividend rate, but it is not the whole story. We would expect managers to take future prospects as well as past achievements into account when setting the payment. [And] . . . that is indeed the case.

## 16.3   THE INFORMATION IN DIVIDENDS . . .

In some countries you cannot rely on the information that companies provide. Passion for secrecy and a tendency to construct multilayered corporate organizations produce asset and earnings figures that are next to meaningless. Some people say that, thanks to creative accounting, the situation is little better for some companies in the United States.

How does an investor in such a world separate marginally profitable firms from the real money makers? One clue is dividends. Investors can't read managers' minds, but they can learn from managers' actions. They know that a firm which reports good earnings and pays a generous dividend is putting its money where its mouth is. We can understand, therefore, why investors would value the information content of dividends and would refuse to believe a firm's reported earnings unless they were backed up by an appropriate dividend policy.

Of course, firms can cheat in the short run by overstating earnings and scraping up cash to pay a generous dividend. But it is hard to cheat in the long run, for a firm that is not making enough money will not have enough cash to pay out. If a firm chooses a high dividend payout without the cash flow to back it up, that firm will ultimately have to reduce its investment plans or turn to investors for additional debt or equity financing. All of these consequences are costly. Therefore, most managers don't increase dividends until they are confident that sufficient cash will flow in to pay them.

There is plenty of evidence that managers do look to the future when they set the dividend payment. For example, Healy and Palepu report that on average earnings jumped 43 percent in the year that companies paid a dividend for the first time.[10] If managers thought that this was a temporary windfall, they might have been cautious about committing themselves to paying out cash. But it looks as if they had good reason to be confident about prospects, for over the next four years earnings grew on average by a further 164 percent.

Since dividends anticipate future earnings, it is no surprise to find that announcements of dividend cuts are usually taken by investors as bad news (stock price typically falls) and that dividend increases are good news (stock price rises). In the case of the dividend initiations studied by Healy and Palepu, the announcement of the dividend resulted in an abnormal rise of 4 percent in the stock price. . . .

## CONTROVERSY ABOUT DIVIDEND POLICY

We have seen that a dividend increase indicates management's optimism about earnings and thus affects the stock price. But the jump in stock price that accompanies an unexpected dividend increase would happen eventually anyway as information about future earnings comes out through other channels. We now ask whether the dividend decision *changes* the value of the stock, rather than simply providing a signal of stock value.

One endearing feature of economics is that it can always accommodate not just two, but three opposing points of view. And so it is with the controversy about dividend policy. On the right there is a conservative group which believes that an increase in dividend payout increases firm value. On the left, there is a radical group which believes that an increase in payout reduces value. And in the center there is a middle-of-the-road party which claims that dividend policy makes no difference.

The middle-of-the-road party was founded in 1961 by Miller and Modigliani (always referred to as "MM" or "M and M"), when they published a theoretical paper showing the irrelevance of dividend policy in a world without taxes, transaction costs, or other market imperfections.[12] . . .

In their classic 1961 article MM argued as follows: Suppose your firm has settled on its investment program. You have worked out how much of this program can be financed from borrowing, and you plan

**10.** See R. Healy and K. Palepu, "Earnings Information Conveyed by Dividend Initiations and Omissions," Journal of Financial Economics 21 (1988), pp. 149–175. Not everyone agrees that dividend changes predict future earnings. See, for example, S. Benartzi, R. Michaely, and R. Thaler, "Do Changes in Dividends Signal the Future or the Past?" Journal of Finance 52 (July 1997), pp. 1007–1034.

**12.** M.H. Miller and F. Modigliani: "Dividend Policy, Growth and the Valuation of Shares," *Journal of Business*, 34: 411–433 (October 1961).

to meet the remaining funds requirement from retained earnings. Any surplus money is to be paid out as dividends.

Now think what happens if you want to increase the dividend payment without changing the investment and borrowing policy. The extra money must come from somewhere. If the firm fixes its borrowing, the only way it can finance the extra dividend is to print some more shares and sell them. The new stockholders are going to part with their money only if you can offer them shares that are worth as much as they cost. But how can the firm do this when its assets, earnings, investment opportunities and, therefore, market value are all unchanged? The answer is that there must be a *transfer of value* from the old to the new stockholders. The new ones get the newly printed shares, each one worth less than before the dividend change was announced, and the old ones suffer a capital loss on their shares. The capital loss borne by the old shareholders just offsets the extra cash dividend they receive. . . .

Does it make any difference to the old stockholders that they receive an extra dividend payment plus an offsetting capital loss? It might if that were the only way they could get their hands on cash. But as long as there are efficient capital markets, they can raise the cash by selling shares. Thus the old shareholders can "cash in" either by persuading the management to pay a higher dividend or by selling some of their shares. In either case there will be a transfer of value from old to new shareholders. The only difference is that in the former case this transfer is caused by a dilution in the value of each of the firm's shares, and in the latter case it is caused by a reduction in the number of shares held by the old shareholders. . . .

Because investors do not need dividends to get their hands on cash, they will not pay higher prices for the shares of firms with high payouts. Therefore firms ought not to worry about dividend policy. They should let dividends fluctuate as a by-product of their investment and financing decisions. [This conclusion is known as the MM dividend-irrelevance proposition.] . . .

We believe—and it is widely believed—that MM's conclusions follow from their assumption of perfect and efficient capital markets. Nobody claims their model is an exact description of the so-called real world. Thus the dividend controversy finally boils down to arguments about imperfections, inefficiencies, or whether stockholders are fully rational.

[One reason that some or many corporations may pay high dividends in the real world is that there] is a natural clientele for high-payout stocks. For example, some financial institutions are legally restricted from holding stocks lacking established dividend records. Trusts and endowment funds may prefer high-dividend stocks because dividends are regarded as spendable "income," whereas capital gains are "additions to principal," which cannot be spent.

There is also a natural clientele of investors who look to their stock portfolios for a steady source of cash to live on. In principle this cash could be easily generated from stocks paying no dividends at all; the investor could just sell off a small fraction of his or her holdings from time to time. But it is simpler and cheaper for AT & T to send a quarterly check than for its stockholders to sell, say, one share every 3 months. AT & T's regular dividends relieve many of its shareholders of transaction costs and considerable inconvenience. . . .

If it is true that nobody gains or loses from shifts in dividend policy, why do shareholders often clamor for higher dividends? One possible explanation is that they don't trust managers to spend retained earnings wisely and they fear that the money will be plowed back into building a larger empire rather than a more profitable one. In this case the dividend decision is mixed up with the firm's investment and operating decisions. The dividend increase may lead to a rise in the stock price not because investors like dividends but because they want management to run a tighter ship.

————

## (b) JUDICIAL REVIEW OF DIVIDEND POLICY

————

## (1) PUBLICLY HELD CORPORATIONS WITH A CONTROLLING SHAREHOLDER

————

### SINCLAIR OIL CORP. v. LEVIEN

[See Chapter 9, supra]

————

## (2) CLOSE CORPORATIONS

————

## SMITH v. ATLANTIC PROPERTIES, INC.

[See Chapter 6, supra]

———

# SECTION 2.   LIMITATIONS ON DIVIDENDS UNDER CREDITORS' RIGHTS LAW

Traditionally, dividends have been regulated by two very different, overlapping, sets of legal rules. The first set of rules is located in creditor's rights (or fraudulent-conveyance) law. These rules center on, but are not limited to, the concept of insolvency, and emphasize the liability of *shareholders* for the *receipt* of improper dividends. The second set of rules is located in state corporation law. These rules emphasize the liability of *directors* for the *payment* of improper dividends. Limitations on dividends under the law of creditor's rights will be considered in this Section. Limitations on dividends under corporation law will be considered in Section 3.

———

## N.Y. BUS. CORP. LAW §§ 102(a)(8), 510(a), (b)

[See Statutory Supplement]

———

## UNIFORM FRAUDULENT TRANSFER ACT §§ 1, 2, 4, 5

[See Statutory Supplement]

———

## BANKRUPTCY CODE §§ 101(32), 548(a)

[See Statutory Supplement]

———

## BACKGROUND NOTE ON CREDITORS' RIGHTS LAW

1. *Definition*. Creditors' rights law imposes several limitations on transfers of assets without adequate consideration. The most prominent limits turns on the concept of insolvency. Insolvency limits on transfers are based on the transferor's financial condition in terms of either (i) its inability to pay its debts as they become due, or (ii) whether its liabilities exceed its assets. Thus, there are two broad definitions of the term *insolvency*.

The first definition—inability to pay debts as they become due—is embodied in most corporate dividend statutes, such as N.Y.Bus.Corp. Law § 102(a)(8). This is known as the *equity meaning* of insolvency, because it was the test generally applied by the equity courts, which had jurisdiction over insolvent estates before the enactment of the bankruptcy statute.

The second definition of insolvency—liabilities in excess of assets—is embodied in the Bankruptcy Code and the Uniform Fraudulent Transfer Act. This second definition is known as the *bankruptcy meaning* of insolvency.[1]

> The difference between these two conceptions can be very great. The equity insolvency test is concerned with current liquidity of the going enterprise; the emphasis of the bankruptcy sense of insolvency is upon liquidation of the enterprise. It is easily possible for an enterprise to be short of cash and other liquid means of payment while at the same time holding illiquid assets of great value; such an enterprise may well fail the equity insolvency test. It is also a quite possible occurrence for an enterprise to have a large current cash flow while steadily operating at a loss and suffering a continuing erosion of its asset base; in time, such an enterprise will fail to meet the bankruptcy test of insolvency.

> Those with any familiarity with accounting will recognizes that the equity insolvency test is concerned with the income and cash flow statements of the enterprise while the bankruptcy insolvency test is focused on the balance sheet of the enterprise. For this reason, the bankruptcy insolvency test is frequently referred to as the "balance sheet" or "net worth" test.

B. Manning & J. Hanks, Legal Capital 64 (3d ed. 1990).

2. *Application of Fraudulent Conveyance Laws to Dividends.* There is some academic controversy concerning whether fraudulent-conveyance laws are applicable to dividends. However, the cases, while few, uniformly hold that dividends are subject to those laws. See Barbara Black, Corporate Dividends and Stock Repurchases § 4.05[6][b] (1998).

3. *Insolvency Under the Dividend Statutes.* Many corporate-law dividend statutes explicitly incorporate an insolvency limitation on the payment of dividends. See, e.g., N.Y.Bus.Corp.Law § 510. Others, like the California statute and the Revised Model Business Corporation Act, do not. The Official Comment to RMBCA § 6.40 states that "[t]he Revised Model Business Corporation Act establishes the validity of distributions from the corporate law standpoint under section 6.40

---

**1.** Under the Bankruptcy Code, the test for whether a debtor can be put into involuntary bankruptcy turns principally on whether the debtor is insolvent in the equity sense. See 11 U.S.C.A. § 303(h). However, once a debtor has been put into bankruptcy, the bankruptcy trustee's right to avoid a pre-bankruptcy transfer turns in large part on whether at the time of the transfer the debtor was insolvent in the bankruptcy sense. See 11 U.S.C.A. §§ 101(32), 548.

The bankruptcy meaning of insolvency is itself susceptible to different nuances, as may be seen by comparing 11 U.S.C.A. § 101(32) with UFTA § 2(a).

and determines the potential liability of directors for improper distributions under sections 8.30 and 8.33. The federal Bankruptcy Act and state fraudulent conveyance statutes, on the other hand, are designed to enable the trustee or other representative to recapture for the benefit of creditors funds distributed to others in some circumstances. In light of these diverse purposes, it was not thought necessary to make the tests of section 6.40 identical to the tests for insolvency under these various statutes." Cal.Corp.Code § 506(d), which governs the liability of shareholders who have received improper dividends, provides that "[n]othing contained in this section affects any liability which any shareholder may have under [the Uniform Fraudulent (Transfer) Act.]."

4. *Unreasonably Small Capital.* Another important limitation on transferor under the UFTA and cognate Acts is that a transfer without adequate consideration is prohibited if it would leave the transferor with unreasonably small capital.

## SECTION 3.   LIMITATIONS ON DIVIDENDS UNDER TRADITIONAL CORPORATE STATUTES

### (a) INTRODUCTORY NOTE

1. *In General.* The dividend-policy cases, like Dodge v. Ford, supra, concern the issue, when may a corporation be *compelled* to pay dividends. Most of the law of dividends, however, centers on *limitations* on a corporation's power to pay dividends. These limitations may be thought of as financial, in the narrow sense that they are not based on judicial determinations of sound dividend policy, but instead turn on quantified tests. Under traditional statutes, however, the limitations involve concepts that are typically of little or no relevance in modern financial theory.

2. *Who Does Corporate Dividend Law Protect?* A preliminary issue raised by the corporate law of dividends is, who does this body of law protect? The class of persons protected by creditors' rights law is clear—creditors. The classes of persons protected by the corporate dividend statutes has not always been clear.

Obviously, one group of persons who might be protected by these statutes is creditors. As stated in D. Kehl, Corporate Dividends (1941), "With the liability of corporate stockholders . . . limited to the amount of capital subscribed . . . it soon became apparent that the original capital should be permanently devoted to the needs of the corporation as at least a partial substitute for the unlimited personal liability existing in individual enterprise." But then, "If the creation of a capital fund was not to defeat its purpose, safeguards against its withdrawal by repayment to shareholders in the guise of dividends, or otherwise, were indispensable. Historically, the principal objective of dividend law has therefore been the preservation of a minimum of assets as a safeguard in assuring the payment of creditors' claims."

In addition to creditors, some of the corporate dividend statutes are also designed to protect the preferences of preferred shareholders.

Finally, at one time it was thought that the corporate dividend statutes were intended to protect common shareholders, partly on the ground that excessive dividends might injure the corporate enterprise, and partly on the ground that dividends out of capital might mislead shareholders into thinking that the corporation was earning money when in fact it wasn't.

Today, the concept that the corporate dividend statutes protect common shareholders is not generally accepted. Furthermore, although the protection that the statutes give to preferred shareholders may sometimes be significant, many corporations have no preferred shareholders. That leaves the protection of creditors. As the following materials will show, however, creditors get very little protection from the traditional dividend statutes.

3.  *Legal Capital and Par Value*. Preliminarily, corporate dividend statutes can be divided into two broad classes—traditional and modern. The traditional statutes need to be understood against the background of the concept of *legal capital*. That concept, in turn, can only be understood against the background of a concept known as *par* or *par value*.

a.  *Par value*. Originally, the par value of a share was the price at which it was expected that the share would be issued (sold) by the corporation. Thus in the paradigm case, a share that carried a $100 par value would be issued for $100. Eventually, a practice emerged under which the par value of stock was not the price at which the stock was to be issued, but a purely nominal amount. For example, stock that was to be issued at $100 might carry a par value of only $1, or even less. Such stock is known as *low-par value* stock. Still later, the statutes were amended to allow the issuance of *no-par value* stock—that is, stock that did not carry any par value at all.

b.  *Legal capital*. *Legal capital* is the sum of (i) the par value of all par-value stock, and (ii) such additional amounts as the board assigns to capital either in connection with the issuance of low-par or no-par stock, or thereafter. Legal capital (or *stated capital*) is a legal construct, with little or no economic reality. *Economic capital* is the amount that the owners of an enterprise have invested in the enterprise, directly or indirectly. When stock was issued at its par value, the concepts of economic and legal capital were tied together. The advent of low-par and no-par stock severed that tie. Because the concept of legal capital is tied to par value, it has become artificial. Nevertheless, the concept still remains important under the traditional dividend statutes.

4.  *Capital-Impairment and Earned-Surplus Statutes*. The traditional dividend statutes generally fall into two basic patterns: *capital-impairment* (or *balance-sheet*) statutes and *earned-surplus* statutes.

The capital-impairment statutes center on whether the corporation's assets exceed its liabilities plus its capital. The *earned-surplus* statutes center on the corporation's accumulated profits. The next two sections concern capital-impairment and earned-surplus statutes, respectively. Thereafter, two leading modern statutes, which take new approaches, will be considered.

5. *Structure of the Traditional Statutes*. Most traditional corporate dividend statutes begin with an insolvency test. There are three possible reasons why these statutes employ an insolvency test, which would be applicable in any event under creditors' rights law. First, it has not always been entirely clear whether creditors' rights law applies to dividends. Second, creditors' rights law emphasize the liability of transferees (in the case of corporations, shareholders) for improper distributions. In contrast, the corporate dividend statutes emphasize the liability of directors. Third, the basic creditors' rights laws—the Bankruptcy Code and the Uniform Fraudulent Transfers Act and cognate statutes—turn on the bankruptcy meaning of insolvency. In contrast, a dividend statute may employ either the equity meaning of insolvency, or both the bankruptcy and the equity meanings.

After beginning with an insolvency test, the traditional dividend statutes add a second basic test, which is frequently subject to important exceptions. The most common traditional second basic test is a capital-impairment or balance-sheet test. Under this test, a dividend cannot be paid if, before or after payment of the dividend, the corporation's assets are or would be less than the sum of its liabilities plus its capital or, in some cases, the sum of liabilities, capital, and liquidation preferences. (In contrast, under the bankruptcy meaning of the insolvency test, a dividend may be paid as long as after the payment the corporation's assets will exceed its liabilities.) Capital-impairment statutes can be conceptualized in two, functionally identical ways: as prohibiting dividends out of capital, or as permitting dividends only out of surplus.

The alternative traditional second basic test is the earned-surplus test. The capital-impairment test will be considered in Section 4(b) infra; the earned-surplus test will be considered in Section 4(c), infra.

---

## (b) TRADITIONAL STATUTES—PART I: CAPITAL-IMPAIRMENT STATUTES

---

## (1) THE BASIC CAPITAL–IMPAIRMENT TEST AND ITS MEANING

---

### DEL. GEN. CORP. LAW §§ 141(e), 154, 170

[See Statutory Supplement]

---

**N.Y. BUS. CORP. LAW §§ 102(a)(9), (12), (13), 506, 510**

[See Statutory Supplement]

---

# Klang v. Smith's Food & Drug Centers, Inc.

Supreme Court of Delaware, 1997.
702 A.2d 150.

■ Before VEASEY, C.J., WALSH, HOLLAND, HARTNETT and BERGER, JJ., constituting the Court en Banc.

■ VEASEY, CHIEF JUSTICE:

This appeal calls into question the actions of a corporate board in carrying out a merger and self-tender offer. Plaintiff in this purported class action alleges that a corporation's repurchase of shares violated the statutory prohibition against the impairment of capital. . . .

No corporation may repurchase or redeem its own shares except out of "surplus," as statutorily defined, or except as expressly authorized by provisions of the statute not relevant here. Balance sheets are not, however, conclusive indicators of surplus or a lack thereof. Corporations may revalue assets to show surplus, but perfection in that process is not required. Directors have reasonable latitude to depart from the balance sheet to calculate surplus, so long as they evaluate assets and liabilities in good faith, on the basis of acceptable data, by methods that they reasonably believe reflect present values, and arrive at a determination of the surplus that is not so far off the mark as to constitute actual or constructive fraud.

We hold that, on this record, the Court of Chancery was correct in finding that there was no impairment of capital and there were no disclosure violations. Accordingly, we affirm.

## Facts

Smith's Food & Drug Centers, Inc. ("SFD") is a Delaware corporation that owns and operates a chain of supermarkets in the Southwestern United States. Slightly more than three years ago, Jeffrey P. Smith, SFD's Chief Executive Officer, began to entertain suitors with an interest in acquiring SFD. At the time, and until the transactions at issue, Mr. Smith and his family held common and preferred stock constituting 62.1% voting control of SFD. Plaintiff and the class he purports to represent are holders of common stock in SFD.

On January 29, 1996, SFD entered into an agreement with The Yucaipa Companies ("Yucaipa"), a California partnership also active in the supermarket industry. Under the agreement, the following would take place:

> (1) Smitty's Supermarkets, Inc. ("Smitty's"), a wholly-owned subsidiary of Yucaipa that operated a supermarket chain in Arizona, was to merge into Cactus Acquisition, Inc. ("Cactus"), a subsidiary of SFD, in exchange for which SFD would deliver to

Yucaipa slightly over 3 million newly-issued shares of SFD common stock;

(2) SFD was to undertake a recapitalization, in the course of which SFD would assume a sizable amount of new debt, retire old debt, and offer to repurchase up to fifty percent of its outstanding shares (other than those issued to Yucaipa) for $36 per share; and

(3) SFD was to repurchase 3 million shares of preferred stock from Jeffrey Smith and his family.

SFD hired the investment firm of Houlihan Lokey Howard & Zukin ("Houlihan") to examine the transactions and render a solvency opinion. Houlihan eventually issued a report to the SFD Board replete with assurances that the transactions would not endanger SFD's solvency, and would not impair SFD's capital in violation of 8 *Del.C.* § 160. On May 17, 1996, in reliance on the Houlihan opinion, SFD's Board determined that there existed sufficient surplus to consummate the transactions, and enacted a resolution proclaiming as much. On May 23, 1996, SFD's stockholders voted to approve the transactions, which closed on that day. The self-tender offer was over-subscribed, so SFD repurchased fully fifty percent of its shares at the offering price of $36 per share.

### Disposition in the Court of Chancery

This appeal came to us after an odd sequence of events in the Court of Chancery. On May 22, 1996, the day before the transactions closed, plaintiff Larry F. Klang filed a purported class action in the Court of Chancery against Jeffrey Smith and his family, various members of the SFD Board, Yucaipa, Yucaipa's managing general partner Ronald W. Burkle, Smitty's and Cactus.... [Plaintiff] contended that the stock repurchases violated 8 *Del.C.* § 160[2] by impairing SFD's capital....

After defendants answered the amended complaint, plaintiff took full discovery. The Court of Chancery heard plaintiff's motion to have the transactions rescinded, and released a Memorandum Opinion dismissing plaintiff's claims in full.

### Plaintiff's Capital–Impairment Claim

A corporation may not repurchase its shares if, in so doing, it would cause an impairment of capital, unless expressly authorized by

---

**2.** Section 160(a) provides:

(a) Every corporation may purchase, redeem, receive, take or otherwise acquire, own and hold, sell, lend exchange, transfer or otherwise dispose of, pledge, use and otherwise deal in and with its own shares; provided, however, that no corporation shall:

(1) Purchase or redeem its own shares of capital stock for cash or other property when the capital of the corporation is impaired or when such purchase or redemption would cause any impairment of the capital of the corporation, except that a corporation may purchase or redeem out of capital any of its own shares which are entitled upon any distribution of its assets, whether by dividend or in liquidation, to a preference over another class or series of its stock, or, if no shares entitled to such a preference are outstanding, any of its own shares, if such shares will be retired upon their acquisition and the capital of the corporation reduced in accordance with §§ 243 and 244 of this title.

Section 160. A repurchase impairs capital if the funds used in the repurchase exceed the amount of the corporation's "surplus," defined by 8 *Del.C.* § 154 to mean the excess of net assets over the par value of the corporation's issued stock.[5]

Plaintiff asked the Court of Chancery to rescind the transactions in question as violative of Section 160. As we understand it, plaintiff's position breaks down into two analytically distinct arguments. First, he contends that SFD's balance sheets constitute conclusive evidence of capital impairment. He argues that the negative net worth that appeared on SFD's books following the repurchase compels us to find a violation of Section 160. Second, he suggests that even allowing the Board to "go behind the balance sheet" to calculate surplus does not save the transactions from violating Section 160. In connection with this claim, he attacks the SFD Board's off-balance-sheet method of calculating surplus on the theory that it does not adequately take into account all of SFD's assets and liabilities. Moreover, he argues that the May 17, 1996 resolution of the SFD Board conclusively refutes the Board's claim that revaluing the corporation's assets gives rise to the required surplus. We hold that each of these claims is without merit.

### SFD's balance sheets do not establish a violation of 8 *Del.C.* § 160

In an April 25, 1996 proxy statement, the SFD Board released a pro forma balance sheet showing that the merger and self-tender offer would result in a deficit to surplus on SFD's books of more than $100 million. A balance sheet the SFD Board issued shortly after the transactions confirmed this result. Plaintiff asks us to adopt an interpretation of 8 *Del.C.* § 160 whereby balance-sheet net worth is controlling for purposes of determining compliance with the statute.[6] Defendants do not dispute that SFD's books showed a negative net worth in the wake of its transactions with Yucaipa, but argue that corporations should have the presumptive right to revalue assets and liabilities to comply with Section 160.

Plaintiff advances an erroneous interpretation of Section 160. We understand that the books of a corporation do not necessarily reflect the current values of its assets and liabilities. Among other factors, unrealized appreciation or depreciation can render book numbers inaccurate. It is unrealistic to hold that a corporation is bound by its balance sheets for purposes of determining compliance with Section 160. Accordingly, we adhere to the principles of *Morris v. Standard Gas & Electric Co.*[7] allowing corporations to revalue properly its assets and liabilities to show a surplus and thus conform to the statute.

---

**5.** Section 154 provides, "Any corporation may, by resolution of its board of directors, determine that only a part of the consideration . . . received by the corporation for . . . its capital stock . . . shall be capital. . . . The excess . . . of the net assets of the corporation over the amount so determined to be capital shall be surplus. Net assets means the amount by which total assets exceed total liabilities. Capital and surplus are not liabilities for this purpose."

**6.** *See, e.g., Wright v. Heizer Corp.,* N.D.Ill., 503 F.Supp. 802, 810 (1980); *In re Kettle of Fried Chicken of America, Inc.,* 513 F.2d 807, 811 (6th Cir.1975).

**7.** *Morris v. Standard Gas & Electric Co.,* Del.Ch., 63 A.2d 577 (1949).

It is helpful to recall the purpose behind Section 160. The General Assembly enacted the statute to prevent boards from draining corporations of assets to the detriment of creditors and the long-term health of the corporation.[8] That a corporation has not yet realized or reflected on its balance sheet the appreciation of assets is irrelevant to this concern. Regardless of what a balance sheet that has not been updated may show, an actual, though unrealized, appreciation reflects real economic value that the corporation may borrow against or that creditors may claim or levy upon. Allowing corporations to revalue assets and liabilities to reflect current realities complies with the statute and serves well the policies behind this statute.

### The SFD Board appropriately revalued corporate assets to comply with 8 *Del.C.* § 160.

Plaintiff contends that SFD's repurchase of shares violated Section 160 even without regard to the corporation's balance sheets. Plaintiff claims that the SFD Board was not entitled to rely on the solvency opinion of Houlihan, which showed that the transactions would not impair SFD's capital given a revaluation of corporate assets. The argument is that the methods that underlay the solvency opinion were inappropriate as a matter of law because they failed to take into account all of SFD's assets and liabilities. In addition, plaintiff suggests that the SFD Board's resolution of May 17, 1996 itself shows that the transactions impaired SFD's capital, and that therefore we must find a violation of 8 *Del.C.* § 160. We disagree, and hold that the SFD Board revalued the corporate assets under appropriate methods. Therefore the self-tender offer complied with Section 160, notwithstanding errors that took place in the drafting of the resolution.

On May 17, 1996, Houlihan released its solvency opinion to the SFD Board, expressing its judgment that the merger and self-tender offer would not impair SFD's capital. Houlihan reached this conclusion by comparing SFD's "Total Invested Capital" of $1.8 billion—a figure Houlihan arrived at by valuing SFD's assets under the "market multiple" approach—with SFD's long-term debt of $1.46 billion. This comparison yielded an approximation of SFD's "concluded equity value" equal to $346 million, a figure clearly in excess of the outstanding par value of SFD's stock. Thus, Houlihan concluded, the transactions would not violate 8 *Del.C.* § 160.

Plaintiff contends that Houlihan's analysis relied on inappropriate methods to mask a violation of Section 160. Noting that 8 *Del.C.* § 154 defines "net assets" as "the amount by which total assets exceeds total liabilities," plaintiff argues that Houlihan's analysis is erroneous as a matter of law because of its failure to calculate "total assets" and "total liabilities" as separate variables. In a related argument, plaintiff claims that the analysis failed to take into account all of SFD's liabilities, *i.e.*, that Houlihan neglected to consider current liabilities in its comparison of SFD's "Total Invested Capital" and long-term debt. Plaintiff contends that the SFD Board's resolution proves that adding

---

**8.** *See Pasotti v. United States Guard-    ian Corp.*, 156 A. 255, at 257 (Del.Ch.1931).

current liabilities into the mix shows a violation of Section 160. The resolution declared the value of SFD's assets to be $1.8 billion, and stated that its "total liabilities" would not exceed $1.46 billion after the transactions with Yucaipa. As noted, the $1.46 billion figure described only the value of SFD's long-term debt. Adding in SFD's $372 million in current liabilities, plaintiff argues, shows that the transactions impaired SFD's capital.

We believe that plaintiff reads too much into Section 154. The statute simply defines "net assets" in the course of defining "surplus." It does not mandate a "facts and figures balancing of assets and liabilities" to determine by what amount, if any, total assets exceeds total liabilities.[9] The statute is merely definitional. It does not require any particular method of calculating surplus, but simply prescribes factors that any such calculation must include. Although courts may not determine compliance with Section 160 except by methods that fully take into account the assets and liabilities of the corporation, Houlihan's methods were not erroneous as a matter of law simply because they used Total Invested Capital and long-term debt as analytical categories rather than "total assets" and "total liabilities."

We are satisfied that the Houlihan opinion adequately took into account all of SFD's assets and liabilities. Plaintiff points out that the $1.46 billion figure that approximated SFD's long-term debt failed to include $372 million in current liabilities, and argues that including the latter in the calculations dissipates the surplus. In fact, plaintiff has misunderstood Houlihan's methods. The record shows that Houlihan's calculation of SFD's Total Invested Capital is already net of current liabilities. Thus, subtracting long-term debt from Total Invested Capital does, in fact, yield an accurate measure of a corporation's net assets.

The record contains, in the form of the Houlihan opinion, substantial evidence that the transactions complied with Section 160. Plaintiff has provided no reason to distrust Houlihan's analysis. In cases alleging impairment of capital under Section 160, the trial court may defer to the board's measurement of surplus unless a plaintiff can show that the directors "failed to fulfill their duty to evaluate the assets on the basis of acceptable data and by standards which they are entitled to believe reasonably reflect present values."[10] In the absence of bad faith or fraud on the part of the board, courts will not "substitute [our] concepts of wisdom for that of the directors."[11] Here, plaintiff does not argue that the SFD Board acted in bad faith. Nor has he met his burden of showing that the methods and data that underlay the board's analysis are unreliable or that its determination of surplus is so far off the mark as to constitute actual or constructive fraud.[12]

**9.** *See Farland v. Wills*, Del.Ch., 1 Del. J.Corp.L. 467, 475 (1975).

**10.** *Morris*, 63 A.2d at 582.

**11.** *Id.* at 583.

**12.** We interpret 8 *Del.C.* § 172 to entitle boards to rely on experts such as Houlihan to determine compliance with 8 *Del.C.* § 160. Plaintiff has not alleged that the SFD Board failed to exercise reasonable care in selecting Houlihan, nor that rendering a solvency opinion is outside Houlihan's realm of competence. Compare 8 *Del.C.* § 141(e) (providing that directors may rely in good faith on records, reports, experts, etc.).

Therefore, we defer to the board's determination of surplus, and hold that SFD's self-tender offer did not violate 8 *Del.C.* § 160.

On a final note, we hold that the SFD Board's resolution of May 17, 1996 has no bearing on whether the transactions conformed to Section 160. The record shows that the SFD Board committed a serious error in drafting the resolution: the resolution states that, following the transactions, SFD's "total liabilities" would be no more than $1.46 billion. In fact, that figure reflects only the value of SFD's long-term debt. Although the SFD Board was guilty of sloppy work, and did not follow good corporate practices, it does not follow that Section 160 was violated. The statute requires only that there exist a surplus after a repurchase, not that the board memorialize the surplus in a resolution. The statute carves out a class of transactions that directors have no authority to execute, but does not, in fact, require any affirmative act on the part of the board. The SFD repurchase would be valid in the absence of any board resolution. A mistake in documenting the surplus will not negate the substance of the action, which complies with the statutory scheme. . . .

The judgment of the Court of Chancery is affirmed.

———

## NOTE ON KLANG v. SMITH'S FOOD & DRUG CENTERS, INC.

1. *Applicability of Klang to Dividends. Klang* concerned a repurchase of the corporation's stock, rather than a dividend. Although certain problems are unique to repurchases—see Section 8, infra—under almost every dividend statute the test for the legality of a repurchase is substantially the same as the test for the legality of a dividend. Accordingly, *Klang* governs the payment of dividends under the Delaware statute, as well as the repurchase of stock.

2. *The Scholarly Debate.* Beginning in the 1940s, there was a long debate in the scholarly literature on whether a capital-impairment test permitted the payment of dividends up to the difference between the *actual value* of the corporation's assets and its liabilities and capital, or only up to the difference between the corporation's assets and its liabilities and capital *as shown on the corporation's balance sheet.* The debate was largely triggered by the leading case of Randall v. Bailey, 23 N.Y.S.2d 174 (Sup.Ct. 1940), aff'd, 288 N.Y. 280, 43 N.E.2d 43 (1942), in which the New York courts took essentially the same position as that later taken by *Klang.* Despite the *post-Randall v. Bailey* debate, the weight of authority favored the rule of *Randall v. Bailey. Klang* probably puts the debate to rest for practical purposes.

———

## (2) EXCEPTIONS TO THE BASIC CAPITAL–IMPAIRMENT TEST

### (A)  *The Current–Earnings Test; Nimble Dividends*

### DEL. GEN. CORP. LAW § 170
[See Statutory Supplement]

Under a few statutes, like that of Delaware, dividends can be paid out of current earnings even if capital is or would be impaired. Such dividends are known as *nimble dividends*. The term "nimble" is used to describe such dividends because they can be paid only if directors are sufficiently *nimble* to declare the dividends before the close of the relevant period or within a short time thereafter, since under the statutes the dividend can be paid only out of *current* profits.

One justification that has been put forward for permitting dividends out of current profits, even when capital is impaired, is that this technique allows the corporation to continue regular dividends on its preferred stock. Another is that a corporation that has suffered heavy losses may need to attract new capital to remain viable, and may be unable to attract new capital if it cannot pay dividends.

Both justifications are thin. Essentially, the ability to pay nimble dividends, in states that permit such dividends, seems to be an erosion—one of many—in the idea that capital should be preserved to protect creditors.

### (B)  *Dividends out of Capital Surplus*

### N.Y. BUS. CORP. LAW §§ 102(a)(9), (13), (14), 510, 516, 520
[See Statutory Supplement]

### DEL. GEN. CORP. LAW §§ 154, 170, 242(a)(3), 244
[See Statutory Supplement]

**BACKGROUND NOTE**

*Surplus* is the difference between assets and capital. One major component of surplus consists of *earned surplus*—total accumulated earnings, minus total distributions. Earned surplus is essentially equivalent to *retained earnings*.

A second major component of surplus is *capital surplus*. Broadly speaking, capital surplus is that portion of surplus that is derived from sources other than corporate earnings, such as amounts paid for stock in excess of the stock's par value. In theory, the permissibility of dividends out of capital surplus marks the major difference between the capital-impairment and earned-surplus tests: Under a balance-sheet test, dividends can be paid out of capital surplus unless specifically prohibited, because such dividends do not impair capital. In contrast, under an earned-surplus test, dividends can be paid out of capital surplus only if specifically permitted, because capital surplus is not earned surplus. In practice, however, as will be seen, the two tests converge.

Two of the most important types of capital surplus are *paid-in surplus* and *reduction surplus*.

1. *Paid-in Surplus*. Paid-in surplus is the excess of (i) the total sale price of newly issued stock, over (ii) that portion of the sale price that constitutes par value or is otherwise allocated by the board to stated capital. This type of surplus is a byproduct of the low-par and no-par phenomena, because it does not arise if stock is issued at par value. In an economic sense, paid-in surplus constitutes capital, because it is part of the shareholders' initial equity investment. Nevertheless, the capital-impairment statutes routinely permit dividends out of paid-in surplus.

2. *Reduction Surplus*. Reduction surplus is the amount by which stated capital is reduced through corporate action pursuant to statutory authority. There are a number of techniques for reducing capital and thereby creating reduction surplus. The most significant of these techniques is to amend the certificate of incorporation to reduce the par value of the corporation's stock. Such a reduction creates a new surplus fund equal to the amount by which stated capital has been reduced. This fund is called reduction surplus, and is a subcategory of capital surplus.

The capital-impairment statutes routinely permit dividends out of both paid-in and reduction surplus, with no significant safeguards for creditors beyond those imposed by the insolvency test. The payment of dividends out of capital surplus seems anomalous under a capital-impairment statute, in which the emphasis is placed on preservation of capital. The power of the corporation to reduce capital, and pay dividends out of the resulting reduction surplus, creates a gaping breach in the purported wall set up by dividend law to protect the interests of creditors.

———

## (c) TRADITIONAL STATUTES—PART II: EARNED-SURPLUS STATUTES

---

### NOTE ON THE EARNED-SURPLUS TEST

The prior version of the Model Act employed a test for dividends that centered on whether a corporation had *earned surplus*. Earned surplus was defined as "the portion of ... surplus ... equal to the balance of ... net profits, income, gains and losses from the date of incorporation ... after deducting subsequent distributions to shareholders and transfers to stated capital and capital surplus made out of earned surplus." William Hackney comments as follows:

> In attempting to formulate statutory language limiting dividends to income, two distinct approaches were found possible.
>
> One is, like the capital-impairment restriction, a balance-sheet test. The surplus of net assets in excess of capital is obtained and then analyzed and any which is not paid-in or other capital surplus is deemed accumulated income.
>
> The second approach ... is to take the balance of all the corporate income statements to date and deduct dividends and other transfers therefrom, with the remainder being earned surplus.
>
> The Model Act definition, it seems, utilizes the aggregate-income-statement method of arriving at earned surplus. It does not use the balance sheet as a source of reference but directs one to take the balance of net profits, income, gains and losses over a period of time.[1]

Despite the focus on earned surplus, the prior version of the Model Act, and the statutes that adopted the Act, also permitted dividends out of capital surplus if the dividend was permitted by the articles of incorporation or approved by the shareholders, was identified as a distribution from capital, there were no accrued dividends on an issue of cumulative preferred stock, and the dividend did not impair the liquidation preference of preferred stock. In practice, therefore, the earned surplus test tended to converge with the capital-impairment test.

As Hackney points out, "The net result [of earned-surplus statutes based on the old Model Act] is an apparent limitation of the funds available for dividends to earned surplus, but actually, in so far as real protection to creditors or preferred stockholders is concerned, there is a complete eradication of the concept of common capital as a cushion protecting the senior interests." Hackney, The Financial Provisions of

---

**1.** Hackney, The Financial Provisions of the Model Business Corporations Act, 70    Harv.L.Rev. 1357, 1365–66 (1957).

the Model Business Corporation Act, 70 Harv.L.Rev. 1357, 1389 (1957).

The current version of the Model Act has dropped the earned-surplus approach. That approach is now followed by only a few statutes.

# SECTION 4.   CONTRACTUAL RESTRICTIONS ON THE PAYMENT OF DIVIDENDS

------

## BACKGROUND NOTE

It should be obvious by now that the traditional dividend statutes provide little protection to creditors beyond that already afforded by the law of creditors' rights. These statutes are so liberal in allowing capital surplus to be created, either through the use of no-par or low-par capitalization when stock is originally issued, or thereafter through a reduction of capital, that corporations can usually make routine distributions even in the absence of retained earnings.

Involuntary creditors, trade creditors, and short-term lenders must normally take the protection of dividend law as they find it. Institutional lenders, however, who provide large amounts of money over a long period of time, have the power to impose contractual restrictions on dividends beyond the weak limits imposed by corporation law, and often do so. Similar restrictions are often extracted by underwriters in connection with bonds and preferred stock issued to the public. Indeed, as a practical matter, it may be said that much of the modern law of dividends is contractual rather than statutory. The practical question is usually not whether a dividend is prohibited by statute, but whether it is prohibited by arrangements with lending institutions or provisions agreed upon in connection with bond or preferred-stock financing.

------

## FORM OF BOND INDENTURE PROVISION
## RESTRICTING DIVIDENDS

[See Statutory Supplement]

------

## SECTION 5.  THE MODERN DIVIDEND STATUTES

### CAL. CORP. CODE §§ 114, 166, 500–503, 507
[See Statutory Supplement]

### REV. MODEL BUS. CORP. ACT §§ 1.40(6), 6.40
[See Statutory Supplement]

### NOTE ON THE MODERN DIVIDEND STATUTES

California's dividend provisions, enacted in 1977, marked a sweeping break with traditional dividend statutes. Until that time, the foundation of most statutes was a legal concept—stated capital. In contrast, the foundation of the California statute is a set of economic realities: retained earnings, asset-liability ratios, liquidation preferences, and an insolvency test. The Revised Model Business Corporation Act followed suit in breaking with the traditional statutes, although it employed a much different approach than the California statute. Among other things, these statutes eliminate the concept of par value, for all practical purposes. As stated in the Comment to Model Act § 6.21, "Since shares need not have a par value, under section 6.21 there is no minimum price at which specific shares must be issued and therefore there can be no 'watered stock' liability for issuing shares below an arbitrarily fixed price."

### KUMMERT, STATE STATUTORY RESTRICTIONS ON FINANCIAL DISTRIBUTIONS BY CORPORATIONS TO SHAREHOLDERS
(pt. II), 59 Wash.L.Rev. 185, 282–84 (1984). "[The California and Revised Model Business Corporation Act approaches] have some remarkable similarities. [Both] proceed from a common assessment of the inadequacies of the concept of legal capital to abolish not only the statutory underpinnings of the concept (the notion of par value and accounting rules for consideration received for shares), but also the series of exceptions (nimble dividends, depletion dividends, and special repurchases of shares) and fictions (treasury shares) erected because of the existence of the concept. [Both] subject transfers of cash or property, or incurrences of indebtedness, by a corporation without consideration to its shareholders to a single set of restrictions, regardless of the form in which the transfer, or incurrence, occurs. [Both] address applications of the restrictions to such transfers, or incurrences, where the transferor, or obligor, is either the parent, or the subsidiary, of another corporation. Finally, drafters of each of the

systems based their efforts on the premise that statutory systems founded on legal capital were essentially misleading insofar as they led creditors and senior security holders to believe that such systems operated to protect their interests.

"[D]espite these similarities, the [California and RMBCA] systems can be clearly distinguished on the basis of their respective responses to that possible misrepresentation. The California series attempts to rectify the misrepresentation by promulgating rules that will provide creditors and senior shareholders with the type of protection they *thought* they were getting from the legal capital system. On the other hand, the Amended Model Act [attempts] to rectify the misrepresentation by promulgating rules that will provide creditors and senior shareholders with the level of protection that the drafters perceived such groups *actually received* from the legal capital system. This variance in fundamental goals in turn produces the significant differences between the Acts on such issues as the relative freedom directors have and the status in the event of financial difficulty of debt issued on repurchase of shares."

----

Another difference between the California and Model Act approaches is that the California statute is in effect an economic counterpart of the earned-surplus test, while the Model Act is in effect an economic counterpart of the capital-impairment test.

## SECTION 6. REPURCHASE BY A CORPORATION OF ITS OWN STOCK

### N.Y. BUS. CORP. LAW §§ 513, 515

[See Statutory Supplement]

----

### DEL. GEN. CORP. LAW § 160(a)

[See Statutory Supplement]

----

### REV. MODEL BUS. CORP. ACT §§ 1.40(6), 6.40

[See Statutory Supplement]

----

### CAL. CORP. CODE § 510(a)

[See Statutory Supplement]

----

## NOTE ON FINANCIAL LIMITATIONS ON A REPURCHASE BY A CORPORATION OF ITS OWN STOCK

1. *General Rule.* When a corporation purchases shares of its own stock, corporate assets flow out to shareholders. Accordingly, from the perspective of creditors a repurchase of stock is economically indistinguishable from a dividend. Ideally, therefore, the financial limitations on repurchases should generally be the same as those for dividends. Thus the California statute and the Model Act treat repurchases and dividends together under the heading, "distributions." Most other statutes provide that, with specified exceptions, a corporation can expend funds to purchase its own stock only if it could pay a dividend in the same amount.

2. *Exceptions.* Despite the general parity in the treatment of dividends and repurchases, most of the traditional statutes permit a corporation to purchase its own stock out of capital for certain specified purposes. The most common such purposes are (i) eliminating fractional shares, (ii) collecting or compromising a shareholder's indebtedness to the corporation, (iii) paying dissenting shareholders for their shares pursuant to the exercise of appraisal rights, and (iv) redeeming or purchasing redeemable stock. See e.g., Del.Gen.Corp. Law § 160(a)(1); N.Y.Bus.Corp.Law § 513(b), (c). The last of these exceptions, which is probably the most important, is usually supported on the grounds that redeemable stock is temporary by the terms of its creation, so that senior interests will not rely on the cushion provided by the capital such shares have contributed; that the exception facilitates refunding of higher-dividend-rate preferred with lower-dividend-rate preferred (redeemable stock is almost invariably preferred); and that abuse is unlikely because the board, which must make a decision to redeem, normally represents the interests of common, not preferred.

# CHAPTER XIV

# THE PUBLIC DISTRIBUTION OF SECURITIES

---

## SECTION 1. INTRODUCTION

The law governing the public distribution of securities is extremely intricate. The purpose of this Chapter is to examine the structure of the Securities Act, and the most important concepts and rules in this area. Many details and qualifications are left to coverage in Securities Regulation courses.

---

## (a) AN OVERVIEW OF THE SECURITIES MARKETS

---

### ROSS, WESTERFIELD, & JORDAN, FUNDAMENTALS OF CORPORATE FINANCE

See Chapter 5, supra.

---

## (b) AN OVERVIEW OF THE SECURITIES ACT

---

## Securities and Exchange Commission, the Work of the SEC 1997

### SECURITIES ACT OF 1933

This "truth in securities" law has two basic objectives:

● To require that investors be provided with material information concerning securities offered for public sale; and

● To prevent misrepresentation, deceit, and other fraud in the sale of securities.

A primary means of accomplishing these objectives is disclosure of financial information by registering offers and sales of securities. Most offerings of debt and equity securities issued by corporations, limited partnerships, trusts, and other issuers must be registered. Federal and most other domestic government debt securities are exempt. Certain securities and transactions qualify for exemptions from registration provisions; these exemptions are discussed below.

PURPOSE OF REGISTRATION

Registration is intended to provide adequate and accurate disclosure of material facts concerning the company and the securities it proposes to sell. Thus, investors may make a realistic appraisal of the merits of the securities and then exercise informed judgment in determining whether or not to purchase them.

Registration requires, but does not guarantee, the accuracy of the facts represented in the registration statement and prospectus. However, the law does prohibit false and misleading statements under penalty of fine, imprisonment, or both. Investors who purchase securities and suffer losses have important recovery rights under the law if they can prove that there was incomplete or inaccurate disclosure of material facts in the registration statement or prospectus. If such misstatements are proven, the following could be liable: the issuing company, its responsible directors and officers, the underwriters, controlling interests, the sellers of the securities, and others. These rights must be asserted in an appropriate federal or state court (not before the Commission, which has no power to award damages).

Registration of securities does not preclude the sale of stock in risky, poorly managed, or unprofitable companies. In fact, it is unlawful to represent that the Commission approves or disapproves of securities on their merits. The only standard which must be met when registering securities is adequate and accurate disclosure of required material facts concerning the company and the securities it proposes to sell. The fairness of the terms, the issuing company's prospects for successful operation, and other factors affecting the merits of investing in the securities (whether price, promoters' or underwriters' profits, or otherwise) have no bearing on the question of whether or not securities may be registered.

THE REGISTRATION PROCESS

The Commission has registration forms for different types of companies. These provide essential facts while minimizing the burden and expense of complying with the law. In general, registration forms call for

- a description of the company's properties and business;
- a description of the security to be offered for sale and its relationship to the company's other capital securities;
- information about the management of the company; and
- financial statements certified by independent public accountants.

Registration statements and prospectuses on securities become public immediately upon filing with the SEC. However, it is unlawful to sell the securities until the effective date. The act provides that most registration statements shall become effective on the 20th day after filing (or on the 20th day after filing the last amendment). At its discretion, the Commission may advance the effective date if deemed appropriate if it benefits the interests of investors and the public, [considering] the adequacy of publicly available information, and the ease with which the facts about the new offering can be disseminated and understood.

Registration statements are subject to examination for compliance with disclosure requirements. If a statement appears to be materially incomplete or inaccurate, the registrant usually is informed by letter and given an opportunity to file correcting or clarifying amendments.

However, the Commission may conclude that material deficiencies in some registration statements appear to stem from a deliberate attempt to conceal or mislead, or that the deficiencies do not lend themselves to correction through the informal letter process. In these cases, the Commission may decide that it is in the public interest to conduct a hearing to develop the facts by evidence and determine if a "stop order" should be issued to refuse or suspend effectiveness of the statement. The Commission may issue stop orders after the sale of securities has been commenced or completed. A stop order is not a permanent bar to the effectiveness of the registration statement or to the sale of the securities. If amendments are filed correcting the statement in accordance with the stop order decision, the order must be lifted and the statement declared effective.

Although any losses suffered in the purchase of securities are not restored to investors by the stop order, the Commission's order precludes future public sales. Also, the decision and the evidence on which it is based may serve to notify investors of their rights and aid them in their own recovery suits.

## EXEMPTIONS FROM REGISTRATION

In general, registration requirements apply to securities of both U.S. and foreign companies or governments sold in U.S. securities markets. There are, however, certain exemptions. Among these are:

- private offerings to a limited number of persons or institutions who have access to the kind of information that registration would disclose and who do not propose to redistribute the securities;

- offerings restricted to residents of the state in which the issuing company is organized and doing business;

- securities of municipal, state, federal, and other governmental instrumentalities as well as charitable institutions and banks;

- "small issues" not exceeding certain specified amounts made in compliance with SEC regulations; and

- offerings of "small business investment companies" made in accordance with SEC regulations of the Commission.

Whether or not the securities are registered, antifraud provisions apply to all sales of securities involving interstate commerce or the mails.

The "small issue exemption" was adopted by Congress primarily as an aid to small business. The law provides that offerings of securities of certain sizes may be exempt from the full registration, subject to provisions designed to protect investors. Regulation A permits certain domestic and Canadian companies to make exempt offerings. A similar regulation is available for offerings under $5 million by small business investment companies licensed by the Small Business Administration. Regulation D permits certain companies to make exempt offerings under $1 million with only minimal federal restrictions; more extensive disclosure requirements and other conditions apply for offerings exceeding that amount.

Exemptions are available when certain specified conditions are met. These conditions include use of an offering circular containing certain basic information in the sale of the securities. . . .

---

## SEC, Q & A: Small Business and The SEC
pp. 8–9, 1993.

### How does my small business "go public"?

Section 5 of the Securities Act requires that a registration statement be filed with the SEC before securities are offered for sale to the public. It also prohibits the sale of those securities until the registration statement becomes "effective." (Although registration statements become public immediately upon filing with the Commission, it is illegal to sell the securities until the effective date.) The basic registration statement consists of two principal parts:

- Part I is the prospectus (the legal offering or "selling" document), which must be furnished to all purchasers of the securities. Your company—the "issuer" of the securities—is required to put in the printed prospectus the essential facts regarding its business operations, financial condition, and management. The prospectus must be made available to everyone who buys the new issue, and also to anyone who is made an offer to purchase the securities.

- Part II contains additional information available at the SEC for inspection by the public. (Copies of all disclosure documents filed with the SEC may be obtained by mail, for a nominal copying charge.)

### Basic Registration of Securities

The basic registration form is Form S–1. It requires companies to disclose, among other things:

- A description of the company's business;

- Its properties;

- Material transactions between the company and its officers and directors;
- Competition;
- Identification of officers and directors and their remuneration;
- Certain pending legal proceedings;
- The plan for distributing the securities; and
- The intended use of the proceeds.

It is not prepared as a fill-in-the-blank form like a tax return but is similar to a brochure, with information provided in a narrative format. There are also detailed requirements concerning financial statements, including the requirement that such statements be audited by an independent certified public accountant.

In addition to the information expressly required by the form, the company must also provide any other information necessary to make the statements complete and not misleading. If sufficient adverse or risk factors exist concerning the offering and the issuer, they must also be set forth prominently in the prospectus, usually in the beginning. Examples of these factors are:

- Lack of business operating history;
- Adverse economic conditions in a particular industry;
- Lack of market for the securities offered; and
- Dependence upon key personnel.

---

## (c) An Overview of the Underwriting Process

---

## L. Loss & J. Seligman, Fundamentals of Securities Regulation 55–66

3d ed. 1995.

### A.  DISTRIBUTION TECHNIQUES

The registration and prospectus provisions of the Securities Act of 1933 can be understood—and their effectiveness evaluated—only on the background of the techniques by which securities are distributed in the United States. [Among these are strict or "old-fashioned" underwriting, firm-commitment underwriting, and best-efforts underwriting.] . . . .

### 1.  Strict or "Old–Fashioned" Underwriting

Under the traditional English system of distribution—which is no longer common in that country—the issuer did not sell to an investment banking house for resale to the public, either directly or through a group of dealers. Instead a designated "issuing house" advertised the issue and received applications and subscriptions from the public on the issuer's behalf after an announced date. When sufficient applications had been received, an announcement was made that "the lists are closed," and the issuer proceeded to allot the securities directly to the applicants or subscribers, using various methods of proration in the event of an oversubscription. Securities firms normally subscribed to new issues not for their own accounts with a view to resale at a profit, but only as brokers for the accounts of their customers. Before the public offering was thus made, the issue was "underwritten" in order to ensure that the company would obtain the amount of funds it required.

This was underwriting in the strict insurance sense. For a fee or premium, the underwriter agreed to take up whatever portion of the issue was not purchased by the public within a specified time....

This method of distribution is called in the United States "strict" or "old-fashioned" or "standby" underwriting. It is seldom if ever used here except in connection with offerings to existing stockholders by means of warrants or rights....

### 2.   Firm–Commitment Underwriting

For some time, the most prevalent type of underwriting has been the "firm-commitment" variety. It is not, technically, underwriting in the classic insurance sense. But its purpose and effect are much the same in that it assures the issuer of a specified amount of money at a certain time (subject frequently to specified conditions precedent in the underwriting contract) and shifts the risk of the market (at least in part) to the investment bankers. The issuer typically sells the entire issue outright to a group of securities firms, represented by one or several "managers" or "principal underwriters" or "representatives." They, in turn, sometimes sell at a differential to a "selling group" of dealers, [who] sell at another differential to the public. In a very limited sense the process is comparable to the merchandising of beans or automobiles or baby rattles. The issuer is the manufacturer of the securities; the members of the underwriting group are the wholesalers; and the members of the selling group are the retailers. But it is not quite so simple. In most firm-commitment underwritings, securities of particular issuers are distributed not continually but once in a long time, and then in a large batch. And the securities market is quite a different animal from the market for canned beans....

... By the turn of the century it was common in the case of large offerings for a single investment banker to do the "origination"—that is, carry on the preliminary negotiations with the issuer, make the investigations deemed necessary, and then purchase the issue from the issuer. The banker was chosen on the basis of past relationships with the issuer and past performance. The "origination" stage was followed by the process of "syndication": In order to spread the commitment, the originating banker would immediately sell the issue to a small "original purchase group." That group would in turn sell to a larger "banking group" ... [T]hese groups were not designed primarily to do the actual distributing; often the members of the groups were not organized for retailing purposes. The public sale would be effected, for the account of whichever group last bought the issue, by the manager (the originating banker) through an organization of employees and agents, which would sometimes include those members of the purchase and banking groups who were geared for retail distribution.

With the increase in the number and size of securities issues during the First World War, as well as the development of coast-to-coast telephone and wire systems, both groups tended to grow in membership and, in order to facilitate the actual mechanics of distribution, it became customary to add still another step to the elaborate process: Instead of the originating banker's selling through agents and employees, a much larger and more dispersed "selling group" or "selling syndicate" would take the issue from the banking group; those members of the earlier group or groups with distributive facilities would join this new group; and it, too, would be managed by the originating banker....

The passage of the Securities Act of 1933 made for a simplification of this system. Under the statute only negotiations between the issuer and "underwriters" are permitted before the filing of the registration statement. Until then, the securities may not be offered to the public or even to dealers who are not "underwriters" within the statutory definition. And until the actual effective date of the registration statement, no sales or contracts may be made except with underwriters. This, in practice, means that there is usually a short period (a few hours at most) between the signing of the underwriting contract and the effective date of the registration statement during which whoever is committed to purchase at a fixed price cannot legally shift his or her liability against a possible market decline. To protect the underwriter until the closing (usually one week later) the "market out" clause in the underwriting contract was developed.

Although the use of this clause is by no means universal it is not considered "cricket" to take advantage of it. It typically provides that the manager of the underwriting group (or the representatives of the group) may terminate the agreement if before the date of public offering (or before the date of the closing or settlement between underwriters and issuer) the issuer or any subsidiary sustains a material adverse change, trading in the securities is suspended, minimum or maximum prices or government restrictions on securities trading are put into effect, a general banking moratorium is declared, or, in the judgment of the managing underwriter (or, alternatively, the representatives of the underwriters or a majority in interests of the several underwriters), material changes in "general economic, political, or financial conditions" or the effect of international conditions on financial markets in the United States makes it impracticable or inadvisable to market the securities at specified public offering price. This clause is much broader than the traditional *force majeure* provision. Another result of the Securities Act and the former transfer taxes has been a tendency to reduce the number of transfers between groups and to enlarge the number of "underwriters" who bear the initial risk. In effect, the originating banker and the purchase and banking groups have all been combined into a single "underwriting syndicate or group." . . .

### 3.   Best–Efforts Underwriting

Companies that are not well established are not apt to find an underwriter that will give a firm commitment and assume the risk of distribution. Of necessity, therefore, they customarily distribute their securities through firms that merely undertake to use their best efforts. Paradoxically, this type of distribution is also preferred on occasion by companies that are so well established that they can do without any underwriting commitment, thus saving on cost of distribution. The securities house, instead of buying the issue from the company and reselling it as principal, sells it for the company as agent; and its compensation takes the form of an agent's commission rather than a merchant's or dealer's profit. There may still be a selling group to help in the merchandising. But its members likewise do not buy from the issuer; they are subagents. This, of course, is not really underwriting; it is simply merchandising. . . .

---

## SECTION 2.   WHAT CONSTITUTES A "SECURITY"

---

### SECURITIES ACT § 2(1)

[See Statutory Supplement]

---

## McGinty, What is a Security?

1993 Wisc.L.Rev. 1033, 1037–39.

In drafting the definition of security, Congress faced two opposing problems. On the one hand, if it defined "security" to include only arrangements with the same names as instruments traded on securities exchanges (like "stock" and "bonds"), shady promoters could escape the securities laws simply by labeling their investment schemes with unusual names. On the other hand, if Congress defined "security" overbroadly (for example, to include "any . . . evidence of indebtedness"), the securities laws could apply to I.O.U.s given between friends or to notes given by parents to a private school for the duration of their child's enrollment. The former approach would exclude arrangements that should be included, thus frustrating Congress's purpose of protecting investors. The latter approach would include arrangements that should not be included, impose significant unnecessary transaction costs, burden the federal judiciary and federalize numerous issues better left to state law. Congress, for its part, drafted the definition of "security" broadly enough to sweep in devious investment schemes bearing innocuous titles. The courts, for their part, have attempted to construe "security" broadly enough to include such schemes, and yet narrowly enough to exclude arrangements whose names fortuitously suggest a security but whose economic realities do not. . . .

Some of the terms that Congress used to define security—such as "investment contract"—lack an established meaning outside judicial opinions and so create elasticity. Other more standard terms such as "stock" or "notes" have accepted meanings within the securities industry, but can also be used in circumstances where one would rationally think no security exists. Because the definitional paragraph begins with the proclamation, "The term 'security' means *any* note, stock . . ." and the other included instruments, the unqualified "any" suggests that all instruments bearing a name listed in the definitional paragraph should be covered, even a note given by one neighbor to another.

Some courts and commentators have argued that the context clause [that is, the introductory clause to Section 2, which provides that "unless the context otherwise requires" the terms in Section 2 have the meanings given in that Section] permits courts to exclude arrangements that possess the standard names but that are not really securities. Yet the statute nowhere defines or even suggests the scope of the context clause's qualification. Thus, construing the definitional section presents two unappetizing choices. If courts restrict the definitional section to the definitional paragraph alone, the logical result is over-inclusiveness and mindless literalism. If the definitional section includes the context clause, the statute is threatened with unbounded judicial discretion. . . .

-----

## Reves v. Ernst & Young

Supreme Court of the United States, 1990.
494 U.S. 56, 110 S.Ct. 945, 108 L.Ed.2d 47.

■ JUSTICE MARSHALL delivered the opinion of the Court.

This case presents the question whether certain demand notes issued by the Farmer's Cooperative of Arkansas and Oklahoma are "securities" within the meaning of § 3(a)(10) of the Securities Exchange Act of 1934. We conclude that they are.

I

The Co–Op is an agricultural cooperative that, at the time relevant here, had approximately 23,000 members. In order to raise money to support its general business operations, the Co–Op sold promissory notes payable on demand by the holder. Although the notes were uncollateralized and uninsured, they paid a variable rate of interest that was adjusted monthly to keep it higher than the rate paid by local financial institutions. The Co–Op offered the notes to both members and non-members, marketing the scheme as an "Investment Program." Advertisements for the notes, which appeared in each Co–Op newsletter, read in part: "YOUR CO–OP has more than $11,000,000 in assets to stand behind your investments. The Investment is not Federal [sic] insured but it is . . . Safe . . . Secure . . . and available when you need it." . . . Despite these assurances, the Co–Op filed for bankruptcy in 1984. At the time of the filing, over 1,600 people held notes worth a total of $10 million.

After the Co–Op filed for bankruptcy, petitioners, a class of holders of the notes, filed suit against Arthur Young & Co., the firm that had audited the Co–Op's financial statements (and the predecessor to respondent Ernst & Young). Petitioners alleged, *inter alia*, that Arthur Young had intentionally failed to follow generally accepted accounting principles in its audit, specifically with respect to the valuation of one of the Co–Op's major assets, a gasohol plant. Petitioners claimed that Arthur Young violated these principles in an effort to inflate the assets and net worth of the Co–Op. Petitioners maintained that, had Arthur Young properly treated the plant in its audits, they would not have purchased demand notes because the Co–Op's insolvency would have been apparent. On the basis of these allegations, petitioners claimed that Arthur Young had violated the antifraud provisions of the 1934 Act as well as Arkansas' securities laws.

Petitioners prevailed at trial on both their federal and state claims, receiving a $6.1 million judgment. Arthur Young appealed, claiming that the demand notes were not "securities" under either the 1934 Act or Arkansas law, and that the statutes' antifraud provisions therefore did not apply. A panel of the Eighth Circuit, agreeing with Arthur Young on both the state and federal issues, reversed. Arthur Young & Co. v. Reves, 856 F.2d 52 (1988). We granted certiorari to address the federal issue, 490 U.S. ___, 109 S.Ct. 3154, 104 L.Ed.2d 1018 (1989), and now reverse the judgment of the Court of Appeals.

## II

### A

This case requires us to decide whether the note issued by the Co–Op is a "security" within the meaning of the 1934 Act. Section 3(a)(10) of that Act is our starting point:

> "The term 'security' means any note, stock, treasury stock, bond, debenture, certificate of interest or participation in any profit-sharing agreement or in any oil, gas, or other mineral royalty or lease, any collateral-trust certificate, preorganization certificate or subscription, transferable share, investment contract, voting-trust certificate, certificate of deposit, for a security, any put, call, straddle, option, or privilege on any security, certificate of deposit, or group or index of securities (including any interest therein or based on the value thereof), or any put, call, straddle, option,

or privilege entered into on a national securities exchange relating to foreign currency, or in general, any instrument commonly known as a 'security'; or any certificate of interest or participation in, temporary or interim certificate for, receipt for, or warrant or right to subscribe to or purchase, any of the foregoing; but shall not include currency or any note, draft, bill of exchange, or banker's acceptance which has a maturity at the time of issuance of not exceeding nine months, exclusive of days of grace, or any renewal thereof the maturity of which is likewise limited." 48 Stat. 884, as amended, 15 U.S.C. § 78c(a)(10).

The fundamental purpose undergirding the Securities Acts is "to eliminate serious abuses in a largely unregulated securities market." United Housing Foundation, Inc. v. Forman, 421 U.S. 837, 849, 95 S.Ct. 2051, 2059, 44 L.Ed.2d 621 (1975). In defining the scope of the market that it wished to regulate, Congress painted with a broad brush. It recognized the virtually limitless scope of human ingenuity, especially in the creation of "countless and variable schemes devised by those who seek the use of the money of others on the promise of profits," SEC v. W.J. Howey Co., 328 U.S. 293, 299, 66 S.Ct. 1100, 1103, 90 L.Ed. 1244 (1946), and determined that the best way to achieve its goal of protecting investors was "to define 'the term 'security' in sufficiently broad and general terms so as to include within that definition the many types of instruments that in our commercial world fall within the ordinary concept of a security.'" Forman, supra, 421 U.S., at 847–848, 95 S.Ct., at 2058–2059 (quoting H.R.Rep. No. 85, 73d Cong., 1st Sess., 11 (1933)). Congress therefore did not attempt precisely to cabin the scope of the Securities Act.[1] Rather, it enacted a definition of "security" sufficiently broad to encompass virtually any instrument that might be sold as an investment.

Congress did not, however, "intend to provide a broad federal remedy for all fraud." Marine Bank v. Weaver, 455 U.S. 551, 556, 102 S.Ct. 1220, 1223, 71 L.Ed.2d 409 (1982). Accordingly, "[t]he task has fallen to the Securities and Exchange Commission (SEC), the body charged with administering the Securities Acts, and ultimately to the federal courts to decide which of the myriad financial transactions in our society come within the coverage of these statutes." Forman, supra, 421 U.S., at 848, 95 S.Ct., at 2059. In discharging our duty, we are not bound by legal formalisms, but instead take account of the economics of the transaction under investigation. See, e.g., Tcherepnin v. Knight, 389 U.S. 332, 336, 88 S.Ct. 548, 553, 19 L.Ed.2d 564 (1967) (in interpreting the term "security," "form should be disregarded for substance and the emphasis should be on economic reality"). Congress' purpose in enacting the securities laws was to

---

**1.** We have consistently held that "[t]he definition of a security in § 3(a)(10) of the 1934 Act, is virtually identical [to the 1933 Act's definition] and, for present purposes, the coverage of the two Acts may be considered the same." United Housing Foundation, Inc. v. Forman, 421 U.S. 837, 847, n. 12, 95 S.Ct. 2051, 2058, n. 12, 44 L.Ed.2d 621 (1975) (citations omitted). We reaffirm that principle here.

regulate *investments,* in whatever form they are made and by whatever name they are called.

A commitment to an examination of the economic realities of a transaction does not necessarily entail a case-by-case analysis of every instrument, however. Some instruments are obviously within the class Congress intended to regulate because they are by their nature investments. In Landreth Timber Co. v. Landreth, 471 U.S. 681, 105 S.Ct. 2297, 85 L.Ed.2d 692 (1985), we held that an instrument bearing the name "stock" that, among other things, is negotiable, offers the possibility of capital appreciation, and carries the right to dividends contingent on the profits of a business enterprise is plainly within the class of instruments Congress intended the securities laws to cover. *Landreth Timber* does not signify a lack of concern with economic reality; rather, it signals a recognition that stock is, as a practical matter, always an investment if it has the economic characteristics traditionally associated with stock. Even if sparse exceptions to this generalization can be found, the public perception of common stock as the paradigm of a security suggests that stock, in whatever context it is sold, should be treated as within the ambit of the Acts. Id., at 687, 693, 105 S.Ct., at 2302, 2305.

We made clear in *Landreth Timber* that stock was a special case, explicitly limiting our holding to that sort of instrument. Id., at 694, 105 S.Ct., at 2304. Although we refused finally to rule out a similar *per se* rule for notes, we intimated that such a rule would be unjustified. Unlike "stock," we said, " 'note' may now be viewed as a relatively broad term that encompasses instruments with widely varying characteristics, depending on whether issued in a consumer context, as commercial paper, or in some other investment context." Ibid. (citing Securities Industry Assn. v. Board of Governors, FRS, 468 U.S. 137, 149–153, 104 S.Ct. 2979, 2985–88, 82 L.Ed.2d 107 (1984)). While common stock is the quintessence of a security, *Landreth Timber,* supra, 471 U.S., at 693, 105 S.Ct., at 2305, and investors therefore justifiably assume that a sale of stock is covered by the Securities Acts, the same simply cannot be said of notes, which are used in a variety of settings, not all of which involve investments. Thus, the phrase "any note" should not be interpreted to mean literally "any note," but must be understood against the backdrop of what Congress was attempting to accomplish in enacting the Securities Acts.[2]

Because the *Landreth Timber* formula cannot sensibly be applied to notes, some other principle must be developed to define the term "note." A majority of the Courts of Appeals that have considered the issue have adopted, in varying forms, "investment versus commercial"

---

**2.** An approach founded on economic reality rather than on a set of *per se* rules is subject to the criticism that whether a particular note is a "security" may not be entirely clear at the time it is issued. Such an approach has the corresponding advantage, though, of permitting the SEC and the courts sufficient flexibility to ensure that those who market investments are not able to escape the coverage of the Securities Acts by creating new instruments that would not be covered by a more determinate definition. One could question whether, at the expense of the goal of clarity, Congress overvalued the goal of avoiding manipulation by the clever and dishonest. If Congress erred, however, it is for that body, and not this Court, to correct its mistake.

approaches that distinguish, on the basis of all of the circumstances surrounding the transactions, notes issued in an investment context (which are "securities") from notes issued in a commercial or consumer context (which are not). See, e.g., Futura Development Corp. v. Centex Corp., 761 F.2d 33, 40–41 (C.A.1 1985); McClure v. First Nat. Bank of Lubbock, Texas, 497 F.2d 490, 492–494 (C.A.5 1974); Hunssinger v. Rockford Business Credits, Inc., 745 F.2d 484, 488 (C.A.7 1984); Holloway v. Peat, Marwick, Mitchell & Co., 879 F.2d 772, 778–779 (C.A.10 1989), cert. pending sub nom. Peat Marwick Main & Co., No. 89–532.

The Second Circuit's "family resemblance" approach begins with a presumption that *any* note with a term of more than nine months is a "security." See, e.g., Exchange Nat'l Bank of Chicago v. Touche Ross & Co., 544 F.2d 1126, 1137 (C.A.2 1976). Recognizing that not all notes are securities, however, the Second Circuit has also devised a list of notes that it has decided are obviously not securities. Accordingly, the "family resemblance" test permits an issuer to rebut the presumption that a note is a security if it can show that the note in question "bear[s] a strong family resemblance" to an item on the judicially crafted list of exceptions, id., at 1137–1138, or convinces the court to add a new instrument to the list. See, e.g., Chemical Bank v. Arthur Andersen & Co., 726 F.2d 930, 939 (C.A.2 1984).

In contrast, the Eighth and District of Columbia Circuits apply the test we created in SEC v. W.J. Howey Co., 328 U.S. 293, 66 S.Ct. 1100, 90 L.Ed. 1244 (1946), to determine whether an instrument is an "investment contract" to the determination whether an instrument is a "note." Under this test, a note is a security only if it evidences "(1) an investment; (2) in a common enterprise; (3) with a reasonable expectation of profits; (4) to be derived from the entrepreneurial or managerial efforts of others." Arthur Young & Co. v. Reves, 856 F.2d at 54. Accord Baurer v. Planning Group, Inc., 215 U.S.App.D.C. 384, 391–393, 669 F.2d 770, 777–779 (1981). See also Underhill v. Royal, 769 F.2d 1426, 1431 (C.A.9 1985) (setting forth what it terms a "risk capital" approach that is virtually identical to the *Howey* test).

We reject the approaches of those courts that have applied the *Howey* test to notes; *Howey* provides a mechanism for determining whether an instrument is an "investment contract." The demand notes here may well not be "investment contracts," but that does not mean they are not "notes." To hold that a "note" is not a "security" unless it meets a test designed for an entirely different variety of instrument "would make the Acts' enumeration of many types of instruments superfluous," *Landreth Timber*, 471 U.S., at 692, 105 S.Ct., at 2305, and would be inconsistent with Congress' intent to regulate the entire body of instruments sold as investments. . . .

The other two contenders—the "family resemblance" and "investment versus commercial" tests—are really two ways of formulating the same general approach. Because we think the "family resemblance" test provides a more promising framework for analysis, however, we adopt it. The test begins with the language of the statute; because the

Securities Acts define "security" to include "any note," we begin with a presumption that every note is a security.[3] We nonetheless recognize that this presumption cannot be irrebuttable. As we have said ... Congress was concerned with regulating the investment market, not with creating a general federal cause of action for fraud. In an attempt to give more content to that dividing line, the Second Circuit has identified a list of instruments commonly denominated "notes" that nonetheless fall without the "security" category. See *Exchange Nat. Bank,* supra, at 1138 (types of notes that are not "securities" include "the note delivered in consumer financing, the note secured by a mortgage on a home, the short-term note secured by a lien on a small business or some of its assets, the note evidencing a 'character' loan to a bank customer, short-term notes secured by an assignment of accounts receivable, or a note which simply formalizes an open-account debt incurred in the ordinary course of business (particularly if, as in the case of the customer of a broker, it is collateralized)"); *Chemical Bank,* supra, at 939 (adding to list "notes evidencing loans by commercial banks for current operations").

We agree that the items identified by the Second Circuit are not properly viewed as "securities." More guidance, though, is needed. It is impossible to make any meaningful inquiry into whether an instrument bears a "resemblance" to one of the instruments identified by the Second Circuit without specifying what it is about *those* instruments that makes *them* non-"securities." Moreover, as the Second Circuit itself has noted, its list is "not graven in stone," ibid., and is therefore capable of expansion. Thus, some standards must be developed for determining when an item should be added to the list.

An examination of the list itself makes clear what those standards should be. In creating its list, the Second Circuit was applying the same factors that this Court has held apply in deciding whether a transaction involves a "security." First, we examine the transaction to assess the motivations that would prompt a reasonable seller and buyer to enter into it. If the seller's purpose is to raise money for the general use of a business enterprise or to finance substantial investments and the buyer is interested primarily in the profit the note is expected to generate, the instrument is likely to be a "security." If the note is exchanged to facilitate the purchase and sale of a minor asset or consumer good, to correct for the seller's cash-flow difficulties, or to advance some other commercial or consumer purpose, on the other hand, the note is less sensibly described as a "security." See, e.g., *Forman,* 421 U.S., at 851, 95 S.Ct., at 2060 (share of "stock" carrying a right to subsidized housing not a security because "the inducement to purchase was solely to acquire subsidized low-cost living space; it was

---

**3.** The Second Circuit's version of the family resemblance test provided that only notes *with a term of more than nine months* are presumed to be "securities". See supra, at 950. No presumption of any kind attached to notes of less than nine months duration. The Second Circuit's refusal to extend the presumption to *all* notes was apparently founded on its interpretation of the statutory exception for notes with a maturity of nine months or less. Because we do not reach the question of how to interpret that exception ... we likewise express no view on how that exception might affect the presumption that a note is a "security."

not to invest for profit"). Second, we examine the "plan of distribution" of the instrument, SEC v. C.M. Joiner Leasing Corp., 320 U.S. 344, 353, 64 S.Ct. 120, 124, 88 L.Ed. 88 (1943), to determine whether it is an instrument in which there is "common trading for speculation or investment," id., at 351, 64 S.Ct., at 123. Third, we examine the reasonable expectations of the investing public: The Court will consider instruments to be "securities" on the basis of such public expectations, even where an economic analysis of the circumstances of the particular transaction might suggest that the instruments are not "securities" as used in that transaction. . . . Finally, we examine whether some factor such as the existence of another regulatory scheme significantly reduces the risk of the instrument, thereby rendering application of the Securities Acts unnecessary. See, e.g., Marine Bank, 455 U.S., at 557–559, and n. 7, 102 S.Ct., at 1224–1225, and n. 7.

We conclude, then, that in determining whether an instrument denominated a "note" is a "security," courts are to apply the version of the "family resemblance" test that we have articulated here: a note is presumed to be a "security," and that presumption may be rebutted only by a showing that the note bears a strong resemblance (in terms of the four factors we have identified) to one of the enumerated categories of instrument. If an instrument is not sufficiently similar to an item on the list, the decision whether another category should be added is to be made by examining the same factors.

### B

Applying the family resemblance approach to this case, we have little difficulty in concluding that the notes at issue here are "securities." *Ernst & Young* admits that "a demand note does not closely resemble any of the Second Circuit's family resemblance examples." Brief for Respondent 43. Nor does an examination of the four factors we have identified as being relevant to our inquiry suggest that the demand notes here are not "securities" despite their lack of similarity to any of the enumerated categories. The Co–Op sold the notes in an effort to raise capital for its general business operations, and purchasers bought them in order to earn a profit in the form of interest.[4] Indeed, one of the primary inducements offered purchasers was an interest rate constantly revised to keep it slightly above the rate paid by local banks and savings and loans. From both sides, then, the transaction is most naturally conceived as an investment in a business enterprise rather than as a purely commercial or consumer transaction.

---

**4.** We emphasize that by "profit" in the context of notes, we mean "a valuable return on an investment," which undoubtedly includes interest. We have, of course, defined "profit" more restrictively in applying the *Howey* test to what are claimed to be "investment contracts." See, e.g., *Forman*, 421 U.S., at 852, 95 S.Ct., at 2060 ("[P]rofit" under the *Howey* test means either "capital appreciation" or "a participation in earnings"). To apply this restrictive definition to the determination whether an instrument is a "note" would be to suggest that notes paying a rate of interest not keyed to the earning of the enterprise are not "notes" within the meaning of the Securities Acts. Because the *Howey* test is irrelevant to the issue before us today, . . . we decline to extend its definition of "profit" beyond the realm in which that definition applies.

As to the plan of distribution, the Co–Op offered the notes over an extended period to its 23,000 members, as well as to non-members, and more than 1,600 people held notes when the Co–Op filed for bankruptcy. To be sure, the notes were not traded on an exchange. They were, however, offered and sold to a broad segment of the public, and that is all we have held to be necessary to establish the requisite "common trading" in an instrument. See, e.g., *Landreth Timber,* supra (stock of closely held corporation not traded on any exchange held to be a "security"); *Tcherepnin,* 389 U.S., at 337, 88 S.Ct., at 553 (nonnegotiable but transferable "withdrawable capital shares" in savings and loan association held to be a "security"); *Howey,* 328 U.S., at 295, 66 S.Ct., at 1101 (units of citrus grove and maintenance contract "securities" although not traded on exchange).

The third factor—the public's reasonable perceptions—also supports a finding that the notes in this case are "securities". We have consistently identified the fundamental essence of a "security" to be its character as an "investment." . . . The advertisements for the notes here characterized them as "investments," . . . and there were no countervailing factors that would have led a reasonable person to question this characterization. In these circumstances, it would be reasonable for a prospective purchaser to take the Co–Op at its word.

Finally, we find no risk-reducing factor to suggest that these instruments are not in fact securities. The notes are uncollateralized and uninsured. Moreover, unlike the certificates of deposit in *Marine Bank,* . . . which were insured by the Federal Deposit Insurance Corporation and subject to substantial regulation under the federal banking laws, and unlike the pension plan in Teamsters v. Daniel, 439 U.S. 551, 569–570, 99 S.Ct. 790, 801–802, 58 L.Ed.2d 808 (1979), which was comprehensively regulated under the Employee Retirement Income Security Act of 1974, 88 Stat. 829, 29 U.S.C. § 1001 et seq., the notes here would escape federal regulation entirely if the Acts were held not to apply.

The court below found that "[t]he demand nature of the notes is very uncharacteristic of a security," 856 F.2d, at 54, on the theory that the virtually instant liquidity associated with demand notes is inconsistent with the risk ordinarily associated with "securities." This argument is unpersuasive. Common stock traded on a national exchange is the paradigm of a security, and it is as readily convertible into cash as is a demand note. The same is true of publicly traded corporate bonds, debentures, and any number of other instruments that are plainly within the purview of the Acts. The demand feature of a note does permit a holder to eliminate risk quickly by making a demand, but just as with publicly traded stock, the liquidity of the instrument does not eliminate risk [altogether]. Indeed, publicly traded stock is even more readily liquid than are demand notes, in that a demand only eliminates risk when and if payment is made, whereas the sale of a share of stock through a national exchange and the receipt of the proceeds usually occur simultaneously.

We therefore hold that the notes at issue here are within the term "note" in § 3(a)(10).

### III

[In Part III of its opinion, the Court held that whether notes have a maturity not exceeding nine months, for purposes of the exclusion for short-term instruments at the end of Section 3(a)(10), is a question of federal law, and that as a matter of federal law the demand notes at issue in *Reves* did not fall within that exclusion.]

### IV

For the foregoing reasons, we conclude that the demand notes at issue here fall under the "note" category of instruments that are "securities" under the 1933 and 1934 Acts. We also conclude that, . . . these demand notes do not fall within the exclusion [for short-term notes]. Accordingly, we reverse the judgment of the Court of Appeals and remand the case for further proceedings consistent with this opinion.

*So ordered.*

[Justice Stevens concurred in the Court's opinion. Chief Justice Rehnquist and Justices White, O'Connor, and Scalia concurred in Part II of the Court's opinion, but dissented from Part III on the ground that the notes at issue fell within the short-term exclusion.]

## SECTION 3.   WHAT CONSTITUTES A "SALE" AND AN "OFFER TO SELL"

---

### SECURITIES ACT §§ 2(a)(3), 3(a)(9); SECURITIES ACT RULE 145

[See Statutory Supplement]

---

### NOTE ON THE MEANING OF "SALE" AND "OFFER TO SELL"

The term "sale" or "sell" is defined in section 2(a)(3) of the Securities Act to include "every contract of sale or disposition of a security or interest in a security, for value." The term "offer to sell," "offer for sale," or "offer" is defined to include "every attempt or offer to dispose of, or solicitation of an offer to buy, a security or interest in a security, for value." The use of the word "includes" rather than "means" emphasizes the breadth of these definitions, and the courts have also interpreted the terms broadly "to include ingenious methods employed to obtain money from members of the public to finance ventures." S.E.C. v. Addison, 194 F.Supp. 709, 722 (N.D.Tex.1961)

Under Rubin v. United States, 449 U.S. 424, 101 S.Ct. 698, 66 L.Ed.2d 633 (1981), a pledge is an offer or a sale for purposes of the 1933 Act.

## SECTION 4.   THE REQUIREMENT OF REGISTRATION

___

## (a) THE BROAD SWEEP OF SECTION 5

___

### SECURITIES ACT §§ 2(10), 5

[See Statutory Supplement]

___

### NOTE ON SECTION 5

The structure of the Securities Act is exceptionally intricate. The key provision is section 5. Section 5(a) provides:

> Unless a registration statement is in effect as to a security, it shall be unlawful for any person, directly or indirectly—
>
> (1) to make use of any means or instruments of transportation or communication in interstate commerce or of the mails to sell such security through the use or medium of any prospectus or otherwise; or
>
> (2) to carry or cause to be carried through the mails or in interstate commerce, by any means or instruments of transportation, any such security for the purpose of sale or for delivery after sale.

Section 5(c) provides:

> It shall be unlawful for any person, directly or indirectly, to make use of any means or instruments of transportation or communication in interstate commerce or of the mails to offer to sell or offer to buy through the use or medium of any prospectus or otherwise any security, unless a registration statement has been filed as to such security. . . .

Section 2(10) defines a "prospectus" to mean "any prospectus, notice, circular, advertisement, letter, or communication, written or by radio or television, which offers any security for sale or confirms the sale of any security," subject to certain exceptions.

Putting section 2(10) together with section 5(a) and (c), if any person proposes to sell a security by any means of communication in interstate commerce or by mail, or sends a security through the mail for purposes of sale, or offers to buy or sell a security by such means, the security must be registered, unless an exemption applies. On its face, therefore, section 5 prohibits virtually every sale of a security, no matter how trivial, and no matter who the seller, unless the security is registered under the Act. Other provisions of the Act, however, carve out a variety of exemptions for large classes of securities and transactions. By virtue of the exemptions, these securities and transactions do not require registration, despite the sweeping language of section 5. The balance of this Section will consider exemptions based on either (1) the number and character of the offerees, (2) the size of the offering, (3) the intrastate nature of an offering, or (4) the absence of an issuer, underwriter, or dealer.

---

## (b) PRIVATE PLACEMENTS

---

### SECURITIES ACT § 4(2)

[See Statutory Supplement]

---

## S.E.C. v. Ralston Purina Co.

Supreme Court of the United States, 1953.
346 U.S. 119, 73 S.Ct. 981, 97 L.Ed. 1494.

■ MR. JUSTICE CLARK delivered the opinion of the Court.

Section 4(1) of the Securities Act of 1933 exempts "transactions by an issuer not involving any public offering"[1] from the registration requirements of § 5. We must decide whether Ralston Purina's offerings of treasury stock to its "key employees" are within this exemption. On a complaint brought by the Commission under § 20(b) of the Act seeking to enjoin respondent's unregistered offerings, the District Court held the exemption applicable and dismissed the suit. The Court of Appeals affirmed. The question has arisen many times since the Act was passed; an apparent need to define the scope of the private offering exemption prompted certiorari. 345 U.S. 903, 73 S.Ct. 643.

Ralston Purina manufactures and distributes various feed and cereal products. Its processing and distribution facilities are scattered

---

**1.** 48 Stat. 77, as amended, 48 Stat.   This is now § 4(2).]
906, 15 U.S.C. § 77d, 15 U.S.C.A. § 77d. [Ed.

throughout the United States and Canada, staffed by some 7,000 employees. At least since 1911 the company has had a policy of encouraging stock ownership among its employees; more particularly, since 1942 it has made authorized but unissued common shares available to some of them. Between 1947 and 1951, the period covered by the record in this case, Ralston Purina sold nearly $2,000,-000 of stock to employees without registration and in so doing made use of the mails.

In each of these years, a corporate resolution authorized the sale of common stock "to employees . . . who shall, without any solicitation by the Company or its officers or employees, inquire of any of them as to how to purchase common stock of Ralston Purina Company." A memorandum sent to branch and store managers after the resolution was adopted, advised that "The only employees to whom this stock will be available will be those who take the initiative and are interested in buying stock at present market prices." Among those responding to these offers were employees with the duties of artist, bakeshop foreman, chow loading foreman, clerical assistant, copywriter, electrician, stock clerk, mill office clerk, order credit trainee, production trainee, stenographer, and veterinarian. The buyers lived in over fifty widely separated communities scattered from Garland, Texas, to Nashua, New Hampshire and Visalia, California. The lowest salary bracket of those purchasing was $2,700 in 1949, $2,435 in 1950 and $3,107 in 1951. The record shows that in 1947, 243 employees bought stock, 20 in 1948, 414 in 1949, 411 in 1950, and the 1951 offer, interrupted by this litigation, produced 165 applications to purchase. No records were kept of those to whom the offers were made; the estimated number in 1951 was 500.

The company bottoms its exemption claim on the classification of all offerees as "key employees" in its organization. Its position on trial was that "A key employee . . . is not confined to an organization chart. It would include an individual who is eligible for promotion, an individual who especially influences others or who advises others, a person whom the employees look to in some special way, an individual, of course, who carries some special responsibility, who is sympathetic to management and who is ambitious and who the management feels is likely to be promoted to a greater responsibility." That an offering to all of its employees would be public is conceded.

The Securities Act nowhere defines the scope of § 4(1)'s private offering exemption. Nor is the legislative history of much help in staking out its boundaries. The problem was first dealt with in § 4(1) of the House Bill, H.R. 5480, 73d Cong., 1st Sess., which exempted "transactions by an issuer not with or through an underwriter; . . ." The bill, as reported by the House Committee, added "and not involving any public offering." H.R.Rep. No. 85, 73d Cong., 1st Sess. 1. This was thought to be one of those transactions "where there is no practical need for [the bill's] application or where the public benefits are too remote." Id., at 5.[5] The exemption as thus delimited became law.[6] It assumed its present shape with the deletion of "not with or through an underwriter" by § 203(a) of the Securities Exchange Act of 1934, 48 Stat. 906, a change regarded as the elimination of superfluous language. H.R.Rep. No. 1838, 73d Cong., 2d Sess. 41.

Decisions under comparable exemptions in the English Companies Acts and state "blue sky" laws, the statutory antecedents of federal securities legislation, have made one thing clear—to be public, an offer need not be open to the whole world. In Securities and Exchange Comm'n v. Sunbeam Gold Mines Co., 95 F.2d 699 (9th Cir.1938), this point was made in dealing with an offering to the stockholders of two corporations about to be merged. Judge Denman observed that:

> "In its broadest meaning the term 'public' distinguishes the populace at large from groups of individual members of the public segregated because of some common interest or characteristic. Yet such a distinction is inadequate for practical purposes; manifestly, an offering of securities to all redheaded men, to all residents of Chicago or San Francisco, to all existing stockholders of the General Motors Corporation or the American Telephone & Telegraph Company, is no less 'public', in every realistic sense of the word, than an unrestricted offering to the world at large. Such an offering, though not open to everyone who may choose to apply, is none the less 'public' in character, for the means used to select the particular individuals to whom the offering is to be made bear no sensible relation to the purposes for which the selection is made.... To determine the distinction between 'public' and 'private' in any particular context, it is essential to examine the circumstances under which the distinction is sought to be established and to consider the purposes sought to be achieved by such distinction." 95 F.2d at 701.

The courts below purported to apply this test. The District Court held, in the language of the *Sunbeam* decision, that "The purpose of the selection bears a 'sensible relation' to the class chosen," finding that "The sole purpose of the 'selection' is to keep part stock ownership of the business within the operating personnel of the business and to spread ownership throughout all departments and activities of the business." The Court of Appeals treated the case as involving "an offering, without solicitation, of common stock to a selected group of key employees of the issuer, most of whom are

---

**5.** " * * * the bill does not affect transactions beyond the need of public protection in order to prevent recurrences of demonstrated abuses." Id., at 7. In a somewhat different tenor, the report spoke of this as an exemption of "transactions by an issuer unless made by or through an underwriter so as to permit an issuer to make a specific or an isolated sale of its securities to a particular person, but insisting that if a sale of the issuer's securities should be made generally to the public that that transaction shall come within the purview of the Act." Id., at 15, 16.

**6.** The only subsequent reference was an oblique one in the statement of the House Managers on the Conference Report: "Sales of stock to stockholders become subject to the act unless the stockholders are so small in number that the sale to them does not constitute a public offering." H.R.Rep. No. 152, 73d Cong., 1st Sess. 25.

already stockholders when the offering is made, with the sole purpose of enabling them to secure a proprietary interest in the company or to increase the interest already held by them.''

Exemption from the registration requirements of the Securities Act is the question. The design of the statute is to protect investors by promoting full disclosure of information thought necessary to informed investment decisions. The natural way to interpret the private offering exemption is in light of the statutory purpose. Since exempt transactions are those as to which "there is no practical need for [the bill's] application," the applicability of § 4(1) should turn on whether the particular class of persons affected need the protection of the Act. An offering to those who are shown to be able to fend for themselves is a transaction "not involving any public offering."

The Commission would have us go one step further and hold that "an offering to a substantial number of the public" is not exempt under § 4(1). We are advised that "whatever the special circumstances, the Commission has consistently interpreted the exemption as being inapplicable when a large number of offerees is involved." But the statute would seem to apply to a "public offering" whether to few or many.[11] It may well be that offerings to a substantial number of persons would rarely be exempt. Indeed nothing prevents the commission, in enforcing the statute, from using some kind of numerical test in deciding when to investigate particular exemption claims. But there is no warrant for superimposing a quantity limit on private offerings as a matter of statutory interpretation.

The exemption, as we construe it, does not deprive corporate employees, as a class, of the safeguards of the Act. We agree that some employee offerings may come within § 4(1), e.g., one made to executive personnel who because of their position have access to the same kind of information that the act would make available in the form of a registration statement. Absent such a showing of special circumstances, employees are just as much members of the investing "public" as any of their neighbors in the community. Although we do not rely on it, the rejection in 1934 of an amendment which would have specifically exempted employee stock offerings supports this conclusion. The House Managers, commenting on the Conference Report, said that "the participants in employee" stock-investment plans may be in as great need of the protection afforded by availability of information concerning the issuer for which they work as are most other members of the public." H.R.Rep. No. 1838, 73d Cong., 2d Sess. 41.

Keeping in mind the broadly remedial purposes of federal securities legislation, imposition of the burden of proof on an issuer who would plead the exemption seems to us fair and reasonable. Schlem-

---

**11.** See Viscount Sumner's frequently quoted dictum in Nash v. Lynde, " 'The public' . . . is of course a general word. No particular numbers are prescribed. Anything from two to infinity may serve: perhaps even one, if he is intended to be the first of a series of subscribers, but makes further proceedings needless by himself subscribing the whole.'' [1929] A.C. 158, 169.

mer v. Buffalo, R. & P.R. Co., 1907, 205 U.S. 1, 10, 27 S.Ct. 407, 408, 51 L.Ed. 681. Agreeing, the court below thought the burden met primarily because of the respondent's purpose in singling out its key employees for stock offerings. But once it is seen that the exemption question turns on the knowledge of the offerees, the issuer's motives, laudable though they may be, fade into irrelevance. The focus of inquiry should be on the need of the offerees for the protections afforded by registration. The employees here were not shown to have access to the kind of information which registration would disclose. The obvious opportunities for pressure and imposition make it advisable that they be entitled to compliance with § 5.

Reversed.

■ THE CHIEF JUSTICE and MR. JUSTICE BURTON dissent.

■ MR. JUSTICE JACKSON took no part in the consideration or decision of this case.

————

## NOTE ON DORAN v. PETROLEUM MANAGEMENT CORP.

Doran v. Petroleum Management Corp., 545 F.2d 893 (5th Cir. 1977) provides the following gloss on *Ralston Purina*:

> This court has in the past identified four factors relevant to whether an offering qualifies for the [private placement] exemption. The consideration of these factors, along with the policies embodied in the 1933 Act, structure the inquiry. . . . The relevant factors include the number of offerees and their relationship to each other and the issuer, the number of units offered, the size of the offering, and the manner of the offering. Consideration of these factors need not exhaust the inquiry, nor is one factor's weighing heavily in favor of the private status of the offering sufficient to ensure the availability of the exemption. Rather, these factors serve as guideposts to the court in attempting to determine whether subjecting the offering to registration requirements would further the purposes of the 1933 Act. . . .
>
> > . . . *The Number of Offerees*
>
> Establishing the number of persons involved in an offering is important both in order to ascertain the magnitude of the offering and in order to determine the characteristics and knowledge of the persons thus identified.
>
> The number of offerees, not the number of purchasers, is the relevant figure in considering the number of persons involved in an offering . . . A private placement claimant's failure to adduce any evidence regarding the number of offerees will be fatal to the claim. . . . The number of offerees is not itself a decisive factor in determining the availability of the private offering exemption. Just as an offering to few may be public, so an offering to many may be private. *SEC v.*

> *Ralston Purina Co., supra,* 346 U.S. at 125, 73 S.Ct. at 984–
> 85. Nevertheless, "the more offerees, the more likelihood
> that the offering is public." *Hill York Corp. v. American
> International Franchises, Inc., supra,* 448 F.2d 680 at
> 688. . . .

———

## SEC, Q & A: Small Business and the SEC
pp. 14–15, 1993.

### Private Offering Exemption

Section 4(2) of the Securities Act provides exemption from registration for "transactions by an issuer not involving any public offering." There has been much uncertainty as to the precise limits of this private offering exemption. Generally, sales to persons who have access to information about the company and are able to fend for themselves (such as those directly managing the business) fall within the intended scope of the exemption. These are known as "sophisticated investors." As the number of purchasers increase and their relationship to the company and its management becomes more remote, however, it becomes more difficult for an issuer to demonstrate that the transaction does, in fact, qualify for the exemption.

To qualify the offering under this exemption, it is necessary that the persons to whom your company sells the security:

• Have sufficient knowledge and experience in financial and business matters that they are capable of evaluating the risks and merits of the investment (the "sophisticated investor"), or are able to bear the economic risk of the investment;

• Have access to the type of information normally provided in a prospectus; and

• Agree not to resell or distribute the securities.

In addition, your offering may not be made by any form of public solicitation or general advertising.

You should be aware that if the security is offered for sale to even one person who does not meet the necessary conditions, the entire offering may be in violation of the Securities Act.

The SEC has adopted Rule 506, another "safe harbor" rule, which provides objective standards upon which business people may rely in order to be certain they meet the requirements of this exemption. [Rule 506 is a part of Regulation D, which is described more fully below—ed.]

———

## (c) LIMITED OFFERINGS

———

## SECURITIES ACT §§ 2(15), 3(b), 4(2), 4(6)

[See Statutory Supplement]

---

## SECURITIES ACT RULE 215; REGULATION D (RULES 501–508)

[See Statutory Supplement]

---

# D. Ratner, Securities Regulation in a Nutshell 57–58

6th ed. 1998.

[Securities Act] § 3(b) authorizes the SEC, "by rules and regulations," to exempt offerings, not exceeding a specified dollar amount, when it finds that registration is not necessary "by reason of the small amount involved or the limited character of the public offering." The dollar limit has been periodically raised by Congress from its initial level of $100,000, the most recent increase coming in 1980 and raising the limit from $2 million to the present level of $5 million. Under this authority, the Commission has adopted a number of rules providing exemptions for certain specialized kinds of offerings, as well as the general exemption in Regulation A. . . .

. . . Also in 1980, Congress added a new § 4(6) to the 1933 Act, exempting any offering of not more than $5 million made solely to "accredited investors" (defined to include specified types of institutions and other classes of investors that the SEC might specify by rule).

These developments set the stage for the coordination of the private offering and small offering exemptions in a new Regulation D.

---

# SEC, Q & A: Small Business and the SEC

pp. 16–21, 1993.

## Regulation D

Under Sections 4(2) and 3(b) of the Securities Act, the SEC in March, 1982, adopted Regulation D to coordinate the various limited offering exemptions and to streamline the existing requirements applicable to private offers and sales of securities. The Regulation establishes three exemptions from registration in Rules 504, 505, and 506.

## Rule 504

Rule 504, which provides an exemption for non-reporting companies unless they are "blank check" issuers, for sales of securities up to $1,000,000, stipulates that:

● The sale of up to $1,000,000 of securities in a 12–month period is permitted;

- No limitation is placed on the number of persons purchasing securities;

- The offering may be made with general solicitation or general advertising;

- The securities received in the offering are not "restricted securities"; and

- A Form D notice be filed with SEC headquarters within 15 days after the first sale of securities under the Rule.

Unlike Rules 505 and 506, Rule 504 does not mandate that specified disclosure be provided to purchasers. Nonetheless, the businessperson should take care that sufficient information is provided to meet the full disclosure obligations which exist under the antifraud provisions of the securities laws.

## Rule 505

Rule 505 was adopted by the SEC to provide small businesses more flexibility in raising capital than under Rule 504—but without the uncertainty of determining the quality of the purchasers that generally is involved in using Rule 506. Rule 505 provides issuers a limited offering exemption for sales of securities totaling up to $5 million in any 12–month period.

Rule 505 contains certain restrictions regarding "accredited investors" and non-accredited persons. The term "accredited investor" includes:

- Banks, insurance companies, registered investment companies, business development companies, or small business investment companies;

- Certain employee benefit plans for which investment decisions are made by a bank, insurance company, or registered investment adviser;

- Any employee benefit plan (within the meaning of Title 1 of the Employee Retirement Income Security Act) with total assets in excess of $5 million;

- Charitable organizations, corporations or partnerships with assets in excess of $5 million;

- Directors, executive officers, and general partners of the issuer;

- Any entity in which all the equity owners are accredited investors;

- Natural persons with a net worth of at least $1 million;

- Any natural person with an income in excess of $200,000 in each of the two most recent years or joint income with a spouse in excess of $300,000 for those years and a reasonable expectation of the same income level in the current year; and

● Trusts with assets of at least $5 million, not formed to acquire the securities offered, and whose purchases are directed by a sophisticated person.

There is no specific information the issuer must furnish to accredited investors. However, non-accredited investors must be advised of and furnished, upon request, all material information furnished to accredited investors, as well as certain specified information.* ...

● The issuer must also be available to answer questions by prospective purchasers about the issuer or the offering.

Further restrictions under Rule 505 include:

● The total offering price of each issue of securities may not exceed $5 million.

● The offering may not be made by means of general solicitation or general advertising.

● The issuer may sell the securities to an unlimited number of "accredited investors" and to 35 non-accredited persons. There are no requirements of "sophistication" or "wealth" for persons to whom the securities are sold.

● A company must take any necessary steps to ensure that the purchasers are acquiring securities for investment only, not for resale. The securities are thus "restricted" and investors must be informed that they may not be able to sell for at least two years.

● The issuer is not required to file any offering materials with the Commission. Fifteen days after the first sale in the offering, the issuer must file a notice of sales on Form D. The notice also contains an undertaking under this Rule for the issuer to furnish the Commission, upon its staff's request, any information given to non-accredited purchasers in connection with the offering.

## Rule 506

Offers and sales of securities by an issuer that satisfy the conditions stated below are deemed transactions not involving any public offering within the meaning of Section 4(2) of the Securities Act. For an offering to be considered exempt from the registration requirements, Rule 506 stipulates:

● There is no ceiling on the amount of money which may be raised.

● No general solicitation or general advertising is permitted.

● The issuer may sell its securities to an unlimited number of accredited investors and 35 non-accredited purchasers. Unlike Rule 505, all non-accredited purchasers (either alone or with a purchaser representative) must be sophisticated—that is, have

---

* The Commission has under consideration proposed rule revisions which would change information and financial statement requirements for purposes of Rules 505 and 506 of Regulation D. These changes had not been adopted as of the publication date of this brochure. (Footnote by SEC.)

sufficient knowledge and experience in financial and business matters to render them capable of evaluating the merits and risks of the prospective investment.

● The term "accredited investor" is defined as above under Rule 505.

● There is no specific information which the issuer must furnish to accredited investors. However, non-accredited investors must be advised of and furnished, upon request, all material information furnished to accredited investors, as well as certain specified information.

● The information requirements are generally the same as those on the registration form the issuer would be entitled to use. If the issuer cannot obtain audited financial statements without unreasonable effort or expense, then financial statements may be provided in accordance with the special treatment described under Rule 505 above.

● The securities sold are "restricted" under the same stipulations in Rule 505.

● A company is required to file a notice of the offering on Form D at SEC headquarters within 15 days after the first sale in the offering. There is no requirement to file the offering memorandum with the Commission.

### Accredited Investor Exemption: Section 4(6)

The Small Business Investment Incentive Act of 1980 created a new statutory exemption from registration under the Securities Act for transactions involving offers and sales of securities by any issuer solely to one or more "accredited investors." Under Section 4(6):

● The total offering price of each issue of securities under the exemption may not exceed the limit on small offerings set by Section 3(b) the Securities Act, which currently is $5 million per issue.

● The offering may not be made by means of any form of advertising or public solicitation.

● The term "accredited investor" is defined to include the same individuals and entities as included for purposes of Rules 505 and 506.

● The issuer is required to file a notice of sales on Form D with the Commission 15 days after the initial sale is made in reliance on the exemption.

● The Section 4(6) exemption does not contain any specific disclosure requirements. The issuer is cautioned however, that, as in the case of the other exemptions, Section 4(6) does not exempt the issuer from the antifraud provisions of the securities laws.

**D. RATNER, SECURITIES REGULATION IN A NUTSHELL** 61 (6th ed. 1998). "Offerings complying with the terms of Rule 504 or 505 are deemed to be exempt under [Securities Act] § 3(b); offerings pursuant to Rule 506, since they may exceed $5 million, cannot be exempt under § 3(b) and are considered to be non-public offerings under § 4(2). Rule 506 is not the exclusive means of making a non-public offering; the Preliminary Note to Regulation D states specifically that failure to satisfy all the terms and conditions of Rule 506 shall not raise any presumption that the exemption provided by § 4(2) is not available."

———

## NOTE ON THE SIGNIFICANCE OF EXEMPTIONS

It's important to keep in mind that a provision exempting securities from registration under Section 5 does not necessarily mean that a seller or offeror of those securities is not required to provide the buyers with information. Some exemptions explicitly require the seller to provide information very much like that required in a registration statement. For example, Regulation A (discussed below in Section 4(d)) requires an elaborate Offering Circular, and Regulation D requires the provision of registration-like information in certain cases. Other exemptions implicitly require the provision of information. For example, a distribution is unlikely to qualify as a private placement unless the offerees have had access to the kind of information that would have been disclosed under a registration statement. Accordingly, when sales are made under Section 4(2) or Rule 506 through investment bankers, the issuer typically supplies an information statement that provides prospectus-like disclosure.

If an offeror of securities has to provide information comparable to that in a registration statement, what is the benefit of an exemption? First, *comparable* information may cost less to assemble and provide than the full information required in a registration statement. Second, an information statement may not require clearance by the SEC, as does a registration statement. Third, certain liability provisions of the Securities Act are keyed into registration, and therefore do not apply to an information statement. See Section 7, infra.

———

## (d) REGULATION A

———

## SECURITIES ACT § 3(b); SECURITIES ACT REG. A [RULES 251–263]

[See Statutory Supplement]

———

## SEC, Q & A: Small Business and the SEC

pp. 15–16, 1993.

### . . . Regulation A

Section 3(b) of the Securities Act gives the SEC authority to exempt from registration certain offerings where the securities to be offered involve relatively small dollar amounts. Under this provision, the SEC has adopted Regulation A, a conditional exemption for certain public offerings not exceeding $5 million in any 12–month period. An offering statement (consisting of a notification, offering circular, and exhibits) must be filed with the SEC Regional Office in the region where the company's principal business activities are conducted. Although Regulation A is technically an exemption from the registration requirements of the Securities Act, it is often referred to as a "short form" of registration since the offering circular (similar in content to a prospectus) must be supplied to each purchaser and the securities issued are freely tradeable in an after-market. The principal advantages of Regulation A offerings, as opposed to full registration on either Form S–1 or SB–2, are

- Required financial statements are simpler and need not be audited; and

- There are no periodic SEC reporting requirements (other than sales reports following the sale of the securities) unless the issuer has more than $5 million in total assets and more than 500 shareholders.

- There are three permitted offering circular formats under Regulation A, one of which is a simplified question-and-answer document. This style of disclosure is useful to potential investors and may offer significant benefits to the issuer in the time expended and the costs of preparation.

All types of companies which are not reporting under the Exchange Act may use Regulation A, except "blank check" companies (i.e., those with the business of seeking an unspecified business) and investment companies registered or required to be registered under the Investment Company Act of 1940. In most cases, Regulation A may also be used by shareholders for the resale of up to $1.5 million of securities.

---

## Securities Act Release No. 33–6949 (1992)

### [Small Business Initiatives] . . .

A. *Regulation A*

As adopted, the dollar ceiling for a Regulation A offering is now $5 million in any 12–month period, including no more than $1.5 million in non-issuer resales. . . .

B.  *"Testing the Waters"*

As discussed in the [Proposing] Release, one of the major impediments to a Regulation A financing for a small start-up or developing company with no established market for its securities, is the cost of preparing the mandated offering statement. The full costs of compliance would be incurred without knowing whether there will be any investor interest in the company.

To remedy this situation, the Commission proposed for the first time to permit companies relying on the Regulation A exemption to "test the waters" for potential interest in the company prior to filing and delivery of the mandated offering statement. All test the water documents are required to be submitted to the Commission at the time of first use. The proposal was enthusiastically endorsed by private sector commenters as a necessary and appropriate solution to a significant regulatory impediment to small business financing, and, as drafted, is consistent with investor protection interests.

A number of refinements have been included in the test the water provisions in response to public comment. First, while the Regulation continues to require that the "testing of the waters" begin with a written solicitation of interest submitted to the Commission at the time of first use, the rules have been revised to make clear that submission of the document is not a condition to the exemption. Failure to comply with the requirement is a grounds for Commission suspension of the exemption.

As proposed, the written test the water document was a free writing subject to the inclusion of two mandated statements—first, that no funds were being solicited or would be accepted, and secondly that a detailed offering document would follow. Some commenters suggested that even these few items should be deleted, while others suggested additional requirements or specific prescription of the content.

The rule as adopted continues to provide for free writing with the inclusion of the following items:

1.  a statement that no money is being solicited, or will be accepted; that no sales can be made until delivery and qualification of the offering circular, and that indications of interest involve no obligation or commitment of any kind; and

2.  a brief, general identification of the company's business, products and chief executive officer.

The rule has been revised to make clear that inclusion of these statements in the soliciting document is not a condition to the exemption, but failure to include the statements is a basis for Commission suspension of the exemption. . . .

Once the offering statement required by Regulation A is filed with the Commission, the issuer may not continue to use its written "test the waters" solicitation materials. The rule requires that at least 20 calendar days elapse between the last use of the solicitation of interest document or broadcast and any sale of securities in the Regulation A offering. Compliance with the rules limiting the use of the test the water documents after filing of the offering statement is not a condition to the exemption, but [noncompliance] is a violation of the rule and is a basis for Commission suspension of the exemption....

---

## (e) THE INTRASTATE EXEMPTION

---

### SECURITIES ACT § 3(a)(11); SECURITIES ACT RULE 147

[See Statutory Supplement]

---

## SEC, Q & A: Small Business and The SEC

pp. 13–14, 1993.

### Intrastate Offering Exemption

Section 3(a)(11) of the Securities Act is generally known as the "intrastate offering exemption." It exempts from registration any security which is part of an issue offered and sold only to residents of a single state or territory and the issuer is both a resident of and doing business within that state or territory. This exemption is intended to facilitate the local financing of local business operations. In order to qualify for the intrastate offering exemption, your company must:

- Be incorporated in the state where it is making the offering;

- Carry out a significant amount of its business in that state; and

- Make offers and sales only to residents of that state.

Although there is no fixed limit on the size of the offering or the number of purchasers, your company has the obligation to determine the residence of each purchaser. If any of the securities are offered or sold to one out-of-state purchaser, the exemption may be lost. In addition, if any of the securities are resold by an original resident purchaser to a person resident outside the state within nine months after the offering by the issuer is completed, the entire transaction may be in violation of the Securities Act. Therefore, there is usually no significant after-market for any securities issued in an intrastate offering during the nine-month period following the initial sale. Consequently, they must normally be sold at a discount.

It is difficult for you as an issuer to rely on the intrastate exemption unless your company knows the purchasers and the sale is directly negotiated with them. A company with some of its assets outside the state, or deriving a substantial portion of its revenues outside the state where it proposes to offer its securities, will probably have a difficult time justifying the exemption.

The SEC has adopted Rule 147, a "safe harbor" rule, which may be followed by companies to be certain they meet the requirements for this exemption. It is possible, however, that transactions not meeting all requirements of Rule 147 may still qualify for the exemption.

---

## (f) TRANSACTIONS NOT INVOLVING AN ISSUER, UNDERWRITER, OR DEALER

---

### SECURITIES ACT §§ 2(11), 4(1), 4(3)
[See Statutory Supplement]

---

### INTRODUCTORY NOTE

Securities Act section 5 broadly prohibits the sale of unregistered securities by any person, subject to the various exemptions under the Act. Section 4(1) of the Act exempts, from section 5's prohibition, transactions by any person other than an issuer, underwriter, or dealer. In effect, therefore, section 5 is applicable only to sales by an issuer, a dealer, or an underwriter.

Section 2(a)(4) defines an *issuer* as "every person who issues or proposes to issue any security."

Section 2(a)(12) defines a *dealer* as "any person who engages either for all or part of his time, directly or indirectly, as agent, broker, or principal, in the business of offering, buying, selling, or otherwise dealing or trading in securities issued by another person." However,section 4(3) exempts most transactions by dealers.

Since the definition of issuer is fairly straightforward, and since most transactions by dealers are empted under section 4(3), the difficult problems in applying section 4(1) concern the meaning of "underwriters" for purposes of that section. Persons who are underwriters for this purpose are known as *statutory underwriters*. The paradigm case of an underwriter is an investment professional who distributes stock on behalf of an issuer. However, section 2(a)(11) defines "underwriter" so as to pick up transactions that don't look anything like that paradigm:

> The term "underwriter" means any person who has purchased from an issuer with a view to, or offers or sells for an issuer in connection with, the distribution of any security, or participates or has a direct or indirect participation in any such undertaking,

or participates or has a participation in the direct or indirect underwriting of any such undertaking; but such term shall not include a person whose interest is limited to a commission from an underwriter or dealer not in excess of the usual and customary distributors' or sellers' commission. As used in this paragraph the term "issuer" shall include, in addition to an issuer, any person directly or indirectly controlling or controlled by the issuer, or any person under direct or indirect common control with the issuer.

The balance of the present Section will explicate Section 2(a)(11) of the Securities Act by considering:

(1) The meaning and implications of the terms, "offers or sells for an issuer in connection with ... the distribution of any security" and "purchased from an issuer with a view to ... the distribution of any security."

(2) The meaning and implications of the terms, "any person directly or indirectly controlling ... the issuer."

(3) Rules 144 and 144A.

------

## (1) WHO IS A STATUTORY UNDERWRITER

------

### NOTE ON THE MEANING OF TERM "OFFERS OR SELLS FOR AN ISSUER IN CONNECTION WITH ... THE DISTRIBUTION OF ANY SECURITY"

The language in section 2(a)(11), "offers or sells for an issuer in connection with ... the distribution of any security," has been very broadly construed. Perhaps the most notable case is SEC v. Chinese Consolidated Benevolent Ass'n., 120 F.2d 738 (2d Cir.1941), cert. denied 314 U.S. 618, 62 S.Ct. 106, 86 L.Ed. 497. The defendant had sold unregistered Chinese government bonds in the United States at the beginning of World War II. The defendant claimed it was not underwriter within the meaning of then-section 2(11) because it had no agreement with the Chinese government to sell the bonds, and was not compensated for selling the bonds, but instead acted out of loyalty to China. Held, the defendant was nevertheless an underwriter:

> Under section 4(1) the defendant is not exempt from registration requirements if it is "an underwriter". The court below reasons that [the defendant] is not to be regarded as an underwriter since it does not sell or solicit offers to buy "for an issuer in connection with, the distribution" of securities. In other words, it seems to have been held that only solicitation authorized by the issuer in connection with the distribution of the Chinese bonds would satisfy the definition of underwriter contained in Section 2(11) and that defendant's activities were never for the Chinese government but only for the purchasers of the bonds. Though the

defendant solicited the orders, obtained the cash from the purchasers and caused both to be forwarded so as to procure the bonds, it is nevertheless contended that its acts could not have been for the Chinese government because it had no contractual arrangement or even understanding with the latter. But the aim of the Securities Act is to have information available for investors. This objective will be defeated if buying orders can be solicited which result in uninformed and improvident purchasers. It can make no difference as regards the policy of the act whether an issuer has solicited orders through an agent, or has merely taken advantage of the services of a person interested for patriotic reasons in securing offers to buy. The aim of the issuer is to promote the distribution of the securities, and of the Securities Act is to protect the public by requiring that it be furnished with adequate information upon which to make investments. Accordingly the words "[sell] for an issuer in connection with the distribution of any security" ought to be read as covering continual solicitations, such as the defendant was engaged in, which normally would result in a distribution of issues of unregistered securities within the United States. Here a series of events were set in motion by the solicitation of offers to buy which culminated in a distribution that was initiated by the defendant. We hold that the defendant acted as an underwriter.

120 F.2d at 740–41.

———

## NOTE ON THE MEANING OF THE TERM "ANY PERSON WHO HAS PURCHASED FROM AN ISSUER WITH A VIEW TO . . . DISTRIBUTION"

Section 2(a)(11) also includes within the term "underwriter," for purposes of that section, a person "who has purchased from an issuer with a view to . . . distribution." Even a person who is not an underwriter in the normal usage of that term may be a statutory underwriter under this provision. Assume that P has purchased securities from an issuer in a private placement. If P purchased the securities with the intent to offer or resell them through a distribution—as opposed to having purchased with an "investment intent"—he is an underwriter under section 2(a)(11). The classic case is that in which P has purchased unregistered securities under the private-placement exemption, and then quickly turned around and re-offered the securities to a number of buyers.

In Gilligan, Will & Co. v. S.E.C., 267 F.2d 461 (2d Cir.1959), cert. denied 361 U.S. 896, 80 S.Ct. 200, 4 L.Ed.2d 152, Gilligan, a partner in Gilligan Will, purchased $100,000 of a $3,000,000 private placement of Crowell–Collier convertible debentures for his own account, representing that he purchased for investment. Notwithstanding these representations, Gilligan quickly sold $45,000 of the debentures to Louis Alter, made offers to two other potential purchasers (selling $5,000 of debentures to one of them) and placed the remaining debentures in a Gilligan Will trading account. Ten months later, Gilligan, Alter, and the Gilligan Will firm converted their debentures into common stock and sold the stock at a profit on the American Stock Exchange. Gilligan and Alter later subscribed to an additional $200,000 of debentures, which they similarly converted to common stock. Gilligan Will also was active in selling $200,000 of the debentures to a mutual fund, and as a result of this transaction other parties received warrants to purchase Crowell–Collier stock.

Gilligan and Gilligan Will argued that since the conversion and sales occurred more than ten months after the purchase of the debentures, the Commission was bound to find that the debentures so converted had been held for investment, and were not purchased with a view to distribution. In answer to this contention the court noted that

> ... Petitioners concede that if such sales were intended at the time of purchase, the debentures would not then have been held as investments; but [they argue] that the stipulation reveals that the sales were undertaken only after a change of the issuer's circumstances as a result of which petitioners, acting as prudent investors, thought it wise to sell. The catalytic circumstances were the failure, noted by Gilligan, of Crowell–Collier to increase its advertising space as he had anticipated it would. We agree with the Commission that in the circumstances here presented the intention to retain the debentures only if Crowell–Collier continued to operate profitably was equivalent to a "purchase ... with a view to ... distribution" within the statutory definition of underwriters in § 2(11). To hold otherwise would be to permit a dealer who speculatively purchases an unregistered security in the hope that the financially weak issuer had, as is stipulated here, "turned the corner," to unload on the unadvised public what he later determines to be an unsound investment without the disclosure sought by the securities laws, although it is in precisely such circumstances that disclosure is most necessary and desirable. . . .

***

**D. RATNER, SECURITIES REGULATION IN A NUTSHELL 73–74** (6th ed. 1998). "One unresolved question is whether a person who has purchased securities from the issuer in a non-public transaction can resell those securities in another *private* transaction, and, if so, what limitations apply to such resales. Since this situation is not technically covered by either § 4(1) or § 4(2), it is sometimes said to be covered by the '§ 4(1½) exemption.' "

***

## (2) SALES BY CONTROLLING PERSONS

***

## NOTE ON OFFERS OR SALES CONTROLLING PERSONS

A distribution of unregistered securities by a person who is in control of an issuer is comparable in many respects to a sale by the issuer itself. Accordingly, distributions by controlling persons are not exempt under section 4(1). This result is reached circuitously. Under the last sentence of Section 2(a)(11), a person is an underwriter if he offers or sells securities for a person who *controls* the issuer, "in connection with ... the distribution of any security." (Under Securities Act Rule 405, "[t]he term 'control' ... means the possession, direct or indirect, of the power to direct or cause the direction of the management and policies of a person, whether through the ownership of voting securities, by contract, or otherwise.")

The applicability of the principle that a distribution on behalf of a controlling person is not exempt from section 5 is often complicated by the issue whether a particular sale on behalf of a controlling person constitutes a "distribution," and whether the sale comes within the exemption in section 4(4) for "brokers' transactions executed upon customers' orders on any exchange or in the over-the-counter market but not the solicitation of such orders."

In In the Matter of Ira Haupt & Co., 23 S.E.C. 589 (1946), Ira Haupt & Company, a brokerage firm, sold approximately 93,000 shares of the unregistered common stock of Park & Tilford, Inc. for the accounts of David A. Schulte and a corporation and trust controlled by Schulte. The sales were made in small lots over the course of approximately six months, pursuant to Schulte's instructions to sell 200–share blocks from his personal holdings at "59 and every quarter up," and up to 73,000 shares for the trust "at $80 per share or better." The price of the stock rose sharply from $57 to $98 per share during this period, because of the announcement that a whiskey dividend would be distributed in kind to the shareholders of Park & Tilford. (A dividend in liquor was especially welcome during the wartime shortage.) Schulte was aware of the planned dividend at the time he placed his sell order with Ira Haupt.

The Schulte interests initially held over 90 percent of the common stock of Park & Tilford, and it was therefore conceded that they controlled Park & Tilford. Accordingly, it was clear that Ira Haupt was selling the securities for a person "controlling the issuer" as contemplated by the last sentence of then section 2(11). Ira Haupt nevertheless denied that it was a statutory underwriter for purposes of the transactions because the sales were not effected "in connection with ... the distribution of any security."

At the outset, the Commission noted that although the term "distribution" is not defined in the Act, it had previously been held to comprise "the entire process by which in the course of a public offering the block of securities is dispersed and ultimately comes to rest in the hands of the investing public." The Commission further remarked:

We find no validity in the argument that a predetermination of the precise number of shares which are to be publicly dispersed is an essential element of a distribution. Nor do we think that a "distribution" loses its character as such merely because the extent of the offering may depend on certain conditions such as the market price. . . . Such offerings are not any less a "distribution" merely because their precise extent cannot be predetermined. . . .

The Commission concluded that

. . . [Ira Haupt] was selling for the Schulte interests, controlling shareholders of Park & Tilford, in connection with the distribution of their holdings in the stock and was, therefore, an "underwriter" within the meaning of the Act.

Thus, the exemption of section 4(1) was not applicable to the transactions.

----

### (3) RULES 144 AND 144A

----

### SECURITIES ACT RULE 144

[See Statutory Supplement]

----

The wide ambit given to the meaning of the term underwriter, together with the coverage of sales by controlling persons, made it difficult for controlling persons, and persons holding restricted securities, to know when they could safely trade unregistered shares. The SEC has sought to meet this problem by providing safe harbors for certain such sales under Rules 144 and 144A.

----

## Securities Act Release No. 5223 (1973) [Notice of Adoption of Rule 144]. . . .

. . . [T]he Commission is of the view that "distribution" is the significant concept in interpreting the statutory term "underwriter." In determining when a person is deemed not to be engaged in a distribution several factors must be considered.

First, the purpose and underlying policy of the Act to protect investors requires, in the Commission's opinion, that there be adequate current information concerning the issuer, whether the resales of securities by persons result in a distribution or are effected in trading transactions. Accordingly, the availability of the rule is conditioned on the existence of adequate current public information.

Secondly, a holding period prior to resale is essential, among other reasons, to assure that those persons who buy under a claim of a Section 4(2) exemption have assumed the economic risks of investment, and therefore, are not acting as conduits for sale to the public of unregistered securities, directly or indirectly, on behalf of an issuer. It should be noted that there is nothing in Section 2(11) which places a time limit on a person's status as an underwriter. The public has the same need for protection afforded by registration whether the securities are distributed shortly after their purchase or after a considerable length of time.

A third factor, which must be considered in determining what is deemed not to constitute a "distribution," is the impact of the particular transaction or transactions on the trading markets. It is consistent with the rationale of the Act that Section 4(1) be interpreted to permit only routine trading transactions as distinguished from distributions. Therefore, a person reselling securities under Section 4(1) of the Act must sell the securities in such limited quantities and in such a manner so as not to disrupt the trading markets. The larger the amount of securities involved, the more likely it is that such resales may involve methods of offering and amounts of compensation usually associated with a distribution rather than routine trading transactions. Thus, solicitation of buy orders or the payment of extra compensation are not permitted by the rule.

In summary, if the sale in question is made in accordance with all the provisions of the rule, . . . any person who sells restricted securities shall be deemed not to be engaged in a distribution of such securities and therefore not an underwriter thereof. The rule also provides that any person who sells restricted or other securities on behalf of a person in a control relationship with the issuer shall be deemed not to be engaged in a distribution of such securities and therefore not to be an underwriter thereof, if the sale is made in accordance with all the conditions of the rule.

———

### RULE 144A

[See Statutory Supplement]

———

## Securities Act Release No. 6862 (1990) [Rule 144A]

RESALE OF RESTRICTED SECURITIES; CHANGES TO METHOD OF DETERMINING HOLDING PERIOD OF RESTRICTED SECURITIES UNDER RULES 144 AND 145.

. . . NEW RULE 144A . . .

### A.  General

Rule 144A sets forth a non-exclusive safe harbor from the registration requirements of Section 5 of the Securities Act for the resale of restricted securities to specified institutions by persons other than the issuer of such securities. The transactions covered by the safe harbor are private transactions that, on the basis of a few objective standards, can be defined as outside the purview of Section 5, without the necessity of undertaking the more usual analysis under Sections 4(1) and 4(3) of the Securities Act.

By providing that transactions meeting its terms are not "distributions," the Rule essentially confirms that such transactions are not subject to the registration provisions of the Securities Act....

### C. Eligible Purchasers

### 1. Types of Institutions Covered

... [E]xcept for registered broker-dealers, to be a "qualified institutional buyer" an institution must in the aggregate own and invest on a discretionary basis at least $100 million in securities of issuers that are not affiliated with the institution....

### D. Information Requirement ...

As adopted, availability of the Rule is conditioned upon the holder and a prospective purchaser designated by the holder having the right to obtain from the issuer, upon the holder's request to the issuer, certain basic financial information, and upon such prospective purchaser having received such information at or prior to the time of sale, upon such purchaser's request to the holder or the issuer. This information is required only where the issuer does not file periodic reports under the Exchange Act, ... and does not furnish home country information to the Commission pursuant to Rule 12g3–2(b)....

---

## NOTE ON EXEMPTED SECURITIES

The exemptions considered in this Section relate to types of *transactions,* and for the most part provide an exemption only from section 5. The Securities Act also exempts certain types of *securities* from the provisions of *the entire Act.* These exemptions are to be found in sections 3(a)(1)–(a)(8). They include U.S. government, state, and municipal securities (section 3(a)(2)), certain short-term paper (section 3(a)(3)), and bankruptcy trustee certificates (section 3(a)(7)).

---

## SECTION 5. MECHANICS OF REGISTRATION

---

### SECURITIES ACT FORMS S–1, S–2, AND S–3

[See Statutory Supplement]

---

## NOTE ON THE MECHANICS OF REGISTRATION

Assuming that securities must be registered, the registration process is begun by filing with the SEC a registration statement on the applicable form. The basic forms are S–1, S–2, and S–3, but there are many other forms for special situations.

In general, the registration statement must describe such matters as the characteristics of the securities; the character and size of the business enterprise; its capital structure, financial history, and earnings; underwriters' commissions; the names of persons who participate in the direction, management, or control of the business; their security holdings and remuneration, including options; payments to promoters made within two years or intended to be made in the near future; acquisitions of property not in the ordinary course of business, and the interests of directors, officers, and principal stockholders therein; pending or threatened legal proceedings; and the purpose to which the proceeds of the offering are to be applied. The registration statement must include the issuer's financial statements, certified by independent accountants.

The Commission is empowered to prevent the sale of securities to the public on the basis of statements that contain inaccurate or incomplete information. The Staff of the Division of Corporate Finance usually notifies the registrant, by an informal letter of comment, of respects in which the registration statement apparently fails to conform to these requirements. The registrant is afforded an opportunity to file an amendment before the statement becomes effective. However, in certain cases, such as where the deficiencies in a registration statement appear to stem from careless disregard of applicable requirements or a deliberate attempt to conceal or mislead, the Commission either institutes an investigation to determine whether "stop-order" proceedings should be instituted, or immediately issues such an order.

The minimum waiting period between the time of filing the registration statement and the time it may become effective is twenty days. This waiting period is designed to provide investors with an opportunity to become familiar with the proposed offering. Information disclosed in the registration statements is disseminated during the waiting period by means of the preliminary prospectus, which presents in summary form the more important of the required disclosures.

---

## NOTE ON THE INTEGRATION OF DISCLOSURE UNDER THE 1933 AND 1934 ACTS

Within recent years, the content of the registration forms has been dramatically affected by the concept of integration. The Securities Exchange Act of 1934 requires *periodic disclosure* by issuers whose stock is registered under that Act. For example, such issuers must file an annual 10–K report, which includes financial statements and various other information; must annually distribute a proxy statement, or the equivalent, containing information on such matters as remuneration of directors and officers and conflict-of-interest transactions; and must file timely 8–K reports whenever certain material events have occurred. In contrast, the Securities Act of 1933 requires only *transactional disclosure*—that is, disclosure only in connection with specific public distributions. Until the late 1970s, the disclosure schemes of the two Acts proceeded on separate courses. At that time, the Commission undertook a program of integrating the two disclosure schemes. Partly, this was accomplished by a uniform Regulation, S–K, which provides equivalent definitions and disclosure requirements for comparable issues under the two Acts. Partly, it was accomplished by stratifying issuers into three classes, and reducing the amount of disclosure required in registration statements under the 1933 Act filed for issuers that are already making periodic disclosure under the 1934 Act, and issuers as to whom a great deal of information is likely to be publicly available even apart from the 1934 Act's disclosure requirements.

---

## Securities Act Release No. 6331 (1981)
[REGISTRATION FORMS]

### ... II. Overview

Under the proposed registration statement framework, registrants would be classified into three categories: (1) companies which are widely followed by professional analysts; (2) companies which have been subject to the periodic reporting system of the Exchange Act for three or more years, but which are not widely followed; and (3) companies which have been in the Exchange Act reporting system for less than three years. The first category would be eligible to use proposed Form S–3, which relies on incorporation by reference of Exchange Act reports and contains minimal disclosure in the prospectus. This form is predicated on the Commission's belief that the market operates efficiently for these companies, i.e., that the disclosure in Exchange Act reports and other communications by the registrant, such as press releases, has already been disseminated and accounted for by the market place. The second category would be eligible for Form S–2, which represents a combination of incorporation by reference of Exchange Act reports and presentation in the prospectus or in an annual report to security holders of certain information. The third category would use Form S–1, which requires complete disclosure of information in the prospectus and does not permit incorporation by reference. . . .

Proposed Form S–3 recognizes the applicability of the efficient market theory to the registration statement framework with respect to those registrants which usually provide high quality corporate reports, including Exchange Act reports, and whose corporate information is broadly disseminated, because such companies are widely followed by professional analysts and investors in the market place. Because these registrants are widely followed, the disclosure set forth in the prospectus may appropriately be limited, without the loss of investor protection, to information concerning the offering and material facts which have not been disclosed previously. The abbreviated disclosure is made possible by the use of incorporation by reference of the registrant's Exchange Act information into the prospectus. Because of the abbreviated disclosure, the utility of proposed Form S–3 is limited to widely followed companies.... The proposed float requirement is designed to correlate the use of abbreviated Form S–3 to widely followed registrants.

... [P]roposed Form S–2 is designed for improved readability by streamlining disclosure requirements and allowing certain disclosure obligations to be satisfied either through the delivery of the annual report to security holders or by presentation of comparable updated information in the prospectus. More specifically, the financial statements, management's discussion and analysis and the brief business description required by proposed Form S–2 are identical to those already presented in the annual report to security holders....

Finally, proposed Form S–1 ... would be used to register securities when no other form is authorized or prescribed and would be used by companies in the Exchange Act reporting system for less than three years, such as new issuers. To ensure that adequate information concerning these registrants is readily available to investors, proposed Form S–1 requires delivery of a more lengthy and comprehensive prospectus than either proposed Form S–2 or Form S–3....

### III.   Synopsis ...

A.   *Eligibility Rules for Use of Forms S–3, S–2 and S–1 ...*

1.   *Form S–3*

The eligibility requirements for use of Form S–3 are broken down into two classifications, "Registrant Requirements" and "Transaction Requirements." A registrant first must meet the Registrant Requirements (which are identical for Forms S–3 and S–2) and then must meet at least one of the Transaction Requirements before it can use Form S–3. ...

2.   *Form S–2*

... [T]he Registrant Requirements of Form S–3 also constitute virtually the entire eligibility requirements for the use of Form S–2....

3.   *Form S–1*

... [T]his more comprehensive form must be used by first time filers and others who have only been filing reports for a short period of time....

c. *Disclosure Provisions*

In proposed Forms S–1, S–2 and S–3, the Commission has developed a Securities Act registration system which identifies the information material to investment decisions in the context of all public offerings and then determines in what form and to whom issuers must disseminate such information. The material information will be required to be part of all Securities Act registration statements, regardless of the form used, through incorporation by reference in some cases. Differences among the forms primarily involve dissemination, i.e., the extent to which the required information must be presented in the prospectus, or may be presented in other documents delivered with the prospectus and incorporated by reference, or may be simply incorporated by reference from information contained in the Exchange Act continuous reporting system.

Generally, it is the issuer-oriented part of the information material to a public offering, as opposed to the transaction-specific information, which, depending on the form available, may be satisfied otherwise than through full prospectus presentation. This information includes the basic package of information about the issuer which the Commission believes is material to investment decisions in all contexts and thus is also required to be presented in annual reports to the Commission on Form 10–K and in annual reports to security holders. Information about the offering will not have been reported on in any other disclosure document or otherwise have been publicly disseminated and thus will be required to be presented in all cases....

2. *Incorporation by Reference*

The technique of incorporation by reference of Exchange Act disclosure documents is central to the integrated Securities Act registration system represented by proposed Forms S–1, S–2 and S–3. Proposed Form S–3 relies on incorporation by reference to replace prospectus presentation of information about the issuer of the securities being registered. Proposed Form S–2 uses incorporation by reference to allow streamlining of the prospectus presentation of issuer-specific information. Proposed Form S–1 uses no incorporation by reference and instead requires full disclosure about the issuer of the securities to be presented in the prospectus....

3. *Disclosure Requirements by Form*

a. *Form S–3*

Proposed Form S–3 provides the shortest form for Securities Act registration. The prospectus would be required to present [certain] items calling for information about the offering....

Information concerning the registrant would be incorporated by reference from Exchange Act reports, which would be available to investors on request. The documents required to be incorporated are the latest annual report on Form 10–K and all other reports filed pursuant to Section 13(a) or 15(d) of the Exchange Act since the end of the fiscal year covered by the Form 10–K, including all Section 13(d) or 15(d) reports filed subsequent to effectiveness of the registration statement and prior to termination of the offering. Unless there has been a material change in the registrant's affairs which has not been reported in an Exchange Act filing, the prospectus would not be required to present any information concerning the registrant. . . .

### b. *Form S–2*

Proposed Form S–2 provides a simplified form for registration by certain registrants. While it requires delivery of information about the registrant in addition to delivery of the same information about the offering as required by Form S–3, proposed Form S–2 significantly streamlines the registrant-specific disclosure by making the required level of disclosure delivered to investors that of the annual report to security holders pursuant to Rule 14a–3 rather than that of the annual report on Form 10–K. Required information about the registrant includes the basic information package components (market price and dividend data, selected financial data, financial statements and management's discussion and analysis) and such other items (brief descriptions of business, segments, supplementary financial information) as are required to be included in the annual report to security holders pursuant to Rule 14a–3. Moreover, registrants are granted the option of providing this information either by presenting it in the prospectus or by delivering the latest annual report to security holders along with the prospectus. Finally, the registrant's latest annual report on Form 10–K and periodic reports on Form 10–Q and Form 8–K must be incorporated by reference into the prospectus, and made available upon request, to round out the information provided about the registrant. . . .

If the Form S–2 registrant elects the alternative of delivering its annual report, it must incorporate certain information in that document by reference and describe in the prospectus any material changes in its affairs since the end of the latest fiscal year reported in the delivered annual report. In addition, it must provide updating information but may avoid duplication of previously reported quarterly information because updating may be accomplished by any one of three means: (1) including in the prospectus such financial and other information as would be required to be reported in a report on Form 10–Q; (2) delivering a copy of the latest Form 10–Q with the prospectus and annual report; (3) delivering a copy of the latest informal quarterly report to shareholders if such report contained the same required information. . . .

### c. *Form S–1*

Proposed Form S–1 presents a simple format. Full disclosure of all material information about the offering and the registrant is required to be presented in the prospectus itself. No incorporation by reference to any Exchange Act documents is allowed. Proposed Form S–1 looks entirely to Regulation S–K for its non-financial substantive disclosure provisions. First, like proposed Forms S–2 and S–3, proposed Form S–1 requires prospectus presentation of the offering-oriented items of § 229.500 of Regulation S–K and the description of securities (proposed Item 202 of Regulation S–K). In addition, the proposed Form S–

1 prospectus must include the same information about the registrant as is required to be reported in an annual report on Form 10–K. This information includes, in addition to the basic information package with respect to the registrant, the full Regulation S–K descriptions of business, properties and legal proceedings as well as the Regulation S–K disclosures with respect to management and security holders. . . .

---

## SECURITIES ACT RULES 176, 415

[See Statutory Supplement]

---

# Securities Act Release No. 6276 (1981) [Shelf Registration]

. . . The last sentence of Section 6(a) of the Securities Act provides: "A registration statement shall be deemed effective only as to the securities specified therein as proposed to be offered." . . . [The Commission has interpreted] that sentence to prohibit the registration of securities for a delayed or postponed offering, commonly referred to as "shelf" offering or registration.

In the absence of any specific legislative comment upon the meaning of the last sentence of Section 6(a) of the Securities Act, as enacted by Congress in 1933, early opinions of the Commission and its staff interpreted the provision as requiring that a registration statement be effective only as to those securities proposed to be offered "in the proximate future". . . . This general prohibition against shelf registration was designed to effectuate the clear policy underlying the last sentence of Section 6(a) that "the registration statements and prospectuses on which they rely, so far as is reasonably possible, provide current information." This interpretation was, in turn, premised upon the assumption that the registration of securities which are to be offered at "some remote future time" gives "the appearance of a registered status" without providing its true substance—accurate and current information.

In practice, the Commission has never adhered to such an absolute prohibition [and] . . . . such registration has been permitted for several types of offerings. . . .

After substantial experience with [several] types of shelf registration, the Commission is not aware of major abuses that have harmed investors. In addition, the integration of the Securities Act and Exchange Act disclosure systems provides an increasingly efficient basis for updating disclosure in securities offerings. Shelf registrations can utilize integration effectively thereby facilitating the development of important new capital raising techniques. Accordingly, the Commission believes that a restrictive policy on shelf registration is not appropriate or necessary for the protection of investors. The Commission is proposing . . . that its stated prohibition of shelf registration be replaced with proposed Rule [415]. . . .

_____

## SECTION 6.   DUTIES AND PROHIBITIONS WHEN A SECURITY IS IN REGISTRATION

_____

### INTRODUCTORY NOTE

Assuming that a registration statement must be filed, the issuer, underwriter, and broker-dealers come under a variety of duties and prohibitions. To analyze these duties and prohibitions, it is necessary to separately consider three time periods. First, the period before registration (the "prefiling period"). Second, the period between the time the registration statement is filed and the time it becomes effective (the "waiting period"). Third, the period after the registration statement becomes effective (the "post-effective period").

Note that the term "in registration" is used to mean "the entire process of registration, at least from the time an issuer reaches an understanding with the broker-dealer which is to act as managing underwriter prior to the filing of a registration statement and the period of 40 to 90 days during which dealers must deliver a prospectus." Securities Act Release No. 5180 n. 1 (1971).

_____

## (a)  OVERVIEW

_____

### Securities Act Release No. 4697 (1964) [Offers and Sales of Securities by Underwriters and Dealers]

In view of recent comments in the press concerning the rights and obligations of, and limitations on, dealers in connection with distributions of registered securities, the Commission takes this opportunity to explain the operation of section 5 of the Securities Act of 1933 with particular reference to the limitations upon, and responsibilities of, underwriters and dealers in the offer and sale of an issue of securities prior to and after the filing of a registration statement.

The discussion below assumes that the offering is not exempt from the registration requirements of the Act and, unless otherwise stated, that the mails or facilities of interstate or foreign commerce are used.

### The Period Before the Filing of a Registration Statement

Section 5 of the Securities Act prohibits both offers to sell and offers to buy a security before a registration statement is filed. Section 2(3) of the Act, however, exempts preliminary negotiations or agreements between the issuer or other person on whose behalf the distribution is to be made and any underwriter or among underwriters. Thus, negotiation of the financing can proceed during this period but neither the issuer nor the underwriter may offer the security either to investors or to dealers, and dealers are prohibited from offering to buy the securities during this period.[1] Consequently, not only may no steps be taken to form a selling group but also dealers may not seek inclusion in the selling group prior to the filing.

It should be borne in mind that publicity about an issuer, its securities or the proposed offering prior to the filing of a registration statement may constitute an illegal offer to sell. Thus, announcement of the underwriter's identity should be avoided during this period. Experience shows that such announcements are very likely to lead to illegal offers to buy. This subject will not be further discussed in this release since it has been extensively considered elsewhere.[2]

These principles, however, are not intended to restrict the normal communications between an issuer and its stockholders or the announcement to the public generally of information with respect to important business and financial developments. Such announcements are required in the listing agreements used by stock exchanges, and the Commission is sensitive to the importance of encouraging this type of communication. In recognition of this requirement of certain stock exchanges, the Commission adopted Rule 135, which permits a brief announcement of proposed rights offerings, proposed exchange offerings, and proposed offerings to employees as not constituting an offer of a security for the purposes of section 5 of the Act.

### The Period After the Filing and Before the Effective Date

After the registration statement is filed, and before its effective date, offers to sell the securities are permitted but no written offer may be made except by means of a statutory prospectus. For this purpose the statutory prospectus includes the preliminary prospectus provided for in Rule 433 as well as the summary prospectus provided for in Rules 434 and 434A. In addition the so-called "tombstone" advertisement permitted by Rule 134 may be used.

---

**1.** The reason for this provision was stated in the House Report on the bill as originally enacted as follows:

"... Otherwise, the underwriter ... could accept them in the order of their priority and thus bring pressure upon dealers, who wish to avail themselves of a particular security offering, to rush their orders to buy without adequate consideration of the nature of the security being offered." H.R.Report No. 85, 73rd Cong., 1st Sess. (1933), p. 11.

**2.** See Securities Act Release No. 3844 (1957); Carl M. Loeb, Rhoades & Co., 38 S.E.C. 843 (1959); First Maine Corporation, 38 S.E.C. 882 (1959).

During the period after the filing of a registration statement, the freedom of an underwriter or dealer expecting to participate in the distribution, to communicate with his customers is limited only by the antifraud provisions of the Securities Act and the Securities Exchange Act, and by the fact that written offering material other than a statutory prospectus or tombstone advertisement may not be used. In other words, during this period "free writing" is illegal. The dealer, therefore, can orally solicit indications of interest or offers to buy and may discuss the securities with his customers and advise them whether or not in his opinion the securities are desirable or suitable for them. In this connection a dealer proposing to discuss an issue of securities with his customers should obtain copies of the preliminary prospectus in order to have a reliable source of information. This is particularly important where he proposes to recommend the securities, or where information concerning them has not been generally available. The corollary of the dealer's obligation to secure the copy is the obligation of the issuer and managing underwriters to make it readily available. Rule 460 provides that as a condition to acceleration of the effective date of a registration statement, the Commission will consider whether the persons making the offering have taken reasonable steps to make the information contained in the registration statement available to dealers who may participate in the distribution.

It is a principal purpose of the so-called "waiting period" between the filing date and the effective date to enable dealers and, through them, investors to become acquainted with the information contained in the registration statement and to arrive at an unhurried decision concerning the merits of the securities. Consistently with this purpose, no contracts of sale can be made during this period, the purchase price may not be paid or received and offers to buy may be cancelled.

### The Period After the Effective Date

When the registration statement becomes effective oral offerings may continue and sales may be made and consummated. A copy of the final statutory prospectus must be delivered in connection with any written offer or confirmation or upon delivery of the security, whichever first occurs. Supplemental sales literature ("free writing") may be used if it is accompanied or preceded by a prospectus. However, care must be taken to see that all such material is at the time of use not false or misleading under the standards of section 17(a) of the Act. If the offering continues over an extended period, the prospectus should be current under the standards of section 10(a)(3). All dealers trading in the registered security must continue to employ the prospectus for the period referred to in section 4.

———

## (b) THE PRE–FILING PERIOD

---

### SECURITIES ACT §§ 2(a)(3), 5

[See Statutory Supplement]

---

### NOTE ON THE PRE–FILING PERIOD

Under section 5(a) of the 1933 Act:

Unless a registration statement is in effect as to a security, it shall be unlawful for any person, directly or indirectly—(1) to make use of any means or instruments of transportation or communication in interstate commerce or of the mails to sell such security through the use or medium of any prospectus or otherwise; or (2) to carry or cause to be carried through the mails or in interstate commerce, by any means or instruments of transportation, any such security for the purpose of sale or for delivery after sale.

Under section 5(a)(c):

It shall be unlawful for any person, directly or indirectly, to make use of any means or instruments of transportation or communication in interstate commerce or of the mails to offer to sell or offer to buy through the use or medium of any prospectus or otherwise any security, unless a registration statement has been filed as to such security. . . .

Under section 2(a)(3):

The term "sale" or "sell" shall include every contract of sale or disposition of a security or interest in a security, for value. The term "offer to sell", "offer for sale", or "offer" shall include every attempt or offer to dispose of, or solicitation of an offer to buy, a security or interest in a security, for value.

There is an important exception to section 2(a)(3):

The terms defined in [§ 2(a)(3)] and the term "offer to buy" as used in subsection (c) of section 5 shall not include preliminary negotiations or agreements between an issuer . . . and any underwriter or among underwriters who are or are to be in privity of contract with an issuer. . . .

Putting together §§ 5(a), 5(c), and 2(a)(3), neither a sale nor an oral or written offer to sell securities to be registered may be made during the prefiling period, except for preliminary negotiations between the issuer and the underwriter and between underwriters. The prohibition against offers in the prefiling period extends not only to formal offers, but to "gun-jumping"—unusual publicity by the issuer or a prospective underwriter that is in effect a preliminary step in the selling effort. On the other hand, if a corporation is already publicly held, blocking the normal flow of information would adversely affect the integrity of the market for the securities that are already outstanding. The cases and rules governing the prefiling period attempt to reconcile the undesirability of gun-jumping with the desirability of maintaining the normal flow of information concerning corporations that are already publicly held.

---

### SECURITIES ACT RULES 135, 137, 139

[See Statutory Supplement]

---

## Securities Act Release No. 5180 (1971)

GUIDELINES FOR THE RELEASE OF INFORMATION BY ISSUERS WHOSE SECURITIES ARE IN REGISTRATION

The Commission today took note of situations when issuers whose securities are "in registration" may have refused to answer legitimate inquiries from stockholders, financial analysts, the press or other persons concerning the company or some aspect of its business. The Commission hereby emphasizes that there is no basis in the securities acts or in any policy of the Commission which would justify the practice of non-disclosure of *factual* information by a publicly held company on the grounds that it has securities in registration under the Securities Act of 1933 ("Act"). Neither a company in registration nor its representatives should instigate publicity for the purpose of facilitating the sale of securities in a proposed offering. . . .

. . . It has been asserted that the increasing obligations and incentives of corporations to make timely disclosures concerning their affairs creates a possible conflict with statutory restrictions on publication of information concerning a company which has securities in registration. As the Commission has stated in previously issued releases this conflict may be more apparent than real. Disclosure of factual information in response to inquiries or resulting from a duty to make prompt disclosure under the antifraud provisions of the securities acts or the timely disclosure policies of self-regulatory organizations, at a time when a registered offering of securities is contemplated or in process, can and should be effected in a manner which will not unduly influence the proposed offering.

### *Statutory Requirements*

In order for issuers and their representatives to avoid problems in responding to inquiries, it is essential that such persons be familiar with the statutory requirements governing this area. Generally speaking, Section 5(c) of the Act makes it unlawful for any person directly or indirectly to make use of any means or instruments of interstate commerce or of the mails *to offer to sell* a security unless a registration statement has been filed with the Commission as to such security. Questions arise from time to time because many persons do not realize that the phrase "offer to sell" is broadly defined by the Act and has been liberally construed by the courts and Commission. For example, the publication of information and statements, and publicity efforts, made in advance of a proposed financing which have the effect of conditioning the public mind or arousing public interest in the issuer or in its securities constitutes an offer in violation of the Act. The same holds true with respect to publication of information which is part of a selling effort between the filing date and the effective date of a registration statement. . . .

### *Guidelines*

The Commission strongly suggests that all issuers establish internal procedures designed to avoid problems relating to the release of corporate information when in registration. As stated above, issuers and their representatives should not initiate publicity when in registration, but should nevertheless respond to legitimate inquiries for factual information about the company's financial condition and business operations. Further, care should be exercised so that, for example, predictions, projections, forecasts, estimates and opinions concerning value are not given with respect to such things, among other, as sales and earnings and value of the issuer's securities.

It has been suggested that the Commission promulgate an all inclusive list of permissible and prohibited activities in this area. This is not feasible for the reason that determinations are based upon the particular facts of each case. However, the Commission as a matter of policy encourages the flow of factual information to shareholders and the investing public. Issuers in this regard should:

1. Continue to advertise products and services.

2. Continue to send out customary quarterly, annual and other periodic reports to stockholders.

3. Continue to publish proxy statements and send out dividend notices.

4. Continue to make announcements to the press with respect to factual business and financial developments; *i.e.,* receipt of a contract, the settlement of a strike, the opening of a plant, or similar events of interest to the community in which the business operates.

5. Answer unsolicited telephone inquiries from stockholders, financial analysts, the press and others concerning factual information.

6. Observe an "open door" policy in responding to unsolicited inquiries concerning factual matters from securities analysts, financial analysts, security holders, and participants in the communications field who have a legitimate interest in the corporation's affairs.

7.   Continue to hold stockholder meetings as scheduled and to answer shareholders' inquiries at stockholder meetings relating to factual matters.

In order to curtail problems in this area, issuers in this regard should avoid:

1.   Issuance of forecasts, projections, or predictions relating but not limited to revenues, income, or earnings per share.

2.   Publishing opinions concerning values.

In the event a company publicly releases material information concerning new corporate developments during the period that a registration statement is pending, the registration statement should be amended at or prior to the time the information is released. If this is not done and such information is publicly released through inadvertence, the pending registration statement should be promptly amended to reflect such information. . . .

----

## (c)  THE WAITING PERIOD

----

### SECURITIES ACT §§ 2(a)(10), 5, 8, 10; SECURITIES ACT RULES 134, 152c–8, 430, 431, 460

[See Statutory Supplement]

----

### NOTE ON THE WAITING PERIOD

1.   Section 8 of the 1933 Act provides that "Except as hereinafter provided, the effective date of a registration statement shall be the twentieth day after the filing thereof or such earlier date as the Commission may determine. . . ."

Accordingly, there is always a waiting period between the time at which a registration statement is filed and the time at which it is effective. Section 5(a) prohibits *sales* unless a registration is effective, thereby prohibiting sales during the waiting period. Section 5(c) prohibits offers "[making] use of any means of interstate commerce to offer to sell ... through the use or medium of any prospectus or otherwise any security, unless a registration statement has been filed," but does not prohibit offers, as such, during the waiting period. However, section 5(b) prohibits the transmission of "any prospectus relating to any securities with respect to which a registration statement has been filed ... unless such prospectus meets the requirements of section 10." Section 2(a)(10) defines "prospectus" very broadly to mean "any prospectus, notice, circular, advertisement, letter, or communication, written or by radio or television, which offers any security for sale or confirms the sale of any security."

The combined effect of sections 5 and 2(a)(10) on issuers, underwriters and dealers, is that during the waiting period: (1) *sales* are not permissible; (2) *oral offers* are permissible, and (3) writings relating to the securities are permissible only if they specifically permitted by statute or rule.

2.   What writings *are* permitted during the waiting period?

In theory, a *final prospectus* (also sometimes known as a *section 10(a) prospectus* or a *statutory prospectus*) is permissible. In practice, however, use of a final prospectus during this period is impossible, because a final prospectus must include certain information that is usually not decided upon until the waiting period is over.

However, certain other writings are permissible.

(a) *Preliminary prospectus.* Section 10(b) of the Securities Act provides that:

> In addition to the prospectus permitted or required in subsection (a), the Commission shall by rules or regulations deemed necessary or appropriate in the public interest or for the protection of investors permit the use of a prospectus for the purposes of subsection (b)(1) of section 5 which omits in part or summarizes information in the prospectus specified in subsection (a).

Pursuant to section 10(b), the Commission has promulgated Rule 430, which provides that

> A form of prospectus filed as a part of the registration statement shall be deemed to meet the requirements of section 10 of the Act for the purpose of section 5(b)(1) thereof prior to the effective date of the registration statement, provided such form of prospectus contains substantially the information required by the Act and the rules and regulations thereunder to be included in a prospectus meeting the requirements of section 10(a) of the Act for the securities being registered, or contains substantially that information except for the omission of information with respect to the offering price, underwriting discounts or commissions, discounts or commissions to dealers, amount of proceeds, conversion rates, call prices, or other matters dependent upon the offering price.

The writing permitted under section 10(b) and Rule 430 is known as a *preliminary prospectus* or *red herring* (so-called because of a red legend that appears on the cover page).

(b) *Summary prospectus.* Under Rule 431, certain issuers can use a *summary prospectus* during the waiting period. Under that Rule:

> ... A summary prospectus shall contain the information specified in the instructions as to summary prospectuses in the form used for registration of the securities to be offered. Such prospectus may include any other information the substance of which is contained in the registration statement except as other-

wise specifically provided in the instructions as to summary prospectuses in the form used for registration.

(c) *Tombstone ads.* Under section 2(a)(10)(b), an ad can be used during the waiting period, if the ad states only from whom a written prospectus, meeting the requirements of section 10, may be obtained, and does no more than identify the security, state the price, state by whom orders will be executed, and contain such other information as the Commission may prescribe. Such an ad is known as a *tombstone ad*, because of its spare nature and typical black border.

(d) *Identifying statement.* Under section 2(a)(10)(b) and Rule 134, an *identifying statement*—in effect, an expanded tombstone ad— can be used during the waiting period. Under Rule 134, certain information, in addition to that specified in section 2(a)(10)(b) for tombstone ads, may be included in an identifying statement.

In short, during the waiting period, issuers, underwriters, and dealers can reach potential customers in writing only by a preliminary prospectus, a summary prospectus, a tombstone ad, or an identifying statement. Any other kind of writing—known as *free writing*—is prohibited.

# (d) THE POST-EFFECTIVE PERIOD

**SECURITIES ACT §§ 2(3), 2(10), 4(3), 5, 10;
SECURITIES ACT RULES 153, 174, 427**

[See Statutory Supplement]

## NOTE ON THE POST-EFFECTIVE PERIOD

After the registration statement has become effective there is no prohibition on either offers or sales, as such. Accordingly, *free writings*—writings other than those permitted during the waiting period— are permitted, with an important limitation. The limitation is that under sections 2(10) and 5(b)(1), no writings may be distributed concerning a security as to which a registration is in effect unless prior to, or at the same time, a section 10 prospectus has been delivered.

Furthermore, under section 5(b)(2) if a registration statement is in effect as to a security, a section 10 prospectus must precede or accompany any securities sold. A section 10 prospectus must also precede or accompany any confirmation of a sale of registered securities, so that a sale cannot be effectively closed without delivery of a section 10 prospectus.

How long do these restrictions last?

Sales of registered securities by an *issuer* must always be accompanied by a section 10 prospectus.

All *underwriters* of an offering, and all *dealers* who were participants in the distribution, are subject to the prospectus-delivery requirement as long as they are offering an unsold allotment of the original public offering. Dealers are also subject to the prospectus-delivery requirement, whether or not they are selling an unsold allotment, during a specified period after commencement of the offering.

However, section 4(4) of the Securities Act provides that "broker's transactions executed upon customers' orders on any exchange or in the over-the-counter market" are exempted from the prospectus-delivery requirement. This exemption "permits individuals to sell their securities through a broker in an ordinary brokerage transaction, during the period of distribution or while a stop order is in effect, without regard to the registration and prospectus requirements of section 5." In the Matter of Ira Haupt & Co., 23 S.E.C. 589 (1946).

## SECTION 7.   LIABILITIES UNDER THE SECURITIES ACT

### SECURITIES ACT §§ 11, 12, 17, 21d(g), 27A; SECURITIES ACT RULES 175, 176

[See Statutory Supplement]

## NOTE ON LIABILITIES UNDER THE SECURITIES ACT

The Securities Act contains four basic liability provisions: Sections 11, 12(a)(1), 12(a)(2), and 17(a).

1. *Section 17(a).* Section 17(a) is a general antifraud provision, whose applicability does not turn on whether there has been a violation of section 5, the registration provision. Section 17(a) is highly comparable to rule 10b–5, because rule 10b–5 was modeled on section 17(a). However, rule 10b–5 regulates both sellers and buyers, while section 17(a) regulates only sellers. On the other hand, section 17(a) applies to "offers" while rule 10b–5 does not.

Scienter is a necessary element of a violation of section 17(a)(1), but not of sections 17(a)(2) or 17(a)(3). Aaron v. S.E.C., 446 U.S. 680, 100 S.Ct. 1945, 64 L.Ed.2d 611 (1980).

There is no private right of action under section 17(a). See, e.g., Finkel v. Stratton Corp., 962 F.2d 169, 174–75 (2d Cir.1992).

2. *Section 12(a)(2).* Section 12(a)(2) provides that, subject to certain conditions, any person who offers or sells a security by means

of a prospectus or oral communication is liable to the purchaser for rescission or damages, if the prospectus or oral communication includes a material misstatement or has a material omission. Thus section 12(a)(2), like section 17(a), is an antifraud provision. Unlike section 17(a), section 12(a)(2) explicitly gives buyers a private right of action. Gustafson v. Alloyd Co., 513 U.S. 561, 115 S.Ct. 1061, 131 L.Ed.2d 1 (1995). However section 12(a)(2) applies only to securities sold in public offerings by issuers or their controlling shareholders. *Gustafson*, supra.

The principal conditions to the seller's liability under section 12(a)(2) are as follows: (1) The buyer must not have known the truth. (2) If the misstatement involves a forward-looking statement, the buyer has available the safe harbor provided by section 27A and rule 175. (3) The seller is not liable if and to the extent he proves that any or all of the amount that the buyer could otherwise have recovered arose from factors other than the misstatement or omission. (This reflects the concept of "loss causation," discussed in Chapter 10.)

The buyer's recovery is limited to the return of the purchase price (plus interest, but minus the amount of any income received), unless he has resold the security. If the buyer has resold the security, he is entitled to the difference between the price he paid for the security and the price at which he resold the security.

To get relief under section 12(a)(2) the buyer must show a false statement or material omission. There is no requirement that the plaintiff relied on the misstatement or omission. He need only show that he did not know the truth. Once the buyer shows that an omission was material, or that a material statement was false, the seller has the burden of showing that he did not know and "in the exercise of reasonable care could not have known" of the untruth or omission. In effect, therefore, section 12(a)(2) makes the seller liable for negligence in connection with a misrepresentation or omission, and puts the burden of proof on the seller to show that he was not negligent.

3.  *Section 12(a)(1)*. Section 12(a)(1) gives buyers a private right of action against sellers who violate section 5 of the 1933 Act—that is, for the most part, against sellers who either (1) sell securities that are required to be, but are not, registered, or (2) sell securities without delivering a required section 10 prospectus or deliver a prospectus that does not satisfy section 10. A seller's liability under section 12(a)(1) is strict. The buyer does not need to show fraud or even a material misstatement or omission in the registration statement. However, the remedy under section 12(a)(1) is limited to buyers who are in privity with—that is, who purchased directly from—the seller in question.

The basic remedy under section 12(a)(1) is rescission. However, a buyer who sold the stock before she brought suit can sue for the difference between the price that she paid for the stock and the price at which she sold it.

The term "seller" in section 12(a)(1) is broadly construed to mean any person who successfully solicits a purchase and who is motivated at least in part by a desire to serve his own financial interests or those of the owner of the securities. Pinter v. Dahl, 486 U.S. 622, 108 S.Ct. 2063, 100 L.Ed.2d 658 (1988).

4. *Section 11*. Section 11 gives buyers a private right of action for material misstatements or omissions in a registration statement, subject to certain conditions and defenses. A variety of persons may be potentially liable under section 11, including the issuer, the directors and certain officers of the issuer, the underwriters, and experts (such as accountants) who have taken responsibility for some portion of the registration statement.

Section 11 does not require privity: any person who has purchased the security in question, either in the original distribution or later, can bring suit. However, liability under section 11 extends only to the securities issued under the registration statement. Accordingly, a buyer who purchased the same class of securities as those registered, but cannot trace the securities she purchased back to the registration statement, cannot bring suit under section 11 even though the securities she purchased were economically identical to the securities issued under the registration statement. Barnes v. Osofsky, 373 F.2d 269 (2d Cir.1967). (However, such a buyer might be able to bring suit under Rule 10b–5.)

Section 11 does not require the buyer to show reliance or causation. However, it is defense that the buyer knew the truth at the time he acquired the security. Under section 27A of the 1933 Act, under certain circumstances there is no liability under section 11 for forward-looking statements.

Damages under section 11 are limited to the difference between the original offering price and the value of the securities at the time of suit. Furthermore, under a proviso to section 11(e), if the defendant proves that any portion (or all) of the damages is based on factors other than the relevant misstatement or omission, that portion of the damages cannot be recovered. This proviso is sometimes referred to as "negative causation." Essentially, it is a form of loss causation, with the burden of proof on the defendant.

An issuer is strictly liable under section 11. Persons other than the issuer (such as directors of the issuer, or experts) can escape liability by establishing what is known as the *due diligence defense*. Under this defense:

A non-expert, as to the nonexpertised portions of the registration statement, and an expert, as to the expertised portions, will not be liable if "he had, after reasonable investigation, reasonable ground to believe" that the relevant statements were true and that there were no material omissions.

As to the expertised portions of the registration statement, a nonexpert will not be liable if "he had no reasonable ground to believe" that the statements made by the expert were untrue or contained material omissions.

Thus section 11, like section 12(a)(2), adopts a negligence standard, with the burden of proof on the defendants to show that they were not negligent. There is a difference in the formulations of the negligence standards in sections 11 and 12(a)(2), and it is not clear whether this means that there are differences in the investigation required to satisfy the defendant's burden of proof under the two sections. See Sanders v. John Nuveen & Co., Inc., 619 F.2d 1222 (7th Cir.1980), cert. denied 450 U.S. 1005, 101 S.Ct. 1719, 68 L.Ed.2d 210 (1981) (opinion of Justice Powell, dissenting from denial of certiorari).

-----

## SECTION 8.   BLUE SKY LAWS

-----

### NOTE ON BLUE SKY LAWS

Prior to the entry of the federal government into the field of securities regulation in 1933, almost all of the states had adopted statutes designed to protect the public from "speculative schemes which have no more basis than so many feet of 'blue sky.' " Hall v. Geiger–Jones Co., 242 U.S. 539, 550, 37 S.Ct. 217, 220–21, 61 L.Ed. 480, 489 (1917).

At present, all states have blue-sky laws in effect. The blue-sky laws vary tremendously in coverage, approach and impact. Three basic methods of regulation are employed, which are sometimes referred to as the *fraud*, *dealer-registration*, and *securities-registration* methods. Most states have adopted all three methods to varying extents, but the methods are embodied in different forms, and the governing standards and procedures vary widely from state to state.

1. *The Fraud Method.* The fraud method simply makes certain practices, usually described by some form of the word "fraud," grounds for criminal prosecution, suspension of trading, or both. The blue-sky administrator normally has broad investigatory powers, but those powers are usually exercised only where there has been complaint or where there are suspicious circumstances. Probably for this reason, the fraud method is not thought to be sufficient in itself.

2. *The Dealer-Registration Method.* The dealer-registration method requires dealers (including issuers, brokers, and salesmen) to register as a prerequisite to trading in securities within a state's borders. The amount, detail, and nature of the information required to register varies widely. In a majority of states, registration may be denied or revoked for cause. The blue-sky administrator sometimes has considerable discretion in determining whether a dealer will be permitted to do business within the state.

3.   *The Securities-Registration Method.* The securities-registration method prohibits dealing in an issue of securities until the issue has been qualified under a designated statutory standard, and in accordance with a designated statutory procedure. This method is sometimes referred to as *merit regulation*, because in contrast to registration under the Securities Act, the blue-sky administrator can deny registration on the ground that the securities issue lacks merit, even though full disclosure has been made. The standards and procedures vary considerably from state to state. In general, the standards and procedures are aimed at unseasoned speculative securities that are to be offered to the general public.

The securities-registration or merit-regulation method encompasses three basic approaches.

a.   *The qualifying approach.* Under the *qualifying* approach, trading in an issue of non-exempt securities is permitted only if an affirmative administrative determination has been made that the issue meets a designated statutory standard, such as "fair, just and equitable." More specific standards are usually imposed on issues of particularly unsafe kinds.

b.   *The Notification approach.* Under the *notification* approach, which is often available for seasoned securities, registration becomes effective after a designated period following notice to the blue-sky administrator of the proposed new issuance, unless the administrator moves to block it.

c.   *The Coordination approach.* The *coordination* approach is similar to the notification approach, but is available only for issues registered under the federal Securities Act. The information submitted to the blue-sky administrator basically consists of copies of the material filed with the SEC. In the absence of adverse action by the administrator, the state registration becomes effective at the moment the federal registration statement becomes effective.

4.   *Federal Preemption.* In 1996, section 18 of the Securities Act was amended to preclude states from requiring Blue Sky registration of securities that are designated in section 18 as "covered securities." Covered securities, which section 18 exempts from state registration requirements, include (i) Securities listed on the New York Stock Exchange, the American Stock Exchange, and the Nasdaq's National Market System. (ii) Securities offered only to "qualified purchasers," as defined by the SEC. (iii) Certain securities whose sale is exempt from registration under the Securities Act.

Under section 18, therefore, the reach of the blue-sky laws has been substantially reduced. The states now can only apply merit-regulation registration requirements to securities that are not "covered securities" under section 18. The states can, however, continue to bring fraud proceedings, and to require filing, even in respect to covered securities, solely for purposes of notice, coordination, and—most significantly—filing-fee charges.

# INDEX

References are to Pages.

**DERIVATIVE ACTIONS**

**DISCLOSURE, DUTY OF**—Cont'd
Information rights of shareholders. See
    Shareholders and Shareholders'
    Rights, this index
Insider Trading, this index
Misstatements of corporate financial conditions, 642 et seq.
Ratification by shareholders of self-interest transaction, required disclosures, 464 et seq.
Self-interested transactions, 446 et seq.
Statutory regulation, 455
Stock option compensation plans, present value, 464 et seq.
Timing of, business judgment as to, 558

**DISHONESTY**
See Loyalty, Duty of, this index

**DISREGARD OF CORPORATE ENTITY**
See Piercing Corporate Veil, this index

**DISSOLUTION**
Close corporations
    Deadlock
        Generally, 319
        Custodians, judicial appointment of, 321
    Effectiveness of remedy, 336
    Four stages of legal treatment of, 337
    Oppression, 322 et seq.
Distributions on, 878
Freezeouts, 779
Oppression
    Generally, 322 et seq.

**DIVIDENDS AND DISTRIBUTIONS**
Generally, 878 et seq.
Bad faith, close corporations, 245 et seq.
Bondholders' rights and dividend payments, 897
Capital impairment statutes
    Generally, 887 et seq.
    Current earnings test, 894
    Earned surplus statutes, 896
    Exceptions, 894 et seq.
    Nimble dividends, 894
    Wasting assets corporations, 894
Capital surplus, dividends from, 895
Capitalization requirements and fraudulent transfer restrictions, 885
Changes in dividends, 878
Close corporations, 245 et seq.
Compensation characterized as. Compensation, this index
Contractual restrictions on dividends, 897
Creditors rights and dividend payments
    Generally, 883
    Contractual restrictions, 897
Current earnings test, capital impairment statutes and, 894
Dissolution distributions, 878
Earned surplus
    Generally, 895
    Statutes, 886
Four approaches of managers, 878
Fraudulent transfers, 187, 883

**DIVIDENDS AND DISTRIBUTIONS**—Cont'd
Freezeouts of minority shareholders, 245 et seq.
Inadequate capitalization and piercing of corporate veil, 175
Insolvency and dividends, 883
Judicial review of dividend policy, 882 et seq.
Legal capital restrictions, 886
Limited liability companies, 358
Nimble dividends, 894
Paid-in surplus, 895
Par value and dividends, 886
Piercing doctrine and unlimited distributions, 173
Policies, dividend, 878 et seq.
Reduction surplus, 895
Refusal to declare dividends, tax implications, 291
Repurchase of shares
    Capital impairment statutes, 893
    Dividends distinguished, 900
    Financial limitations, 900 et seq.
Social responsibility and maximization of profits, 98 et seq.
Statutory limitations on dividends, 885 et seq.
Surplus and, 895
Tax implications of refusal to declare dividends, 291
Waste of assets, distribution attacked as, 386 et seq.
Wasting assets corporations, 894

**DUTIES**
Care, Duty of, this index
Disclosure, Duty of, this index
Fiduciary Duties, this index
Law, Duty to Obey, this index
Loyalty, Duty of, this index

**EFFICIENT CAPITAL MARKETS HYPOTHESIS (ECMH)**
See Markets, this index

**ENTERPRISE LIABILITY**
Generally, 7

**ENTITY STATUS**
Characteristics of corporate form, 67

**EQUITABLE SUBROGATION**
Shareholder claims, 186

**ESTOPPEL**
Agency by, 9
Corporation by, 82 et seq.
Ultra vires and, 87

**EXECUTIVE COMPENSATION**
See Compensation, this index

**FIDUCIARY DUTIES**
See also Loyalty, Duty of, this index
Agency Relationships, this index
Close corporation shareholders, 284 et seq.
Employee shareholders fiduciary obligations to, 284 et seq., 292

1—56662—906—3

90000

9 781566 629065